THE CAMBRIDGE FACTFINDER

Edited by
DAVID CRYSTAL

THE CAMBRIDGE FACTFINDER

Edited by
DAVID CRYSTAL

CAMBRIDGE
UNIVERSITY PRESS

Published by the Press Syndicate of the University of Cambridge
The Pitt Building, Trumpington Street, Cambridge CB2 1RP
40 West 20th Street, New York, NY 10011-4211
10 Stamford Road, Oakleigh, Victoria 3166, Australia

First published in 1993

Typeset by Flairplan Phototypesetting Ltd, Ware, UK, Prestige Typographics Ltd, Bury St Edmunds, UK and Desktype Image Creation Ltd, Cambridge, UK

Printed in Great Britain at The Bath Press, Avon

A catalogue record for this book is available from the British Library

Library of Congress cataloging in publication data available

ISBN 0 521 45306 2 hardback

ABOUT THIS BOOK

The Cambridge Factfinder contains more facts than any other book of its kind. We also believe it is much easier to use than other such books. What might seem at first the most simple of books - a collection of bits of information for use in the home, at school or in the office - is actually the product of much hard thinking about how best to organize the information, and, indeed, what the nature of this information is.

What is a fact?

> Something that has really occurred or is actually the case; something certainly known to be of this character; hence a particular truth known by actual observation or authentic testimony, as opposed to what is merely inferred, or to a conjecture or fiction; a datum of experience, as opposed to the conclusions which may be based upon it.

This definition, one of the longest in the *Oxford English Dictionary*, gives a hint of the difficulty involved in saying what exactly counts as a 'fact' and thus of the difficulties facing any editor who has to decide what should be included in a book of them. At first glance, the answer is obvious: there are facts about objects and animals (what are the characteristics of X?), people (who is X?), places (where is X?), and times (when did X happen?), and these facts can be numerical (how many X? how often did X happen?), verbal (how to describe X?), and tabular (how to classify X?)

At second glance, the situation becomes more complicated (and more interesting). There are facts about fictions (X in mythology or literature) and fictions about facts (disputes over the longest or largest X). There are situations where we cannot decide whether something is fiction or fact (the changing politics of country X). There are near-facts (estimates of X), transient facts (world records about X), qualified facts (the majority of X), arguable facts (the most important X), politically-biased facts (the growth or decline of X), and contrived facts (neat classifications of X). A factbook must not ignore these awkward and marginal cases, but having included them it must always remember to warn readers if 'there's something they should know' before swallowing a 'fact' whole. Examples of this advice are given on p. 42 (about longest rivers) and p. 406 (about saints' days). Many bitter arguments (such as those which arise out of a disputed answer in a quiz game) could be avoided if more attention were paid to this issue.

What isn't a fact?

On the other hand, certain notions are not part of a factbook. Definitions of words, for example, really have no place. It is a fact that there was a major tsunami in the Sea of Japan in 1983 (p. 28). However, if you don't know what a tsunami is, you had best look the word up in a dictionary. Nor do explanations of concepts have any place in a factbook. If, to continue the example, you are unclear of how a tsunami is formed, then you had better look this up in an encyclopedia. A factbook is not intended to do the job of a glossary, a manual, or a textbook.

Nor is a fact a single, isolated piece of information. An enquirer may have a single question in mind, and want a single fact for an answer, but any factbook worth its salt should show how this enquiry fits into a broader frame of reference. No fact exists in isolation. Everything is part of a pattern. It is therefore important to show the pattern. A factbook should say to a reader: 'You asked about X, and here's the answer - but don't forget there's also Y and Z, which can help you understand X further. And, while you're here, have a look at Y and Z anyway, as they're interesting too.' A good factbook, once entered, should put questions in perspective, and also be difficult to leave. There should be a strong temptation to stay awhile, and browse. In *The Cambridge Factfinder*, the organization of information into fields of meaning, sequenced logically, and grouped hierarchically, provides both motivation and means. If the job is done well, answering factual questions proves to be the least trivial of pursuits.

Selecting the facts

A factbook could, in theory, be any size, from a few dozen to thousands of pages. Whatever the size, two considerations are paramount. There should be a balance between the various areas of knowledge covered; and there should be a pragmatic principle at work by which the editor tries to answer those questions which readers are most likely to ask.

Balance is relatively easy to achieve, by devising a scheme which works systematically through the various well-recognized domains of enquiry. In *The Cambridge Factfinder*, this is handled by starting with the most general perspective (the Universe) and finding a coherent path (one of many possible) through physical, biological, historical, geographical, and social domains.

Justifying the selection within each domain is less simple, and any editor has to fall back on the well-tried principle that 'one can please all of the people some of the time ...' In the present case, the task was much aided by the experience of running the *Cambridge Encyclopedia* Datasearch project since 1990. This project enables readers of the *Encyclopedia* to interrogate its database to obtain further information about topics which interest them. By keeping a record of the types of enquiry, it has proved possible to develop a sharpened sense of the kinds of things people want to know about. Examining the question-lists of innumerable pub quiz competitions, and other such games, has provided a further dimension.

Finding your way about

A factbook should be as accurate and as up-to-date as the state of knowledge permits, and *The Cambridge Factfinder* team has made every effort to ensure that these criteria are met. Full use has been made of the database compiled for *The Cambridge Encyclopedia*, which is continually being updated. The comprehensive coverage of the *Encyclopedia* has helped to guarantee the breadth of the present project; and the many specialized reference books in the Cambridge list have proved to be of great value in developing the project's depth of detail. Directly or indirectly, over 250 experts have been involved in generating the information which the *Factfinder* contains.

But it is no use having marvellously up-to-date and accurate facts if readers cannot find them. Critical to the success of any factbook, therefore, is an appropriate means of information retrieval. This is where most factbooks fall down. They may advertise that there are 'hundreds of thousands of facts' within their covers, but if it proves impossible to find the answer to a simple question without having to spend several minutes combing through the pages, the factbook has to be judged a failure. The solution is simple: proper indexing, with a preparedness to set aside sufficient space so that the project gets the index it deserves.

There are, broadly speaking, two ways into a factbook, and both are represented in *The Cambridge Factfinder*:

- One way suits the person who is interested in a general area of knowledge, and who wishes to explore it systematically. This person may not have a specific question in mind, only a vague uncertainty or need for clarification. Often a precise question does not become apparent until a range of possible answers is presented. Such enquirers need a thematic guide to the factbook, where the various types of information are presented conceptually, with as much logical order relating the concepts as it is possible to impose. The logic underlying *The Cambridge Factfinder* is shown on p. ix. Using this information, it should be possible to 'home in' quickly on a broad area, and then to focus on a chosen topic.

- The other way suits the person who does have a precise question in mind - a who, a what, a when, a where. For this person, a thematic approach is of relatively little value. If you wish to find out a fact about the *gull*, for example, you want to be able to go immediately to where in the book this item is located, and not waste time searching for it unfruitfully under such a heading as *sea birds* (it is in fact a shore bird). Similarly, under which heading would you look for information about a particular thing or person? (Does the *Tay Bridge* appear under Communications, Scotland or UK? Is *Leonardo da Vinci* under sculptors, architects, or painters?) All of this uncertainty is avoided through the expedient of an in-depth letter-by-letter index, with appropriate cross-references to handle alternative points of entry. Thus, in the index to this book, *Tay Bridge* is under T and *Leonardo da Vinci* is under L (with cross-references from D and V). The headings are there, too (*bridges* under *B* etc.), as an alternative route to themes and sub-themes. The index of *The Cambridge Factfinder* is far and away the most comprehensive ever prepared for a book of this kind, and it is space well-used.

In short, the opening pages present in a thematic way the various fields or systems of information dealt with in this book. The closing pages present in an alphabetical way the items those systems contain. This dual perspective has been called, in lexicography, an 'index-to-system' approach, and it is the first time that it has been used to its full potential in a factbook. Such an approach adds coherence, increases speed of item look-up, makes the information more accessible, and promotes flexibility by providing alternative routes to answering a question. I hope that, after using the book, it is an opinion that readers will share.

Acknowledgement

A book of this kind is the product of thousands of person-hours of preparatory editorial and design work. I have had the privilege of working with a team of in-house editors – Paul James, Kendall Clarke, Pauline Graham, and Alyson Jones – who have had the onerous task of compiling the bulk of the tabular material, and an in-house designer – Geoff Staff – who has had the unenviable task of supervising the transition from edited copy to printed page. Their contribution to The Cambridge Factfinder has been fundamental, and it is a pleasure to have this opportunity to acknowledge it.

David Crystal

Editor
David Crystal

Illustrators
David Brogan
George Kilgour
John Marshall
Joanna Cameron
European Map Graphics Ltd

Cartography
European Map Graphics Ltd

Design
Sally Jeffery

AREAS OF KNOWLEDGE

This page shows how *The Cambridge Factfinder* is divided into broad areas of knowledge. Also indicated (in roman numerals) are the pages where you will find a much more detailed breakdown of each section in the Table of Contents which follows. For really specific queries, you should use the Index at the back of the book.

TABLE OF CONTENTS

THE UNIVERSE

THE COSMOS

Star distances

Star	Distance (l y)[a]
Proxima Centauri	4.24
Alpha Centauri A	4.34
Alpha Centauri B	4.34
Barnard's Star	5.97
Wolf 359 (CN Leonis)	7.80
Lalande 21185	8.19
UV Ceti A	8.55
UV Ceti B	8.55
Sirius A	8.67
Sirius B	8.67
Ross 154	9.52
Ross 248 (HH Andromedae)	10.37
Epsilon Eridani	10.63
Ross 128 (Fl Virginis)	10.79
L 789–6	11.12
GX Andromedae	11.22
GQ Andromedae	11.22
61 Cygnus A	11.22
61 Cygnus B	11.22
HD 173739	11.25
Epsilon Indi	11.25
Tau Ceti	11.41

[a]l y = light years.

Star magnitudes

Star	Proper name	Magnitude	Distance (l y)[a]
Alpha Canis Majoris	Sirius	−1.47	8.7
Alpha Carinae	Canopus	−0.71	98
Alpha Boötis	Arcturus	−0.06	36
Alpha Centauri	Rigil Kentaurus	+0.01	4.3
Alpha Lyrae	Vega	0.03	26
Alpha Aurigae	Capella	0.05	45
Beta Orionis	Rigel	0.14	815
Alpha Canis Minoris	Procyon	0.34	11
Alpha Orionis	Betelgeuse	0.41	520
Alpha Eridani	Achernar	0.49	118
Beta Centauri	Hadar	0.61	490
Alpha Aquilae	Altair	0.75	16
Alpha Tauri	Aldebaran	0.78	68
Alpha Virginis	Spica	0.91	220
Alpha Scorpii	Antares	0.92	520
Alpha Piscis Austrini	Fomalhaut	1.15	23
Beta Geminorum	Pollux	1.16	35
Alpha Cygni	Deneb	1.26	1600
Beta Crucis	Mimosa	1.28	490
Alpha Leonis	Regulus	1.33	85
Alpha Crucis	Acrux	1.39	370

[a]l y = light years.

The constellations

Latin name	English name
Andromeda	Andromeda
Antlia	Air Pump
Apus	Bird of Paradise
Aquarius (Z)	Water Bearer
Aquila	Eagle
Ara	Altar
Aries (Z)	Ram
Auriga	Charioteer
Boötes	Herdsman
Caelum	Chisel
Camelopardalis	Giraffe
Cancer (Z)	Crab
Canes Venatici	Hunting Dogs
Canis Major	Great Dog
Canis Minor	Little Dog
Capricornus (Z)	Sea Goat
Carina	Keel
Cassiopeia	Cassiopeia
Centaurus	Centaur
Cepheus	Cepheus
Cetus	Whale
Chamaeleon	Chameleon
Circinus	Compasses
Columba	Dove
Coma Berenices	Berenice's Hair
Corona Australis	Southern Crown
Corona Borealis	Northern Crown
Corvus	Crow
Crater	Cup
Crux	Southern Cross
Cygnus	Swan
Delphinus	Dolphin
Dorado	Swordfish
Draco	Dragon
Equuleus	Little Horse
Eridanus	River Eridanus
Fornax	Furnace
Gemini (Z)	Twins
Grus	Crane
Hercules	Hercules
Horologium	Clock
Hydra	Sea Serpent
Hydrus	Water Snake
Indus	Indian
Lacerta	Lizard
Leo (Z)	Lion
Leo Minor	Little Lion
Lepus	Hare
Libra (Z)	Scales
Lupus	Wolf
Lynx	Lynx
Lyra	Harp
Mensa	Table
Microscopium	Microscope
Monoceros	Unicorn
Musca	Fly
Norma	Level
Octans	Octant
Ophiuchus	Serpent Bearer
Orion	Orion
Pavo	Peacock
Pegasus	Winged Horse
Perseus	Perseus
Phoenix	Phoenix
Pictor	Easel
Pisces (Z)	Fishes
Piscis Austrinus	Southern Fish
Puppis	Ship's Stern
Pyxis	Mariner's Compass
Reticulum	Net
Sagitta	Arrow
Sagittarius (Z)	Archer
Scorpius (Z)	Scorpion
Sculptor	Sculptor
Scutum	Shield
Serpens	Serpent
Sextans	Sextant
Taurus (Z)	Bull
Telescopium	Telescope
Triangulum	Triangle
Triangulum Australe	Southern Triangle
Tucana	Toucan
Ursa Major	Great Bear
Ursa Minor	Little Bear
Vela	Sails
Virgo (Z)	Virgin
Volans	Flying Fish
Vulpecula	Fox

Z = zodiac constellation.

The northern sky

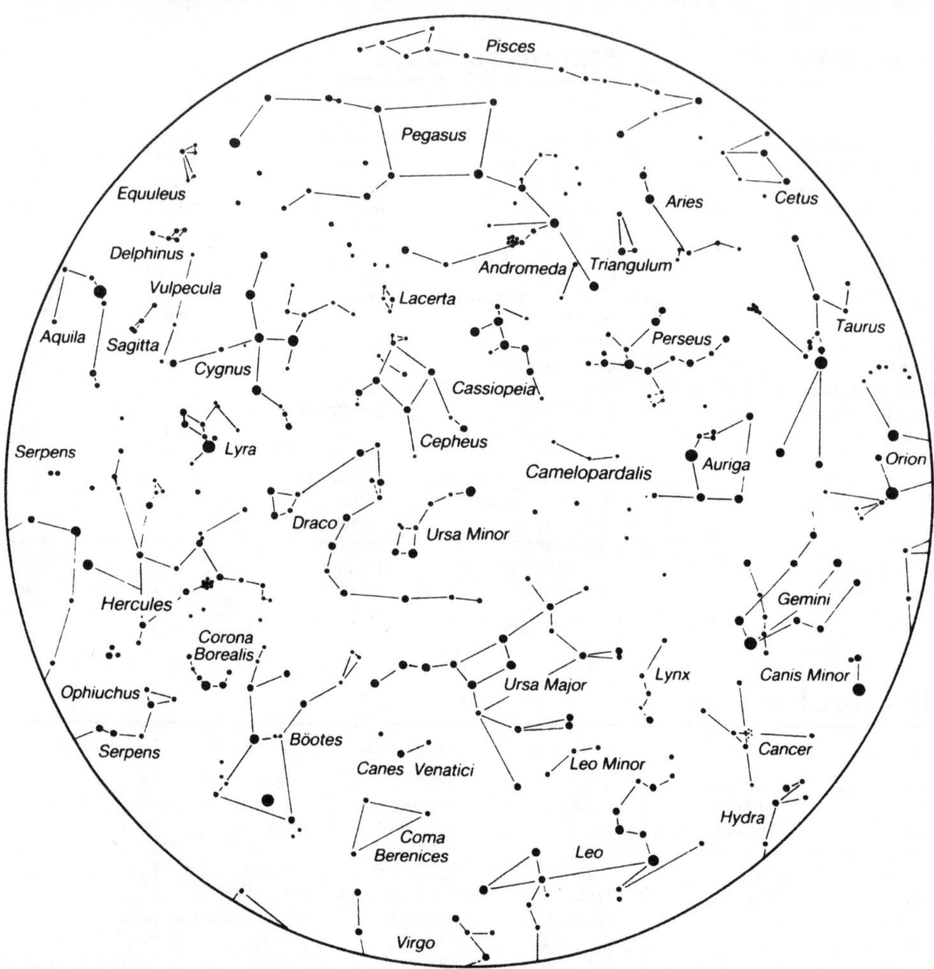

'Alpha' stars within constellations[a]

Name	Constellation	Name	Constellation	Name	Constellation
Achernar	Eridanus	Ankaa	Phoenix	Fomalhaut	Piscis Austrinus
Acrux	Crux	Antares	Scorpius	Hamal	Aries
Acubens	Cancer	Arcturus	Boötes	Kaïtain	Pisces
Al Giedi	Capricornus	Arneb	Lepus	Kitalpha	Equuleus
Al Rijil	Centaurus	Atria	Triangulum Australe	Markab	Pegasus
Aldebaran	Taurus	Betelgeuse	Orion	Men	Lupus
Alderamin	Cepheus	Canopus	Carina	Menkar	Cetus
Alkes	Crater	Capella	Auriga	Mirphak	Perseus
Alkhiba	Corvus	Castor	Gemini	Phakt	Columba
Alnair	Grus	Choo	Ara	Polaris	Ursa Minor
Alphard	Hydra	Cor Caroli	Canes Venatici	Praecipua	Leo Minor
Alphekka	Corona Borealis	Deneb	Cygnus	Procyon	Canis Minor
Alpheratz	Andromeda	Diadem	Coma Berenices	Rasalgethi	Hercules
Altair	Aquila	Dubhe	Ursa Major	Rasalhague	Ophiuchus

[a]'Alpha' denotes the brightest star in a constellation.

The southern sky

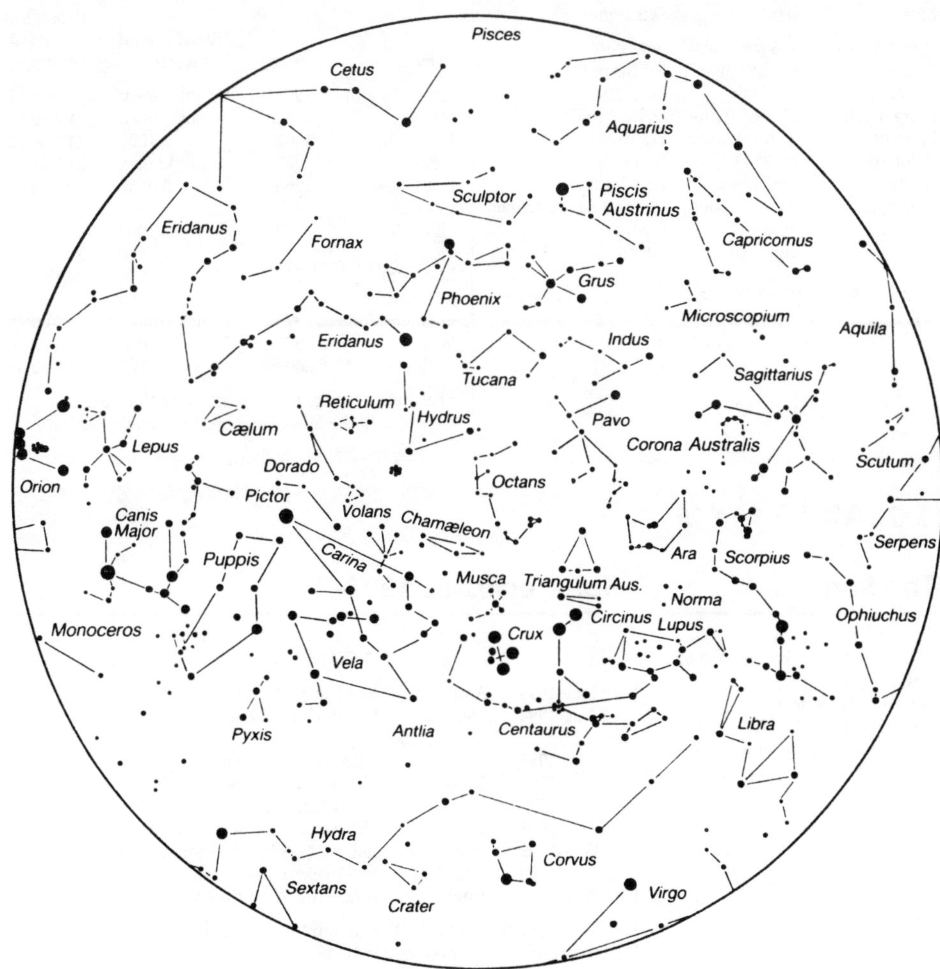

'Alpha' stars within constellations[a] (continued)

Name	Constellation	Name	Constellation	Name	Constellation
Rasalmothallah	Triangulum	Shedir	Cassiopeia	Thuban	Draco
Regulus	Leo	Sirius	Canis Major	Unukalhai	Serpens
Rukbat	Sagittarius	Spica	Virgo	Vega	Lyra
Sadalmelik	Aquarius	Svalocin	Delphinus	Zubenelgenubi	Libra

[a]'Alpha' denotes the brightest star in a constellation.

Meteor showers

Name	*Dates*	*Star region*
Quadrantids	1–6 Jan	Beta Boötis
Lyrids	19–22 Apr	Nu Herculis
Eta Aquarids	1–8 May	Eta Aquarii
Delta Aquarids	15 Jul–10 Aug	Delta Aquarii
Perseids	27 Jul–17 Aug	Eta Persei
Orionids	15–25 Oct	Nu Orionis
Leonids	14–20 Nov	Zeta Leonis
Andromedids	26 Nov–4 Dec	Gamma Andromedae
Geminids	9–13 Dec	Castor
Ursids	20–22 Dec	Kocab

Historic comets

Name	*First seen*	*Period of orbit (in years)*	*Date of last perihelion[a] passage*
Arend-Roland	1957	not known	8 Apr 57
Mrkos	1957	not known	1 Aug 57
Humason	1962	3 000	14 May 62
Ikeya	1963	not known	21 Mar 63
Ikeya–Seki	1965	879.88	21 Oct 65
Tago–Sato–Kosaka	1969	420 000	21 Dec 69
Bennett	1970	1 680	20 Mar 70
Kohoutek	1973	75 000	28 Dec 73
Kobayashi–Berger–Milon	1975	not known	5 Sep 75
West	1976	500 000	25 Feb 76
Halley	240 BC	76.1	9 Feb 86

[a]'Perihelion' refers to the position of the closest approach to the Sun of an object in an elliptical orbit.

SOLAR SYSTEM

The Sun

Age 4 500 000 000 years
Diameter 1 392 000 km/864 950 mi
Mass 2×10^{30} kg
Mean density 1.4 g/cm^3
Luminosity 3.9×10^{27} kW
Effective surface temperature 5 770 K
Average orbital velocity 107 210 kph/66 620 mph

Solar eclipses 1994–9

Date	*Extent of eclipse*	*Visible from parts of*[a]
10 May 1994	Annular[b]	Mid-Pacific, N America, N Africa
3 Nov 1994	Total	Indian Ocean, S Atlantic, S America, Mid-Pacific
29 Apr 1995	Annular[b]	S Pacific, S America
24 Oct 1995	Total	Middle East, S Asia, S Pacific
9 Mar 1997	Total	C & N Asia, Arctic
26 Feb 1998	Total	Mid-Pacific, C America, N Atlantic
22 Aug 1998	Annular[b]	Indonesia, S Pacific, Indian Ocean
16 Feb 1999	Annular[b]	Indian Ocean, Australia
11 Aug 1999	Total	N Atlantic, N Europe, Middle East, N India

[a] The eclipse begins in the first area named. [b] In an annular eclipse a ring-shaped part of the Sun remains visible.

Planetary data (1)

Planet	*Distance from sun maximum million km*	*maximum million mi*	*minimum million km*	*minimum million mi*	*Sidereal period*[a]	*Axial rotation (equatorial)*	*Diameter (equatorial) km*	*Diameter (equatorial) mi*
Mercury	69.4	43.0	46.8	29.0	88 d	58d 16h	4 878	3 031
Venus	109.0	67.6	107.6	66.7	224.7 d	243 d	12 104	7 521
Earth	152.6	94.6	147.4	91.4	365.26 d[b]	23 h 56 m 4 s	12 756	7 927
Mars	249.2	154.5	207.3	128.5	687 d	24 h 37 m 23 s	6 794	4 222
Jupiter	817.4	506.8	741.6	459.8	11.86 y	9 h 50 m 30 s	142 800	88 700
Saturn	1 512	937.6	1 346	834.6	29.46 y	10 h 14 m	120 000	74 600
Uranus	3 011	1 867	2 740	1 699	84.01 y	16–28 h[c]	52 000	32 300
Neptune	4 543	2 817	4 466	2 769	164.79 y	18–20 h[c]	48 400	30 000
Pluto	7 346	4 566	4 461	2 766	247.7 y	6 d 9 h	1 145	711

[a]'Sidereal period' refers here to the period of revolution around the Sun with respect to the stars.

[b] precisely 365 d 5 h 48 m 46 s [c] Different latitudes rotate at different speeds. y: years d: days h: hours m: minutes s: seconds km: kilometres mi: miles

Planetary data (2)

Mercury
Atmosphere hydrogen, helium, neon; *satellites* 0; *features* lunar-like crust, crustal faulting, small magnetic field.

Venus
Atmosphere carbon dioxide; *satellites* 0; *features* shrouded in clouds, 70% rolling plains, 10% highlands, 20% lowlands, craters.

Earth
Atmosphere nitrogen, oxygen; *satellites* 1; *features* liquid water oceans filling lowland regions between continents, permanent ice caps at each pole, unique in supporting life, magnetic field.

Mars
Atmosphere carbon dioxide; *satellites* 2; *features* cratered uplands, lowland plains, massive volcanic regions.

Jupiter
Atmosphere hydrogen, methane; *satellites* 16; *features* covered by clouds, craters, volcanic features, dark ring of dust, magnetic field.

Saturn
Atmosphere hydrogen, helium; *satellites* 18 (the exact number is not yet determined, but could be 18 or more); *features* several cloud layers, magnetic field, thousands of rings.

Uranus *Atmosphere* methane, helium, hydrogen; *satellites* 15; *features* clouds, layers of mist, magnetic field, c. 11 rings.

Neptune
Atmosphere methane, hydrogen; *satellites* 2; *features* unable to detect telescopically from Earth.

Pluto
Atmosphere methane; *satellites* 1; *features* unable to detect telescopically from Earth, thought to be partially covered with frozen methane.

The 'asteroid belt' is found mainly in a large series of orbits lying between Mars and Jupiter.

Planetary satellites

	Year discovered	*Distance from planet* km	mi	*Diameter* km	mi
Earth					
Moon	–	384 000	238 000	3 476	2 155
Mars					
Phobos	1877	938 000	583 000	27	17
Deimos	1877	2 346 000	1 458 000	15	9
Jupiter					
Metis	1979	128 000	79 000	40	25
Adrastea	1979	129 000	80 000	24	15
Amalthea	1892	181 000	112 000	270	168
Thebe	1979	222 000	138 000	100	60
Io	1610	422 000	262 000	3 650	5 850
Europa	1610	671 000	417 000	3 400	1 925
Ganymede	1610	1 070 000	665 000	5 260	3 270
Callisto	1610	1 883 000	1 170 000	4 800	3 000
Leda	1974	11 110 000	6 904 000	20	12
Himalia	1904	11 480 000	7 134 000	180	110
Lysithea	1938	11 720 000	7 283 000	40	25
Elara	1905	11 740 000	7 295 000	80	50
Ananke	1951	21 200 000	13 174 000	30	19
Carme	1938	22 600 000	14 044 000	40	25
Pasiphae	1908	23 500 000	14 603 000	50	30
Sinope	1914	23 700 000	14 727 000	40	25
Saturn					
Atlas	1980	138 000	86 000	40	25
1980 S27	1980	139 000	86 000	100	60
1980 S26	1980	142 000	88 000	100	60
Epimetheus	1980	151 000	94 000	140	90
Janus	1980	151 000	94 000	200	120
Mimas	1789	186 000	116 000	390	240
Enceladus	1789	238 000	148 000	500	310
Calypso	1980	295 000	183 000	30	19
Telesto	1980	295 000	183 000	24	15
Tethys	1684	295 000	183 000	1 050	650
Dione	1684	377 000	234 000	1 120	700
Dione B	1982	378 000	235 000	15	9
Rhea	1672	527 000	327 000	1 530	950
Titan	1655	1 222 000	759 000	5 150	3 200
Hyperion	1848	1 481 000	920 000	400	250
Iapetus	1671	3 560 000	2 212 000	1 440	900
Phoebe	1898	12 950 000	8 047 000	160	100
Uranus					
Miranda	1948	130 000	81 000	400	250
Ariel	1851	191 000	119 000	1 300	800
Umbriel	1851	266 000	165 000	1 100	700
Titania	1787	436 000	271 000	1 600	1 000
Oberon	1787	583 000	362 000	1 600	1 000

A further ten satellites at distances from 50 000–86 000 km, and with diameters 15–170 km, were discovered in 1986.

Neptune					
Triton	1846	355 000	221 000	3 800	2 400
Nereid	1949	5 510 000	3 424 000	300	190
Pluto					
Charon	1978	20 000 000	12 500 000	1 000	620

The near side of the Moon

The lunar 'maria'[a]

Latin name	*English name*	*Latin name*	*English name*
Lacus Somniorum	Lake of Dreams	Mare Serenitatis	Sea of Serenity
Mare Australe	Southern Sea	Mare Smythii	Smyth's Sea
Mare Crisium	Sea of Crises	Mare Spumans	Foaming Sea
Mare Fecunditatis	Sea of Fertility	Mare Tranquillitatis	Sea of Tranquillity
Mare Frigoris	Sea of Cold	Mare Undarum	Sea of Waves
Mare Humboldtianum	Humboldt's Sea	Mare Vaporum	Sea of Vapours
Mare Humorum	Sea of Humours	Oceanus Procellarum	Ocean of Storms
Mare Imbrium	Sea of Showers	Palus Epidemiarum	Marsh of Epidemics
Mare Ingenii	Sea of Geniuses	Palus Putredinis	Marsh of Decay
Mare Marginis	Marginal Sea	Palus Somnii	Marsh of Sleep
Mare Moscoviense	Moscow Sea	Sinus Adstuum	Bay of Heats
Mare Nectaris	Sea of Nectar	Sinus Iridum	Bay of Rainbows
Mare Nubium	Sea of Clouds	Sinus Medii	Central Bay
Mare Orientale	Eastern Sea	Sinus Roris	Bay of Dew

[a]'Maria' refers to the lowland areas of the moon flooded by lava 3.5 billion years ago.

The far side of the Moon

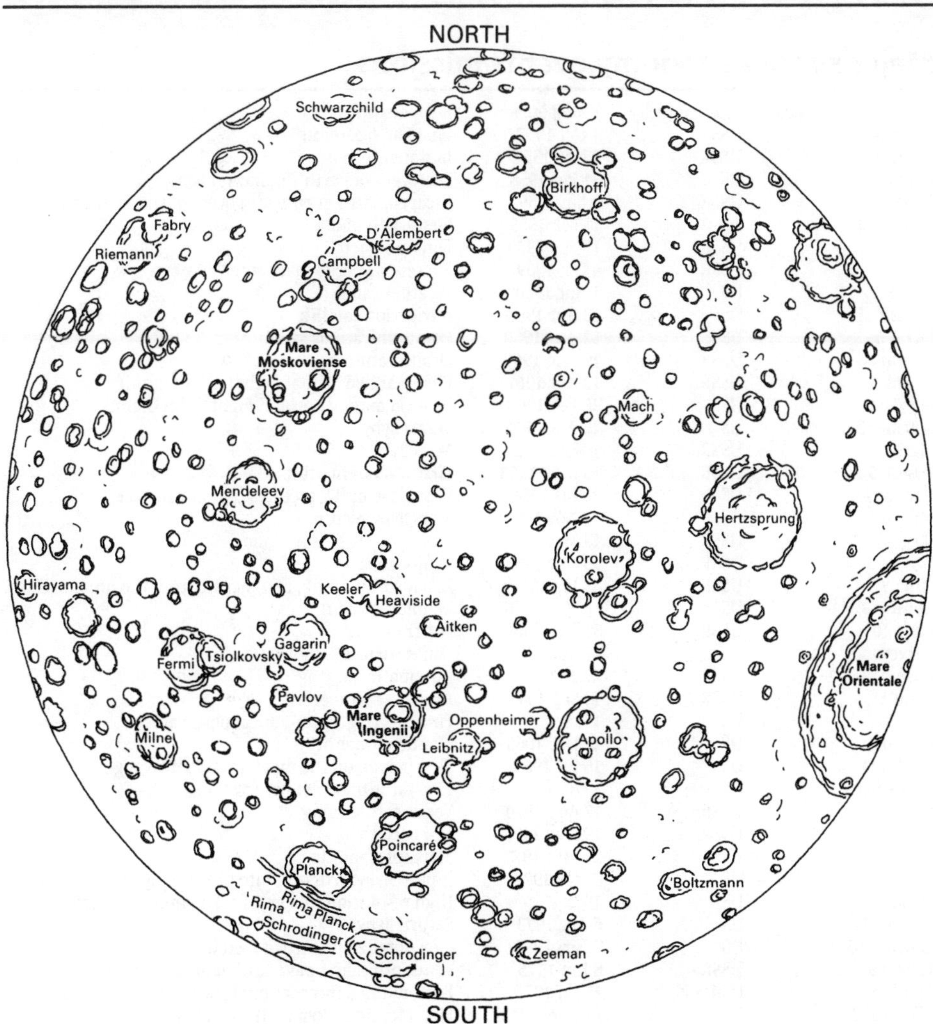

Lunar eclipses 1993–2000

Date	*Extent of eclipse*	*Time of mid-eclipse*	*Where visible*
4 Jun 1993	Total	13.02	Pacific, Australia, SE Asia
29 Nov 1993	Total	06.26	N and S America
25 May 1994	Partial	03.32	C and S America, part of N America, W Africa
15 Apr 1995	Partial	12.19	Pacific, Australia, SE Asia
4 Apr 1996	Total	00.11	Africa, SE Europe, S America
27 Sep 1996	Total	02.55	C and S America, part of N America, W Africa
24 Mar 1997	Partial	04.41	C and S America, part of N America, W Africa
16 Sep 1997	Total	18.47	S Africa, E Africa, Australia
28 Jul 1999	Partial	11.34	Pacific, Australia, SE Asia
21 Jan 2000	Total	04.45	N America, part of S America, SW Europe, W Africa
16 Jul 2000	Total	13.57	Pacific, Australia, SE Asia

The universe

SPACE EXPLORATION

Major space astronomy events/missions

Name of event/mission	*Country/agency*	*Year of launch*	*Event description*
Sputnik 1	USSR	4 Oct 1957	First Earth satellite
Sputnik 2	USSR	3 Nov 1957	Biosatellite
Explorer 1	US	31 Jan 1958	Discovery of Earth's radiation belts
Luna 1	USSR	2 Jan 1959	Escaped Earth gravity; discovery of the solar wind
Vanguard 2	US	17 Feb 1959	First Earth photo
Luna 2	USSR	12 Sep 1959	Lunar impact
Luna 3	USSR	4 Oct 1959	First lunar photo (dark side)
TIROS 1	US	1 Apr 1960	Weather satellite
Transit 1B	US	13 Apr 1960	Navigation satellite
ECHO 1	US	12 Aug 1960	Communications satellite
Sputnik 5	USSR	19 Aug 1960	Orbited animals
Vostok 1	USSR	12 Apr 1961	First manned orbital flight (Yuri Gagarin)
Mercury	US	20 Feb 1962	First US manned orbital flight (John Glenn)
Mariner 2	US	26 Aug 1962	Venus flyby
Mars 1	USSR	1 Nov 1962	Mars flyby
Vostok 6	USSR	16 June 1963	First woman in orbit
Ranger 7	US	28 Jul 1964	First close-up TV pictures of lunar surface
Mariner 4	US	28 Nov 1964	Mars flyby pictures
Voskhod 2	USSR	18 Mar 1965	First spacewalk (AA Leonov)
Venera 3	USSR	16 Nov 1965	Venus impact
Luna 9	USSR	31 Jan 1966	Lunar soft landing; first picture from the lunar surface
Gemini 8	US	16 Mar 1966	Manned docking
Luna 10	USSR	31 Mar 1966	Lunar orbiter
Surveyor 3	US	17 Apr 1967	Lunar surface sampler
Cosmos 186/188	USSR	22/28 Oct 1967	Automatic docking
Zond 5	USSR	14 Sep 1968	Animals moon orbit
OAO 2	US	1968	First orbiting astronomical observatory
Apollo 8	US	21 Dec 1968	Manned lunar orbit
Apollo 11	US	16 Jul 1969	First person on the moon (Neil Armstrong)
Copernicus	US	1970	First far ultra-violet observatory
Venera 7	USSR	17 Aug 1970	Venus soft landing
Mars 2	USSR	19 May 1971	Mars orbit
Mars 3	USSR	28 May 1971	Mars soft landing
Pioneer 10	US	3 Mar 1972	Jupiter flyby; crossed Pluto orbit; escaped Solar System
Skylab	US	1973	High resolution images of solar corona in X-rays
Pioneer 11	US	6 Apr 1973	Saturn flyby
Mariner 10	US	3 Nov 1973	First detailed picture of Mercury
Venera 9	USSR	8 Jun 1975	Venus orbit; first picture of Venusian surface
Apollo/Soyuz	US/USSR	15 Jul 1975	First manned international cooperative mission
Viking 1, 2	US	Aug/Sep 1975	First pictures taken on the Martian surface
Voyager 1, 2	US	Aug/Sep 1977	First images of Jupiter, Saturn, Uranus and Neptune
IUE	US/UK/ESA	1978	First international space observatory
ISEE C	US	12 Aug 1978	Comet intercept
STS 1	US	12 Apr 1981	First launch of 'Columbia' space shuttle
STS 6	US	4 Apr 1983	First launch of 'Challenger'
Soyuz T 9	USSR	27 Jun 1983	Construction in space
STS 9	US	28 Nov 1983	First flight of the ESA spacelab
STS 41 D	US	30 Aug 1984	First launch of 'Discovery'
STS 51 A	US	8 Nov 1984	Recovery of satellites 'Westar 6' and 'Palapa B2'
Vega 1	USSR	15 Dec 1984	Halley flyby
STS 51 J	US	3 Oct 1985	First launch of 'Atlantis'
Giotto	ESA	1986	First high resolution image of Halley's nucleus
STS 26	US	29 Sep 1988	First launch after 'Challenger' disaster
Magellan	US	5 May 1989	Global radar map of Venus
STS 34	US	18 Oct 1989	Galileo launch
Muses A	Japan	24 Jan 1990	Two satellites placed in orbit round the moon
STS 31	US/ESA	24 Apr 1990	Launch of Hubble Space Telescope
STS 41	US/ESA	6 Oct 1990	Launch of 'Ulysses'; first flight above the solar poles
STS 37	US	5 Apr 1991	Launch of Compton Gamma Ray Observatory

(ESA = European Space Agency)

Satellite launch centres

Country	*Launch base*	*Organisation responsible*	*First launch*
USA	Cape Canaveral	US Air Force/NASA	31 Jan 1958 (Explorer 1)
	Kennedy Space Center	NASA	9 Nov 1967 (Apollo 4)
	Vandenberg AFB	US Air Force/SAMTO/NASA	28 Feb 1959 (Discoverer 1)
	Wallops Island	NASA Goddard Space Flight Center	16 Feb 1961 (Explorer 9)
CIS	Kapustin Yar, or Volgograd cosmodrome	Ministry of Defence/Academy of Sciences/Intercosmos	16 Mar 1962 (Cosmos 1)
	Plesetsk, or Northern cosmodrome	Ministry of Defence/Academy of Sciences	17 March 1966 (Cosmos 112)
	Tyuratam Leninsk, or Baikonur cosmodrome	Ministry of Defence/Academy of Sciences	4 Oct 1957 (Sputnik 1)
Australia	Woomera Range	WRE/British DTI/ELDO	29 Nov 1967 (Wresat)
China	Jiuquan SLC	Ministry of Defence/MOA	24 Apr 1970 (SKW1/Tungfanghung)
	Xichang SLC	MOA	29 Jan 1984 (STW1)
France	Guianan Space Centre at Kouru	CNES/ESA/Arianespace	10 March 1970 (Dial)
	Hammaguir/Colombia Bechar	CIEES/CNES	26 Nov 1965 (A1 'Asterix')
India	SHAR/Sriharikota Range	ISRO	18 Jul 1980 (Rohini RS1)
Italy	San Marco platform	CRA/University of Rome	26 Apr 1967 (San Marco 2)
Japan	Kagoshima Space Centre	ISAS/University of Tokyo	11 Feb 1970 (Ohsumi)
	Tanegashima Space Centre	Nasda	9 Sep 1975 (ETS1/Kiku)
Under construction in the 1990s			
Brazil	Alcantara Launch Centre	Ministry of Aeronautics/COBAE/CTA	planned for mid 1990s
Sweden	Esrange, Kiruna	Swedish Space Corporation	during the late 1990s

International space launchers

The major launch vehicles in use and some of their important predecessors. The data refer to lift capacity (given in kg/lb, in most cases to the nearest hundred) and year of launch.

LEO: low Earth orbit (c. 200 km/125 mi)
GEO: geosynchronous Earth orbit (36 000 km/22 500 mi)
ETO: elliptical transfer orbit (intermediate between LEO and GEO)

CIS

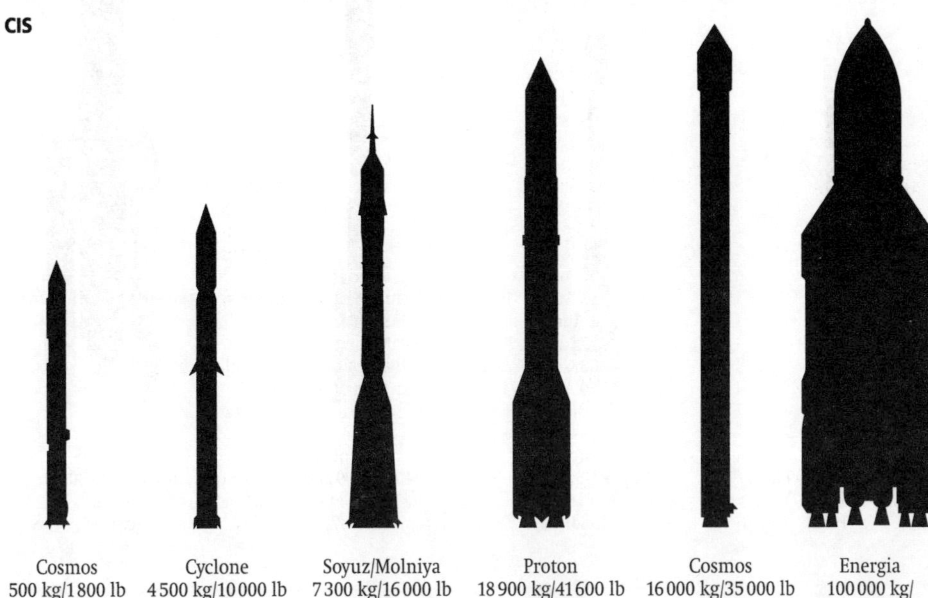

Cosmos 500 kg/1800 lb to LEO (1964)

Cyclone 4 500 kg/10 000 lb to LEO (1966)

Soyuz/Molniya 7 300 kg/16 000 lb to LEO 1 600 kg/3 500 lb to ETO (1960)

Proton 18 900 kg/41 600 lb to LEO 1 600 kg/3 500 lb to GEO (1965)

Cosmos 16 000 kg/35 000 lb to LEO (1985)

Energia 100 000 kg/ 220 000 lb to LEO (1987)

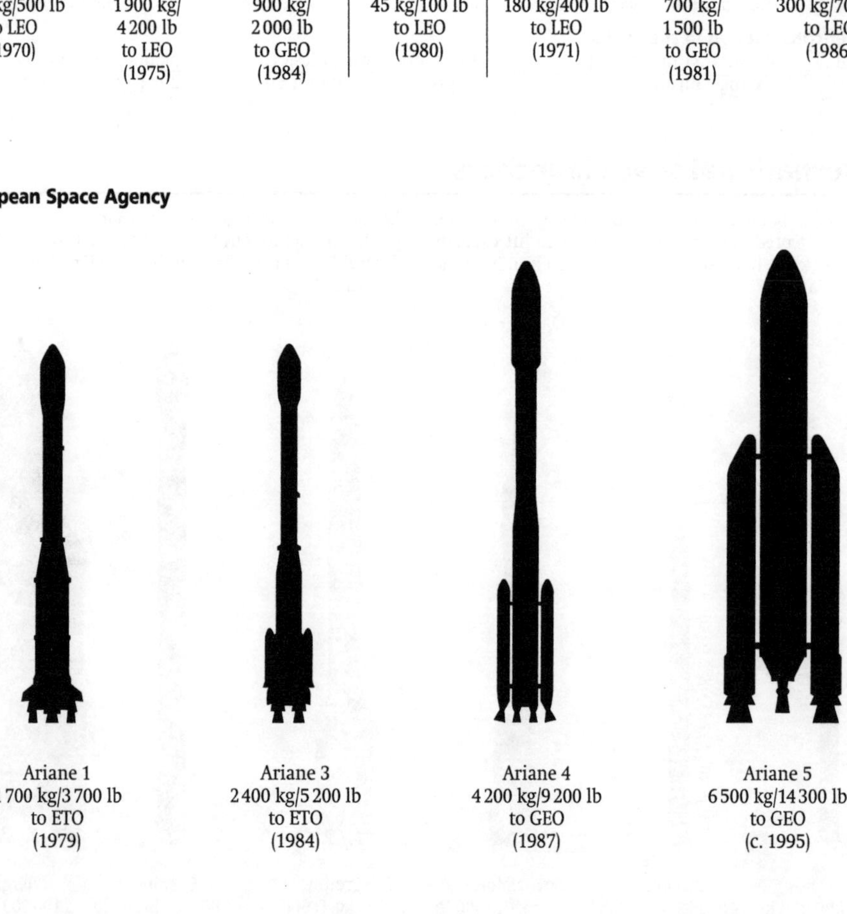
China
India
Japan
Long March 1
225 kg/500 lb
to LEO
(1970)
Long March 2
1 900 kg/
4 200 lb
to LEO
(1975)
Long March 3
900 kg/
2 000 lb
to GEO
(1984)
SLV-3
45 kg/100 lb
to LEO
(1980)
MU-3
180 kg/400 lb
to LEO
(1971)
N-2
700 kg/
1 500 lb
to GEO
(1981)
H-1
300 kg/700 lb
to LEO
(1986)
European Space Agency
Ariane 1
1 700 kg/3 700 lb
to ETO
(1979)
Ariane 3
2 400 kg/5 200 lb
to ETO
(1984)
Ariane 4
4 200 kg/9 200 lb
to GEO
(1987)
Ariane 5
6 500 kg/14 300 lb
to GEO
(c. 1995)

United States of America

Scout
800 kg/400 lb
to LEO
(1960)

Delta
1 700 kg/3 700 lb
to LEO
(1960)

Scout
270 kg/600 lb
to LEO
(1979)

Space Shuttle
24 400 kg/53 700 lb
to LEO
(1981)

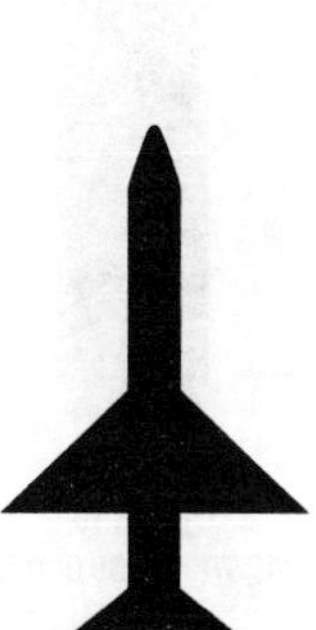

Pegasus
455 kg/1 000 lb
to LEO
(1990)

Taurus
1450 kg/3200 lb
to LEO
(1992)

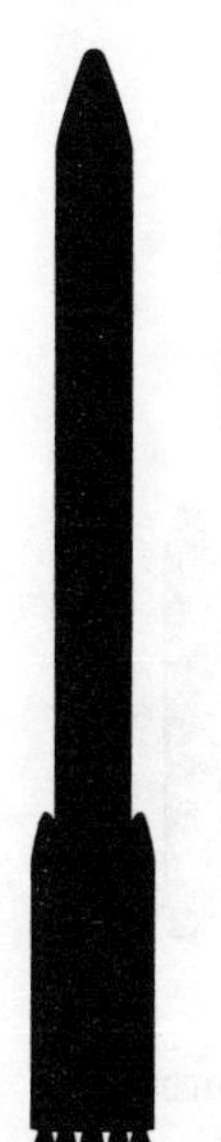

Delta II - 6925
3 990 kg/8 780 lb
to LEO
(1989)

Delta II - 7925
5045 kg/11 100 lb
to LEO
(1990)

United States of America (continued)

Atlas
1700 kg/3 700 lb
to LEO
(1963)

Atlas E
820 kg/1 800 lb
to LEO
(1974)

Atlas I
5 580 kg/12 300 lb
to LEO
(1990)

Atlas II
6 395 kg/14 100 lb
to LEO
(1991)

Atlas IIA
6 760 kg/14 900 lb
to LEO
(1991)

Atlas IIAS
8 390 kg/18 500 lb
to LEO
(1993)

Titan 3B
3 900 kg/8 600 lb
to LEO
(1966)

Titan 34D
13 600 kg/30 000 lb
to LEO
(1984)

Titan II SLV
1 905 kg/4 200 lb
to LEO
(1988)

Titan III
14 515 kg/32 000 lb
to LEO
(1989)

Titan IV
17 700 kg/39 000 lb
to LEO
(1989)

THE EARTH

HISTORY

The developing world

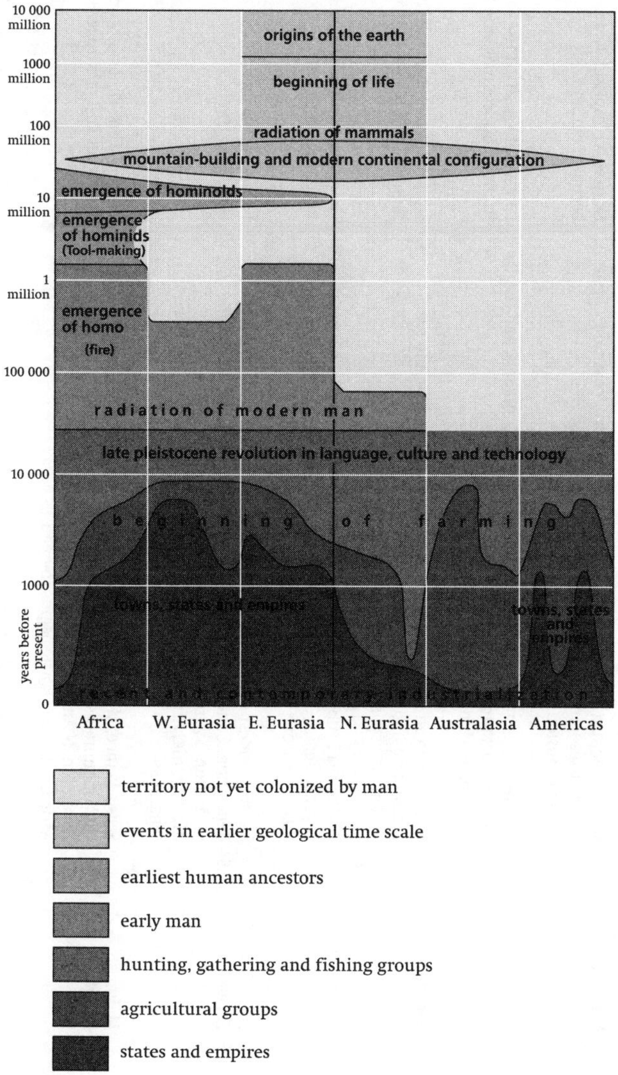

Africa W. Eurasia E. Eurasia N. Eurasia Australasia Americas

- territory not yet colonized by man
- events in earlier geological time scale
- earliest human ancestors
- early man
- hunting, gathering and fishing groups
- agricultural groups
- states and empires

Major ice age periods

A schematic presentation of the major glacial periods (black) in the Earth's history. It is likely that a number of glaciations occurred within each epoch. Note the change in scale on the time axis at 1 000 million years ago.

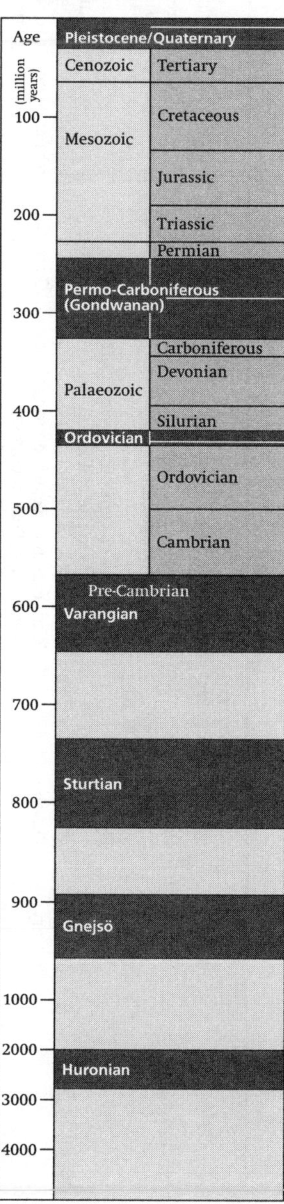

Geological time scale

Eon	*Era*	*Period*	*Epoch*	*Million years before present*	*Geological events*	*Sea life*	*Land life*
Phanerozoic	Cenozoic	Quaternary	Holocene		Glaciers recede. Sea level rises. Climate becomes more equable.	As now.	Forests flourish again. Humans acquire agriculture and technology.
				0.01			
			Pleistocene		Widespread glaciers melt periodically causing seas to rise and fall.	As now.	Many plant forms perish. Small mammals abundant. Primitive humans established.
				2.0			
		Tertiary	Pliocene		Continents and oceans adopting their present form. Present climatic distribution established. Ice caps develop.	Giant sharks extinct. Many fish varieties.	Some plants and mammals die out. Primates flourish.
				5.1			
			Miocene		Seas recede further. European and Asian land masses join. Heavy rain causes massive erosion. Red Sea opens.	Bony fish common. Giant sharks.	Grasses widespread. Grazing mammals become common.
				24.6			
			Oligocene		Seas recede. Extensive movements of Earth's crust produce new mountains (eg Alpine–Himalayan chain).	Crabs, mussels, and snails evolve.	Forests diminish. Grasses appear. Pachyderms, canines, and felines develop.
				38.0			
			Eocene		Mountain formation continues. Glaciers common in high mountain ranges. Greenland separates. Australia separates.	Whales adapt to sea.	Large tropical jungles. Primitive forms of modern mammals established.
				54.9			
			Paleocene		Widespread subsidence of land. Seas advance again. Considerable volcanic activity. Europe emerges.	Many reptiles become extinct.	Flowering plants widespread. First primates. Giant reptiles extinct.
				65			
	Mesozoic	Cretaceous	Late Early	 97.5	Swamps widespread. Massive alluvial deposition. Continuing limestone formation. S America separates from Africa. India, Africa and Antarctica separate.	Turtles, rays, and now-common fish appear.	Flowering plants established. Dinosaurs become extinct.
				144			
		Jurassic	Malm Dogger Lias	 163 188	Seas advance. Much river formation. High mountains eroded. Limestone formation. N America separates from Africa. Central Atlantic begins to open.	Reptiles dominant.	Early flowers. Dinosaurs dominant. Mammals still primitive. First birds.
				213			
		Triassic	Late Middle	 231	Desert conditions widespread. Hot climate slowly becomes warm and wet.	Ichthyosaurs, flying fish, and crustaceans appear.	Ferns and conifers thrive. First mammals, dinosaurs, and flies.

			Early	243	Break up of Pangea into supercontinents Gondwana (S) and Laurasia (N).		
				248			
	Paleozoic	Permian	Late Early	 258	Some sea areas cut off to form lakes. Earth movements form mountains. Glaciation in southern hemisphere.	Some shelled fish become extinct.	Deciduous plants. Reptiles dominant. Many insect varieties.
				286			
		Carboniferous	Pennsylvanian Mississippian	 320	Sea-beds rise to form new land areas. Enormous swamps. Partly-rotted vegetation forms coal.	Amphibians and sharks abundant.	Extensive evergreen forests. Reptiles breed on land. Some insects develop wings.
				360			
		Devonian	Late Middle Early	 374 387	Collision of continents causing mountain formation (Appalachians, Caledonides, and Urals). Sea deeper but narrower. Climatic zones forming. Iapetus ocean closed.	Fish abundant. Primitive sharks. First amphibians.	Leafy plants. Some invertebrates adapt to land. First insects.
				408			
		Silurian	Pridoli Ludlow Wenlock Llandovery	 414 421 428	New mountain ranges form. Sea level varies periodically. Extensive shallow sea over the Sahara.	Large vertebrates.	First leafless land plants.
				438			
		Ordovician	Ashgill Caradoc Llandeilo Llanvirn Arenig Tremadoc	 448 458 468 478 488	Shore lines still quite variable. Increasing sedimentation. Europe and N America moving together.	First vertebrates. Coral reefs develop.	None.
				505			
		Cambrian	Merioneth St David's Caerfai	 525 540	Much volcanic activity, and long periods of marine sedimentation.	Shelled invertebrates. Trilobites.	None.
				590			
Proterozoic	Precambrian	Vendian			Shallow seas advance and retreat over land areas. Atmosphere uniformly warm.	Seaweed. Algae and invertebrates.	None.
				650			
		Riphean	Late Middle Early	900 1300	Intense deformation and metamorphism.	Earliest marine life and fossils.	None.
				1600			
		Early Proterozoic			Shallow shelf seas. Formation of carbonate sediments and 'red beds'.	First appearance of stromatolites.	None.
				2500			
Archaean		Archaean (Azoic)			Banded iron formations. Formation of the Earth's crust and oceans.	None.	None.
				4600			

STRUCTURE

The Earth

Age 4 500 000 000 years
Area 509 600 000 sq km/197 000 000 sq mi
Mass 6.0 × 10^{24} kg
Land surface 148 000 000 sq km/57 000 000 sq mi (c. 29% of total area)
Water surface 361 000 000 sq km/140 000 000 sq mi (c. 71% of total area)
Circumference (equator) 40 076 km/24 902 mi
Circumference (meridian) 40 000 km/24 860 mi
Diameter (equator) 12 757 km/7 927 mi
Diameter (meridian) 12 714 km/7 900 mi
Period of axial rotation 23 h 56 m 4.0996 s
Lithosphere 80 km/50 mi thick
Thickness of upper mantle 700 km/430 mi
Thickness of lower mantle 2 200 km/1 370 mi
Thickness of outer core 2 250 km/1 400 mi
Radius of inner core 3 480 km/2 160 mi
Density of core 13.09 g/cm^3
Temperature at core 4 500 °C

The structure of the Earth

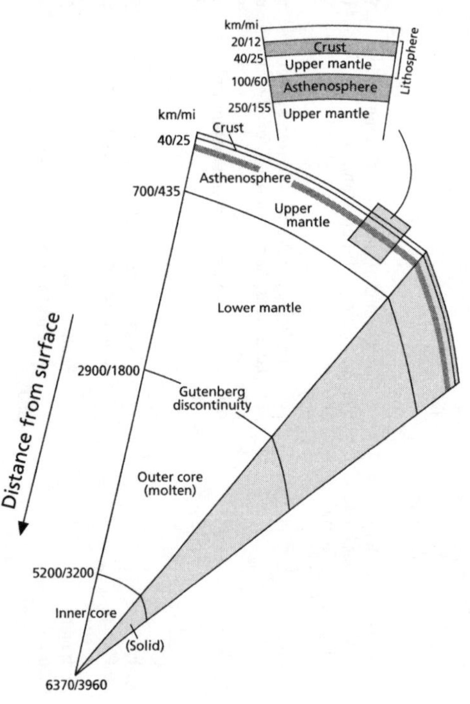

Earth's crust composition

This pie chart shows percentages of the most abundant elements in the Earth's crust.

a Oxygen 46.6%
b Silicon 27.72%
c Aluminium 8.13%
d Iron 5.0%
e Calcium 3.63%
f Sodium 2.83%
g Potassium 2.59%
h Magnesium 2.09%
i Other elements 1.41%

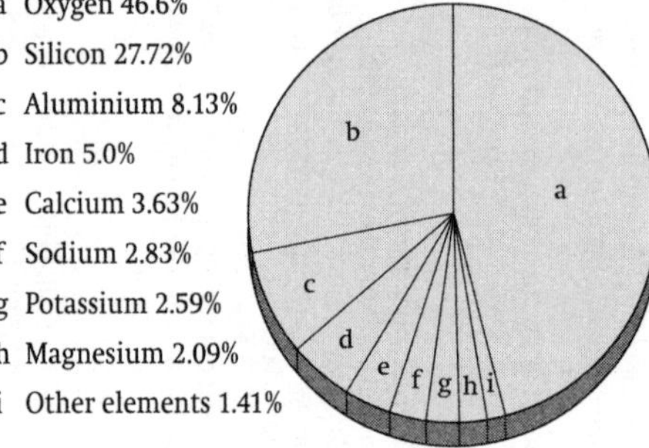

Mineral composition of rocks

Mineral component (%)	*Type of rock* Granite	Basalt	Amphibolite	Schist	Shale	Sandstone	Limestone
Quartz	30			32	17	97	3
Alkali feldspar	60	5				1	1
Plagioclase	5	45	42	18			
Pyroxene		40					
Amphibole			50				
Olivine		5					
Biotite	4		5	7			
Muscovite				38	1	1	
Magnetite	1	5	3	3	1	1	1
Staurolite				2			
Clay minerals					80		1
Calcite					1		94

Chemical composition of rocks

Oxide component (%)	*Type of rock* Granite	Basalt	Amphibolite	Schist	Shale	Sandstone	Limestone
SiO_2	70.8	49.0	49.3	63.3	62.4	94.4	5.2
TiO_2	0.4	1.0	1.2	1.4	1.1	0.1	0.1
Al_2O_3	14.5	18.2	16.9	17.9	16.6	1.1	0.8
Fe_2O_3	1.6	3.2	3.6	3.6	3.2	0.4	0.3
FeO	1.8	6.0	6.8	2.6	2.1	0.2	0.2
MgO	0.9	7.6	7.0	1.6	2.5	0.1	7.9
CaO	1.8	11.0	9.5	1.9	1.7	1.6	42.6
Na_2O	3.3	2.5	2.9	1.3	0.9	0.1	0.1
K_2O	4.0	0.9	1.1	3.1	3.0	0.2	0.3
H_2O	0.8	0.4	1.5	2.6	5.2	0.3	0.7
CO_2					1.0	1.1	41.6

Mohs' scale of hardness

Friedrich Mohs (1773–1839) introduced a simple definition of hardness, according to which one mineral is said to be harder than another if the former scratches the latter. The Mohs' scale is based on a series of common minerals, arranged in order of increasing hardness.

Mineral	*Composition*	*Simple hardness test*	*Hardness*
Talc	$Mg_3Si_4O_{10}(OH)_2$	Crushed by finger nail	1
Gypsum	$CaSO_4 2H_2O$	Scratched by finger nail	2
Calcite	$CaCO_3$	Scratched by copper coin	3
Fluorite	CaF_2	Scratched by glass	4
Apatite	$Ca_5(PO_4)_3F$	Scratched by penknife	5
Orthoclase (feldspar)	$KAlSi_3O_8$	Scratched by quartz	6
Quartz	SiO_2	Scratched by steel file	7
Topaz	$Al_2SiO_4F_2$	Scratched by corundum	8
Corundum	Al_2O_3	Scratched by diamond	9
Diamond	C		10

World minerals map

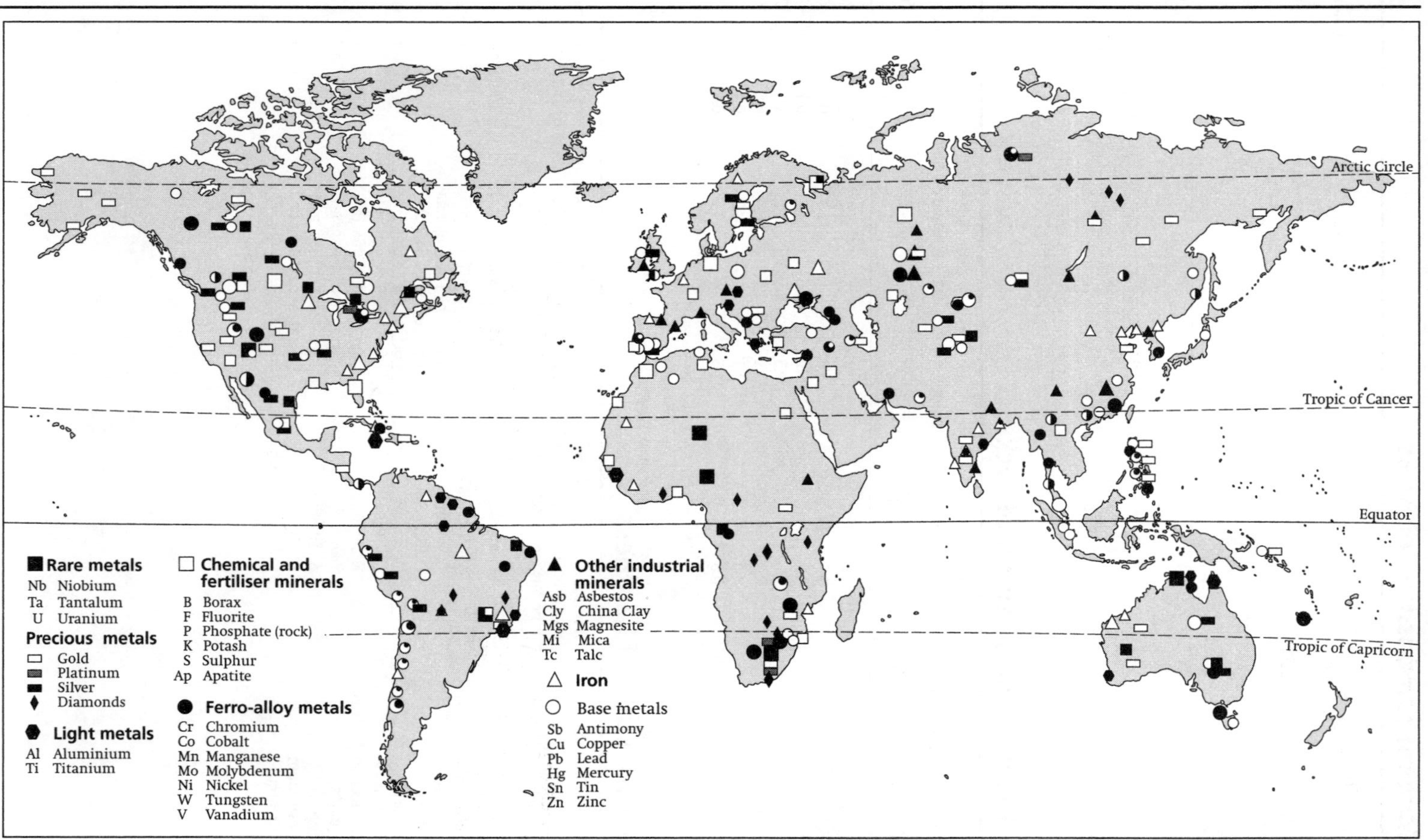

Continental drift

240 million years ago
The single supercontinent Pangea is formed, with a single superocean, Panthalassa.

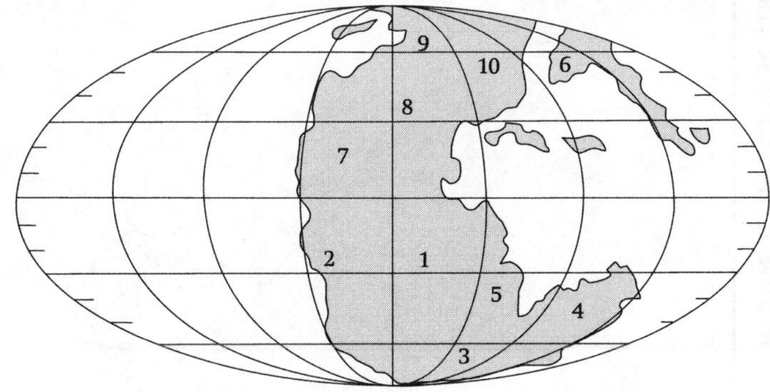

120 million years ago
Tethys, a broad gulf, divides Pangea into two huge landmasses: Laurasia in the north; Gondwana in the south.

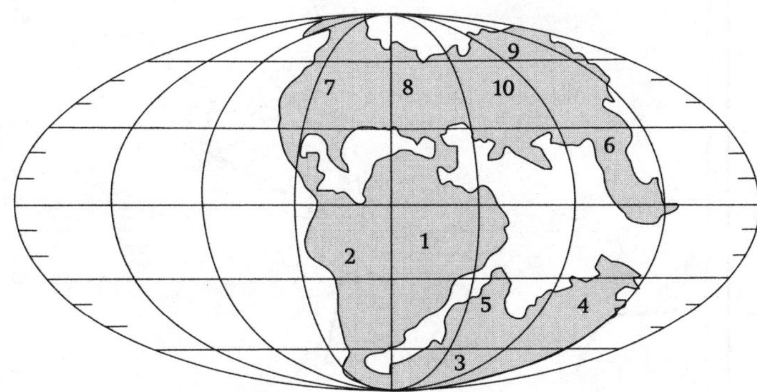

60 million years ago
Laurasia and Gondwana have split to begin to form the continents as we know them today.

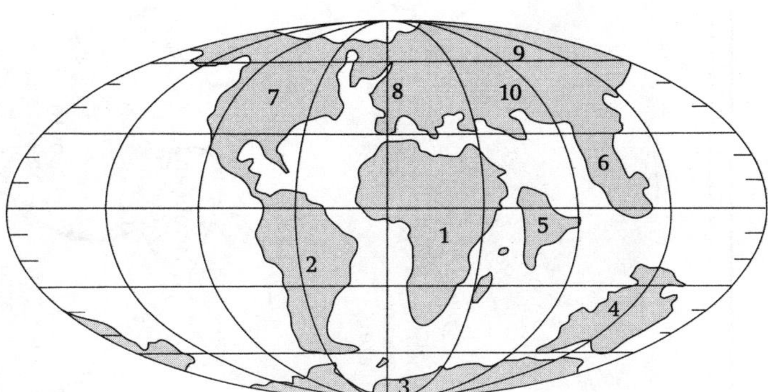

Major lithospheric plates

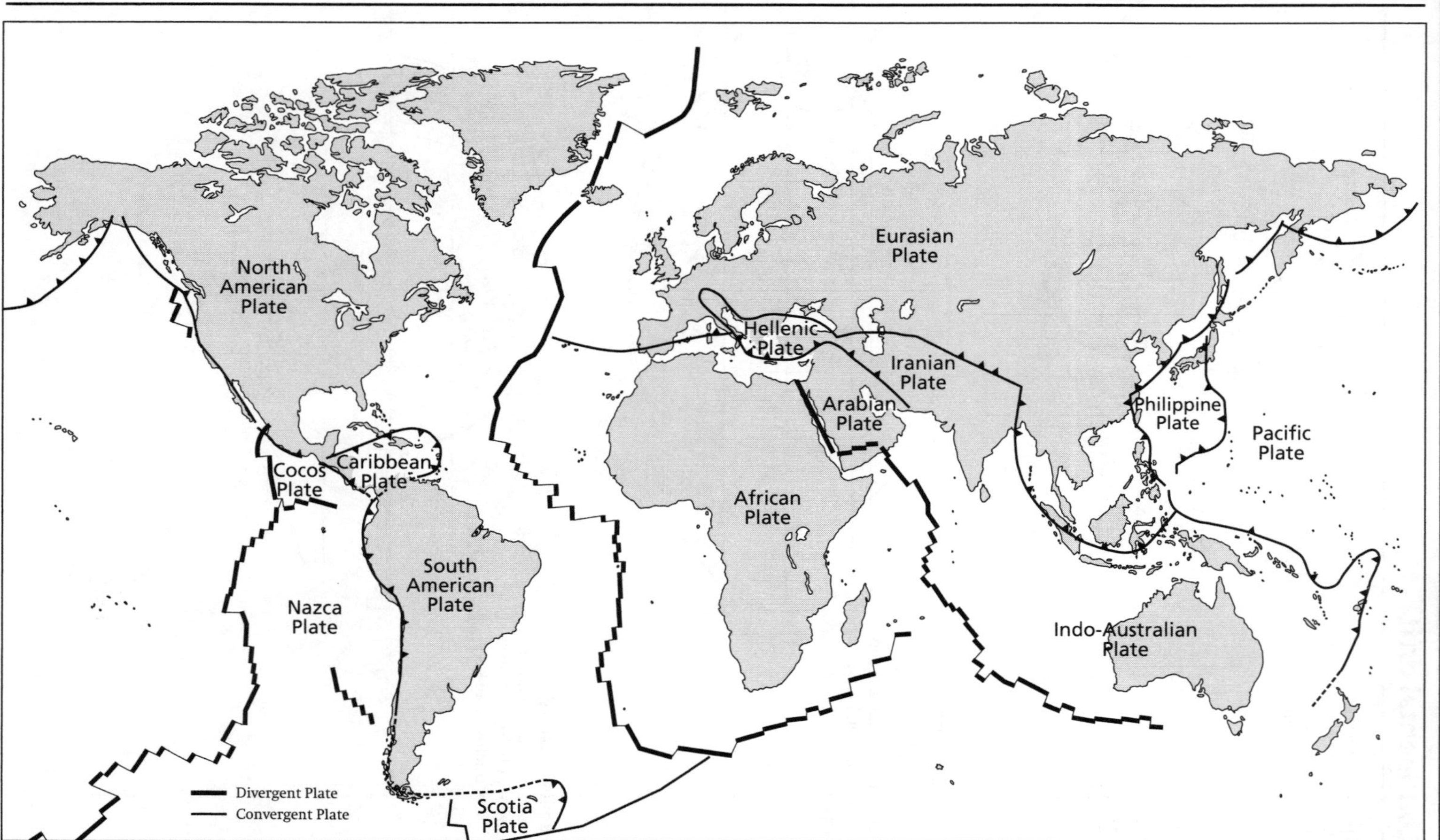

Earthquake distribution

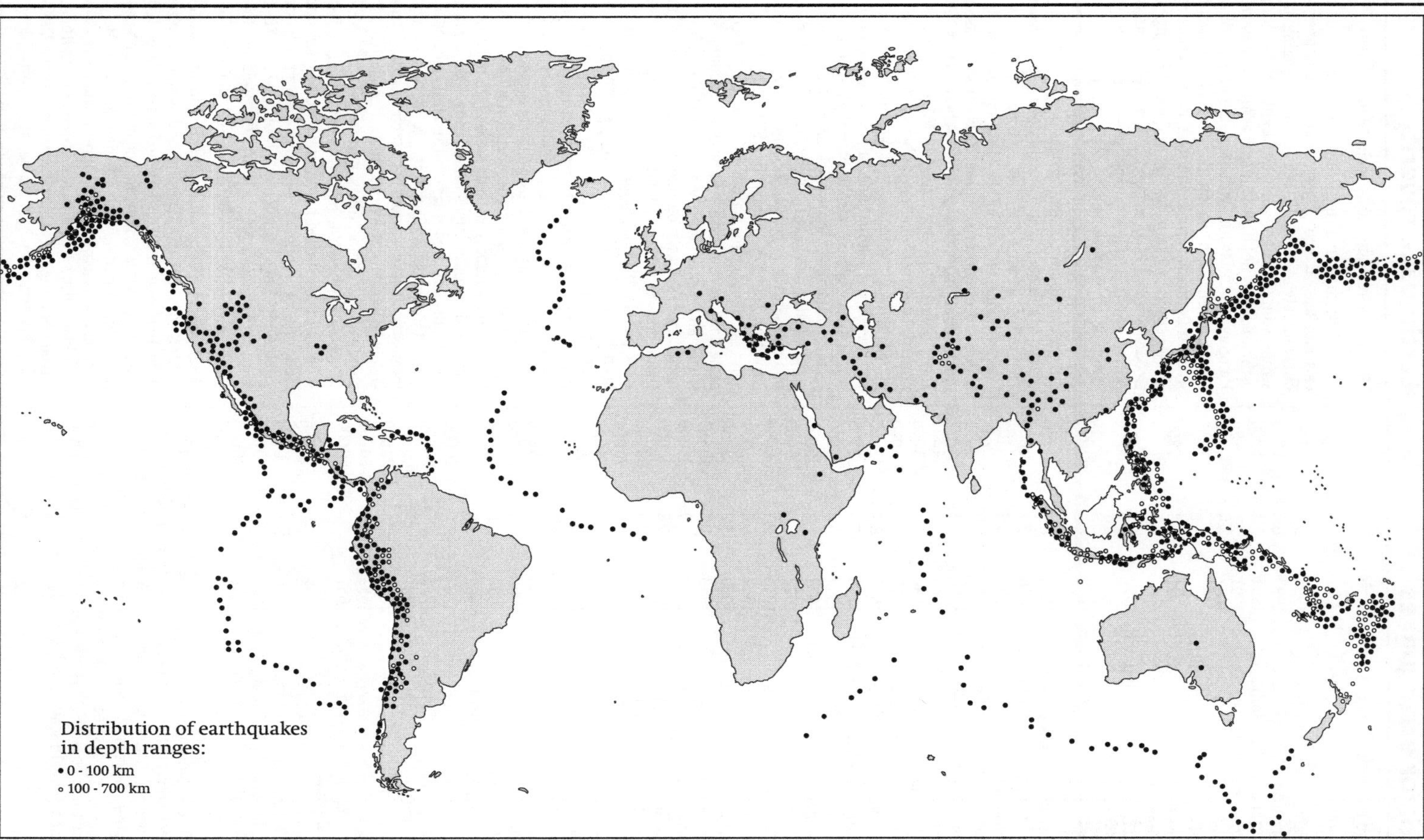

Major earthquakes

All magnitudes on the Richter scale[a]

Location	*Country*	*Year*	*Magnitude*	*Deaths*
Cairo	Egypt	1992	5.9	500
Erzincan	Turkey	1992	6.2	2000
Uttar Pradesh	India	1991	6.1	1000
Costa Rica/Panama		1991	7.5	80
Georgia	CIS	1991	7.2	100
Hindu Kush Mts	Afghanistan/ Pakistan	1991	6.8	1300
Cabanatuan, Luzon	Philippines	1990	7.7	1653
Caspian Sea area	Iran	1990	7.7	40000
Moyobamba	Peru	1990	5.8	90
Carpathian Mts	Romania	1990	6.6	70
Luzon Island	Philippines	1990	7.7	1600
San Francisco	USA	1989	6.9	100
Armenia	CIS	1988	7.0	25000
Mexico City	Mexico	1985	8.1	7200
Naples	Italy	1980	7.2	4500
El Asnam	Algeria	1980	7.3	5000
Tabas	Iran	1978	7.7	25000
Tangshan	China	1976	8.2	242000
Guatemala City	Guatemala	1976	7.5	22778
Kashmir	Pakistan	1974	6.3	5200
Managua	Nicaragua	1972	6.2	5000
Tehran	Iran	1972	6.9	5000
Chimbote	Peru	1970	7.7	66000
Anchorage	USA	1964	8.5	131
Agadir	Morocco	1960	5.8	12000
Ashkhabad	CIS	1948	7.3	19800
Erzincan	Turkey	1939	7.9	23000
Chillan	Chile	1939	7.8	30000
Quetta	India	1935	7.5	60000
Gansu	China	1932	7.6	70000
Nan-Shan	China	1927	8.3	200000
Kanto	Japan	1923	8.3	143000
Gansu	China	1920	8.6	180000
Avezzano	Italy	1915	7.5	30000
Messina	Italy	1908	7.5	120000
Valparaiso	Chile	1906	8.6	20000
San Francisco	USA	1906	8.3	500
Calabria	Italy	1783		50000
Lisbon	Portugal	1755		70000
Calcutta	India	1737		300000
Hokkaido	Japan	1730		137000
Catania	Italy	1693		60000
Caucasia, Shemaka	CIS	1667		80000
Shensi	China	1556		830000
Chihli	China	1290		100000
Cilicia	Turkey	1268		60000
Corinth	Greece	856		45000
Antioch	Turkey	526		250000

[a]The Richter scale is a logarithmic scale, devised in 1935 by geophysicist Charles Richter, for representing the energy released by earthquakes. A figure of 2 or less is barely perceptible, while an earthquake measuring over 5 may be destructive. More relevant as a measure of earthquake strength is the intensity, for which the modified Mercalli scale is widely used.

Earthquake severity

Modified Mercalli intensity scale (1956 revision)

I Not felt; marginal and long-period effects of large earthquakes. **II** Felt by persons at rest, on upper floors or favourably placed. **III** Felt indoors; hanging objects swing; vibration like passing of light trucks; duration estimated; may not be recognized as an earthquake. **IV** Hanging objects swing; vibration like passing of heavy trucks, or sensation of a jolt like a heavy ball striking the walls; standing cars rock; windows, dishes, doors rattle; glasses clink; crockery clashes; in the upper range of IV, wooden walls and frames creak. **V** Felt outdoors; direction estimated; sleepers wakened; liquids disturbed, some spilled; small unstable objects displaced or upset; doors swing, close, open; shutters, pictures move; pendulum clocks stop, start, change rate. **VI** Felt by all; many frightened and run outdoors; persons walk unsteadily; windows, dishes, glassware break; knick-knacks, books, etc, fall off shelves; pictures off walls; furniture moves or overturns; weak plaster and masonry D crack; small bells ring (church, school); trees, bushes shake visibly, or heard to rustle. **VII** Difficult to stand; noticed by drivers; hanging objects quiver; furniture breaks; damage to masonry D, including cracks; weak chimneys broken at roof line; fall of plaster, loose bricks, stones, tiles, cornices, also unbraced parapets and architectural ornaments; some cracks in masonry C; waves on ponds, water turbid with mud; small slides and caving in along sand or gravel banks; large bells ring; concrete irrigation ditches damaged. **VIII** Steering of cars affected; damage to masonry C and partial collapse; some damage to masonry B; none to masonry A; fall of stucco and some masonry walls; twisting, fall of chimneys, factory stacks, monuments, towers, elevated tanks; frame houses move on foundations if not bolted down; loose panel walls thrown out; decayed piling broken off; branches broken from trees; changes in flow or temperature of springs and wells; cracks in wet ground and on steep slopes. **IX** General panic; masonry D destroyed; masonry C heavily damaged, sometimes with complete collapse; masonry B seriously damaged; general damage to foundations; frame structures, if not bolted, shift off foundations; frames racked; serious damage to reservoirs; underground pipes break; conspicuous cracks in ground; in alluviated areas sand and mud ejected, earthquake fountains, sand craters. **X** Most masonry and frame structures destroyed with their foundations; some well-built wooden structures and bridges destroyed; serious damage to dams, dikes, embankments; large landslides; water thrown on banks of canals, rivers, lakes, etc; sand and mud shifted horizontally on beaches and flat land; rails bent slightly. **XI** Rails bent greatly; underground pipelines completely out of service. **XII** Damage nearly total; large rock masses displaced; lines of sight and level distorted; objects thrown into the air.

Note *Masonry A* Good workmanship, mortar and design; reinforced, especially laterally, and bound together by using steel, concrete etc; designed to resist lateral forces. *Masonry B* Good workmanship and mortar; reinforced, but not designed in detail to resist lateral forces. *Masonry C* Ordinary workmanship and mortar; no extreme weakness like failing to tie in at corners, but neither reinforced nor designed against horizontal forces. *Masonry D* Weak materials, such as adobe; poor mortar; low standards of workmanship; weak horizontally.

Major volcanoes and eruptions

Name	*Location*	*Height* *m*	*ft*	*Major eruptions (year/s)*	*Last eruption (year)*
Aconcagua	Argentina	6960	22831	Extinct	
Ararat	Turkey	5198	18350	Extinct	Holocene
Awu	Sangihe Is	1327	4355	1711, 1856, 1892	1968
Bezymianny	Russia	2800	9186	1955–6	1984
Coseguina	Nicaragua	847	1598	1835	1835
El Chichón	Mexico	1349	4430	1982	1982
Erebus	Antarctica	4023	13200	1947, 1972, 1986	1991
Etna, Mt	Italy	3236	10625	AD 122, 1169, 1329, 1536, 1669, 1928, 1964, 1971, 1986	1992
Fuji	Japan	3776	12388	1707	1707
Galunggung	Java	2180	7155	1822, 1918	1982
Hekla	Iceland	1491	4920	1693, 1845, 1947–8, 1970	1981
Helgafell	Iceland	215	706	1973	1973
Hudson	Chile	1740	5742	1971, 1973	1991
Jurullo	Mexico	1330	4255	1759–74	1774
Katmai	Alaska	2298	7540	1912, 1920, 1921	1931
Kilauea	Hawaii	1247	4100	1823–1924, 1952, 1955, 1960, 1967–8, 1968–74, 1983–7, 1988, 1991	1992
Kilimanjaro	Tanzania	5930	19450	Extinct	Pleistocene
Klyuchevskoy	Russia	4850	15910	1700–1966, 1984	1985
Krakatoa	Sumatra	818	2685	1680, 1883, 1927, 1952–3, 1969	1980
La Soufrière	St Vincent	1232	4048	1718, 1812, 1902, 1971–2	1979
Laki	Iceland	500	1642	1783	1784
Lamington	Papua New Guinea	1780	5844	1951	1956
Lassen Peak	USA	3186	10453	1914–15	1921
Mauna Loa	Hawaii	4172	13685	1859, 1880, 1887, 1919, 1950, 1984	1987
Mayon	Philippines	2462	8084	1616, 1766, 1814, 1897, 1968	1978
Nyamuragira	Zaire	3056	10026	1921–38, 1971, 1980, 1984	1988
Paricutín	Mexico	3188	10460	1943–52	1952
Pelée, Mont	Martinique	1397	4584	1902, 1929–32	1932
Pinatubo	Philippines	1758	5770	1391	1991
Popocatépetl	Mexico	5483	17990	1920	1943
Rainer, Mt	USA	4392	14416	1st-c BC, 1820	1882
Ruapehu	New Zealand	2796	9175	1945, 1953, 1969, 1975	1986
St Helens, Mt	USA	2549	8364	1800, 1831, 1835, 1842–3, 1857, 1980	1987
Santorini/ Thera	Greece	556	1824	1470 BC, 197 BC, AD 46, 1570–3, 1707–11, 1866–70	1950
Stromboli	Italy	931	3055	1768, 1882, 1889, 1907, 1930, 1936, 1941, 1950, 1952, 1986	1990
Surtsey	Iceland	174	570	1963–7	1967
Taal	Philippines	1448	4752	1911, 1965, 1969	1977
Tambora	Sumbawa	2868	9410	1815	1880
Tarawera	New Zealand	1 149	3770	1886	1973
Unzen, Mt	Japan	1360	4462	1360, 1791	1991
Vesuvius	Italy	1289	4230	AD 79, 472, 1036, 1631, 1779, 1906	1944
Vulcano	Italy	502	1650	Antiquity, 1444, 1730–40, 1786, 1873, 1888–90	1890

Major tsunamis

Tsunamis are long-period ocean waves produced by movements of the sea floor associated with earthquakes, volcanic explosions, or landslides. They are also referred to as *seismic sea waves*, and in popular (but not technical) oceanographic use as *tidal waves*.

Location of source	*Year*	*Height* *m*	*ft*	*Location of deaths/damage*	*Deaths*
Sea of Japan	1983	15	49	Japan, Korea	107
Indonesia	1979	10	32	Indonesia	187
Celebes Sea	1976	30	98	Philippine Is	5000
Alaska	1964	32	105	Alaska, Aleutian Is, California	122
Chile	1960	25	82	Chile, Hawaii, Japan	1260
Aleutian Is	1957	16	52	Hawaii, Japan	0
Kamchatka	1952	18.4	60	Kamchatka, Kuril Is, Hawaii	Many
Aleutian Is	1946	32	105	Aleutian Is, Hawaii, California	165
Nankaido (Japan)	1946	6.1	20	Japan	1997
Kii (Japan)	1944	7.5	25	Japan	998
Sanriku (Japan)	1933	28.2	93	Japan, Hawaii	3000
E Kamchatka	1923	20	66	Kamchatka, Hawaii	3
S Kuril Is	1918	12	39	Kuril Is, Russia, Japan, Hawaii	23
Sanriku (Japan)	1896	30	98	Japan	27122
Sunda Strait	1883	35	115	Java, Sumatra	36000
Chile	1877	23	75	Chile, Hawaii	Many
Chile	1868	21	69	Chile, Hawaii	25000
Hawaii	1868	20	66	Hawaii	81
Japan	1854	6	20	Japan	3000
Flores Sea	1800	24	79	Indonesia	4–500
Ariake Sea	1792	9	30	Japan	9745
Italy	1783	?	?	Italy	30000
Ryukyu Is	1771	12	39	Ryukyu Is	11941
Portugal	1775	16	52	W Europe, Morocco, W Indies	60000
Peru	1746	24	79	Peru	5000
Japan	1741	9	30	Japan	1000 +
SE Kamchatka	1737	30	98	Kamchatka, Kuril Is	?
Peru	1724	24	79	Peru	?
Japan	1707	11.5	38	Japan	30000
W Indies	1692	?	?	Jamaica	2000
Banda Is	1629	15	49	Indonesia	?
Sanriku (Japan)	1611	25	82	Japan	5000
Japan	1605	?	?	Japan	4000
Kii (Japan)	1498	?	?	Japan	5000

Recent hurricanes

A hurricane (H) is an intense, often devastating, tropical storm which occurs as a vortex spiralling around a low pressure system. Wind speeds are high – above 75 mph. Hurricanes originate over tropical oceans and move in a W or NW direction in the northern hemisphere, and SW in the southern hemisphere, losing energy as they reach land. They are also known as *typhoons* in the western N Pacific and *cyclones* in the Bay of Bengal.

Name	*Location*	*Year*	*Deaths*	*Damage (US $bn)*
H Andrew	S Florida	1992	30	7.3
H Iniki	Kauai, Hawaii	1992	3	1.0
H Bob	NE USA	1991	17	1.5
Cyclone	Bangladesh	1991	200 000	
H Hugo	S Carolina	1989	49	7.0
H Gilbert	Caribbean, Mexico	1988	318	5.0
H Joan	Caribbean	1988	216	
H Elena	Mississippi, Alabama, NW Florida	1985	2	1.25
H Gloria	E USA	1985	15	0.9
H Juan	Louisiana	1985	12	1.5
H Kate	Florida	1985	16	0.3
Cyclone	Bangladesh	1985	11 000	
H Alicia	N Texas	1983	18	2.0
H Allen	S Texas	1980	235	0.3
H David	Florida	1979	2 400	0.3
H Frederic	Alabama, Mississippi	1979	31	2.3
H Eloise	NW Florida	1975	100	0.49
H Carmen	Louisiana	1974	1	0.15
H Fifi	Honduras, C America	1974	10 000	1.0
Cyclone Tracey	Darwin, Australia	1974	65	1.0
H Agnes	E Coast, USA	1972	122	2.1
Cyclone	Bangladesh	1970	300 000	0.086

ATMOSPHERE

Layers of the atmosphere

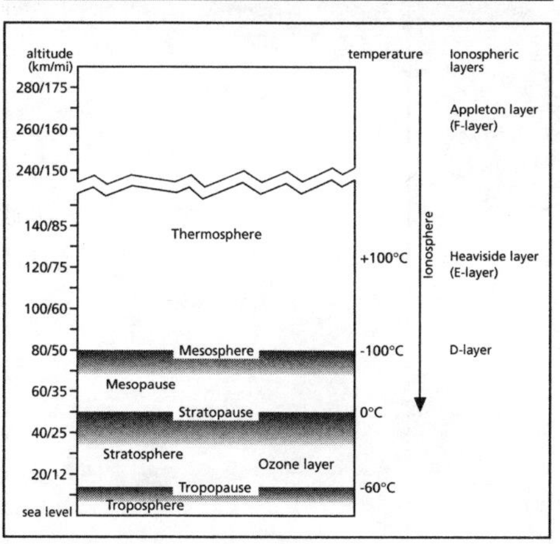

The composition of dry air at sea level

Gas	*Per cent by volume*
Nitrogen (N_2)	78.08
Oxygen (O_2)	20.95
Argon (Ar)	0.93
Carbon dioxide (CO_2)	0.031
Neon (Ne)	0.0018
Helium (He)	0.000 52
Krypton (Kr)	0.000 11
Xenon (Xe)	0.000 0087
Hydrogen (H_2)	0.000 05
Methane (CH_4)	0.000 2
Nitric oxide (NO)	0.000 05
Ozone (O_3)	0.000 002 (winter) 0.000 007 (summer)

CLIMATE

World temperatures

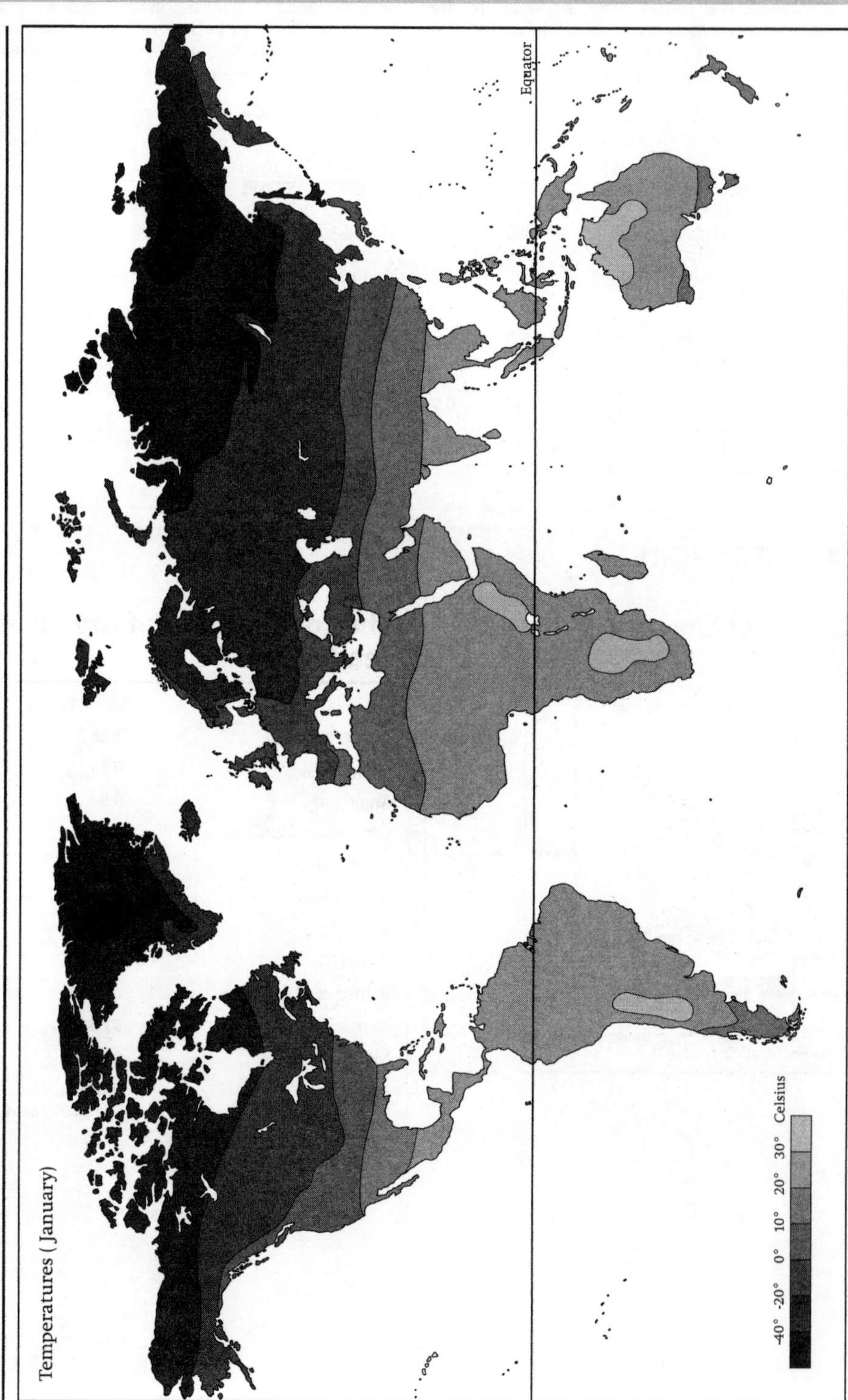

The Earth

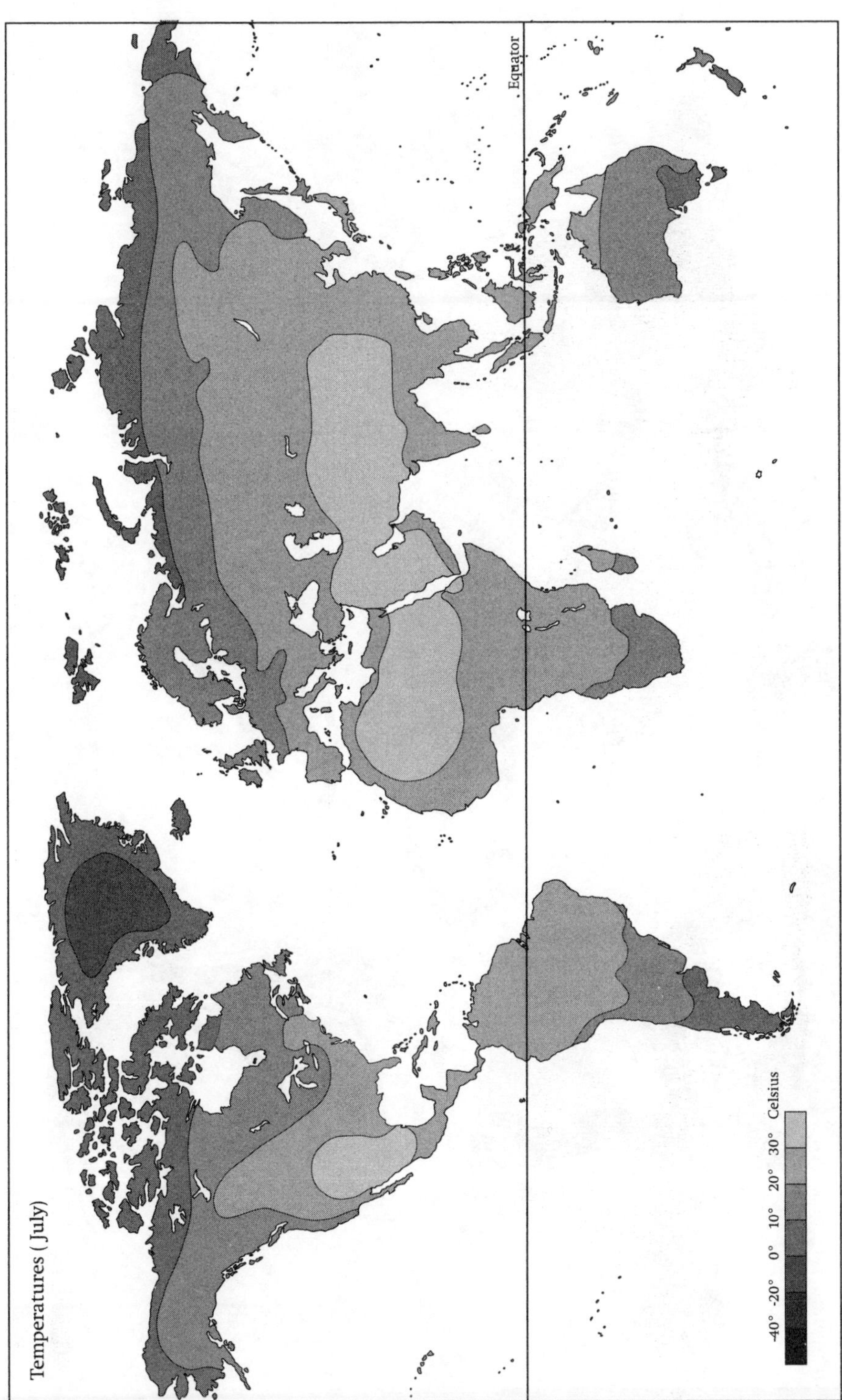

World precipitation

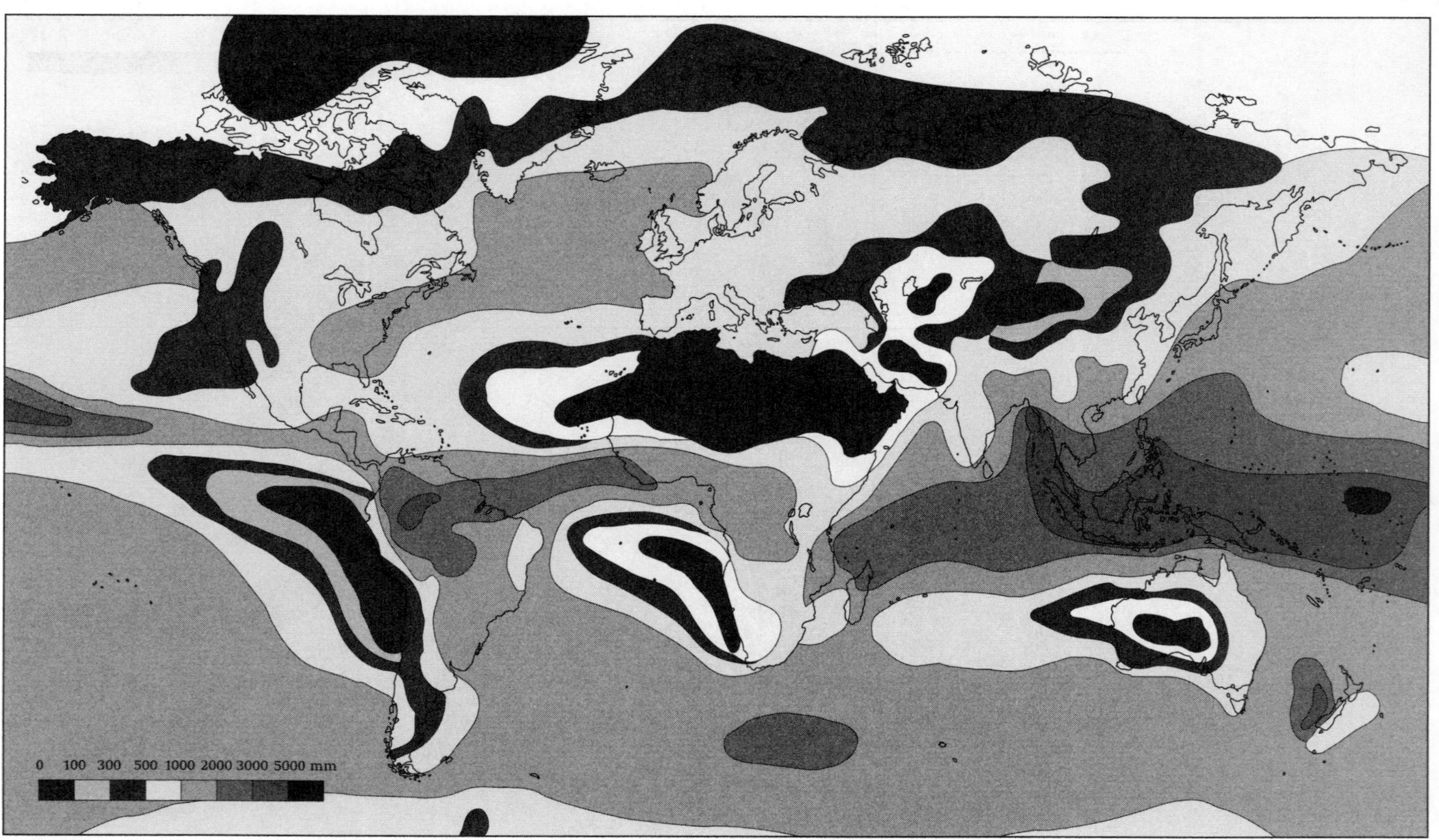

Meteorological records

Hottest place	Dallol, Ethiopia	34°C / 94°F (annual mean)
Coldest place	Pole of Cold, Antarctica	–58°C / –72°F (annual mean)
Driest place	Arica-Antofagasta, Pacific coast, Chile	0.1 mm / 0.004 in (annual mean rainfall)
Wettest place	Tutenendo, Columbia	11770 mm / 463.5 in (annual mean rainfall)
Windiest place	Commonwealth Bay, George V Coast, Antarctica	320 kph/231 mph (maximum wind speed)

Cloud types

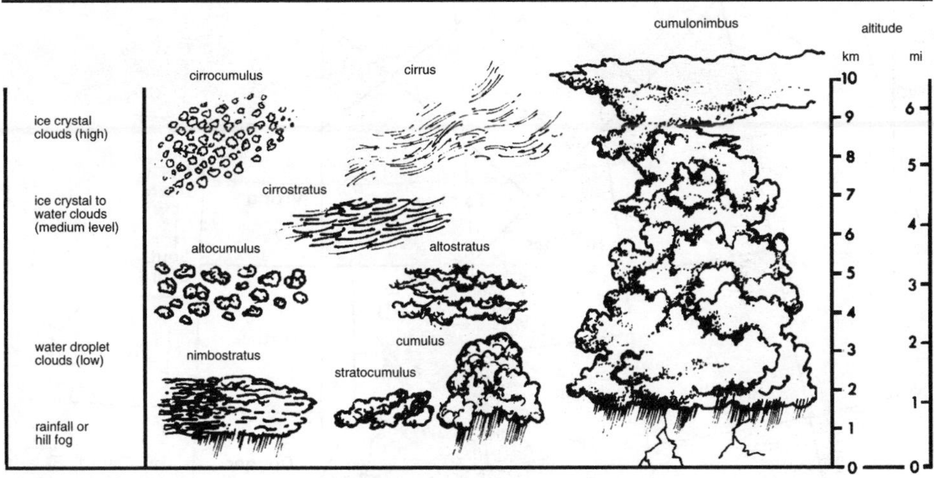

Depression

Plan view of the six idealized stages in the development and final occlusion of a depression along the polar front in the northern hemisphere. Stage 4 shows a well-developed depression system and stage 5 shows the occlusion. The cross-section is taken along the line AB in stage 4. The cloud types are:

Cb – cumulonimbus;
As – altostratus;
Ac – altocumulus;
Cs – cirrostratus;
Ns – nimbostratus;
Ci – cirrus.

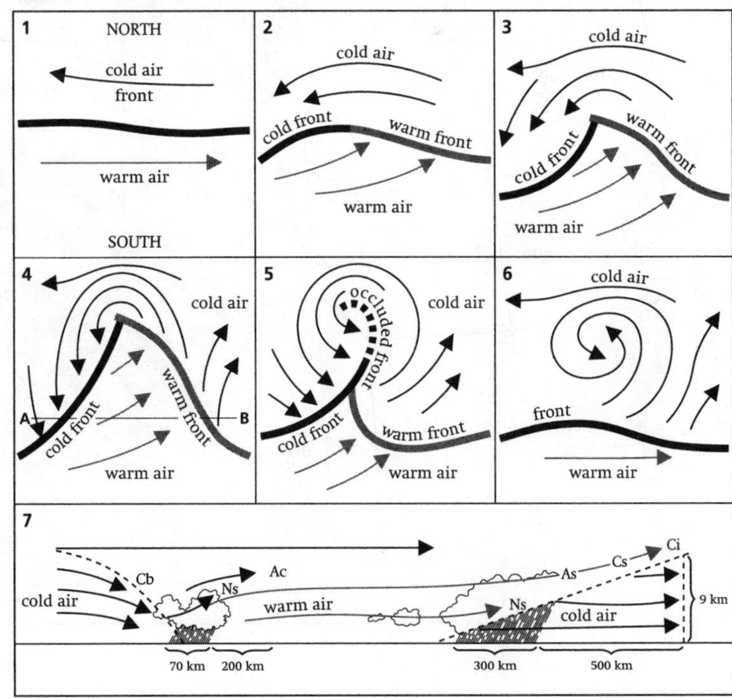

Meteorological sea areas

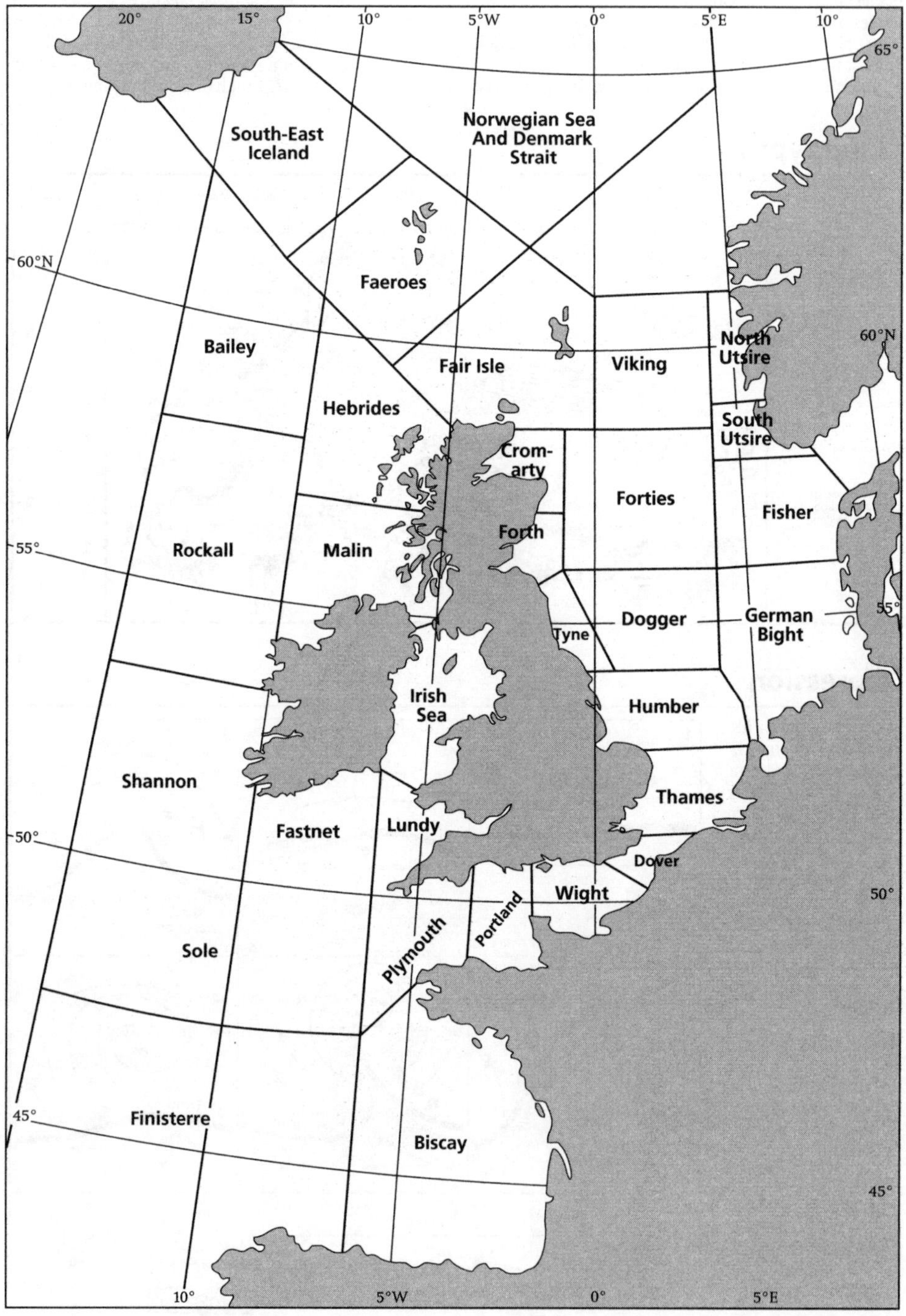

The Earth

Wind force and sea disturbance

Beaufort number	*m/s*	*Wind speed kph*	*mph*	*Wind name*	*Observable wind characteristics*
0	1	<1	<1	Calm	Smoke rises vertically
1	1	1–5	1–3	Light air	Wind direction shown by smoke drift but not by wind vanes
2	2	6–11	4–7	Light breeze	Wind felt on face: leaves rustle: vanes moved by wind
3	4	12–19	8–12	Gentle breeze	Leaves and small twigs in constant motion: wind extends light flag
4	7	20–28	13–18	Moderate	Raises dust, loose paper: small branches moved
5	10	29–38	19–24	Fresh	Small trees begin to sway
6	12	39–49	25–31	Strong	Large branches in motion: difficult to use umbrellas
7	15	50–61	32–38	Near gale	Whole trees in motion: difficult to walk against wind
8	18	62–74	39–46	Gale	Breaks twigs off trees: impedes progress
9	20	75–88	47–54	Strong gale	Slight structural damage caused
10	26	89–102	55–63	Storm	Trees uprooted: considerable damage occurs
11	30	103–17	64–72	Violent storm	Widespread damage
12–17	>33	>118	>73	Hurricane	

Sea disturbance number (Beaufort)	*Average wave height m*	*ft*	*Observable sea characteristics*
0 (0)	0	0	Sea like a mirror
0 (1)	0	0	Ripples like scales
1 (2)	0.3	0–1	More definite wavelets
2 (3)	0.3–0.6	1–2	Large wavelets: crests beginning
3 (4)	0.6–1.2	2–4	Small waves becoming longer: fairly frequent white horses
4 (5)	1.2–2.4	4–8	Moderate waves with longer form: many white horses: some foam spray
5 (6)	2.4–4	8–13	Large waves forming: more white foam crests: spray
6 (7)	4–6	13–20	Sea heaps up: streaks of white foam blown along
6 (8)	4–6	13–20	Moderately high waves of greater length: well-marked streaks of foam
6 (9)	4–6	13–20	High waves: dense streaks of foam: sea begins to roll: spray affects visibility
7 (10)	6–9	20–30	Very high waves with overhanging crests: generally white appearance of surface: heavy rolling
8 (11)	9–14	30–45	Exceptionally high waves: long white patches of foam: poor visibility: ships lost to view behind waves
9 (12–17)	14	>45	Air filled with foam and spray: sea completely white; very poor visibility

SURFACE

World physical map

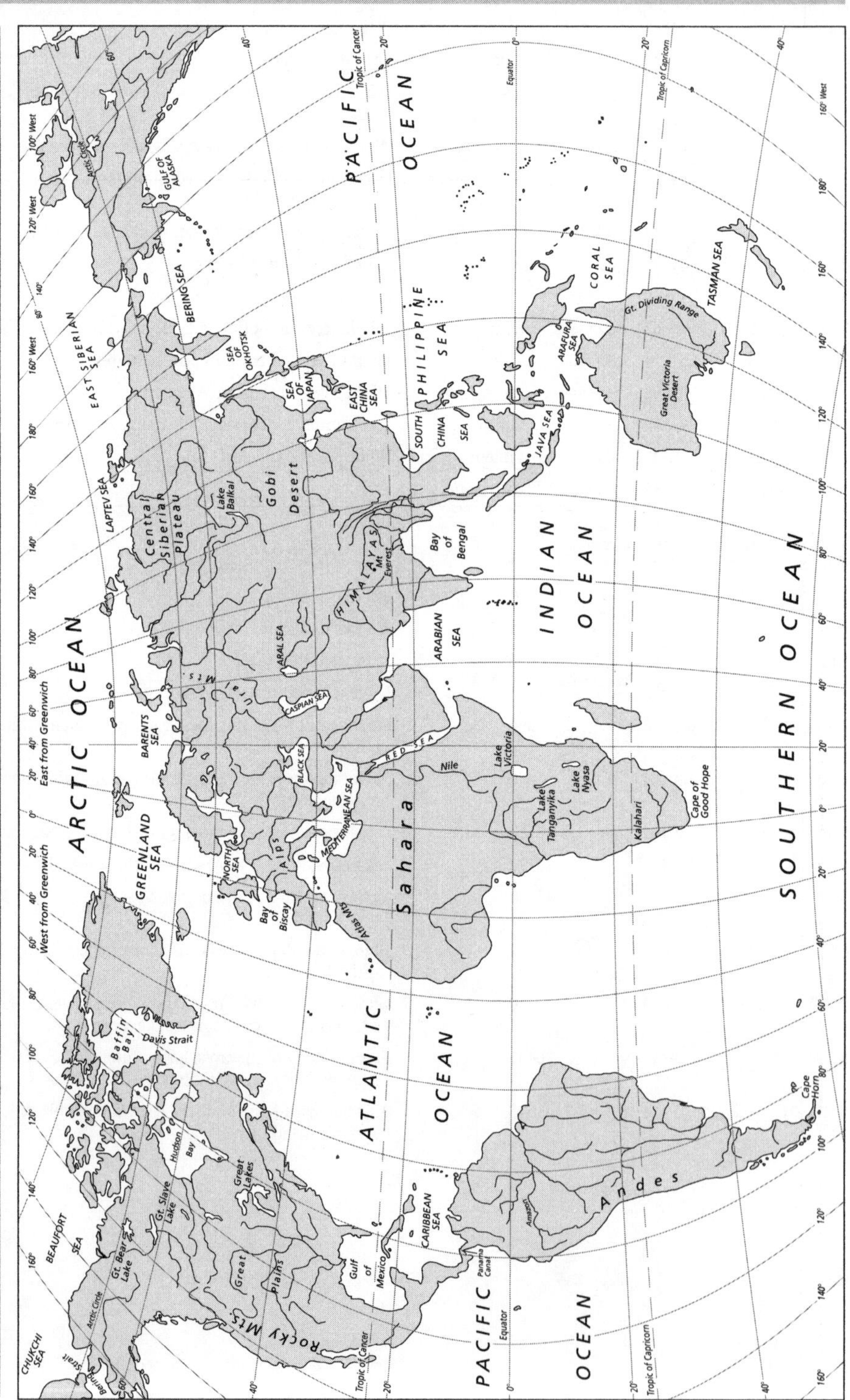

Major ocean surface currents

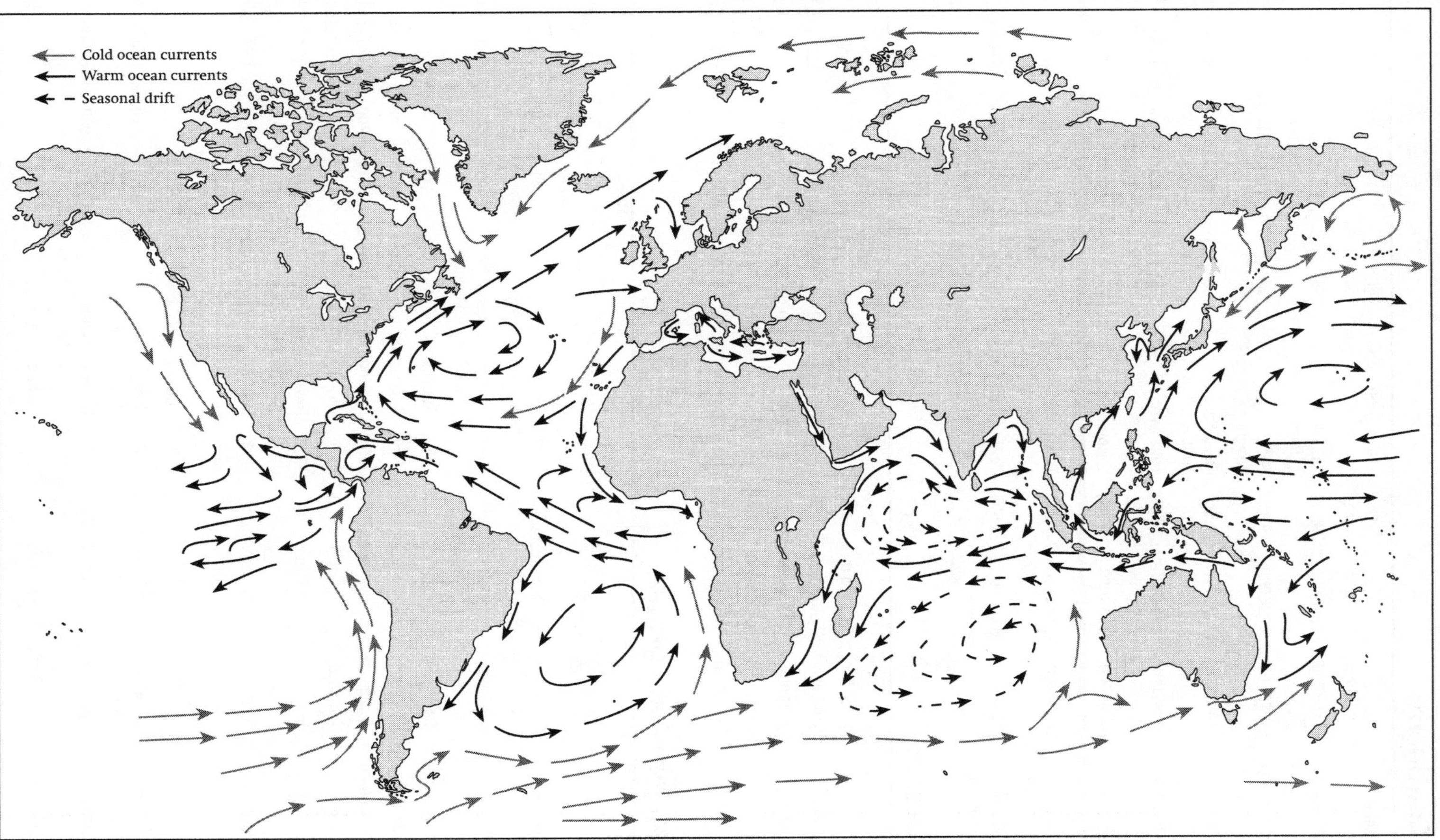

Continents

Name	Area sq km	Area sq mi	% of total	Lowest point below sea level	m	ft	Highest elevation	m	ft
Africa	30 293 000	11 696 000	(20.2%)	Lake Assal, Djibouti	156	512	Kilimanjaro, Tanzania	5 895	19 340
Antarctica	13 975 000	5 396 000	(9.3%)	Bently subglacial trench	2 538	8 327	Vinson Massif	5 140	16 864
Asia	44 493 000	17 179 000	(29.6%)	Dead Sea, Israel/Jordan	400	1 312	Mt Everest, China/Nepal	8 848	29 028
Oceania	8 945 000	3 454 000	(6%)	Lake Eyre, S Australia	15	49	Puncak Jaya, Indonesia	5 030	16 500
Europe	10 245 000	3 956 000	(6.8%)	Caspian Sea, Russia	29	94	Elbrus, Russia	5 642	18 510
North America	24 454 000	9 442 000	(16.3%)	Death Valley, California	86	282	Mt McKinley, Alaska	6 194	20 320
South America	17 838 000	6 887 000	(11.9%)	Peninsular Valdez, Argentina	40	131	Aconcagua, Argentina	6 960	22 831

Oceans

Name	Area sq km	Area sq mi	% of total	Average depth m	Average depth ft	Greatest depth	m	ft
Arctic	13 986 000	5 400 000	(3%)	1 330	4 300	Eurasia Basin	5 122	16 804
Atlantic	82 217 000	31 700 000	(24%)	3 700	12 100	Puerto Rico Trench	8 648	28 372
Indian	73 426 000	28 350 000	(20%)	3 900	12 800	Java Trench	7 725	25 344
Pacific	181 300 000	70 000 000	(46%)	4 300	14 100	Marianas Trench	11 040	36 220

Major island groups

Name	Country	Sea/Ocean	No. of islands	Main islands	Area sq km	Area sq mi	Inhabitants
Aeolian	Italy	Mediterranean	7	Stromboli, Lipari, Vulcanö, Salina	90	30	10 208 (1981)
Åland	Finland	Gulf of Bothnia	6 080	Eckerö, Lemland, Vardö, Lumparland	1 500	570	23 239 (1983)
Aleutian	USA	Pacific	150	Andreanof, Adak	1 800	6 800	7 768 (1980)
Alexander	Canada	Pacific	11 000	Baranof, Prince of Wales	na	na	32 586 (1980)
Andaman	India	Bay of Bengal	300+	N Andaman, S Andaman	8 300	3 200	188 254 (1981)
Azores	Portugal	Atlantic	9	São Miguel, Flores	2 300	900	243 410 (1981)
Bahamas	Bahamas	Atlantic	700	New Providence, Grand Bahama	13 900	5 400	254 685 (1991)
Balearic	Spain	Mediterranean	5	Mallorca, Menorca, Ibiza	5 000	1 900	655 909 (1981)
Bismarck	Papua New Guinea	Pacific	2 000	New Britain, New Ireland, Admiralty Island	49 700	19 200	314 308 (1980)
Bijagos	Guinea-Bissau	Atlantic	15	Orango, Formoza, Caravela, Roxa	50	30	25 713 (1979)
Canary	Spain	Atlantic	7	Tenerife, Gomera, Lanzarote, Las Palmas	7 300	2 800	1 615 000 (1986)
Cape Verde	Cape Verde	Atlantic	10	Barlavento group, Sotavento group	4 000	1 500	383 000 (1991)

Name	Country	Sea/Ocean	No. of islands	Main islands	Area sq km	Area sq mi	Inhabitants
Caroline	USA	Pacific	680	Yop, Pohnpei, Truk	1300	500	97400 (1983)
Channel	UK	English Channel	4	Guernsey, Jersey, Sark, Alderney	200	80	145000 (1986)
Commander	Russia	Bering Sea	4	Bering, Medny	1800	700	na
Comoros	Republic of Comoros	Mozambique Channel	4	Grand Mohore, Anjouan, Moheli, Mayotte	1900	700	463000 (1990)
Cook	New Zealand	Pacific	15	Palmerston, Rarotonga, Mangaia	240	90	17185 (1986)
Cyclades	Greece	Aegean	c 220	Andros, Mikonos, Paros	2600	990	88458 (1981)
Dodecanese	Greece	Aegean	12	Rhodes, Kos	2700	1000	145071 (1981)
Falkland	UK	Atlantic	200	W Falkland, E Falkland, S Georgia	12200	4700	2121 (1991)
Faroe	Denmark	Atlantic	22	Strømø, Østerø	1400	540	478000 (1990)
Fiji	Fiji	Pacific	844	Viti Levu, Vanua Levu	18330	7080	744000 (1991)
Galapagos	Ecuador	Pacific	16	Santa Cruz, Santiago	7800	3010	6119 (1982)
Gotland	Sweden	Baltic	2	Gotland, Fårö	3140	1210	55895 (1983)
Greenland	Denmark	N Atlantic, Arctic	2	Greenland, Disko	2175600	840000	56000 (1990)
Hawaiian	USA	Pacific	8	Hawaii, Oahu	16760	6470	1083000 (1987)
Hebrides	UK	Atlantic	10+	Lewis, Skye, Mull		na	44344 (1981)
Indonesia	Indonesia	Pacific	13677	Java, Sumatra	1900240	735810	193000000 (1991)
Ionian	Greece	Aegean	7	Kerkira, Levkas	2300	890	182651 (1981)
Japan	Japan	Pacific	1000+	Honshu, Hokkaido, Kyushu, Shikoku	370000	145000	124017000 (1991)
Juan Fernandez	Chile	Pacific	3	Mas a Tierra, Santa Clara	180	70	516 (1982)
Kuril	Russia/Japan	Pacific	56	Shumsu, Iturup	15600	6000	15000 (1970)
Laccadive	India	Arabian Sea	27	Laccadive, Amaindivi	30	10	40237 (1981)
Lofoten	Norway	Norwegian Sea	5	Hinnoy, Austvagoy	1420	550	26241 (1970)
Madeira	Portugal	Atlantic	4	Madeira	790	310	252844 (1981)
Malaysia	Federation of Malaysia	Pacific/ Indian	20000	Borneo, New Guinea, Sumatra	2470250	955700	17981000 (1991)
Maldives	Republic of Maldives	Indian	1190	Male	300	120	226000 (1991)
Malta	Republic of Malta	Mediterranean	5	Malta, Gozo	320	120	354000 (1991)
Mariana	Common-wealth of Mariana Islands	Pacific	14	Saipan, Tinian, Rota	470	180	43345 (1990)
Marquesas	France	Pacific	10	Nukultiva	1190	460	6548 (1983)
Marshall	Marshall Islands	Pacific	1200+	Bikini	180	70	38000 (1989)
Mascarene	France	Indian	3	Réunion, Mauritius, Rodrigues	na	na	1475700 (1982)
Melanesia		Pacific	na	Solomon, Bismark, Fiji, New Guinea	540000	210000	4677000 (1986)
Micronesia		Pacific	na	Caroline, Gilbert, Marshalls, Kiribati	3270	1260	358700 (1986)

Major island groups (continued)

Name	Country	Sea/Ocean	No. of islands	Main islands	Area sq km	Area sq mi	Inhabitants
New Hebrides	Republic of Vanuatu	Pacific	72	Espiritu Santo	14760	5700	147000 (1990)
New-foundland	Canada	Atlantic	na	Prince Edward	405720	156650	580000 (1986)
New Zealand	New Zealand	Pacific	4+	North, South	268050	103500	3291300 (1985)
Nicobar	India	Bay of Bengal	300+	Great Nicobar	8300	3200	188254 (1981)
Novaya Zemlya	Russia	Arctic	5	North, South	81300	31400	400 est. (1983)
Orkney	UK	North Sea	20	Mainland, Ronaldsay	980	380	19056 (1981)
Philippines	Republic of the Philippines	Pacific	7100	Luzon, Mindanao, Samar	300680	110680	65758000 (1991)
Polynesia		Pacific	na	Hawaii, Tonga, Kiribati, Easter, Samoa	17200	10700	61480000 (1990)
Queen Charlotte	Canada	Pacific	150	Prince Rupert	9800	3800	5884 (1981)
São Tomé and Príncipe	Republic of São Tomé & Príncipe	Atlantic	2	São Tomé, Príncipe	970	370	128000 (1991)
Scilly	UK	English Channel	140	St Mary's, St Martin's	20	10	1900 (1987)
Seychelles	Republic of Seychelles	Indian	115	Mahé, La Digue	450	170	68000 (1991)
Shetland	UK	North Sea	100	Mainland, Unst	1400	550	27277 (1981)
Society	France	Pacific	2	Tahiti	1500	590	152129 (1983)
Solomon	Solomon Islands	Pacific	6+	New Georgia, San Cristobal	27560	10640	347000 (1991)
South Orkney	UK	Atlantic	2	Coronation, Laurie	620	240	uninhabited
Sri Lanka	Republic of Sri Lanka	Indian	2	Sri Lanka, Mannar	65610	25200	17423000 (1991)
Taiwan	Republic of China	China Sea/Pacific	na	Taiwan	36000	25300	20658000 (1991)
Tasmania	Australia	Tasman Sea	5+	Tasmania, King Flinders, Bruny	67600	26200	432600 (1983)
Tierra del Fuego	Argentina/Chile	Pacific			73700	28500	29392 (1980)
Tristan da Cunha	UK	Atlantic	5	Gough, Inaccessible, Nightingale	100	40	325 (1982)
Tuamotu	France	Pacific	80	Rangiroa, Hao, Fakarava	800	320	uninhabited
Tuvalu	Tuvalu	Pacific		Funafuti Atoll, Nanumea	30	10	9317 (1991)
Virgin	USA	Caribbean	50+	St Croix, St Thomas	340	130	101809 (1990)
Virgin	UK	Caribbean	36	Tortola, Virgin Gorda	150	60	13000 (1990)
Zanzibar	Tanzania	Indian	3	Zanzibar, Tumbatu	1600	640	571000 (1985)

na – data not available

Considerable variation will be found among sources giving area estimates for island groups, because of the difficulty in deciding where the group boundary line should lie. All estimates above 100 sq km have been rounded to nearest 10, and all above 1000 to the nearest 100.

Largest seas

Name	Area[a] sq km	sq mi
Coral Sea	4791000	1850200
Arabian Sea	3863000	1492000
S China (Nan) Sea	3685000	1423000
Mediterranean Sea	2516000	971000
Bering Sea	2304000	890000
Bay of Bengal	2172000	839000
Sea of Okhotsk	1590000	614000
Gulf of Mexico	1543000	596000
Gulf of Guinea	1533000	592000
Barents Sea	1405000	542000
Norwegian Sea	1383000	534000
Gulf of Alaska	1327000	512000
Hudson Bay	1232000	476000
Greenland Sea	1205000	465000
Arafura Sea	1037000	400000
Philippine Sea	1036000	400000
Sea of Japan	978000	378000
E Siberian Sea	901000	348000
Kara Sea	883000	341000
E China Sea	664000	256000
Andaman Sea	565000	218000
North Sea	520000	201000
Black Sea	508000	196000
Red Sea	453000	175000
Baltic Sea	414000	160000
Arabian/Persian Gulf	238000	92200
Gulf of St Lawrence	238300	92000

Oceans are excluded.
[a]Areas are rounded to nearest 1000 sq km/sq mi.

Largest islands

Name	Area[a] sq km	sq mi
Australia	7692300	2969200
Greenland	2175600	830780
New Guinea	790000	305000
Borneo	737000	285000
Madagascar	587000	227600
Baffin	507000	196000
Sumatra	425000	164900
Honshu (Hondo)	228000	88000
Great Britain	219000	84400
Victoria, Canada	217300	83900
Ellesmere, Canada	196000	75800
Celebes	174000	67400
South I, New Zealand	151000	58200
Java	129000	50000
North I, New Zealand	114000	44200
Newfoundland	109000	42000
Cuba	110860	42790
Luzon	105000	40400
Iceland	103000	40000
Mindanao	94600	36500
Novaya Zemlya (two islands)	90600	35000
Ireland	70280	27100
Hokkaido	78500	30300
Hispaniola	77200	29800
Sakhalin	75100	29000

[a]Areas are rounded to the nearest three significant digits.

Largest lakes

Name/location	Area[a] sq km	sq mi
Caspian Sea, Iran/CIS	371000	143240[b]
Superior, USA/Canada	82260	31760[c]
Aral Sea, Kazakhstan	64500	24900[b]
Victoria, E Africa	62940	24300
Huron, USA/Canada	59580	23000[c]
Michigan, USA	58020	22400
Tanganyika, E Africa	32000	12350
Baikal, Russia	31500	12160
Great Bear, Canada	31330	12100
Great Slave, Canada	28570	11030
Erie, USA/Canada	25710	9920[c]
Winnipeg, Canada	24390	9420
Malawi/Nyasa, E Africa	22490	8680
Balkhash, Kazakhstan	18300	7000[b]
Ontario, Canada	19270	7440[c]
Ladoga, Russia	18130	7000
Chad, W Africa	10000–26000	4000–10000
Maracaibo, Venezuela	13010	5020[d]
Patos, Brazil	10140	3920[d]
Onega, Russia	9800	3800
Rudolf, E Africa	9100	3500
Eyre, Australia	8800	3400[d]
Titicaca, Peru	8300	3200

[a]Areas are given to the nearest 10 sq km/sq mi. The Caspian and Aral Seas, being entirely surrounded by land, are classified as lakes. [b]Salt lakes [c]Average of areas given by Canada and USA [d]Salt lagoons

Largest deserts

Name/location	Area[a] sq km	sq mi
Sahara, N Africa	8600000	3320000
Arabian, SW Asia	2330000	900000
Gobi, Mongolia and NE China	1166000	450000
Patagonian, Argentina	673000	260000
Great Victoria, SW Australia	647000	250000
Great Basin, SW USA	492000	190000
Chihuahuan, Mexican	450000	175000
Great Sandy, NW Australia	400000	150000
Sonoran, SW USA	310000	120000
Kyzyl-Kum, Kazakhstan/Uzbekistan	300000	115000
Takla Makan, N China	270000	105000
Kalahari, SW Africa	260000	100000
Kara-Kum, Turkmenia	260000	100000
Kavir, Iran	260000	100000
Syrian, Saudi Arabia/Jordan/ Syria/Iraq	260000	100000
Nubian, Sudan	260000	100000
Thar, India/Pakistan	200000	77000
Ust'-Urt, Kazakhstan/Uzbekistan	160000	62000
Bet-Pak-Dala, Kazakhstan	155000	60000
Simpson, C Australia	145000	56000
Dzungaria, China	142000	55000
Atacama, Chile	140000	54000
Namib, SE Africa	134000	52000
Sturt, SE Australia	130000	50000
Bolson de Mapimi, Mexico	130000	50000
Ordos, China	130000	50000
Alashan, China	116000	45000

[a]Desert areas are very approximate, because clear physical boundaries may not occur.

Highest mountains

Name	Height[a] m	ft	Location
Everest	8850	29030	China–Nepal
K2	8610	28250	Kashmir–Jammu
Kangchenjunga	8590	28170	India–Nepal
Lhotse	8500	27890	China–Nepal
Kangchenjunga S Peak	8470	27800	India–Nepal
Makalu I	8470	27800	China–Nepal
Kangchenjunga W Peak	8420	27620	India–Nepal
Llotse E Peak	8380	27500	China–Nepal
Dhaulagiri	8170	26810	Nepal
Cho Oyu	8150	26750	China–Nepal
Manaslu	8130	26660	Nepal
Nanga Parbat	8130	26660	Kashmir–Jammu
Annapurna I	8080	26500	Nepal
Gasherbrum I	8070	26470	Kashmir–Jammu
Broad-highest	8050	26400	Kashmir–Jammu
Gasherbrum II	8030	26360	Kashmir–Jammu
Gosainthan	8010	26290	China
Broad-middle	8000	26250	Kashmir–Jammu
Gasherbrum III	7950	26090	Kashmir–Jammu
Annapurna II	7940	26040	Nepal
Nanda Devi	7820	25660	India
Rakaposhi	7790	25560	Kashmir
Kamet	7760	25450	India
Ulugh Muztagh	7720	25340	Tibet
Tirich Mir	7690	25230	Pakistan
Muz Tag Ata	7550	24760	China
Communism Peak	7490	24590	Tajikistan
Pobedy Peak	7440	24410	China–kyrgyzstan
Aconcagua	6960	22830	Argentina
Ojos del Salado	6910	22660	Argentina–Chile

[a]Heights are given to the nearest 10 m/ft.

Highest waterfalls

Name	Height m	ft	Location
Angel (upper fall)	807	2648	Venezuela
Itatinga	628	2060	Brazil
Cuquenan	610	2000	Guyana–Venezuela
Ormeli	563	1847	Norway
Tysse	533	1749	Norway
Pilao	524	1719	Brazil
Ribbon	491	1612	USA
Vestre Mardola	468	1535	Norway
Roraima	457?	1500?	Guyana
Cleve-Garth	450?	1476?	New Zealand

Distances are given for individual leaps.

Deepest caves

Name/location	Depth m	ft
Jean Bernard, France	1494	4900
Snezhnaya, Russia	1340	4397
Puertas de Illamina, Spain	1338	4390
Pierre-Saint-Martin, France	1321	4334
Sistema Huautla, Mexico	1240	4067
Berger, France	1198	3930
Vqerdi, Spain	1195	3921
Dachstein-Mammuthöhle, Austria	1174	3852
Zitu, Spain	1139	3737
Badalona, Spain	1130	3707
Batmanhöhle, Austria	1105	3626
Schneeloch, Austria	1101	3612
GES Malaga, Spain	1070	3510
Lamprechtsofen, Austria	1024	3360

Longest rivers

Name	Outflow	Length[a] km	mi
Nile–Kagera–Ruvuvu–Ruvusu–Luvironza	Mediterranean Sea (Egypt)	6690	4160
Amazon–Ucayali–Tambo–Ene–Apurimac	Atlantic Ocean (Brazil)	6570	4080
Mississippi–Missouri–Jefferson–Beaverhead–Red Rock	Gulf of Mexico (USA)	6020	3740
Chang Jiang (Yangtze)	E China Sea (China)	5980	3720
Yenisey–Angara–Selenga–Ider	Kara Sea (Russia)	5870	3650
Amur–Argun–Kerulen	Tartar Strait (Russia)	5780	3590
Ob–Irtysh	Gulf of Ob, Kara Sea (Russia)	5410	3360
Plata–Parana–Grande	Atlantic Ocean (Argentina–Uruguay)	4880	3030
Huang Ho (Yellow)	Yellow Sea (China)	4840	3010
Congo (Zaire)–Lualaba	Atlantic Ocean (Angola–Zaire)	4630	2880
Lena	Laptev Sea (Russia)	4400	2730
Mackenzie–Slave–Peace–Finlay	Beaufort Sea (Canada)	4240	2630
Mekong	S China Sea (Vietnam)	4180	2600
Niger	Gulf of Guinea (Nigeria)	4100	2550

[a]Lengths are given to the nearest 10 km/mi, and include the river plus tributaries comprising the longest watercourse.

The Earth's largest drainage basins

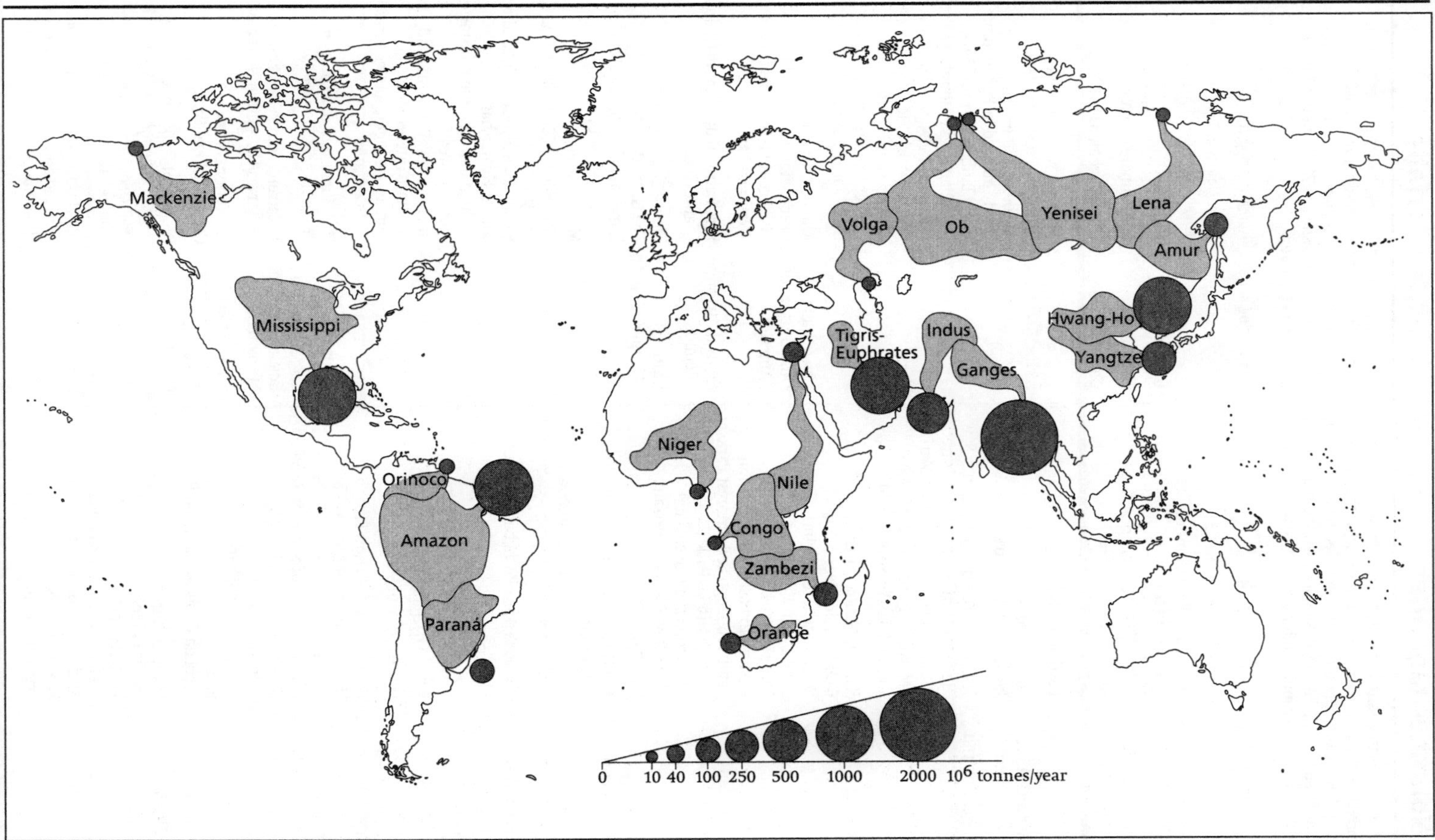

World heritage sites

A world heritage site is a site (natural or cultural) recognized by the international community (in the shape of the World Heritage Convention founded by the General Conference of UNESCO in 1972) as possessing universal value, and thus coming under a collective responsibility.

A country nominates a site to the Convention, and a decision on whether to include it in the world heritage list is made by an 21-member international committee. There are now 378 sites – 276 cultural, 87 natural and 15 mixed – in 86 States.

Contracting state	*Name of property*
Albania	Butrinti
Algeria	Al Qal'a of Beni Hammad Tassili n'Ajjer M'Zab Valley Djemila Tipasa Timgad Kasbah of Algiers
Argentina	Los Glaciares Iguazu National Park
Argentina and Brazil	Jesuit Missions of the Guaranis: San Ignacio Mini, Santa Ana, Nuestra Señora de Loreto and Santa Maria Mayor (Argentina), ruins of Sao Miguel das Missões (Brazil)
Australia	Kakadu National Park Great Barrier Reef Willandra Lakes Region Tasmanian Wilderness Lord Howe Island Group Australian East Coast Temperate and Sub-Tropical Rainforest Parks Uluru National Park Wet Tropics of Queensland Shark Bay, Western Australia Fraser Island
Bangladesh	The Historic Mosque City of Bagerhat Ruins of the Buddhist Vihara at Paharpur
Belarus/Poland	Belovezhskaya Pushcha/Bialowieza Forest
Benin	Royal Palaces of Abomey
Bolivia	City of Potosi Jesuit Missions of the Chiquitos Historic city of Sucre
Brazil	Historic town of Ouro Preto Historic centre of the town of Olinda Historic centre of Salvador de Bahia Sanctuary of Bom Jesus do Congonhas Iguaçu National Park Brasilia Serra da Capivara National Park
Bulgaria	Boyana Church Madara Rider Thracian tomb of Kazanlak Rock-hewn churches of Ivanovo Ancient city of Nessebar Rila Monastery Srebarna Nature Reserve Pirin National Park Thracian tomb of Sveshtari
Cambodia	Angkor
Cameroon	Dja Faunal Reserve
Canada	L'Anse aux Meadows National Historic Park Nahanni National Park Dinosaur Provincial Park Anthony Island Head-Smashed-In Buffalo Jump Wood Buffalo National Park Canadian Rocky Mountains Parks (Burges Shale, previously inscribed on the World Heritage List, is part of this site) Quebec (historic area) Gros Morne National Park
Canada and United States of America	Kluane National Park/Wrangell–Saint Elias National Park and Preserve, and Glacier Bay National Park
Central African Republic	Parc national du Manovo-Gounda Saint Floris
China (People's Rep. of)	Mount Taishan The Great Wall Imperial Palace of the Ming and Qing Dynasties Mogao Caves The Mausoleum of the First Qin Emperor Peking Man Site at Zhoukoudian Mount Huangshan Wulingyuan scenic and historic interest area Jiuzhaigou Valley scenic and historic interest area Huanglong scenic and historic interest area
Colombia	Port, fortresses and group of monuments, Cartagena
Costa Rica/ Panama	Talamanca Range-La Amistad Reserves/La Amistad National Park
Côte d'Ivoire	Tai National Park Como National Park
Croatia	Old city of Dubrovnik Historical complex of Split with the Palace of Diocletian Plitvice Lakes National Park
Cuba	Old Havana and its fortifications Trinidad and the Valley de los Ingenios

Contracting state	*Name of property*
Cyprus	Paphos
	Painted churches in the Troodos region
Czech and Slovak Federal Republics	Historic centre of Prague
	Historic centre of Cesky Krumlov
	Historic centre of Telc
Dominican Republic	Colonial city of Santo Domingo
Ecuador	Galapagos Islands
	City of Quito
	Sangay National Park
Egypt	Memphis and its necropolis – the Pyramid fields from Giza to Dahshur
	Ancient Thebes with its necropolis
	Nubian monuments from Abu Simbel to Philae
	Islamic Cairo
	Abu Mena
Ethiopia	Simen National Park
	Rock-hewn churches, Lalibela
	Fasil Ghebbi, Gondar Region
	Lower valley of the Awash
	Tiya
	Aksum
	Lower valley of the Omo
Finland	Old Rauma
	Fortress of Suomenlinna
France	Mont-Saint-Michel and its bay
	Chartres Cathedral
	Palace and park of Versailles
	Vézelay, church and hill
	Decorated grottoes of the Vézère Valley
	Palace and park of Fontainebleau
	Château and estate of Chambord
	Amiens Cathedral
	The Roman theatre and its surroundings and the 'Triumphal Arch' of Orange
	Roman and romanesque monuments of Arles
	Cistercian abbey of Fontenay
	Royal Saltworks of Arc-et-Senans
	Place Stanislas, Place de la Carrière and Place d'Alliance in Nancy
	Church of Saint-Savin sur Gartempe
	Cape Girolata, Cape Porto and Scandola Nature Reserve in Corsica
	Pont du Gard (Roman aqueduct)
	Strasbourg – Grande Ile
	Paris, banks of the Seine
	Cathedral of Notre-Dame, former Abbey of Saint-Remi and Tau Palace, Cathedral of Reims
	Bourges Cathedral
Germany	Aachen Cathedral
	Speyer Cathedral
	Würzburg Residence with the court gardens and Residence Square
	Pilgrimage church of Wies

Contracting state	*Name of property*
	The Castles of Augustusburg and Falkenlust at Brühl
	St Mary's Cathedral and St Michael's Church at Hildesheim
	Roman monuments, cathedral and Liebfrauen-Church in Trier
	Hanseatic city of Lübeck
	Palaces and parks of Potsdam and Berlin
	Abbey and Altenmünster of Lorsch
	Mines of Rammelsberg and the historic town of Goslar
Ghana	Forts and castles, Volta, Greater Accra, Central and Western Regions
	Ashante traditional buildings
Greece	Temple of Apollo Epicurius at Bassae
	Archaeological site of Delphi
	The Acropolis, Athens
	Mount Athos
	Meteora
	Paleochristian and Byzantine monuments of Thessalonika
	Archaeological site of Epidaurus
	Mediaeval city of Rhodes
	Archaeological site of Olympia
	Mystras
	Delos
	Monasteries of Daphni, Hossios Lukas, and Nea Moni of Chios
	Pythagoreion and Heraion of Samos
Guatemala	Tikal National Park
	Antigua Guatemala
	Archaeological park and ruins of Quirigua
Guinea and Côte d'Ivoire	Mount Nimba Strict Nature Reserve
Haiti	National History Park – Citadel, Sans Souci, Ramiers
Holy See	Vatican City
Honduras	Maya site of Copan
	Rio Platano Biosphere Reserve
Hungary	Budapest, the banks of the Danube with the district of Buda Castle
	Hollokö
India	Ajanta Caves
	Ellora Caves
	Agra Fort
	Taj Mahal
	The Sun Temple, Konarak
	Group of monuments at Mahabalipuram
	Kaziranga National Park
	Manas Wildlife Sanctuary
	Keoladeo National Park
	Churches and convents of Goa
	Khajuraho group of monuments
	Group of monuments at Hampi
	Fatehpur Sikri
	Group of monuments at Pattadakal
	Elephanta Caves

World heritage sites (continued)

Contracting state	*Name of property*
	Brihadisvara Temple, Thanjavur Sundarbans National Park Nanda Devi National Park Buddhist monuments at Sanchi
Indonesia	Komodo National Park Ujung Kulon National Park Borobudur Temple compound Prambanan Temple compound
Iran	Tchogha Zanbil Persepolis Meidan Emam, Esfahan
Iraq	Hatra
Italy	Rock Drawings in Valcamonica The Church and Dominican convent of Santa Maria delle Grazie with 'The Last Supper' by Leonardo da Vinci Historic centre of Florence Venice and its lagoon Piazza del Duomo, Pisa Historic centre of San Gimignano
Italy/Holy See (each according to its jurisdiction)	Historic Centre of Rome, the properties of the Holy See in that city enjoying extraterritorial rights, and San Paolo fuori la Mura
Jordan*	Old City of Jerusalem and its walls Petra Quseir Amra
Lebanon	Anjar Baalbek Byblos Tyr
Libyan Arab Jamahiriya	Archaeological site of Leptis Magna Archaeological site of Sabratha Archaeological site of Cyrene Rock-art sites of Tadrart Acacus Old town of Ghadamès
Madagascar	Tsingy Bemaraha Strict Nature Reserve
Malawi	Lake Malawi National Park
Mali	Old towns of Djenné Timbuktu Cliff of Bandiagara (Land of the Dogons)
Malta	Hal Saflieni Hypogeum City of Valetta Megalithic temples of Malta
Mauritania	Banc d'Arguin National Park
Mexico	Sian Ka'an Pre-Hispanic city and national park of Palenque Historic centre of Mexico City and Xochimilco Pre-Hispanic city of Teotihuacan Historic centre of Oaxaca and archaeological site of Monte Alban Historic centre of Puebla Historic town of Guanajuato and adjacent mines Pre-Hispanic city of Chichen-Itza Historic centre of Morelia El Tajin, Pre-Hispanic City
Morocco	Medina of Fez Medina of Marrakesh Ksar of Aït-Ben-Haddou
Mozambique	Island of Mozambique
Nepal	Sagarmatha National Park Kathmandu Valley Royal Chitwan National Park
New Zealand	Te Wahipounamu – South West New Zealand (Westland/Mount Cook National Park and Fiordland National Park, previously inscribed on the World Heritage List, are part of this site) Tongariro National Park
Niger	Aïr-Ténéré Reserve
Norway	Urnes Stave Church Bryggen Røros Rock drawings of Alta
Oman	Bahla Fort Archaeological sites of Bat, Al-Khutm, and Al-Ayn
Pakistan	Archaeological ruins of Moenjodaro Taxila Buddhist ruins of Takht-i-Bahi and neighbouring city remains at Sahr-i-Bahlol Historical monuments of Thatta Fort and Shalamar Gardens in Lahore
Panama	The fortifications on the Caribbean side of Portobelo-San Lorenzo Darien National Park
Peru	City of Cuzco Historic sanctuary of Machu Picchu Chavin (archaeological site) Huascaran National Park Chan Chan Archaeological Zone Manu National Park Rio Abiseo National Park Historic centre of Lima
Poland	Kraków's historic centre Wieliczka Salt Mine Auschwitz Concentration Camp Historic centre of Warsaw Old city of Zamość
Portugal	Central zone of the Town of Angra do Heroismo in the Azores Monastery of the Hieronymites and Tower of Belem in Lisbon

* The Old City of Jerusalem was annexed by Israel in 1967, but this claim has not been recognised by the UN.

Contracting state	Name of property
	Monastery of Batalha Convent of Christ in Tomar Historic centre of Evora Monastery of Alcobaça
Romania	Danube Delta
Russian Federation	Historic centre of Saint Petersburg and related groups of monuments[a] Khizi Pogost[a] Kremlin and Red Square in Moscow[b] Historic monuments of Novgorod and surroundings Cultural and historic ensemble of Solovetsky Islands The White Monuments of Vladimir and Suzdal
Senegal	Island of Gorée Niokolo-Koba National Park Djoudj National Bird Sanctuary
Seychelles	Aldabra Atoll Vallée de Mai Nature Reserve
Slovenia	Skocjan Caves
Spain	The Mosque of Córdoba The Alhambra and the Generalife, Granada Burgos Cathedral Monastery and site of the Escorial, Madrid Parque Güell, Palacio Güell and Casa Mila, in Barcelona Altamira Cave Old town of Segovia and its aqueduct Churches of the Kingdom of the Asturias Santiago de Compostela (Old Town) Old town of Avila with its extra muros churches Mudejar architecture of Teruel Historic city of Toledo Garajonay National Park Old town of Cáceres The Cathedral, the Alcazar and the Archivo de Indias, in Seville Old city of Salamanca Poblet Monastery
Sri Lanka	Sacred city of Anuradhapura Ancient city of Polonnaruva Ancient city of Sigiriya Sinharaja Forest Reserve Sacred city of Kandy Old town of Galle and its fortifications Golden Temple of Dambulla
Sweden	Royal Domain of Drottningholm
Switzerland	Convent of Saint Gall Benedictine convent of Saint John at Müstair Old city of Berne
Syrian Arab Republic	Ancient city of Damascus Ancient city of Bosra Site of Palmyra Ancient city of Aleppo
Thailand	Thungyai-Huai Kha Khaeng wildlife sanctuaries Historic town of Sukhothai and associated historic towns Historic city of Ayutthaya and associated historic towns Ban Chiang archaeological site
Tunisia	Medina of Tunis Site of Carthage Amphitheatre of El Djem Ichkeul National Park Punic town of Kerkuane and its necropolis Medina of Sousse Kairouan
Turkey	Historic areas of Istanbul Göreme National Park and the rock sites of Cappadocia Great Mosque and hospital of Divrigi Hattusha Nemrut Dag Xanthos-Letoon Hierapolis-Pamukkale
Ukraine	Kiev: Saint Sophia Cathedral and related monastic buildings, and Lavra of Kiev-Pechersk
United Kingdom	The Giant's Causeway and Causeway Coast Durham Castle and Cathedral Ironbridge Gorge Studley Royal Park including the ruins of Fountains Abbey Stonehenge, Avebury and associated sites The castles and town walls of King Edward in Gwynedd Saint Kilda Blenheim Palace City of Bath Hadrian's Wall Palace of Westminster, Abbey of Westminster, and Saint Margaret's Church Henderson Island The Tower of London Canterbury Cathedral, Saint Augustine's Abbey, and Saint Martin's Church
United Republic of Tanzania	Ngorongoro Conservation Area Ruins of Kilwa Kisiwani and ruins of Songo Mnara Serengeti National Park Selous Game Reserve Kilimanjaro National Park
United States of America	Mesa Verde Yellowstone Grand Canyon National Park Everglades National Park

World heritage sites (continued)

Contracting state	*Name of property*
	Independence Hall
	Redwood National Park
	Mammoth Cave National Park
	Olympic National Park
	Cahokia Mounds state historic site
	Great Smoky Mountains National Park
	La Fortaleza and San Juan historic site in Puerto Rico
	The Statue of Liberty
	Yosemite National Park
	Chaco Culture National Historical Park
	Monticello and University of Virginia in Charlottesville
	Hawaii Volcanoes National Park
	Pueblo de Taos
Uzbekistan	Itchan Kala[ab]
Yemen	Old walled city of Shibam
	Old city of Sana'a
Yugoslavia	Stari Ras and Sopocani
	Ohrid Region with its cultural and historical aspect and its natural environment (situated in Macedonia)
	Natural and culturo-historical region of Kotor
	Durmitor National Park
	Studenica Monastery
Zaire	Virunga National Park
	Garamba National Park
	Kahuzi-Biega National Park
	Salonga National Park
Zambia/Zimbabwe	Victoria Falls/Mosi-oa-Tunya
Zimbabwe	Mana Pools National Park, Sapi, and Chewore Safari Areas
	Great Zimbabwe National Monument
	Khami Ruins National Monument

[a]The nominations related to these cultural sites were submitted in 1989 by the USSR. [b]Since the formation of the Commonwealth of Independent States, in place of the USSR, UNESCO has not received, to date, a declaration by Uzbekistan as to whether it is, or is not, a party to the World Heritage Convention.

National Parks in England and Wales

Name (Date of designation)	*Location*	*Area* *sq km*	*sq mi*
Brecon Beacons (1957)	Powys, Dyfed, Gwent, Mid Glamorgan	1351	522
Dartmoor (1951)	Devon	954	368
Exmoor (1954)	Somerset, Devon	693	268
Lake District (1951)	Cumbria	2292	885
Northumberland (1956)	Northumberland	1049	405
North York Moors (1952)	North Yorkshire, Cleveland	1436	554
Peak District (1951)	Derbyshire, Staffordshire, South Yorkshire, Cheshire, West Yorkshire, Greater Manchester	1438	555
Pembrokeshire Coast (1952)	Dyfed	584	225
Snowdonia (1951)	Gwynedd	2142	817
Yorkshire Dales (1954)	N Yorkshire, Cumbria	1769	683

National Parks in the USA

Park (Date authorized)	Location	Area hectares	acres
Arcadia (1916)	SE Maine	15 770	38 971
Arches (1929)	E Utah	29 695	73 379
Badlands (1929)	SW South Dakota	98 461	243 302
Big Bend (1935)	W Texas	286 565	708 118
Biscayne (1968)	SE Florida	72 900	180 128
Bryce Canyon (1923)	SW Utah	14 502	35 835
Canyonlands (1964)	SE Utah	136 610	337 570
Capitol Reef (1937)	S Utah	97 895	214 904
Carlsbad Caverns (1923)	SE New Mexico	18 921	46 755
Channel Islands (1938)	S California	100 910	249 354
Crater Lake (1902)	SW Oregon	64 869	160 290
Denali (1917)	S Alaska	1 645 248	4 065 493
Everglades (1934)	S Florida	566 075	1 398 800
Gates of the Arctic (1978)	N Alaska	2 854 000	7 052 000
Glacier (1910)	NW Montana	410 188	1 013 595
Glacier Bay (1925)	SE Alaska	1 569 481	3 878 269
Grand Canyon (1908)	NW Arizona	493 059	1 218 375
Grand Teton (1929)	NW Wyoming	125 661	310 516
Great Smoky Mountains (1926)	N Tennessee	210 550	520 269
Guadalupe Mountains (1966)	W Texas	30 875	76 293
Haleakala (1916)	Hawaii	11 956	28 655
Hawaii Volcanoes (1916)	Hawaii	92 745	229 177
Hot Springs (1832)	Central Arkansas	2 358	5 826
Isle Royale (1931)	NW Michigan	231 398	571 796
Katmai (1918)	SW Alaska	1 792 810	4 430 125
Kenai Fjords (1978)	S Alaska	229 457	567 000
Kings Canyon (1940)	E California	186 211	460 136
Kobuk Valley (1978)	N Alaska	692 000	1 710 000
Lake Clark (1978)	S Alaska	987 000	2 439 000
Lassen Volcanic (1907)	N California	43 047	106 372
Mammoth Cave (1926)	Central Kentucky	21 230	52 452
Mesa Verde (1906)	SW Colorado	21 078	52 085
Mount Rainier (1899)	SW Washington	95 265	235 404
North Cascades (1968)	N Washington	204 277	504 781
Olympic (1909)	NW Washington	370 250	914 890
Petrified Forest (1906)	E Arizona	37 835	93 493
Redwood (1915)	NW California	44 280	109 415
Rocky Mountain (1915)	Central Colorado	106 762	263 809
Sequoia (1890)	E California	162 885	402 488
Shenandoah (1926)	Virginia	78 845	194 826
Theodore Roosevelt (1947)	W North Dakota	28 497	70 416
Virgin Islands (1956)	Virgin Islands	5 947	14 695
Voyageurs (1971)	N Minnesota	88 678	219 128
Wind Cave (1903)	SW South Dakota	11 449	28 292
Wrangell-St Elias (1978)	SE Alaska	3 297 000	8 147 000
Yellowstone (1872)	Idaho, Montana, Wyoming	898 350	2 219 823
Yosemite (1890)	E California	307 932	760 917
Zion (1909)	SW Utah	59 308	146 551

ENVIRONMENT

CLIMATE

The climate system

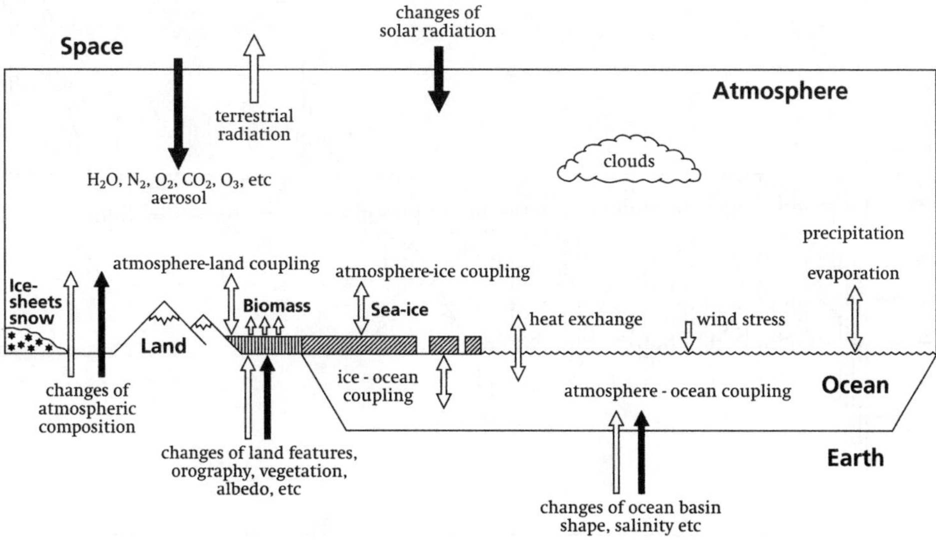

Schematic illustration of the climate system components and interactions (from Houghton, J.T. (ed), 1984, *The global climate*; Cambridge University Press).

Climate alterations produced by cities

Element	*Compared to rural environs*
contaminants	
condensation nuclei	10 times more
particulates	10 times more
gaseous admixtures	5–25 times more
radiation	
total on horizontal surface	0–20% less
ultraviolet, winter	30% less
ultraviolet, summer	5% less
sunshine duration	5–15% less
cloudiness	
clouds	5–10% more
fog, winter	100% more
fog, summer	30% more
precipitation	
amounts	5–15% more
days with less than 5 mm	10% more
snowfall, inner city	5–10% less
snowfall, lee of city	10% more
thunderstorms	10–15% more
temperature	
annual mean	0.5–30°C more
winter minimums (average)	1–2°C more
summer maximums	1–3°C more
heating degree days	10% less
relative humidity	
annual mean	6% less
winter	2% less
summer	8% less
wind speed	
annual mean	20–30% less
extreme gusts	10–20% less
calm	5–20% more

Temperature change

Global-mean combined land-air and sea-surface temperatures, 1861–1989, relative to the average for 1951–80.

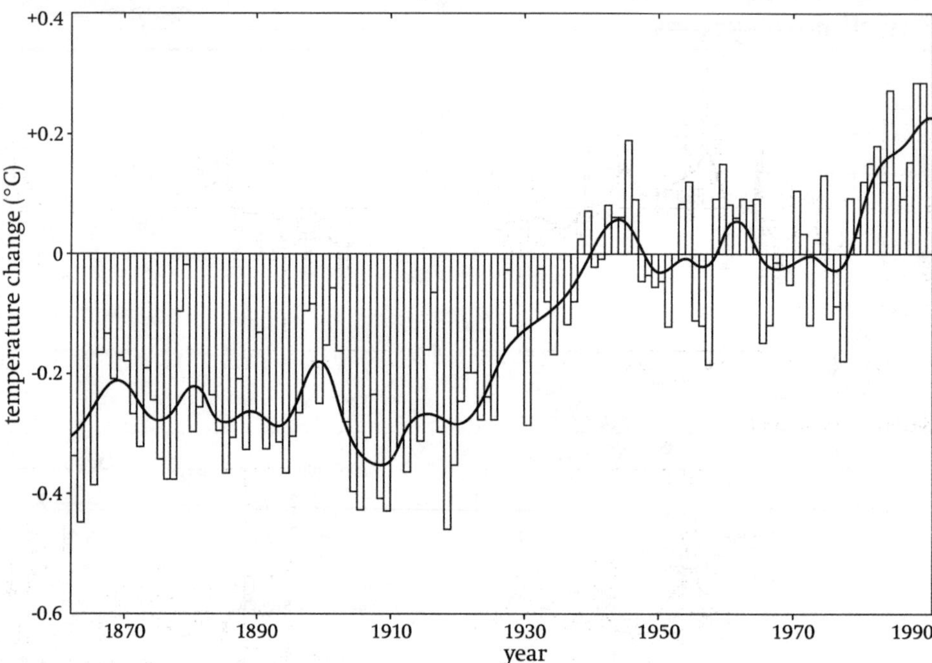

Global mean surface temperature during the last 120 years.

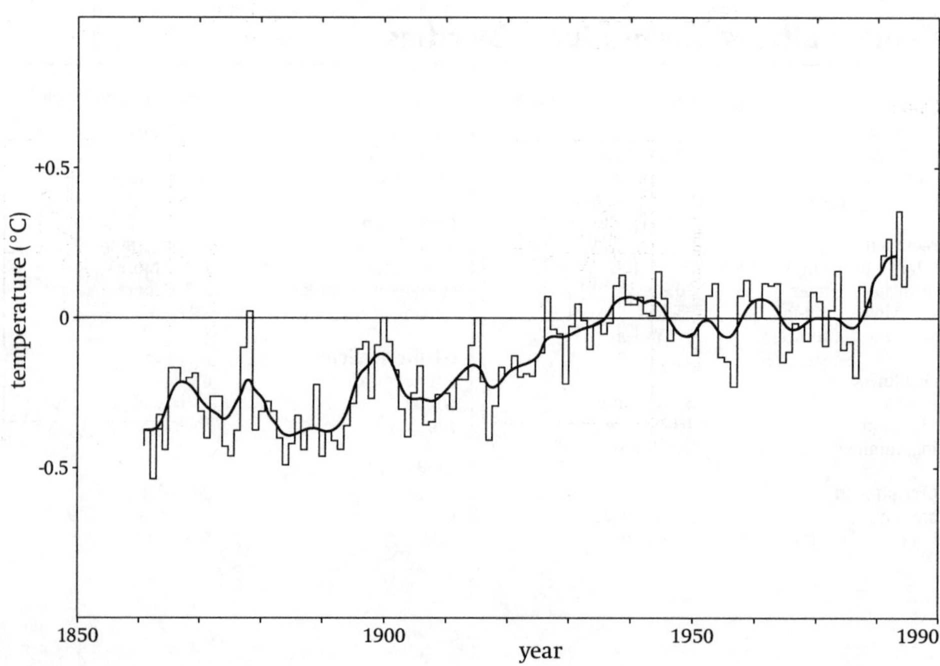

Changes of maximum (day-time) and minimum (night-time) temperatures.

United States

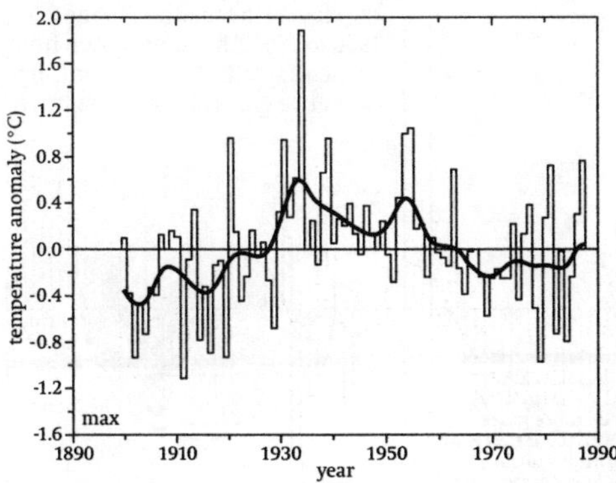

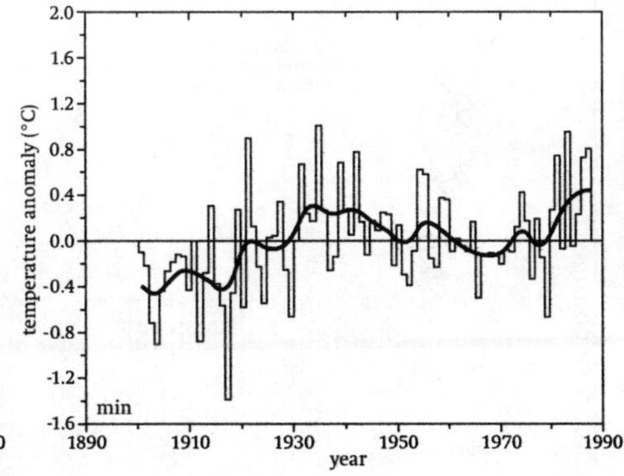

South-eastern Australia

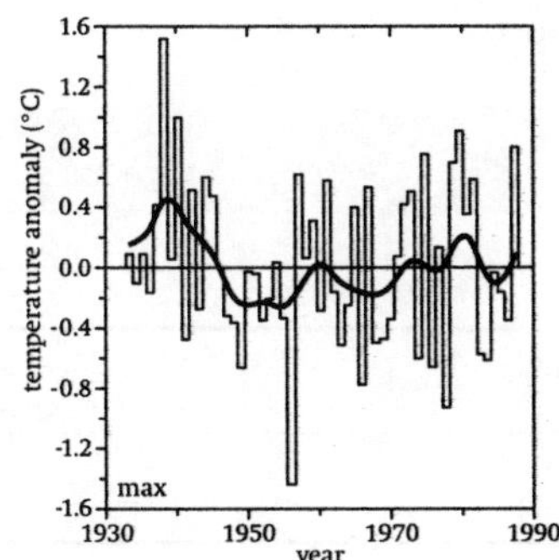

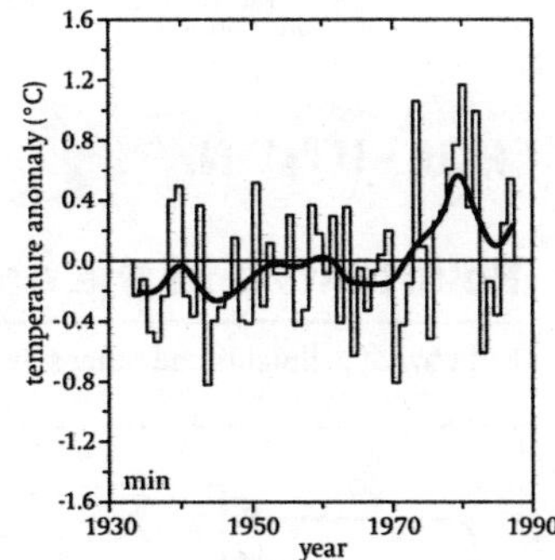

China

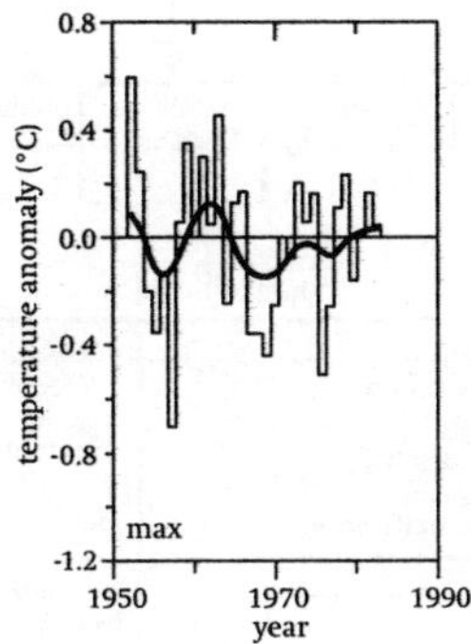

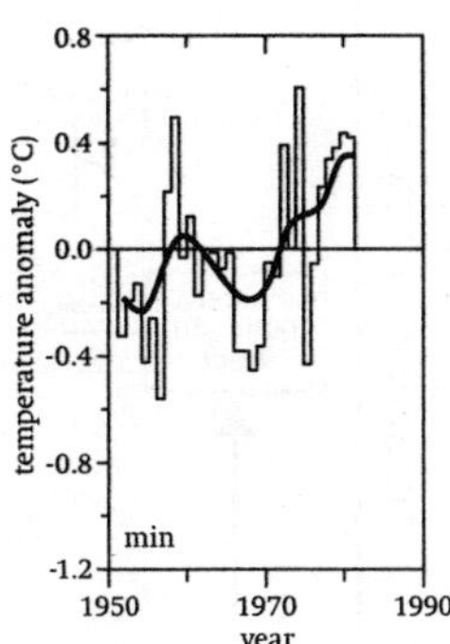

The greenhouse effect

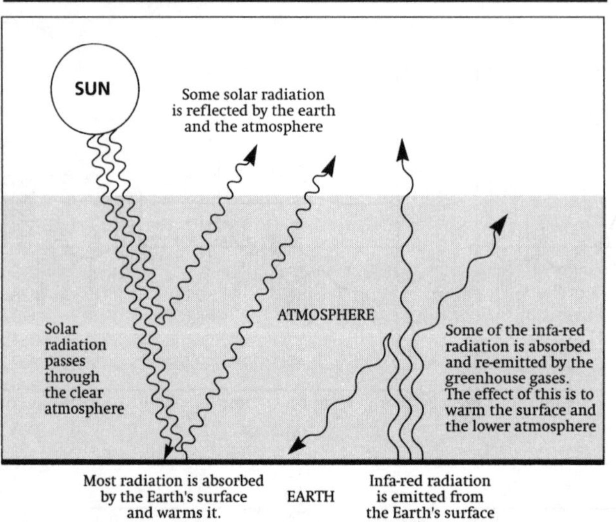

Greenhouse gases

The contribution from each of the human-made greenhouse gases to the change in radiative forcing from 1980 to 1990. The contribution from ozone may also be significant, but cannot be quantified at present.

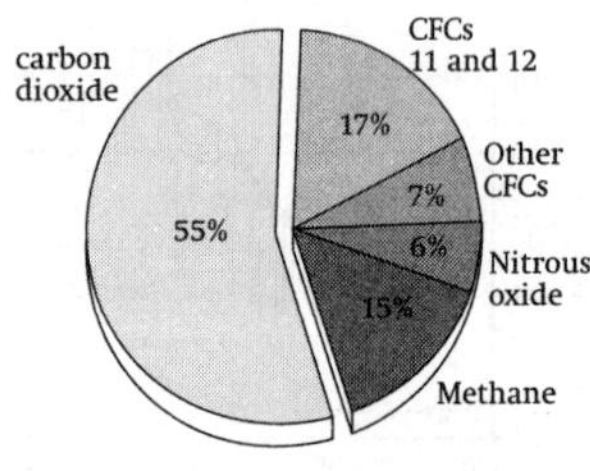

POLLUTION

Pollutants and the ecosystem

Pathways of pollutants and other substances in ecosystems.

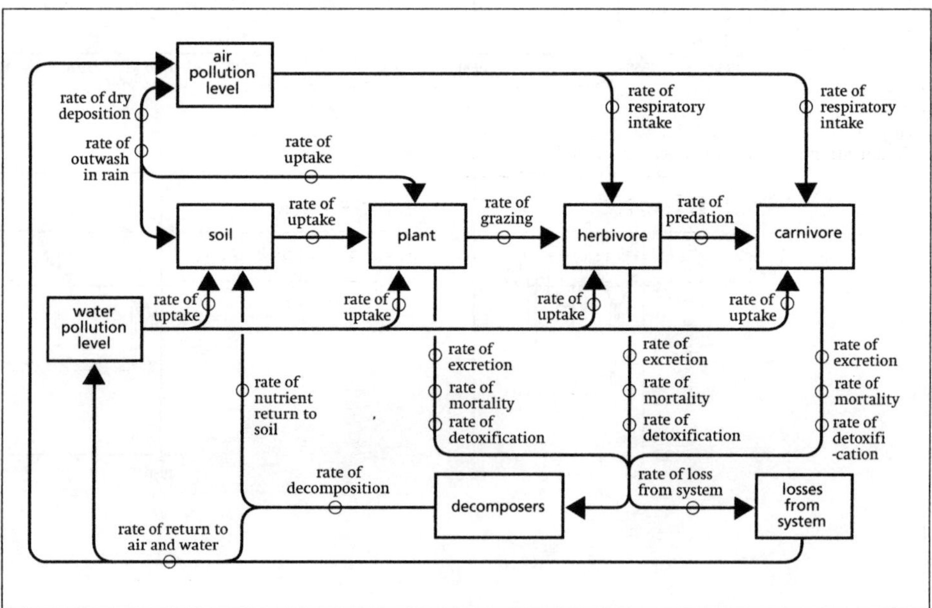

Carbon dioxide

Carbon dioxide emissions from energy use, selected OECD* countries, 1971–1989[a]

million tonnes Carbon

	1971	*1975*	*1980*	*1985*	*1986*	*1987*	*1988*	*1989*
Canada	97.3	113.6	130.0	120.6	118.8	122.8	131.1	135.5
USA	1239.5	1274.7	1410.0	1364.8	1359.1	1413.3	1463.9	1480.0
Japan	225.6	261.8	272.0	260.4	257.9	252.6	280.2	288.0
Australia	48.8	56.4	66.0	66.4	66.3	70.2	71.0	76.3
New Zealand	4.5	5.4	5.0	6.7	6.9	7.0	7.5	7.9
Austria	15.1	15.1	17.0	16.5	16.7	17.1	16.7	17.0
Belgium	36.8	36.5	39.0	31.1	32.0	32.5	33.0	33.6
Denmark	17.5	16.1	18.0	18.3	18.2	18.6	17.7	16.2
Finland	15.0	15.6	19.0	17.3	17.7	19.6	17.8	18.4
France	129.9	130.7	144.0	112.7	108.7	108.8	106.1	110.8
Germany	291.9	279.6	304.5	291.4	294.7	292.6	289.3	281.9
Greece	8.5	11.8	15.0	18.2	18.0	19.5	20.9	22.7
Iceland	0.5	0.5	0.0	0.5	0.5	0.5	0.5	0.6
Ireland	6.3	6.1	7.0	7.3	7.7	8.0	7.9	8.1
Italy	97.7	102.4	112.0	105.4	106.8	111.3	112.4	117.3
Luxembourg	3.9	3.4	3.0	2.6	2.6	2.5	2.5	2.7
Netherlands	46.8	48.3	53.0	49.8	51.9	52.7	53.3	53.5
Norway	7.5	7.6	9.0	8.8	10.2	9.6	8.8	10.6
Portugal	5.7	6.9	8.0	8.8	9.7	9.8	10.5	13.0
Spain	36.7	48.1	57.0	56.4	57.4	57.6	58.5	63.2
Sweden	27.4	26.9	25.0	22.8	22.8	22.2	22.1	21.4
Switzerland	11.9	11.2	12.0	12.4	13.1	12.4	12.6	12.1
Turkey		24.2	28.0	35.8	38.6	41.3	39.8	43.8
UK	188.5	171.7	169.0	160.5	163.3	165.7	164.9	164.0
North America	1336.8	1388.3	1540.0	1485.4	1477.9	1536.1	1595.0	1615.5
Australia	53.3	61.8	71.0	73.1	73.2	77.2	78.5	84.2
OECD Europe	960.2	962.7	1039.5	976.6	990.6	1002.3	995.3	1010.9
EC	870.2	861.6	925.5	862.5	871.0	879.6	877.0	887.0
OECD	2575.9	2674.6	2922.5	2795.5	2799.6	2868.2	2929.0	2998.6
World [b]	4379.7	4811.5	5528.4	5801.9	5900.0	6080.8	6255.9	

[a] Anthropogenic carbon dioxide emissions from energy use only. Oil held in international marine bunkers is included. Quantities are assigned to the country in which these bunkers are situated. Oil and gas for non-energy purposes are excluded.
[b] World emissions estimated using a simplified method compared to that used for OECD countries.
* Organization for Economic Cooperation and Development (see note page 73)

Geographic distribution of carbon emissions

Geographic distribution of the emissions of carbon from combustion of fossil fuels in 1980.

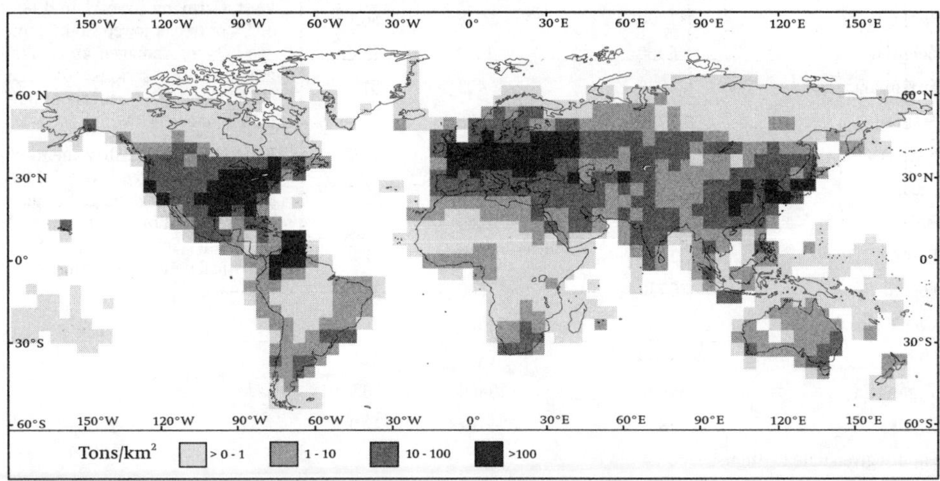

Changes in greenhouse gases pollution

Concentrations of carbon dioxide and methane after remaining relatively constant up to the eighteenth century, have risen sharply since then due to human activities. Concentrations of nitrous oxide have increased since the mid-18th-c, especially in the last few decades. CFCs were not present in the atmosphere before the 1930s.

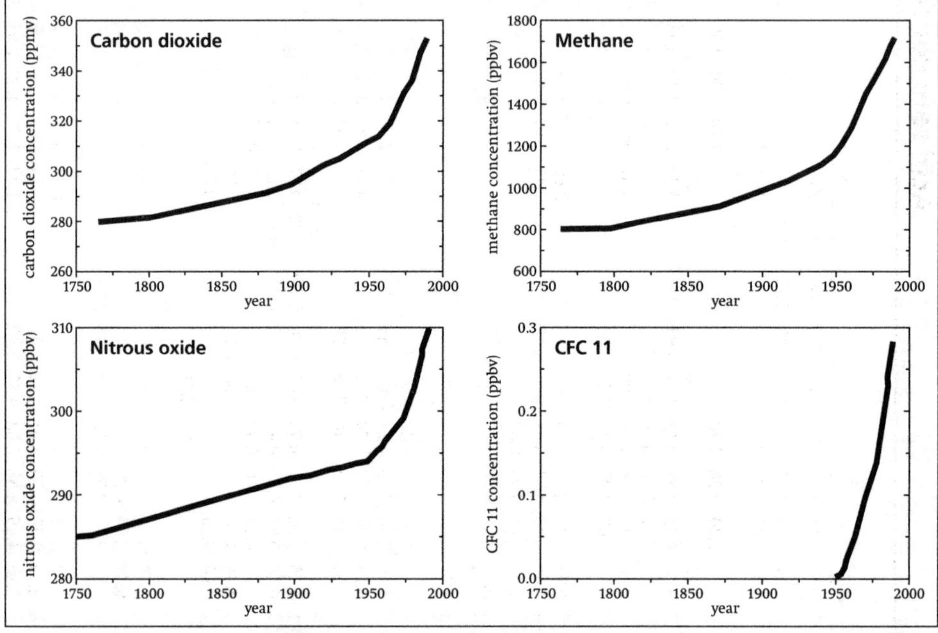

Acid rain damage to forests in Europe

Country	*Forest expanse (sq km)*	*Extent of damage*[a] *(sq km)*	*Percentage damaged*
Finland	194 000	67 900	35.0
Norway	83 330	4 100	4.9
Sweden	265 000	10 600	4.0
West Germany	73 230	38 240	51.9
Netherlands	3 090	1 548	50.1
Belgium	6 160	1 110	18.0
Luxembourg	820	423	51.6
France	150 750	2 796	1.85
Switzerland	12 000	4 320	36.0
Austria	375 400	9 600	24.2
Italy	63 630	3 180	5.0
East Germany	29 000	3 500	12.0
Poland	86 770	22 730	26.2[b]
Czechoslovakia	46 000	12 500	26.1
Hungary	16 700	1 837	11.0
Yugoslavia	95 000	10 400	10.9
Totals	1 500 880	194 784	12.9

Figures given date to August 1986.

[a] Four classes of damage are generally recognised, viz. slight damage, medium to serious damage, critical damage with trees actually dying, and complete damage with trees dead (conforming to needle/leaf loss of 11–25%, 26–60%, 61–90%, and 100%). In West Germany as of late 1985, 32.7% of trees showed slight damage (63% of damaged area), 17% medium to serious damage (32.8%), and 2.2% critical or complete damage (4.2%).

[b] In late 1986 the Polish Academy of Sciences estimated around 50%. Extensive forest damage has also been reported in western parts of the former Soviet Union, but no statistical details are available.

Acid rain concentrations

Concentrations in acid precipitation, selected areas, 1975–90

		pH								*SO^{2-}_4 (mg/l)*								*NO_3 (mg/l)*							
Country	*Areas*	*1975*	*1980*	*1985*	*1986*	*1987*	*1988*	*1989*	*1990*	*1975*	*1980*	*1985*	*1986*	*1987*	*1988*	*1989*	*1990*	*1975*	*1980*	*1985*	*1986*	*1987*	*1988*	*1989*	*1990*
Canada	Great Lakes	4.40	4.40	4.23	4.20	4.31	4.33	4.31	4.34	6.53	3.61	2.65	2.57	2.52	2.49	2.49	2.36	3.16	2.59	2.24	1.99	2.17	2.11	2.44	1.86
USA	Great lakes		4.42	4.53	4.52	4.50					2.65	2.09	2.25	2.18					1.63	1.35	1.42	1.46			
Japan	Kanto District	3.90	4.30							7.80	4.40							5.30	2.70						
	Tokyo			5.00	5.00	5.50						2.30	3.20	3.20						1.20	2.20	2.50			
Austria	Illmitz		4.47				5.30				6.03				4.26				2.83				2.75		
Belgium	Offagne		5.96	5.61	5.29	5.84	5.23	5.03			5.13	4.62	3.78	3.12	2.67	2.94			5.30	2.92	2.30	2.26	2.26	2.57	
	Bruxelles			5.26	5.15	4.68	4.84	4.81				6.51	6.12	5.88	5.13	5.73				3.10	3.10	3.28	2.97	3.76	
Denmark	Tange		4.43	4.48	4.66	4.54	4.48				2.66	1.18	0.84	1.04	0.90				1.41	0.69	0.51	0.62	0.53		
Finland	Uto, Ahtari, Virolahti	4.79	4.63	4.46	4.49	4.54	4.52	4.45		2.95	4.12	3.67	3.93	3.30	3.57	2.20					2.52	2.04	2.48	2.17	
France	Vert-Le-Petit		4.58	4.64	4.99	4.54	4.90				5.24	4.38	4.17	4.59	3.06				3.69	4.11	3.85	4.47	2.13		
	Carpentras	5.40	5.30	5.70	5.50	4.90	5.40	6.10		6.05	5.65	5.16	5.73	5.91	5.15	2.75		1.66	2.47	1.61	1.83	3.26	2.81	1.61	
Germany	Rheinland	4.20	4.20	4.40	4.40	4.50						5.48	4.93	6.30											
	Deuselbach			4.36	4.42	4.46	4.55	4.46				3.33	2.65	2.52	2.55	2.68				2.49	1.99	2.15	2.16	2.54	
Iceland	Irafoss		5.22				5.32				0.93				1.20								0.44		
Ireland	Valentia		4.63				5.39				1.86				4.98								0.44		
Italy	Ispra						4.23								4.02								3.85		
Luxembourg	National					5.07	5.23	4.68						4.03	3.90	3.41						2.01	2.11	2.67	
Netherlands	National		4.46	4.71	4.68	4.62	4.66	4.63			6.16	5.43	5.59	4.61	4.06	4.65			3.08	2.81	3.27	2.98	2.40	2.47	
	Limburg		4.36	4.60	4.65	4.72	4.99				9.04	8.00	7.69	5.70	7.33				4.81	3.68	3.83	4.26	4.03		
	North Holland		4.34	4.76	4.49	4.24	4.54	4.76			7.65	7.16	7.05	7.16	7.86	11.06				3.34	2.66	3.06	4.16	2.01	
Norway	National	4.47	4.36	4.41	4.36	4.45	4.38																		
	Birkenes	4.27	4.16	4.24	4.26	4.38	4.25	4.27	4.40	1.01	1.23	0.98	1.01	0.74	0.83	0.90	0.72	0.49	0.57	0.58	0.60	0.43	0.58	0.76	0.47
	Skreadalen	4.55	4.54	4.48	4.51	4.54	4.55	4.56	4.63	0.57	0.48	0.59	0.53	0.47	0.41	0.43	0.37	0.18	0.21	0.32	0.29	0.28	0.28	0.28	0.22
	Background											0.52	0.60	0.49	0.45					0.25	0.29	0.22	0.25		
Portugal	Braganca		6.22	5.30		5.10	5.50	5.60			1.60	1.00			0.86	0.73			0.21	0.30			0.04	0.08	
	Faro		6.70	6.70							1.90	1.00							0.21	1.21					
Spain	La Cartuja						6.22								3.81								2.83		
	Roquetas						6.38								3.51								1.02		
Sweden	Rorvik	4.40	4.20	4.22	4.10	4.10	4.04	4.08		4.38	3.52	4.29	4.98	3.90	4.29	3.96		2.60	3.03	3.49	3.76	2.52	3.54	3.50	
	Goteburg	4.16		4.27	4.50	4.50				7.81	9.59	7.97	6.09	4.74				3.69	3.33	4.46	5.26	4.29			
Switzerland	Payerne				4.94	4.90	4.88	4.78	5.11				2.58	1.86	1.98	3.75	2.28				1.68	1.59	1.64	3.14	1.99
	Duebendorf							4.58	4.64							3.54	2.67							3.36	2.61
UK	Inverpolly		4.70	5.30	5.22	5.10					1.30	0.91							0.37	0.56	0.50	0.50			
	Eskdalemuir	4.33	4.24	4.72	4.69	4.68	4.63	4.79			2.50	1.49	1.50	1.41	1.89	1.38			1.24	0.93	0.86	1.00	1.06	1.02	
Yugoslavia	Puntijarka		5.06	5.33	5.20	5.10	5.02	5.03			5.86	4.45	4.58	3.33	4.27	5.95			1.22	1.77	1.99	2.04	2.65	4.48	

Environment

Traffic pollution

Road traffic volumes: total vehicles, selected OECD* countries, 1970–89

billion veh.-km

	1970	*1975*	*1980*	*1981*	*1982*	*1983*	*1984*	*1985*	*1986*	*1987*	*1988*	*1989*
Canada	125.9	171.4	205.5	201.8	204.2	204.1	202.4	201.0	206.8	216.5	220.8	225.1
USA	1787.3	2104.1	2418.6	2425.4	2538.2	2634.1	2745.2	2840.0	2937.2	3072.9	3243.0	3307.4
Japan	226.0	286.3	389.1	394.7	402.6	408.9	415.5	447.0	465.0	471.1	511.8	520.7
Australia	79.0	98.0	114.7	118.8	125.2	128.7	132.7	137.5	139.9	144.2	148.6	152.9
New Zealand	13.2	15.7	16.5	16.7	17.6	19.0	18.2	18.6	19.3	20.4	20.9	21.5
Austria	21.9	30.1	35.4	35.9	36.1	36.4	37.7	38.3	39.4	49.7	51.9	54.2
Belgium	33.3	38.3	45.8	46.3	46.8	46.5	46.8	47.1	48.2	49.7	51.4	52.2
Denmark	23.0	25.3	26.3	26.6	26.3	27.2	28.3	29.7	31.6	33.3	34.9	36.0
Finland	19.3	24.4	26.8	27.3	28.2	29.1	29.9	31.2	32.4	34.3	36.5	38.7
France	208.0	260.7	298.0	309.0	313.0	318.0	321.0	328.1	345.0	376.0	399.0	414.0
West Germany	234.2	279.9	340.8	326.5	337.8	341.0	350.8	351.1	375.1	396.1	416.5	427.0
Greece	9.2	13.3	20.4	21.6	23.2	24.9	26.6	28.6	30.4	32.2	34.2	36.0
Iceland	0.7	1.0	1.2	1.2	1.3	1.4	1.4	1.5	1.6	1.7	1.8	1.7
Ireland	10.7	12.1	18.5	19.0	17.6	17.7	18.3	18.8	19.3	19.9	21.1	23.0
Italy	146.4	184.6	226.6	235.2	248.7	239.5	247.9	257.8	265.0	278.7	286.1	297.2
Luxembourg	1.5	1.7	2.2	2.3	2.3	2.4	2.5	2.5	2.8	2.9	3.0	3.1
Netherlands	48.3	55.7	70.3	69.9	68.9	71.7	74.2	74.4	78.2	82.2	87.4	89.4
Norway	10.7	14.7	16.6	16.6	17.2	17.6	18.2	19.5	20.6	21.2	21.2	21.2
Portugal	9.4	15.5	21.2	23.2	24.8	26.4	27.7	27.9	29.4	30.4	31.6	32.8
Spain	35.1	55.5	74.6	72.0	73.2	73.9	75.8	75.1	82.6	85.9	92.8	100.0
Sweden	35.1	41.6	44.2	44.3	44.7	46.0	46.9	48.0	50.7	52.6	59.0	60.8
Switzerland	25.0	30.5	36.8	38.4	39.6	40.6	41.2	42.3	43.3	44.4	45.1	47.5
Turkey	6.1	13.4	14.8	15.3	16.0	16.8	18.6	19.1	19.0	20.9	22.3	23.4
UK	178.9	206.0	241.7	245.2	252.4	257.9	268.3	274.0	285.0	310.7	327.5	356.7
Yugoslavia	10.8	20.9	29.5	30.8	32.3	33.2	34.4	33.0	34.8	35.6	36.1	36.9
North America	1913.2	2275.6	2624.1	2627.2	2742.3	2838.2	2947.6	3041.1	3144.0	3289.4	3463.8	3532.6
Australia	92.1	113.7	131.3	135.5	142.8	147.7	150.9	156.1	159.2	164.6	169.5	174.4
OECD* Europe	1056.9	1304.3	1562.2	1575.9	1618.1	1634.9	1682.3	1714.9	1799.5	1922.7	2023.3	2115.1
EC	938.1	1148.6	1386.3	1396.8	1435.0	1447.0	1488.3	1515.2	1592.5	1698.0	1785.5	1867.5
OECD*	3288.3	3979.8	4706.7	4733.2	4905.9	5029.7	5196.3	5359.1	5567.7	5847.8	6168.5	6342.9

Pesticide pollution

Consumption of pesticides, selected OECD* countries, late 1980s

tonnes (active ingredients)

	Year	*Pesticides total*	*Insecticides*	*Fungicides*	*Herbicides*	*Other pesticides*
Canada	1985	39259	3172	2823	30181	3083
USA	1984	373333				
Japan	1985	83096	45018	18662	19416	
Austria	1986	6069	500	2426	3053	90
Belgium	1984	13263	1160	5337	6767	
Denmark	1988	5774	189	1179	3988	419
Finland	1987	2006	128	101	1599	178
France	1988	92500	6600	49800	36100	
West Germany	1987	29857	1220	9206	16967	2464
Greece	1984	35124	3249	27397	2611	1867
Iceland	1983	5	1	2	2	
Ireland	1984	2250	107	497	1647	
Italy	1988	196097	36494	111873	31 110	16621
Netherlands	1989	19146	745	4052	3330	11019
Norway	1986	1514	47	144	1188	134
Portugal	1988	12907	887	10193	1428	399
Spain	1989	134150				
Sweden	1986	5715	216	916	4432	151
Switzerland	1988	2412	253	1561	577	21
Turkey	1989	34649	18647	5884	6133	3985
UK	1982	40300	1480	4780	28100	5900

Amount of waste generated

Amounts of waste generated, by source, selected countries, late 1980s

1000 tonnes

	Year	*Municipal*	*Industrial*	*Energy production*	*Agriculture*	*Mining*	*Demolition wastes*	*Dredge spoils*	*Sewage sludge*	*Others*
Canada	1989	16400	61000	12400	48000	10529	1540	7540	500	38500
USA	1986	208760	760000	99247	150566	14000	31500		10400	
Japan	1988	48283	312271	19828	62690	26017	57886		2001	
Austria	1983	2700	13258	707		466	390	2100	1350	
Belgium	1988	3470	26700	1069	53000	7069	680	4805	687	2830
Denmark	1985	2400	2400	1532			1500		1263	300
Finland	1987	2500	10500	950	23000	21600	2000	420	153	
France	1989	17000	50000		400000	10000			620	2800
West Germany	1987	19483	61424	11702		9488	11826		1750	
Greece	1989	3147	4304	7680	90	3900				1200
Ireland	1984	1100	1580	130	22000	1930	240		570	860
Italy	1989	17300	39978		29830	57000	34374		3500	1985
Luxembourg	1990	170	1300				4000		15	
Netherlands	1988	6900	6687	1482	86000	121	7700	16000	252	664
Norway	1989	2000	2186		18000	9000	2000		100	
Portugal	1987	2350	662	260	202	3900				
Spain	1988	12546	5108		45000	18000			10000	
Sweden	1989	2650	4000	550	21000	28000	3000	600	372	3895
Switzerland	1989	2850					3000		260	
Turkey	1989	19500								
UK	1989	20000	50000	14000	250000	23000	25000	37000	30000	21000
Yugoslavia	1989		7164		20597					
OECD*		423000	1430000							

Industrial and hazardous waste

Industrial waste, hazardous and special waste, total amount generated by type

1000 tonnes

	Year	*Chemical waste*	*Non-chemical waste*	*Total*	*Hazardous and special waste*[a]
Canada	1980		196	61000	3290
USA	1986	105400		760000	238327
Japan	1985			312271	666
Austria	1983	525	12733	13258	400
Belgium	1989			26700	915
Denmark	1988			2400	112
Finland	1987			10500	230
France	1989			50000	3000
West Germany	1987	10218	51206	61424	14210
Greece	1989	423	3881	4304	423
Ireland	1984			1580	20
Italy	1989			39978	3640
Luxembourg	1990			1300	742
Netherlands	1988	624	6063	6687	1500
Norway	1989	2186			200
Portugal	1987	530	133	662	165
Spain	1987			5108	1708
Sweden	1980	500	3500	4000	500
Switzerland	1989				400
UK	1989			50000	2220
Yugoslavia	1989			7164	
OECD*	1989			1430000	303000

[a] The total amount of special waste is 18 million tonnes

* *Source*: Organization for Economic Cooperation and Development (see note page 73)

Water pollution

Water quality of lakes, annual mean concentration of phosphorus and nitrogen, selected lakes, 1970-late 1980s

		Total phosphorus (mgP/l)					*Total nitrogen (mgN/l)*				
Country	*Lake*	*1970*	*1975*	*1980*	*1985*	*late 1980s*	*1970*	*1975*	*1980*	*1985*	*late 1980s*
Canada	Ontario	0.022	0.022	0.017	0.013	0.010	0.226	0.283	0.308	0.572	0.218
	Erie	0.017	0.023	0.011	0.012			0.278	0.163		
USA	Cayuga (NY)	0.020	0.020				0.370	0.510			
	W. Twin (Ohio)	0.150	0.100				1.930				
Japan	Biwa (North)	0.009	0.005	0.009	0.007	0.008	0.200	0.290	0.270	0.260	0.290
	Biwa (South)	0.013	0.015	0.017	0.020	0.017	0.270	0.400	0.330	0.360	0.350
	Kasumigaura		0.040	0.080	0.060	0.074		1.200	1.000	1.200	1.200
Austria	Mondsee		0.029	0.025	0.014	0.010					
	Ossiachersee		0.015	0.010	0.016	0.034					
Denmark	Knud Soe		0.060	0.050	0.042	0.025		2.000	3.000	2.900	3.000
Finland	Paeaejaervi	0.013	0.014	0.010	0.014	0.013	0.900	1.150	1.350	1.100	1.400
	Paeijaenne	0.010	0.011	0.009	0.008	0.007	0.500	0.460	0.460	0.510	0.520
	Yli-kitka		0.005	0.006	0.007	0.006		0.180	0.170	0.260	0.220
Germany	Bodensee	0.061	0.099	0.099	0.071	0.069	0.755	0.763	0.856	0.875	1.566
Ireland	Ennel		0.089	0.029	0.032	0.010		0.270	0.470	0.340	0.200
	Derg		0.025	0.020	0.060			0.840	1.200	1.260	
Italy	Maggiore		0.026	0.036	0.019				0.770		
	Como		0.068	0.078	0.052		0.640	0.710	0.800	0.800	
	Garda		0.009	0.020	0.011		0.310	0.300	0.390	0.350	
	Orta			0.011	0.006		13.000	9.620	9.500	7.110	
Netherlands	Ijssel		0.350	0.350	0.290	0.240		4.025	4.385	4.140	3.950
Norway	Mjoesa	0.010	0.010	0.009	0.007	0.010	0.400	0.400	0.500	0.432	0.430
	Randsfjorden			0.004		0.006			0.514		0.460
Portugal	Ria de Aveiro			0.015	0.026						
Spain	Castrejon			5.790	4.805	3.158					
	Alcantara		0.387	0.428	0.141	0.251		1.341	2.864		
Sweden	Maelaren	0.029	0.024	0.034	0.031	0.024	0.918	0.735	0.708	0.859	0.688
	Vaettern	0.008	0.009	0.009	0.006	0.005	0.594	0.562	0.625	0.681	0.730
Switzerland	Leman	0.104	0.082	0.090	0.073	0.058			0.660	0.730	0.709
	Constance	0.055	0.078	0.077	0.066	0.039		0.861	0.900	0.930	0.970
Turkey	Kurtbogazi			0.110	0.200	0.060			0.430	0.360	0.280
	Sapanca			0.030	0.030	0.060			0.942	0.617	0.370
	Altinapa			0.030	0.150	0.150			1.550	0.549	1.810
UK	Neagh		0.095	0.107	0.114	0.106		1.180	1.580	1.920	1.303
	Lomond			0.009	0.009	0.002			0.300	0.290	0.160

Consequences of water pollution

Cultural or accelerated eutrophication caused by sewage and nitrate fertiliser run-off into lakes.

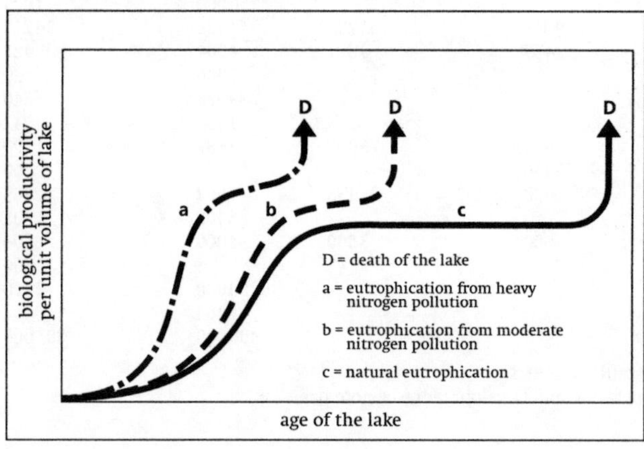

DEFORESTATION

Forests of the world, areas and carbon stocks

Forest type	*Area (millions sq km)*	*Carbon stocks in plants (gigatons, or billion metric tons, of carbon)*	*Carbon stocks in detritus and soil (gigatons, or billion metric tons, of carbon)*
Tropical forests (both evergreen, and in primary form)	8.6	202	288
Temperate-zone forests	8.2	65	161
Boreal forests	11.7	127	247
Woodland and shrublands	12.8	57	59
Rest of Earth's land surface	103.3	109	720
Totals	144.6	560	1475

World distribution of various types of forest

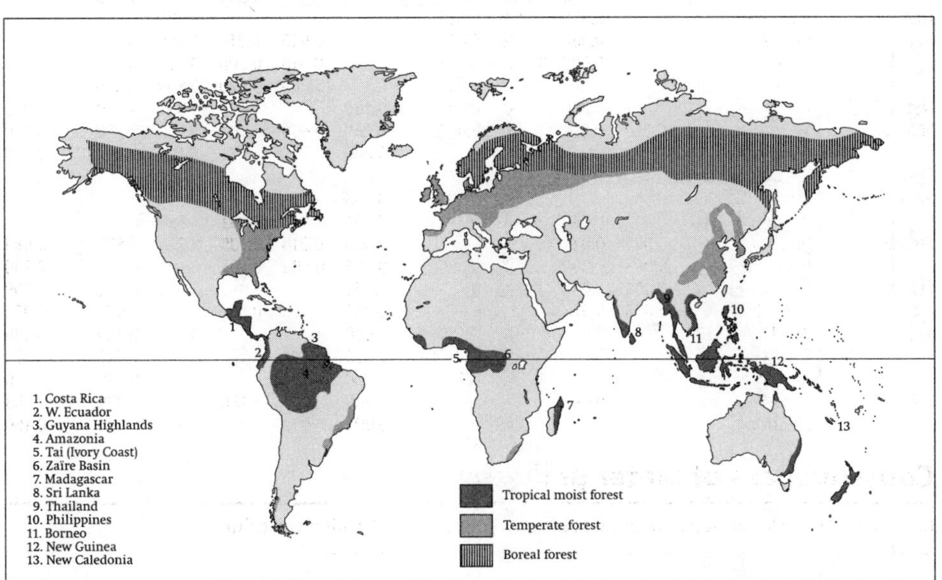

Forest depletion and growth, selected countries, 1970–89

	Annual depletion (1000 m³)												Annual growth (1000 m³)				Intensity of use			
	Harvest				Losses				Total								Harvested/Annual growth			
	1970	1980	1985	1989	1970	1980	1985	1989	1970	1980	1985	1989	1970	1980	1985	1989	1970	1980	1985	1989
Canada	121 400	158 800	143 700	156 000		24 600	143 800	138 100		181 100	287 500	294 100		305 300	338 000	363 400		00.52	0.43	0.43
USA	397 372	402 923	482 522		113 976	115 902	129 918		511 320	518 824	612 440		67 516	736 780	763 851		0.59	0.55	0.63	
Japan	65 996	42 932	42 067	38 554	390	2 100	1 286	1 050	66 386	45 032	43 353	39 604			115 500				0.36	
Australia	13 700		16 300												42 000				0.39	
New Zealand	8 478	10 776	9 626											5 000	17 556			2.16	0.55	
Austria	15 100		15 200	13 408				3 178				16 586		19 298			0.81	0.78		
Belgium	3 200		2 800												5 000				0.56	
Denmark	2 109	2 138	2 249	2 163									1 935	2 851			1.09	0.75		
Finland	51 990	53 740	48 880	48 869	6 710	5 960	6 320	6 257	58 700	59 700	55 200	55 127	57 150	62 800	68 380	73 522	0.91	0.86	0.71	0.66
France	32 300	34 380	35 000	37 000	16 700	18 500	37 700	37 000	49 000	52 880	72 700	74 000		64 500	74 700	76 500		0.53	0.47	0.48
West Germany	28 196	30 327	31 219	31 819			14 550	353			45 769	32 172	34 000		42 000		0.88		0.71	
Greece	35 000		2 900												3 600				0.81	
Ireland	380	527	953		2	7	53		382	534	1 006		1 903	2 370	2 710		0.20	0.22	0.35	
Italy	6 942	7 712	9 383		200	200	250		7 142	7 912	9 633		13 070	12 080	11 667		0.53	0.64	0.80	
Luxembourg							140								1 000					
Netherlands	1 200		1 500														0.98	0.87		
Norway	8 500	9 100	9 400	11 800	1 100	1 400	1 800	2 000	9 600	10 500	11 200	13 800	14 500	15 700	16 600	18 300	0.59	0.58	0.57	0.64
Portugal	10 700	9 500	2 435			1 840	8 602				11 037				7 000				0.35	
Spain	6 192	7 661	9 512	11 529										16 674	24 000			0.46	0.40	
Sweden	63 600	53 000	59 600	59 000	8 000	8 000	4 500	5 300	71 600	61 000	64 100	64 300	78 700	81 700	97 200	99 200	0.81	0.65	0.61	0.59
Switzerland	4 210	4 690	4 410	4 800											6 000		0.91		0.74	
Turkey	17 789	23 243	18 124	14 500					17 789	23 243	18 124	14 500	22 135	22 135	22 135	22 135	0.80	1.05	0.82	0.66
UK	3 600	4 660	5 170	6 505					3 000	4 660	5 170	6 505	5 700	10 720		15 415	0.63	0.43		0.42
Yugoslavia	14 797	19 149	22 428	21 540	4 625	4 470	4 844	3 568	18 283	23 619	27 272	25 108	21 088	29 351	29 351	29 351	0.70	0.65	0.76	0.73

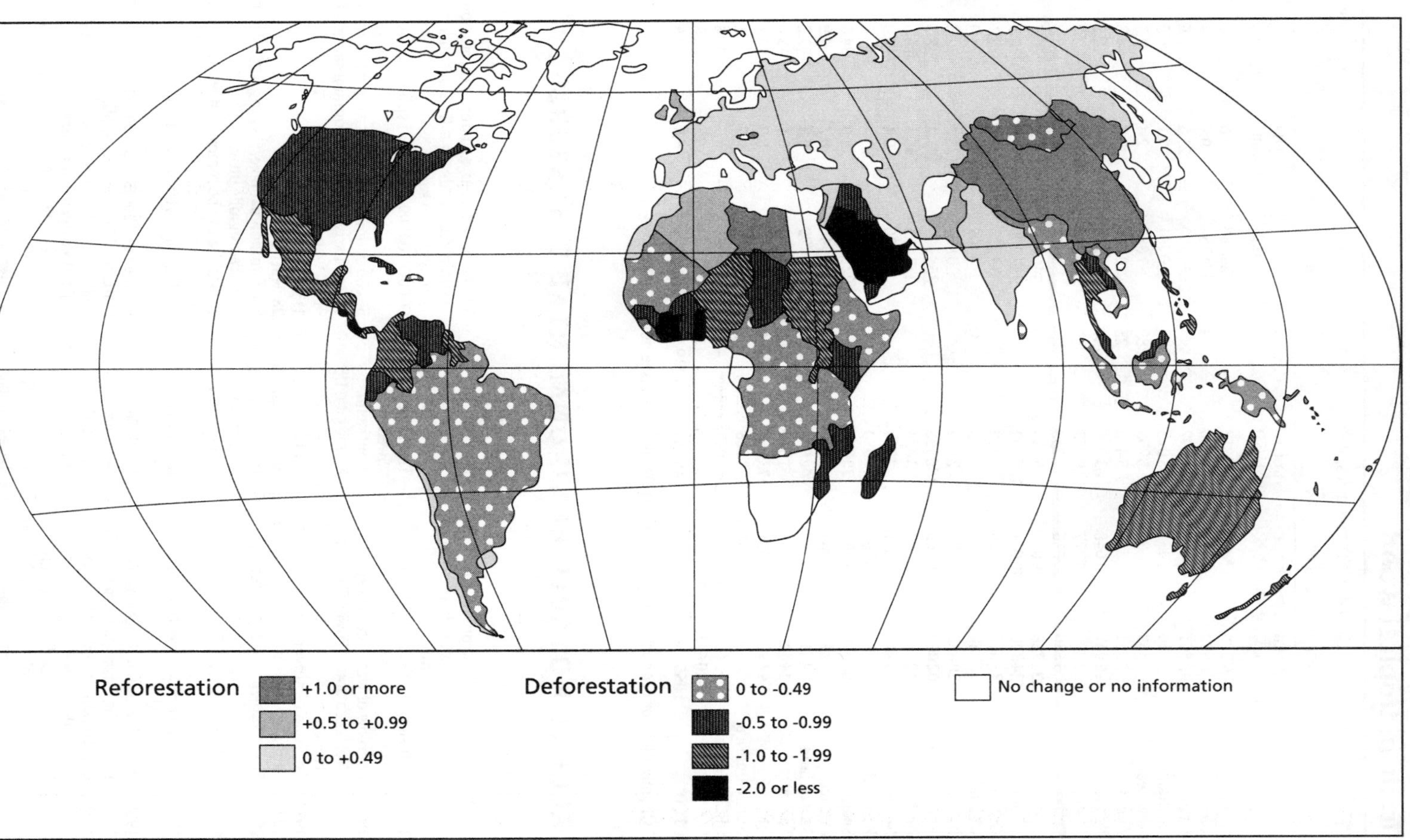
Annual percentage change in forest and woodland area, 1974–84
Reforestation
+1.0 or more
+0.5 to +0.99
0 to +0.49
Deforestation
0 to -0.49
-0.5 to -0.99
-1.0 to -1.99
-2.0 or less
No change or no information

Trade in tropical wood

Trade in tropical wood, selected OECD* countries, 1988

	Imports of cork and wood from				*Total*		
	Africa (1000 US$)	*Latin America (1000 US$)*	*Far East (1000 US$)*	*Oceania (1000 US$)*	*(1000 US$)*	*per capita (US$/cap.)*	*% of total imports*
Canada	208	7359	17212	9	24788	1.0	3.7
USA	6832	96472	71176	84	174564	0.7	5.4
Japan	42861	12688	2475697	120444	2651690	21.6	32.6
Australia	34	1434	93023	5670	100161	6.1	26.5
New Zealand	359	31	5208	2289	7887	2.4	41.3
Austria	3961	176	15478	25	19640	2.6	4.3
Belgium	16447	1648	63536	147	81778	1.2	12.5
Denmark	2994	1777	9373		14144	2.8	3.7
Finland	5630	686	2133		8449	1.7	3.3
France	221788	9001	115993	26	346808	6.2	36.7
West Germany	124320	10061	157909		292290	4.8	18.9
Greece	33045	120	160		33325	2.0	23.1
Iceland	44	268	95		407		1.9
Ireland	20433	7992	2409		30834	123.3	32.8
Italy	202060	19868	136103		358031	101.2	18.5
Netherlands	42132	8489	173034		223655	596.4	26.5
Norway	1419	2221	2760		6400	0.4	2.0
Portugal	105925	8361	550		114836	27.3	61.6
Spain	168476	32397	25005		225878	21.9	34.5
Sweden	5241	2009	3696		10946	0.3	1.9
Switzerland	4112	75	2612		6799	0.8	2.2
Turkey	14441	6	1529		15976	2.4	12.6
UK	42997	98881	173668	244	315790	5.9	13.1
North America	7040	103831	88388	93	199352	0.7	5.1
OECD* Europe	1015465	204036	886043	442	2105986	6.7	17.8
EC	980617	198595	857740	417	2037369	7.3	20.8
OECD*	1065759	322020	3548359	128938	5065076	6.5	20.8

* Organization for Economic Cooperation and Development (see note page 73)

RECENT NOTABLE ENVIRONMENTAL DISASTERS

Date	*Event*	*Location*	*Consequence*
1957	Fire in Windscale plutonium production reactor. Ignited three tonnes of uranium	Cumbria	Spread of radioactive material throughout Britain. Official death toll 39 but this is strongly contested.
1970	Collision of the tanker *Othello*	Tralhavet Bay, Sweden	60000–100000 tons of oil spilled.
1971	Overflow of water storage space at Northern States Power Company's reactor	Monticello, Minnesota, US	50000 gallons of radioactive waste dumped into Mississippi River. Contamination of St Paul water system.
1972	Collision of tanker *Sea Star*	Gulf of Oman	115 000 tons of oil spilled.
1974	Explosion of container of cyclohexane	Flixborough, UK	28 deaths.
1975	Fire at Brown's Ferry reactor	Decatur, Alabama, US	$100 million damage. Cooling water level lowered significantly.
1976	Leak of toxic gas TCDD	Seveso, Italy	Topsoil had to be removed in worst contaminated areas.
1976	The supertanker the *Urquiola* is grounded	La Coruña, Spain	Spillage of 100000 tons of oil.
1977	Well blow-out at Ecofisk oil field.	North Sea	Spillage of 8200000 gallons of oil.
1977	Fire on the *Hawaiian Patriot*	Northern Pacific	Spillage of 99 000 tons of oil.
1978	Cyprus tanker, the *Amoco Cadiz*, is grounded	Portshall, France	Spillage of 65562000 gallons of oil. Pollution of 160 km/99 mi of French coast.
1979	Uranium released from secret nuclear fuel plant	Erwin, Tennessee, US	Approximately 1000 people contaminated
1979	Collision of *Burmah Agate*	Galveston Bay, Texas	Spillage of 10700000 gallons of oil.

Date	Event	Location	Consequence
1979	Release of radioactive steam after water pump breaks down	Three Mile Island	Pollution by radioactive gases. Partial core meltdown in reactor.
1979	Blowout in Ixtoc oil well	Gulf of Mexico	600 000 tons of oil spilled.
1979	Collision of the *Atlantic Empress* and *Aegean Captain*	Trinidad and Tobago	300 000 tons of oil spilled.
1980	Chemical spill due to Sandez factory fire	Basel, Switzerland	Rhine polluted 200 km/124 mi.
1983	Fire on the *Castillo de Beliver*	Cape Town, South Africa	Spillage of 250 000 tons of oil.
1983	Blow-out in Nowruz oil field	Persian Gulf	Spillage of 176 400 000 gallons of oil.
1984	Union Carbide pesticide plant leaks toxic gas	Bhopal, India	Death of 2 352 people officially. Unofficially, an estimated 10 000 died.
1986	Explosion of nuclear reactor	Chernobyl, Ukraine	Official death toll 50. Radioactive cloud spread across Europe contaminating farmland. Long-term effects on inhabitants of surrounding areas are not yet ascertainable
1987	Abandoned radiotherapy unit containing radioactive material leaks	Goiana, Brazil	Radioactive contamination affected 249 people.
1988	Accident at water treatment works results in aluminium sulphate being flushed into local rivers	Camelford, Cornwall	Local people suffer from stomach and skin disorders. Thousands of fish killed.
1989	*Exxon Valdez* tanker is grounded on Bligh Reef	Prince William Sound, Alaska	Spillage of 10 080 000 gallons of oil and 1 170 km/1 162 mi of Alaskan coastline polluted. More than 3 600 sq km/1 390 sq mi contaminated. Thousands of birds and animals killed.
1989	Explosion in hull of Iranian supertanker, *Khark 5*	Atlantic Ocean, north of Canary Islands	Spillage of 19 000 000 gallons of crude oil and 370 km/230 mi oil slick, almost reaching Morocco.
1991	Greek tanker, *Kiriki*, breaks up	Cervantes, W Australia	Spillage of 5 880 000 gallons of crude oil and pollution of conservation and fishing areas.
1991	Oil fields set alight by Iraqi forces during the Gulf War	Kuwait	Spillage estimated between 25 000 000–130 000 000 gallons. Air pollution and potential increase in acid rain.
1992	Greek oil tanker, the *Aegean Sea*, runs aground and catches fire	La Coruña, Spain	Spillage of an estimated 16 million gallons (8 000 tons) of crude oil, creating a slick 12 mi long and 1 mi wide and causing contamination of 50 mi of Spanish coastline. Serious pollution of sealife and clam and oyster fisheries.
1993	Break-up of tanker, the *Braer*, on the rocks of Pitful Head	Shetlands, Scotland	Oil slick contained to 200–300 yards but serious pollution of fishing grounds and fish farms, as well as sea animals and birds.

FLORA AND FAUNA

Threatened species

Threatened animal species in selected OECD* countries (early 1980s)

Country	Mammals	Birds	Reptiles	Amphibians	Fishes
Mediterranean countries					
France	58(57)[a]	155(58)	19(39)	18(53)	20(27)
Italy	13(13)	60(14)	24(52)	13(46)	70(14)
Spain[b]	53(53)	142(37)	20(41)	18(78)	12(9)
European non-Mediterranean countries					
Austria	38(46)	121(60)	[c]	[c]	54(59)
Denmark	14(29)	41(22)	0(0)	3(21)	17(10)
Finland	21(34)	15(7)	1(20)	0(0)	4(7)
West Germany	44(47)	98(22)	9(75)	11(58)	40(23)
Hungary	14([c])	83([c])	4([c])	1([c])	2([c])
Netherlands	29(48)	85(33)	6(86)	10(67)	11(22)

Threatened species (continued)

Country	*Mammals*	*Birds*	*Reptiles*	*Amphibians*	*Fishes*
Norway	10(14)	28(10)	1(20)	1(20)	[c]
United Kingdom	26(51)	51(26)	2(33)	2(33)	18(49)
North America					
Canada	6(6)	10(2)	2(6)	2(4)	15(2)
United States	35(8)	69(6)	25(7)	8(4)	44(2)
Oceania					
Australia	40(13)	36(5)	8(1)	6(4)	[c]
New Zealand	14(21)	16(6)	7(19)	[c]	3(0)

[a] Numbers given are total number of threatened species in each taxonomic group. Numbers in parentheses are the threatened species expressed as a percentage of the total number of species known to exist in a particular country.
[b] Data for Spain refer to peninsular Spain and the Balearics only.
[c] Estimates not available. 'Threatened' refers to the sum of the number of species in both 'endangered' and 'vulnerable' categories, which are roughly analogous to US 'endangered' and 'threatened' categories, respectively.
* Organization for Economic Cooperation and Development (see note page 73)

Extinction of birds and mammals

Species and subspecies of mammals and birds extinct since 1600

Location	*Mammals*	*Birds*
Continents		
Africa	11	0
Asia	11	6
Australia	22	0
Europe	7	0
North America	22	8
South America	0	2
Total	73	16
Pelagic	1	0
Islands		
Continental		
Africa	0	2
Asia	4	0
Australia	0	2
North America	4	3
Oceanic		
Pacific Ocean		
Galapagos	4	0
Baja California islands	0	8
Hawaii	0	24
New Zealand	0	16
Chatham	absent	5
Lord Howe	0	8
Norfolk	absent	6
Cebu (Philippines)	0	11
Bonin, Ryukyu	0	10
Other	0	21
Indian Ocean		
Madagascar	1	2
Christmas	3	0
Mascarenes	0	14
Seychelles	0	2
Atlantic Ocean		
West Indies	22	15
Other	1	5
Mediterranean	2	1
Total, all islands	41	155
Total, all locations	115	171

This tabulation omits numerous island birds believed to have become extinct after 1600 but known only from recently reported subfossil bones.

Threatened plant species

Country/region	*Species*	*Rare and threatened taxa*	*Extinct taxa since 1700*	*Endangered taxa*
Australia	25 000	1 716	117	215
Europe	11 300	1 927	20	117
New Zealand	2 000	186	4	42
South Africa	23 000	2 122	39	107
USSR	21 100	653	~20	~160
United States (Continental)	20 000	2 050	90	?
Worldwide[a]	250 000	25 000	5 050	15 000[b]

[a]Estimated from various sources.
[b]Includes 4 000 species from Pacific coastal Ecuador and 3 000 from Atlantic Coastal Brazil.

Tropical marine areas under threat

Habitat	*Reason*
mangroves	
Niger River delta, Nigeria	Exploited for timber, fuel, fodder and urban expansion.
Kenya and Tanzania	Cleared for fuelwood, building materials and tourist resorts.
Indus River mouth, Pakistan	Overexploitation for fuel, fodder and building material.
Sundarbans, India and Bangladesh	Overexploitation for fuel, fodder, timber and fishponds.
Malaysia and Gulf of Thailand	Destruction for fish and shellfish ponds and agricultural land.
Philippines	Destruction for timber, tannin, fuelwood and fish and shellfish ponds.
Indonesia	Massive destruction for logging and woodchip industries, fish and shellfish ponds and for building materials and fuelwood.
Queensland, Australia	Town and tourist development.
US south coast, Texas to Florida	Over-development of coastline for urban expansion, resorts, housing estates. Also used as rubbish dumps.
Panama	Cleared for fish and shrimp ponds.
Ecuador	Cleared for fish and shrimp ponds.
Caribbean	All mangrove stands disturbed. Main threats: tourism and coastal land development.
seagrasses	
East Africa	Under threat from heavy sedimentation of shallow coastal waters caused by erosion of agricultural lands.
Southeast Asia	Under threat from loss of mangroves, coastal development, urban expansion and bucket dredging for tin.
Caribbean and Gulf of Mexico	Under threat from dredge and fill operations, loss of mangroves, coastal development for tourism, oil production.
Coral reefs	
East Africa	Coral mining for building materials, blast fishing, tourist trade and sedimentation.
The Gulf	Oil and industrial pollution, sedimentation.
Thailand and Malaysia	Tourist resorts, bucket dredging for tin, over-fishing.
Philippines	Blast fishing, coral mining, collection for tourist trade and use of poisons.
Southern Japan–Ryukyu Archipelago	Destroyed by coastal development and sedimentation.
Indonesia	Destroyed by blast fishing, coral mining, tourist trade and coastal development.
South Pacific	Tourism, sedimentation from coastal development.
Wider Caribbean	Collection for tourist trade, coastal development, mangrove destruction/sedimentation and damage by boat anchors.

CONSERVATION

Protected areas – national parks

National parks, selected OECD* countries, 1990

	Number of sites	*Total size (sq km)*	*Percent of territory (%)*	*Protected area per 1000 inhabitants (ha/1000 cap.)*
Canada	237	309 529	3.1	1179.2
USA	59	202 320	2.2	81.3
Japan	15	12 991	3.4	10.6
Australia	339	275 551	3.6	1639.5
New Zealand	11	21 011	7.8	628.5
Finland	17	3 541	1.0	71.3
France	5	2 613	0.5	4.7
West Germany	1	131	0.1	0.2
Greece	8	526	0.4	5.2
Iceland	3	1 801	1.7	711.9
Ireland	3	225	0.3	6.4
Italy	3	1 259	0.4	2.2
Netherlands	1	54	0.1	0.4
Norway	17	19 102	5.9	451.9

Protected areas – national parks (continued)

	Number of sites	*Total size (sq km)*	*Percent of territory (%)*	*Protected area per 1000 inhabitants (ha/1000 cap.)*
Portugal	2	994	1.1	9.6
Spain	9	1228	0.2	3.2
Sweden	15	5892	1.3	69.4
Switzerland	1	169	0.4	2.5
Turkey	11	1944	0.2	3.5
UK	1	41		0.1
Yugoslavia	17	4055	1.6	17.0
OECD*	758	860 922	2.7	103.5
World	1392	3 092 274	2.3	58.4

* Organization for Economic Cooperation and Development (see note page 73)

Environmental programmes

CLIMAP	Climatic Applications Project (WMO)
COADS	Comprehensive Ocean Air Data Set
GAW	Global Atmospheric Watch
ERBE	Earth Radiation Budget Experiment
ERS	Earth Resources Satellite
GEWEX	Global Energy and Water Cycle Experiment
GMCC	Geophysical Monitoring of Climatic Change
ICRCCM	Intercomparison of Radiation Codes in Climate Models
IGAC	International Global Atmospheric Chemistry Programme
IGBP	International Geosphere-Biosphere Programme
ISCCP	International Satellite Cloud Climatology Project
JGOFS	Joint Global Ocean Flux Study
SAGE	Stratospheric Aerosol and Gas Experiment
TOGA	Tropical Ocean and Global Atmosphere
WCRP	World Climate Research Programme
WOCE	World Ocean Circulation Experiment

Multilateral conventions concerning the environment

No.	*Subject*	*Type*[a]	*Place and date*	*No. of OECD country signatures*	*No. of OECD ratifications or accessions*	*Entry into force*
	Sea pollution					
1–1.	Prevention of pollution of the sea by oil (OILPOL)	Conv.	London, 1954	15	19	26.7.1958
1–2.	Limitation of liability of owners of sea-going ships	Conv.	Brussels, 1957	14	15	31.5.1968
1–3.	Pollution of the North Sea by oil	Agr.	Bonn, 1969	8	8	9.8.1969
1–4.	Civil liability for oil pollution damage (CLC)	Conv.	Brussels, 1969	15	19	19.6.1975
1–4a.	Protocol to amend No 1–4	Prot.	London, 1984	10	3	pending
1–5.	Intervention on the high seas in case of oil pollution (INTERVENTION)	Conv.	Brussels, 1969	18	17	6.5.1975
1–5a.	Protocol to No. 1–5 (substances other than oil)	Prot.	London, 1973	8	14	30.3.1983
1–6.	Cooperation against pollution of the sea by oil	Agr.	Copenhagen, 1971	4	4	16.10.1971
1–7.	International fund for compensation for oil pollution damage (FUND)	Conv.	Brussels, 1971	12	15	16.10.1978
1–7a.	Protocol to No. 1–7 (FUND)	Prot.	London, 1976	3	11	pending
1–7b.	Protocol to No. 1–7 (FUND)	Prot.	London, 1984		2	pending
1–8.	Prevention of marine pollution by dumping from ships and aircraft	Conv.	Oslo, 1972	20	20	7.4.1974
1–9.	Prevention of marine pollution by dumping of wastes + other matter (LDC)	Conv.	London, Mexico, Moscow, Washington, 1972	22	21	30.8.1975
1–10.	Prevention of pollution from ships (MARPOL)	Conv.	London, 1973	11	5	pending
1–10a.	Protocol to No. 1–10 (MARPOL PROT) (segregated ballast)	Prot.	London, 1978	8	15	2.10.1983

No.	Subject	Type[a]	Place and Date	No. of OECD Country Signatures	No. of OECD Ratifications or Accessions	Entry into Force
1-11.	Protection of the marine environment of the Baltic Sea	Conv.	Helsinki, 1974	4	4	3.5.1980
1.12.	Prevention of marine pollution from land-based sources	Conv.	Paris, 1974	13 (+EC)	11 (+EC)	6.5.1978
1-13.	Protection of the Mediterranean Sea against pollution	Conv.	Barcelona, 1976	5 (+EC)	5 (+EC)	12.2.1978
1-13a.	Protocol to No. 1-13 (dumping from ships and aircraft)	Prot.	Barcelona, 1976	5 (+EC)	5 (+EC)	12.2.1978
1-13b.	Protocol to No. 1-13 (pollution by oil/cooperation in emergency cases)	Prot.	Barcelona, 1976	5 (+EC)	5 (+EC)	12.2.1978
1-13c.	Protocol to No. 1-13 (protection against land-based sources)	Prot.	Athens, 1980	4 (+EC)	2 (+EC)	17.6.1983
1-14.	Limitation of liability for maritime claims (LLMC)	Conv.	London, 1976	8	8	1.12.1986
1-15.	Law of the Sea	Conv.	Montego Bay, 1982	24 (+EC)	1	pending
1-16.	Protocol concerning Mediterranean specially protected areas	Prot.	Geneva, 1982	4		pending
1-17.	Coop. in dealing with pollution of the North Sea by oil + other subst.	Agr.	Bonn, 1983	8	(+EC)	pending
1-18.	Protection + development of the wider Caribbean region	Conv.	Cartagena, 1983	4 (+EC)	0	pending
1-18a.	Protocol to No. 1-18 (oil spills)	Prot.	Cartagena, 1983			pending
1-18b.	Protocol to No. 1-18 (specially protected areas and wild life)	Prot.	1990			
1-19.	Protection of the natural resources and environment of the South Pacific	Conv.	Noumea, 1986		3	pending
	Nuclear					
2-1.	Third party liability for nuclear energy	Conv.	Paris, 1960	16	14	1.4.1968
2-1a.	Protocol to No. 2-1.	Prot.	Paris, 1982	17	13	7.10.1988
2-2.	Liability of operators of nuclear ships	Conv.	Brussels, 1962	5 (+EC)	2	pending
2-3.	Supplementary to No. 2-1 (third party liability for nuclear energy)	Conv.	Brussels, 1963	13	11	4.12.1974
2-3a.	Additional protocol to No. 2-3	Prot.	Paris, 1982	13	10	pending
2-4.	Banning nuclear weapons tests in the atmosphere, outer space, and under water	Conv.	Moscow, 1963	23	23	10.10.1963
2-5.	Prohibition of nuclear weapons on the seabed, ocean floor, and sub-soil	Conv.	London, Moscow, Washington, 1971	22	22	18.5.1972
2-6.	Civil liability in maritime carriage of nuclear material	Conv.	Brussels, 1971	10	8	15.7.1975
2-7.	Early notification of a nuclear accident	Conv.	Vienna, 1986	22	8	27.10.1986
2-8.	Assistance in the case of a nuclear accident of radiological emergency	Conv.	Vienna, 1986	21	4	26.2.1987
2-9.	Joint Protocol relating to the application of the Vienna Convention and the Paris Convention	Prot.	Vienna, 1988	15	1	pending
	Flora and Fauna					
3-1.	Preservation of fauna and flora	Conv.	London, 1933	6	4	14.1.1936
3-2.	Regulation of whaling	Conv.	Washington, 1946	7	17	10.11.1948
3-3.	Conservation of the living resources of the South East Atlantic	Conv.	Rome, 1969	6	7	24.10.1971
3-4.	Wetlands of international importance especially as waterfowl habitat	Conv.	Ramsar, 1971	13	22	21.12.1975
3-5.	Protection of world cultural and natural heritage	Conv.	Paris, 1972	17	17	17.12.1975
3-6.	Antarctic seals	Conv.	London, 1972	8	7	23.11.1972
3-7.	Polar bears	Agr.	Oslo, 1973	4	4	26.5.1976
3-8.	Fishing and conservation of the living resources in the Baltic Sea	Conv.	Gdansk, 1973	4	EEC	28.7.1974

Multilateral conventions concerning the environment (continued)

No.	Subject	Type[a]	Place and Date	No. of OECD Country Signatures	No. of OECD Ratifications or Accessions	Entry into Force
3-9.	International trade in endangered species	Conv.	Washington, 1973	17	20	1.7.1975
3-10.	Future multilateral cooperation in the North West Atlantic fisheries	Conv.	Ottawa, 1978	6 (+EC)	3 (+EC)	1.1.1979
3-11.	European wild life and natural habitats	Conv.	Bern, 1979	18 (+EC)	17 (+EC)	1.6.1982
3-12.	Conservation of migratory species of wild animals	Conv.	Bonn, 1979	13 (+EC)	12 (+EC)	1.11.1983
3-13.	Conservation of antarctic marine living resources	Conv.	Canberra, 1980	9 (+EC)	9 (+EC)	7.4.1982
	Air Pollution					
4-1.	Long range transboundary air pollution	Conv.	Geneva, 1979	21 (+EC)	21 (+EC)	16.3.1983
4-1a.	Protocol to 4-1 on the reduction of sulphur emissions or their transboundary fluxes by 30%	Prot.	Helsinki, 1985	13	12	2.9.1987
4-1b.	Protocol to 4-1 concerning the control of emissions of nitrogen oxides or their transboundary fluxes	Prot.	Sofia, 1988	14	4	pending
4-2.	Transfrontier cooperation	Conv.	Madrid, 1980	9	11	22.12.1981
4-3.	Protection of the ozone layer	Conv.	Vienna, 1985	17 (+EC)	23 (+EC)	1.1.1989
4-4.	Protocol to 4-4	Prot.	Montreal, 1987	17 (+EC)	23 (+EC)	1.1.1989
	Rhine Pollution					
5-1.	Protection of the Rhine against pollution	Agr.	Bonn, 1963	5 (+EC)	5 (+EC)	1.5.1965
5-2.	Rhine chloride pollution	Conv.	Bonn, 1976	4	4	1985
5-3.	Protection of the Rhine against chemical pollution	Conv.	Bonn, 1976	5 (+EC)	5 (+EC)	1.2.1979
	Miscellaneous					
6-1.	International carriage of dangerous goods by road (ADR)	Agr.	Geneva, 1957	14		29.1.1968
6-2.	Restriction of use of detergents	Agr.	Strasbourg, 1968	9	10	16.2.1971
6-2a.	Protocol amending No. 6-2	Prot.	Strasbourg, 1983	5	3	1.11.1984
6-3.	International liability for damage caused by space objects	Conv.	London, Moscow, Washington, 1972	15	22	17.8.1972
6-4.	Nordic environmental protection	Conv.	Stockholm, 1974	4	4	5.10.1976
6-5.	Prohibition of military use of environmental modification techniques	Conv.	Geneva, 1977	19	11	5.10.1978
6-6.	Protection of workers against air pollution, noise + vibration (ILO 148)	Conv.	Geneva, 1977		6	11.7.1979
6-7.	Control of transboundary movements of hazardous wastes and their disposal	Conv.	Basel, 1989			
6-8.	Civil liability for damage caused during carriage of dangerous goods by road, rail, and inland navigation vessels (CRTD)	Conv.	Geneva, 1990			

[a] Abbreviations: Agr.– Agreement; Conv. – Convention; Prot. – Protocol.

Waste recycling activities

Recovery rates, selected countries, 1975–1989

	Percentage %								
	Paper and Cardboard				*Glass*				
	1975	*1980*	*1985*	*1989*	*1975*	*1980*	*1985*	*1987*	*1989*
Canada		18.0	18.0	23.0		12.0	12.0		
USA	15.4		20.0		2.9		8.0		
Japan	39.6	48.1	49.6			35.3	47.2	54.4	
Australia			31.8				17.0		
New Zealand			19.0				53.0		
Austria		30.0	36.8			20.0	38.0	44.0	
Belgium	8.7	14.7				33.0	42.0	39.0	
Denmark	28.4	25.6	31.3	29.7		8.0	53.9	55.0	
Finland	29.0	35.0	39.0	40.0		10.0	21.0	25.0	
France	31.7	37.0	41.3	45.7		20.0	26.0	26.1	28.5
West Germany	34.2	33.9	43.6	43.0	7.7	24.0	35.5	39.4	42.3
Ireland	22.0	15.0				8.0	7.0	8.0	
Italy						20.0	25.0	38.0	
Netherlands	42.0	45.5	50.3	58.4		41.0	53.0	62.0	55.2
Norway	23.8	21.9	21.1	23.2					10.0
Portugal		38.0					10.0	14.0	
Spain		38.1	44.1				13.1	22.0	
Sweden	30.0	34.0	40.0				20.0		22.0
Switzerland		38.0				36.0	46.0	47.0	
UK	28.0	29.0	27.0	27.0		5.0	12.0	14.0	18.0

* Much of the data in this section comes from the Organization for Economic Cooperation and Development (OECD). **OECD Europe** refers to all EC member countries of OECD, plus Austria, Finland, Iceland, Norway, Sweden, Switzerland and Turkey.
OECD refers to all members of OECD Europe, plus Canada, US, Japan, Australia and New Zealand.

NATURAL HISTORY

CLASSIFICATION OF LIVING ORGANISMS

It has been estimated that between 3 million and 20 million different kinds of organism are alive in the world today. Large numbers of other organisms have become extinct, and some of these are preserved as fossils. Most modern schemes of classification of living organisms are based upon the pioneering work of the Swedish biologist Carl von Linné (in Latin, Carolus Linnaeus, 1707–78), who established the practice of binomial nomenclature, by which all organisms are given two names, traditionally printed in italics. The first name is that of the *genus*, and is common to a group of closely related organisms. The second is that of the *species* and is unique to a particular type of organism. Higher levels of classification show a hierarchy of relationships. These are illustrated here using the human species as an example.

Classification of the human species

Taxonomic level		
Kingdom	Animalia	(animals)
Phylum (division)[a]	Chordata	(chordates)
Subphylum	Vertebrata	(vertebrates)
Class	Mammalia	(mammals)
Order	Primates	
Family	Hominoidea	(hominids)
Genus	*Homo*	
Species	*sapiens*	

[a] In classifiying plants, fungi and bacteria, the term *division* is used rather than phylum.

The five kingdoms

While almost all modern systems of classification use the same basic taxonomic system, there are several different ways of grouping living organisms together. This book uses the popular Whittaker system, which divides the living world into five kingdoms.

Kingdom	*Members of kingdom*
Prokaryotae*	monera, or bacteria
Protocista	algae, protozoans, slime moulds
Fungi	mushrooms, moulds and lichens
Animalia	animals
Plantae	plants

*The kingdom Prokaryotae is sometimes given to include the viruses. Other systems describe viruses as being outside normal systems of classification.

ANIMALS

The animal kingdom is usually divided up into about 30 phyla, which differ enormously in size.

Classification of animals

Phylum	*Common name/examples*	*No of species*	*Comments*
Placozoa	*Trichoplax adhaerens*	1	the only species in the phylum, this is the simplest animal known. No tissues, organs or symmetry
Porifera	sponges	10 000	all aquatic, vast majority in sea-water, 150 in fresh water. No tissues, organs or symmetry
Cnidaria	coelenterates, *hydra,* true jellyfish, corals and sea anemones	9 500	nearly all marine. Radially symmetrical with tissues and organs, have stinging cells (nematocysts) on tentacles
Ctenophora	comb jellies, sea gooseberries	90	aquatic, transparent
Mesozoa	mesozoans	50	small, worm-like organisms
Platyhelminthes	flatworms, flukes, tapeworms	15 000	ribbon shaped and soft-bodied, the least complex of the animals that have heads
Nemertina	ribbon worms or proboscis worms	900	characteristic feature is long, sensitive anterior proboscis, used to explore the environment and capture prey
Gnasthostomulida	jaw worms or gnasthostomulids	80	microscopic marine worms
Gastrotricha	gastrotrichs	400	aquatic microscopic animals with cilia on their bodies

Classification of animals (continued)

Phylum	*Common name/examples*	*No of species*	*Comments*
Rotifera	rotifers or wheel animals	2000	aquatic microscopic animals with their anterior end modified into a ciliary organ called a *corona*, the beating of which resembles a rotating wheel
Kinorhyncha	kinorhynchs	150	small worm-like marine animals
Loricifera	loriciferans	10	tiny marine animals with abdomen covered by a girdle of spiny plates called a *lorica*
Acanthocephala	spiny-headed worms	600	gut parasites of vertebrates, usually of carnivores
Entoprocta	entoprocts	150	small marine animals, mostly sedentary, living in colonies attached to rocks, shells, algae or other animals
Nematoda	nematodes or roundworms	>80000	unsegmented, more or less cylindrical worms which occur free-living in all types of environment, and also as parasites of plants and animals. It has been estimated that there may be as many as 1 million species of nematode in the world (ie vast numbers of undiscovered species). In terms of numbers of individuals, nematodes are the most abundant group of multicellular animals
Nematomorpha	horsehair worms, hair-worms, Gordian worms	240	very long, thin worms which are parasitic in insects and crustaceans as juveniles, and free-living in water as adults
Ectoprocta	ectoprocts	5000	small aquatic animals, mostly colonial
Phoronida	horseshoe worms, phoronids	10	marine worms with as many as 1500 hollow tentacles. Live in tubes which they secrete and strengthen with sand or shell fragments
Brachiopoda	lamp shells	335	bottom-living marine animals with shells with two valves. They thrived during the Paleozoic era – more than 30000 extinct species have been described
Mollusca	molluscs, including snails, slugs (gastropods), clams, mussels, oysters (bivalves), octopus, squid (cephalopoda),	110 000	the second largest phylum of animals, molluscs live in aquatic or moist environments, are soft-bodied and are usually protected by calcareous shell that is secreted by a fold of the body wall called the *mantle*
Priapulida	priapulids	10	small carnivorous marine worms
Sipuncula	peanut worms	>300	unsegmented marine worms, live in crevices or are burrowing
Echiura	spoon worms	140	unsegmented marine worms which burrow in marine deposits
Annelida	annelids, including earthworms, leeches, ragworms	8900	worms with a well-developed coelom, and with the body divided up into a number of more or less similar segments. Terrestrial, freshwater or marine
Tardigrada	water bears, tardigrades	380	minute animals which live in films of water around mosses and other low terrestrial features. Four pairs of stubby legs armed with terminal claws

Phylum	*Common name/examples*	*No of species*	*Comments*
Pentastoma	tongue worms	70	parasitic worms in the respiratory passages of air-breathing vertebrates with a chitinous cuticle that is periodically moulted to allow growth
Onychophora	velvet worms, onychophorans	80	soft-bodied, segmented animals with many paired but unjointed legs. Confined to humid tropics
Arthropoda	arthropods, including crustaceans (shrimps, barnacles, woodlice, crabs), scorpions, mites, ticks, spiders, insects, centipedes and millipedes	>2 000 000	by far the largest animal phylum with more species than all the other phyla combined (more than 800 000 species of insects alone have been described, some zoologists think there may be as many as 10 million). Arthropods are segmented animals with paired, jointed appendages on some or all of their body segments
Pogonophora	beard worms	100	extremely slender gutless, tube-living marine worms
Echinodermata	echinoderms, including starfish, sea urchins, sea cucumbers	6 000	marine, mostly bottom-dwelling animals usually displaying five-fold symmetry. The fluid-filled tube feet are used for locomotion and feeding
Chaetognatha	arrow worms	>100	small, slender torpedo-shaped marine planktonic animals which are voracious carnivores
Hemichordata	hemichordates	90	small soft-bodied animals that inhabit shallow U-shaped burrows in sandy or muddy sea bottoms
Chordata	mammals, birds, amphibians, reptiles, fish, plus a small number of invertebrates	45 000	the best known phylum of Animalia containing all the species which, in the minds of many, are considered 'animals'. Chordates are distinguished by (i) having the walls of their pharynx, at some stage in their life cycle, perforated by gill clefts; (ii) a hollow dorsal nerve cord; (iii) an axial cartilaginous rod – the notochord – lying immediatedly beneath the nerve cord. Most chordates have backbones and are called vertebrates, but two of the three subphyla are small invertebrate groups

ANIMAL RECORDS

Size

This table shows the largest species in the animal kingdom, plus some others of particular interest. Unless otherwise stated: (i) *largest* means bulkiest and heaviest; (ii) the size given is the largest size regularly attained by the species, not that of individual 'record-holders'. (*spp.* = species).

	species	*dimension*	*size (m)*	*comments*
mammals				
cetacea	blue whale *(Balaenoptera musculis)*	length	35	the largest and longest living mammal, and the largest animal ever known
	sperm whale *(Physeter catadon)*	length	25	the largest toothed mammal and the largest marine carnivore[a]
marine carnivores	sperm whale (see above)			
	southern elephant seal *(Mirounga leonina)*	length	6.0	the largest seal

Animal records (continued)

	species	*dimension*	*size (m)*	*comments*
ungulates	African elephant *(Loxodonta africana)*	height	3.2	the largest land mammal
	giraffe *(Giraffa camelopardalis)*	height	5.5	the tallest land mammal
terrestrial carnivores	Kodiak bear *(Ursus arctos middendorffi)*	length	2.4	the largest land carnivore
	Indian tiger *(Panthera tigris tigris)*	length	3.15	the largest member of the cat family
primates	eastern lowland mountain gorilla *(Gorilla gorilla graueri)*	height (standing)	1.88	the largest and tallest primate[b]
rodents	capybara *(Hydrochoerus hydrochoerus)*	length	1.4	the largest rodent
	coypu *(Myocastor coypus)*	length	0.9	
marsupial	red kangaroo *(Megaleia rufa)*	height	2.15	the largest marsupial
birds	ostrich *(Struthio camelus)*	height	2.75	the largest and tallest bird
reptiles	estuarine or saltwater crocodile *(Crocodylus porosus)*	length	4.8	the largest reptile
snakes	anaconda *(Eunectes murinus)*	length	8.5	the largest snake
	reticulated python *(Python reticulatus)*	length	10.0	the longest snake
lizards	Komodo monitor *(Varanus komodoensis)*	length	2.25	the largest lizard
	Salvadori monitor *(Varanus salvadori)*	length	4.75	the longest lizard
amphibians	giant salamander *(Andrias davidianus)*	length	1.2	the largest amphibian
fish				
marine fish	whale shark *(Rhincodon typus)*	length	13	the largest marine fish
freshwater fish	sturgeon *(Acipenseridae spp.)*	length	5.0	the largest freshwater fish
	European catfish *(Siluridae spp.)*	length	4.0	
molluscs	Atlantic giant squid *(Architeuthis dux)*	length	17	the largest mollusc and the largest invertebrate
	Pacific giant octopus *(Octopus dofleini)*	length	10	
crustaceans				
marine	giant spider crab *(Macrocheira kaempferi)*	claw span	2.7	the largest crustacean
	North Atlantic lobster *(Homarus americanus)*	length	1.06	the heaviest crustacean
freshwater	crayfish *(Astacopsis gouldi)*	length	0.6	the largest freshwater crustacean
worms	bootlace worm *(Lineus longissimus)*	length	40	the longest worm
jellyfish	Arctic giant *(Cyanae capillata arctica)*	diameter	2.2	the largest jellyfish
		length of tentacles	35	
insects	Goliath beetle *(Scarabaeidae spp.)*	length	0.11	the largest insect
	Queen Alexandra's birdwing *(Ornithoptera alexandrae)*	wing-span	0.28	the largest butterfly
spiders	goliath bird-eating spider *(Theraphosa leblondi)*	leg-span	0.25	the largest spider

[a] discounting the filter-feeding baleen whales (e.g. the blue whale) which feed on small crustaceans such as krill.

[b] man (*Homo sapiens*) regularly exceeds this height. In fact, the tallest recorded human Robert Pershing Wadlow (1918-40), who measured 2.72m at his death, is probably the tallest ever primate.

Weight

	metric tonnes
blue whale	120
sperm whale	50
right whale	50
whale shark	43
basking shark	40
African elephant	6
white shark	5
elephant seal	4
hippopotamus	3
manta ray	3
white rhinoceros	2
moonfish	2
saltwater crocodile	1.5
American bison	1.5
leatherback turtle	0.8
Kodiak bear	0.74
gorilla	0.35
anaconda	0.23

Speed in the air

	km/h
Mammals	
bat	20–50
birds	
(diving)	
peregrine falcon	360
golden eagle	300
(horizontal flight)	
swift	200
teal	120
oystercatcher	100
swan	90
duck	85
partridge	84
pheasant	60
crane	50
gull	40
crow	40
fish	
flying fish	90
insects	
dragonfly	75
hawkmoth	50
hoverfly	14
bumblebee	11

Speed in water

	km/h
mammals	
dolphin	64
killer whale	55
sea lion	40
birds	
penguin	40
reptiles	
leatherback turtle	35
fish	
sailfish	110
swordfish	90
blue shark	70
tuna	70
salmon	40
trout	37
pike	33

Speed on the ground

	km/h
mammals	
cheetah	110
roe deer	98
antelope	95
lion	80
red deer	78
hare	70
horse	69
zebra	65
greyhound	60
giraffe	50
wolf	45
elephant	40
birds	
ostrich	50
reptiles	
crocodile	13
mamba (snake)	11

Mammals

Order	*Family name*	*Common name/examples*	*No of species*	*Distribution of order*	*General characteristics of order*
Monotremes	Ornithorhynchidae	platypus	1	Australia	lay eggs from which young are hatched
	Tachyglossidae	echidna (spiny-anteater)	2		
Marsupialia	Didelphidae	opossums	65	Australia, S and C America	premature birth of young and continued development outside the womb
	Thylacinidae	Tasmanian wolf	1		
	Dasyuridae	native cats, marsupial mice	48		
	Myrmecobiidae	numbat	1		
	Notoryctidae	marsupial moles	2		
	Peramelidae	bandicoots	22		
	Thylacomyidae	burrowing bandicoots	20		
	Caenolestidae	rat opossums	7		
	Phalangeridae	phalangers, cuscuses	15		
	Burramyidae	pigmy possums, feathertail gliders	6		
	Petauridae	gliding phalangers	25		
	Macropodidae	kangaroos, wallabies	47		
	Phascolarctidae	koala	1		
	Vombatidae	wombats	4		
	Tarsipedidae	honey possum	1		
Insectivora	Erinaceidae	hegdehogs, gymnures	14	Europe, N and S America, Asia, Australia	active mainly at night, do not need to rely on vision for orientation
	Talpidae	moles	22		
	Tenrecidae	tenrecs	20		
	Potamogalidae	otter shrews	3		
	Chrysochloridae	golden moles	11		

Mammals *(continued)*

Order	*Family name*	*Common name/examples*	*No of species*	*Distribution of order*	*General characteristics of order*
	Solenodontidae	solenodon, almiqui	2		
	Soricidae	shrews	291		
	Macroscelididae	elephant shrews	28		
	Tupaiidae	tree shrews	15		
Chiroptera	Pteropodidae	Old World fruit bats, flying foxes	154	Europe, N and S America, Asia, Africa, Australia	insectivorous, nocturnal, migrate annually to and from summer roosts and winter migration sites, use echolocation for orientation, order defined by true flight
	Rhinopomatidae	mouse-tailed bats	3		
	Emballonuridae	sheath-tailed or sac-winged bats	50		
	Nycteridae	slit-faced or hollow-faced bats	13		
	Megadermatidae	false vampires	5		
	Hipposideridae	Old World leaf-nosed bats	60		
	Rhinolophidae	horseshoe bats	70		
	Noctilionidae	bulldog bats	2		
	Mormoopidae	insectivorous bats	9		
	Phyllostomatidae	American leaf-nosed bats	120		
	Desmodontidae	vampire bats	3		
	Natalidae	funnel-eared bats	4		
	Furipteridae	smoky bats	2		
	Thyropteridae	disk-wing bats	2		
	Myzopodidae	Old World sucker-footed bats	1		
	Vespertilionidae	common bats	290		
	Mystacinidae	New Zealand short-tailed bats	1		
	Molossidae	free-tailed bats	90		
Rodentia	Aplodontidae	mountain beaver or sewellel	1	Europe, Asia, N and S America, Africa, Australia	one pair of upper and lower incisors which grow throughout life, broadly herbivorous, gnawing mechanism, clawed digits
	Sciuridae	squirrels, chipmunks, marmots	250		
	Cricetidae	field mice, deer mice, voles, lemmings, muskrats	560		
	Muridae	Old World rats and mice	450		
	Heteromyidae	mice, pocket mice, kangaroo rats	75		
	Geomyidae	pocket gophers	40		
	Zapodidae	jumping and birch mice	10		
	Dipodidae	jerboas	25		
	Spalacidae	mole rats	3		
	Rhizomyidae	bamboo rats, African mole rats	18		
	Octodontidae	octodonts, degus	7		
	Echimyidae	spiny rats, rock rats	40		
	Ctenomyidae	tuco-tucos	26		
	Abrocomidae	abrocomes or chinchilla rats	2		
	Chinchillidae	chinchillas, viscachas	6		
	Capromyidae	hutias, coypus	10		
	Dasyproctidae	pacas, agoutis	13		
	Dinomyidae	pacarana or Branick's paca	1		
	Caviidae	cavies, guinea pigs, maras	12		
	Hydrochoeridae	capybaras	2		
	Erethizontidae	New World porcupines	8		
	Petromuridae	rock or dassie rat	1		
	Thryonomyidae	cane rats	2		
	Bathyergidae	blesmols or African mole rats	9		
	Hystricidae	Old World porcupines	15		
	Castoridae	beavers	2		
	Anomaluridae	scaly-tailed squirrels	7		
	Ctenodactylidae	gundis	8		
	Pedetidae	Cape jumping hare or springhaas	1		
	Gliridae	dormice	20		

Order	*Family name*	*Common name/examples*	*No of species*	*Distribution of order*	*General characteristics of order*
	Seleveniidae	jumping dormouse	1		
Edentata	Myrmecophagidae Bradypodidae Dasypodidae	anteaters tree sloths armadillos	3 5 20	S and N America	reduced dentition, long sticky tongue, powerful clawed forefeet
Lagomorpha	Ochotonidae Leporidae	pikas hares, rabbits	14 46	Asia, N America, Europe, S Africa, S America, Australia	herbivorous, well-developed incisors which grow continuously from roots, elongation of the limbs distally
Carnivora	Canidae Ursidae Otariidae Procyonidae Mustelidae Phocidae Felidae Viverridae Hyaenidae	dogs, foxes, wolves, jackels bears, giant panda eared seals, walrus racoons, coatis, lesser panda weasels, otters, skunks, badgers, mink earless seals cats civets, mongooses, genet hyenas	35 7 15 15 65 20 35 70 4	Europe, Asia, N America, S America, Africa, Australia	high level of intelligence, highly developed sense of smell, varied dentition, well-developed carnassials
Cetacea	Balaenidae Eschrichtiidae Balaenopteridae Platanistidae Delphinidae Phocoenidae Monodontidae Physeteridae Hyperoodontidae (formerly Ziphiidae) Stenidae	right whales grey whale rorquals, humpbacks river dolphins dolphins, killer whales porpoises beluga, narwhal sperm whales beaked whales long-snouted dolphins	3 1 8 4 30 6 2 3 15 4	S America, Africa, N America, Europe, Asia, Antarctica, Australia	breathe through blowholes, tapered body, develop young internally and give birth at sea, long breeding period, hearing is major sense, migrate seasonally
Proboscidea	Elephantidae	African elephant, Asian elephant	2	Africa, Asia	bulky bodies and elongated snout, each toe has heavy hoof nail, no canine teeth, herbivorous
Sirenia	Dugongidae Trichechidae	dugong manatees	1 3	Australia, S America, Africa	herbivorous, totally aquatic, torpedo-shaped bodies, tough almost hairless skin, body contains much fat
Perissodactyla	Equidae Tapiridae Rhinocerotidae	horses, asses, zebras, donkeys tapirs rhinoceroses	7 4 5	Africa, Europe, Asia	herbivorous, high-crowned grinding teeth
Artiodactyla	Tragulidae Antilocapridae Giraffidae Cervidae Bovidae Camelidae Suidae Tayassuidae Hippopotamidae	chevrotains pronghorn giraffe, okapi deer cattle, goats, sheep, antelopes, gazelles camels, llamas pigs peccaries hippopotamuses	4 1 2 35 110 4 8 3 2	Asia, Africa, C and S America	ruminants, herbivorous, cloven-hoofed, moderately large brain, migrate seasonally

Mammals (continued)

Order	*Family name*	*Common name/examples*	*No of species*	*Distribution of order*	*General characteristics of order*
Primates	Lemuridae	lemurs	14	Africa, Asia, S America (man is distributed worldwide)	omniverous, multi-purpose dentition, large brain, body position upright, five-digit hands and feet, stereoscopic vision
	Cheirogaleidae	dwarf lemurs, mouse lemurs	4		
	Indriidae	indrii, sifaka, avali	4		
	Daubentoniidae	aye aye (lemur)	1		
	Lepilmuridae	sportive lemurs	2		
	Galagidae	galagos	7		
	Lorisidae	lorises, pottos, bushbabies	12		
	Tupaiidae	tree shrews	17		
	Tarsiidae	tarsiers	3		
	Callitrichidae	tamarins, marmosets	15		
	Cebidae	New World monkeys	30		
	Cercopithecidae	Old World monkeys	72		
	Hylobatidae	gibbons, siamang	7		
	Pongidae	great apes: gorilla, chimpanzee, orangutan	10		
	Hominidae	man	1		

Length of pregnancy in some mammals

animal	*gestation period*[a]
camel	406
cat	62
cow	280
chimpanzee	237
dog	62
dolphin	276
elephant, African	640
ferret	42
fox	52
giraffe	395–425
goat	151
guinea pig	68
hamster	16
hedgehog	35–40
horse	337
human	266
hyena	110
kangaroo	40
lion	108
mink	50
monkey, rhesus	164
mouse	21
opossum	13
orangutan	245–275
pig	113
rabbit	32
rat	21
reindeer	215–245
seal, northern fur	350
sheep	148
skunk	62
squirrel, grey	44
tiger	105–109
whale	365

[a] average number of days

Birds

Order	*Family*	*Common name*	*No of species*	*Distribution of family*	*General characteristics of order*
Struthioniformes	Struthionidae	ostrich	1	Africa	the ostrich is the world's largest living bird. Swift-running, flightless and gregarious, ground-nesting, feeds on vegetable matter.
Rheiformes	Rheidae	rheas	2	S America	swift-running, flightless ground-nesting birds which feed on vegetation and insects. Ostrich-like with short wings and no tailfeathers.
Casuariiformes	Casuariidae	cassowaries	3	Australia	large, flightless, running birds with three toes and rough, hair-like plumage.
	Dromaiidae	emu	1		

Order	*Family*	*Common name*	*No of species*	*Distribution of family*	*General characteristics of order*
Apterygiformes	Apterygidae	kiwis	3	New Zealand	small-eyed, flightless, tailless birds with vestigial wings. They nest in burrows, are mainly small, nocturnal, insectivorous and forest-dwelling.
Tinamiformes	Tinamidae	tinamous	45	S and C America	terrestrial, ground-nesting birds that can fly but do so rarely. They have patterned plumage, feed on vegetation, and live in grassland, brush and forest.
Sphenisciformes	Spheniscidae	penguins	16	Antarctica, Australia, Africa, S America	black and white, flightless, aquatic birds. They nest in burrows or on the ground and are good swimmers, living off fish, squid and crustacea. Walk upright or glide on their stomachs. Specially adapted feet feature a highly efficient heat-exchange mechanism to ensure survival in cold climates.
Gaviformes	Gaviidae	divers or loons	4	N America, Eurasia	black and brown diving birds which breed on inland lakes and nest on the ground. They eat fish, insects etc. and winter on sea coasts. Clumsy on land, their legs are adapted for swimming and diving.
Podicipediformes	Podicipedidae	grebes	20	Africa, Europe, Asia, Australia, N and S America	large grey and brown short-winged diving birds with partly webbed feet. They eat fish and nest on the water. They inhabit freshwater lakes in the summer and sea coasts in winter. Some are migratory.
Procellariiformes	Diomedeidae	albatrosses	14	Africa, Asia, N and S America, Australia, Antarctica	generally long-winged, partly webbed-toed seabirds which feed on fish and nest on isolated islands and cliffs. Secrete oil in self-defence.
	Procellariidae	petrels, fulmars, shearwaters	55		
	Hydrobatidae	storm petrels	20		
	Pelecanoididae	diving petrels	4		
Pelecaniformes	Pelecanidae	pelicans	7	all continents	diverse order of diving birds, found in marine and freshwater coastal habitats worldwide. They nest on cliffs or in trees, have a diet of mostly fish and are generally web-toed.
	Sulidae	gannets, boobies	9	N Atlantic, S Africa, Australasia	
	Phaethontidae	tropicbirds	3	tropical oceans	
	Phalacrocoracidae	cormorants	29	worldwide	
	Fregatidae	frigatebirds	5	tropical oceans	
	Anhingidae	darters	4	N and S America, Africa, Asia, Australasia	

Birds (continued)

Order	*Family*	*Common name*	*No of species*	*Distribution of family*	*General characteristics of order*
Ciconiiformes	Ardeidae	herons, bitterns	60	worldwide except N America and Eurasia	upright, wading birds with specialised bills. Their toes are sometimes webbed and the middle claw is often serrated, or pectinate, for preening.
	Scopidae	hammerhead	1	SW Arabia, Sub-Saharan Africa	
	Balaenicipitidae	whale-headed stork	1	Africa	
	Ciconiidae	storks	17	N America, Eurasia	
	Threskiornithidae	spoonbills, ibises	31	worldwide	
	Phoenicopteridae	flamingos	5	tropical zones	
Anseriformes	Anatidae	ducks, geese, swans	147	worldwide except Antarctica	marsh-dwelling waders which eat vegetation and nest on the ground.
	Anhimidae	screamers	3	S America	
Falconiformes	Cathartidae	vultures (New World)	7	Americas	birds of prey, or raptors. Expert fliers, they have hooked beaks and talons, and are generally large, heavily feathered birds with excellent eyesight (eight times better than human sight) and good hearing.
	Sagittariidae	secretary-bird	1	Sub-Saharan Africa	
	Pandionidae	osprey	1	worldwide	
	Falconidae	falcons, caracaras	60	worldwide except Antarctica	
	Accipitridae	kites, Old World vultures, harriers, hawks, eagles, buzzards	217	worldwide except Antarctica	
Galliformes	Megapodidae	megapodes	9	E Indies, Malaysia, New Guinea, Australia	the Galliformes, or gamebirds, have short rounded wings ill-adapted for sustained flight. They have large feet and claws, and are usually omnivorous in diet. The male plumage is often brilliant. Many are endangered owing to habitat destruction and over-hunting.
	Cracidae	guans, curassows, chachalacas	42	Americas	
	Tetraonidae	grouse	16	Eurasia, America	
	Phasianidae	pheasants, quail, partridge	180	worldwide, except N Eurasia and S America	
	Numididae	guineafowl	7	Sub-Saharan Africa	
	Meleagrididae	turkeys	2	N and S America	
Gruiformes	Mesitornithidae	mesites	3	Madagascar	diverse order of ground-feeding birds generally with brown or grey plumage and long, rounded wings.
	Turnicidae	buttonquails, hemipodes	16	Sub-Saharan Africa, Mediterranean, China, Philippines, Australia	
	Perdionomidae	plains wanderer or collared hemipode	1	Australia	
	Gruidae	cranes	15	all continents except S America and Antarctica	
	Aramidae	limpkin	1	Americas	
	Psophiidae	trumpeters	3	S America	
	Rallidae	rails	129	worldwide	
	Heliornithidae	finfoots	3	tropical America, tropical Africa and SE Asia	
	Rhynochetidae	kagu	1	New Caledonia	
	Eurypygidae	sunbittern	1	S America	
	Cariamidae	seriemas	2	S America	
	Otididae	bustards	22	Africa, Eurasia, Australia	

Order	Family	Common name	No of species	Distribution of family	General characteristics of order
Charadriiformes (Sub-order Charadrii)	Jacanidae	jacanas or lily-trotters	7	Americas, Africa, SE Asia, N Australia	diverse order of mostly small to medium-sized shorebirds and seabirds. They generally have long, narrow wings which can act as aquatic paddles.
	Rostratulidae	painted snipe	2	S America, SE Asia, Australia	
	Haematopodidae	oystercatchers	6	all continents	
	Charadriidae	plovers, lapwings	62	worldwide	
	Scolopacidae	sandpipers	81	all continents	
	Recurvirostridae	avocets, stilts	7	all continents	
	Phalaropodidae	phalaropes	3	N Eurasia, N America	
	Dromadidae	crab plover	1	Indian ocean coastlines	
	Burhinidae	stonecurlews or thick-knees	9	all continents except N America	
	Glareolidae	pratincoles, coursers	17	Eurasia, Africa, Australia	
	Thinocoridae	seed snipe	4	S America	
	Chionididae	sheathbills	2	Antarctica	
(Sub-order Lari)	Stercorariidae	skuas, jaegers	6	worldwide	
	Laridae	gulls	45	worldwide	
	Sternidae	terns, noddies	42	worldwide	
	Rynchopidae	skimmers	3	tropical Africa, SE Asia, eastern N America, C and S America	
(Sub-order Alcae)	Alcidae	auks	22	Northern hemisphere	
Columbiformes	Pteroclididae	sandgrouse	16	Africa, S Europe, Asia	small to medium-sized arboreal and terrestial birds with thick, heavy plumage.
	Columbidae	pigeons, doves	300	worldwide except Antarctica	
Psittaciformes	Psittacidae	parrots, lories, cockatoos, lovebirds, macaws, budgerigars	330	all continents except Antarctica	the parrots have zygodactyl toes: two pointing forward, and two backward, enabling them to climb and hold objects. They have strong, hooked bills – (with mobile upper mandible) used for cracking nuts, holding things and climbing – as a 'third foot'. Often colourful, they nest in trees and on ledges and have a largely vegetarian diet.
Cuculiformes	Musophagidae	turacos	22	Sub-Saharan Africa	diverse order of arboreal and terrestial birds. The cuckoos are brood parasites, relying on other species to raise their young.
	Cuculidae	cuckoos, anis, roadrunner, coucals	128	worldwide	
	Opisthocomidae	hoatzin	1	S America	
Strigiformes	Strigidae	(typical) owls	124	worldwide except Antarctica	the owls are nocturnal raptors found in grassland and woodland habitats,

Birds (continued)

Order	*Family*	*Common name species*	*No of of family*	*Distribution of order*	*General characteristics*
	Tytonidae	barn owls	10	worldwide except C Asia, New Zealand and Antarctica	usually nesting in cavities. Their large, forward-facing eyes peer out of a facial disc and give them binocular vision. Owls can turn their heads in either direction more than 180°, and also have acute hearing.
Caprimulgiformes	Caprimulgidae	nightjars or goatsuckers	70	open habitats in temperate and tropical regions	these are generally insectivorous. Some hibernate and many are migratory. They have wide, gaping mouths with hooked beaks, large eyes and short legs with weak feet. Many species are two-coloured, featuring grey and red phases.
	Podargidae	frogmouths	12	SE Asia, Australia	
	Aegothelidae	owlet-nightjars	8	Australia, SE Asia	
	Nyctibiidae	potoos	5	S America	
	Steatornithidae	oilbird	1	S America	
Apodiformes	Apodidae	swifts	80	worldwide	aerial birds that depend on their flying skills for food. Swifts areinsectivorous and migratory. While on the wing they feed, mate, collect nest material, drink and even, in some species, pass the night at high altitudes. Hummingbirds feed on nectar, supplemented with insects.
	Hemiprocnidae	crested swifts	3	SE Asia	
	Trochilidae	hummingbirds	320	Americas	
Coliiformes	Coliidae	mousebirds or colies	6	Sub-Saharan Africa	these acrobatic, highly social birds live in scrub and bushes, feeding on fruit and vegetation – often becoming agricultural pests.
Trogoniformes	Trogonidae	trogons	35	America, Asia, Sub-Saharan Africa	colourful, sedentary, arboreal birds that feed on fruit and insects. They nest in tree cavities and termite mounds.
Coraciiformes	Alcedinidae	kingfishers	87	worldwide	the three anterior toes on these birds are united, an adaptation for perching and tree-climbing. Many are brightly coloured, some are social. All nest in cavities, digging holes in, for example, earth banks or rotten trees.
	Todidae	todies	5	W Indies	
	Momotidae	motmots	8	S America	
	Meropidae	bee-eaters	24	Africa, Eurasia, Australia	
	Leptosomatidae	cuckoo-roller	1	Madagascar, Comoros Islands	
	Coraciidae	rollers	16	Africa, Eurasia, Australia	
	Upupidae	hoopoe	1	Africa, Eurasia	
	Phoeniculidae	woodhoopoes	6	Sub-Saharan Africa	
	Bucerotidae	hornbills	45	Sub-Saharan Africa, SE Asia	

Order	*Family*	*Common name*	*No of species*	*Distribution of family*	*General characteristics of order*
Piciformes	Galbulidae	jacamars	15	S America	these birds are zygodactylous (see Psittaciformes). Colourful and arboreal, they feed on vegetation and insects, and nest in holes.
	Bucconidae	puffbirds	30	S America	
	Capitonidae	barbets	76	America, Sub-Saharan Africa, SE Asia	
	Indicatoridae	honeyguides	15	Sub-Saharan Africa, Himalayas, SE Asia	
	Ramphastidae	toucans	40	S America	
	Picidae	woodpeckers, piculets, wrynecks	200	Worldwide	
Passeriformes (Sub-order Eurylaimi)	Eurylaimidae	broadbills	14	Africa, Asia	around 5 200 species, well over half of all birds, belong to the order Passeriformes, the perching birds or passerines. The order includes the most familiar garden birds – tits, chickadees, robins and sparrows - as well as other species found in virtually all land habitats. No passerine is a true water bird, though the dippers come close. Most are small or medium-sized birds (the largest species are the raven and the Australian lyrebird) The perching feet have four well-developed, separate toes. They are very vocal, singing birds. The male is often more brightly coloured than the female. Most are opportunistic feeders, being dependent on high-energy foods such as seeds and insects. Monogamy is the norm.
(Sub-order Menurae)	Menuridae	lyrebirds	2	SE Australia	
	Atrichornithidae	scrub-birds	2	W and E Australia	
(Sub-order Tyranni)	Furnariidae	ovenbirds	220	C and S America	
	Dendrocolaptidae	woodcreepers	48	S America	
	Formicariidae	antbirds	230	S America	
	Tyrannidae	tyrant flycatchers	375	Americas	
	Pittidae	pittas	29	Africa, SE Asia, Australia	
	Pipridae	manakins	53	S America	
	Cotingidae	cotingas	65	S America	
	Conopophagidae	gnateaters	9	S America	
	Rhinocryptidae	tapaculos	29	S America	
	Oxyruncidae	sharpbill	1	S America	
	Phytotomidae	plantcutters	3	S America	
	Xenicidae	New Zealand wrens	4	New Zealand	
	Philepittidae	sunbird astites	4	Madagascar	
(Sub-order Oscines)	Hirundinidae	swallows, martins	74	worldwide	
	Alaudidae	larks	75	all continents	
	Motacillidae	wagtails, pipits	54	worldwide	
	Pycnonotidae	bulbuls	120	S Asia, Africa	
	Laniidae	shrikes	69	N America, Africa, Eurasia	
	Campephagidae	cuckoo-shrikes	72	Africa, Australia, S and E Asia	
	Irenidae	leafbirds	14	S and E Asia	
	Prionopidae	helmet shrikes	9	Sub-Saharan Africa	
	Vangidae	vanga shrikes	13	Madagascar, Comoros	
	Bombycillidae	waxwings, silky flycatchers	8	N Eurasia, S America	
	Dulidae	palmchat	1	S America	
	Cinclidae	dippers	5	N Africa, Eurasia, W America	
	Troglodytidae	wrens	60	NW Africa, Eurasia, N and S America	
	Mimidae	mockingbirds	30	Americas	

Birds (continued)

Order	*Family*	*Common name*	*No of species*	*Distribution of family*	*General characteristics of order*
	Subfamilies of the family Muscicapidae				
	Prunellidae	accentors	13	N Africa, Eurasia, S Asia	
	Turdinae	thrushes	305	worldwide	
	Timaliinae	babblers	252	Africa, S Asia, Australasia, N America	
	Sylviinae	warblers (Old World)	350	worldwide	
	Muscicapinae	flycatchers (Old World)	155	Australasia	
	Malurinae	fairy-wrens	26	Australia, New Guinea	
	Paradoxornithinae	parrotbills	19	Asia, Europe	
	Monarchinae	monarch flycatchers	133	Sub-Saharan Africa, S Asia, Australasia	
	Orthonychinae	logrunners	20	SE Asia, Australia	
	Acanthizinae	Australian warblers	65	SE Asia, Australasia	
	Rhipidurinae	fantail flycatchers	39	SE Asia, Australasia	
	Pachycephalinae	thickheads	46	SE Asia, Australasia	
	Paridae	tits	46	Africa, Eurasia, N America	
	Aegithalidae	long-tailed tits	7	Eurasia, N America	
	Remizidae	penduline tits	10	Africa, Eurasia, N America	
	Sittidae	nuthatches	21	N America, Eurasia, N Africa, Australia	
	Climacteridae	Australasian treecreepers	8	Australia, New Guinea	
	Certhiidae	holarctic treecreepers	5	Eurasia, Africa, N America	
	Rhabdornithidae	Philippine treecreepers	2	Philippines	
	Zosteropidae	white-eyes	85	Sub-Saharan Africa, S and E Asia, Australasia	
	Dicaeidae	flowerpeckers	50	SE Asia, Australasia	
	Pardalotidae	pardalotes or diamond eyes	5	Australia	
	Nectariniidae	sunbirds, spiderhunters	116	Old World tropics, Africa to Australia	
	Meliphagidae	honeyeaters	169	Australasia, S Africa	
	Ephthianuridae	Australian chats	5	Australia	
	Subfamilies of the family Emberizidae				
	Emberizinae	Old World buntings, New World sparrows	281	worldwide except SE Asia and Australasia	
	Catambly-rhynchinae	plush-capped finch	1	S America	
	Thraupinae	tanagers, honeycreepers	233	Americas	
	Cardinalinae	cardinal grosbeaks	37	S America	
	Tersininae	swallow tanager	1	S America	
	Parulidae	wood warblers	119	Americas	

Order	Family	Common name	No of species	Distribution of family	General characteristics of order
	Vireonidae	vireos, pepper shrikes	43	Americas	
	Icteridae	American blackbirds	94	Americas	
	Subfamilies of the family Fringillidae				
	Fringillinae	fringilline finches	3	Eurasia, Canary Islands	
	Carduelinae	cardueline finches	122	worldwide except Australia	
	Drepanidinae	Hawaiian honeycreepers	23	Hawaiian Islands	
	Estrildidae	waxbills	124	Africa, S Asia, Australia	
	Subfamilies of the family Ploceidae				
	Ploceinae	true weavers	95	Africa, S Asia	
	Viduinae	widow birds	10	Sub-Saharan Africa	
	Bubalornithinae	buffalo weavers	3	Sub-Saharan Africa	
	Passerinae	sparrow weavers, sparrows	37	Africa, Eurasia	
	Sturnidae	starlings	106	Africa, Eurasia, Australia, New Zealand	
	Oriolidae	orioles, figbirds	28	Africa, Eurasia, Australia	
	Dicruridae	drongos	20	Sub-Saharan Africa, S Asia, N and E Australia	
	Callaeidae	New Zealand wattlebirds	3	New Zealand	
	Grallinidae	magpie larks	2	Australia	
	Corcoracidae	Australian mudnesters	2	E Australia	
	Artamidae	wood swallows	10	SE Asia, Australia	
	Cracticidae	bell magpies	9	New Guinea, Australia	
	Ptilonorhynchidae	bowerbirds	18	New Guinea, Australia	
	Paradisaeidae	birds of paradise	43	New Guinea, Australia	
	Corvidae	crows, magpies, jays	113	worldwide	

Incubation and fledgling periods in some common birds

Bird family	Incubation period (days)	Fledgling period (days)
Hole nesters		
bee-eaters	20	23
hornbills	35	46
kingfishers	22	29
owls	30	30
rollers	18	28
swifts	20	44
Open nesters		
anis	13	11
cuckoos	12	22
passerines	13	13
pigeons	15	17
turacos	17	28
Seabirds		
wandering albatross	78	280
fulmar	49	49
gannet	44	90
king penguin	53	360
adelie penguin	33	51
giant petrel	59	108
storm petrel	41	63
shag	30	53
common tern	23	30
sandwich tern	23	35

Bird family Incubation Fledgling

Largest wingspan

	metres
albatross	3.6
white pelican	3.6
marabou stork	3.3
Andean condor	3.2
hooping swan	3.0
bearded vulture	3.0
bald vulture	2.8
grey crane	2.5
golden eagle	2.5
white stork	1.8
grey heron	1.7
gannet	1.7
seagull	1.7

Natural history

Life history features of some well-known birds

Species	Maximum recorded age (years)	Annual adult mortality (%)	Age of first breeding (years)	No. of eggs	Body weight (g)
blue tit	10	70	1	12–14	11
European robin	13	52	1	4–6	18
song sparrow	8	44	1	4–6	30
house sparrow	12	50	1	3–6	30
European starling	20	50	1–2	4–6	80
American robin	10	48	1	4–6	100
European blackbird	20	42	1	3–5	80–110
barn swallow	16	63	1	4–6	20
common swift	21	15	2	2–3	36–50
tawny owl	18	26	2	2–4	680–750
mourning dove	17	55	1	2	140
woodpigeon	16	36	1	2	450–550
Atlantic puffin	22	5	4	1	350–550
black-legged kittiwake	21	14	4–5	2–3	300–500
herring gull	36	6	3–5	3	750–1 250
curlew	32	26	2	4	575–800
redshank	17	31	1–2	4	110–155
lapwing	23	32	1–2	4	200–300
avocet	25	22	2–3	4	250–400
pheasant	8	58	1–2	8–15	900–1 400
kestrel	17	34	1–2	4–6	190–240
buzzard	26	19	2–3	2–4	550–1 200
osprey	32	18	2–3	2–3	1 200–2 000
mallard	29	48	1–2	9–13	850–1 400
tufted duck	15	46	1–2	8–11	550–900
eider	18	20	2–3	4–6	1 200–2 800
barnacle goose	23	9	3	3–5	1 400–1 600
mute swan	22	10	3–4	5–8	10 000–12 000
grey heron	25	30	2	4–5	1 600–2 000
white stork	26	21	3–5	3–5	3 000–3 500
shag	21	16	3–4	3–4	1 750–2 250
short-tailed shearwater	31	5	5–8	1	530
royal albatross	36	3	8–10	1	8 300
yellow-eyed penguin	18	10	2–4	2	5 200

Reptiles

Order	Family	Common name	No of species	Distribution	General characteristics of order
Chelonia	Dermatemydidae	Central American river turtle	1	C America, Mexico	aquatic and terrestial reptiles – turtles, terrapins and tortoises. These have a rigid body shell comprising a dorsal carapace and a ventral plastron, into which most species draw their head and legs for protection. The jaws are beaked, without teeth.
	Chelydridae	common and alligator snapping turtles	2	N and S America	
	Kinosternidae	mud and musk turtles	21	tropical regions	
	Testudinidae	tortoises	40	all continents except Australia	
	Platysternidae	big-headed turtle	1	SE Asia	
	Emydidae	common turtle	76	abundant in northern hemisphere	
	Cheloniidae	sea turtles	5	worldwide	
	Dermochelyidae	leatherback turtle	1	worldwide	
	Carettochelyidae	New Guinea plateless turtle	1	New Guinea	
	Trionychidae	soft-shell turtles	20	all continents except S America and Australia	
	Pelomedusidae	side-necked turtles	14	Africa, S America	

Order	Family	Common name	No of species	Distribution	General characteristics of order
	Chelyidae	snake-necked turtles	31	Australia, S America	
Rhynchocephalia	Sphenodontidae	tuatara	1	New Zealand	primitive nocturnal reptile, feeds on snails, worms, occasionally small lizards and birds.
Squamata (sub-order Sauria)	Gekkonidae	geckos	650	worldwide	the Squamata are a large and very diverse order comprising three suborders, Sauria (lizards), Serpentes or Ophidia (snakes) and Amphisbaenia (worm lizards). This order contains the great majority of living reptiles.
	Pygopodidae	flap-footed lizards	15	Australia, New Guinea	
	Dibamidae	burrowers	3	Philippines, Vietnam, New Guinea	
	Iguanidae	iguanas	600	N and S America, W Indies, Galapagos, Fiji, Madagascar	
	Agamidae	agamid lizard	300	tropical regions worldwide	
	Chameleontidae	Old World chameleons	85	Africa, W Asia, India	lizards vary in size from a few centimetres (some geckos) to about 3 metres in length (the Komodo dragon). They feed as herbivores, insectivores or as predators of small vertebrates. The skull is made up of several separate mobile elements (a form of modification known as cranial kinesis). Limbs may be reduced in burrowing forms.
	Scincidae	skinks	800	worldwide except polar regions	
	Cordylidae	girdle-tailed lizards	50	S Africa, Madagascar	
	Lacertidae	Old World terrestrial lizards	150	Europe, Asia, Africa	
	Teiidae	whiptail lizards	200	tropical regions	
	Anguidae	glass lizards, alligator lizards, galliwasps	67	Americas	
	Anniellidae	California legless lizards	2	California	
	Xenosauridae		4	Mexico, China	
	Helodermatidae	gila monster lizard, bearded lizard	2	N America, Mexico	
	Varanidae	monitor lizards	30	tropical regions	
	Lanthanotidae	earless monitor lizard	1	Borneo	
	Xantusiidae	night lizards	12	C America, Cuba	
(sub-order Serpentes)	Typhlopidae	blind snakes, worm snakes	200	tropical regions	snakes have no limbs, have long, cylindrical scaly bodies, lidless eyes and highly mobile jaws (cranial kinesis). They eat animals (or eggs), killing by suffocation, by biting or by venom, and cannot chew. They moult their skin several times each year.
	Letotyphlopidae	slender blind snakes	40	N and S America, SW Asia, Africa	
	Xenopeltidae	sunbeam snake	1	India	
	Uropeltidae	shieldtail snakes	50	S Asia	
	Boidae	pythons, boas, woodsnakes	60	tropical regions	
	Acrochordidae	wart snakes	2	Australia, E Indies, SE Asia	
	Colubridae	terrestrial, arboreal and aquatic snakes	>1500	worldwide	
	Viperidae	vipers, rattlesnakes, moccasins	180	Europe, Asia, Africa, not Australia	
	Elapidae	cobras, mambas, coral snakes	170	Asia, Africa, N and S America	
	Hydrophiidae	sea snakes	50	Indian and Pacific oceans	

Reptiles (continued)

Order	Family	Common name	No of species	Distribution	General characteristics of order
(sub-order Amphisbaenia)	Amphisbaenidae	worm lizards	100	Africa, C and S America, SE Asia and Seychelle Islands	small, limbless burrowing lizards with concealed eyes and wedge-shaped skulls to aid with digging. They eat small animals.
Crocodilia	Alligatoridae	alligators, caiman	7	S America, Africa, Asia,	small to very large (7 metres) carnivorous, amphibious reptiles. Heavy cylindrical body armoured with bony plates, elongated snout, webbed toes, powerful tail, mainly nocturnal.
	Crocodilidae	true crocodile	13	Australia	
	Gavialidae	gavial or gharial	1	India	

Amphibians

Order	Family	Common name	No of species	Distribution	General characteristics of order
Trachystomata		sirens	3	N America	aquatic, eel-like amphibians, no hindlimbs, forelimbs tiny, without external eyes or ears.
Gymnophiona		caecilians	160	C and S America, Africa, SE Asia, Seychelle Islands	caecilians are limbless, worm-like subterranean amphibians with annuli (rings) along length of body.
Urodela or Caudata	Hynobiidae	Asiatic salamanders	30	N Asia (from Ural Mountains to Japan and Taiwan)	the tailed amphibians – salamanders and newts. Adults aquatic or terrestial, occasionally arboreal, eggs and larvae primitively aquatic. Feed on slow-moving invertebrates (worms, slugs and snails).
	Cryptobranchidae	giant salamanders, hellbenders	3	N America, China and Japan	
	Sirenidae	sirens, dwarf sirens	3	SE United States, Mexico	
	Proteidae	olm	1	Balkan peninsula	
	Necturidae	mud puppies	5	N America	
	Amphiumidae	congo eels	3	SE United States	
	Salamandridae	salamanders and newts	42	Europe, N Africa, Middle East, S Asia, N America	
	Ambystomatidae	mole salamanders, axolotl	33	N America	
	Plethodontidae	lungless salamanders	210	Americas, S Europe	
Anura	Leiopelmatidae	primitive frogs	4	New Zealand, N America	the frogs and toads. Tail absent, hindlimbs enlarged for jumping. Adults aquatic or terrestial, occasionally arboreal or burrowing. Eggs
	Discoglossidae	fire-bellied toads, midwife toads	8	Europe, Asia, N America, Philippines	
	Rhinophrynidae	burrowing toad	1	C America	
	Pipidae	tongueless frogs	14	Africa, S America	

Order	Family	Common name	No of species	Distribution	General characteristics of order
	Pelobatidea	spadefoots	59	Europe, Asia, N America, Australia	and larvae (tadpoles) typically aquatic, but reproductive strategies vary. Largely insectivorous. (Smooth wet-skinned species of Anura are usually known as frogs, rough dry-skinned species as toads, but there is no technical difference between the two).
	Myobatrachidae	terrestrial, arboreal and aquatic frogs	95	New Guinea, Australia, South Africa	
	Rhinodermatidae	mouth-breeding frog	1	S America	
	Leptodactylidae	terrestrial neotropical frogs	650	Americas Caribbean	
	Bufonidae	true toads	235	worldwide	
	Brachycephalidae	terrestrial toads	2	Brazil	
	Dendrobatidae	arrow-poison frogs	70	C and S America	
	Pseudidae	fully aquatic frogs	5	S America	
	Centrolenidae	leaf frogs	60	C and S America	
	Hylidae	tree frogs	400	worldwide	
	Ranidae	true frogs	850	Worldwide	
	Sooglossidae	terrestrial frogs	3	Seychelle Islands	
	Microhylidae	narrow-mouthed frogs	230	Africa, Asia, N and S America, Australia	

Fishes

There have been many different systems of fish classification, and today there is still much debate about taxonomy. Most systems divide the world of fishes into three: the jawless fishes, the cartilagenous fishes and the bony fishes. This table lists some of the best-known types of fish.

Order	Common name	No. of species	Distribution	General characteristics of order
Class Agnatha *(jawless fishes)*				
Cyclostomata	lampreys	30	cool, fresh, and coastal waters of all continents, except Africa	eel-shaped body; well-developed dorsal and caudal fins; horny teeth; feed on the blood of other fishes; only breed in fresh water
	hagfishes	30	cold, marine bottom waters, equatorial oceans	soft-skinned; nearly cylindrical; eyes vestigial, covered by skin; feed on dead or moribund fishes or invertebrates; locate food by scent; only breed in marine water.
Class Chondrichthyes *(fishes with a cartilage skeleton)*				
Selachii	sharks	>200	tropical and temperate zones; particularly New Zealand, S Africa	large group of predatory fishes belonging to nineteen separate families; streamlined bodies; highly sensitive sense of smell; attacks on humans very rare, usually occur in water warmer than 21 °C (70 °F); an exception, however, is the white shark, which is also the most dangerous; others include hammerheads (very mobile using rudder effect of head), tiger and sand sharks; largest are the whale and basking sharks.

Fishes (continued)

Order	*Common name*	*No. of species*	*Distribution*	*General characteristics of order*
Batoidei	rays, skates, stingrays	>300	all oceans from tropical to temperate latitudes	bottom dwellers, preying on other animals on sea floor; differ externally from sharks having gill openings confined to lower surface; eyes on dorsal surface; many armed with thorns, tubercles or prickles; stingrays live in shallow, coastal waters; if provoked, will lash back its tail; electric rays are sluggish, stun invertebrates and fish by shocks produced from electric organs. Skates lie on bottom, often partially buried; rise in pursuit of prey, particularly herring; trap victims by swimming over them and settling upon them; their egg cases ('mermaid's purses') are often washed ashore.
Class Osteichthyes *(fishes with a bony skeleton)*				
Dipnoi	lungfishes	6	freshwater; Australia, Africa, N America	voracious, eating aquatic animals, including own species; most grow to substantial size; sac-shaped, pneumatic organs that lie along alimentary tract whose structure and function are like primitive lungs of amphibians.
Acipenseriformes	sturgeons	25	marine and freshwater; Europe, Asia, N America	braincase mostly cartilaginous; ground feeding by dragging tactile, whisker-like barbels over bottom; toothless mouth with protractile lips surrounded by taste buds; food fish for man, source of caviar.
	paddlefishes	2	marine and freshwater; China and N America	braincase mostly cartilaginous; feed by straining plankton through gill system; elongated, paddle-shaped snout composed entirely of cartilage, measuring one third of the total body length.
Polypteriformes	bichirs or reedfishes	11	tropical swamps and rivers in C Africa	inhabit edges of streams and flood plains, concealed by day, forage for worms, insect larvae, small fishes by night.
Elopiformes	bonefishes	4	coastal and deep waters of warm oceans	specialized bottom feeders; grubs with snout for worms and shellfish which it crushes with rounded palatal teeth.
	tarpons	2	warm coastal waters Atlantic	fast-swimming predator; swim bladder lung-like, partially compartmented, highly vascularized; obligate air breathers, can die from asphyxiation if prevented from reaching surface.
	ladyfish	6	warm coastal waters circumtropical	fast-swimming predators; appear to 'roll' at sea surface apparently for intake of air; open duct to swim bladder when air is taken through mouth.

Order	Common name	No. of species	Distribution	General characteristics of order
Anguilliformes	eels	>500	marine and freshwater; of Europe and N America; some in shallow water or deep sea	elongate, cylindrical body form; carnivorous until maturity; morays and congers inhabit rock crevices, others form vast colonies of individuals in tropical reef areas; return to sea to spawn.
Clupeiformes	herrings	190	virtually worldwide in marine waters, and in many bodies of freshwater	teeth usually absent or weakly developed; single schools of herring estimated to include many millions.
	anchovies	200	widespread in surface coastal waters of tropical and temperate seas; a few anadromous (returning to fresh water to spawn)	snout projects beyond very wide mouth; upper and lower jaws usually armed with rows of minute teeth; found in large schools, some spreading over 100 metres, contracting to writhing sphere of thousands of fishes only a few metres across at approach of a predator.
Osteoglossiformes	bony tongues	6	freshwater; rivers and lakes, turbid waters or regions with dense aquatic vegetation	strongly toothed jaws; large mouth; well developed swim bladder; some species, upper portion of ear (for balance) completely separated from lower part (for hearing).
	freshwater butterfly fish	1	freshwater; Africa	greatly expanded wing-like pectoral fins (behind gills) which are used for short flights to the air, either to escape predators or to catch insects.
Salmoniformes	salmons, trouts, chars, smelts, graylings, whitefishes	150	widespread, marine or freshwater. Salmon common in N Atlantic; return to freshwater to breed	trim, fusiform body; powerful caudal (tail) muscles; commonly migrate upstream to spawn; very important food fishes.
	pikes, mudminnows	10	freshwater; northern hemisphere	long bodies; dorsal and anal fins positioned posteriorly, adipose fin absent.
Ostariophysi	carps, minnows, barbs, suckers, loaches	3 500	fresh to brackish waters: Africa, S and C America, Eurasia	small to medium-sized fishes; upper jaw protractile, jaw teeth usually absent. Body covered in scales.
	catfishes	2 500	low saline, brackish freshwater or marine	order of small to very large freshwater fishes; oral incubation of eggs by some species; most active at night or under conditions of reduced light.
Characiformes	tetras, darters piranhas	>1 300	freshwater: S & C America, Africa	mostly small, colourful fishes; upper jaw projectile, jaws bearing teeth; of prime importance in aquarium trade.
Paracanthopterygii	toadfishes	45	primarily marine, mainly tropical and temperate shallow waters along continental coasts; occasionally freshwater	generally have two dorsal fins; nine venomous species restricted to coast and rivers of C and S America.
	trout-perches	8	all freshwater, N America	live under conditions of dim light; can be found in clear water of the Great Lakes at depths of about 35 fathoms.
	codfishes	800	primarily marine, shallow water, some deep sea types, worldwide distribution; particularly N Atlantic	largest of order, growing to about 2 metres in length and attain weights that may exceed 90 kilograms (200 pounds); migrate over long distances, gathering in late winter and early spring to spawn, each species goes to particular area.

Fishes (continued)

Order	*Common name*	*No. of species*	*Distribution*	*General characteristics of order*
Atheriniformes	flying fishes	50	surface marine waters, worldwide	surface fishes of the open ocean where they breed; capable of leaping or skipping on surface to escape predators; tail (caudal) fin usually asymmetrical, lower lobes longer than body so while out of water lower lobe vibrates as a scull driving fish along.
	needlefishes and garfishes	25	mostly temperate and tropical marine, a few freshwater	pelagic (inhabiting the open ocean); predatory habit highly developed; long, formidable toothed jaws elongated into strongly toothed beak; breed near shore.
	cyprinodonts	500	tropical and subtropical distribution, including hot springs of Africa and America	diminutive; many important as experimental animals in biological research; among hardiest of fish, some surviving in rigorous environments, including water temperatures in hot springs approaching coagulation point of protoplasm.
Gasterosteiformes	sticklebacks	11	fresh, brackish, and marine waters of northern hemisphere	small, scaleless fishes; short jaws armed with sharp teeth; body more nearly fusiform (tapered at both ends).
	tube snout	1	NE Pacific Ocean	elongated, slender, cylindrical body tipped by prolonged snout; small toothed mouth has hinged upper jaw; scale-less body armoured with series of embedded bony plates.
	sea horses	24	widely distributed; marine	bony rings instead of scales; use coiled tail to grip seaweed and other plants/objects; propulsion by means of dorsal fin (midline of back); tiny pectoral fin used for steering; rise or settle to another depth by changing air volume within the bladder.
Scorpaeniformes	scorpion fishes, rockfishes, redfishes, turkeryfishes, gunards	330	tropical, temperate, and northern seas	live on coral or rocky bottom; many possess remarkable degree of concealing coloration and shape; dorsal fin spines long and numerous; head spiny; body scaly; some with venom glands on fin spines.
Perciformes				the order Perciformes, the perch-like species, is the largest group of fishes, comprising about 7000 species in 150 families.
	perches	125	freshwater temperate species	possess numerous short, fine, pointed teeth; prefer quiet waters; pike-perches semi-migratory, prefer quiet, running waters.

Order	Common name	No. of species	Distribution	General characteristics or order
	tunas	40	open waters of tropics and warm seas of world	may travel across entire Pacific Ocean from California coast to Japan, or reverse, to spawn; one of the larger predatory perciforms; carnivorous; well-developed vascular system under skin associated with sustained high-speed swimming and a body temperature a few degrees higher than surrounding water.
	marlins	7	worldwide in warm seas	greatest game fishes of the ocean; black marlin is the largest at 900 kg (2 000 lb).
Pleuronectiformes	flatfishes	2	Indo-Pacific and Africa	asymmetrical; found in depths up to 1 000 metres (3 300 feet), most occur on continental shelf in less than 200 metres of water; swim by undulating movement of body and fins; lie on bottom, generally covered by sand or mud, with only eyes protruding; eyes can be raised, lowered and moved independently.
	flounders	300+	marine and freshwater, tropic and temperate seas	either right-eyed (dextral) or left-eyed (sinistral); asymmetrical; feed primarily on crustaceans, other bottom invertebrates and small fish; when feeding lie motionless and then pounce on close prey.
	soles	100+	tropic and temperate seas, some freshwater	asymmetrical; strongly compressed; eyes, usually small, on one side (dextral); mouth curved downward; caudal fin with numerous rays.
Tetraodontiformes	box fishes	25	prominent around coral reefs, open sand and grassy flats; worldwide	carapace closed behind anal and usually behind dorsal fin; no ventral keel; blow jet of water out of mouth onto sand bottom to expose burrowing invertebrates.
	puffer fishes	7	prominent around coral reefs, open sand and grassy flats; worldwide	poisonous flesh, at least during certain seasons of year; most of highly poisonous substance contained in viscera; flesh can be eaten if professionally cleaned.
	ocean sunfishes	3	prominent around coral reefs, open sand and grassy flats; tropical and subtropical oceans worldwide	massive, crushing jaws and teeth; feed extensively on soft-bodied invertebrates, such as jellyfishes.

Insects

Order	Common name	No. of species	Distribution	General characteristics of order
Collembola	springtails	2 000	worldwide	blind, primitively wingless insects with entognathous mouthparts (ie contained within an invagination of the head). They leap by means of a forked springing organ on the underside of the abdomen.
Diplura	diplurans	660	worldwide	small, slender, blind, whitish insects with entognathous mouthparts, found in damp soil, under logs and stones.

Insects (continued)

Order	*Common name*	*No. of species*	*Distribution*	*General characteristics of order*
Protura	proturans	120	worldwide	primitively wingless, white, blind, no antennae, reduced mouthparts, found under bark, stones or rotting vegetation.
Thysanura	bristletails, silverfish	600	worldwide	primitive wingless insects found amongst decaying wood etc., in human habitations, and in association with ants and termites; feed on fungi, lichens, algae, pollen or decaying vegetable matter.
Ephemeroptera	mayflies	2000	worldwide, except Antarctica	some species carnivorous, but majority are herbivorous, life cycle consists of four stages. Nymph can live for two weeks to two years; the adults are winged and non-feeding, living from 2 to 72 hours, during which time they mate.
Odonata	dragonflies, damselflies	5000	worldwide	carniverous, often brightly coloured; aquatic larvae, adults have powerful predatory mouthparts and two pairs of richly veined wings. Larvae feed on aquatic larvae, tadpoles, worms and small fish, adults on flying insects.
Orthoptera	grasshoppers, locusts, crickets	24000	worldwide	wings, when present, number four, chewing mouthparts, mostly plant feeders. Hindlimbs usually specialized for jumping; many species produce sounds by rubbing together forewings. Of immense economic importance.
Phasmida (Phasmoptera)	stick insects, leaf insects	2500	tropical areas	arboreal, nocturnal, feed on plant juices, camouflage and mimicry highly developed.
Blattaria	cockroaches	3700	worldwide	depressed body, long legs, forewings hard or leathery, hindwings membranous, but may be reduced or absent. Typically live on the ground, under stones or in litter and wood debris. Some are household pests.
Embioptera	webspinners	200	tropical regions	inhabit extensive galleries or labyrinths of silk on bark, litter, moss, lichens or within the soil. Body slender, legs short, females and some males wingless.
Zoraptera	zorapterans	20	tropical regions	tiny insects resembling slender termites.
Dermaptera	earwigs	1500	worldwide	feed as scavengers or predators with large pincers variously used for predation, defence, courtship and grooming. Wings frequently reduced or absent.
Mantodea	mantids, mantises	1800	tropical and subtropical areas	predatory insects in which body shape is highly adapted for camouflage; head very mobile, eyes large; in some species female eats male headfirst during copulation.
Isoptera	termites or white ants	2000	Europe, Australia, Asia, N America	cellulose-eating, social insects that construct nests which vary in size from a few centimetres to several metres. Caste system includes morphologically distinct soldiers and workers.
Phthiraptera	sucking lice (Anoplura), biting lice (Mallophaga), booklice and barklice (Psocoptera)	3400	worldwide	parasites of birds or mammals, eyes reduced or absent, reduced antennae, mouthparts mandibulate or piercing.

Order	*Common name*	*No. of species*	*Distribution*	*General characteristics of order*
Thysanoptera	thrips	5000	tropical regions	fringed wings, bristles on body wall; mouthparts specialized for piercing and sucking. Feed on plant juices, fungi, spores, pollen, or body fluids of other arthropods. Some species hibernate in winter in cold climates.
Homoptera	cicadas, hoppers, whiteflies, aphids, scale insects	45000	worldwide	plant feeders with mouth parts adapted for sucking plant sap; wings number two or four when present. Many are crop pests.
Hemiptera	true bugs	35000	worldwide	sucking mouthparts adapted to pierce plant or animal tissue; most species terrestrial, a few aquatic; well-developed compound eyes; scent glands usually present. Many are crop pests
Neuroptera	alderflies, dobsonflies (Megaloptera), lacewings (Plannipennia), snakeflies (Raphidiodea)	4500	worldwide	biting mouthparts, two pairs of similar wings. Alderflies, dobsonflies have aquatic larvae. Snakeflies arboreal, characterised by elongate and highly mobile thorax
Trichoptera	caddisflies	7000	worldwide	moth-like, wings covered with hairs, long antennae, large compound eyes, larvae almost exclusively aquatic.
Lepidoptera	butterflies, moths, skippers	138000	worldwide	two pairs of wings, covered by dustlike scales, four stages of life, day-flying, herbivorous, complete metamorphisis occurs (larvae are caterpillars). Adults typically with slender coiled sucking proboscis.
Coleoptera	beetles, weevils	250000	worldwide	two pairs of wings, front pair modified into horny covers, antennae variable, large compound eyes, mouthparts adapted for chewing, hard outer skeleton, complete metamorphosis.
Hymenoptera	ants, bees, sawflies, wasps	130000	worldwide except polar regions	pollinators of wild and cultivated flowering plants, some species have complex social organization, complete metamorphosis, four membranous wings, mouthparts adapted for chewing and sucking, larvae usually maggot-like.
Strepsiptera	stylopids	400	worldwide	parasites of other insects, male winged, female wingless and larvae-like.
Mecoptera	scorpion flies	450	mostly tropical and subtropical area	inhabit moist forests feeding on nectar or preying on other insects.
Diptera	true flies	150 000	worldwide	forewings membranous, hindwings modified as minute club-like balancing organs (halteres). Feed on plant and animal juices or other insects, two wings, sucking mouthparts, some pupae aquatic. Many are disease vectors, though many are also beneficial as pollinators.
Siphonaptera	fleas	1 750	worldwide	wingless, parasitic, mouthparts adapted to piercing and sucking, larvae elongated and often enclosed in cocoons. Feed mainly on mammals, but also some birds. Disease vectors.

PLANTS

Classification of plants

Phylum	*Common name/examples*	*No of species*	*Comments*
Bryophyta	liverworts (*Hepaticae*) hornworts (*Anthocerotae*) mosses (*Musci*)	24 000	small plants living in moist habitats (their sperm must swim through water to reach their eggs). Reproduce by spores.
Psilophyta	whiskferns	12	simple vascular plants lacking true roots and, in some species, leaves. Reproduce by spores.
Lycopodophyta	club mosses	1 000	small, terrestrial or epiphytic (ie grow on other plants); needle or scale-like leaves arranged spirally on stem. Reproduce by spores.
Sphenophyta or Equisetophyta	horsetails, scouring rushes	20	primarily found in moist, muddy habitats; stems creeping underground and producing erect annual or perennial stems with tiny leaves whorled into sheaves around stem. Jointed hollow stems and rough, ribbed texture caused by the mineral silica. Reproduce by spores.
Filicinophyta or Pteridophyta	ferns	12 000	vascular plants which reproduce by spores; stems mostly creeping, large leaves (megaphylls) with branching veins. The most complex, diverse and abundant of the plant phyla that do not form seeds.
Cycadophyta	cycads	100	evergreen perennial shrubs or trees with stems that are usually unbranched but thickened by some secondary growth. Palm-like or fern-like compound leaves; they contain symbiotic cyanobacteria in special roots.
Ginkgophyta	ginkgo, maidenhair tree	1	native to China but cultivated worldwide, the ginkgo is a tall tree with deciduous fan-shaped leaves; the only living descendant of a once-large group.
Coniferophyta or Pinatae	conifers	550	by far the most familiar of the gymnosperms (plants having naked seeds); usually evergreen shrubs or trees with simple needle-like leaves, spirally arranged. Commercially important for timber, pulp, turpentine and resin products.
Gnetophyta	gnetophytes (cone-bearing desert plants)	70	cone-bearing desert plants. Resemble flowering plants in many ways; were once thought to be a link between conifers and angiosperms.
Angiospermophyta or Magnoliophyta	angiosperms, flowering plants	>230 000	the dominant land vegetation of the Earth, including nearly every familiar tree, shrub or garden plant that produces flowers and seeds. Characterised by the aggregation of sexual reproductive structures with specialized shoots (flowers), which typically comprise four kinds of modified leaves: sepals, petals, stamens (male organs) and carpels (female organs).

World vegetation map

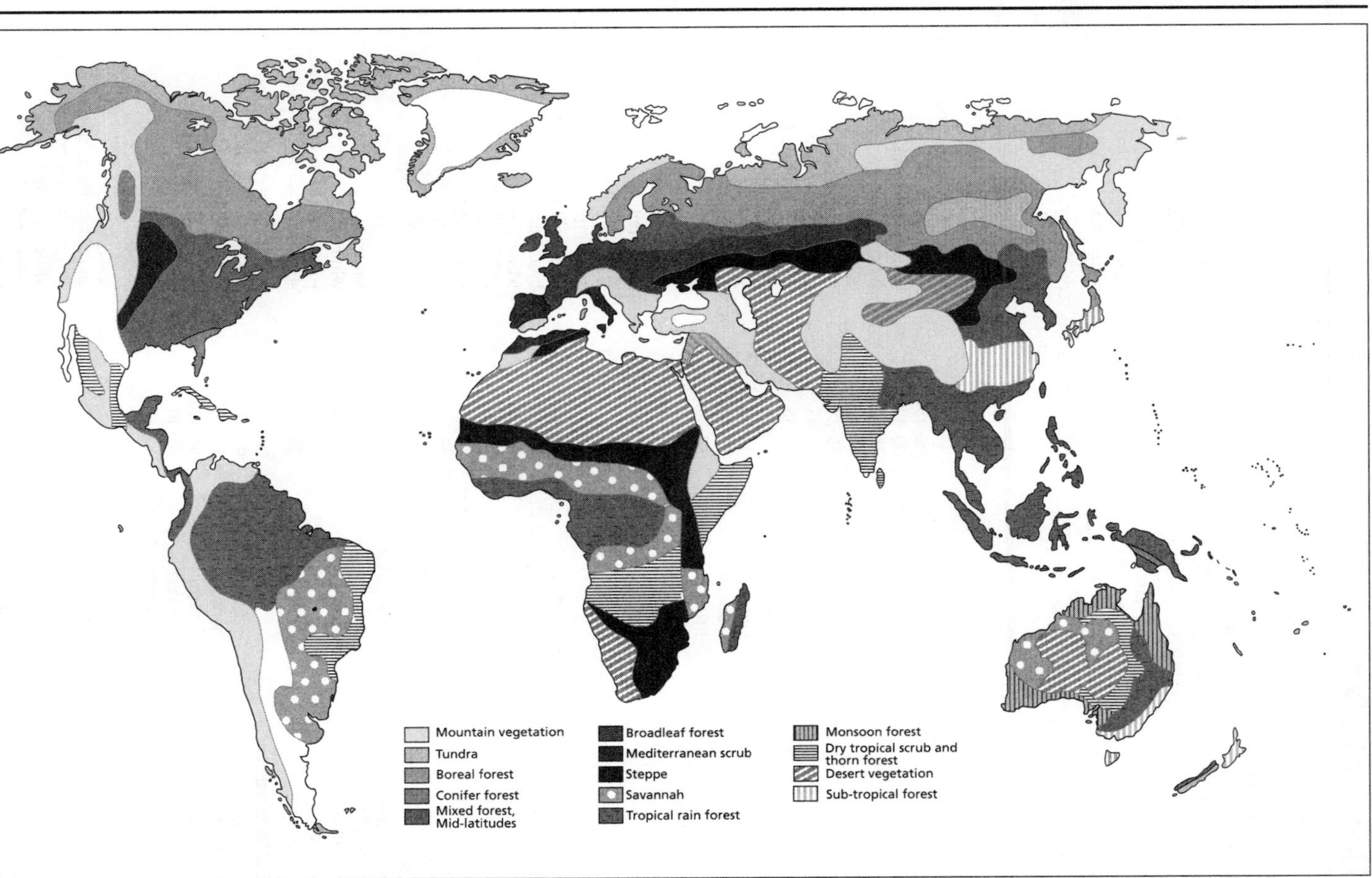

Natural history

Flowering plants

Common name	*Latin name*	*Height (cm)*	*Colour*
Annuals and biennials			
baby's breath	*Gypsophila*	30–45	white, pink
begonia	*Begonia*	15–45	pink, white, red
black-eyed Susan	*Thunbergia*	120–300	yellow
busy Lizzie	*Impatiens*	15–30	white, pink, red, orange, mauve
Canterbury bell	*Campanula*	45–75	purple, white
chrysanthemum	*Chrysanthemum*	45–60	yellow, red, white
corn cockle	*Agrostemma*	75	pale lilac
cornflower	*Centaurea*	30–75	blue, pink
dahlia	*Dahlia*	30–60	white, red, yellow
daisy	*Bellis*	8–15	white, pink, red
flower of an hour	*Hibiscus*	60	cream
forget-me-not	*Myosotis*	15–30	blue
foxglove	*Digitalis*	90–150	purple
godetia	*Godetia*	20–60	pink, orange
heliotrope	*Heliotropium*	45	white, dark blue, purple
hollyhock	*Althea*	90–150	pink
larkspur	*Delphinium*	30–120	white, pink, red, blue
morning glory	*Ipomoea*	180–360	blue, purple, red
nasturtium	*Tropaeolum*	30–180	yellow, orange
pansy	*Viola*	15–25	violet, yellow
petunia	*Petunia*	15–45	pink, red ,blue, white
phlox	*Phlox*	15–45	pink, red, white, yellow
poppy	*Papaver*	15–90	red, pink, white
pot marigold	*Calendula*	15–30	yellow, orange
snapdragon	*Antirrhinum*	90–120	crimson, scarlet
sunflower	*Helianthus*	60–300	yellow
sweet alyssum	*Alyssum*	8–15	white, purple, lilac, pink
sweet pea	*Lathyrus*	30–240	orange, crimson
sweet William	*Dianthus*	30–60	white, red
wallflower	*Cheiranthus*	20–60	crimson, white, purple, orange, cream
Bulbs			
begonia	*Begonia*	30–45	pink, yellow, white, cream
bluebell	*Scilla*	8	blue, purple
crocus	*Crocus*	8–10	white, purple, yellow
cyclamen	*Cyclamen*	8–15	red, pink, white
daffodil	*Narcissus*	15–30	yellow, white
freesia	*Freesia*	15	white, red, yellow, pale blue
hyacinth	*Hyacinthus*	8–15	yellow, white, blue, pink, violet, red
iris	*Iris*	15–30	blue, yellow, white, purple
lily of the valley	*Convallaria*	20	white
snowdrop	*Galanthus*	13	white
star of Bethlehem	*Ornithogalum*	15–30	white
sword lily	*Gladiolus*	90–125	yellow, red, pink, peach, orange
tulip	*Tulipa*	20–80	red, yellow, white, purple, peach
Border perennials			
campion	*Lychnis*	90	red, pink
Chinese bellflower	*Platycodon*	15–30	white, pink, pale blue
clematis	*Clematis*	90–125	blue, white
columbine	*Aquilegia*	60–90	yellow, red, blue
crane's-bill	*Geranium*	45	violet, pink
lady's mantle	*Alchemilla*	45	yellow
lamb's ear	*Stachys*	45	lilac, pink
lupin	*Lupinus*	90–125	pink, lilac, white, blue
michaelmas daisy	*Aster*	60–125	pink, white, crimson, blue
peony	*Paeonia*	60	white, pink, red
primrose	*Primula*	15–60	yellow, red, lilac
red hot poker	*Kniphofia*	75–155	orange-red
Solomon's seal	*Polygonatum*	60–90	cream
speedwell	*Veronica*	45–155	blue, pink, white
violet	*Viola*	10–15	violet, white, lilac, pink

Shrubs

Common name	Latin name	Height (cm)	Colour
azalea	*Rhododendron*	180	pink, red, white, yellow
bay laurel	*Laurus*	610	yellow
broom	*Genista*	210	yellow
butterfly bush	*Buddleia*	250	purple, white, mauve
camellia	*Camellia*	180–250	red, pale pink, white, bright pink
fatsia	*Fatsia*	300	white
firethorn	*Pyracantha*	370	red, yellow
fuchsia	*Fuchsia*	180	red
gorse	*Ulex*	180	yellow
heather	*Erica*	20–60	white, purple, yellow
holly	*Ilex*	1 500	red
honeysuckle	*Lonicera*	210–300	pink, cream
hydrangea	*Hydrangea*	90–150	pale blue, white, pink, purple
japonica	*Chaenomeles*	120–190	red, white
jasmine	*Jasminum*	300	yellow
lavender	*Lavandula*	90	blue
lilac	*Syringa*	370	purple, white, lavender, lilac
magnolia	*Magnolia*	150–610	white, red
myrtle	*Myrtus*	300	white
oleaster	*Elaeagnus*	230–300	white
periwinkle	*Vinca*	20–25	white, blue
rhododendron	*Rhododendron*	180	red, purple, pink, white
silk tassel bush	*Garrya*	275	white
veronica	*Hebe*	30–300	blue, white
viburnum	*Viburnum*	180–300	white, pink, red, blue
winter sweet	*Chimonanthus*	275	yellow

Trees

Common name	Latin name	Varieties	Height (m)
alder	*Alnus*	common, Italian, golden leaf	20
Antarctic beech	*Nothofagus*	false beech	12
ash	*Fraxinus*	common, raywood, manna	18
avocado	*Persia*	Americana, *drymifolia*	18
bamboo	*Bambusoidae*	*dendrocalamus strictus, bambusa arundinacea*	36
baobab	*Andansonia*	*digitata, gregorii*	9–12
beech	*Fagus*	Dawyck, fern-leaved, weeping, copper, golden	30
birch	*Betula*	silver, Swedish	10
coconut palm	*Cocus nucifera*	coconut palm	30
cypress	*Chamaecyparis*	Lawson cypress	30–36
elm	*Ulmus*	wych, Dutch, English, weeping, Chinese	27–36
false acacia	*Robinia*	*frisia, pseudoacacia*	18
flame tree	*Delonix regia*	flame tree	15
flowering cherries	*Prunus*	ornamental almond, ornamental plum, ornamental peach, ornamental cherry	6–12
flowering crab	*Malus*	John Downie, golden hornet, Japanese, Montreal beauty, profusion, Van Eseltine, *lemoinei*	6–15
golden rain	*Laburnum*	common, scotch, *vosii*	4
gum	*Eucalyptus*	gum, snow gum	15
handkerchief	*Davidia*	*involucrata*	15
hawthorn	*Crataegus*	*monogyna*, Paul's scarlet, *crusgalli, orientalis, prunifolia*	4
hazel	*Corylus*	common, *aurea*, corkscrew, filbert, giant, *purpurea*	3–9
honey locust	*Gleditsia*	sunburst, *elegantissima*	7
hornbeam	*Carpinus*	common	12
horse chestnut	*Aesculus*	red, common	18
Indian bean	*Catalpa*	Indian bean, *aurea*	6
Judas	*Cercis*	Judas, white Judas	4
juniper	*Juniperus*	*communis, virginiana, sabina, chinensis, phoenicea, horizontales, thuinfera*	3-6

Trees (continued)

Common name	*Latin name*	*Varieties*	*Height (m)*
larch	*Larix*	European, golden	24–30
lime	*Tilia*	common, large-leaved, American	24–27
mango	*Mangifera indica*	mango	18
maple	*Acer*	field, Norway, purple Norway, sycamore	6–9
mountain ash	*Sorbus*	rowan, Joseph rock, Swedish whitebeam	15
mulberry	*Morus*	black mulberry	6
oak	*Quercus*	English, sessile, Turkey, red, holm, willow	24
ornamental pear	*Pyrus*	*pendula*	6
palm	*Palmae*	sugar, cohune, *palmyra*, silver, coconut, *carnaulsa*, doum, coco de mer, date, royal, cabbage	20
paulownia	*Paulownia*	*tomentosa*	7
pea	*Caragana*	*pendula*, dwarf	4
pine	*Pinus*	scots, Corsican, Austrian, Monterey	18–36
plane	*Platanus*	London plane	24
poplar	*Populus*	white, grey, *aurora*, *Italica*, aspen	24
pride of India	*Koelreuteria*	*paniculata*	6
sweet chestnut	*Castanea*		30
sweet gum	*Liquidambar*	*styraciflua*	45
tree of heaven	*Ailanthus*	*altissima*	20
tulip	*Liriodendron*	*tulipifera*	35
tupelo	*Nyssa*	*sylvatica*	9
walnut	*Juglans*		30
willow	*Salix*	golden, weeping, American, Kilmarnock, purple, corkscrew	3–9
yew	*Taxus baccata*	common, Irish	4–15

Plants as foodstuffs

Temperate fruits

Common name	*Latin name*	*Family*
apple	*Malus pumila*	Rosaceae
pear	*Pyrus communis*	Rosaceae
quince	*Cydonia vulgaris*	Rosaceae
peach, nectarine	*Prunus persica*	Rosaceae
sweet cherry	*P. avium*	Rosaceae
sour cherry, cooking cherry morello	*P. cerasus*	Rosaceae
plum	*P. domestica*	Rosaceae
bullace, damson	*P. insititia*	Rosaceae
gage, greengage	*P. insititia*	Rosaceae
mirabelle	var *italica*	Rosaceae
	var *syriaca*	Rosaceae
cherry plum	*P. cerasifera*	Rosaceae
Japanese plum	*P. salicina*	Rosaceae
American plum	*P. americana*	Rosaceae
apricot	*P. armeniaca*	Rosaceae
medlar	*Mespilus germanica*	Rosaceae
raspberry	*Rubus idaeus*	Rosaceae
American red raspberry	*R. ideaus* var *strigosus*	Rosaceae
black raspberry	*R. occidentalis*	Rosaceae
backberry, bramble	*R. fruticosus*	Rosaceae
evergreen blackberry	*R. laciniatus*	Rosaceae
cloudberry	*R. chamaemorus*	Rosaceae
pacific dewberry	*R. ursinus*	Rosaceae
loganberry boysenberry, veitchberry	*R. x loganbaccus*	Rosaceae
wineberry	*R. phoenicolasius*	Rosaceae
strawberry	*Fragaria × ananassa* (= *F. virginiana* × *F. chiloensis*)	Rosaceae
gooseberry	*Ribes uva-crispa* (= *R. grossularia*)	Rosaceae
blackcurrent	*R. nigrum*	Rosaceae
redcurrent	*R. rubrum*	Rosaceae
fig	*Ficus carica*	Moraceae
olive	*Olea europaea*	Oleaceae
mulberry, black mulberry	*Morus nigra*	Moraceae
red mulberry	*M. rubra*	Moraceae
grape	*Vitis vinifera*	Vitaceae
frost grape	*V. riparia, V. vulpina*	Vitaceae
bush or sand grape	*V. rupestris*	Vitaceae
fox or skunk grape	*V. labrusca*	Vitaceae
muscadine, bullace grape	*V. rotundifolia*	Vitaceae
bilberry	*Vaccinium myrtillus*	Ericaceae
cranberry	*V. oxycoccus, V. macrocarpon*	Ericaceae
cowberry	*V. vitis-idaea*	Ericaceae
lowbush blueberry	*V. angustifolium*	Ericaceae
highbush blueberry	*V. corymbosum*	Ericaceae
strawberry tree	*Arbutus unedo*	Ericaceae
Chinese gooseberry, kiwiberry	*Actinidia chinensis*	Actinidiaceae

Tropical and subtropical fruits

Common Name	*Latin name*	*Family*
sweet orange	*Citrus sinensis*	Rutaceae
sour, Seville or bitter orange	*C. aurantium*	Rutaceae
lime	*C. aurantiifolia*	Rutaceae
lemon	*C. limon*	Rutaceae
rangpur lime, mandarin lime	*C.* x *limonia*	Rutaceae
shaddock, pummelo	*C. maxima*	Rutaceae
citron	*C. medica*	Rutaceae
king orange	*C.* x *nobilis*	Rutaceae
grapefruit	*C.* x *paradisi*	Rutaceae
mandarin, satsuma, tangerine, clementine	*C. reticulata*	Rutaceae
kumquat	*Fortunella japonica*	Rutaceae
loquat, Japanese medlar	*Eriobotrya japonica*	Rosaceae
breadfruit	*Artocarpus altilis*	Moraceae
jackfruit	*A. heterophyllus*	Moraceae
cherimoya	*Annona cherimolia*	Annonaceae
custard apple, bullock's heart	*A. reticulata*	Annonaceae
soursop, guanabana	*A. muricata*	Annonaceae
sugarapple, sweetsop	*A. squamosa*	Annonaceae
banana, edible plantain	*Musa acuminata, M.* x *paradisiaca*	Musaceae
fehi banana	*M. fehi*	Musaceae
avocado, aguacate alligator pear	*Persaea americana* (= *P. gratissima*)	Lauraceae
coconut	*Cocos nucifera*	Palmae
date	*Phoenix dactylifera*	Palmae
pineapple	*Ananas comosus*	Bromeliaceae
mango	*Mangifera indica*	Anacardiaceae
cashew apple	*Anacardium occidentale*	Anacardiaceae
granadilla, passion fruit	*Passiflora edulis*	Passifloraceae
sweet granadilla	*P. ligularis*	Passifloraceae
yellow granadilla	*P. laurifolia*	Passifloraceae
sweet calabash	*P. maliformis*	Passifloraceae
curuba	*P. mollissima*	Passifloraceae
giant granadilla	*P. quadrangularis*	Passifloraceae
papaw, pawpaw	*Carica papaya*	Caricaceae
durian	*Durio zibethinus*	Bombacaceae
mangosteen	*Garcinia mangostana*	Guttiferae
rambutan	*Nephelium lappaceum*	Sapindaceae
longan	*Euphoria longan*	Sapindaceae
akee	*Blighia sapida*	Sapindaceae
guava	*Psidium guajava*	Myrtaceae
cape gooseberry	*Physalis peruviana*	Solanaceae
tomatillo, jamberry	*P. ixocarpa*	Solanaceae
mammey apple, mammee	*Mammea americana*	Guttiferae
sapodilla	*Manilkara sapota*	Sapotaceae
sapote	*Pouteria sapota* (= *Calocarpoum sapota)*	Sapotaceae
tamarind	*Tamarindus indica*	Leguminosae
carambola, caramba, blimbing, bilimbi	*Averrhoa carambola*	Oxalidaceae
persimmon	*Diospyros kaki*	Ebenaceae
pomegranate	*Punica granatum*	Punicaceae
litchi, lychee	*Litchi chinensis*	Sapindaceae

Vegetables

Common name	*Latin name*	*Family*
Brassicas		
cabbage, spring		Cruciferae
cabbage, savoy		Cruciferae
cauliflower		Cruciferae
broccoli, calabrese	*Brassica oleracea*	Cruciferae
kale		Cruciferae
brussel sprouts		Cruciferae
turnip, swede	*Brassica campestris*	Cruciferae
pak-choi	*Brassica campestris* subspecies *chinensis*	Cruciferae
pe-tsai	*Brassica campestris* subspecies *pekinensis*	Cruciferae
Leaf and stem vegetables		
asparagus	*Asparagus officinalis*	Liliaceae
wild asparagus	*A. acutifolius*	Liliaceae
chives	*Allium schoenoprasum*	Liliaceae
celery	*Apium graveolens*	Umbelliferae
fennel	*Foeniculum vulgare* var *vulgare*	Umbelliferae
Florence fennel, finocchio	*F. vulgare* var *azoricum*	Umbelliferae
chicory, asparagus chicory, witloof, belgian endive	*Cichorium intybus*	Compositae
radicchio, red verona chicory, treviso chicory, castelfranco chicory	*Cichorium intybus*	Compositae
grumolo, broad-leaved chicory	*Cichorium intybus*	Compositae
endive, escarolle, batavian endive	*Cichorium endivia*	Compositae
lettuce, cabbage lettuce, cos lettuce	*Lactuca sativa*	Compositae
wild lettuce	*Lactuca taraxaciflora*	Compositae
spinach, summer or round-seeded, winter or prickly-seeded	*Spinacia oleracea*	Chenopodiaceae
spinach beet	*Beta vulgaris* var *cicla*	Chenopodiaceae
seakale beet, swiss chard	*Beta vulgaris* var *cicla*	Chenopodiaceae

Leaf and stem vegetables (continued)

Common name	Latin name	Family
orache	*Atriplex hortensis*	Chenopodiaceae
New Zealand spinach	*Tetragonia expansa*	Aizoaceae
amaranth spinach	*Amaranthus caudatus, A. hybridus, A. tricolor*	Amaranthaceae
sea kale	*Crambe maritima*	Cruciferae
bamboo shoots	*Bambusa arundinacea B. beecheyana, B. vulgaris, Phyllostachys dulcis, P. pubescens etc*	Gramineae
globe artichoke	*Cynara scolymus*	Compositae
cardoon	*Cynara cardunculus*	Compositae
okra, gumbo, lady's fingers	*Hibiscus esculentus (= Abelmoschus esculentus)*	Malvaceae
jew's mallow	*Corchorus olitorius*	Tiliaceae
jute	*C. capsularis*	Tiliaceae
water spinach	*Ipomoea aquatica*	Convolvulaceae
rhubarb, garden	*Rheum rhabarbarum*	Polygonaceae
Root vegetables		
radish	*Raphanus sativus*	Cruciferae
winter radish	*R. sativus* cv *'Longipinnatus'*	Cruciferae
black salsify	*Scorzonera hispanica*	Compositae
salsify, oyster plant	*Tragopogon porrifolius*	Compositae
carrot	*Daucus carota* subspecies *sativus*	Umbelliferae
parsnip	*Pastinaca sativa*	Umbelliferae
celeriac, turnip-rooted celery	*Apium graveolens* var *rapaceum*	Umbelliferae
arracacha	*Arracacia xanthorrhiza*	Umbelliferae
turnip-rooted parsley, hamburg parsley	*Petroselinum crispum* var *tuberosum*	Umbelliferae
chervil, turnip-rooted	*Chaerophyllum bulbosum*	Umbelliferae
Jerusalem artichoke	*Helianthus tuberosus*	Compositae
Chinese artichoke	*Stachys tuberifera*	Labiatae
oca	*Oxalis tuberosa*	Oxalidaceae
ulluco, ullucu	*Ullucus tuberosus*	Basellaceae
anu, anyu	*Tropaeolum tuberosum*	Tropaeolaceae
yam bean	*Pachyrhizus erosus*	Leguminosae
yam bean, potato bean	*P. tuberosus*	Leguminosae
sacred or East Indian lotus	*Nelumbo nucifera*	Nymphaeaceae
kaffir potato, hausa potato	*Plectranthus (Coleus) esculentus*	Labiatae
onion	*Allium cepa*	Liliaceae
shallot	*A. cepa* var *aggregatum (= A. ascalonicum)*	Liliaceae
Welsh onion, Japanese onion	*A. fistulosum*	Liliaceae
garlic	*A. sativum*	Liliaceae
leek	*A. porrum*	Liliaceae

Fruit vegetables

Common name	Latin name	Family
tomato	*Lycopersicum esculentum*	Solanaceae
aubergine	*Solanum melongena*	Solanaceae
cucumber	*Cucumis sativa*	Cucurbitaceae
gherkin	*C. anguria*	Cucurbitaceae
bitter gourd, bitter cucumber	*Momordica charantia*	Cucurbitaceae
bottle gourd, calabash gourd white gourd	*Lagenaria siceraria*	Cucurbitaceae
snake gourd	*Trichosanthes cucumerina*	Cucurbitaceae
wax, ash gourd	*Benincasa hispida*	Cucurbitaceae
chayote, christophine pumpkins, marrows, squashes	*Sechium edule*	Cucurbitaceae
breadfruit	*Artocarpus altilis*	Moraceae
jackfruit	*A. heterophyllus*	Moraceae
pepper, sweet pepper	*Capsicum annuum*	Solanaceae
avocado, alligator pear	*Persea americana*	Lauraceae

Root crops

Common name	Latin name	Family
Temperate		
turnip	*Brassica campestris* ssp *rapifera*	Cruciferae
swede, rutabaga	*Brassica napus* var *napobrassica*	Cruciferae
mangel, mangel-wurzel, mangold	*Beta vulgaris* ssp *vulgaris*	Chenopodiaceae
beet, sugarbeet beetroot	*Beta vulgaris* ssp *vulgaris*	Chenopodiaceae
potato	*Solanum tuberosum*	Solanaceae
Tropical		
sweet potato	*Ipomoea batatas*	Convolvulaceae
topee-tambu	*Calathea alloula*	Marantaceae
cassava, manihot	*Manihot esculenta*	Euphorbiaceae
taro, tanier cocoyams, arrowroots		
yam, white Guinea	*Dioscorea rotundata*	Dioscoreaceae
yam, yellow Guinea	*D. cayenensis*	Dioscoreaceae
yam, greater	*D. alata*	Dioscoreaceae
yam, bitter	*D. dumetorum*	Dioscoreaceae
yam, Asiatic	*D. esculenta*	Dioscoreaceae
yam, American	*D. trifida*	Dioscoreaceae

Legumes and pulses

Common name	Latin name	Part consumed
Cool temperate and warm temperate		
garden pea	*Pisum sativum*	seeds, young pods
field pea	*P. arvense*	seeds
asparagus pea winged pea	*Tetragonolobus purpureus*	
French, kidney haricot, green, runner, string, salad, wax bean	*Phaseolus vulgaris*	young pods, seeds
runner, scarlet runner	*P. coccineus*	young pods
butter, sieva, civet Madagascar, Carolina sewee bean	*P. lunatus*	seeds
Lima bean	*P. limensis*	seeds
soybean	*Glycine max* (*G. soja*)	seeds sprouts, oil
lentil	*Lens culinaris*	seeds
broad bean	*Vicia faba*	seeds
lupin	*Lupinus albus* *L. pilosus* *L. luteus* *L. mutabilis*	seeds
carob bean, locust bean, St John's bread	*Ceratonia siliqua*	pods
Tropical		
tepary bean	*Phaseolus acutifolius* var *latifolius*	seeds
cluster bean, guar	*Cyamopsis tetragonolobus*	young pods, seeds
goa bean, asparagus pea	*Psophocarpus tetragonolobus*	young pods
winged pea	*P. palmettorum*	young pods
yam bean, chopsui potato	*Pachyrhizus erosus* *P. tuberosus*	young pods roots
lablab, hyacinth	*Dolichos lablab*	Pods, seeds
Madras gram, horse gram	*D. biflorus*	seeds
chick pea	*Cicer arietinum*	seeds
bambara groundnut, kaffir pea	*Voandzeia subterranea*	seeds
Kersting's groundnut	*Kerstingiella geocarpa*	seeds
tamarind	*Tamarindus indica*	pulp from pods, seeds
moth bean	*Vigna aconitifolia*	seeds
adzuki bean	*V. angularis*	seeds
cowpea	*Vigna unguiculata*	seeds
black-eyed pea	subspecies *unguiculata*	seeds
yard long bean	subspecies *sesquipedalis*	pods
black gram	*Vigna mungo* (*Phaseolus mungo*)	seeds, young pods
green gram, mung bean	*V. radiata* (*Phaseolus aureus*)	seeds pods, sprouts
rice bean	*V. umbellata*	seeds
jack bean	*Canavalia ensiformis*	young pods, seeds
sword bean	*C. gladiata*	young pods, seeds
groundnut	*Arachis hypogaea*	seeds, oil
pigeon pea, Cajan congo pea, red gram	*Cajanus cajan*	seeds
African locust bean	*Parkia filicoidea* *P. biglobosa*	seeds, pulp of pod
yam bean	*Sphenostylis stenocarpa*	seeds

Main cereal crops

Common name	Latin name
wheat	*Triticum*
wild emmer	*T. diococcoides*
cultivated emmer	*T. diococcum*
einkorns	*T. monococcum* var *monococcum*, *T. m.* var *boeoticum*
hard (durum)	*T. durum*
turgidum	*T. turgidum*
bread	*T. aestivum* var *aestivum*
spelt	*T. spelta*
club	*T. compactum*
barley	*Hordeum vulgare*
two-rowed	*H. distichum*
six-rowed	*H. hexastichum*
rye	*Secale cereale*
maize	*Zea mays*
rice	*Oryza sativa*
African rice	*O. glaberrima*
oats	*Avena*
hexaploid	*A. sativa*, *A. byzantina* *A. nuda*
tetraploid	*A. abyssinica*
diploid	*A. strigosa*, *A. brevis*
sorghum	*Sorghum bicolor*
millets	
finger or African	*Eleusine coracana*
bulrush, pearl, bajra,	*Pennisetum americanum*
common, proso	*Panicum miliaceum*
Japanese barnyard, sanwa	*Echinachloa frumentacea*
foxtail, German, Italian	*Setaria italica*
teff	*Eragrostis tef*
fonio, fundi	*Digitaria* species
koda, kodo	*Paspalum scrobiculatum*

Sugar and starch crops

Common name	Latin name	Family
Sugar plants		
sugar cane	*Saccharum officinarum*	Gramineae
sugar beet	*Beta vulgaris*	Chenopodiaceae
sugar maple	*Acer saccharum*	Aceraceae
black maple	*A. nigrum*	Aceraceae
barley (germinating)	*Hordeum vulgare*	Gramineae

Sugar and starch crops (continued)

Common name	*Latin name*	*Family*
sweet sorghum, sorgo	*Sorghum bicolor*	Gramineae
wild date palm	*Phoenix sylvestris*	Palmae
palmyra palm	*Borassus flabellifer*	Palmae
toddy palm, sago palm, jaggery palm	*Caryota urens*	Palmae
coconut palm	*Cocos nucifera*	Palmae
gomuti palm, sugar palm	*Arenga pinnata*	Palmae
honey palm, syrup palm	*Jubaea chilensis*	Oleaceae
nypa palm	*Nypa fruticans*	Oleaceae
manna ash	*Fraxinus ornus*	Oleaceae

Starch plants

Common name	*Latin name*	*Family*
potato	*Salanum tuberosum*	Solanaceae
cassava, manioc	*Manihot esculenta*	Euphorbiaceae
arrowroot	*Maranta arundinacea*	Marantaceae
Queensland arrowroot	*Canna edulis*	Cannaceae
taro	*Colocasia esculenta*	Araceae
giant taro	*Alocasia macrorrhiza*	Araceae
dasheen	*Colocasia esculenta* var *globifera*	Araceae
giant swamp taro	*Cyrtosperma chamissonis* (*C. edule*)	Araceae
tanier, cocoyam	*Xanthosma atrovirens* *X. sagittifolium* *X. violaceum*	Araceae
East Indian arrowroot	*Curcuma angustifolia*	Zingiberaceae
Fijian arrowroot, Tahitian arrowroot	*Tacca leontopetaloides* (*T. pinnatifida*)	Taccaceae
greater Asiatic yam	*Dioscorea alata*	Dioscoreaceae
white Guinea yam	*D. rotundata*	Dioscoreaceae
yellow Guinea yam	*D. cayenensis*	Dioscoreaceae
air potato	*D. bulbifera*	Dioscoreaceae
cush-cush, yampee	*D. trifida*	Dioscoreaceae
sago palm	*Metroxylon rumphii* *M. sagu*	Palmae
sago palm, gomuti palm	*Arenga pinnata*	Palmae
American cabbage palm, caribee palm	*Oreodoxa oleracea* *Roystonea oleracea*	Palmae Palmae
kaffir bread	*Encephalartos caffer*	Zamiaceae
bread tree	*E. altensteinii*	Zamiaceae
sago palm, queen sago	*Cycas circinalis*	Cycadaceae
Japanese sago palm	*C. revoluta*	Cycadaceae
maize	*Zea mays*	Gramineae
wheat	*Triticum* species	Gramineae
rice	*Oryza sativa*	Gramineae

Edible nuts

Common name	*Latin name*	*Main areas of cultivation*
hazelnut, cob European filbert	*Corylus avellana*	Turkey, Italy, Spain, France, England, Oregon
giant filbert	*C. maxima* (*C. americana*)	(as above)
Turkish cobnut	*C. colurna*	Turkey
sweet chestnut	*Castanea sativa*	S Europe, N America
American chestnut	*C. dentata*	N America
Japanese chestnut	*C. crenata*	Japan, N America
Chinese chestnut	*C. mollissima*	China, Korea, N America
almond	*Prunus amygdalus* (= *P. dulcis*)	Mediterranean, SW Asia, N America
sweet almond	var *amygdalus*	America
bitter almond	var *amara*	
walnut	*Juglans regia*	Europe, Asia N America
black walnut, eastern walnut	*J. nigra*	N America
butternut	*J. cinerea*	N America
Japanese walnut	*J. ailanthifolia*	Japan, N America
Chinese walnut	*J. cathayensis*	China, N America
pecan	*Carya illinoinensis*	N America
shagbark hickory	*C. ovata*	N America
shellbark hickory	*C. laciniosa*	N America
brazil nut, paranut	*Bertholletia excelsa*	Amazon region (wild)
sapucaia, sapucaya	*Lecythis sabucayo*	S America (wild)
monkey nut	*L. usitata*	S America (wild)
cashew nut	*Anacardium occidentale*	tropical S America, India, E Africa
coconut	*Cocos nucifera*	India, Sri Lanka, Malaysia, Indonesia, Philippines

Natural history

Common name	Latin name	Main areas of cultivation
macadamia nut, Australia, or Queensland nut, (smooth shell)	*Macadamia integrifolia*	Australia, California
macadamia nut (rough shell)	*M. tetraphylla*	Australia, California
Moreton bay chestnut	*Castanospermum australe*	Australia (wild)
oysternut	*Telfairia pedata*	E Africa
peanut, ground nut	*Arachis hypogaea*	India, tropical Africa, China
pilt nut	*Canarium luzonicum* *C. ovatum*	Philippines
Java almond	*C. commune*	Java
pistachio	*Pistacia vera*	E Mediterranean, India, S USA
betel nut	*Areca catechu*	Old World tropics
kola	*Cola nitida*	W Africa, Caribbean
	C. acuminata	W Africa, Brazil
water chestnut	*Trapa natans* *T. bicornis* *T. maximowiczii*	E Asia, Malaysia, India
pine nut, pine kernel	*Pinus pinea*	Mediterranean
	P. pinaster	Mediterranean
Swiss stone pine	*P. cembra*	Europe
Mexican stone pine	*P. cembroides*	Mexico

Herbs and spices

Common name	Latin name	Forms	Area of origin
anise	*Pimpinella anisum*	seeds, leaves	Middle East, now Southern Russia, Turkey, India, parts of Europe
basil	*Ocimum basilicum*	leaves	Europe
bay	*Laurus nobilis*	leaves	Mediterranean
bergamot	*Monarda didyma*	flowers, leaves	N America
caraway	*Carum carvi*	seeds (ground), leaves, tap roots	temperate Asia, Europe and N America
cardamom	*Elettaria cardomomum*	pods, seeds (dried)	India, Middle East
chervil	*Anthriscus cerfolium*	leaves	S Russia, now Europe
chilli	*Capsicum annuum*	whole (fresh or dried)	N America, Europe
chives	*Allium schoenoprasum*	stems, flowers	Europe
cinnamon	*Cinnamomum zeylanicum*	bark (dried or ground)	Sri Lanka
cloves	*Eugenia aromatica*	buds (whole and ground)	SE Asia, Indonesia, Madagascar, Tanzania, Sri Lanka, Malaysia, Grenada
coriander	*Coriandrum sativum*	leaves, seeds (ground)	S Europe, Middle East
cumin	*Cuminum cyminum*	seeds (whole and ground)	the East, India, Egypt, Arabia
dill	*Anethum graveolens*	leaves, seeds	Scandinavia, Germany, C and E Europe
fennel	*Foeniculum vulgare*	leaves, stalks, seeds	Southern Europe
ginger	*Zingiber officinale*	root	tropical Asia, Middle East, Southern Europe
juniper	*Juniperus communis*	berries	Southern Europe
lovage	*Levisticum officinale*	leaves, seeds, stems	Europe
marjoram	*Origanum majorana*	leaves	Mediterranean regions
mint	*Mentha*	leaves	Europe, Middle East
mustard	*Brassica nigra* *Brassica juncea* *Brassica alba*	seeds	Europe, (white mustard - Mediterranean region)
nutmeg	*Myristica fragrans*	whole, ground	SE Asia
Oregano	*Oregano vulgare*	leaves	Mediterranean regions
paprika	*Capsicum tetragonum*	fresh (whole), dried (ground)	Mexico, Spain, Morocco, Hungary
parsley	*Petroselinum crispum*	leaves	Southern Europe, now all world's temperate regions
poppy seeds	*Papaver somniferum*	seeds	Middle East, India, N America, Europe
rosemary	*Rosmarinus officinalis*	leaves, flowers	Mediterranean region
saffron	*Crocus sativus*	flowers (dried and ground)	Mediterranean countries, particularly Spain

Herbs and spices (continued)

Common name	*Latin name*	*Forms*	*Area of origin*
sage	*Salvia officinalis*	leaves	N Mediterranean coast
sassafras	*Sassafrass albidum, Sassafrass officinalis*	leaves, bark (dried)	N America
sesame seeds	*Sesamum indicum*	seeds	Africa, India, China
sorrel	*Rumex acetosa, Rumex scutatus*	leaves	Europe, particularly France
tamarind	*Tamarindus indica*	pulp	E Africa, Southern Asia
tansy	*Chrysanthemum vulgare*	leaves	Europe
tarragon	*Artemisia dracunculus*	leaves	Siberia, now Europe
thyme	*Thymus vulgaris*	leaves	Mediterranean regions
turmeric	*Curcuma longa*	root (whole or ground)	India, China, Middle East
vanilla	*Vanilla plainfolia*	pods	S Mexico, Madagascar, C America, Puerto Rico, Réunion

FUNGI

Phylum	*No. of species*	*Class*	*Examples*	*Characteristics of class*
Zygomycota	600	Mucorales	black bread mould *(Rhizopus stolonifer)* *Mucor*	many saprozoic on dung or organic debris. Others parasites of invertebrates, other fungi and plants.
		Entomophthorales	*Basidiobolus*	most parasites of animals, mainly insects.
		Zoopagales	*Cochlonema* *Endocochlus*	parasites of amoebas, nematodes and other small animals.
Ascomycota	15 000	Hemiascomycetae	yeasts e.g. Baker's Yeast *(Saccharomyces cerevisiae)*	morphologically simple. Short mycelia or none at all.
		Euascomycetae	morels, truffles *(Tuber)*, most fungal partners in lichens *Neurospora*	largest and best known class of Ascomycota.
		Loculoascomycetae	*Mycosphaerella* *Elsinoe*	many are parasites of economically important food plants.
		Laboulbeniomycetae	*Rhizomyces* *Amorphomyces*	parasites of insects.
Basidiomycota	25 000	Heterobasiciomycetae	jelly fungi, rusts and smuts	
		Homobasidiomycetae	common mushrooms, shelf fungi, coral fungi puffballs, earthstars, stinkhorns, bird's nest fungi	contains most of the fungi known as mushrooms and toadstools.
Deuteromycota (Fungi Imperfecti)	25 000	Sphaeropsida	*Clypeoseptoria aparothospermi*	
		Melanconia	*Cryptosporium lunasporum*	
		Monilia	*Penicillium* *Candida albicans*	pathogenic yeasts, other yeasts that do not form asci or basidia.
		Mycelia Sterilia	*Rhizoctonia*	

HUMAN BEINGS

EARLY HUMANS

Evolution of early humans

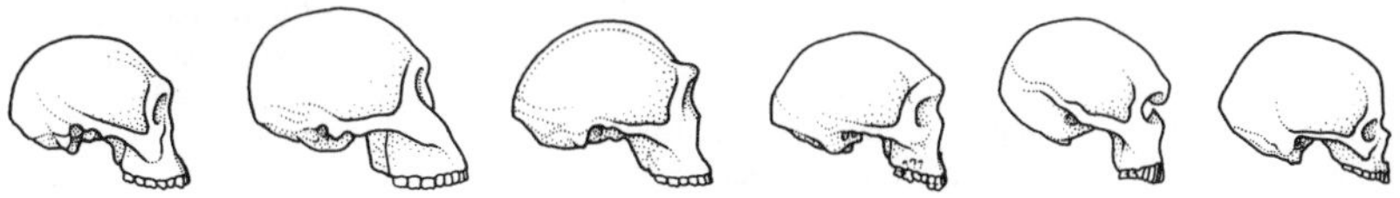

	Homo habilis *(small)*	Homo habilis *(large)*	Homo erectus	*'Archaic* Homo sapiens'	*Neanderthals*	*Early modern* Homo sapiens
Height (m)	c. 1	c. 1.5	1.3–1.5	?	1.5–1.7	1.6–1.85
Physique	Relatively long arms	Robust but 'human' skeleton	Robust but 'human' skeleton	Robust but 'human' skeleton	As 'archaic *H. sapiens*', but adapted for cold	Modern skeleton; ?adapted for warmth
Brain size (ml)	500–650	600–800	750–1 250	1 100–1 400	1 200–1750	1 200–1700
Skull form	Relatively small face; nose developed	Larger, flatter face	Flat, thick skull with large occipital and brow ridge	Higher skull; face less protruding	Reduced brow ridge; thinner skull; large nose; midface projection	Small or no brow ridge; shorter, high skull
Jaws/teeth	Thinner jaw; smaller, narrow molars	Robust jaw; large narrow molars	Robust jaw in larger individuals; smaller teeth than *H. habilis*	Similar to *H. erectus* but teeth may be smaller	Similar to 'archaic *H. sapiens*'; teeth smaller except for incisors; chin development in some	Shorter jaws than Neanderthals; chin developed; teeth may be smaller
Distribution	Eastern (+ southern?) Africa	Eastern Africa	Africa, Asia and Indonesia (+ Europe?)	Africa, Asia and Europe	Europe and western Asia	Africa and western Asia
Known date (years ago)	2–1.6 million	2–1.6 million	1.8–0.3 million	400 000–100 000	150 000–30 000	130 000–60 000

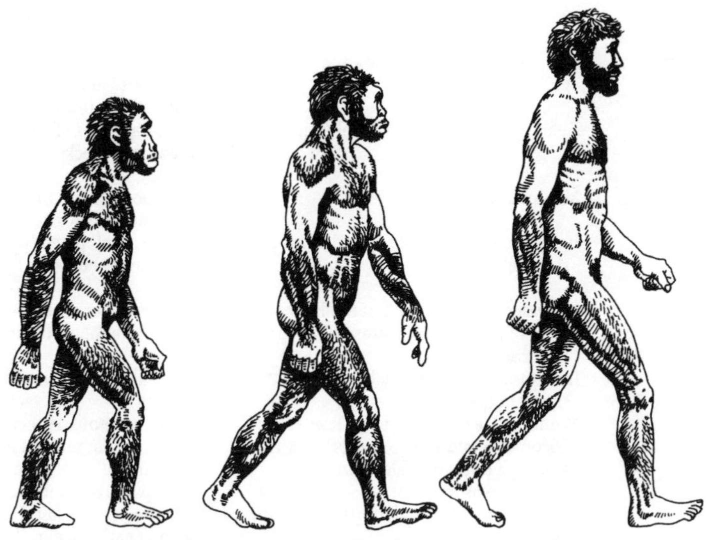

Homo habilis *Homo erectus* *Homo sapiens*

Human beings

Human beings

Early human behaviour and ecology

Hominids and time periods (years ago)	*Inference*	*Nature of the evidence*
A. Hominid ancestors ?8–5 million	Equatorial African origin	Humans are genetically closest to African apes, which today are distributed across equatorial Africa; earliest hominid fossils are in eastern Africa
B. Earliest hominids 5–3 million	Habitually bipedal on the ground; occasionally arboreal	Postcranial anatomy of fossils from Hadar in Ethiopia (but disagreements about similarity to modern human bipedalism and degree of arboreality)
	Inhabited a mosaic of grassland, woodland and thick shrub	Faunas from Laetoli in Tanzania, Hadar and Makapansgat in South Africa
3–2 million	Occupation of open savannas	Fossil pollen and fauna
	Emphasis on a fibrous plant diet in robust australopithecines	Microwear on teeth; large teeth and jaws
	First known manufacture of stone tools	Tools from Ethiopia, Kenya, Malawi, Zaire dated between 2.5 and 2.0 million years
C. Plio-Pleistocene hominids 2.0–1.5 million (Stone technology and changes in diet, brain size, etc. are usually associated with *Homo*)	Increased commitment to bipedalism on the ground	Postcranial anatomy associated with archaic *Homo* established
	Increased dexterity related to tool use and toolmaking, and possibly foraging	Anatomy of hand bones and characteristics of stone tools and cores
	Stones and animal bones carried repeatedly to specific sites	Earliest known complex sites with many stone artifacts and fossils
	Use of tools to procure and process food	Bone and stone tools with distinctive traces of use
	Dietary increase in protein and fat from large animals	Cut marks made by stone tools on animal bones
	Scavenging and possible hunting of large animals; processing of animals at specific spots	Limb bones of animals concentrated at undisturbed archaeological sites
	Increased cognitive capacities associated with making tools, foraging, social arrangements and/or developing linguistic skills	Increase in brain size from about a third to a half that of modern humans
	Changes in maturation rate	Implied by brain size increase and possible changes in tooth development
	Increased mobility and predator defence	Large stature evident in skeletal remains of early *Homo erectus* from West Turkana in Kenya
D. Early Pleistocene hominids 1.5–0.1 million	Occupation of new habitats and geographic zones	Sites occur in previously unoccupied areas of eastern Africa; first appearance of hominids outside Africa
	Definite preconception of tool form	Biface handaxes of consistent shape made from rocks of varying original shape
	Manipulation of fire	Indications of fire differentially associated with archaeological sites
	Increased levels of activity and stress on skeletons	Massive development of postcranial and cranial bones
E. Late Pleistocene hominids 100 000–35 000 (Neanderthals)	Increased sophistication of toolkit and technology; still slow rate of change to tool assemblage	Larger number of stone-tool types than before; complex preparation of cores
	Intentional burial of dead and suggestions of ritual	Preservation of skeletons, some with objects
	Maintenance of high activity levels (locomotor endurance; powerful arms) and high levels of skeletal stress (eg teeth used as tools)	Robust skeletons, especially thick leg bones and large areas for muscle attachment on arm bones; prominent wear patterns on incisor teeth
35 000–10 000 (fully modern *Homo sapiens*)	Decreased levels of activity and stress on skeleton	Decrease in skeletal robusticity (also seen in early modern humans before 35 000 years ago)

Hominids and time periods (years ago)	*Inference*	*Nature of the evidence*
	Enhanced technological efficiency	Innovations in stone- and bone-tool production (eg blades and bone points)
	Innovations in hunting and other foraging activities, including systematic exploitation of particular animal species	Evidence of spearthrower and harpoon, and trapping and netting of animals; animal remains in archaeological middens
	Colonisation of previously uninhabited zones	For example, sites in tundra in Europe and Asia; colonisation of the Americas (Australasia was probably first inhabited around 50 000 years ago)
	Elaboration of artistic symbolic expression and notation	Engraving, sculpting and painting of walls and figurines; repetitive marks on bones; jewellery
	Surge of technological and cultural differentiation and change	Variation in toolkits over space and time
	Harvesting and first cultivation of grains; first domestication of animals	Evidence of seeds and fauna from sites dating to the end of the Pleistocene

THE BODY

DNA

DNA or deoxyribonucleic acid contains the genetic information for most living organisms. Each human cell contains about 2 m/6.6 ft of DNA supercoiled on itself so that it fits in the cell nucleus (less than 10 μm in diameter).

DNA consists of four 'bases' (adenine [A], guanine [G], thymine [T] and cytosine [C]), a sugar (2-deoxy-D-ribose) and phosphoric acid, arranged in the famous double helical structure discovered by geneticists James Watson and Francis Crick in 1953. In the helical structure, A pairs only with T, and G only with C.

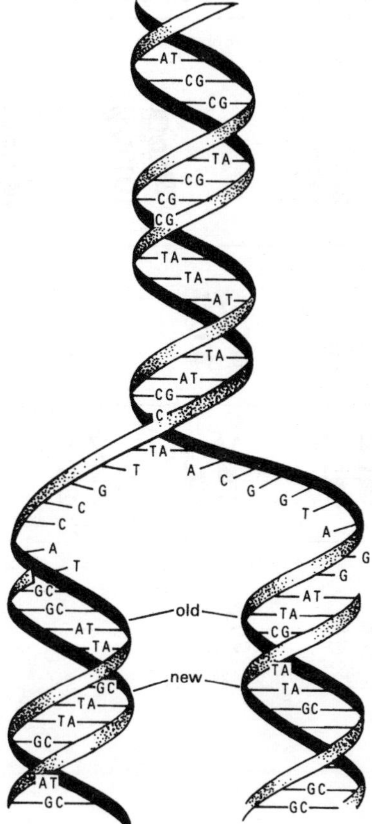

DNA structure and replication, following Watson and Crick. The two strands of the double helix separate, and a daughter strand is laid down alongside each with a constitution determined by the base sequence of its parent strand.

The genetic code

The four DNA bases A, G, T and C, like the letters of the alphabet, can be used to store information. This genetic information is passed on via RNA or ribonucleic acid (consisting of the four bases adenine, guanine, cytosine and uracil [U]) and instructs the cell to create specific amino acids, which are joined together to form proteins.

A group of three DNA or RNA bases is known as a triplet or codon, and codes for a particular amino acid. Information is passed from DNA to RNA by complementary pairing: A only pairs with U, and G only with C.

Genetic code in RNA triplets

1st base		*2nd base*			*3rd base*
	U	C	A	G	
U	Phenylalanine	Serine	Tyrosine	Cysteine	U
	Phenylalanine	Serine	Tyrosine	Cysteine	C
	Leucine	Serine	—[a]	—[a]	A
	Leucine	Serine	—[a]	Tryptophan	G
C	Leucine	Proline	Histidine	Arginine	U
	Leucine	Proline	Histidine	Arginine	C
	Leucine	Proline	Glutamine	Arginine	A
	Leucine	Proline	Glutamine	Arginine	G
A	Isoleucine	Threonine	Asparagine	Serine	U
	Isoleucine	Threonine	Asparagine	Serine	C
	Isoleucine	Threonine	Lysine	Arginine	A
	Methionine	Threonine	Lysine	Arginine	G
G	Valine	Alanine	Aspartic acid	Glycine	U
	Valine	Alanine	Aspartic acid	Glycine	C
	Valine	Alanine	Glutamic acid	Glycine	A
	Valine	Alanine	Glutamic acid	Glycine	G

[a] Chain termination

The human chromosomes

The 46 human chromosomes, showing the banding patterns characteristic of each, grouped according to convention.

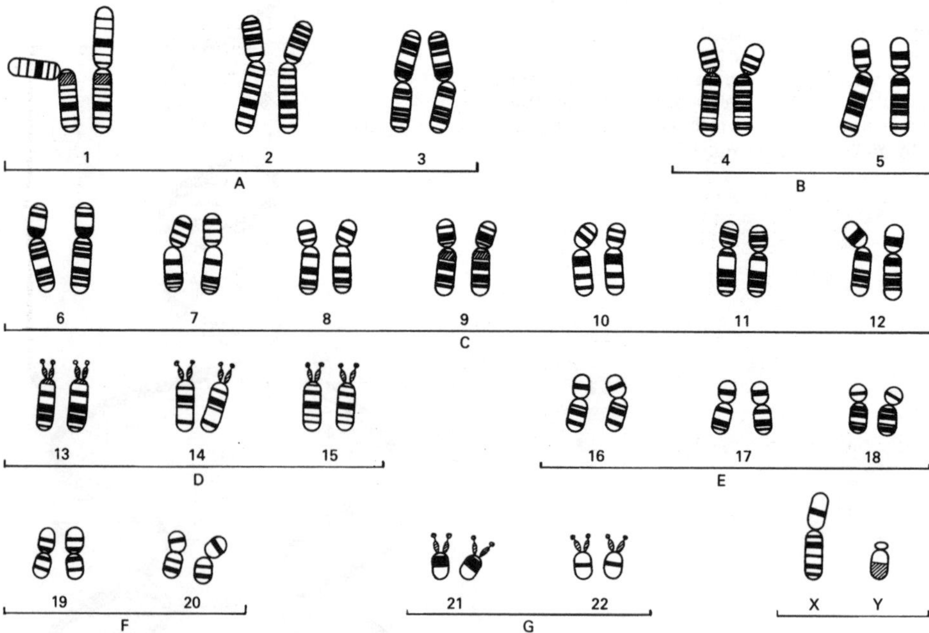

The human skeleton

The bones of the skeleton are often divided into two groups: the axial skeleton comprises the bones of the vertebral column, skull, ribs, and sternum; and the appendicular skeleton comprises the remainder.

1 Skull, displaying the frontal bone, and the front parts of the parietal and temporal bones **2** Maxilla **3** Mandible **4** Clavicle **5** Humerus **6** Radius **7** Ulna **8** Sternum **9** Scapula (obscured in this view by the upper ribs) **10** Ribs **11** Vertebral column, displaying (from above to below) cervical, thoracic, lumbar, sacral, and coccygeal vertebrae **12** Ilium **13** Sacrum **14** Coccyx **15** Femur **16** Fibula **17** Tibia **18** Bones of the hand, comprising the eight carpals, the five metacarpals, the three phalanges in each finger, and the two phalanges in the thumb **19** Bones of the foot, comprising the seven tarsals, the five metatarsals, the two phalanges in the big toe, and the three phalanges in the other toes

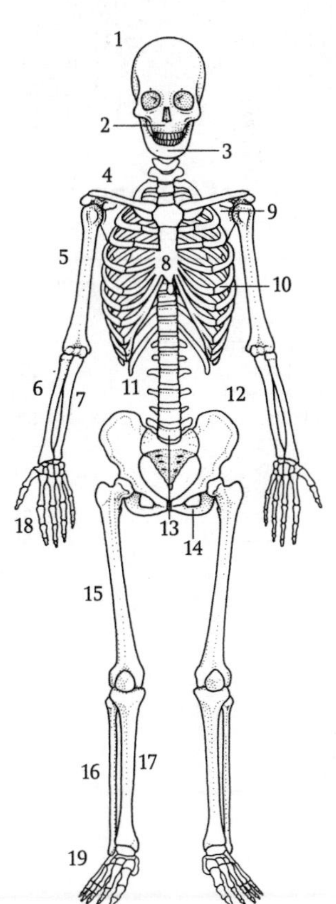

Bones of the human body

	Skull	
1	Occipital	
2	Parietal – 1 pair	
1	Sphenoid	
1	Ethmoid	
2	Inferior nasal conchae	
1	Frontal – 1 pair, fused	
2	Nasal – 1 pair	
2	Lacrimal – 1 pair	
2	Temporal – 1 pair	
2	Maxilla – 1 pair	
2	Zygomatic – 1 pair	
1	Vomer	
2	Palatine – 1 pair	
1	Mandible – 1 pair, fused (jawbone)	
22		

	The ears	
2	Malleus (hammer)	ossicles
2	Incus (anvil)	ossicles
2	Stapes (stirrups)	ossicles
6		

	Vertebrae
7	Cervical
12	Thoracic
5	Lumbar
1	Sacral – 5, fused to form the sacrum
1	Coccyx – between 3 and 5, fused
26	

	Vertebral ribs
14	Ribs, 'true' – 7 pairs
10	Ribs, 'false' – 5 pairs of which 2 pairs are floating
24	

	Sternum (breastbone)
1	Manubrium
1	'The body' (sternebrae)
1	Xiphisternum
3	

1	Hyoid (in the throat)

	Pectoral girdle
2	Clavicle – 1 pair (collar bone)
2	Scapula (including coracoid) – 1 pair (shoulder blade)
4	

	Upper extremity (each arm)		
1	Humerus		
1	Radius	forearm	
1	Ulna	forearm	
	Carpus:		hand
1	Scaphoid	wrist	hand
1	Lunate	wrist	hand
1	Triquetral	wrist	hand
1	Pisiform	wrist	hand
1	Trapezium	wrist	hand
1	Trapezoid	wrist	hand
1	Capitate	wrist	hand
1	Hamate	wrist	hand
5	Metacarpals		hand
	Phalanges:		hand
2	First digit	fingers	hand
3	Second digit	fingers	hand
3	Third digit	fingers	hand
3	Fourth digit	fingers	hand
3	Fifth digit	fingers	hand
30			

	Pelvic girdle
2	Ilium, ischium and pubis (combined) – 1 pair of hip bones, innominate

	Lower extremity (each leg)		
1	Femur (thighbone)		
1	Tibia		
1	Fibula		
1	Patella (kneebone)		
	Tarsus:	ankle	foot
1	Talus	ankle	foot
1	Calcaneus	ankle	foot
1	Navicular	ankle	foot
1	Cuneiform medial	ankle	foot
1	Cuneiform, intermediate	ankle	foot
1	Cuneiform, lateral	ankle	foot
1	Cuboid	ankle	foot
5	Metatarsals		foot
	Phalanges:		foot
2	First digit	toes	foot
3	Second digit	toes	foot
3	Third digit	toes	foot
3	Fourth digit	toes	foot
3	Fifth digit	toes	foot
30			

	Total
22	Skull
6	The ears
26	Vertebrae
24	Vertebral ribs
3	Sternum
1	Throat
4	Pectoral girdle
60	Upper extremity (arms) – 2 × 30
2	Hip bones
60	Lower extremity (legs) – 2 × 30
208	

Muscles and internal organs

In human beings the musculature normally accounts for some 40% of the total body weight. There are 639 named muscles in the human anatomy.

1 Trapezius muscle
2 Deltoid muscles
3 Triceps muscles (the biceps, at the front of the arm, cannot be seen from this view)
4 Latissimus dorsi muscle
5 Gluteus maximus muscle (largest muscle in the body)
6 Kidney
7 Trachea
8 Lungs
9 Heart
10 Liver (only a small part of the liver can be seen in this illustration)
11 Stomach
12 Spleen
13 Colon
14 Small intestine
15 Appendix
16 Bladder

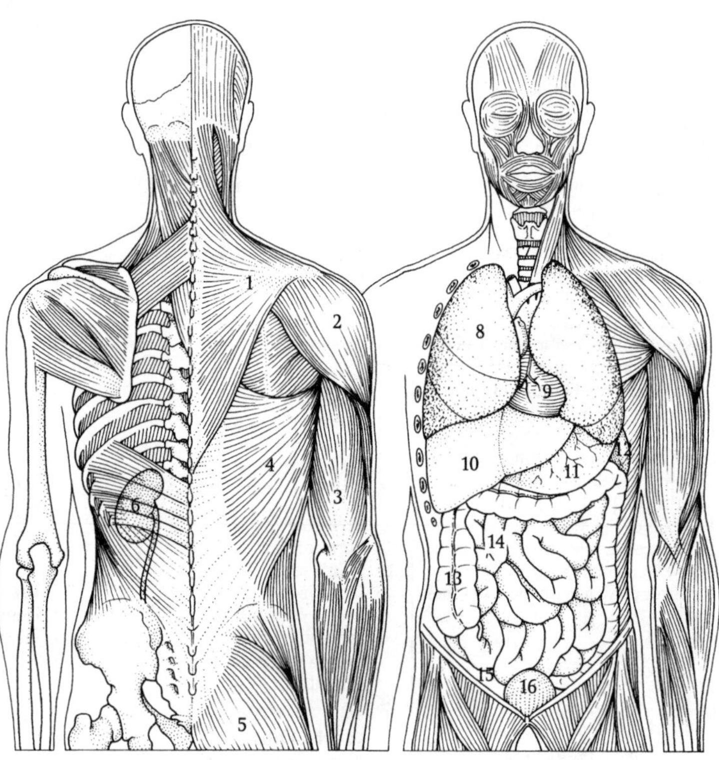

The heart

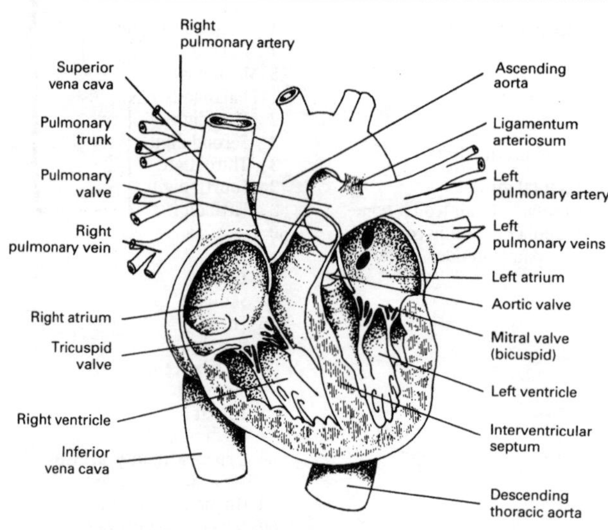

Normal human pulse rates

	Beats per minute
Foetus *in utero*	150
New born (full term)	140
First year	120
Second year	110
5 years	100
10 years	90
20 years	71
50 years	72
70 years	75
>80	78

The composition of blood

In an average human being blood accounts for 7–8% of body weight. Blood consists of:

Plasma: Water (90%), proteins (7%), nutrients, salts, nitrogen waste, carbon dioxide, hormones

Red blood cells (erythrocytes), 54% of which is haemoglobin. Normal count = 4–6 million per cu mm

White blood cells (leukocytes). Normal count = 4500–11000 per cu mm

Platelets (thrombocytes). Normal count = 150000–300000 per cu mm

The brain in section

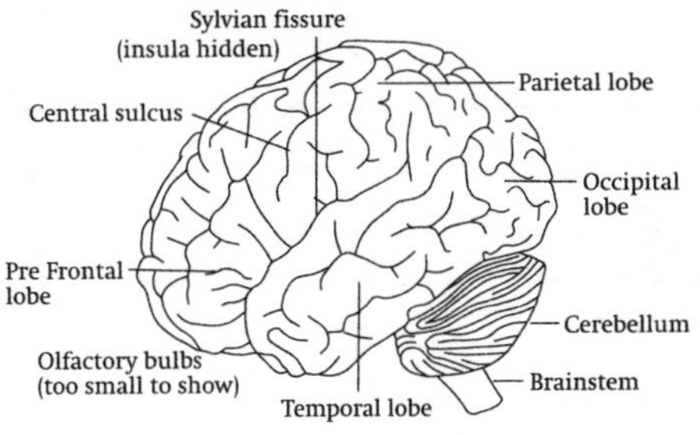

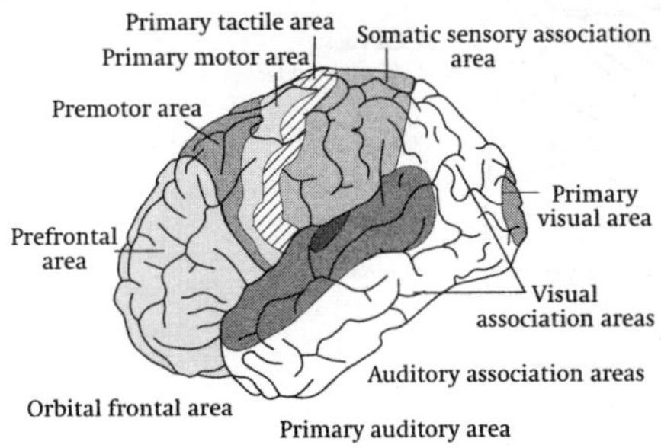

The ear

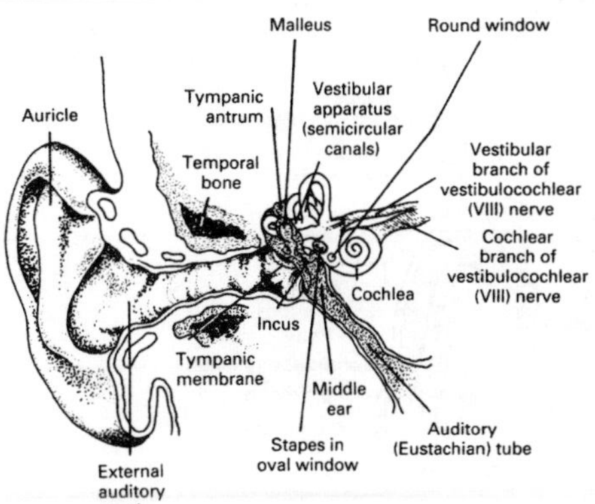

The eye

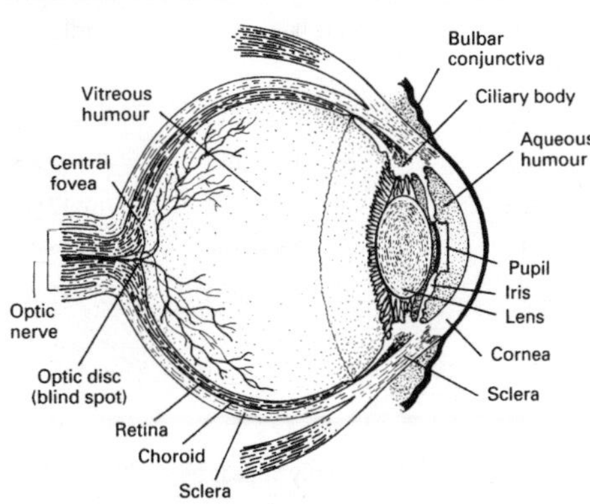

Normal eye

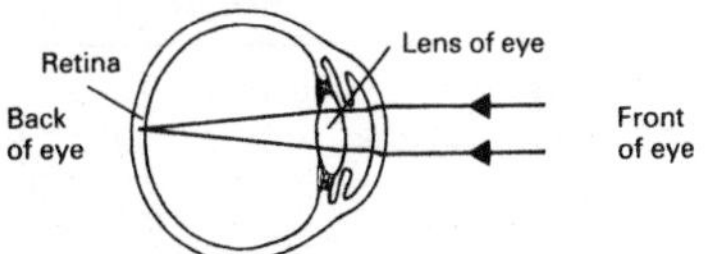

The image is in focus on the retina without a correcting lens in front.

Short-sighted or near-sighted eye (Myopia)

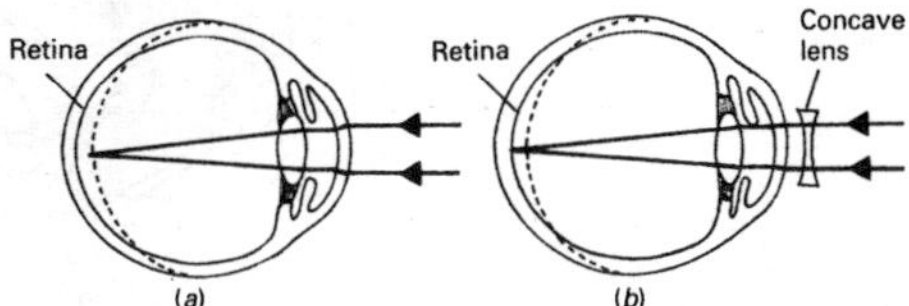

(*a*) The eye is too long and the image is not in focus on the retina. (*b*) The use of a concave lens brings the image into focus.

Long-sighted or far-sighted eye (Hypermetropia)

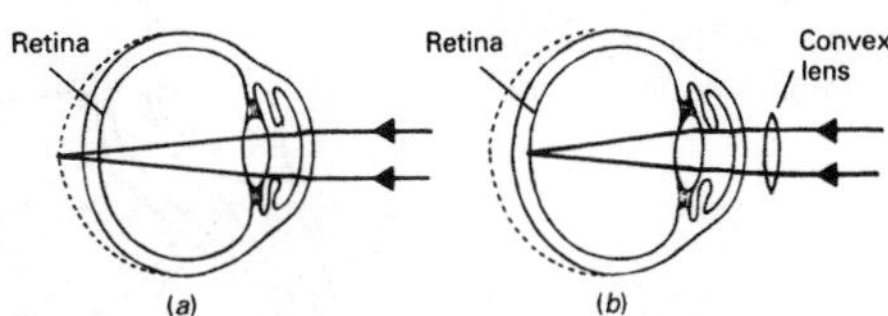

(*a*) The eye is too short and the image is not in focus on the retina. (*b*) The use of a convex lens brings the image into focus.

The approximate times of eruption and shedding of teeth

	Eruption	*Shed*
Milk		
Incisor 1	6–10 months	6–7 years
Incisor 2	8–12 months	7–8 years
Canine	16–22 months	10–12 years
Molar 1	13–19 months	9–11 years
Molar 2	25–33 months	10–12 years

	Eruption
Permanent	
Incisor 1	7–8 years
Incisor 2	8–9 years
Canine	10–12 years
Premolar 1	10–11 years
Premolar 2	11–12 years
Molar 1	6–7 years
Molar 2	12 years
Molar 3	17–21 years

Note: The lower teeth usually appear before the equivalent upper teeth.

The reproductive organs

Main female organs of reproduction and surrounding structures

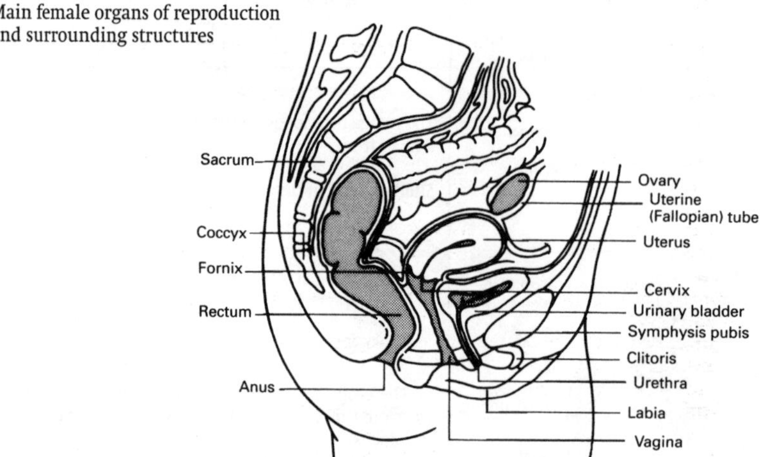

Main male organs of reproduction and surrounding structures

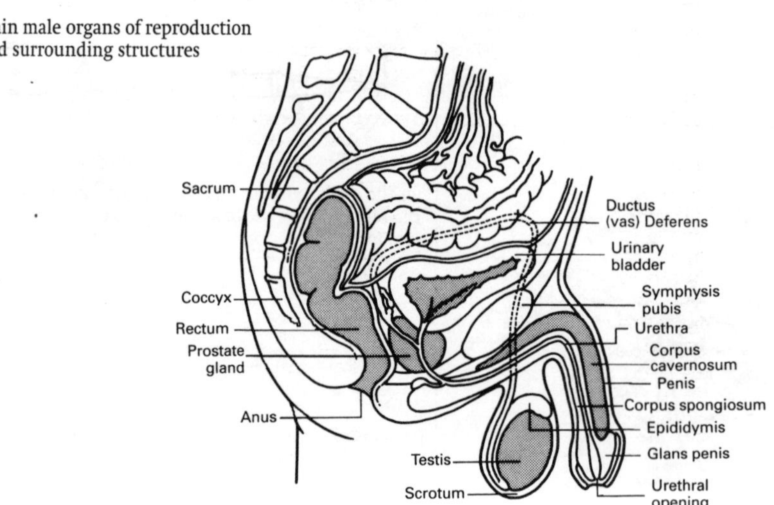

DISEASE

Communicable diseases

Name	*Cause*	*Transmission*	*Incubation period*
AIDS (Acquired Immune Deficiency Syndrome)	Human Immuno-deficiency Virus (HIV)	Sexual relations, sharing of syringes, blood transfusion	Several years
Brucellosis	*Brucellus abortus* or *B meliteusis* bacteria	Cattle or goats	3–6 years
Chickenpox (varicella)	Varicella-zoster virus (US) Herpes zoster virus (UK)	Infected persons; articles contaminated by discharge from mucous membranes	10–21 days
Cholera	*Vibrio cholerae* bacterium	Contaminated water and seafood	A few hours – 5 days
Common cold	Numerous viruses	Respiratory droplets of infected person	1–4 days
Diphtheria	*Corynebacterium diphtheriae* bacillus	Respiratory secretions and saliva of infected persons or carriers	2–6 days
Encephalitis	Viruses	Bite from infected mosquito	4–21 days
Gas gangrene	Clostridia bacteria	Soil or soil-contaminated articles	1–4 days
Gonorrhoea	*Neisseria gonorrhoeae* bacterium	Urethral or vaginal secretions of infected persons	3–8 days
Hepatitis A (infectious)	Hepatitis A virus	Contaminated food and water	15–50 days
Hepatitis B (serum type B)	Hepatitis B virus	Infected blood; parenteral injection	6 weeks – 6 months
Infectious mononucleosis (US) Glandular fever (UK)	Epstein-Barr virus	Saliva; direct oral contact with infected person	2–6 weeks
Influenza	Numerous viruses (types A, B, C)	Direct contact; respiratory droplets, possibly airborne	1–4 days
Legionnaires' disease	*Legionella pneumophila* bacterium	Water droplets in infected humidifiers, cooling towers	1–3 days
Leprosy	*Mycobacterium leprae* bacillus	Droplet infection (minimally contagious)	Variable
Malaria	*Plasmodium* protozoa	Bite from infected mosquito	6–37 days
Measles (rubeola)	Rubeola virus	Droplet infection	10–15 days
Meningitis	Various bacteria (bacterial meningitis) and viruses (viral meningitis)	Respiratory droplets	Varies with causative agent
Mumps	Virus	Direct contact with infected persons; respiratory droplets and oral secretions	14–21 days
Paratyphoid fevers	*Salmonella* bacteria	Ingestion of contaminated food and water	1–14 days
Pneumonia	*Streptococcus pneumoniae* bacterium	Droplet infection	1–3 weeks
Poliomyelitis	Polio viruses	Direct contact with nasopharyngeal secretions of infected persons, vomit	7–21 days
Rabies	Virus	Bite from rabid animal	10 days–6 months
Rubella (German measles)	Rubella virus	Direct contact or droplet spread of nasopharyngeal secretion	14–21 days
Scarlet fever	Group A hemolytic *Streptococcus* bacteria	Direct or indirect contact with infected persons, or droplet infection	1–5 days
Shingles	*see chickenpox*	*see chickenpox*	
Smallpox (variola)	Poxvirus variola	Direct contact, droplet	7–14 days
Syphilis	*Treponema pallidum* bacterium	Sexual relations, contact with open lesions, blood transfusion	10–90 days
Tetanus (lockjaw)	*Clostridium tetani* bacillus	Animal faeces and soil	3–21 days
Tuberculosis	*Mycobacterium tuberculosis* bacillus	Droplet spread; ingestion from contaminated milk	Variable
Typhoid fever	*Salmonella typhi* bacillus	Contaminated food and water	7–21 days
Whooping cough (pertussis)	*Bordetella pertussis* bacterium	Droplet spread	10–21 days
Yellow fever	Arbovirus	Bite from infected mosquito	3–6 days

The geography of HIV infection

Although sub-Saharan Africa still has by far the most infections (some 6 million adults may be harbouring HIV), other regions are catching up fast. By the mid-1990s, the number of people infected in Asia could rise to 3 million, most of them in India and Thailand. (Early 1992 figures.)

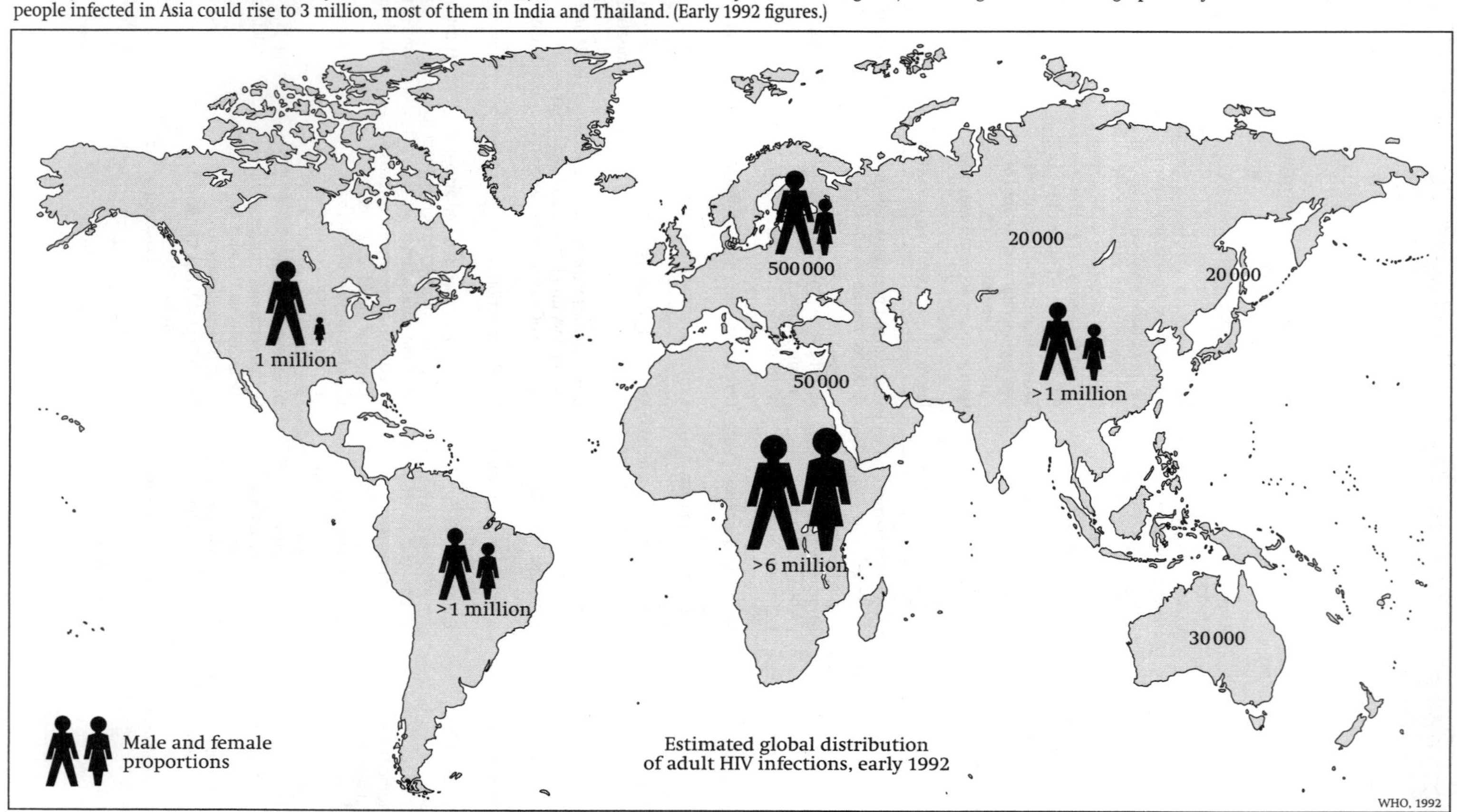

The occurrence of coronary heart disease

Age-standardized rates of mortality for men and women aged 40–49 in 1985.

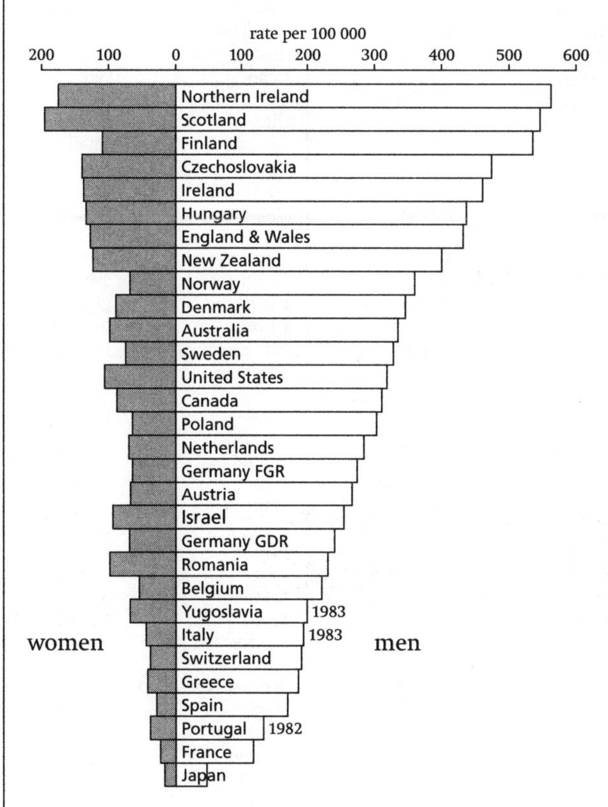

Estimates of most frequent cancers worldwide (1980)

Males

	Number[a]	%
1. Lung	513.6	15.8
2. Stomach	408.8	12.6
3. Colon/rectum	286.2	8.8
4. Mouth/pharynx	257.3	7.9
5. Prostate	235.8	7.3
6. Oesophagus	202.1	6.2
7. Liver	171.7	5.3
8. Bladder	167.7	5.2
9. Lymphoma	139.9	4.3
10. Leukaemia	106.9	3.3

Females

	Number[a]	%
1. Breast	572.1	18.4
2. Cervix	465.6	15.0
3. Colon/rectum	285.9	9.2
4. Stomach	260.6	8.4
5. Corpus uteri	148.8	4.8
6. Lung	146.9	4.7
7. Ovary	137.6	4.4
8. Mouth/pharynx	121.2	3.9
9. Oesophagus	108.2	3.5
10. Lymphoma	98.0	3.2

Both sexes

	Number[a]	%
1. Stomach	669.4	10.5
2. Lung	660.5	10.4
3. Breast	572.1	9.0
4. Colon/rectum	572.1	9.0
5. Cervix	465.6	7.3
6. Mouth/pharynx	378.5	6.0
7. Oesophagus	310.4	4.9
8. Liver	251.2	4.0
9. Lymphoma	237.9	3.7
10. Prostate	235.8	3.7
11. Bladder	219.4	3.5
12. Leukaemia	188.2	3.0

[a] in thousands

Phobias

An A to Z of phobias arranged by technical term

Technical term	Everyday name	Technical term	Everyday name	Technical term	Everyday name
Acero-	sourness	Elektro-	electricity	Nelo-	glass
Achulo-	darkness	Entomo-	insects	Neo-	newness
Acro-	heights	Eoso-	dawn	Nephelo-	clouds
Aero-	air	Eremo-	solitude	Noso- (patho-)	disease
Agora-	open spaces	Erete-	pins	Ocho-	vehicles
Aichuro-	points	Ereuthro-	blushing	Odonto-	teeth
Ailouro-	cats	Ergo-	work	Oiko-	home
Akoustico-	sound	Geno-	sex	Olfacto-	smell
Algo-	pain	Geuma-	taste	Omato-	eyes
Amaka-	carriages	Grapho-	writing	Oneiro-	dreams
Amatho-	dust	Gymnoto-	nudity	Ophido-	snakes
Andro-	men	Gyno-	women	Ornitho-	birds
Anemo-	wind	Hamartio-	sin	Ourano-	heaven
Angino-	narrowness	Hapto-	touch	Pan- (panto)-	everything
Anthropo-	man	Harpaxo-	robbers	Partheno-	girls
Antlo-	flood	Hedono-	pleasure	Patroio-	heredity
Apeiro-	infinity	Haemato-	blood	Penia-	poverty
Arachno-	spiders	Helmintho-	worms	Phasmo-	ghosts
Astheno-	weakness	Hodo-	travel	Phobo-	fears
Astra-	astral	Homichlo-	fog	Photo-	light
Ate-	ruin	Horme-	shock	Pnigero-	smothering
Aulo-	flute	Hydro-	water	Poine-	punishment
Aurora-	Northern Lights	Hypegia-	responsibility	Poly-	many things
Bacilli-	microbes	Hypno-	sleep	Poto-	drink
Baro-	gravity	Ideo-	ideas	Pterono-	feathers
Baso-	walking	Kakorraphia-	failure	Pyro-	fire
Batracho-	reptiles	Karagalo-	ridicule	Rypo-	soiling
Belone-	needles	Keno-	void	Satano-	Satan
Bronto-	thunder	Kineso-	motion	Sela-	flashes
Cheima-	cold	Klepto-	stealing	Sidero-	stars
Chiono-	snow	Kopo-	fatigue	Sito-	food
Chrometo-	money	Kristallo-	ice	Sperma- (spermato-)	germs
Chrono-	duration	Lalio-	stuttering	Stasi-	standing
Chrystallo-	crystals	Linono-	string	Stygio- (hade-)	hell
Claustro-	closed spaces	Logo-	words	Syphilo-	syphilis
Cnido-	stings	Lysso- (mania-)	insanity	Thalasso-	sea
Cometo-	comets	Mastigo-	flogging	Thanato-	death
Cromo-	colour	Mechano-	machinery	Thasse-	sitting
Cyno-	dogs	Metallo-	metals	Theo-	God
Demo-	crowds	Meteoro-	meteors	Thermo-	heat
Demono-	demons	Miso-	contamination	Toxi-	poison
Dermato-	skin	Mono-	one thing	Tremo-	trembling
Dike-	injustice	Musico-	music	Triskaideka-	thirteen
Dora-	fur	Muso-	mice	Zelo-	jealousy
Eisoptro-	mirror	Necro-	corpses	Zoo-	animals
				Xeno-	strangers

An A to Z of phobias arranged by everyday name

Everyday name	*Technical term*
Air	aero-
Animals	zoo-
Astral	astra-
Birds	orthino-
Blood	hemato-
Blushing	ereuthro-
Carriages	amaka-
Cats	ailouro-
Closed spaces	claustro-
Clouds	nephelo-
Cold	cheima-
Colour	cromo-
Comets	cometo-
Contamination	miso-
Corpses	necro-
Crowds	demo-
Crystals	chrystallo-
Darkness	achluo-
Dawn	eoso-
Death	thanato-
Demons	demono-
Disease	noso- (patho-)
Dogs	cyno-
Dreams	oneiro-
Drinks	poto-
Duration	chrono-
Dust	amatho-
Electricity	elektro-
Everything	pan- (panto-)
Eyes	omato-
Failure	kakorrphia-
Fatigue	kopo-
Fears	phobo-
Feathers	pterono-
Fire	pyro-
Flashes	sela-
Flogging	mastigo-
Flood	antlo-
Flute	aulo-
Fog	homichlo-
Food	sito-
Fur	dora-
Germs	sperma- (spermato-)
Ghosts	phasmo-
Girls	partheno-
Glass	nelo-
God	theo-
Gravity	baro-
Heat	thermo-
Heaven	ourano-
Heights	acro-
Hell	stygio- (hade-)
Heredity	patroio-
Home	oiko-
Ice	kristallo-
Ideas	ideo-
Infinity	apeiro-
Injustice	dike-
Insanity	lysso- (mania-)
Insects	entomo-
Jealousy	zelo-
Light	photo-
Machinery	mechano-
Man	anthropo-
Many things	poly-
Men	andro-
Metals	metallo-
Meteors	meteoro-
Mice	muso-
Microbes	bacilli-
Mirrors	eisoptro-
Money	chrometo-
Motion	kineso-
Music	musico-
Narrowness	angino-
Needles	belone-
Newness	neo-
Northern Lights	aurora-
Nudity	gymnoto-
One thing	mono-
Open spaces	agora-
Pain	algo-
Pins	erete-
Pleasure	hedono-
Points	aichuro-
Poison	toxi-
Poverty	penia-
Punishment	poine-
Reptiles	batracho-
Responsibility	hypegia-
Ridicule	katagalo-
Robberies	harpaxo-
Ruin	ate-
Satan	Satano-
Sea	thalasso-
Sex	geno-
Shock	horme-
Sin	hamartio-
Sitting	thasso-
Skin	dermato-
Sleep	hypno-
Smell	olfacto-
Smothering	pnigero-
Snakes	ophidio-
Snow	chiono-
Soiling	rypo-
Solitude	eremo-
Sound	akoustico-
Sourness	acero-
Spiders	arachno-
Standing	stasi-
Stars	sidero-
Stealing	klepto-
Stings	cnido-
Strangers	xeno-
String	linono-
Stuttering	lalio-
Syphilis	syphilo-
Taste	geuma-
Teeth	odonto-
Thirteen	triskaideka-
Thunder	bronto- (tonitro-)
Touch	hapto-
Travel	hodo-
Trembling	tremo-
Vehicles	ocho-
Void	keno-
Walking	baso-
Water	hydro-
Weakness	astheno-
Wind	anemo-
Women	gyno-
Words	logo-
Work	ergo-
Worms	helmintho-
Writing	grapho-

Commonly used drugs

Common name	*Drug type*	*Use*	*Comments*
Adrenaline	Sympathomimic Vasoconstrictor Bronchodilator	Counteracts cardiac arrest, relieves severe allergic reactions and controls symptoms of asthma	Constricts blood vessels and is used to control bleeding in surgery
Anabolic steroids	Male sex hormones	Increase muscle bulk and body growth. Help increase production of blood cells in some forms of anaemia	Risk of serious side effects. Abused by some athletes to improve performance
Aspirin	Analgesic Anti-inflammatory Anti-platelet	Relieves pain, reduces fever, helps prevent blood clots from forming	Introduced by Hermann Dresser, 1893 Can cause irritation to the stomach and even bleeding
Beta blockers	Beta blockers	Treat angina, hypertension and irregular heart rhythms. Can also prevent migraines	Minor side effects of reduced circulation and reduced capacity for strenuous exercise
Chloral hydrate	Sleeping drug	Short-term treatment of insomnia	Suitable for use by children
Cimetidine	Anti-ulcer drug	Reduces level of acid and pepsin and promotes healing of stomach and duodenal ulcers	Also affects actions of certain enzymes in the liver Prescribed only when possibility of stomach cancer has been ruled out
Codeine	Narcotic analgesic	Relieves mild pain. Also effective cough suppressant	Introduced at turn of century. Can be habit-forming, but addiction seldom occurs if drug used for limited period
Cortisone	Corticosteroid	Treatment of rheumatoid arthritis. Anti-inflammatory drug	Discovered by Edward Calvin Kendall, 1934, as adrenal cortisone extracts
Co-trimoxazole	Antibacterial	Treats respiratory, constipating and urinary tract infections	Can have side effects of nausea and vomiting
Diazepam	Benzodiazepine anti-anxiety drug	Treats anxiety, insomnia. Also prescribed as muscle relaxant	Can be habit-forming if taken over a long period
Digoxin	Digitalis drug	Slows down rate of heart. Controls tiredness, breathlessness and fluid retention	Treatment must be monitored carefully
Ethambutol	Antituberculosis	Used with other tuberculosis drugs it helps boost their effects	Side effect can be eye damage
Frusemide	Loop diuretic	Treats fluid retention caused by heart failure and some liver and kidney disorders	Discovered 1960
Ibuprofen	Analgesic Anti-inflammatory	Treats symptoms of rheumatoid arthritis as well as headaches and menstrual pain	Few side effects and does not cause bleeding in the stomach
Insulin	Drug for diabetes	Supplements or replaces natural insulin in diabetes mellitus	Isolated by Frederick Banting, C H Best, 1921 Only effective treatment of juvenile diabetes
Magnesium hydroxide	Antacid	Neutralizes stomach acid. Also acts as laxative	
Morphine	Narcotic analgesic	Relieves severe pain	Discovered by Friedrich Serturner, 1805 Derives from opium and can be addictive
Paracetamol/ Acetaminophen	Analgesic	Relieves bouts of mild pain and fever. Does not cause damage to stomach	First used by Joseph von Mering, 1893 Large doses can be toxic and an overdose can cause serious damage to liver and kidneys
Penicillin	Antibiotic	Treats many common infections	Discovered by Alexander Fleming, 1928 Can cause allergic reactions
Pethidine	Narcotic analgesic	Used particularly to relieve pain in childbirth. Effect short-lasting	Introduced by Hoechst, 1939 Habit-forming if taken over long period of time
Phenylpropan-olamine	Decongestant	Relieves nasal congestion in colds and hay fever	Can raise the heart rate and cause palpitations

Common name	Drug type	Use	Comments
Quinidine	Anti-arrhythmic drug	Treats abnormal heart rhythms	Can cause allergic reactions
Quinine	Antimalarial drug	Treatment for malaria and leg cramps	Discovered by P J Pelletier, J B Caventou, 1818 Now rarely prescribed due to side effects of headaches, nausea, hearing loss and blurred vision
Ranitidine	Anti-ulcer drug	Prevents gastric and duodenal ulcers. Reduces amount of acid produced by stomach	Prescribed only when possibility of stomach cancer has been ruled out
Salbutamol/ Albutero	Bronchodilator	Treats asthma, bronchitis and emphysema	Little stimulant effect on heart rate and blood pressure. Gives rapid relief and is more effective if inhaled rather than taken by mouth
Sodium bicarbonate	Antacid	Relieves indigestion and discomfort caused by peptic ulcers. Relieves pain from urinary tract infections	If given by injection can also be effective in treatment of acidity of the blood
Temazepam	Benzodiazepine sleeping drug	Short-term treatment of insomnia	Can be habit-forming
Terfenadine	Antihistamine	Treats allergic rhinitis, particularly hay fever	Little or no sedative effect on the nervous system
Testosterone	Male sex hormone	Increases fertility in men with testicular disorders. Also used to induce puberty in cases of hormone deficiency	Can interfere with growth or cause over-rapid sexual development
Tetracycline	Antibiotic	Treats pneumonia, bronchitis and chest infections	Common side effects are nausea and vomiting

Commonly abused drugs

Name	Common name	Effects	Comments
Alcohol	Booze, drink	Acts as central nervous system depressant, so reduces anxiety, concentration impaired, reactions slowed	Long-term effects include liver disease (cirrhosis, liver cancer, hepatitis), heart disease, inflammation of stomach. Alcoholics have above average chance of developing dementia
Amphetamines	Uppers, speed, bennies	Promote feelings of alertness, increase in speech and physical activity	Can produce toxic effects, mood swings, circulatory and cardiac disturbances, feelings of paranoia, hallucinations, convulsions
Barbiturates (Nembutal, Seconal, Amytal)	Barbs, reds, downers	Calm the nerves, induce sleep, hypnotic effect	Highly addictive, overdose is lethal, can induce state of coma, often fatal if taken with alcohol
Benzodiazepines	Tranquillizers	Reduce mental activity and anxiety, slow body's reactions, reduce alertness	Can cause dependency. Withdrawal symptoms occur on stopping the drug – anxiety, insomnia, panic attacks, head-aches and palpitations
Cocaine	Coke, crack, ice, snow (Crack is a blend of cocaine, baking powder and water)	Increased blood pressure, heart rate, breathing and body temperature, feelings of euphoria, illusions of increased sensory awareness and mental and physical strength, decrease in hunger, pain and need for sleep	Regular use can cause anxiety, insomnia, weight loss, increased paranoia and psychosis. Crack is highly addictive and has more intense effects than cocaine. Increased risk of abnormal heart rhythms, high blood pressure, stroke and death. Long-term consequences in clude mental deterioration, personality changes, paranoia or violent behaviour
Heroin	Junk, smack	Induces euphoria, relieves pain and often induces sleep	Highly addictive, overdose can result in death, serum hepatitis is common, skin abscesses, inflammation of the veins, constipation, respiratory depression
Lysergic acid diethylamide	LSD, acid	Hallucinations, vision alters, rise in temperature and heart-beat, flashbacks	Long-term use causes anxiety and depression, impaired memory and attention span, difficulty with abstract thinking

Commonly abused drugs (continued)

Name	*Common name*	*Effects*	*Comments*
Marijuana	Grass, pot, weed, dope	Increase in heartbeat, heightens senses, feelings of euphoria and relaxation	Reduces the ability to perform tasks requiring concentration, slows reactions and impairs coordination
MDMA	Ecstasy, E	Mental relaxation, increased sensitivity to stimuli, sometimes hallucinations	High doses have amphetamine-like effects. Can produce severe or fatal reactions, sometimes after only one dose
Mescaline	Peyote, cactus buttons	Induces hallucinations, affects sensations and perceptions	Loss of control of normal thought processes; long-term depression and anxiety; can induce 'breaks from reality'
Methadone		Induces sleep and feeling of relaxation	Addictive, overdose can result in death
Nicotine		Stimulates the nervous system, increases concentration, relieves tension and fatigue, increases heart rate and blood pressure	Taken regularly can cause increase in fatty acids in bloodstream, increases risk of heart disease and circulatory problems, can also increase risk of peptic ulcers. Increased risk of lung, throat and mouth cancers from tobacco smoke
Nitrites	Poppers	Give the user a rapid high, felt as rush of energy. Heart rate increases, feelings of dizziness and nausea. High doses can cause fainting	Lasting physical damage, in the form of cardiac problems, can occur
Phencyclidine	PCP, Angel dust	Feeling of euphoria, floating sensation, numbness, change in user's perception of the body, visual disturbances	Can produce violent behaviour against the user or others, schizophrenic-like psychosis which can last for days or weeks
Solvents		Lightheadedness, dizziness and drowsiness. Large doses can lead to loss of consciousness	Some products can seriously disrupt heart rhythm or cause heart failure and sometimes death. Aerosols can cause suffocation by coating the lungs. Risk of death also from depression of the breathing mechanism. Long-term misuse leads to kidney and liver damage

NUTRITION

Ideal weights for men and women, over 25 years of age

Women Height (cm)	*Ideal weight (kg)*	*Men* Height (cm)	*Ideal weight (kg)*
153	53.9–46.3	155	63.9–53.5
155	55.3–47.6	157	65.3–54.8
157	57.1–48.9	160	67.1–56.2
160	58.9–50.3	162	68.9–57.6
162	61.2–51.7	165	70.8–58.9
165	63.0–53.5	168	73.0–60.8
168	64.8–55.3	170	75.3–62.6
170	66.7–57.1	173	77.1–65.4
173	68.5–58.9	175	78.9–66.2
175	70.3–60.8	178	81.2–68.0
178	72.1–62.6	180	83.5–69.8
180	73.9–64.4	183	86.7–71.6
183	75.7–66.2	185	87.9–73.5
185	77.6–68.0	188	90.2–75.7
188	79.3–69.8	190	92.5–78.0
		193	94.8–80.3

Composition of foods

Figures (approximate) per 100 g of food

Food	*Protein (g)*	*Carbohydrates (g)*	*Fat (g)*	*Fibre (g)*	*Energy value (calories[a])*
Meat, poultry, fish					
Bacon, back, grilled	15	2	24	0	271
Bacon, streaky, grilled	16	2	27	0	308
Beef, minced	31	0	16	0	221
Beef, rump steak, grilled	30	0	12	0	218
Chicken, meat only, roast	19	0	4	0	142
Cod, cooked	19	0	1	0	94
Crab, cooked	18	1	5	0	129
Haddock, cooked	19	0	1	0	96
Ham, lean	22	0	5	0	168
Lamb chop, boned, grilled	24	0	29	0	353
Liver, cooked	20	6	13	0	254
Lobster, cooked	20	trace	3	0	119
Mackerel, cooked	25	0	11	0	188
Mussels, cooked	17	0	1	0	86
Pork chop, boned, grilled	28	0	24	0	328
Prawns, cooked	18	0	1	0	107
Salmon, cooked	20	0	13	0	196
Tuna, canned in brine	28	0	1	0	118
Turkey, meat only, roast	36	0	3	0	140
Vegetables					
Asparagus, cooked	2	4	trace	1	18
Aubergine/Egg-plant, cooked	1	4	trace	2	14
Beans, broad, cooked	4	66	1	4	46
Beans, dried white, cooked	8	21	7	25	118
Beans, green, cooked	2	5	trace	4	25
Beetroot, cooked	1	7	trace	2	43
Broccoli, cooked	3	5	trace	4	26
Brussel sprouts, cooked	4	6	trace	3	18
Cabbage, cooked	2	trace	trace	2	11
Cabbage, raw	2	5	trace	3	25
Carrots, cooked	1	5	trace	3	20
Carrots, raw	1	6	trace	3	25
Cauliflower, cooked	2	4	trace	2	22
Celery, raw	1	2	trace	2	36
Chick peas, dry	20	50	6	15	320
Corn (on the cob)	3	21	1	5	91
Courgettes/Zucchini, cooked	1	3	trace	1	14
Cucumber, raw	1	3	trace	trace	15
Leeks, cooked	1	7	0	4	25
Lentils, cooked	8	19	trace	4	106
Lettuce, raw	1	3	trace	1	12
Mushrooms, raw	3	4	trace	2	14
Onions, raw	2	9	trace	1	38
Parsnip, cooked	1	17	trace	4	50
Peas, fresh cooked	5	4	trace	5	54
Pepper, green, raw	1	5	trace	1	14
Pepper, red, raw	1	7	trace	1	20
Potatoes, baked in skin	3	21	trace	2	86
Potatoes, boiled in skin	2	17	trace	2	75
Spinach, cooked	3	4	trace	6	23
Swede, cooked	1	4	trace	3	18
Turnip, cooked	1	5	trace	2	14
Fruit					
Apples	trace	15	trace	2	38
Apricots, dried	5	67	1	24	182
Apricots, raw	1	13	trace	2	25
Avocados	2	6	16	2	221
Bananas	1	22	trace	2	85

[a] Multiply calories by 4.187 to convert to kilojoules

Composition of foods (continued)

Food	*Protein (g)*	*Carbohydrates (g)*	*Fat (g)*	*Fibre (g)*	*Energy value (calories[a])*
Blackberries	1	13	1	7	29
Blackcurrants	2	14	trace	9	29
Cherries	1	17	trace	1	70
Dates	2	73	1	7	214
Figs, dried	4	69	1	19	214
Grapefruit	1	11	trace	trace	41
Grapes	1	16	1	1	69
Melon, honeydew	1	5	trace	1	21
Melon, water	trace	5	trace	1	21
Nectarines	1	17	trace	2	64
Oranges, peeled	1	12	trace	2	49
Peaches	1	8	trace	1	38
Pears	1	15	trace	2	61
Pineapple	trace	14	trace	1	46
Prunes	1	77	trace	14	136
Raisins	3	77	trace	7	246
Raspberries	1	14	1	7	25
Strawberries	1	8	1	2	37
Tomatoes	1	5	trace	1	14
Dairy products					
Butter, salted	1	trace	82	0	740
Cheese, Brie	19	2	23	0	314
Cheese, Cheddar	25	2	32	0	414
Cheese, cottage	17	2	4	0	96
Cheese, Edam	30	trace	23	0	314
Cream, double	2	3	48	0	446
Milk, cow's, skimmed	4	5	trace	0	36
Milk, cow's, whole	4	5	4	0	65
Yogurt, skimmed milk	3	5	2	0	50
Yogurt, whole milk	3	5	3	0	62
Grain products					
Flour, white	9	80	1	4	350
Flour, wholemeal	13	56	2	10	318
Oatmeal, cooked	2	10	1	7	399
Oats, porridge	10	70	7	7	377
Pasta, dry	12	71	2	4	353
Rice, brown, cooked	3	26	1	1	129
Rice, white, cooked	3	33	trace	1	121
Legumes, nuts & seeds					
Almonds	19	20	54	15	564
Brazil nuts	14	11	67	9	618
Peanuts, fresh	26	19	48	8	571
Walnuts	15	16	64	5	525
Miscellaneous					
Biscuit, chocolate digestive	6	64	25	4	506
Biscuit, digestive	7	62	23	5	486
Chocolate bar, plain	4	63	29	0	510
Crisps	6	40	37	11	517
Egg, boiled	13	1	12	0	163
Honey	trace	82	0	0	289
Jam	1	79	trace	1	261
Margarine	trace	1	80	0	730
Oil, vegetable	0	0	100	0	900
Orange juice	1	10	trace	0	45
Sugar	0	100	0	0	394

[a]Multiply calories by 4.187 to convert to kilojoules

Main types of vitamin

Fat soluble vitamins

Vitamin	*Chemical name*	*Precursor*	*Main symptom of deficiency*	*Dietary source*
A	Retinol	Beta-carotene	Xerophthalmia (eye disease)	Retinol: milk, butter, cheese, egg yolk, liver and fatty fish Carotene: green vegetables, yellow and red fruits and vegetables, especially carrots
D	Cholecalciferol	UV-activated 7-dehydro-cholesterol	Rickets; osteomalacia	Fatty fish, margarine, and some fortified milks
K	Phytomenadione		Haemorrhagic problems	Green leafy vegetables and liver
E	Tocopherols		Multiple effects	Vegetable oils

Water soluble vitamins

Vitamin	*Chemical name*	*Main symptom of deficiency*	*Dietary source*
C	Ascorbic acid	Scurvy	Citrus fruits, potatoes, green leafy vegetables
B-vitamins			
B_1	Thiamine	Beri-beri	Seeds and grains: widely distributed
B_2	Riboflavin	Failure to thrive	Liver, milk, cheese, yeast
–	Nicotinic acid	Pellagra	Meat, fish, cereals, pulses
B_6	Pyridoxine	Dermatitis; neurological disorders	Cereals, liver, meat, fruits, leafy vegetables
B_{12}	Cyanocobalamin	Anaemia	Meat, milk, liver
–	Folic acid	Anaemia	Liver, green vegetables
–	Pantothenic acid	Dermatitis	Widespread
–	Biotin	Dermatitis	Liver, kidney, yeast extracts

Main trace minerals

Mineral	*Main symptom of deficiency*	*Dietary source*	*% of total body weight*
Calcium	Rickets in children; osteoporosis in adults	Milk, butter, cheese, sardines, green leafy vegetables, citrus fruits	2.5
Chromium	Adult-onset diabetes	Brewer's yeast, black pepper, liver, wholemeal bread, beer	<0.01
Copper	Anaemia; Menkes' syndrome	Green vegetables, fish, oysters, liver	<0.01
Fluorine	Tooth decay; possibly osteoporosis	Fluoridated drinking water, seafood, tea	<0.01
Iodine	Goitre; cretinism in new-born children	Seafood, salt-water fish, seaweed, iodized salt, table salt	<0.01
Iron	Anaemia	Liver, kidney, green leafy vegetables, egg yolk, dried fruit, potatoes, molasses	0.01
Magnesium	Irregular heart beat; muscular weakness; insomnia	Green leafy vegetables (eaten raw), nuts, whole grains	0.07
Manganese	Not known in humans	Legumes, cereals, green leafy vegetables, tea	<0.01
Molybdenum	Not known in humans	Legumes, cereals, liver, kidney, some dark green vegetables	<0.01
Phosphorus	Muscular weakness; bone pain; loss of appetite	Meat, poultry, fish, eggs, dried beans and peas, milk products	1.1
Potassium	Irregular heart beat; muscular weakness; fatigue; kidney and lung failure	Fresh vegetables, meat, orange juice, bananas, bran	0.10
Selenium	Not known in humans	Seafood, cereals, meat, egg yolk, garlic	<0.01
Sodium	Impaired acid-base balance in body fluids (very rare)	Table salt, other naturally occurring salts	0.10
Zinc	Impaired wound healing; loss of appetite; impaired sexual development	Meat, whole grains, legumes, oysters, milk	<0.01

Food additives

The prefix 'E' stands for European and indicates that an additive is accepted as safe all over the European Community. It was introduced by the Food Labelling Regulations of 1984 and is used by food manufacturers in member states of the EC.

Any number without the prefix 'E' has been approved by the UK, but not yet by the European Community.

Also listed (without numbers) are additives with a long history of use in the food industry for which formal EC approval is either pending or deemed unnecessary.

In the United States, additives require approval by the US Food and Drug Administration (FDA).

Antioxidants

Stop fatty foods from going rancid and protect fat-soluble vitamins from the harmful effects of oxidation.

E300 L-ascorbic acid – *fruit drinks; also used to improve flour and bread dough*
E301 Sodium L-ascorbate
E302 Calcium L-ascorbate
E304 6-0-Palmitoyl-L-ascorbic acid (ascorbyl palmitate) – *scotch eggs*
E306 Extracts of natural origin rich in tocopherols – *vegetable oils*
E307 Synthetic alpha-tocopherol – *cereal-based baby foods*
E308 Synthetic gamma-tocopherol
E309 Synthetic delta-tocopherol
E310 Propyl gallate – *vegetable oils; chewing gum*
E311 Octyl gallate
E312 Dodecyl gallate
E320 Butylated hydroxyanisole (BHA) – *soup mixes; cheese spread*
E321 Butylated hydroxytoluene (BHT) – *chewing gum*
E322 Lecithins – *low fat spreads; also used as an emulsifier in chocolate*
Diphenylamine
Ethoxyquin – *used to prevent 'scald' (a discolouration) on apples and pears*

Preservatives

Protect against microbes which cause spoilage and food poisoning. They also increase storage life of foods.

E200 Sorbic acid – *soft drinks; fruit yoghurt; processed cheese slices*
E201 Sodium sorbate
E202 Potassium sorbate
E203 Calcium sorbate – *frozen pizza; flour confectionery*
E210 Benzoic acid
E211 Sodium benzoate
E212 Potassium benzoate
E213 Calcium benzoate
E214 Ethyl 4-hydroxybenzoate (ethyl para-hydroxybenzoate)
E215 Ethyl 4-hydroxybenzoate, sodium salt (sodium ethyl para-hydroxybenzoate)
E216 Propyl 4-hydroxybenzoate (propyl para-hydroxybenzoate).
E217 Propyl 4-hydroxybenzoate, sodium salt (sodium propyl para-hydroxybenzoate)
E218 Methyl 4-hydroxybenzoate (methyl para-hydroxybenzoate)
E219 Methyl 4-hydroxybenzoate, sodium salt (sodium methyl para-hydroxybenzoate) – *beer, jam, salad cream, soft drinks, fruit pulp, fruit-based pie fillings, marinated herring and mackerel*
E220 Sulphur dioxide
E221 Sodium sulphite
E222 Sodium hydrogen sulphite (sodium bisulphite)
E223 Sodium metabisulphite
E224 Potassium metabisulphite
E226 Calcium sulphite
E227 Calcium hydrogen sulphite (calcium bisulphite) – *dried fruit, dehydrated vegetables, fruit juices and syrups, sausages, fruit-based dairy desserts, cider, beer and wine; also used to prevent browning of raw peeled potatoes and to condition biscuit doughs*
E228 Potassium bisulphite – *wines*
E230 Biphenyl (diphenyl)
E231 2-Hydroxybiphenyl (orthophenylphenol)
E232 Sodium biphenyl-2-yl oxide (sodium orthophenylphenate) – *surface treatment of citrus fruit*
E233 2-(Thiazol-4-yl) benzimidazole (thiabendazole) – *surface treatment of bananas*
234 Nisin – *cheese, clotted cream*
E239 Hexamine (hexamethylenetetramine) – *marinated herring and mackerel*
E249 Potassium nitrite
E250 Sodium nitrite
E251 Sodium nitrate
E252 Potassium nitrate – *bacon, ham, cured meats, corned beef and some cheeses*
E280 Propionic acid
E281 Sodium propionate
E282 Calcium propionate
E283 Potassium propionate – *bread and flour confectionery, Christmas pudding*

Colours

Make food more colourful, compensate for colour lost in processing.

E100 Curcumin – *flour confectionery, margarine*
E101 Riboflavin – *sauces*
101(a) Riboflavin-5'-phosphate
E102 Tartrazine – *soft drinks*
E104 Quinoline yellow
E110 Sunset Yellow FCF – *biscuits*
E120 Cochineal – *alcoholic drinks*
E122 Carmoisine – *jams and preserves*
E123 Amaranth
E124 Ponceau 4R – *dessert mixes*
E127 Erythrosine BS – *glacé cherries*
128 Red 2G – *sausages*
E131 Patent Blue V
E132 Indigo Carmine
133 Brilliant Blue FCF – *canned vegetables*
E140 Chlorophyll
E141 Copper complexes of chlorophyll and chlorophyllins
E142 Green S – *pastilles*
E150 Caramel – *beer, soft drinks, sauces, gravy browning*
E151 Black PN
E153 Carbon Black (vegetable carbon) – *liquorice*

154 Brown FK – *kippers*
155 Brown HT – *chocolate cake*
E160(a) *Alpha*-carotene; *beta*-carotene; *gamma*-carotene – *margarine, soft drinks*
E160(b) Annatto; bixin; norbixin – *crisps/potato chips*
E160(c) Capsanthin; capsorubin
E160(d) Lycopene
E160(e) *Beta*-apo-8'-carotenal
E160(f) Ethyl ester of beta-apo-8'-carotenoic acid
E161(a) Flavoxanthin
E161(b) Lutein
E161(c) Cryptoxanthin
E161(d) Rubixanthin
E161(e) Violaxanthin
E161(f) Rhodoxanthin
E161(g) Canthaxanthin
E162 Beetroot Red (betanin) – *ice-cream, liquorice*
E163 Anthocyanins – *yogurt*
E171 Titanium dioxide – *sweets*
E172 Iron oxides; iron hydroxides
E173 Aluminium
E174 Silver
E175 Gold – *cake decorations*
E180 Pigment Rubine (lithol rubine BK)
Methyl violet – *used for the surface marking of raw or unprocessed meat*
Paprika – *canned vegetables*
Turmeric – *soup*

Sweeteners

There are two types of sweeteners; intense sweeteners and bulk sweeteners. Intense sweeteners have a sweetness many times that of sugar and are therefore used at very low levels. They are marked with * in the following list. Bulk sweeteners have about the same sweetness as sugar and are used at the same sort of levels as sugar.

*Acesulfame potassium – *canned foods, soft drinks, table-top sweeteners*
*Aspartame – *soft drinks, yogurts, dessert and drink mixes, sweetening tablets*
Hydrogenated glucose syrup
Isomalt
Lactitol
E421 Mannitol – *sugar-free confectionery*
*Saccharin
*Sodium saccharin
*Calcium saccharin – *soft drinks, cider, sweetening tablets, table-top sweeteners*
E420 Sorbitol; sorbitol syrup – *sugar-free confectionery, jams for diabetics*
*Thaumatin – *table-top sweeteners, yogurt*
Xylitol – *sugar-free chewing gum*

Emulsifiers and stabilisers

Enable oils and fats to mix with water in foods; add to smoothness and creaminess of texture; retard baked goods going stale.

E400 Alginic acid – *ice-cream; soft cheese*
E401 Sodium alginate – *cake mixes*
E402 Potassium alginate
E403 Ammonium alginate
E404 Calcium alginate
E405 Propane-1, 2-diol alginate (propylene glycol alginate) – *salad dressings; cottage cheese*
E406 Agar – *ice-cream*
E407 Carrageenan – *quick setting jelly mixes; milk shakes*
E410 Locust bean gum (carob gum) – *salad cream*
E412 Guar gum – *packet soups and meringue mixes*
E413 Tragacanth – *salad dressings; processed cheese*
E414 Gum arabic (acacia) – *confectionery*
E415 Xanthan gum – *sweet pickle; coleslaw*
416 Karaya gum – *soft cheese; brown sauce*
432 Polyoxyethylene (20) sorbitan monolaurate (Polysorbate 20)
433 Polyoxyethylene (20) sorbitan mono-oleate (Polysorbate 80)
434 Polyoxyethylene (20) sorbitan monopalmitate (Polysorbate 40)
435 Polyoxyethylene (20) sorbitan monostearate (Polysorbate 60)
436 Polyoxyethylene (20) sorbitan tristearate (Polysorbate 65) – *bakery products; confectionery creams*
E440 (i) Pectin
E440 (ii) Amidated pectin
Pectin extract – *jams and preserves*
442 Ammonium phosphatides – *cocoa and chocolate products*
E460 Microcrystalline cellulose – *grated cheese*
Alpha-cellulose (powdered cellulose) – *slimming bread*
E461 Methylcellulose – *low fat spreads*
E463 Hydroxypropylcellulose
E464 Hydroxypropylmethylcellulose – *edible ices*
E465 Ethylmethylcellulose – *gateaux*
E466 Carboxymethylcellulose, sodium salt (CMC) – *jelly; gateaux*
E470 Sodium, potassium and calcium salts of fatty acids – *cake mixes*
E471 Mono- and di-glycerides of fatty acids – *frozen desserts*
E472(a) Acetic acid esters of mono- and di-glycerides of fatty acids – *mousse mixes*
E472(b) Lactic acid esters of mono- and di-glycerides of fatty acids – *dessert topping*
E472(c) Citric acid esters of mono- and di-glycerides of fatty acids – *continental sausages*
E472(d) Tartaric acid esters of mono- and di-glycerides of fatty acids
E472(e) Mono- and di-acetyltartaric acid esters of mono- and di-glycerides of fatty acids – *bread; frozen pizza*
E472(f) Mixed acetic and tartaric acid esters of mono- and di-glycerides of fatty acids
E473 Sucrose esters of fatty acids
E474 Sucroglycerides – *edible ices*
E475 Polyglycerol esters of fatty acids – *cakes and gateaux*
E476 Polyglycerol esters of polycondensed fatty acids of castor oil (polyglycerol polyricinoleate) – *chocolate-flavour coatings for cakes*
E477 Propane-1, 2-diol esters of fatty acids – *instant desserts*
E481 Sodium stearoyl-1-2-lactylate – *bread, cakes and biscuits.*
E482 Calcium stearoyl-1-2-lactylate – *gravy granules*
E483 Stearyl tartrate
491 Sorbitan monostearate
492 Sorbitan tristearate
493 Sorbitan monolaurate
494 Sorbitan mono-oleate
495 Sorbitan monopalmitate – *cake mixes*
Extract of quillaia – *used in soft drinks to promote foam*

Food additives (continued)

Oxidatively polymerised soya bean oil
Polyglycerol esters of dimerised fatty acids of soya bean oil – *emulsions used to grease bakery tins*

Others

Acids, anti-caking agents, anti-foaming agents, bases, buffers, bulking agents, firming agents, flavour modifiers, flour improvers, glazing agents, humectants, liquid freezants, packaging gases, propellants, release agents, sequestrants and solvents.

E170 Calcium carbonate – *base, firming agent, release agent, diluent; nutrient in flour*
E260 Acetic acid
E261 Potassium acetate
E262 Sodium hydrogen diacetate
262 Sodium acetate – *acid/acidity regulators (buffers) used in pickles, salad cream and bread; they contribute to flavour and provide protection against mould growth*
E263 Calcium acetate – *firming agent; also provides calcium which is useful in quick-set jelly mix*
E270 Lactic acid – *acid/flavouring protects against mould growth; salad dressing, soft margarine*
E290 Carbon dioxide – *carbonating agent/packaging gas and propellant; used in fizzy drinks*
296 DL-malic acid; L-malic acid
297 Fumaric acid – *acid/flavouring; used in soft drinks, sweets, biscuits, dessert mixes and pie fillings*
E325 Sodium lactate – *buffer, humectant; used in jams, preserves, sweets, flour confectionery*
E326 Potassium lactate – *buffer; jams, preserves and jellies*
E327 Calcium lactate – *buffer, firming agent; canned fruit, pie filling*
E330 Citric acid
E331 Sodium dihydrogen citrate (monosodium citrate); disodium citrate; trisodium citrate
E332 Potassium dihydrogen citrate (monopotassium citrate); tripotassium citrate
E333 Monocalcium citrate; dicalcium citrate; tricalcium citrate – *acid/flavourings, buffers, sequestrants, emulsifying salts (calcium salts are firming agents); used in soft drinks, jams, preserves, sweets, UHT cream, processed cheese, canned fruit, dessert mixes, ice-cream*
E334 L-(+)-tartaric acid
E335 Monosodium L-(+)-tartrate; disodium L-(+)-tartrate
E336 Monopotassium L-(+)-tartrate (cream of tartar); dipotassium L-(+)-tartrate
E337 Potassium sodium L-(+)-tartrate – *acid/flavourings, buffers, emulsifying salts, sequestrants; used in soft drinks, biscuit creams and fillings, sweets, jams, dessert mixes and processed cheese*
E338 Orthophosphoric acid (phosphoric acid) – *acid/flavourings; soft drinks, cocoa*
E339 Sodium dihydrogen orthophosphate; disodium hydrogen orthophosphate; trisodium orthophosphate
E340 Potassium dihydrogen orthophosphate; dipotassium hydrogen orthophosphate; tripotassium orthophosphate – *buffers, sequestrants, emulsifying salts; used in dessert mixes, non-dairy creamers, processed cheese*
E341 Calcium tetrahydrogen diorthophosphate; calcium hydrogen orthophosphate; tricalcium diorthophosphate – *firming agent, anti-caking agent, raising agent; cake mixes, baking powder, dessert mixes*
350 Sodium malate; sodium hydrogen malate
351 Potassium malate – *buffers, humectants; used in jams, sweets, cakes, biscuits*
352 Calcium malate; calcium hydrogen malate – *firming agent in processed fruit and vegetables*
353 Metatartaric acid – *sequestrant used in wine*
355 Adipic acid – *buffer/flavouring; sweets, synthetic cream desserts*
363 Succinic acid – *buffer/flavouring; dry foods and beverage mixes*
370 1,4-heptonolactone – *acid, sequestrant; dried soups, instant desserts*
375 Nicotinic acid – *colour stabiliser and nutrient; bread, flour, breakfast cereals*
380 Triammonium citrate – *buffer, emulsifying salt; processed cheese*
381 Ammonium ferric citrate – *dietary iron supplement; bread*
385 Calcium disodium ethylenediamine-NNN'N'-tetra-acetate (calcium disodium EDTA) – *sequestrant; canned shellfish*
E422 Glycerol – *humectant, solvent; cake icing, confectionery*
E450(a) Disodium dihydrogen diphosphate; trisodium diphosphate; tetrasodium diphosphate; tetrapotassium diphosphate
E450(b) Pentasodium triphosphate; pentapotassium triphosphate
E450(c) Sodium polyphosphates, potassium polyphosphates – *buffers, sequestrants, emulsifying salts, stabilisers, texturisers, raising agents; used in whipping cream, fish and meat products, bread, processed cheese, canned vegetables*
500 Sodium carbonate; sodium hydrogen carbonate (bicarbonate of soda); sodium sesquicarbonate
501 Potassium carbonate; potassium hydrogen carbonate – *bases, aerating agents, diluents; used in jams, jellies, self-raising flour, wine, cocoa*
503 Ammonium carbonate; ammonium hydrogen carbonate – *buffer, aerating agent; cocoa, biscuits*
504 Magnesium carbonate – *base, anti-caking agent; wafer biscuits, icing sugar*
507 Hydrochloric acid
508 Potassium chloride – *gelling agent, salt substitute; table salt replacement*
509 Calcium chloride – *firming agent in canned fruit and vegetables*
510 Ammonium chloride – *yeast food in bread*
513 Sulphuric acid
514 Sodium sulphate – *diluent for colours*
515 Potassium sulphate – *salt substitute*
516 Calcium sulphate – *firming agent and yeast food; bread*
518 Magnesium sulphate – *firming agent*
524 Sodium hydroxide – *base; cocoa, jams and sweets*

525 Potassium hydroxide – *base; sweets*
526 Calcium hydroxide – *firming agent, neutralising agent; sweets*
527 Ammonium hydroxide – *diluent and solvent for food colours, base; cocoa*
528 Magnesium hydroxide – *base; sweets*
529 Calcium oxide – *base; sweets*
530 Magnesium oxide – *anti-caking agent; cocoa products*
535 Sodium ferrocyanide
536 Potassium ferrocyanide – *anti-caking agents in salt; crystallisation aids in wine*
540 Dicalcium diphosphate – *buffer, neutralising agent; cheese*
541 Sodium aluminium phosphate – *acid, raising agent; cake mixes, self-raising flour, biscuits*
542 Edible bone phosphate – *anti-caking agent*
544 Calcium polyphosphates – *emulsifying salt; processed cheese*
545 Ammonium polyphosphates – *emulsifier, texturiser; frozen chicken*
551 Silicon dioxide (silica) – *anti-caking agent; skimmed milk powder, sweeteners*
552 Calcium silicate – *anti-caking agent, release agent; icing sugar, sweets*
553(a) Magnesium silicate synthetic; magnesium trisilicate – *anti-caking agent; sugar confectionery*
553(b) Talc – *release agent; tabletted confectionery*
554 Aluminium sodium silicate
556 Aluminium calcium silicate
558 Bentonite
559 Kaolin
570 Stearic acid – *anti-caking agents*
572 Magnesium stearate – *emulsifier, release agent; confectionery*
575 D-glucono-1, 5-lactone (glucono delta-lactone) – *acid, sequestrant; cake mixes, continental sausages*
576 Sodium gluconate
577 Potassium gluconate – *sequestrants*
578 Calcium gluconate – *buffer, firming agent, sequestrant; jams, dessert mixes*
620 L-glutamic acid
621 Sodium hydrogen L-glutamate (monosodium glutamate; MSG)
622 Potassium hydrogen L-glutamate (monopotassium glutamate)
623 Calcium dihydrogen di-L-glutamate (calcium glutamate)
627 Guanosine 5'-disodium phosphate (sodium guanylate)
631 Inosine 5'-disodium phosphate (sodium inosinate)
635 Sodium 5'-ribonucleotide – *flavour enhancers used in savoury foods and snacks, soups, sauces and meat products*
636 Maltol
637 Ethyl maltol – *flavourings/flavour enhancers used in cakes and biscuits*
900 Dimethylpolysiloxane – *anti-foaming agent*
901 Beeswax
903 Carnauba wax – *glazing agents used in sugar and chocolate confectionery*
904 Shellac – *glazing agent used to wax apples*
905 Mineral hydrocarbons – *glazing/coating agent used to prevent dried fruit sticking together*
907 Refined microcrystalline wax – *release agent; chewing gum*
920 L-cysteine hydrochloride
925 Chlorine
926 Chlorine dioxide
927 Azodicarbonamide – *flour treatment agents used to improve the texture of bread, cake and biscuit doughs*

Aluminium potassium sulphate – *firming agent; chocolate-coated cherries*
2-Aminoethanol – *base; caustic lye used to peel vegetables*
Ammonium dihydrogen orthophosphate; diammonium hydrogen othophosphate – *buffer, yeast food*
Ammonium sulphate – *yeast food*
Benzoyl peroxide – *bleaching agent in flour*
Butyl stearate – *release agent*
Calcium heptonate – *firming agent sequestrant; prepared fruit and vegetables*
Calcium phytate – *sequestrant; wine*
Dichlorodifluoromethane – *propellant and liquid freezant used to freeze food by immersion*
Diethyl ether – *solvent*
Disodium dihydrogen ethylenediamine-NNN'N'-tetra-acetate (disodium dihydrogen EDTA) – *sequestrant; brandy*
Ethanol (ethylalcohol)
Ethyl acetate
Glycerol mono-acetate (monoacetin)
Glycerol di-acetate (diacetin)
Glycerol tri-acetate (triacetin) – *solvents used to dilute and carry food colours and flavourings*
Glycine – *sequestrant, buffer, nutrient*
Hydrogen
Nitrogen – *packaging gases*
Nitrous oxide – *propellant used in aerosol packs of whipped cream*
Octadecylammonium acetate – *anti-caking agent in yeast foods used in bread*
Oxygen – *packaging gas*
Oxystearin – *sequestrant, fat crystallisation inhibitor; salad cream*
Polydextrose – *bulking agent; reduced and low calorie foods*
Propan-1, 2-diol (propylene glycol)
Propan-2-ol (isopropyl alcohol) – *solvents used to dilute colours and flavourings*
Sodium heptonate – *sequestrant; edible oils*
Spermaceti
Sperm oil – *release agents*
Tannic acid – *flavouring, clarifying agent; beer wine and cider*

The world's top wine producers

Country	*Percentage of total world wine production*	*Quantity (thousand tonnes)*
Italy	20.6	5980
France	20.3	5891
Spain	10.4	3030
Argentina	6.9	2000
USSR	6.5	1900
Germany	4	1165
Romania	3.4	1000
South Africa	3.2	944
Portugal	2.9	845

Figures date from 1989

Grape varieties

Although there are now over 4000 named varieties of grape, only a small number have a truly distinctive flavour and are capable of producing great wine. These *classic grapes* form the basis of an international category of wine.

The *major varieties* are those grapes which are also fairly widespread across the international wine market but are considered less distinctive than the classic grapes.

Australia

Classic grapes
RED
Cabernet Sauvignon
Pinot Noir
Syrah
WHITE
Riesling
Chardonnay
Sémillon

Major varieties
Muscat de Frontignan
Muscadelle

Areas
Adelaide Hills
Barossa Valley
Clare Valley
Coonawarra
Corowa-Rutherglen
Upper Hunter Valley
Lower Hunter Valley
Margaret River
Mount Barker
Mount Frankland
Padthaway
Yarra Valley

Central Europe

Classic grapes
RED
Cabernet Sauvignon
Pinot Noir
Merlot
WHITE
Riesling
Chardonnay
Sauvignon Blanc

Major varieties
Austria
Gewürztraminer
Müller-Thurgau
Muscat Ottonel
Pinot Gris
Pinot Blanc
Silvaner
Welschriesling

Bulgaria
Aligoté
Gewürztraminer

Czechoslovakia
Gewürztraminer
Pinot Blanc
Silvaner
Welschriesling

Hungary
Cabernet Franc
Gewürztraminer
Pinot Gris
Pinot Blanc
Silvaner
Welschriesling

Romania
Aligoté
Cabernet Franc
Gewürztraminer
Muscat Ottonel
Pinot Gris
Welschriesling

Russian Federation
Aligoté
Gewürztraminer
Muscat Ottonel

Yugoslavia (formerly)
Cabernet Franc
Gewürztraminer
Malvasia
Muscat Ottonel
Pinot Blanc
Pinot Gris
Welschriesling

France

Alsace
Classic grapes
RED
Pinot Noir
WHITE
Riesling

Major varieties
Gewürztraminer
Muscat
Pinot Gris

Areas
Brand
Eichberg
Geisberg
Gloeckelberg
Goldert Hatschbourg
Hengst
Kastelberg
Kessler
Kirchberg de Barr
Kirchberg de Ribeauville
Kitterle
Moenchberg
Saering
Schloss Rosacker
Sommerberg
Spiegel
Wiebelsberg

Bordeaux
Classic grapes
RED
Cabernet Sauvignon
Merlot
WHITE
Sémillon
Sauvignon Blanc

Major varieties
Cabernet Franc
Colombard

Merlot Blanc
Muscadelle
Trebbiano (Ugni Blanc)

Areas
Côtes de Blaye
Côtes de Bourg
Entre-deux-mers
Fronsac
Graves
Médoc
Pomerol
Sauternes
St-Emilion

Burgundy
Classic grapes
RED
Pinot Noir
WHITE
Chardonnay
Sauvignon Blanc

Major varieties
Gamay
Aligoté

Areas
Beaujolais
Chablis
Côte de Beaune
Côte Chalonnaise
Côte de Nuits
Hautes Côtes de Beaune
Hautes Côtes de Nuits
Maconnais

Champagne
Classic grapes
RED
Pinot Noir
WHITE
Chardonnay

Major varieties
Meunier

Areas
Ambonnay
Avize
Ay
Beaumont-sur-Vesle
Bisseuil
Bouzy
Champillon
Chigny-les-Roses
Chouilly
Cramant
Cuis
Cumieres
Dizy-Magenta
Grauves
Hautvillers
Le Mesnil-sur-Oger
Louvois
Mailly
Mareuil-sur-Ay
Montbre
Mutigny
Oger
Pierry
Puisieulx
Rilly-la-Montagne
Sillery
Tauxieres-Mutry
Tours-sur-Marne
Trepail
Vertus
Verzenay
Verzy
Villers-Marmery

Loire
Classic grapes
RED
Cabernet Sauvignon
Pinot Noir
WHITE
Chardonnay
Sauvignon Blanc
Chenin Blanc

Areas
Anjou
Anjou-Côteaux de la Loire
Anjou Gamay
Bonnezeaux
Bourgueil
Champigny
Côteaux de L'Aubance
Côteaux du Layon
Côteaux de Saumur
Jasnières
Menetou-Salon
Muscadet
Muscadet des Coteaux de la Loire
Muscadet de Sèvre-et-Maine
Pouilly Fumé
Pouilly-sur-Loire
Quarts de Chaume
Quincy
Reuilly
Rose d'Anjou
Sancerre
Saumur
Savennieres
Touraine
Vouvray-Montlouis

The Midi
Classic grapes
RED
Cabernet Sauvignon
Syrah
Merlot
WHITE
Chardonnay
Sauvignon Blanc
Chenin Blanc

Major varieties
Garnacha
Carignan
Cinsaut
Garnacha Blanca

Areas
Aude
Bouches-du-Rhone
Gard
Herault
Pyrenees-Orientales
Var
Vaucluse

Germany

Around eighty per cent of German vineyard produce is white wine. The predominant grape is the Riesling but listed below are also major local varieties which are significant in terms of both quantity and quality. They are listed in the order of the most widely planted variety per region.

Ahr
Pinot Noir
Blauer Portugieser
Riesling
Müller-Thurgau
Kerner

Baden
Pinot Noir
Pinot Gris
Chasselas
Riesling
Silvaner
Pinot Blanc
Blauer Portugieser

Franken
Müller-Thurgau
Silvaner
Riesling
Pinot Noir
Blauer Portugieser
Perle
Rieslaner

Hessische Bergstrasse
Riesling
Müller-Thurgau
Silvaner
Pinot Noir
Blauer Portugieser

Mittelrhein
Riesling
Müller-Thurgau
Kerner
Silvaner
Pinot Noir
Blauer Portugieser

Mosel-Saar-Ruwer
Riesling
Müller-Thurgau
Wiesser Elbling
Kerner

Nahe
Müller-Thurgau
Riesling
Silvaner
Kerner
Blauer Portugieser
Pinot Noir

Grape varieties (continued)

Rheingau
Riesling
Müller-Thurgau
Pinot Noir
Silvaner
Blauer Portugieser

Rheinhessen
Müller-Thurgau
Silvaner
Scheurebe
Kerner
Riesling
Morio-Muscat
Blauer Portugieser
Pinot Noir

Rheinpfalz
Müller-Thurgau
Riesling
Kerner
Silvaner
Morio-Muscat
Blauer Portugieser
Scheurebe
Pinot Noir
Gewürztraminer

Württemberg
Riesling
Blauer Trollinger
Müller-Thurgau
Kerner
Silvaner
Blauer Portugieser
Schwarzriesling
Pinot Noir
Pinot Gris

Italy

Classic grapes
RED
Cabernet Sauvignon
Pinot Noir
Merlot
WHITE
Riesling
Chardonnay
Sauvignon Blanc

Major varieties
Barbera
Cabernet Franc
Carignan
Cinsaut
Garnacha
Muscat of Alexandria
Muscat Blanc
Muscat Blanc à Petits Grains
Nebbiolo
Pinot Blanc
Pinot Gris
Sangiovese
Trebbiano
Welschriesling

Areas
Friuli-Venezia Giulia
Lombardia
Piemonte
Trentino/Alto Adige
Veneto

New Zealand

Classic grapes
RED
Cabernet Sauvignon
Pinot Noir
WHITE
Riesling
Chardonnay
Sauvignon Blanc
Chenin Blanc

Major varieties
Gamay
Gewürztraminer
Müller-Thurgau
Palomino
Silvaner

Areas
Auckland
Canterbury
Hawke's Bay
Marlborough
Nelson
Northland
Poverty Bay
Waikato

South Africa

Classic grapes
RED
Cabernet Sauvignon
Pinot Noir
Syrah
Merlot
WHITE
Riesling
Chardonnay
Sémillon
Sauvignon Blanc
Chenin Blanc

Major varieties
Cinsaut
Colombard
Muscat of Alexandria
Muscat Blanc
Muscat Blanc à Petits Grains
Palomino
Trebbiano

Areas
Malmesbury
Montagu
Olifants River
Paarl
Robertson
Stellenbosch
Worcester

South America

Classic grapes
RED
Cabernet Sauvignon
Pinot Noir
Syrah
Merlot
WHITE
Riesling
Chardonnay
Sémillon
Sauvignon Blanc
Chenin Blanc

Major varieties
Argentina
Barbera
Cabernet Franc
Gewürztraminer
Muscat à Petits Grains
Tempranillo
Trebbiano

Brasil
Trebbiano

Chile
Cabernet Franc
Carignan
Gewürztraminer
Muscat of Alexandria
Muscat à Petits Grains
Pinot Blanc

Mexico
Carignan
Colombard
Gamay
Garnacha
Palomino
Pinot Gris
Tempranillo
Trebbiano

Uruguay
Barbera
Nebbiolo
Pinot Blanc

Spain and Portugal

Spain and Portugal grow few of the international classic grapes and are better known as exporters of their own locally grown grape varieties, such as the Palomino, Tempranillo and Carignan.

Major varieties
Carignan
Garnacha
Malvasia
Palomino
Tempranillo

Areas
Algarve
Alicante

Bairrada
Bucelas
Carcavelos
Carineria
Colares
Dao
Douro
Jumilla
La Mancha
Malaga
Montilla-Moriles
Navarra
Penedes
Rioja (Alta, Alavesa, Baja)
Setubal
Tarragona
Valdepenas
Vinho Verde

USA

California
Major varieties grown in the region

Central Valley
Barbera
Carignan
Cinsaut
Emerald Riesling*
Flora
Garnacha
Muscat Blanc à Petits Grains
Palomino
Trebbiano
Zinfandel*

Mendocino, Lake
Carignan
Gamay Beaujolais
Garnacha
Gewürztraminer
Trousseau Gris
Zinfandel

Monterey, San Benito
Carignan
Colombard
Emerald Riesling
Folle Blanche
Gamay Beaujolais
Garnacha
Gewürztraminer
Melon de Bourgogne
Muscat Blanc à Petits Grains
Silvaner
Zinfandel

Napa
Cabernet Franc
Gamay Beaujolais
Gewürztraminer
Trousseau Gris
Zinfandel

San Luis Obispo, Santa Barbara
Gewürztraminer
Silvaner
Zinfandel

Sonoma
Carignan
Gamay Beaujolais
Gewürztraminer
Melon de Bourgogne
Muscadelle
Zinfandel

S California
Garnacha
Palomino
Zinfandel

*denotes quality grape varieties bred in California

Idaho
Major varieties
Gewürztraminer

Washington
Major varieties
Cabernet Franc
Garnacha
Gewürztraminer
Muscat Blanc à Petits Grains

HISTORY

THE CALENDAR

Perpetual calendar 1801–2000

The calendar for each year is given under the corresponding letter below.

1801 I	1821 C	1841 K	1861 E	1881 M	1901 E	1921 M	1941 G	1961 A	1981 I
1802 K	1822 E	1842 M	1862 G	1882 A	1902 G	1922 A	1942 I	1962 C	1982 K
1803 M	1823 G	1843 A	1863 I	1883 C	1903 I	1923 C	1943 K	1963 E	1983 M
1804 B	1824 J	1844 D	1864 L	1884 F	1904 L	1924 F	1944 N	1964 H	1984 B
1805 E	1825 M	1845 G	1865 A	1885 I	1905 A	1925 I	1945 C	1965 K	1985 E
1806 G	1826 A	1846 I	1866 C	1886 K	1906 C	1926 K	1946 E	1966 M	1986 G
1807 I	1827 C	1847 K	1867 E	1887 M	1907 E	1927 M	1947 G	1967 A	1987 I
1808 L	1828 F	1848 N	1868 H	1888 B	1908 H	1928 B	1948 J	1968 D	1988 L
1809 A	1829 I	1849 C	1869 K	1889 E	1909 K	1929 E	1949 M	1969 G	1989 A
1810 C	1830 K	1850 E	1870 M	1890 G	1910 M	1930 G	1950 A	1970 I	1990 C
1811 E	1831 M	1851 G	1871 A	1891 I	1911 A	1931 I	1951 C	1971 K	1991 E
1812 H	1832 B	1852 J	1872 D	1892 L	1912 D	1932 L	1952 F	1972 N	1992 H
1813 K	1833 E	1853 M	1873 G	1893 A	1913 G	1933 A	1953 I	1973 C	1993 K
1814 M	1834 G	1854 A	1874 I	1894 C	1914 I	1934 C	1954 K	1974 E	1994 M
1815 A	1835 I	1855 C	1875 K	1895 E	1915 K	1935 E	1955 M	1975 G	1995 A
1816 D	1836 L	1856 F	1876 N	1896 H	1916 N	1936 H	1956 B	1976 J	1996 D
1817 G	1837 A	1857 I	1877 C	1897 K	1917 C	1937 K	1957 E	1977 M	1997 G
1818 I	1838 C	1858 K	1878 E	1898 M	1918 E	1938 M	1958 G	1978 A	1998 I
1819 K	1839 E	1859 M	1879 G	1899 A	1919 G	1939 A	1959 I	1979 C	1999 K
1820 N	1840 H	1860 B	1880 J	1900 C	1920 J	1940 D	1960 L	1980 F	2000 N

A

January

S	M	T	W	T	F	S
1	2	3	4	5	6	7
8	9	10	11	12	13	14
15	16	17	18	19	20	21
22	23	24	25	26	27	28
29	30	31				

February

S	M	T	W	T	F	S
			1	2	3	4
5	6	7	8	9	10	11
12	13	14	15	16	17	18
19	20	21	22	23	24	25
26	27	28				

March

S	M	T	W	T	F	S
			1	2	3	4
5	6	7	8	9	10	11
12	13	14	15	16	17	18
19	20	21	22	23	24	25
26	27	28	29	30	31	

April

S	M	T	W	T	F	S
						1
2	3	4	5	6	7	8
9	10	11	12	13	14	15
16	17	18	19	20	21	22
23	24	25	26	27	28	29
30						

May

S	M	T	W	T	F	S
	1	2	3	4	5	6
7	8	9	10	11	12	13
14	15	16	17	18	19	20
21	22	23	24	25	26	27
28	29	30	31			

June

S	M	T	W	T	F	S
				1	2	3
4	5	6	7	8	9	10
11	12	13	14	15	16	17
18	19	20	21	22	23	24
25	26	27	28	29	30	

July

S	M	T	W	T	F	S
						1
2	3	4	5	6	7	8
9	10	11	12	13	14	15
16	17	18	19	20	21	22
23	24	25	26	27	28	29
30	31					

August

S	M	T	W	T	F	S
		1	2	3	4	5
6	7	8	9	10	11	12
13	14	15	16	17	18	19
20	21	22	23	24	25	26
27	28	29	30	31		

September

S	M	T	W	T	F	S
					1	2
3	4	5	6	7	8	9
10	11	12	13	14	15	16
17	18	19	20	21	22	23
24	25	26	27	28	29	30

October

S	M	T	W	T	F	S
1	2	3	4	5	6	7
8	9	10	11	12	13	14
15	16	17	18	19	20	21
22	23	24	25	26	27	28
29	30	31				

November

S	M	T	W	T	F	S
			1	2	3	4
5	6	7	8	9	10	11
12	13	14	15	16	17	18
19	20	21	22	23	24	25
26	27	28	29	30		

December

S	M	T	W	T	F	S
					1	2
3	4	5	6	7	8	9
10	11	12	13	14	15	16
17	18	19	20	21	22	23
24	25	26	27	28	29	30
31						

B (leap year)

January

S	M	T	W	T	F	S
1	2	3	4	5	6	7
8	9	10	11	12	13	14
15	16	17	18	19	20	21
22	23	24	25	26	27	28
29	30	31				

February

S	M	T	W	T	F	S
			1	2	3	4
5	6	7	8	9	10	11
12	13	14	15	16	17	18
19	20	21	22	23	24	25
26	27	28	29			

March

S	M	T	W	T	F	S
				1	2	3
4	5	6	7	8	9	10
11	12	13	14	15	16	17
18	19	20	21	22	23	24
25	26	27	28	29	30	31

April

S	M	T	W	T	F	S
1	2	3	4	5	6	7
8	9	10	11	12	13	14
15	16	17	18	19	20	21
22	23	24	25	26	27	28
29	30					

May

S	M	T	W	T	F	S
		1	2	3	4	5
6	7	8	9	10	11	12
13	14	15	16	17	18	19
20	21	22	23	24	25	26
27	28	29	30	31		

June

S	M	T	W	T	F	S
					1	2
3	4	5	6	7	8	9
10	11	12	13	14	15	16
17	18	19	20	21	22	23
24	25	26	27	28	29	30

July

S	M	T	W	T	F	S
1	2	3	4	5	6	7
8	9	10	11	12	13	14
15	16	17	18	19	20	21
22	23	24	25	26	27	28
29	30	31				

August

S	M	T	W	T	F	S
			1	2	3	4
5	6	7	8	9	10	11
12	13	14	15	16	17	18
19	20	21	22	23	24	25
26	27	28	29	30	31	

September

S	M	T	W	T	F	S
						1
2	3	4	5	6	7	8
9	10	11	12	13	14	15
16	17	18	19	20	21	22
23	24	25	26	27	28	29
30						

October

S	M	T	W	T	F	S
	1	2	3	4	5	6
7	8	9	10	11	12	13
14	15	16	17	18	19	20
21	22	23	24	25	26	27
28	29	30	31			

November

S	M	T	W	T	F	S
				1	2	3
4	5	6	7	8	9	10
11	12	13	14	15	16	17
18	19	20	21	22	23	24
25	26	27	28	29	30	

December

S	M	T	W	T	F	S
						1
2	3	4	5	6	7	8
9	10	11	12	13	14	15
16	17	18	19	20	21	22
23	24	25	26	27	28	29
30	31					

Perpetual calendar 1801–2000 (continued)

C

January

S	M	T	W	T	F	S
	1	2	3	4	5	6
7	8	9	10	11	12	13
14	15	16	17	18	19	20
21	22	23	24	25	26	27
28	29	30	31			

February

S	M	T	W	T	F	S
				1	2	3
4	5	6	7	8	9	10
11	12	13	14	15	16	17
18	19	20	21	22	23	24
25	26	27	28			

March

S	M	T	W	T	F	S
				1	2	3
4	5	6	7	8	9	10
11	12	13	14	15	16	17
18	19	20	21	22	23	24
25	26	27	28	29	30	31

April

S	M	T	W	T	F	S
1	2	3	4	5	6	7
8	9	10	11	12	13	14
15	16	17	18	19	20	21
22	23	24	25	26	27	28
29	30					

May

S	M	T	W	T	F	S
		1	2	3	4	5
6	7	8	9	10	11	12
13	14	15	16	17	18	19
20	21	22	23	24	25	26
27	28	29	30	31		

June

S	M	T	W	T	F	S
					1	2
3	4	5	6	7	8	9
10	11	12	13	14	15	16
17	18	19	20	21	22	23
24	25	26	27	28	29	30

July

S	M	T	W	T	F	S
1	2	3	4	5	6	7
8	9	10	11	12	13	14
15	16	17	18	19	20	21
22	23	24	25	26	27	28
29	30	31				

August

S	M	T	W	T	F	S
			1	2	3	4
5	6	7	8	9	10	11
12	13	14	15	16	17	18
19	20	21	22	23	24	25
26	27	28	29	30	31	

September

S	M	T	W	T	F	S
						1
2	3	4	5	6	7	8
9	10	11	12	13	14	15
16	17	18	19	20	21	22
23	24	25	26	27	28	29
30						

October

S	M	T	W	T	F	S
	1	2	3	4	5	6
7	8	9	10	11	12	13
14	15	16	17	18	19	20
21	22	23	24	25	26	27
28	29	30	31			

November

S	M	T	W	T	F	S
				1	2	3
4	5	6	7	8	9	10
11	12	13	14	15	16	17
18	19	20	21	22	23	24
25	26	27	28	29	30	

December

S	M	T	W	T	F	S
						1
2	3	4	5	6	7	8
9	10	11	12	13	14	15
16	17	18	19	20	21	22
23	24	25	26	27	28	29
30	31					

D (leap year)

January

S	M	T	W	T	F	S
	1	2	3	4	5	6
7	8	9	10	11	12	13
14	15	16	17	18	19	20
21	22	23	24	25	26	27
28	29	30	31			

February

S	M	T	W	T	F	S
				1	2	3
4	5	6	7	8	9	10
11	12	13	14	15	16	17
18	19	20	21	22	23	24
25	26	27	28	29		

March

S	M	T	W	T	F	S
					1	2
3	4	5	6	7	8	9
10	11	12	13	14	15	16
17	18	19	20	21	22	23
24	25	26	27	28	29	30
31						

April

S	M	T	W	T	F	S
	1	2	3	4	5	6
7	8	9	10	11	12	13
14	15	16	17	18	19	20
21	22	23	24	25	26	27
28	29	30				

May

S	M	T	W	T	F	S
			1	2	3	4
5	6	7	8	9	10	11
12	13	14	15	16	17	18
19	20	21	22	23	24	25
26	27	28	29	30	31	

June

S	M	T	W	T	F	S
						1
2	3	4	5	6	7	8
9	10	11	12	13	14	15
16	17	18	19	20	21	22
23	24	25	26	27	28	29
30						

July

S	M	T	W	T	F	S
	1	2	3	4	5	6
7	8	9	10	11	12	13
14	15	16	17	18	19	20
21	22	23	24	25	26	27
28	29	30	31			

August

S	M	T	W	T	F	S
				1	2	3
4	5	6	7	8	9	10
11	12	13	14	15	16	17
18	19	20	21	22	23	24
25	26	27	28	29	30	31

September

S	M	T	W	T	F	S
1	2	3	4	5	6	7
8	9	10	11	12	13	14
15	16	17	18	19	20	21
22	23	24	25	26	27	28
29	30					

October

S	M	T	W	T	F	S
		1	2	3	4	5
6	7	8	9	10	11	12
13	14	15	16	17	18	19
20	21	22	23	24	25	26
27	28	29	30	31		

November

S	M	T	W	T	F	S
					1	2
3	4	5	6	7	8	9
10	11	12	13	14	15	16
17	18	19	20	21	22	23
24	25	26	27	28	29	30

December

S	M	T	W	T	F	S
1	2	3	4	5	6	7
8	9	10	11	12	13	14
15	16	17	18	19	20	21
22	23	24	25	26	27	28
29	30	31				

E

January

S	M	T	W	T	F	S
		1	2	3	4	5
6	7	8	9	10	11	12
13	14	15	16	17	18	19
20	21	22	23	24	25	26
27	28	29	30	31		

February

S	M	T	W	T	F	S
					1	2
3	4	5	6	7	8	9
10	11	12	13	14	15	16
17	18	19	20	21	22	23
24	25	26	27	28		

March

S	M	T	W	T	F	S
					1	2
3	4	5	6	7	8	9
10	11	12	13	14	15	16
17	18	19	20	21	22	23
24	25	26	27	28	29	30
31						

April

S	M	T	W	T	F	S
	1	2	3	4	5	6
7	8	9	10	11	12	13
14	15	16	17	18	19	20
21	22	23	24	25	26	27
28	29	30				

May

S	M	T	W	T	F	S
			1	2	3	4
5	6	7	8	9	10	11
12	13	14	15	16	17	18
19	20	21	22	23	24	25
26	27	28	29	30	31	

June

S	M	T	W	T	F	S
						1
2	3	4	5	6	7	8
9	10	11	12	13	14	15
16	17	18	19	20	21	22
23	24	25	26	27	28	29
30						

July

S	M	T	W	T	F	S
	1	2	3	4	5	6
7	8	9	10	11	12	13
14	15	16	17	18	19	20
21	22	23	24	25	26	27
28	29	30	31			

August

S	M	T	W	T	F	S
				1	2	3
4	5	6	7	8	9	10
11	12	13	14	15	16	17
18	19	20	21	22	23	24
25	26	27	28	29	30	31

September

S	M	T	W	T	F	S
1	2	3	4	5	6	7
8	9	10	11	12	13	14
15	16	17	18	19	20	21
22	23	24	25	26	27	28
29	30					

October

S	M	T	W	T	F	S
		1	2	3	4	5
6	7	8	9	10	11	12
13	14	15	16	17	18	19
20	21	22	23	24	25	26
27	28	29	30	31		

November

S	M	T	W	T	F	S
					1	2
3	4	5	6	7	8	9
10	11	12	13	14	15	16
17	18	19	20	21	22	23
24	25	26	27	28	29	30

December

S	M	T	W	T	F	S
1	2	3	4	5	6	7
8	9	10	11	12	13	14
15	16	17	18	19	20	21
22	23	24	25	26	27	28
29	30	31				

F (leap year)

January

S	M	T	W	T	F	S
		1	2	3	4	5
6	7	8	9	10	11	12
13	14	15	16	17	18	19
20	21	22	23	24	25	26
27	28	29	30	31		

February

S	M	T	W	T	F	S
					1	2
3	4	5	6	7	8	9
10	11	12	13	14	15	16
17	18	19	20	21	22	23
24	25	26	27	28	29	

March

S	M	T	W	T	F	S
						1
2	3	4	5	6	7	8
9	10	11	12	13	14	15
16	17	18	19	20	21	22
23	24	25	26	27	28	29
30	31					

April

S	M	T	W	T	F	S
		1	2	3	4	5
6	7	8	9	10	11	12
13	14	15	16	17	18	19
20	21	22	23	24	25	26
27	28	29	30			

May

S	M	T	W	T	F	S
				1	2	3
4	5	6	7	8	9	10
11	12	13	14	15	16	17
18	19	20	21	22	23	24
25	26	27	28	29	30	31

June

S	M	T	W	T	F	S
1	2	3	4	5	6	7
8	9	10	11	12	13	14
15	16	17	18	19	20	21
22	23	24	25	26	27	28
29	30					

July

S	M	T	W	T	F	S
		1	2	3	4	5
6	7	8	9	10	11	12
13	14	15	16	17	18	19
20	21	22	23	24	25	26
27	28	29	30	31		

August

S	M	T	W	T	F	S
					1	2
3	4	5	6	7	8	9
10	11	12	13	14	15	16
17	18	19	20	21	22	23
24	25	26	27	28	29	30
31						

September

S	M	T	W	T	F	S
	1	2	3	4	5	6
7	8	9	10	11	12	13
14	15	16	17	18	19	20
21	22	23	24	25	26	27
28	29	30				

October

S	M	T	W	T	F	S
			1	2	3	4
5	6	7	8	9	10	11
12	13	14	15	16	17	18
19	20	21	22	23	24	25
26	27	28	29	30	31	

November

S	M	T	W	T	F	S
						1
2	3	4	5	6	7	8
9	10	11	12	13	14	15
16	17	18	19	20	21	22
23	24	25	26	27	28	29
30						

December

S	M	T	W	T	F	S
	1	2	3	4	5	6
7	8	9	10	11	12	13
14	15	16	17	18	19	20
21	22	23	24	25	26	27
28	29	30	31			

G

January

S	M	T	W	T	F	S
			1	2	3	4
5	6	7	8	9	10	11
12	13	14	15	16	17	18
19	20	21	22	23	24	25
26	27	28	29	30	31	

February

S	M	T	W	T	F	S
						1
2	3	4	5	6	7	8
9	10	11	12	13	14	15
16	17	18	19	20	21	22
23	24	25	26	27	28	

March

S	M	T	W	T	F	S
						1
2	3	4	5	6	7	8
9	10	11	12	13	14	15
16	17	18	19	20	21	22
23	24	25	26	27	28	29
30	31					

April

S	M	T	W	T	F	S
		1	2	3	4	5
6	7	8	9	10	11	12
13	14	15	16	17	18	19
20	21	22	23	24	25	26
27	28	29	30			

May

S	M	T	W	T	F	S
				1	2	3
4	5	6	7	8	9	10
11	12	13	14	15	16	17
18	19	20	21	22	23	24
25	26	27	28	29	30	31

June

S	M	T	W	T	F	S
1	2	3	4	5	6	7
8	9	10	11	12	13	14
15	16	17	18	19	20	21
22	23	24	25	26	27	28
29	30					

July

S	M	T	W	T	F	S
		1	2	3	4	5
6	7	8	9	10	11	12
13	14	15	16	17	18	19
20	21	22	23	24	25	26
27	28	29	30	31		

August

S	M	T	W	T	F	S
					1	2
3	4	5	6	7	8	9
10	11	12	13	14	15	16
17	18	19	20	21	22	23
24	25	26	27	28	29	30
31						

September

S	M	T	W	T	F	S
	1	2	3	4	5	6
7	8	9	10	11	12	13
14	15	16	17	18	19	20
21	22	23	24	25	26	27
28	29	30				

October

S	M	T	W	T	F	S
			1	2	3	4
5	6	7	8	9	10	11
12	13	14	15	16	17	18
19	20	21	22	23	24	25
26	27	28	29	30	31	

November

S	M	T	W	T	F	S
						1
2	3	4	5	6	7	8
9	10	11	12	13	14	15
16	17	18	19	20	21	22
23	24	25	26	27	28	29
30						

December

S	M	T	W	T	F	S
	1	2	3	4	5	6
7	8	9	10	11	12	13
14	15	16	17	18	19	20
21	22	23	24	25	26	27
28	29	30	31			

H (leap year)

January

S	M	T	W	T	F	S
			1	2	3	4
5	6	7	8	9	10	11
12	13	14	15	16	17	18
19	20	21	22	23	24	25
26	27	28	29	30	31	

February

S	M	T	W	T	F	S
						1
2	3	4	5	6	7	8
9	10	11	12	13	14	15
16	17	18	19	20	21	22
23	24	25	26	27	28	29

March

S	M	T	W	T	F	S
1	2	3	4	5	6	7
8	9	10	11	12	13	14
15	16	17	18	19	20	21
22	23	24	25	26	27	28
29	30	31				

April

S	M	T	W	T	F	S
			1	2	3	4
5	6	7	8	9	10	11
12	13	14	15	16	17	18
19	20	21	22	23	24	25
26	27	28	29	30		

May

S	M	T	W	T	F	S
					1	2
3	4	5	6	7	8	9
10	11	12	13	14	15	16
17	18	19	20	21	22	23
24	25	26	27	28	29	30
31						

June

S	M	T	W	T	F	S
	1	2	3	4	5	6
7	8	9	10	11	12	13
14	15	16	17	18	19	20
21	22	23	24	25	26	27
28	29	30				

July

S	M	T	W	T	F	S
			1	2	3	4
5	6	7	8	9	10	11
12	13	14	15	16	17	18
19	20	21	22	23	24	25
26	27	28	29	30	31	

August

S	M	T	W	T	F	S
						1
2	3	4	5	6	7	8
9	10	11	12	13	14	15
16	17	18	19	20	21	22
23	24	25	26	27	28	29
30	31					

September

S	M	T	W	T	F	S
		1	2	3	4	5
6	7	8	9	10	11	12
13	14	15	16	17	18	19
20	21	22	23	24	25	26
27	28	29	30			

October

S	M	T	W	T	F	S
				1	2	3
4	5	6	7	8	9	10
11	12	13	14	15	16	17
18	19	20	21	22	23	24
25	26	27	28	29	30	31

November

S	M	T	W	T	F	S
1	2	3	4	5	6	7
8	9	10	11	12	13	14
15	16	17	18	19	20	21
22	23	24	25	26	27	28
29	30					

December

S	M	T	W	T	F	S
		1	2	3	4	5
6	7	8	9	10	11	12
13	14	15	16	17	18	19
20	21	22	23	24	25	26
27	28	29	30	31		

I

January

S	M	T	W	T	F	S
				1	2	3
4	5	6	7	8	9	10
11	12	13	14	15	16	17
18	19	20	21	22	23	24
25	26	27	28	29	30	31

February

S	M	T	W	T	F	S
1	2	3	4	5	6	7
8	9	10	11	12	13	14
15	16	17	18	19	20	21
22	23	24	25	26	27	28

March

S	M	T	W	T	F	S
1	2	3	4	5	6	7
8	9	10	11	12	13	14
15	16	17	18	19	20	21
22	23	24	25	26	27	28
29	30	31				

April

S	M	T	W	T	F	S
			1	2	3	4
5	6	7	8	9	10	11
12	13	14	15	16	17	18
19	20	21	22	23	24	25
26	27	28	29	30		

May

S	M	T	W	T	F	S
					1	2
3	4	5	6	7	8	9
10	11	12	13	14	15	16
17	18	19	20	21	22	23
24	25	26	27	28	29	30
31						

June

S	M	T	W	T	F	S
	1	2	3	4	5	6
7	8	9	10	11	12	13
14	15	16	17	18	19	20
21	22	23	24	25	26	27
28	29	30				

July

S	M	T	W	T	F	S
			1	2	3	4
5	6	7	8	9	10	11
12	13	14	15	16	17	18
19	20	21	22	23	24	25
26	27	28	29	30	31	

August

S	M	T	W	T	F	S
						1
2	3	4	5	6	7	8
9	10	11	12	13	14	15
16	17	18	19	20	21	22
23	24	25	26	27	28	29
30	31					

September

S	M	T	W	T	F	S
		1	2	3	4	5
6	7	8	9	10	11	12
13	14	15	16	17	18	19
20	21	22	23	24	25	26
27	28	29	30			

October

S	M	T	W	T	F	S
				1	2	3
4	5	6	7	8	9	10
11	12	13	14	15	16	17
18	19	20	21	22	23	24
25	26	27	28	29	30	31

November

S	M	T	W	T	F	S
1	2	3	4	5	6	7
8	9	10	11	12	13	14
15	16	17	18	19	20	21
22	23	24	25	26	27	28
29	30					

December

S	M	T	W	T	F	S
		1	2	3	4	5
6	7	8	9	10	11	12
13	14	15	16	17	18	19
20	21	22	23	24	25	26
27	28	29	30	31		

J (leap year)

January

S	M	T	W	T	F	S
				1	2	3
4	5	6	7	8	9	10
11	12	13	14	15	16	17
18	19	20	21	22	23	24
25	26	27	28	29	30	31

February

S	M	T	W	T	F	S
1	2	3	4	5	6	7
8	9	10	11	12	13	14
15	16	17	18	19	20	21
22	23	24	25	26	27	28
29						

March

S	M	T	W	T	F	S
	1	2	3	4	5	6
7	8	9	10	11	12	13
14	15	16	17	18	19	20
21	22	23	24	25	26	27
28	29	30	31			

April

S	M	T	W	T	F	S
				1	2	3
4	5	6	7	8	9	10
11	12	13	14	15	16	17
18	19	20	21	22	23	24
25	26	27	28	29	30	

May

S	M	T	W	T	F	S
						1
2	3	4	5	6	7	8
9	10	11	12	13	14	15
16	17	18	19	20	21	22
23	24	25	26	27	28	29
30	31					

June

S	M	T	W	T	F	S
		1	2	3	4	5
6	7	8	9	10	11	12
13	14	15	16	17	18	19
20	21	22	23	24	25	26
27	28	29	30			

July

S	M	T	W	T	F	S
				1	2	3
4	5	6	7	8	9	10
11	12	13	14	15	16	17
18	19	20	21	22	23	24
25	26	27	28	29	30	31

August

S	M	T	W	T	F	S
1	2	3	4	5	6	7
8	9	10	11	12	13	14
15	16	17	18	19	20	21
22	23	24	25	26	27	28
29	30	31				

September

S	M	T	W	T	F	S
			1	2	3	4
5	6	7	8	9	10	11
12	13	14	15	16	17	18
19	20	21	22	23	24	25
26	27	28	29	30		

October

S	M	T	W	T	F	S
					1	2
3	4	5	6	7	8	9
10	11	12	13	14	15	16
17	18	19	20	21	22	23
24	25	26	27	28	29	30
31						

November

S	M	T	W	T	F	S
	1	2	3	4	5	6
7	8	9	10	11	12	13
14	15	16	17	18	19	20
21	22	23	24	25	26	27
28	29	30				

December

S	M	T	W	T	F	S
			1	2	3	4
5	6	7	8	9	10	11
12	13	14	15	16	17	18
19	20	21	22	23	24	25
26	27	28	29	30	31	

K

January

S	M	T	W	T	F	S
					1	2
3	4	5	6	7	8	9
10	11	12	13	14	15	16
17	18	19	20	21	22	23
24	25	26	27	28	29	30
31						

February

S	M	T	W	T	F	S
	1	2	3	4	5	6
7	8	9	10	11	12	13
14	15	16	17	18	19	20
21	22	23	24	25	26	27
28						

March

S	M	T	W	T	F	S
	1	2	3	4	5	6
7	8	9	10	11	12	13
14	15	16	17	18	19	20
21	22	23	24	25	26	27
28	29	30	31			

April

S	M	T	W	T	F	S
				1	2	3
4	5	6	7	8	9	10
11	12	13	14	15	16	17
18	19	20	21	22	23	24
25	26	27	28	29	30	

May

S	M	T	W	T	F	S
						1
2	3	4	5	6	7	8
9	10	11	12	13	14	15
16	17	18	19	20	21	22
23	24	25	26	27	28	29
30	31					

June

S	M	T	W	T	F	S
		1	2	3	4	5
6	7	8	9	10	11	12
13	14	15	16	17	18	19
20	21	22	23	24	25	26
27	28	29	30			

July

S	M	T	W	T	F	S
				1	2	3
4	5	6	7	8	9	10
11	12	13	14	15	16	17
18	19	20	21	22	23	24
25	26	27	28	29	30	31

August

S	M	T	W	T	F	S
1	2	3	4	5	6	7
8	9	10	11	12	13	14
15	16	17	18	19	20	21
22	23	24	25	26	27	28
29	30	31				

September

S	M	T	W	T	F	S
			1	2	3	4
5	6	7	8	9	10	11
12	13	14	15	16	17	18
19	20	21	22	23	24	25
26	27	28	29	30		

October

S	M	T	W	T	F	S
					1	2
3	4	5	6	7	8	9
10	11	12	13	14	15	16
17	18	19	20	21	22	23
24	25	26	27	28	29	30
31						

November

S	M	T	W	T	F	S
	1	2	3	4	5	6
7	8	9	10	11	12	13
14	15	16	17	18	19	20
21	22	23	24	25	26	27
28	29	30				

December

S	M	T	W	T	F	S
			1	2	3	4
5	6	7	8	9	10	11
12	13	14	15	16	17	18
19	20	21	22	23	24	25
26	27	28	29	30	31	

L (leap year)

January

S	M	T	W	T	F	S
					1	2
3	4	5	6	7	8	9
10	11	12	13	14	15	16
17	18	19	20	21	22	23
24	25	26	27	28	29	30
31						

February

S	M	T	W	T	F	S
	1	2	3	4	5	6
7	8	9	10	11	12	13
14	15	16	17	18	19	20
21	22	23	24	25	26	27
28	29					

March

S	M	T	W	T	F	S
		1	2	3	4	5
6	7	8	9	10	11	12
13	14	15	16	17	18	19
20	21	22	23	24	25	26
27	28	29	30	31		

April

S	M	T	W	T	F	S
					1	2
3	4	5	6	7	8	9
10	11	12	13	14	15	16
17	18	19	20	21	22	23
24	25	26	27	28	29	30

May

S	M	T	W	T	F	S
1	2	3	4	5	6	7
8	9	10	11	12	13	14
15	16	17	18	19	20	21
22	23	24	25	26	27	28
29	30	31				

June

S	M	T	W	T	F	S
			1	2	3	4
5	6	7	8	9	10	11
12	13	14	15	16	17	18
19	20	21	22	23	24	25
26	27	28	29	30		

July

S	M	T	W	T	F	S
					1	2
3	4	5	6	7	8	9
10	11	12	13	14	15	16
17	18	19	20	21	22	23
24	25	26	27	28	29	30
31						

August

S	M	T	W	T	F	S
	1	2	3	4	5	6
7	8	9	10	11	12	13
14	15	16	17	18	19	20
21	22	23	24	25	26	27
28	29	30	31			

September

S	M	T	W	T	F	S
				1	2	3
4	5	6	7	8	9	10
11	12	13	14	15	16	17
18	19	20	21	22	23	24
25	26	27	28	29	30	

October

S	M	T	W	T	F	S
						1
2	3	4	5	6	7	8
9	10	11	12	13	14	15
16	17	18	19	20	21	22
23	24	25	26	27	28	29
30	31					

November

S	M	T	W	T	F	S
		1	2	3	4	5
6	7	8	9	10	11	12
13	14	15	16	17	18	19
20	21	22	23	24	25	26
27	28	29	30			

December

S	M	T	W	T	F	S
				1	2	3
4	5	6	7	8	9	10
11	12	13	14	15	16	17
18	19	20	21	22	23	24
25	26	27	28	29	30	31

M

January

S	M	T	W	T	F	S
						1
2	3	4	5	6	7	8
9	10	11	12	13	14	15
16	17	18	19	20	21	22
23	24	25	26	27	28	29
30	31					

February

S	M	T	W	T	F	S
		1	2	3	4	5
6	7	8	9	10	11	12
13	14	15	16	17	18	19
20	21	22	23	24	25	26
27	28					

March

S	M	T	W	T	F	S
		1	2	3	4	5
6	7	8	9	10	11	12
13	14	15	16	17	18	19
20	21	22	23	24	25	26
27	28	29	30	31		

April

S	M	T	W	T	F	S
					1	2
3	4	5	6	7	8	9
10	11	12	13	14	15	16
17	18	19	20	21	22	23
24	25	26	27	28	29	30

May

S	M	T	W	T	F	S
1	2	3	4	5	6	7
8	9	10	11	12	13	14
15	16	17	18	19	20	21
22	23	24	25	26	27	28
29	30	31				

June

S	M	T	W	T	F	S
			1	2	3	4
5	6	7	8	9	10	11
12	13	14	15	16	17	18
19	20	21	22	23	24	25
26	27	28	29	30		

July

S	M	T	W	T	F	S
					1	2
3	4	5	6	7	8	9
10	11	12	13	14	15	16
17	18	19	20	21	22	23
24	25	26	27	28	29	30
31						

August

S	M	T	W	T	F	S
	1	2	3	4	5	6
7	8	9	10	11	12	13
14	15	16	17	18	19	20
21	22	23	24	25	26	27
28	29	30	31			

September

S	M	T	W	T	F	S
				1	2	3
4	5	6	7	8	9	10
11	12	13	14	15	16	17
18	19	20	21	22	23	24
25	26	27	28	29	30	

October

S	M	T	W	T	F	S
						1
2	3	4	5	6	7	8
9	10	11	12	13	14	15
16	17	18	19	20	21	22
23	24	25	26	27	28	29
30	31					

November

S	M	T	W	T	F	S
		1	2	3	4	5
6	7	8	9	10	11	12
13	14	15	16	17	18	19
20	21	22	23	24	25	26
27	28	29	30			

December

S	M	T	W	T	F	S
				1	2	3
4	5	6	7	8	9	10
11	12	13	14	15	16	17
18	19	20	21	22	23	24
25	26	27	28	29	30	31

N (leap year)

January

S	M	T	W	T	F	S
						1
2	3	4	5	6	7	8
9	10	11	12	13	14	15
16	17	18	19	20	21	22
23	24	25	26	27	28	29
30	31					

February

S	M	T	W	T	F	S
		1	2	3	4	5
6	7	8	9	10	11	12
13	14	15	16	17	18	19
20	21	22	23	24	25	26
27	28	29				

March

S	M	T	W	T	F	S
			1	2	3	4
5	6	7	8	9	10	11
12	13	14	15	16	17	18
19	20	21	22	23	24	25
26	27	28	29	30	31	

April

S	M	T	W	T	F	S
						1
2	3	4	5	6	7	8
9	10	11	12	13	14	15
16	17	18	19	20	21	22
23	24	25	26	27	28	29
30						

May

S	M	T	W	T	F	S
	1	2	3	4	5	6
7	8	9	10	11	12	13
14	15	16	17	18	19	20
21	22	23	24	25	26	27
28	29	30	31			

June

S	M	T	W	T	F	S
				1	2	3
4	5	6	7	8	9	10
11	12	13	14	15	16	17
18	19	20	21	22	23	24
25	26	27	28	29	30	

July

S	M	T	W	T	F	S
						1
2	3	4	5	6	7	8
9	10	11	12	13	14	15
16	17	18	19	20	21	22
23	24	25	26	27	28	29
30	31					

August

S	M	T	W	T	F	S
		1	2	3	4	5
6	7	8	9	10	11	12
13	14	15	16	17	18	19
20	21	22	23	24	25	26
27	28	29	30	31		

September

S	M	T	W	T	F	S
					1	2
3	4	5	6	7	8	9
10	11	12	13	14	15	16
17	18	19	20	21	22	23
24	25	26	27	28	29	30

October

S	M	T	W	T	F	S
1	2	3	4	5	6	7
8	9	10	11	12	13	14
15	16	17	18	19	20	21
22	23	24	25	26	27	28
29	30	31				

November

S	M	T	W	T	F	S
			1	2	3	4
5	6	7	8	9	10	11
12	13	14	15	16	17	18
19	20	21	22	23	24	25
26	27	28	29	30		

December

S	M	T	W	T	F	S
					1	2
3	4	5	6	7	8	9
10	11	12	13	14	15	16
17	18	19	20	21	22	23
24	25	26	27	28	29	30
31						

The seasons

N hemisphere	*S hemisphere*	*Duration*
Spring	Autumn	From vernal/autumnal equinox (c. 21 Mar) to summer/winter solstice (c. 21 Jun)
Summer	Winter	From summer/winter solstice (c. 21 Jun) to autumnal/spring equinox (c. 23 Sept)
Autumn	Spring	From autumnal/spring equinox (c. 23 Sept) to winter/summer solstice (c. 21 Dec)
Winter	Summer	From winter/summer solstice (c. 21 Dec) to vernal/autumnal equinox (c. 21 Mar)

Wedding anniversaries

In many Western countries, different wedding anniversaries have become associated with gifts of different materials. There is some variation between countries.

1st	Cotton	14th	Ivory
2nd	Paper	15th	Crystal
3rd	Leather	20th	China
4th	Fruit, flowers	25th	Silver
5th	Wood	30th	Pearl
6th	Sugar	35th	Coral
7th	Copper, wool	40th	Ruby
8th	Bronze, pottery	45th	Sapphire
9th	Pottery, willow	50th	Gold
10th	Tin	55th	Emerald
11th	Steel	60th	Diamond
12th	Silk, linen	70th	Platinum
13th	Lace		

Year equivalents

Jewish[a] (AM)	*Islamic[b] (H)*	*Hindu[c] (SE)*
5750 (30 Sep 1989–19 Sep 1990)	1410 (4 Aug 1989–23 Jul 1990)	1911 (22 Mar 1989–21 Mar 1990)
5751 (20 Sep 1990–8 Sep 1991)	1411 (24 Jul 1990–12 Jul 1991)	1912 (22 Mar 1990–21 Mar 1991)
5752 (9 Sep 1991–27 Sep 1992)	1412 (13 Jul 1991–1 Jul 1992)	1913 (22 Mar 1991–20 Mar 1992)
5753 (28 Sep 1992–15 Sep 1993)	1413 (2 Jul 1992–20 Jun 1993)	1914 (21 Mar 1992–21 Mar 1993)
5754 (16 Sep 1993–5 Sep 1994)	1414 (21 Jun 1993–9 Jun 1994)	1915 (22 Mar 1993–21 Mar 1994)
5755 (6 Sep 1994–24 Sep 1995)	1415 (10 Jun 1994–30 May 1995)	1916 (22 Mar 1994–21 Mar 1995)
5756 (25 Sep 1995–13 Sep 1996)	1416 (31 May 1995–18 May 1996)	1917 (22 Mar 1995–20 Mar 1996)
5757 (14 Sep 1996–1 Oct 1997)	1417 (19 May 1996–8 May 1997)	1918 (21 Mar 1996–21 Mar 1997)
5758 (2 Oct 1997–20 Sep 1998)	1418 (9 May 1997–27 Apr 1998)	1919 (22 Mar 1997–21 Mar 1998)
5759 (21 Sep 1998–10 Sep 1999)	1419 (28 Apr 1998–16 Apr 1999)	1920 (22 Mar 1998–21 Mar 1999)
5760 (11 Sep 1999–29 Sep 2000)	1420 (17 Apr 1999–5 Apr 2000)	1921 (22 Mar 1999–21 Mar 2000)

Gregorian equivalents are given in parentheses and are AD (= Anno Domini).

[a] Calculated from 3761 BC, said to be the year of the creation of the world. AM = Anno Mundi.

[b] Calculated from AD 622, the year in which the Prophet went from Mecca to Medina. H = Hegira.

[c] Calculated from AD 78, the beginning of the Saka era (SE), used alongside Gregorian dates in Government of India publications since 22 Mar 1957. Other important Hindu eras include: Vikrama era (58 BC), Kalacuri era (AD 248), Gupta era (AD 320), and Harsa era (AD 606).

Month equivalents

Gregorian equivalents to other calendars are given in parentheses; the figures refer to the number of solar days in each month.

Gregorian	*Jewish*	*Islamic*	*Hindu*
(Basis: Sun)	(Basis: Moon)	(Basis: Moon)	(Basis: Moon)
January (31)	Tishri (Sep–Oct) (30)	Muharram (Sep–Oct) (30)	Caitra (Mar–Apr) (29 or 30)
February (28 or 29)	Heshvan (Oct–Nov) (29 or 30)	Safar (Oct–Nov) (29)	Vaisakha (Apr–May) (29 or 30)
March (31)	Kislev (Nov–Dec) (29 or 30)	Rabi I (Nov–Dec) (30)	Jyaistha (May–Jun) (29 or 30)
April (30)	Tevet (Dec–Jan) (29)	Rabi II (Dec–Jan) (29)	Asadha (Jun–Jul) (29 or 30)
May (31)	Shevat (Jan–Feb) (30)	Jumada I (Jan–Feb) (30)	Dvitiya Asadha *certain leap years*
June (30)	Adar (Feb–Mar) (29 or 30)	Jumada II (Feb–Mar) (29)	Svrana (Jul–Aug) (29 or 30)
July (31)	Adar Sheni *leap years only*	Rajab (Mar–Apr) (30)	Dvitiya Sravana *certain leap years*
August (31)	Nisan (Mar–Apr) (30)	Shaban (Apr–May) (29)	Bhadrapada (Aug–Sep) (29 or 30)
September (30)	Iyar (Apr–May) (29)	Ramadan (May–Jun) (30)	Asvina (Sep–Oct) (29 or 30)
October (31)	Sivan (May–Jun) (30)	Shawwal (Jun–Jul) (29)	Karttika (Oct–Nov) (29 or 30)
November (30)	Tammuz (Jun–Jul) (29)	Dhu al-Qadah (Jul–Aug) (30)	Margasirsa (Nov–Dec) (29 or 30)
December (31)	Av (Jul–Aug) (30)	Dhu al-Hijjah (Aug–Sep) (29 or 30)	Pausa (Dec–Jan) (29 or 30)
	Elul (Aug–Sep) (29)		Magha (Jan–Feb) (29 or 30)
			Phalguna (Feb–Mar) (29 or 30)

Names of the months

Month	Name origin
January	Janus, the two-faced god of gates
February	Februa, day of purification (February 15)
March	Mars, god of War
April	Apru, Etruscan goddess of love
May	Maia, eldest daughter of Atlas
June	Juno, wife of Jupiter
July	Julius Caesar
August	Augustus, adopted son of Julius Caesar
September	The seventh month of the earlier Roman calendar
October	The eighth month of the earlier Roman calendar
November	The ninth month of the earlier Roman calendar
December	The tenth month of the earlier Roman calendar

Months: associations

In many Western countries, the months are traditionally associated with gemstones and flowers. There is considerable variation between countries. The following combinations are widely recognized in North America and the UK.

	Gemstone	Flower
January	Garnet	Carnation, snowdrop
February	Amethyst	Primrose, violet
March	Aquamarine, bloodstone	Jonquil, violet
April	Diamond	Daisy, sweet pea
May	Emerald	Hawthorn, lily of the valley
June	Alexandrite, moonstone, pearl	Honeysuckle, rose
July	Ruby	Larkspur, water lily
August	Peridot, sardonyx	Gladiolus, poppy
September	Sapphire	Aster, morning glory
October	Opal, tourmaline	Calendula, cosmos
November	Topaz	Chrysanthemum
December	Turquoise, zircon	Holly, narcissus, poinsettia

Names of the days

Sunday	Sun day
Monday	Moon day
Tuesday	Tiw's day (God of battle)
Wednesday	Woden's or Odin's day (God of poetry and the dead)
Thursday	Thor's day (God of thunder)
Friday	Frigg's day (Goddess of married love)
Saturday	Saturn's day (God of fertility and agriculture)

Chinese animal years and times 1984–2007

Chinese	English	Years		Time of day (hours)
Shu	Rat	1984	1996	2300–0100
Niu	Ox	1985	1997	0100–0300
Hu	Tiger	1986	1998	0300–0500
T'u	Hare	1987	1999	0500–0700
Lung	Dragon	1988	2000	0700–0900
She	Serpent	1989	2001	0900–1100
Ma	Horse	1990	2002	1100–1300
Yang	Sheep	1991	2003	1300–1500
Hou	Monkey	1992	2004	1500–1700
Chi	Cock	1993	2005	1700–1900
Kou	Dog	1994	2006	1900–2100
Chu	Boar	1995	2007	2100–2300

Chinese agricultural calendar

(Basis: Sun and Moon)

Fortnight

Li Chun ('Spring Begins')
Yu Shui ('Rain Water')
Jing Zhe ('Excited Insects')
Chun Fen ('Vernal Equinox')
Qing Ming ('Clear and Bright')
Gu Yu ('Grain Rains')
Li Xia ('Summer Begins')
Xiao Man ('Grain Fills')
Mang Zhong ('Grain in Ear')
Xia Zhi ('Summer Solstice')
Xiao Shu ('Slight Heat')
Da Shu ('Great Heat')
Li Qiu ('Autumn Begins')
Chu Shu ('Limit of Heat')
Bai Lu ('White Dew')
Qui Fen ('Autumn Equinox')
Han Lu ('Cold Dew')
Shuang Jiang ('Frost Descends')
Li Dong ('Winter Begins')
Xiao Xue ('Little Snow')
Da Xue ('Heavy Snow')
Dong Zhi ('Winter Solstice')
Xiao Han ('Little Cold')
Da Han ('Severe Cold')

Zodiac

Spring signs

Aries, the Ram
(Mar 21–Apr 19)

Taurus, the Bull
(Apr 20–May 20)

Gemini, the Twins
(May 21–Jun 20)

Summer signs

Cancer, the Crab
(Jun 21–Jul 22)

Leo, the Lion
(Jul 23–Aug 22)

Virgo, the Virgin
(Aug 23–Sep 22)

Autumn signs

Libra, the Balance
(Sep 23–Oct 22)

Scorpio, the Scorpion
(Oct 23–Nov 21)

Sagittarius, the Archer
(Nov 22–Dec 21)

Winter signs

Capricorn, the Goat
(Dec 22–Jan 19)

Aquarius, the
Water Bearer
(Jan 20–Feb 18)

Pisces, the Fishes
(Feb 19–Mar 20)

WORLD CHRONOLOGY

There are remarkably few events which have an obligatory place in any summary of world affairs. Judgments about the significance of an event are inevitably bound up with a country's cultural and social history, and are affected by a person's interests and tastes – all of which are inherent in any selection. The chief purpose of a chronological summary, however, is not to make authoritative decisions about significance (even if that were possible), but to present a series of events in such a way that interesting or informative relationships emerge. When a wide range of contexts is surveyed, including science and the arts alongside political history and world exploration, the (sometimes unexpected) contemporaneous juxtapositions can add a fresh dimension to our awareness of historical facts.

BC

c.9000 First walled city founded at Jericho.
c.6000 Çatal Hüyük flourishes in Anatolia.
c.3500 Sumerian civilization flourishes.
c.3500 Pictographic writing in Sumer.
c.3500 Earliest Chinese cities.
c.3500 Megalithic tombs in north-west Europe.
c.3500 Flax used for textiles in Middle East.
c.3100 Dynastic period begins in Egypt.
c.3000 Temple constructed at Uruk.
c.2680 Beginning of Old Kingdom in Egypt.
c.2590 Cheops begins Great Pyramid in Egypt.
c.2500 Beginning of Indus Valley civilization (to c.1500).
c.2500 Canaanite tribes settle in Palestine.
c.2500 Use of papyrus by Egyptians.
c.2300 Mesopotamian empire established.
c.2200 Beginning of Xia dynasty in China.
c.2100 Construction of ziggurat at Ur.
c.2000 Hittites invade Anatolia.
c.2000 Construction of Babylon.
c.2000 Beginning of Minoan civilization in Crete (to c.1450).
c.2000 Completion of Stonehenge.
1991 Beginning of Middle Kingdom in Egypt.
c.1860 Development of early Semitic alphabet.
c.1780 Hammurabi of Babylon promulgates legal code.
c.1650 Hyksos invasion of Egypt.
c.1600 Beginning of Mycenaean civilization in Greece.
1567 Beginning of New Kingdom in Egypt.
c.1500 Composition of the Vedas begun in India.
c.1360 Amenhotep IV (Akhenaton) establishes worship of Sun God.
c.1300 Construction of Temple of Abu Simbel for Rameses II.
c.1260 Archaeological dating of Trojan War.
c.1200 Olmec civilization begins to flourish in Mexico.
1175 Egypt divided into Upper and Lower Kingdoms.
c.1100 Phoenicians develop alphabetic script.
c.1066 Zhou dynasty in China.
c.1000 Israelite kingdoms established by David and Solomon.
c.1000 Building of the Temple in Jerusalem begins.
c.850 Homer writes *Iliad* and *Odyssey*.
814 Traditional year of the foundation of Carthage.
c.800 Beginning of period of composition of the Upanishads.
776 First Olympic Games in Greece.
753 Traditional year of the foundation of Rome.
671 Assyrian conquest of Egypt.
c.650 Iron technology in China.
c.650 Earliest Latin inscriptions.
621 Laws of Draco in Athens.
c.600 Age of Greek lyric poetry.
586 Babylonian captivity of the Jews.
581 First Phythian Games.
581 Building of Shwe Dagon Pagoda, Myanmar.
c.550 Cyrus the Great begins expansion of Persian Empire.
c.550 Abacus developed by Chinese.
c.530 Pythagoras founds school in Greece.
c.530 Temple of Apollo built at Corinth.
521 Darius the Great divides Persian Empire into satrapies.
c.520 Death of Lao Zi, founder or Taoism.
509 Foundation of Roman Republic.
490 Persians defeated by Athenians at Marathon.
c.483 Death of Siddhartha Gautama, founder of Buddhism.
480 Persians defeat Greeks at Thermopylae.
480 Greeks destroy Persian fleet at Salamis.
479 Death of Confucius.
462 Pericles' reforms in Athens.
c.460 Construction of Temple of Zeus at Olympia.
456 Death of Aeschylus.
450 Codification of Roman law (the Twelve Tables).
433 Completion of Parthenon at Athens.
431 Beginning of Peloponnesian War (until 404).
425 Death of Herodotus.
406 Death of Sophocles.
403 Overthrow of the Thirty Tyrants in Athens.
c.377 Death of Hippocrates.
c.370 Plato opens Academy in Athens.
359 Philip of Macedon becomes King of Macedonia.
c.350 Tomb of Mausolus completed.
c.350 Hill fort constructed at Maiden Castle, England.
347 Death of Plato.
336 Assassination of Philip of Macedon.
329 Alexander the Great reaches India.
322 Death of Aristotle.
310 Epicurus opens school of philosophy at Mitylene.
304 Foundation of Ptolemaic dynasty in Egypt.
c.300 Euclid teaching in Alexandria.
c.290 Foundation of library at Alexandria.
264 First Punic War begins (to 241).
c.250 Writing of the Septuagint.
238 Hamilcar begins conquest of Spain.
221 Qin dynasty unifies China.
221 Beginning of Great Wall of China.
218 Second Punic War begins (to 201).
218 Hannibal invades Italy from the north.
212 Death of Archimedes.
206 Han dynasty in China.
205 Scipio completes conquest of Spain.
168 Revolt of the Maccabees against Antiochus IV.
146 Romans destroy Corinth.
c.110 Opening of Silk Road across Central Asia.
c.100 Dionysius Thrax writes first Greek grammar.
51 Cleopatra becomes Queen of Egypt.

c.50 Julius Caesar writes account of Gallic Wars.
46 Adoption of Julian calendar.
44 Assassination of Julius Caesar.
43 Death of Cicero.
31 Beginning of Roman Empire.
30 Death of Antony and Cleopatra.
19 Death of Virgil.
6 Annexation of Judaea by Rome.
c.5 Birth of Jesus of Nazareth.

AD

5 Cunobelinus recognized by Romans as King of Britain.
14 Death of Augustus.
25 Han dynasty restored in China.
26 Pontius Pilate made procurator of Judaea.
27 Baptism of Jesus Christ.
c.30 Jesus of Nazareth crucified in Jerusalem.
c.34 Conversion of Saul of Tarsus.
43 Roman invasion of Britain.
46 St Paul begins missionary journeys.
54 Nero made emperor in Rome.
61 Defeat of British revolt under Boudicca.
64 Great Fire of Rome.
c.64 Saints Peter and Paul martyred at Rome.
c.65 Foundation of Glastonbury Abbey.
70 Jewish revolt, and destruction of Temple at Jerusalem.
79 Destruction of Pompeii by Vesuvius eruption.
80 Colosseum completed at Rome.
96 Persecution of Christians by Domitian.
c.100 Roman Empire at its peak.
c.105 Paper manufacture begins in China.
120 Earliest Chinese dictionary, by Hsu Shen.
122 Hadrian begins building of wall in Britain.
132 Jewish rebellion and dispersion.
c.150 Buddhism reaches China.
c.150 Ptolemy devises his theory of astronomy.
c.200 Compilation of Mahabharata.
c.200 Codification of Mishnah completed.
220 End of Han dynasty in China.
224 Beginning of Sassanid dynasty in Persia.
238 Gothic invasions of Roman Empire.
265 Six Dynasties in China (to 581).
286 Diocletian divides Empire into West and East.
285 Confucianism reaches Japan.
c.300 Rise of Mayan civilization in Mesoamerica.
312 Constantine unites Roman Empire.
313 Christianity recognized in Roman Empire.
319 Development of Arianism.
320 Chandragupta I founds Gupta Empire in N India.
325 Council of Nicaea formulates Nicene Creed.
330 Capital of Roman Empire moves to Constantinople.
c.350 Gothic Bible produced.
c.350 Fortification of London.
360 Picts and Scots attack Britain.
c.370 Hunnish invasions in Europe.
396 Last Olympic Games of classical times.
404 Latin translation of the Bible by St Jerome (Vulgate).
410 Visigoths sack Rome.
432 St Patrick begins mission to Ireland.
438 Theodosian Code of Roman law.
449 Angles, Saxons, and Jutes invade Britain.
455 Vandals sack Rome.
476 Last Western Roman emperor deposed.
480 End of Gupta Empire in N India.
481 Accession of Clovis I, founder of the Frankish kingdom.
c.515 St Benedict devises monastic rule.
534 Justinian introduces legal code.
552 Buddism introduced into Japan.
c.563 St Columba founds monastery at Iona.
597 St Augustine lands in Britain.
602 Foundation of Archbishopric of Canterbury.
618 Beginning of Tang dynasty in China.
622 Hegira of Mohammed.
625 Mohammed begins dictation of Koran.
632 Death of Mohammed.
641 Arabs begin conquest of North Africa.
664 Synod of Whitby decides date of Easter.
691 Dome of the Rock completed in Jerusalem.
710 Nara becomes capital of Japan.
711 Muslim invasion of Spain.
c.730 Printing begins in China.
732 Arab expansion in Europe stopped by Battle of Poitiers.
735 Death of St Bede.
749 Beginning of Abbasid caliphate.
762 Death of Li Bo, Chinese poet.
762 Foundation of Baghdad.
771 Accession of Charlemagne as King of the Franks.
774 Charlemagne conquers north Italy.
787 Beginning of Viking raids in Britain.
800 Charlemagne crowned Emperor in Rome.
828 Egbert of Wessex recognized as overlord of England.
c.860 Newspaper printed in China.
866 Danish kingdom established in England.
871 Accession of King Alfred the Great in England.
878 Alfred defeats Danes at Edington.
c.900 School of medicine founded at Salerno.
907 Five Dynasties era in China.
910 Foundation of Cluny Abbey.
960 Sung dynasty in China.
967 Fujiwara period begins in Japan.
987 Accession of Capetians in France.
990 Completion of Great Mosque at Córdoba.
c.1000 Inca Empire expands in Peru.
c.1000 Vikings reach America (Vinland).
c.1000 Iron Age settlement in Zimbabwe.
1014 Vikings defeated in Ireland at Clontarf.
1016 Canute made King of England.
1037 Death of Avicenna.
1040 Duncan, King of Scots, killed by Macbeth.
c.1050 Invention of moveable type in China.
1054 Schism between Western and Eastern Christianity.
1065 Consecration of Westminster Abbey.
1066 Norman Conquest of England.
1086 Domesday Book completed.
1094 El Cid defeats the Moors at Valencia.
1096 First Crusade begins (to 1099).
1099 Church of Holy Sepulchre built in Jerusalem.
c.1100 Toltec capital built in Mexico.
1113 Foundation of the Knights Hospitallers of St John of Jerusalem.
1147 Second Crusade begins (to 1148)
c.1150 Angkor Wat temple built in Cambodia.
c.1150 Yoruba city states in Nigeria.
1154 Angevins rule in England and France.
c.1155 Beginnings of Paris University.
1156 Foundation of Moscow.

World chronology (continued)

1163 Building of Nôtre Dame Cathedral, Paris, begins.
1170 Assassination of Thomas à Becket at Canterbury.
1175 Muslim Empire founded in India.
1187 Saladin captures Jerusalem.
1189 Third Crusade begins (to 1192).
1191 Crusaders capture Acre.
1195 Building of Chartres Cathedral begins.
c.1200 Rise of Mali Empire in West Africa.
1202 Fourth Crusade begins (to 1204)
1204 Crusaders capture Constantinople.
1206 Genghis Khan begins Mongol invasion of Asia.
1211 Delhi Sultanate begins under Iltutmish.
1212 The Children's Crusade.
1215 Magna Carta signed at Runnymede.
1215 Dominican Order of friars founded.
1217 Fifth Crusade begins (to 1221).
1228 Sixth Crusade begins (to 1229).
1236 Mongols conquer Russia.
1242 Alexander Nevsky defeats Teutonic Order.
1248 Seventh Crusade begins (to 1254).
1250 Beginning of Mamluk rule in Egypt.
1260 Ghibellines defeat Guelphs at Montaperti.
1261 Greek rule restored in Constantinople.
1264 Kublai Khan founds Yuan dynasty in China.
1270 Eighth Crusade begins (to 1272).
1271 Marco Polo first visits China.
1274 Death of St Thomas Aquinas.
1276 Edward I begins Welsh wars.
1280 Death of Albertus Magnus.
c.1290 Invention of spectacles.
1291 Knights of St John driven from Acre to Cyprus.
1291 Swiss Confederation begins.
1292 Death of Roger Bacon.
1294 Death of Kublai Khan.
c.1300 Foundation of Ottoman Empire.
1300 Rise of Benin Empire in Nigeria.
1302 First meeting of French estates general.
1306 Scots revolt under Robert Bruce.
1309 Papacy moves to Avignon (to 1377).
1311 Guild of Mastersingers founded at Mainz.
c.1313 Invention of cannon.
1314 Scots defeat English at Bannockburn.
1321 Death of Dante.
1337 Hundred Years War begins between France and England.
1339 Building of Kremlin in Moscow.
c.1344 Aztecs build capital at Tenochtitlan.
1346 Edward III defeats French at Crécy.
1347 Black Death arrives in Europe (to 1351).
1353 Ottoman invasion of Europe begins.
1356 English defeat French at Poitiers.
1368 Ming dynasty in China.
1369 Timur (Tamerlane) begins conquest of Asia.
1371 House of Stewart ascends to Scottish throne.
1374 Death of Petrarch.
1377 Poll tax first introduced in England.
1378 Great Schism begins in West.
1380 Wycliffe's translation of the Bible appears.
1381 Peasants' Revolt in England.
1397 Union of Denmark, Norway, and Sweden.
1399 Death of John of Gaunt.
1399 Henry IV deposes Richard II.
1400 Death of Chaucer.
1403 Henry IV defeats Percys at Shrewsbury.
1411 Foundation of the Guildhall in London.
1415 Defeat of French by Henry V at Agincourt.
1417 End of Great Schism.
1427 Defeat of Hussites in Bohemia.
1431 Joan of Arc burned at Rouen.
c.1445 Gutenberg introduces printing in Europe.
1450 Jack Cade's rebellion in England.
1453 End of Hundred Years War.
1453 Turks capture Constantinople.
1455 Wars of the Roses begin (to 1485).
1460 Death of Henry the Navigator.
1471 First European observatory at Nuremburg.
1475 Caxton prints first book in English.
1479 Union of Aragon and Castile under Ferdinand and Isabella.
1485 Henry Tudor defeats Richard III at Bosworth.
1486 Portuguese reach Angola.
1487 Diaz sails around Cape of Storms (Good Hope).
1492 Columbus reaches America.
1492 Jews expelled from Spain.
1492 Revolt of Perkin Warbeck in England (to 1499).
1497 Cabot reaches Newfoundland.
1498 Columbus reaches South America.
1498 Vasco da Gama reaches India.
1499 Vespucci reaches Venezuela.
1500 Cabral reaches Brazil.
1506 Rebuilding of St Peter's, Rome, begins.
1508 Michelangelo begins painting of Sistine Chapel, Vatican (to 1512).
1509 Accession of Henry VIII.
1509 Watch invented in Nuremberg.
1513 Balboa reaches Pacific Ocean.
1513 Ponce de Leon reaches Florida.
1517 Luther nails theses to church door at Wittenburg.
1517 Coffee introduced to Europe.
1519 Cortés begins conquest of Aztecs.
1519 Death of Leonardo da Vinci.
1520 Magellan reaches Pacific Ocean.
1520 Death of Raphael.
1521 Books begin to be printed at Cambridge.
1525 Tyndale's English translation of New Testament published.
1526 Foundation of Mughal dynasty in India.
1531 Pizarro captures Inca capital.
1534 Henry VIII breaks with Rome.
1534 Ignatius Loyola founds Society of Jesus (Jesuits).
1535 Miles Coverdale publishes first complete Bible in English.
1536 Statute of Union between England and Wales.
1536 Suppression of monasteries begins in England.
1536 Cartier claims Canada for France.
1536 Akbar the Great defeats Hindus at Panipat.
1536 Death of Erasmus.
1539 Death of Nanak, founder of Sikhism.
1539 Publication of the Great Bible in England.
1539 Word *encylopaedia* first used by Thomas Elyot.
1541 John Calvin founds church at Geneva.
1543 Copernicus publishes *Of the Revolution of Celestial Bodies*.
1545 Council of Trent begins (to 1563).
1546 Agricola makes first scientific classification of minerals.
1549 Book of Common Prayer issued.
1558 England loses Calais to the French.
1558 Accession of Elizabeth I of England.

1559 Acts of Supremacy and Uniformity in England.
1560 Nicot brings tobacco into France.
1562 Netherlands revolt against Spain.
1562 Wars of Religion begin in France (to 1598).
1564 Death of Michelangelo.
1564 Birth of Shakespeare.
1569 Union of Lublin unites Lithuania to Poland.
1569 Fitzmaurice's rebellion in Ireland.
1569 Mercator Chart introduced.
1571 Turks defeated at Lepanto.
1571 Thirty-Nine Articles adopted in England.
1572 St Bartholomew's Day massacre in France.
1572 Beginning of Dutch rebellion against Spain.
1576 First theatre opens in England, at Shoreditch.
1577 Drake leaves on world voyage.
1581 Independence of United Provinces (Netherlands).
1582 Introduction of Gregorian Calendar in Italy.
1584 Raleigh sends first expendition to Virginia.
1587 Execution of Mary, Queen of Scots.
1587 First European Academy, in Italy.
1588 Defeat of Spanish Armada by England.
1589 Foundation of Bourbon dynasty in France.
1594 Death of Palestrina.
1600 British and Dutch East India companies founded.
1600 Gilbert writes on electricity and magnetism.
1603 Accession of James VI of Scotland as James I of England.
1603 Tokugawa shogunate begins in Japan (to 1868).
1605 Discovery of Gunpowder Plot in London.
1607 Jamestown settlement in America.
1608 French found Quebec.
1610 Galileo records rings of Saturn and moons of Jupiter.
1610 Arrival of tea in Europe from China.
1611 Authorized Version of the Bible issued.
1614 Publication of Napier's book on logarithms.
1615 Inigo Jones becomes surveyor-general in England.
1616 Death of Shakespeare.
1616 Baffin discovers Baffin Bay.
1617 Jonson made first poet laureate.
1618 Thirty Years War begins (to 1648).
1620 Puritans reach New England in *Mayflower*.
1622 Invention of the slide rule.
1624 Richelieu becomes First Minister in France.
1625 Dutch found New Amsterdam.
1627 Maratha kingdom founded in India.
1628 Harvey publishes treatise on circulation of the blood.
1629 Capture of Quebec by English from French.
1629 Colony of Massachusetts founded.
1632 Shah Jahan begins building of Taj Mahal (to 1654).
1635 Death of Lope de Vega.
1636 Foundation of Harvard University.
1638 Scottish Covenant drawn up.
1638 First printing press set up in America.
1640 English Long Parliament assembles.
1640 Stage-coaches introduced into England.
1641 Grand Remonstrance passed against Charles I.
1642 Tasman sights Tasmania (Van Dieman's Land).
1642 Beginning of English Civil War.
1643 Death of Monteverdi.
1643 Torricelli invents barometer.
1643 New England Confederation of colonies formed.
1644 Qing dynasty founded in China.
1645 Charles I defeated at Naseby.
1645 Tasman circumnavigates Australia.
1647 Pascal constructs first calculating machine.
1648 Peace of Westphalia ends Thirty Years War.
1648 Wars of the Frondes begin in France (to 1653).
1649 Execution of Charles I of England.
1650 Von Guericke invents air pump.
1652 First Anglo-Dutch War.
1652 Dutch found Cape Colony.
1653 Cromwell appointed Lord Protector in England.
1660 Restoration of monarchy in England.
1660 Royal Society founded in London.
1660 Pepys begins his diary (1669).
1661 Louis XIV assumes absolute power in France.
1661 Bank of Sweden issues world's first banknotes.
1662 Boyle states gas law.
1662 Death of Pascal.
1664 English rename New Amsterdam as New York.
1665 Great Plague of London at its height.
1666 Great Fire of London.
1669 Death of Rembrandt.
1670 Hudson's Bay Trading Company given Royal Charter.
1673 Death of Molière.
1674 Death of Milton.
1675 Wren begins new St Paul's Cathedral (finished 1710).
1678 Popish Plot in England.
1679 Discovery of Niagara Falls.
1681 Penn granted patent for land in North America.
1681 La Salle explores Mississippi.
1681 First (oil) street lamps in London.
1682 Halley observes 'his' comet.
1687 Newton publishes his *Principia*.
1688 William of Orange invited to England.
1688 Lloyd's coffee-house in London begins to be used as insurance centre.
1689 Grand Alliance against Louis XIV.
1690 James II defeated by William III at the Boyne.
1690 Foundation of Calcutta.
1694 Establishment of Bank of England.
1696 Accession of Peter I (the Great) as sole Tsar of Russia.
1699 Death of Racine.
1700 Beginning of Great Northern War (to 1721).
1701 Tull invents horse-drawn seeding drill.
1701 Foundation of Yale University.
1702 War of Spanish Succession begins (to 1713).
1702 England's first daily newspaper issued, *The Daily Courant*.
1703 Foundation of St Petersburg.
1704 French defeated by Marlborough at Blenheim.
1705 Introduction of ship's wheel to replace tiller.
1707 Act of Union unites England and Scotland.
1707 Death of Aurungzebe.
1709 Swedes defeated by Peter the Great at Poltava.
1714 Beginning of Hanoverian dynasty in England (George I).
1714 Fahrenheit invents mercury thermometer.
1715 Jacobite rebellion in Britain.
1721 Rifle introduced into America.
1730 Founding of Methodism by John and Charles Wesley.
1735 Linnaeus publishes *Systema naturae*.
1738 Bernoulli states law of hydrodynamics.
1739 War of Jenkins's Ear between Britain and Spain.
1740 War of Austrian Succession (to 1748).

World chronology (continued)

1741 Wrought iron first used in bridge construction.
1742 First performance of Handel's *Messiah*.
1743 French explorers reach Rocky Mountains.
1745 Jacobite rebellion in Britain.
1746 Franklin begins his research into electricity.
1747 Foundation of Afghanistan.
1750 Death of Bach.
1750 Lacaille draws up star catalogue.
1751 Diderot begins work on *Encyclopédie* (to 1776).
1752 Gregorian Calendar adopted in Britain.
1754 Black identifies carbon dioxide.
1755 Publication of Johnson's *Dictionary*.
1756 Beginning of Seven Years War (to 1763).
1756 Black Hole of Calcutta.
1757 British defeat French at Plassey.
1759 Quebec captured by Wolfe.
1759 Death of Handel.
1760 Identification of hydrogen by Cavendish.
1762 Publication of Rousseau's *Social Contract*.
1764 Watt invents separate condenser for steam engine.
1767 Mason–Dixon line established.
1768 Cook's first voyage to the Pacific.
1768 Arkwright introduces spinning frame in England.
1769 Birth of Napoleon.
1770 Bruce finds source of Blue Nile.
1770 Cook arrives in Botany Bay.
1771 Scheele discovers oxygen.
1772 First partition of Poland between Russian and Austria.
1772 Bridgewater Canal finished in England.
1773 Boston Tea Party.
1774 Accession of Louis XVI of France.
1774 Formulation of the rules of cricket.
1774 First commercial steam engine produced by Watt and Boulton.
1775 US War of Independence begins (to 1783).
1776 American Declaration of Independence.
1776 Publication of Adam Smith's *Wealth of Nations*.
1778 Bramah invents water-closet.
1778 Death of Voltaire.
1779 Crompton produces spinning mule.
1781 British surrender to Washington at Yorktown.
1781 Publication of Kant's *Critique of Pure Reason*.
1781 Herschell discovers Uranus.
1781 Messier produces star catalogue.
1783 Britain recognizes independence of American colonies.
1783 United Empire Loyalists settle in Canada.
1783 Montgolfier brothers ascend in a balloon.
1784 Cort introduces puddling process for iron.
1784 First official mail coach, Bristol–London.
1785 Cartwright patents power loom.
1786 Klaproth discovers uranium.
1788 British found colony in Australia.
1788 Lavoisier shows air to be a mixture of oxygen and nitrogen.
1789 French Revolution begins.
1789 Washington becomes first president of USA.
1789 Mutiny on the *Bounty*.
1789 US Post Office established.
1790 Galvani carries out electrical experiments.
1790 First table of chemical elements presented by Lavoisier.
1790 Foundation of Washington.
1790 Cartwright introduces steam-powered loom.
1791 Bill of Rights ratified by US Congress.
1791 Unsuccessful flight of Louis XVI.
1791 Death of Mozart.
1791 Paine publishes first part of *The Rights of Man*.
1792 Foundation of French Republic.
1793 French Revolutionary Wars begin (to 1799).
1793 Execution of Louis XVI.
1793 Whitney patents cotton gin.
1794 End of 'Reign of Terror' in France.
1795 Park explores Niger River.
1795 Directory established in France.
1795 First settlements in New Zealand.
1796 Jenner discovers smallpox vaccine.
1796 Senefelder invents lithography.
1797 MacArthur introduces merino sheep to Australia.
1798 Napoleon invades Egypt.
1798 Irish rebellion suppressed.
1798 Nelson defeats French at Aboukir Bay.
1798 Wordsworth and Coleridge publish *Lyrical Ballads*.
1798 Malthus publishes *Essay on the Principle of Population*.
1799 Death of Washington.
1799 Napoleon becomes First Consul.
1799 Beethoven writes first symphony.
1800 Act of Union between England and Ireland.
1800 Volta makes first battery.
1801 Trevithick builds steam carriage.
1801 First paddle steamer used in Scotland.
1802 Peace of Amiens between England and France.
1803 Beginning of Napoleonic Wars (to 1815).
1803 Louisiana Purchase in USA.
1804 Napoleon made Emperor.
1805 British defeat French and Spanish at Trafalgar.
1807 Abolition of slave trade in British Empire.
1808 Independence movements begin in South America.
1808 Peninsular War begins (to 1814).
1809 Death of Haydn.
1810 Chile and Mexico declare independence from Spain.
1810 Dalton presents basis of atomic theory.
1811 Avogrado formulates hypothesis on gas molecules.
1811 Krupp founds ironworks at Essen.
1812 Napoleon invades Russia.
1812 War between Britain and USA (to 1814).
1812 Luddite riots in England.
1812 Invention of cylinder printing press.
1815 Defeat of Napoleon at Battle of Waterloo.
1815 Congress of Vienna.
1816 Argentina declares independence from Spain.
1816 Laennec invents stethoscope.
1818 Defeat of Marathas by British in India.
1819 Florida Purchase in USA.
1819 Foundation of Singapore.
1819 Peterloo Massacre at Manchester.
1820 War of Greek Independence begins (to 1828).
1822 Foundation of Liberia for freed slaves.
1822 First photographic image made by Niepce.
1823 Monroe Doctrine formulated.
1823 First Ashanti War (to 1866).
1824 Death of Byron.
1825 First passenger steam railway in England.

1825 Opening of the Erie Canal.
1827 Faraday becomes professor at Royal Institution.
1827 Death of Beethoven.
1828 Webster's *Dictionary* published in America.
1829 Catholic Emancipation Act in Britain.
1829 Braille invents system of touch-reading for blind.
1829 Henry invents electromagnetic motor.
1829 First Oxford and Cambridge Boat Race.
1829 Stephenson constructs the *Rocket*.
1830 July Revolution in France.
1830 Independence of Belgium.
1831 Darwin begins voyage on the *Beagle*.
1832 First Reform Act in Britain.
1832 First railway constructed in USA.
1832 Death of Goethe.
1833 First steam crossing of Atlantic by SS *Royal William*.
1834 German customs union (*Zollverein*) officially founded.
1834 McCormick patents harvesting machine.
1835 Colt patents revolver.
1835 Beginning of construction of Great Western Railway in England.
1835 Foundation of Melbourne.
1835 Morse develops telegraph in USA.
1836 Boer Great Trek in South Africa.
1836 Siege of the Alamo in Texas.
1837 Pitman introduces his shorthand system.
1838 Anti-Corn Law League founded in Manchester.
1839 First Opium War between Britain and China (to 1842).
1839 First Grand National steeplechase in Liverpool.
1840 Marriage of Queen Victoria and Prince Albert.
1840 Introduction of penny postage stamps in Britain.
1840 Bicycle invented in Scotland.
1841 Act of Union joins Upper and Lower Canada.
1841 British annexation of New Zealand.
1842 British annexation of Hong Kong.
1842 Khyber Pass massacre.
1843 Opening of Brunel's tunnel under the Thames.
1845 US annexation of Texas.
1846 Britain repeals Corn Laws.
1846 Mexican War begins (to 1848).
1846 Oregon Treaty defines US–Canadian boundary.
1846 Foundation of Smithsonian Institution in Washington, DC.
1846 Howe invents sewing machine.
1847 Mormons emigrate to Utah.
1848 Revolutionary movements throughout Europe.
1848 Abdication of Louis Philippe in France.
1848 Communist Manifesto published.
1848 Yale invents cylinder lock.
1848 Gold discovered in California.
1849 Death of Chopin.
1849 Punjab annexed by Britain.
1849 Livingstone begins explorations in Africa.
1851 Taiping rebellion in China (to 1865).
1851 Great Exhibition in London.
1851 First publication of *New York Times*.
1852 Louis Napoleon becomes Emperor of France.
1852 Otis invents lift with automatic brake.
1852 Wells Fargo & Co founded in USA.
1854 Beginning of Crimean War (to 1856).
1854 Haussmann begins reconstruction of Paris.
1855 Livingstone reaches Victoria Falls.
1856 Introduction of Bessemer process for steel.
1857 Indian Mutiny.
1858 Laying of first Atlantic cable.
1858 Speke and Burton reach Lake Tanganyika.
1859 Movement for unification of Italy begins (to 1870).
1859 Publication of Darwin's *The Origin of Species*.
1859 De Lesseps begins work on Suez Canal.
1859 First American oil-wells drilled in Pennsylvania.
1860 Garibaldi's Expedition of the Thousand.
1861 American Civil War begins (to 1865).
1861 Emancipation of Russian serfs.
1861 Germ theory of disease proposed by Pasteur.
1862 Bismarck appointed Prime Minister of Prussia.
1862 Gatling patents machine gun.
1863 Lincoln's Gettysburg Address.
1863 Beginning of underground railway in London.
1864 Paraguayan War begins (to 1870).
1864 Foundation of Red Cross in Geneva.
1865 American Civil War ends.
1865 Assassination of Lincoln.
1865 Lewis Carroll publishes *Alice in Wonderland*.
1866 Prussia defeats Austria in Seven-Weeks War.
1866 Winchester introduces repeating rifle.
1866 Mary Baker Eddy founds Christian Science movement.
1866 Mendel proposes laws of inheritance.
1867 US purchase of Alaska from Russia.
1867 Establishment of Dominion of Canada.
1867 Dual Monarchy established in Austria–Hungary.
1867 Publication of Marx's *Das Kapital*.
1867 Nobel produces dynamite.
1867 South African diamond fields discovered.
1868 Meiji Restoration in Japan.
1869 Opening of Suez Canal.
1869 Completion of first trans-continental railway in USA.
1869 Mendeleyev draws up table of elements.
1870 Franco-Prussian War begins (to 1871).
1870 Papal infallibility declared.
1870 Death of Dickens.
1871 German Empire proclaimed.
1871 Third Republic begins in France.
1872 Monet's 'Impression: Sunrise' gives name to Impressionists.
1873 Sholes and Glidden design first commercial typewriter.
1873 Maxwell publishes treatise on electricity and magnetism.
1875 Gilbert and Sullivan produce their first operetta.
1876 Custer defeated at Battle of Little Big Horn.
1876 Bell invents telephone.
1876 Otto devises four-stroke cycle gas engine.
1877 Queen Victoria proclaimed Empress of India.
1877 Edison invents the phonograph.
1879 War of the Pacific begins (to 1883).
1879 Zulu War in South Africa.
1879 Woolworths opens first store.
1880 First Boer War (to 1881).
1881 Death of Dostoevsky.
1881 Pasteur develops immunization against anthrax.
1882 Phoenix Park murders in Dublin.
1882 Koch discovers tuberculosis bacillus.
1882 Mahdi proclaimed as Messiah in Sudan.
1883 Opening of Brooklyn Bridge, New York.
1883 Death of Wagner.
1883 Krakatoa volcanic explosion.

World chronology (continued)

1884 Germany acquires South-West Africa.
1884 Discovery of gold in Transvaal.
1885 Belgium acquires Congo.
1885 Death of Gordon at Khartoum.
1885 Foundation of Indian National Congress.
1885 Benz builds his first motor cars in Germany.
1885 Completion of Canadian Pacific Railway.
1886 Partition of East Africa by Germany and Britain.
1886 Foundation of Johannesburg.
1886 Daimler produces motorcycle.
1886 Statue of Liberty erected in the USA.
1887 French establish Indo-Chinese Union.
1887 Michelson–Morley experiment on relative velocity of light.
1887 Goodwin invents celluloid film.
1887 Invention of pneumatic tyre by Dunlop.
1887 Hertz discovers electromagnetic waves.
1887 First book on Esperanto published.
1888 Tesla makes alternating-current motor.
1888 Eastman produces Kodak camera.
1889 Foundation of British South Africa Company.
1889 Eiffel completes Tower in Paris.
1889 First skyscraper in America (in Chicago).
1890 Dismissal of Bismarck.
1890 Death of Van Gogh.
1891 Beginning of Trans-Siberian Railway.
1893 Death of Tchaikovsky.
1893 Lumière brothers invent cinematograph.
1894 Beginning of Sino-Japanese War (to 1895).
1894 Opening of Blackpool Tower.
1894 Opening of Manchester Ship Canal.
1894 Launch of first steam-turbine ship (*Turbinia*).
1895 Röntgen discovers X-rays.
1895 Marconi invents wireless telegraphy.
1895 Wood begins Promenade Concerts in London.
1896 Italians defeated by Ethiopians at Battle of Adowa.
1896 Jameson Raid in South Africa.
1896 Establishment of Nobel Prizes.
1896 Becquerel discovers radioactivity.
1897 Death of Brahms.
1897 First Women's Institute, in Canada.
1897 Joseph Thomson discovers the electron.
1897 Diesel demonstrates compression-ignition engine.
1898 The Curies isolate radium.
1898 Spanish–American War.
1898 Hundred Days of Reform in China.
1898 USA annexes Hawaii.
1898 Howard proposes garden city concept.
1899 Second Boer War begins (to 1902).
1899 Permanent Court of Arbitration established in The Hague.
1900 Boxer uprising in China.
1900 Planck proposes quantum theory.
1900 Freud publishes *The Interpretation of Dreams*.
1901 Establishment of Commonwealth of Australia.
1901 Marconi transmits wireless signals across the Atlantic.
1902 Caruso makes first gramophone record.
1903 Panama Canal Zone leased to USA.
1903 Wright brothers make their first flight.
1903 Ford founds motor company.
1903 Russell publishes *Principles of Mathematics*.
1904 Beginning of Russo-Japanese War (to 1905).
1904 Construction of first engine-powered lifeboat.
1905 Revolution in Russia against Tsar.
1905 Einstein presents theory of special relativity.
1906 Major earthquake in San Francisco.
1906 Foundation of Rolls-Royce Ltd in England.
1906 Death of Ibsen.
1907 Dominion of New Zealand established.
1907 Cubist exhibition in Paris.
1907 Discovery of principal blood groups.
1908 Young Turks revolution.
1908 Baden-Powell founds Boy Scout movement.
1908 First Model T Ford made.
1908 Great meteorite falls in Siberia.
1909 Diaghilev launches Ballets Russes.
1909 Peary reaches North Pole.
1909 Blériot makes first cross-Channel flight.
1910 Foundation of Union of South Africa.
1910 Beginning of Mexican revolution (to 1917).
1910 Annexation of Korea by Japan.
1910 Constitutional Crisis in Britain.
1910 Ehrlich invents salvarsan as cure for syphilis.
1910 Death of Tolstoy.
1911 Chinese Revolution.
1911 Rutherford propounds theory of atomic structure.
1911 Amundsen first to reach South Pole.
1912 Beginning of Balkan Wars (to 1913).
1912 Sinking of SS *Titanic*.
1912 Republic of China established under Sun Yat-sen.
1912 Hess discovers cosmic rays.
1914 First Charlie Chaplin films.
1914 Opening of Panama Canal.
1914 First World War begins (to 1918).
1916 Einstein presents general theory of relativity.
1916 Battle of the Somme.
1916 Irish rebellion (to 1921).
1917 US Expeditionary Force in Europe.
1917 Russian Revolution.
1917 Civil war in Russia (to 1922).
1917 Balfour Declaration promises Jews a home in Palestine.
1918 End of First World War.
1918 Fourteen Points statement by President Wilson.
1918 Women over 30 given right to vote in Britain.
1919 May 4th movement in China.
1919 Foundation of Soviet Republic.
1919 Amritsar massacre in India.
1919 Bauhaus movement established in Germany.
1919 Alcock and Brown make first Atlantic air crossing.
1919 First woman MP in House of Commons (Lady Astor).
1919 Hitler founds National Socialist German Workers' Party.
1919 Spartacist rising in Berlin crushed.
1920 League of Nations established.
1920 Radio broadcasting begins.
1921 Treaty partitions Ireland.
1922 USSR established.
1922 Mussolini in power in Italy.
1922 Banting and Best isolate insulin.
1922 BBC makes first regular broadcasts.
1922 Tomb of Tutankhamun discovered in Egypt.
1923 Munich putsch by Hitler.
1923 Republic proclaimed in Turkey.
1923 Major earthquake in Japan.

1924 Death of Lenin.
1925 Hitler publishes *Mein Kampf*.
1926 General Strike in Britain.
1926 Jiang Jieshi (Chiang Kai-shek) leads movement for reunification of China.
1926 Baird demonstrates television.
1927 Talking pictures begin.
1927 Lindbergh first solo flight across Atlantic.
1927 Duke Ellington begins playing at the Cotton Club.
1928 Fleming discovers penicillin.
1928 Walt Disney introduces Mickey Mouse.
1929 Wall Street crash.
1929 Lateran Treaty establishes Vatican as state.
1930 Amy Johnson solo flight, England to Australia.
1931 Creation of republic in Spain.
1931 Japanese occupy Manchuria.
1931 Empire State Building built in New York.
1932 Foundation of Kingdom of Saudi Arabia.
1932 Chaco War between Paraguay and Bolivia (to 1935).
1933 Roosevelt introduces New Deal.
1933 Hitler becomes Chancellor of Germany.
1933 Reichstag Fire in Berlin.
1933 Prohibition repealed in the USA.
1933 Discovery of polythene.
1934 Long March of Chinese Communists begins (to 1935).
1934 Discovery of nuclear fission.
1935 Italian invasion of Abyssinia (Ethiopia).
1936 Beginning of Spanish Civil War (to 1939).
1936 Anti-Comintern Pact between Japan and Germany.
1936 Arab revolt in Palestine.
1936 British constitutional crisis over Edward VIII.
1936 Keynes publishes his economic theory.
1936 First public television transmissions in Britain.
1936 *Queen Mary*'s maiden voyage.
1936 Crystal Palace destroyed by fire.
1937 War between Japan and China begins.
1937 Picasso paints 'Guernica'.
1937 Golden Gate Bridge completed in San Francisco.
1937 *Hindenburg* zeppelin destroyed by fire in USA.
1937 Jet engine tested.
1938 Germany occupies Austria.
1938 Munich Agreement.
1938 Discovery of nylon.
1938 Carlson makes first xerographic print.
1939 Germany invades Czechoslovakia and Poland.
1939 Second World War begins.
1940 Evacuation of Dunkirk.
1940 Battle of Britain.
1940 Plutonium obtained by bombardment of uranium.
1941 Germany invades Russia.
1941 Japanese attack Pearl Harbor.
1941 Death of James Joyce.
1941 Orson Wells makes *Citizen Kane*.
1942 Construction of first nuclear reactor.
1942 Defeat of Germany at El Alamein.
1942 American defeat of Japan at Midway.
1942 Anglo-American landings in North Africa.
1943 Surrender of German army at Stalingrad.
1943 Capitulation of Italy.
1944 D-Day landing in Normandy.
1944 Perón in power in Argentina.
1944 Education Act in Britain.
1945 Atom bombs dropped on Japan.
1945 Second World War ends.
1945 Yalta Conference.
1945 Nuremberg War Crimes Tribunal opens.
1945 United Nations established.
1945 Republic of Yugoslavia established under Tito.
1946 Civil War in China (to 1949).
1946 Civil War in Indo-China (to 1954).
1946 Construction of first electronic digital computer.
1947 First supersonic flight.
1947 Independence of India and Pakistan.
1947 Greek Civil War (to 1949).
1947 Marshall Plan for European reconstruction.
1947 Dead Sea Scrolls found in Palestine.
1947 Dior introduces 'New Look'.
1948 Creation of State of Israel.
1948 Communist rule established in Czechoslovakia.
1948 Berlin airlift.
1948 Formation of Organization of American States.
1948 First Arab–Israeli War.
1948 Invention of the transistor.
1948 Creation of World Council of Churches.
1948 Assassination of Gandhi.
1948 Apartheid policy begins in South Africa.
1948 Creation of World Health Organization.
1948 Kinsey report on sexual behaviour published.
1949 Formation of NATO.
1949 Communist victory in China.
1949 Creation of West and East Germany.
1949 Communist rule established in Hungary.
1950 Beginning of Korean War (to 1953).
1951 Nuclear power stations introduced.
1951 Festival of Britain.
1951 First turbo-jet airliner (*Comet*).
1952 Mau Mau rebellion begins in Kenya.
1952 Military revolt in Egypt.
1952 Contraceptive pill introduced.
1952 Accession of Elizabeth II of Britain.
1952 Detonation of first hydrogen bomb.
1953 Death of Stalin.
1953 Edmund Hillary and Sherpa Tensing conquer Everest.
1953 Watson and Crick show DNA molecule structure.
1954 Independence of Cambodia and Laos.
1954 Nationalist revolt in Algeria.
1954 Nasser in power in Egypt.
1954 Vietnam divided into North and South.
1954 Independent Television Authority set up in Britain.
1955 Formation of Warsaw Pact.
1955 Enosis (Greek unity) crisis in Cyprus (to 1959).
1956 Gomulka in power in Poland.
1956 Soviet forces crush Hungarian revolt.
1956 Second Arab–Israeli War.
1956 Suez Crisis.
1956 Neutrino experimentally observed.
1956 Rock-and-roll music era begins.
1957 Independence of Ghana.
1957 Treaty of Rome forms European Economic Community.
1957 Launch of first space satellite (*Sputnik 1*).
1957 Civil Rights violence at Little Rock, Arkansas.
1958 Fifth Republic formed in France under de Gaulle.
1958 Introduction of stereo recordings.
1959 Formation of European Free Trade Association.
1959 Castro in power after Cuban revolution.

World chronology (continued)

1959 First photograph of dark side of the Moon (*Luna 3*).
1959 First section of Britain's first motorway opened.
1960 Independence of many African states.
1960 Sharpeville massacre in South Africa.
1960 Kennedy becomes US president.
1960 Development of the laser.
1961 Berlin Wall built.
1961 South Africa becomes republic.
1961 Gagarin becomes first man in space (*Vostok 1*).
1962 Second Vatican Council begins (to 1965).
1962 Independence of Algeria.
1962 Cuban missile crisis.
1963 Assassination of Kennedy.
1963 Tereshkova becomes first woman in orbit.
1963 Beatles become internationally known.
1964 Publication of *Thoughts of Chairman Mao*.
1964 Civil Rights Bill in USA.
1964 Foundation of Palestine Liberation Organization.
1965 War between India and Pakistan.
1965 Unilateral declaration of independence by Rhodesia (Zimbabwe).
1966 Cultural Revolution in China.
1966 First lunar soft landing (*Luna 9*).
1966 Assassination of Verwoerd in Cape Town, South Africa.
1967 Civil war in Nigeria, and secession of Biafra (to 1970).
1967 Third Arab–Israeli War ('Six-Day War').
1967 Oil tanker *Torrey Canyon* disaster.
1967 Barnard carries out first heart transplant operation.
1968 Soviet invasion of Czechoslovakia.
1968 Student protest movement in many countries.
1968 Assassination of Martin Luther King, Jr.
1968 First manned lunar orbit (*Apollo 8*).
1968 Discovery of pulsars.
1969 First man on the moon (Neil Armstrong).
1969 Nixon becomes US president.
1969 Outbreak of troubles in Northern Ireland.
1970 Boeing 747 'jumbo' jets introduced.
1971 East Pakistan becomes Bangladesh.
1971 Policy of détente introduced by USA with USSR and China.
1971 Decimal currency introduced into UK.
1972 Pocket calculators introduced.
1973 Fourth Arab–Israeli War.
1973 Britain joins European Economic Community.
1973 US forces withdraw from South Vietnam.
1973 Major famine in Ethiopia.
1973 Death of Picasso.
1974 Turkish invasion of Cyprus.
1974 Haile Selassie deposed in Ethiopia.
1974 Strategic Arms Limitation Treaty signed.
1974 Resignation of Nixon after Watergate scandal.
1974 First 'test-tube babies'.
1975 End of Vietnam War.
1975 Civil war begins in Lebanon.
1975 Death of Franco.
1975 Dutch Elm disease widespread.
1975 *Apollo–Soyuz* space project.
1975 Domestic videorecorders introduced.
1975 Floppy disks introduced.
1976 Death of Mao Zedong.
1976 *Concorde* supersonic airliner begins transatlantic flights.
1976 First Bantustan established in South Africa (Transkei).
1977 Military coup in Pakistan.
1977 Carter becomes US president.
1977 Death of Elvis Presley.
1977 Launch of *Voyager* missions to outer planets.
1978 Camp David Treaty between Egypt and Israel.
1978 John Paul II becomes Pope.
1979 Former President Bhutto executed in Pakistan.
1979 Amin expelled from Uganda.
1979 Civil war in Nicaragua.
1979 Islamic Republic established in Iran under Khomeini.
1979 Invasion of Afghanistan by USSR.
1979 Vietnam invades Cambodia.
1979 Saddam Hussein becomes president of Iraq.
1979 Thatcher becomes British prime minister.
1979 Walkman portable cassette player introduced.
1980 Death of Tito.
1980 Black majority rule in Zimbabwe.
1980 Major famine in East Africa.
1980 Creation of Solidarity union in Poland.
1980 Beginning of Iran–Iraq War (to 1988).
1980 Reagan becomes US president.
1980 Humber Bridge completed.
1980 Introduction of videodisk.
1980 Growth of Green movement in Europe.
1980 Assassination of John Lennon in New York.
1980 Borg wins Wimbledon for fifth successive year.
1980 Eruption of Mt St Helens in USA.
1981 Martial law in Poland.
1981 Assassination of Sadat of Egypt.
1981 Hunger strikers die in Northern Ireland.
1981 First re-usable space shuttle flight.
1981 Race riots in British cities.
1981 First reports of AIDS.
1981 IBM personal computer system introduced.
1982 War between Britain and Argentina over Falkland Islands.
1982 PLO expelled from Beirut.
1982 Israel withdraws from Sinai Peninsula.
1982 Draft treaty to control CFCs.
1982 Introduction of compact discs.
1983 Global warming effect demonstrated.
1983 US proposes 'star wars' missile programme.
1984 Assassination of Indira Gandhi.
1985 Gorbachev in power in USSR.
1985 Halley comet intercepted.
1986 Chernobyl nuclear power disaster.
1986 State of emergency in South Africa.
1986 US bombing of Libya.
1986 Waldheim becomes President of Austria.
1986 *Glasnost* and *perestroika* advocated by Gorbachev.
1986 *Challenger* space shuttle disaster.
1986 Hole in ozone layer reported.
1986 Iran-*contra* scandal in USA.
1987 World population passes 5 thousand million.
1989 Bush becomes US president.
1989 Soviet army completes withdrawal from Afghanistan.
1989 Solidarity prime minister elected in Poland (Mazowiecki).
1989 Tiananmen Square demonstration in Beijing.

1989 Death of Ayatollah Khomeini in Iran.
1989 Opening of Berlin Wall.
1989 End of Communist rule in Czechoslovakia.
1989 Invasion of Panama by USA.
1989 Execution of Ceausescu in Romania.
1989 Death of Emperor Hirohito of Japan.
1989 De Klerk becomes President of South Africa.
1990 Reunification of Germany.
1990 Resignation of Thatcher in Britain.
1990 Independence of Armenia.
1990 Walesa becomes President of Poland.
1990 Independence of Lithuania.
1990 Release of Mandela from prison in South Africa.
1990 Invasion of Kuwait by Iraq.
1990 De Klerk begins dismantling of South African apartheid system.
1991 Gulf War (Operation Desert Storm).
1991 Civil war begins in Yugoslavia.
1991 Mandela elected President of African National Congress.
1991 Independence of Baltic States recognized by USSR.
1991 Independence of Croatia, Macedonia, Slovenia.
1991 Independence of remaining republics of former Soviet Union.
1991 Formation of Commonwealth of Independent States.
1991 Resignation of Gorbachev in Russia.
1991 Yeltsin becomes Russian president.
1992 Independence of Bosnia and Herzegovina.
1992 Boutros Ghali becomes UN secretary-general.
1993 Division of Czechoslovakia into Czech and Slovak Republics.
1993 Clinton becomes US president.

Seven wonders of the Ancient World

Name	*Date built*	*History*
Egyptian Pyramids	More than 4000 years ago	Oldest of the ancient wonders and the only one surviving today Served as tombs for Egyptian pharoahs
Colossus of Rhodes	c.305–292 BC	32 m (105 ft) high bronze statue of the sun god Helius Destroyed by an earthquake in 224 BC
Hanging Gardens of Babylon	6th century BC	Series of terraces of trees and flowers along the banks of the Euphrates Built by Nebuchadnezzar II (also known in the Book of Daniel as Nebuchadrezzar)
Mausoleum at Halicarnassus, Asia Minor	4th century BC	Tomb of Mausolus built by his widow. Destroyed by an earthquake before the 15th century
Pharos of Alexandria	c.270 BC	The world's first known lighthouse at the entrance of Alexandria harbour in Egypt. 122 m (400 ft) high In ruins by 15th century
Statue of Zeus at Olympia	5th century BC	9 m (30 ft) high wooden statue of Greek god Zeus covered with gold and ivory. Designed by Athens sculptor Phidias. Destroyed by fire AD 475
Temple of Artemis at Ephesus, Asia Minor	6th century BC	Marble temple in honour of goddess of hunting and the moon. Rebuilt in 4th century BC but destroyed by Goths in 3rd century AD

Dynasties of China

Name	*Date*	*History*
Xia	c.2200–c.1523 BC	Emperor Yu Land reclaimed, bronze weapons made, grain cultivated, first use of written symbols
Shang or Yin	c.1480–1050 BC	First historic dynasty Agricultural society with class system First Chinese calendar Age of bronze casting
Zhou	c.1066–221 BC	Classical age Laws in place Money economy
Qin (Ch'in)	221–206 BC	Rule by Shi Huang-ti Unification of country begun Feudalism replaced by bureaucratic government Large part of Great Wall built
Han	206 BC–AD 220	Bureaucratic state based on Confucianism Buddhism introduced
Three Kingdoms (San-kuo)	AD 220–265	Divided into three states Wei, Shu, Wu Increased importance of Buddhism and Taoism
Tsin	265–420	Founded by Wei general N China ruled by series of barbarian dynasties
Sui	581–618	Country reunified and central government established Canal system constructed
Tang	618–907	Period of territorial expansion Buddhism suppressed Age of great poets, sculptors and painters
Five Dynasties and Ten Kingdoms	907–960	Period of hardship with wars and official corruption First printing of paper money
Song (Sung)	960–1279	Great changes socially and intellectually Confucianism superceeds Taoism and Buddhism Central bureaucracy reformed Cultivation of tea and cotton on a large scale
Yuan	1279–1368	Founding of Mongol dynasty by Kubla Khan Confucianism out of favour End of dynasty in S China Riots in Mongolia
Ming	1368–1644	Mongols expelled Confucianism reinstated Porcelain production flourishes Great developments in architecture, the novel and drama
Ch'ing (Manchu)	1644–1912	Decline of central authority Increase in European trade China divided into spheres of influence by foreign powers Last Chinese monarchy

Dynasties of Ancient Egypt

Period	*Dynasty*	*Date*	*Major rulers*	*History*
Early Dynastic Period	I	3110–2884 BC	Menes	Unification of Upper and Lower Egypt
	II	2884–2780 BC		Memphis founded
Old Kingdom	III	2780–2680 BC	Snefru	Step Pyramid built
	IV	2680–2565 BC	Khufu (Cheops), Khafre, Menkaure	Age of the great pyramids
	V	2565–2420 BC		
	VI	2420–2258 BC	Pepi I, Pepi II	

Period	Dynasty	Date	Major rulers	History
First Intermediate Period	VII, VIII	2258–2225 BC		Egypt divided politically Control by local monarchs
	IX, X	2225–2134 BC		Capital at Heracleopolis
	XI	2134–c.2000 BC	Mentuhotep II	Capital at Thebes Reunification
Middle Kingdom	XII	2000–1786 BC	Amenemhet I, Sesostris I, Amenemhet II, Sesostris II, Amenemhet III, Amenemhet IV	Conquest of Nubia
Second Intermediate Period	XIII–XVII	1786–1570 BC	Hyksos	Egypt liberated by Theban dynasty
New Kingdom	XVIII	1570–c.1342 BC	Amenhotep I, Thutmose I, II, III, IV, Akhenaton Tutankhamun	Period of empire building – extends from Syria to Southern Sudan Capital city Thebes Extensive building programme
	XIX	c.1342–1200 BC	Ramses I, Ramses II	
	XX	1200–1085 BC	Ramses III	New Kingdom declines
	XXI	1085–945 BC		Egypt divided – Amun rule in Thebes and pharaohs in Tanis
	XXII	945–745 BC	Sheshonk I	Libyan dynasty
	XXIII	745–718 BC		Nubian dynasty with invasion of Piankhi
	XXIV	718–712 BC		
	XXV	712–663 BC	Taharka	Invasion by Assyria – foreign domination follows
	XXVI	663–525 BC	Necho	
	XXVII	525–405 BC	Achaemenids of Persia, Darius II	Egypt revolts
	XXVIII, XXIX, XXX	405–332 BC	Nekhtnebf I	Last native dynasties, ending with conquest of Alexander the Great Capital at Sais, Mendes, then Sebennytos

Rulers of the Roman Empire

Name	Dates	History
Augustus	27 BC–AD 14	Grandnephew of Julius Caesar
Tiberius	AD 14–37	Stepson of Augustus
Gaius Caesar (Caligula)	37–41	Grandnephew of Tiberius
Claudius I	41–54	Uncle of Caligula
Nero	54–68	Stepson of Claudius
Galba	68–69	Proclaimed emperor by soldiers
Otho	69	Military commander
Vespasian	69–79	Military commander
Titus	79–81	Son of Vespasian
Domitian	81–96	Son of Vespasian
Nerva	96–98	Elected interim ruler
Trajan	98–117	Adopted son of Nerva
Hadrian	117–138	Ward of Trajan
Antoninus Pius	138–161	Adopted by Hadrian
Marcus Aurelius	161–180	Adopted by Antoninus Pius
Lucius Verus	161–169	Adopted by Antoninus Pius and ruled together with Marcus Aurelius
Commodus	180–192	Son of Marcus Aurelius
Pertinax	193	Proclaimed emperor by the Praetorian guard
Didius Julianus	193	Bought office from the Praetorian guard
Septimus Severus	193–211	Proclaimed emperor
Caracalla	211–217	Son of Severus
Geta	211–212	Son of Severus and ruled together with Caracalla
Macrinus	217–218	Proclaimed emperor by soldiers
Heliogabalus (Elagabalus)	218–222	Cousin of Caracalla
Alexander Severus	222–235	Cousin of Heliogabalus
Maximin	235–238	Proclaimed emperor by soldiers
Gordian I and Gordian II, Balbinus, Pupienus	238	Proclaimed by senate and all ruled together
Gordian III	238–244	Son of Gordian II
Philip	244–249	Assassin of Gordian III
Decius	249–251	Proclaimed emperor by soldiers
Hostilianus	251	Son of Decius
Gallus	251–253	Military commander
Aemilianus	253	Military commander

Rulers of the Roman Empire (continued)

Name	*Dates*	*History*
Valerian	253–260	Military commander
Gallienus	253–268	Son of Valerian Co-emperor with his father and later emperor in his own right
Claudius II	268–270	Military commander
Aurelian	270–275	Chosen by Claudius as successor
Tacitus	275–276	Chosen by senate
Florianus	276	Half brother of Tacitus
Probus	276–282	Military commander
Carus	282–283	Proclaimed by the Praetorian guard
Carinus	283–285	Son of Carus
Numerianus	283–284	Son of Carus and ruled together with Carinus
Diocletian	284–305	Military commander Ruled together with Maximian and Constantius Empire divided
Maximian	286–305	Appointed by Diocletian
Constantius I	305–306	Successor of Diocletian
Galerius	305–310	Emperor with Constantius
Maximin	308–313	Nephew of Galerius
Licinius	308–324	Appointed emperor in West by Galerius
Maxentius	306–312	Son of Maximin
Constantine I (the Great)	306–337	Son of Constantius
Constantine II	337–340	Son of Constantine I
Constans	337–350	Son of Constantine I
Constantius II	337–361	Son of Constantine I
Magnentius	350–353	Usurped Constans' throne
Julian	361–363	Nephew of Constantine I
Jovian	363–364	Elected by the army
Valentinian I	364–375	Proclaimed by the army Ruled in the West
Valens	364–378	Brother of Valentinian I Ruled in the East
Grantian	375–383	Son of Valentinian I Co-ruler in West with Valentinian II
Maximus	383–388	Usurper in the West
Valentinian II	375–392	Son of Valentinian I
Eugenius	392–394	Usurper in West
Theodosius I (the Great)	375–395	Appointed ruler in the East by Gratian. Last ruler of united empire
Arcadius	395–408	Son of Theodosius I Emperor in East
Theodosius II	408–450	Son of Arcadius Emperor in East
Marcian	450–457	Brother-in-law of Theodosius II Emperor in East
Leo I	457–474	Chosen by senate Emperor in East
Leo II	474	Grandson of Leo I Emperor in East
Honorius	395–423	Son of Theodosius I Emperor in West
Maximus	409–411	Usurper in Spain Emperor in West
Constantius III	421	Named joint emperor by Honorius Emperor in West
Valentinian III	425–455	Nephew of Honorius and son of Constantius III Emperor in West
Petronius Maximus	455	Bribed his way into office Emperor in West
Avitus	455–456	Placed in office by Goths Emperor in West
Majorian	457–461	Puppet emperor of Ricimer Emperor in West
Libius Severus	461–465	Puppet emperor of Ricimer Emperor in West
Anthemius	467–472	Appointed by Ricimer and Leo I Emperor in West
Olybrius	472	Appointed by Ricimer Emperor in West
Glycerius	473–474	Appointed by Leo I Emperor in West
Julius Nepos	474–475	Appointed by Leo I Emperor in West
Romulus Augustus	475–476	Placed in office by his father Orestes Emperor in West

The Roman Empire in the 1st century AD

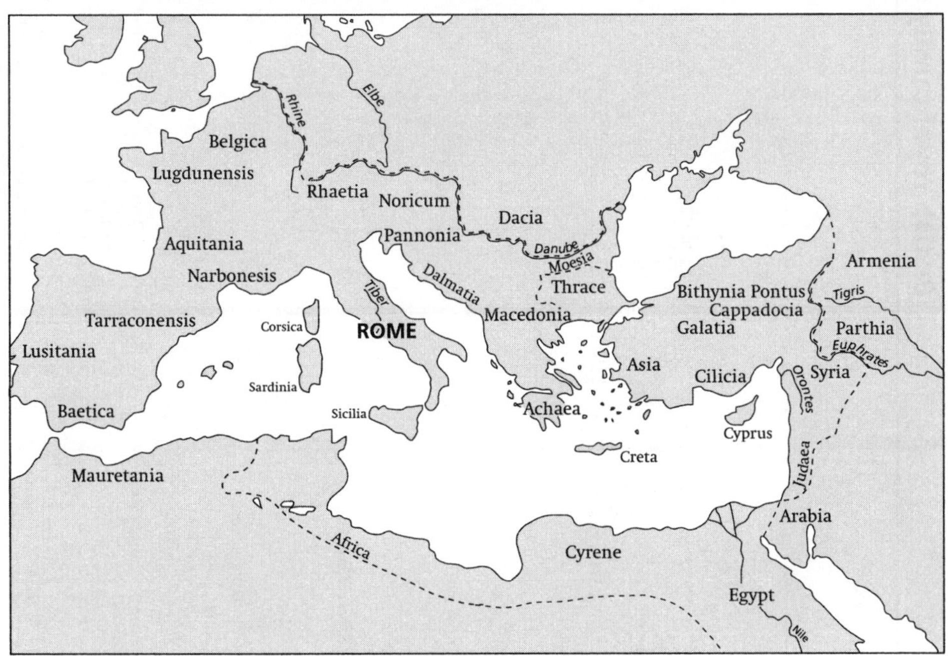

Chief Roman roads in Britain

British royal family tree

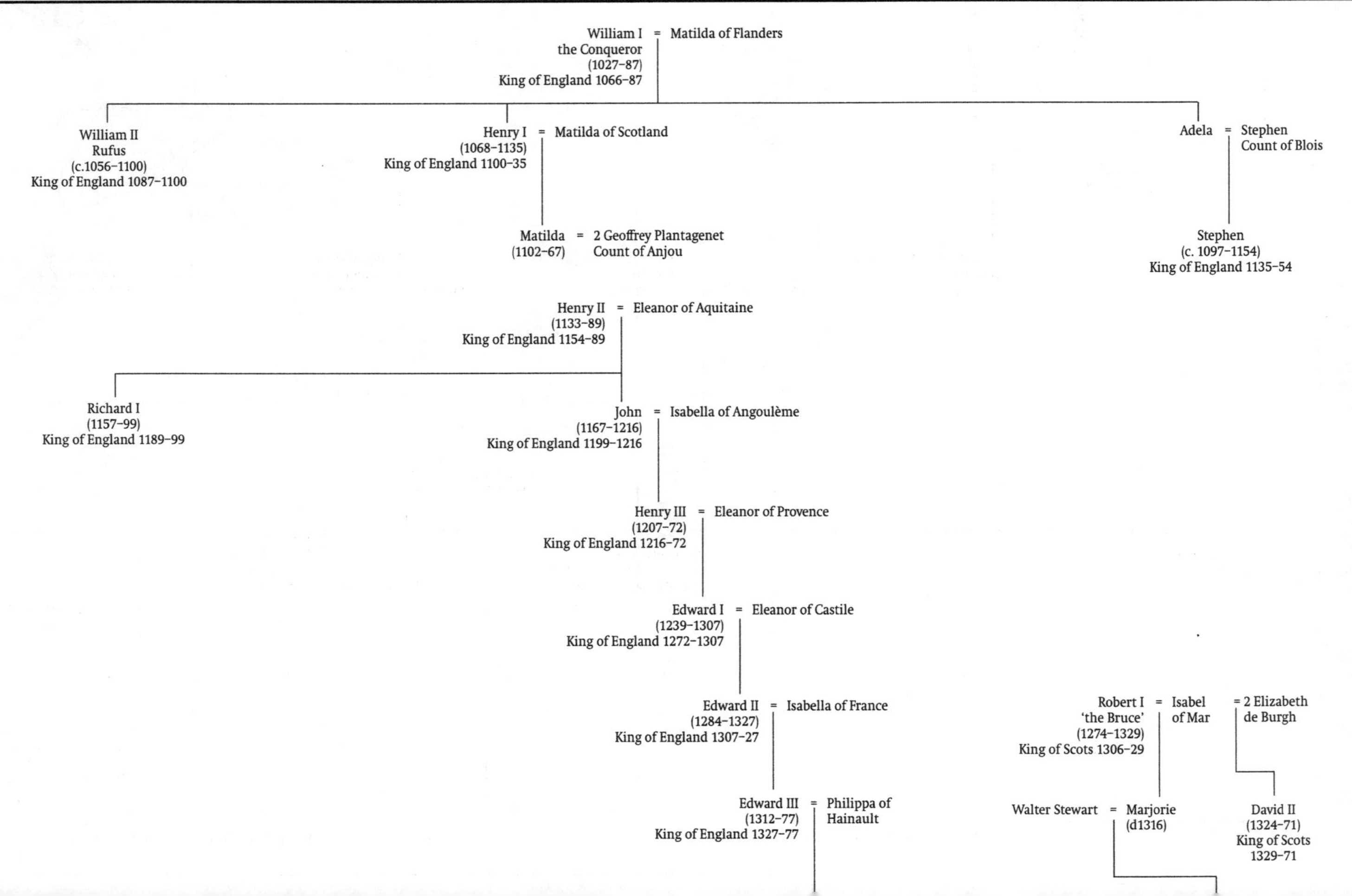

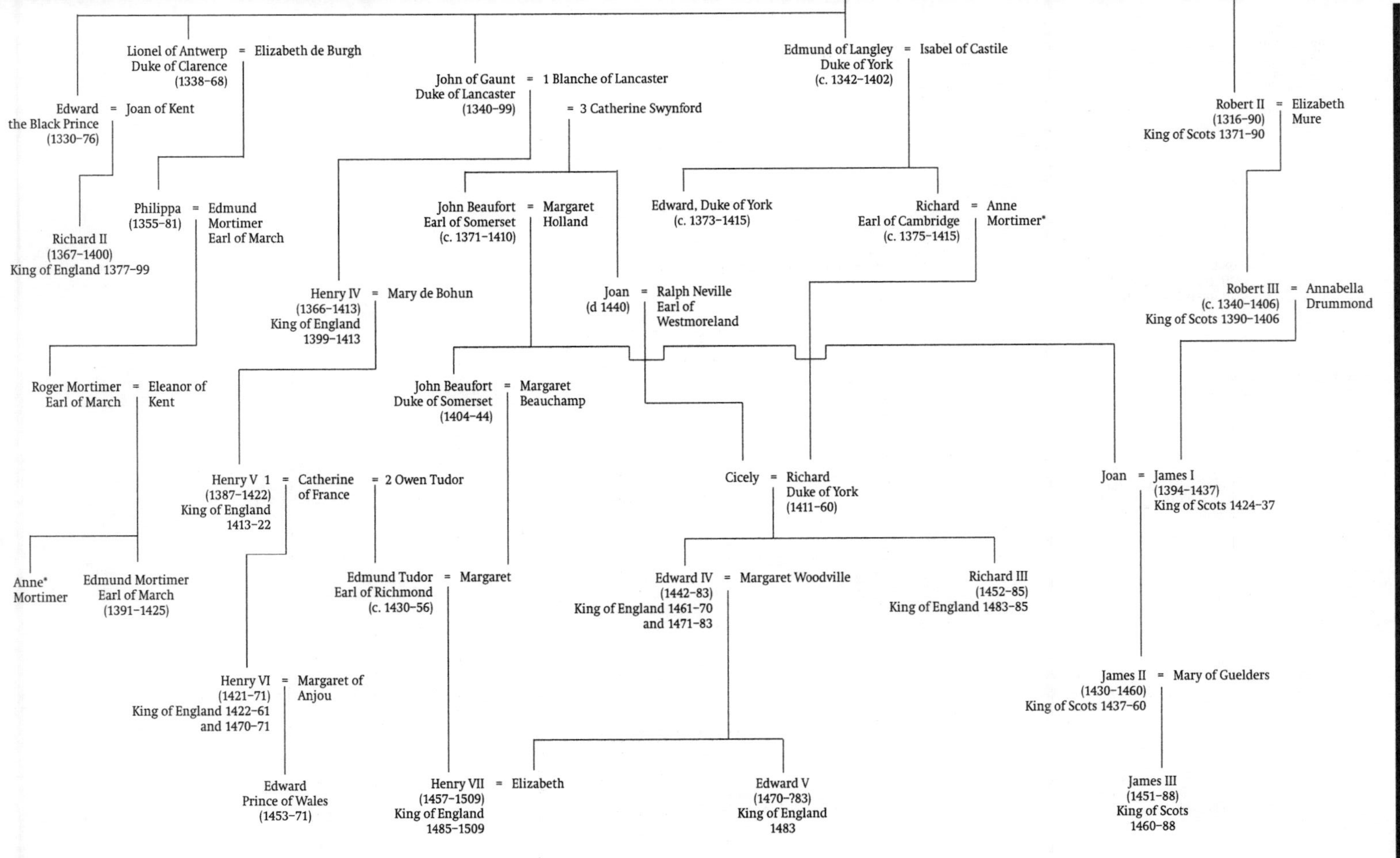

Asterisks denote the same person occurring in a different part of the tree
1 denotes first marriage, 2 second marriage, 3 third marriage

British royal family tree (continued)

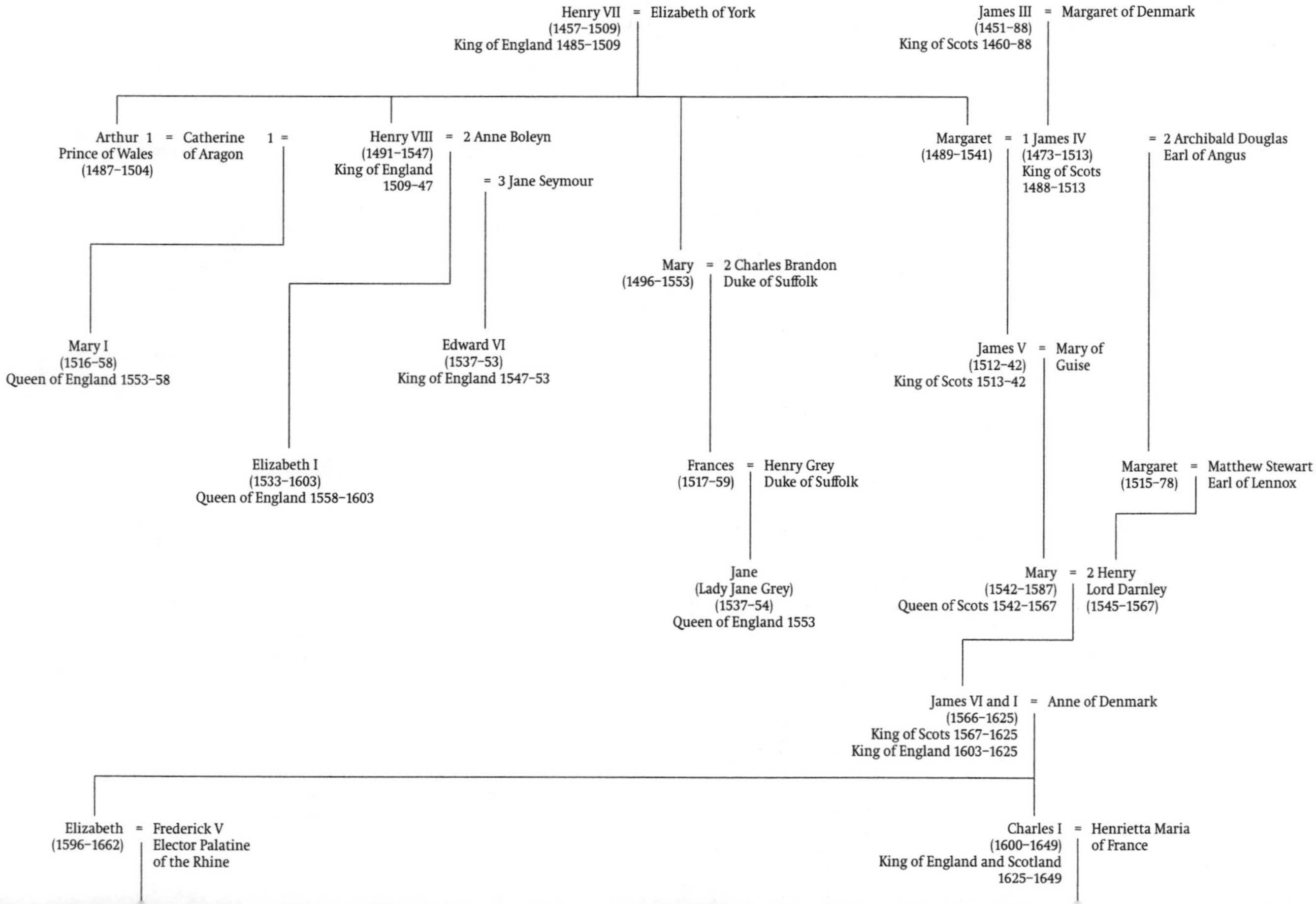

- Henry VII (1457–1509) King of England 1485–1509 = Elizabeth of York
  - Arthur (1487–1504) Prince of Wales = 1 Catherine of Aragon
  - Henry VIII (1491–1547) King of England 1509–47
    - = 1 Catherine of Aragon
      - Mary I (1516–58) Queen of England 1553–58
    - = 2 Anne Boleyn
      - Elizabeth I (1533–1603) Queen of England 1558–1603
    - = 3 Jane Seymour
      - Edward VI (1537–53) King of England 1547–53
  - Mary (1496–1553) = 2 Charles Brandon, Duke of Suffolk
    - Frances (1517–59) = Henry Grey, Duke of Suffolk
      - Jane (Lady Jane Grey) (1537–54) Queen of England 1553
  - Margaret (1489–1541)
    - = 1 James IV (1473–1513) King of Scots 1488–1513 (son of James III (1451–88) King of Scots 1460–88 = Margaret of Denmark)
      - James V (1512–42) King of Scots 1513–42 = Mary of Guise
        - Mary (1542–1587) Queen of Scots 1542–1567 = 2 Henry, Lord Darnley (1545–1567)
          - James VI and I (1566–1625) King of Scots 1567–1625, King of England 1603–1625 = Anne of Denmark
            - Elizabeth (1596–1662) = Frederick V, Elector Palatine of the Rhine
            - Charles I (1600–1649) King of England and Scotland 1625–1649 = Henrietta Maria of France
    - = 2 Archibald Douglas, Earl of Angus
      - Margaret (1515–78) = Matthew Stewart, Earl of Lennox
        - Henry, Lord Darnley (see above)

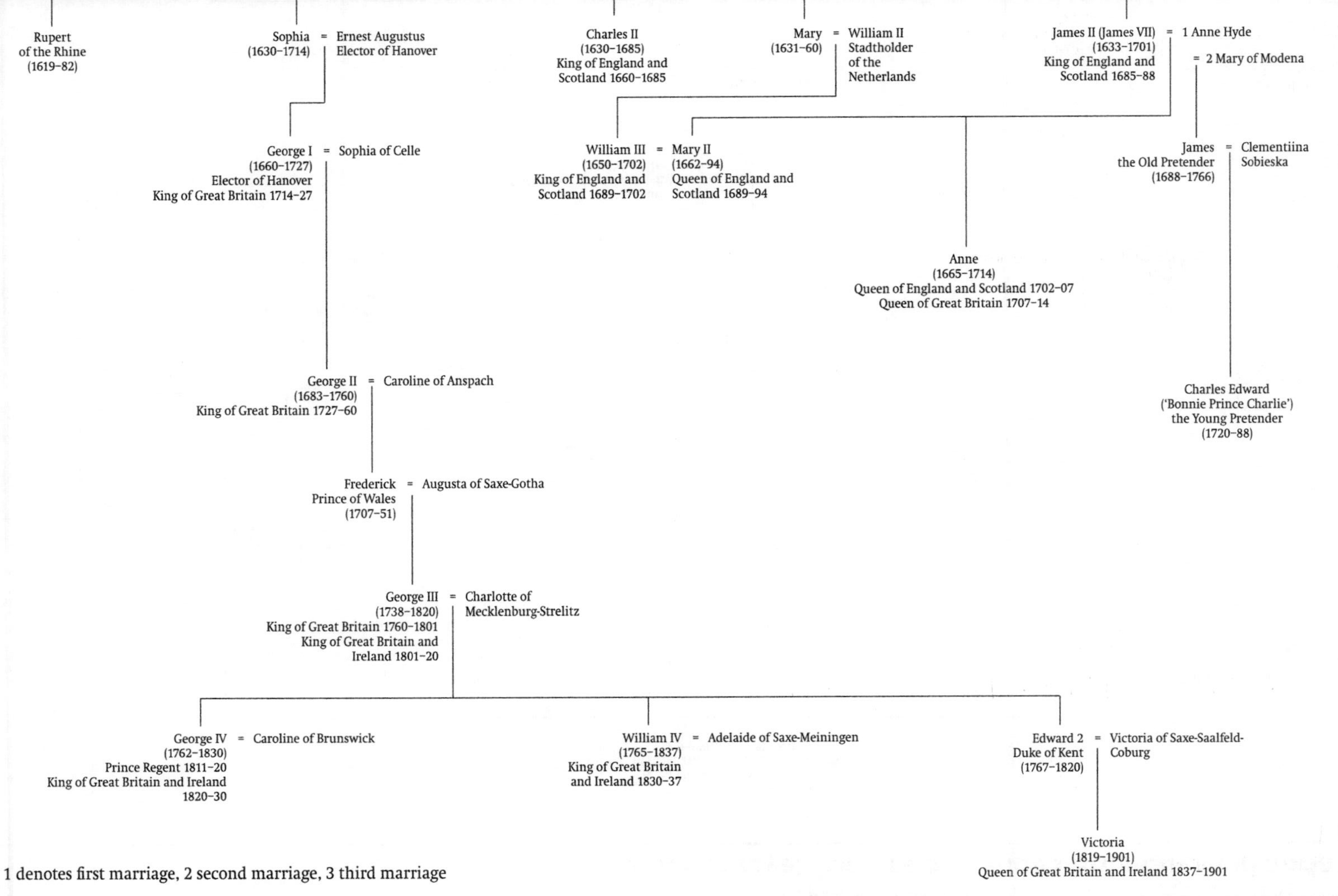

1 denotes first marriage, 2 second marriage, 3 third marriage

European royal families descended from Queen Victoria

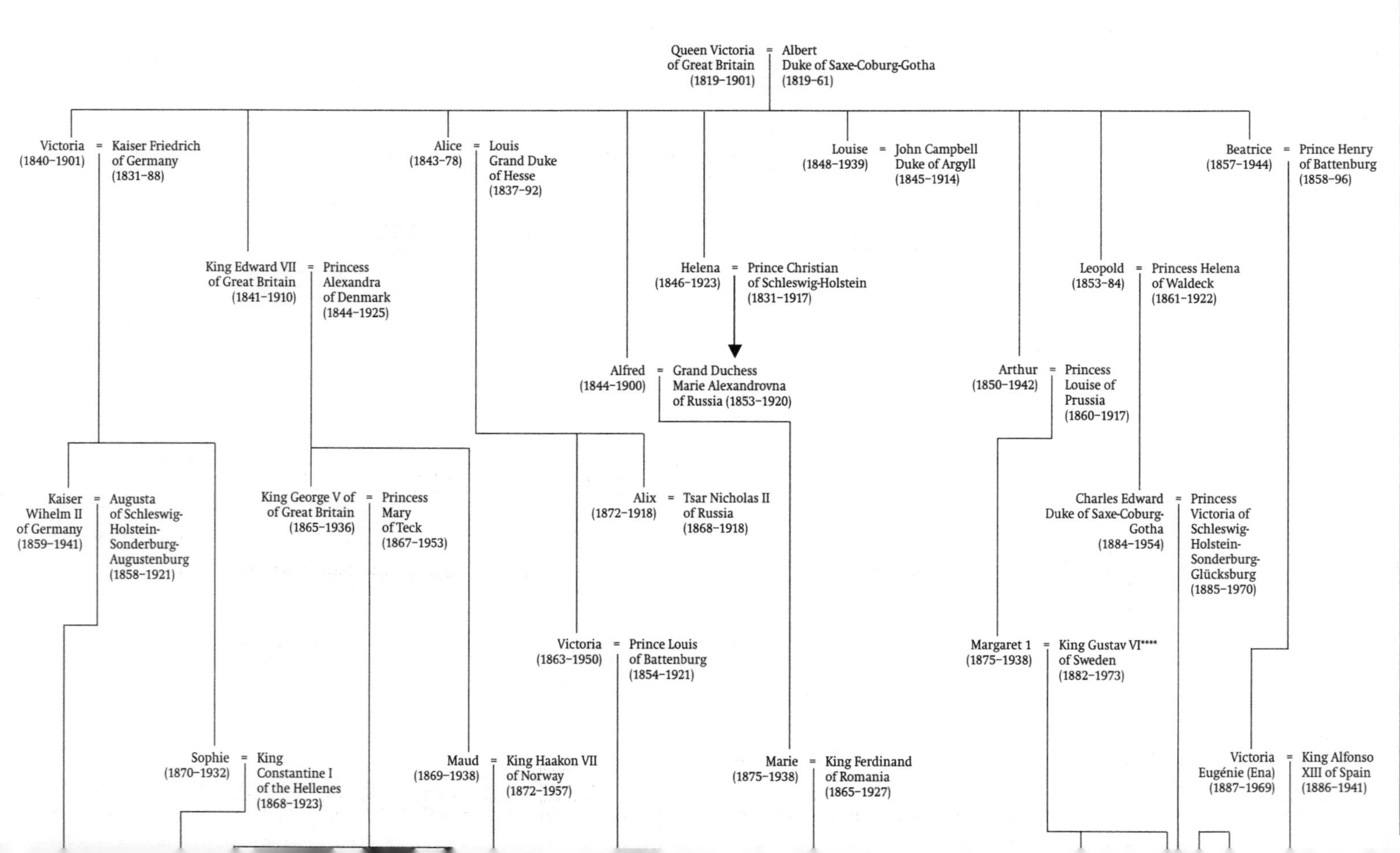

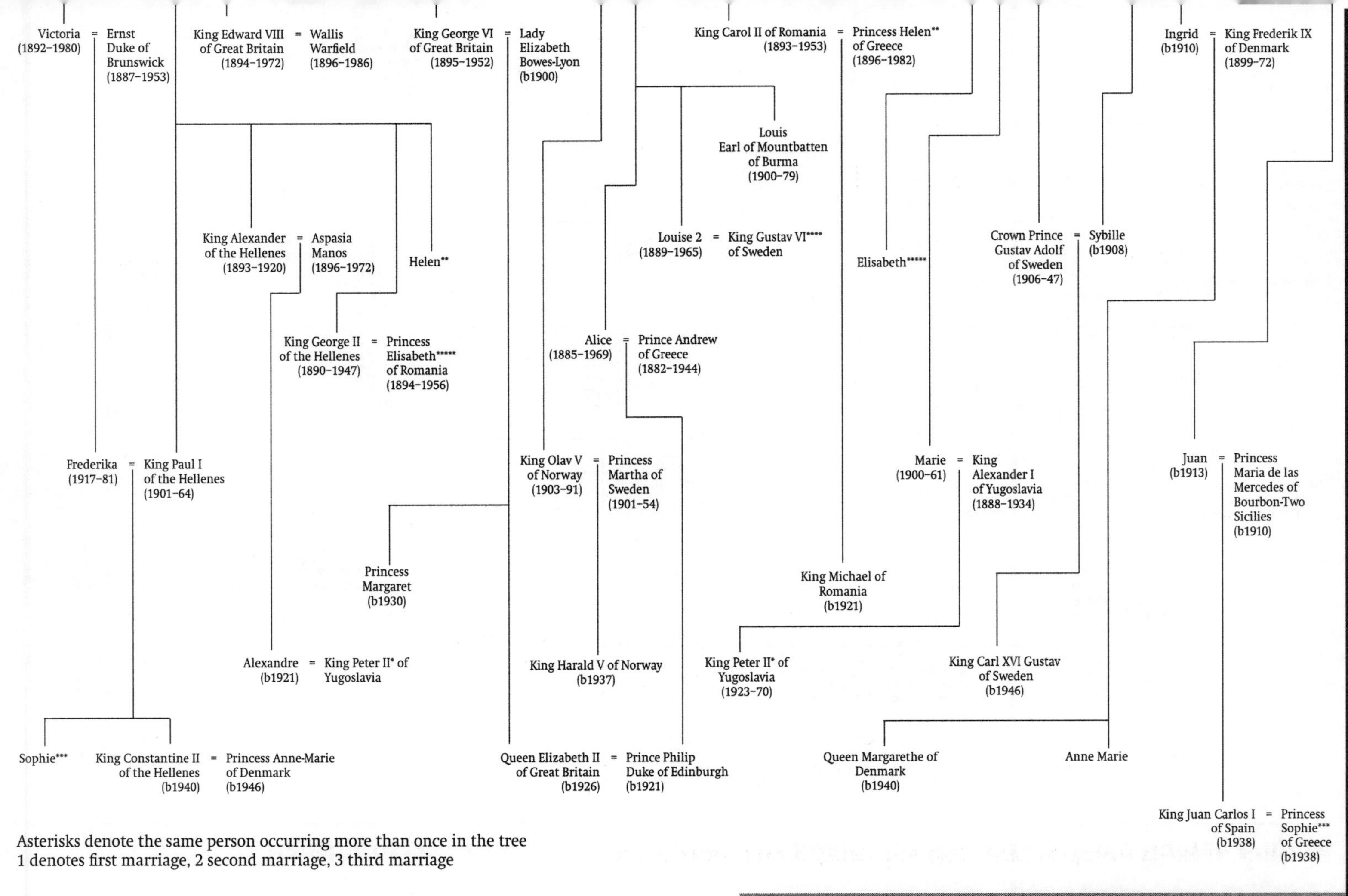

Victoria (1892–1980) = Ernst Duke of Brunswick (1887–1953)
King Edward VIII of Great Britain (1894–1972) = Wallis Warfield (1896–1986)
King George VI of Great Britain (1895–1952) = Lady Elizabeth Bowes-Lyon (b1900)
King Carol II of Romania (1893–1953) = Princess Helen** of Greece (1896–1982)
Ingrid (b1910) = King Frederik IX of Denmark (1899–72)
Louis Earl of Mountbatten of Burma (1900–79)
King Alexander of the Hellenes (1893–1920) = Aspasia Manos (1896–1972)
Helen**
Louise 2 (1889–1965) = King Gustav VI**** of Sweden
Elisabeth*****
Crown Prince Gustav Adolf of Sweden (1906–47) = Sybille (b1908)
King George II of the Hellenes (1890–1947) = Princess Elisabeth***** of Romania (1894–1956)
Alice (1885–1969) = Prince Andrew of Greece (1882–1944)
Frederika (1917–81) = King Paul I of the Hellenes (1901–64)
King Olav V of Norway (1903–91) = Princess Martha of Sweden (1901–54)
Marie (1900–61) = King Alexander I of Yugoslavia (1888–1934)
Juan (b1913) = Princess Maria de las Mercedes of Bourbon-Two Sicilies (b1910)
Princess Margaret (b1930)
King Michael of Romania (b1921)
Alexandre (b1921) = King Peter II* of Yugoslavia
King Harald V of Norway (b1937)
King Peter II* of Yugoslavia (1923–70)
King Carl XVI Gustav of Sweden (b1946)
Sophie***
King Constantine II of the Hellenes (b1940) = Princess Anne-Marie of Denmark (b1946)
Queen Elizabeth II of Great Britain (b1926) = Prince Philip Duke of Edinburgh (b1921)
Queen Margarethe of Denmark (b1940)
Anne Marie
King Juan Carlos I of Spain (b1938) = Princess Sophie*** of Greece (b1938)
Asterisks denote the same person occurring more than once in the tree
1 denotes first marriage, 2 second marriage, 3 third marriage

Hapsburgs, Bourbons and the thrones of Spain, France and the Holy Roman Empire

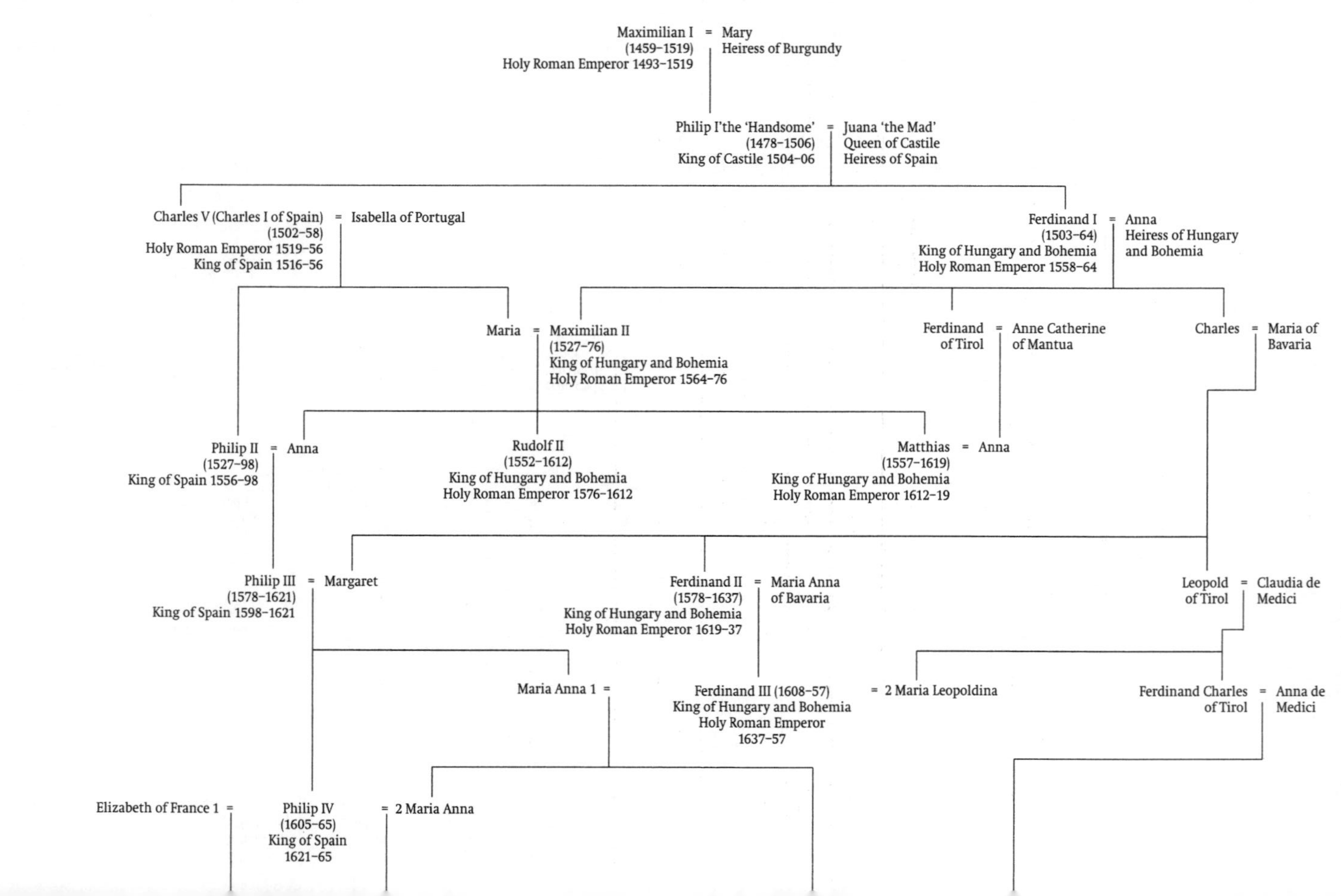

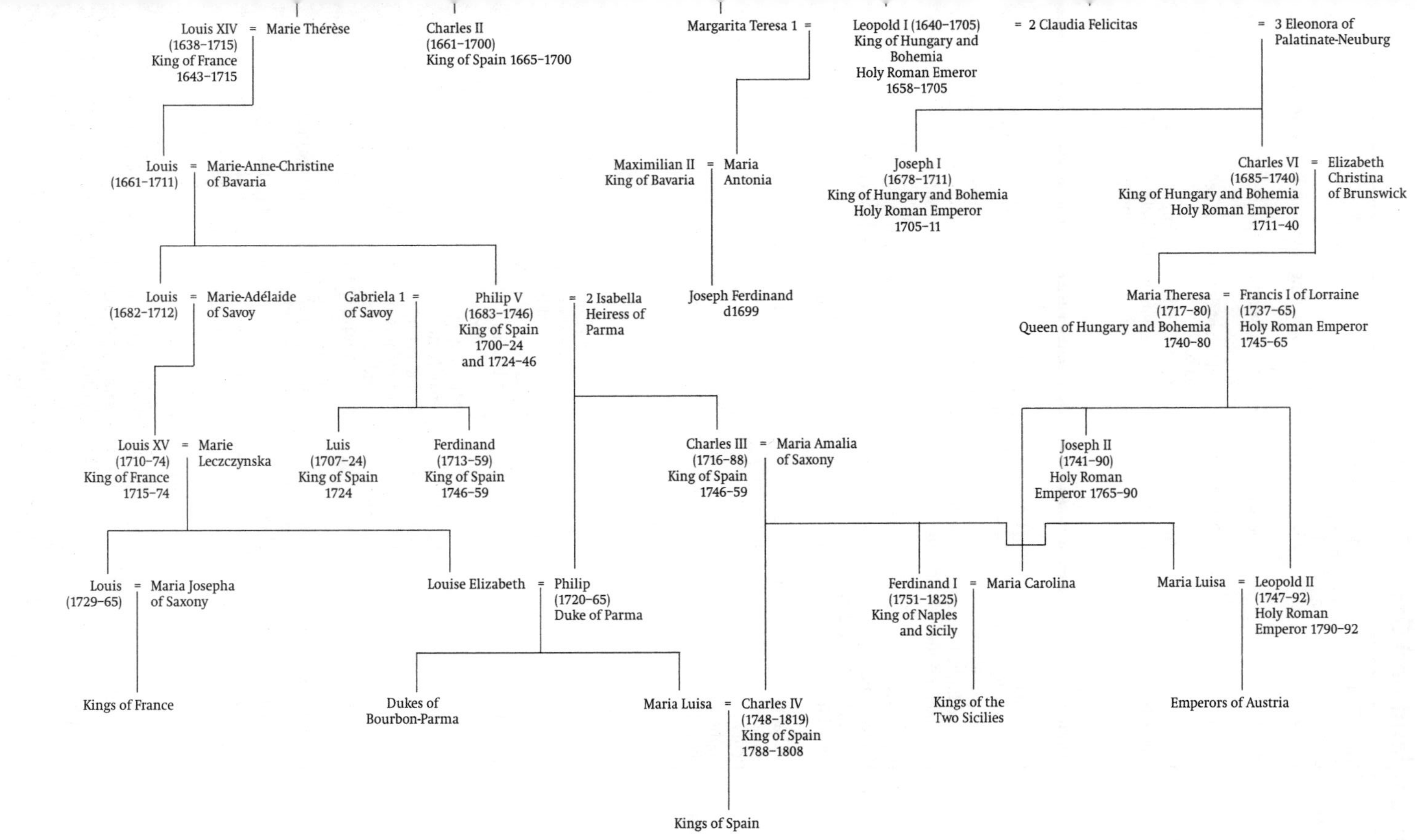

1 denotes first marriage, 2 second marriage, 3 third marriage

Rulers of England and Great Britain

Period	*Name of ruler*	*Dates of rule*	*History*
Saxons and Danes	Egbert	802–39	King of Essex.
	Ethelwulf	839–58	Son of Egbert. King of Wessex, Sussex, Kent, Essex.
	Ethelbald	858–60	Son of Ethelwulf. Displaced his father as King of Wessex.
	Ethelbert	860–5	Second son of Ethelwulf. United Kent and Wessex.
	Ethelred	865–71	Third son of Ethelwulf. King of Wessex.
	Alfred (the Great)	871–99	Fourth son of Ethelwulf. Defeated the Danes.
	Edward (the Elder)	899–924	Son of Alfred. United England and claimed Scotland.
	Athelstan (the Glorious)	924–39	Son of Edward. King of Mercia, Wessex.
	Edmund	939–46	Third son of Edward. King of Wessex, Mercia.
	Edred	946–55	Fourth son of Edward.
	Edwy (the Fair)	955–9	Eldest son of Edmund. King of Wessex.
	Edgar (the Peaceful)	959–75	Younger son of Edmund. Ruled all England.
	Edward (the Martyr)	975–8	Son of Edgar. Murdered by step-mother.
	Ethelred II (the Unready)	978–1016	Second son of Edgar.
	Edmund (Ironside)	1016	Son of Ethelred II. King of London.
	Canute	1016–35	The Dane. Became ruler by conquest.
	Harold I (Harefoot)	1037–40	Illegitimate son of Canute.
	Hardecanute	1040–2	Son of Canute by Emma. King of Denmark.
	Edward (the Confessor)	1042–66	Younger son of Ethelred II.
	Harold II	1066	Brother-in-law of Edward the Confessor. Last Saxon King.
House of Normandy	William I (the Conqueror)	1066–87	Became ruler by conquest.
	William II (Rufus)	1087–1100	Third son of William I.
	Henry I	1100–35	Youngest son of William I.
House of Blois	Stephen	1135–54	Grandson of William I.
House of Plantagenet	Henry II	1154–89	Grandson of Henry I.
	Richard I (Coeur de Lion)	1189–99	Third son of Henry II. Crusader
	John	1199–1216	Youngest son of Henry II. Signed Magna Carta 1215.
	Henry III	1216–72	Son of John.
	Edward I (Longshanks)	1272–1307	Son of Henry III.
	Edward II	1307–27	Son of Edward I. Deposed by parliament.
	Edward III	1327–77	Son of Edward II.
	Richard II	1377–99	Grandson of Edward III. Deposed.
House of Lancaster	Henry IV	1399–1413	Grandson of Edward III.
	Henry V	1413–22	Son of Henry IV. Victor of Battle of Agincourt 1415.
	Henry VI	1422–61	Son of Henry V.
		1470–71	Second period of rule.
House of York	Edward IV	1461–70	Great-grandson of Edward III.
		1471–83	Second period of rule.
	Edward V	1483	Son of Edward IV. Murdered in Tower of London.
	Richard III (Crookback)	1483–5	Brother of Edward IV. Fell at Bosworth Field.
House of Tudor	Henry VII	1485–1509	Descendant of Edward III.
	Henry VIII	1509–47	Son of Henry VII. Created Church of England.
	Edward VI	1547–53	Son of Henry VIII (by Jane Seymour).
	Mary I	1553–8	Daughter of Henry VIII (by Catherine of Aragon).
	Elizabeth I	1558–1603	Younger daughter of Henry VIII (by Anne Boleyn).
House of Stuart	James I/James VI of Scotland	1603–25	Descendant of Henry VII. First King of Great Britain (official in 1607 with the Act of the Union).
	Charles I	1625–49	Son of James I. Beheaded.
Commonwealth	Oliver Cromwell	1649–60	Lord Protector.
	Richard Cromwell (son)	1658–9	Lord Protector.
House of Stuart	Charles II	1660–85	Son of Charles I.
	James II	1685–88	Younger son of Charles I. Deposed.
	William III	1689–1702	Grandson of Charles I.

Period	Name of ruler	Dates of rule	History
	Mary II	1689–94	Daughter of James II. Ruled together with William III.
	Anne	1702–14	Younger daughter of James II.
House of Hanover	George I	1714–27	Great-grandson of James I.
	George II	1727–60	Only son of George I.
	George III	1760–1820	Grandson of George II.
	George IV	1820–30	Eldest son of George III.
	William IV	1830–7	Third son of George III.
	Victoria	1837–1901	Granddaughter of George III.
House of Saxe-Coburg	Edward VII	1901–10	Son of Victoria.
House of Windsor	George V	1910–36	Son of Edward VII.
	Edward VIII	1936	Eldest son of George V. Abdicated.
	George VI	1936–52	Second son of George V.
	Elizabeth II	1952–	Daughter of George VI.

MAJOR WARS OF MEDIEVAL AND MODERN TIMES

War	Dates	History
Norman Conquest of England	1066	France (William the Conqueror)–England (Harold II) Battle of Hastings (14 Oct 1066). Most decisive battle on English soil which led to the successful conquest by the Normans. Harold II died in battle Began rule of a dynasty of Norman Kings and almost complete replacement of English nobility by Normans, Bretons, and Flemings
The Crusades	1095–1272	Christians–Turks Holy Wars authorized by the Pope, fought against infidels in the East, heretics who threatened Catholic unity, and against Christian lay powers who opposed the Papacy
Conquests of Genghis Khan	1190–1227	Mongols–N China, Kara–Chitai Empire Subjugation of hostile tribes – Naimans, Tanguts, and Turkish Uigurs
War of the Sicilian Vespers	1282–1302	Sicily–France Massacre of the French in Sicily marked the beginning of revolt of Sicilians against Charles of Anjou War of Sicilian Vespers ensued. Angevins supported by papacy, Italian Guelphs and Philip II of France, while Aragonese helped by Italian Ghibellines. James II ascended to throne, made peace with papacy, France, and Angevins (to whom he renounced Sicily) by Treaty of Anagni
Hundred Years' War	1337–1453	England–France Edward III claimed French throne in 1340 and style himself 'King of England and France'. Traditional rivalries exploded into a dynastic struggle. 1415 Battle of Agincourt – Henry V led overwhelming victory over French. 1417 English then began systematic conquest of Normandy, a task beyond their resources. Evicted from Guyenne (1453) which reduced England's French territories to Calais (lost in 1558) and the Channel Islands. However, the title of King of France was not relinquished until 1801
Fall of Constantinople	1453	Turks–Byzantine Empire Collapse of the Byzantine Empire. Since 1261, when Constantinople had been retaken from Latin rule by Michael VII Paleologus, the Byzantine Empire had been threatened by growing power of Ottoman Turks in Asia Minor. 1422 Ottoman Sultan of Turkey Murad II laid siege to the city. This failed but attempt thirty years later by Mehmed II succeeded. Constantinople fell 1453. Last Byzantine emperor Constantine XI Paleologus died in battle
Wars of the Roses	1455–85	Civil wars in England Between two rival factions of the House of Plantagenet – York (white rose) and Lancaster (red rose). Began when Richard, Duke of York, claimed protectorship of crown after King Henry VI's mental breakdown and ended with Henry Tudor's defeat of Richard III in Battle of Bosworth. Wars escalated by gentry and by aristocratic feuds

Major wars of medieval and modern times (continued)

War	*Dates*	*History*
French Wars of Religion	1562–98	Catholics–Huguenots Caused by growth of Calvinism, noble factionalism, and weak royal government. From 1550s Calvinist or Huguenot numbers increased, fostered by missionary activities of Geneva. Noble factions of Bourbons, Guise, and Montmorency were split by religion as well as by family interests. Civil wars were encouraged by Philip II's support of Catholic Guise faction and by Elizabeth I's aid to Huguenots. They ended when Henry of Navarre returned to Catholicism and crushed the Guise Catholic League
Thirty Years' War	1618–48	France–Habsburg rulers Power struggle between Kings of France and Habsburg rulers of Holy Roman Empire and Spain. War fuelled by conflict between Calvinism and Catholicism, and also by the underlying constitutional conflict between Holy Roman Emperor and the German Princes. With Frederick V's defeat (1620) and intervention by other powers (such as Sweden, Denmark, and France) the conflict intensified and spread. Spain collapsed and left the emperor isolated. Peace negotiations opened and ended German war at the Peace of Westphalia
Bishops' Wars	1639–40	Scotland–England Two wars between Charles I and Scotland caused by Charles I's unpopular policies towards the Scottish kirk. Resulted in English defeats and bankruptcy for Charles who was then forced to call the Short and Long Parliaments in 1640, bringing to an end his personal rule
English Civil Wars	1642–51	Charles I–Parliamentarians Parliamentary opposition to Royal policies. First battle at Edgehill (Oct 1642) but neither side victorious. Royalists then threatened London, the Parliamentarians stronghold. By autumn the North and West were in their hands. Crucial event was 1643 alliance of Parliament with the Scots. This increased military strength helped the parliamentarians, led by Oliver Cromwell, defeat the Royalists at Marston Moor. 1646 saw end of first civil war with Charles' surrender to the Scots at Newark in May. 1646–48 negotiations between parliament and King began. Aug 1647 army presented King with Head of Proposals asking for religious tolerance and parliamentary control of the armed forces. Charles made secret pact with the Scots, promising to establish Presbyterianism in England. Scots invaded England and were only repulsed in Battle of Preston. Around 100,000 men died in the two wars (1 in 10 of the adult male population). Charles brought to trial by Cromwell (who was also signatory of his death warrant) and executed Jan 1649
War of League of Augsburg	1688–97	Louis XIV–European Alliance. The third major war of Louis XIV of France in which his expansionist plans were blocked by the alliance led by England, United Provinces (of the Netherlands) and Austrian Habsburgs. Issue underlying war was the balance of power between Bourbon and Habsburg dynasties. War began when French marched into the Palatinate while Austria was defeating Turks in the East. Grand alliance of United Provinces, England, Saxony, Bavaria, and Spain, all fearful of French annexations, joined together against France. The war was costly and lengthy. Louis XIV opened negotiations for peace 1696 and in 1697 Treaty of Rijswijk drawn up. Did not resolve conflict between Habsburgs and Bourbons, nor English and French, both of which erupted again only four years later in the Spanish Succession
War of Spanish Succession	1701–14	Alliance–Louis XIV Alliance of British, Dutch, and Habsburg Emperor against French, supported by Spanish. War arose out of conflict as to succession to throne of Spain following death of childless Charles II. Claimants were England, Dutch Republic and France. When alliance collapsed the war was concluded by Treaties of Utrecht which divided inheritance among the powers, Britain's imperial power grew at the expense of France and Spain
War of Jenkin's Ear	1739–43	Britain–Spain Began in 1739 but then merged into War of the Austrian Succession.

War	Dates	History
		Anti-Spanish feeling in Britain provoked war as Captain Robert Jenkins claimed Spanish coastguards in the Caribbean cut off his ear
War of Austrian Succession	1740–8	Prussia–Austria Struggle for mastery of German states. Hostilities prompted by Frederick II of Prussia's seizure of Habsburg province of Silesia. French allied with Bavaria and Spain and later Saxony and Prussia. Austria was supported by Britain who feared France's hegemony in Europe which would threaten Britain's colonial and commercial empire. After 1744 this developed into a colonial conflict between Britain and the Franco-Spanish bloc. Peace concluded only by Treaty of Aix-la-Chapelle (1748) which preserved Austrian inheritance but also confirmed Prussian inheritance of Silesia
Seven Years' War	1756–63	A major European conflict rooted in the rivalry between Austria and Prussia and the imminent colonial struggle between Britain and France in the New World and the Far East. Hostilities in N America (1754) pre-dated the Diplomatic Revolution in Europe (1756), which created two opposing power blocs: Austria, France, Russia, Sweden, and Saxony against Prussia, Britain, and Portugal. British maritime superiority countered Franco-Spanish naval power and prevented an invasion by the French. The European war, precipitated by Prussia's seizure of Saxony, was marked by many notable pitched land battles. Saved from total defeat when Russia switched sides, Frederick II of Prussia retained Silesia in 1763
US War of Independence	1775–83	American settlers–Britain Insurrection of thirteen of Britain's N American colonies. Began as civil war but America was later joined by France (1778), Spain (1779), and Netherlands (1780). America rejected Britain's offer of peace in the civil war conflicts and declared independence. Britain ultimately defeated
French Revolutionary Wars	1792–1802	A series of campaigns between France and neighbouring European states hostile to the Revolution and to French hegemony, merging ultimately with the Napoleonic Wars
Napoleonic Wars	1800–15	Fought to preserve French hegemony in Europe. Initially a guarantee for political, social, and economic changes of the Revolution, but increasingly became manifestation of Napoleon's territorial ambitions. War began with Napoleon's destruction of the Second Coalition (1800). Britain resumed hostilities 1803 prompting Napoleon to prepare for invasion and encouraging the formation of a Third Coalition. Britain retained naval superiority but Napoleon established territorial domination with the invasions of Spain (1808) and Russia (1812). French finally overwhelmed by the Fourth Coalition and war ended with the Battle of Waterloo (1815)
Peninsular War	1808–14	France–Britain Struggle for the Iberian peninsula which began as Spanish revolt against imposition of Napoleon's brother, Joseph, as King of Spain, but developed into bitter conflict, with British forces under Wellington liberating Spain (1811). Following Napoleon's Moscow campaign (1812) French resources were overextended, enabling Wellington's army to invade SW France (1813–14)
Greek War of Independence	1821–8	Greece–Turkey Greece fought alone until 1825 when her cause was seconded by Britain, Russia, and later France. Turks defeated and Greece's independence guaranteed by her allies
Crimean War	1853–6	Fought in Crimean Peninsula by Britain and France against Russia. Origins lay in the Russian successes against the Turks in the Black Sea area, and the British and French desire to prevent further Russian expansion westward which threatened the Mediterranean and overland routes to India. Major battles were fought at the River Alma (Sep 1854), Balaclava (1854), and Inkermann (Nov 1854). Fall of Russian fortress at Sebastopol (Sep 1855) led to negotiations for peace. Finally agreed in Paris 1856 that Russia would cede South Bessarabia to Moldavia
American Civil War	1861–5	Conflict between Republicans and Confederates. Dealt with two great issues; the nature of the Federal Union and the relative power of the states and central government; and the existence of Black slavery. When Lincoln and the Republican Party's election demonstrated

Major wars of medieval and modern times (continued)

War	Dates	History
		that the South could no longer expect to control the high offices of state, eleven Southern states withdrew from the Union and established the Confederate States of America. War broke out (12 Apr 1861) when the Southern batteries opened fire on a Union emplacement in the harbour of Charlottesville. Lincoln at first defined the issue as preservation of the Union, without any reference to slavery, but he broadened the war aims (Jan 1861) proclaiming the emancipation of all slaves in areas then under arms against the government. The winning strategy began in 1863 when the Republican General Grant won control of the whole Mississippi valley, isolating the western confederate states from the rest. After several fierce battles (Gettysburg, Fredericksburg, and the Chattanooga campaign) the South's position became untenable and General Lee, leader of the Confederate forces, abandoned the Confederate capital in Apr 1865 and finally capitulated at Appomattox Court House. The last surrender took place on 26 May
Franco-Prussian War	1870	Marked the end of French hegemony in Europe and the foundation of a German empire. In Napoleon III's ambition to conquer Prussia, Bismarck saw an opportunity to bring the S German states into unit with the Prussian-led N German states and build a strong German empire. Conflict was sparked off by disputed candidature for the French throne. The Ems Telegram, sent by Wilhelm I of Prussia refusing the French conditions, succeeded in provoking the French to declare war five days later. After only four weeks the French found themselves trapped at Metz. Main French army tried to relieve them but were surrounded and trapped by Germans at Sedan. French army, with Napoleon III and Macmahon, surrendered. French resistance continued with the new government and the Germans then began to besiege Paris. Paris surrendered Jan 1871. Treaty of Frankfurt drawn up. Germany annexed Alsace and Lorraine, imposed a high war indemnity on France and occupied northern territory until indemnity paid
Boer Wars	1880–1, 1899–1902	Wars fought by Britain for the mastery of South Africa. British had made several attempts to re-incorporate the Boers into a South African confederation. First war ended with defeat of British at Majuba Hill and the signing of the Pretoria and London conventions in 1881 and 1884. Second Boer War (1899–1902) can be divided into three phrases – series of Boer successes, counter-offensives by British which captured Pretoria, period of guerilla warfare. Boers effectively won the peace. Retained control of 'native affairs', won back representative government in 1907 and federated South Africa on their own terms (1910). Nevertheless, British interests in South Africa remained protected
World War 1	1914–18	Origins lay in reaction of other great powers to ambitions of German Empire. The political tensions divided Europe into two camps – the Triple Alliance (Britain, France, and Russia) and the Triple Entente (Germany, Austria-Hungary, and Italy) Catalyst to war was the assassination of heir to Habsburg throne, Franz Ferdinand, in Bosnia. Austria declared war on Serbia. Germany then declared war on Russia and France and invaded neutral Belgium. This brought the British into the war on the side of the French. Japan joined Britain as did Italy in 1915. Germany was joined by Turkey (1914) and Bulgaria (1915). Military campaigns centre on France and Belgium in W Europe. First battle of Ypres prevented the Germans from reaching the ports. By end 1914 static line of defence had been established from Belgian coast to Switzerland. Position of stalemate reached. 1916 allies launched offensive for the W front but stopped by Germans who attacked French at Verdun. To relieve situation Battle of the Somme was launched but proved indecisive. Spring 1918 Germany launched major offensive on West but was driven back by the allies with help from USA. By November armistice was signed with allies having recaptured Belgium and nearly all French territory. Treaty of Versailles drawn up 1919 assigning responsibility for causing the

War	Dates	History
		war to Germany and establishing her liability for reparations payments. Germany lost all overseas territories and considerable territory in Poland. Rhineland demilitarized and occupied by allied forces. Germany called treaty a 'Diktat' and its harshness was bitterly resented throughout the interwar years.
Spanish Civil War	1936–9	Republicans–Nationalists (led by General Franco) Both sides attracted foreign assistance; Republic from the USSR and the International Brigades and the Nationalists from Fascist Italy and Nazi Germany. Nationalist victory due to balance of foreign aid, to nonintervention on part of the Western democracies and to greater internal unity in the Nationalist army under Franco.
World War 2	1939–45	Allies (Britain and British Commonwealth, China, France, USA, USSR)–Axis Powers (Germany, Italy, Japan) Origins lay in three different conflicts which merged after 1941: Germany's desire for expansion, Japan's struggle against China, conflict between Japanese and US interests in the Pacific. War in Europe caused by German unwillingness to accept Treaty of Versailles, which was systematically dismantled aided by the allied policy of appeasement. Increased German aggression finally resulted in the invasion of Czechoslovakia, after which Britain and France abandoned policy of appeasement and pledged support to Poland which was now threatened. Germany signed alliance with Russia and invaded Poland. Britain and France then declared war on Germany. Little fighting took place but Germany proceeded to occupy Norway and Denmark. German Blitzkrieg tactics (a combination of tank warfare and airpower) brought about the surrender of Holland in four days, Belgium in three weeks, and France in seven weeks. After failed attempt to gain air supremacy over Britain (Battle of Britain) the invasion of Britain was postponed. Germany then moved east into Greece and Yugoslavia. British military efforts were concentrated against Italy in Mediterranean and N Africa. Allied forces finally ejected German and Italian forces in mid-1943, invaded Sicily and Italy itself and forced Italy to make a separate peace. June 1941 Germany invaded her ally Russia and advanced towards Moscow, Leningrad, and the Volga. After two years of occupation and the Battle of Stalingrad in winter 1942–3 (a major turning point in the allied campaign) they were driven out. Allies launched a second front through invasion of Normandy and Paris was liberated in August. Allies advanced into Germany and linked with the Russians on the River Elbe. Germans surrendered unconditionally at Rheims 7 May 1945. Japan's desire for expansion led to her attack on Pearl Harbor, Hawaii, and US declared war on Japan next day (8 Dec 1941). In reply, Germany and Italy declared war on US. Not until June 1942 did naval victories halt Japanese advance. Fighting continued until 1945 when US dropped two atomic bombs on Hiroshima and Nagasaki (6 and 9 Aug). Japan then surrendered
First Indochinese War	1946–54	Vietnam–France Vietnam controlled by France as colony 1883–1939 and then as a possession 1930–45. Ho Chi Minh proclaimed its independence on 2 Sep 1945 and French opposed the move. Ho Chi Minh led guerrilla warfare against French which ended in Vietnamese victory at Dien Bien Phu in May 1954. Agreement signed in Geneva providing temporary division of the country at the 17th parallel of latitude between the communist-dominated North and the US-supported South. Activities of procommunist rebels would lead to the second Vietnam War.
Korean War	1950–3	Communists and non-Communists Communist North invaded South after series of border clashes. UN forces intervened driving the invaders back to Chinese frontier. China entered conflict and with N Koreans occupied Seoul. UN forces counterattacked and retook territory south of 38th parallel.
Suez War	1956	Britain, France, Israel–Egypt. In July 1956 Egyptian President Abdel Nasser nationalized the Suez Canal following American and British decision not to finance construction of the Aswan Dam. When diplomacy failed France and England planned military action to

Major Wars of Medieval and Modern Times (continued)

War	*Dates*	*History*
		regain control of the canal, allied with Israel. In Oct Israel invaded Egypt. England and France ordered Israel to leave and also landed at Port Said, apparently to enforce the UN ceasefire. Growing opposition at home, hostile position of USA, and the threatened intervention of the Soviets forced them to withdraw. The outcome of the incident was Israel regaining shipping rights to the canal, though France and England lost influence in the area
Vietnam War	1956–75	The war between communist North Vietnam and non-communist South Vietnam, also known as the Second Indochinese War. The Geneva settlement had left North Vietnam under communist rule, and the South ruled first by the emperor Bas Dai (until 1955) and then by Ngo Dinh Diem's dictatorial regime. From 1961, US aid and numbers of 'military advisers' increased considerably. From 1964, US aircraft bombarded the North, and by 1968 over 500,000 troops were involved. These troops were withdrawn in 1973, and hostilities ceased in 1975 when the North's victory was completed with the capture of Saigon (renamed Ho Chi Minh City)
Six Day War	1967	Syrian bombings of Israeli villages intensified early 1967. Israeli air force shot down six Syrian planes. In retaliation Abdel Nasser mobilised Egyptian forces near Sinai border. Israel defeated Egyptian forces and established air superiority. War cost Arabs Old City of Jerusalem, Sinai and Gaza Strip, West Bank, and the Golan Heights
Cambodian War	1970–5	Cambodia, S Vietnam, US–N Vietnam, Viet Cong, Khmer Rouge. Cambodia had achieved independence in 1953, under Prince Norodom Sihanouk. He assumed position of neutrality in Vietnam war and allowed Vietnamese communists sanctuary in Cambodia. In 1970 he was deposed by coup and US and S Vietnam forces invaded Cambodia to destroy communist sanctuaries. New Cambodian government faced growing threat from Cambodian communists (Khmer Rouge). US launched series of raids by which it hoped to halt Khmer activity but, after five years of civil war, Phnom Penh fell to Khmer Rouge. In 1979 Vietnamese forces invaded and installed a puppet government
Iran–Iraq War	1980–8	After the Islamic Revolution in Iran, the Iranians accused Baghdad of encouraging the Arabs of Iran's Khuzestan province to demand autonomy. Iraq also feared Iranian provocation of its own large Sh'ite population. Border fighting followed and Iraqi forces advanced into Iran (Sep 1980). Peace finally agreed in 1988 after deaths of around half a million on each side. Iraq accepted Iran's terms in 1990
Falklands War	1982	Britain–Argentina Argentinian invasion of the islands governed by Britain since 1933. War ended after three months in Argentinian surrender
Gulf War	1991	Iraq–US led allies (29 member coalition) War caused by Iraqi invasion of Kuwait and failure to comply with UN resolution calling for withdrawal. Hostilities suspended after 43 days of fighting when Iraq accepted the UN resolution
Yugoslavian Civil War	1991–	Declarations of independence by Slovenia, Macedonia, and Croatia considered illegal by central government. Confrontation between Croatia and Serb-dominated national army developed into civil war. Germany's recognition of the states of Croatia and Slovenia in the middle of December led to Serbian acceptance of peace plan at the end of that month. 10 000 UN peace-keeping soldiers deployed in Croatia. In Apr 1992 the UN then recognised independence of Bosnia-Herzegovina. Serbia still continued to battle the secessionists. May saw beginning of bombardment of Sarajevo, followed by bombardment of Dubrovnik at the end of that month. This brought about UN resolution to ban all exports to Yugoslavia. By July an estimated 700 000 people had been driven out of Bosnia since beginning of war, all due to Serbs policy of 'ethnic cleansing' (aimed at driving Muslims out of areas shared with ethnic Serbs). In August the UN authorized use of military force to insure humanitarian aid getting through to Bosnia. In Sept Yugoslavia expelled from the UN.

The main crusades to the East

	Background	*Leader(s)*	*Outcome*
First Crusade (1096–9)	Proclaimed by Urban II to aid the Greeks against the Seljuk Turks in Asia Minor, liberate Jerusalem and the Holy Land from Seljuk domination, and safeguard pilgrim routes to the Holy Sepulchre.	Bohemond I Godfrey of Bouillon Raymond, Count of Toulouse Robert, Count of Flanders Robert Curthose, Duke of Normandy Stephen, Count of Blois	Capture of Nicaea in Anatolia (Jun 1097); Turks vanquished at Battle of Dorylaeum (Jul 1097); capture of Antioch in Syria (Jun 1098), Jerusalem (Jul 1099). Godfrey of Bouillon became ruler of the new Latin kingdom of Jerusalem, and defeated the Fatimids of Egypt near Ascalon in Palestine (Aug 1099). Three other crusader states were founded: Antioch, Edessa, Tripoli.
Second Crusade (1147–8)	Proclaimed by Eugenius III to aid the crusader states after the Muslim reconquest of Edessa (1144).	Conrad III of Germany Louis VII of France	German army heavily defeated by Turks near Dorylaeum (Oct 1147), and the French at Laodicea (Jan 1148); Damascus in Syria invested, but siege abandoned after four days (Jul 1148). The crusaders' military reputation was destroyed, and the Syrian Muslims united against the Latins.
Third Crusade (1189–92)	Proclaimed by Gregory VIII after Saladin's defeat of the Latins at the Battle of Hattin (Jul 1187) and his conquest of Jerusalem (Oct 1187). (By 1189 all that remained of the kingdom of Jerusalem was the port of Tyre.)	Frederick I Barbarossa Philip II Augustus of France Richard I of England	Cyprus conquered from Greeks (May 1191), and established as new crusader kingdom (survived until 1489); capture of Acre in Palestine (Jul 1191); Saladin defeated near Arsuf (Sep 1191); three-year truce guaranteeing safe conduct of Christian pilgrims to Jerusalem. Most cities and castles of the Holy Land remained in Muslim hands.
Fourth Crusade (1202–4)	Proclaimed by Innocent III to recover the Holy Places	Boniface of Montferrat	Despite papal objections, crusade diverted from Egypt or Palestine (1) to Zara, a Christian town in Dalmatia, conquered for Venetians (Nov 1202); (2) to Byzantium, where embroilment in dynastic struggles led to sack of Constantinople (Apr 1204) and foundation of Latin Empire of Constantinople (survived until 1261). The crusading movement was discredited; the Latins in Palestine and Syria were hardly helped at all; the Byzantine empire never fully recovered; and the opportunity was lost of a united front between the Latins and Greeks against the Muslims.
Fifth Crusade (1217–21)	Proclaimed by Innocent III when a six-year truce between the kingdom of Jerusalem and Egypt expired.	Andrew II of Hungary John of Brienne, King of Jerusalem Leopold, Duke of Austria	Three indecisive expeditions against Muslims in Palestine (1217); capture of Damietta in Egypt after protracted siege (May 1218–Nov 1219), further conquests attempted, but crusaders forced to relinquish Damietta (Aug 1221) and withdrew

The main crusades to the East (continued)

	Background	*Leader(s)*	*Outcome*
Sixth Crusade (1228–9)	Emperor Frederick II, who first took the Cross in 1215, married the heiress to the kingdom of Jerusalem in 1225. Excommunicated by Gregory IX for delaying his departure, he finally arrived at Acre in Sep 1228.	Frederick II	Negotiations with Egyptians secured Jerusalem and other places, including Bethlehem and Nazareth (Feb 1229); Frederick crowned King of Jerusalem in church of Holy Sepulchre (Mar 1229). Jerusalem was held until recaptured by the Khorezmian Turks in 1244.
Seventh Crusade (1248–54)	Proclaimed by Innocent IV after the fall of Jerusalem and defeat of the Latin army near Gaza by the Egyptians and Khorezmians (1244).	Louis IX of France	Capture of Damietta (June 1249); defeat at Mansurah (Feb 1250); surrender of crusaders during attempted withdrawal. Damietta relinquished and large ransoms paid (May 1250). Louis spent four years in Palestine, refortifying Acre, Caesarea, Joppa and Sidon, and fruitlessly attempting to regain Jerusalem by alliances with the Mameluks and Mongols
Eighth Crusade (1270–2)	Proclaimed after the Mameluk conquest of Arsuf, Caesarea, Haifa (1265). Antioch and Joppa (1268).	Charles of Anjou, King of Naples-Sicily Edward of England (later Edward I) Louis IX of France	Attacked Tunisia in N Africa (Jul 1270); Louis died in Aug; Charles concluded treaty with Tunis and withdrew; Edward negotiated 11 years' truce with Mameluks in Palestine. By 1291 the Latins had been driven from the Holy Land.

The American Civil War

1859

16 Oct	John Brown's raid on Harper's Ferry

1860

6 Nov	Abraham Lincoln elected President
20 Dec	Secession of seven Southern states

1861

4 Feb	Announcement of the Confederated States of America – Jefferson Davis named as President
4 Mar	Inauguration of Lincoln as President
12 Apr	Southern Bombardment of Fort Sumter
21 Jul	First Battle of Bull Run

1862

6 Apr	Battle of Shiloh
29–30 Aug	Second Battle of Bull Run
17 Sep	Battle of Antietam
22 Sep	Preliminary Emancipation Proclamation
13 Dec	Battle of Fredericksburg

1863

1 Jan	Emancipation Proclamation
2 May	Battle of Chancellorsville – death of Stonewall Jackson
3 Jul	Battle of Gettysburg
4 Jul	Fall of Vicksburg
19–20 Sep	Battle of Chickamauga
24–25 Nov	Battle of Chattanooga

1864

1 Sep	Fall of Atlanta
15–16 Dec	Battle of Nashville

1865

9 Apr	Surrender of Confederate forces at Appomatox
14 Apr	Assassination of Lincoln

Circumnavigations of the world

Exploration and discovery

Great explorers

Name	*Dates*	*Nationality*	*Major voyages of exploration*
Amundsen, Roald	1872–1928	Norwegian	1911 voyage to the South Pole
Baffin, William	1584–1622	English	1616 explores Baffin Bay
Balboa, Vasco Núñez de	1475–1517	Spanish	1513 reaches the Pacific Ocean
Bougainville, Louis de	1729–1811	French	1766 begins circumnavigation of the globe
Cabral, Pedro Álvarez	c. 1467–1520	Portuguese	1500 reaches Brazil
Cartier, Jacques	1491–1557	French	1534 explores the coast of N America
Cook, James	1728–79	English	1769 maps coast of New Zealand and Australia 1770 lands at Botany Bay 1774 reaches S Georgia and the Sandwich Islands 1778 explores islands now known as Hawaii
Davis, John	c. 1550–1605	English	1585 expedition to Greenland; discovers the Davis Strait
Diaz, Bartolomeu	c. 1450–1500	Portuguese	1488 sails round Cape of Good Hope
Diaz, Dinís	c. 15th century	Portuguese	1446 reaches Cape Verde and Senegal
Drake, Francis	c. 1540–96	English	1580 completes circumnavigation of the globe
Gama, Vasco da	c. 1469–1525	Portuguese	1497 sails round Cape of Good Hope 1498 explores coast of Madagascar and discovers sea route to India
Gomes, Diogo	c. 1440–84	Portuguese	1469 crosses the equator
Hillary, Edmund	1919–	New Zealander	1953 first ascent of Mount Everest, with Norgay Tenzing
Hudson, Henry	c. 1565–1611	English	1610 discovers Hudson's Bay
Livingstone, David	1813–73	English	1841 reaches Lake Ngami 1855 reaches the Victoria Falls
López de Cárdenas, García		Spanish	1540 reaches the Grand Canyon
Magellan, Ferdinand	c. 1480–1521	Portuguese	1520 discovers the Strait of Magellan 1521 explores the Philippines
Mendoza, Pedro de	1487–1537	Spanish	1536 founds Buenos Aires
Nansen, Fridtjof	1861–1930	Norwegian	1888 crosses Greenland
Peary, Robert	1856–1920	American	1909 successful voyage to reach North Pole
Raleigh, Walter	1552–1618	English	1595 explores Orinoco River 1617 explores Guiana
Saussure, Horace	1740–99	Swiss	1787 first ascent of Mont Blanc
Scott, Robert Falcon	1868–1912	English	1912 reaches South Pole
Shackleton, Ernest	1874–1922	English	1914 leads expedition to Antarctica
Stanley, Henry Morton	1841–1904	English	1875 traces Congo to the Atlantic
Tasman, Abel Janszoon	1603–c. 1659	Dutch	1642 reaches Tasmania and New Zealand
Tenzing, Norgay	1914–86	Nepalese	1953 first ascent of Mount Everest, with Edmund Hillary
Verrazano, Giovanni da	1485–1528	Italian	1524 reaches New York Bay and the Hudson River
Vespucci, Amerigo	1454–1512	Italian	1499 discovers mouth of River Amazon 1501 explores coast of S America

Colonialism (Imperialism)

The main era of imperialism was the period 1880–1914, when many European powers sought to gain territories in Africa and Asia. The motivation was, many suggest, economic, and territories were taken normally by force and subjected to rule by the imperial power. It is only in the twentieth century that colonialism has become generally regarded as illegitimate.

Colonial powers in 1914

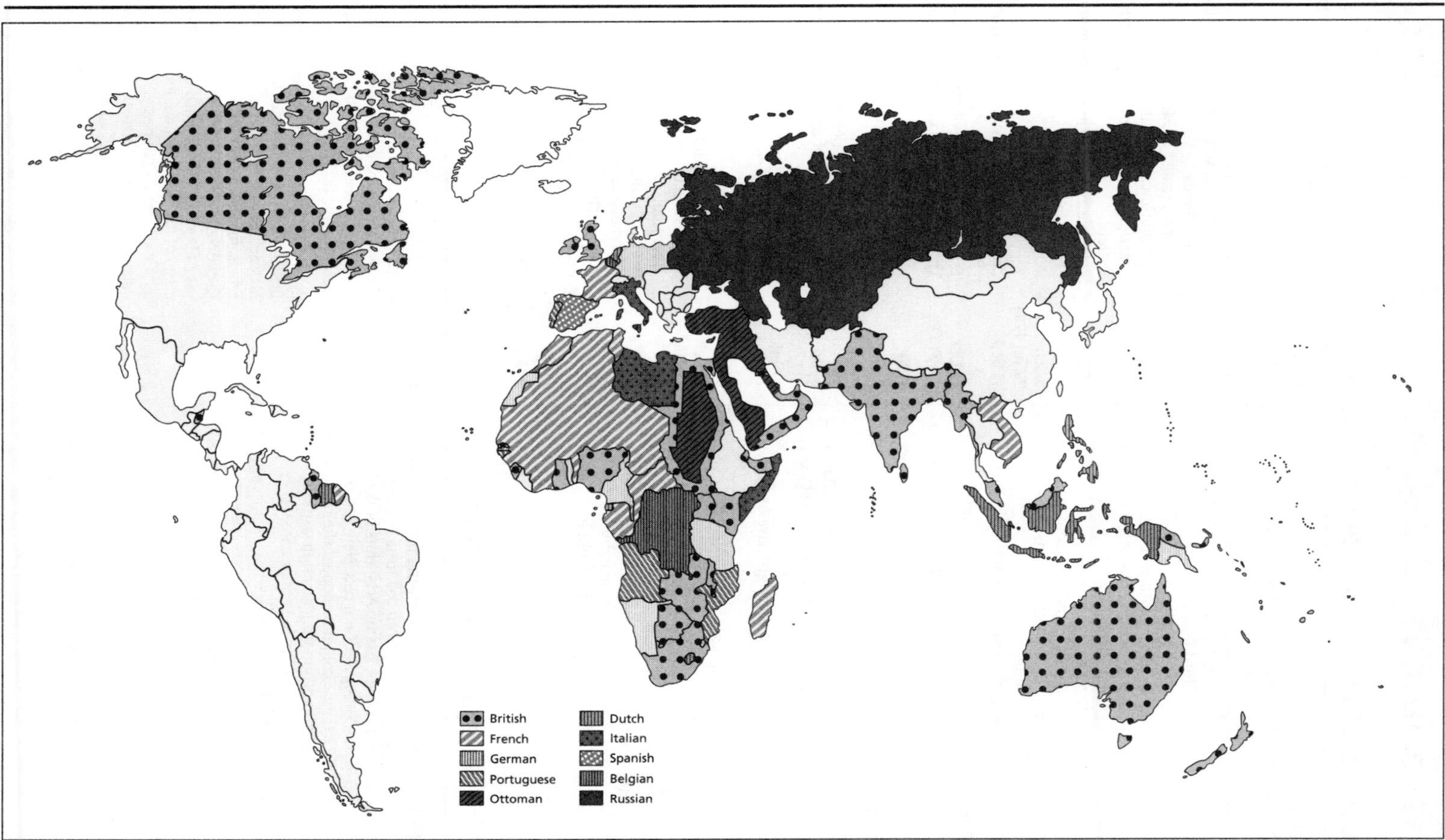

REVOLUTIONS

Events of the French Revolution, 1789–99

1789

Mar–May	Election of deputies to the Estates General
5 May	Opening of the Estates General
17 Jun	Title of National Assembly adopted by the Third Estate
Jul	The 'Great Fear'
14 Jul	Seizing of the Bastille in Paris
4 Aug	Abolition of the feudal regime
26 Aug	Declaration of the Rights of Man and Citizens
Oct	Foundation of the Club des Jacobins
5–6 Oct	Louis XVI brought to Paris from Versailles
19 Oct	National Assembly installed in Paris

1790

19–23 Jun	Abolition of hereditary nobility and titles
July	Foundation of the Club des Cordeliers

1791

20–21 Jun	Flight of the King to Varennes
16 Jul	Foundation of the Club des Feuillants
13 Sep	Acceptance of the Constitution by the King
Oct	Formation of the Legislative Assembly

1792

9–10 Aug	Attack of the Tuileries. Functions of the King suspended
12 Aug	King and royal family imprisoned in the Temple
2–6 Sep	Massacre of nobles and clergy in prisons
21 Sep	Abolition of the monarchy
22 Sep	Proclamation of the Republic

1793

17 Jan	National Convention votes for the death of the King
21 Jan	Execution of the King
1 Feb	Declaration of war against England and Netherlands
Mar	Tribunal created in Paris (later called the Revolutionary Tribunal)
6 Apr	Creation of the Committee of Public Safety
27 Jul	Robespierre elected to the Committee of Public Safety
5 Sep–27 Jul 1794	Reign of Terror
11 Sep	Creation of the Revolutionary Army of Paris
16 Oct	Trial and execution of Marie Antoinette
24–31 Oct	Trial and execution of the Girondins

1794

5 Apr	Execution of the Cordeliers, including Danton
24 Mar	Execution of the Hébertists
8 Jun	Inaugural Feast of the Supreme Being and of Nature
27 Jul	(9 Thermidor) Fall of Robespierre
19 Nov	Closure of the Club des Jacobins

1795

21 Feb	Separation of Church and State
31 May	Suppression of the Revolutionary Tribunal
8 Jun	Death of Louis XVII in the Temple
5 Oct	(13 Vendémiaire) Royalists crushed by Bonaparte
27 Oct–4 Nov	Institution of the Directory

1799

9 Nov	(18 Brumaire) Abolition of the Directory

The American Revolution

1765 Stamp Act crisis. Following the imposition of taxes on American colonists by the British Parliament (Stamp Acts) riots broke out. At the Stamp Act Congress, New York 7–25 Oct, nine colonies adopted the Declaration of Rights opposing taxation without representation in Parliament. Acts withdrawn 17 Mar 1766

1767 Townshend Acts imposed taxes on five categories of goods (glass, lead, paper, paint and tea) imported into the American colonies. Repeal of all taxes, except that on tea, in 1770

1770

5 Mar Boston massacre. First bloodshed of the American Revolution when British troops fired on rioting crowd at Boston customs house, killing five

1773

16 Dec Boston Tea Party. Valuable cargo of tea thrown overboard by rebellious American colonists protesting British Parliament's 'Tea Act' (Apr 1773)

1774 The 'Intolerable Acts' are passed by the British Parliament in order to punish Massachussetts, considered the leader of rebels, for the Boston Tea Party. Involved the curtailing of self-rule and barred the use of Boston harbour until the destroyed cargo of tea had been paid for

5 Sep–26 Oct First Continental Congress (a body of delegates from the thirteen colonies which assumed the duties of a national government), held in Philadelphia, protested British measures and called for civil disobedience

1775

18 Apr — Advance of British on Concord to destroy military stores of rebel American patriots

19 Apr — Beginning of fighting at Lexington and Concord

17 Jun — Battle of Bunker Hill, Massachussetts; technically an American defeat though British suffered high casualties

1776

7 Jun — Proposal in Continental Congress to declare independence from Britain

2 Jul — Resolution adopted

4 Jul — Approval of Declaration of Independence

27 Aug — British defeat of Washington in Battle of Long Island

15 Sep — British occupation of New York City

1777

3 Jan — Defeat of Lord Cornwallis by Washington at Battle of Princeton. Continental Congress adopted Stars and Stripes as flag of the United States

11 Sep — Battle of Brandywine. American retreat enabled British to occupy Philadelphia

17 Oct — Battle of Saratoga. British, under General John Burgoyne, forced to surrender

15 Nov — Articles of Confederation and Perpetual Union adopted by Continental Congress

1778

6 Feb — Assistance of the American patriots by French fleet after France and US sign treaty of aid

18 Jun — British evacuation from Philadelphia

1781

26 Sep — Arrival of joint American and French forces in Williamsburg near Yorktown where British forces, under Cornwallis, had retreated

6–19 Oct — Battle of Yorktown. Beginning odf siege of Yorktown, Virginia. British troops heavily outnumbered by joint American and French forces. Eventual surrender of Cornwallis on 19 Oct

1782

Mar — Agreement by new British cabinet to recognize independence of United States of America

30 Nov — Preliminary agreement signed in Paris

Events of the Russian Revolution

1916

End — Internal state of Russia precarious. Tsar politically isolated and universally unpopular

1917

Beginning — Bolsheviks, under Lenin's leadership, cultivate feelings of discontent and organise strikes

February Revolution — On March 8th government of Tsar Nicholas II introduces bread and flour rationing in Petrograd. Mass strike begins. On third day of protest police begin firing on striking workers

12 Mar — The Petrograd Soviet of workers and the Duma form a 'Provisional Committee', later to become a 'Provisional Government'

15 Mar — Tsar Nicholas II abdicates

Mar–May — Conflict in the dual power begins to emerge.
Disagreement on whether to continue the war (WWI) and war aims

Apr — Lenin returns from exile in Switzerland
Change of Bolshevik policy in supporting the provisional government
April Theses. Lenin advocates overthrow of provisional government and government by the soviets for the working class. Also advocated redistribution of land to peasants and signature of peace treaty with Germany. Policy of 'All Power to the Soviet'

Jun — Demonstrations called by the Petrograd Soviet to outmanoeuvre the Bolsheviks. Bolshevik support still strong
The July Days. Kronstradt sailors supporting Bolsheviks demonstrate in Petrograd. Demonstrators fired on and chaos followed. Prime Minister Lvov forced to resign and replaced by Kerensky (links to the Soviet). Bolsheviks held responsible for bloodshed and their newspapers closed and warrants for arrest of leaders issued. Lenin and Stalin fled. Trotsky and Kamenev imprisoned

Sep — Kornilov Affair – General Kornilov tries to move on Petrograd with his troops, under pretext of restoring order. Kerensky appeals to Bolsheviks for help in defeating Kornilov. Lenin recognised the opportunity and formed a Red Guard of Bolshevik soldiers and workers, set up Military Revolutionary Committee. Most of Kornilov's troops deserted, Kornilov arrested and Bolsheviks support increased further

26 October — October Revolution. Bolsheviks agree to make seizure of power 'the order of the day'. Kerensky mobilises troops too late and they are defeated by troops loyal to the Bolsheviks. Insurrection, led by Trotsky, now begins. All main public buildings occupied. Kerensky flees. Bolsheviks assume power and effect series of radical reforms

1989: Revolutionary year

15 Jan	Czechoslovakia: pro-democracy demonstration in Prague attacked by police
19 Jan	USSR: defence cuts announced
20 Jan	USSR: nuclear cuts announced for Eastern Europe
29 Jan	Hungary: statement by radical Communist Party member Imre Pozsgay, that the events of 1956 were not a counter-revolution, but a 'popular uprising'
3 Feb	Paraguay: President Stroessner deposed by the army
6 Feb	Poland: Solidarity begins official talks with the government
15 Feb	Afghanistan: withdrawal of Soviet army completed
22 Feb	Czechoslovakia: Dissident author Vaclav Havel jailed for nine months
14 Apr	USSR: demonstrators shot in Tbilisi; Georgian leadership resigns
17 Apr	Poland: ban on Solidarity lifted
20 Apr	China: student demonstration broken up by police in Beijing (Peking)
25 Apr	USSR: hardliners purged from Central Committee
27 Apr	China: major demonstration in Tiananmen Square, Beijing
20–22 May	China: army halted by large numbers of demonstrators
26 May	China: purge of moderates from government
30 May	China: statue of Democracy and Freedom erected in Tiananmen Square
2 Jun	China: army moves against demonstrators
3 Jun	Iran: death of Ayatollah Khomeini
4 Jun	China: army crushes student demonstrators, with undisclosed number of dead
4 Jun	Poland: free elections promised
17 Jun	Hungary: body of Imre Nagy disinterred and reburied in Bucharest
21 Aug	Czechoslovakia: demonstration to mark 21 years since crushing of the Prague Spring
23 Aug	USSR: human chain formed across Estonia, Latvia, and Lithuania, on 50th anniversary of Soviet annexation
24 Aug	Poland: Solidarity prime minister elected, Tadeusz Mazowiecki
10 Sep	Hungary: border opened with Austria; thousands of East Germans travel across Hungary to the West
19 Sep	Hungary: free elections promised
3 Oct	East Germany: closes border, as thousands more leave for the West
9 Oct	East Germany: large demonstrations in Leipzig
15 Oct	South Africa: release of Walter Sisulu and several other political prisoners
18 Oct	East Germany: resignation of Erich Honecker, replaced by Egon Krenz
26 Oct	USSR: Gorbachev speech endorses developments in Eastern Europe
31 Oct	East Germany: half a million demonstrators in Leipzig
1 Nov	East Germany: border reopened to Czechoslovakia
3 Nov	East Germany: East Germans permitted to travel across Czechoslovakia into West Germany without special formalities
9 Nov	East Germany: opening of the Berlin Wall
10 Nov	Bulgaria: Todor Zhivkov deposed
14 Nov	Namibia: elections won by South West Africa People's Organization
17 Nov	Czechoslovakia: major demonstration in Prague, violently put down by police
19 Nov	East Germany: visit of West German Chancellor Kohl
21 Nov	Czechoslovakia: meeting between Prime Minister Ladislav Adamec and leaders of the demonstration
24 Nov	Czechoslovakia: resignation of Communist Party leadership
30 Nov	Czechoslovakia: Communist Party gives up its leading role
1 Dec	Vatican City: meeting between the Pope and President Gorbachev (USSR)
3 Dec	Mediterranean: meeting between Presidents Bush (USA) and Gorbachev; announcement of the end of the Cold War
4 Dec	USSR: formal condemnation of 1968 invasion of Czechoslovakia
6 Dec	East Germany: resignation of Egon Krenz
7 Dec	Czechoslovakia: resignation of Adamec
10 Dec	Czechoslovakia: noncommunist government appointed
11 Dec	Bulgaria: free elections promised
14 Dec	South Africa: talks between President de Klerk and Nelson Mandela (African National Congress)
14 Dec	Chile: dictatorship ended with the election of Patricio Aylwin as President
17 Dec	Romania: many demonstrators killed in Timisoara
17 Dec	Brazil: first President elected for nearly 30 years, Fernando Collor de Mello
20 Dec	Panama: invasion by USA; General Noriega deposed
21 Dec	Romania: major demonstration in Bucharest, with criticism of President Nicolae Ceausescu
22 Dec	Romania: Ceausescu deposed
25 Dec	Romania: execution of Ceausescu and his wife, Elena
28 Dec	Czechoslovakia: election of Alexander Dubcek as Chairman of the Czech parliament
29 Dec	Czechoslovakia: election of Vaclav Havel as President

POLITICAL LEADERS AND RULERS

Australia

Chief of State: British monarch, represented by Governor General

Prime Minister

1901–3 Edmund Barton *Prot*
1903–4 Alfred Deakin *Prot*
1904 John Christian Watson *Lab*
1904–5 George Houstoun Reid *Free*
1905–8 Alfred Deakin *Prot*
1908–9 Andrew Fisher *Lab*
1909–10 Alfred Deakin *Fusion*
1910–13 Andrew Fisher *Lab*
1913–14 Joseph Cook *Lib*
1914–15 Andrew Fisher *Lab*
1915–17 William Morris Hughes *Nat Lab*
1917–23 William Morris Hughes *Nat*
1923–9 Stanley Melbourne Bruce *Nat*
1929–32 James Henry Scullin *Lab*
1932–9 Joseph Aloyslus Lyons *Un*
1939 Earle Christian Grafton Page *Co*
1939–41 Robert Gordon Menzies *Un*
1941 Arthur William Fadden *Co*
1941–5 John Joseph Curtin *Lab*
1945 Francis Michael Forde *Lab*
1945–9 Joseph Benedict Chifley *Lab*
1949–66 Robert Gordon Menzies *Lib*
1966–7 Harold Edward Holt *Lib*
1967–8 John McEwen *Co*
1968–71 John Grey Gorton *Lib*
1971–2 William McMahon *Lib*
1972–5 (Edward) Gough Whitlam *Lab*
1975–83 John Malcolm Fraser *Lib*
1983–91 Robert James Lee Hawke *Lab*
1991– Paul Keating *Lab*

Co Country; *Free* Free Trade; *Lab* Labor; *Lib* Liberal; *Nat* Nationalist; *Nat Lab* National Labor; *Prot* Protectionist; *Un* United

Canada

Chief of State: British monarch, represented by Governor General

Prime Minister

1867–73 John Alexander MacDonald *Con*
1873–8 Alexander Mackenzie *Lib*
1878–91 John Alexander MacDonald *Con*
1891–2 John J C Abbot *Con*
1892–4 John Sparrow David Thompson *Con*
1894–6 Mackenzie Bowell *Con*
1896 Charles Tupper *Con*
1896–1911 Wilfrid Laurier *Lib*
1911–20 Robert Laird Borden *Con*
1920–1 Arthur Meighen *Con*
1921–6 William Lyon Mackenzie King *Lib*
1926 Arthur Meighen *Con*
1926–30 William Lyon Mackenzie King *Lib*
1930–5 Richard Bedford Bennett *Con*
1935–48 William Lyon Mackenzie King *Lib*
1948–57 Louis Stephen St Laurent *Lib*
1957–63 John George Diefenbaker *Con*
1963–8 Lester Bowles Pearson *Lib*
1968–79 Pierre Elliott Trudeau *Lib*
1979–80 Joseph Clark *Con*
1980–4 Pierre Elliott Trudeau *Lib*
1984 John Napier Turner *Lib*
1984–93 (Martin) Brian Mulroney *Con*
1993– Kim Campbell *Con*

Con Conservative; *Lib* Liberal

France

Prime Minister

1815 Charles-Maruice, Prince de Talleyrand-Perigord
1815–18 Armand-Emmanuel Vignerot-Duplessis, Duc de Richlieu
1818–19 Jean Joseph, Marquis Dessolle
1819–20 Duc Élie Decazes
1820–1 Armand-Emmanuel Vignerot-Duplessis, Duc de Richlieu
1821–9 Guillaume-Aubin, Comte de Villèle
1829–30 Auguste, Prince de Polignac
1830–1 Jacques Lafitte
1831–2 Casimir Périer
1832–4 Nicolas Soult
1834 Etienne, Comte Gérard
1834 Napoléon Joseph Maret, Duc de Bassano
1834–5 Étienne Mortier, Duc de Trévise
1835–6 Achille, Duc de Broglie
1836 Adolphe Thiers
1836–9 Louis, Comte Molé
1839–40 Nicolas Soult
1840 Adolphe Thiers
1840–7 Nicolas Soult
1847–8 François Guyzot
1848 Jacques Charles Dupont de L'Eure
1848 Louis-Eugène Cavaignac
1848–9 Odilon Barrot
1849–70 *No Prime Minister*

Third Republic

1870–1 Jules Favre
1871–3 Jules Dufaure
1873–4 Albert, Duc de Broglie
1874–5 Ernest Louis Courtot de Cissey
1875–6 Louis Buffet
1876 Jules Dufaure
1876–7 Jules Simon
1877 Albert, Duc de Broglie
1877 Gaetan de Grimaudet de Rochebouét
1877–9 Jules Dufaure
1879 William H Waddington
1879–80 Louis de Freycinet
1880–1 Jules Ferry
1881–2 Léon Gambetta
1882 Louis de Freycinet
1882–3 Eugène Duclerc
1883 Armand Fallières
1883–5 Jules Ferry
1885–6 Henri Brisson
1886 Louis de Freycinet
1886–7 René Goblet
1887 Maurice Rouvier
1887–8 Pierre Tirard
1888–9 Charles Floquet
1889–90 Pierre Tirard
1890–2 Louis de Freycinet
1892 Émile Loubet
1892–3 Alexandre Ribot
1893 Charles Dupuy
1893–4 Jean Casimir-Périer
1894–5 Charles Dupuy
1895 Alexandre Ribot
1895–6 Léon Bourgeois
1896–8 Jules Méline
1898 Henri Brisson
1898–9 Charles Dupuy
1899–1902 Pierre Waldeck-Rousseau
1902–5 Emile Combes
1905–6 Maurice Rouvier
1906 Jean Sarrien
1906–9 Georges Clemenceau
1909–11 Aristide Briand
1911 Ernest Monis
1911–12 Joseph Caillaux
1912–13 Raymond Poincaré
1913 Aristide Briand
1913 Jean Louis Barthou
1913–14 Gaston Doumergue
1914 Alexandre Ribot
1914–15 René Viviani
1915–17 Aristide Briand
1917 Alexandre Ribot
1917 Paul Painlevé
1917–20 Georges Clemenceau
1920 Alexandre Millerand
1920–1 Georges Leygues
1921–2 Aristide Briand
1922–4 Raymond Poincaré

Political leaders and rulers (continued)

1924 Frédéric François-Marsal
1924–5 Édouard Herriot
1925 Paul Painlevé
1925–6 Aristide Briand
1926 Édouard Herriot
1926–9 Raymond Poincaré
1929 Aristide Briand
1929–30 André Tardieu
1930 Camille Chautemps
1930 André Tardieu
1930–1 Théodore Steeg
1931–2 Pierre Laval
1932 André Tardieu
1932 Édouard Herriot
1932–3 Joseph Paul-Boncour
1933 Édouard Daladier
1933 Albert Sarrault
1933–4 Camille Chautemps
1934 Édouard Daladier
1934 Gaston Doumergue
1934–5 Pierre Étienne Flandin
1935 Fernand Bouisson
1935–6 Pierre Laval
1936 Albert Sarrault
1936–7 Léon Blum
1937–8 Camille Chautemps
1938 Léon Blum
1938–40 Édouard Daladier
1940 Paul Reynaud
1940 Philippe Pétain

Vichy Government
1940–4 Philippe Pétain

Provisional Government of the French Republic
1944–6 Charles de Gaulle
1946 Félix Gouin
1946 Georges Bidault

Fourth Republic
1946–7 Léon Blum
1947 Paul Ramadier
1947–8 Robert Schuman
1948 André Marie
1948 Robert Schuman
1948–9 Henri Queuille
1949–50 Georges Bidault
1950 Henri Queuille
1950–1 René Pleven
1951 Henri Queuille
1951–2 René Pleven
1952 Edgar Faure
1952–3 Antoine Pinay
1953 René Mayer
1953–4 Joseph Laniel
1954–5 Pierre Mendès-France
1955–6 Edgar Faure
1956–7 Guy Alcide Mollet
1957 Maurice Bourgès-Maunoury
1957–8 Félix Gaillard
1958 Pierre Pflimin
1958–9 Charles de Gaulle

Fifth Republic
1959–62 Michel Debré
1962–8 Georges Pompidou
1968–9 Maurice Couve de Murville
1969–72 Jacques Chaban Delmas
1972–4 Pierre Mesmer
1974–6 Jacques René Chirac
1976–81 Raymond Barre
1981–4 Pierre Mauroy
1984–6 Laurent Fabius
1986–8 Jacques René Chirac
1988–91 Michael Rocard
1991–2 Edith Cresson
1992–3 Pierre Bérégovoy
1993– Edouard Balladur

President

Third Republic
1870–1 *Commune*
1871–3 Louis Adolphe Thiers
1873–9 Marie Edmé de Mac-Mahon
1879–87 Jules Grévy
1887–94 Sadi Carnot
1894–5 Jean Paul Pierre Casimir-Périer
1895–9 François Félix Faure
1899–1906 Émile Loubet
1906–13 Armand Fallières
1913–20 Raymond Poincaré
1920 Paul Deschanel
1920–4 Alexandre Millerand
1924–31 Gaston Doumergue
1931–2 Paul Doumer
1932–40 Albert Lebrun
1940–45 *German occupation*
1945–7 *No President*

Fourth Republic
1947–54 Vincent Auriol
1954–8 René Coty

Fifth Republic
1958–69 Charles de Gaulle
1969–74 Georges Pompidou
1974–81 Valéry Giscard d'Estaing
1981– François Mitterand

Germany

Chancellor
1871–90 Otto von Bismarck
1890–4 Georg Leo, Graf von Caprivi
1894–1900 Chlodwic, Fürst zu Hohenlohe-Schillingfürst
1900–09 Bernard Heinrich, Prince von Bülow
1909–17 Theobald von Bethmann Hollweg
1917–18 Georg von Herfling
1918 Prince Max of Baden
1918 Friedrich Ebert
1919–20 Philipp Scheidemann
1920 Hermann Müller
1920–1 Konstantin Fehrenbach
1921–2 Karl Joseph Wirth
1922–3 Wilhelm Cuno
1923 Gustav Stresemann
1923–5 Wilhelm Marx
1925–6 Hans Luther
1926–8 Wilhelm Marx
1928–9 Hermann Müller
1929–32 Heinrich Brüning
1932–3 Franz von Papen
1933–45 Adolf Hitler (from 1934 *Führer*)

German Democratic Republic (East Germany)

President
1949–60 Wilhelm Pieck

Chairman of the Council of State
1960–73 Walter Ulbricht
1973–6 Willi Stoph
1976–89 Erich Honecker
1989 Egon Krenz
1989–90 Gregor Gysi *General Secretary as Chairman*

Premier
1949–64 Otto Grotewohl
1964–73 Willi Stoph
1973–6 Horst Sindermann
1976–89 Willi Stoph
1989–90 Hans Modrow
1990 Lothar de Maizière

The German Democratic Republic ceased to exist as a separate state and East Germany became part of the German Federal Republic in 1990.

German Federal Republic (until 1990 West Germany)

President
1949–59 Theodor Heuss
1959–69 Heinrich Lübke
1969–74 Gustav Heinemann
1974–9 Walter Scheel
1979–84 Karl Carstens
1984– Richard, Baron von Weizsäcker

Chancellor
1949–63 Konrad Adenauer
1963–6 Ludwig Erhard
1966–9 Kurt Georg Kiesinger
1969–74 Willy Brandt
1974–82 Helmut Schmidt
1982– Helmut Kohl

Russia and the Union of Soviet Socialist Republics

RUSSIA

Grand Duke of Moscow

House of Riurik
1283–1303 Daniel
1303–25 Yuri
1325–41 Ivan I Kalita
1341–53 Semeon
1353–9 Ivan II
1359–89 Dmitri I Donskoy

1389–1425 Vasily I
1425–62 Vasily II
1462–72 Ivan II 'the Great'

Ruler of all Russia
House of Riurik
1472–1505 Ivan III 'the Great'
1505–33 Vasily III
1533–47 Ivan IV 'the Terrible'

Tsar of Russia
House of Riurik
1547–84 Ivan IV 'the Terrible'
1584–98 Fedor I
1598–1605 Boris Godunov
1605 Fedor II
1605–06 Dmitri II (the 'false Dmitri')
1606–10 Vasily IV Shuisky
1610–13 *Civil war*

House of Romanov
1613–45 Mikhail (Michael Romanov)
1645–76 Alexei I Milhailovitch
1676–82 Fedor III
1682–1725 Peter I 'the Great' *Joint ruler to 1676*
1682–96 Ivan V *Joint ruler*
1725–7 Catherine I
1727–30 Peter II
1730–40 Anna Ivovna
1740–1 Ivan VI
1741–62 Elizabeth Petrovna
1762 Peter III
1762–96 Catherine II 'the Great'
1796–1801 Paul
1801–25 Alexander I
1825–55 Nicholas I
1855–81 Alexander II 'the Liberator'
1881–94 Alexander III
1894–1917 Nicholas II

Soviet Union
President
1917 Lev Borisovich Kamenev
1917–19 Yakov Mikhailovich Sverlov
1919–46 Mikhail Ivanovich Kalinin
1946–53 Nikolai Mikhailovich Shvernik
1953–60 Klimenti Efremovich Voroshilov
1960–4 Leonid Ilyich Brezhnev
1964–5 Anastas Ivanovich Mikoyan
1965–77 Nikolai Viktorovich Podgorny
1977–82 Leonid Ilyich Brezhnev
1982–3 Vasily Vasiliyevich Kuznetsov *Acting*
1983–4 Yuri Vladimirovich Andropov
1984 Vasily Vasiliyevich Kuznetsov *Acting*
1984–5 Konstantin Ustinovich Chernenko
1985 Vasily Vasiliyevich Kuznetsov *Acting*
1985–8 Andrei Andreevich Gromyko
1988–90 Mikhail Sergeevich Gorbachev

Executive President
1990–1 Mikhail Sergeevich Gorbachev

Russian Federation
President
1991– Boris Nikolayevich Yeltsin

United Kingdom
Prime Minister
1721–42 Robert Walpole, Earl of Oxford *Whig*
1742–3 Spencer Compton, Earl of Wilmington *Whig*
1743–54 Henry Pelham *Whig*
1754–6 Thomas Pelham (Pelham-Hollies), Duke of Newcastle *Whig*
1756–7 William Cavendish, 1st Duke of Devonshire *Whig*
1757–62 Thomas Pelham (Pelham-Hollies), Duke of Newcastle *Whig*
1762–3 John Stuart, 3rd Earl of Bute *Tory*
1763–5 George Grenville *Whig*
1765–6 Charles Watson Wentworth, 2nd Marquis of Rockingham *Whig*
1766–7 William Pitt, 1st Earl of Chatham *Whig*
1767–70 Augustus Henry Fitzroy, 3rd Duke of Grafton *Whig*
1770–82 Frederick, 8th Lord North *Tory*
1782 Charles Watson Wentworth, 2nd Marquis of Rockingham *Whig*
1782–3 William Petty, 2nd Earl of Shelburne *Whig*
1783 William Henry Cavendish, Duke of Portland *Coal*
1783–1801 William Pitt *Tory*
1801–4 Henry Addington *Tory*
1804–6 William Pitt *Tory*
1806–7 William Wyndham Grenville, 1st Baron Grenville *Whig*
1807–9 William Henry Cavendish, Duke of Portland *Coal*
1809–12 Spencer Perceval *Tory*
1812–27 Robert Banks Jenkinson, 2nd Earl of Liverpool *Tory*
1827 George Canning *Tory*
1827–8 Frederick John Robinson, 1st Earl of Ripon *Tory*
1828–30 Arthur Wellesley, 1st Duke of Wellington *Tory*
1830–4 Charles Grey, 2nd Earl Grey *Whig*
1834 William Lamb, 2nd Viscount Melbourne *Whig*
1834–5 Robert Peel *Con*
1835–41 William Lamb, 2nd Viscount Melbourne *Whig*
1841–6 Robert Peel *Con*
1846–52 Lord John Russell, 1st Earl Russell *Lib*
1852 Edward Geoffrey Smith Stanley, 14th Earl of Derby *Con*
1852–5 George Hamilton-Gordon, 4th Earl of Aberdeen *Peelite*
1855–8 Henry John Temple, 3rd Viscount Palmerston *Lib*
1858–9 Edward Geoffrey Smith Stanley, 14th Earl of Derby *Con*
1859–65 Henry John Temple, 3rd Viscount Palmerston *Lib*
1865–6 Lord John Russell, 1st Earl Russell *Lib*
1866–8 Edward Geoffrey Smith Stanley, 14th Earl of Derby *Con*
1868 Benjamin Disraeli *Con*
1868–74 William Ewart Gladstone *Lib*
1874–80 Benjamin Disraeli *Con*
1880–5 William Ewart Gladstone *Lib*
1885–6 Robert Arthur James Gascoyne-Cecil, 5th Marquis of Salisbury *Con*
1886 William Ewart Gladstone *Lib*
1886–92 Robert Gascoyne-Cecil, 5th Marquis of Salisbury *Con*
1892–4 William Ewart Gladstone *Lib*
1894–5 Archibald Philip Primrose, 5th Earl of Rosebery *Lib*
1895–1902 Robert Gascoyne-Cecil, 5th Marquis of Salisbury *Con*
1902–5 Arthur James Balfour *Con*
1905–8 Henry Campbell-Bannerman *Lib*
1908–15 Herbert Henry Asquith *Lib*
1915–16 Herbert Henry Asquith *Coal*
1916–22 David Lloyd-George *Coal*
1922–3 Andrew Bonar Law *Con*
1923–4 Stanley Baldwin *Con*
1924 James Ramsay MacDonald *Lab*
1924–9 Stanley Baldwin *Con*
1929–31 James Ramsay MacDonald *Lab*

Political leaders and rulers (continued)

1931–5 James Ramsay MacDonald *Nat*
1935–7 Stanley Baldwin *Nat*
1937–40 (Arthur) Neville Chamberlain *Nat*
1940–5 Winston Leonard Spencer Churchill *Coal*
1945–51 Clement Richard Atlee *Lab*
1951–5 Winston Churchill *Con*
1955–7 (Robert) Anthony Eden, 1st Earl of Avon *Con*
1957–63 (Maurice) Harold Macmillan *Con*
1963–4 Alexander Frederick (Alec) Douglas-Home, Baron Home of the Hirsel *Con*
1964–70 (James) Harold Wilson *Lab*
1970–4 Edward Richard George Heath *Con*
1974–6 (James) Harold Wilson *Lab*
1976–9 (Leonard) James Callaghan *Lab*
1979–90 Margaret Hilda Thatcher *Con*
1990– John Major *Con*

Coal Coalition; *Con* Conservative; *Lab* Labour; *Lib* Liberal; *Nat* Nationalist

United States of America
President
Vice President in parentheses

1789–97 George Washington (1st) (John Adams)
1797–1801 John Adams (2nd) *Fed* (Thomas Jefferson)
1801–9 Thomas Jefferson (3rd) *Dem-Rep* (Aaron Burr, 1801–5) (George Clinton, 1805–9)
1809–17 James Madison (4th) *Dem-Rep* (George Clinton, 1809–12) *No Vice President* 1812–13 (Elbridge Gerry, 1813–14) *No Vice President* 1814–17
1817–25 James Monroe (5th) *Dem-Rep* (Daniel D Tompkins)
1825–9 John Quincy Adams (6th) *Dem-Rep* (John Caldwell Calhoun)
1829–37 Andrew Jackson (7th) *Dem* (John Caldwell Calhoun, 1829–32) *No Vice President* 1832–3 (Martin Van Buren, 1833–7)
1837–41 Martin Van Buren (8th) *Dem* (Richard Mentor Johnson)
1841 William Henry Harrison (9th) *Whig* (John Tyler)
1841–5 John Tyler (10th) *Whig* *No Vice President*
1845–9 James Knox Polk (11th) *Dem* (George Mifflin Dallas)
1849–50 Zachary Taylor (12th) *Whig* (Millard Fillmore)
1850–3 Milard Fillmore (13th) *Whig* *No Vice President*
1853–7 Franklin Pierce (14th) *Dem* (William Rufus King, 1853) *No Vice President* 1853–7
1857–61 James Buchanan (15th) *Dem* (John C Brechinridge)
1861–5 Abraham Lincoln (16th) *Rep* (Hannibal Hamlin, 1861–5) (Andrew Johnson, 1865)
1865–9 Andrew Johnson (17th) *Dem-Nat* *No Vice President*
1869–77 Ulysses Simpson Grant (18th) *Rep* (Schuyler Colfax, 1869–73) (Henry Wilson, 1873–5) *No Vice President* 1875
1877–81 Rutherford Birchard Hayes (19th) *Rep* (William A Wheeler)
1881 James Abram Garfield (20th) *Rep* (Chester Alan Arthur)
1881–5 Chester Alan Arthur (21st) *Rep* *No Vice President*
1885–9 Stephen Grover Cleveland (22nd) *Dem* (Thomas A Hendricks, 1885) *No Vice President* 1885–9
1889–93 Benjamin Harrison (23rd) *Rep* (Levi Parsons Morton)
1893–7 Stephen Grover Cleveland (24th) *Dem* (Adlai Ewing Stevenson)
1897–1901 William McKinley (25th) *Rep* (Garret A Hobart, 1897–9) *No Vice President* 1899–1901 (Theodore Roosevelt, 1901)
1901–9 Theodore Roosevelt (26th) *Rep* *No Vice President* 1901–5 (Charles W Fairbanks, 1905–9)
1909–13 William Howard Taft (27th) *Rep* (James S Sherman, 1909–12) *No Vice President* 1912–13
1913–21 Thomas Woodrow Wilson (28th) *Dem* (Thomas R Marshall)
1921–3 Warren G Harding (29th) *Rep* (Calvin Coolidge)
1923–9 Calvin Coolidge (30th) *Rep* *No Vice President* 1923–5 (Charles Gates Dawes, 1925–9)
1929–33 Herbert Clark Hoover (31st) *Rep* (Charles Curtis)
1933–45 Franklin Delano Roosevelt (32nd) *Dem* (John N Garner, 1933–41) (Henry Agard Wallace, 1941–5) (Harry S Truman, 1945)
1945–53 Harry S Truman (33rd) *Dem* *No Vice President* 1945–9 (Alben W Barkley, 1949–53)
1953–61 Dwight David Eisenhower (34th) *Rep* (Richard Milhous Nixon)
1961–3 John Fitzgerald Kennedy (35th) *Dem* (Lyndon Baines Johnson)
1963–9 Lyndon Baines Johnson (36th) *Dem* *No Vice President* 1963–5 (Hubert Horatio Humphrey, 1965–9)
1969–74 Richard Milhous Nixon (37th) *Rep* (Spiro Theodore Agnew, 1969–73) *No Vice President* Oct–Dec 1973 (Gerald Rudolph Ford, 1973–4)
1974–7 Gerald Rudolph Ford (38th) *Rep* *No Vice President* Aug–Dec 1974 (Nelson Aldrich Rockefeller 1974–7)
1977–81 James Earl (Jimmy) Carter (39th) *Dem* (Walter Frederick Mondale)
1981–9 Ronald Wilson Reagan (40th) *Rep* (George Herbert Walker Bush)
1989–92 George Herbert Walker Bush (41st) *Rep* (J Danforth (Dan) Quayle)
1992– William Jefferson (Bill) Clinton (42nd) *Dem* (Albert Arnold Gore, Jr)

Dem Democrat; *Fed* Federalist; *Nat*; National Union; *Rep* Republican

HUMAN GEOGRAPHY

Political map of the world

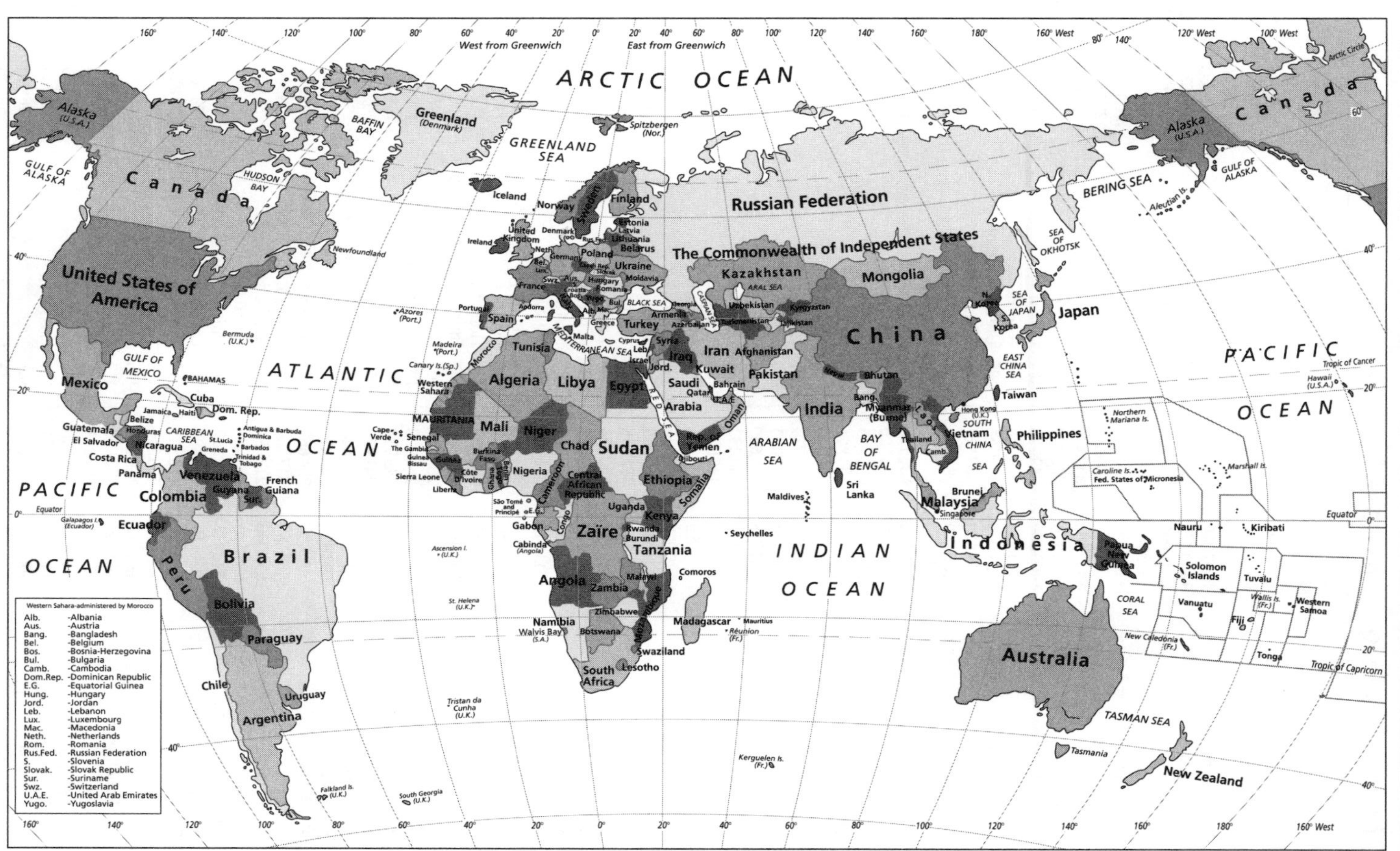

The world's largest nations by area

	Nation	*Area* sq km	*Area* sq mi
1	Russian Federation	17§075 400	6 591 100
2	Canada	9 971 500	3 848 900
3	China, People's Republic of	9 597 000	3 704 000
4	United States	9 160 454	3 535 935
5	Brazil	8 511 965	3 285 618
6	Australia	7 692 300	2 969 228
7	India	3 166 829	1 222 396
8	Argentina	2 780 092	1 073 115
9	Kazakhstan	2 717 300	1 048 878
10	Sudan, The	2 504 530	966 749
11	Algeria	2 460 500	949 753
12	Zaïre	2 343 950	904 765
13	Saudi Arabia	2 331 000	899 766
14	Mexico	1 978 800	763 817
15	Indonesia	1 906 240	735 809
16	Libya	1 758 610	678 823
17	Iran	1 648 000	636 128
18	Mongolia	1 566 500	604 800
19	Peru	1 285 216	496 225
20	Chad	1 284 640	495 871
21	Angola	1 245 790	480 875
22	Mali	1 240 192	478 714
23	South Africa	1 233 404	476 094
24	Ethiopia	1 221 918	471 660
25	Niger	1 186 408	457 953
26	Colombia	1 140 105	440 080
27	Bolivia	1 098 580	424 052
28	Mauritania	1 029 920	397 549
29	Egypt	1 001 449	386 559
30	Tanzania	939 652	362 706
31	Nigeria	923 768	356 574
32	Venezuela	912 050	352 051
33	Namibia	823 144	317 734
34	Pakistan	803 943	310 322
35	Mozambique	789 800	304 863
36	Turkey	779 452	300 868
37	Chile	756 626	292 058
38	Zambia	752 613	290 509
39	Somalia	686 803	265 106
40	Myanmar (Burma)	678 576	261 930
41	Afghanistan	647 497	249 934
42	Central African Republic	626 780	241 937
43	Ukraine	603 700	233 028
44	Madagascar	592 800	228 821
45	Botswana	582 096	224 689
46	Kenya	564 162	217 766
47	France	551 000	212 686
48	Yemen	531 570	205 186
49	Thailand	513 115	198 062
50	Spain	504 750	194 833
51	Turkmenistan	488 100	188 400
52	Cameroon	475 439	183 519
53	Papua New Guinea	462 840	178 656
54	Uzbekistan	447 400	172 696
55	Iraq	434 925	167 881
56	Sweden	411 479	158 830
57	Morocco	409 200	157 951
58	Paraguay	406 750	157 000
59	Zimbabwe	391 090	150 961
60	Japan	381 945	147 431
61	Germany	357 868	138 136
62	Congo	341 945	132 000
63	Finland	338 145	130 524
64	Malaysia	329 749	127 283
65	Vietnam	329 566	127 212
66	Norway	323 895	125 023
67	Côte d'Ivoire	320 633	123 764
68	Poland	312 612	120 668
69	Italy	301 225	116 273
70	Oman	300 000	115 800
71	Burkina Faso	274 540	105 972
72	Ecuador	270 699	104 490
73	New Zealand	270 534	104 426
74	Gabon	267 667	103 319
75	Guinea	246 048	94 974
76	United Kingdom	244 755	94 475
77	Ghana	238 686	92 133
78	Uganda	238 461	92 046
79	Romania	237 500	91 675
80	Laos	236 800	91 405
81	Philippines	229 679	115 676
82	Guyana	214 969	82 978
83	Belarus	207 600	80 134
84	Kyrgyzstan	198 500	76 621
85	Senegal	196 840	75 980
86	Syria	185 180	71 479
87	Cambodia	181 035	68 879
88	Uruguay	176 215	68 018
89	Tunisia	164 150	63 362
90	Suriname	163 265	63 020
91	Nicaragua	148 000	57 128
92	Nepal	145 391	56 121
93	Bangladesh	143 998	55 583
94	Tajikistan	143 100	55 200
95	Greece	131 957	50 935
96	North Korea	122 098	47 130
97	Malawi	118 484	45 735
98	Liberia	113 370	43 800
99	Benin	112 622	43 472
100	Honduras	112 088	43 266
101	Bulgaria	110 912	42 812
102	Cuba	110 860	42 792
103	Guatemala	108 889	42 031
104	Iceland	103 000	40 000
105	Yugoslavia*	102 173	39 438
106	South Korea	98 913	38 180
107	Jordan	96 188	37 129
108	Hungary	93 036	35 912
109	Portugal	88 500	34 200
110	Azerbaijan	86 600	33 428
111	Austria	83 854	32 368
112	United Arab Emirates	83 600	32 300
113	Czech Republic	78 864	30 441
114	Panama	77 082	29 753
115	Sierre Leone	72 325	27 917
116	Ireland	70 282	27 129
117	Georgia	69 700	26 900
118	Sri Lanka	65 610	25 325
119	Lithuania	65 200	25 167
120	Latvia	63 700	24 600
121	Togo	56 600	21 848
122	Croatia	56 540	21 825
123	Bosnia-Herzegovina	51 129	19 736
124	Costa Rica	51 022	19 694
125	Slovak Republic	49 035	18 927

Human geography

	Nation	Area sq km	sq mi
126	Dominican Republic	48 442	18 699
127	Bhutan	46 600	18 000
128	Estonia	45 100	17 409
129	Denmark	43 076	16 627
130	Switzerland	41 228	15 914
131	Guinea-Bissau	36 260	13 996
132	Taiwan	36 000	13 896
133	Netherlands, The	33 929	13 097
134	Moldova	33 700	13 008
135	Belgium	30 540	11 788
136	Lesotho	30 460	11 758
137	Armenia	29 800	11 500
138	Albania	28 748	11 097
139	Equatorial Guinea	28 051	10 828
140	Burundi	27 834	10 744
141	Haiti	27 750	10 712
142	Solomon Islands	27 556	10 637
143	Rwanda	26 338	10 166
144	Macedonia, former Yugoslav Republic of	25 713	9 925
145	Djibouti	23 310	8 998
146	Belize	22 963	8 864
147	El Salvador	21 476	8 290
148	Israel	20 770	8 017
149	Slovenia	20 251	7 817
150	Fiji	18 333	7 076
151	Kuwait	17 818	6 878
152	Swaziland	17 363	6 702
153	Vanuatu	14 763	5 698
154	Bahamas, The	13 934	5 378
155	Qatar	11 437	4 415
156	Jamaica	10 957	4 229
157	Lebanon	10 452	4 034
158	Gambia, The	10 402	4 015
159	Cyprus	9 251	3 571
160	Brunei	5 765	2 225
161	Trinidad and Tobago	5 128	1 979
162	Cape Verde	4 033	1 557
163	Western Samoa	2 842	1 097
164	Luxembourg	2 586	998
165	Mauritius	1 865	720
166	Comoros	1 862	719
167	São Tomé and Príncipe	963	372
168	Dominica	751	290
169	Kiribati	717	277
170	Bahrain	678	262
171	Tonga	646	249
172	Singapore	618	238
173	St Lucia	616	238
174	Andorra	468	181
175	Antigua and Barbuda	442	171
176	Barbados	430	166
177	St Vincent and the Grenadines	390	150
178	Grenada	344	133
179	Malta	316	122
180	Maldives	300	116
181	St Kitts and Nevis	269	104
182	Liechtenstein	160	62
183	San Marino	61	23
184	Tuvalu	26	10
185	Nauru	21.3	8.2
186	Monaco	1.95	0.75

This list is not exhaustive, particularly among the smaller nations. Differences of status of many of the 'nations' listed also make direct comparisons difficult.

*Yugoslavia in this context consists of the states of Montenegro and Serbia only.

The world's largest nations by population

	Nation	Population total (1990–2) estimates
1	China, People's Republic of	1 133 682 501
2	India	866 000 000
3	United States	255 600 000
4	Indonesia	193 000 000
5	Brazil	150 368 000
6	Russian Federation	148 800 000
7	Japan	124 017 000
8	Pakistan	117 490 000
9	Bangladesh	107 992 140
10	Mexico	90 007 000
11	Nigeria	88 500 000
12	Germany	79 632 000
13	Vietnam	69 200 000
14	Philippines	65 758 000
15	Turkey	59 200 000
16	Iran	59 051 000
17	Italy	57 772 000
18	United Kingdom	57 533 000
19	Thailand	56 814 000
20	France	56 681 000
21	Egypt	54 451 000
22	Ethiopia	53 131 000
23	Ukraine	52 100 000
24	South Korea	43 134 000
25	Myanmar (Burma)	42 112 000
26	South Africa	40 600 000
27	Spain	39 384 000
28	Zaïre	37 900 000
29	Poland	37 799 000
30	Colombia	32 978 000
31	Argentina	32 646 000
32	Canada	27 400 000
33	Sudan, The	27 220 000
34	Tanzania	26 869 000
35	Morocco	26 181 000
36	Algeria	25 798 000
37	Kenya	25 241 000
38	Romania	23 397 000
39	North Korea	22 937 000
40	Peru	22 361 000
41	Uzbekistan	21 300 000
42	Taiwan	20 658 000
43	Nepal	19 611 000
44	Iraq	19 524 000
45	Venezuela	18 900 000
46	Malaysia	17 981 000
47	Saudi Arabia	17 869 000
48	Uganda	17 500 000
49	Sri Lanka	17 423 000
50	Australia	16 850 540
51	Kazakhstan	16 700 000
52	Afghanistan	16 600 000
53	Mozambique	16 142 000
54	Ghana	15 336 000
55	Netherlands, The	15 231 000
56	Chile	13 173 000
57	Syria	12 965 000
58	Cameroon	12 700 000
59	Côte d'Ivoire	12 657 000
60	Madagascar	12 185 000
61	Ecuador	10 780 000
62	Cuba	10 603 000
63	Hungary	10 588 000
64	Yemen	10 400 000
65	Yugoslavia*	10 400 000
66	Portugal	10 387 000
67	Czech Republic	10 362 000
68	Angola	10 301 000
69	Belarus	10 300 000
70	Greece	10 300 000
71	Zimbabwe	10 300 000
72	Belgium	9 968 000
73	Guatemala	9 700 000

The world's largest nations by population (continued)

	Nation	*Population total (1990–2) estimates*
74	Malawi	9 438 000
75	Bulgaria	8 990 000
76	Burkina Faso	8 776 000
77	Cambodia	8 592 000
78	Sweden	8 564 000
79	Tunisia	8 400 000
80	Zambia	8 400 000
81	Mali	8 338 000
82	Niger	8 154 000
83	Senegal	7 952 000
84	Rwanda	7 902 000
85	Guinea	7 800 000
86	Austria	7 730 000
87	Somalia	7 555 000
88	Dominican Republic	7 384 000
89	Bolivia	7 356 000
90	Azerbaijan	7 236 000
91	Switzerland	6 783 000
92	Haiti	6 286 000
93	Chad	5 678 000
94	Burundi	5 450 000
95	El Salvador	5 418 000
96	Georgia	5 400 000
97	Slovak Republic	5 274 335
98	Denmark	5 139 000
99	Finland	4 991 000
100	Tajikistan	4 969 000
101	Honduras	4 949 000
102	Benin	4 883 000
103	Israel	4 882 000
104	Croatia	4 600 000
105	Paraguay	4 500 000
106	Kyrgyzstan	4 400 000
107	Bosnia-Herzegovina	4 364 574
108	Libya	4 350 000
109	Moldova	4 341 000
110	Sierra Leone	4 274 000
111	Norway	4 273 000
112	Laos	4 113 000
113	Papua New Guinea	3 913 000
114	Togo	3 810 000
115	Turkmenistan	3 809 000
116	Nicaragua	3 751 000
117	Lithuania	3 700 000
118	Ireland	3 509 000
119	Armenia	3 500 000
120	New Zealand	3 429 000
121	Jordan	3 412 000
122	Lebanon	3 384 000
123	Albania	3 303 000
124	Uruguay	3 100 000
125	Costa Rica	3 015 000
126	Central African Republic	2 875 000
127	Singapore	2 756 000
128	Liberia	2 730 000
129	Latvia	2 700 000
130	United Arab Emirates	2 500 000
131	Jamaica	2 489 000
132	Panama	2 426 000
133	Congo	2 326 000
134	Mongolia	2 247 000
135	Macedonia, former Yugoslav Republic of	2 033 964
136	Kuwait	2 024 000
137	Mauritania	1 995 000
138	Slovenia	1 962 600
139	Lesotho	1 801 000
140	Estonia	1 600 000
141	Oman	1 534 000
142	Namibia	1 520 000
143	Bhutan	1 476 000
144	Trinidad and Tobago	1 300 000
145	Botswana	1 289 000
146	Gabon	1 170 000
147	Mauritius	1 083 000
148	Guinea-Bissau	1 000 000
149	Gambia, The	901 000
150	Swaziland	859 000
151	Guyana	800 000
152	Fiji	744 000
153	Cyprus	568 000
154	Djibouti	541 000
155	Bahrain	518 000
156	Qatar	518 000
157	Comoros	463 000
158	Suriname	402 000
159	Luxembourg	388 000
160	Cape Verde	383 000
161	Equatorial Guinea	360 000
162	Malta	354 000
163	Solomon Islands	347 000
164	Brunei	259 000
165	Iceland	259 000
166	Barbados	258 000
167	Bahamas, The	254 685
168	Maldives	226 000
169	Vanuatu	200 000
170	Western Samoa	200 000
171	Belize	189 462
172	St Lucia	153 075
173	São Tomé and Príncipe	128 000
174	St Vincent and the Grenadines	114 000
175	Tonga	102 000
176	Grenada	100 000
177	Dominica	86 000
178	Antigua and Barbuda	80 600
179	Kiribati	71 000
180	Andorra	51 000
181	St Kitts and Nevis	44 100
182	Monaco	29 712
183	Liechtenstein	28 700
184	San Marino	23 000
185	Nauru	9 333
186	Tuvalu	9 317

This list is not exhaustive, particularly among the smaller nations.

All population figures provided are the last available authoritative estimates for each country and range from 1990 to 1992. For the exact year for each figure, see individual country entries.

*Yugoslavia in this context consists of the states of Montenegro and Serbia only.

World population estimates

Date (AD)	*Millions*
1	200
1000	275
1250	375
1500	420
1700	615
1800	900
1900	1 625
1920	1 860
1930	2 070
1940	2 295
1950	2 500
1960	3 050
1970	3 700
1975	4 080
1980	4 450
1985	4 845
1986	4 936
1987	5 023
1988	5 111
1989	5 201
1990	5 246
1991	5 385
1992	5 480
2000	6 100
2050	11 000

Estimates for 2000 and 2050 are United Nations 'medium' estimates. They should be compared with the 'low' estimates for these years of 5 400 and 8 500 and 'high' estimates of 7 000 and 13 000, respectively.

World population density

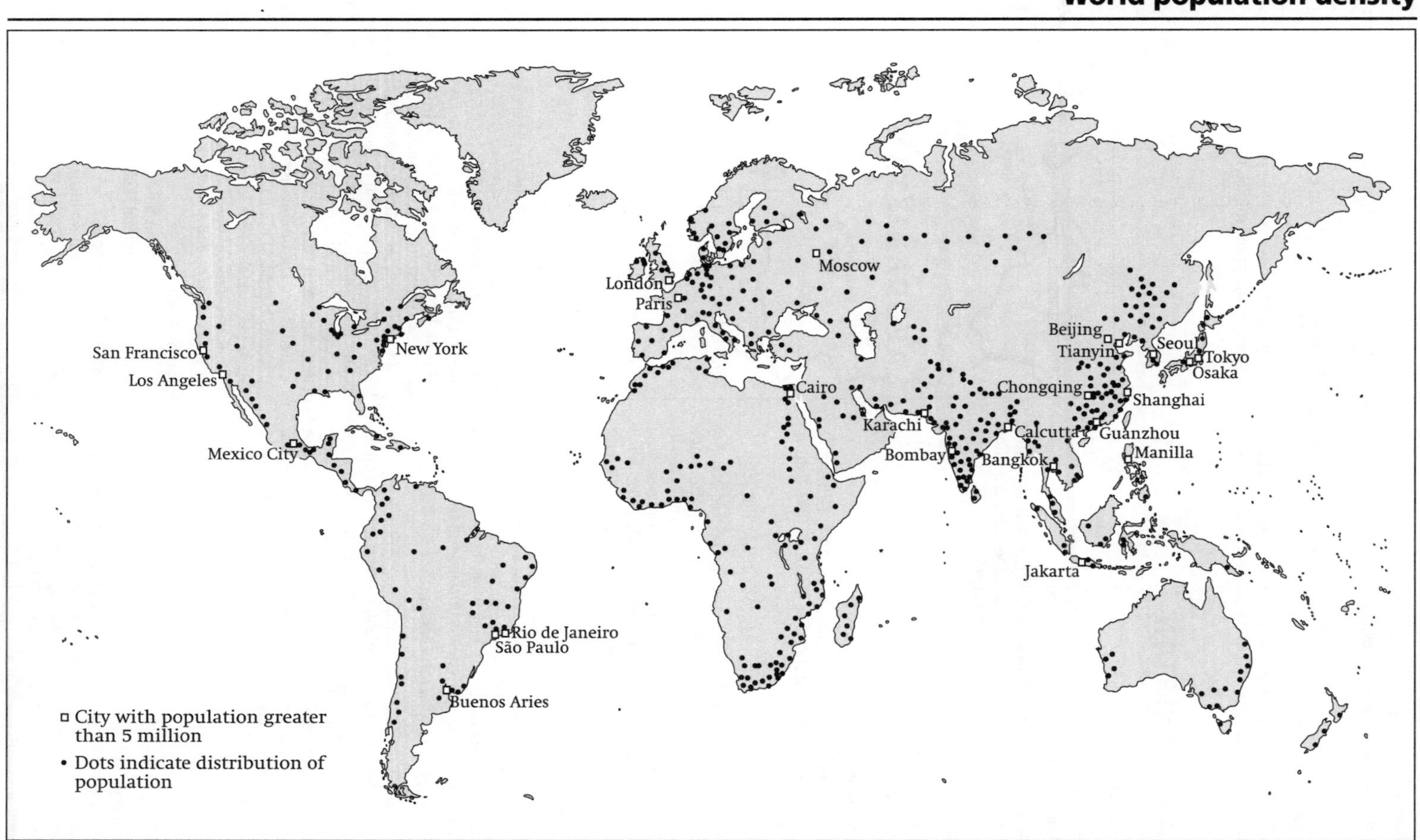

Notes

All population figures provided are the latest available authoritative figures. Estimates are indicated using the suffix 'e'.

Gross Domestic Product (GDP) and Gross National Product (GNP) figures are provided in US $ in millions (mln) or billions (bln = 1 000 mln).

In the majority of cases, the Head of State/Head of Government given are those in office since 1990. Unless stated, the head of state refers to the president and the head of government to the prime minister.

AFGHANISTAN

Local name Afghānestān

Timezone GMT + 4.5

Area 647 497 sq km/249 934 sq mi

Population total (1990e) 16 600 000, plus an estimated 2.5 million members of nomadic tribes, and 2 million living in Pakistan and Iran as refugees

Status Democratic republic

Date of independence 1919

Capital Kabul

Languages Pushtu, Dari

Ethnic groups Pathans (50%), Tajik (20%), Uzbek (9%), Hazara (9%), Chahar Aimak (3%), Turkmen (2%), Baluchi (1%)

Religions Muslim (Sunni 84%, Shi'ite Muslim 15%)

Physical features Mountainous, landlocked country centred on and divided E–W by the Hindu Kush mountain range which reach heights of over 7 000 m/24 000 ft; three distinctive regions: fertile valley of Herat in NW; arid uplands to the S; and 129 495 sq km/50 000 sq mi of desert in the SW plateau, (including the Rigestan Desert); Amu Darya (Oxus) R forms N border.

Climate Continental climate, summers warm everywhere except on highest peaks; rain mostly during spring and autumn; average annual rainfall 338 mm/13.25 in; winters generally cold, with much snow at higher altitudes (central highlands have a sub-polar climate); at lower levels desert or semi-arid climate.

Currency 1 Afghani (Af) = 100 puls

Economy Traditionally based on agriculture, especially wheat, fruit and vegetables, maize, barley, cotton, sugar-beet, sugar cane, sheep, cattle, goats; natural-gas production in the N, largely for export; most sectors have been affected by civil war, especially sugar, carpets and textiles; natural resources also include oil, coal, copper, sulphur, lead, zinc, iron, salt, and precious and semi-precious stones, many of these resources remain untapped owing to inaccessibility; main trading partners, Eastern European and CIS countries, Japan and China.

GDP (1989) $3 bln, per capita $200

History Nation first formed, 1747, under Ahmed Shah Durrani; seen as a bridge between India and the Middle East; Britain tried but failed to gain control during a series of Afghan Wars (the last in 1919); independence declared after World War 1, 1919; feudal monarchy survived until after World War 2, when the constitution became more liberal under several Soviet-influenced five-year economic plans; king deposed, 1973, and a republic formed; new constitution, 1977; coup (1979) brought to power Hafizullah Amin, which led to invasion by USSR forces and establishment of Babrak Karmal as head of state; new constitution, 1987, provided for an executive president, bicameral National Assembly, and Council of Ministers; Soviet withdrawal implemented 1988–9; new regime met with heavy guerrilla resistance from the Mujahadeen (Islamic fighters); resignation of President Najibullah, April 1992; Islamic State of Afghanistan declared, 1992; continuing unrest and disunity among Mujahadeen groups, hindering implementation of UN-backed peace plans; Dec 1992, a recently created constituent assembly elected Burhanuddin Rabbani as president for two years and also appointed a parliament.

Head of State
1987–92 Mohammad Najibullah
1992– Burhanuddin Rabbani

Head of Government
1989–90 Sultan Ali Keshtmand
1990–2 Fazl Haq Khaleqiar
1992–3 Abdul Sabur Fareed
1993– *to be announced*

ALBANIA

Local name Shqipëri

Timezone GMT + 1

Area 28 748 sq km/11 097 sq mi

Population total (1991e) 3 303 000

Status Republic

Date of independence 1912

Capital Tiranë

Languages Albanian (official) (Gheg and Tosk, the main dialects), Greek

Ethnic groups Albanian (96%), Greek (2%), Macedonian, Vlach, Gypsy, Bulgarian

Religions Muslim (Sunni 70%), Roman Catholic (5%), Greek Orthodox (2%) (before April 1991, Albania was constitutionally atheist)

Physical features Mountainous country, relatively inaccessible and untravelled; geologically active – earthquakes severe and relatively frequent; N Albanian Alps rise to 2692 m/8 832 ft; mountainous highlands (N, S and E) account for c.70% of the land; coastal lowland in the W is agricultural; rivers include the Drin i zi, Shkumbin, Seman, Vijosë; 45% of land is forested; 25% of land is arable, mostly grain-producing; c.20% is permanent pasture land.

Climate Mediterranean climate, hot and dry on the plains in summer; average annual temperatures, 8–9°C (Jan), 24–5°C (Jul); thunderstorms frequent; mild, damp, and cyclonic winters.

Currency 1 Lek (L) = 100 qintars

Economy Seventh five-year plan (1981–5) focused on industrial expansion, especially in oil (new sources were located), mining, chemicals, natural gas; hydroelectric power plans for several rivers (eg the Koman hydroelectric complex on the Drin i zi R); agricultural product processing, textiles, oil products, cement; main crops are wheat, sugar-beet, maize, potatoes, fruit, grapes, oats; all industry is nationalised; progressive transformation of farm co-operatives into state farms; chromate, low-grade iron ore and soft coal are exported; other natural resources are crude petroleum, asphalt, lignite (brown coal), phosphorus, bauxite and precious metals.

GNP (1991) $4.0 bln, (1987) per capita $1 300

History Albanians descended from Illyrians, who occupied W Balkan peninsula c.1000 BC; King Argon and, after him, his wife Teuta, conquered many territories, provoking the military might of Rome; despite Roman occupation and invasions by Visigoths, Slavs, and Huns, the Albanians were one of the few peoples to retain their Illyrian language and customs; Turkish invasions began in 14th-c; independence followed the end of Turkish rule, 1912; Italian forces occupied the country, 1914–20; Albania became a republic, 1925, and a monarchy, 1928, under King Zog I; occupied by Germany and Italy during World War 2; a new republic was instigated, 1946, headed by Enver Hoxha (until 1985); dispute with the Soviet Union, 1961, led to withdrawal from Warsaw Pact, 1968, but close links with China maintained; People's Socialist Republic instituted, 1976; renamed Republic of Albania, 1991; first free elections, 1991, gave a decisive majority to the Communists, but general strike and demonstrations forced government to resign; Communist party renamed itself the Socialist Party, but the Democratic Party was elected in 1992 elections; People's Assembly (supreme legislative body) elects the president and Council of Ministers.

Head of State

1991–2 Fatos Nano *Provisional*
1992– Sali Berisha

Head of Government

(People's Socialist Republic)
1981–91 Adil Carcani
(Republic of Albania)
1991 Ylli Bufi
1991–2 Vilson Ahmeti
1992– Alexander Meksi

ALGERIA

Local names Al-Jazā'ir (Arabic), Algérie (French)

Timezone GMT + 1

Area 2 460 500 sq km/949 753 sq mi

Population total (1991e) 25 798 000

Status Democratic republic

Date of independence 1962

Capital Algiers (Alger)

Languages Arabic (official), Berber, French

Ethnic groups Arab (75%), Berber (25%)

Religions Muslim (Sunni 99%), Roman Catholic (0.5%)

Physical features Mountainous area in N Africa; mountains rise in a series of ridges and plateaux to the Atlas Saharien; Ahaggar Mts in the far S, rising to 2 918 m/9 573 ft at Mt Tahat; 85% of land is Saharan desert.

Climate Mediterranean in N, with cool, rainy winters and hot dry summers; average annual temperatures 12°C (Jan), 25°C (Jul); average annual rainfall 400–800 mm/15.8–31.5 in (mostly Nov–Mar); essentially rainless Saharan climate in S.

Currency 1 Algerian Dinar (AD, DA) = 100 centimes

Economy Petroleum products account for about 30% of national income; natural gas liquification; jointly built with Italy first trans-Mediterranean gas pipeline; agriculture mainly on N coast; wheat, barley, oats, grapes, citrus fruits, vegetables, food processing, textiles, clothing.

GNP (1989) $53.1 bln, per capita $2 170

History Islamic Berber empires followed collapse of Numidian, Roman, Vandal and Byzantine rule; Turkish invasion, 16th-c; French colonial campaign in 19th-c led to French control, 1902; guerrilla war (1954–62) with French forces by the National Liberation Front (FLN) led to independence, 1962; first president of the republic, Ahmed Ben Bella, replaced after coup in 1965; new constitution, 1976; military took control of government, 1992, and a state of emergency was declared; legislative power is shared by the president and National Assembly.

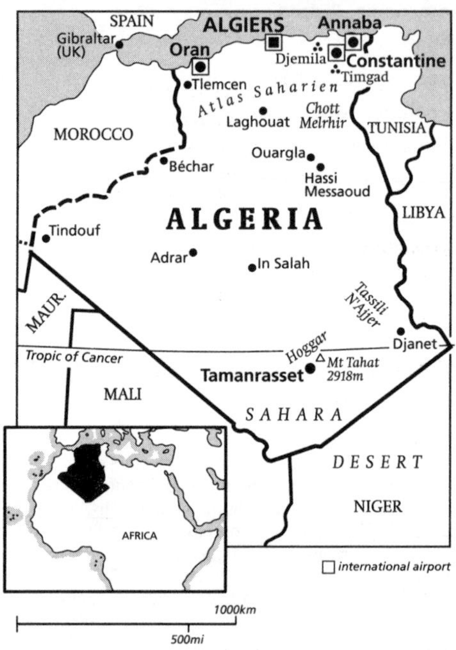

Head of State

1978–92	Chadli Benjedid
1992	Mohamed Boudiaf
1992–	Ali Kafi

Head of Government

1984–91	Mouloud Hamrouche
1991–2	Sid Ahmed Ghozali
1992–	Belaid Abdesselam

AMERICAN SAMOA >> UNITED STATES OF AMERICA

ANDORRA

Local name Vallée d'Andorre (French), Valls d'Andorra (Spanish)

Timezone GMT + 1

Area 468 sq km/181 sq mi

Population total (1991e) 51 000

Status Autonomous co-principality of France and Spain

Capital Andorra-la-Vella

Languages Catalan (official), French, Spanish

Ethnic groups Catalan (50%), Andorran (29%), French (8%), Portuguese (7%)

Religion Roman Catholic (94%)

Physical features Mountainous country, located on the S slopes of the C Pyrénées between France and Spain; reaching 2 942 m/9 665 ft at Coma Pedrosa; occupying two valleys (del Norte and del Orient) of the R Valira.

Climate Alpine climate; heavy snow in winter, warm summers; average annual temperature 2°C (Jan), 19°C (Jul); lowest average monthly rainfall, 34 mm/1.34 in (Jan).

Currency 1 French Franc (Fr) = 100 centimes, 1 Peseta (Pta, Pa) = 100 céntimos

Economy No restriction on currency exchange, and no direct value-added taxes, therefore marketing centre for goods imported from Europe and Asia; commerce, agriculture; skiing at five mountain resorts; in recent years, textiles, publishing, leather, mineral water, tourism.

GDP (1990e) $727 mln, per capita $14 000

History One of the oldest states in Europe, under the joint protection of France and Spain since 1278; Co-Princes of Principality are the President of France and the Bishop of Urgel; General Council of the Valley appoints the head of the government.

Heads of State (Co-Princes)
(President of France)
1981– François Mitterand
(Bishop of Urgel, Spain)
1971– Joan Martí Alanís

Head of Government (Chief Executive)
1989– Óscar Ribas Reig

ANGOLA

Local name Angola

Timezone GMT + 1

Area 1 245 790 sq km/480 875 sq mi

Population total (1991e) 10 301 000

Status Republic

Date of independence 1975

Capital Luanda

Languages Portuguese (official), Bantu languages, including Ovimbundu, Kimbundu, Bakongo and Chokwe

Ethnic groups Ovimbundu (37%), Mbundu (22%), Bakongo (13%), Lunda-Tchokwe (5%), also Nganguela, Nyaneka-Humbe, Herero, Ambo and Portuguese

Religions Traditional religions (47%), Roman Catholic (38%), Protestant (15%)

Physical features Located in SW Africa; narrow coastal plain; in S and E the planalto central (central plateau, continuation of great SW African plateau), covers c.60% of the country; in N, highland plateau, mean elevation 1200 m/4 000 ft; highest point, Serro Môco 2 619 m/8 592 ft; coastal desert in W; in the E, upland escarpments; c.40% of land forested.

Climate Tropical plateau climate; at Huambo, on the plateau, average annual rainfall 1 450 mm/57 in; rainfall varies greatly from SW to NE (negligible rainfall on SW coastal desert caused by Benguela current); average daily temperatures 24–29°C; temperature much reduced on the coast, which is semi-desert as far N as Luanda.

Currency 1 New Kwanza (kw, kz) = 100 Iweis

Economy Reserves of several minerals; extraction and refining of oil (mainly off the coast of Cabinda Province) provides over 75% of current export earnings; diamond exporter; large producer of honey; principal livestock, cattle, goats, pigs, and sheep; agriculture and fishing (mackerel and sardines) industries small; several airfields and railways.

GDP (1990e) $4 700 mln, per capita $600

Angola (continued)

History Became a Portuguese colony after exploration, 1483; slave trade flourished, causing friction and war (in early 17th-c, c.10 000 slaves were exported from Luanda annually); boundaries formally defined during the Berlin West Africa Congress (1884–5); became an overseas province of Portugal, 1951; Portuguese finally withdrew, 1975, and the People's Republic of Angola achieved full independence; civil war followed independence involving three internal factions – the Marxist MPLA (Popular Movement for the Liberation of Angola), UNITA (the National Union for the Total Independence of Angola), and the FNLA (National Front for the Liberation of Angola); Cuban combat troops arrived, 1976, at request of MPLA; at the end of 1988, Geneva agreement linked arrangements for independence of Namibia with withdrawal of Cuban troops, and the cessation of South African attacks and support for UNITA; peace agreement, 1991; established a one-party state, governed by a president, Council of Ministers, and National People's Assembly; adopted the name Republic of Angola, and first multi party legislative elections held, Sep 1992.

Head of State

1975–9 Antonio Agostinho Neto
1979– José Eduardo dos Santos

Head of Government

1991–2 Fernando José Frana Van Dúnem
1992– Marcolino José Carlos Moco

ANGUILLA >> UNITED KINGDOM

ANTIGUA and BARBUDA

Local name Antigua and Barbuda

Timezone GMT – 4

Area 442 sq km/171 sq mi Antigua: 280 sq km/108 sq mi; Barbuda: 161 sq km/62 sq mi; Redonda: 1 sq km/0.4 sq mi

Population total (1991e) 80 600

Status Independent republic within the Commonwealth

Date of Independence 1981

Capital St John's (on Antigua)

Language English (official)

Ethnic groups African descent (92%), Portuguese, Lebanese, and British (4%)

Religions Anglican (80%), Roman Catholic (10%)

Physical features Group of three islands in the Leeward group of the Lesser Antilles, E Caribbean; W part of Antigua rises to 405 m/ 1 328 ft at Boggy Peak; Barbuda is a flat coral island reaching only 44 m/144 ft at its highest point, with a large lagoon on its W side; Redonda is an uninhabited, volcanic island, rising to 305 m/ 1 000 ft at its highest point.

Climate Tropical; temperatures ranging from 24°C (Aug–Sep); mean annual rainfall 1 000 mm/40 in.

Currency 1 East Caribbean Dollar (EC$) = 100 cents

Economy Tourism; sugar (40% of national income, marked decline in 1960s, now recovering), cotton.

GDP (1989e) $353.5 mln, per capita $5 500

History Antigua claimed for Spain by Columbus, 1493; colonized by British, 1632; ceded to Britain, 1667; Barbuda colonized from Antigua, 1661; administered as part of the Leeward Is Federation, 1871–1956; an associated state of the UK, 1967; independence achieved, 1981; legislative power is vested in a bicameral parliment; governor-general appoints the prime minister and cabinet.

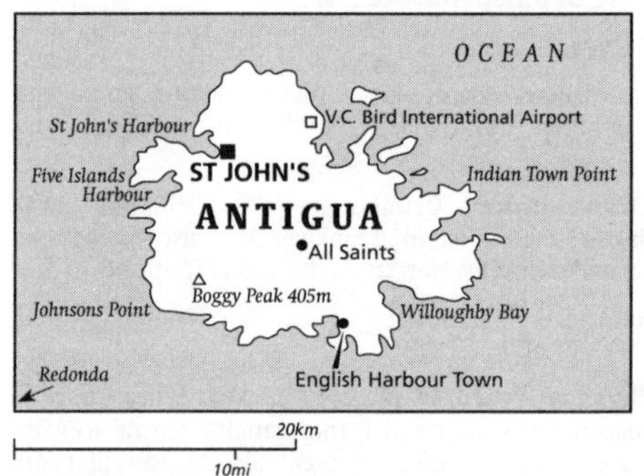

Head of State

(British monarch represented by Governor-General)
1981– Sir Wilfred E Jacobs

Head of Government

1981– Vere Cornwall Bird

ANTILLES, NETHERLANDS >> NETHERLANDS

ARGENTINA

Local name Argentina

Timezone GMT - 3

Area American continent: 2780092 sq km/1073115 sq mi on Antarctic continent: 964250 sq km/372200 sq mi

Population total (1991e) 32646000

Status Republic

Date of independence 1816

Capital Buenos Aires

Language Spanish (official)

Ethnic groups European origin (c.85%), Mestizo European/Indian origin (15%)

Religions Roman Catholic (90%), Protestant (2%)

Physical features Argentina can be divided into four regions: sub-tropical NE plains, the Pampa, Patagonia, and the Andes; Andes stretch the entire length of Argentina (N–S), forming the boundary with Chile (highest peak, Aconcagua 6 960 m/22 831 ft); uneven, semi-desert, arid steppes in the S (Patagonia); grassy, treeless Pampa to E; N Argentina is drained by the Paraguay, Paraná, and Uruguay rivers, which join in the R Plate estuary; island of Tierra del Fuego off the S tip.

Climate Moderately humid sub-tropical climate in the NE; average annual temperature 16°C; average annual rainfall 500–1 000 mm/20–40 in; semi-arid in interior S lowlands; Pampa temperate, dry in W and humid in E, with temperatures ranging from tropical to moderately cool; S directly influenced by strong prevailing westerlies.

Currency 1 Peso = 10 000 australs

Economy Major contribution to economy from agricultural produce and meat processing; deposits of oil and natural gas, chiefly off the coast of Patagonia; important reserves of iron ore, coal, copper, lead, zinc, gold, silver, uranium, and manganese.

GDP (1990) $70.1 bln, per capita $2 162

History Pre-colonially, nomadic Indian hunters lived in S, and Inca farmers in NW; after a long battle the country was settled in the 16th-c by the Spanish; declared independence as the federal Republic of Argentina, 1816, and United Provinces of the Río de la Plata established; dictatorship of Juan Manuel de Rosas, 1829–52; federal constitution, 1853; ranchers' oligarchy, 1916, was ended by military coup, 1930; acquisition of the Gran Chaco after war with Paraguay, 1865–70; considerable European settlement since the opening up of the Pampas in the 19th-c; Juan Perón elected president (1946 and 1973), eventually suceeded by his wife Isabel (Martínez de Perón) who was deposed, 1976; attempt to control the Falkland Is (1982) failed following war with the UK; successive military governments, until federal constitution reestablished, 1983, with election of Raúl Alfonsín; governed by a president and a bicameral National Congress, with a Chamber of Deputies and a Senate.

Head of State/Government

1983–8	Raúl Alfonsín
1989–	Carlos Saúl Menem

ARMENIA

Local name Armenia

Timezone GMT + 3

Area 29 800 sq km/11 500 sq mi

Population total (1992e) 3 500 00

Status Republic

Date of independence 1991

Capital Yerevan

Language Armenian (official)

Ethnic groups (1991) Armenian (90%), Azer (3%), Kurd (2%), Russian (2%) (ethnic conflict since 1990 makes accurate statistical analysis impossible)

Religions Christian (Armenian Church), Russian Orthodox

Physical features Mountainous region in S Transcaucasia, rising to 4 090 m/13 418 ft at Mt Aragats (W); rivers include Razdan and Vorotan; largest mountain lake, Sevan, 1 401 sq km/541 sq mi; main source of irrigation system and hydroelectric power.

Armenia (continued)

Climate Varies with elevation; chiefly dry and continental with considerable regional variation.

Currency 1 Rouble (R) = 100 kopecks

Economy Large mineral resources, chiefly copper; also molybdenum, gold, silver; electrical equipment and machinery, chemicals, textiles, cognac; agriculture based on fruits, wheat, wine grapes, cotton, and tobacco.

GDP Not available

History Proclaimed a Soviet Socialist Republic, 1920; constituent republic of the USSR, 1936; civil war over Nagorno-Karabakh began, 1989; declaration of independence, 1990; independence recognised, joined CIS, 1991; ongoing conflict with Azerbaijan over disputed enclave of Nagorno-Karabakh.

Head of State
1991– Levon Ter-Petrosian

Head of Government
1991– Gagik Arutynian

ARUBA >> NETHERLANDS, THE

AUSTRALIA

Local name Australia

Timezone GMT + 8 (Western Australia); GMT + 10 (New South Wales, Queensland, Tasmania, Victoria, Australian Capital Territory); GMT + 9.5 (South Australia, Northern Territory)

Area 7 692 300 sq km/2 969 228 sq mi

Population total (1991) 16 850 540

Status Independent state within the Commonwealth

Date of independence 1901

Capital Canberra

Language English (official)

Ethnic groups European descent (95%), Aboriginal (1.5%)

Religions Anglican (30%), Roman Catholic (25%)

Physical features Smallest continent; consists largely of plains and plateaux, most of which average 600 m/ 2 000 ft above sea-level; four main regions: Western Craton (or Western Shield), the Great Artesian Basin, the Great Dividing Range (or Eastern Uplands), and the Flinders-Mt Lofty ranges; W Australian Plateau occupies nearly half of the country; MacDonnell Ranges lie in the centre, highest point Mt Liebig, 1 524 m/5 000 ft; most of the plateau is dry, barren desert; Nullarbor Plain in the S, is crossed by the Trans-Australian Railway; Great Dividing Range parallel to the Great Barrier Reef, rising to 2 228 m/7 310 ft at Mt Kosciusko, Australia's highest point; Great Barrier Reef off NE coast stretches for over 1 900 km/ 1 200 mi; island of Tasmania rises to 1 617 m/5 305 ft at Mt Ossa, separated from the mainland by the Bass Strait; the longest river is the Murray, chief tributaries, the Darling, Murrumbidgee, and Lachlan; Lake Eyre, 8 800 sq km/ 3 400 sq mi; c.18% of area is forested; c.6% is arable.

Climate More than a third of Australia receives under 260 mm/10 in mean annual rainfall; less than a third receives over 500 mm/20 in; prolonged drought and frequent heatwaves in many areas; average daily temperature 26–34°C (Nov) and 19–31°C (Jul) in N; rainfall varies from 286 mm/15.2 in (Jan) to zero (Jul); fertile land with a temperate climate and reliable rainfall only in the lowlands and valleys near the E and SE coast, and a small part of the SW corner; Tasmania and Mt Kosciusko have snow fields in winter.

Currency 1 Australian Dollar ($A) = 100 cents

Economy Free enterprise economy; world's largest wool producer, and a top exporter of veal and beef; most important crop, wheat; major mineral producer, discoveries of petroleum reserves, bauxite, nickel, lead, zinc, copper, tin, uranium, iron ore, and other minerals in early 1960s; manufacturing industry expanded rapidly since 1945, especially engineering, shipbuilding, car manufacture, metals, textiles, clothing, chemicals, food processing, and wine; self-sufficient in lumber; marine fishing (especially tuna) is important; tourism and winter sports.

GDP (1990) $311 bln, per capita $18 054

History Aboriginal people thought to have arrived in Australia from SE Asia c.40 000 years ago; first European visitors were the Dutch, who explored the Gulf of Carpentaria, 1606 and settled, 1616; became known as New Holland, 1644; Captain James Cook arrived in Botany Bay, 1770, and claimed the E coast for Britain; New South Wales established as a penal colony, 1788; gold discovered in New South Wales and Victoria, 1851, and in Western Australia, 1892; transportation of convicts to E Australia ended, 1840, but continued until 1853 in Tasmania, and 1868 in Western Australia; during this period the

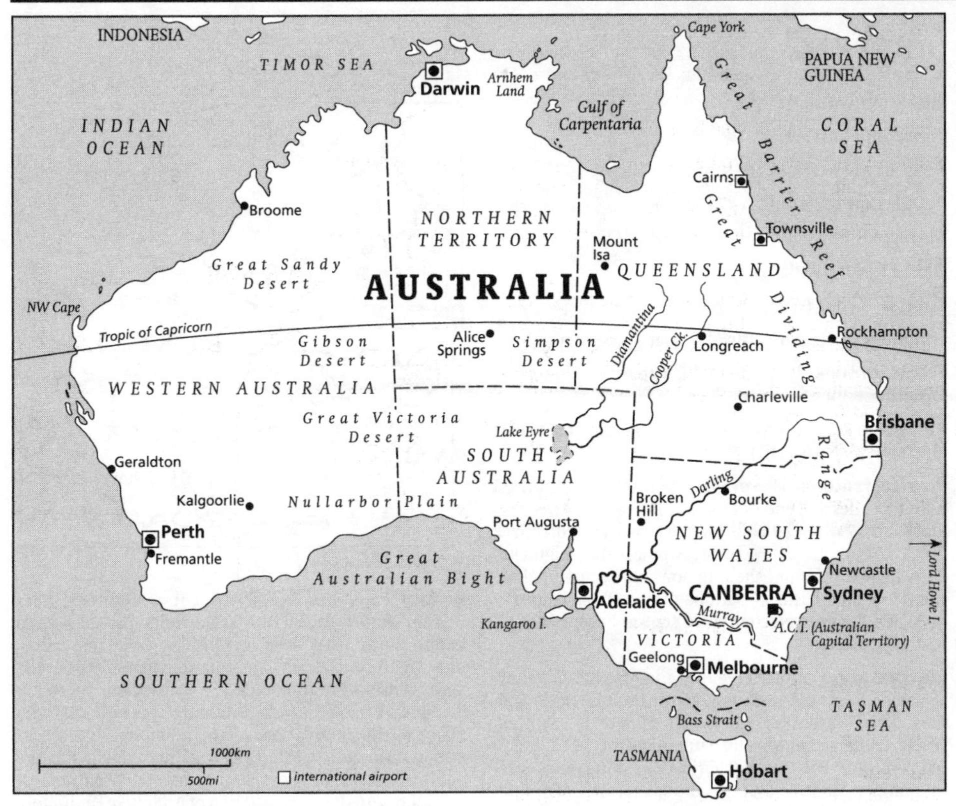

colonies drafted their own constitutions and set up governments: New South Wales (1855), Tasmania and Victoria (1856), South Australia (1857), Queensland (1860), and Western Australia (1890); Commonwealth of Australia established, 1901 with Canberra subsequently chosen as capital, 1901; policy of preventing immigration by non-Whites remained in force from the end of the 19th-c until 1974; Northern Territory self-governing since 1978; divided into six states and two territories; each state has its own legislature, government and constitution; legislature comprises a bicameral federal parliament with a prime minister and cabinet; British monarch is head of state, represented by a governor-general.

Head of State

(British monarch represented by Governor-General)
1952– Bill Hayden

Head of Government

1983–91 Robert Hawke
1991– Paul Keating

>> Political leaders and rulers

Australian states

Name	*Area sq km*	*sq mi*	*State capital*
Australian Capital Territory	2 400	930	Canberra
New South Wales	801 400	309 400	Sydney
Northern Territory	1 346 200	519 800	Darwin
Queensland	1 727 200	666 900	Brisbane
South Australia	984 000	379 900	Adelaide
Tasmania	67 800	26 200	Hobart
Victoria	227 600	87 900	Melbourne
Western Australia	2 525 500	975 000	Perth

External territories

Name	*Area sq km*	*sq mi*	*Population total*	*Date under Australian administration*
The Ashmore & Cartier Islands	3.0	2.0	Uninhabited	1931
Australian Antarctic Territory	6 043 852.0	2 332 927.0	Uninhabited	1936
Christmas Island	155.0	60.0	(1990e) 1 300	1958
Cocos (Keeling) Islands	14.2	5.5	(1990) 613	1955
Coral Sea Island	2.0*	0.8*	Uninhabited	1969
Heard Island & McDonald Islands	412.0	159.0	Uninhabited	1947
Norfolk Island	35.0	13.0	(1991) 1 912	1913

* Land figure only. Islands cover 1 000 000 sq km/286 000 sq mi of ocean

AUSTRIA

Local name Österreich

Timezone GMT + 1

Area 83 854 sq km/32 368 sq mi

Population total (1991e) 7 730 000

Status Republic

Date of independence 1955

Capital Vienna (Wien)

Languages German (official), Croatian, Slovene

Ethnic groups Austrian (99%), Croatian, Slovakian, Turkish, German

Religions Roman Catholic (85%), Protestant (12%), Muslim (1%), Jewish (1%)

Physical features One of most mountainous countries in Europe; lies at E end of the Alps; highest point, Grossglockner, 3 797 m/12 457 ft; largest lake, Neusiedler See; divided into three regions: Alpine, the highland Bohemian Massif, and the hilly lowland region, including the Vienna basin; R Danube drains whole country; most densely forested country in central Europe (40% of land is forested).

Climate Three climatic regions: the Alps (often sunny in winter, but cloudy in summer), the Danube valley and Vienna basin (driest region), and the SE, a region of often severe winters but warmer summers; average annual temperature − 2°C (Jan), 20°C (Jul) in Vienna; most rain in summer months; average annual rainfall 868 mm/34 in; winters cold, especially with winds from the E or NE; humid, continental climate in NE.

Currency 1 Schilling (S, Sch) = 100 Groschen

Economy Mixed free market; principal agricultural areas to the N of the Alps, and along both sides of the Danube; principal crops, cereals; dairy cattle and pigs; wine industry; wide range of metal and mineral resources; tourism (summer and winter); well-developed transportation networks; river ports at Linz and Vienna; airports at Vienna, Graz, Linz, Klagenfurt, Salzburg, Innsbruck; much of Austria's power produced hydroelectrically.

GDP (1991e) $163 bln, per capita $21 087

History Early Iron-Age settlement at Hallstatt; later Illyrian settlers driven out by the Celts; part of Roman Empire until 5th-c, then occupied by Germanic tribes, most significantly Bavarians; Charlemagne drove out the Slavic Avars who also settled in the region; became a duchy and passed to the Habsburg family, 1282, who made it the foundation of their Empire; Hungarian nationalism and Habsburg defeats in 19th-c led to the dual monarchy of Austria–Hungary, 1867; nationalist protest resulted in assassination of Archduke Ferdinand, 1914, and World War 1, which ended the Austrian Empire; republic established, 1918; annexed by the German Reich in 1938 (the *Anschluss*) and named Ostmark; occupied by British, American, French, and Russian troops from 1945; obtained independence, 1955; neutrality declared, since when Austria has been a haven for many refugees; governed by a Federal Assembly; Federal President appoints a Federal Chancellor.

Head of State (Federal President)
1986–92 Kurt Waldheim
1992– Thomas Klestil

Head of Government (Federal Chancellor)
1986– Franz Vranitzky

AZERBAIJAN

Local name Azerbaijan

Timezone GMT + 3

Area 86 600 sq km/33 428 sq mi

Population total (1992e) 7 236 000

Status Republic

Date of independence 1991

Capital Baku

Languages Azeri (official), Russian

Ethnic groups Azeri (83%), Russian (6%), Armenian (6%) (ethnic conflict since 1990 makes accurate statistical analysis impossible)

Religion Shi'ite Muslim

Physical features Mountainous country in E Transcaucasia; 10% of country is above 1 494 m/4 900 ft; 40% of land is lowland, 396–1 494 m/1 300–4 900 ft; Bazar-Dyuzi rises to 4 480 m/14 698 ft; rivers include the Kara and Araks.

Climate Central and eastern Azerbaijan is dry and subtropical with mild winters and long, hot summers (often as hot as 43°C); SE is humid with annual rainfall of 1 193–1 396 mm/47–55 in.

Currency 1 Rouble (R) = 100 kopecks

Economy Once the former Soviet Union's most important oil-producing region, but now in decline; manufacturing industries include building materials, chemicals, textiles; mineral resources include natural gas, iron, copper, lead, zinc; exports include cotton, wheat, tobacco.

GDP Not available

History Proclaimed a Soviet Socialist Republic, 1920; constituent republic of the USSR, 1936; declaration of independence, 1991; became a member of UN, 1992; ongoing conflict with Armenia over disputed enclave of Nagorno-Karabakh.

Head of State

1991–2 Ayaz Mutalibov
1992 Yagub Mamedov *Interim*
1992–3 Abulfaz Elchibey
1993– Geidar Aliyev *Acting*

Head of Government

1991–2 Gasan Gasanov
1992–3 Feirus Mustafayev
1993 Rakhim Guseinov
1993– Suret Guseinov *Acting*

AZORES >> PORTUGAL

BAHAMAS

Local name Bahamas

Timezone GMT – 5

Area 13 934 sq km/5 378 sq mi

Population total (1991) 254 685

Status Independent state within the Commonwealth

Date of independence 1973

Capital Nassau

Language English (official)

Ethnic groups African (85%), European/N American descent (15%)

Religions Baptist (29%), Anglican (29%), Roman Catholic (23%)

Physical features Coral archipelago of 700 islands and 2 400 uninhabited cays, forming a chain extending c.800 km/500 mi SE from the coast of Florida; population centres on the two oceanic banks of Little and Great Bahama; highest point, Mt Alvernia, 120 m/394 ft.

Climate Sub-tropical; average temperatures 21°C (Jan) and 27°C (Jul); mean annual rainfall 750–1 500 mm/30–60 in; hurricanes frequent (Jun–Nov).

Currency 1 Bahamian Dollar (BA$, B$) = 100 cents

Economy Market economy based on tourism; important financial centre (no income tax); oil refining, fishing, rum and liqueur distilling, cement, pharmaceuticals.

GDP (1990e) $2.8 bln, per capita $11 055

History Visited by Columbus, 1492, but first permanent European settlement not until 1647 by British and Bermudan religious refugees; British Crown Colony, 1717; independence, 1973; governed by a bicameral parliament.

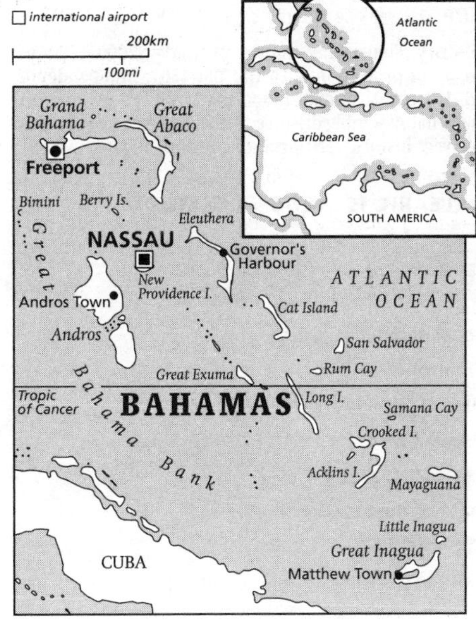

Head of State

(British monarch represented by Governor-General)
1988– Sir Henry Taylor

Head of Government

1973–92 Sir Lynden O Pindling
1992– Hubert Alexander Ingraham

BAHRAIN

Local name Al-Bahrayn

Timezone GMT + 3

Area 678 sq km/262 sq mi

Population total (1991e) 518 000

Status Independent state

Date of independence 1971

Capital Al Manama

Languages Arabic (official), Farsi, Urdu and English

Ethnic groups Bahraini Arab (63%), Asian (13%), Arab (10%), Iranian (6%)

Religions Shi'ite Muslim (60%), Sunni Muslim (40%)

Physical features Island of Bahrain c.48 km/30 mi long, 13–16 km/8–10 mi wide, area 562 sq km/217 sq mi; highest point Jabal Du Khan, 135 m/443 ft; largely bare and infertile.

Climate Temperate (Dec–Mar); hot and humid (particularly Jun–Sep); cool N/NE winds with a little rain (Dec–Mar), average annual rainfall 35 mm/1.4 in; average annual temperature 19°C (Jan), 36°C (Jul).

Currency 1 Bahrain Dinar (BD) = 1 000 fils

Economy Major centre for oil trading, banking and commerce.

GDP (1989e) $3.4 bln, per capita $7 300

History Flourishing centre of trade, 2000–1800 BC; treaty of protection with the UK, 1861; independence, 1971; a constitutional monarchy governed by an emir; National Assembly dissolved, 1975 and has not yet been revived; historic territorial dispute with Qatar over the Hawar Is began with the brief occupation of Fasht al-Dibal by Qatari troops, 1986; Bahrain joined UN coalition during the Iraqi invasion of Kuwait, 1990.

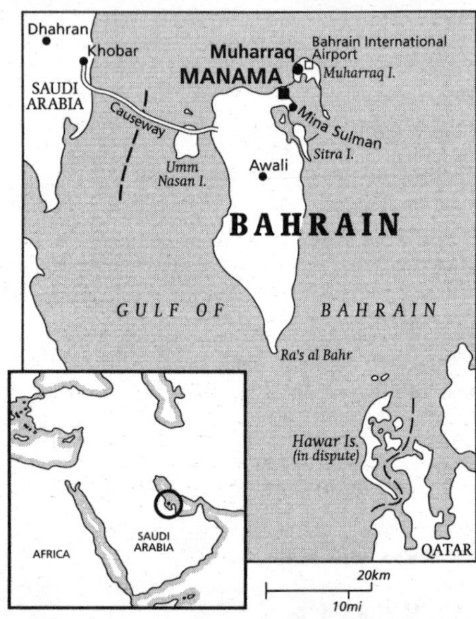

Head of State (Emir)
1971– Shaikh Isa bin Sulman al-Khalifa

Head of Government
1971– Shaikh Khalifa bin Sulman al-Khalifa

BALEARIC ISLANDS >> SPAIN

BANGLADESH

Local name Bangladesh

Timezone GMT + 6

Area 143 998 sq km/55 583 sq mi

Population total (1991) 107 992 140

Status Republic

Date of independence 1971

Capital Dhaka

Languages Bengali (official), also local dialects and English are widely spoken

Ethnic groups Bengali (98%), Bihari (1%), tribal: Garo, Khasi, Santal (1%)

Religions Muslim (86%), Hindu (12%), Buddhist (1%), small Christian majority

Physical features Mainly a vast, low-lying alluvial plain, cut by a network of rivers, canals, swamps, and marshes; main rivers the Ganges (Padma), Brahmaputra (Jamuna), and Meghna, joining in the S to form the largest delta in the world; subject to frequent flooding; Chittagong Hill Tracts in the E, rise to 1 200 m/3 900 ft.

Climate Tropical climate; monsoon season (Jun–Oct).

Currency 1 Taka (TK) = 100 poisha

Economy Agriculture, especially rice (employs 86% of population); supplies 80% of the world's jute; paper, aluminium, textiles, glass, shipbuilding, fishing, natural gas.

GDP (1990e) $20.2 bln, per capita $180

History Part of the State of Bengal until Muslim East Bengal created, 1905, separate from Hindu West Bengal; reunited, 1911; partitioned again, 1947, with West Bengal remaining in India and East Bengal forming East Pakistan; rebellion in 1971 led to independence as the People's Republic of Bangladesh; political unrest led to suspension of constitution, and assassination of first president, Sheikh Mujib, 1975; further coups, 1975, 1977, and 1982; constitution restored, 1986; last military dictator, Hossain Mohammad Ershad, overthrown, 1990; constitutional amendments, 1991, restricted powers of president to ceremonial and restored full powers to unicameral legislature, *Jatiya Sangsad*.

Head of State

1983–90 Hossain Mohammad Ershad
1990–1 Shehabuddin Ahmed *Acting*
1991– Abdur Rahman Biswas

Head of Government

1989–91 Kazi Zafar Ahmed
1991– Begum Khaleda Zia

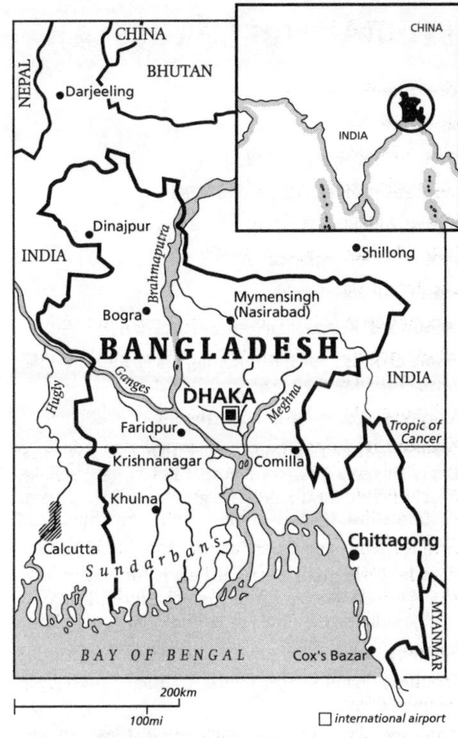

BARBADOS

Local name Barbados

Timezone GMT – 4

Area 430 sq km/166 sq mi

Population total (1991e) 258 000

Status Independent state within the Commonwealth

Date of independence 1966

Capital Bridgetown

Language English (official)

Ethnic groups African (80%), mixed race (16%)

Religions Anglican (40%), Protestant (15%), Roman Catholic (4%)

Physical features Small, triangular island in the Atlantic Ocean; length 32 km/20 mi (NW–SE), rising to 340 m/1 115 ft at Mt Hillaby; ringed by a coral reef.

Climate Tropical climate, with average annual temperature 27°C; mean annual rainfall 1 420 mm/56 in.

Currency 1 Barbados Dollar (Bds$) = 100 cents

Economy Market economy based on tourism and sugar cane; cotton, bananas; natural gas; textiles.

GDP (1990e) $1400 mln, per capita $5405

History Colonized by the British, 1627; self-government, 1961; independent within the Commonwealth, 1966; executive power rests with the prime minister, appointed by a governor-general; Senate, and House of Assembly.

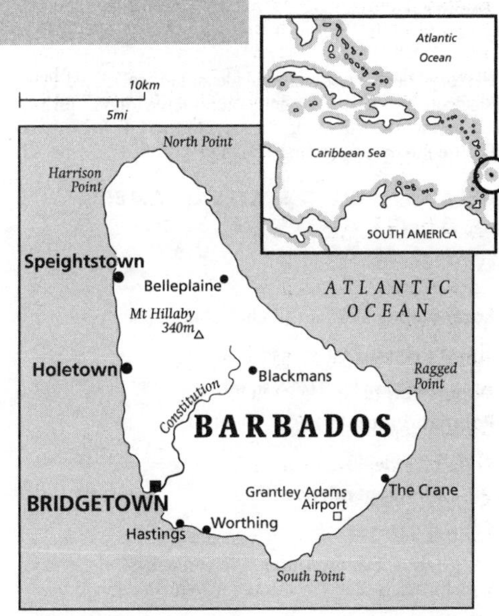

Head of State

(British monarch represented by Governor-General)
1984–90 Hugh Springer
1990– Dame Nita Barrow

Head of Government

1987– L Erskine Sandiford

BELARUS (BELORUSSIA)

Local name Belarus

Timezone GMT + 3

Area 207 600 sq km/80 134 sq mi

Population total (1992e) 10 300 000

Status Republic

Date of independence 1991

Capital Minsk (Mensk)

Languages Belorussian (official), Russian

Ethnic groups (1989) Belorussian (78%), Russian (13%), Polish (4%), Ukrainian (3%), Jewish (1%)

Religions Roman Catholic, Orthodox

Physical features Hilly lowlands with marshes, swamps; Dzyarzhynskaya Mt rises 346 m/1 135 ft; largest lake, Narach; Belaruskaya Hrada, largest glacial ridge, runs NW into Minsk Upland; rivers include the Pripyat and Dnepr; Pripyat marshes in S.

Climate Varies from maritime near Baltic, to continental and humid; average annual temperatures, 18°C (Jul), −6°C (Jan); average annual rainfall 550–700 mm/22–28 in.

Currency Belorussian Rouble = 100 kopecs (in parallel with the Russian Rouble); currency coupons for food, alcohol, tobacco

Economy Main exports include textiles, timber, chemical products, fertilizers, electrical goods; valuable resource peat marshes.

GDP Not available

History Neolithic remains widespread; colonized by E Slavic tribes, 5th-c; Mongols conquered Slavs, 13th-c; Catherine the Great of Russia acquired E Belorussia (White Russia) in the first Polish partition, 1772; gained Minsk, 1793, and the remainder, 1795; W Belorussia ceded to Poland, 1921, as part of the Treaty of Riga which ended Soviet–Polish War; regained by Soviet Union as part of Nazi–Soviet Non-aggression Pact, 1939, and Belorussia became Belorussian Soviet Socialist Republic; admitted to UN, 1945; declared independence, 1991; co-founder of Commonwealth of Independent States (CIS), 1991.

Head of State

1991– Stanislav Shushkevich

Head of Government

1991– Vyacheslav Kebich

BELAU >> UNITED STATES OF AMERICA

BELGIUM

Local names Belgique (French), België (Flemish)

Timezone GMT + 1

Area 30 540 sq km/11 788 sq mi

Population total (1991e) 9 968 000

Status Kingdom

Date of independence 1830

Capital Brussels

Languages Flemish/Dutch (56%), French (32%), German (1%); (Brussels officially bilingual Flemish/French)

Ethnic groups Flemish (Teutonic origin) (55%), Walloon (French Latin) (33%)

Religions Roman Catholic (75%), Muslim (1%), Protestant (0.4%)

Physical features Mostly low-lying, with some hills in the SE region (Ardennes), average elevation 300–500 m/1 000–1 600 ft; large areas of fertile soil, intensively cultivated for many centuries; main river systems linked by complex network of canals; low-lying, dune-fringed coastline.

Climate Cool and temperate with strong maritime influences; average annual temperatures 2°C (Jan), 18°C (Jul) in Brussels; average annual rainfall 825 mm/35 in.

Currency 1 Belgian Franc (BFr) = 100 centimes

Economy One of the earliest countries in Europe to industrialize, using rich coalfields of the Ardennes; Flanders textile industry; long-standing centre for European trade; major iron and steel industry, with wide range of metallurgical and engineering products; agriculture mainly livestock; full economic union (Benelux Economic Union) between Belgium, Netherlands, and Luxembourg, 1948; Brussels is the headquarters of several major international organizations, including the Commission of the EC.

GDP (1990) $144.8 bln, per capita $14 600

History Part of the Roman Empire until 2nd-c; then became part of the Frankish Empire following Celt and Germanic invasions; ruled by the Habsburgs from 1477 until the Peace of Utrecht, 1713, when sovereignty passed to Austria; conquered by the French, 1794; part of the French Republic and Empire until 1815, then united with the Netherlands; Belgian rebellion against Dutch rule, 1830, led to recognition as an independent kingdom under Leopold of Saxe-Coburg; occupied by Germany in both World Wars; became a constitutional monarchy with bicameral parliament; political tension between Walloons in S and Flemings in N, 1980; federal constitution divided Belgium into the autonomous regions of Flanders, Wallonia, and Brussels, 1989; constitutional monarch has limited powers; Chamber of Deputies and a Senate.

Head of State (Monarch)
1950–93 Baudouin I
1993– Albert II

Head of Government
1981–92 Wilfried Martens
1992– Jean-Luc Dehaene

BELIZE

Local name Belice (Spanish)

Timezone GMT – 6

Area 22 963 sq km/8 864 sq mi

Population total (1992) 189 462

Status Independent state within the Commonwealth

Date of independence 1981

Capital Belmopan

Languages English (official), Spanish, Garifuna, Maya

Ethnic groups Creole (38%), mestizo (33%), Mayan (10%), Carib (7%)

Religions Roman Catholic (62%), Protestant (30%)

Physical features Located in C America; extensive coastal plain; swampy in the N, fertile in the S; Maya Mts extend almost to the E coast, rising to 1 120 m/ 3 674 ft at Victoria Peak; Belize R flows W–E; inner coastal waters protected by world's second longest barrier reef.

Climate Generally sub-tropical, but tempered by trade winds; average annual temperature 24°C (Jan), 27°C (Jul); variable rainfall; average annual rainfall 1 290 mm/50 in (N), 4 445 mm/175 in (S); hurricanes frequent.

Currency 1 Belize Dollar (Bz$) = 100 cents

Economy Developing free market economy based on timber and forest products, more recently on agriculture.

GDP (1990) $290 mln, per capita $1 320

History Evidence of early Mayan settlement; colonized in the 17th-c by shipwrecked British sailors and disbanded soldiers from Jamaica; created a British colony, 1862; administered from Jamaica until 1884; internal self-government, 1964; changed name from British Honduras to Belize, 1973; full independence, 1981; Guatemalan claims over Belize territory have led to a continuing British military presence; bicameral National Assembly, comprising of a House of Representatives and a Senate.

Head of State
(British monarch represented by Governor-General)
1981– Dame Minita Elvira Gordon

Head of Government
1989– George Cadle Price

BENIN

Local name Bénin

Timezone GMT + 1

Area 112 622 sq km/43 472 sq mi

Population total (1991e) 4 883 000

Status Republic

Date of independence 1960

Capital Porto Novo (nominal), Cotonou (political and economic)

Languages French (official), Fon (47%), Adja (12%), Bariba (10%), Yoruba (9%), Fulani (6%), Somba (5%), Aizo (5%)

Ethnic groups Fon (40%), Yoruba (10%), Bariba (20%), minority of Fulani nomads

Religions Traditional beliefs (c.70%), Christian (15%), Muslim (13%)

Physical features Located in N Africa; rises from a 100 km/62 mi-long, sandy coast with lagoons to low-lying plains; savannah plateau, c. 400 m/1 300 ft, in N, descend to forested lowlands in S fringing the Bight of Benin; Atakora Mts rise to over 500 m/1 600 ft in NW; rivers included Ouémé, Alibori and Mekrou; Pendjari National Park in NW.

Climate Tropical climate divided into three zones: in the S, rain throughout the year, especially during the Guinea Monsoon (May–Oct); in C, two rainy seasons (peaks in May–Jun and Oct); in the N, one rainy season (Jul–Sep); dry season in N (Oct–Apr), hot, with low humidity, subject to the dry harmattan wind from the NE.

Currency 1 CFA Franc (CFAFr) = 100 centimes

Economy Agriculture, especially palm oil products, cashew nuts, maize, cassava, rice, cotton, coffee; no known natural resources in commercial quantity; small offshore oilfield.

GDP (1991) $1.7 bln, per capita $400

History Pre-colonially a collection of small, warring principalities, including the Fon Kingdom of Dahomey (founded 17th-c); Portuguese colonial activities centred on slave trade; subjugated by French becoming the French Protectorate of Dahomey, 1892; territory within French West Africa, 1904; independence, 1960; Marxist-Leninist regime gained power, 1972; name changed from Dahomey to the People's Republic of Benin, 1975; Marxism -Leninism abandoned, 1989, and a new multi party constitution approved, 1990; changed name to Republic of Benin, 1990; multi party elections held, 1991; president elected for five-year term, and a National Assembly.

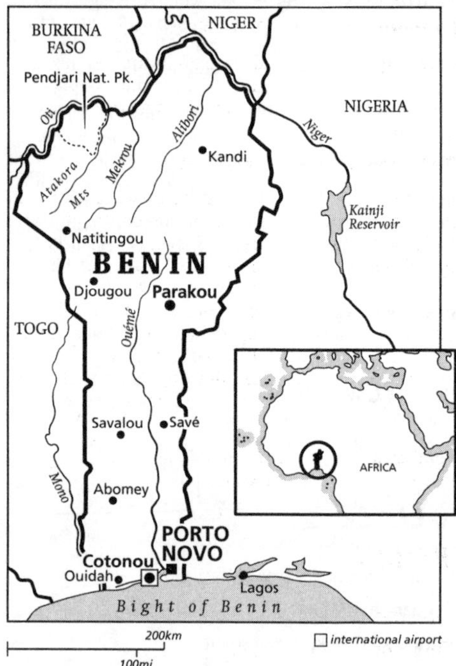

Head of State

1990–1 Ahmed Kerekou
1991– Nicéphore Soglo

Head of Government

1990–1 Nicéphore Soglo

BERMUDA >> UNITED KINGDOM

BHUTAN

Local name Druk-Yul

Timezone GMT + 5.5

Area 46 600 sq km/18 000 sq mi

Population total (1991e) 1 476 000

Status Kingdom

Capital Thimphu

Languages Dzongkha (official) (60%), Nepalese (25%), English

Ethnic groups Bhote (60%), Gurung (15%), Assamese (13%)

Religions Mahayana Buddhist (75%), Hindu (20%), Muslim (5%)

Physical features High peaks of E Himalayas in the N, over 7 000m/23 000 ft; forested mountain ridges with fertile valleys descend to low foothills in the S; rivers include Wong Chu, Manas; permanent snowfields in the mountains; sub-tropical forest in S.

Climate Affected by altitude; snow capped in glaciated N; average monthly temperatures 4°C (Jan), 17°C (Jul); torrential rain common, average 1 000 mm/40 in (C valleys) and 5 000 mm/200 in (S).

Currency 1 Ngultrum (Nu) = 100 chetrum

Economy Largely based on agriculture, mainly rice, wheat, maize, mountain barley, potatoes, vegetables, fruit (especially oranges); timber (large area of plantation forest).

GDP (1989) $273 mln, per capita $199

History British involvement since treaty of 1774 with the East India Company; S part of the country annexed, 1865; Anglo-Bhutanese Treaty signed, in which Britain agreed not to interfere in internal affairs of Bhutan, 1910; similar treaty (Indo-Bhutan Treaty of Friendship) signed with India, 1949; governed by a maharajah from 1907, now addressed as King of Bhutan; National Assembly (*Tsogdu*) established, 1953; constitutional monarchy with power shared between the king, Council of Ministers, National Assembly, and the monastic head of the kingdom's Buddhist priesthood.

Head of State/Government (Monarch)
1972– Jigme Singye Wangchuk

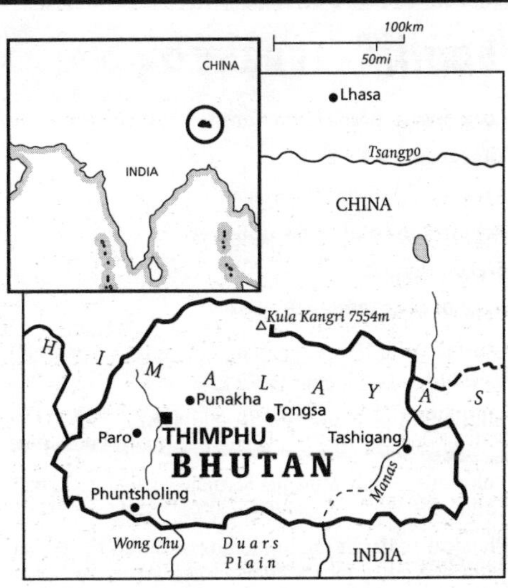

BOLIVIA

Local name Bolivia

Timezone GMT – 4

Area 1 098 580 sq km/424 052 sq mi

Population total (1991e) 7 356 000

Status Republic

Date of independence 1825

Capital La Paz (administrative), Sucre (legal)

Languages Spanish, Quechua, Aymará (all used officially)

Ethnic groups Mestizo (31%), Quechua (30%), Aymará (25%)

Religions Roman Catholic (95%), Baha'i (3%)

Physical features Landlocked country, bounded W by the Cordillera Occidental of the Andes, rising to 6 542 m/21 463 ft at Sajama; separated from the Cordillera Real to the E by the flat, 400 km/250 mi-long Altiplano plateau, 3 600 m/11 800 ft; major lakes, Titicaca and Poopó.

Climate Varies with altitude, ranging from consistently warm (26°C) and damp conditions (1 800 mm/71 in of rainfall per year) in NE rainforests of Amazon Basin, to drought conditions in S; over 500 m/16 404 ft conditions become sub-polar.

Currency 1 Boliviano (Bs) = 100 centavos

Economy Dependent on minerals for foreign exchange; silver largely exhausted, but replaced by tin (a fifth of world supply); oil- and natural-gas pipelines to Argentina and Chile; illegally-produced cocaine.

GDP (1990) $4.8 bln, per capita $690

History Part of Inca Empire, conquered by Spanish in 16th-c; independence after war of liberation, 1825; much territory lost after wars with neighbouring countries; several changes of government and military coups between 1964–82; returned to civilian rule, 1982; governed by a bicameral Congress and elected president and a cabinet.

Head of State/Government
1982–5 Hernán Siles Suazo
1985–9 Victor Paz Estenssoro
1989– Jaime Paz Zamora

BOSNIA–HERZEGOVINA

Local name Bosna i Hercegovina

Timezone GMT + 2

Area 51 129 sq km/19 736 sq mi

Population total (1991) 4 364 574

Status Republic

Date of independence 1992

Capital Sarajevo

Language Serbo-Croat

Ethnic groups (Pre-civil war) Slav (44%), Serbian (31%), Croatian (17%)

Religions Sunni Muslim, Serbian Orthodox, Roman Catholic

Physical features Mountainous region in the Balkan peninsula noted for its stone gorges, lakes, rivers, and mineral springs; reaches heights of 1 800 m/6 000 ft above sea level; principal rivers are Bosna, Una, Drina, Neretva and Sava; in the SW lies the dry, limestone plateau (karst).

Climate Ranges from Mediterranean to mildly continental; sirocco wind brings rain from SW; strong NE wind (*bora*) affects coastal area in winter.

Currency 1 Dinar (D, Dn) = 100 paras

Economy Highly industrialized, particularly iron and steel; large cellulose factory at Banja Luka; forestry strong in Bosnia; inflation rate high; war (1992–3) disrupted all economic activity.

GDP Not available

History Annexed by Austria, 1908; Serbian opposition to the annexation led to the murder of Archduke Francis Ferdinand and World War 1; ceded to Yugoslavia, 1918; declaration of sovereignty, 1991; Bosnian Serbs proclaimed three autonomous regions (Bosanska Krajina, Romanija, and Northern Bosnia), 1991; declaration of independence, 1992, led to ongoing military conflict between formerly integrated communities of Bosnians, Croats, and Serbs; UN peace-keeping forces deployed, and air-exclusion ('no-fly') zone imposed, 1992.

Head of State

1992– Alija Izetbegovic

Head of Government

1992 Jure Pelivan
1992– Mile Akmadzic

BOTSWANA

Local name Botswana

Timezone GMT + 2

Area 582 096 sq km/224 689 sq mi

Population total (1991e) 1 289 000

Status Independent republic within the Commonwealth

Date of independence 1966

Capital Gaborone

Languages English (official), Tswana

Ethnic groups Tswana (75%), Shona (12%), San (Bushmen) (3%), Khoikhoin (Hottentot) (3%), Ndebele (1%)

Religions Traditional beliefs (49%), Protestant (29%), African Christian (12%), Roman Catholic (9%)

Physical features Landlocked S African republic; undulating, sand-filled plateau, part of the S African Plateau; mean elevation c.1 000 m/3 300 ft; the N–S plateau divides country into two regions: hilly grasslands (velt) to E, and Okavango Swamps to W; most of the population lives in fertile, hilly E; SE terrain hilly, 1 402 m/ 4 600 ft; dry scrubland, savannah and the Kalahari Desert in W; salt lakes in N.

Climate Largely sub-tropical; rainfall in N and E almost totally in summer (Oct–Apr); average annual temperature 26°C (Jan), 13°C (Jul) in Gaborone; average annual rainfall 450 mm/17.7 in.

Currency 1 Pula (P, Pu) = 100 thebes

Economy Mainly subsistence farming, especially livestock; continual problems of drought and disease; some crops, especially sorghum; main minerals, nickel, diamonds (jointly mined by the government and De Beers Consolidated Mines of South Africa), cobalt; tourism, especially wildlife observation; principal trading partners members of South African Customs Union; Central Kalahari Game Reserve (54 388 sq km/21 000 sq mi) attracts tourists.

GDP (1990) $3.1 bln, per capita $2 500

History San (Bushmen) were the earliest inhabitants, followed by Sotho peoples who migrated to Botswana c.1600; explored by Europeans, 1801; visited by missionaries during 19th-c; London Missionary Society established a mission on the Kuruman R, 1813; Ndebele raided Botswana; Boers arrived, 1835; gold was discovered, 1867; under British protection, 1885; S became a Crown Colony, then part of Cape Colony, 1895; N became the Bechuanaland Protectorate; self-government, 1964; independence and change of name to Botswana, 1966; governed by a legislative National Assembly, president, and cabinet; House of Chiefs considers chieftaincy matters but has no right of veto.

Head of State/Government
1980– Quett K J Masire

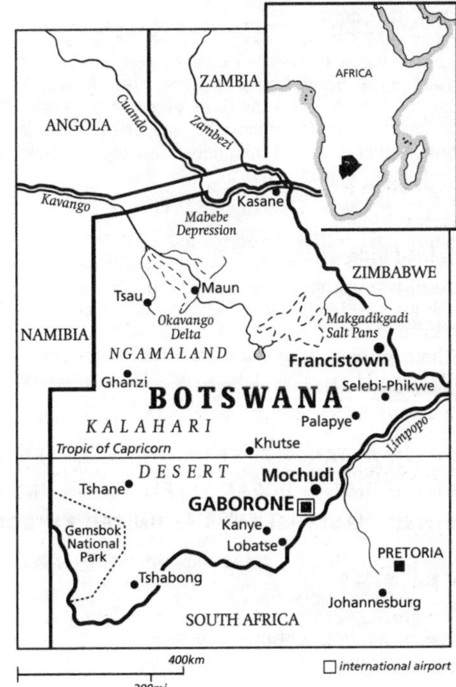

BRAZIL

Local name Brasil

Timezone GMT – 2 (Atlantic Islands); GMT – 3 (E); GMT – 4 (mid-W); GMT – 5 (extreme W)

Area 8 511 965 sq km/3 285 618 sq mi

Population total (1990e) 150 368 000

Status Republic

Date of independence 1822

Capital Brasília

Language Portuguese (official)

Ethnic groups White (55%), mixed (38%), Black (6%)

Religions Roman Catholic (89%), Protestant, Spiritualist

Physical features Located in E and C South America; low-lying Amazon basin in the N; where forest canopy cleared, soils susceptible to erosion; Brazilian plateau in the C and S, average height 600–900 m/2 000–3 000 ft; Guiana Highlands (S) contain Brazil's highest peak, Pico da Neblina, 3 014 m/9 888 ft; eight river systems, notably the Amazon (N), the São Francisco (C), the Paraguay, Paraná (S); 30% of population concentrated on a thin coastal strip on the Atlantic, c.100 km/325 mi wide.

Climate Almost entirely tropical, equator passing through the N region, and Tropic of Capricorn through the SE; Amazon basin, annual rainfall 1 500–2 000 mm/60–80 in; no dry season; average midday temperatures 27°–32°C; dry region in the NE, susceptible to long

droughts; hot, tropical climate on narrow coastal strip, with rainfall varying greatly N–S; S states have a seasonal temperate climate.

Currency 1 Cruzeiro (Cr$) = 100 centavos

Economy One of the world's largest farming countries, agriculture employing 35% of the population; world's

Brazil (continued)

largest exporter of coffee, second largest exporter of cocoa and soya beans; iron ore reserves (possibly world's largest); timber reserves the third largest in the world, but continuing destruction of the Amazon rainforest is causing much concern; road network being extended through the Amazon rainforest.

GDP (1990) $388 bln, per capita $2 540

History Claimed for the Portuguese by Pedro Alvares Cabral in 1500, first settlement at Salvador da Bahia; King of Portugal moved seat of government to Brazil, 1808; his son, Dom Pedro, declared himself emperor, 1818; independence established, 1822; Dom Pedro forced to abdicate, 1831 and was succeeded by his 14-year-old son, Dom Pedro II, 1840; abolition of slavery, 1888, persuaded former slave-owners in declining sugar plantation areas to join Republican opposition to the king, who was overthrown in the coup of 1889; ruled by dictator, Getúlio Vargas, 1930–45; Vargas deposed by military, and liberal republic restored, 1946; he was returned to office in 1950, but committed suicide in 1954; capital moved from Rio de Janeiro to Brasília, 1960; another coup in 1964 led to a military-backed presidential regime; President da Costa e Silva resigned and military junta took control, 1969; new elections, 1985; new constitution approved, transferring power from the president to the congress, 1988; bicameral National Congress.

Head of State/Government

1985–90	José Sarney
1990–2	Fernando Collor de Mello
1992–	Itamar Franco

BRITISH ANTARCTIC TERRITORY >> UNITED KINGDOM

BRITISH INDIAN OCEAN TERRITORY >> UNITED KINGDOM

BRITISH VIRGIN ISLANDS >> UNITED KINGDOM

BRUNEI

Local name Negara Brunei Darussalam

Timezone GMT + 8

Area 5 765 sq km/2 225 sq mi

Population total (1990e) 259 000

Status Independent state

Date of independedce 1984

Capital Bander Seri Begawan

Languages Malay (official), English

Ethnic groups Malay (65%), Chinese (20%)

Religions Sunni Muslim (65%), Buddhist (12%), Christian (9%)

Physical features Swampy coastal plain; equatorial rainforest covers 75% of land area; rivers include Belait, Tutong and Brunei; mountainous tract on Sarawak border, average height 500 m/1 640 ft.

Climate Tropical; high temperatures and humidity and no marked seasons; average daily temperature 24–30°C; average annual rainfall 2 540 mm/100 in on coast, doubling in the interior.

Currency 1 Brunei Dollar (Br$) = 100 cents

Economy Largely dependent on oil (discovered 1929) and gas resources.

GDP (1989) $3.1 bln, per capita $9 600

History Formerly a powerful Muslim sultanate, with dominion over all of Borneo, its neighbouring islands, and parts of the Philippines by early 16th-c; under British protection, 1888; occupied by Japanese, 1941; liberated and reverted to former status as a British residency, 1945; internal self-government, 1971; full independence, 1984; a constitutional monarchy with the Sultan as head of state, who presides over a Council of Cabinet Ministers, Religious Council and a Privy Council.

international airport

Head of State/Government (Sultan)

1967–	Muda Hassanal Bolkiah Mu'izzadin Waddaulah

BULGARIA

Local name Bălgarija

Timezone GMT + 2

Area 110 912 sq km/42 812 sq mi

Population total (1992e) 8 990 000

Status Republic

Date of independence 1908

Capital Sofia

Languages Bulgarian (official), Turkish

Ethnic groups Bulgarian (85%), Turkish (9%)

Religions Bulgarian Orthodox (85%), Muslim (13%)

Physical features Traversed W–E by the Balkan Mts, averaging 2 000 m/6 500 ft; in the SW, Rhodope Mts, rising to 3 000 m/9 600 ft; rivers include Maritsa, Iskur and Danube.

Climate Continental climate, with hot summers, cold winters; average annual temperatures −2°C (Jan), 21°C (Jul); average annual rainfall 635 mm/25 in.

Currency 1 Lev (Lv) = 100 stotinki

Economy Mainly agricultural produce; coal, iron ore; offshore oil (Black Sea), natural gas; tourism; tobacco, wine exports.

GNP (1990) $47.3 bln, per capita $5 300

History Bulgars crossed the Danube in the 7th-c; their empire continually at war with Byzantines until destroyed by Turks in the 14th-c; remained under Turkish rule, 1396–1878; full independence, 1908; became a kingdom, 1908–46; aligned with Germany in World Wars; occupied by USSR, 1944; Socialist People's Republic founded, 1946; unicameral National Assembly established, 1971; proclaimed Republic of Bulgaria, 1990; new constitution, 1991, with a directly elected president, and 250-member National Assembly.

Head of State

1989–90 Petar Mladenov
1990– Zhelyu Zhelev

Head of Government

1990–1 Dimitar Popov
1991–2 Filip Dimitrov
1992– Lyuben Berov

BURKINA FASO

Local name Burkina Faso

Timezone GMT

Area 274 540 sq km/105 972 sq mi

Population total (1992e) 8 776 000

Status Republic

Date of independence 1960

Capital Ouagadougou

Languages French (official), with Moré, Mossi, Mande, Fulani, Lobi and Bobo also spoken

Ethnic groups Mossi (48%), over 50 other groups

Religions Traditional beliefs (45%), Muslim (43%), Christian (12%)

Physical features Landlocked republic in W Africa; low-lying plateau, falling away to the S; tributaries of the

Burkina Faso (continued)

Volta and Niger unnavigable in dry season; wooded savannahs in S; semi-desert in N.

Climate Tropical; average annual rainfall 894 mm/35 in; dry season (Dec–May), rainy season (Jun–Oct); average annual temperature 24°C (Jan), 28°C (Jul) in Ouagadougou; violent storms (Aug); subject to drought conditions.

Currency 1 CFA Franc (CFAFr) = 100 centimes

Economy Based on agriculture, largely at subsistence level; millet, corn, rice, livestock, peanuts, sugar cane, cotton.

GDP (1989) $1.7 bln, per capita $205

History Mossi empire in 18th–19th-c; Upper Volta created by French, 1919; abolished, 1932, with most land joined to Ivory Coast; original borders reconstituted, 1947; autonomy within French community, 1958; independence, 1960, with several military coups since; changed name from Upper Volta to Burkina Faso ('land of upright men'), 1984; end of military rule, 1991, after a draft constitution was adopted by national referendum; governed by a president elected on a seven-year mandate, and a 107-member National Assembly.

Head of State
1984–7 Thomas Sankara *Chairman*
1987– Blaise Compaoré

Head of Government
1992– Youssouf Ouedraogo

BURMA >> MYANMAR

BURUNDI

Local name Burundi

Timezone GMT + 2

Area 27 834 sq km/10 744 sq mi

Population total (1990e) 5 450 000

Status Republic

Date of independence 1962

Capital Bujumbura

Languages French and Kirundi (official), Swahili

Ethnic groups Hutu (82%), Tutsi (14%), Twa Pygmy (1%)

Religions Roman Catholic (62%), traditional beliefs (32%)

Physical features Located in C Africa; lies across Nile–Congo watershed; interior plateau, c.1 500 m/5 000 ft; highest point, Mt Karonje 2 685 m/8 809 ft; river Ruzizi forms part of NW frontier with Zaïre and links Lake Kivu in Rwanda, with Lake Tanganyika in S and E; river Malagarazi valley in E.

Climate Equatorial; moderately wet; dry season (Jun–Sep); average annual temperature 23°C; average annual rainfall at Bujumbura, 850 mm/33.5 in.

Currency 1 Burundi Franc (BuFr, FBu) = 100 centimes

Economy Mainly agriculture; cash crops include coffee, cotton, tea; light consumer goods, shoes, blankets; reserves of rare-earth metals.

GDP (1989) $1.2 bln, per capita $220

History Ruled by the Tutsi kingdom, 16th-c ; occupied by Germany, 1890, and included in German East Africa, 1890; League of Nations mandated territory, administered by Belgians, 1919; joined with Rwanda to become the UN Trust Territory of Ruanda-Urundi, 1946; independence, 1962; full republic following the overthrow of the monarchy, 1966; civil war, 1972; military coup, 1976; new constitution provided a National Assembly, 1981; Assembly dissolved and constitution suspended after 1987 coup; Military Council for National Salvation disbanded, 1990; new constitution, 1992.

Head of State
1987– Pierre Buyoya *Military Junta*

Head of Government
1988– Adrien Sibomana

CAMBODIA

Local name Cambodia

Timezone GMT + 7

Area 181 035 sq km/69 879 sq mi

Population total (1990e) 8 592 000

Status State

Date of independence 1953

Capital Phnom Penh

Languages Khmer (official), French

Ethnic groups Khmer (93%), Chinese (3%), Cham (2%)

Religions Theravada Buddhist (88%), Muslim (2%)

Physical features Republic of S Indo-China, SE Asia; crossed E by floodplain of Mekong R; Chaîne des Cardamomes mountain range 160 km/100 mi across Thailand border, rising to 1 813 m/5 948 ft at Phnom Aural; Tonle Sap (Great Lake) in NW.

Climate Tropical monsoon climate, with a wet season (May–Sep); high temperatures in lowland region throughout the year; average annual temperature 21°C (Jan), 29°C (Jul); average annual rainfall 5 000 mm/71 in (SW), 1 300 mm/51 in (interior lowlands).

Currency 1 Riel (CRl) = 100 sen

Economy Most of population employed in subsistence agriculture, rice and corn; industrial development disrupted by the civil war.

GDP (1989) $890 mln, per capita $130

History Originally part of Fou-Nan Kingdom, then part of the Khmer Empire, 7th-c; in dispute with Vietnamese and Thais from 15th-c; French Protectorate, 1863; part of Indo-China, 1887; independence, 1953; Prince Sihanouk deposed, Khmer Republic formed, 1970; fighting throughout the country involved troops from N and S Vietnam and the USA; surrender of Phnom Penh to the Khmer Rouge, country renamed Kampuchea, 1975; attempt to reform economy on co-operative lines by Pol Pot (1975–8) caused the deaths of an estimated three million people; further fighting 1977–8; Phnom Penh captured by the Vietnamese, causing Khmer Rouge to flee, 1979; 1981 constitution established a Council of State and Council of Ministers; name of Cambodia restored, 1989; Vietnamese troops completed withdrawal, 1989; UN peace plan agreed, with ceasefire and return of Sihanouk as head of state, 1991; administrative power currently held by State of Cambodia (SOC) government; free elections scheduled for Sep 1993.

Head of State

1975–6	Prince Norodom Sihanouk
1976–81	Khieu Samphan
1981–91	Heng Samrin
1991–	Prince Norodom Sihanouk

Head of Government (Chair of the SOC Council of Ministers)

1976–9	Pol Pot
1979–81	Khieu Samphan
1981–5	Chan Si
1985–	Hun Sen

CAMEROON

Local name Cameroun

Timezone GMT + 1

Area 475 439 sq km/183 519 sq mi

Population total (1992e) 12 700 000

Status Republic

Date of independence 1960

Capital Yaoundé

Languages French and English (official), 24 major African languages including Fang, Bamileke, Luanda, Fulani, Tika, Maka

Ethnic groups Highlanders (31%), Equatorial Bantu (19%), Kirdi (11%), Fulani (10%)

Religions Christian (40%), traditional beliefs (39%), Muslim (21%)

Physical features Located in W Africa; equatorial forest, with low coastal plain, C plateau 1 300 m/4 200;

Cameroon (continued)

W forested and mountainous, Mt Cameroon, 4 070 m/ 13 353 ft (active volcano and the highest peak in W Africa); low savannah, semi-desert towards L Chad; rivers include Sanaga and Dja.

Climate Rain all year in equatorial S; daily temperature in Yaoundé, 27–30°C; average annual rainfall 4 030 mm/159 in.

Currency 1 CFA Franc (CFAFr) = 100 centimes

Economy Agriculture (employs c.80% of workforce); world's fifth largest producer of cocoa; tourism, especially to national parks.

GDP (1991) $11.6 bln, per capita $1 010

History First explored by Portuguese navigator Fernando Po, later by traders from Spain, Netherlands, and Britain; German protectorate of Kamerun, 1884; divided into French and British Cameroon, 1919; confirmed by League of Nations mandate, 1922; UN trusteeships, 1946; French Cameroon independent as Republic of Cameroon, 1960; N sector of British Cameroon voted to become part of Nigeria, S sector part of Cameroon; became Federal Republic of Cameroon, with separate parliaments, 1961; federal system abolished, 1972, and name changed to United Republic of Cameroon; changed name to the Republic of Cameroon, 1984; legislation adopted for a multi party system, 1990; governed by a president, executive prime minister, cabinet, and National Assembly.

Head of State
1982– Paul Biya

Head of Government
1991–2 Sadou Hayatou
1992– Simon Achidi Achu

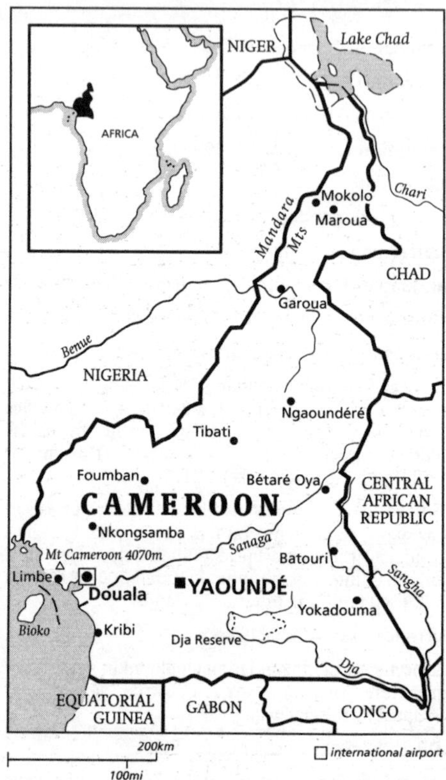

CANADA

Local name Canada

Timezone GMT W – 9, to E – 3

Area 9 971 500 sq km/3 848 900 sq mi

Population total (1992e) 27 400 000

Status Independent nation within the Commonwealth

Date of independence 1867 (Dominion of Canada)

Capital Ottawa

Languages English and French (official)

Ethnic groups British origin (45%), French origin (29%), other European, Indian and Inuit (23%)

Religions Roman Catholic (49%), United Church (18%), Anglican (12%)

Physical features Dominated in the NE by the Canadian Shield; flat prairie country S and W of the Shield, stretching to the Western Cordillera, which includes the Rocky, Cassiar, and Mackenzie Mts; Coast Mts flank a rugged, heavily indented coastline; Mt Logan in the Yukon, 5 950 m/19 521 ft, is the highest peak in Canada; major rivers, the Mackenzie (W), and St Lawrence (E); Great Bear, 31 330 sq km/11 030 sq mi, and Great Slave, 28 570 sq km/11 030 sq mi, lakes in NW Territories.

Climate N coast permanently ice-bound or obstructed by ice floes, but for Hudson Bay (frozen c.9 months each year); mild winters and warm summers on Pacific coast and around Vancouver Island; average annual rainfall 145 mm/57 in.

Currency 1 Canadian Dollar (C$, Can$) = 100 cents

Economy Traditionally based on natural resources and agriculture; world's second largest exporter of wheat; world's largest producer of asbestos, zinc, silver, nickel; second largest producer of potash, gypsum, molybdenum, sulphur; hydroelectricity, oil (especially Alberta), natural gas; major industrial development in recent decades.

GDP (1990) $516 bln, per capita $19 500

History Evidence of Viking settlement c.1000; Newfoundland claimed for England, 1583; Champlain founded Québec, 1608; Hudson's Bay Company founded, 1670; conflict between British and French in late 17th-c; Britain gained large areas from Treaty of Utrecht, 1713;

after Seven Years' War, during which British General James Wolfe captured Québec from Louis Montcalm's forces, 1759, Treaty of Paris gave Britain almost all France's possessions in N America; province of Québec created, 1774; migration of loyalists from USA after War of Independence led to division of Québec into Upper and Lower Canada; reunited as Canada, 1841; Dominion of Canada created (1867) by confederation of Québec, Ontario, Nova Scotia, and New Brunswick; Rupert's Land and Northwest Territories bought from Hudson's Bay Company, 1869–70; joined by Manitoba (1870), British Columbia (1871), Prince Edward I (1873), Alberta and Saskatchewan (1905), and Newfoundland (1949); recurring political tension in recent decades arising from French-Canadian separatist movement in Québec; Canada Act, 1982, gave Canada full responsibility for constitution; bicameral federal parliament includes Senate and a House of Commons; British monarch is head of state, represented by a governor-general.

Head of State

(British monarch represented by Governor-General)
1990– Ramon John Hnatyshyn

Head of Government

1984–93 Brian Mulroney
1993– Kim Campbell

>> Political leaders and rulers

Canadian provinces and territories

Name	*Area* sq km	*Area* sq mi	*Capital*
Alberta	661 190	255 285	Edmonton
British Columbia	947 800	365 945	Victoria
Manitoba	649 950	250 945	Winnipeg
New Brunswick	73 440	28 355	Fredericton
Newfoundland	405 720	156 648	St John's
Northwest Territories	3 426 320	1 322 902	Yellowknife
Nova Scotia	55 490	21 424	Halifax
Ontario	1 068 580	412 578	Toronto
Prince Edward Island	5 660	2 185	Charlottetown
Québec	1 540 680	594 856	Québec City
Saskatchewan	652 380	251 883	Regina
Yukon Territory	483 450	186 660	Whitehorse

CANARY ISLANDS >> SPAIN

CAPE VERDE

Local name Cabo Verde

Timezone GMT – 1

Area 4 033 sq km/1 557 sq mi

Population total (1991e) 386 000

Status Republic

Date of independence 1975

Capital Praia (on São Tiago Island)

Languages Portuguese (official), Crioulo (Portuguese-based creole)

Ethnic groups Creole (mulatto) (60%), African (28%), European (2%)

Religion Roman Catholic (80%), others (20%)

Physical features Island group in the Atlantic Ocean off W Coast of Africa, c.500 km/310 mi W of Dakar, Senegal; Barlavento (windward) group in N; Sotavento (leeward) group in S; mostly mountainous islands of volcanic origin; highest peak, Pico do Cano, 2 829 m/ 9 281 ft; active volcano on Fogo I; fine sandy beaches on most islands.

Climate Arid climate; located at N limit of tropical rain belt, low and unreliable rainfall (Aug–Sep); small temperature range throughout year; average annual temperature 23°C; average annual rainfall 250 mm/10 in.

Currency 1 Escudo (CVEsc) = 100 centavos

Economy Suffering because of drought; substantial emigration in early 1970s; c.70% of workforce are farmers occupying irrigated inland valleys; increase in fishing since 1975.

GDP (1989) $281 mln, per capita $760

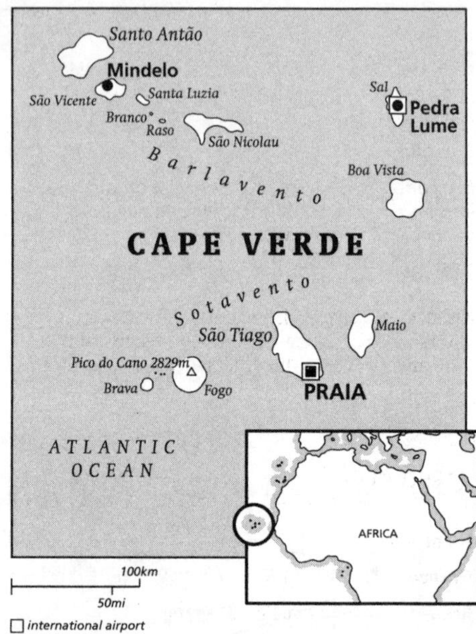

History Colonized by Portuguese in 15th-c, also used as a penal colony; administered with Portuguese Guinea until 1879; overseas province of Portugal, 1951; independence, 1975; governed by a president, Council of Ministers, and People's National Assembly; multi party elections held, 1991.

Head of State

1975–91 Aristides Pereira
1991– Antonio Mascarenhas Monteiro

Head of Government

1975–91 Pedro Pires
1991– Carlos Viega

CAYMAN ISLANDS >> UNITED KINGDOM

CENTRAL AFRICAN REPUBLIC

Local name République Centrafricaine

Timezone GMT + 1

Area 626 780 sq km/241 937 sq mi

Population total (1990e) 2 875 000

Status Republic

Date of independence 1960

Capital Bangui

Languages French (official), Sangho

Ethnic groups Baya (34%), Banda (28%), Sara (10%), over 80 other groups

Religions Christian (50%), (Protestant 25%, Roman Catholic 25%), also Muslim and traditional beliefs

Physical features Located in C Africa; plateau forming a watershed between Chad and Congo river basins;

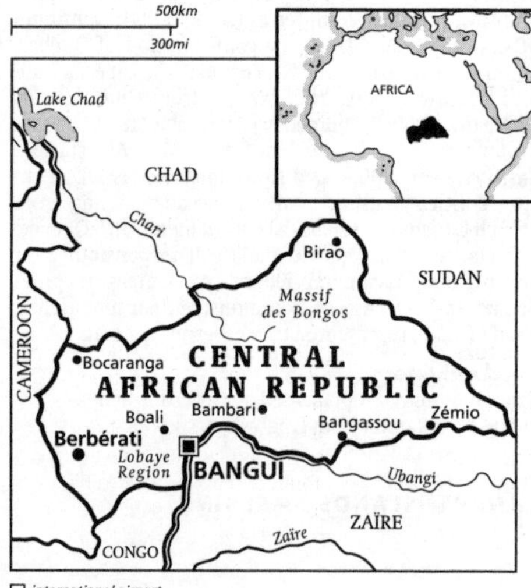

Massif des Bongos rises 1 400 m/4 593 ft in NW; granite ranges of Mont Karre, 1 220 m/4 003 ft in W.

Climate Tropical; single rainy season in N (May–Sep); average annual rainfall 875–1 000 mm/34–39 in; more equatorial climate in S, rainfall 1 500–2 000 mm/60–80 in.

Currency 1 CFA Franc (CFAFr) = 100 centimes

Economy Agriculture (employs c.85% of working population); also sawmilling, brewing, diamond splitting, leather and tobacco processing.

GDP (1990e) $1.3 bln, per capita $440

History Part of French Equatorial Africa (Ubangi Shari); autonomous republic within the French community, 1958; independence, 1960; coup deposed country's first president, David Dacko, 1965; Jean-Bédel Bokassa declared himself emperor for life, and country's name changed to the Central African Empire, 1976; Bokassa deposed and country reverted to a republic, 1979; military coup established Committee for National Recovery, 1981–5; Committee dissolved and National Assembly established, 1987; movement toward multi party democracy, 1991; elections scheduled for 1993.

Head of State
1960–6 David Dacko
1966–79 Jean-Bédel Bokassa (*from 1977*, Emperor Bokassa I)
1979–81 David Dacko
1981– André Kolingba

Head of Government
1991–2 Edouard Frank
1992– Thimothée Malendoma

CHAD

Local name Tchad

Timezone GMT + 1

Area 1 284 640 sq km/495 871 sq mi

Population total (1990e) 5 678 000

Status Republic

Date of independence 1960

Capital N'Djamena

Languages Arabic and French (official), many local languages spoken

Ethnic groups Sara, Bagirmi, and Kreish (30%); Sudanic Arab (26%), Teda (17%), Masalit, Maba, Mimi (6%), over 200 groups

Religions Muslim (50%), Christian (Roman Catholic 21%, Protestant 12%), and local religions

Physical features Landlocked in C Africa; mostly arid, semi-desert plateau at edge of Sahara Desert; average altitude of 200–500 m/650–1 650 ft; Tibesti Mts (N) rise to 3 415 m/11 204 ft at Emi Koussi; rivers in S, (Chari and Logone) flow NW to Lake Chad.

Climate Tropical, moderately wet in S (May–Oct): hot, arid N, almost rainless; C plain hot, dry, with brief rainy season (Jun–Sep).

Currency 1 CFA Franc (CFAFr) = 100 centimes

Economy Severely damaged in recent years by drought, locusts, and civil war; export of cotton, kaolin, animal products; salt mined around L Chad.

GDP (1989e) $1.1 bln, per capita $205

History Part of French Equatorial Africa, 1908; colonial status, 1920; independence, 1960; Libyan troops occupied the Aozou Strip in extreme N, 1973; fighting between Libyan-supported rebels and French-supported government until cease-fire agreed, 1987; new constitution established a National Assembly, 1989; replaced by a Provisional Council of the Republics, 1991; Chad and Libya presented their individual territorial claims to Aozou Strip, 1990; president Habré ousted by coup and new constitution adopted, 1991; progress towards a multi party system and future presidential and general elections, 1992.

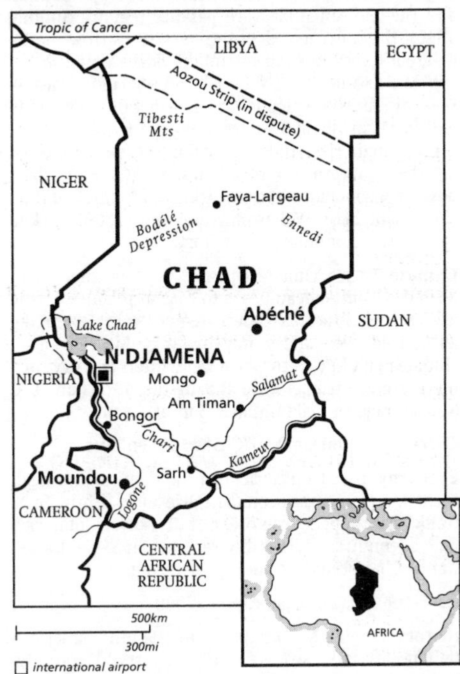

Head of State
1982–90 Hissne Habré
1990– Idriss Déby *Interim*

Head of Government
1991–2 Jean Alingue Bawoyeu
1992– Joseph Yodemane

CHANNEL ISLANDS >> UNITED KINGDOM

CHILE

Local name Chile

Timezone GMT - 4

Area 756 626 sq km/292 058 sq mi (excluding territory claimed in Antarctica)

Population total (1990e) 13 173 000

Status Republic

Date of independence 1818

Capital Santiago

Language Spanish (official)

Ethnic groups Mestizo (92%), Indian (6%), European (2%)

Religions Roman Catholic (89%), Protestant (10%), small Jewish and Muslim minority

Physical features Coastal Cordillera, Pampa Central, and the Chilean Andes are parallel regions running almost the entire length of the country; narrow coastal belt, backed by Andean mountain ridges rising in the NW to 6 880 m/22 572 ft at Ojos del Salado; Atacama Desert in far NW which is rich in minerals; arable land and forest in the S; S Andes still experiences volcanic activity; main river, the Bío-Bío; Punta Arenas is located on the southern tip of Chile's mainland; Chilean possessions include a rock measuring 424 m/1 390 ft on Horn Island in the Wollaston group, and 1 250 000 sq km/ 482 628 sq mi of Antarctic territory.

Climate Varied climate (spans 37° of latitude, with altitudes from Andean peaks to coastal plain); extreme aridity in N Atacama Desert, temperatures averaging 20°C; cold, wet, and windy in far S; Mediterranean climate in C Chile, with warm wet winters and dry summers; average temperature at Santiago, 19°C (Jan), 8°C (Jul); average annual rainfall 375 mm/14.8 in.

Currency 1 Chilean Peso (Ch$) = 100 centavos

Economy Based on agriculture and mining; wheat, corn, potatoes, sugar beet, fruit, livestock; fishing in N, timber in S; copper, iron ore, nitrates, silver, gold, coal, molybdenum; oil and gas discovered in far S (1945); steel, wood pulp, cellulose, mineral processing.

GDP (1991) $32 bln, per capita $2 500

History Originally occupied by South American Indians; arrival of Spanish in 16th-c; part of Viceroyalty of Peru; independence from Spain declared, 1810, with a provisional government set up in Santiago; Spain reasserted its authority, 1814; the patriot leader, Bernardo O'Higgins, escaped and returned with the military help of José de San Martín, to defeat the Spanish at Chacabuco, 1817; O'Higgins became the first president and independence was declared, 1818; border disputes with Bolivia, Peru, and Argentina brought Chilean victory in War of the Pacific, 1879–84; economic unrest in late 1920s led to military dictatorship under Carlos Ibáñez until 1931; Marxist coalition government of Salvador Allende Gossens ousted, 1973, and replaced by military junta under Augusto Pinochet Ugarte, which banned all political activity; constitution providing for eventual return to democracy came into effect, 1981; plebiscite held in 1988 resulted in a defeat for Pinochet's candidacy as president beyond 1990, and limited political reforms; National Congress restored, comprising a Senate and a Chamber of Deputies, 1990.

Head of State/Government

1973–90 Augusto Pinochet Ugarte
1990– Patricio Aylwin Azócar

CHINA

Local name Zhongguo

Timezone GMT + 8

Area 9 597 000 sq km/3 704 000 sq mi (also claims island of Taiwan)

Population total (1990) 1 133 682 501

Status People's republic

Capital Beijing (Peking)

Languages Standard Chinese (Putonghua) or Mandarin, also Yue (Cantonese), Wu, Minbei, Minnan, Xiang, Gan and Hakka

Ethnic groups Han Chinese (93%), over 50 minorities, including Chuang, Manchu, Hui, Miao, Uighur, Hani, Kazakh, Tai and Yao

Religions Officially atheist; widespread Confucianism and Taoism (20%), Buddhism (6%)

Physical features Over two-thirds of country are upland hills, mountains, and plateaux; highest mountains in the W, where the Tibetan plateau rises to average altitude of 4 000 m/13 000 ft; Mt Everest rises to 8 848 m /29 028 ft on the Nepal–Tibet border; land descends to desert /semi-desert of Sinkiang and Inner Mongolia (NE); broad and fertile plains of Manchuria (NE); further E and S, Sichuan basin, drained by Yangtze R (5 980 km/ 3 720 mi in length); Huang He (Yellow) R runs for 4 840 km/3 010 mi; heavily populated S plains and E coast, with rich, fertile soils.

Climate Varied, with seven zones: (1) NE China: cold winters, with strong N winds, warm and humid summers, unreliable rainfall; (2) C China: warm and humid summers, sometimes typhoons or tropical cyclones on coast; (3) S China: partly within tropics, wettest area in summer, frequent typhoons; (4) SW China: summer temperatures moderated by altitude, winters mild with little rain; (5) Xizang autonomous region: high plateau surrounded by mountains, winters severe with frequent light snow and hard frost; (6) Xinjiang and W interior: arid desert climate, cold winters, rainfall well distributed throughout year; (7) Inner Mongolia: extreme continental climate, cold winters, warm summers.

Currency 1 Renminbi Yuan (RMBY, $, Y) = 10 jiao = 100 fen

Economy Since 1949, economy largely based on heavy industry; more recently, light industries; special economic zones set up to attract foreign investment; rich mineral deposits; largest oil-producing country in Far East; major subsistence crops include rice, grain, beans, potatoes, tea, sugar, cotton.

China (continued)

GDP (1989e) $413 bln, per capita $370

History Chinese civilization believed to date from the Xia dynasty (2200–1799 BC); Qin dynasty (221–206 BC) unified warring states and provided system of centralized control; expansion W during Western and Eastern Han dynasties (206 BC–AD 220), and Buddhism introduced from India; split into Three Kingdoms (Wei, Shu, Wu, 220–65); from 4th-c, series of N dynasties set up by invaders, with several dynasties in S; gradually reunited during the Sui (581–618) and Tang (618–907) dynasties; partition into the Five Dynasties (907–60); Song (Sung) dynasty (960–1279), remembered for literature, philosophy, and inventions; Kublai Khan established Mongol Yuan dynasty which ruled China, 1279–1368; visits by Europeans, such as Marco Polo, 13th–14th-c; Ming dynasty (1368–1644) increased contacts with West; overthrown by Manchus, who ruled China, 1644–1911, under the Qing dynasty, and enlarged empire to include Manchuria, Mongolia, Tibet, Taiwan; opposition to foreign imports led to Opium Wars 1839–42, 1858–60; Sino-Japanese War, 1895; Boxer Rising, 1900; Republic of China, founded by Sun Yatsen, 1912; unification under Jiang Jieshi (Chiang Kai-shek), who made Nanjing capital, 1928; conflict between Nationalists and Communists led to the Long March, 1934–5, with Communists moving to NW China under Mao Zedong (Mao Tse-tung); Nationalist defeat by Mao and withdrawal to Taiwan, 1949; People's Republic of China proclaimed, 1949, with capital at Beijing; first Five-Year Plan (1953–7) period of nationalization and collectivization; Great Leap Forward, 1958–9, emphasized local authority and establishment of rural communes; Cultural Revolution initiated by Mao Zedong, 1966; many policies reversed after Mao's death, 1976, and drive towards rapid industrialization and wider trade relations with West; since 1980, Deng Xiaoping became the dominant figure within the ruling Chinese Communist Party; he retired from his last official post, 1990, but still remains the most influential figure in Chinese politics; governed by elected National People's Congress who elect a State Council.

Head of State
1988– Yang Shangkun

Head of Government
1987– Li Peng

COLOMBIA

Local name Colombia

Timezone GMT – 5

Area 1 140 105 sq km/440 080 sq mi

Population total (1990e) 32 978 000

Status Republic

Date of independence 1819

Capital Bogotá

Language Spanish (official)

Ethnic groups Mestizo (58%), Amerindian (10%), European descent (20%)

Religion Roman Catholic (95%), other (5%)

Physical features Located in NW South America, includes several island possessions (Providencia, San Andrés and Mapelo); Andes run N–S dividing narrow coastal plains from forested lowlands of Amazon basin; Cordillera Central rises 5 000 m/16 000 ft to the high peak of Nev. de Huila, 5 750 m/18 865 ft; rivers include Vaupés, Magdalena, Cauca and Guaviare.

Climate Hot, humid coastal plains (NW and W); annual rainfall over 2 500 mm/100 in; drier period on Caribbean coast (Dec–Apr); hot, humid tropical lowlands in E.

Currency 1 Colombian Peso (Col$) = 100 centavos

Economy Virtually self-sufficient in food; major crops include coffee, bananas, cotton; leather; gold, silver, emeralds, coal, oil; widespread illegal cocaine trafficking.

GDP (1990e) $43 bln, per capita $1 300

History Spanish occupation from early 16th-c, displacing Amerindian peoples; governed by Spain within Viceroyalty of Peru, later Viceroyalty of New Granada; independence, 1819, after the campaigns of Simón Bolívar; union with Ecuador, Venezuela, and Panama as Gran Colombia, 1821–30; civil war in 1950s; considerable political unrest in 1980s; new constitution, 1991; governed by a president, bicameral Congress and cabinet.

Head of State/Government
1978–82 Julio César Turbay Ayala
1982–6 Belisario Betancur
1986–90 Virgilio Barco Vargas
1990– César Gaviria Trujillo

COMMONWEALTH OF INDEPENDENT STATES, THE (CIS)

A multilateral group of independent states which were once members of the USSR; the CIS was formed in December, 1991; membership includes all the states that once comprised the USSR, with the exceptions of the Baltic States (Latvia, Lithuania and Estonia), and Georgia; and the partial exceptions of Azerbaijan and Moldova which have observer status only.

CIS >> ARMENIA, BELARUS, KAZAKHSTAN, KYRGYZSTAN, RUSSIA, TAJIKISTAN, TURKMENISTAN, UKRAINE, UZBEKISTAN

COMOROS

Local name Comores

Timezone GMT + 3

Area 1 862 sq km/719 sq mi

Population total (1990e) 463 000

Status Federal Islamic republic

Date of independence 1975

Capital Moroni (on Njazidja Island)

Languages Arabic, French (official), Kiswahili

Ethnic groups Comorian (97%), Makua (2%)

Religions Sunni Muslim (86%), Roman Catholic (14%)

Physical features Located in the Mozambique Channel between mainland Africa and Madagascar; a group of three volcanic islands, Njazidja (Grande Comore), Nzwani (Anjouan), and Mwali (Mohéli); largest island, Njazidja, with an active volcano, Mt Kartala, 2 361 m/ 7 746 ft.

Climate Tropical; dry season (May–Oct), hot, humid season (Nov–Apr); average temperatures, 20°C (Jul), 28°C (Nov).

Currency 1 Comorian Franc (CFr) = 100 centimes

Economy Largely agricultural economy; vanilla, copra, cacao, sisal, coffee, cloves, vegetable oils, perfume.

GDP (1990e) $245 mln, per capita $530

History Under French control, 1843–1912; French overseas territory, 1947; internal political autonomy, 1961; unilateral independence declared, 1975; Mayotte, island in the archipelago, has remained under French rule; established as a Federal Islamic Republic, 1978; a one-party state, governed by a president, a Council of Ministers, and a unicameral Federal Assembly.

Head of State/Government

1976–8 Ali Soilih
1978–89 Ahmed Abdallah Abderemane
1989– Said Mohammed Djohar

Map >> MADAGASCAR

CONGO

Local name Congo

Timezone GMT + 1

Area 341 945 sq km/132 000 sq mi

Population total (1990e) 2 326 000

Status Republic

Date of independence 1960

Capital Brazzaville

Language French (official), with local languages, including Kongo and Téké

Ethnic groups Kongo (45%), Sangha (15%), Téké (20%)

Religions Roman Catholic (54%), Protestant (25%), local traditional beliefs

Physical features Niari valley rises to 1 040 m/3 412 ft at Mont de la Lékéti; mainly covered by dense grassland, mangrove, and tropical rainforest; rivers include Sangha and Alima in N.

Climate Hot, humid equatorial climate; annual rainfall 1 250–1 750 mm/50–70 in; annual daily temperature, 28–33°C in Brazzaville; dry season (Jun–Sep).

Currency 1 CFA Franc (CFAFr) = 100 centimes

Economy Mainly agriculture and forestry; sugar cane, coffee, cocoa, palm oil, tobacco; oil, timber, diamonds; sugar-refining.

GDP (1989e) $2.26 bln, per capita $1 050

History Visited by Portuguese, 14th-c; part of French Equatorial Africa, known as 'Middle Congo', 1908–58; independence as Republic of Congo, 1960; military coup created first Marxist state in Africa, renamed People's Republic of the Congo, 1968; Congolese Labour Party (PCT), the single ruling party in Congo, renounced Marxism, 1990; transitional government formed, 1991, and country renamed the Republic of Congo; new constitution, 1992, recognized a multi party system; executive authority vested in the president who elects a prime minister and cabinet.

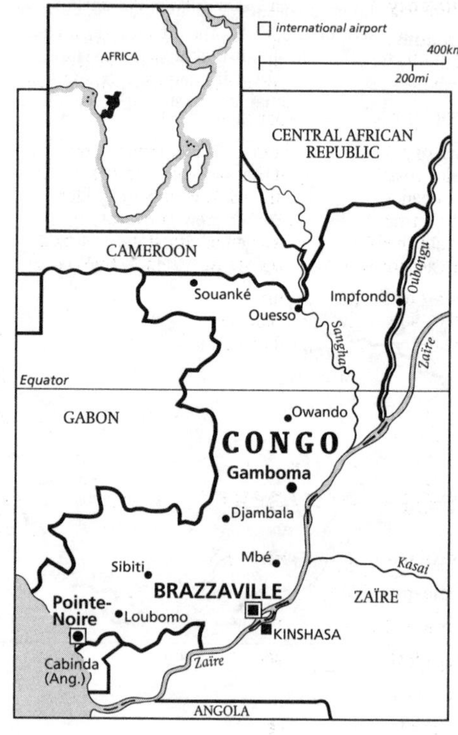

Head of State

1979–92 Denis Sassou-Nguesso
1992– Pascal Lissouba

Head of Government

1991–2 André Milongo
1992 Stephane Bongho-Nouarra
1992– Claude Antoine Dacosta

COOK ISLANDS >> NEW ZEALAND

CORSICA >> FRANCE

COSTA RICA

Local name Costa Rica

Timezone GMT – 6

Area 51 022 sq km/19 694 sq mi

Population total (1990e) 3 015 000

Status Republic

Date of independence 1821

Capital San José

Language Spanish (official)

Ethnic groups European (87%), mestizo (7%), black/mulatto (3%), E Asian (mostly Chinese) (2%), Amerindian (1%)

Religions Roman Catholic (85%), Protestant (15%)

Physical features Second smallest republic in C America; formed by series of volcanic ridges; Cordillera de Guanacaste (NW), Cordillera Central and Cordillera de Talamanca; highest peak, Chirripó Grande, 3 819 m/12 529 ft; C plateau; swampy land near coast rising to tropical forest.

Climate Tropical; small temperature range; abundant rainfall; dry season (Dec–May); average annual temperature, 26–28°C.

Currency 1 Costa Rican Colón (CR¢) = 100 céntimos

Economy Primarily agriculture, mainly coffee (especially in Meseta Central), bananas, sugar, cattle; silver, bauxite; exploration for oil in collaboration with Mexico.

GDP (1990e) $5.5 bln, per capita $1 810

History Visited by Columbus, 1402; named Costa Rica ('rich coast') in the belief that vast gold treasures existed; independence from Spain, 1821; member of Federation of Central America, 1824–39; new constitution, 1949, established Costa Rica as a democratic state; governed by an executive president, Legislative Assembly, and cabinet.

Head of State/Government

1986–90 Oscar Arias Sánchez
1990– Rafael Angel Calderón Fournier

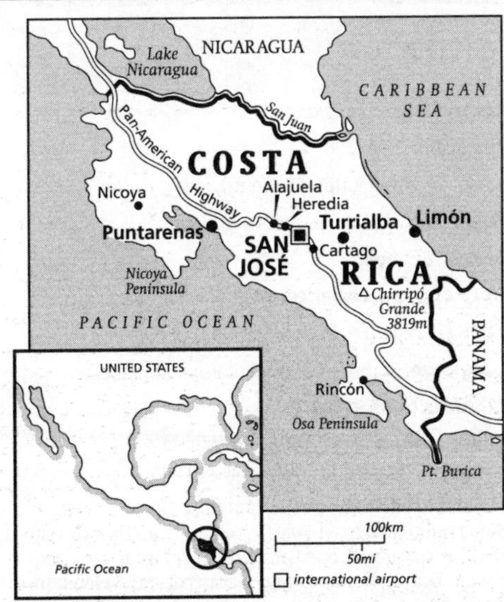

CÔTE D'IVOIRE

Local name Côte d'Ivoire

Timezone GMT

Area 320 633 sq km/123 764 sq mi

Population total (1990e) 12 657 000

Status Republic

Date of independence 1960

Capital Yamoussoukro (formerly Abidjan)

Languages French (official), Akan, Kru

Ethnic groups Akan (41%), Kru (17%), Voltaic (16%), Malinke (15%), Southern Mande (10%)

Religions Traditional beliefs (65%), Muslim (23%), Christian (12%)

Physical features Sandy beaches and lagoons backed by broad forest-covered coastal plain; Mt Nimba massif in NW, 1 752 m /5 748 ft; rivers include Comoé, Sassandra and Bandama.

Climate Tropical, varying with distance from coast; average annual rainfall at Yamoussoukro, 2 100 mm/83 in; average annual temperatures 25–27°C.

Currency 1 CFA Franc (CFAFr) = 100 centimes

Economy Largely based on agriculture (employs c.82% of the population); palm oil, rice, maize, ground nuts, bananas; world's largest cocoa producer, third largest coffee producer.

GDP (1989) $9.5 bln, per capita $820

History Explored by Portuguese, 15th-c; declared a French protectorate, 1889; colony, 1893; territory within French West Africa, 1904; independence, 1960; constitution provides for a multi party system, however opposition parties only allowed to function since 1990; post of prime minister created, 1990; governed by a National Assembly, executive president, and a Council of Ministers.

Head of State

1960– Félix Houphouët-Boigny

Head of Government

1990– Alassane D Ouattara

CROATIA

Local name Hrvatska

Timezone GMT + 1

Area 56 540 sq km/21 825 sq mi

Population total (1992e) 4 600 000

Status Republic

Date of independence 1992

Capital Zagreb

Language Serbo-Croat (with Roman alphabet)

Ethnic groups (1990) Croat (75%), Serb (12%), Slovenes (1%)

Religions Roman Catholic, Eastern Orthodox

Physical features Fertile Pannonian Plain in C and E; mountainous, barren coastal region near Dinaric Alps; Adriatic coast to W; one third of country is forested; main rivers, Drava, Danube, and Sava; coastal Velebit and Velika Kapela ranges reach heights of 2 200 m/7 200 ft; islands include Korčula, Lošinj, Dugi Otok and Cres.

Climate Continental in Pannonian Basin, average temperatures, 19°C (Jul), −1°C (Jan); average annual rainfall 750 mm/30 in; Mediterranean climate on Adriatic coast, average temperatures 24°C (Jul), 6°C (Jan).

Currency Kruna

Economy Agriculture; corn, oats, sugar-beet, potatoes, meat and dairy products; tourism on Adriatic coast; electrical engineering; metal-working; machinery manufacture; lumber; aluminium, textiles, petroleum refining, chemicals and rubber; natural resources include bauxite, coal, copper, iron; all economic activity adversely affected by war of independence.

GDP Not available

History Slavic Croat tribes (Chrobati, Hrvati) migrated to White Russia (now Ukraine) during 6th-c AD; converted to Christianity between 7th and 9th-c and adopted Roman alphabet; Frankish and Byzantine invaders were repelled, and Croat kingdom reached its peak during 11th-c; Lázló I of Hungary claimed Croatian throne, 1091; Turkish defeat of Hungary, 1526, placed Pannonian Croatia under Ottoman rule, the rest of Croatia elected Ferdinand of Austria as their king and fought Turkey; Croatia and Slovenia became part of Hungary until collapse of Austria-Hungary, 1918; formed the Kingdom of Serbs, Croats and Slovenes with Montenegro and Serbia, 1918; changed name to Yugoslavia, 1929; proclaimed an independent state during occupation by the Axis Powers, 1941–5; became a republic of Yugoslavia again, 1945; nationalist upsurges during 1950s against Communist rule culminated in a bloody war with Serbian-dominated Yugoslav army, 1991; declaration of independence, 1991; UN peacekeeping forces sent in to protect Serb minority in Croatia, 1992; autonomy claimed by Serb dominated Krajina area; UN peacekeeping forces deployed, 1992; continued fighting between Croatian forces and Bosnian Serbs in the civil war in Bosnia-Hercegovina.

Head of State
1991– Franjo Tudjman

Head of Government
1991–2 Franjo Greguric
1992– Hrvoje Sarinic

CUBA

Local name Cuba

Timezone GMT − 5

Area 110 860 sq km/42 792 sq mi

Population total (1990e) 10 603 000

Status Republic

Date of independence 1902

Capital Havana

Language Spanish (official)

Ethnic groups Mulatto (50%), Spanish (37%), African origin (11%)

Religions Roman Catholic (40%), Protestant (3%), Afro-Cuban syncretist (2%), non-religious (55%), (Castro regime discourages religious practice)

Physical features Archipelago in the Caribbean Sea, comprising the island of Cuba, Isla de la Juventud, and c.1600 islets and cays; main island of Cuba, 1250 km/777 mi; three mountainous regions range E–W, the Oriental, including Cuba's highest peak, Pico Turquino, 2005 m/6578 ft, Central and Occidental ranges; longest river is Rio Cauto in E.

Climate Subtropical climate, warm and humid; average annual temperature, 25°C; dry season (Nov–Apr); mean annual rainfall, 1375 mm/54 in; hurricanes (Jun–Nov).

Currency 1 Cuban Peso (Cub$) = 100 centavos

Economy World's second largest sugar producer (accounting for 75% of export earnings); world's fifth largest producer of nickel; fish, coffee, tobacco, citrus fruits, rice.

GNP (1990e) $20.9 bln, per capita $2000

History Visited by Columbus, 1492; Spanish colony until 1898, following revolution under José Martí with support of USA; independence, 1902; struggle against dictatorship of General Batista led by Fidel Castro Ruz was finally successful, 1959, and a Communist state established; invasion of Cuban exiles with US support, defeated at Bay of Pigs, 1961; US naval blockade, after Soviet installation of missile bases discovered in Cuba (Cuban Missile Crisis), 1962; Communist Party of Cuba established as the sole legal party, 1965; president of the State Council is head of state; State Council, appointed by National Assembly of People's Power.

Head of State/Government

1956–76 Osvaldo Dorticós Torrado
1976– Fidel Castro Ruz

CYPRUS

Local names Kipros (Greek), Kibris (Turkish)

Timezone GMT + 3

Area 9251 sq km/3571 sq mi

Population total (1990e) 568000

Status Republic

Date of independence 1960

Capital Nicosia

Languages Greek and Turkish (official), English

Ethnic groups Greek (78%), Turkish (18%), other (4%)

Religions Greek Orthodox (78%), Sunni Muslim (18%), other Christian (4%)

Physical features Third largest island in Mediterranean; Kyrenia Mts extend 150 km/90 mi along N coast, Mt Kyparissovouno, 1 024 m/3 360 ft; forest-covered Troödos Mts in SW, rising to 1951 m/6401 ft at Mt Olympus; fertile alluvial Mesaoria plain extends across island centre; SE plateau region slopes towards indented coastline, with several long, sandy beaches; major rivers include the Pedios, Karyota and Kouris.

Climate Mediterranean, with hot, dry summers and warm, wet winters; average annual rainfall ranges from 300–400 mm/12–16 in on the Mesaoria Plain to 1200 mm/47 in in the Troödos Mts; mean daily temperatures, in Nicosia 10°C (Jan), 28°C (Jul); temperatures range from 22°C on Troödos Mts, to 29°C on Central plain (Jul–Aug); snow on higher land in winter.

Currency 1 Cyprus Pound (£C) = 100 cents

Economy Main exports include cement, clothing, footwear, citrus, potatoes, grapes, wine; tourism also recovering (now accounting for c.15% of national income); Famagusta (chief port prior to 1974 Turkish invasion) now under Turkish occupation, and declared closed by Cyprus government; Turkish Cypriot economy heavily dependent on agriculture.

Cyprus (continued)

GDP (1990) $5.3 bln, per capita $7585

History Recorded history of 4000 years, rulers included Greeks, Ptolemies, Persians, Romans, Byzantines, Arabs, Franks, Venetians, Turks (1571–1878), and British; British Crown Colony, 1925; Greek Cypriot demands for union with Greece (*enosis*) led to guerrilla warfare, under Grivas and Makarios, and four-year state of emergency, 1955–9; independence, 1960; with Britain retaining sovereignty over bases at Akrotiri and Dhekelia; Greek–Turkish fighting throughout 1960s, with UN peacekeeping force sent in, 1964; Greek Junta engineered coup d'état, 1972; Turkish invasion, 1974, led to occupation of over a third of the island; island divided into two parts by the Attila Line, cutting through Nicosia where it is called the Green Line; almost all Turks now live in N sector (37% of island); governed by a president (head of state), elected by the Greek community, and House of Representatives; Turkish members ceased to attend in 1983, when the Turkish community declared itself independent (as 'Turkish Republic of Northern Cyprus' with Rauf Denktas as president, recognised only by Turkey); UN peace proposals rejected, 1984; summit meeting between Kyprianou (Greek president of Cyprus) and Denktas failed, 1985; President Georgios Vassiliou renewed talks with Denktas, 1988; peace talks abandoned, 1989; new president, Glafkos Clirides, 1993.

Head of State/Government
1988–93 Georgios Vassiliou
1993– Glafkos Clirides

CZECHOSLOVAKIA >> CZECH REPUBLIC; SLOVAK REPUBLIC

CZECH REPUBLIC

Local name Ceskà republika

Timezone GMT + 1

Area 78 864 sq km/30 441 sq mi

Population total (1990e) 10 362 000

Status Republic

Date of independence 1993

Capital Prague

Languages Czech (official), with Hungarian and Slovak widely spoken

Ethnic groups Czech (94%), Slovak (4%), Hungarian, Polish, German and Ukrainian minorities

Religions Roman Catholic, Protestant

Physical features Landlocked in C Europe; Bohemian Massif, average height, 900 m/2 953 ft, surrounds the Bohemian basin in W; Elbe-Moldau river system flows N into E Germany; fertile Danube plain in S Vltava valley of Moravia divides Czech from Slovak Republic; c.40% land is arable

Climate Continental, with warm, humid summers and cold, dry winters; average annual temperatures 2°C (Jan), 19°C (Jul) in Prague; average annual rainfall, 483 mm/19 in.

Currency 1 Koruna (Kčs) = 100 haler

Economy Steel production around Ostrava coalfields; machinery, iron, glass, chemicals, motor vehicles, cement; wheat, sugar beet, potatoes, rye, corn, barley.

GDP Not yet available

History Originally ruled by Austrian Habsburgs; Czech lands united with Slovakia to form separate state of Czechoslovakia, 1918; occupied by Germany, 1938; government in exile in London during World War 2; Czechoslovakian independence with loss of some territory to USSR, 1946; communist rule imposed by Russia following 1948 coup; attempt at liberalization by Dubcek terminated by intervention of Warsaw Pact troops, 1968; fall from power of the Communist Party, 1989; 1992 agreement to divide Czechoslovakia into its constituent republics, Czech and Slovak, by Jan 1993; Czech Republic now comprises former provinces of Bohemia, Silesia, and Moravia.

Head of State/Government
1993– Vaclav Klaus

DENMARK

Local name Danmark

Timezone GMT + 1

Area 43 076 sq km/16 627 sq mi (excluding Greenland and Faroe Islands)

Population total (1990e) 5 139 000

Status Kingdom

Capital Copenhagen

Language Danish (official)

Ethnic groups Danish (97%), Turkish (0.5%), other Scandinavian (0.4%)

Religions Evangelical Lutheran (97%), Roman Catholic (0.5%), Jewish (0.1%)

Physical features Consists of most of the Jutland peninsula, several islands in the Baltic Sea, and some of the N Frisian Is in the North Sea; coastline 3 400 km/ 2 100 mi; uniformly low-lying; no large rivers and few lakes; shoreline indented by many lagoons and fjords, largest is Lim Fjord.

Climate Modified by Gulf Stream; cold and cloudy winters, warm and sunny summers; average annual temperatures range from 0.5°C (Jan) to 17°C (Jul); average annual rainfall 800 mm/32 in.

Currency 1 Danish Krone (Dkr) = 100 øre

Economy Lack of raw materials has resulted in development of processing industries; intensive agriculture; wide range of food processing; machinery, textiles, furniture, electronics; dairy products; joined European Economic Community, 1973.

GDP (1990) $78 bln, per capita $15 200

History Part of Viking kingdoms, 8th–10th-c; Danish Empire under Canute, 11th-c; joined with Sweden and Norway under Queen Margrethe of Denmark, 1389; Sweden separated from union, 16th-c, followed by

Norway, 1814; Schleswig-Holstein lost to Germany, 1864; N Schleswig returned after plebiscite, 1920; occupied by Germany during World War 2; Iceland independent, 1944; Greenland and Faroe Is remain dependencies; constitutional monarchy since 1849; unicameral system adopted, 1953; legislative power lies with the monarch and the Diet jointly.

Head of State (Monarch)
1972– Margrethe II

Head of Government
1982– Poul Schlüter

FAROE ISLANDS (FAEROE)

Local name Faerøerne (Danish)

Timezone GMT

Area 1 400 sq km/540 sq mi

Population total (1989e) 47 800

Status Self-governing region of Denmark

Capital Tórshavn

Languages Faroese (official, derived from Old Norse), Danish

Religion Evangelical Lutheran

Physical features Group of 22 sparsely vegetated volcanic islands in the N Atlantic between Iceland and the Shetland Is; 17 inhabited; largest islands, Strømø, Østerø, Vagø, Suderø, Sandø and Bordø.

Climate Mild winters, overcast cool summers.

Currency 1 Danish Krone (Dkr) = 100 øre

Economy Main produce fish, crafts, potatoes; Denmark provides an annual economic subsidy.

GNP (1986) per capita $16 800

History Settled by Norse, 8th-c; part of Norway, 11th-c; passed to Denmark, 1380; self-governing region of Denmark since 1948; parliament restored, 1852; unicameral parliament (*Lagting*) consists of 34 members.

Head of State (Monarch)
1972– Margrethe II

Head of Government
1988– Atli Dam

Denmark (continued)

GREENLAND (Kalaalit Nunaat)

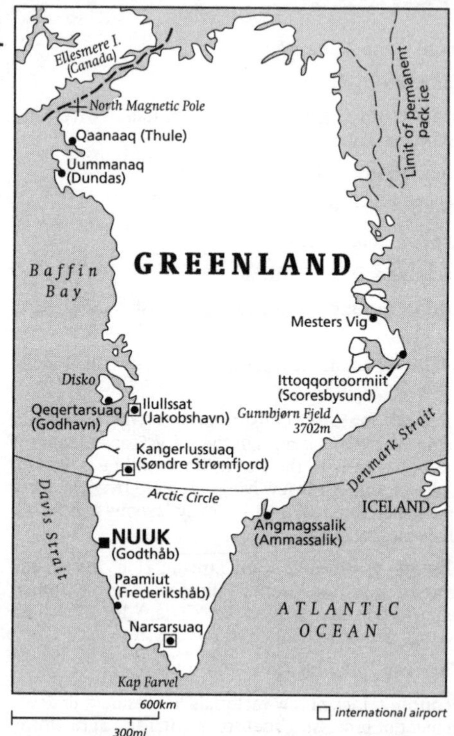

Local names Kalaalit Nunaat (Greenlandic), Grønland (Danish), Kalâtdlit-Nunât (Inuit)

Timezone GMT – 3

Area 2 175 600 sq km/839 781 sq mi

Population total (1990e) 55 900

Status Self-governing province of Denmark

Capital Nuuk (Godthåb)

Languages Danish (official), Inuit

Ethnic groups Largely Inuit (Eskimo), with Danish admixtures

Religions Lutheran, Shamanist

Physical features Located in N Atlantic and Arctic Oceans; largely covered by an ice-cap (up to 4 300 m/14 000 ft thick); coastal mountains rise to 3 702 m/12 145 ft at Gunnbjørn Fjeld (SE); less than 5% of island is inhabitable.

Climate Arctic to subarctic.

Currency 1 Danish Krone (Dkr) = 100 øre

Economy Largely dependent on fishing from ice-free SW ports; hunting for seal and fox furs in N and E; reserves of lead, zinc, molybdenum, uranium, coal, cryolite.

GDP Not available

History Settled by seal-hunting Eskimos from N America c.2500 BC; Norse settlers in SW, 12th–15th-c AD; explored by Frobisher and Davis, 16th-c; Danish colony, 1721; self-governing province of Denmark, 1979; elected Provincial Council sends two members to the Danish Parliament.

Head of State (Monarch)
1972– Margrethe II

Head of Government
1987– Jonathan Motzfeldt

DJIBOUTI

Local name Jumhouriyya Djibouti

Timezone GMT + 3

Area 23 310 sq km/8 998 sq mi

Population total (1991e) 541 000

Status Republic

Date of independence 1977

Capital Djibouti

Language Arabic (official)

Ethnic groups Somali (60%), Afar (20%), Arab (mostly Yemeni) (6%), European (4%), other refugees (10%)

Religions Muslim (94%), Christian (Roman Catholic 4%, Protestant 1%, Orthodox 1%)

Physical features Located in NE Africa; series of plateaux dropping down from mountains to flat, low-lying, rocky desert; fertile coastal strip around the Gulf of Tadjoura; highest point, Moussa Ali, rising to 2020 m/6 627 ft in the N.

Climate Semi-arid climate, with hot season (May–Sep); very high temperatures on coastal plain all year round; average temperatures 26°C (Jan), 36°C (Jul); slightly lower humidity and temperatures in interior highlands; low rainfall, average annual rainfall 130 mm/5 in.

Currency 1 Djibouti Franc (DF, DjFr) = 100 centimes

Economy Crop-based agriculture possible only with irrigation; livestock raising among nomadic population; some fishing on coast; Port of Djibouti provides an important transit point for Red Sea trade, particularly for Ethiopia; small industrial sector.

GDP (1989e) $344 mln, per capita $1 030

History French colonial interest in mid-19th-c; annexed by France as French Somaliland, 1896; French Overseas Territory, following World War 2; French Territory of the

Afars and the Issas, 1967; independence, 1977; political parties combined to form People's Progress Assembly (RPP) as single ruling party, 1979; overwhelming majority voted in favour of a multi party constitution, 1992; governed by a president, a legislative chamber, an executive prime minister, and a Council.

Head of State
1977– Hassan Gouled Aptidon

Head of Government
1978– Barkat Gourad Hamadou

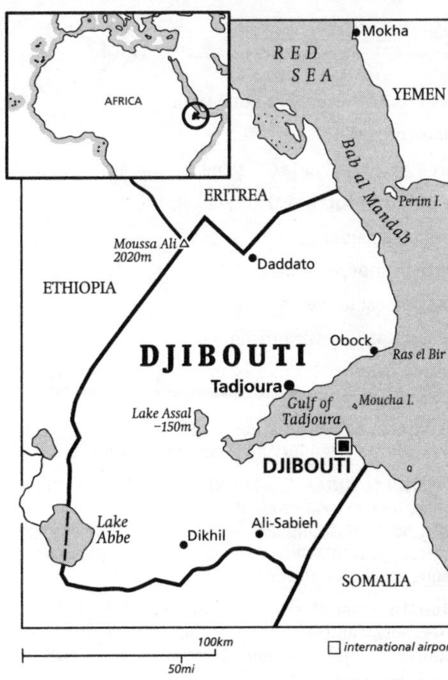

DOMINICA

Local name Dominica

Timezone GMT – 4

Area 751 sq km/290 sq mi

Population total (1991e) 86 000

Status Independent republic within the Commonwealth

Date of independence 1978

Capital Roseau

Languages English (official), with French widely spoken

Ethnic groups African or mixed African-European descent (97%), Amerindian (2%)

Religions Christian (Roman Catholic 77%, Protestant 16%)

Physical features Island in the Windward group of the West Indies; c.50 km/30 mi long and 26 km/16 mi wide, rising to 1 447 m/4 747 ft at Morne Diablotin; volcanic origin; central ridge, with several rivers; 67% of land area forested.

Climate Warm and humid tropical climate; temperatures ranging 26–32°C; rainy season (Jun–Oct); heavy rainfall, varies from 1 750 mm/69 in average on the coast, to 6 250 mm/246 in inland.

Currency 1 East Caribbean Dollar (EC$) = 100 cents

Economy Agriculture; tourism; coconut-based products, cigars, citrus fruits (notably limes), bananas, coconuts, bay oil.

GDP (1989) $153 mln, (1985) per capita $1 090

History Visited by Columbus, 1493; colonization attempts by French and British in 18th-c; British Crown Colony, 1805; part of Federation of the West Indies, 1958–62; independent republic within the Commonwealth, 1978; governed by a House of Assembly, president, prime minister, and cabinet.

Head of State
1984– Clarence Augustus Seignoret

Head of Government
1980– Mary Eugenia Charles

DOMINICAN REPUBLIC

Local name República Dominicana

Timezone GMT - 4

Area 48 442 sq km/18 699 sq mi

Population total (1991) 7 384 000

Status Republic

Date of independence 1844

Capital Santo Domingo

Language Spanish (official)

Ethnic groups Spanish, or mixed Spanish and Indian descent

Religions Roman Catholic (92%), other (mostly Evangelical Protestant and followers of voodoo) (8%)

Physical features Crossed NW–SE by Cordillera Central, with many peaks over 3 000 m/10 000 ft; Pico Duarte, 3 175 m/10 416 ft, highest peak in the Caribbean; wide coastal plain in E; main rivers include Yaque del Sur, Yaque del Norte and the Yuna (E).

Climate Tropical maritime climate with rainy season (May–Nov); Santo Domingo, average temperature 24°C (Jan), 27°C (Jul); annual rainfall 1 400 mm/55 in; hurricanes (Jul-Nov).

Currency 1 Dominican Peso (RD$, DR$) = 100 centavos

Economy Mainly agriculture, especially sugar, cocoa; tourism expanding with new resort complexes on N coast.

GDP (1990) $7.1 bln, (1991) per capita $998

History Visited by Columbus, 1492; Spanish colony, 16th-17th-c; E province of Santo Domingo remained Spanish after partition of Hispaniola, 1697; taken over by Haiti on several occasions; independence from Haiti, 1844, as Dominican Republic; occupied by USA, 1916–24; comprises of 26 provinces and a National District which contains the capital; governed by a president and a National Congress (Senate and Chamber of Deputies).

Head of State/Government

1982–6 Salvador Jorge Blanco
1986– Joaquín Videla Balaguer

ECUADOR

Local name Ecuador

Timezone GMT - 5

Area 270 699 sq km/104 490 sq mi (including the Galápagos Islands, 7 812 sq km/3 015 sq mi)

Population total (1990e) 10 780 000

Status Republic

Date of independence 1830

Capital Quito

Languages Spanish (official), with Quechua also spoken

Ethnic groups Indian (25%), Mestizo (55%), Spanish (10%), African (10%)

Religions Roman Catholic (94%), other (6%)

Physical features Located in NW S America; includes the Galápagos Is, Ecuadorean island group on the equator 970 km/600 mi W of S American mainland; coastal plain in the W, descending from rolling hills (N) to broad lowland basin; Andean uplands in C rising to snow-capped peaks which include Cotopaxi, 5 896 m/19 343 ft;

forested alluvial plains in the E, dissected by rivers flowing from the Andes towards the Amazon (source of the Amazon located in Peru).

Climate Hot and humid, wet equatorial climate; rain throughout year (especially Dec–Apr); average annual rainfall 1 115 mm/44 in; average annual temperatures, 15°C (Jan), 14°C (Jul).

Currency 1 Sucre (Su, S/.) = 100 centavos

Economy Agriculture (employs c.50% of population); beans, cereals, livestock; bananas, coffee, fishing (especially shrimps); petrochemicals, steel, cement, pharmaceuticals; oil piped from the Oriente basin in E to refineries at Esmeraldas.

GDP (1990) $10.9 bln, (1989) per capita $1 040

History Formerly part of Inca Empire; taken by Spanish, 1527; within Viceroyalty of New Granada; independent, 1822; joined with Panama, Colombia, and Venezuela to form Gran Colombia; left union, to become independent republic, 1830; highly unstable political history; comprises 21 provinces, including the Galápagos Is, each administered by a governor; governed by a president and a unicameral National Congress.

Head of State/Government
1988–92 Rodrigo Borja Cevallos
1992– Sixto Durán Ballén

EGYPT

Local name Misr

Timezone GMT + 2

Area 1 001 449 sq km/386 559 sq mi

Population total (1991e) 54 451 000

Status Republic

Date of independence 1922

Capital Cairo

Language Arabic (official)

Ethnic group Population mainly of E Hamitic origin (90%)

Religions Sunni Muslim (c.90%), minority largely Coptic Christian (c.10%)

Physical features R Nile flows N from Sudan, dammed S of Aswan, creating L Nasser; huge delta N of Cairo, 250 km/150 mi across and 160 km/100 mi N–S; narrow Eastern Desert, sparsely inhabited, between Nile and Red Sea; broad Western Desert, covering over two-thirds of the country; Sinai Peninsula (S), desert region with mountains rising to 2 637 m/8 651 ft at Gebel Katherîna, Egypt's highest point; 90% of population lives on Nile floodplain (c.3% of country's area).

Climate Mainly desert climate, except for 80 km/50 mi wide Mediterranean coastal fringe; very hot on coast where dust-laden khamsin wind blows N from Sahara (Mar–Jun); Alexandria, average maximum daily temperatures 18–30°C; elsewhere rainfall less than 50 mm/12 in.

Currency 1 Egyptian Pound (E£, LE) = 100 piastres

Economy Agriculture on floodplain of R Nile accounts for about a third of national income; building of Aswan High Dam extended irrigated cultivation; a major tourist area.

GDP (1990e) $37 bln, per capita $700

History Neolithic cultures on R Nile from c.6000 BC; Pharaoh dynasties from c.3100 BC; Egyptian power greatest during the New Empire period, 1576–1085 BC; became Persian province, 6th-c BC; conquered by Alexander the Great, 4th-c BC; Ptolemaic Pharaohs ruled Egypt until 30 BC; conquered by Arabs, AD 672; Suez Canal constructed, 1869; revolt, 1879, put down by British,

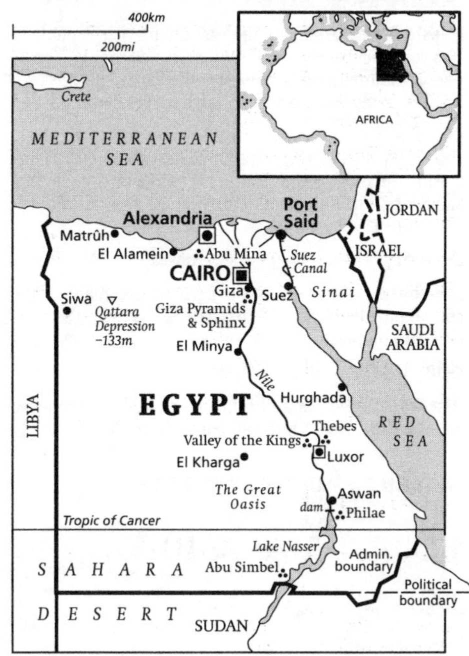

international airport

1882; British protectorate, 1914; declared independence, 1922; King Farouk deposed by Nasser, 1952; Egypt declared a republic, 1953; attack on Israel followed by Israeli invasion in 1967; Suez Canal remained blocked 1967–75; changed name to Arab Republic of Egypt, 1971; Yom Kippur War, 1973, against Israel; Israel returned disputed Taba Strip, 1989; participated in Gulf War with US-led coalition, 1991; governed by a People's National Assembly, president, prime minister, and Council of Ministers.

Head of State
1981– Mohammed Hosni Mubarak

Head of Government
1986– Atif Sidqi

EL SALVADOR

Local name El Salvador

Timezone GMT – 6

Area 21 476 sq km/8 290 sq mi

Population total (1991e) 5 418 000

Status Republic

Date of independence 1841

Capital San Salvador

Language Spanish (official)

Ethnic groups Spanish-Indian (89%), Indian, (mostly Pipil) (5%)

Religions Roman Catholic (93%), other (mostly Evangelical Protestant) (7%)

Physical features Smallest of C America republics; two volcanic ranges run E–W; narrow coastal belt in S, rises to mountains in N; highest point, Santa Ana, 2 381 m/7 812 ft; many volcanic lakes; earthquakes common.

Climate Varies greatly with altitude; hot tropical on coastal lowlands; single rainy season (May–Oct); temperate uplands; average annual temperature at San Salvador, 24°C (Jul), 22°C (Jan); average annual rainfall, 1 775 mm/170 in.

Currency 1 Colón (ES¢) = 100 centavos

Economy Largely based on agriculture; main crops coffee and cotton; sugar, maize, balsam (world's main source); chemicals, rubber, rubber goods, oil products.

GDP (1990) $5.1 bln, per capita $940

History Originally part of the Aztec kingdom; conquest by Spanish, 1526; independence from Spain, 1821; member of the Central American Federation until its dissolution, 1839; independent republic, 1841; war with Honduras, 1965, 1969; considerable political unrest in 1970s and 80s, with guerrilla activity directed against the US-supported government; civil war, 1979–91; peace plan agreed, 1991; governed by a president, and Council of Ministers; unicameral Legislative Assembly.

Head of State/Government

1984–9 José Napoleón Duarte
1989– Alfredo Cristiani Burkard

ENGLAND >> UNITED KINGDOM

EQUATORIAL GUINEA

Local name Guinea Ecuatorial

Timezone GMT + 1

Area 26 016 sq km/10 042 sq mi (mainland area) 28 051 sq km/10 828 sq mi (total area)

Population total (1991e) 360 000

Status Republic

Date of independence 1968

Capital Malabo

Language Spanish (official)

Ethnic groups Mainland population, mainly Fang (83%), Bubi (10%), Ndowe (4%), Annobonés (2%), Bujeba (1%)

Religions Roman Catholic (80%), traditional beliefs (5%)

Physical features Located in WC Africa, comprising the mainland area (Río Muni) and several islands in the Gulf of Guinea; mainland rises sharply from a narrow coast of mangrove swamps towards the heavily forested African plateau; Bioko, fertile volcanic island in NW,

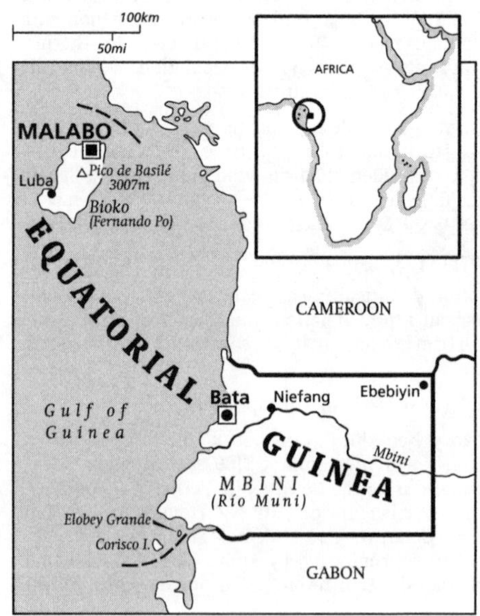

contains Guinea's highest point, Pico de Basilé, 3 007 m/ 9 865 ft.

Climate Hot and humid equatorial climate; average maximum daily temperature, 29–32°C; average annual rainfall c.2 000 mm/80 in.

Currency 1 CFA Franc (CFA Fr) = 100 centimes

Economy Largely based on agriculture; cocoa, coffee, timber, bananas, cassava, palm oil, sweet potatoes.

GDP (1989e) $149 mln, (1989) per capita $430

History First visited by Europeans in 15th-c; island of Fernando Po claimed by Portugal, 1494–1788; occupied by Britain, 1781–1843; rights to the area acquired by Spain, 1844; independence, 1968; military coup, 1975; governed by Supreme Military Council headed by a president; new constitution, 1991.

Head of State/Government

1968–79 Francisco Macias Nguema
1979– Teodoro Obiang Nguema Mbasogo

ESTONIA

Local name Eesti

Timezone GMT + 2

Area 45 100 sq km/17 409 sq mi

Population total (1990e) 1 600 000

Status Republic

Date of independence 1991

Capital Tallinn

Languages Estonian (official), also Russian

Ethnic groups Estonian (65%), Russian (28%), Ukrainian (3%), Belorussian (2%)

Religions Evangelical Lutheran, with Orthodox minority

Physical features Consists of mainland area and c.800 islands (including the Baltic island of Saaremaa); S covered with morainal hills, C with elongated glacial hills usually arrayed in the direction of glacial movement; most lakes and rivers drain either E into Lake Peipus, N into the Gulf of Finland or a few W into Gulf of Riga.

Climate Mild climate; average annual temperatures 23–25°C (Feb) and 17°C (Jul); average annual rainfall 650 mm/26 in.

Currency 1 Kroon = 100 centts

Economy Major industries, agricultural machinery, electric motors; agricultural produce of grain, vegetables; livestock.

GDP (1991e) $10.8 bln, per capita not available

History Ceded to Russia, 1721; independence, 1918; proclaimed a Soviet Socialist Republic, 1940; occupied by Germany in World War 2; resurgence of nationalist movement in the 1980s; declared independence, 1991; 105-member parliament; 495-member Congress of Estonia.

Head of State

1991–2 Arnold Rüütel
1992– Lennart Meri

Head of Government

1991–2 Edgar Savisaar
1992 Tiit Vahi
1992– Mart Laar

ETHIOPIA

Local name Ityopiya

Timezone GMT + 3

Area 1 221 918 sq km/471 660 sq mi

Population total (1991e) 53 131 000

Status Republic

Capital Addis Ababa

Language Amharic (official)

Ethnic groups Galla (40%), Amhara and Tigray (32%)

Religions Muslim (45%), Ethiopian Orthodox (37%), traditional beliefs (11%)

Physical features Located in NE Africa; dominated by mountainous C plateau, mean elevation 1 800–2 400 m/6–8 000 ft; split diagonally by the Great Rift Valley; highest point, Ras Dashen Mt, 4 620 m/15 157 ft; crossed E–W by Blue Nile; Danakil Depression (NE) dips to 116 m/381 ft below sea level.

Climate Tropical climate, moderated by higher altitudes; distinct wet season (Apr–Sep); hot, semi-arid NE and SE lowlands receive less than 500 mm/20 in of rainfall annually; severe droughts in 1980s caused widespread famine, deaths, and resettlement.

Currency 1 Ethiopian Birr (Br) = 100 cents

Economy One of the world's poorest countries; over 80% of population employed in agriculture, especially subsistence farming; production severely affected by drought; distribution of foreign aid hindered by internal civil war and poor local organization.

GDP (1991) $6.6 bln, per capita $130

History Oldest independent country in sub-Saharan Africa; first Christian country in Africa; Eritrea occupied by Italy, 1882; Abyssinian (former name of Ethiopia) independence recognized by League of Nations, 1923; Haile Selassie became emperor, 1930, and began programme of modernization and reform; Italian invasion, 1935; annexation as Italian East Africa, 1936–41; Italians forced from Ethiopia by the Allies, and Haile Selassie returned to power, 1941; military coup 1974; ongoing conflict with Somalia over Ogaden region; internal conflict with regional separatist Eritrean and Tigrean forces; transfer of power to People's Democratic Republic, 1987; government overthrown by separatist forces, 1991; Council of Representatives formed; movement towards independence for Eritrea, which has functioned as an autonomous region since the fall of the government, 1991; Eritrea formally recognized as an independent state, May 1993.

Head of State

1987–91 Mengistu Haile Mariam
1991– Meles Zenawi

Head of Government

1991– Tamirat Layne

FAROE ISLANDS >> DENMARK

FALKLAND ISLANDS >> UNITED KINGDOM

FIJI

Local name Viti

Timezone GMT + 11

Area 18 333 sq km/7 076 sq mi

Population total (1991e) 744 000

Status Republic

Date of independence 1970

Capital Suva (on Viti Levu Island)

Language English (official)

Ethnic groups Indigenous Fijians (44%), Indian (51%)

Religions Native Fijians, mainly Christian (Methodist c.85%, Roman Catholic 12%); Indo-Fijians, mainly Hindu (c.70%) and Muslim (25%)

Physical features Melanesian group of 844 islands and islets in the SW Pacific Ocean; highest peak, Tomaniivi (Mt Victoria) on Viti Levu, 1 324 m/4 344 ft; most smaller islands consist of limestone, little vegetation; Great Sea Reef stretches 500 km/300 mi along W fringe; dense tropical forest on wet, windward side (SE); mainly treeless on dry, leeward side.

Climate Tropical oceanic climate, high humidity; average annual temperature 27°C, ranging from 35°C (Dec–Apr), 16°C (Jun–Sep); heavy rainfall; occasional hurricanes.

Currency 1 Fiji Dollar (F$) = 100 cents

Economy Agriculture; sugar cane (accounts for over two-thirds of export earnings); bananas, ginger, gold, silver, limestone, timber; major tourist area.

GDP (1990) $1.3 bln, per capita $1 840

History Visited by Tasman, 1643, and by Cook, 1774; British colony, 1874; independence within the Commonwealth, 1970; 1987 election brought to power an Indian-dominated coalition, which led to military coups (May and Sep), and proclamation of a republic outside the Commonwealth; civilian government restored, Dec 1987; new constitution, 1990; bicameral parliament of a nominated Senate and an elected House of Representatives.

Head of State
1987– Penaia Ganilau

Head of Government
1987–92 Kamisese Mara
1992– Sitiveni Rabuka

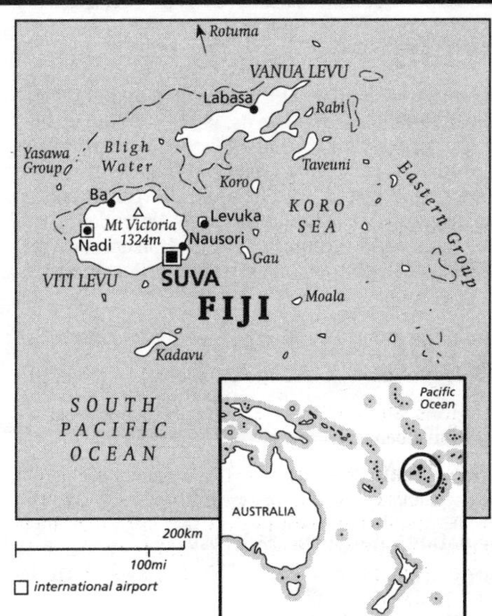

FINLAND

Local name Suomi (Finnish)

Timezone GMT + 2

Area 338 145 sq km/130 524 sq mi

Population total (1991e) 4 991 000

Status Republic

Date of independence 1917

Capital Helsinki

Languages Finnish and Swedish (official), also Saame (Lappish)

Ethnic groups Finnish (94%), Swedish, Lappish, Russian minorities

Religions Lutheran (90%), Finnish/Greek Orthodox

Physical features Low-lying, glaciated plateau, average height 150 m/500 ft; highest peak Haltiatunturi, 1 328 m/4 357 ft, on NW border; over 60 000 shallow lakes in SE, providing a system of inland navigation; over a third of the country is located N of the Arctic Circle; archipelago of Saaristomeri (SW), with over 17 000 islands; including Åland Is (Ahvenanmaa) (SW); forest covers 65% of the country, water covers 10%.

Climate Extreme N of the Arctic Circle; average annual temperatures −30°C (Jan), 27°C (Jul); half annual precipitation falls as snow; sun does not go down beyond the horizon for over 70 days during summer; average temperatures −6°C (Jan), 17°C (Jul) at Helsinki; average annual rainfall 618 mm/24 in.

Currency 1 Markka (FMk) = 100 penni

Economy Traditional focus on forestry, farming; rapid economic growth since 1950s; metals, clothing, chemicals; copper, iron ore mining; wide use of hydroelectric power.

GDP (1990) $77 bln, per capita $15 500

History Ruled by Sweden from 1157 until ceded to Russia, 1809; Grand Duchy of the Russian Czar, 19th-c;

Finland (continued)

independent republic, 1917; parliamentary system created, 1928; invaded by Soviets, 1939–40, (Winter War); lost territory to USSR, including Petsamo and Porkkala peninsula, 1944; signed a friendship treaty with Soviet Union, 1948 (renewed 1955, 1970 and 1983) undertaking to resist any attack made on the Soviet Union launched through Finnish territory; Harri Holkeri became Finland's first post-war conservative prime minister, 1987; governed by a single-chamber House of Representatives and president assisted by a Council of State.

Head of State
1982– Mauno Koivisto

Head of Government
1987–91 Harri Holkeri
1991– Esko Aho

FRANCE

Local name France

Timezone GMT + 1

Area 551 000 sq km/212 686 sq mi

Population total (1991e) 56 681 000

Status Republic

Capital Paris

Languages French (official), Breton, Occitan and Alsatian are also spoken

Ethnic groups Celtic and Latin origin (91%), Breton, Catalan, and large immigrant population (including Portuguese, Algerian, Moroccan and Arab minorities)

Religions Roman Catholic (90%), Protestant (4%), Muslim (3%), Jewish (1%)

Physical features Bounded S and E by large mountain ranges, notably (interior) the Massif Central, Jura and Alps (E), rising to 4 807 m/15 771 ft at Mont Blanc, and the Pyrénées (S); chief rivers include Loire (longest at 1 020 km/633 mi), Rhône, Seine, Garonne; 60% of land is arable.

Climate Mediterranean climate in S, with warm, moist winters and hot, dry summers; average temperatures, 3°C (Jan), 18°C (Jul); continental climate in E; average annual rainfall 786 mm/31 in.

Currency 1 French Franc (Fr) = 100 centimes

Economy Main industries include wine, fruit, cheese; perfume, textiles and clothing; steel, chemicals, machinery, cars and aircraft; natural resources of coal, iron ore, bauxite, timber; tourism important.

GDP (1990) $873 bln, per capita $15 500

History Celtic-speaking Gauls dominant by 5th-c BC; part of Roman Empire, 125 BC to 5th-c AD; feudal monarchy founded by Hugh Capet, 987; Plantagenets of England acquired several territories, 12th-c; lands gradually recovered in Hundred Years' War, 1337–1453, apart from Calais (regained, 1558); Capetian dynasty followed by the Valois, from 1328, and the Bourbons, from 1589; Wars of Religion, 1562–95; monarchy overthrown by the French Revolution, 1789; First Republic declared, 1792; First Empire, ruled by Napoleon, 1804–14; monarchy restored, 1814–48; Second Republic, 1848–52, and Second Empire, 1852–70, ruled by Louis Napoleon; Third Republic, 1870–1940; great political instability between World Wars, with several governments holding office for short periods; occupied by Germany 1940–4, with pro-German government at Vichy, and Free French in London under de Gaulle; Fourth Republic, 1946; war with Indo-China, 1946–54; conflict in Algeria, 1954–62; Fifth Republic, 1958; governed by a president, appointed prime minster, Council of Ministers; bicameral National Assembly and Senate.

international airport

Head of State
Fifth Republic
1969–74 Georges Pompidou
1974–81 Valéry Giscard d'Estaing
1981– François Mitterand

Head of Government
Fifth Republic
1991–2 Edith Cresson
1992–3 Pierre Bérégovoy
1993– Edouard Balladur

>> Political leaders and rulers

Internal Collective Territory
Island of Corsica in the Mediterranean Sea; area 8 680 sq km/3 350 sq mi; capital, Ajaccio; GMT + 1

Regions of France

Overseas departments

Name	Area sq km	sq mi	capital	GMT
Guadeloupe	1779	687	Basse-Terre	– 4
Martinique	1079	416	Fort-de-France	– 4
Guiana	90909	35091	Cayenne	– 3.5
Réunion	2512	970	St Denis	+ 4
St Pierre et Miquelon	240	93	St Pierre	– 3
Mayotte	374	144	Dzaoudzi	+ 3

Overseas territories

Name	Area sq km	sq mi	capital/ chief centre	GMT
New Caledonia	18575	7170	Nouméa	+ 11
French Polynesia	3941	1521	Papeete	– 6
Wallis and Futuna	274	106	Matu Utu	+ 12
Southern and Antarctic Territories	10100	3900	Port-aux-Français	

GABON

Local name Gabon

Timezone GMT + 1

Area 267667 sq km/103319 sq mi

Population total (1991e) 1079000

Status Republic

Date of independence 1960

Capital Libreville

Languages French (official), Fang, Myene, Bateke, and other Bantu dialects spoken

Ethnic groups c.40 Bantu tribes, (Fang 30%, Eshira 25%, Bateke and Bapounou 10%) and c.10% expatriate Africans and Europeans

Religions Christian (96%) (Roman Catholic 65%, Protestant 19%, other 12%), traditional beliefs

Physical features Located in W Africa, lies on the equator for 880 km/550 mi W–E; land rises towards the African central plateau, cut by several rivers, notably the Ogooué and N'Gounié; highest point, Mont Iboundji, 980 m/3215 ft.

Climate Typical equatorial climate, hot, wet, and humid; mean annual temperature, 27°C; annual average rainfall, 1250–2000 mm/50–80 in inland.

Currency 1 CFA Franc (CFAFr) = 100 centimes

Economy Small area of land under cultivation, but employing 65% of population; coffee, cocoa, palm oil, rubber; timber extraction; rapid economic growth since independence, largely because of offshore oil, natural gas, and minerals; manganese, uranium, iron ore.

GDP (1991) $5.3 bln, per capita $4400

History Visited by Portuguese, 15th-c; under French control from mid-19th-c; slave ship captured by the French, 1849, the liberated slaves forming the settlement of Libreville; occupied by France, 1885; one of four territories of French West Africa, 1910; independence, 1960; multi party elections held, 1990; new constitution, 1991; governed by a president, an appointed Council of Ministers, and a legislative National Assembly.

Head of State

1960–7 Léon M'ba

1967– Omar (Bernard-Albert, *to 1973*) Bongo

Head of Government

1975–90 Léon Mébiame (Mébiane)

1990– Casimir Oyé M'ba

GAMBIA, THE

Local name Gambia

Timezone GMT

Area 10 402 sq km/4 015 sq mi

Population total (1991e) 860 000

Status Independent republic within the Commonwealth

Date of independence 1965

Capital Banjul

Languages English (official), also Madinka, Wolof and Fula

Ethnic groups Madinka (40%), Fula (19%), Wolof (15%), Dyola (10%), Sonike (8%)

Religions Muslim (85%), Christian (14%), traditional local beliefs (1%)

Physical features Located in W Africa, surrounded, except for coastline, by Senegal; strip of land 322 km/200 mi E–W along the R Gambia; flat country, not rising above 90 m/295 ft; c.25% of land is arable.

Climate Tropical climate; average temperatures, 23°C (Jan), 27°C (Jul), rising upland to over 40°C; rainy season (Jun–Sep) with high humidity and high night temperatures; rainfall decreasing inland.

Currency 1 Dalasi (D, Di) = 100 butut

Economy Agriculture, especially groundnuts; cotton, rice, millet, sorghum, fruit, vegetables, livestock; groundnut processing, brewing, soft drinks, agricultural machinery assembly, metal working, clothing, tourism.

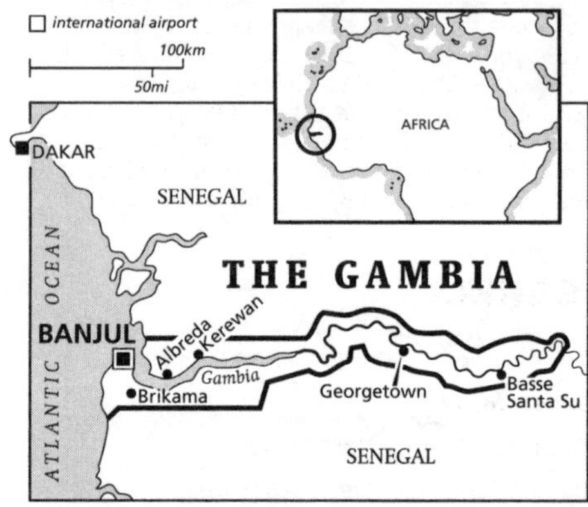

GDP (1990) $196 mln, per capita $230

History Visited by Portuguese, 1455; settled by English in 17th-c; independent British Crown Colony, 1843; independent member of Commonwealth, 1965; republic, 1970; joined Confederation of Senegambia, 1982–9; signed treaty of friendship with Senegal, 1991; governed by a House of Representatives, a president and cabinet.

Head of State/Government

1965– Dawda Kairaba Jawara

GEORGIA

Local name Georgia

Timezone GMT + 3

Area 69 700 sq km/26 900 sq mi

Population total (1990e) 5 400 000

Status Republic

Date of independence 1991

Capital Tbilisi

Languages Georgian (official), also Russian

Ethnic groups Georgian (69%), Armenian (9%), Russian (7%), Azerbaijani (5%), Ossetian (3%), Abkhazian (2%)

Religion Georgian Church, independent of the Russian Orthodox Church since 1917

Physical features Mountainous country in C and W Transcaucasia; contains the Greater Caucasus (N) and Lesser Caucasus (S); highest point in the republic, Mt Shkhara, 5 203 m/17 070 ft; chief rivers, the Kura and Rioni; c.39% of land is forested.

Climate Great Caucasus in N borders temperate and subtropical climatic zones; average temperatures 1–3°C (Jan), 25°C (Jul) in E Transcaucasia; humid, subtropical climate with mild winters in W; Mediterranean climate with humid winters, dry summers in N Black Sea region.

Currency (1992) 1 Rouble (R) = 100 kopecks

Economy Kakhetia region famed for its orchards and wines; holiday resorts, spas on the Black Sea; manganese, coal, iron and steel, oil refining; tea, fruits, tung oil, tobacco, vines, silk, textiles, food processing.

GDP Not available

History Proclaimed a Soviet Socialist Republic, 1921; linked with Armenia and Azerbaijan as Transcaucasian Republic, 1922–36; made a constituent republic within the Soviet Union, 1936; declaration of independence, 1991; quest for regional autonomy led to declaration of secession by S Ossetia, 1991, and declaration of independence by Abkhazia, 1992; failed to join new Commonwealth of Independent States (CIS), 1991; President Gamsakhurdia overthrown in civil war, Jan 1992, brought military council to power; parliament dismissed and powers transferred to a State Council headed by Shevardnadze, 1992; new interim constitution, 1992; head of state holds executive power, advised by Cabinet of Ministers.

Head of State

1991–2 Zviad Gamsakhurdia
1992 Military Council
1992– Eduard Shevardnadze (Chairman of State Council) *Interim*

Head of Government

1992– Tengiz Sigua

GERMANY

Local name Bundesrepublik Deutschland

Timezone GMT + 1

Area 357 868 sq km/138 136 sq mi

Population total (1991e) 79 548 000

Status Federal republic

Capital Berlin

Languages German (official)

Ethnic groups German (93%), Turkish (2%), Yugoslav (1%), Italian (1%), other European Community (3%)

Religions Lutheran (55%), Roman Catholic (38%), Muslim (3%)

Physical features Lowland plains rise SW through C uplands and Alpine foothills to the Bavarian Alps; highest peak, the Zugspitze, 2 962 m/9 718 ft; C uplands include the Rhenish Slate Mts, Black Forest, and Harz Mts; Rhine crosses the country S–N; complex canal system links chief rivers, Elbe, Weser, Danube, Rhine and Main.

Climate Oceanic influences strongest in NW, where winters are mild, stormy; elsewhere continental climate; lower winter temperatures in E and S, with considerable snowfall; average annual temperatures −0.5°C (Jan) to 19°C (Jul); average annual rainfall 600–700 mm/23–27 in.

Currency 1 Deutsche Mark (DM) = 100 Pfennige

Economy Economically powerful member of EC, (accounts for 30% of European Community output); substantial heavy industry in NW, wine in Rhine and Moselle valleys; increasing tourism, especially in the S; leading manufacturer of vehicles, electrical and electronic goods; much less development in the E, after the period of socialist economy; following unification, a major socio-economic division emerged between W and E, leading to demonstrations in the E provinces, 1991.

GDP (1991) $1 157 bln, per capita $14 600

History Ancient Germanic tribes united in 8th-c within the Frankish Empire of Charlemagne; elective monarchy after 918 under Otto I, with Holy Roman Empire divided into several hundred states; after Congress of Vienna, 1814–15, a confederation of 39 states under Austria; under Bismarck, Prussia succeeded Austria as the leading German power; union of Germany and foundation of the second Reich, 1871, with King of Prussia as hereditary German Emperor; aggressive foreign policy, eventually leading to World War 1; after German defeat, second Reich replaced by democratic Weimar Republic; world economic crisis led to collapse of Weimar Republic and rise of National Socialist movement, 1929; Adolph Hitler became dictator of the totalitarian Third Reich, 1933; acts of aggression led to World War 2 and a second defeat for Germany, with collapse of the German political regime; partition of Germany, 1945, with occupation zones given to UK, USA, France, and USSR, who formed a Control Council; USSR withdrew from the Control Council, 1948, dividing Germany into W and E: W Germany controlled by the three remaining powers, UK, USA and France; E administered by USSR.

West Germany (former Federal Republic of Germany) Area 249 535 sq km/96 320 sq mi; Population total (1990) 62 679 035; including West Berlin; established in 1949; gained full sovereignty, 1954; entered NATO, 1955; founder member of the European Economic

Germany (continued)

Community, 1957; federal system of government, built around 10 provinces (*Länder*) with considerable powers; two-chamber legislature, consisting of Federal Diet (*Bundestag*) and Federal Council (*Bundesrat*).
East Germany (former German Democratic Republic) Area 108 333 sq km/41 816 sq mi; Population total (1990) 16 433 796; administered by USSR after 1945 partition, and Soviet model of government established, 1949; anti-Soviet demonstrations put down, 1953; recognized by USSR as an independent republic, 1954; flow of refugees to West Germany continued until 1961, largely stopped by the Berlin Wall built along zonal boundary, dividing western sectors of Berlin from eastern, 1961; governed by the People's Chamber, a single-chamber parliament (*Volkskammer*) which elected Council of State, Council of Ministers, and National Defence Council; movement for democratic reform culminated, Nov 1989, in the opening and removal of the Wall and other border crossings to the West, and a more open government policy; first free all-German elections since 1932 held, Mar 1990, paved the way for a currency union with West Germany, Jul 1990, and full political unification, Oct 1990.
United Germany The 10 provinces of West Germany joined by the five former East German provinces abolished after World War 2 (Brandenburg, Mecklenburg-West, Pomerania, Saxony, Saxony-Anhalt, Thuringia), along with unified Berlin; West German electoral system adopted in East Germany; first national elections, Dec 1990.

Länder of Germany

Head of State
1990– Richard von Weizsäcker

Head of Government (Federal Chancellor)
1990– Helmut Kohl

>> Political leaders and rulers

GHANA

Local name Ghana

Timezone GMT

Area 238 686 sq km/92 133 sq mi

Population total (1991e) 15 616 000

Status Republic

Date of independence 1957

Capital Accra

Languages English (official), Akan, Mossi, Ewe, Ga, Gurma, Yoruba

Ethnic groups c.75 tribal groups, including Akan (44%), Mole-Dagbani (16%), Ewe (13%), and Ga (8%)

Religions Christian (43%), traditional local beliefs (38%), Muslim (12%)

Physical features Located in W Africa; low-lying plains inland, leading to the Ashanti plateau (W) and R Volta basin (E), dammed to form L Volta; mountains (E) rise to 885 m/2903 ft at Mt Afadjado; Ashanti plateau in W and Akwapin Toto Mts in E.

Climate Tropical climate, including a warm dry coastal belt (SE), a hot, humid SW corner, and a hot, dry savannah (N); average temperatures 27°C (Jan), 25°C (Jul) in Accra.

Currency 1 Cedi (¢) = 100 pesewas

Economy Agriculture; cocoa (world's leading producer) provides two-thirds of export revenue; tourism; commercial reserves of oil, diamonds, gold, manganese, bauxite, timber.

GDP (1990e) $5 080 mln, per capita $410

History Visited by Europeans in 15th-c; centre of slave trade, 18th-c; modern state created by union of two former British territories, British Gold Coast (Crown Colony, 1874) and British Togoland merged to form Ghana and declared independence, 1957; independent republic within the Commonwealth, 1960; first British colony in Africa to achieve independence; 1979; constitution provides for a parliament, executive president, cabinet, and Council of State; series of military coups (1966, 1972, 1979, 1982) led to the creation of a Provisional National Defence Council, which rules by decree; new multi party constitution, 1992, allowing for a directly elected executive president and legislature.

Head of State/Government
(Chairman of the Provisional National Defence Council)
1981– Jerry John Rawlings

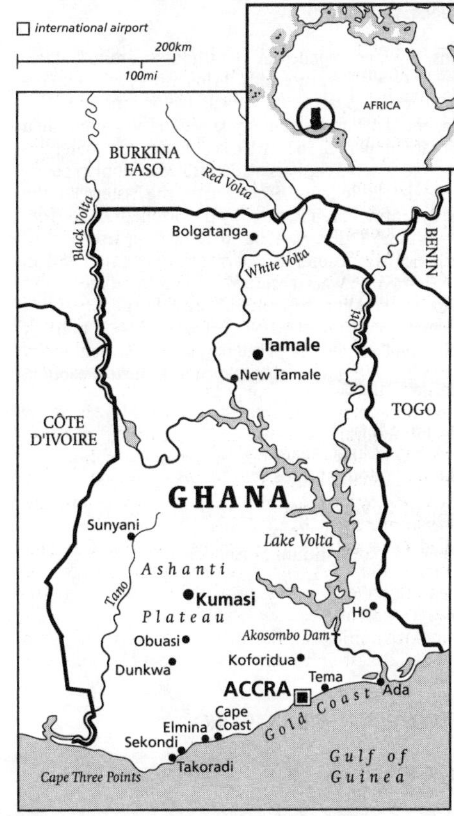

GIBRALTAR >> UNITED KINGDOM

GREECE

Local name Ellás

Timezone GMT + 2

Area 131 957 sq km/50 935 sq mi

Population total (1992e) 10 300 000

Status Republic

Date of independence 1830

Capital Athens (Athínai)

Languages Greek (official), English and French widely spoken

Ethnic groups Greek (98%), Albanian, Slav, Turkish minorities, and others (2%)

Religions Christian (98%) (Greek Orthodox 97.5%, Roman Catholic 0.4%, Protestant 0.1%), Muslim, Judaism and others (2%)

Physical features Located in SE Europe, occupying the S part of the Balkan peninsula and numerous islands in the Aegean and Ionian seas; mainland includes the Peloponnese (S), connected via the narrow Isthmus of Corinth; over 1 400 islands (only 169 inhabited), including Crete, the largest, 8 336 sq km/3 218 sq mi, Rhodes, Milos, Corfu, Lesbos and Kos; nearly 80% of Greece is mountainous or hilly; Pindus Mts run N to S; highest point, Mt Olympus, 2 917 m/9 570 ft; principal rivers include the Néstos, Strimón, Arakhthos; c.30% of land is arable or under permanent cultivation; c.20% is forested.

Climate Mediterranean climate for coast and islands, with mild, rainy winters and hot, dry summers; rainfall almost entirely in winter; island of Corfu receives maximum rainfall 1 320 mm/52 in; severe winters in mountains; average annual temperatures 9°C (Jan), 28°C (Jul) in Athens.

Currency 1 Drachma (Dr) = 100 lepta

Economy Strong service sector accounts for c.55% of national income; agriculture based on cereals, cotton, tobacco, fruit, figs, raisins, wine, olive oil, vegetables; major tourist area, especially on islands; world's largest shipping fleet (under own and other flags); member of the EC, 1981.

GDP (1990) $76 bln, per capita $7 650

History Prehistoric civilization culminated in the Minoan-Mycenean culture of Crete; Dorians invaded from the N, 12th-c BC; Greek colonies established along N and S Mediterranean and on the Black Sea; many city-states on mainland, notably Sparta and Athens; Persian inva-

Greece (continued)

sions, 5th-c BC, repelled at Marathon, Salamis, Plataea, Mycale; Greek literature and art flourished, 5th-c BC; conflict between Sparta and Athens (Peloponnesian War) weakened both and hegemony passed to Thebes, and then Macedon under Philip II, 4th-c BC; his son, Alexander the Great, conquered the Persian Empire; Macedonian power broken by the Romans, 197 BC; part of the Eastern Roman and Byzantine empires; ruled by the Ottoman Turks from 15th-c until 19th-c; national reawakening led to independence as kingdom, 1830; territorial gains after Balkan and First World Wars; absorbed over 1 mln refugees after defeat in Asia Minor, 1922; republic established, 1924–35; German occupation 1941–4; civil war, 1944–9; military coup, 1967; abolition of monarchy, 1969; democracy restored, 1974; governed by a prime minister; cabinet, unicameral parliament, and president.

Head of State

1985–90 Christos Sartzetakis
1990– Konstantinos Karamanlis

Head of Government

1989–90 Xenofon Zolotas
1990– Konstantinos Mitsotakis

GREENLAND >> DENMARK

GRENADA

Local name Grenada

Timezone GMT – 4

Area 344 sq km/133 sq mi

Population total (1992e) 100 000

Status Independent state within the Commonwealth

Date of independence 1974

Capital St George's

Languages English (official), French patois

Ethnic groups African descent (84%), mixed (12%), E Indian (3%), European (1%)

Religions Roman Catholic (64%), Protestant (21%)

Physical features Most southerly of the Windward Is, E Caribbean; comprises the main island of Grenada, 34 km/21 mi long, 19 km/12 mi wide, and the S Grenadines; Grenada volcanic in origin, with a ridge of mountains along its entire length; highest point, Mt St Catherine, rising to 840 m/2 756 ft; many rivers and lakes, including Grand Étang.

Climate Sub-tropical climate; average annual temperature 23°C; wet season (Jun–Dec); annual rainfall varies from 1 270 mm/150 in (coast) to 5 000 mm/200 in (interior); lies within Caribbean hurricane zone.

Currency 1 East Caribbean Dollar (EC$) = 100 cents

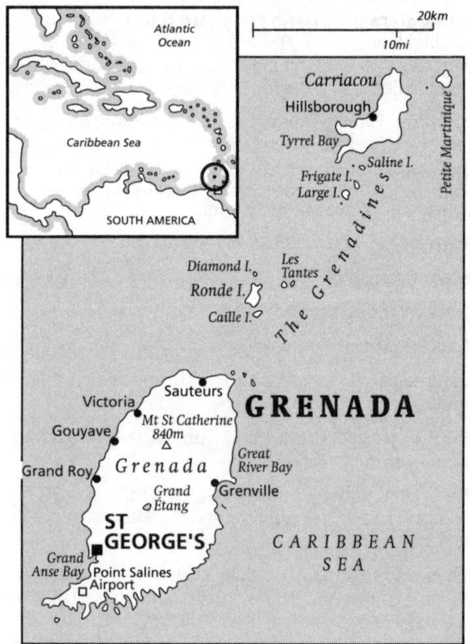

Economy Economy based on agriculture, notably fruit, vegetables, cocoa, nutmegs, bananas, mace; processing of agricultural products and their derivatives.

GDP (1990e) $119 mln, per capita $1 400

History Visited by Columbus and named Concepción, 1498; settled by French, mid-17th-c; ceded to Britain, 1763; retaken by France, 1779; ceded again to Britain, 1783; British Crown Colony, 1877; independence, 1974; popular people's revolution, 1979; Prime Minister Maurice Bishop killed during further uprising, 1983; a group of Caribbean countries requested US involvement, and troops invaded the island, Oct 1983, to restore stable government; governed by a Senate, House of Representatives, prime minister, and cabinet.

Head of State

(British monarch represented by Governor-General)

1978– Sir Paul Scoon

Head of Government

1989–90 Ben Jones *Acting*

1990– Nicholas Braithwaite

GUADELOUPE >> FRANCE

GUAM >> UNITED STATES OF AMERICA

GUATEMALA

Local name Guatemala

Timezone GMT - 6

Area 108 889 sq km/42 031 sq mi

Population total (1992e) 9 700 000

Status Republic

Date of independence 1838

Capital Guatemala City

Languages Spanish (official), c.40% speak Indian dialects, including Quiche, Cakchiquel and Kekchi

Ethnic groups Amerindian (45%), Ladino (45%)

Religions Roman Catholic (75%), Protestant (25%)

Physical features Northernmost of the C American republics; over two-thirds mountainous, with large forested areas; narrow Pacific coastal plain, rising steeply to highlands of 2 500–3 000 m/8 000–10 000 ft; many volcanoes on S edge of highlands; low undulating tableland of El Petén to the N.

Climate Humid tropical climate on lowlands and coast; average annual temperatures 17°C (Jan), 21°C (Jul) in Guatemala City; rainy season (May–Oct); average annual rainfall 1 316 mm /51.8 in; area subject to hurricanes and earthquakes.

Currency 1 Quetzal (Q) = 100 centavos

Economy Agricultural products account for c.65% of exports, chiefly coffee, bananas, cotton, sugar; on higher ground, wheat, maize, beans; cotton, sugar cane, rice, beans on the Pacific coastal plain.

GDP (1990) $11.1 bln, per capita $1 180

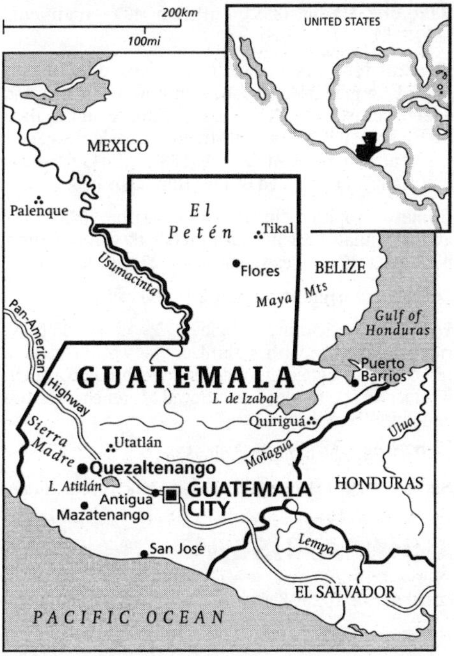

History Mayan and Aztec civilizations before Spanish conquest, 1523–4; independence as part of the Federation of Central America, 1821; independence as the Republic of Guatemala, 1838; 1985 constitution provides for the election of a president (who appoints a cabinet), and a National Assembly; a claim is still made over Belize to the East.

□ *international airport*

Head of State/Government

1986–91 Marco Vinicio Cerezo Arévalo

1991– Jorge Serrano Elias

GUIANA >> FRANCE

GUINEA

Local name Guinée

Timezone GMT

Area 246 048 sq km/94 974 sq mi

Population total (1992e) 7 800 000

Status Republic

Date of independence 1958

Capital Conakry

Languages French (official), Fulani, Malinké, Susu, Kissi, Kpelle

Ethnic groups Fulani (40%), Malinké (25%), Susu (11%), Kissi (6%), Kpelle (5%)

Religions Muslim (85%), Christian (10%), traditional beliefs (5%)

Physical features Located in W Africa; coast characterized by mangrove forests, rising to a forested and widely cultivated narrow coastal plain; Fouta Djallon massif beyond, c.900 m/ 3 000 ft; higher peaks near Senegal frontier include Mt Tangue, 1 537 m/5 043 ft; savannah plains in E; forested Guinea Highlands in S.

Climate Tropical climate; wet season (May–Oct); annual rainfall 4 923 mm/194 in at Conakry; average temperature 32 °C (dry season) on coast, 23 °C (wet season).

Currency 1 Guinean Franc (GFr) = 100 cauris

Economy Agriculture (employs 75% of population); rich in minerals, with a third of the world's bauxite reserves; gold, diamonds; independence brought a fall in production as a result of withdrawal of French expertise and investment.

GDP (1989) $2.7 bln, per capita $380

History Part of Mali empire, 16th-c; French protectorate, 1849; governed with Senegal as Rivières du Sud; separate colony, 1893; constituent territory within French West Africa, 1904; overseas territory, 1946; independent republic, 1958; death of Sékou Touré, Guinea's first president (1961–84); coup in 1984 established a Military Committee for National Recovery (CMRN); CMRN replaced by a mixed military and civilian Transitional Committee of National Recovery (CTRN), 1991; governed by a president and a Council of Ministers; new constitution approved, 1990.

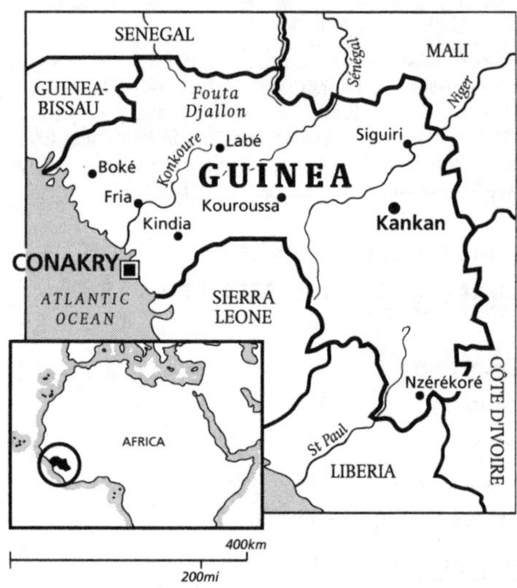

Head of State/Government

1961–84 Ahmed Sékou Touré
1984– Lansana Conté

GUINEA-BISSAU

Local name Guiné-Bissau

Timezone GMT

Area 36 260 sq km/13 996 sq mi

Population total (1992e) 1 000 000

Status Republic

Date of independence 1974

Capital Bissau

Languages Portuguese (official), Criolo, Balante

Ethnic groups Balante (30%), Fulani (20%), Manjaca (14%), Mandingo (13%), Pepel (10%)

Religions Traditional beliefs (65%), Muslim (30%), Christian (5%)

Physical features Located in W Africa; indented coast backed by forested coastal plains; main rivers, Geba and Cacheu; low-lying with savannah-covered plateaux (S, E), rising to 310 m/1 017 ft on the Guinea border; includes the heavily-forested Bijagós archipelago located in the Atlantic Ocean off the shores of the mainland.

Climate Tropical climate, hot and humid; wet season (Jun–Oct); average annual rainfall at Bissau, 1 950 mm/76.8 in; average annual temperature 24°C (Jan), 27°C (Jul) in Bissau.

Currency 1 Guinea-Bissau Peso (GBP, PG) = 100 centavos

Economy Based on agriculture, especially rice, maize, beans, peanuts, coconuts, palm oil, groundnuts, shrimps, fish, timber; reserves of petroleum, bauxite, phosphate.

GDP (1989) $154 mln, (1991) per capita $160

History Visited by Portuguese, 1446; Portuguese colony, 1879; overseas territory of Portugal, 1952; independence, 1974; military coup, 1980; governed by a president and Council of Ministers; new constitution, 1984; National Assembly elects Council of State; president of the Council of State is also the head of government; introduction of a multi party system, 1991.

Head of State/Government

1980–4 João Bernardo Vieira (President of the Military Council)

1984– João Bernardo Vieira (President of the State Council)

GUYANA

Local name Guyana

Timezone GMT – 3.5

Area 214 969 sq km/82 978 sq mi

Population total (1992e) 800 000

Status Co-operative republic

Date of independence 1966

Capital Georgetown

Languages English (official), Hindi, Urdu, Amerindian dialects

Ethnic groups E Indian (51%), mixed African (31%), Amerindian (5%) (Carib 4%, Arawak 1%)

Religions Christian (57%), Hindu (33%)

Physical features Located on N coast of S America; inland forest covers c.85% of land area; highest peak, Mt Roraima, rising to 2 875 m/9 432 ft in the Pakaraima Mts (W); main rivers, the Essequibo, Rupununi, and Courantyne, with many rapids and waterfalls in upper courses.

Climate Equatorial climate in the lowlands; hot, wet, with constant high humidity; average annual temperature 26°C (Jan), 27°C (Jul) in Georgetown; two seasons of high rainfall (May–Jul, Nov–Jan); average annual rainfall 2 175 mm/87 in.

Currency 1 Guyana Dollar (G$) = 100 cents

Economy High unemployment, influenced by labour unrest, low productivity, and high foreign debt; economy largely based on sugar, rice, bauxite, shrimps, livestock, cotton, molasses, timber.

GDP (1989) $248 mln, (1987) per capita $380

History Sighted by Columbus, 1498; settled by the Dutch, late 16th-c; several areas ceded to Britain, 1815; consolidated as British Guiana, 1831; independence, 1966; Co-operative republic within the Commonwealth, 1970; governed by a president who holds executive power and appoints a prime minister, and a National Assembly, elected every five years.

Head of State/Government

1985–92 Hugh Desmond Hoyte

1992– Cheddi Jagan

Prime Minister and First Vice-President

1985–92 Hamilton Green

Human geography

HAITI

Local name Haïti

Timezone GMT – 5

Area 27 750 sq km/10 712 sq mi

Population total (1991e) 6 286 000

Status Republic

Date of independence 1804

Capital Port-au-Prince

Languages French (official), with Creole French widely spoken

Ethnic groups African descent (95%), European (mulatto) (5%)

Religions Roman Catholic (80%), Protestant (10%)

Physical features Consists of two mountainous peninsulas Massif du Nord (N) and Massif de la Hotte (S), separated by a deep structural depression, the Plaine du Cul-de-Sac; highest peak, La Selle, 2 680 m/8 793 ft; includes islands of Gonâve (W) and Tortue (N).

Climate Tropical climate; average annual temperatures 25°C (Jan) 29°C (Jul) in Port-au-Prince; wet season (May–Sep); average annual rainfall for N coast and mountains 1 475–1 950 mm/58–77 in, but only 500 mm/20 in on W side; hurricanes common.

Currency 1 Gourde (G, Gde) = 100 centimes

Economy Based on agriculture; large plantations grow coffee, sugar, sisal, rice, bananas, corn, sorghum, cocoa; sugar refining, textiles, flour milling, cement, bauxite; tourism; light assembly industries.

GDP (1990e) $2.7 bln, per capita $440

History Visited by Columbus, 1492; created when W third of island ceded to France as Saint-Domingue, 1697; slave rebellion followed by independence as Haiti, 1804; united with Santo Domingo (Dominican Republic), 1822–44; under US occupation, 1915–34; Duvalier family had absolute power, 1957–86; after 1986 coup, new constitution provided for a bicameral National Congress consisting of a Senate and National Assembly; military coup, 1992, forced Jean-Bertrand Aristide to flee country, and a provisional government was created; Marc Bazin resigned as head of army-backed coalition government, 1993; talks between deposed president Aristide and coup leader Cédras reached deadlock, Jun 1993.

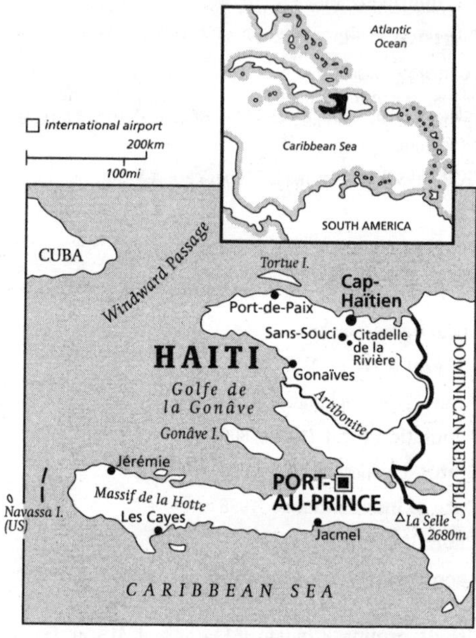

Head of State

1990	Ertha Pascal-Trouillot *Interim*
1990–1	Jean-Bertrand Aristide
1991	Raoul Cédras *Military Junta*
1991–2	Joseph Nerette *Interim*
1992–	Marc Bazin

Head of Government

1992–3	Marc Bazin

HONDURAS

Local name Honduras

Timezone GMT – 6

Area 112 088 sq km/43 266 sq mi

Population total (1991e) 4 949 000

Status Republic

Date of independence 1821

Capital Tegucigalpa

Languages Spanish (official), a number of Indian dialects are also spoken by aboriginal population

Ethnic groups Spanish-Indian origin (90%), Indian (7%)

Religions Roman Catholic (85%), Protestant (mainly Fundamentalist, Moravian and Methodist) (10%)

Physical features Coastal lands (S) separated from Caribbean coastlands by mountains running NW–SE; S plateau rises to 2 849 m/9 347 ft at Cerro de las Minas; also includes Bay Is in the Caribbean Sea and nearly 300 islands in the Gulf of Fonseca.

Climate Tropical climate in coastal areas, temperate in C and W; average annual temperatures 19°C (Jan), 23°C (Jul) in Tegucigalpa; two wet seasons in upland areas (May–Jul, Sep–Oct).

Currency 1 Lempira (L, La) = 100 centavos

Economy Agriculture (provides a third of national income), forestry, mining, cattle raising; bananas, coffee, beef, cotton, tobacco, sugar; exports of silver, lead and zinc; offshore oil exploration in the Caribbean.

GDP (1990e) $4.9 bln, (1989) per capita $960

History Centre of Mayan culture, 4th–9th-c; settled by the Spanish, early 16th-c, and became province of Guatemala; independence from Spain, 1821; joined Federation of C America; independence, 1838; several military coups in 1970s; a democratic constitutional republic, governed by a president and a National Assembly.

Head of State/Government

1982–6 Roberto Suazo Córdova
1986–9 José Azcona Hoyo
1989– Rafael Callejas

HONG KONG >> UNITED KINGDOM

HUNGARY

Local name Magyarország

Timezone GMT + 1

Area 93 036 sq km/35 912 sq mi

Population total (1991e) 10 588 000

Status Republic

Date of independence 1918

Capital Budapest

Language Hungarian (Magyar) (official)

Ethnic groups Magyar (96%), German (2%), Slovak (1%), Romanian and Yugoslav minorities

Religions Roman Catholic (67%), Calvinist (20%), Lutheran (5%)

Physical features Drained by the R Danube (flows N–S) and its tributaries; crossed (W) by a low spur of the Alps; highest peak, Kékestető, 1 014 m/3 327 ft; frequent flooding, especially in the Great Plains (E); 54% of land is arable, 18% forested.

Climate Fairly extreme continental climate due to landlocked position; average annual temperature 0°C (Jan), 21°C (Jul) in Budapest; wettest in spring and early summer; average annual rainfall 600 mm/23.6 in; cold winters, R Danube sometimes frozen over for long periods; frequent fogs.

Currency 1 Forint (Ft) = 100 fillér

Economy Large-scale nationalization as part of centralized planning strategy of the new republic, 1946–9; greater independence to individual factories and farms, from 1968; grain, potatoes, sugar beet, fruit, wine; coal, bauxite, lignite; metallurgy, engineering, chemicals, textiles, food processing.

GNP (1990e) $60.9 bln, per capita $5 800

History Kingdom formed under St Stephen I, 11th-c; conquered by Turks, 1526; part of Habsburg Empire,

17th-c; Austria and Hungary reconstituted as a dual monarchy, 1867; republic, 1918; communist revolt led by Béla Kun, 1919; monarchical constitution restored, 1920; new republic with communist government, 1949; uprising crushed by Soviet forces, 1956; during 1989, pressure for political change towards a multi party system; multi party elections, 1990, saw an end to communist rule; governed by a National Assembly which elects a Presidential Council and Council of Ministers.

Head of State

1989–90 Mátyás Szűrös
1990– Árpád Göncz

Head of Government

1988–90 Miklós Németh
1990– József Antall

ICELAND

Local name Ísland

Timezone GMT

Area 103 000 sq km/40 000 sq mi

Population total (1991e) 259 000

Status Republic

Date of independence 1944

Capital Reykjavík

Language Icelandic (official)

Ethnic groups Homogeneous (96%), with European minorities

Religions Protestant (95%) (Evangelical Lutheran 93%, other Lutheran 2%), Roman Catholic (1%), non-religious (1%)

Physical features Several active volcanoes, including Hekla, 1 491 m/4 920 ft, Helgafell 215 m/706 ft, and Surtsey 174 m/570 ft; famous for its geysers; many towns heated by subterranean hot water; heavily indented coastline with many long fjords; high ridges rise to 2 119 m/6 952 ft at Hvannadalshnúkur (SE); several large snowfields and glaciers.

Climate Changeable, summers cool and cloudy, mild winters; average annual temperature 1 °C (Jan), 11 °C (Jul); Reykjavík generally ice-free throughout year; average monthly rainfall reaches 94 mm/3.7 in (Oct).

Currency 1 Króna (Kr, SK) = 100 aurar

Economy Based on inshore and deep-water fishing (75% of national income); stock and dairy farming, potatoes, greenhouse vegetables; aluminium, diatomite; tourism.

GDP (1990) $4.2 bln, per capita $16 300

History Settled by the Norse, 9th-c; world's oldest parliament (*Althing*), 10th-c; union with Norway, 1262; union with Denmark, 1380; independent kingdom in personal union with Denmark, 1918; independent republic, 1944; extension of the fishing limit around Iceland in 1958 and 1975 precipitated the 'Cod War' disputes with the UK; governed by a bicameral parliament (*Althing*), president, prime minister, and cabinet.

Head of State

1980– Vigdís Finnbogadóttir

Head of Government

1988–91 Steingrímur Hermannsson

1991– Davíd Oddsson

INDIA

Local name Bhārat (Hindi)

Timezone GMT + 5.5

Area 3 166 829 sq km/1 222 396 sq mi

Population total (1991e) 866 000 000

Status Republic

Date of independence 1947

Capital New Delhi

Languages Hindi and English (official), others include Urdu, Panjabi, Gujarati, Marathi, Bengali, Oriya, Kashmiri, Assamese, Kannada, Malayalam, Sindhi, Tamil and Telugu

Ethnic groups Indo-Aryan (72%), Dravidian (25%), with Mongoloid and other minorities

Religions Hindu (83%), Muslim (11%), Christian (2%), Sikh (2%), Buddhist (1%)

Physical features Seventh largest country in the world, located in S Asia; includes Andaman and Nicobar Is in the Bay of Bengal, and Laccadive Is in the Indian Ocean; folded mountain ridges and valleys in N, highest peaks over 7 000 m/23 000 ft; C river plains of the Ganges, Yamuna, Ghaghari, and Brahmaputra to the S; control measures needed to prevent flooding; Thar Desert in NW bordered by semi-desert areas; Deccan Plateau in the S peninsula, with hills and wide valleys, bounded by the Western and Eastern Ghats; coastal plains, important areas of rice cultivation.

Climate Dominated by the Asiatic monsoon; rains come from the SW (Jun–Oct); rainfall decreases E–W on the N plains, with desert conditions in extreme W; tropical in S even in cool season; average annual temperature 14°C (Jan), 31°C (Jul) in New Delhi; average annual rainfall 640 mm/25.2 in; cyclones and storms on SE coast (especially Oct–Dec).

Currency 1 Indian Rupee (Re, Rs) = 100 paisa

Economy Agriculture employs over two-thirds of the labour force; tea, rice, wheat, coffee, sugar cane, cotton, jute, oil seed, maize, pulses, milk; floods and drought cause major problems; considerable increase in industrial production since independence; iron, steel, oil products, chemicals, fertilizers, chromite, barites, oil, natural gas; tourism.

GDP (1990e) $220 830 mln, per capita $290

History Indus civilization emerged c.2500 BC, destroyed in 1500 BC by the Aryans, who developed the Brahmanic caste system; Mauryan Emperor Asoka unified most of India, and established Buddhism as the state religion, 3rd-c BC; spread of Hinduism, 2nd-c BC; Muslim influences during 7th–8th-c, with sultanate established at Delhi; Mughal Empire established by Babur, 1526, extended by Akbar and Aurangzeb; Portuguese, French, Dutch, and British footholds in India, 18th-c; conflict between France and Britain, 1746–63; development of British interests represented by the East India Company; British power established after the Indian Mutiny crushed, 1857; movement for independence, late 19th-c; Government of India Act, 1919, allowed election of Indian ministers to share power with appointed British governors; further Act, 1935, allowed election of independent provincial governments; passive resistance campaigns of Mohandas Gandhi from 1920s; independence granted, 1947, on condition that a Muslim state be established (Pakistan); Indian states later reorganised on a linguistic basis; Pakistan–India war over disputed territory in Kashmir and Jammu, 1948; federal democratic republic within the Commonwealth, 1950; Hindu–Muslim hostility, notably in 1978, and further India–Pakistan conflict in 1965 and 1971; separatist movements continue, especially relating to Sikh interests in the Punjab; suppression of militant Sikh movement in 1984 led to assassination of Indira Gandhi; Rajiv Gandhi assassinated, 1991; each of the 25 states administered by a governor appointed by the president; each state has an Assembly; president, advised by a Council of Ministers, appoints a prime minister; parliament comprises the president, an Upper House and a House of the People.

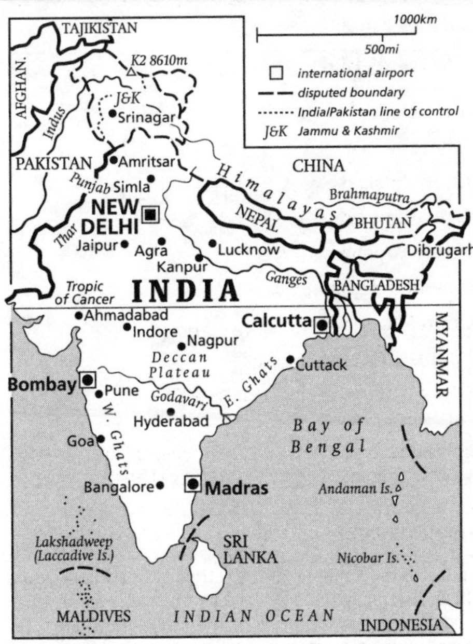

Head of State

1987–92 Ramaswami Venkataraman
1992– Shankar Dayal Sharma

Head of Government

1989–90 Vishwanath Pratap Singh
1990–1 Chandra Shekhar
1991– P V Narasimha Rao

INDONESIA

Local name Indonesia

Timezone GMT + 7 to + 9

Area 1 906 240 sq km/735 809 sq mi

Population total (1991e) 193 000 000

Status Republic

Date of independence 1945

Capital Jakarta

Languages Bahasa Indonesia (official), English, Dutch and Javanese widely spoken

Ethnic groups Madurese (40%), Javanese (33%), Sudanese (15%), Bahasa Indonesian (12%)

Religions Muslim (78%), Christian (9%) (Roman Catholic 6%, Protestant 2%), Hindu (2%), Buddhist (1%)

Physical features World's largest island group of 13 677 islands and islets, of which c.6 000 are inhabited; five main islands, Sumatra, Java, Kalimantan (two-thirds of Borneo I), Sulawesi, Irian Jaya (W half of New Guinea I); characterized by mountainous volcanic landscape and equatorial rainforest; over 100 volcanic peaks on Java, 15 active.

Climate Hot and humid equatorial climate; dry season (Jun–Sep), rainy season (Dec–Mar); average annual temperature 26°C (Jan), 27°C (Jul) in Jakarta; average annual rainfall 1 775 mm/69 in.

Currency 1 Indonesian Rupiah (Rp) = 100 sen

Economy Mainly agrarian, notably rice; oil, natural gas, and petroleum products from Borneo and Sumatra account for nearly 60% of national income; small manufacturing industry.

GDP (1990e) $94 bln, per capita $490

History Settled in early times by Hindus and Buddhists whose power lasted until the 14th-c; Islam introduced, 14th–15th-c; Portuguese settlers, early 16th-c; Dutch East India Company established, 1602; Japanese occupation in World War 2; independence proclaimed with Sukarno as president, 1945; changed name from Netherlands East

Indonesia (continued)

Indies to the Republic of the United States of Indonesia, 1949; federal system replaced by unified control, 1950, and the unitary Republic of Indonesia proclaimed (W New Guinea remained under Dutch control until 1963 and is now called Irian Jaya); military coup, 1966; governed by a president elected by a People's Consultative Assembly, and advised by a cabinet and several advisory agencies; separatist movements in Irian Jaya and East Timor; United Nations refuses to recognize Indonesian sovereignty in East Timor.

Head of State/Government
1968– T N J Suharto

IRAN

Local name Īrān

Timezone GMT + 3.5

Area 1 648 000 sq km/636 128 sq mi

Population total (1991e) 59 051 000

Status Islamic republic

Date of independence 1925

Capital Teheran

Languages Farsi (Persian) (official), several minority languages including Kurdish, Baluchi, Luri, and Turkic (including Afshari, Shahsavani and Turkish)

Ethnic groups Persian (63%), Turkic (18%), other Iranian (13%), Kurdish (3%), Arab and other Semitic (3%)

Religions Muslim (Shi'ite 92%, Sunni 5%), Zoroastrian (2%), Jewish, Baha'i and Christian (1%)

Physical features Largely composed of a vast arid C plateau, average elevation 1 200 m/4 000 ft; bounded N by the Elburz Mts, rising to 5 670 m/18 602 ft at Mt Damavand; Zagros Mts in W and S.

Climate Mainly a desert climate, hot and humid on Arabian Gulf; average annual temperatures 2°C (Jan), 30°C (Jul) in Teheran; average annual rainfall 246 mm/9.7 in; frequent earthquakes.

Currency 1 Iranian Rial (RIs, RI) = 100 dinars

Economy World's fourth largest oil producer, but production severely disrupted by 1978 revolution, Iran–Iraq War and Gulf War, 1991; agriculture and

forestry (employs a third of population); natural gas, iron ore, copper, coal, salt; textiles, sugar refining, petrochemicals; traditional handicrafts (especially carpets).

GDP (1990) $80 bln, per capita $1 400

History Early centre of civilization, dynasties including the Achaemenids and Sassanids; ruled by Arabs, Turks, and Mongols until the Sasavid dynasty, 16th–18th-c, and the Qajar dynasty, 19th–20th-c; military coup, 1921, with independence under Reza Shah Pahlavi, 1925; changed name from Persia to Iran, 1935; protests against Shah's regime in 1970s led to revolution, 1978; exile of Shah and proclamation of Islamic Republic under Ayatollah Khomeini, 1979; Islamic Cultural Revolution under Khomeini saw a return to strict observance of Muslim principles and traditions; occupation of US embassy in Teheran, 1979–81; Iran–Iraq War following invasion of Iraq, 1980–8; overall authority exercised by appointed spiritual leader; post of prime minister abolished, 1989; governed by a president and Consultative Assembly (*Majlis*).

Leader of the Islamic Republic
1979–89 Ayatollah Khomeini
1989– Ayatollah Sayed Ali Khamenei

Head of State/Government
1981–9 Sayed Ali Khamenei
1989– Ali Akbar Hashemi Rafsanjani

IRAQ

Local name Al-'Īrāq

Timezone GMT + 3

Area 434 925 sq km/167 881 sq mi

Population total (1991e) 19 524 000

Status Republic

Date of independence 1932

Capital Baghdad

Languages Arabic (official), also English, Kurdish, Persian, Turkish and Assyrian spoken

Ethnic groups Arab (79%), Kurd (largely in NE) (16%), Persian (3%), Turkish (2%)

Religions Muslim (95%) (Shi'ite 63%, Sunni 32%), Christian (3%)

Physical features Comprises the vast alluvial tract of the Tigris–Euphrates lowland (ancient Mesopotamia); Tharthar and Euphrates rivers divided by Al Jazirah plain, flow over dense swampland and join to form the navigable Shatt al-Arab; mountains (NE) rise to over 3 000 m/ 9 800 ft; desert in other areas.

Climate Mainly arid climate; summers very hot and dry; winters often cold; average annual temperature 10°C (Jan), 35°C (Jul) in Baghdad; average annual rainfall 140 mm/15.5 in.

Currency 1 Iraqi Dinar (ID) = 1 000 fils

Economy World's second largest producer of oil, but production severely disrupted during both Gulf Wars (several oil installations destroyed); natural gas, oil refining, petrochemicals, cement, textiles; dates, cotton, winter wheat, rice, sheep, cattle.

GDP (1989) $35 bln, per capita $1 950

History Part of the Ottoman Empire from 16th-c until World War I; captured by British forces, 1916; British-mandated territory, 1921; independence under Hashemite dynasty, 1932; monarchy replaced by military rule, and Iraq declared a republic, 1958; since 1960s, Kurdish nationalists in NE fighting to establish a separate state; invasion of Iran, 1980, led to the Iran–Iraq War, lasting until ceasefire, 1988; invasion and annexation of Kuwait, Aug 1990, led to the 1991 Gulf War (Jan–Feb); UN sanctions imposed on Iraq, 1991, and successful land, sea and air offensive by UN ended war; rebellions against the government by Kurds (N Iraq) and Shi'ites (S Iraq) quelled, however, UN forced to impose a no-fly zone over S Iraq to protect Shi'ites, and a security zone in N Iraq to protect Kurdish refugees, 1992; governed by Revolutionary Command Council, which elects a president and shares legislative authority with National Assembly; Kurdish regional assembly has limited powers of legislation.

□ international airport

Head of State/Government
1968–79 Said Ahmad Hassan al Bakr
1979– Sadam Hussein at-Takriti

IRELAND, REPUBLIC OF

Local name Éire (Gaelic)

Timezone GMT

Area 70 282 sq km/27 129 sq mi

Population total (1990e) 3 509 000

Status Republic (occupying S, C, and NW Ireland; bounded NE by Northern Ireland, part of the UK)

Capital Dublin

Languages Irish Gaelic and English (official)

Ethnic groups Celtic (94%), small English minority

Religions Roman Catholic (95%), Anglican (Church of Ireland) (3%), Presbyterian (1%)

Physical features Mountainous landscapes in W, part of Caledonian system of Scandinavia and Scotland with quartzite peaks weathered into conical mountains such as Croagh Patrick, 765 m/2 510 ft; landscape of ridges and valleys in SW, rising towards Macgillycuddy's Reek Mts; lowlands in E drained by slow-moving rivers such as the Shannon (S), Liffey (E), and Slaney (SE).

Climate Mild and equable climate; average annual temperature 5°C (Jan), 15°C (Jul); rainfall heaviest in W, often over 3 000 mm/120 in.

Currency 1 Irish Pound/Punt (1£, IR£) = 100 new pence

Economy Primarily agriculture (two-thirds of country covered by improved agricultural land); forestry developed since 1950s; fishing; food, drink, tobacco, textiles; recent growth in light engineering; synthetic fibres, electronics, pharmaceuticals; several peat-fired power stations; Kinsale natural gas field near Cork; major tourist area; member of the EC, 1973.

GDP (1990) $33.9 bln, per capita $9690

History Occupied by Goidelic-speaking Celts during the Iron Age; conversion to Christianity by St Patrick, 5th-c; SE attacked by Vikings, c.800; Henry II of England declared himself lord of Ireland, 1171, but English influence restricted to area round Dublin (the Pale); Henry VIII took the title 'King of Ireland', 1542; Catholic rebellion during English Civil War suppressed by Oliver Cromwell, 1649–50; supporters of deposed Catholic King James II defeated by William III at Battle of the Boyne, 1690; struggle for Irish freedom developed in 18th–19th-c, including such revolutionary movements as Wolfe Tone's United Irishmen, 1796–8, and later Young Ireland, 1848, and the Fenians, 1866–7; Act of Union, 1801; Catholic Relief Act enabling Catholics to sit in parliament, 1829; Land Acts, 1870–1903, attacking Irish poverty; population reduced by half during famine, 1846; Home Rule Bills introduced by Gladstone, 1886, 1893; third Home Rule Bill passed in 1914, but never came into effect because of World War I; armed rebellion, 1916; republic proclaimed by Sinn Fein, 1919; partition proposed by Britain, 1920; treaty signed giving dominion status, 1921; right of Northern Ireland to opt out was exercised, and frontier agreed, 1925; renamed Éire, 1937; left Commonwealth, 1949; Anglo-Irish Agreement signed, 1985; a president (*Uachtarán na h'Éireann*) elected for seven years; prime minister (*Taoiseach*); National Parliament (*Oireachtas*) includes a House of Representatives (*Dail Éireann*) and a Senate (*Seanad Eireann*).

Head of State

1976–90 Patrick J Hillery
1990– Mary Robinson

Head of Government

1987–92 Charles Haughey
1992– Albert Reynolds

Counties of Ireland

County	Area sq km	sq mi	Population (1986)	Admin. centre
Carlow	896	346	40 988	Carlow
Cavan	1 891	730	53 965	Cavan
Clare	3 188	1 231	91 344	Ennis
Cork	7 459	2 880	412 735	Cork
Donegal	4 830	1 865	129 664	Lifford
Dublin	922	356	1 021 449	Dublin
Galway	5 939	2 293	178 552	Galway
Kerry	4 701	1 815	124 159	Tralee
Kildare	1 694	654	116 247	Naas
Kilkenny	2 062	796	73 186	Kilkenny
Laoighis (Leix)	1 720	664	53 284	Portlaoise
Leitrim	1 526	589	27 035	Carrick
Limerick	2 686	1 037	164 569	Limerick
Longford	1 044	403	31 496	Longford
Louth	821	317	91 810	Dundalk
Mayo	5 398	2 084	115 184	Castlebar
Meath	2 339	903	103 881	Trim
Monaghan	1 290	498	52 379	Monaghan
Offaly	1 997	771	59 835	Tullamore
Roscommon	2 463	951	54 592	Roscommon
Sligo	1 795	693	56 046	Sligo
Tipperary	4 254	1 642	136 619	Clonmel
Waterford	1 869	710	91 151	Waterford
Westmeath	1 764	681	63 379	Mullingar
Wexford	2 352	908	102 552	Wexford
Wicklow	2 025	782	94 542	Wicklow

ISLE OF MAN >> UNITED KINGDOM

ISRAEL

Local names Yisra'el (Hebrew), Isrā'īl (Arabic)

Timezone GMT + 2

Area 20 770 sq km/8 017 sq mi (within boundaries defined by 1949 armistice agreements)

Population total (1990e) 4 882 000 (excluding E Jerusalem and Israeli settlers in occupied territories)

Status State

Date of independence 1948

Capital Jerusalem

Languages Hebrew and Arabic (official), also European languages spoken

Ethnic groups Jewish (83%), Arab (11%)

Religions Jewish (85%), Muslim (11%), Christian and others (4%)

Physical features Extends 420 km/261 mi N–S; width varies from 20 km/12 mi to 116 km/72 mi; mountainous interior, rising to 1 208 m/3 963 ft at Mt Meron; mountains near Galilee (Lake Tiberius) and Samaria in the West Bank, dropping E to below sea-level in the Jordan–Red Sea rift valley; R Jordan forms part of E border; Dead Sea, between Israel and Jordan, −400 m/ −1 286 ft below sea level, is the largest lake and has no outlet; Negev desert (S) occupies c.60% of the country's area.

Climate Mediterranean climate in N and C, with hot, dry summers and warm, wet winters; average annual temperature 9°C (Jan), 23°C (Jul) in Jerusalem; rainfall 528 mm/21 in.

Currency 1 New Israeli Shekel (NIS) = 100 agorot

Economy Over 90% of exports are industrial products; major tourist area, primarily to the religious centres; copper, potash, phosphates, citrus fruits, cotton, sugar beet, bananas, beef and dairy products; a world leader in agrotechnology, with areas of intensive cultivation; the *kibbutz* system produces c.40% of food output, but in recent years has turned increasingly towards industry.

GNP (1990) $46.5 bln, per capita $10 500

History Zionist movement founded by Theodor Herzl, end of 19th-c; thousands of Jews returned to Palestine, then part of the Ottoman Empire; Britain given League of Nations mandate to govern Palestine and establish Jewish national home there, 1922; British evacuated Palestine, and Israel proclaimed independence, 1948; invasion by Arab nations, resulting in armistice, 1949; Israel gained control of the Gaza Strip, Sinai Peninsula (as far as the Suez Canal), West Bank of the R Jordan (including E sector of Jerusalem), and the Golan Heights in Syria, during the Six-Day War, 1967; Camp David conference between Egypt and Israel, 1978; Israeli withdrawal from Sinai, 1979; invasion of Lebanon, forcing the PLO to leave Beirut, 1982–5; renewed tension with uprising of Arabs in occupied territories (the *intifada*) since 1988; missile attacks by Iraq in Gulf War, 1991; a parliamentary democracy with a prime minister and a cabinet, and a unicameral parliament (*Knesset*); president elected for a maximum of two 5-year terms.

Head of State

1978–83 Yitzhak Navon
1983– Chaim Herzog

Head of Government

1988–92 Yitzhak Shamir
1992– Yitzhak Rabin

ITALY

Local name Italia

Timezone GMT + 1

Area 301 225 sq km/116 273 sq mi

Population total (1991e) 57 772 000

Status Republic

Capital Rome

Languages Italian (official), with German spoken in the Trentino-Alto Adige, French in Valle d'Aosta, and Slovene in Trieste-Gorizia

Ethnic groups Homogeneous (98%), with German–Italian, French–Italian, and Slovene–Italian minorities

Religions Roman Catholic (83%), non-religious (14%)

Physical features Comprises the boot-shaped peninsula extending south into the Mediterranean Sea, as well as Sicily, Sardinia and some smaller islands; Italian peninsula extends c.800 km/500 mi SE from the Lombardy plains; Apennines rise to peaks above 2 000 m/6 500 ft; Alps form a border in N; broad, fertile Lombardo-Venetian plain in basin of R Po; several lakes at foot of the Alps, including Maggiore, Como, and Garda; flat and marshy on Adriatic coast (N); coastal mountains descend steeply to the Ligurian Sea on the Riviera (W); Mt Vesuvius, 1 289 m/4 230 ft and Vulcano, 502 m/1 650 ft are also active volcanoes; island of Sicily separated from the mainland by the 4 km/2.5 mi wide Strait of Messina includes the volcanic cone of Mt Etna, 3 326 m/10 625 ft.

Regions of Italy

Climate Warm and temperate in S; hot and sunny summers, short cold winters; average annual temperatures 7°C (Jan), 25°C (Jul); average annual rainfall 657 mm/26 in; cold, wet, often snowy in higher peninsular areas; Mediterranean climate in coastal regions; Adriatic coast colder than the W coast, and receives less rainfall.

Currency 1 Italian Lira (L, Lit) = 100 centesimi

Economy Industry largely concentrated in N; machinery, iron and steel; tourism; poorer agricultural region in S; Po valley a major agricultural region, wheat, maize, sugar, potatoes, rice, beef, dairy farming; foothills of the Alps, apples, peaches, walnuts, wine; further S, citrus fruits, vines, olives, tobacco.

GDP (1990) $844 bln, per capita $14 600

History Inhabited by the Etruscans (N), Latins (C), and Greeks (S) in pre-Roman times; most regions part of the Roman Empire by 3rd-c BC; invaded by barbarian tribes in 4th-c AD; last Roman emperor deposed, 476; ruled by the Lombards and by the Franks under Charlemagne, who was crowned Emperor of the Romans in 800; part of the Holy Roman Empire under Otto, 962; conflict between popes and emperors throughout Middle Ages; dispute between Guelphs and Ghibellines, 12th-c; divided among five powers, 14th–15th-c (Kingdom of Naples, Duchy of Milan, republics of Florence and Venice, the papacy); major contribution to European culture through the Renaissance; numerous republics set up after the French Revolution; Napoleon crowned King of Italy, 1805; upsurge of liberalism and nationalism (*Risorgimento*) in 19th-c; unification achieved under Victor Emmanuel II of Sardinia, aided by Cavour and Garibaldi, by 1870; fought alongside Allies in World War I; Fascist movement brought Mussolini to power, 1922; conquest of Abyssinia, 1935–6, and Albania, 1939; alliance with Hitler in World War 2 led to the end of the Italian Empire; monarchy abolished, became a democratic republic, 1946;

parliament consists of a Chamber of Deputies and a Senate; President of the Republic is head of state and appoints a prime minister; continued political instability, with over 45 governments in power since the formation of the republic.

Head of State
1985–92 Francesco Cossiga
1992– Oscar Luigi Scalfaro

Head of Government
1989–92 Giulio Andreotti
1992– Giuliano Amato

JAMAICA

Local name Jamaica

Timezone GMT – 5

Area 10 957 sq km/4 229 sq mi

Population total (1991e) 2 489 000

Status Independent state within the Commonwealth

Date of independence 1962

Capital Kingston

Languages English (official), with Jamaican Creole widely spoken

Ethnic groups African (76%), Afro-European (15%), East Indian and Afro-Indian (3%), White (3%), Chinese and Afro-Chinese (1%)

Religions Christian (Protestant 56%, Roman Catholic 5%), non-religious (17%)

Physical features Third largest island in the Caribbean; maximum length, 234 km/145 mi; width, 35–82 km/22–51 mi; mountainous and rugged, particularly in the E, where the Blue Mt Peak rises to 2 256 m/ 7 401 ft; over 100 small rivers, several used for hydroelectric power.

Climate Humid, tropical climate at sea-level; more temperate at higher altitudes; average annual temperature 24°C (Jan), 27°C (Jul); mean annual rainfall 1 980 mm/ 70 in; virtually no rainfall on S and SW plain; lies within the hurricane belt.

Currency 1 Jamaican Dollar (J$) = 100 cents

Economy Plantation agriculture (still employs about a third of workforce); sugar, bananas, citrus fruits, coffee, cocoa, ginger, coconuts; bauxite (world's second largest producer); cement, fertilizer, textiles, rum, chemical products; tourism.

GDP (1990) $3.9 bln, per capita $150

History Visited by Columbus, 1494; settled by Spanish, 1509; West African slave labour imported for work on sugar plantations from 1640; British occupation, 1655; self-government, 1944; independence, 1962; governor-general appoints prime minister and cabinet; bicameral parliament consists of House of Representatives and a Senate.

Head of State
(British monarch represented by Governor-General)
1991– Howard Cooke

Head of Government
1989–1992 Michael Norman Manley
1992– Percival Patterson

JAPAN

Local name Nihon (Nippon)

Timezone GMT + 9

Area 381 945 sq km/147 431 sq mi

Population total (1991e) 124 017 000

Status Monarchy

Capital Tokyo

Language Japanese (official)

Ethnic groups Japanese (99%), with Korean minorities

Religions Shintoist (40%), Buddhist (39%), Christian (4%)

Physical features Island state comprising four large islands (Hokkaido, Honshu, Kyushu, Shikoku) and several small islands; consists mainly of steep mountains with many volcanoes; Hokkaido (N) central range runs N–S, rising to over 2 000 m/6 500 ft, falling to coastal uplands and plains; Honshu, the largest island, comprises parallel arcs of mountains bounded by narrow coastal plains; includes Mt Fuji, 3 776 m/12 388 ft; heavily populated Kanto plain in E; Shikoku and Kyushu (SW) consist of clusters of low cones and rolling hills,

Japan (continued)

mostly 1 000–2 000 m/3 000–6 000 ft; Ryukyu chain of volcanic islands to the S, largest Okinawa.

Climate Oceanic climate, influenced by the Asian monsoon; heavy winter rainfall on W coasts of Honshu and in Hokkaido; short, warm summers in N, and severe winters, with heavy snow; variable winter weather throughout Japan, especially in N and W; typhoons in summer and early autumn; mild and almost subtropical winters in S Honshu, Shikoku, and Kyushu; average annual temperatures 5°C (Jan), 25°C (Jul) in Tokyo.

Currency 1 Yen (¥, Y) = 100 sen

Economy Limited natural resources, (less than 20% of land under cultivation); intensive crop production (principally of rice); timber, fishing, engineering, shipbuilding, textiles, chemicals; major industrial developments since 1960s especially in computing, electronics, and vehicles.

GNP (1990) $2.1 trillion, per capita $17 100

History Originally occupied by the Ainu; developed into small states, 4th-c; culture strongly influenced by China, 8th–12th-c; ruled by feudal shoguns until power passed to the emperor, 1867; limited contact with the West until the Meiji Restoration, 1868; successful war with China, gained Formosa (Taiwan) and S Manchuria, 1894–5; war with Russia, 1904–5, Russia ceded southern half of Sakhalin; formed alliance with Britain, 1902; Korea annexed, 1910; joined allies in World War 1, 1914; received German Pacific islands as mandates, 1919; war with China, occupied Manchuria, 1931–2; renewed fighting, 1937; entered World War 2 with surprise attack on the US fleet at Pearl Harbour, Hawaii, 1941; occupied British and Dutch possessions in SE Asia, 1941–2; pushed back during 1943–5; atomic bombs dropped on Hiroshima and Nagasaki by allied forces, 1945, ended World War 2 with Japanese surrender; allied control commission took power, and Formosa and Manchuria returned to China; Emperor Hirohito became figurehead ruler, 1946; full sovereignty regained, 1952; joined United Nations, 1958; strong economic growth in 1960s; regained Bonin, Okinawa and Volcano Islands, 1972; a constitutional

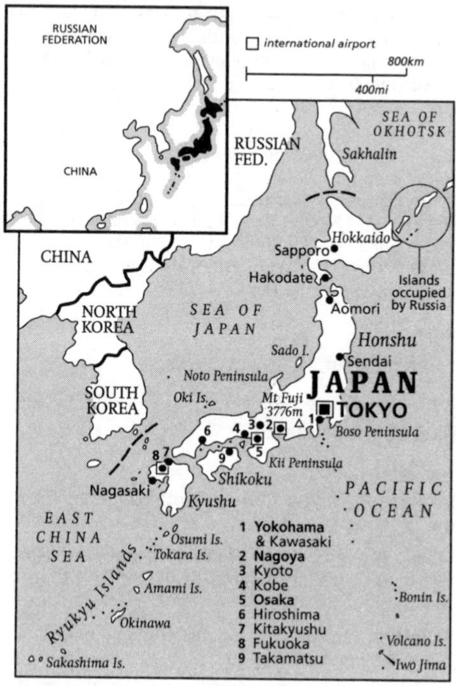

monarchy with an emperor as head of state; prime minister, cabinet; bicameral Diet (*Kokkai*), with a House of Representatives and a House of Councillors.

Head of State (Emperor)

1989– Akihito

Head of Government (Prime Minister)

1989–91 Toshiki Kaifu
1991–3 Kiichi Miyazawa
1993– Morihiro Hosokawa

JORDAN

Local name Al'Urdun

Timezone GMT + 2

Area 96 188 sq km/37 129 sq mi (including 6 644 sq km/2 565 sq mi in the West Bank)

Population total (1991e) 3 412 000

Status Hashemite kingdom

Date of independence 1946

Capital Amman

Language Arabic (official)

Ethnic groups Arab (99%), Circassian, Armenian, Turkish, Kurd minorities

Religions Muslim (Sunni 95%), Christian (including Roman Catholic, Anglican, Coptic, Greek Orthodox and Evangelical Lutheran) (5%)

Physical features Located in Middle East, divided N–S by Red Sea–Jordan rift valley, much lying below sea level; lowest point, −400 m/−1 312 ft at the Dead Sea; highest point, Jebel Ram, 1 754 m/5 754 ft; land levels out to the Syrian desert (E); c.90% of Jordan is desert.

Climate Mediterranean; hot, dry summers, cool, wet winters; desert area uniformly hot, sunny; rainfall below 200 mm/8 in; average annual temperatures 8°C (Jan), 25°C (Jul) in Amman.

Currency 1 Jordan Dinar = 1 000 fils

Economy Oil, cement, potash, phosphate (world's third largest exporter), light manufacturing; cereals, vegetables, citrus fruits, olives.

GDP (1987) $4.3 bln, (1988) per capita $1 127

History Part of Roman Empire; Arab control, 7th-c; part of Turkish Empire, 16th-c until World War 1; area divided into Palestine (W of R Jordan) and Transjordan (E of R Jordan), administered by Britain; independence as Transjordan, 1946; British mandate over Palestine ended, 1948; renamed Jordan, 1949; Israeli control of West Bank after Six-Day War, 1967; civil war, following attempts by Jordanian army to expel Palestinian guerrillas from West Bank, 1970–1; claims to the West Bank ceded to the Palestine Liberation Organisation, 1974; links with the West Bank cut, PLO established a government in exile, 1988; martial law formally abolished by King Hussein, 1992, and ban on political parties lifted; monarch is head of state and appoints a prime minister, who selects a Council of Ministers; parliament consists of Senate and House of Representatives.

Head of State (Monarch)

1952 – Hussein II

Head of Government

1991 Taher al-Masri

1991– Sharif Zaid bin Shaker

Golan Heights and West Bank occupied by Israel since 1967

KAZAKHSTAN

Local name Kazakhstan

Timezone GMT + 5

Area 2 717 300 sq km/1 048 878 sq mi

Population total (1992e) 16 700 000

Status Republic

Date of independence 1991

Capital Almaty (Alma-Ata)

Languages Kazakh (official), Russian and German

Ethnic groups Kazakh (40%), Russian (37%), German (6%), Ukrainian (5%)

Religions Muslim (Sunni), Christian (Russian Orthodox, Protestant)

Kazakhstan (continued)

Physical features Bounded E by China and W by Caspian Sea; second largest republic in former USSR; mountain ranges in E and SE; steppeland (N) gives way to desert (S); lowest elevation near the E shore of the Caspian Sea, 132 m/1 433 ft below sea-level; main rivers, the Irtysh, Syr Darya, Ural, and Ili; largest lake, L Balkhash; space launch centre at Tyuratam, near Baikonur.

Climate Continental; hot summers, extreme winters; wide range of temperatures, from −17°C in N and C ranges, to −3°C in S (Jan), 20°C in N, 29°C in S (Jul); strong, dry winds common in NW.

Currency (1992) 1 Rouble (R) = 100 kopecks

Economy Coal, iron ore, bauxite, copper, nickel, oil; oil refining, metallurgy, heavy engineering, chemicals, leatherwork, footwear, food processing; cotton, fruit, grain, sheep.

GNP (1992e) $41.7 bln, per capita $2 470

History Under the control of the Mongols, 13th-c; gradually under Russian rule, 1730–1853; became constituent republic of USSR, 1936; independence movement, 1990–1; independence declared, 1991, and joined new Commonwealth of Independent States (CIS); joined the CSCE (Conference on Security and Cooperation in Europe), 1992.

Head of State
1991– Nursultan A Nazarbayev

Head of Government
1991– Sergei Tereshchenko

KENYA

Local name Kenya

Timezone GMT + 3

Area 564 162 sq km/217 766 sq mi

Population total (1991e) 25 241 000

Status Republic

Date of independence 1963

Capital Nairobi

Languages English and Swahili (official), with many local languages spoken

Ethnic groups Kikuyu (21%), Luhya (14%), Luo (13%), Kalenjin (11%), Kamba (11%), Kisii (6%), Meru (6%)

Religions Christian (66%) (Roman Catholic 28%, Protestant 38%), local beliefs (26%), Muslim (6%)

Physical features Crossed by the Equator; SW plateau rises to 600–3 000 m/2 000–10 000 ft, includes Mt Kenya, 5 200 m/17 058 ft; Great Rift Valley (W) runs N–S; dry, arid semi-desert in the N, generally under 600 m/2 000 ft; rivers include Tana and Athi; L Turkana in NW.

Climate Tropical climate on coast, with high temperatures and humidity; average annual temperature 18 °C (Jan), 16°C (Jul) in Nairobi; average annual rainfall 958 mm/38 in.

Currency 1 Kenyan shilling (KSh) = 100 cents

Economy Agriculture (accounts for c.35% of national income); coffee, tea, cashew nuts, rice, wheat, maize, sugar cane; textiles, chemicals, cement, oil refining, tobacco, rubber; reserves of soda ash, salt, limestone, lead, gemstones, silver, gold; 14 national parks attract large numbers of tourists.

GDP (1990) $8.5 bln, per capita $380

History Very early fossil hominids found in the region by anthropologists; coast settled by Arabs, 7th-c; Portuguese control, 16th–17th-c; British control as East African Protectorate, 1895; British colony, 1920; independence movement led to Mau Mau rebellion, 1952–60; independence within the Commonwealth, 1963; declared Republic of Kenya, 1964; first leader, Jomo Kenyatta; anti-government riots for the approval of multi party politics, 1990; constitutional amendments passed, 1992; governed by a president with a unicameral National Assembly.

Head of State/Government
1978 – Daniel Arap Moi

KIRIBATI

Local name Kiribati

Timezone GMT – 12

Area 717 sq km/277 sq mi

Population total (1990e) 71 100

Status Republic

Date of independence 1979

Capital Bairiki (on Tarawa Atoll)

Languages English (official) and Gilbertese

Ethnic groups Micronesian, small Polynesian and non-Pacific minorities

Religions Roman Catholic (54%), Kiribati Protestant (39%), Baha'i (2%), Seventh-day Adventist (2%), Morman (2%)

Physical features Group of 33 low-lying islands scattered over c.3 000 000 sq km/1 200 000 sq mi of the C Pacific Ocean; comprises the Gilbert Is Group, Phoenix Is, and eight of the eleven Line Islands, including Christmas I; islands seldom rise to more than 4 m/13 ft; usually consist of a reef enclosing a lagoon.

Climate Maritime equatorial climate in central islands, tropical further N and S; periodic drought in some islands; wet season (Nov–Apr); subject to typhoons; average annual temperatures 28°C (Jan), 27°C (July) in Tarawa; average annual rainfall 1 977 mm/78 in.

Currency 1 Australian Dollar ($A) = 100 cents

Economy 50% of land under permanent cultivation; main exports include fish, particularly tuna, phosphates, copra, coconuts, bananas, pandanus, breadfruit, papaya, sea fishing.

GDP (1990) $36 mln, (1988) per capita $430

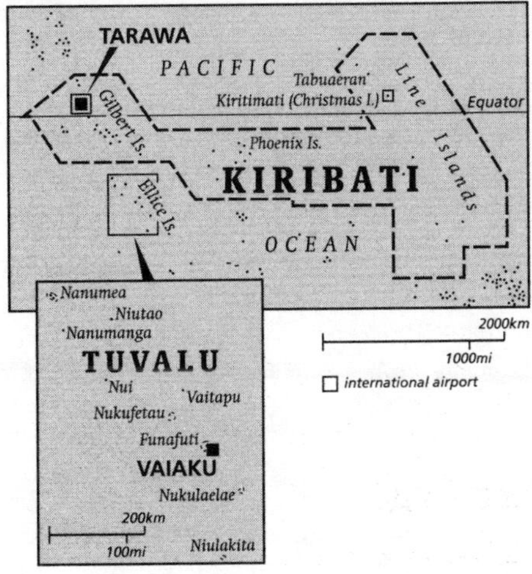

History Gilbert and Ellice Is proclaimed a British protectorate, 1892; became a Crown Colony, 1916; occupied by Japan during World War II, but driven out by US forces; Ellice Is severed links with Gilbert Is to form separate dependency of Tuvalu, 1975; Gilbert Is independence as Kiribati, 1979; a sovereign and democratic republic, with a president and an elected House of Assembly.

Head of State/Government

1979–91	Ieremia T Tabai
1991–	Teatao Teannaki

KOREA, NORTH

Local name Chŏson Minjujuŭi In'min Konghwaguk

Timezone GMT + 9

Area 122 098 sq km/47 130 sq mi

Population total (1990e) 22 937 000

Status Democratic people's republic

Date of independence 1948

Capital Pyongyang

Language Korean (official)

Ethnic groups Korean (99.8%), Chinese (0.2%)

Religions Atheist or non-religious (68%), Buddhist (2%), Christian (1%)

Physical features Located in E Asia, in the N half of the Korean peninsula; separated from South Korea to the S by a demilitarized zone of 1 262 sq km/487 sq mi; volcanic peak of Mount Paek-tu rises 2 744 m/9 003 ft in NE; Yalu river valley marks Korean-Chinese border in NW; fertile Chaeryong and Pyongyang plains in SW; 74% of land is forested, 18% is arable.

Climate Temperate; warm summers, severely cold winters; often rivers freeze for up to 3–4 months in winter; average annual temperatures –8°C (Jan), 24°C (Jul); average annual rainfall 916 mm/26 in.

Currency 1 Won (NKW) = 100 chon

Economy Agriculture (employs c.48% of workforce generally on large-scale collective farms); rice, maize, vegetables, livestock, wheat, barley, bean, tobacco; timber, fishing; severely affected during the Korean War, but rapid recovery with Soviet and Chinese aid; machine building, mining, chemicals, textiles.

GNP (1988) $20 bln, per capita $2 180

History (See KOREA, SOUTH history); formally annexed by Japan, 1910; N area occupied by Soviet troops following invasion by US and Russian troops and the dividing of the country into N and S, 1945; Democratic People's Republic of Korea declared, 1948; Korean War, 1950–3; demilitarized zone established, 1953; friendship and mutual assistance treaty signed with China, 1961; unsuccessful reunification talks, 1980; became a member of UN, 1991; non-aggression agreement signed

Korea, North (continued)

with S Korea, 1991; governed by a president and a Supreme People's Assembly.

Head of State

1972– Kim Il-sung

Head of Government

1988–92 Yon Hyong-muk
1992– Kang Song San

KOREA, SOUTH

Local name Taehan-Min'guk

Timezone GMT + 9

Area 98 913 sq km/38 180 sq mi

Population total (1991e) 43 134 000

Status Republic

Date of independence 1948

Capital Seoul

Language Korean (official)

Ethnic groups Korean (99.9%), Chinese (0.1%)

Religions Buddhist (18%), Christian (Protestant 41%, Roman Catholic 3%), Confucianist (1%)

Physical features Occupies the S half of the Korean peninsula; bordered N by North Korea, from which it is separated by a demilitarized zone at 38°N; Taebaek Sanmaek Mt range runs N–S along the E coast; descends to broad, undulating coastal lowlands; rivers include Naktong and Han; c.3 000 islands off the W and S coasts; largest island is Cheju do, which contains Korea's highest peak, Hallasan, 1 950 m/6 398 ft.

Climate Extreme continental climate, cold winters, hot summers; average annual temperatures −5°C (Jan), 25°C (Jul); average annual rainfall 1 250 mm/49 in.

Currency 1 Won (W) = 100 chon

Economy Light consumer goods, with a shift towards heavy industries; petrochemicals, textiles, electrical machinery, steel, ships, fish; one of the world's largest deposits of tungsten; only a fifth of land suitable for cultivation; rice, wheat, barley, grain, pulses, tobacco.

GNP (1990) $238 bln, per capita $5 600

History Originally split into three rival kingdoms,

united in 668 AD by the Silla dynasty; succeeded by the Koryo dynasty, 935 AD; Yi dynasty, 1392–1910; independence recognized by China, 1895; annexation by Japan, 1910; entered by Russia (from N) and USA (from S) to enforce the Japanese surrender, dividing the country in N and S at the 38th parallel, 1945; declared Republic of Korea, 1948; North Korean forces invaded, 1950; UN forces assisted South Korea in stopping the advance, 1950–3; military coup, 1961; assassination of Park Chung Hee, 1979; became a member of UN, 1991; non-aggresion pact signed with N Korea, 1991; governed by a president, a State Council, and a National Assembly.

Head of State
1988–93 Roh Tae-woo
1993– Kim Young Sam

Head of Government
1988–90 Kang Young-hoon
1990–1 Ro Jai-bong
1991–2 Chung Won-shik
1992–3 Hyun Soong Jong
1993– Hwang In Sung

KUWAIT

Local name Dowlat al Kuwait (Arabic)

Timezone GMT + 3

Area 17 818 sq km/6 878 sq mi

Population total (1991e) 2 024 000

Status Independent state

Date of independence 1961

Capital Kuwait City

Language Arabic (official)

Ethnic groups Kuwaiti (42%), non-Kuwaiti Arab (40%), Asian (3%)

Religions Muslim (90%), Christian (8%), Hindu (2%)

Physical features Consists of mainland and nine offshore islands; terrain flat or gently undulating, rising SW to 271 m/889 ft; Wadi al Batin on W border with Iraq; low ridges in NE generally stony with sparse vegetation.

Climate Hot and dry climate; summer temperatures very high, often above 45°C (Jul–Aug); humidity often over 90%; sandstorms common all year; average annual temperature 14°C (Jan), 37°C (Jul) in Kuwait City; average annual rainfall 111 mm/4 in.

Currency 1 Kuwaiti Dinar (KD) = 1 000 fils

Economy Oil discovered, 1938, and before the Gulf War provided 95% of government revenue; active programme of economic diversification; petrochemicals, fertilizers, construction materials, asbestos, batteries; agriculture gradually expanding; dates, citrus fruits, timber, livestock.

GDP (1989) $19.9 bln, per capita $19 700

History Port founded in 18th-c; British protectorate, 1914; full independence from Britain, 1961; invasion and annexation by Iraq (Aug 1990), leading to Gulf War (Jan–Feb 1991), with severe damage to Kuwait City, Kuwaiti government-in-exile in Saudi Arabia; Kuwait liberated with the aid of UN forces, 1991, and government returned from exile; new Cabinet formed headed by Crown Prince as prime minister; large refugee emigration; major post-war problems, including burning of Kuwaiti oil wells by Iraq and pollution of Gulf waters by oil; Emir is head of state, governing through an appointed prime minister and Council of Ministers.

Head of State (Emir)
1978– Jabir al-Ahmad al-Jabir

Head of Government (Prime Minister)
1978– Saad al-Abdallah al-Salim

KYRGYZSTAN

Local name Kyrgyzstan

Timezone GMT + 5

Area 198 500 sq km/76 621 sq mi

Population total (1990e) 4 400 000

Status Republic

Date of independence 1991

Capital Bishkek (formerly Frunze)

Language Kyrgyz (official)

Ethnic groups Kyrgyz (52%), Russian (21%), other (27%)

Religion Sunni Muslim (chief religion)

Physical features Located in C Asia, bounded SE and E by China; largely occupied by the Tien Shan Mts; highest point within the republic at Pik Pobedy, 7 439 m/24 406 ft; chief river, the Naryn; largest lake, L Issyk-Kul.

Climate Typical desert climate in N, W, and SE; hot, dry summers in valleys; mean annual temperature −18°C (Jan), 28°C (Jul).

Currency (1992) 1 Rouble (R) = 100 kopecks

Economy Metallurgy; machines; coal; natural gas; textiles, food processing, gold; wheat, cotton, tobacco, animal husbandry.

GNP (1992e) $6.9 bln, per capita $1 550

History Part of an independent Turkestan republic,

1917–24; proclaimed a constituent republic of the USSR, 1936; state of emergency declared in Bishkek, Askar Akayev chosen by Supreme Soviet as state president, 1990; declaration of independence, 1991, and joined new Commonwealth of Independent States (CIS); joined the CSCE (Conference on Security and Cooperation in Europe), 1992.

Head of State/Government

1990– Askar Akayev

LAOS

Local name Lao

Timezone GMT + 7

Area 236 800 sq km/91 405 sq mi

Population total (1991e) 4 113 000

Status Republic

Date of independence 1949

Capital Vientiane

Languages Lao (official), French and tribal languages

Ethnic groups Laotian (60%), hill tribes (35%)

Religions Buddhist (58%), animist (largely the Lao-Theung) (34%), Christian (2%)

Physical features Landlocked country on the Indo-Chinese peninsula; dense jungle and rugged mountains (E), rising to 2 751 m/9 025 ft on Vietnamese border, and 2 820 m/9 252 ft at Phou Bia on the Xieng Khouang plateau; Mekong R flows NW–SE, fertile Mekong flood-plains in W; 4% of land is arable, 58% forested.

Climate Monsoonal climate; average annual rainfall 1 715 mm/67.5 in; (heaviest, May–Sep); average annual temperature 21°C (Jan), 27°C (Jul) in Vientiane.

Currency (1992) 1 Kip (Kp) = 100 at

Economy Agricultural economy suffered severely in

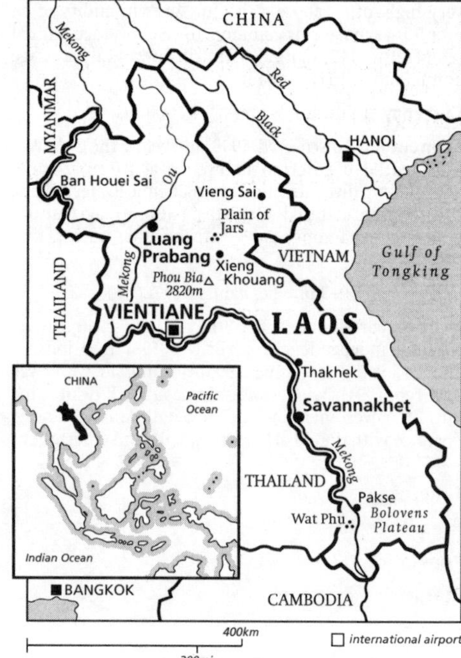

the civil war; rice, coffee, tobacco, cotton, spices, opium; tin, iron ore, potash; forestry, rubber, cigarettes, matches; textiles.

GDP (1990) $600 mln, per capita $150

History Visited by Europeans, 17th-c; French protectorate, 1893; occupied by Japanese in World War 2; independence from France, 1949; civil war, 1953–75, between the Lao government, supported by the USA, and the communist-led Patriotic Front *(Pathet Lao)*, supported by North Vietnam; monarchy abolished and communist republic established, 1975; headed by a president and governed by a prime minister.

Head of State

1987–91 Phoumi Vongvichit
1991–2 Kaysone Phomvihane
1992– Nouhak Phoumsavan

Head of Government

1975–91 Kaysone Phomvihane
1991– Khamtay Siphandon

LATVIA

Local name Latvija (Latvian)

Timezone GMT + 2

Area 63 700 sq km/24 600 sq mi

Population total (1990e) 2 700 000

Status Republic

Date of independence 1991

Capital Riga

Language Latvian (official)

Ethnic groups Latvian (52%), Russian (34%), Belorussian (5%), Ukrainian (4%), Polish (2%), Lithuanian (1%)

Religions Predominantly Evangelical Lutheran, with Orthodox and Roman Catholic minorities

Physical features Flat, glaciated region; highest point, central Vidzeme (Livonia) elevation, 312 m/1 024 ft; over 40% forested; coastline ranges over 472 km/293 mi; wooded lowland, marshes, lakes; NW coast indented by the Gulf of Riga; chief river, the Daugava.

Climate Mild climate, with high humidity; only c.30–40 days of sunshine annually; summers cool and rainy; average mean temperature −2°C (Jan), 17°C (Jul); average annual rainfall 700–800 mm/28–31 in.

Currency (1991) 1 Latvian Rouble (R) = 100 kopecks (new currency planned: lat)

Economy Machine-building, metalworking, electrical engineering, electronics, chemicals, furniture, food processing, fishing, timber, paper and woollen goods, meat and dairy products.

GDP Not available

History Incorporated into USSR, 1721; independent state, 1918–40; proclaimed a Soviet Socialist Republic, 1940; occupied by Germany in World War 2; USSR regained control, 1944; nationalism overt from 1988; coalition government elected, 1989; declared independence, 1991; Congress of Latvia instituted and granted United Nations membership, 1991.

Head of State

1991–3 Anatolijs Gorbunovs
1993– Guntis Ulmanis

Head of Government

1991– Ivars Godmanis

LEBANON

Local names Al-Lubnān (Arab), Liban (French)

Timezone GMT + 2

Area 10 452 sq km/4 034 sq mi

Population total (1991e) 3 384 000

Status Republic

Date of independence 1941

Capital Beirut

Languages Arabic (official), French, English and Armenian also spoken

Ethnic groups Arab (83%), Palestinian (9%), Armenian (5%), Syrian, Kurdish, Turkish and Greek (3%)

Religions Muslim (c.75%), Christian (c.25%), also c.17 religious sects including Armenian, Greek, Roman Catholic, Alawite, Druze and Jewish

Lebanon (continued)

Physical features Narrow coastal plain rises gradually E to the Lebanon Mts (Jebel Liban) rising to 3 087 m/ 10 128 ft at Qornet es Saouda; arid E slopes fall abruptly to the fertile El Beqaa plateau, average elevation 1 000 m/ 3 300 ft; Anti-Lebanon range (Jebel esh Sharqi) in the E; R Litani flows S between the two ranges.

Climate Mediterranean climate, varying with altitude; hot, dry summers, warm, moist winters; average annual temperatures 13°C (Jan), 27°C (Jul); average annual rainfall 920 mm/36 in; much drier and cooler in the Bekaa valley.

Currency 1 Lebanese Pound/Livre (LL, £L) = 100 piastres

Economy Commercial and financial centre of the Middle East until the civil war, which severely damaged economic infrastructure and reduced industrial and agricultural production; oil refining, textiles, chemicals, food processing; citrus fruits, apples, grapes, bananas, sugar beet, olives, wheat; tourism has virtually collapsed.

GDP (1990) $3.3 bln, per capita $1 000

History Part of the Ottoman Empire from 16th-c; after the massacre of (Catholic) Maronites by (Muslim) Druzes in 1861, Maronite area around Jabal Lubnan granted special autonomous status; Greater Lebanon, based on this area, created in 1920 under French mandate; Muslim coastal regions incorporated, despite great opposition; constitutional republic, 1926; independence, 1941; Palestinian resistance units established in Lebanon by late 1960s despite government opposition, including the Palestine Liberation Organization (PLO); several militia groups developed in the mid-1970s; following terrorist attacks, Israel invaded S Lebanon, 1978 and 1982; heavy Israeli bombardment of Beirut forced the withdrawal of Palestinian forces, 1982; unilateral withdrawal of Israeli and Syrian forces from Lebanon brought clashes between the Druze (backed by Syria) and Christian Lebanese militia; ceasefire announced in late 1982, broken many times since; Syrian troops entered Beirut in 1988 in an attempt to restore order; release of Western hostages taken by militant groups began, 1990; timetable for militia disarmament introduced, 1991; constitution (in semi-suspension since 1988) provides for a Council of Ministers, president (a Maronite Christian), prime minister (a Sunni Muslim), cabinet, and parliament, equally divided between Christians and Muslims.

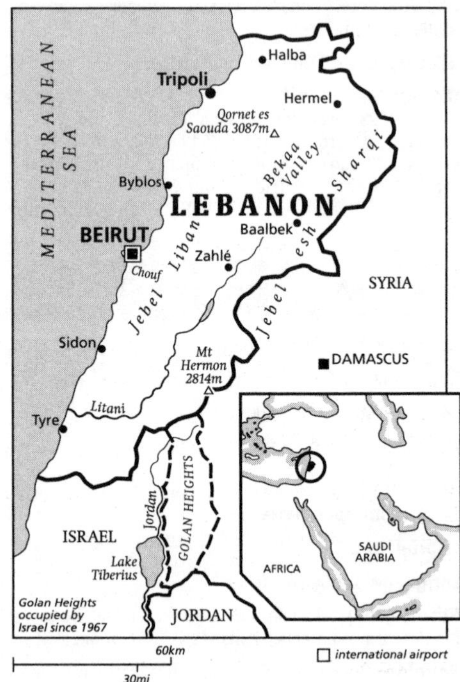

Head of State

1989– Elias Hrawi

Head of Government

1990 Selim al-Hoss
1990–92 Umar Karami
1992 Rashid al-Solh
1992– Rafiq al-Hariri

LESOTHO

Local name Lesotho

Timezone GMT + 3

Area 30 460 sq km/11 758 sq mi

Population total (1991e) 1 801 000

Status Independent kingdom within the Commonwealth

Date of independence 1960

Capital Maseru

Languages Lesotho (Sesotho) and English (official), Zulu, Afrikaans, French, Xhosa also spoken

Ethnic groups Sotho (99%), Zulu, Tembu and Fingo tribes, European and Asian minorities

Religions Roman Catholic (44%), Protestant (mostly Lesotho Evangelical) (30%), Anglican (12%), other Christian (8%), traditional beliefs (6%)

Physical features S African kingdom completely bounded by South Africa; Drakensberg Mts in NE and E, highest peak Thabana-Ntlenyana, 3 482 m/11 424 ft; serious soil erosion, especially in W; main rivers, the Orange and the Caledon; mountainous land, particularly in SW with the Maloti Mountain range.

Climate Mild, dry winters; warm summer season (Oct–Apr); average annual temperatures 15°C (Jan), 25°C (Jul); average annual rainfall 725 mm/28.5 in (Oct–Apr).

Currency 1 Loti (*plural* Maloti) (M, LSM) = 100 lisente

Economy Economy based on intensive agriculture and contract labour working in South Africa; wheat, peas, beans, barley, cattle; diamonds, textiles, pharmaceuticals; jewellery, crafts, wool, mohair.

GDP (1990) $420 mln, per capita $240

History Originally inhabited by hunting and gathering bushmen; Bantu arrived 16th-c, and Basotho nation established; incorporated in Orange Free State, 1854; under British protection as Basutoland, 1869; independence, 1960; declared Kingdom of Lesotho, 1966, as a hereditary monarchy within the Commonwealth; constitution suspended and country ruled by Council of Ministers, 1970–86; prime minister deposed by coup and political activity banned, 1986, with Military Council as effective ruling body; King Moshoeshoe dethroned by military council, 1990, and replaced by eldest son; Ramaema took over as Chairman of the Military Council following bloodless coup, 1991; civilian government introduced and role of prime minister recreated to replace Chairman of Military Council, Jun 1993.

Head of State (Monarch)
1966–90 Moshoeshoe II
1990– Letsie III

Head of Government (Chairman of Military Council until 1993, now Prime Minister)
1986–91 Justin Metsing Lekhanya
1991–93 Elias Tutsoane Ramaema
1993– Ntsu Mokhehle

LIBERIA

Local name Liberia

Timezone GMT

Area 113 370 sq km/43 800 sq mi

Population total (1991e) 2 730 000

Status Republic

Date of independence 1847

Capital Monrovia

Languages English (official) with 20 dialects/languages of Niger-Congo spoken

Ethnic groups Indigenous tribes (including Kpelle, Bassa, Gio, Kru, Gola, Kissi, Vai and Bella) (95%), Americo-Liberians (repatriated slaves from the USA) (5%)

Religions Traditional animist beliefs (70%), Muslim (20%), Christian (10%)

Physical features Low coastal belt with lagoons, beaches and mangrove marshes; land rises inland to mountains, reaching 1 752 m/5 748 ft at Mt Nimba; rivers include Mano, Moro, St Paul, St John, Cess, Duoubé and Cavalla.

Climate Equatorial climate; high temperatures, abundant rainfall; high humidity during rainy season (Apr–Sep), especially on coast; average annual temperatures 26°C (Jan), 24°C (Jul); average annual rainfall 5 138 mm/202 in.

Currency 1 Liberian Dollar (L$) = 100 cents

Economy Based on minerals, especially iron ore; two-thirds of the population rely on subsistence agriculture; rubber, timber, palm oil, rice, cassava, coffee, cocoa, coconuts; large merchant fleet, including the registration of many foreign ships.

GNP (1989) $1.0 bln, per capita $440

Liberia (continued)

History Mapped by the Portuguese, 15th-c; created as a result of the activities of several US philanthropic societies, wishing to establish a homeland for former slaves; founded in 1822; constituted as the Free and Independent Republic of Liberia, 1847; military coup and assassination of president, 1980, established a People's Redemption Council, with a chairman and a cabinet; new constitution, 1984, with an elected Senate and House of Representatives; civil war, followed by arrival of West African peacekeeping force, 1990; interim Government of National Unity installed.

Head of State/Government

1986–90 Samuel K Doe

1990– Amos Sawyer *Acting*

LIBYA

Local name Lībiyā

Timezone GMT + 1

Area 1 758 610 sq km/678 823 sq mi

Population total (1991e) 4 350 000

Status Republic

Date of independence 1951

Capital Tripoli

Languages Arabic (official), with English and French widely spoken

Ethnic groups Berber and Arab (96%), Greek, Maltese, Italian, Egyptian, Pakistani, Turk, Indian and Tunisian minorities (3%)

Religions Sunni Muslim (96%), Christian (Roman Catholic, Anglican, Coptic Orthodox) (3%), Jewish (1%)

Physical features Mainly low-lying Saharan desert or semi-desert; 93% of land is contained in the arid Saharan plateau; land rises (S) to over 2 000 m/6 500 ft in the Tibesti massif; highest point, Pic Bette, 2 286 m/7 500 ft; comparatively fertile region in Gefara plain and Jabal Nafusah plateau in Tripolitania region.

Climate Mediterranean climate on coast; rainy season (Oct–Mar) in NW and NE upland regions; average annual temperature 11°C (Jan), 27°C (Jul) in Tripoli; average annual rainfall 400 mm/15.7 in.

Currency 1 Libyan Dinar (LD) = 1 000 dirhams

Economy Former agricultural economy; barley, olives, fruit, dates, almonds, tobacco; relatively poor until economy transformed by discovery of oil and natural gas, 1959; petroleum processing; iron, steel, aluminium; textiles; nomadic farming in S.

GNP (1989) $24 bln, (1986) per capita $5 500

History Controlled by Phoenicians, Carthaginians, Greeks, Vandals, and Byzantines; Arab domination during 7th-c; Turkish rule from 16th-c; Italians gained control, 1911; named Libya by the Italians, 1934; heavy fighting during World War 2, followed by British and French control; independent Kingdom of Libya, 1951; military coup established a republic under Muammar al-Gaddafi, 1969; governed by a Revolutionary Command Council; foreign military installations closed down in early 1970s; Libyan troops occupied Aozou Strip, 1973; strained relations with other countries due to controversial activities, including alleged organization of international terrorism; diplomatic relations severed by UK after the murder of a policewoman in London, 1984; Tripoli and Benghazi bombed by US Air Force in response to alleged terrorist activity, 1986; Libya and Chad presented their individual territorial claims to Aozou Strip, 1990.

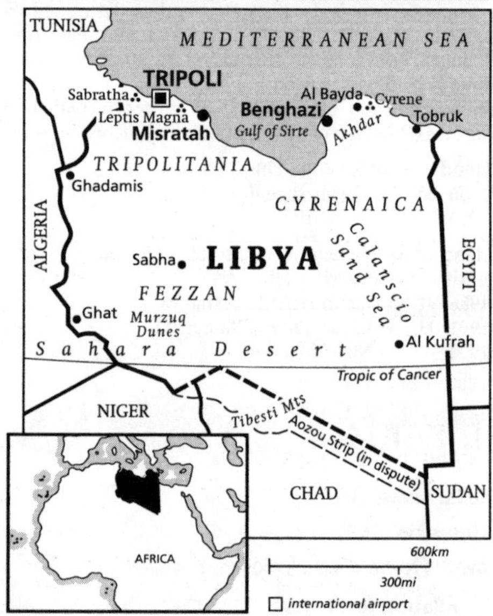

Head of State/Government

1969– Muammar al-Gaddafi

LIECHTENSTEIN

Local name Liechtenstein

Timezone GMT + 1

Area 160 sq km/62 sq mi

Population total (1990e) 28 700

Status Independent principality

Date of independence 1719

Capital Vaduz

Language German (official)

Ethnic groups Liechtensteiner (64%), Swiss (16%), Austrian (8%), German (4%)

Religions Roman Catholic (87%), Protestant (9%)

Physical features Alpine principality, located in C Europe; fourth smallest country in the world; land boundary 76 km/47 mi; bounded W by the R Rhine; mean altitude, 450 m/1 475 ft; forested mountains rise to 2 599 m/8 527 ft in the Grauspitz; Samina River flows N.

Climate Mild, equable climate; temperatures range from −15°C (Jan), 20–28°C (Jul); average annual rainfall 1 050–1 200 mm/41–47 in.

Currency 1 Swiss Franc (SFr, SwF) = 100 centimes

Economy Industrial sector developing since 1950s; export-based, centred on specialized and high-tech production; metal-working, engineering, chemicals, pharmaceuticals; international banking and finance; tourism.

GDP (1987) $1 bln, per capita $32 000

History Became a sovereign state, 1342; independent principality within Holy Roman Empire, 1719; part of Holy Roman Empire until 1806; became a sovereign state, 1342; adopted Swiss currency, 1921; united with Switzerland in a customs union, 1923; became a member of UN, 1990; joined European Free Trade Association (EFTA), 1991; constitutional monarchy ruled by hereditary princes of the House of Liechtenstein; governed by prime minister, four councillors, and unicameral parliament.

Head of State (Monarch)
1989– Hans Adam II

Head of Government
1978– Hans Brunhart

LITHUANIA

Local name Lietuva

Timezone GMT + 2

Area 65 200 sq km/25 167 sq mi

Population total (1990e) 3 700 000

Status Republic

Date of independence 1991

Capital Vilnius

Language Lithuanian (official)

Ethnic groups Lithuanian (80%), Russian (9%), Polish (7%), Belorussian (2%)

Religions Roman Catholic, small minority of Evangelical Lutherans and Evangelical Reformists

Physical features Glaciated plains cover much of the area; central lowlands with gentle hills in W and higher terrain in SE; highest point, Jouzapine in the Asmenos Hills, 294 m/964 ft; 25% forested; some 3 000 small lakes mostly in E and SE; complex sandy dunes on Kursiu Marios lagoon; chief river, the Nemunas.

Climate Continental climate, affected by maritime weather of W Europe and continental E; Baltic Sea influences a narrow coastal zone; average annual temperatures −5°C (Jan), 16°C (Jul); average annual rainfall 630 mm/25 in.

Currency (1991) 1 Rouble (R) = 100 kopecks
(new currency planned: litas)

Economy Electrical engineering, computer hardware, instruments, machine tools, ship building; synthetic fibres, fertilizers, plastics, food processing, oil refining; cattle, pigs, poultry, grain, potatoes, vegetables.

GDP Not available

History United with Poland, 1385–1795; intensive russification led to revolts, 1905, 1917; occupied by Germany in both World Wars; proclaimed a republic, 1918; annexed by the USSR, 1940; growth of nationalist movement in the late 1980s; declared independence, 1990, but not recognised until 1991.

Head of State
1991–2 Vytautas Landsbergis
1992– Algirdas Brazauskas

Head of Government
1991–2 Gediminas Vagnorius
1992 Aleksandras Abisala
1992– Bronislovas Lubys

LUXEMBOURG

Local names Lëtzebuerg (Letz), Luxembourg (French), Luxemburg (German)

Timezone GMT + 1

Area 2586 sq km/998 sq mi

Population total (1991e) 388000

Status Grand Duchy

Date of independence 1867

Capital Luxembourg

Languages French, German, Letzeburgesch

Ethnic groups Luxemburger (73%), Portuguese (9%), Italian (5%), French (3%), Belgian (3%), German (2%)

Religions Roman Catholic (97%), Protestant (2%), Jewish (1%)

Physical features Divided into the two natural regions of Ardennes (Ösling) (N); forest in N, and Gutland in S, flatter, average height 250 m/820 ft; principal rivers include the Sûre, Our and Moselle.

Climate Mild climate, influenced by warm S wind (*Fröhn*); average annual temperatures 0.7°C (Jan), 18°C (Jul) in Luxembourg; average annual rainfall, 1050–1200 mm/41–47 in.

Currency 1 Luxembourg Franc (LFr) = 100 centimes

Economy Important international centre based in city of Luxembourg; iron and steel, food processing; chemicals, tyres, metal products; mixed farming, dairy farming; wine; forestry; tourism.

GDP (1990) $6.9 bln, per capita $18000

History Made a Grand Duchy by the Congress of Vienna, 1815; granted political autonomy, 1838; recognized as a neutral independent state, 1867; occupied by Germany in both World Wars; joined Benelux economic union, 1948; neutrality abandoned on joining NATO, 1949; a hereditary monarchy with the Grand Duke as head of state; Parliament consists of Chamber of Deputies and State Council; head of government is the Minister of State.

Head of State (Grand Dukes and Duchesses)

1919–64	Charlotte (*in exile, 1940–44*)
1964–	Jean

Head of Government

1984–	Jacques Santer

MACAO >> PORTUGAL

MACEDONIA, FORMER YUGOSLAV REPUBLIC OF

Local name Makedonija

Timezone GMT + 2

Area 25713 sq km/9925 sq mi

Population total (1991) 2033964

Status Republic

Date of independence 1991

Capital Skopje

Language Macedonian (Slavic language belonging to the Indo-European family)

Ethnic groups (1981) Macedonian Slav (67%), Albanian (21%), Turk (4%), Serbian (3%), Bulgarian and Greek minorities

Religions Macedonian Orthodox Christian, Muslim

Physical features Landlocked, mountainous region, bordered by Serbia, Bulgaria, Greece and Albania; divided from Greek Macedonia by the Kožuf and Nidže ranges, highest point, Korab, 2764 m/9068 ft; main rivers, Struma and Vardar.

Climate Continental; average annual temperatures 0°C (Jan), 24°C (Jul); often heavy winter snowfalls; average annual rainfall 500 mm/20 in.

Currency (1992) Dinar

Economy Agriculture; wheat, barley, corn, rice, tobacco; sheep, cattle; mining of minerals, iron ore, lead, zinc, nickel; steel, chemicals, textiles.

GDP Not available

History Part of Macedonian, Roman and Byzantine Empires; settled by Slavs in 6th-c; conquered by Bulgars,

7th-c; and by Serbia, 14th-c; incorporated into Serbia after the Balkan Wars; united, 1918, in what later became Yugoslavia, but continuous demands for autonomy persisted; occupied by Bulgaria during World War 2, 1941–44; declaration of independence, 1991; international discussions continue over the name under which the country will be accorded international recognition (the adjacent province of Greece bears the name Macedonia).

Head of State
1991– Kiro Gligorov

Head of Government
1991– Branko Crvenkovski

MADAGASCAR

Local name Madagasikara

Timezone GMT + 3

Area 592 800 sq km/228 821 sq mi

Population total (1991e) 12 185 000

Status Republic

Date of independence 1960

Capital Antananarivo

Languages Malagasy (official), with French widely spoken

Ethnic groups Malagasy (99%) (including Merina 26%, Betsimisaraka 15%, Betsileo 12%)

Religions Traditional animist beliefs (52%), Christian (40%) (Roman Catholic 26%, Protestant 23%), Muslim (7%)

Physical features World's fifth largest island, length (N–S) 1 580 km/982 mi; dissected N–S by a ridge of mountains (Tsaratananan Range), rising to 2 876 m/9 436 ft at Maromokotra; cliffs (E) drop down to a coastal plain through tropical forest; terraced descent (W) through savannah to coast, heavily indented in N.

Climate Tropical, variable rainfall; average annual rainfall 1 000–1 500 mm/40–60 in, higher in tropical coastal region; average annual temperatures 21 °C (Jan), 15 °C (Jul).

Currency 1 Madagascar Franc (FMG, MgFr) = 100 centimes

Economy Chiefly agricultural economy; rice, manioc, coffee, sugar, vanilla, cotton, peanuts, tobacco, livestock; food processing, tanning, cement, soap, paper, textiles, oil products; graphite, chrome, coal, ilmenite.

GDP (1990) $2.5 bln, per capita $200

History Settled by Indonesians, 1st-c AD and by African

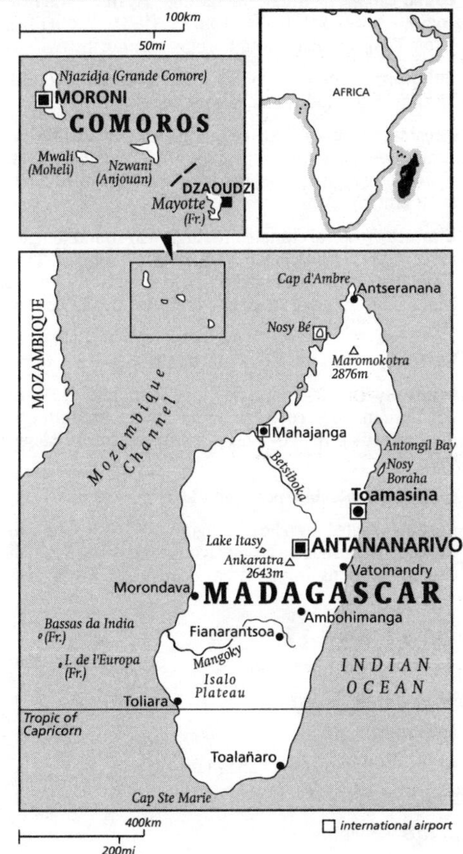

Madagascar (continued)

traders, 8th-c; visited by Portuguese, 16th-c; French established trading posts, late 18th-c; claimed as a protectorate by the French, 1895; autonomous overseas French territory (Malagasy Republic), 1958; independence, 1960; became Madagascar, 1977; governed by a president, who appoints a Council of Ministers and is guided by a Supreme Revolutionary Council; National People's Assembly elected every five years.

Head of State
1975– Didier Ratsiraka

Head of Government
1991– Guy Willy Razanamasy

MADEIRA (ISLANDS) >> PORTUGAL

MALAWI

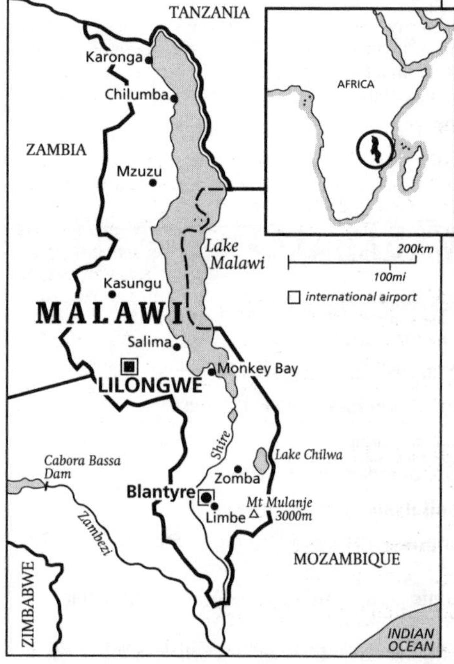

Local name Malawi (Malaêi)

Timezone GMT + 2

Area 118 484 sq km/45 735 sq mi

Population total (1991e) 9 438 000

Status Republic

Date of independence 1964

Capital Lilongwe

Languages English and Chichewa (official)

Ethnic groups Maravi (including Nyanja, Chewa, Tonga, Tumbuka) (60%), Lomwe (18%), Yao (13%), Ngoni (7%), also Asian and European minorities

Religions Protestant (55%), Roman Catholic (20%), Muslim (20%), traditional animist beliefs (3%)

Physical features Crossed N–S by the Great Rift Valley; contains Africa's third largest lake, L Malawi; main river, Shire; Shire highlands (S) rise to nearly 3 000 m/10 000 ft at Mt Mulanje.

Climate Tropical climate in S; high year-round temperatures, 28–37°C; average annual temperatures 23°C (Jan), 16°C (Jul) in Lilongwe; average annual rainfall, 740 mm/30 in; more moderate temperatures in central areas.

Currency 1 Kwacha (MK) = 100 tambala

Economy Based on agriculture (employs 90% of population); tobacco, sugar, tea, cotton, groundnuts, maize; textiles, matches, cigarettes, beer, spirits, shoes, cement.

GDP (1990) $1.6 bln, per capita $175

History Visited by the Portuguese 17th-c; European contact established by David Livingstone, 1859; Scottish church missions in the area; claimed as the British Protectorate of Nyasaland, 1891; British colony, 1907; in the 1950s joined with N and S Rhodesia to form the Federation of Rhodesia and Nyasaland; independence, 1964; republic, 1966; governed by a president, cabinet and National Assembly.

Head of State/Government
1966– Hastings Kamuzu Banda

MALAYSIA

Local name Malaysia

Timezone GMT + 8

Area 329 749 sq km/127 283 sq mi

Population total (1991e) 17 981 000

Status Republic

Date of independence 1957

Capital Kuala Lumpur

Languages Bahasa Malaysia (Malay) (official), also Chinese, English and Tamil widely spoken

Ethnic groups Malay (59%), Chinese (32%), Indian (9%)

Religions Muslim (53%), Buddhist (17%), Chinese folk-religionist (12%), Hindu (7%), Christian (6%)

Physical features Independent federation of states located in SE Asia, comprising 11 states and a federal territory in Peninsular Malaysia, and the E States of Sabah and Sarawak on the island of Borneo; mountain chain of granite and limestone running N–S, rising to Mt Tahan, 2 189 m/7 182 ft; peninsula length 700 km/435 mi, width up to 320 km/200 mi; mostly tropical rainforest and mangrove swamp; Mt Kinabalu on Sabah, Malaysia's highest peak, 4 094 m/13 432 ft.

Climate Tropical climate strongly influenced by monsoon winds; high humidity; average annual rainfall in the peninsula, 260 mm/10 in (S), 800 mm/32 in (N); average daily temperatures, 21–32°C in coastal areas, 12–25°C in mountains.

Currency 1 Malaysian Dollar/Ringgit (M$) = 100 cents

Economy Discovery of tin in the late 19th-c brought European investment; rubber trees introduced from Brazil; minerals including iron ore, bauxite; oil, natural gas; electronic components, electrical goods; tourism.

GDP (1990) $43 bln, per capita $2 460

History Part of Srivijaya Empire, 9th–14th-c; Hindu and Muslim influences, 14th–15th-c; Portugal, the Netherlands and Britain vied for control from the 16th-c; Singapore, Malacca and Penang formally incorporated into the British Colony of the Straits Settlements, 1826; British protection extended over Perak, Selangor, Negeri Sembilan and Pahang, constituted into the Federated Malay States, 1895; protection treaties with several other states (Unfederated Malay States), 1885–1930; occupied by Japanese in World War 2; Federation of Malaya, 1948; independence, 1957; constitutional monarchy of Malaysia, 1963; Singapore withdrew from the Federation, 1965; governed by a bicameral federal parliament; head of state is a monarch elected for five years by his fellow sultans; advised by a prime minister and cabinet.

Head of State (Sultan)

1989– Azlan Muhibuddin Shah

Head of Government

1981– Mahathir bin Mohamad

MALDIVES

Local name Divehi Jumhuriya

Timezone GMT + 5.5

Area 300 sq km/116 sq mi

Population total (1991e) 226 000

Status Independent republic within the Commonwealth

Date of independence 1965

Capital Malé

Languages Divehi (official), Arabic, Hindi and English widely spoken

Ethnic groups Sinhalese (Dravidian extraction mainly), also Arab, Negrito, African influences

Religion Almost 100% Sunni Muslim

Physical features Island archipelago in the Indian Ocean; comprises c.1 190 islands (202 inhabited) in a chain of 20 coral atolls; many small and low-lying with sandy beaches fringed with coconut palms; none of the islands rising above 1.8 m/5 ft; 10% of land is arable, 3% forested.

Climate Generally warm and humid; wet season created by SW monsoons (Apr–Oct), dry season by NE monsoon (Dec–Mar); average annual rainfall, 2 100 mm /83 in; average daily temperature 22°C.

Currency 1 Rufiyaa (MRf, Rf) = 100 laaris

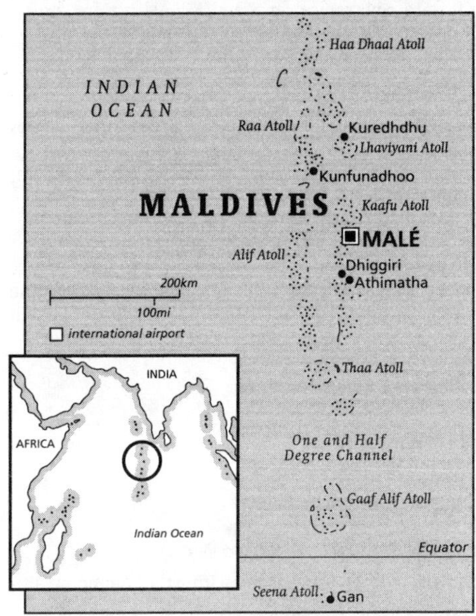

Economy Agriculture; breadfruit, banana, mango, cassava, sweet potato, millet; fishing, shipping, tourism.

Maldives (continued)

GDP (1989) $136 mln, per capita $670

History Former dependency of Ceylon (Sri Lanka); British protectorate, 1887–1965; became a Republic within the Commonwealth, 1953; Sultan restored, 1954; independence outside the Commonwealth, 1965; rejoined Commonwealth, 1982; governed by a president, a ministers' *Majlis* (cabinet), and a citizens' *Majlis* of 48 members elected for five years.

Head of State/Government

1978– Maumoon Abdul Gayoom

MALI

Local name Mali

Timezone GMT

Area 1 240 192 sq km/478 714 sq mi

Population total (1991e) 8 338 000

Status Republic

Date of independence 1960

Capital Bamako

Languages French (official), local languages (including Bambara) widely spoken

Ethnic groups Mande (Bambara, Malinke, Sarakole) (50%), Peul (Fulani nomads) (17%), Voltaic (including Senufo, Bura, Senouto, Minianka) (12%), Songhai (6%), Tuareg and Moor (5%)

Religions Muslim (90%), traditional animist beliefs (9%), Christian (1%) (Roman Catholic 0.5%, Protestant 0.5%)

Physical features Landlocked country on the fringe of the Sahara; lower part of the Hoggar massif (N); arid plains 300–500 m/1 000–1 600 ft; mainly savannah land in the S; main rivers, the Niger and Bani; featureless desert land (N).

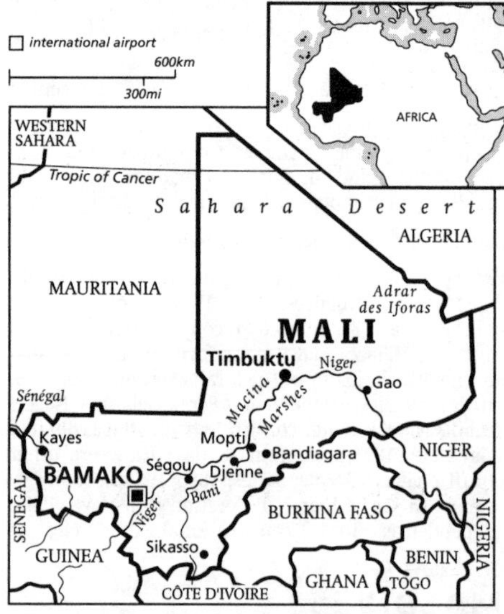

Climate Subtropical in S and SW, with rainy season (Jun–Oct); average rainfall c.1 000 mm/140 in; average annual temperatures 24°C (Jan), 27°C (Jul) in Bamako.

Currency 1 CFA Franc (CFAFr) = 100 centimes

Economy Mainly subsistence agriculture; crops severely affected by drought conditions; fishing, livestock, food processing, textiles, leather, cement; some tourism.

GDP (1989) $2 bln, per capital $250

History Mediaeval state controlling the trade routes between savannah and Sahara, reaching its peak in the 14th-c; governed by France, 1881–95; territory of French Sudan (part of French West Africa) until 1959; partnership with Senegal as the Federation of Mali, 1959; separate independence, 1960; under 1979 constitution (suspended, 1991) governed by a president elected every six years, and a National Assembly.

Head of State

1969–91 Moussa Traoré
1991–2 *Military Junta* (Amadou Toumani Touré)
1992– Alpha Oumar Konaré

Head of Government

1988–91 *No Prime Minister*
1991–2 Soumana Sacko
1992– Younoussi Toure

MALTA

Local name Malta

Timezone GMT + 2

Area 316 sq km/122 sq mi

Population total (1991e) 354 000

Status Independent republic within the Commonwealth

Date of independence 1964

Capital Valletta

Languages English and Maltese (official)

Ethnic groups Maltese (mixed Arabic, Sicilian, Norman, Spanish, English, Italian racial origin) (95%), English (2%)

Religions Roman Catholic Apostolic (97%), Anglican Communion (2%)

Physical features Archipelago, comprising the islands of Malta (246 sq km/95 sq mi), Gozo (67 sq km/26 sq mi), and Comino (2.7 sq km/1 sq mi), with the uninhabited islets of Cominotto, Filfla and St Paul; highest point, 252 m/830 ft, on island of Malta; well-indented coastline with natural harbours, rocky coves, no rivers.

Climate Mediterranean, hot, dry summers, cool, rainy winters; rainy season (Oct–Mar); average annual rainfall 578 mm/22.7 in; average annual temperatures 13 °C (Jan), 26 °C (Jul) in Valletta.

Currency 1 Maltese Lira (LM) = 100 cents

Economy Tourism; ship repair (naval dockyards now converted to commercial use); developing as a trans-shipment centre for the Mediterranean; tobacco, plastic and steel goods, paints, detergents; potatoes, tomatoes, oranges, grapes.

GDP (1989) $2.3 bln, per capita $6 564

History Controlled at various times by Phoenicia, Greece, Carthage and Rome; conquered by Arabs, 9th-c; given to the Knights Hospitallers, 1530; British Crown Colony, 1815; important strategic base in both World Wars; for its resistance to heavy air attacks, the island was awarded the George Cross, 1942; achieved independence, 1964; republic, 1974; British military base closed, 1979; governed by a president, prime minister, cabinet and House of Representatives.

Head of State
1989– Vincent Tabone

Head of Government
1987– Edward Fenech-Adami

MARIANA ISLANDS, NORTHERN >> UNITED STATES OF AMERICA

MARSHALL ISLANDS

Timezone GMT + 12

Area c.180 sq km/70 sq mi

Population total (1991e) 49 000

Status Republic

Date of independence 1986

Capital Dalap-Uliga-Darrit (municipality on Majuro Atoll)

Languages Marshallese (Kajin-Majol) (official), English and Japanese also spoken

Ethnic group Micronesian (99%)

Religions Christian (Protestant 90%, Roman Catholic 8%)

Physical features Archipelago in C Pacific Ocean; c.925 km/800 mi in length; comprising 34 islands, including Kwajalein and Jaluit, and 870 reefs; two parallel chains of coral atolls, Ratik (E) and Ralik (W), extending c.925 km/800 mi in lenth; volcanic islands, rise no more than a few metres above sea level.

Climate Hot and humid; wet season (May–Nov); typhoon season (Dec–Mar); average annual temperature 27°C.

Currency 1 US Dollar ($, US$) = 100 cents

Economy Farming; fishing; tropical agriculture; coconuts, tomatoes, melons, breadfruit.

GDP (1989) $63 mln, per capita $1 500

History Explored by the Spanish, 1529; part of UN Trust Territory of the Pacific, 1949–78, administered by the USA; US nuclear weapon tests held on Bikini and Eniwetak atolls, 1946–62; self-governing republic, 1979; compact of free association with the USA, 1986, with US recognizing independence of Marshall Islands; trusteeship ended, 1990; governed by a president, elected by a parliament.

Head of State/Government
1987– Amata Kabua

MARTINIQUE >> FRANCE

MAURITANIA

Local names Mūritāniyā (Arabic), Mauritanie (French)

Timezone GMT

Area 1 029 920 sq km/397 549 sq mi

Population total (1991e) 1 995 000

Status Islamic republic

Date of independence 1960

Capital Nouakchott

Mauritania (continued)

Languages Arabic (official), French and local languages also spoken

Ethnic groups Moor (30%), Black (30%), mixed (40%)

Religions Sunni Muslim (99%), Roman Catholic (1%)

Physical features Saharan zone in N comprises two-thirds of the country; coastal zone has minimal rainfall; Sahelian zone, with savannah grasslands; Sénégal R zone, the chief agricultural region; highest point, Kediet Ijill, 915 m/3 002 ft in the NW.

Climate Dry, tropical climate, with sparse rainfall; average annual temperatures 22°C (Jan), 28°C (Jul) in Nouakchott; rainy season (May–Sep) in S, with occasional tornadoes; average annual rainfall 158 mm/6.2 in.

Currency 1 Ouguiya (U, UM) = 5 khoums

Economy Subsistence agriculture (employs 80% of population); crop success constantly under threat from drought; livestock, cereals, vegetables, dates; mining of iron ore, copper and gypsum.

GDP (1989) $953 mln, per capita $490

History Visited by Portuguese, 15th-c; French protectorate within French West Africa, 1903; French colony, 1920; independence, 1960; military coup, 1979; new constitution, 1991; became a republic, 1992; governed by an executive president (6-year term), who appoints a prime minister, National Assembly, and Senate.

Head of State
1984– Moaouia Ould Sidi Mohammed Taya

Head of Government
1991– Sidi Mohammed Ould Boubaker

MAURITIUS

Local name Mauritius

Timeone GMT + 4

Area 1 865 sq km/720 sq mi

Population total (1991e) 1 083 000

Status Republic within the Commonwealth

Date of independence 1968

Capital Port Louis

Languages English (creole-English) (official), French, Hindi, Urdu, Bojpoori and Hakka also spoken

Ethnic groups Indo-Mauritian (68%), Creole (27%), Sino-Mauritian (3%), Franco-Mauritian (2%)

Religions Hindu (53%), Roman Catholic (26%), Muslim (13%), Protestant (4%)

Physical features Comprises the main island, 20 adjacent islets and the dependencies of Rodrigues I, Agalega I, and Cargados Carajos Is (St Brandon Is); volcanic main island; highest peak, 826 m/2 710 ft, Piton de la Petite Rivière Noire; dry, lowland coast with wooded savannah, mangrove swamp, and (E) bamboo; surrounded by coral reefs enclosing lagoons and sandy beaches.

Climate Humid tropical-maritime climate; average annual temperatures 23°C (Jan), 27°C (Jul) in Port Louis;

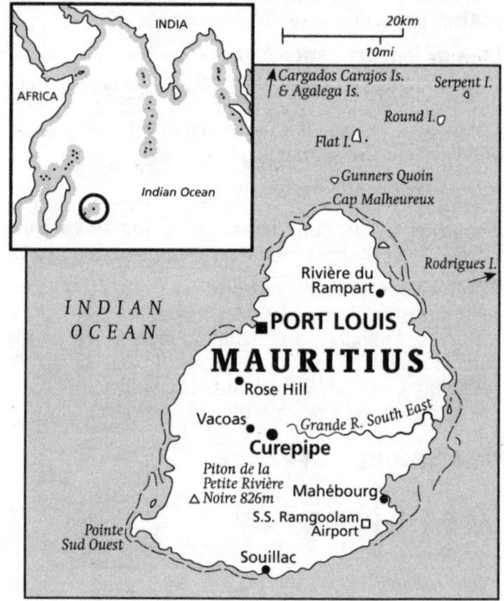

average annual rainfall 1 000 mm/39 in; lies within Indian cyclone belt.

Currency 1 Mauritian Rupee (MR, MauRe) = 100 cents

Economy Sugar-cane (employs over 25% of the work-force); clothing; diamond-cutting, watches, rum, fertilizer; tea, tobacco, vegetables; fishing; tourism.

GDP (1989) $2 bln, per capita $1 950

History Visited by the Portuguese and Dutch, 16th-c; settled by the French, 1722; ceded to Britain, 1814; governed jointly with Seychelles as a single colony until 1903; independent sovereign state within the Commonwealth, 1968; links with British monarchy broken, 1992, became a republic, remaining within the Commonwealth; president (ceremonial post) is elected by the National Assembly; prime minister appoints the Council of Ministers; unicameral National Assembly.

Head of State

1992 Veerasamy Ringadoo
1992– Cassam Uteem

Head of Government

1982– Aneerood Jugnauth

MAYOTTE >> FRANCE

MEXICO

Local name México

Timezone GMT – 8 to – 6

Area 1 978 800 sq km/763 817 sq mi

Population total (1991e) 90 007 000

Status Republic

Date of independence 1821

Capital Mexico City

Languages Spanish (official), indigenous languages

Ethnic groups Indian-Spanish (mestizo) (60%), Amerindian (30%), White (9%)

Religions Roman Catholic (97%), Protestant (3%)

Physical features Narrow coastal plains; land rises steeply to C plateau, c.2 400 m/7 800 ft; volcanic peaks to S, notably Citlaltépetl, 5 699 m/18 697 ft; limestone lowlands of the Yucatán peninsula stretch into the Gulf of Mexico (SE); region subject to earthquakes.

Climate Tropical climate in S; severe, arid conditions N and W; average annual temperatures 13°C (Jan), 16°C (Jul) in Mexico City; average annual rainfall 747 mm /29.4 in.

Currency 1 Mexican Peso (Mex$) = 100 centavos

Economy Wide range of mineral exports; major discoveries of oil and natural gas in the 1970s (now world's fourth largest producer); fluorite and graphite (world's leading producer); large petrochemical industry.

GDP (1990) $236 bln, per capita $2 680

History Centre of Indian civilizations for over 2 500 years; Gulf Coast Olmecs based at La Venta, Zapotecs at Monte Albán near Oaxaca, Mixtecs at Mitla, Toltecs at Tula, Maya in the Yucatán, Aztecs at Tenochtitlán; Spanish arrival, 1516; Vice-royalty of New Spain established; struggle for independence from 1810; federal republic, 1824; lost territory to the USA, 1836, and after the Mexican War, 1846–8; civil war, 1858–61; occupation of Mexico City by French forces in 1863–7; revolution, 1910–7; financial crisis, 1982–4, foreign debt estimated c.$800 000 mln; major earthquake in Mexico City, 1985, killed c.7 000; governed by a president, cabinet, and bicameral Congress with Senate and Chamber of Deputies.

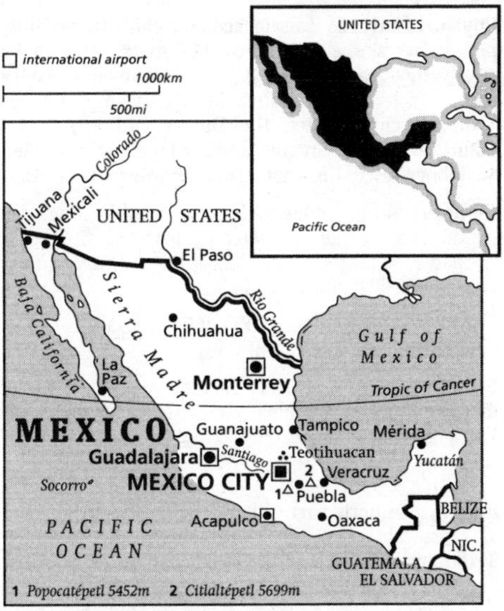

Head of State/Government

1988– Carlos Salinas de Gortari

MICRONESIA >> UNITED STATES OF AMERICA

MOLDOVA

Local name Moldova

Timezone GMT + 2

Area 33 700 sq km/13 008 sq mi

Population total (1992e) 4 341 000

Status Republic

Date of independence 1991

Capital Kishinev

Languages Moldovan (official), Ukrainian also spoken

Ethnic groups Moldovan (64%), Ukrainian (14%), Russian (13%), Gagauzi (4%), Jewish (2%)

Religions Christian (mainly Russian Orthodox, also Baptist and Roman Catholic)

Physical features Landlocked area consisting of hilly plains, average elevation of 147 m/482 ft, cut by river valleys, ravines, and gullies; uplands in C, Kodry Hills, reach highest point, Mt Balaneshty, 429 m/1 409 ft; chief rivers, the Dnestr and Prut; level plain of Bel'tsy Steppe and uplands (N); eroded Medobory-Toltry limestone ridges border R Prut (N).

Climate Warm, moderately continental; long dry periods in S; average annual temperatures −5°C (N), −3°C (S) (Jan), 20°C (N), 23°C (S) (Jul); average annual rainfall 450–550 mm/18–22 in.

Currency (1992) 1 Rouble (R) = 100 kopecks (new currency planned: leu)

Economy Main exports include wine, tobacco, food-canning, machinery, electrical engineering, knitwear, textiles, fruit.

GDP Not available

History Formerly part of Romania (the region known as Bessarabia); W part remained in Romania, Bessarabia in E became the Moldavian Soviet Socialist Republic, 1940; occupied by Romania, who allied with Germany in World War 2; recaptured by USSR, 1944; Moldavian language granted official status, 1989, leading to tension between ethnic Russians and Moldovans; declaration of independence, 1991, joined new Commonwealth of Independent States (CIS); tension due to separatist pressure from Gagauz and Dnestr Russian minorities, 1990–1; admitted to Conference on Security and Cooperation in Europe (CSCE), 1992; governed by a president, prime minister and Supreme Soviet (380-seat legislative body).

Head of State

1991– Mircea Snegur

Head of Government

1991–2 Valeriu Muravschi
1992– Andrei Sangheli

MONACO

Local name Monaco

Timezone GMT + 1

Area 1.95 sq km/0.75 sq mi

Population total (1991e) 29 712

Status Principality

Capital Monaco-Ville

Languages French (official), English, Italian and Monegasque also spoken

Ethnic groups French (58%), Italian (16%), Monegasque (16%)

Religion Roman Catholic (95%)

Physical features Located on Mediterranean Riviera, close to the Italian frontier with France; surrounded landward by the French department of Alpes-Maritimes; steep and rugged landscape; area available for commercial development has been extended by land reclaimed from sea.

Climate Mediterranean; warm, dry summers, mild, wet winters; average annual temperatures 10°C (Jan), 23°C (Jul); average annual rainfall 758 mm/30 in.

Currency 1 French Franc (Fr) = 100 centimes

Economy Tourism; chemicals, printing, textiles, plastics.

GDP Not available

History Under the protection of France since the 17th-c, apart from a period under Sardinia, 1815–61; 1911 constitution ended power of Prince as an absolute ruler; constitution of 1911 suspended, 1959; new constitution adopted, 1962; governed by a prince as head of state, a minister of state, heading a Council of Government, and a National Council.

Head of State (Prince)
1949– Rainier III

Head of Government (Minister of State)
1986–91 Jean Ausseil
1991– Jacques Dupont

Map >> FRANCE

MONGOLIA

Local name Mongol Ard Uls

Timezone GMT + 7 (W), + 8 (C), + 9 (E)

Area 1 566 500 sq km/604 800 sq mi

Population total (1991e) 2 247 000

Status State

Date of independence 1911

Capital Ulan Bator

Languages Khalka (official), Russian and Chinese spoken by respective minorities

Ethnic groups Mongol (Khalka, Dorbed, Buryat, Dariganga) (90%), Kazakh (4%), Russian (2%), other (4%)

Religions Formerly Tibetan Buddhist (now only a single monastry remains in Ulan Bator); unreliable data on current situation as a result of religious suppression in 20th-c

Physical features Landlocked mountainous country; highest point, Tavan-Bogdo-Uli, 4 373 m/14 347 ft; high ground mainly in W, with mountains lying NW–SE to form Mongolian Altai chain; lower SE area runs into the Gobi Desert; lowland plains; mainly arid grasslands.

Climate Extreme continental climate, with hard and long-lasting frosts in winter; arid desert conditions prevail in the S; average annual temperatures −26°C (Jan), 16°C (Jul); average annual rainfall 208 mm/18.2 in.

Currency 1 Tugrik (Tug) = 100 möngö

Economy Traditionally a pastoral nomadic economy; series of 5-year plans aiming for an agricultural-industrial economy; 70% of agricultural production derived from cattle raising; foodstuffs, animal products; coal, gold, uranium, lead.

GDP (1990) $2.2 bln, per capita $1 000

History Originally the homeland of nomadic tribes,

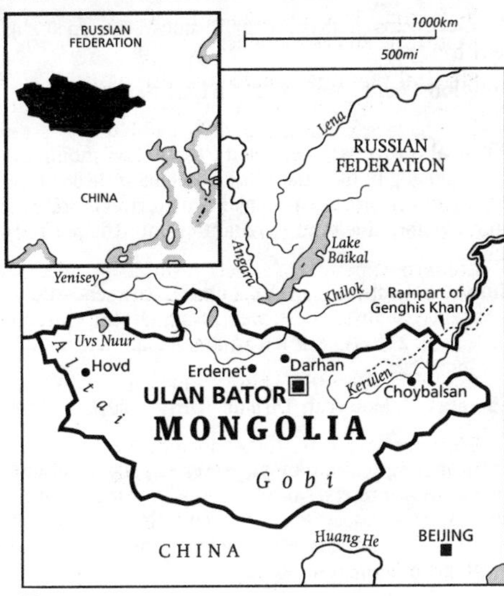

which united under Genghis Khan in the 13th-c to become part of the great Mongol Empire; assimilated into China, and divided into Inner and Outer Mongolia; Outer Mongolia declared itself an independent monarchy, 1911; changed name to Mongolian People's Republic, 1924, not recognized by China until 1946; governed by a Great People's Khural (parliament), a Council of Ministers, and a Presidium; chairman of Presidium is head of state; changed name to State of Mongolia, 1992, and new constitution established.

Head of State
1990– Punsalmaagiyn Ochirbat

Head of Government
1990–2 Dashiyn Byambasuren
1992– Puntsagiyn Jasray

MONTSERRAT >> UNITED KINGDOM

MOROCCO

Local name Al-Magrib

Timezone GMT

Area 409 200 sq km/157 951 sq mi

Population total (1991e) 26 181 000

Status Kingdom

Date of independence 1956

Capital Rabat

Languages Arabic (official), Berber, Spanish and French also widely spoken

Ethnic groups Arab-Berber (99%), non-Moroccan (0.7%), Jewish (0.2%)

Religions Sunni Muslim (98%), Christian (1%), Jewish (0.2%)

Physical features Dominated by a series of mountain ranges, rising in the Atlas Mts (S) to 4 165 m/13 664 ft at Jebel Toubkal; broad coastal plain; main rivers, Drâ'ar (S and SW) and Moulouya (N) draining into the Mediterranean.

Climate Mediterranean climate on N coast; semi-arid in S; Sahara virtually rainless; average annual temperatures 13°C (Jan), 22°C (Jul) in Rabat; average annual rainfall 564 mm/22.2 in.

Currency 1 Moroccan Dirham (DH) = 100 Moroccan francs

Economy Agriculture (employs over 50% of population); largest known reserves of phosphate in world; fishing, textiles, cement, soap, tobacco, chemicals, paper, timber products; tourism centred on the four imperial cities and the warm Atlantic resorts.

GDP (1990) $25.4 bln, per capita $990

History N coast occupied by Phoenicians, Carthaginians, and Romans since 12th-c BC; invasion by Arabs, 7th-c AD; conflicting French and Spanish interest in the region in 19th-c; Treaty of Fez, 1912, established Spanish Morocco (capital, Tétouan) and French Morocco (capital, Rabat); Tangier became an international zone, 1923–56; protectorates gained independence, 1956; became Kingdom of Morocco, 1957; Spanish withdrew from former Spanish Sahara (Western Sahara), 1975; Morocco laid claim to this area using the 'Green March' as a gesture of peaceful occupation; Mauritania withdrew from southern third of territory, 1979, leaving Morocco fighting with the Polisario for the whole of Western Sahara; ceasefire agreement signed, 1990; a 'constitutional' monarchy, but the king presides over his appointed cabinet, which is led by a prime minister; unicameral Chamber of Representatives. >> WESTERN SAHARA

Head of State (Monarch)
1961– King Hassan II

Head of Government
1985–92 Azzedine Laraka
1992– Mohammed Karim Lamrani

MOZAMBIQUE

Local name Moçambique

Timezone GMT + 2

Area 789 800 sq km/304 863 sq mi

Population total (1991e) 16 142 000

Status Republic

Date of independence 1975

Capital Maputo

Languages Portuguese (official), Swahili and Bantu dialects widely spoken

Ethnic groups Makua/Lomwe (52%), Thonga (23%), Malawi (12%), Shona (6%), Yao (3%)

Religions Local animist beliefs (60%), Christian (majority Roman Catholic) (30%), Muslim (10%)

Physical features Located in SE Africa; main rivers, the Zambezi and Limpopo provide irrigation and hydroelectricity; savannah plateau inland, mean elevation 800–1 000 m/2 699–4 000 ft; highest peak, Mt Binga, 2 436 m/7 992 ft; S of Zambezi is low-lying coast with sandy beaches and mangroves; low hills of volcanic origin inland, Zimbabwe plateau further N.

Climate Tropical with high humidity; rainy season

(Dec–Mar); drought conditions in S; average annual temperatures 26°C (Jan), 18°C (Jul) in Maputo; average annual rainfall 560 mm/30 in.

Currency 1 Metical (Mt, MZM) = 100 centavos

Economy Badly affected by drought (1981–4), internal strife and lack of foreign exchange; agriculture (employs c.85% of population); cashew nuts, tea, cotton, sugar cane, copra, sisal, groundnuts, fruit, rice, cereals, tobacco; forestry; livestock; reserves of gemstones and minerals.

GDP (1989) $1.6 bln, per capita $110

History Originally inhabited by Bantu peoples from the N, 1st–4th-c AD; coast settled by Arab traders; visited by Portuguese explorers by late 15th-c; part of Portuguese Africa since 1751; Mozambique Portuguese East Africa, late 19th-c; overseas province of Portugal, 1951; independence movement formed in 1962, the Frente de Libertação de Moçambique (FRELIMO), with armed resistance to colonial rule; independence as the People's Republic of Mozambique, 1975; continuing civil war, with first peace talks in 1990; socialist one-party state, 1975–90; new constitution and change of name to Republic of Mozambique, 1990; peace accord signed between Chissanó (president of Mozambique) and Dhlakama (leader of the Renamo-Mozambique National Resistance), 1992; president (term of 5 years) rules with an Assembly of the Republic.

Head of State
1986– Joaquim Alberto Chissanó

Head of Government
1986– Mario de Graça Machungo

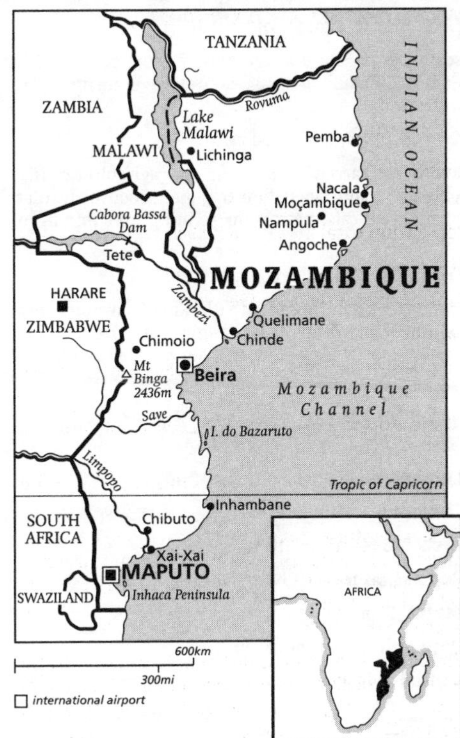

MYANMAR (BURMA)

Local name Pyidaungsu Myanma Naingngandaw

Timezone GMT + 6.5

Area 678 576 sq km/261 930 sq mi

Population total (1991e) 42 112 000

Status Union

Date of independence 1948

Capital Yangon (Rangoon)

Languages Burmese (official), also tribal languages spoken

Ethnic groups Burman (Tibeto-Chinese) (72%), Shan (9%), Karen (7%), Chinese (3%), Indian (2%)

Religions Theravada Buddhist (85%), animist, Muslim, Hindu, Christian minorities (15%)

Physical features Bordered in the N, E, and W by mountains rising (N) to Hkakabo Razi, 5 881 m/19 294 ft, located on Chinese frontier, forming part of Kumon Range; Chin Hills (W) descend into upland forests of the Arakan-Yoma range (S); principal rivers, Irrawaddy, Salween and Sittang.

Climate Tropical monsoon climate; equatorial on coast; humid temperate in extreme N; SW monsoon season (Jun–Sep); cool, dry season (Nov–Apr); hot, dry

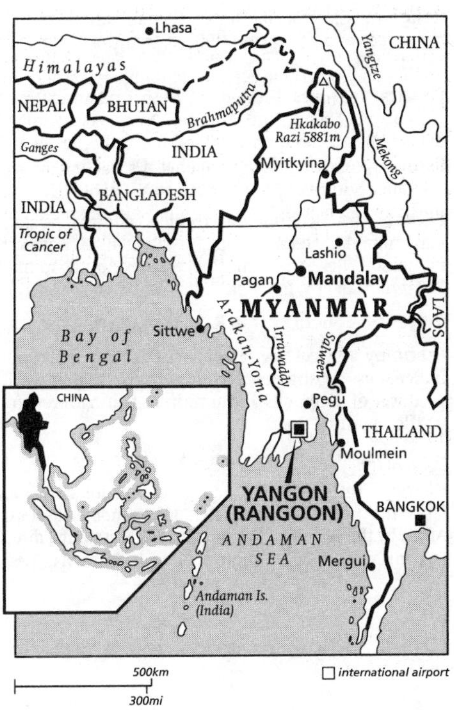

Myanmar (Burma) (continued)

season (May–Sep); average annual temperatures 23°C (Jan), 27°C (Jul) in Yangon; average annual rainfall 2616 mm/103 in.

Currency 1 Kyat (K) = 100 pyas

Economy Largely dependent on agriculture; rice, pulses, sugar cane; forestry (hardwoods); textiles, pharmaceuticals, petroleum refining and mining of minerals.

GDP (1990) $16.8 bln, per capita $408

History First unified in 11th-c by King Anawrahta; invasion by Kubla Khan, 1287; second dynasty established under King Tabinshweti, 1486, but plagued by internal disunity and wars with Siam from 16th-c; new dynasty under King Alaungpaya, 1752; annexed to British India following Anglo-Burmese wars (1824–86); separated from India, 1937; occupied by Japanese in World War 2; independence as Union of Burma under Prime Minister U Nu, 1948; military coup under U Ne Win, 1962; single-party socialist republic, 1974; army coup, 1988, leading to formation of a State Law and Order Restoration Council, headed by a chairman; name changed to Union of Myanmar, 1989 and renamed capital Yangon.

Head of State/Government

1988–92 Saw Maung
1992– General Than Shwe

NAMIBIA

Local name Namibia

Timezone GMT + 2

Area 823 144 sq km/317 734 sq mi

Population total (1991e) 1 520 000

Status Republic

Date of independence 1990

Capital Windhoek

Languages English (official), Afrikaans, German, local languages

Ethnic groups African (chiefly Ovambo) (85%), White (7%), mixed (8%)

Religions Christian (Lutheran, Roman Catholic, Dutch Reformed and Anglican) (90%), traditional animist beliefs (10%)

Physical features Located in SW Africa; Namib Desert runs parallel along the Atlantic Ocean coast; inland plateau, mean elevation 1 500 m/5 000 ft; highest point, Brandberg, 2 606 m/8 550 ft; Kalahari Desert to the E and S; Orange R forms S frontier with South Africa.

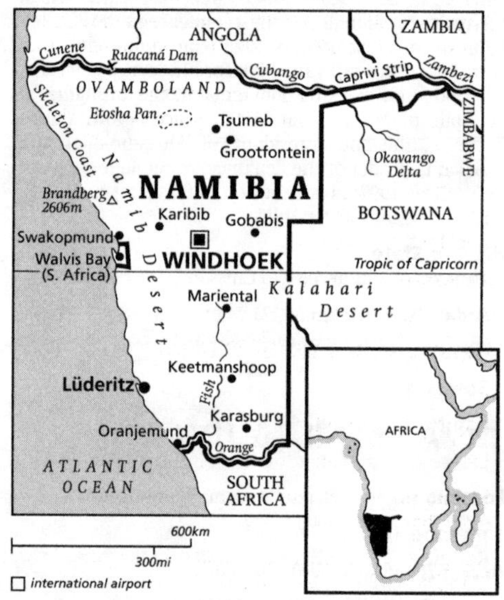

Climate Arid, continental tropical climate; average maximum daily temperature, 20–30°C; 49°C (Nov–Apr) in coastal desert (Namib); average annual rainfall 360 mm/14 in at Windhoek.

Currency 1 South African Rand (R) = 100 cents

Economy Agriculture (employs c.60% of population); indigenous subsistence farming in N; major world producer of diamonds and uranium; fishing; brewing; textiles; plastics.

GNP (1990) $1.8 bln, per capita $1 240

History Visited by British and Dutch missionaries from late 18th-c; German protectorate, 1884; mandated to South Africa by the League of Nations, 1920; UN assumed direct responsibility, 1966, changing name to Namibia, 1968, and recognizing the Southwest Africa People's Organization (SWAPO) as representative of the Namibian people, 1973; South Africa continued to administer the area as Southwest Africa; SWAPO commenced guerrilla activities, 1966; bases established in S Angola, involving Cuban troops in 1970s; interim administration installed by South Africa, 1985; full independence, 1990; governed by president, prime minister and cabinet, and elected National Assembly.

Head of State

1990– Sam Nujoma

Head of Government

1990– Hage Geingob

NAURU

Local name Naeoro (Nauruan)

Timezone GMT + 12

Area 21.3 sq km/8.2 sq mi

Population total (1991e) 9333

Status Republic

Date of independence 1968

Capital Yaren District (No official capital)

Languages Nauruan (official), English

Ethnic groups Nauruans (62%), Pacific islanders (26%), Asian (9%), Caucasian (3%)

Religions Christian (Nauruan Protestant, Roman Catholic)

Physical features Small isolated island in WC Pacific Ocean, 4 000 km/2 500 mi NE of Sydney, Australia; ground rises from sandy beaches to give fertile coastal belt, c.100–300 m/300–1 000 ft wide, the only cultivable soil; central plateau inland, highest point 65 m/213 ft; mainly phosphate-bearing rocks.

Climate Tropical, hot and humid; average annual temperatures 27°C (Jan), 28°C (Jul); average annual rainfall 1 524 mm/60 in; monsoon season (Nov–Feb).

Currency 1 Australian Dollar ($A) = 100 cents

Economy Based on phosphate mining, now limited reserves; coconuts, some vegetables; tourism; tax haven.

GNP (1989) $60 mln, per capita not available

History Under German administration from 1880s to 1914; after 1919, League of Nations mandate, administered by Australia; occupied by Japan, 1942–5; independence movement, 1960s; self-government, 1966; full independence, 1968; 18-member unicameral parliament, elected every 3 years; parliament elects a president, who appoints a cabinet.

Head of State/Government
1989– Bernard Dowiyogo

NEPAL

Local name Nepāl

Timezone GMT + 5.5

Area 145391 sq km/56121 sq mi

Population total (1991e) 19611000

Status Kingdom

Capital Kathmandu

Languages Nepali (official), Maithir, Bhojpuri

Ethnic groups Nepalese (58%), Bihari (19%), Tamang (4%), Tharu (3%), Newar (3%)

Religions Only official Hindu state in the world: Hindu (90%), Buddhist (5%), Muslim (3%), Christian (0.2%)

Physical features Landlocked, rises steeply from the Ganges basin in India; high fertile valleys in the 'hill country' at 1 300 m/4 300 ft, notably the Vale of Kathmandu (a world heritage site); dominated by the Himalayas (glaciated), highest peak, Mt Everest, 8 848 m/29 028 ft.

Climate Varies from subtropical lowland with hot, humid summers and mild winters, to an alpine climate over 3 300 m/10 800 ft, with permanently snow-covered peaks; average annual temperatures 0°C (Jan), 24°C (Jul) in Kathmandu; monsoon season (Jun–Sep); average annual rainfall 1 428 mm/56 in.

Currency 1 Nepalese Rupee (NRp, NRs) = 100 paise/pice

Economy Agriculture (employs 90% of population); rice, jute, cereals, sugar cane; agricultural and forest based goods; carpets; garments, handicrafts; hydroelectric power developing; tourism increasingly important.

GDP (1990) $3.1 bln, per capita $160

History Originally a group of independent hill states, united in 18th-c; parliamentary system introduced, 1959; replaced by village councils (*panchayats*), 1960; a constitutional monarchy ruled by hereditary king; period of unrest, 1990, followed by reduction of king's powers, a new constitution and fresh elections, 1991; king now rules with a Council of Ministers, a bicameral parliament consisting of an elected House of Representatives and a National Council.

Head of State (Monarch)
1972– Birendra Bir Bikram Shah Deva

Head of Government
1990 Lokendra Bahadur Chand
1990–1 Krishna Prasad Bhattarai
1991– Giriga Prasad Koirala

NETHERLANDS, THE

Local name Nederland

Timezone GMT + 1

Area 33 929 sq km/13 097 sq mi

Population total (1991e) 15 231 000

Status Kingdom

Date of independence 1830

Capital Amsterdam

Language Dutch (official)

Ethnic groups Dutch (Germanic/Gallo-Celtic descent) (99%), Indonesian/Surinamese (1%)

Religions Roman Catholic (40%), Protestant (Dutch Reformed Church and other Protestant churches) (31%)

Physical features Generally low and flat, except SE where hills rise to 321 m/1 053 ft; much of coastal area below sea-level, reaching lowest point −6.7 m/−19.7 ft N of Rotterdam; protected by coastal dunes and artificial dykes; highest point, Vaalserberg in SE; 27% of land area is below sea-level, an area inhabited by c.60% of population.

Climate Cool, temperate maritime climate, with continental influences; average annual temperatures 2°C (Jan), 17°C (Jul); average annual rainfall exceeds 700 mm/27 in, evenly distributed throughout the year.

Currency 1 Guilder (Gld)/ Florin (f) = 100 cents

Economy Rotterdam and newly-constructed Europort are the major European ports of transshipment, handling goods for EC member countries; Amsterdam is a world diamond centre; world's largest exporter of dairy produce; highly intensive agriculture; horticulture; engineering, chemicals, oil products, natural gas, high technology and electrical goods; fishing; tourism.

GDP (1990) $218 bln, per capita $14 600

History Part of Roman Empire to 4th-c AD; part of Frankish Empire by 8th-c; incorporated into the Holy Roman Empire; lands passed to Philip II, who succeeded to Spain and the Netherlands, 1555; attempts to stamp out Protestantism led to rebellion, 1572; seven N provinces united against Spain, 1579; United Provinces independence, 1581; overrun by the French, 1795–1813, who established the Batavian Republic; united with Belgium as the Kingdom of the United Netherlands until 1830, when Belgium withdrew; neutral in World War 1; occupied by Germany, World War 2, with strong Dutch resistance; joined with Belgium and Luxembourg to form the Benelux economic union, 1948; conflict over independence of Dutch colonies in SE Asia in late 1940s; joined NATO, 1949; independence granted to former colonies, Indonesia, 1949, with the addition of W New Guinea, 1963, and Suriname, 1975; a parliamentary democracy under a constitutional monarchy; government led by a prime minister; States General (Staten-Generaal) consists of a 75-member First Chamber, and a 150-member Second Chamber.

Head of State (Monarch)

1980– Beatrix

Head of Government

1982– Ruud F M Lubbers

ARUBA

Timezone GMT

Area 193 sq km/74.5 sq mi

Population total (1991e) 60 000

Status Self-governing region of the Netherlands

Date of independence Planned for 1996

Capital Oranjestad

Languages Dutch (official) with Papiamento, English and Spanish widely spoken

Ethnic groups Large majority of mixed European/Caribbean Indian descent

Religions Christian (Roman Catholic and Protestant), small Hindu, Muslim, Confucian and Jewish minorities

Physical features Island in the Caribbean, the westernmost of the Lesser Antilles, N of Venezuela; flat, rocky terrain, dry, with little vegetation.

Climate Dry, tropical, with little seasonal temperature variation; average annual temperature 27°C; annual rainfall often falls to below 488 mm/19 in; lies just outside the Caribbean hurricane belt.

Currency 1 Aruban Guilder/Florin = 100 cents

Economy Lack of natural resources limits agriculture and manufacturing; depends heavily on thriving tourist industry.

GDP (1989) $1 168 mln, per capita not available

History Claimed by Dutch, 1634, but remained undeveloped; construction of an oil refinery brought employment and prosperity, 1929; acquired full internal self-government within kingdom of the Netherlands, 1954, as part of the Netherlands Antilles; growing resentment led to a campaign for Aruba's independence; closure of oil refinery, 1985; obtained separate status from the Netherlands Antilles with full internal autonomy, 1986, pending full independence in 1996; sovereign of the Netherlands is head of state, represented by a governor-general, a Council of Ministers and a unicameral legislature.

Head of State
(Dutch monarch represented by Governor-General)
1986– Felipe B Tromp

Head of Government
1986–89 Henry Eman
1989– Nelson Oduber

Map >> VENEZUELA

NETHERLANDS ANTILLES

Local name Nederlandse Antillen

Timezone GMT – 4

Area 993 sq km/383 sq mi

Population total (1989e) 183 000

Status Self-governing region of the Netherlands

Capital Willemstad (on Curaçao Island)

Languages Dutch (official), Papiamento, English and Spanish widely spoken

Ethnic groups Large majority of mixed European/Caribbean Indian descent

Religions Christian (mainly Roman Catholic)

Physical features Islands in the Caribbean Sea, comprising the Southern group (Leeward Is) of Curaçao and Bonaire, 60–110 km/37–68 mi N of the Venezuelan coast, and the Northern group (Windward Is) of St Maarten, St Eustatius and Saba; terrain generally hilly, with volcanic interiors.

Climate Tropical maritime climate; average annual temperature 28°C; average annual rainfall varies from 500 mm/20 in (S) to 1 000 mm/39.4 in (N); Northern group subject to hurricanes (Jul–Oct).

Currency 1 Netherland Antilles Guilder/Florin = 100 cents

Economy Based on refining of crude oil imported from Venezuela; aim of industrial diversification; ship repairing; tourism.

History Visited by Columbus, initially claimed for Spain; small-scale Spanish colonization in Curaçao, 1511; occupied by Dutch settlers, 17th-c; acquired full internal self-government within Kingdom of the Netherlands, 1954; Aruba separated from the other islands, 1986; sovereign of the Netherlands is head of state, represented by a governor, a Council of Ministers and a unicameral legislature.

Head of State
(Dutch monarch represented by Governor-General)
1983–90 Rene Romer
1990– Jaime Saleh

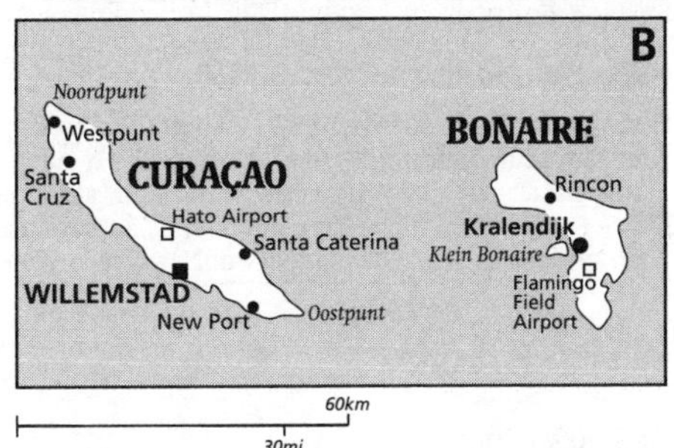

Head of Government
1988– Maria Liberia Peters

NEW CALEDONIA >> FRANCE

NEW ZEALAND

Local name Aotearoa (Maori)

Timezone GMT + 12

Area 270 534 sq km/104 426 sq mi

Population total (1991e) 3 449 700

Status Independent member of the Commonwealth

Date of independence 1947

Capital Wellington

Languages English and Maori (official)

Ethnic groups European (mainly British, Australian and Dutch) (87%), Maori (9%)

Religions Christian (59%) (Anglican 25%, Presbyterian 18%, Roman Catholic 16%)

Physical features Consists of two principal islands (North and South) separated by the Cook Strait, and several minor islands; North Island mountainous in the centre with many hot springs; peaks rise to 2 797 m/ 9 176 ft at Mt Ruapehu; South Island mountainous for its whole length, rising in the Southern Alps to 3 764 m/ 12 349 ft at Mt Cook, New Zealand's highest point (however, in 1991, Mt Cook transformed by a massive landslide that lowered its summit by 11 m to 3 753 m/12 313 ft); many glaciers and mountain lakes; largest area of level lowland is the Canterbury Plain, E side of South Island; L Taupo, largest natural lake, occupies an ancient volcanic crate; major lakes include Te Anau and Wakatipu.

Climate Cool, temperate climate, almost subtropical in extreme N; mean temperature range, 18 °C in N, 9 °C in S; lower temperatures in South Island; highly changeable weather, all months moderately wet; average annual temperature 16–23 °C (Jan), 8–13 °C (Jul) in Auckland; average annual rainfall 1 053 mm/41 in; subject to periodic subtropical cyclones.

Currency 1 New Zealand Dollar ($NZ) = 100 cents

Economy Farming, especially sheep and cattle; one of the world's major exporters of dairy produce; third largest exporter of wool; kiwi fruit, venison; textiles; timber, food processing; substantial coal and natural gas reserves; hydroelectric power; tourism.

GDP (1991) $40 bln, per capita $12 200

History Settled by Maoris from E Polynesia by c.1000 AD; first European sighting by Abel Tasman, 1642, named Staten Landt; later known as Nieuw Zeeland, after the Dutch Province; visited by Captain Cook, 1769; first European settlement, 1792; dependency of New South Wales until 1841; outbreaks of war between immigrants and Maoris, 1860–70; Dominion of New Zealand, 1907; independent within the Commonwealth, 1947; governed by a prime minister, cabinet and unicameral, 95-member House of Representatives; elections every 3 years.

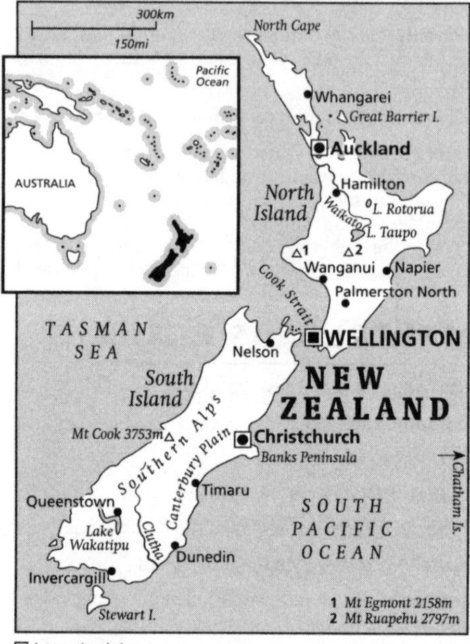

□ international airport

Head of State

(British monarch represented by Governor-General)

1990– Dame Catherine Tizard

Head of Government

1984–89 David Russell Lange
1989–90 Geoffrey Palmer
1990– James Brendan Bolger

Overseas territories

Name	Area sq km	Area sq mi	Capital	Population total
Cook Islands	238	92	Avarua	(1986) 17 185
Niue	263	101	Alofi	(1991) 2 239
Tokelau	10	4	Nukunonu	(1991) 1 578
Ross Dependency	3 540	159 626	–	uninhabited

NICARAGUA

Local name Nicaragua

Timezone GMT – 6

Area 148 000 sq km/57 128 sq mi

Population total (1991e) 3 751 000

Status Republic

Date of independence 1821

Capital Managua

Languages Spanish (official), indigenous Indian languages and English (creole-English)

Ethnic groups Mestizo (69%), White (17%), Black (9%), Indian (Sumu, Mikito, Ramaguie peoples) (5%)

Religions Roman Catholic (95%), Protestant (5%)

Physical features Mountainous W half, with volcanic

ranges rising to over 2 000 m/6 500 ft (NW); two large lakes, Lake Nicaragua and Lake Managua, behind the coastal mountain range; rolling uplands and forested plains to the E; many short rivers flow into the Pacific Ocean and the lakes.

Climate Tropical climate; average annual temperatures, 26°C (Jan), 30°C (Jul) at Managua; rainy season (May–Nov), high humidity; average annual rainfall 1 140 mm/45 in.

Currency 1 New Córdoba (C$) = 100 centavos

Economy Agriculture (accounts for over two-thirds of total exports); cotton, coffee, sugar cane, rice, corn, tobacco; oil, natural gas; gold, silver, chemicals, textiles.

GDP (1990) $1.7 bln, per capita $470

History Colonized by Spaniards, early 16th-c; independence from Spain, 1821; left the Federation of Central America, 1838; dictatorship under Anastasio Somoza, 1938; Sandinista National Liberation Front seized power, 1979, and established a socialist junta of national reconstruction; under the 1987 constitution, a president and a 96-member Constituent Assembly are elected for 6-year terms; former supporters of the Somoza government (the Contras), based in Honduras and supported by the USA, carried out guerilla activities against the junta from 1979; ceasefire and disarmament agreed, 1990.

Head of State/Government

1984–90 Daniel Ortega Saavedra
1990– Violeta Barrios de Chamorro

NIGER

Local name Niger

Timezone GMT + 1

Area 1 186 408 sq km/457 953 sq mi

Population total (1991e) 8 154 000

Status Republic

Date of independence 1960

Capital Niamey

Languages French (official) with Hausa, Songhai, Fulfulde, Tamashek and Arabic widely spoken

Ethnic groups Hausa (54%), Djerma and Songhai (22%), Fulani (9%), Tuareg (8%), Beriberi (4%), Arab (2%)

Religions Muslim (80%), traditional beliefs and small Christian minority (primarily Roman Catholic) (20%)

Physical features Occupies S fringe of Sahara Desert, on a high plateau; Hamada Mangueni plateau (far N); Aïr massif (C); Ténéré du Tafassasset desert (E); W Talk desert (C and N); water in quantity found only in the SW (R Niger) and SE (L Chad).

Climate One of the hottest countries in the world; average annual temperature 16 °C (Jun–Oct), 41 °C (Feb–May); rainy season in S (Jun–Oct); rainfall decreases N to almost negligible levels in desert areas; average annual rainfall at Niamey, 554 mm/22 in.

Currency 1 CFA Franc (CFAFr) = 100 cents

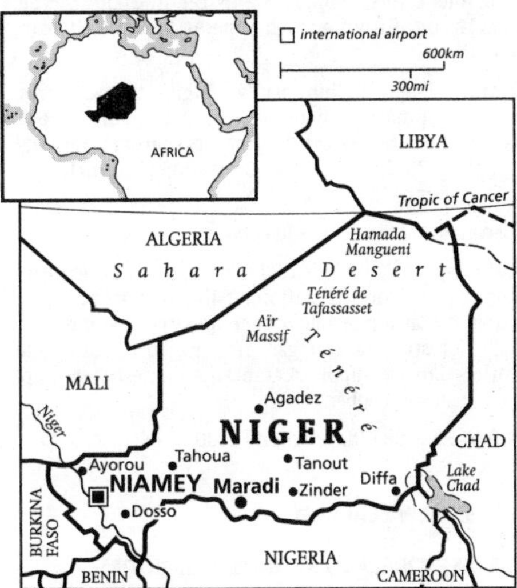

Economy Dominated by agriculture and mining; production badly affected by severe drought conditions in 1970s; uranium, tin, phosphates, coal, salt, natron; building materials, textiles, food processing.

GDP (1989) $2.1 bln, per capita $290

Niger (continued)

History Occupied by the French, 1883–99; territory within French West Africa, 1904; independence, 1960; military coup, 1974; governed by a Higher Council for National Orientation led by a President who appoints a Council of Ministers; elected National Assembly, 1989; constitution suspended, 1991; multi party constitution adopted, 1992.

Head of State

1987– Ali Saibou

Head of Government

1990–1 Aliou Mahamidou
1991– Amadou Cheiffou *Interim*

NIGERIA

Local name Nigeria

Timezone GMT + 1

Area 923 768 sq km/356 574 sq mi

Population total (1991) 88 500 000

Status Republic

Date of independence 1960

Capital Abuja

Languages English (official), Hausa, Yoruba, Ibo and other Niger-Congo dialects widely used

Ethnic groups Over 250 tribal groups, notably Hausa and Fulani, Yoruba and Ibo (65%); Kanuri, Tiv, Edo, Nupe and Ibidio (25%)

Religions Muslim (50%), Christian (34%), indigenous animist beliefs (10%)

Physical features Long, sandy shoreline with mangrove swamp, dominated by R Niger delta; undulating area of tropical rainforest and oil palm bush behind a coastal strip; open woodland and savannah further N; numerous rivers, notably the Niger and the Benue; Gotel Mts on SE frontier, highest point, Mt Vogel, 2 024 m/6 640 ft.

Climate Tropical; uniformly high temperatures; average annual temperatures 21–7°C (Jan), 25–6°C (Jul); dry season in the N (Oct–Apr); average annual rainfall 1 836–2 497 mm/54–98 in; subject to influence of the Saharan Harmattan in N.

Currency 1 Naira (N) = 100 kobo

Economy Oil (provides c.90% of exports); agriculture (employs 50% of population); palm oil, groundnuts, cotton, cassava, rice, sugar cane, tobacco; fishing, livestock, forestry; natural gas, tin, iron ore, columbite (world's largest supplier), tantalite, limestone; pulp, paper, textiles, rubber.

GDP (1990) $28 bln, per capita $230

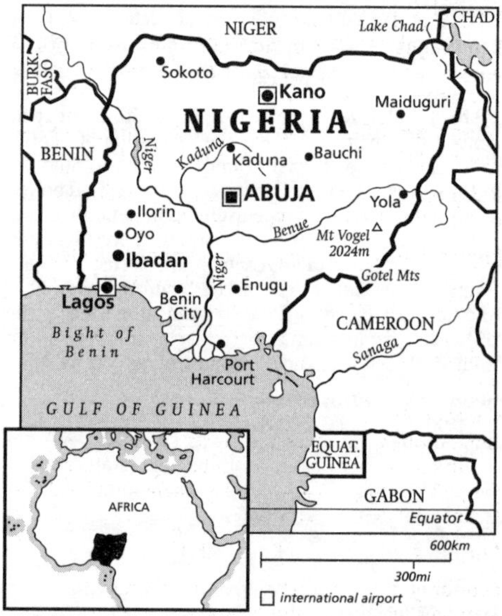

History Centre of the Nok culture, 500 BC–AD 200; Muslim immigrants, 15th–16th-c; British colony at Lagos, 1861; protectorates of N and S Nigeria, 1900; amalgamated as the Colony and Protectorate of Nigeria, 1914; federation, 1954; independence, 1960; federal republic, 1963; military coup, 1966; E area formed Republic of Biafra, 1967; civil war, and surrender of Biafra, 1970; military coups 1983 and 1985; a president rules with an Armed Forces Ruling Council, which appoints a Council of Ministers.

Head of State/Government

1983–4 Mohammadu Buhari
1985– Ibrahim B Babangida

NIUE >> NEW ZEALAND

NORTHERN IRELAND >> UNITED KINGDOM

NORTH KOREA >> KOREA, NORTH

NORTHERN MARIANA ISLANDS >> UNITED STATES OF AMERICA

NORWAY

Local name Norge

Timezone GMT + 1

Area 323 895 sq km/125 023 sq mi

Population total (1991e) 4 273 000

Status Kingdom

Date of independence 1905

Capital Oslo

Languages Norwegian (official) (in the varieties of Bokmål and Nynorsk), Lappish and Finnish speaking minorities

Ethnic groups Germanic (Nordic, Alpine, Baltic descent) (97%), Sami/Lapp minority in far N

Religions Evangelical Lutheran (94%), Baptist, Pentecostalist, Methodist and Roman Catholic (6%)

Physical features Mountainous country; Kjölen Mts form the N part of the boundary with Sweden; Jotunheimen range in SC Norway; much of the interior over 1 500 m/5 000 ft; numerous lakes, the largest being L Mjøsa, 368 sq km/142 sq mi; irregular coastline with many small islands and long deep fjords.

Climate Arctic winter climate in interior highlands, snow, strong winds and severe frosts; comparatively mild conditions on coast; average annual temperatures −4°C (Jan), 17°C (Jul) in Oslo; average annual rainfall 683 mm /27 in; rainfall heavy on W coast.

Currency 1 Norwegian Krone (NKr) = 100 øre

Economy Based on extraction and processing of raw materials, using plentiful hydroelectric power; oil and natural gas from North Sea fields; land under cultivation, less than 3%; productive forests covered 21% of land area, 1985.

GDP (1990) $74 bln, per capita $17 400

History A united kingdom achieved by St Olaf in the 11th-c, whose successor, Cnut, brought Norway under Danish rule; united with Sweden and Denmark, 1389; annexed by Sweden as a reward for assistance against Napoleon, 1814; growing nationalism resulted in independence, 1905; declared neutrality in both World Wars, but occupied by Germany, 1940–4; joined NATO, 1949; joined European Free Trade Association, 1960; a limited, hereditary monarchy; government led by a prime minister; parliament (*Storting*) comprises upper (*Lagting*) and lower (*Odelsting*) chambers.

Head of State (Monarch)

1957–91 Olav V
1991– Harald V

Head of Government

1989–90 Jan P Syse
1990– Gro Harlem Brundtland

OMAN

Local name 'Umān

Timezone GMT + 4

Area 300 000 sq km/115 800 sq mi

Population total (1991e) 1 534 000

Status Sultanate

Date of independence 1951

Capital Muscat

Languages Arabic (official), English, Baluchi (and other Mahri languages), Urdu and Indian dialects also spoken

Ethnic groups Arab, with small Baluchi, Iranian, Indian, Pakistani and W European minorities

Religions Ibadhi Muslim (75%), Sunni Muslim, Shi'a Muslim and Hindu (25%)

Physical features Located on the SE corner of the Arabian peninsula; the tip of the Musandam peninsula in the Strait of Hormuz is separated from the rest of the country by an 80 km/50 mi strip belonging to the United Arab Emirates; several peaks in the Hajjar Mt range, Jabal Akhdar ridge rises to 3 000 m/10 000 ft; vast sand desert in NE; Dhofar uplands in SW.

Oman (continued)

Climate Desert climate, hot and arid; hot, humid on coast (Apr–Oct); average annual temperature 22°C (Jan), 33°C (Jul); light monsoon rains in S (Jun–Sep); average annual rainfall 99 mm/3.9 in.

Currency 1 Rial Omani (RO) = 1 000 baizas

Economy Oil discovered, 1964, now provides over 90% of government revenue; natural gas an important source of industrial power; c.70% of the population relies on agriculture; alfalfa, wheat, tobacco, fruit, vegetables, fishing.

GDP (1989) $7.7 bln, per capita not available

History Dominant maritime power of the W Indian Ocean in 16th-c; independent from UK, 1951; separatist tribal revolt, 1964, led to a police coup that installed the present Sultan, 1970; opened airbases to Western forces, following Iraqi invasion of Kuwait, 1990; independent state ruled by a sultan who is both head of state and premier, and who appoints a Cabinet and Consultative Council, which replaced the Consultative Assembly, 1992.

Head of State/Government (Sultan)
1932–70 Said bin Taimur
1970– Qaboos bin Said

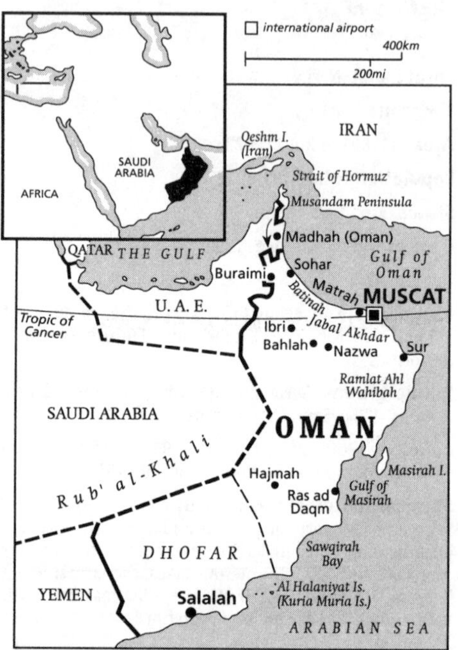

PAKISTAN

Local name Pākistān

Timezone GMT + 5

Area 803 943 sq km/310 322 sq mi

Population total (1991e) 117 490 000

Status Republic

Date of independence 1947

Capital Islamabad

Languages Urdu and English (official), Punjabi, Sindhi, Pashto, Urdu, Baluchi and Brahvi mainly spoken

Ethnic groups Punjabi (66%), Sindhi (13%), Baluchi (3%), Pathan and Muhajir minorities, also Afghan refugees in W Pakistan

Religions Muslim (97%) (Sunni 77%, Shi'a 20%), Christian, Hindu, Parsee, Buddhist minorities

Physical features R Indus flows from Himalayas to Karachi, forming a vast, fertile, densely populated alluvial floodplain in E; bounded N and W by mountains rising to 8 611 m/28 250 ft at K2, and 8 126 m/26 660 ft at Nanga Parbat; mostly flat plateau, low-lying plains and arid desert to the S; major rivers include Jhelum, Chenab, Indus and Sutlej.

Climate Continental, with many temperature variations; dominated by the Asiatic monsoon; severe winters in mountainous regions; average annual temperatures 10°C (Jan), 32°C (Jul) in Islamabad; average annual rainfall 900 mm/35 in; rainy season (Jun–Oct).

Currency 1 Pakistan Rupee (PRs, Rp) = 100 paisa

Economy Agriculture (employs 55% of labour force); cotton production important, supporting major spinning, weaving and processing industries; sugar cane; textiles; natural gas; tobacco; salt; uranium.

GDP (1990) $43 bln, per capita $380

History Remains of Indus Valley civilization over 4 000 years ago; Muslim rule under the Mughal Empire, 1526–1761; British rule over most areas, 1840s; separated from India to form a state for the Muslim minority, 1947; consisted of West Pakistan (Baluchistan, North-West Frontier, West Punjab, Sind) and East Pakistan (East Bengal), physically separated by 1 610 km/1 000 mi; occupied Jammu and Kashmir, 1949 (disputed territory with India, and the cause of wars in 1965 and 1971); proclaimed an Islamic republic, 1956; differences between E and W Pakistan developed into civil war, 1971; E Pakistan became an independent state (Bangladesh); military coup, 1977; Benazir Bhutto became first woman premier of a modern Islamic state, 1988; governed by an elected president and a bicameral federal parliament.

Head of State

1988– Ghulam Ishaq Khan

Head of Government

1988–90 Benazir Bhutto
1990 Ghulam Mustafa Jatoi
1990– Mian Mohammad Nawaz Sharif

PALAU >> UNITED STATES OF AMERICA

PANAMA

Local name Panamá

Timezone GMT – 5

Area 77 082 sq km/29 753 sq mi

Population total (1991e) 2 476 000

Status Republic

Date of independence 1903

Capital Panama City

Languages Spanish (official), English and indigenous languages (including Cuna, Chibchan, Choco)

Ethnic groups Mestizo (mixed Spanish-Indian) (70%), West Indian (14%), White (10%), Indian (6%)

Religions Christian (Roman Catholic 93%, Protestant 6%), Jewish, Muslim and Baha'i minorities

Physical features Mostly mountainous; Serranía de Tabasará (W) rises to 3 475 m/11 401 ft at Volcán Baru; Azuero peninsula (Peninsula de Azuero) in the S; lake-studded lowland cuts across the isthmus; dense tropical forests on the Caribbean coast; Panama Canal, 82 km/51 mi long, connects Pacific and Atlantic oceans.

Climate Tropical, with uniformly high temperatures; average annual temperature 26°C (Jan), 27°C (Jul) in Panama City; dry season (Jan–Apr) only; average annual rainfall 1 770 mm/69.7 in.

Currency 1 Balboa (B, Ba) = 100 cents

Economy Canal revenue (accounts for 80% of country's wealth); great increase in banking sector since 1970; attempts to diversify include oil refining, cigarettes, paper products; tourism; copper, gold, silver; bananas, coffee, cacao, sugar cane.

GDP (1990) $4.8 bln, per capita $1 980

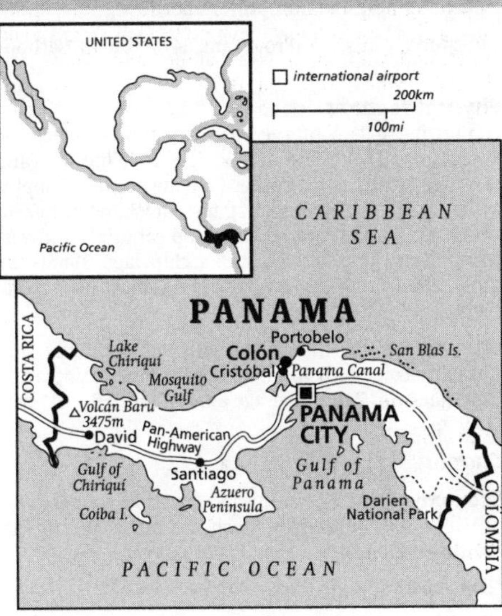

History Visited by Columbus, 1502; under Spanish colonial rule until 1821; joined the Republic of Greater Colombia; separation from Colombia after a US-inspired revolution, 1903; assumed sovereignty of the 8 km/5 mi-wide Canal zone, previously administered by the USA, 1979; military were the ruling force led by Manuel Noriega, 1983–9; US invasion, 1989, deposed Noriega and installed Guillermo Endara Galimany as president; governed by a president, cabinet, and unicameral Legislative Assembly.

Head of State/Government

1989– Guillermo Endara

PAPUA NEW GUINEA

Local name Papua New Guinea

Timezone GMT + 10

Area 462 840 sq km/178 656 sq mi

Population total (1991e) 3 913 000

Status Independent state within the Commonwealth

Date of independence 1975

Capital Port Moresby

Languages Pidgin English and Motu (official parliamentary languages), Tok Pisin and c.750 indigenous languages spoken

Ethnic groups Papuan (80%), Melanesian (15%), Polynesian, Chinese and European minorities

Religions Christian (Protestant 64%, Roman Catholic 33%), local beliefs

Physical features Island group in SW Pacific Ocean, comprising E half of the island of New Guinea, the Bismarck and Louisiade archipelagos, the Trobriand and D'Entrecasteaux Is, and other off-lying groups; complex system of mountains, highest point, Mt Wilhelm, 4 509 m /14 793 ft; mainly covered with tropical rainforest; vast mangrove swamps along coast; archipelago islands are mountainous, mostly volcanic and fringed with coral reefs.

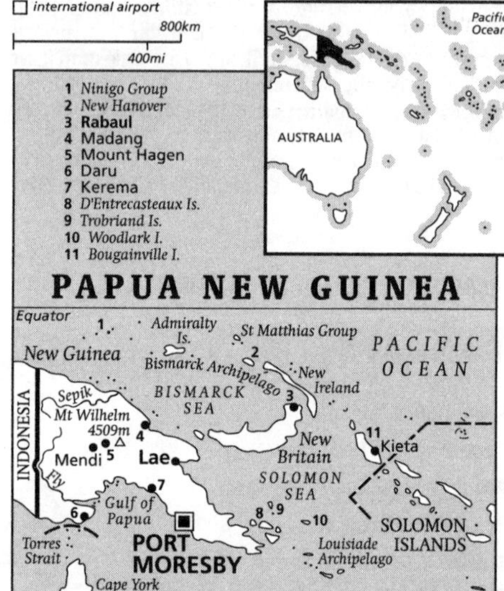

Climate Typical monsoon, with temperatures and humidity constantly high; average annual temperature 28°C (Jan), 26°C (Jul); average annual rainfall 1 011 mm /39.9 in.

Currency 1 Kina (K) = 100 toea

Economy Farming, fishing and forestry (engages c.75% of workforce); vegetables, sugar, peanuts; natural gas; brewing; tourism.

GDP (1989) $2.7 bln, per capita $725

History British protectorate in SE New Guinea, 1884; some of the islands under German protectorate, 1884; German New Guinea in NE, 1899; German colony annexed by Australia in World War 1; Australia mandated to govern both British and German areas, 1920; combined as the United Nations Trust Territory of Papua and New Guinea, 1949; independence within the Commonwealth, 1975; a governor-general represents the British Crown; governed by a prime minister and cabinet, with a unicameral National Parliament.

Head of State

(British monarch represented by Govenor-General)

1991– Wiwa Korowi

Head of Government

1988–92 Rabbie Namiliu

1992– Paias Wingti

PARAGUAY

Local name Paraguay

Timezone GMT – 3/4

Area 406 750 sq km/157 000 sq mi

Population total (1992e) 4 500 000

Status Republic

Date of independence 1811

Capital Asunción

Languages Spanish (official), but Guaraní also spoken

Ethnic groups Mestizo (mixed Spanish-Guaraní Indian) (95%), Amerindian, Black, European and Asian minorities

Religions Roman Catholic (97%), Mennonite, Baptist/ Anglican minorities

Physical features Landlocked, in C South America; divided into two regions by the R Paraguay; Gran Chaco in the W, mostly cattle country or scrub forest; more fertile land in the E; Paraná plateau at 300–600 m/ 1 000–2 000 ft, mainly wet, treeless savannah.

Climate Tropical NW, with hot summers, warm winters; temperate in SE; average annual temperatures 27°C (Jan), 18°C (Jul) in Asunción; average annual rainfall 1 316 mm/52 in.

Currency 1 Guaraní (₲) = 100 céntimos

Economy Agriculture (employs 40% of the labour force); oilseed, cotton, wheat, tobacco, corn, rice, sugar cane; pulp, timber, textiles, cement, glass.

GDP (1990) $4.7 bln, per capita $1 100

History Originally inhabited by Guaraní Indians; arrival of the Spanish, 1537; arrival of Jesuit missionaries, 1609; independence from Spain, 1811; War of the Triple

Alliance against Brazil, Argentina and Uruguay, 1864–70; Chaco War with Bolivia, 1932–5; civil war, 1947; General Alfredo Stroessner seized power, 1954, forced to stand down following a coup in 1989; new constitution, creating post of Vice-President, 1992; governed by a president, appointed Council of Ministers, and a bicameral National Congress.

Head of State/Government
1989– Andres Rodriguez

PERU

Local name Perú

Timezone GMT - 5

Area 1 285 216 sq km/496 225 sq mi

Population total (1991e) 22 361 000

Status Republic

Date of independence 1821

Capital Lima

Languages Spanish and Quechua (official), Aymará also spoken

Ethnic groups South American Indian (45%), Mestizo (mixed Indian and European) (37%), White (15%), Black, Japanese and Chinese (3%)

Religions Roman Catholic (90%), Anglican, Methodist, Peruvian Baha'i minorities

Physical features Arid plains and foothills on the coast, with areas of desert and fertile river valleys; Central Sierra, average altitude 3 000 m/10 000 ft, contains 50% of the population; highest peak, Mt Huascarán, 6 768 m/22 204 ft, in W; forested Andes and Amazon basin (E), with major rivers flowing to the Amazon.

Climate Mild temperatures all year on coast; dry, arid desert in the S; typically wet, tropical climate in Amazon basin; average annual temperatures 23°C (Jan), 17°C (Jul) in Lima; average annual rainfall 48 mm/1.9 in.

Currency 1 New Sol = 100 centavos

Economy One of the world's leading producers of silver, zinc, lead, copper, gold, iron ore; 80% of Peru's oil extracted from the Amazon forest; cotton, potatoes, sugar, olives; tourism, especially to ancient sites.

GDP (1989) $19.3 bln, (1990) per capita $898

History Highly developed Inca civilization; arrival of Spanish, 1531; Vice-royalty of Peru established; independence declared, 1821; frequent border disputes in 19th-c (eg War of the Pacific, 1879–83); several military coups; terrorist activities by Maoist guerrillas; bicameral Congress consists of a Senate and a National Chamber of Deputies; an elected president appoints a Council of Ministers.

Head of State/Government
1985–90 Alan García Pérez
1990– Alberto Keinya Fujimori

PHILIPPINES

Local name Filipinas

Timezone GMT + 8

Area 299 679 sq km/115 676 sq mi

Population total (1991e) 65 758 000

Status Republic

Date of independence 1946

Capital Manila

Languages Tagalog (Filipino), and English (official), over 87 local languages, including Cebuano, Ilocano, Bicol and Samar-Leyte

Ethnic groups Tagalog (Filipino) with Chinese, Spanish and American minorities

Religions Roman Catholic (83%), Protestant (9%), Muslim (5%), Buddhist (3%)

Physical features An archipelago of more than 7 100 islands and islets, NE of Borneo; largest island, Luzon 108 172 sq km/41 754 sq mi; Mindanao, 94 227 sq km/36 372 sq mi, has active volcano Apo, 2 954 m/9 690 ft, and mountainous rainforest; Mount Pinatubo volcano, 1 758 m/5 770 ft, situated 90 km/56 mi NW of Manila; largely mountainous islands.

Climate Tropical, maritime; warm and humid throughout year; average annual temperature 25°C (Jan), 28°C (Jul) in Manila; average annual rainfall 2 083 mm/82 in; frequent typhoons and occasional earth tremors and tsunamis (tidal waves).

Currency 1 Philippine Peso (PP, ₱) = 100 centavos

Economy Farming (employs c.50% of workforce); rice, pineapples, mangos, vegetables, livestock, sugar, tobacco, rubber, coffee; oil, copper, gold; textiles; vehicles; tourism.

GNP (1990) $45.2 bln, per capita $700

History Claimed for Spain by Magellan, 1521; ceded to the USA after the Spanish-American War, 1898; became a self-governing Commonwealth, 1935; occupied by the Japanese in World War 2; independence, 1946; communist guerrilla activity in N; Muslim separatist movement in S; martial law following political unrest, 1972–81; exiled political leader Benigno Aquino assassinated on returning to Manila, 1983; coup in 1986 ended the 20-year rule of President Ferdinand Marcos; new constitution, 1987; attempted coup, 1989, with continuing political unrest; eruption of Mount Pinatubo, 1991; governed by a president and a bicameral legislature, comprising a Senate and a House of Representatives.

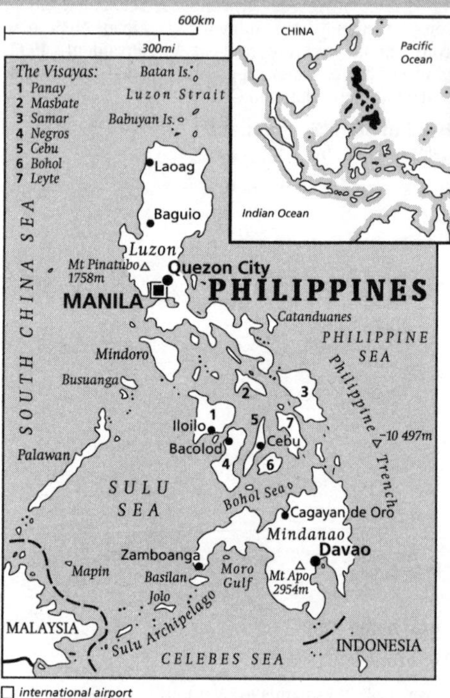

☐ international airport

Head of State/Government

1986–92 Maria Corazon Aquino
1992– Fidel Ramos

PITCAIRN ISLANDS >> UNITED KINGDOM

POLAND

Local name Polska

Timezone GMT + 1

Area 312 612 sq km/120 668 sq mi

Population total (1991e) 37 799 000

Status Republic

Date of independence 1918

Capital Warsaw

Language Polish (official)

Ethnic groups Polish (99%), Ukrainian, Belorussian and Jewish minorities

Religions Roman Catholic (95%), small Jewish and Muslim minorities

Physical features Part of the great European plain, with the Carpathian and Sudetes Mts (S) rising in the High Tatra to 2 499 m/8 199 ft at Mt Rysy; Polish plateau in N, cut by the Bug, San and Wisla (Vistula) rivers; richest coal basin in Europe in the W (Silesia); flat Baltic coastal area; forests cover 20% of land.

Climate Continental climate, with severe winters, hot summers; average annual temperatures −4°C (Jan), 19°C (Jul) in Warsaw; average annual rainfall 550 mm/22 in.

Currency 1 Złoty (Zl) = 100 groszy

Economy Nearly 50% of the land under cultivation; major producer of coal; zinc, lead, sulphur; shipbuilding, machinery, vehicles, electrical equipment; textiles.

GDP (1990) $158 bln, per capita $4 200

History Emergence as a powerful Slavic group, 11th-c; united with Lithuania, 1569; divided between Prussia, Russia and Austria, 1772, 1793, 1795; semi-independent state after Congress of Vienna, 1815; incorporated into the Russian Empire; after World War 1, declared an independent Polish state, 1918; partition between Germany and the USSR, 1939; invasion by Germany, 1939; major resistance movement, and a government in exile during World War 2; People's Democracy established under Soviet influence, 1944; rise of independent trade union, Solidarity, 1980; state of martial law imposed, 1981–3; loss of support for communist government and major success for Solidarity in 1989 elections; proclaimed Polish Republic, 1989, and constitution amended to provide for a bicameral National Assembly.

Head of State
1989–9 Wojciech Jaruzelski
1990– Lech Walesa

Head of Government
1989–91 Tadeusz Mazowiecki
1991 Jan Krzysztof Bielecki
1991–2 Jan Olszewski
1992 Waldemar Pawlak
1992–3 Hanna Suchocka
Elections scheduled for Sep, 1993

POLYNESIA, FRENCH >> FRANCE

PORTUGAL

Local name Portugal

Timezone GMT

Area 88 500 sq km/34 200 sq mi

Population total (1991e) 10 387 000

Status Republic

Capital Lisbon

Languages Portuguese (official), with many dialectal variations

Ethnic groups Homogeneous (Mediterranean stock), with small African minority

Religions Roman Catholic (97%), Protestant (1%), Muslim minority

Physical features Located on W side of Iberian peninsula; includes semi-autonomous Azores and Madeira Is; chief mountain range, the Serra da Estrêla (N), rising to 1 991 m/6 532 ft; main rivers, Douro, Tagus, Guadiana, are the lower courses of rivers beginning in Spain.

Climate Cool, maritime climate in N; warmer Mediterranean type in S; most rainfall in winter; average annual temperature 11°C (Jan), 22°C (Jul) in Lisbon; average annual rainfall 686 mm/27 in.

Currency 1 Escudo (Esc) = 100 centavos

Economy Several labour-intensive areas, including textiles, leather, wood products, cork, ceramics; timber;

Portugal (continued)

wine, fish; chemicals, electrical machinery, steel, shipbuilding; minerals, cereals, pulses, fruit, olive oil; c.20% of land is forested.

GDP (1990) $57 bln, per capita $5 580

History Became a kingdom under Alphonso I, 1139; major period of world exploration and beginning of Portuguese Empire, 15th-c; under Spanish domination, 1580–1640; invaded by the French, 1807; island of Azores granted semi-autonomy, 1895; monarchy overthrown and republic established, 1910; dictatorship of Dr Salazar, 1932–68; military coup, 1974, followed by 10 years of political unrest under 15 governments; island of Madeira gained partial autonomy, 1980; Macao is still administered by Portugal; joined EC, 1985; governed by a president, elected for five years, a prime minister and Council of Ministers, and a 250-member unicameral Assembly of the Republic, elected every four years.

Head of State
1986– Mário Alberto Nobre Lopez Soares

Head of Government
1986– Aníbal Cavaço Silva

AZORES

Local name Ilhas dos Açôres

Timezone GMT – 1

Area 2 300 sq km/900 sq mi

Population total (1990) 252 000

Status Semi-autonomous region of Portugal

Capital Ponta Delgada (on São Miguel Island)

Physical features Island archipelago of volcanic origin, 1 400–1 800 km/870–1 100 mi W of mainland Portugal; three widely separated groups of nine islands; Flores and Corvo (NW), Terceira, Graciosa, São Jorge, Faial (Fayal), Pico (C), and Santa Maria with the Formigas Islands and São Miguel, the principal island (E); highest point, Pico, 2 351 m/7 713 ft; volcanic terrain.

Economy Agriculture; grain, fruit, tea, tobacco, wine.

History Settled by the Portugese, 1439; under Spanish rule, 1580–1640; new constitution established, 1832, when islands were grouped into three administrative districts; given limited autonomous administration, 1895; has no central government, but a General Council.

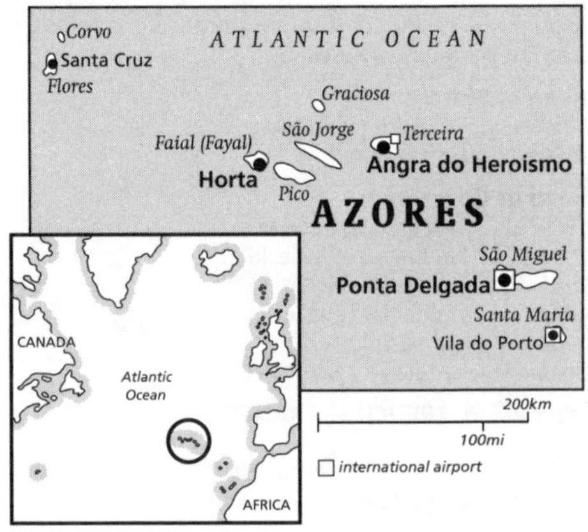

MADEIRA (Islands)

Local name Ilha de Madeira

Timezone GMT

Area 813 sq km/314 sq mi

Population total (1990) 275 000

Status Semi-autonomous region of Portugal

Capital Funchal (on Madeira Island)

Physical features Main island in an archipelago off the coast of N Africa, 990 km/615 mi SW of Lisbon; consists of Madeira, Porto Santo and three uninhabited islands; highest point, Pico Ruivo de Santana, 1 861 m/6 106 ft on Madeira.

Economy Agriculture; sugar cane, fruit, fishing, Madeira (a fortified wine); embroidery, crafts; tourism.

History
Occupied by the Portuguese, 16th-c; occupied by Britain, 1801, and 1807–14; gained partial autonomy, 1980, but remains a Portuguese overseas territory; locally elected government, and Assembly.

MACAO

Local name Macáu

Timezone GMT + 8

Area 16 sq km/6 sq mi

Population total (1991e) 399 000

Status Territory under Portguese administration

Capital Nome de Deus de Macau

Languages Portuguese and Cantonese (official), with English generally spoken

Ethnic group Chinese (99%)

Religions Roman Catholic, Buddhist

Physical features Flat, maritime tropical peninsula in SE China; also includes the nearby islands of Taipa and Colôane; on the Pearl R delta, 64 km/40 mi W of Hong Kong; ferry links with Hong Kong.

Climate Subtropical; cool winters, warm summers.

Currency 1 Pataca = 100 avos

Economy Textiles, electronics, toys, tourism, fishing.

History Portuguese trade with China began in 16th-c; Macao became a Portuguese colony, 1557; right of permanent occupation granted to Portugal by the Sino-Portuguese treaty, 1887; Portugal changed Macao's status from overseas province to a 'territory under Portuguese administration', 1974; Sino-Portuguese negotiations on the transfer of administration began 1986; in 1987 Portugal and China agreed that Macao would revert to China in 1999, when it will become a 'special administrative region' of China; governor appointed by Portugal; Legislative Assembly.

Head of State/Government (Governor)
1987– Carlos Melancia

Map >> CHINA

PUERTO RICO >> UNITED STATES OF AMERICA

QATAR

Local name Qatar

Timezone GMT + 3

Area 11 437 sq km/4 415 sq mi

Population total (1991e) 518 000

Status Independent state

Date of independence 1971

Capital Doha

Languages Arabic (official), English

Ethnic groups Arab (40%), Pakistani (18%), Indian (18%), Iranian (10%)

Religion Sunni Muslim (95%)

Physical features Low-lying state on the E coast of the Arabian Peninsula, comprising the Qatar Peninsula and numerous small offshore islands; the peninsula, 160 km/100 mi long and 34 km–50 mi wide, slopes gently from the Dukhan Heights 98 m/321 ft, to the E shore; barren terrain, mainly sand and gravel; coral reefs offshore.

Climate Desert climate; average temperatures 23°C (Jan), 35°C (Jul); high humidity; sparse rainfall; average annual rainfall 62 mm/2.4 in.

Currency 1 Qatar Riyal (QR) = 100 dirhams

Economy Based on oil; offshore gas reserves thought to be an eighth of known world reserves; oil refineries, petrochemicals, liquefied natural gas, fertilizers, steel, cement, ship repairing, engineering; fishing.

GDP (1988) $6.6 bln, (1990) per capita $12 500

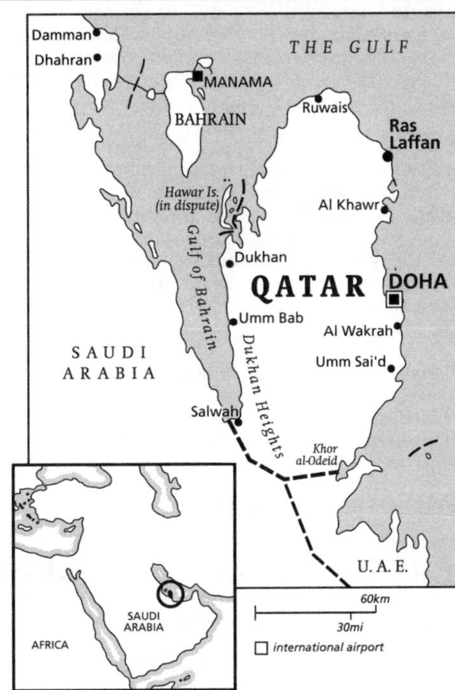

History British protectorate after Turkish withdrawal, 1916; independence, 1971; palace coup brought Khalifah bin Hamad to power, 1972; historic territorial dispute with Bahrain over Hawar Is following brief occupation of Fasht-al Dibal (a coral reef being reclaimed from sea by Bahrain) by Qatari troops; a hereditary monarchy, with an emir who is both head of state and prime minister; Council of Ministers assisted by a 30-member nominated Consultative Council.

Head of State/Government (Emir)
Family name: al-Thani
1971–2 Ahmad bin Ali
1972– Khalifa bin Hamad

RÉUNION >> FRANCE

ROMANIA

Local name Romãnia

Timezone GMT + 2

Area 237 500 sq km/91 675 sq mi

Population total (1991e) 23 397 000

Status Republic

Date of independence 1918

Capital Bucharest

Languages Romanian (official), with French, Hungarian and German widely spoken

Ethnic groups Romanian (89%), Hungarian (7%), German (2%), Ukrainian, Serb, Croat, Russian, Turk and Gypsy (2%)

Religions Eastern Orthodox Christian (80%), Roman Catholic (6%), Calvinist, Lutheran, Baptist (4%)

Physical features Carpathian Mts form the heart of the country; highest peak, Negoiu, 2 548 m/8 359 ft; crossed by many rivers; c.3 500 glacial ponds, lakes and coastal lagoons; over 25% of land is forested.

Climate Continental, with cold, snowy winters and warm summers; winters can be severe; mildest along the Black Sea coast; average annual temperatures range from 7°C (N), to 11°C (S), −3°C (Jan), 24°C (Jul); average annual rainfall 579 mm/22.8 in.

Currency 1 Leu (plural lei) = 100 bani

Economy Gradual change from agricultural to industrial economy (since World War 2); state owns nearly 37% of farm land, mainly organized as collectives and state farms; wheat, maize, sugar beet, fruit, potatoes; livestock; oil, natural gas; iron and steel, metallurgy, engineering, chemicals, textiles, electronics, timber; tourism.

GDP (1990) $69 bln, per capita $3 000

History Formed from the unification of Moldavia and Wallachia, 1862; monarchy created, 1866; Transylvania, Bessarabia, and Bucovina united with Romania, 1918; support given to Germany in World War 2; occupied by Soviet forces, 1944; monarchy abolished and People's Republic declared, 1947; Socialist Republic declared, 1965; increasingly independent from the USSR from the 1960s; leading political force was the Romanian Communist Party, led by dictator Nicolae Ceaucescu; popular uprising due to violent repression of protest led to the overthrow of the Ceaucescu regime, 1989; new constitution, 1991, gave executive power to a directly elected president, who elects a prime minister and cabinet; Chamber of Deputies and a Senate.

Head of State

1989– Ion Iliescu

Head of Government

1989–91 Petre Roman
1991–2 Theodor Stolojan
1992– Nicolae Vacaroiu

ROSS DEPENDENCY >> NEW ZEALAND

RUSSIA (RUSSIAN FEDERATION)

Local name Rossiyskaya (Rossiyskaya Federatsiya)

Timezone GMT ranges from + 3 to + 13

Area 17 075 400 sq km/6 591 100 sq mi

Population total (1992e) 148 800 000

Status Republic

Date of independence 1991

Capital Moscow

Languages Russian (official), and c.100 different languages

Ethnic groups Russian (82%), Tatars (3%), Ukrainian (3%)

Religions Christian (Russian Orthodox 25%), nonreligious (60%), Muslim

Physical features Occupying much of E Europe and N Asia; consists of c.75% of the area of the former USSR and contains over 50% of its population; vast plains dominate the W half; Ural Mts separate the E European Plain (W) from the W Siberian Lowlands (E); E of the R Yenisey lies the C Siberian Plateau; N Siberian Plain further E; Caucasus on S frontier; Lena, Ob, Severnaya Dvina, Pechora, Yenisey, Indigirka, and Kolyma rivers flow to the Arctic Ocean; Amur, Argun, and rivers of the Kamchatka

Peninsula flow to the Pacific Ocean; Caspian Sea basin includes the Volga and Ural rivers; over 20 000 lakes, the largest being the Caspian Sea, L Taymyr, L Baikal.

Climate Half of country covered by snow for 6 months of year; coldest region, NE Siberia, average annual temperature −46 °C (Jan), 16 °C (Jul); summers in rest of country generally short and hot; average annual temperature −18–9 °C (Jan), 16–24 °C (Jul) in Moscow; average annual rainfall 500–750 mm/ 20–30 in.

Currency Rouble (R)

Economy Oil fields in W Siberia (provide 50% of country's petroleum); series of 5-year plans since 1928 promoted industry; heavy industry products include chemicals, construction materials, machine tools and steel-making; mining, major producer of iron ore, manganese, natural gas, nickel and platinum, also coal, copper, gold, zinc, tin, lead; agriculture, primarily wheat, fruit, vegetables, tobacco, cotton, sugar beet; textiles; timber.

GDP Not available
Former USSR GNP (1989) 1 064 000 mln, per capita $3 800

History Conquered by Mongols, 13th-c; Ivan IV (the Terrible) became first ruler to be crowned Tsar, 1547; Time of Trouble, 1604–13; under Peter the Great, territory expanded to the Baltic Sea and St Petersburg founded as capital, 1703; Napoleon invasion failed, 1812; Crimean War, 1853–6; emancipation of the serfs, 1861; assassination of Alexander II, 1881; Balkan War with Turkey, 1877–8; Russo-Japanese War, 1904–5; establishment of a parliament (Duma) with limited powers, 1906; Russia allied with Britain and France, World War I; revolution overthrew Nicholas II, Bolsheviks (Communists) seized power under the dictatorship of Lenin, 1917; Russia forced to withdraw from War; renamed the Russian Soviet Federated Socialist Republic, 1918, and Moscow was reinstated as the capital; Russia became part of the Union of Soviet Socialist Republics (USSR), established, 1922; death of Lenin, 1924; Trotsky deported in 1928 by which time Stalin acquiring dictatorial power; USSR fought with the Allies against Germany in World War II; from 1946 development of the Cold War between East and West; troops intervene in Afghanistan, 1979; radical reform of the system under the leadership of Gorbachev, 1985–91; first contested elections in Soviet history held, and the end of the Cold War announced, 1989; troops withdrawn from Afghanistan, 1989; during war over Nagorno Karabakh troops sent to Azerbaijan to defuse situation, 1990; declarations of sovereignty made by Baltic republics, recognized by Russian leadership, but not by USSR; Yeltsin first elected president of Russian Republic, 1991; coup attempt to remove Gorbachev (president of USSR) from power failed, August 1991; his position, however, undermined by Yeltsin who encouraged the rapid dissolution of the Soviet Union and banished communist structures; Yeltsin began negotiations for the formation of a new confederal Commonwealth of Independent States (CIS); Gorbachev resigned and USSR dissolved, end December 1991; Russian Republic became independent and a founder member of the CIS in 1991; legislative power exercised by Congress of People's Deputies and the bicameral Supreme Soviet; as a preliminary to a new Russian constitution, a Federal Treaty was signed by the 21 republics which are constituent parts of the Russian Federation, March 1992.

Head of State

1991– Boris Yeltsin

Head of Government

1991–2 Yegor Gaidar *Acting*
1992– Victor Chernomyrdin *Interim*

>> Political Leaders and Rulers

RWANDA

Local name Rwanda

Timezone GMT + 2

Area 26 338 sq km/10 166 sq mi

Population total (1991e) 7 902 000

Status Republic

Date of independence 1962

Capital Kigali

Languages French and Kinyarwanda (official), with Kiswahili widely used in commerce

Ethnic groups Hutu (84%), Tutsi (14%), Pygmoid Twa (1%)

Religions Roman Catholic (65%), local indigenous beliefs (17%), Protestant (9%), Muslim (9%)

Physical features Landlocked in C Africa; mountainous, with many of the highest mountains formed by volcanoes; highest point Karisimbi, 4 507 m/14 787 ft, in the Virunga range; W third drains into L Kivu and then the R Congo, remainder drains towards the R Nile; L Kivu and Ruzizi river form W border as part of Africa's Great Rift Valley.

Climate Tropical climate, influenced by high altitude; average annual temperature 19°C (Jan), 21°C (Jul) in Kigali; average annual rainfall 1 000 mm/40 in in Kigali; two wet seasons (Oct–Dec, Mar–May); highest rainfall in the W, decreasing in the C uplands and to the N and E.

Currency 1 Rwanda Franc (RF) = 100 centimes

Economy Based largely on agriculture; coffee, tea, pyrethrum, maize, beans, livestock; minerals; plastic goods, textiles.

GDP (1989) $2.1 bln, per capita $310

History In the 16th-c the Tutsi tribe moved into the country and took over from the Hutu, forming a monarchy; German protectorate, 1899; mandated with Burundi to Belgium as the Territory of Ruanda-Urundi, 1919; United Nations Trust Territory administered by Belgium, after World War 2; unrest in 1959 led to a Hutu revolt and the overthrow of Tutsi rule; independence, 1962; military coup, 1973; return to civilian rule, 1980; further fighting, 1990; governed by a National Development Council of 70 members, a president, and a Council of Ministers; new constitution providing for a multi party democracy, 1991, and introduced the post of prime minister.

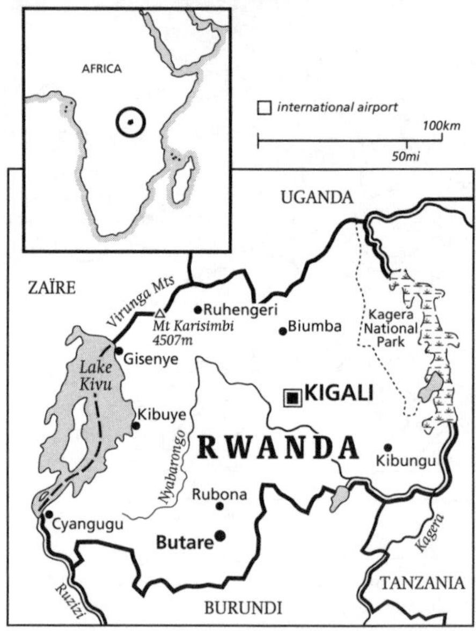

Head of State

1973– Juvenal Habyarimana

Head of Government

1991–2 Sylvestre Nsanzimana

1992– Dismas Nsengiyaremye

SAINT HELENA AND DEPENDENCIES >> UNITED KINGDOM

SAINT KITTS AND NEVIS

Local name Saint Christopher (Kitts) and Nevis

Timezone GMT – 4

Area 269 sq km/104 sq mi

Population total (1991e) 40 293

Status Independent state within the Commonwealth

Date of independence 1983

Capital Basseterre

Languages English (official), with creole-English widely spoken

Ethnic groups Black African descent (94%), mulatto (3%), White (1%)

Religions Christian (Anglican 36%, Methodist 32%, other Protestant 8%, Roman Catholic 11%)

Physical features Located in the N Leeward Is, E Caribbean; comprises the islands of St Christopher (St Kitts), Nevis and Sombrero; volcanic origin with mountain ranges rising to 1 156 m/3 793 ft at Mt Misery; Nevis dominated by a central peak rising to 985 m/3 232 ft.

Climate Tropical, warm climate; average annual temperature 26°C; average annual rainfall 1 375 mm/54 in; low humidity, modified by sea winds; hurricanes possible (Jul–Oct).

Currency 1 East Caribbean Dollar (EC$) = 100 cents

Economy Sugar and its products (supply 60% of total exports); copra, cotton, electrical appliances, footwear, garments, tourism.

GDP (1988) $97 mln, per capita not available

History St Kitts was the first British colony in the W

Indies, 1623; control disputed between France and Britain, 17th–18th-c; ceded to Britain, 1783; St Kitts and Nevis united in 1882; area gained full internal self-government, 1967; Anguilla declared itself independent from the control of St Kitts, which led to British troops intervention, 1969; island reverted to being a British dependent territory, 1971 and was formally separated from St Kitts-Nevis, 1980; independence of St Kitts-Nevis, 1983; British monarch is represented by a governor-general; governed by a prime minister and two legislative chambers; island of Nevis has its own legislature (the Nevis Island Assembly), and executive, which has exclusive responsibility for the island's internal administration.

Head of State
(British monarch represented by Governor-General)
1983– Sir Clement Athelston Arrindell

Head of Government
1983– Kennedy Alphonse Simmonds

SAINT LUCIA

Local name Saint Lucia

Timezone GMT - 4

Area 616 sq km/238 sq mi

Population total (1991e) 153 075

Status Independent state within the Commonwealth

Date of independence 1979

Capital Castries

Languages English (official), with French patois widely spoken

Ethnic groups African descent (90%), mixed (6%), East Indian (3%), Caucasian (1%)

Religions Christian (Roman Catholic 90%, Protestant 7%, Anglican 3%)

Physical features Second largest of the Windward Is, E Caribbean; volcanic island; forested mountainous centre rising to 950 m/3 117 ft at Mt Gimie; sulphurous springs of Qualibou and twin peaks of Gros and Petit Pitons (SW).

Climate Tropical climate; average temperature 26°C; wet season (May–Aug), dry season (Jan–Apr); average annual rainfall 1 500 mm/59 in (lowlands), 3 500 mm/138 in (mountainous zone).

Currency 1 East Caribbean Dollar (EC$) = 100 cents

Economy Tourism (fastest-growing sector of the economy); bananas, cocoa, copra, citrus fruits, coconut oil; garments, textiles, electronic components; oil refining and transshipment.

GDP (1989) $267 mln, per capita $1 810

History Reputedly visited by Columbus, 1502; disputed ownership between England and France, 17th–18th-c; British Crown Colony, 1814; full internal autonomy, 1967; independence, 1979; British monarch represented by a governor-general; House of Assembly, elected every five years, and a Senate.

Head of State
(British monarch represented by Governor-General)
1988– Stanislaus A James

Head of Government
1982– John George Melvin Compton

Map >> VENEZUELA

SAINT PIERRE AND MIQUELON >> FRANCE

SAINT VINCENT AND THE GRENADINES

Local name Saint Vincent and the Grenadines

Timezone GMT - 4

Area 390 sq km/150 sq mi

Population total (1991e) 114 000

Status Independent state within the Commonwealth

Date of independence 1979

Capital Kingstown

Languages English (official), with French patois widely spoken

Ethnic groups Black African descent (82%), mixed (14%), White, Asian and Amerindian minorities

Religions Christian (Anglican 42%, Methodist 21%, Roman Catholic 12%)

Physical features Island group of the Windward Is, E Caribbean, comprising the island of St Vincent and the N Grenadine Is; St Vincent volcanic in origin; highest peak, Soufrière, active volcano 1 234 m/4 048 ft (N), most recent eruption, 1979.

Climate Tropical climate, average annual temperature, 25°C; average annual rainfall 1 500 mm/60 in (coast), 3 800 mm/150 in (interior).

Currency 1 East Caribbean Dollar (EC$) = 100 cents

Economy Based on agriculture; bananas, arrowroot (world's largest producer), coconuts, spices, sugar cane; food processing, textiles; tourism.

GDP (1989) $146 mln, per capita $1 315

History Visited by Columbus, 1498; British control, 1763; part of West Indies Federation, 1958–62; achieved internal self-govenment, 1969; independence, 1979; British sovereign represented by a governor-general; a prime minister leads a unicameral National Assembly.

Head of State
(British monarch represented by Governor-General)
1989– David Jack

Head of Government
1984– James FitzAllan Mitchell

Map >> VENEZUELA

SALVADOR >> EL SALVADOR

SAMOA, AMERICAN >> UNITED STATES OF AMERICA

SAMOA, WESTERN >> WESTERN SAMOA

SAN MARINO

Local name San Marino

Timezone GMT + 1

Area 61 sq km/23 sq mi

Population total (1991e) 23 000

Status Republic

Capital San Marino

Language Italian (official)

Ethnic groups Sanmarinesi (San Marino citizens) (87%), Italian (12%)

Religion Roman Catholic (95%)

Physical features Landlocked in C Italy; smallest republic in the world, land boundaries, 34 km/21 mi; ruggedly mountainous, centred on the limestone ridges of Monte Titano, 793 m/2 602 ft, and the valley of the R Ausa.

Climate Temperate climate, with cool winters, warm summers, average annual temperatures −6°C (Jan), 26°C (Jul); moderate rainfall; average annual rainfall 880 mm /35 in.

Currency 1 Italian Lira (L, Lit)/1 San Marino Lira = 100 centesimi

Economy Wheat, grapes, cheese, livestock; postage stamps, tourism, textiles, pottery; chemicals, paints, wine.

GDP (1990) $393 mln, per capita not available

History Founded by a 4th-c Christian saint as a refuge against religious persecution; treaty of friendship with the Kingdom of Italy, preserving independence, 1862; in World War 2, followed Italy and declared war on Britain, 1940; declared neutrality shortly before Italian surrender, 1943; governed by an elected 60-member unicameral parliament (the Grand and General Council) and an 11-member Congress of State; parliament elects two of its members every six months to act as captains-regent (Capitani Reggenti), with the functions of head of state.

Head of State/Government (Captains-Regent)

Oct 1992–Mar 1993 Romeo Morri/Marino Zanotti
Apr 1993–Sep 1993 Patricia Busignani/Salvatore Tonelli

Map >> ITALY

SÃO TOMÉ AND PRÍNCIPE

Local name São Tomé e Príncipe

Timezone GMT + 1

Area 963 sq km/372 sq mi

Population total (1991e) 128 000

Status Democratic republic

Date of independence 1975

Capital São Tomé

Languages Portuguese (official), with a number of creoles spoken

Ethnic groups Portuguese-African descent, African minority

Religions Roman Catholic (80%), Seventh Day Adventist and Evangelical Protestant

Physical features Equatorial volcanic islands in the Gulf of Guinea, off the coast of Equatorial Guinea, W Africa; comprises São Tomé, Príncipe, and several smaller islands; São Tomé, (area 845 sq km/ 326 sq mi), greatest height, 2 024 m/6 640 ft, Pico de São Tomé in central volcanic uplands; heavily forested.

Climate Tropical climate; average annual temperature 27°C (coast), 20°C (mountains); rainy season (Oct–May); annual average rainfall 500–1 000 mm/20–40 in.

Currency 1 Dobra (Db) = 100 centimos

Economy Based on agriculture (employs c.70% of population); cocoa, copra, palm kernels, coffee, wine, fishing; plans to restructure economy, 1985, with greater involvement in commerce, banking and tourism.

GDP (1989) $46 mln, per capita $384

History Visited by the Portuguese, 1469–72; Portuguese colony, 1522; resistance to Portuguese rule led to riots, 1953, and the formation of an overseas liberation movement based in Gabon; independence, 1975; sole legal party was the Movement for the Liberation of São Tomé and Príncipe, until new constitution, 1990, approved multi party democratic system and created a National Assembly; criticism of economic reforms forced Trovoada to dismiss the government, Apr 1992, and appoint a new prime minister.

Head of State

1975–91 Manuel Pinto da Costa
1991– Miguel Trovoada

Head of Government

1991–2 Daniel Daio
1992– Norberto José d'Alva Costa Alegre

SAUDI ARABIA

Local name Al-'Arabīyah as Sa'ūdīyah (Arabic)

Timezone GMT + 3

Area 2 331 000 sq km/899 766 sq mi

Population total (1991e) 17 869 000

Status Kingdom

Capital Riyadh (Ar-Riyād)

Language Arabic (official)

Ethnic groups Arab (90%), Afro-Asian (10%)

Religions Muslim (Sunni 85%, Shi'ite 15%), small Christian minority

Physical features Comprises four-fifths of the Arabian peninsula; Red Sea coastal plain bounded E by mountains; highlands in SW contain Jebel Abha, Saudi Arabia's highest peak, 3 133m/10 279 ft; Arabian peninsula slopes gently N and E towards oil rich Al Hasa plain on the Arabian Gulf; interior comprises two extensive areas of sand desert, the An Nafud (N) and Rub' al-Khali (the Great Sandy Desert) (S); salt flats numerous in E lowlands; large network of wadis drains NE; 95% of land is arid or semi-arid desert.

Climate Hot, dry climate; average temperatures 21°C (N), 26°C (S), rise to 50°C in the interior; night frosts common in N and highlands; Red Sea coast hot and humid; average annual temperatures 14°C (Jan), 33°C (Jul) in Riyadh; average annual rainfall 100 mm/4 in.

Currency 1 Saudi Arabian Riyal (SAR, SRls) = 100 halalah

Economy Oil discovered in 1930s; now the world's leading oil exporter (reserves account for c.25% of world's known supply); rapidly developing construction industry; large areas opened up for cultivation in 1980s; agriculture; wheat, dates, livestock; pilgrimage trade.

GDP (1989) $79 bln, per capita $4 800

History Famed as the birthplace of Islam, a centre of pilgrimage to the holy cities of Mecca, Medina, and Jedda; modern state founded by Ibn Saud who by 1932 united the four tribal provinces of Hejaz (NW), Asir (SW), Najd (C), and Al Hasa (E); governed as an absolute monarchy based on Islamic law and Arab Bedouin tradition; king (official title: Custodian of the Two Holy Mosques (Mecca and Medina)) is head of state and prime minister, assisted by a Council of Ministers; there is no parliament; royal decree, 1992, provided for the creation of a 60-member Consultative Council to be appointed every 4 years.

Head of State/Government (Monarch)
Family name: Al-Saud
1982– Fahd ibn Abdul Aziz

SCOTLAND >> UNITED KINGDOM

SENEGAL

Local name Sénégal (French)

Timezone GMT

Area 196 840 sq km/75 980 sq mi

Population total (1991e) 7 952 000

Status Republic

Date of independence 1960

Capital Dakar

Languages French (official), with various ethnic languages spoken

Ethnic groups Wolof (36%), Fulani (17%), Serer (17%), Toucouleur (9%), Diola (9%), Mandingo (9%), European and Lebanese (1%)

Religions Sunni Muslim (90%), Roman Catholic (5%), local beliefs (3%)

Physical features Located in W Africa; extensive low-lying basin of savannah and semi-desert vegetation to the N; sand dunes along coastline; dunes and mangrove forests in S, where land rises to around 500 m/1 600 ft; lowland savannah and semi-desert regions of N drain into R Sénégal, which forms the N and NE boundary with Mauritania and Mali.

Climate Tropical climate; rainy season (Jun–Sep); high humidity levels and high night-time temperatures, especially on the coast; average temperature, 22–28°C; average annual rainfall 541 mm/21 in at Dakar.

Currency 1 CFA Franc (CFAFr) = 100 centimes

Human geography

Senegal (continued)

Economy Agriculture (employs c.75% of workforce); groundnuts, cotton, sugar, millet, sorghum, maize, livestock; minerals, iron ore, gold; oil, natural gas; fishing, timber; textiles, chemicals; shipbuilding and repairing; tourism.

GDP (1989) $4.7 bln, per capita $615

History Part of the Mali Empire, 14th–15th-c; French established a fort at Saint-Louis, 1659; incorporated as a territory within French West Africa, 1902; autonomous state within the French community, 1958; joined with French Sudan as independent Federation of Mali, 1959; withdrew in 1960 to become a separate independent republic; joined with The Gambia to form the Confederation of Senegambia, 1982–9; Confederation collapsed, 1989, following violent clashes between Senegalese and Mauritanians; governed by a president (elected for a 5-year term), prime minister, cabinet and 120-member National Assembly.

Head of State
1981– Abdou Diouf

Head of Government
1991– Habib Thiam

SEYCHELLES

Local name Seychelles

Timezone GMT + 4

Area 453 sq km/175 sq mi

Population total (1991e) 68 000

Status Republic

Date of independence 1976

Capital Victoria (on Mahé Island)

Languages Creole (official since 1981), French and English

Ethnic groups Seychellois (Asian, African and European admixtures), Malagasy (3%), Chinese (2%), English (1%)

Religions Roman Catholic (90%), Anglican (8%), other (2%)

Physical features Island group in SW Indian Ocean, N of Madagascar, comprising 115 islands; main islands include Mahé (largest), Praslin and La Digue; islands fall into two main groups, a compact group of 41 mountainous islands rising steeply from the sea, highest point 906 m/2 972 ft on Mahé; and a group of low-lying coralline islands and atolls to the SW, flat, waterless and mostly uninhabited.

Climate Tropical climate; average annual temperature 27°C (Jan), 26°C (Jul); wet humid season (Dec–May); average annual rainfall 2 375 mm/93.5 in.

Currency 1 Seychelles Rupee (SR) = 100 cents

Economy Agriculture; fruit, vegetables, livestock, cinnamon, copra; brewing, plastics, steel fabricated goods, fishing; tourism.

GDP (1989) $285 mln, per capita $4 170

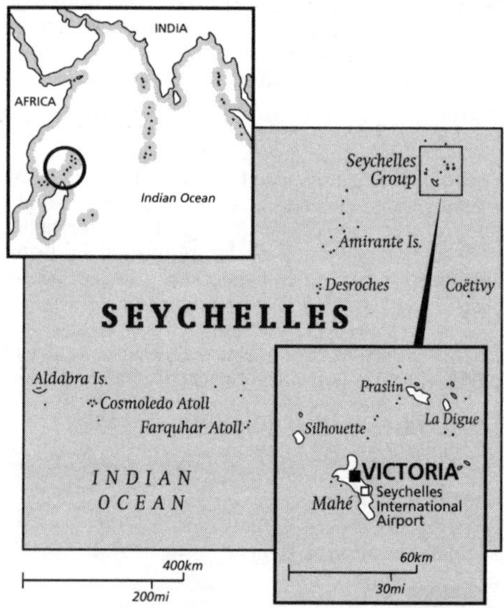

History Colonized by the French, 1768; captured by Britain, 1794; incorporated as a dependency of Mauritius, 1814; separate Crown Colony, 1903; independent republic within the Commonwealth, 1976; constitution, 1979, established a one-party state; governed by a president, elected for a 5-year term, Council of Ministers, and unicameral National Assembly; legislation legalizing the activity of opposition parties adopted, 1991.

Head of State/Government
1977– France-Albert René

SIERRA LEONE

Local name Sierra Leone

Timezone GMT

Area 72 325 sq km/27 917 sq mi

Population total (1991e) 4 274 000

Status Republic

Date of independence 1961

Capital Freetown

Languages English (official), with Krio widely spoken

Ethnic groups African origin (99%) (including Mendes, Temnes, Limbas, Korankos and Lokos)

Religions Local beliefs (70%), Sunni Muslim (25%), Christian (Protestant 6%, Roman Catholic 2%)

Physical features Low narrow coastal plain in W Africa; rises to an average height of 500 m/1 600 ft in the Loma Mts (E), highest point, Loma Mansa, 1 948 m/6 391 ft; Tingi Mts rise to 1 853 m/6 079 ft (SE); principal rivers include the Great Scarcies, Rokel, Gbangbaia, Jong and Sewa.

Climate Equatorial climate; temperatures uniformly high throughout the year; average annual temperature 27°C; rainy season (May–Oct); highest rainfall on coast; average annual rainfall 3 436 mm/135 in at Freetown.

Currency 1 Leone (Le) = 100 cents

Economy Mining (most important sector of the economy); diamonds (represent c.60% of exports); bauxite, gold, titanium, iron ore and other mineral and metal ores; subsistence agriculture (employs over 70% of population); rice, coffee, cocoa, citrus fruits; timber; food processing.

GDP (1989) $1.3 bln, per capita $325

History First visited by Portuguese navigators and British slave traders; land bought from local chiefs by English philanthropists who established settlements for freed slaves, 1780s; British Crown Colony, 1808; hinterland declared a British protectorate, 1896; independence declared within the Commonwealth as a constitutional monarchy, 1961; period of military rule, 1967–8; became a republic, 1971; established as a one-party state, 1978; new constitution, 1991, allowing for multi party politics, and interim government formed until general elections; interrupted by military coup, 1992, government overthrown, House of Representatives dissolved, and Supreme Council of State (SCS) and Civilian Council of State Secretaries (Cabinet) established.

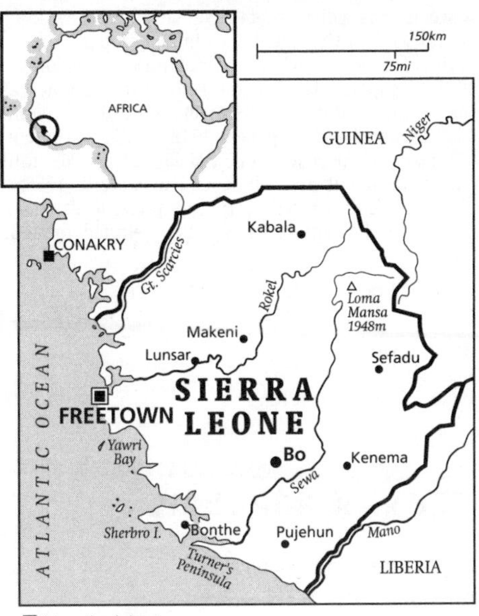

Head of State/Government

1985–92 Joseph Saidu Momoh
1992– Valentine Strasser

SINGAPORE

Local name Singapore

Timezone GMT + 8

Area 618 sq km/238 sq mi

Population total (1991e) 2 756 000

Status Republic

Date of independence 1965

Capital Singapore City

Languages English, Malay, Chinese and Tamil (official)

Ethnic groups Chinese (77%), Malay (15%), Indian (6%)

Religions Chinese population mainly Buddhists, Malay mainly Muslim, also Taoist, Christian and Hindu minorities

Physical features Located at the S tip of the Malay Peninsula, SE Asia; consists of the island of Singapore and c.50 adjacent islets; linked to Malaysia by a causeway across the Johor Strait; Singapore Island is low-lying, rising to 177 m/581 ft at Bukit Timah; Seletar River drains N–E; deep-water harbour (SE).

Climate Equatorial climate; high humidity; no clearly defined seasons; average annual temperature range, 21–34°C; average annual rainfall, 2 438 mm/96 in.

Currency 1 Singapore Dollar/Ringgit (S$) = 100 cents

Economy Major transshipment centre (one of world's largest ports); oil refining; rubber, food processing, chemicals, electronics; ship repair; financial services; fishing.

Singapore (continued)

GDP (1990) \$34.6 bln, (1988) per capita \$12700

History Originally part of the Sumatran Sri Vijaya kingdom; leased by the British East India Company, on the advice of Sir Stamford Raffles, from the Sultan of Johore, 1819; Singapore, Malacca, and Penang incorporated as the Straits Settlements, 1826; British Crown Colony, 1867; occupied by the Japanese, 1942–5; self-government, 1959; part of the Federation of Malaya from 1963 until its establishment as an independent state in 1965; a prime minister, elected every four years, leads a unicameral parliament of 81 members, elected for four years.

Head of State
1985– Wee Kim Wee

Head of Government
1959–90 Lee Kuan Yew
1990– Goh Chok Tong

SLOVAK REPUBLIC

Local name Slovenska republiká

Timezone GMT + 1

Area 49035 sq km/18927 sq mi

Population total (1991) 5274335

Status Republic

Date of independence 1993

Capital Bratislava

Languages Slovak (official), with Czech and Hungarian widely spoken

Ethnic groups Slovak (87%), Hungarian (11%), Czech (1%), with German, Polish and Ukrainian minorities

Religions Roman Catholic (70%), Protestant

Physical features Dominated by the Carpathian Mountains, consisting of a system of E–W ranges separated by valleys and basins; ranges include the Low Tatras of the Inner Carpathians, 1829 m/6000 ft, and the highest point, Gerlachovsky Peak, 2655 m/8710 ft in the Tatra Mts (N); main rivers include the Danube, Vah, Hron; national parks at Pieniny, Low and High Tatra.

Climate Continental climate; warm humid summers, cold dry winters; snow remains on the mountains for 130 days of the year; average annual temperature −4°C (Jan), 18°C (Jul) in Bratislava; average annual rainfall 500–650 mm/20–30 in.

Currency 1 Slovak Crown = 100 halers

Economy Agricultural region, especially cereals, wine, fruit; steel production in Košice; heavy industry suffering since previously dependent on state subsidies.

GDP Not available

History Settled in 5th–6th-c by Slavs; part of Great Moravia, 9th-c; part of Magyar Empire from 10th-c; became part of Kingdom of Hungary, 11th-c; united with Czech lands to form the separate state of Czechoslovakia, 1918; under German control, 1938–9; Slovakia became a separate republic under German influence, 1939; Czechoslovakia regained its independence, 1945; under Communist rule following 1948 coup; attempt at liberalization by Dubcek terminated by intervention of Warsaw Pact troops, 1968; from 1960s, Slovaks revived efforts to gain recognition for Slovak rights; fall from power of Communist party, 1989; 1992 agreement to divide Czechoslovakia into its constituent republics, led to declaration of independence of Slovak Republic, 1993.

Head of State
1993– Michal Kovac

Head of Government
1993– Vladimir Meciar

SLOVENIA

Local name Slovenija

Timezone GMT + 2

Area 20 251 sq km/7 817 sq mi

Population total (1991e) 1 974 000

Status Republic

Date of independence 1991

Capital Ljubljana

Languages Slovene, Serbo-Croat

Ethnic group Slovene (90%)

Religions Roman Catholic, Protestant, some Eastern Orthodox

Physical features Mountainous republic between Austria and Croatia; Slovenian Alps (NW) rise to 2 863 m/ 9 393 ft at Triglav in the Julian Alps (Julijske Alpe); rivers include Sava, Savinja and Drava; chief port, Koper.

Climate Continental climate; more Mediterranean in W; average annual temperature −1°C (Jan), 19°C (Jul) in Ljubljana; average annual rainfall 1 600 mm/63 in.

Currency (1991) 1 Slovene Tolar = 100 paras

Economy Agriculture; maize, wheat, sugar beet, potatoes, livestock, wine, timber, lignite; textiles; large iron and steel plants; vehicles; coal, lead, mercury mining in W.

GDP Not available

History Settled by Slovenes, 6th–8th-c; later controlled by Slavs and Franks; part of the Austro-Hungarian Empire until 1918; people's republic within Yugoslavia, 1946; declaration of full sovereignty, 1990; declaration of independence from Yugoslavia as the Republic of Slovenia, 1991; opposed by central government, brief period of fighting upon the intervention of the federal army who withdrew, Aug 1991; tricameral legislature replaced by a bicameral National Assembly, consisting of 90-seat Chamber of Deputies and a 40-member State Council; Chamber of Associated Labour abolished and a new constitution reduced the role of the president, Dec 1991.

Head of State

1991– Milan Kucan

Head of Government

1991–2 Lojze Peterle
1992– Janez Drnovsek

SOLOMON ISLANDS

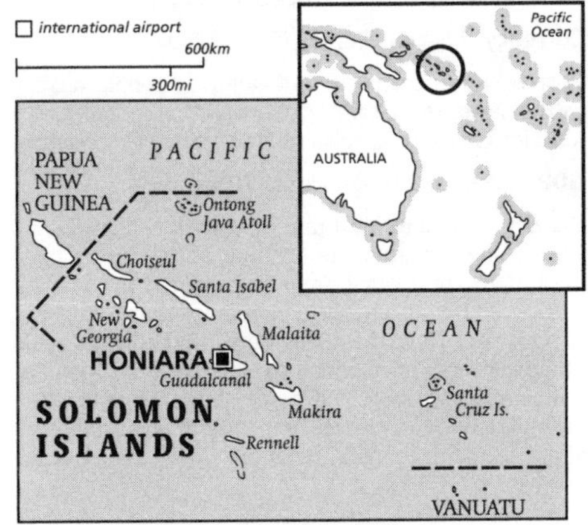

Local name Solomon Islands

Timezone GMT + 11

Land area 27 556 sq km/10 637 sq mi

Population total (1991e) 347 000

Status Independent state within the Commonwealth

Date of independence 1978

Capital Honiara

Languages English (official), with pidgin English and c.80 local languages also spoken

Ethnic groups Melanesian (93%), Polynesian (4%), Micronesian (1.5%), European (1%), Chinese (0.5%)

Religions Christian (95%) (Protestant 41%, Anglican 34%, Roman Catholic 19%)

Physical features Archipelago of several hundred islands in the SW Pacific Ocean, stretching c.1 400 km/ 870 mi, between Papua New Guinea (NW) and Vanuatu

Solomon Islands (continued)

(SE); six main islands, Choiseul, Guadalcanal, Malaita, New Georgia, San Cristobal (now Makira), Santa Isabel; highest point, Mt Makarakomburu, 2 477 m/8 126 ft, on Guadalcanal (largest island); large islands have forested mountain ranges and coastal belts; Anuta, Fataka and Tikopia islands are volcanic.

Climate Equatorial climate; high humidity; average annual temperature 27°C; maximum rainfall Nov–Apr; average annual rainfall, c.3500 mm/138 in; periodic cyclones.

Currency 1 Solomon Islands Dollar (SI$) = 100 cents

Economy Based on agriculture; forestry, livestock, fisheries, taro, rice, bananas, yams, copra, oil palm, rice; milling, fish processing; crafts.

GDP (1989) $156 mln, per capita $570

History Visited by the Spanish, 1568; S Solomon Is placed under British protection, 1893; outer islands (Santa Cruz group) added to the protectorate, 1899; scene of fierce fighting in World War 2; achieved internal self-government, 1976; independence, 1978; British monarch is represented by a governor-general; prime minister leads a unicameral National Parliament of 38 members elected for four years.

Head of State
(British monarch represented by Governor-General)
1988– Sir George Lepping

Head of Government
1989– Solomon Mamaloni

SOMALIA

Local name Somaliya

Timezone GMT + 3

Area 686 803 sq km/265 106 sq mi

Population total (1991e) 6 709 000

Status Republic

Date of independence 1960

Capital Mogadishu

Languages Somali, Arabic (official)

Ethnic groups Somali (85%), Bantu (15%), with Arab, European and Asian minorities

Religions Sunni Muslim (99%), small Christian minority

Physical features Occupies the E Horn of Africa, where dry coastal plain broadens to the S, and rises inland to a plateau c.1 000 m/3 300 ft; forested mountains on the Gulf of Aden coast rise to 2 416 m/7 926 ft at Mt Shimbiris; main rivers, Jubba and Webi Shabeelle.

Climate Predominantly arid; average daily maximum temperatures 28–32°C in Mogadishu; average annual rainfall 490 mm/19.3 in; heavier rainfall (Apr–Sep) on E coast; serious, persistent threat of drought.

Currency 1 Somali Shilling (SoSh) = 100 cents

Economy Agriculture (c.70% nomadic people raising cattle, sheep, goats, camels); bananas, sugar, spices, cotton, rice, citrus fruits, tobacco, iron ore; textiles; fishing.

GDP (1989) $1.7 bln, per capita $170

History Settled by Muslims, 7th-c; Italian, French, and British interests after the opening of the Suez Canal, 1869; after World War 2, Somalia formed by the amalgamation of Italian and British protectorates; independence, 1960; from the 1960s, territorial conflict with Ethiopia over Ogaden which has a large Somali population; military coup, 1969; peace agreement with Ethiopia, 1989; governed by a president, Council of Ministers, and People's Assembly; new constitution

approved, 1990; NE region seceded as Somaliland Republic, 1991; civil war, 1991–2, forced UN troops to intervene to safeguard food supplies for starving population, 1992.

Head of State
1980–91 Mohammed Siad Barre
1991– Ali Mahdi Muhammed *Interim*

Head of Government
1987–90 Mohammed Ali Samater
1990–1 Mohammed Hawadie Madar
1991– Umar Arteh Ghalib

SOUTH AFRICA

Local name Suid-Afrika (Afrikaans)

Timezone GMT + 2

Area 1 233 404 sq km/476§094 sq mi

Population total (1991e) 40 600 000

Status Republic

Date of independence 1961

Capitals Cape Town (legislative); Pretoria (administrative); Bloemfontein (judicial)

Languages English and Afrikaans (official), many African languages spoken, including Xhosa, Zulu and Sesotho

Ethnic groups Black African (70%), White (18%), Asian (3%), Coloured (9%)

Religions Christian (most Whites and Coloureds and c.60% Africans), traditional beliefs, Hindu, Muslim, and Judaist minorities

Physical features Occupies the S extremity of the African plateau, comprising the four provinces of Cape, Natal, Orange Free State and Transvaal; also includes six non-independent national states of Gazankulu, Lebowa, QwaQwa, KwaZulu, KaNgwane, and KwaNdebele; fringed by fold mountains and a lowland coastal margin to the W, E, and S; N interior comprises the Kalahari Basin, scrub grassland and arid desert; Great Escarpment rises E to 3 482 m/11 424 ft at Thabana-Ntlenyana; Orange R flows W to meet the Atlantic; chief tributaries, Vaal and Caledon rivers.

Climate Subtropical in E; average annual temperature 4°C (Jan), 17°C (Jul) in Cape Town; average annual rainfall 1 008 mm/39.7 in Durban; dry moistureless climate on W coast; desert region further N, annual average rainfall less than 30 mm/1.2 in.

Currency 1 Rand (R) = 100 cents

Economy Industrial growth as a result of 19th-c gold (c.50% of export income) and diamond discoveries; grain, wool, sugar, tobacco, cotton, citrus fruit, dairy products, livestock, fishing; motor vehicles, machinery, chemicals, fertilizers, textiles, clothes, metal products, electronics, computers, tourism.

GDP (1990) $101 bln, per capita $2 600

History Originally inhabited by Khoisan tribes; Portuguese reached the Cape of Good Hope, late 15th-c; settled by Dutch, 1652; arrival of British, 1795; British annexation of the Cape, 1814; Great Trek by Boers NE across the Orange R to Natal, 1836; first Boer republic founded, 1839; Natal annexed by the British, 1846, but the Boer republics of Transvaal (founded 1852) and Orange Free State (1854) were recognized; South African Wars, 1880–1, 1899–1902; Transvaal, Natal, Orange Free State, and Cape Province joined as the Union of South Africa, a dominion of the British Empire, 1910; sovereign state within the Commonwealth, 1931–61; independent republic, 1961; independence granted by South Africa to Transkei (1976), Bophuthatswana (1977), Venda (1979) and Ciskei (1981), not recognized internationally; politics dominated by treatment of non-White majority following the apartheid (racial segregation) policy after 1948; continuing racial violence and strikes led to a state of emergency, 1986, and several countries imposed economic and cultural sanctions; progressive dismantling of apartheid system by F W de Klerk from 1990; Black Nationalist leader, Nelson Mandela was freed after more than 27 years in prison, and the African National Congress was unbanned, 1990; readmitted into international sport, USA lifted trade and investment sanctions, 1991; most remaining apartheid legislation abolished, 1991; governed by a tricameral parliament comprising a House of Assembly (for Whites), a House of Representatives (for Coloureds), and a House of Delegates (for Asians); 60-member President's Council.

Head of State/Government

1989– Frederik Willem de Klerk

South African States

Name	*Area* sq km	sq mi	*State capital*
Cape Province (Kaapprovinsie)	641 379	247 636	Cape Town
Natal	91 355	35 272	Pietermaritzburg
Orange Free State (Oranje Vrystaat)	127 993	49 418	Bloemfontein
Transvaal	262 499	101 351	Pretoria
Independent Black Homelands			
Bophuthatswana	44 000	17 000	Mmabatho
Ciskei	7 700	3 000	Bisho
Transkei	42 200	16 300	Umtata
Venda	6 500	2 500	Thohoyandou
Non-independent Black Homelands (National States)			
Gazankulu	6 561	2 533	Giyani
KaNgwane	3 823	1 476	Nyamasane
KwaNdebele	2 860	1 100	Siyabuswa
KwaZulu	30 151	11 642	Uluni
Lebowa	22 503	8 688	Lebowakgom
QwaQwa	502	194	Phuthaditjhaba

SOUTH GEORGIA >> UNITED KINGDOM

SOUTH KOREA >> KOREA, SOUTH

SOUTH SANDWICH ISLANDS >> UNITED KINGDOM

SPAIN

Local name España (Spanish)

Timezone GMT + 1

Area 504 750 sq km/194 833 sq mi

Population total (1991e) 39 384 000

Status Kingdom

Capital Madrid

Languages Spanish (official) with Catalan, Galician and Basque also spoken in their respective regions

Ethnic groups Spanish (Castilian, Valencian, Andalusian, Asturian) (73%), Catalan (16%), Galician (8%), Basque (2%)

Religions Roman Catholic (99%), other Christian (including Anglican, Baptist, Evangelical, Mormon, Jehovah's Witnesses) and Muslim minorities

Physical features Located in SW Europe, occupying four-fifths of the Iberian peninsula; includes the Canary Is, Balearic Is, several islands off the coast of N Africa, as well as the Presidios of Ceuta and Melilla in N Morocco; mostly a furrowed C plateau (the Meseta, average height 700 m/2 300 ft) crossed by mountains; Andalusian or Baetic Mts (SE) rise to 3 478 m/11 411 ft at Mulhacén; Pyrénées (N) rise to 3 404 m/11 168 ft at Pico de Aneto; rivers run E–W, notably the Tagus, Ebro, Guadiana, Miño, Duero, Guadalquivir, Segura, and Júcar.

Climate Continental climate in the Meseta and Ebro Basin, with hot summers, cold winters, low rainfall; highest rainfall in the mountains; S Mediterranean coast has warmest winter temperatures on European mainland; average annual temperatures 5°C (Jan), 25°C (Jul) in Madrid; average annual rainfall 419 mm/16.5 in.

Currency 1 Peseta (Pta, Pa) = 100 céntimos

Economy Traditional agricultural economy gradually being supplemented by varied industries; textiles, iron, steel, shipbuilding, electrical appliances, cars, wine; forestry; fishing; tourism; zinc and other mineral ores; cereals, olives, almonds, pomegranates; member of EC, 1986.

GDP (1990) $435 bln, per capita $11 100

History Early inhabitants included Iberians, Celts, Phoenicians, Greeks, and Romans; Muslim domination from the 8th-c; Christian reconquest completed by 1492; a monarchy since the unification of the Kingdoms of Castile, León, Aragón, and Navarre, largely achieved by 1572; 16th-c exploration of the New World, and the growth of the Spanish Empire; period of decline after the Revolt of the Netherlands, 1581, and the defeat of the Spanish Armada, 1588; War of the Spanish Succession, 1701–14; Peninsular War against Napoleon, 1808–14; war with the USA in 1898 led to the loss of Cuba, Puerto Rico, and remaining Pacific possessions; dictatorship under Primo de Rivera (1923–30), followed by exile of the King and establishment of the Second Republic (1931); military revolt headed by Franco in 1936 led to civil war and a Fascist dictatorship; Prince Juan Carlos of Bourbon nominated to succeed Franco, 1969; acceded, 1975; under 1978 constitution, the Kingdom of Spain is a constitutional monarchy; monarch appoints the prime minister; governed by a bicameral parliament (Cortes Generales) comprising a Congress of Deputies and a Senate; there has been a move towards local government autonomy with the creation of 17 self-governing regions.

Head of State (Monarch)
1975– Juan Carlos I

Head of Government
1982– Felipe González Márquez

BALEARIC ISLANDS

Local name Islas Baleares

Area 5 014 sq km/1 935 sq mi

Population total (1989e) 750 967

Status Province of Spain

Capital Palma de Mallorca

Physical features Archipelago of five major islands and 11 islets in the Mediterranean, near the E coast of Spain; E group of islands consists of Mallorca (Majorca), Menorca, Cabrera; Ibiza and Formentera (W group); popular tourist resorts.

Climate Continental; average annual temperatures 11 °C (Jan), 25 °C (Jul); average annual rainfall 347 mm/14 in.

Currency 1 Peseta (Pta, Pa) = 100 céntimos

Economy Tourism; fruit, wine, grain, cattle, fishing, textiles, chemicals, cork, timber.

CANARY ISLANDS

Local name Islas Canarias

Area 7 273 sq km/2 807 sq mi

Population total (1989e) 1 557 533

Status Forms two provinces of Spain

Chief town Las Palmas

Physical features Island archipelago, located in the Atlantic, 100 km/60 mi off the NW coast of Africa; includes the islands of Tenerife, La Palma, Gomera, Hierro, Grand Canary (Gran Canaria), Fuerteventura, Lanzarote and several uninhabited islands; major ports, Las Palmas, Santa Cruz; volcanic and mountainous, the Pico de Teide rises to 3 718 m/12 198 ft on Tenerife; tourist resorts on main islands.

Climate Continental; average annual temperature 18 °C (Jan), 24 °C (Jul); average annual rainfall 196 mm/8 in.

Currency 1 Peseta (Pta, Pa) = 100 céntimos

Economy Tourism; agriculture, fishing, canning, textiles, leatherwork, footwear, cork, timber, chemical and metal products.

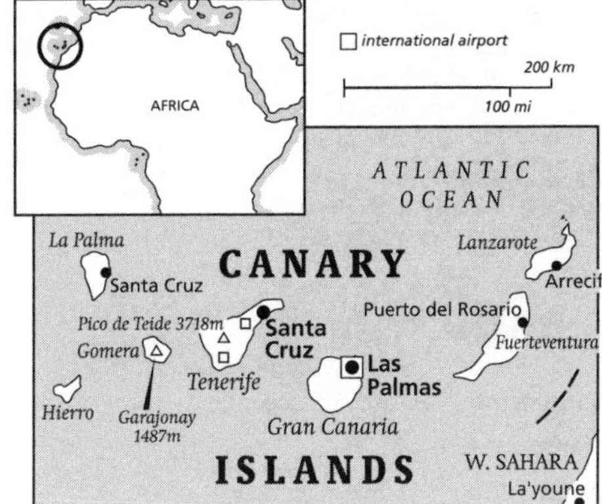

SRI LANKA

Local name Sri Lanka

Timezone GMT + 5.5

Area 65 610 sq km/25 325 sq mi

Population total (1991e) 17 423 000

Status Republic

Date of independence 1972

Capital Sri-Jayawardenapura (since 1983); (former capital, Colombo)

Languages Sinhala, Tamil (official), English also spoken

Ethnic groups Sinhalese (74%), Tamil (18%), Muslim (7%), Burgher, Malay and Veddha (1%)

Religions Buddhist (69%), Hindu (15%), Christian (8%), Muslim (8%)

Sri Lanka (continued)

Physical features Island state in the Indian Ocean; separated from the Indian sub-continent by the Palk Strait, linked by a series of coral islands known as Adam's Bridge; low-lying areas in N and S, surrounding SC uplands; highest peak, Pidurutalagala, 2524 m/8281 ft; coastal plain fringed by sandy beaches and lagoons; c.50% of land is tropical monsoon forest or open woodland.

Climate Equatorial, tropical climate; modified temperatures in interior according to altitude; average annual temperature 27°C in Sri-Jayawardenapura; average annual rainfall 2527 mm/99.5 in; greatest rainfall on SW coast and in the mountains; monsoon season (Dec–Feb) in NE, dry, semi-arid for rest of year.

Currency 1 Sri Lanka Rupee (SLR, SLRs) = 100 cents

Economy Agriculture (employs 46% of labour force); rice, rubber, tea, coconuts, spices, sugar cane; timber, fishing; graphite, coal, precious and semi-precious stones; electricity produced largely by water power; textiles, chemicals, paper.

GDP (1990) $6.6 bln, per capita $380

History Visited by the Portuguese, 1505; taken by the Dutch, 1658; British occupation, 1796; British colony, 1802; Tamil labourers brought in from S India during colonial rule, to work on coffee and tea plantations; Dominion status, 1948; changed former name of Ceylon and became the independent republic of Sri Lanka, 1972; governed by a president and a National State Assembly; acute political tension exists between the Buddhist Sinhalese majority and the Hindu Tamil minority, who wish to establish an independent state in the N and E; considerable increase in racial violence in the area during the 1980s; state of emergency declared, 1983.

Head of State

1989–93	Ranasinghe Premadasa
1993–	Dingiri Banda Wijedunga

Head of Government

1989–93	Dingiri Banda Wijedunga
1993–	Ranil Wickremasinghe

SUDAN, THE

Local name As-Sūdān (Arabic)

Timezone GMT + 2

Area 2504530 sq km/966749 sq mi

Population total (1991e) 27220000

Status Republic

Date of independence 1956

Capital Khartoum

Languages Arabic (official), local languages, including Darfurian, Nilotic and Nilo-Hamitic, are also spoken

Ethnic groups Black (52%), Arab (39%), Beja (6%)

Religions Muslim (Sunni 70%), traditional animist beliefs (20%), Christian (5%)

Physical features Largest country on the African continent, astride the middle reaches of the R Nile; E edge formed by Nubian Highlands and an escarpment rising c.2000 m/6500 ft on the Red Sea; Imatong Mts (S) rise to 3187 m/10456 ft at Kinyeti, highest point in Sudan;

Darfur Massif in the W; White Nile flows N to meet the Blue Nile at Khartoum.

Climate Tropical, continental; desert conditions in NW, with temperatures rarely falling below 24°C; hottest months (Jul–Aug); sandstorms common; average annual temperature 23°C (Jan), 32°C (Jul) in Khartoum; average annual rainfall 157 mm/6.2 in.

Currency 1 Sudanese pound (LSd, £S) = 100 piastres

Economy Dominated by agriculture (employs c.75% of population); commercial farming (N) and livestock farming (S); large-scale irrigation schemes, fed by dams; major famines, especially 1984–5, 1990–1; gum arabic (80% of world supply); reserves of copper, lead, iron ore, chromite, manganese, gold; development hindered by poor transport system.

GDP (1990) $8.5 bln, per capita $330

History Christianized, 6th-c; Muslim conversion from 13th-c; Egyptian control of N Sudan, early 19th-c; Mahdi unified W and C tribes in a revolution, 1881; fall of Khartoum, 1885; combined British-Egyptian offensive, 1898, leading to a jointly administered condominium; independence, 1956; period of military rule following coup, 1985; drought and N-S rivalry have contributed to years of instability and several coups; a transitional constitution of 1987 provided for a president, prime minister, Council of Ministers and Legislative Assembly; military coup, 1989, suspended constitution and dissolved National Assembly which was replaced by a Revolutionary Command Council; continuing civil war between N and S, 1990.

Head of State/Government
1989– Omar Hassan Ahmad al-Bashir

SURINAME

Local name Suriname

Timezone GMT – 3

Area 163 265 sq km/63 020 sq mi

Population total (1991e) 402 000

Status Republic

Date of independence 1975

Capital Paramaribo

Languages Dutch (official), Hindu and Javanese (native languages), Sranan Tongo, Chinese and Spanish also spoken

Ethnic groups Hindustani (East Indian) (37%), Creole (31%), Javanese (15%), Amerindian (3%), Chinese (2%), European (1%)

Religions Hindu (27%), Protestant (25%), Roman Catholic (23%), Muslim (20%), indigenous beliefs (5%)

Physical features Located in NE South America; natural regions, range from coastal lowland through savannah to mountainous upland; coastal strip covered by swamp; highland interior (S) overgrown with dense tropical forest; highest point, Juliana Top, 1 230 m/4 035 ft, in SC; seven major rivers including Marowijne (E), Corantijn (W) and Suriname.

Climate Equatorial tropical, uniformly hot and humid; two rainy seasons (May–Jul, Nov–Jan); average annual temperatures 22–33°C in Paramaribo; average monthly rainfall 310 mm/12.2 in (N), 67 mm/2.6 in (S).

Currency 1 Suriname Guilder/Florin (SGld, F) = 100 cents

Economy Based on agriculture and mining, but hindered by lack of foreign exchange; bauxite mining (provides c.80% of export income); sugar cane, rice, citrus fruits, coffee, bananas, oil palms, cacao, fishing; vast timber resources.

GDP (1989) $1.3 bln, per capita $3 400

History Sighted by Columbus, 1498; first settled by the British, 1651; taken by the states of Zeeland, 1667; captured by the British, 1799; restored to the Netherlands, 1818 and remained part of Netherland West Indies as

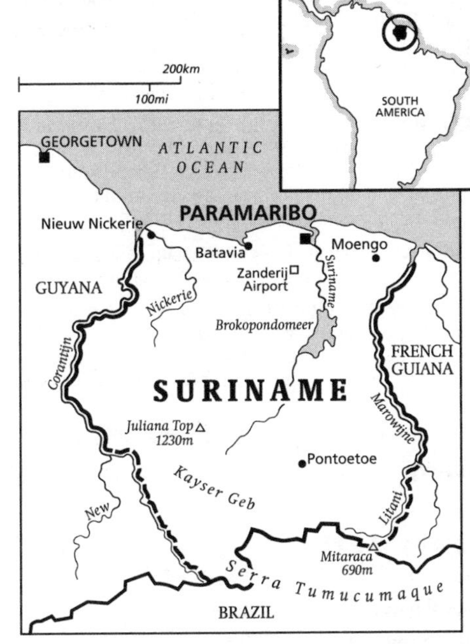

Dutch Guiana; independence as the Republic of Suriname, 1975; emigration of c.40% of population to the Netherlands, following independence; military coup, 1980; ban on political activities lifted, 1985; 1987 constitution provides for a National Assembly, and a president elected by the Assembly.

Head of State (President)
1990–1 Johan Kraag
1991– Runaldo Venetiaan

Head of Government (Vice-President)
1988–90 Henck Arron
1990–1 Jules Wijdenbosch
1991– Jules Adjodhia

SWAZILAND

Local name Swaziland

Timezone GMT + 2

Area 17 363 sq km/6 702 sq mi

Population total (1991e) 859 000

Status Kingdom

Date of independence 1968

Capital Mbabane

Languages English and Siswati (official)

Ethnic groups African (97%), European (3%)

Religions Christian (Roman Catholic, Anglican, Methodist and Evangelical Lutheran) (57%), traditional animist beliefs (40%)

Physical features Landlocked, in SE Africa; divided into four topographical regions, mountainous Highveld (W), highest point Emblembe, 1 862 m/6 109 ft; heavily populated Middleveld (C), descending to 600–700 m/ 2 000–3 000 ft; rolling, bush-covered Lowveld (E), irrigated by river systems; Lubombo escarpment, covering 90% of the territory; main rivers, Komati, Usutu, Mbuluzi, flow W–E.

Climate Temperate; tropical in W, with relatively little rain, 500–890 mm/20–35 in; susceptible to drought; subtropical and drier in C; average annual temperature 15°C (Jul), 22°C (Jan) in Mbabane; average annual rainfall 1 402 mm/55 in; rainy season (Nov–Mar).

Currency 1 Lilangeni (plural Emalangeni) (Li, E) = 100 cents

Economy Agriculture (employs 70% of population); maize, groundnuts, beans, sorghum, cotton, tobacco, pineapples, citrus; sugar refining, several hydroelectric schemes; asbestos, iron ore, coal, textiles, cement, paper, chemicals.

GNP (1990) $563 mln, (1989) per capita $900

History Arrival of Swazi in the area, early 19th-c; boundaries with the Transvaal decided, and independence guaranteed, 1881; British agreed to Transvaal administration, 1894; British High Commission territory, 1903; independence as a constitutional monarchy within the Commonwealth, 1968; all political parties are banned under 1978 constitution; governed by a bicameral parliament consisting of a National Assembly and a Senate; the king has considerable executive power, appoints a cabinet and prime minister.

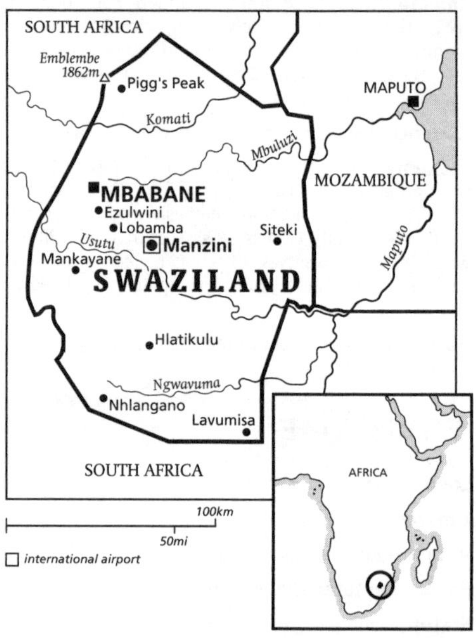

Head of State (Monarch)
1986– Mswati III

Head of Government
1989– Obed Dlamini *Acting*

SWEDEN

Local name Sverige (Swedish)

Timezone GMT + 1

Area 411 479 sq km/158 830 sq mi

Population total (1991e) 8 564 000

Status Kingdom

Capital Stockholm

Languages Swedish (official), Finnish and Lapp in N

Ethnic groups Swedish (91%), Finns, with Polish, Turkish, W German, Chilean, Iranian and other minorities

Religions Lutheran Protestant (93%), Roman Catholic (2%), Scandinavian Jewish minorities

Physical features Occupies the E side of the Scandinavian peninsula; 15% of country lies N of the Arctic Circle; large amount of inland water (9%); chief lakes being Vänern, Vättern, and Mälaren; many coastal islands, notably Gotland and Öland; c.57% forested; Kjölen Mts (W) form much of the boundary with Norway; highest peak, Kebnekaise, 2 111 m/6 926 ft; several rivers flow SE towards the Gulf of Bothnia.

Climate Continental,with cold winters and mild summers; rainfall lowest in NE; winters warmer in SW; enclosed parts of Baltic Sea often freeze in winter and can remain frozen for up to 6 months; continuous daylight in N during Arctic summer produces mean temperatures of −10°C (Jan), 15°C (Jul).

Currency 1 Swedish Krona (Skr) = 100 øre

Economy Gradual shift in the economy from the traditional emphasis on raw materials (timber and iron ore) to advanced technology; transportation equipment, electronics, electrical equipment, chemicals, engineering, steelmaking, non-ferrous metals; hydroelectricity provides 70% of power; wheat, barley, oats, sugar beet, cattle, fishing; tourism.

GDP (1990) $137 bln, per capita $16 200

History Formed from the union of the kingdoms of the Goths and Svears, 7th-c; Danes continued to rule in the extreme S (Skåne) until 1658; united with Denmark and Norway under Danish leadership, 1389; union ended in 1527, following revolt led by Gustavus Vasa; Sweden acquired Norway from Denmark, 1814; union with Norway dissolved, 1905; a neutral country since 1814; Social Democratic Party controlled government, 1932–76 and returned to power, 1982; applied for European Community membership, 1990; a representative and parliamentary democracy, with a monarch as head of state; governed by a prime minister and unicameral parliament (Riksdag) elected every three years.

Head of State (Monarch)
1973– Carl XVI Gustaf

Head of Government
1986–91 Ingvar Carlsson
1991– Carl Bildt

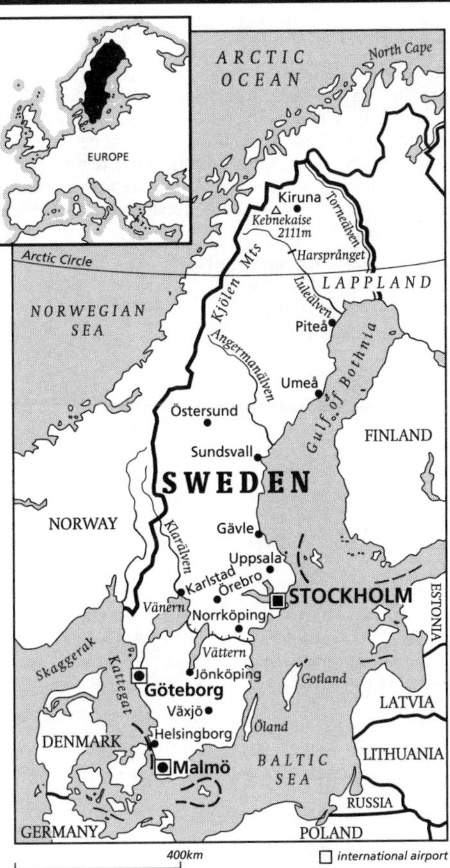

SWITZERLAND

Local names Schweiz (German), La Suisse (French), Svizzera (Italian)

Timezone GMT + 1

Area 41 228 sq km/15 914 sq mi

Population total (1991e) 6 783 000

Status Confederation

Date of independence 1291

Capital Bern (Berne)

Languages German, French, Italian, Romansch (official), Spanish and Turkish also spoken

Ethnic groups (of Swiss nationals) German (74%), French (20%), Italian (4%), Romansch (1%)

Religions Christian (Roman Catholic 49%, Protestant 48%), Jewish minority

Physical features Landlocked, with Alps running roughly E–W in the S; highest peak, Dufourspitze, 4 634 m/15 203 ft; Pre-Alps (NW) average 2 000 m/6 500 ft; sparsely forested Jura Mts run SW–NW; mean altitude of C plateau, 580 m/1 900 ft, fringed with great lakes; chief rivers, the Rhine, Rhône, Inn and tributaries of the Po; c.3 000 sq km/1 160 sq mi of glaciers, notably the Aletsch.

Climate Temperate climate, subject to Atlantic, Mediterranean and E and C European influences; warm summers, with considerable rainfall; perennial snow cover above 3 00m/9 842 ft; average annual temperature 0°C (Jan), 19°C (Jul) in Bern; average annual rainfall 986 mm/39 in; the Föhn (warm wind) noticeable late winter and spring in the Alps.

Currency 1 Swiss Franc (SFr, SwF) = 100 centimes

Economy Increased specialization and development in high-technology products; machinery, precision instruments, watches, drugs, chemicals, textiles; a major financial centre; headquarters of many international organizations; all-year tourist area; dairy farming, wheat, potatoes, sugar beet, grapes, apples.

GDP (1990) $126 bln, per capita $18 700

History Part of the Holy Roman Empire, 10th-c; Swiss Confederation created, 1291; expanded during 14th-c; centre of the Reformation, 16th-c; Swiss independence and neutrality recognized under the Treaty of Westphalia, 1648; conquered by Napoleon, who instituted the

Switzerland (continued)

Helvetian Republic, 1798; organized as a confederation of cantons, 1815; federal constitution, 1848; Red Cross founded, 1863; neutral in both World Wars; helped form European Free Trade Association, 1960; Jura became 23rd canton of Switzerland, 1979; bicameral Federal Association comprising of a Council of States (Ständerat) and a National Council (Nationalrat); president elected yearly by Federal Council.

Head of State/Government

1990	Arnold Koller
1991	Flavio Cotti
1992	René Felber

SYRIA

Local name As-Sūrīyah (Arabic)

Timezone GMT + 2

Area 185 180 sq km/71 479 sq mi

Population total (1991e) 12 965 000

Status Republic

Date of independence 1946

Capital Damascus

Languages Arabic (official), Kurdish, Armenian, Aramaic and Circassian also spoken

Ethnic groups Arab (90%), Kurd, Armenian, Turkish, Circassian and Assyrian

Religions Muslim (Sunni Muslim 74%, Alawite, Druse and other sects 16%), Christian (10%)

Physical features Narrow Mediterranean coastal plain; Jabal al Nusayriyah mountain range rises to c.1 500 m/5 000 ft; steep drop (E) to Orontes R valley; Anti-Lebanon range (SW) rises to 2 814 m/9 232 ft at Mt Hermon; open steppe and desert to the E.

Climate Coastal Mediterranean, hot, dry summers, mild, wet winters; desert or semi-desert climate in 60% of country; annual rainfall below 200 mm/8 in; khamsin wind causes temperatures to rise to 43–49°C; average annual temperatures 7°C (Jan), 27°C (Jul) in Damascus.

Currency 1 Syrian pound (LS, Syr £)= 100 piastres

Economy Oil (most important source of export revenue since 1974); Euphrates dam project (begun 1978) presently supplies 97% of domestic electricity, intended to increase arable land by 6 400 sq km/2 500 sq mi; food processing; textiles; tobacco; cement.

Golan Heights and West Bank occupied by Israel since 1967

GDP (1990) $20 bln, per capita $1 600

History Part of Phoenician Empire; Islam introduced, 7th-c; conquered by Turks, 11th-c; part of Ottoman Empire, 1517; brief period of independence, 1920, then made a French mandate; independence, 1946; merged with Egypt and Yemen to form United Arab Republic, 1958; re-established itself as independent state under present name, 1961; Golan Heights region seized by Israel, 1967; after outbreak of civil war in Lebanon (1975),

Syrian troops sent to restore order, have remained as part of the Arab peace keeping force; from mid-1970s have been increasingly involved in Lebanon; breaking of diplomatic relations with Great Britain, 1986; condemned Iraqi invasion of Kuwait and sent allied forces troops in Gulf War, 1990, restoring relations; accepted US proposals for terms of an Arab-Israeli peace conference, 1991.

Head of State
1971– Hafez al-Assad

Head of Government
1987– Mahmoud Zuabi

TAIWAN

Local name T'aiwan

Timezone GMT + 8

Area 36 000 sq km/13 896 sq mi

Population total (1991e) 20 658 000

Status Republic

Date of independence 1949

Capital Taipei

Languages Mandarin Chinese (official), various dialects including Taiwanese and Hakka also spoken

Ethnic groups Han Chinese (98%), small (Polynesian) aboriginal minority

Religions Taoist, Buddhist, Christian (Protestant and Roman Catholic)

Physical features Consists of Taiwan I and several smaller islands c.130 km/80 mi off the SE coast of mainland China; mountain range runs N–S, covering two-thirds of the island; highest peak, Yu Shan 3 997 m/13 113 ft; low-lying land mainly in the W; crossed by the Tropic of Cancer.

Climate Tropical monsoon-type climate; hot, humid summers, mild, short winters; wet season (May–Sep); typhoons common (Jul–Sep); average daily temperature 12–19°C (Jan), 24–33°C (Jul) in Taipei; average annual rainfall 2 500 mm/98 in.

Currency 1 New Taiwan Dollar (NT$) = 100 cents

Economy Progressed from agriculture to industry since 1950s; high technology, textiles, electronics, plastics, petrochemicals, machinery; natural gas, limestone, marble, asbestos; sugar, bananas, pineapples, citrus fruits, vegetables, tea, fish.

GNP (1990) $150.2 bln, per capita $7 380

History Taiwan (Formosa) visited by the Portuguese, 1590; conquered by Manchus, 17th-c; ceded to Japan following Sino-Japanese War, 1895; returned to China, 1945; Nationalist government moved to Taiwan by Jiang Jieshi (Chang Kai-shek); government still maintains claim to legal jurisdiction over mainland China and continues to designate itself as the Republic of China; protected by US naval forces during Korean War, 1950–3; signed mutual defence pact with USA, 1954–79; end of state of civil war with People's Republic of China declared by President Lee Teng-hui, 1991; governed by a president, who appoints a premier; elections held for a reformed National Assembly, 1991; plans for a new 161 member parliament (Yuan) and a 52 member Control Yuan before end of 1993.

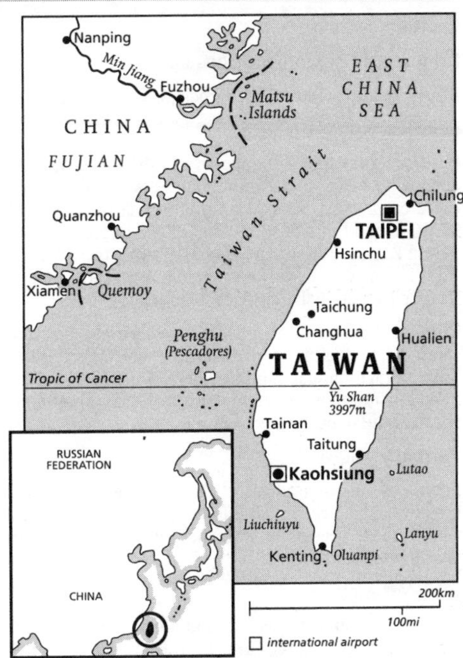

Head of State (President)
1987– Lee Jeng-hui

Head of Government (Premier)
1989–90 Lee Huan
1990– Hau Pei-tsun

TAJIKISTAN (TADZHIKISTAN)

Local name Tojikiston

Timezone GMT + 5

Area 143 100 sq km/55 200 sq mi

Population total (1992e) 4 969 000

Status Republic

Date of independence 1991

Capital Dushanbe

Languages Tajik (official), Russian

Ethnic groups Tajik (59%), Uzbek (23%), Russian (13%)

Religion Sunni Muslim

Physical features Republic in SE Middle Asia; Tien Shan, Gissar-Alai, and Pamir ranges cover over 90% of the area; highest peaks, Communism Peak, 7 495 m/ 24 590 ft, and Lenin Peak, 7 134 m/23 405 ft, located in N part of Pamirs; R Pyandzh flows E–W along the S border till it is joined by R Valksh to form R Amu Darya; lakes include L Kara-Kul (largest) and L Sarez.

Climate Continental; subtropical valley areas, hot, dry summers; annual mean temperature −0.9°C (Jan), 27°C (Jul); average annual rainfall 150–250 mm/6–10 in; in highlands, average mean temperature −3°C (Jan); average annual rainfall 60–80 mm/2–3 in.

Currency Rouble (R)

Economy Oil, natural gas, coal, lead, zinc, machinery, metalworking, chemicals, food processing; cotton, wheat, maize, vegetables, fruit; hot mineral springs and health resorts.

GDP Not available

History Conquered by Persia, and Alexander the Great; invaded by Arabs, 8th-c; Turkish invasion, 10th-c; until mid 18th-c, part of the emirate of Bukhara, which in effect became a protectorate of Russia, 1868; following the Russian Revolution (1917), became part of Turkestan Soviet Socialist Autonomous Republic, 1918; scene of the Basmachi revolt, 1922–3; Tajik Autonomous Soviet Socialist Republic created as part of the Uzbek SSR, 1924; became a Soviet Socialist Republic, 1929; declaration of independence from the Soviet Union, 1991; joined new Commonwealth of Independent States (CIS), 1991; republican Communist Party remained in power until civil war began in Dushanbe, 1992.

Head of State

1991–2	Rakhman Nabiyev
1992	Akbarsho Iskandrov *Chair of the Supreme Soviet*
1992–	Imamoli Rakhmanov *Acting*

Head of Government

1991–2	Abdumalik Abdullojanov *Acting*

TANZANIA

Local name Tanzania

Timezone GMT + 3

Area 939 652 sq km/362 706 sq mi

Population total (1991e) 26 869 000

Status Republic

Date of independence 1961

Capital Dodoma

Languages Swahili and English (official), various tribal languages

Ethnic groups Bantu (99%) (including Nyamwezi and Sukuma 21%, Swahili 9%, Hehet and Bena 6%, Makonde 6%, Haya 6%), Arab, Asian and European minorities

Religions Mainland: Christian (34%), Muslim (33%), traditional animist beliefs (33%); Zanzibar: Muslim (96%), Hindu (4%)

Physical features Largest E African country, just S of the Equator; includes the islands of Zanzibar, Pemba and Mafia; coast fringed by long sandy beaches protected by coral reefs; rises towards a C plateau, average elevation 1 000 m/3 300 ft; Rift Valley branches round L Victoria (N), several high volcanic peaks, notably Mt Kilimanjaro, 5 895 m/ 19 340 ft; extensive Serengeti Plain to the NW; other main lakes, L Tanganyika and L Rukwa.

Climate Tropical; hot, humid climate on coast and offshore islands; average temperatures 27°C (Jan), 23°C (Jul); average annual rainfall 1 000 mm/40 in; hot and dry on C plateau, average annual rainfall 250 mm/10 in; semi-temperate conditions above 1 500 mm/5 000 ft.

Currency 1 Tanzanian Shilling (TSh) = 100 cents

Economy Agriculture; rice, sorghum, coffee, sugar, cloves (most of world's market), coconuts, tobacco, cotton; reserves of iron, coal, tin, gypsum, salt, phosphate, gold, diamonds, oil; tourism.

GDP (1989) $5.9 bln, per capita $240

History Swahili culture developed, 10th–15th-c; Zanzibar became the capital of the Omani empire, 1840s; became a British protectorate, 1890; German East Africa established, 1891; British mandate to administer Tanganyika, 1919; first E African country to gain independence and become a member of the Commonwealth, 1961; republic, 1962; Zanzibar given independence as a constitutional monarchy with Sultan as head of state; Sultan overthrown, 1964, and Act of Union between Zanzibar and Tanganyika led to the United Republic of Tanzania; a one-party state following 1965 constitution; legislation was passed allowing for opposition parties, 1991, following a unanimous vote for a multi party system; governed by a president, a cabinet, and a National Assembly.

Head of State

1985– Ali Hassan Mwinyi

Head of Government

1985–90 Joseph S Warioba
1990– John Malecela

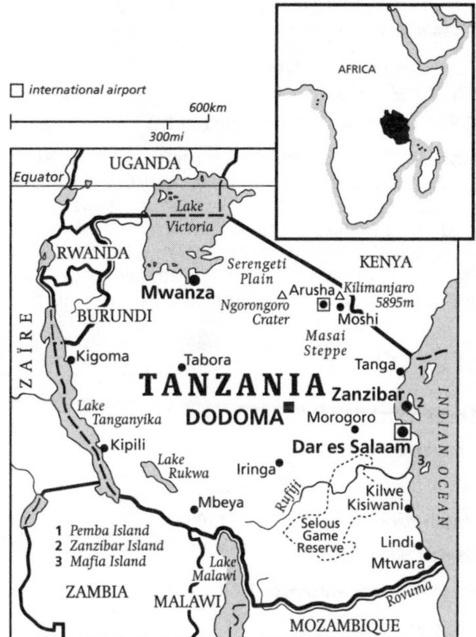

THAILAND

Local name Muang Thai

Timezone GMT + 7

Area 513 115 sq km/198 062 sq mi

Population total (1991e) 56 814 000

Status Kingdom

Capital Bangkok (Krung Thep)

Languages Thai (official), Malay and English also spoken

Ethnic groups Thai (75%), Chinese (14%), Khmer and Mon minorities

Religions Theravada Buddhist (95%), Muslim, Hindu, Sikh and Christian (4%)

Physical features Agricultural region dominated by the floodplain of the Chao Phraya R; NE plateau rises above 300 m/1 000 ft and covers a third of the country; mountainous N region rising to 2 595 m/8 514 ft at Doi Inthanon; narrow, low-lying S region separates the Andaman Sea from the Gulf of Thailand; covered in tropical rainforest, except sparsely vegetated Khorat plateau (NE).

Climate Equatorial climate in the S; tropical monsoon climate in the N and C; high temperatures and humidity; wet season (Jun–Oct); average annual temperature 26 °C (Jan), 28 °C (Jul) in Bangkok; average annual rainfall 1 400 mm/55 in.

Currency 1 Baht (B) = 100 satang

Economy Agriculture; rice, maize, bananas, pineapple, sugar cane, rubber, teak; textiles, electronics, cement, chemicals, food processing, tourism; tin (world's third largest supplier), tungsten (world's second

Thailand (continued)

largest supplier), manganese, antimony, lead, zinc, copper, natural gas.

GNP (1989) $64.4 bln, per capita $1 170

History Evidence of Bronze Age communities, 4000 BC; Thai nation founded, 13th-c; only country in S and SE Asia to have escaped colonization by a European power; occupied by the Japanese in World War 2; 'revolution' brought end to absolute monarchial rule, 1932; followed by periods of military rule interspersed with brief periods of democratic government; 1991 constitution (with amendments) provides for a National Legislative Assembly comprising a House of Representatives, appointed Senate and a cabinet headed by a prime minister; king is head of state.

Head of State (Monarch)
1946– Bhumibol Adulyadej (Rama IX)

Head of Government
1991–2 Anand Panyarachun *Military Junta*
1992 Suchinda Kraprayoon
1992– Chuan Leekpai

TOGO

Local name République Togolaise (French)

Timezone GMT

Area 56 600 sq km/21 848 sq mi

Population total (1991e) 3 810 000

Status Republic

Date of independence 1960

Capital Lomé

Languages French (official), local languages (Ewe, mostly in S, 47%), Hamitic people in N, mostly Voltaic speaking)

Ethnic groups Ewe (35%), Kabyè (22%), Mina (6%), with c.34 other ethnic groups, European and Syrian-Lebanese minorities

Religions Traditional animist beliefs (70%), Christian (20%), Muslim (10%)

Physical features Located in W Africa; land rises from the lagoon coast of the Gulf of Guinea, past low-lying plains to the Atakora Mts running NE–SW in the N; highest peak, Pic Baumann, 986 m/3 235 ft; flat plains in NW; main rivers, Oti, Mono.

Climate Tropical, high temperatures and humidity; wet seasons (Mar–Jul, Oct–Nov); single rainy season in N (Jul–Sep); average annual temperature 27°C (Jan), 24°C (Jul) in Lomé; average annual rainfall 875 mm/34 in; dry Saharan Harmattan blows from NE (Oct–Apr).

Currency 1 CFA Franc (CFAFr) = 100 centimes.

Economy Largely agricultural economy; coffee, cocoa, cotton, cassava, maize, rice, timber; phosphates, bauxite, limestone, iron ore, marble; cement, steel, oil refining, food processing, crafts, textiles, beverages.

GDP (1989) $1.3 bln, per capita $390

History Formerly part of the Kingdom of Togoland; German protectorate, 1884–1914; mandate of the League of Nations, 1922, divided between France (French Togo) and Britain (part of British Gold Coast); trusteeships of the United Nations, 1946; French Togo became an autonomous republic within the French Union, 1956; British Togoland voted to join the Gold Coast (Ghana), 1957; independence, 1960; military coups, 1963, 1967; return to civilian rule, 1980; riots in protest at slow rate of reform, 1991; at the National Conference, Aug 1991, President Eyadema was stripped of all powers, National Assembly was dissolved, and a transitional legislature, the High Council of the Republic, was established in its place; political situation remains unstable.

Head of State/Government
1967–91 Gnassingbe Eyadema
1991– Joseph Kokou Koffigoh *Interim*

TOKELAU >> NEW ZEALAND

TONGA

Local name Tonga

Timezone GMT + 13

Area 646 sq km/249 sq mi

Population total (1991e) 102 000

Status Independent kingdom within the Commonwealth

Date of independence 1970

Capital Nuku'alofa

Languages Tongan and English (official)

Ethnic groups Tongan (98%), other Polynesian, European minorities

Religions Christian (Free Wesleyan Methodists 47%, Roman Catholic 14%, Mormon 9%, Anglican minorities)

Physical features Island group in the SW Pacific Ocean, 2 250 km/1 400 mi NE of New Zealand; consists of 169 islands, 36 inhabited, divided into three main groups, Ha'apai, Tongatapu and Vava'u; Tongatapu, largest island, inhabited by two-thirds of the population; W islands mainly volcanic, some still active; highest point, extinct volcano of Kao, 1 014 m/3 327 ft.

Climate Semi-tropical; average annual temperature 26°C (Jan), 21°C (Jul) in Nuku'alofa; average annual rainfall 1 576 mm/62 in; occasional hurricanes in summer months.

Currency 1 Pa'anga/Tongan Dollar (T$) = 100 seniti

Economy Largely based on agriculture; copra, coconuts, bananas, watermelons, yams, taro, cassava, groundnuts, rice, maize, tobacco, sugar cane; tourism and cottage handicrafts are small, but growing industries.

GDP (1989) $89 mln, per capita $910

History Early settlers were Polynesians; visited by Dutch, early 17th-c; visited by the British explorer, James Cook, 1773; Methodist missionaries converted most of population to Christianity during early 19th-c; Chief Taufa'ahau united the islands and declared himself the first monarch of Tonga, 1945; became a British protectorate, 1899, under its own monarchy; independence, 1970; governed by a sovereign, Privy Council, and a unicameral Legislative Assembly of cabinet members, nobles, and elected people's representatives.

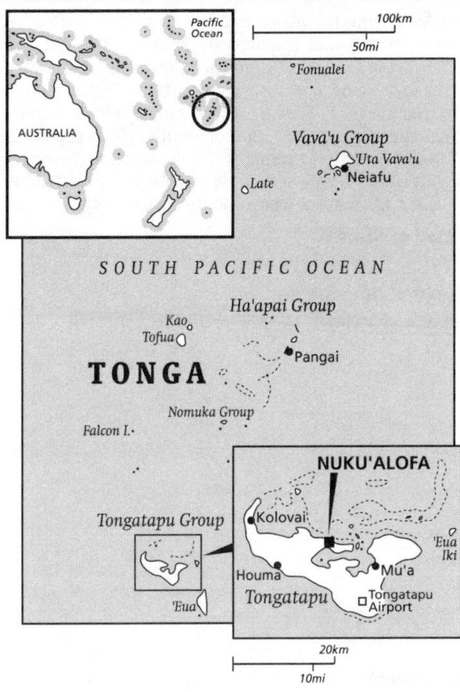

Head of State (Monarch)
1965– Taufa'ahau Tupou IV

Head of Government (Prime Minister)
1970–91 Fatafehi Tu'ipelehake
1991– Baron Vaea

TRINIDAD AND TOBAGO

Local name Trinidad and Tobago

Timezone GMT – 4

Area 5 128 sq km/1 979 sq mi

Population total (1992e) 1 300 000

Status Independent republic within the Commonwealth

Date of independence 1962

Capital Port of Spain

Languages English (official), Hindi, French, Spanish

Ethnic groups African (43%), East Indian (40%), mixed (14%), Chinese (1%)

Religions Christian (Roman Catholic 34%, Protestant 29%), Hindu (25%), Muslim (6%)

Physical features Southernmost islands of the Lesser Antilles, SE Caribbean; Trinidad, area 4 828 sq km/1 864 sq mi, traversed by three mountain ranges (N, C and S), rising to 940 m/3 084 ft at El Cerro del Aripo; drained by Caroni, Ortoire and Oropuche rivers; Tobago, area 300 sq km/116 sq mi, Main Ridge extends along most of island, rising to 576 m/1 890 ft.

Climate Tropical, hot and humid; average annual temperature 29°C; dry season (Jan–May); wet season (Jun–Dec); average annual rainfall 1 270 mm/50 in (SW Trinidad), 2 540 mm/100 in (Tobago mountains).

Currency 1 Trinidad and Tobago Dollar (TT$) = 100 cents

Economy Oil and gas (main industries); industrial complex, W coast of Trinidad; cement, oil refining, petrochemicals; cocoa, coffee, fruit; tourism.

Trinidad and Tobago (continued)

GDP (1989) $4 bln, per capita $3 363

History Trinidad visited by Columbus, 1498; settled by Spain, 16th-c, and acquired by Britain, 1797; Tobago captured by French, 1781 and acquired by Britain, 1802; Tobago became a British colony, 1814; Trinidad and Tobago united as British Crown Colony, 1899; independent member of the Commonwealth, 1962; republic, 1976; governed by a president and bicameral parliament, comprising a Senate and House of Representatives; there is also a 15-member Tobago House of Assembly.

Head of State
1987– Noor Hassanali

Head of Government
1986–91 Arthur Napoleon Raymond Robinson
1991– Patrick Manning

TUNISIA

Local names Tunis (Arabic), Tunisie (French)

Timezone GMT + 1

Area 164 150 sq km/63 362 sq mi

Population total (1992e) 8 400 000

Status Republic

Date of independence 1956

Capital Tunis

Languages Arabic (official), French and Berber widely spoken

Ethnic groups Arab (98%), European (1%), small Jewish minority

Religions Sunni Muslim (98%), Christian (1%), small Jewish minority

Physical features Located in N Africa, on Mediterranean coast; Atlas Mts (NW) rise to 1 544 m/5 065 ft at Jebel Chambi; Majardah river valley is the most fertile area (N); from Tabussah range, land descends across a plateau to the Saharan desert (S) and a coastal plain (E).

Climate Mediterranean in N, with hot, dry summers, mild, rainy winters; extreme desert-continental conditions in S, with little rainfall; average annual temperature 9°C (Jan), 26°C (Jul); average annual rainfall 400 mm/15.7 in.

Currency 1 Tunisian Dinar (TD,D) = 1 000 millèmes

Economy Agriculture (employs c.50% of population, but of declining importance); wheat, barley, grapes; olive oil (world's fourth largest producer); phosphates (fifth largest producer).

GDP (1990e) $10 bln, per capita $1 235

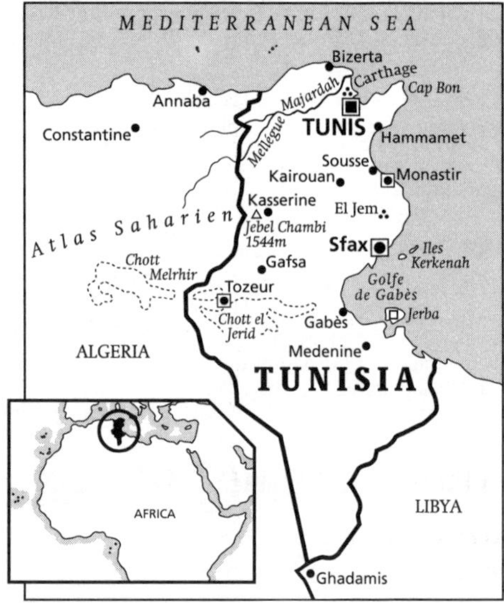

History Ruled by Phoenicians, Carthaginians, Romans, Byzantines, Arabs, Spanish, and Turks; under the control of the Ottoman Empire, 1574; French protectorate, 1883; gained internal self-government, 1955; independence, 1956; monarchy abolished and republic declared, 1957; executive power held by president, who appoints the prime minister and Council of Ministers; unicameral legislature, National Assembly, elected every five years.

Head of State
1987– Zine al-Abidine bin Ali

Head of Government
1989– Hamed Karoui

TURKEY

Local name Türkiye Cumhuriyeti

Timezone GMT + 3

Area 779 452 sq km/300 868 sq mi

Population total (1992e) 59 200 000

Status Republic

Capital Ankara

Languages Turkish (Türkçe) (official), Kurdish and Arabic, Greek, Armenian and Yiddish minorities

Ethnic groups Turkish (85%), Kurd (12%)

Religions Sunni Muslim (98%), Greek Orthodox, Armenian and Jewish minorities

Physical features Lying partly in Europe and partly in Asia, W area (Thrace), E area (Anatolia); Turkish Straits (Dardanelles, Sea of Marmara, Bosporus) connect the Black Sea (NE) and Mediterranean Sea (SW); mountainous area, Taurus Mts, cover the entire S part of Anatolia; highest peak Mt Ararat, 5 165 m/16 945 ft; sources of rivers Euphrates and Tigris in E.

Climate Mediterranean climate on Aegean and Mediterranean coasts, with hot, dry summers, warm, wet winters; mean temperature 19°C (Jul); average annual temperatures 0.3°C (Jan), 23°C (Jul) in Ankara; average annual rainfall 367 mm/14 in.

Currency 1 Turkish Lira (TL) = 100 kurus

Economy Agriculture (employs c.60% of workforce); cotton, tobacco, fruits, nuts, livestock; minerals, textiles, glass and cement; many Turks find work elsewhere in Europe, especially Germany.

GDP (1991) $119 bln, per capita $1 905

History Seljuk sultanate replaced by the Ottoman in NW Asia Minor, 13th-c; Turkish invasion of Europe, first in Balkans, 1375; fall of Constantinople, 1453; empire at its peak under Sulaiman the Magnificent, 16th-c; Young Turks seized power, 1908; Balkan War, 1912–13; allied with Germany during World War 1; republic followed

□ international airport 1 Antakya (Antioch) 2 Iskenderun (Alexandretta) 3 *Ataturk Dam* 4 *Keban Dam*

Young Turk revolution, led by Kemal Atatürk, 1923; policy of westernization and economic development; neutral throughout most of World War 2, then sided with Allies; military coups, 1960, 1980; strained relations with Greece, and invasion of Cyprus, 1974; aided the allied forces during the Gulf War, 1991; constitution provides for a single-chamber National Assembly; a president appoints a prime minister and a Council of Ministers.

Head of State

1989–93 Turgut Özal
1993– Süleyman Demirel

Head of Government

1989–91 Yıldırım Akbulut
1991 Mesut Yılmaz
1991–93 Süleyman Demirel
1993– Tansu Ciller

TURKMENISTAN

Local name Turkmenostan

Timezone GMT + 5

Area 488 100 sq km/188 400 sq mi

Population total (1992e) 3 809 000

Status Republic

Date of independence 1991

Capital Ashkhabad (Ashgabad)

Languages Turkmenian (official), other Turkic languages, Russian

Ethnic groups Turkmen (72%), Russian (10%), Uzbek, Kazakh, Ukrainian minorities

Religion Sunni Muslim

Physical features Kara Kum (Black Sands) desert, area 310 800 sq km/120 000 sq mi, covers c.80% of the country; Turan Plain covers four-fifths of Turkmenistan; foothills in the S; Kopet Dag mountain range is volcanic; other foothills are spurs of the Kugitangtau and Pamir-Alay ranges; rivers Amu Darya and Murghab.

Climate Continental, great variation of temperatures; temperatures range from 50°C (Jul) in KaraKum, to −33°C (Jan) in the Kushka; in the mountains, average annual rainfall 120–250 mm/5–10 in.

Currency Rouble (R) (1993 New currency: Manat)

Economy Mineral resources of oil, natural gas, sulphur, potassium, and salt; oil, gas extraction (main industries); textiles; cotton production; agriculture; raising of Karakul sheep, Turkoman horses, and camels.

Turkmenistan (continued)

GDP Not available

History Part of the ancient Persian empire; ruled by Seljuk Turks during 11th-c; conquered by Genghis Khan and the Mongols during 13th-c; Uzbeks invaded, 15th-c; divided into two: one part belonged to the Khanate of Khiva (which became part of the Russian empire), and the other to the Khanate of Bukhara; Turkistan Autonomous Soviet Socialist Republic formed, 1922; full Soviet Socialist Republic, 1925; declared sovereignty, 1990; independence and membership of Commonwealth of Independent States, 1991; UN membership, 1992; republic consists of five provinces: Ashgabad, Chardjou, Drasnovodsk, Mary, and Tashauz.

Head of State/Government
1992– Saparmurad Niyazov

TURKS AND CAICOS ISLANDS >> UNITED KINGDOM

TUVALU

Local name Tuvalu

Timezone GMT + 12

Area 26 sq km/10 sq mi

Population total (1991e) 9 317

Status Independent state within the Commonwealth

Date of independence 1978

Capital Funafuti (Fongafale)

Languages Tuvaluan, English

Ethnic group Polynesian (96%)

Religions Christian (Protestant Church of Tuvalu, Roman Catholic, Baha'i) (97%), small Muslim minority

Physical features Island group in the SW Pacific, 1 050 km/650 mi off Fiji; comprises nine low-lying coral atolls, running NW–SE in a chain 580 km/360 mi long; consists of the islands of Funafuti, Nukufetau, Nukulailai, Nanumea, Niutao, Nanumanga, Nui, Vaitupu and Niulakita; all low-lying, highest point, 4.6 m/15 ft, on Niulakita.

Climate Hot, humid climate; average annual temperatures 29°C (Jan), 27°C (Jul) in Funafuti; average annual rainfall 4 003 mm/158 in.

Currency 1 Australian Dollar ($A) = 100 cents

Economy Subsistence economy; agriculture, coconuts, copra, tropical fruit; fish; handcrafted products, postage stamps.

GDP (1989e) $4.6 mln, per capita $530

History Invaded by Samoans, 16th-c; British protectorate, as the Ellice Is, 1892; administered as a colony jointly with Gilbert Is (now Kiribati), 1915; American soldiers occupied the Ellice Islands during World War 2, to counter the advance of the Japanese, 1942; separate constitution, following 1974 referendum; independence as a constitutional monarchy within the Commonwealth, 1978; Tuvalu Trust Fund set up by Britain, Australia, New Zealand and South Korea, 1987; British monarch represented by a governor general; governed by a prime minister, cabinet, and unicameral parliament.

Head of State
(British monarch represented by Governor-General)
1978– Toaripi Lauti

Head of Government
1989– Bikenibeu Paeniu

Map >> KIRIBATI

UGANDA

Local name Uganda (Swahili)

Timezone GMT + 3

Area 238 461 sq km/92 046 sq mi

Population total (1992e) 17 500 000

Status Republic

Date of independence 1962

Capital Kampala

Languages English (official), Swahili, Luganda (Ganda), Ateso, and Luo are also spoken

Ethnic groups Ganda, with Bantu, Nilotic and Hamitic minorities

Religions Christian (66%) (Roman Catholic 33%, Protestant 33%), traditional animist beliefs (18%), Muslim (16%)

Physical features Landlocked country in E Africa, mainly plateau, height 900–1 000 m/3 000–3 250 ft; dry savannah or semi-desert in the N; fertile L Victoria basin; highest point in Uganda and Zaïre, Margherita Peak, 5 110 m/16 765 ft; main lakes, Victoria (SE), George and Edward (SW), Albert (W), Kwania and Kyoga (C), Bisina (formerly L Salisbury) (E); main rivers are the upper reaches of R Nile, the Victoria Nile, and the Albert Nile.

Climate Tropical climate; temperatures rarely rise above 29°C, or fall below 15°C (S); average annual temperature 23°C (Jan), 21°C (Jul); average annual rainfall 1 150 mm/45 in.

Currency 1 Uganda Shilling = 100 cents

Economy Agriculture; coffee (over 90% of exports), tea, sugar, cotton; bananas, plantains, cassavas, potatoes, sweet potatoes, maize, sorghum.

GDP (1989) $4.9 bln, per capita $290

History Visited by Arab traders, 1830s; explored by Speke, 1860s; granted to the British East Africa Company, 1888; Kingdom of Buganda became a British protectorate, 1893; other territory included by 1903; independence, 1962; Dr Milton Obote assumed all powers, 1966; coup led by General Idi Amin Dada, 1971; Amin's regime overthrown, 1979; further coup, 1985, overthrew Milton Obote, General Tito Okello became president; National Resistance Movement (NRM) captured Kampala, 1986, and Museveni became president; governed by a president, cabinet, prime minister and National Resistance Council; awaiting drafting of a new constitution.

Head of State

1986– Yoweri Kaguta Museveni

Head of Government

1986–91 Samson B Kisekka
1991– George Cosmas Adyebo

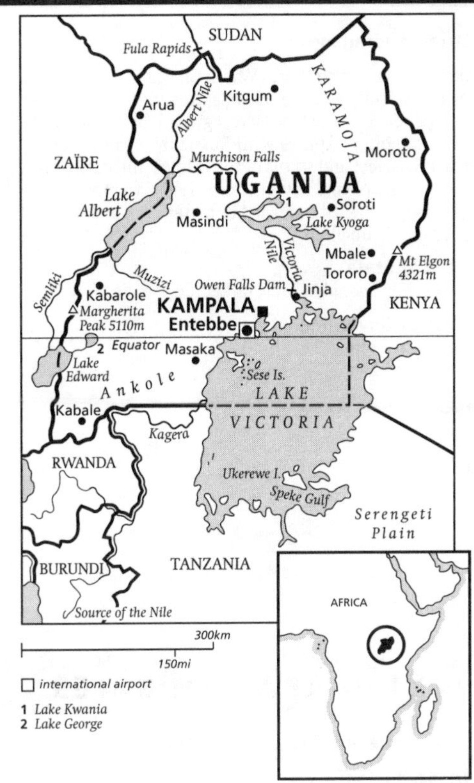

UKRAINE

Local name Ukraina

Timezone GMT + 2

Area 603 700 sq km/233 028 sq mi

Population total (1992e) 52 100 000

Status Republic

Date of independence 1991

Capital Kiev

Languages Ukrainian (official), Russian

Ethnic groups Ukrainian (73%), Russian (22%), Moldovan, Bulgarian and Polish minorities

Religions Orthodox (Autocephalous and Russian) (76%), Roman Catholic (14%), Jewish (2%), Baptist, Mennonite, Protestant and Muslim (8%)

Physical features Most fertile area of former USSR, consisting largely of black soil steppes, forming a substantial part of the East European Plain; borders the Black Sea and Sea of Azov (S); Carpathian Mts, 2 061 m/6 762 ft at Mt Goverla (SW); Crimean Mts (S); main rivers, Dnepr, Yuzhny, and Bug; Donets coalfield, area 25 900 sq km/10 000 sq mi.

Climate Moderate, mild winters, hot summers (SW); average annual temperatures −3°C (Jan), 23°C (Jul); average annual rainfall in Crimea 400–610 mm/16–24 in.

Currency (1992) Roubles replaced with karbovanet coupons, pending introduction of the new Ukrainian currency (the hryvna)

Economy Important industrial bases for iron and steel manufacture, chemical and engineering bases; shipbuilding on Black Sea; agriculture (was the USSR's major wheat producer); wheat, corn, rye, potatoes, cotton, flax, sugar beet; coal and salt deposits in Donets basin.

GNP (1990) $47.6 bln, (1989) per capita $4 700

History Conquered by Mongols, 1240; dominated by Poland, 13–16th-c; applied to Moscow for help fighting Poland in return for sovereignty, 1654; declared independence from Russia, 1918, after Russian Revolution; became a member of the USSR, 1922; suffered

Ukraine (continued)

devastation during World War 2; Chernobyl was the site of the world's worst nuclear accident, 1986; declared independence which was recognized by UN and US, 1991; ongoing disputes with Russia over control of the Black Sea Fleet and status of the Crimea; introduction of border controls and new currency, 1993, in contravention of CIS agreements; governed by a president and 450-seat Supreme Council.

Head of State
1991– Leonid M Kravchuk

Head of Government
1990–2 Vitold P Fokin
1992– Leonid Kuchma

UNITED ARAB EMIRATES

Local name Ittihād al-Imārat al-'Arabīyah

Timezone GMT + 4

Area 83 600 sq km/32 300 sq mi

Population total (1992e) 2 500 000

Status Federation of autonomous emirates

Date of independence 1971

Capital Abu Dhabi

Languages Arabic (official), English, Farsi, Urdu and Hindi also spoken

Ethnic groups Emirian (19%), other Arab (23%), S Asian (50%)

Religions Muslim (Sunni 80%, Shi'ite 16%), Christian (4%), small Hindu minority

Physical features Seven states in EC Arabian peninsula on S shore (Trucial Coast) of the Arabian Gulf; Al Fujairah has a coastline along the Gulf of Oman; salt marshes predominate on coast; barren desert and gravel plain inland; Hajar Mts in Al Fujairah rise to over 1 000 m/3 000 ft in E.

Climate Hot, dry desert climate, extreme summer temperatures exceeding 40°C and limited rainfall; frequent sandstorms; average annual temperatures 23°C (Jan), 42°C (Jul) in Dubai; average annual rainfall 60 mm/2.4 in.

Currency 1 United Arab Emirates Dirham (DH) = 100 fils

Economy Based on oil and gas (main producers, Abu Dhabi, Dubai); important commercial and trading centre; saline water supplies have restricted agriculture to oases and irrigated valleys of Hajar Mts; vegetables, fruits, dates, dairy farming; tourism.

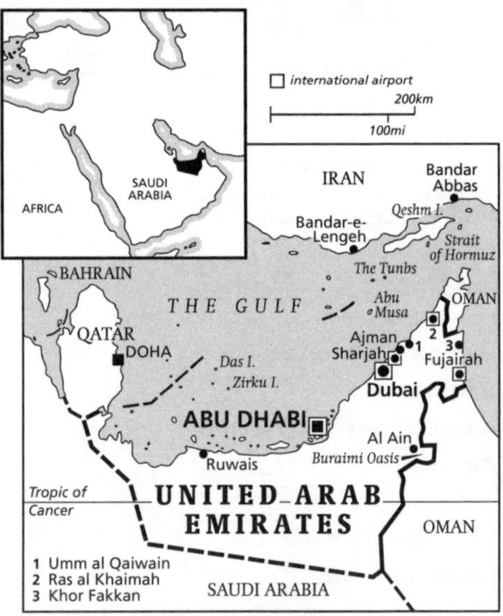

GDP (1989) $27.3 bln, per capita $12 100

History Originally peopled by sea-faring tribes, converted to Islam, 7th-c; Mecca conquered by powerful sheikdom of Carmathians; upon its collapse piracy common, area known as the Pirate Coast; Portuguese explorers arrived, 16th-c; British East India Company arrived, 17th-c; British attacked the coastal ports, 1819–20 and exacted a pledge to renounce piracy in the General Treaty, 1820; became know as Trucial Coast after signing of Treaty of Maritime Peace in Perpetuity, 1853; administered by British India, 1873–1947, and thereafter by London Foreign Office; Trucial States Council formed, 1960; federated and became United Arab Emirates, 1971, comprising seven emirates: Abu Dhabi, Ajman, Dubai, Al Fujairah, Ras al Khaimah, Sharjah and Umm al Qaiwain; Ras al Khaimah joined federation, 1972; governed by Supreme Council of the seven emirate rulers (each of whom is an absolute monarch in own state); BCCI scandal, 1992, adversely affected the federation, which was a major shareholder.

Head of State

1971– Zayed bin Sultan al-Nahyan

Head of Government

1979–90 Rashid bin Said al-Maktoum
1990– Maktoum bin Rashid al-Maktoum

UNITED KINGDOM (UK)

Local names United Kingdom of Great Britain and Northern Ireland, Great Britain, Britain

Timezone GMT

Area 244 755 sq km/94 475 sq mi

Population total (1991) 55 486 800

Status Kingdom

Capital London

Languages English (official), Irish Gaelic, Scots Gaelic (Gallic), Welsh

Ethnic groups English (82%), Scottish (10%), Irish (2%), Welsh (2%), West Indian, Asian and African (2%), Arabic, Turkish and Greek minorities

Religions Christian (90%) (Anglican 63%, Roman Catholic 14%, Presbyterian 4%, Methodist 3%, Baptist 1%, Orthodox 1%, other 6%), Muslim (3%), Sikh (1%), Hindu (1%), Jewish (1%), other (1%)

Physical features Varied landscape, comprising the mountainous Lake District in NW, rocky moors in SW, hilly downs of S and SE, and the low, marshy fenlands of C and E; the Cheviot Hills separate Scotland and England; highest point, Ben Nevis in Scotland, 1 342 m/4 406 ft; the Pennines form a ridge down the middle of England, from Lake District to C; highest point in England and Wales, Mt Snowdon in Wales, 1 085 m/3 560 ft; in N Ireland, the Sperrin Mts and the granite Mourne Mts rise to heights over 610 m/2 000 ft.

Climate Temperate maritime climate; SW airstream determines weather, bringing depressions (causing wet weather) or N winds (bringing drier and colder); some regional diversity, but no world climate systems' boundaries pass through the islands; on average, wetter and slightly warmer in W; rainfall evenly distributed throughout the year; average annual rainfall 1 600 mm/60 in (W), 800 mm/30 in (C and E).

Currency 1 Pound Sterling (£) = 100 pence

Economy Service industries; agriculture, potatoes, wheat, barley, and sugar beets; livestock; large fishing industry; deposits of iron ore; oil and gas from N Sea; coal industry declining; highly developed financial systems; London the commercial and financial centre of Western world; UK one of the world's largest trading nations, relying heavily on imports; exports include machinery, transport equipment, petroleum, chemicals and textiles.

GDP (1990) $858.3 bln, per capita $15 000

History Migrations and settlements resulted in the insular Celtic nation; invaded by Rome in 1 AD; Romans withdrew in the 5th-c; constantly attacked by Scandinavian tribes; defeated by Alfred, 878; united under the kings of Wessex, 10th-c; Edward the Confessor died, 1066, leaving a disputed succession; Norman invasion under William, Duke of Normandy, 1066; Edward I conquered Wales, 1301; Hundred Years' War with France, 1337–1453; recurring plagues of Black Death, 1347–1400, wiped out one third of population; Wars of the Roses, 1455–85, resulted in victory for House of Lancaster; establishment of Church of England and split from Church of Rome, 1533; union with Wales, 1536; coronation of Elizabeth I, 1558; execution of Mary Queen of Scots, 1587; defeat of the Spanish Armada, 1588; English Civil War, 1642–6 and 1648–9; execution of Charles I, 1649; England and Scotland joined by the Act of Union, 1707; 1714–60, development of parliamentary government under Hanoverian kings; revolt of the American colonies, 1775–81; Ireland officially joined to Great Britain, 1801; World War 1, 1914–18; became the United

United Kingdom (continued)

Kingdom of Great Britain and Northern Ireland following the establishment of the Irish Free State, 1922; General Strike, 1926; abdication of Edward VIII, 1936; World War 2, 1939–45; National Health system implemented, 1948; Indian independence, 1947; joined EC, 1973; Falklands War with Argentina, 1982; involvement in Gulf War, 1991; a kingdom with the monarch as head of state; governed by a bicameral parliament, comprising an elected 650-member House of Commons and a House of Lords; a Cabinet is appointed by the prime minister.

Head of State (Monarch)
1952– Elizabeth II

Head of Government
1979–90 Margaret Hilda Thatcher
1990– John Major

>> **Political leaders and rulers**

ENGLAND

Area 130 357 sq km/50 318 sq mi

Population total (1991) 48 068 400

Status Constituent part of the United Kingdom

Capital London

Languages English (official), with c.100 minority languages

Ethnic groups & Religions (*see* UNITED KINGDOM)

Physical features Largest area within the United Kingdom, forming the S part of the island of Great Britain; since 1974 divided into 46 counties; includes the Isles of Scilly, Lundy, and the Isle of Wight; largely undulating lowland, rising (S) to the Mendips, Cotswolds, Chilterns, and North Downs, (N) to the N–S ridge of the Pennines, and (NW) to the Cumbria Mts; drained E by the Tyne, Tees, Humber, Ouse, and Thames Rivers, and W by the Eden, Ribble, Mersey, and Severn Rivers; Lake District (NW) includes Derwent Water, Ullswater, Windermere and Bassenthwaite; linked to Europe by ferry and hovercraft, and (from 1994) the Channel Tunnel.

Economy North Sea oil and gas, coal, tin, china clay, salt, potash, lead ore, iron ore; vehicles, heavy engineering, petrochemicals, pharmaceuticals, textiles, food processing, electronics, telecommunications, publishing, brewing, fishing, livestock, agriculture, horticulture, pottery and tourism.

History (See UNITED KINGDOM)

Counties of England

County	*Area* sq km	sq mi	*Population (1991)*	*Admin Centre*
Avon*	1 345	520	962 000	Bristol
Bedfordshire	1 235	477	534 300	Bedford
Berkshire	1 259	486	752 500	Reading
Buckinghamshire	1 883	727	640 200	Aylesbury
Cambridgeshire	3 409	1 316	669 900	Cambridge
Cheshire	2 328	899	966 500	Chester
Cleveland*	583	225	557 000	Middlesbrough
Cornwall	3 564	1 376	475 200	Truro
Cumbria*	6 810	2 629	489 700	Carlisle
Derbyshire	2 631	1 016	939 800	Matlock
Devon	6 711	2 591	1 040 000	Exeter
Dorset	2 654	1 025	662 900	Dorchester
Durham	2 436	941	604 300	Durham
Essex	3 672	1 418	1 548 000	Chelmsford
Gloucestershire	2 643	1 020	538 800	Gloucester
Greater London*	1 579	610	6 803 100	no central authority
Greater Manchester*	1 287	497	2 561 600	no central authority
Hampshire	3 777	1 458	1 578 700	Winchester
Hereford and Worcester*	3 9261	516	686 000	Worcester
Hertfordshire	1 634	631	989 500	Hertford
Humberside*	3 512	1 356	874 400	Beverley
Isle of Wight	381	147	126 600	Newport
Kent	3 731	1 441	1 538 800	Maidstone
Lancashire	3 063	1 183	1 408 000	Preston
Leicestershire	2 553	986	890 800	Leicester
Lincolnshire	5 915	2 284	592 600	Lincoln
Merseyside* †	652	252	1 441 100	Liverpool
Norfolk	5 368	2 073	759 400	Norwich
Northamptonshire	2 367	914	587 100	Northampton
Northumberland	5 032	1 943	307 100	Morpeth
Nottinghamshire	2 164	836	1 015 500	Nottingham
Oxfordshire	2 608	1 007	579 700	Oxford
Shropshire	3 490	1 347	412 500	Shrewsbury
Somerset	3 451	1 332	469 400	Taunton
Staffordshire	2 716	1 049	1 047 400	Stafford
Suffolk	3 797	1 466	661 900	Ipswich
Surrey	1 679	648	1 035 500	Kingston upon Thames
Sussex, East	1 795	693	716 500	Lewes
Sussex, West	1 989	768	713 600	Chichester
Tyne and Wear* †	540	208	1 125 600	Newcastle upon Tyne

Warwickshire	1981	765	489900	Warwick
West Midlands* †	899	347	2619000	Birmingham
Wiltshire	3481	1344	575100	Trowbridge
Yorkshire, North	8309	3208	720900	Northallerton
Yorkshire, South	1560	602	1292700	Barnsley
Yorkshire, West †	2039	787	2066200	Wakefield

* New counties in 1974 were formed as follows:
Avon: parts of Somerset and Gloucestershire

Cleveland: parts of Durham and Yorkshire

Cumbria: Cumberland, Westmoreland, parts of Lancashire and Yorkshire

Greater London: London and most of Middlesex

Greater Manchester: parts of Lancashire, Cheshire and Yorkshire

Hereford and Worcester: Hereford, most of Worcestershire

Humberside: parts of Yorkshire and Lincolnshire

Merseyside: parts of Lancashire and Cheshire

West Midlands: parts of Staffordshire, Warwickshire and Worcestershire

Tyne and Wear: parts of Northumberland and Durham

† the councils of these metropolitan councils were abolished in 1986

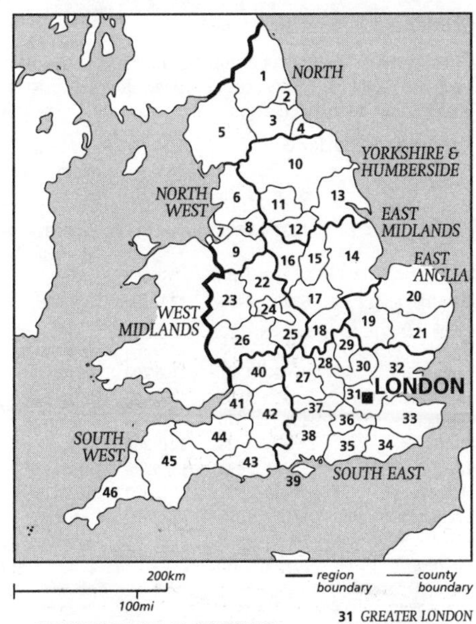

1 NORTHUMBERLAND
2 TYNE & WEAR
3 DURHAM
4 CLEVELAND
5 CUMBRIA
6 LANCASHIRE
7 MERSEYSIDE
8 GREATER MANCHESTER
9 CHESHIRE
10 NORTH YORKSHIRE
11 WEST YORKSHIRE
12 SOUTH YORKSHIRE
13 HUMBERSIDE
14 LINCOLNSHIRE
15 NOTTINGHAMSHIRE
16 DERBYSHIRE
17 LEICESTERSHIRE
18 NORTHAMPTONSHIRE
19 CAMBRIDGESHIRE
20 NORFOLK
21 SUFFOLK
22 STAFFORDSHIRE
23 SHROPSHIRE
24 WEST MIDLANDS
25 WARWICKSHIRE
26 HEREFORD & WORCESTER
27 OXFORDSHIRE
28 BUCKINGHAMSHIRE
29 BEDFORDSHIRE
30 HERTFORDSHIRE
31 GREATER LONDON
32 ESSEX
33 KENT
34 EAST SUSSEX
35 WEST SUSSEX
36 SURREY
37 BERKSHIRE
38 HAMPSHIRE
39 ISLE OF WIGHT
40 GLOUCESTERSHIRE
41 AVON
42 WILTSHIRE
43 DORSET
44 SOMERSET
45 DEVON
46 CORNWALL & ISLES OF SCILLY

SCOTLAND

Area 78742 sq km/30394 sq mi

Population total (1991) 4861854

Status Constituent part of the United Kingdom

Capital Edinburgh

Languages English, Scots Gaelic (Gallic) (known or used by c.80000 residents)

Physical features Comprises the N part of the UK, and includes the island groups of Outer and Inner Hebrides, Orkney and Shetland; divided into Southern Uplands, rising to 843 m/2766 ft at Merrick; Central Lowlands (most densely populated area); and Northern Highlands, divided by the fault line following the Great Glen, and rising to 1342 m/4406 ft at Ben Nevis; W coast heavily indented; several wide estuaries on E coast, primarily Firths of Forth, Tay and Moray; many freshwater lochs in the interior, largest being Loch Lomond, 70 sq km/27 sq mi, and deepest Loch Morar, 310 m/1020 ft.

Economy Based on coal, but all heavy industry declined through the 1980s, with closure of many pits; oil services on E coast; tourism, especially in Highlands; shipbuilding, steel, whisky, textiles, agriculture, forestry.

History Roman attempts to limit incursions of N tribes marked by Antonine Wall and Hadrian's Wall; beginnings of unification, 9th-c; wars between England and Scotland in Middle Ages; Scottish independence declared by Robert Bruce, recognized 1328; Stuart succession, 14th-c; crowns of Scotland and England united, 1603; parliaments united under Act of Union, 1707;

Scotland (continued)

unsuccessful Jacobite rebellions, 1715, 1745; devolution proposal rejected, 1979; since 1974, divided into 12 regions and 53 districts.

Regions of Scotland

Name	*Area sq km*	*Area sq mi*	*Population total (1991)*	*Admin centre*
Borders	4672	1804	103881	Newton St Boswells
Central	2631	1016	268000	Stirling
Dumfries and Galloway	6370	2459	147100	Dumfries
Fife	1307	505	339300	Glenrothes
Grampian	8704	3361	493200	Aberdeen
Highland	25391	9804	209400	Inverness
Lothian	1755	678	723700	Edinburgh
Strathclyde	13537	5225	2218200	Glasgow
Tayside	7493	2893	385300	Dundee
Orkney Is	976	377	19300	Kirkwall
Shetland Is	1433	553	22400	Lerwick
Western Is	2898	1119	31000	Stornoway

WALES

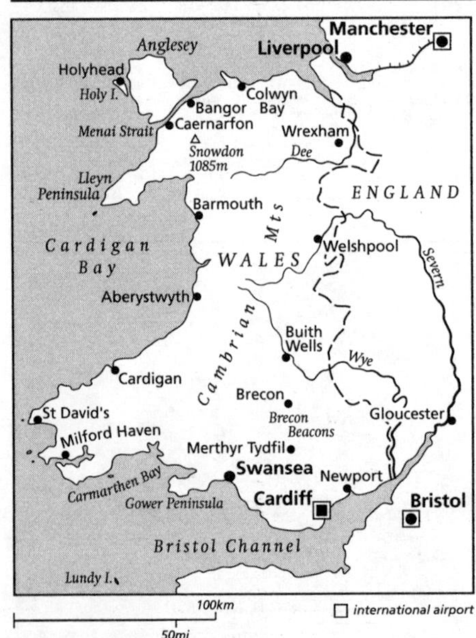

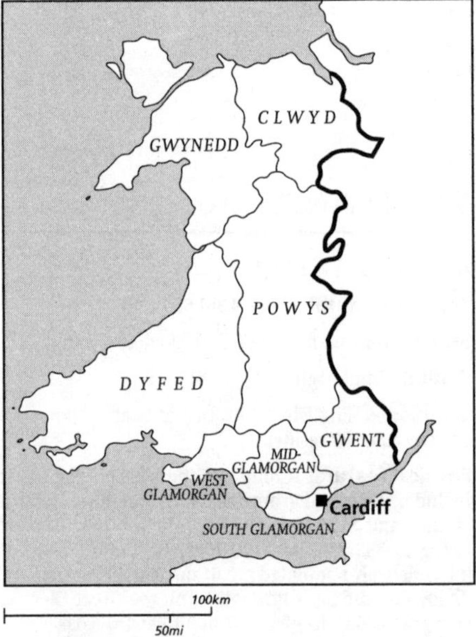

Local name Cymru (Welsh)

Area 20761 sq km/8014 sq mi

Population total (1991e) 2886400

Status Principality (Constituent part of the United Kingdom)

Capital Cardiff

Languages English, Welsh

Physical features Situated on the W coast of the UK, divided into 8 counties since 1974; includes the island of Anglesey off the NW coast; land rises to 1085 m/3560 ft at Snowdon (NW), also Cambrian Mts (C); Brecon Beacons (S); drained by the Severn, Clwyd, Dee, Conwy, Dovey, Taff, Towy and Wye rivers.

Economy Coal; slate, lead, steel; industrialized S valleys and coastal plain; tourism in N and NW; ferries to Ireland at Holyhead, Fishguard; important source of water for England.

History Rhodri Mawr united Wales against Saxons, Norse and Danes, 9th-c; Edward I of England established authority over Wales, building several castles, 12th–

13th-c; Edward I's son created first Prince of Wales, 1301; 14th-c revolt under Owen Glendower; politically united with England by Act of Union, 1535; centre of Nonconformist religion since 18th-c; University of Wales, 1893, with constituent colleges; political nationalist movement (Plaid Cymru) returned first MP, 1966; Welsh television channel; 1979 referendum opposed devolution.

Counties of Wales

Name	Area sq km	Area sq mi	Population total (1991)	Admin centre
Clwyd	2426	937	413800	Mold
Dyfed	5768	2227	350900	Carmarthen
Gwent	1376	531	446900	Cwmbran
Gwynedd	3869	1494	240100	Caernarvon
Powys	5077	1960	118700	Llandrindod Wells
Glamorgan, Mid	1018	393	541600	Cardiff
Glamorgan, South	416	161	405900	Cardiff
Glamorgan, West	817	315	368700	Swansea

NORTHERN IRELAND (ULSTER)

Area 14120 sq km/5450 sq mi

Population total (1991) 1594400

Status Constituent division of the United Kingdom

Capital Belfast

Languages English, Irish Gaelic

Religions Christian (Roman Catholic 28%, Presbyterian 23%, Church of Ireland 19%)

Physical features Occupies the NE part of Ireland, centred on Lough Neagh; Mourne Mts in SE; highest point, Slieve Donard, 847 m/2 786 ft, in the former Co. Down; R Mourne, 82 km/51 mi in length.

Economy Agriculture; service industries, shipbuilding, engineering, chemicals; linen, textiles; economy badly affected by the sectarian troubles since 1969.

History Separate parliament established, 1920, with a 52-member House of Commons and a 26-member Senate; Protestant majority in the population, generally supporting political union with Great Britain; many of the Roman Catholic minority look for union with the Republic of Ireland; violent conflict between the communities broke out, 1969, leading to the establishment of a British army peace-keeping force; sectarian murders and bombings continued both within and outside the province; as a result of the disturbances, parliament was abolished, 1973; powers are now vested in the UK Secretary of State for Northern Ireland; formation of a 78-member Assembly, 1973; replaced by a Constitutional Convention, 1975; Assembly re-formed, 1982, but Nationalist members did not take their seats; under the 1985 Anglo-Irish agreement, the Republic of Ireland was given a consultative role in the government of Northern Ireland; all Northern Ireland MPs in the British Parliament resigned in protest, 1986; continuing controversy in the late 1980s; fresh talks between all main parties and the Irish government, 1992.

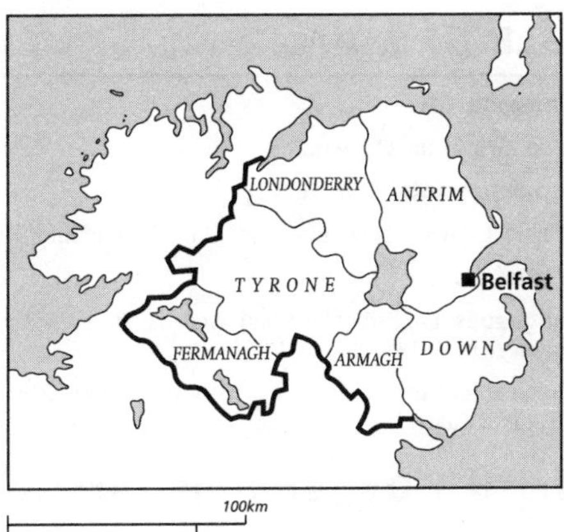

Districts of Northern Ireland

Name	Area sq km	Area sq mi	Population total (1991e)	Admin centre
Antrim	563	217	45400	Antrim
Ards	369	142	65000	Newtownards
Armagh	672	259	51800	Armagh
Ballymena	638	246	56600	Ballymena
Ballymoney	419	162	24200	Ballymoney
Banbridge	444	171	33500	Banbridge
Belfast	140	54	287100	Belfast
Carrickfergus	87	34	33100	Carrickfergus
Castlereagh	85	33	61500	Belfast
Coleraine	485	187	51200	Coleraine
Cookstown	623	240	30900	Cookstown
Craigavon	383	147	75400	Craigavon
Down	646	249	58800	Downpatrick
Dungannon	779	301	45300	Dungannon
Fermanagh	1876	715	54400	Enniskillen
Larne	338	131	29500	Larne
Limavady	587	227	29700	Limavady
Lisburn	444	171	101100	Lisburn
Londonderry/ Derry	382	147	97100	Londonderry/ Derry
Magherafelt	573	221	36100	Magherafelt

Northern Ireland (Ulster) (continued)

Moyle	495	191	14700	Ballycastle
Newry and Mourne	895	346	83100	Newry
Newtownabbey	152	59	74500	Newtownabbey
North Down	73	28	72900	Bangor
Omagh	1129	436	4600	Omagh
Strabane	870	336	35500	Strabane

British Islands

CHANNEL ISLANDS

Timezone GMT

Area 194 sq km/75 sq mi

Population total (1986e) 145000

Status Crown dependency of the United Kingdom

Capital St Helier (on Jersey), St Peter Port (on Guernsey)

Languages English and Norman-French

Physical features Island group of the British Isles in the English Channel, W of Normandy; comprises the islands of Guernsey, Jersey, Alderney, Sark, Herm, Jethou, Brechou and Lihou.

Economy Tourism, fruit, vegetables, flowers, dairy produce, Jersey and Guernsey cattle; used as a tax haven; not part of the European Community.

History Granted to the Dukes of Normandy, 10th-c; only British possession to have been occupied by Germany during World War 2; a dependent territory of the British Crown, with individual legislative assemblies and legal system; divided into the Bailiwick of Guernsey and the Bailiwick of Jersey; Bailiff presides over the Royal Court and the Representative Assembly (the States).

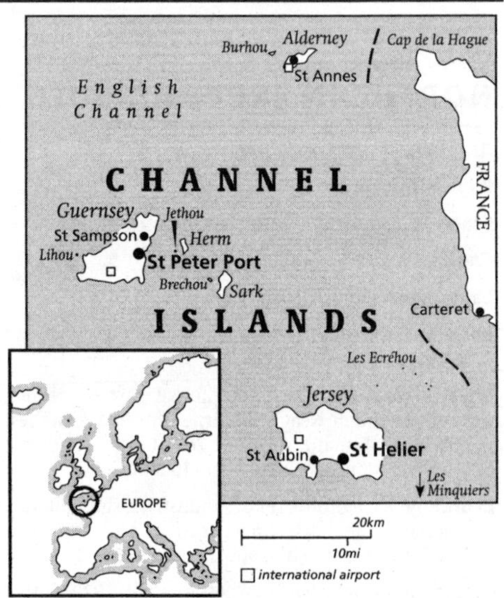

ISLE OF MAN

Timezone GMT

Area 572 sq km/221 sq mi

Population total (1986) 64282

Status Crown dependency of the United Kingdom

Capital Douglas

Languages English (Manx survived as an everyday language until 19th-c)

Physical features Island in the Irish Sea; rises to 620 m/2034 ft at Snaefell.

Economy Tourism, agriculture, fishing, light engineering; used as a tax haven; not part of European Community; annual Tourist Trophy motorcycle races held here.

History Ruled by the Welsh, 6th–9th-c; then by the Scandinavians, Scots, and English; purchased by the British Government between 1765 and 1828; the island has its own parliament, the bicameral Court of Tynwald, which consists of the elected House of Keys and the Legislative Council; acts of the British Parliament do not generally apply to Man.

British Dependent Territories

ANGUILLA

Timezone GMT - 4

Area 91 sq km/35 sq mi

Population total (1992) 8800

Capital The Valley

Physical features Most northerly of the Leeward Is, E Caribbean; also includes Sombrero I and several other offshore islets and cays; low-lying coral island, covered in low scrub and fringed with white coral-sand beaches.

Climate Tropical climate; average annual temperature ranges from 24–30°C; low and erratic annual rainfall, 550–1250 mm/22–50 in; hurricane season (Jul–Oct).

Currency 1 East Caribbean Dollar (EC$) = 100 cents

Economy Tourism, fishing, peas, corn, sweet potatoes, salt, boatbuilding.

History Colonized by English settlers from St Kitts, 1650; ultimately incorporated in the colony of St Kitts-Nevis-Anguilla; separated, 1980; governor appointed by the British sovereign; Legislative Assembly.

BERMUDA

Timezone GMT – 4

Area 53 sq km/20 sq mi

Population total (1990e) 60 000

Capital Hamilton

Physical features Archipelago in W Atlantic, c.900 km/560 mi E of Cape Hatteras, N Carolina; c.150 low-lying coral islands and islets, 20 inhabited, seven linked by causeways and bridges; largest island, (Great) Bermuda; highest point, Gibb's Hill, 78 m/256 ft.

Climate Subtropical climate; generally humid; rain throughout year; warm summers, mild winters.

Currency 1 Bermuda Dollar = 100 cents

Economy Mainly year-round tourism; increasingly an international company business centre; petroleum products, pharmaceuticals, aircraft supplies, boatbuilding, ship repair, vegetables, citrus fruits; fish processing centre.

History Formerly called Somers Is, discovered by Spanish mariner, Juan Bermudez, in early 16th-c; colonized by English settlers, 1612; important naval station, and (to 1862) penal settlement; internal self-government, 1968; movement for independence caused tension in the 1970s, including assassination of the governor-general; bicameral legislature.

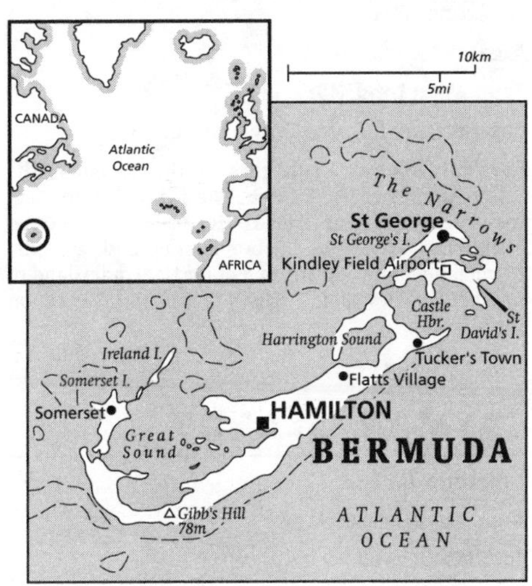

BRITISH ANTARCTIC TERRITORY

British colonial territory, designated 1962; 20°–80°W and S of 60°S; includes South Orkney Is, South Shetland Is, Antarctic Graham Land Peninsula, and the land mass extending to the South Pole; area, 5 700 000 sq km/2 200 000 sq mi; land area covered by ice and fringed by floating ice shelves; population solely of scientists of the British Antarctic Survey; territory administered by a High Commissioner in the Falkland Is.

BRITISH INDIAN OCEAN TERRITORY

British territory, 1 900 km/1 180 mi NE of Mauritius, c.2 300 islands, comprising the Chagos Archipelago; area, 60 sq km/23 sq mi; covering c.54 400 sq km/21 000 sq mi of Indian Ocean; tropical maritime climate, hot and humid; acquired by France, 18th-c; annexed by Britain, 1814; bought by the Crown, 1967; population working on copra plantations were resettled in Mauritius or the Seychelles, 1967–73; construction of a naval and air base by Britain and US started on Diego Garcia, the largest island; population total (1982e) 3 000; no permanent civilian population.

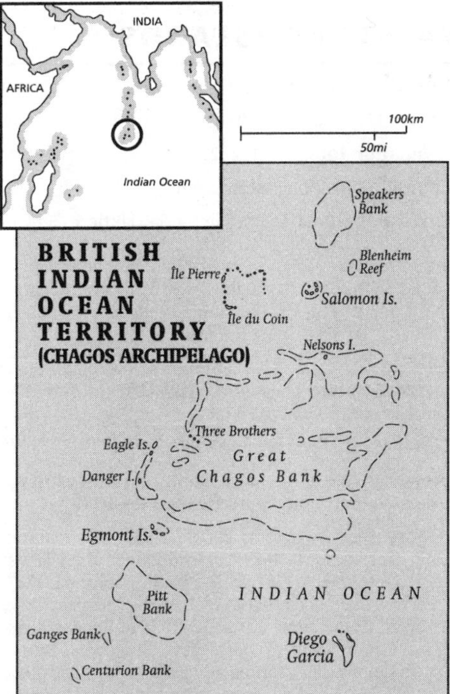

BRITISH VIRGIN ISLANDS

Timezone GMT – 4

Area 153 sq km/59 sq mi

Population total (1987) 12 197

Capital Road Town (on Tortola Island)

Physical features Island group at the NW end of the Lesser Antilles chain, E Caribbean, NE of Puerto Rico; comprises four large islands (Tortola, Virgin Gorda, Anegada, Jost Van Dyke) and over 30 islets and cays; only 16 inhabited; hilly terrain, except for flat coral island of Anegada; highest point, Sage Mt, 540 m/1 772 ft, on Tortola I.

Climate Subtropical climate; average annual temperatures 17–28°C (Jan), 26–31°C (Jul); average annual rainfall 1 270 mm/50 in.

Currency 1 US Dollar (US$) = 100 cents

Economy Tourism (accounts for 50% of national income); construction and stone extraction; rum, paint, gravel livestock, coconuts, sugar cane, fruit and vegetables, fish.

History Tortola colonized by British planters, 1666; constitutional government, 1774; part of the Leeward Is, 1872; separate Crown Colony, 1956; governor represents the British sovereign; Executive Council and Legislative Council.

CAYMAN ISLANDS

Timezone GMT – 5

Area 260 sq km/100 sq mi

Population total (1991e) 27 000

Capital George Town

Physical features Located in W Caribbean, comprising the islands of Grand Cayman, Cayman Brac, and Little Cayman, c.240 km/150 mi S of Cuba; low-lying, rising to 42 m/138 ft on Cayman Brac plateau; ringed by coral reefs.

Climate Tropical climate; average temperatures 24–32°C (May–Oct), 16–24°C (Nov–Apr); average annual rainfall 1 420 mm/56 in; hurricane season (Jul–Nov).

Currency 1 Cayman Island Dollar (CI$) = 100 cents

Economy Tourism; international finance, property development; over 450 banks and trust companies established on the islands; oil transshipment; crafts, jewellery, vegetables, tropical fish.

History Visited by Colombus, 1503; ceded to Britain, 1670; colonized by British settlers from Jamaica; British Crown Colony, 1962; a governor represents the British sovereign, and presides over a Legislative Assembly.

FALKLAND ISLANDS

Timezone GMT – 4

Area c.12 200 sq km/4 700 sq mi

Population total (1991) 2 121

Capital Stanley (on East Falkland)

Physical features Located in the S Atlantic, c.650 km/400 mi NE of the Magellan Strait; consists of East Falkland and West Falkland, separated by the Falkland Sound, with over 200 small islands; hilly terrain, rising to 705 m/2 313 ft at Mt Usborne (East Falkland) and 700 m/2 297 ft at Mt Adam (West Falkland).

Climate Cold, strong westerly winds; low rainfall; narrow temperature range 19°C (Jan), 2°C (Jul); average annual rainfall 635 mm/25 in.

Currency 1 Falkland Pound = 100 pence

Economy Agriculture; oats, sheep; service industries to the continuing military presence in the islands.

History Seen by several early navigators, including Capt John Strong in 1689–90, who named the islands; French settlement, 1764; British base established, 1765; French yielded their settlement to the Spanish, 1767; occupied in the name of the Republic of Buenos Aires, 1820; Britain asserted possession, became a British Crown Colony, 1833; formal annexation, 1908 and 1917; the whole island claimed since independence by Argentina; Falklands War, precipitated by the Argentine

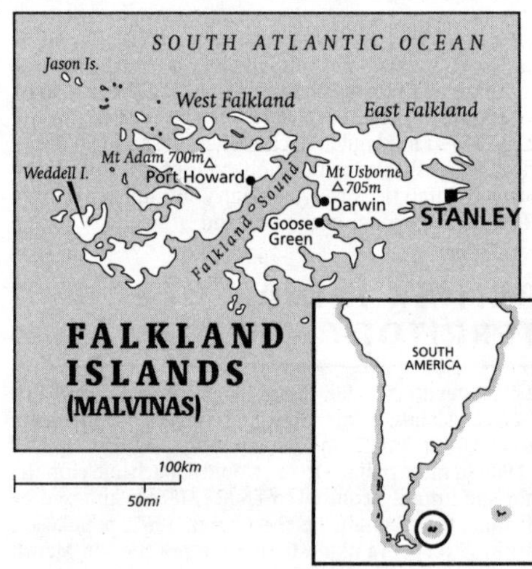

invasion of the islands, Apr 1982, led to the dispatch of the British Task Force and the return of the islands to British rule, Jun 1982; external affairs and defence are the responsibility of the British government, which appoints civil and military commissioners; internal affairs are governed by executive and legislative councils.

SOUTH GEORGIA

British Dependent Territory, located in the S Atlantic, c.500 km/300 mi E of the Falkland Islands; area, c.3 750 sq km/1 450 sq mi; barren, mountainous, snow-covered island, length, 160 km/100 mi; discovered by the London merchant De la Roche, 1675; landing by Captain Cook, 1775; British annexation, 1908 and 1917; burial place of Ernest Shackleton, the British explorer, who died at S Georgia, 1922; sealing and whaling centre until 1965; invaded by Argentina and recaptured by Britain, April 1982; territory administered from the Falkland Islands.

SOUTH SANDWICH ISLANDS

British Dependent Territory; group of small, unihabited islands in the S Atlantic, c.720 km/450sq mi SE of South Georgia; 56°18-59°25S 26°15W; discovered by Captain Cook, 1775; annexed by Britain, 1908 and 1917; administered from the Falkland Islands.

GIBRALTAR

Timezone GMT + 1

Area 5.9 sq km/2.3 sq mi

Population total (1991) 29 613

Capital Gibraltar

Physical features Narrow rocky peninsula rising steeply from the low-lying coast of SW Spain at the E end of the Strait of Gibraltar, 8 km/5 mi from Algeciras; narrows to limestone massif, 'The Rock', height 426 m/1 398 ft, connected to the Spanish mainland by a sandy plain; home of the Barbary apes, the only native monkeys in Europe.

Climate Mediterranean climate, with mild winters, warm summers; average annual temperature range 13–29°C.

Currency 1 Gibraltar Pound = 100 pence

Economy Largely dependent on the presence of British forces; Royal Naval Dockyard converted to a commercial yard, 1985; transshipment trade; fuel supplies to shipping; tourism.

History Settled by Moors, 711; taken by Spain, 1462; ceded to Britain, 1713; Crown Colony, 1830; played a key role in Allied naval operations during both World Wars; proposal to end British rule defeated by referendum, 1967; Spanish closure of frontier, 1969–85; Spain continues to claim sovereignty; British monarch represented by a governor and House of Assembly; military base; important strategic point of control for the W Mediterranean.

HONG KONG

Timezone GMT + 8

Area 1 066.5 sq km/411.7 sq mi

Population total (1992e) 5 700 00

Capital Hong Kong

Languages English and Cantonese (official), with Mandarin widely spoken

Ethnic groups Chinese (98%), including many illegal immigrants from China and refugees from Vietnam; 59% of population born in Hong Kong, 37% in China

Religions Buddhist, Taoist and Confuncianist majorities, Christian, Muslim, Hindu, Sikh and Jewish minorities

Physical features Located off the coast of SE China, on the South China Sea; divided into Hong Kong Island, Kowloon, and New Territories (includes most of the colony's 235 islands); highest point, Tai Mo Shan, 957 m/3 140 ft; hilly terrain, sharply indented coastline; natural harbour between Kowloon and Hong Kong Island; built-up areas on artificially levelled or reclaimed land.

Climate Subtropical climate, with hot, humid summers

Hong Kong (continued)

and cool, dry winters; average annual temperatures 16°C (Jan), 29°C (Jul); average annual rainfall 2 225 mm/ 88 in.

Currency 1 Hong Kong Dollar (HK$) = 100 cents

Economy Based on banking, import-export trade, tourism, shipbuilding, and a diverse range of light industry; an important freeport acting as a gateway to China for the West.

History Ceded to Britain, 1842; New Territories leased to Britain, 1898; occupied by the Japanese in World War 2; British Crown Colony, governor represents the British Crown, advised by an Executive Council; in 1997, Britain's 99-year lease of the New Territories will expire, whereupon Hong Kong will be restored to China; China has designated Hong Kong a special administrative region from 1997; it will remain a freeport, foreign markets will be retained, and the Hong Kong dollar will remain as official currency; however, anxiety over the colony's political future remains.

MONTSERRAT (EMERALD ISLE)

Timezone GMT - 4

Area 106 sq km/41 sq mi

Population total (1991) 12 504

Capital Plymouth

Physical features Volcanic island in the Leeward Is, E Caribbean; mountainous, heavily forested; highest point, Chance's Peak, 914 m/2 999 ft; seven active volcanoes.

Climate Tropical climate, with low humidity; average annual rainfall 1 500 mm/60 in; hurricanes occur (Jun–Nov).

Currency 1 East Caribbean Dollar (EC$) = 100 cents

Economy Tourism (accounts for 25% of national income); cotton, peppers, livestock, electronic assembly, crafts, rum distilling, postage stamps.

History Visited by Colombus, 1493; colonized by English and Irish settlers, 1632; plantation economy based on slave labour; British Crown Colony, 1871; joined Federation of the West Indies, 1958–62; island severely damaged by hurricane Hugo, 1989; British sovereign represented by a governor, with an Executive Council and a Legislative Council.

PITCAIRN ISLANDS

Timezone GMT - 8.5

Area 27 sq km/10 sq mi

Population total (1992) 56

Capital Adamstown

Physical features Volcanic island group in the SE Pacific Ocean, E of French Polynesia; comprises Pitcairn Island, 4.5 sq km/1.7 sq mi, and the uninhabited islands of Ducie, Henderson and Oeno; Pitcairn Island rises to 335 m/1 099 ft.

Climate Equable climate; average annual temperatures 24°C (Jan), 19°C (Jul); average annual rainfall 2 000 mm/ 80 in.

Currency 1 New Zealand Dollar ($NZ) = 100 cents

Economy Postage stamps; tropical and subtropical crops; crafts, forestry.

History Visited by the British, 1767; occupied by nine mutineers from HMS Bounty, 1790; overpopulation led to emigration to Norfolk I, 1856; some returning, 1864; transferred to Fiji, 1952; now a UK Dependent Territory, governed by the High Commissioner in New Zealand.

SAINT HELENA AND DEPENDENCIES

Timezone GMT

Area 122 sq km/47 sq mi

Population total (1991) 6 695

Capital Jamestown (on St Helena Island)

Physical features Volcanic group of islands in the S Atlantic, 1 920 km/1 200 mi from the SW coast of Africa; includes St Helena, Ascension, Gough I, Inaccessible I, Nightingale I and Tristan da Cunha; rugged, volcanic terrain; highest point, Diana's Peak, 823 m/2 700 ft.

Climate Tropical marine; mild, tempered by SE 'trade' winds.

Currency 1 St Helena Pound (£) = 100 pence

Economy Fish (mostly tuna); agriculture, coffee; postage stamps; heavily subsidised by the UK.

History Discovered by the Portuguese on St Helena's feast day, 1502; annexed by the Dutch, 1633; annexed by the East India Company, 1659; Napolean exiled here, 1815–21; Ascension and Tristan da Cunha made dependencies, 1922; evacuated between 1961–3, following volcanic eruption; governed by an executive council and 12-member elected Legislative Council.

TURKS AND CAICOS ISLANDS

Timezone GMT – 5

Area 500 sq km/200 sq mi

Population total (1991) 9983

Capital Grand Turk

Physical features Two island groups comprising c.30 islands and cays, forming the SE archipelago of the Bahamas chain, W Atlantic Ocean; Turk I and Caicos I are separated by 35 km/22 mi; only six of the other islands are inhabited.

Climate Subtropical climate; average annual temperatures 24–7°C (Jan), 29–32°C (Jul); average annual rainfall 525 mm/21 in; occasional hurricanes.

Currency 1 US Dollar ($, US$) = 100 cents

Economy Tourism is a rapidly expanding industry; corn, beans, fishing, fish-processing.

History Visited by the Spanish, 1512; linked formally to the Bahamas, 1765; transferred to Jamaica, 1848; British Crown Colony, 1972; internal self-government, 1976; British sovereign represented by a governor, who presides over a Council.

UNITED STATES OF AMERICA (USA)

Local names United States, America

Timezone GMT – 5 (E coast) to – 8 (W coast)

Area 9160454 sq km/3535935 sq mi

Population total (1992e) 255600000

Status Federal republic

Date of independence 1776

Capital Washington, DC.

Languages English, large Spanish-speaking minority

Ethnic groups European origin (including 6.2% Hispanic) (86.2%), African American (11%), Asian and Pacific (1.6%), Native American, Aleut, and Inuit (0.7%)

Religions Christian (86%) (Protestant 61%, Roman Catholic 25%), atheist (7%), other (5%), Jewish (2%)

Physical features Includes the separate states of Alaska (GMT – 9) and Hawaii (GMT – 10); E Atlantic coastal plain is backed by the Appalachian Mts from the Great Lakes to Alabama, a series of parallel ranges including the Allegheny, Blue Ridge, and Catskill Mts; plain broadens out (S) towards the Gulf of Mexico and into the Florida peninsula; Gulf Plains stretch N to meet the Great Plains from which they are separated by the Ozark Mts; further W, Rocky Mts rise to over 4300 m/14400 ft; highest point in US, Mt McKinley, Alaska, 6194 m/20321 ft; Death Valley, –86 m/–282 ft, is the lowest point; drainage N is into the St Lawrence R or the Great Lakes; in the E, the Hudson, Delaware, Potomac, and other rivers flow E to the Atlantic Ocean; central plains drained by the great Red River-Missouri-Mississippi system and by other rivers flowing into the Gulf of Mexico; main rivers in W, Columbia and Colorado; deserts cover much of Texas, New Mexico, Arizona, Utah and Nevada.

Climate Climate varies from conditions found in hot, tropical deserts (SW), to those typical of Arctic continental regions on the northern Pacific Coast; continental climate on High Plains, with summer dust storms and winter blizzards; temperate continental on Central Plains; continental Mid West and the Great Lakes, with very cold winters; cool temperate in N Appalachians, warm temperate in S; subtropical to warm temperate on the Gulf Coast, with plentiful rainfall and frequent hurricanes and tornadoes; temperate maritime on the Atlantic coast, with heavy snowfall in N; cool temperate

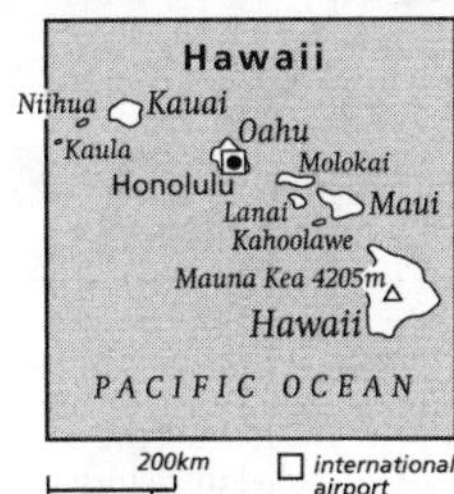

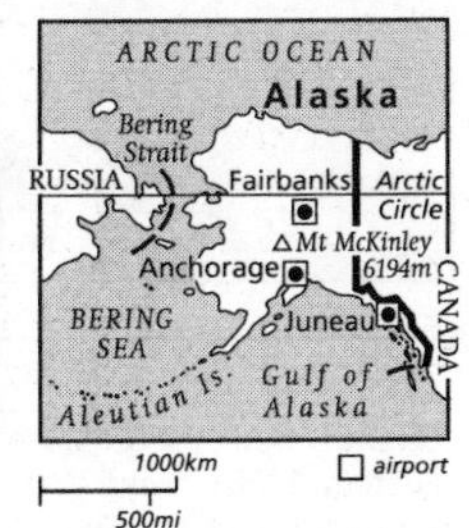

in New England, with warm summers and severe winters; mean annual temperatures range from 29°C in Florida, to –13°C in Alaska; average annual temperatures in Chicago, –3°C (Jan), 24°C (Jul); in Arizona, 11°C (Jan), 32°C (Jul); average annual rainfall in Alabama, 1640 mm/65 in, in Arizona, 180 mm/7 in; hot and humid in Hawaii, with average annual rainfall 1524–5080 mm/60–200 in.

Currency 1 US Dollar ($, US$) = 100 cents

Economy One of the world's most productive industrial nations; highly diversified economy; vast mineral and agricultural resources; major exporter of grains, cereals, potatoes, sugar, and fruit; livestock farming of beef, veal and pork; chief exports include aircraft, cars, machinery, chemicals, military equipment, and non-fuel minerals; advanced system of communications and transportation; leader in space exploration programme of the 1970s.

GDP (1991) $5677.5 bln, per capita $19082

History First settled by groups who migrated from Asia across the Bering Straits over 25000 years ago; explored by the Norse, 9th-c; and by the Spanish, 15th-c, who settled in Florida and Mexico; in the 17th-c, settlements by the British, French, Dutch, Germans, and Swedes; many Black Africans introduced as slaves to work on the plantations; British control during 18th-c after defeat of French in Seven Years' war; revolt of the English-speaking colonies in the War of Independence, 1775–83, resulted in the creation of the United States of America; Louisiana sold to the USA by France, 1803 (the Louisiana Purchase) and the westward movement of settlers began; Florida ceded by Spain, 1819, and further Spanish states joined the Union between 1821–53; 11 Southern states

left the Union over the slavery issue and formed the Confederacy, 1860–1; Civil War, 1861–5, ended in victory for the North, and the Southern states later rejoined the Union; Alaska purchased from Russia, 1867; Hawaiian islands annexed, 1898; several other islands formally associated with the USA, such as Puerto Rico, American Samoa, and Guam; in the 19th-c, arrival of millions of immigrants from Europe and the Far East; more recent arrival of large numbers of Spanish-speaking people, mainly from Mexico and the West Indies; entered World War 1 on the side of the Allies, 1917, and again in World War 2, 1941; became the chief world power opposed to communism, a policy which led to involvement in the Korean War (1950–3) and Vietnam (1956–75); campaign for Black civil rights developed, 1960s, and eventually led to Civil Rights Act (1964); invasion of Grenada, 1983; mid 1980s rapprochement of US and USSR; invasion of Panama, 1989; involvement in Gulf War, 1991; military intervention in Somalia, 1993; Congress consists of 435-member House of Representatives, and a 100-member Senate; a president elected every 4 years by a college of state representatives, appoints an executive cabinet

responsible to Congress; divided into 50 federal states and the District of Columbia; each state having its own two-body legislature and governor.

Head of State/Government (President)
1989–93 George Herbert Walker Bush
1993– William Jefferson Clinton

>> **Political leaders and rulers**

American States

(Timezones: two sets of figures indicate that different zones operate in a state. The second figure refers to Summer Time (Apr–Oct, approximately)
2 Aleutian/Hawaii Standard Time : 3 Alaska Standard Time : 4 Pacific Standard Time : 5 Mountain Standard Time : 6 Central Standard Time : 7 Eastern Standard Time

Name	*Area*		*Capital*	*Time*	*Population*	*Nickname*
	sq km	*sq mi*		*zone*	*figures (1992)*	
Alabama (AL)	133 911	51 705	Montgomery	7/8	4 089 000	Camellia State, Heart of Dixie
Alaska (AK)	1 518 748	586 412	Juneau	3/4	570 000	Mainland State, The Last Frontier
Arizona (AZ)	295 249	114 000	Phoenix	5	3 750 000	Apache State, Grand Canyon State
Arkansas (AR)	137 403	53 187	Little Rock	6/7	2 372 000	Bear State, Land of Opportunity
California (CA)	411 033	158 706	Sacramento	4/5	30 380 000	Golden State
Colorado (CO)	269 585	104 091	Denver	5/6	3 377 000	Centennial State
Connecticut (CT)	12 996	5 018	Hartford	7/8	3 291 000	Nutmeg State, Constitution State
Delaware (DE)	5 296	2 045	Dover	7/8	680 000	Diamond State, First State
District of Columbia (DC)	173.5	67.0	Washington	7/8	606 900	
Florida (FL)	151 934	58 664	Tallahassee	6/7, 7/8	13 277 000	Everglade State, Sunshine State
Georgia (GA)	152 571	58 910	Atlanta	7/8	6 623 000	Empire State of the South, Peach State
Hawaii (HI)	16 759	6 471	Honolulu	2	1 135 000	Aloha State
Idaho (ID)	216 422	83 564	Boise	4/5, 5/6	1 039 000	Gem State
Illinois (IL)	145 928	56 345	Springfield	6/7	11 543 000	Prairie State, Land of Lincoln
Indiana (IN)	93 715.5	36 185	Indianapolis	6/7, 7/8	5 610 000	Hoosier State
Iowa (IA)	145 747	56 275	Des Moines	6/7	2 795 000	Hawkeye State, Corn State
Kansas (KS)	213 089	82 277	Topeka	5/6, 6/7	2 475 000	Sunflower State, Jayhawker State
Kentucky (KY)	104 658	40 410	Frankfort	6/7, 7/8	3 713 000	Bluegrass State
Louisiana (LA)	123 673	47 752	Baton Rouge	6/7	4 252 000	Pelican State, Sugar State, Creole State
Maine (ME)	86 153	33 265	Augusta	7/8	1 235 000	Pine Tree State
Maryland (MD)	27 090	10 460	Annapolis	7/8	4 860 000	Old Line State, Free State
Massachusetts (MA)	21 455	8 284	Boston	7/8	5 996 000	Bay State, Old Colony
Michigan (MI)	151 579	58 527	Lansing	6/7, 7/8	9 368 000	Wolverine State, Great Lake State
Minnesota (MN)	218 593	84 402	St Paul	6/7	4 432 000	Gopher State, North Star State
Mississippi (MS)	123 510	47 689	Jackson	6/7	2 592 000	Magnolia State
Missouri (MO)	180 508	69 697	Jefferson City	6/7	5 158 000	Bullion State, Show Me State
Montana (MT)	380 834	147 046	Helena	5/6	808 000	Treasure State, Big Sky Country
Nebraska (NE)	200 342	77 355	Lincoln	5/6, 6/7	1 593 000	Cornhusker State, Beef State

American States (continued)

Nevada (NV)	286 341	110 561	Carson City	4/5	1 284 000	Silver State, Sagebrush State
New Hampshire (NH)	24 032	9 279	Concord	7/8	1 105 000	Granite State
New Jersey (NJ)	20 167	7 787	Trenton	7/8	7 760 000	Garden State
New Mexico (NM)	314 914	121 593	Santa Fe	5/6	1 548 000	Sunshine State, Land of Enchantment
New York (NY)	127 185	49 108	Albany	7/8	18 058 000	Empire State
North Carolina (NC)	136 407	52 699	Raleigh	7/8	6 737 000	Old North State, Tar Heel State
North Dakota (ND)	180 180	69 567	Bismarck	5/6, 6/7	635 000	Flickertail State, Sioux State
Ohio (OH)	107 040	41 330	Columbus	7/8	10 939 000	Buckeye State
Oklahoma (OK)	181 083	69 919	Oklahoma City	6/7	3 175 000	Sooner State
Oregon(OR)	251 409	97 073	Salem	4/5	2 922 000	Sunset State, Beaver State
Pennsylvania (PA)	117 343	45 308	Harrisburg	7/8	11 961 000	Keystone State
Rhode Island (RI)	3 139	1 212	Providence	7/8	1 004 000	Little Rhody, Plantation State
South Carolina (SC)	80 579	31 113	Columbia	7/8	3 560 000	Palmetto State
South Dakota (SD)	199 723	77 116	Pierre	5/6, 6/7	703 000	Sunshine State, Coyote State
Tennessee (TN)	109 149	42 144	Nashville	6/7, 7/8	4 953 000	Volunteer State
Texas (TX)	691 003	266 807	Austin	5/6, 6/7	17 349 000	Lone Star State
Utah (UT)	219 880	84 899	Salt Lake City	5/6	1 770 000	Mormon State, Beehive State
Vermont (VT)	24 899	9 614	Montpelier	7/8	567 000	Green Mountain State
Virginia (VA)	105 582	40 767	Richmond	7/8	6 286 000	Old Dominion State, Mother of Presidents
Washington (WA)	176 473	68 139	Olympia	4/5	5 018 000	Evergreen State, Chinook State
West Virginia (WV)	62 758	24 232	Charleston	7/8	1 801 000	Panhandle State, Mountain State
Wisconsin (WI)	145 431	56 153	Madison	6/7	4 955 000	Badger State, America's Dairyland
Wyoming (WY)	253 315	97 809	Cheyenne	5/6	460 000	Equality State

United States Formal Dependencies

AMERICAN SAMOA

Local name São Paulo de Loanda (Portuguese)

Timezone GMT - 11

Area 197 sq km/76 sq mi

Population total (1990) 46 773

Capital Pago Pago

Languages English (official), Samoan

Physical features Located in the US Pacific Ocean, some 3 500 km/2 175 mi N of New Zealand; five principal volcanic islands (including Tutuila, Aunu'u, Ofu, Olosega, Ta'u, Rose and Swains I) and two coral atolls; main island, Tutuila, 109 sq km/42 sq mi, rises to 653 m/2 142 ft; islands mostly hilly, with large areas covered by thick bush and forest.

Climate Tropical maritime climate; average annual temperatures 28 °C (Jan), 27 °C (Jul) in Pago Pago; plentiful rainfall; rainy season (Nov–Apr); dry season (May–Oct); average annual rainfall 5 000 mm/200 in.

Economy Principal crops, taro, breadfruit, yams, bananas, coconuts; tuna fishing; local inshore fishing, handicrafts.

History US acquired rights to American Samoa, 1899 and the islands were ceded by their chiefs, 1900–25; now an unincorporated territory of the USA, administered by the Department of the Interior; bicameral legislature established, 1948, comprising the Senate and the House of Representatives.

GUAM

Local name Guam

Timezone GMT + 10

Area 541 sq km/209 sq mi

Population total (1990e) 138 000

Status Unincorporated territory of the United States of America

Capital Agana

Languages Chamorro and English (official), Japanese is also spoken

Ethnic groups Chamorros (42%), Caucasian (24%), Filipino (21%), Micronesian (13%)

Religion Roman Catholic

Physical features Largest and southernmost of the Mariana Islands, covering c.48 km/30 mi in the Pacific Ocean; volcanic island fringed by a coral reef; relatively flat limestone plateau, with narrow coastal plains in N, low rising hills in C and mountains in S; highest point, 406 m/1 332 ft at Mt Lamlam.

Climate Tropical maritime climate; average annual temperature 24–30°C; average annual rainfall 2 125 mm/ 84 in; wet season (Jul–Dec).

Currency 1 US Dollar (US$) = 100 cents

Economy Economy highly dependent on government activities; military installations cover 35% of the island; diversifying industrial and commercial projects; oil refining, dairy products, furniture, watches, copra, processed fish; rapidly growing tourist industry.

History Originally settled by Malay-Filipino peoples; Ferdinand Magellan landed on the island, 1521; claimed for Spain, 1565; rebellion against Spanish missionaries, 1670–95; US consulate established, 1855; ceded to US by Spain after defeat in Spanish-American War, 1898; occupied by Japan, 1941–4; unincorporated territory of the US, Organic Act, 1950; elected governor and a unicameral legislature.

THE COMMONWEALTH OF PUERTO RICO

Local name Puerto Rico

Timezone GMT – 4

Area 8 897 sq km/3 434 sq mi

Population total (1990) 3 522 037

Status Commonwealth

Capital San Juan

Languages Spanish (official), with English widely spoken

Religion Roman Catholic

Physical features Easternmost island of the Greater Antilles; almost rectangular in shape; crossed W–E by mountains, rising to 1 338 m/4 389 ft at Cerro de Punta; coastal plain belt in N; islands of Vieques and Culebra also belong to Puerto Rico.

Climate Tropical maritime climate; average annnual temperature 25°C; high humidity.

Currency 1 US Dollar (US$) = 100 cents

Economy Manufacturing is the most important sector of the economy; food processing, petrochemicals, electrical equipment, pharmaceuticals; textiles, clothing; livestock, tobacco, sugar, pineapples, coconuts; tourism.

History Originally occupied by Carib and Arawak Indians; visited by Columbus, 1493; remained a Spanish colony until ceded to the US, 1898; high levels of emigration to the US, 1940s–50s; became a semi-autonomous Commonwealth in association with US, 1952; executive power is exercised by a Governor; a bicameral Legislative Assembly consists of a Senate and House of Representatives.

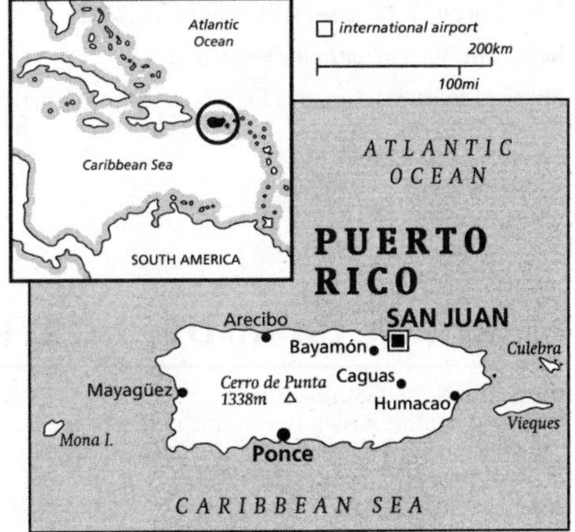

VIRGIN ISLANDS, UNITED STATES

Local name US Virgin Islands

Timezone GMT – 4

Area 342 sq km/132 sq mi

Population total (1990) 101 809 (St Croix 50 139, St Thomas 48 166, St John 3 504)

Status Territory

Capital Charlotte Amalie (on St Thomas Island)

Languages English (official), with Spanish and Creole widely spoken

Ethnic groups West Indian, French, Hispanic

Physical features Nine islands and 75 islets in the Lesser Antilles, Caribbean Sea; three main inhabited islands, St Croix, St Thomas, and St John; volcanic origin,

Virgin Islands, United States (continued)

mostly hilly or rugged and mountainous; highest peak, Crown Mt, 474 m/1 555 ft on St Thomas.

Climate Subtropical climate; average annual temperatures 21–29°C (Dec–Mar), 24–31°C (Jun–Sep); low humidity; rainy season (May–Nov); subject to severe droughts, floods and earthquakes.

Currency 1 US Dollar (US$) = 100 cents

Economy Tourism (chief industry); St Croix industries include oil and alumina products, clocks and watches, textiles, rum, fragrances, petrochemicals; vegetables, fruit, sorghum.

History Originally inhabited by Ciboney Indians, followed by Arawak Indians, then Caribs; discovered by Columbus, 1493; Denmark colonized St Thomas and St John, 1665 and 1718, and bought St Croix from France, 1733; purchased by US, 1916; now an unincorporated territory of the US; a governor heads a unicameral legislature.

MICRONESIA, FEDERATED STATES OF

Timezone GMT + 11

Area 700 sq km/270 sq mi

Population total (1991e) 111 000

Status Republic

Date of independence 1991

Capital Palikir (on Pohnpei Island)

Languages English (official), with several indigenous languages also spoken

Ethnic groups Trukese (41%), Pohnpeian (26%)

Religions Roman Catholic, Protestant

Physical features Group of four states in the W Pacific Ocean (Yap, Truk, Ponape, Kosrae); comprises all the Caroline I except Belau; islands vary from high mountainous terrain to low coral atolls.

Climate Tropical climate, with occasional typhoons; heavy rainfall all year.

Currency 1 US Dollar (US$) = 100 cents

Economy Agriculture; farming and fishing; tropical fruits, coconuts, vegetables; few mineral resources.

GDP Not available

History Settled by Spanish seafarers, 1565; formally annexed by Spain, 1874; sold to Germany, 1899; control mandated to Japan by League of Nations, 1920; American Navy took control following Japan's defeat in World War 2, 1945; part of UN Trust Territory of the Pacific, 1947; compact of free association with the US, 1982; trusteeship ended, 1990; independent state, 1991, under Compact of Free Association, the US continues to control its defence and foreign relations; governed by a president and a National Congress.

Head of State/Government

1991– Bailey Olter

MARIANA ISLANDS, NORTHERN

Located in N Pacific Ocean, area 471 sq km/182 sq mi; limestone southern islands, volcanic northern islands; capital Saipan; population total (1990) 43 345; tropical marine climate; part of UN Trust Territory of the Pacific, 1947; became a self-governing US Commonwealth Territory, 1975; trusteeship ended 1990.

BELAU (PALAU)

Consists of c. 350 Pacific Ocean islands; eight inhabited; area, 494 sq km/ 191 sq mi; population total (1990e) 14 800; capital Koror; part of US Trust Territory of the Pacific, 1947; proclaimed a republic, 1981; Compact of Free Association signed with US, 1982, needs to gain the required 75% support of the voters of Belau before it can be recognized as self-governing; remains the only surviving part of Trust Territory which has not formally achieved independence.

Other American Islands

BAKER, HOWLAND, AND JARVIS ISLANDS

1 500–1 650 mi SW of the Hawaiian group, Pacific Ocean; uninhabited since World War 2; under Interior Department.

JOHNSTON ATOLL
Consists of four small islands, SW of Hawaii: Johnston, Sand, Hikina and Akau; used for military purposes, otherwise uninhabited.

KINGMAN REEF
Uninhabited reef S of Hawaii, under Navy control.

MIDWAY ISLANDS
Atoll and two islands, Eastern and Sand, lying NW of Hawaii, in N Pacific; unpopulated apart from US naval personnel.

PALMYRA
Atoll 1 000 mi S of Hawaii; privately owned; under Interior Department.

WAKE ISLAND
Uninhabited but for US naval personnel, Wake I lies between Guam and Midway I; sister islands, Wilkes and Peale.

NAVASSA
Caribbean island between Jamaica and Haiti, 100 mi S of Guatanámo Bay, Cuba; covers c.3 sq mi and is reserved by US for a lighthouse, administered by US Coast Guard; uninhabited.

URUGUAY

Local name Uruguay

Timezone GMT - 3

Area 176 215 sq km/68 018 sq mi

Population total (1992e) 3 100 000

Status Republic

Date of independence 1828

Capital Montevideo

Language Spanish (official)

Ethnic groups European (mainly Spanish, Italian) (90%), mestizo (8%)

Religions Roman Catholic (66%), Protestant (2%), Jewish (2%), unaffiliated (30%)

Physical features Located in E South America; grass covered plains (S) rise to a high, sandy plateau, traversed SE and NW by the Cuchilla Grande and Cuchilla de Haedo, rising to 501 m/1 644 ft at Cerro Mirados; R Negro flows SW to meet the R Uruguay on the Argentine frontier.

Climate Temperate, with warm summers, mild winters; average annual temperature 10 °C (Jul), 22 °C (Jan) in Montevideo; average annual rainfall 890 mm/35 in; rainy season (Apr–May), occasional droughts.

Currency 1 New Uruguayan Peso (NUr$, UrugN$) = 100 centésimos

Economy Traditionally based on livestock and agriculture; meat, wool, fish, wheat, barley, maize, rice; naturally occurring minerals include granite and marble; hydroelectric power, food processing and packing, light engineering, cement, textiles, leather, steel.

GDP (1990e) $9.2 bln, per capita $2 970

History Originally occupied by Charrúas Indians; visited by the Spanish, 1515; part of the Spanish Viceroyalty of Río de la Plata, 1726; province of Brazil, 1814–25; independence as the Eastern Republic of Uruguay, 1828; unrest caused by Tupamaro guerrillas in late 1960s and early 1970s; military rule until 1985; a president is advised by a Council of Ministers; bicameral legislature consists of a Senate and Chamber of Deputies.

Head of State/Government
1984–90 Julio María Sanguinetti Cairolo
1990– Luis Alberto Lacalle Herrera

USSR (FORMER) >> CIS, LATVIA, LITHUANIA, ESTONIA, GEORGIA

UZBEKISTAN

Local name Ozbekiston Republikasy

Timezone GMT + 6

Area 447 400 sq km/172 696 sq mi

Population total (1992e) 21 300 000

Status Republic

Date of independence 1991

Capital Tashkent

Language Uzbek

Ethnic groups Uzbek (71%), Russian (8%), Tajik (5%), Kazakh (4%)

Religion Sunni Muslim

Physical features Located in C and N Middle Asia; four fifths of area is flat, sandy plain/desert (W); Turan Plain (NW) rises near the Aral Sea to 90 m/300 ft above sea level; delta of major river R Amu Darya forms alluvial plain over C Kara-Kalpak; Sultan-Uizdag Mts rise to 500 m/1 600 ft; Kyzyl Kum broken by hills in SE; lowest point, Mynbulak, −12 m/39 ft; Pskem Mts in E rise to 4 299 m/14 104 ft at Beshtor Peak.

Climate Dry and continental; average annual temperatures in S, −12°C (Jan), 32–40°C (Jul); low rainfall.

Currency Rouble (R)

Economy Deposits of coal, natural gas, oil, gold, lead, copper, and zinc; third largest cotton-growing area in the world; silk, wool; agriculture dependent on irrigated land; abundant orchards and vineyards; industry powered hydroelectrically.

GDP Not available

History Conquered by Alexander the Great, 4th-c; invaded by Mongols under Genghis Khan, 13th-c; Genghis Khan's grandson, Shibaqan, inherited the area; converted to Islam, 14th-c, under the ruler of Kipchak, Uzbek; became part of Tamerlane the Great's empire, 16th-c; conquered by Russia, mid-19th-c; became the Uzbek Republic, 1924, and Uzbekistan Soviet Socialist Republic, 1925; declared independence, 1991, and President Karimov resigned after supporting coup against Gorbachev; Communist party outlawed; joined CIS, 1991; Karimov elected president, with restricted opposition; highest legislative body, 500-seat Supreme Soviet; new constitution adopted, 1992.

Head of State
1991– Islam A Karimov

Head of Government
1991– Abdulhashim Mutalov

VANUATU

Local name Ripablik Blong Vanuatu

Timezone GMT + 11

Area 14 763 sq km/5 698 sq mi

Population total (1992e) 200 000

Status Independent republic within the Commonwealth

Date of independence 1980

Capital Port Vila (on Efate Island)

Languages Bislama, English, and French (official)

Ethnic groups Melanesian (95%), Micronesian, Polynesian, and European minorities

Religions Christian (70%) (Presbyterian 40%, Roman Catholic 15%, Anglican 15%), indigenous beliefs (8%), other (15%)

Physical features Mountainous, volcanic Y-shaped island chain in SW Pacific Ocean, 400 km/250 mi NE of New Caledonia; consisting of 13 islands and 70 islets; two thirds of population occupy the four main islands of Efate, Espiritu Santo, Malekula and Tanna; highest peak, rises to 1 888 m/6 194 ft, on Espiritu Santo; islands comprise raised coral beaches fringed by reefs; several active volcanoes.

Climate Tropical, high temperatures; hot and rainy season (Nov–Apr) when cyclones may occur; average annual temperatures, 27°C (Jan), 22°C (Jul) in Vila; average annual rainfall 2 103 mm/83 in.

Currency 1 Vatu (VT) = 100 centimes

Economy Agriculture; subsistence farming and plantations; yams, breadfruit, taro, copra, beef, cocoa, coffee, timber; manganese, fish processing, foodstuffs, crafts; tourism rapidly increasing, especially from cruise ships.

GDP (1989e) $137 mln, per capita $860

Human geography

History Visited by the Portuguese, 1606; charted and named the New Hebrides by British explorer James Cook, 1774; under Anglo-French administration as the condominium of the New Hebrides, 1906; escaped Japanese occupation during World War 2; independence as the Republic of Vanuatu, 1980; governed by a president, prime minister, and cabinet and a representative Assembly.

Head of State
1989– Frederick Karlomuana Timakata

Head of Government
1980–91 Walter Lini
1991 Donald Kalpokas
1991– Maxime Carlot

Map >> SOLOMON ISLANDS

VATICAN CITY STATE

Local name Stato della Città del Vaticano

Timezone GMT + 1

Area 0.44 sq km/0.17 sq mi

Population total (1991) 778

Status Papal sovereign state

Date of independence 1929

Capital The Holy See, Vatican City

Languages Latin and Italian

Ethnic groups Italian, European, and various minorities

Religion Roman Catholic

Physical features The world's smallest state, situated on the Vatican hill in Rome, on W bank of R Tiber; architectural features include the Vatican Palace and Museum, St Peter's, the Pope's summer villa at Castel Gandolfo, and the Sistine Chapel; three entrances to the city in the care of the Pontifical Swiss Guard, 'The Bronze Doors', the Arch of Charlemagne, or the 'Arch of Bells', and the Via di Porta Angelica.

Climate Mediterranean; average annual temperature 7°C (Jan), 25°C (Jul); average annual rainfall 657 mm/26 in.

Currency 1 Vatican Lira (L, Lit) = 100 centesimi

Economy The state is supported by special collections and donations from Catholic congregations around the world; issues its own stamps, coinage and has own communications and banking systems; tourism; pilgrimages.

Income (1991) income $109 mln, expenses $196 mln

History Papacy's temporal authority exercised from a palace built on Rome's Vatican hill, 1377; extended to much of central Italy by 16th-c; incorporated into the emerging Italian state during the fight to unite Italy, 1860–70; the Lateran Treaty of 1929 recognized the Holy See's sovereignty in the Vatican City State and Catholicism became Italy's state religion; Karol Wojtyla became the first non-Italian pontiff since the 16th-c, 1978; in 1985, a concordat, replacing the Lateran Treaty, affirmed independence of the Vatican, but ended some of its privileges, Roman Catholicism ceased to be the state religion, and Rome lost its status as a 'sacred city'; sovereignty exercised by Pope, who is elected for life by a conclave of the College of Cardinals.

Head of State (Sovereign Pontiff/Pope)
1978– Pope John Paul II (Karol Wojtyla)

Head of Government (Secretary of State)
1990– Cardinal Angelo Sodano

Map >> ITALY

VENEZUELA

Local name República de Venezuela

Timezone GMT – 4

Area 912 050 sq km/352 051 sq mi

Population total (1992e) 18 900 000

Status Republic

Date of independence 1830

Capital Caracas

Languages Spanish (official), Italian, c.25 Indian languages also spoken in the interior

Ethnic groups Mestizo (67%), European (21%), African origin (9%), Indian (2%)

Religions Roman Catholic (96%), Protestant (2%)

Physical features Occupies most of the N coast of S America; Guiana Highlands (SE) cover almost half the country; Venezuelan Highlands in the W and along the coast, highest point, Pico Bolívar 5 007 m/16 411 ft; vast grasslands (*Llanos*) in the Orinoco basin; chief river, Orinoco; largest lake in S America, L Maracaibo, 21 486 sq km/

Human geography

Venezuela (continued)

8 296 sq mi; highest waterfall in the world, Angel Falls 979 m/3 212 ft.

Climate Tropical, generally hot and humid; average annual temperatures 18°C (Jan), 21°C (Jul) in Caracas; one rainy season (Apr–Nov); average annual rainfall 833 mm/33 in.

Currency 1 Bolívar (B) = 100 céntimos

Economy Since 1920s, based on oil from Maracaibo (now provides over 90% of export revenue); aluminium (second-highest source of revenue); iron ore, gold, diamonds; 20% of the land is under cultivation; beef and dairy farming; coffee, cocoa, cotton, rice, tobacco, sugar.

GDP (1990e) $42.4 bln, per capita $2 150

History Originally inhabited by Carib and Arawak; seen by Columbus, 1498; Spanish settlers, 1520; frequent revolts against Spanish colonial rule; independence movement under Simón Bolívar, leading to the establishment of the State of Gran Colombia (Colombia, Ecuador, Venezuela), 1821; independent republic, 1830; governed by an elected two-chamber National Congress, comprising a Senate and a Chamber of Deputies; a president is advised by a Council of Ministers.

Head of State/Government
1989– Carlos Andrés Pérez

VIETNAM

Local name Công Hòa Xã Hôi Chu Nghĩa Viêt Nam (Vietnamese)

Timezone GMT + 7

Area 329 566 sq km/127 212 sq mi

Population total (1992e) 69 200 000

Status Socialist republic

Date of independence 1976

Capital Hanoi

Languages Vietnamese (official), French, Chinese, English, Khmer

Ethnic groups Vietnamese (85–90%), Chinese (3%), various minorities include Khmer, Cham, Hmong, Nung, and Tay, local dialects

Religions Buddhist (principal), Taoist, Confucian, Muslim, Roman Catholic, Hoa Hoa, Cao Dai, Protestant, and animist beliefs

Physical features Occupies a narrow strip along the coast of the Gulf of Tongking and the S China Sea on Indochinese peninsula in SE Asia; highest peak Fan-si-Pan, 3 143 m/10 312 ft; Mekong R delta (S) and Red R delta (N) linked by narrow coastal plain; heavily forested mountains and plateaux.

Climate Tropical, monsoon climate; sub-tropical in N; average annual temperatures 17°C (Jan), 29°C (Jul) in Hanoi; average annual rainfall 1 830 mm/72 in; typhoons and flooding frequent in N and SW.

Currency 1 Dông = 10 hao = 100 xu

Economy Agriculture (employs over 70% of the workforce); however, natural disasters, war and political unrest have adversely affected economy; Vietnam War brought depopulation of the countryside and considerable destruction of forest and farmland; exports include coal, minerals, rice, rubber, sugar cane.

GNP (1990e) $15.2 bln, per capita $230

History Under the influence of China for many centuries; regions of Tongking (N), Annam (C), and Cochin-China (S) united as Vietnamese Empire, 1802; French protectorates established in Cochin-China, 1867, and in Annam and Tongking, 1884; formed the French Indo-Chinese Union with Cambodia and Laos, 1887; occupied by the Japanese in World War 2; communist Viet-Minh League under Ho Chi Minh formed after the War, not recognized by France; Indo-Chinese war, resulting in French withdrawal, 1946–54; 1954 armistice divided the country between the communist 'Democratic Republic' in the N, and the 'State' of Vietnam in the S; civil war led to US intervention on the side of S Vietnam, 1965; fall of Saigon, 1975; reunification as the Socialist Republic of Vietnam, 1976; large numbers of refugees tried to find homes in the W in the late 1970s; Hanoi invaded neighbouring Cambodia, overthrowing hostile Khmer Rouge government, 1978; Chinese responded with invasion of Vietnam in 1979 - greatly increased the number trying to leave the country by sea (Vietnamese boat people); in 1984, Hanoi agreed to talks with US about whereabouts of missing US servicemen; limited troop withdrawals from Laos and Cambodia, 1989; Vietnam supported Cambodian peace agreement, 1991; new constitution, 1992, replaced Council of Ministers with a prime minister and cabinet.

Head of State
1986–91 Nguyen Van Linh
1991–2 Do Muoi
1992– Le Duc Anh

Head of Government
1988–91 Do Muoi
1991– Vo Van Kiet

VIRGIN ISLANDS, BRITISH >> UNITED KINGDOM

VIRGIN ISLANDS, US >> UNITED STATES OF AMERICA

WALLIS AND FUTUNA >> FRANCE

WESTERN SAHARA >> MOROCCO

WESTERN SAHARA

Timezone GMT

Area 2 842 sq km/1 097 sq mi

Population total (1990e) 186 000

Status Under dispute, still officially part of Morocco

Capital Ad Dakhla

Languages Arabic (Hassaniya and Moroccan), French, Berber dialects, Spanish

Ethnic groups Mainly of Arab and Berber descent

Religion Sunni Muslim

Physical features Located in NW Africa, between Morocco (N), Mauritania (S), and Atlantic Ocean (E); low, flat terrain rising to small mountains in S and NE.

Climate Hot, dry desert; limited rainfall; fog and heavy dew produced by cold offshore currents.

Currency 1 Moroccan Dirham (DH) = 100 Moroccan francs

Economy Limited by low rainfall and few natural resources; fishing and phosphate mining are main sources of income.

GDP Not available

History Spanish province known as Spanish Sahara (Western Sahara) since 1884; partitioned by Morocco and Mauritania after its Spanish status ended in 1975; independence proclaimed, 1976, as Saharan Arab Democratic Republic (SADR); Morocco refused to withdraw its claim to the region, resulting in fighting between Morocco and Polisario guerrillas; Mauritania withdraw its claim after signing a peace treaty with the Polisario Front, 1979; SADR admitted to the Organization of African Unity, 1982; UN-supervised talks to decide the region's future began, 1990; Polisario guerrilla warfare stopped under UN ceasefire, Sep 1991; renewed fighting, Feb 1993; UN Security Council approved referendum to determine the country's political future, scheduled end 1993; UN Secretary-General visited for self-determination talks, May-Jun 1993.

Main SADR government leaders *

Head of State
Mohammed Abdelazziz

Head of Government
Mahfoud Ali Beiba

* Officially administered by Morocco and the Moroccan government.

Map >> MOROCCO

WESTERN SAMOA

Local name Samoa i Sisifo (Samoan)

Timezone GMT - 11

Area 2 842 sq km/1 097 sq mi

Population total (1992e) 200 000

Status Independent state within the Commonwealth

Date of independence 1962

Capital Apia

Languages Samoan and English (official)

Ethnic groups Polynesian, with Pacific Islanders, Euronesian, Chinese, and European minorities

Religions Christian (99%) (Protestant 70%, Roman Catholic 20%, other 9%)

Physical features Two large (Upolu, Savai'i) and seven small islands in the South Pacific Ocean, 2 600 km/ 1 600 mi NE of Auckland, New Zealand; formed from ranges of extinct volcanoes, rising to 1 829 m/6 001 ft on Savai'i; last volcanic activity, 1905–11; thick tropical vegetation; several coral reefs along coast.

Climate Tropical climate; cool, dry season (May–Nov), average temperature 22°C; rainy season (Dec–Apr) with temperatures reaching 36°C; average annual rainfall, 2 775 mm/109 in; frequent hurricanes.

Currency 1 Tala (WS$) = 100 sene

Western Samoa (continued)

Economy Largely agricultural subsistence economy; taro, yams, breadfruit, pawpaws, coconuts, cocoa, bananas; tourism increasing; internal transportation system depends largely on roads and ferries; charter air service operates between the two main islands.

GDP (1990e) $115 mln, per capita $620

History Visited by the Dutch, 1772; 1889 commission divided Samoa between Germany (which acquired Western Samoa) and the US (which acquired Tutuila and adjacent small islands, now known as American Samoa); New Zealand granted a League of Nations mandate for Samoa, 1919; UN Trust Territory under New Zealand, 1946; independence, 1962; became a member of the Commonwealth, 1970; governed by a monarch as head of state for life, a prime minister, and a 49-member Legislative Assembly (*Fono*).

Head of State (O le Ao O le Malo)
1963– Malietoa Tanumafili II

Head of Government
1988– Tofilau Eti Alesana

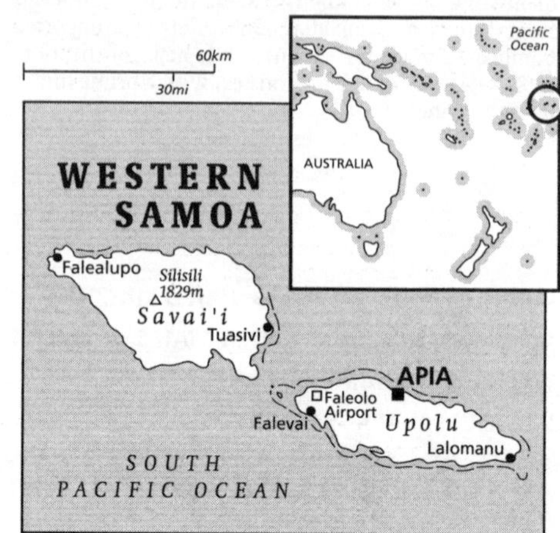

YEMEN

Local name Al-Yaman (Arabic)

Timezone GMT + 3

Area 531 570 sq km/205 186 sq mi

Population total (1992e) 10 400 000

Status Republic

Date of independence 1967

Capitals Sana (political), Aden (commercial)

Languages Arabic (official), English

Ethnic groups Arab (96%), with Indo-Pakistani, Somali, Amhara and Swahili, Persian, Jewish and European minorities

Religions Muslim (Sunni 53%, Shiite 47%), small Christian, Hindu and Yemeni Jew minorities

Physical features Occupies the SW corner of the Arabian peninsula; narrow coastal plain, backed by mountains rising to 3 000–3 500 m/10 000–11 500 ft; highlands, central plateau and maritime range of former South Yemen form the most fertile part of the country; former North Yemen is largely desert and mountainous.

Climate Hot and humid climate; lowland and desert regions in NE receive an average annual rainfall of 100 mm/4 in; hot and humid on Tihamat coastal strip with mean temperature of 29°C; mild and temperate in interior highlands, with cool winters; average annual temperatures 25°C (Jan), 32°C (Jul) in Aden; average annual rainfall, 46 mm/1.8 in.

Currency 1 Yemeni Riyal (YR, YRl) = 100 fils (former N Yemen)
1 Yemeni Dinar (YD) = 1 000 fils (1 Dinar = 26 Riyals) (former S Yemen)

Economy Based on agriculture (largely subsistence) and light industry; cotton has overtaken coffee as chief cash crop; irrigation schemes likely to increase area under cultivation; Qat, a narcotic leaf, now a major enterprise; hides, vegetables, dried fish; crude and refined oil industry; textiles, cement, aluminium, salt.

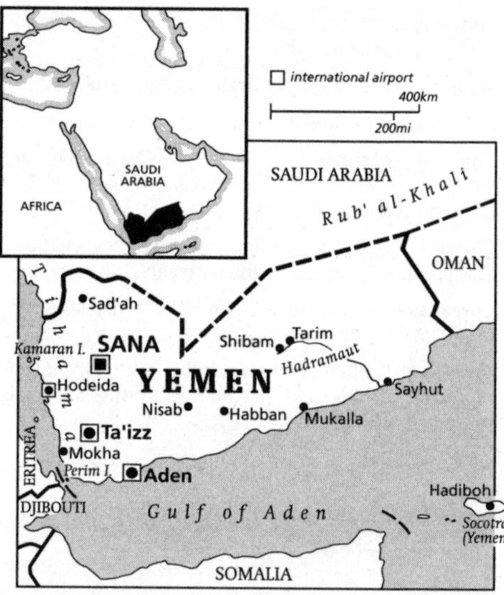

GDP (1990e) $5.3 bln, per capita $545

History Part of the Minaean kingdom, 1200–650 BC; converted to Islam in 7th-c; Turkish occupation, 1538–1630 and 1849–1918; between and after Turkish rule, Yemen under the rule of the Hamid al-Din dynasty; sovereignty of Yemen acknowledged by Saudi Arabia and Britain, 1934; joined Arab League, 1945; Egypt-backed revolution, 1962, resulting in civil war; Yemen Arab Republic (North Yemen) declared, 1962; royalists defeated, 1969; neighbouring People's Republic of South Yemen established, 1967, when Britain ended 129 years of rule in Aden and the Marxist National Liberation Front took over; the People's Republic comprised Aden and 16 of the 20 protectorate states once under British control; renamed People's Democratic Republic of Yemen, 1970; negotiations to merge the two Yemens began in 1979; unification proclaimed and ratified, 1990; new state called Republic of Yemen; former President of North Yemen was declared president of the unified state, and the former president of South Yemen became prime minister; supported Iraq during Gulf War, 1991; elections scheduled for Nov 1992 postponed until Apr 1993; coalition government formed, May 1993; coalition government formed, May 1993; governed by a president, prime minister, House of Representatives and Advisory Council.

Head of State
1990– Ali Abdullah Saleh

Head of Government
1990– Haidar Abu Bakr al-Attas

YUGOSLAVIA

Local name Jugoslavija

Timezone GMT + 2

Area Prior to 1991: 256 409 sq km/98 974 sq mi
Since 1991: 102 173 sq km/39 438 sq mi (comprising the states of Montenegro and Serbia)

Population total Prior to 1991: 23 860 000
Since 1991: (1992e) 10 400 000 (comprising the states of Montenegro and Serbia)

Status Federal Republic

Date of independence Now comprises the republics of Serbia and Montenegro; formerly (to 1991) a federation of six republics (additionally, Bosnia and Herzegovina, Croatia, Macedonia, Slovenia) formerly united in 1918 as an independent Federal Republic

Capital Belgrade (Serbia)

Languages Serbo-Croat, with Albanian and Hungarian also spoken

Ethnic groups Prior to 1991: Serbian (36%), Croatian (20%), Bosnian (10%), Slovene (8%), Albanian (8%), Macedonian (6%), Montenegrin (3%), other (9%)
Since 1991: continuing civil war prevents accurate recording of ethnic group data

Religions Prior to 1991: Serbian Orthodox (35%), Roman Catholic (26%), other Christian (11%), Muslim (10%)
Since 1991: continuing civil war prevents accurate recording of religious groups

Physical features Mountainous country with fertile valleys; Julian and Karawanken Alps rise (N) to 2 863 m/9 393 ft at Triglav; Adriatic fringed by the Dinaric Alps; fertile Danubian plain in NE Serbia; chief river, R Danube, also the Tisza, Drava, Sava and Morava; limestone Karst plateaux in W along coast.

Climate Moderate, continental climate; average annual temperatures 0°C (Jan), 22°C (Jul) in Belgrade; average annual rainfall 610 mm/24 in.

Currency 1 Yugoslav Dinar (D, Din) = 100 paras

Economy Ongoing conflict and escalating violence has crippled the economy of the countries involved; formerly agriculture; corn, wheat, tobacco, sugar beets; mining and manufacturing industries; exports of textiles, leather goods, machinery; natural resources of copper, coal, timber, iron, lead, zinc, bauxite.

GNP Prior to 1991: (1990e) $120.1 bln, per capita $5 040
Since 1991: not available

History Serbs, Croats, and Slovenes united under one monarch, 1918; formation of new state did not quell long-held nationalist feelings; in an attempt to create a sense of common patriotism King Alexander changed the kingdom's name to Yugoslavia, 1929; civil war between Serbian royalists (Chetniks), Croatian nationalists, and Communists; occupied by Germany in World War 2; Federal People's Republic established under Tito, 1945; revised constitution, 1974, instituted a rotating leadership, with the prime minister elected annually; governed by a bicameral Federal Assembly, comprising a Federal Chamber and a Chamber of Republics and Provinces; following a break with the USSR, 1948, the country followed an independent form of communism and a general policy of non-alignment; at the end of the 1980s political disagreement between the federal republics increased; ethnic unrest in Serbia (Kosovo); Slovenian unilateral declaration of independence, 1989, followed by Macedonian and Croatian declarations, 1991, considered illegal by central government; inter-republic talks on Yugoslavia's future, but confrontation between Croatia and Serb-dominated National Army developed into civil war, 1991; Serbian support of Serb guerrillas in Bosnia resulted in UN sanctions, mid-1992; arrival

Yugoslavia (continued)

of UN Protection Force, 1992; Federal Republic of Yugoslavia declared, 1992, consisting of only two of the six republics that made up former Yugoslavia, Montenegro and Serbia; the new state remains unrecognized due to continuing fighting; failure of the Vance-Owen Peace Plan, 1993 leading to increasing uncertainty about the future of a residual Yugoslavia. >> BOSNIA AND HERZEGOVINA, CROATIA, MACEDONIA, SLOVENIA

Head of State

1989–90 Janez Drnovsek
1990–1 Borisav Jovic
1991–2 Stipe Mesic
1992–3 Dobrica Cosic
1993 Milos Radulovic (*Acting*)
1993– Zoron Lilic

Head of Government

1989–91 Ante Markovic
1991–3 Milan Panic
1993– Radoje Kontic

ZAÏRE

Local name République du Zaïre

Timezone GMT + 1 (W) to + 2 (E)

Area 2 343 950 sq km/904 765 sq mi

Population total (1992e) 37 900 000

Status Republic

Date of independence 1960

Capital Kinshasa

Languages French (official), English, with various Bantu dialects (including Swahili, Lingala, Ishiluba, and Kikongo) spoken

Ethnic groups Bantu, with Sudanese, Nilotes, Pygmies, Hamite and Angolan minorities

Religions Christian (70%) (Roman Catholic 50%, Protestant 20%), Kimbanguist (10%), Muslim (10%), traditional beliefs (10%)

Physical features Located in C Africa, land rises E from a low-lying basin to a densely forested plateau; Ruwenzori Mts (NE) rise to 5 110 m/16 765 ft in the Mt Stanley massif; Mitumba Mts further S; Rift Valley chain of lakes, Albert, Edward, Kivu, and Tanganyika; Zaïre R.

Climate Equatorial, hot and humid; average annual temperature, 26°C (Jan), 23°C (Jul) in Kinshasa; average annual rainfall 1 125 mm/44 in; dry coastal region; dry season (May–Sep) S of the equator, (Dec–Feb) N of the equator.

Currency 1 Zaïre (Z) = 100 makuta (singular likuta)

Economy Subsistence farming employs c.80% of population; palm oil, rubber, quinine, fruit, vegetables, tea, cocoa; extensive mineral reserves; world's biggest producer of cobalt, industrial diamonds, copper; coffee, petroleum, cotton, tobacco processing, chemicals, cement.

GDP (1990e) $6.6 bln, per capita $180

History Visited by the Portuguese, 1482; expeditions of Henry Morton Stanley, 1874–7; claimed by King Leopold of Belgium, recognized, 1885; Congo Free State ceded to the state, 1907 and renamed Belgian Congo; independence as the Democratic Republic of the Congo, 1960; shortly after, mineral-rich Katanga (later, Shaba) province claimed independence, leading to civil war; UN peace-keeping force present until 1964; renamed the Republic of Zaïre, 1971; further conflict, 1977–8, as Katangese rebels invaded Shaba province from Angola; President Mobutu announced proposals for the introduction of a new constitution, 1990, including the adoption of a three-party system; dissatisfaction with proposals resulted in boycotting of elections scheduled for 1992; controversial changes to constitution in Apr 1993 gave president power to appoint the prime minister; Birindwa appointed, Mar; ensuing conflict; EC refused to acknowledge Birindwa's premiership, Apr 1993; UN intervention requested; UN mission sent, May 1993; continuing unrest.

Head of State

1965– Mobutu Sese Seko (formerly Joseph Mobutu)

Head of Government

1989–91 Lunda Bululu
1991 Mulumba Lukeji
1991 Etienne Tshisekedi
1991 Bernardin Mungul Diaka
1991–2 Jean Nguza Karl-I-Bond
1992–3 Etienne Tshisekedi
1993– Faustin Birindwa (*Acting*)

ZAMBIA

Local name Zambia

Timezone GMT + 2

Area 752 613 sq km/290 509 sq mi

Population total (1992e) 8 400 000

Status Independent republic within the Commonwealth

Date of independence 1964

Capital Lusaka

Languages English (official), with c.70 local languages (including Tonga, Kaonde, Lunda and Luvale) also spoken

Ethnic groups Bantu (99%), including Bemba Nyanja, Barotse, Mambwe and Swahili peoples

Religions Christian (75%), local beliefs (23%), Muslim and Hindu (1%)

Physical features High plateau in SC Africa, altitude 1 000–1 400 m/3 300–4 600 ft; highest point, 2 067 m/6 781 ft, SE of Mbala; a number of rivers drain southwards to join Zambezi R in N, including R Luangwa; highest waterfall, Kalambo Falls, 221 m/726 ft; man-made L Kariba in S, 440 sq km/170 sq mi.

Climate Warm temperate climate on plateau; tropical in lower valleys; although in C Africa and subequatorial, protected from very high temperatures by altitude; three distinct seasons, hot, dry (Aug–Oct), warm, wet (Nov–Apr), dry, cool (May–Jul); average annual temperatures, 21°C (Jan), 16°C (Jul) in Lusaka; average annual rainfall 836 mm/33 in.

Currency 1 Kwacha (K) = 100 ngwee

Economy Based on copper and cobalt, (provide over 50% of national income); lead, zinc, tobacco, coal, copper, cobalt; corn, tobacco, rice, sugar cane, groundnuts, cotton; sugar refining, glassware, tyres, brewing, oil refining.

GDP (1990) $4.7 bln, per capita $580

History European influence followed Livingstone's discovery of the Victoria Falls, 1855; administered by the British South Africa Company under Rhodes; Northern and Southern Rhodesia declared a British sphere of influence, 1888; became Northern Rhodesia, 1911; British protectorate, 1924; joined with Southern Rhodesia and Nyasaland as the Federation of Rhodesia and Nyasaland, 1953; Federation dissolved, 1963; independence as the Republic of Zambia, 1964; president has executive power and legislative power is held by 150-member National Assembly; new multi party constitution adopted, 1991.

Head of State (President)
1964–91 Kenneth Kaunda
1991– Frederick Chiluba

Head of Government (Vice-President)
1989–91 Malimba Masheke
1991– Levy Mwanawasa

ZIMBABWE

Local name Zimbabwe

Timezone GMT + 2

Area 391 090 sq km/150 961 sq mi

Population total (1992e) 10 300 000

Status Independent republic within the Commonwealth

Date of independence 1980

Capital Harare

Languages English (official), Ndebele and Shona widely spoken

Ethnic groups Bantu (97%) (including Shona 71%, Ndebele 16%), European (2%)

Religions Syncretic Christian/local beliefs (50%), Christian (25%), traditional animist beliefs (24%), small Muslim minority

Physical features Landlocked country in SC Africa; mostly savannah (tropical grassland); Highveld ridge crosses SW to NE to join the Inyanga Mts on Mozambique border, highest point, Mt Inyangani, 2 592 m/8 504 ft; Highveld flanked by lower plateau, Middleveld; Lowveld, altitude, 300 m/1 000 ft, lies NE; tropical hardwood forests (SE); chief rivers, Zambezi, Limpopo, and Sabi.

Climate Subtropical climate, strongly influenced by altitude; average annual temperature 21°C (Jan), 14°C (Jul) in Harare; average annual rainfall 828 mm/33 in; rainfall increases from SW to NE; wet season (Nov–Mar).

Currency 1 Zimbabwe Dollar (Z$) = 100 cents

Zimbabwe (continued)

Economy Agriculture (involves 70% of population), manufacturing and mining; sugar, cotton, livestock; natural resources, gold, copper, chrome, nickel, tin, asbestos; tourism to national parks; major industries in steel, textiles, vehicles, and chemicals.

GDP (1990e) $5.6 bln, per capita $540

History Mediaeval Bantu kingdom, 12–16th-c, with capital at Great Zimbabwe; visited by Livingstone in the 1850s; Southern Rhodesia under British influence in the 1880s as the British South Africa Company under Cecil Rhodes; divided into Northern and Southern Rhodesia, 1911; Southern Rhodesia became a self-governing British colony, 1923; Northern and Southern Rhodesia and Nyasaland formed a multi-racial federation, 1953; independence of Nyasaland and Northern Rhodesia, 1963; opposition to the independence of Southern Rhodesia under African rule resulted in a Unilateral Declaration of Independence (UDI) by the White-dominated government, 1965; economic sanctions and internal guerrilla activity forced the government to negotiate with the main African groups: the Zimbabwe African People's Union (ZAPU), led by Joshua Nkomo, the Zimbabwe African National Union (ZANU), led by Robert Mugabe, and the United African National Council (UANC), led by Bishop Abel Muzorewa; independence as the Republic of Zimbabwe, 1980; since 1987, the post of executive president has combined the posts of head of state and head of government; bicameral legislature replaced, 1990, by new single chamber parliament, the House of Assembly.

Head of State/Government

1987– Robert Gabriel Mugabe

SOCIETY

ANTHROPOLOGY

Nations of the world: general data

In the case of countries that do not use the Roman alphabet (such as the Arabic countries), there is variation in the spelling of names and currencies, depending on the system of transliteration used.

Where more than one language is shown with a country, the status of the languages may not be equal. Some languages have a 'semi-official' status, or are used for a restricted set of purposes, such as trade or tourism.

Population census estimates are for 1990 or later.

English name	*Local name*	*Official name (in English)*	*Capital (English name in parentheses)*	*Language(s)*	*Currency*	*Population*
Afghanistan	Afghānestān	Republic of Afghanistan	Kābul	Dari, Pushtu	1 Afghani (Af) = 100 puls	16 600 000
Albania	Shqipëri	Republic of Albania	Tiranë (Tirana)	Albanian	1 Lek (L) = 100 qintars	3 303 000
Algeria	Al-Jazā'ir (Arabic) Algérie (French)	Democratic and Popular Republic of Algeria	El Djazair (Algiers)	Arabic	1 Algerian Dinar (AD DA) = 100 centimes	25 798 000
Andorra	Andorra	Principality of Andorra; the Valleys of Andorra	Andorra La Vella	Catalan	1 French Franc (Fr) = 100 centimes 1 Peseta (Pta) = 100 céntimos	51 000
Angola	Angola	People's Republic of Angola	Luanda	Portuguese	1 New Kwanza (kw, kz) = 100 lwei	10 301 000
Antigua and Barbuda	Antigua and Barbuda	Antigua and Barbuda	St John's	English	1 East Caribbean Dollar (EC$) = 100 cents	80 600
Argentina	Argentina	Argentine Republic	Buenos Aires	Spanish	1 Austral (A) = 1000 pesos	32 646 000
Armenia	Armenia	Republic of Armenia	Yerevan	Armenian	1 Rouble (R) = 100 Kopecks	3 500 000
Australia	Australia	Commonwealth of Australia	Canberra	English	1 Australian Dollar ($A) = 100 cents	17 341 000
Austria	Österreich	Republic of Austria	Vienna	German	1 Schilling (S, Sch) = 100 Groschen	7 730 000
Azerbaijan	Azerbaijan	Republic of Azerbaijan	Baku	Azerbaijani	1 Rouble (R) = 100 Kopecks	7 236 000
Bahamas	Bahamas	Commonwealth of the Bahamas	Nassau	English	1 Bahamian Dollar (BA$, B$) = 100 cents	254 685
Bahrain	Al-Bahrayn	State of Bahrain	Al-Manāmah (Manama)	Arabic	1 Bahrain Dinar (BD) = 1000 fils	518 000
Bangladesh	Bangladesh	People's Republic of Bangladesh	Dhaka (Dacca)	Bengali	1 Taka (TK) = 100 poisha	107 992 140
Barbados	Barbados	Barbados	Bridgetown	English	1 Barbados Dollar (Bds$) = 100 cents	258 000
Belarus	Belarus	Republic of Belarus	Mensk (Minsk)	Belarussian, Russian	Belarussian rouble	10 300 000
Belgium	Belgique (French) België (Flemish)	Kingdom of Belgium	Bruxelles (Brussels)	Flemish, French, German	1 Belgian Franc (BFr) = 100 centimes	9 968 000
Belize	Belize	Belize	Belmopan	English	1 Belize Dollar (Bz$) = 100 cents	189 462
Benin	Bénin	Republic of Benin	Porto-Novo	French	1 CFA Franc (CFAFr) = 100 centimes	4 883 000
Bhutan	Druk-Yul	Kingdom of Bhutan	Thimbu/Thimphu	Dzongkha	1 Ngultrum (Nu) = 100 chetrum	1 476 000
Bolivia	Bolivia	Republic of Bolivia	La Paz/Sucre	Spanish, Aymara, Quechua	1 Boliviano (Bs) = 100 centavos	7 356 000
Bosnia and Herzegovina	Bosnia i Hercegovina	Republic of Bosnia and Herzgovinia	Sarajevo	Serbo-Croat	1 Dinar (D, Dn) = 100 paras	4 364 574
Botswana	Botswana	Republic of Botswana	Gaborone	English, Setswana	1 Pula (P, Pu) = 100 thebe	1 289 000

Brazil	Brasil	Federative Republic of Brazil	Brasília	Portuguese	1 Cruzeiro (Cr$) = 100 centavos	150 368 000
Brunei	Brunei Darussalam	State of Brunei, Abode of Peace	Bandar Seri Begawan	Malay, English	1 Brunei Dollar (Br$) = 100 cents	259 000
Bulgaria	Bǎlgarija	Republic of Bulgaria	Sofija (Sofia)	Bulgarian	1 Lev (Lv) = 100 stotinki	8 990 000
Burkina Faso	Burkina Faso	Burkina Faso	Ouagadougou	French	1 CFA Franc (CFAFr) = 100 centimes	8 776 000
Burma *see* Myanmar						
Burundi	Burundi	Republic of Burundi	Bujumbura	French, (Ki) Rundi	1 Burundi Franc (BuFr, FBu) = 100 centimes	5 450 000
Cambodia	Cambodia	State of Cambodia	Phnum Pénh (Phnom Penh)	Khmer	1 Riel (CRI) = 100 sen	8 592 000
Cameroon	Cameroun	Republic of Cameroon	Yaoundé	English, French	1 CFA Franc (CFAFr) = 100 centimes	12 700 000
Canada	Canada	Canada	Ottawa	English, French	1 Canadian Dollar (C$, Can$) = 100 cents	27 400 000
Cape Verde	Cabo Verde	Republic of Cape Verde	Praia	Portuguese	1 Escudo (CVEsc) = 100 centavos	383 000
Central African Republic	République Centrafricaine	Central African Republic	Bangui	French	1 CFA Franc (CFAFr) = 100 centimes	2 875 000
Chad	Tchad	Republic of Chad	N'Djamena	Arabic, French	1 CFA Franc (CFAFr) = 100 centimes	5 678 000
Chile	Chile	Republic of Chile	Santiago	Spanish	1 Chilean Peso (Ch$) = 100 centavos	13 173 000
China	Zhongguo	People's Republic of China	Beijing/Peking	Mandarin Chinese	1 Renminbi Yuan (RMBY, $, Y) = 10 jiao = 100 fen	1 133 682 501
Colombia	Colombia	Republic of Colombia	Bogotá	Spanish	1 Colombian Peso (Col$) = 100 centavos	32 978 000
Comoros	Comores	Federal Islamic Republic of the Comoros	Moroni	Arabic, French	1 Comorian Franc (CFr) = 100 centimes	463 000
Congo	Congo	Republic of Congo	Brazzaville	French	1 CFA Franc (CFAFr) = 100 centimes	2 326 000
Costa Rica	Costa Rica	Republic of Costa Rica	San José	Spanish	1 Costa Rican Colón (CR¢) = 100 céntimos	3 015 000
Côte d'Ivoire (Ivory Coast)	Côte d'Ivoire	Republic of Côte d'Ivoire	Abidjan/ Yamoussoukro	French	1 CFA Franc (CFAFr) = 100 centimes	12 657 000
Croatia	Croatia	Republic of Croatia	Zagreb	Serbo-Croat	Kruna	4 600 000
Cuba	Cuba	Republic of Cuba	La Habana (Havana)	Spanish	1 Cuban Peso (Cub$) = 100 centavos	10 603 000
Cyprus	Kipros (Greek) Kibris (Turkish)	Republic of Cyprus	Lavkosia (Nicosia)	Greek, Turkish	1 Cyprus Pound (£C) = 100 cents	568 000
Czech Republic	Česká Republika	Czech Republic	Praha (Prague)	Czech	1 Koruna (Kčs) = 100 haler	10 362 000
Denmark	Danmark	Kingdom of Denmark	København (Copenhagen)	Danish	1 Danish Krone (Dkr) = 100 øre	5 139 000
Djibouti	Djibouti	Republic of Djibouti	Djibouti	Arabic, French	1 Djibouti Franc (DF, DjFr) = 100 centimes	541 000
Dominica	Dominica	Commonwealth of Dominica	Roseau	English	1 East Caribbean Dollar (EC$) = 100 cents	86 000
Dominican Republic	República Dominicana	Dominican Republic	Santo Domingo	Spanish	1 Dominican Peso (RD$, DR$) = 100 centavos	7 384 000

Society

Nations of the world: general data (continued)

English name	*Local name*	*Official name (in English)*	*Capital (English name in parentheses)*	*Official language(s)*	*Currency*	*Population*
Ecuador	Ecuador	Republic of Ecuador	Quito	Spanish	1 Sucre (Su, S/.) = 100 centavos	10 780 000
Egypt	Misr	Arab Republic of Egypt	Al-Qāhirah (Cairo)	Arabic	1 Egyptian Pound (E£, LE) = 100 piastres	54 451 000
El Salvador	El Salvador	Republic of El Salvador	San Salvador	Spanish	1 Colón (ES₡) = 100 centavos	5 418 000
Equatorial Guinea	Guinea Ecuatorial	Republic of Equatorial Guinea	Malabo	Spanish	1 CFA Franc (CFAFr) = 100 centimes	360 000
Estonia	Eesti Estonskaya (Russian)	Republic of Estonia	Tallinn	Estonian, Russian	1 Kroon = 100 cents	1 600 000
Ethiopia	Ityopiya	People's Democratic Republic of Ethiopia	Adis Abeba (Addis Ababa)	Amharic	1 Ethiopian Birr (Br) = 100 cents	53 131 000
Fiji	Fiji	Sovereign Democratic Republic of Fiji	Suva	English	1 Fiji Dollar (F$) = 100 cents	744 000
Finland	Suomi (Finnish) Finland (Swedish)	Republic of Finland	Helsingfors (Helsinki)	Finnish, Swedish	1 Markka (FMk) = 100 penni	4 991 000
France	France	French Republic	Paris	French	1 French Franc (Fr) = 100 centimes	56 681 000
Gabon	Gabon	Gabonese Republic	Libreville	French	1 CFA Franc (CFAFr) = 100 centimes	1 170 000
Gambia, The	Gambia	Republic of the Gambia	Banjul	English	1 Dalasi (D, Di) = 100 butut	901 000
Georgia	Georgia	Republic of Georgia	Tbilisi	Georgian, Armenian, Russian	1 Rouble (R) = 100 kopecks	5 400 000
Germany	Bundesrepublik Deutschland	Federal Republic of Germany	Berlin	German	1 Deutsche Mark (DM) = 100 pfennige	79 632 000
Ghana	Ghana	Republic of Ghana	Accra	English	1 Cedi (¢) = 100 pesewas	15 336 000
Greece	Ellás	Hellenic Republic	Athinai (Athens)	Greek	1 Drachma (Dr) = 100 leptae	10 300 000
Greenland	Kalaallit Nunaat Grønland (Danish)	Greenland	Nuuk	Greenlandic, Danish	1 Danish Krona (DKr) = 100 øre	55 900
Grenada	Grenada	Grenada	St George's	English	1 East Caribbean Dollar (EC$) = 100 cents	100 000
Guatemala	Guatemala	Republic of Guatemala	Guatemala City	Spanish	1 Quetzal (Q) = 100 centavos	9 700 000
Guinea	Guinée	Republic of Guinea	Conakry	French	1 Guinean Franc (GFr) = 100 cauris	7 800 000
Guinea-Bissau	Guiné-Bissau	Republic of Guinea-Bissau	Bissau	Portuguese	1 Guinea-Bissau Peso (GBP, PG) = 100 centavos	1 000 000
Guyana	Guyana	Co-operative Republic of Guyana	Georgetown	English	1 Guyana Dollar (G$) = 100 cents	800 000
Haiti	Haïti	Republic of Haiti	Port-au-Prince	Hatian Creole, French	1 Gourde (G. Gde) = 100 centimes	6 286 000
Holland *see* Netherlands, The						
Honduras	Honduras	Republic of Honduras	Tegucigalpa	Spanish	1 Lempira (L, La) = 100 centavos	4 949 000
Hong Kong	Hsiang Kang (Chinese) Hong Kong (English)	Hong Kong	none	English, Chinese	1 Hong Kong Dollar (HK$) = 100 cents	5 841 000

Hungary	Magyarország	Republic of Hungary	Budapest	Hungarian	1 Forint (Ft) = 100 fillér	10 588 000
Iceland	Ísland	Republic of Iceland	Reykjavik	Icelandic	1 Króna (IKr, ISK) = 100 aurar	259 000
India	Bhārat (Hindi)	Republic of India	New Delhi	Hindi, English	1 Indian Rupee (Re, Rs) = 100 paisa	866 000 000
Indonesia	Indonesia	Republic of Indonesia	Jakarta	Bahasa Indonesia	1 Rupiah (Rp) = 100 sen	193 000 000
Iran	Īrān	Islamic Republic of Iran	Tehrān (Tehran)	Farsi	1 Iranian Rial (Rls, Rl) = 100 dinars	59 051 000
Iraq	Al-' Irāq	Republic of Iraq	Baghdād (Baghdad)	Arabic	1 Iraqi Dinar (ID) = 1000 fils	19 254 000
Ireland	Éire (Gaelic) Ireland (English)	Republic of Ireland	Baile Átha Cliath (Dublin)	Irish, English	1 Irish Pound/Punt (I£, IR£) = 100 pence	3 509 000
Israel	Yisra'el (Hebrew) Isrā' īl (Arabic)	State of Israel	Yerushalayim (Jerusalem)	Hebrew, Arabic	1 New Israeli Shekel (NIS) = 100 agorot	4 822 000
Italy	Italia	Italian Republic	Roma (Rome)	Italian	1 Italian Lira (L, Lit) = 100 centesimi	57 772 000
Ivory Coast *see* Côte d'Ivoire						
Jamaica	Jamaica	Jamaica	Kingston	English	1 Jamaican Dollar (J$) = 100 cents	2 489 000
Japan	Nippon	Japan	Tōkyō (Tokyo)	Japanese	1 Yen (¥, Y) = 100 sen	124 017 000
Jordan	Al'Urdunn	Hashemite Kingdom of Jordan	'Ammān (Amman)	Arabic	1 Jordan Dinar = 1000 fils	3 412 000
Kampuchea *see* Cambodia						
Kazakhstan	Kazakhstan	Republic of Kazakhstan	Alma-Ata	Kazakh, Russian	1 Rouble (R) = 100 kopecks	16 700 000
Kenya	Kenya	Republic of Kenya	Nairobi	Swahili, English	1 Kenyan shilling (KSh) = 100 cents	25 241 000
Kiribati	Kiribati	Republic of Kiribati	Baikiri, on Tarawa	English	1 Australian Dollar ($A) = 100 cents	71 100
Korea, North	Chos on Minjujuui In'min Konghwaguk	Democratic People's Republic of Korea	P'yongyang (Pyongyang)	Korean	1 Won (NKW) = 100 chon	22 937 000
Korea, South	Taehan-Min'guk	Republic of Korea	Soul (Seoul)	Korean	1 Won (W) = 100 chon	43 134 000
Kuwait	Al-Kuwayt	State of Kuwait	Al-Kuwayt (Kuwait City)	Arabic	1 Kuwaiti Dinar (KD) = 1000 fils	2 024 000
Kyrgyzstan	Kirgizstan	Republic of Kyrgyzstan	Bishek	Kirgizian, Russian	1 Rouble (R) = 100 kopecks	4 400 000
Laos	Lao	Lao People's Deomocratic Republic	Viangchan (Vientiane)	Lao	1 Kip (Kp) = 100 at	4 113 000
Latvia	Latvija Latviskaya (Russian)	Republic of Latvia	Riga	Latvian, Russian	1 Rouble (R) = 100 kopecks (new currency planned: lat)	2 700 000
Lebanon	Al-Lubnān	Republic of Lebanon	Bayrūt (Beirut)	Arabic	1 Lebanese Pound/Livre (LL, £L) = 100 piastres	3 384 000
Lesotho	Lesoto	Kingdom of Lesotho	Maseru	Sotho, English,	1 Loti (*pl* Maloti) (M, LSM) = 100 lisente	1 801 000
Liberia	Liberia	Republic of Liberia	Monrovia	English	1 Liberian Dollar (L$) = 100 cents	2 730 000
Libya	Lībiyā	Socialist People's Libyan Arab Jamahiriya	Tarābulus (Tripoli)	Arabic	1 Libyan Dinar (LD) = 1000 dirhams	4 350 000
Liechtenstein	Liechtenstein	Principality of Liechtenstein	Vaduz	German	1 Swiss Franc (SFr, SwF) = 100 centimes	28 700
Lithuania	Lietuva	Republic of Lithuania	Vilnius	Lithuanian, Russian	1 Rouble (R) = 100 kopecks (new currency planned: litas)	3 700 000
Luxembourg	Lëtzebuerg Luxembourg (French) Luxemburg (German)	Grand Duchy of Luxembourg	Luxembourg	French, German, Letzebuergesch	1 Luxembourg Franc (LFr) = 100 centimes	388 000

Society

Nations of the world: general data (continued)

English name	*Local name*	*Official name (in English)*	*Capital (English name in parentheses)*	*Official language(s)*	*Currency*	*Population*
Macedonia	Makedonija	Republic of Macedonia	Skopje	Macedonian	Dinar	2 033 964
Madagascar	Madagasikara	Democratic Republic of Madagascar	Antananarivo	Malagasy, French	1 Madagascar Franc (FMG, MgFr) = 100 centimes	12 185 000
Malawi	Malaŵi	Republic of Malawi	Lilongwe	Chewa, English	1 Kwacha (MK) = 100 tambala	9 438 000
Malaysia	Malaysia	Malaysia	Kuala Lumpur	Malay	1 Malaysian Dollar/Ringgit (M$) = 100 cents	17 981 000
Maldives	Maldive Divehi Jumhuriya	Republic of Maldives	Male	Divehi	1 Rufiyaa (MRf, Rf) = 100 laari	226 000
Mali	Mali	Republic of Mali	Bamako	French	1 CFA Franc (CFAFr) = 100 centimes	8 338 000
Malta	Malta	Republic of Malta	Valletta	Maltese, English	1 Maltese Lira (LM) = 100 cents	354 000
Marshall Islands		Republic of the Marshall Islands	Dalap-Uliga-Darrit, on Majuro	Marshallese, English	1 US Dollar (US $) = 100 cents	49 000
Mauritania	Mauritanie (French) Muritaniya (Arabic)	Islamic Republic of Mauritania	Nouakchott	Arabic	1 Ouguiya (U, UM) = 5 khoums	1 995 000
Mauritius	Mauritius	Mauritius	Port Louis	English	1 Mauritian Rupee (MR, MauRe) = 100 cents	1 083 000
Mexico	México	United Mexican States	Ciudad de México (Mexico City)	Spanish	1 Mexican Peso (Mex$) = 100 centavos	90 007 000
Micronesia		The Federated States of Micronesia	Palikir, on Pohnpei	English	1 US Dollar (US $) = 100 cents	110 000
Moldova	Moldova	Republic of Moldova	Kishinev	Romanian, Russian	1 Rouble (R) = 100 kopecks	4 341 000
Monaco	Monaco	Principality of Monaco	Monaco	French	1 French Franc (F) = 100 centimes	29 712
Mongolia	Mongol Ard Uls	Mongolian People's Republic	Ulaanbaatar (Ulan Bator)	Khalka	1 Tugrik (Tug) = 100 möngös	2 247 000
Morocco	Al-Magrib	Kingdom of Morocco	Rabat	Arabic	1 Dirham (DH) = 100 francs	26 181 000
Mozambique	Moçambique	Republic of Mozambique	Maputo	Portuguese	1 Metical (Mr, MZM) = 100 centavos	16 142 000
Myanmar	Pyidaungsu Myanma Naingngandaw	Union of Myanmar	Yangôn (Rangoon)	Burmese	1 Kyat (K) = 100 pyas	42 112 000
Namibia	Namibia	Republic of Namibia	Windhoek	English	1 South African Rand (R) = 100 cents	1 520 000
Nauru	Naeoro (Nauruan) Nauru (English)	Republic of Nauru	Yaren District	Nauruan, English	1 Australian Dollar ($A) = 100 cents	9 333
Nepal	Nepāl	Kingdom of Nepal	Kathmandu	Nepali	1 Nepalese Rupee (NRp, NRs) = 100 paise/pice	19 611 000
Netherlands, The	Nederland	Kingdom of the Netherlands	Amsterdam/ 's-Gravenhage (The Hague)	Dutch	1 Dutch Guilder (Gld)/Florin (f) = 100 cents	15 231 000
New Zealand	New Zealand (English) Aotearoa (Maori)	New Zealand	Wellington	English, Maori	1 New Zealand Dollar ($NZ) = 100 cents	3 429 000
Nicaragua	Nicaragua	Republic of Nicaragua	Managua	Spanish	1 Córdoba Oro (C$) = 100 centavos	3 751 000
Niger	Niger	Republic of Niger	Niamey	French	1 CFA Franc (CFAFr) = 100 centimes	8 154 000

Nigeria	Nigeria	Federal Republic of Nigeria	Lagos	English	1 Naira (N, ₦) = 100 kobo	88 500 000
Norway	Norge	Kingdom of Norway	Oslo	Norwegian	1 Norwegian Krone (NKr) = 100 øre	4 273 000
Oman	‘Umān	Sultanate of Oman	Masqat (Muscat)	Arabic	1 Rial Omani (RO) = 1000 baizas	1 534 000
Pakistan	Pākistān	Islamic Republic of Pakistan	Islāmābād (Islamabad)	Urdu	1 Pakistan Rupee (PRs, Rp) = 100 paisa	117 490 000
Panama	Panamá	Republic of Panama	Panamá (Panama City)	Spanish	1 Balboa (B, Ba) = 100 cents	2 426 000
Papua New Guinea	Papua New Guinea	Independent State of Papua New Guinea	Port Moresby	English, Tok Pïsin	1 Kina (K) = 100 toea	3 913 000
Paraguay	Paraguay	Republic of Paraguay	Asunción	Spanish	1 Guarani (₲) = 100 céntimos	4 279 000
Peru	Perú	Republic of Peru	Lima	Spanish, Quechua	1 New Sol = 100 centavos	22 361 000
Philippines	Filipinas	Republic of the Philippines	Manila	English, Pilipino	1 Philippine peso (PP, ₱) = 100 centavos	65 718 000
Poland	Polska	Republic of Poland	Warszawa (Warsaw)	Polish	1 Złoty (Zl) = 100 groszy	37 799 000
Portugal	Portugal	Republic of Portugal	Lisboa (Lisbon)	Portuguese	1 Escudo (Esc) = 100 centavos	10 387 000
Puerto Rico	Puerto Rico	Commonwealth of Puerto Rico	San Juan	Spanish, English	1 US Dollar (US$) = 100 cents	3 336 000
Qatar	Qatar	State of Qatar	Ad-Dawhah (Doha)	Arabic	1 Qatar Riyal (QR) = 100 dirhams	445 000
Romania	Romănia	Republic of Romania	București (Bucharest)	Romanian	1 Leu (*pl* lei) = 100 bani	23 397 000
Russia	Rossiyskaya	Russian Federation	Moskva (Moscow)	Russian	1 Rouble (R) = 100 kopecks	148 800 000
Rwanda	Rwanda	Republic of Rwanda	Kigali (Kinya)	Rwanda, French	1 Rwanda Franc (RF) = 100 centimes	7 902 000
Saint Kitts and Nevis	Saint Christopher/Kitts and Nevis	Federation of Saint Kitts and Nevis	Basseterre	English	1 East Caribbean Dollar (EC$) = 100 cents	44 100
Saint Lucia	Saint Lucia	Saint Lucia	Castries	English	1 East Caribbean Dollar (EC$) = 100 cents	153 075
Saint Vincent and the Grenadines	Saint Vincent and the Grenadines	Saint Vincent and the Grenadines	Kingstown	English	1 East Caribbean Dollar (EC$) = 100 cents	114 000
San Marino	San Marino	Most Serene Republic of San Marino	San Marino	Italian	1 Italian Lira (L, Lit) = 100 centesimi	23 000
São Tomé and Príncipe	São Tomé e Príncipe	Democratic Republic of São Tomé and Príncipe	São Tomé	Portuguese	1 Dobra (Db) = 100 centimos	128 000
Saudi Arabia	Al.‘Arabīyah as Sa‘ūdīyah	Kingdom of Saudi Arabia	Ar-Riyād (Riyādh)	Arabic	1 Saudi Arabian Riyal (SAR, SRIs) = 100 halalah	17 869 000
Senegal	Sénégal	Republic of Senegal	Dakar	French	1 CFA Franc (CFAFr) = 100 centimes	7 952 000
Seychelles	Seychelles	Republic of Seychelles	Victoria	Creole French, English, French	1 Seychelles Rupee (SR) = 100 cents	68 000
Sierra Leone	Sierra Leone	Republic of Sierra Leone	Freetown	English	1 Leone (Le) = 100 cents	4 274 000
Singapore	Singapore	Republic of Singapore	Singapore	Chinese, English, Malay, Tamil	1 Singapore Dollar/Ringgit (S$) = 100 cents	2 756 000
Slovakia	Slovenská republika	Republic of Slovakia	Bratislava	Slovakian	Slovak Crown = 100 haler	5 274 335
Slovenia	Slovenija	Republic of Slovenia	Ljubljana	Slovene	1 Slovene Tolar = 100 paras	1 962 600
Solomon Islands	Solomon Islands	Solomon Islands	Honiara	English	1 Solomon Islands Dollar (SI$) = 100 cents	347 000

Nations of the world: general data (continued)

English name	*Local name*	*Official name (in English)*	*Capital (English name in parentheses)*	*Official language(s)*	*Currency*	*Population*
Somalia	Somaliya	Somali Democratic Republic	Muqdisho (Mogadishu)	Arabic, Somali	1 Somali Shilling (SoSh) = 100 cents	7 555 000
South Africa	South Africa (English) Suid-Afrika (Afrikaans)	Republic of South Africa	Pretoria/Cape Town	Afrikaans, English	1 Rand (R) = 100 cents	40 600 000
Spain	España	Kingdom of Spain	Madrid	Spanish	1 Peseta (Pta, Pa) = 100 céntimos	39 384 000
Sri Lanka	Sri Lanka	Democratic Socialist Republic of Sri Lanka	Colombo/Sri Jaya-wardenapura	Sinhala, Tamil	1 Sri Lanka Rupee (SLR, SLRs) = 100 cents	17 423 000
Sudan	As-Sūdān	Republic of the Sudan	Al-Khar tum (Khartoum)	Arabic	1 Sudanese pound (LSd, £S) = 100 piastres	27 220 000
Suriname	Suriname	Republic of Suriname	Paramaribo	Dutch	1 Suriname Guilder/Florin (SGld, F) = 100 cents	402 000
Swaziland	Swaziland	Kingdom of Swaziland	Mbabane	English, Swati	1 Lilangeni (*pl* Emalangeni) (Li, E) = 100 cents	859 000
Sweden	Sverige	Kingdom of Sweden	Stockholm	Swedish	1 Swedish Krona (Skr) = 100 øre	8 564 000
Switzerland	Schweiz (German) Suisse (French) Svizzera (Italian)	Swiss Confederation	Bern (Berne)	French, German, Italian, Romansch	1 Swiss Franc (SFr, SwF) = 100 centimes	6 783 000
Syria	As-Sūrīyah	Syrian Arab Republic	Dimashq (Damascus)	Arabic	1 Syrian pound (LS, Syr) = 100 piastres	12 965 000
Tadzhikistan	Tajikistan	Republic of Tadzhikistan	Duschanbe	Tajik, Uzbek, Russian	1 Rouble (R) = 100 kopecks	4 969 000
Taiwan	T'aiwan	Republic of China	T'aipei (Taipei)	Mandarin Chinese	1 New Taiwan Dollar (NT$) = 100 cents	20 658 000
Tanzania	Tanzania	United Republic of Tanzania	Dar es Salaam	Swahili, English	1 Tanzanian Shilling (TSh) = 100 cents	26 869 000
Thailand	Muang Thai	Kingdom of Thailand	Krung Thep (Bangkok)	Thai	1 Baht (B) = 100 satang	56 814 000
Togo	Togo	Republic of Togo	Lomé	French	1 CFA Franc (CFAFr) = 100 centimes	3 810 000
Tonga	Tonga	Kingdom of Tonga	Nuku'alofa	English, Tongan	1 Pa'anga/Tongan Dollar (T$) = 100 seniti	102 000
Trinidad and Tobago	Trinidad and Tobago	Republic of Trinidad and Tobago	Port of Spain	English	1 Trinidad and Tobago Dollar (TT$) = 100 cents	1 300 000
Tunisia	Tunis (Arabic) Tunisie (French)	Republic of Tunisia	Tunis	Arabic	1 Tunisian Dinar (TD, D) = 1000 milimes	8 400 000
Turkey	Türkiye	Republic of Turkey	Ankara	Turkish	1 Turkish Lira (TL) = 100 kurus	59 200 000
Turkmenistan	Turkmenostan	Republic of Turkmenistan	Ashkhabad	Turkmen, Russian	1 Rouble (R) = 100 kopecks	3 809 000
Tuvalu	Tuvalu	Tuvalu	Fongafale, on Funafuti	English	1 Australian Dollar = 100 cents	9 317
Uganda	Uganda	Republic of Uganda	Kampala	English, Swahili	1 Uganda Shilling = 100 cents	17 500 000
Ukraine	Ukraine	Republic of Ukraine	Kiev	Ukranian, Russian	1 Rouble (R) = 100 Kopecks	52 100 000
United Arab Emirates	Ittiḥād al-Imārāt al-'Arabīyah	United Arab Emirates	Abū Ẓabi (Abu Dhabi)	Arabic	1 Dirham (DH) = 100 fils	2 500 000

United Kingdom	United Kingdom/ (Great) Britain	United Kingdom of Great Britain and Northern Ireland	London	English	1 Pound Sterling (£) = 100 new pence	57 533 000
United States of America	United States of America (USA)	United States of America	Washington, DC	English	1 US Dollar ($, US$) = 100 cents	252 688 000
Uruguay	Uruguay	Oriental Republic of Uruguay	Montevideo	Spanish	1 Uruguayan New Peso (NUr$, UrugN$) = 100 centésimos	3 100 000
Uzbekistan	Uzbekistan	Republic of Uzbekistan	Toshkent	Uzbek, Russian	1 Rouble (R) = 100 kopecks	21 300 000
Vanuatu	Vanuatu	Republic of Vanuatu	Port Vila	English, French, Bislama	1 Vatu (VT) = 100 centimes	200 000
Venezuela	Venezuela	Republic of Venezuela	Caracas	Spanish	1 Bolívar (B) = 100 céntimos	18 900 000
Vietnam	Viêt-nam	Socialist Republic of Vietnam	Ha-noi (Hanoi)	Vietnamese	1 Dông = 10 hao = 100 xu	69 200 000
Western Samoa	Western Samoa (English) Samoa i Sisifo (Samoan)	Independent State of Western Samoa	Apia	English, Samoan	1 Tala (WS$) = 100 sene	200 000
Yemen	Al-Yaman	Republic of Yemen	Sana/Aden	Arabic	1 Yemeni Riyal (YR, YRI) = 100 fils 1 Yemeni Dinar (YD) = 1000 fils	10 400 000
Yugoslavia *See* Croatia, Bosnia and Herzegovina, Macedonia, Slovenia						
Zaire	Zaïre	Republic of Zaire	Kinshasa	French	1 Zaïre (Z) = 100 makuta (*sing.* likuta)	37 900 000
Zambia	Zambia	Republic of Zambia	Lusaka	English	1 Kwacha (K) = 100 ngwee	8 400 000
Zimbabwe	Zimbabwe	Republic of Zimbabwe	Harare	English	1 Zimbabwe Dollar (Z$) = 100 cents	10 300 000

Tribal peoples and their ways of life

The population figures here must be taken as a very rough guide. An exact enumeration is impossible, because of the difficulty of census-taking in many areas, the problem of defining who is and is not 'tribal', and the fact that available figures have been collected at different dates with different biases.

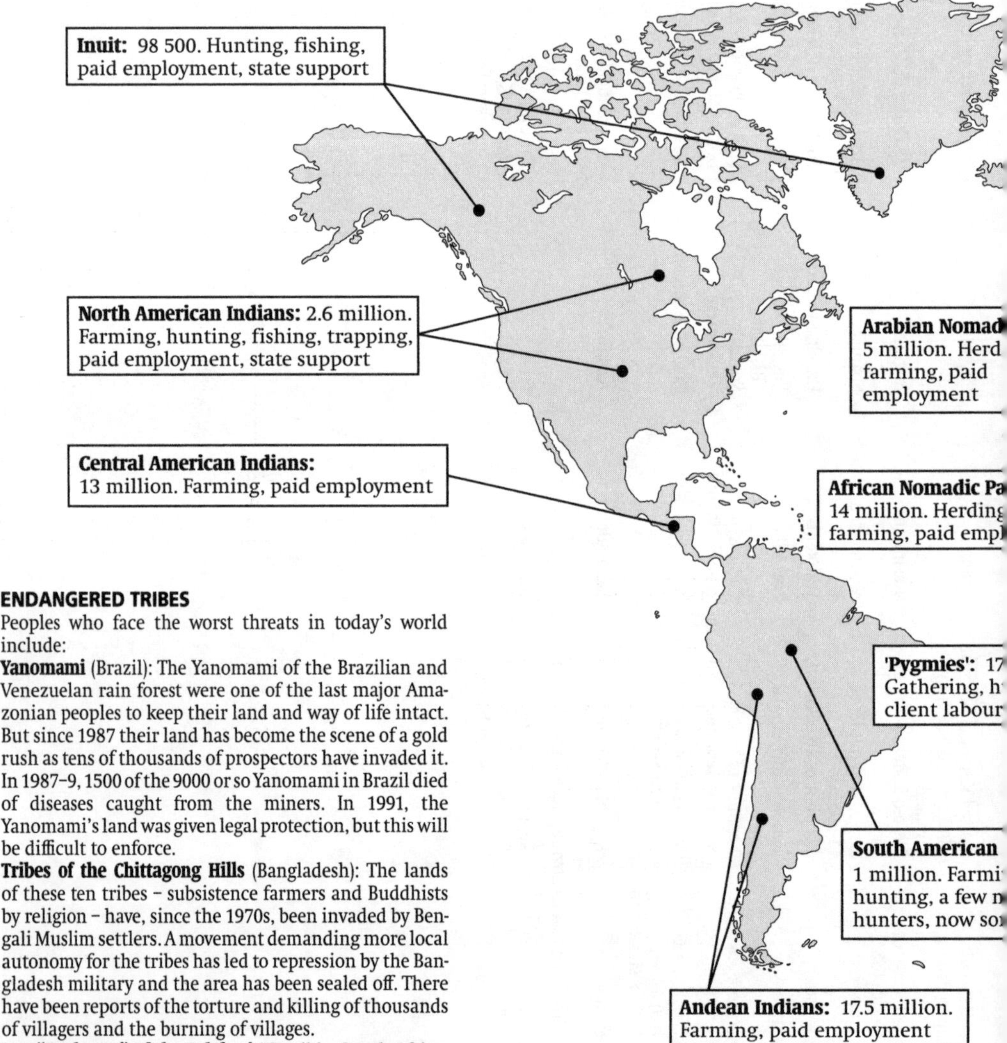

ENDANGERED TRIBES

Peoples who face the worst threats in today's world include:

Yanomami (Brazil): The Yanomami of the Brazilian and Venezuelan rain forest were one of the last major Amazonian peoples to keep their land and way of life intact. But since 1987 their land has become the scene of a gold rush as tens of thousands of prospectors have invaded it. In 1987–9, 1500 of the 9000 or so Yanomami in Brazil died of diseases caught from the miners. In 1991, the Yanomami's land was given legal protection, but this will be difficult to enforce.

Tribes of the Chittagong Hills (Bangladesh): The lands of these ten tribes – subsistence farmers and Buddhists by religion – have, since the 1970s, been invaded by Bengali Muslim settlers. A movement demanding more local autonomy for the tribes has led to repression by the Bangladesh military and the area has been sealed off. There have been reports of the torture and killing of thousands of villagers and the burning of villages.

San ('Bushmen') of the Kalahari (Namibia, South Africa, Botswana, and Angola): The group of peoples known as Bushmen, San, and other names has been hunted and exploited for centuries by both blacks and whites. Farms, ranches, and game parks now occupy most of their former hunting grounds. Today, in spite of romantic images perpetuated by the media, almost none follow the old hunter-gatherer way of life. Most are now farm labourers for little or no pay, or depend on government handouts. Some are attempting to remain independent by taking up subsistence farming and herding.

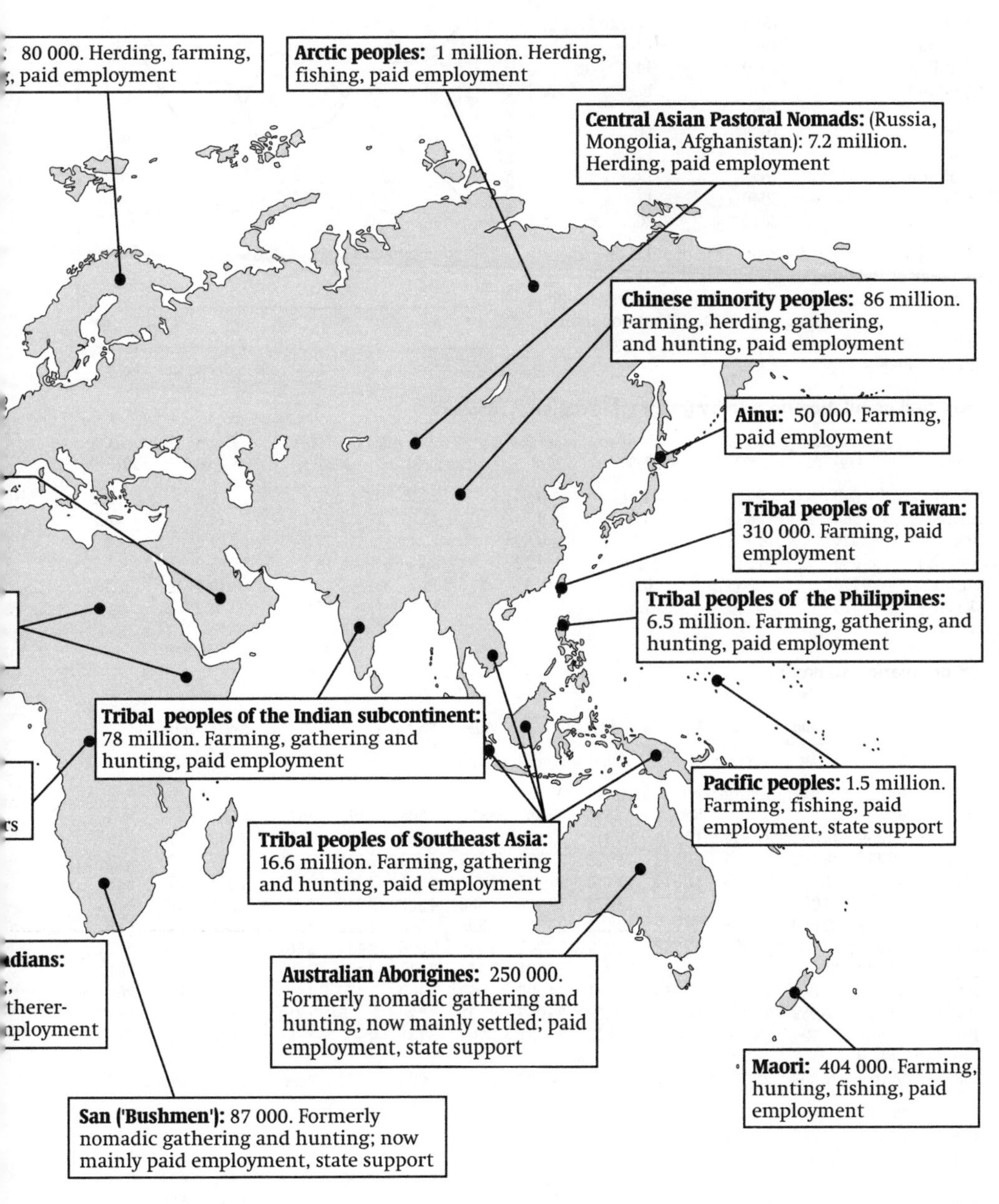

80 000. Herding, farming,
, paid employment
Arctic peoples: 1 million. Herding, fishing, paid employment
Central Asian Pastoral Nomads: (Russia, Mongolia, Afghanistan): 7.2 million. Herding, paid employment
Chinese minority peoples: 86 million. Farming, herding, gathering, and hunting, paid employment
Ainu: 50 000. Farming, paid employment
Tribal peoples of Taiwan: 310 000. Farming, paid employment
Tribal peoples of the Philippines: 6.5 million. Farming, gathering, and hunting, paid employment
Tribal peoples of the Indian subcontinent: 78 million. Farming, gathering and hunting, paid employment
Pacific peoples: 1.5 million. Farming, fishing, paid employment, state support
Tribal peoples of Southeast Asia: 16.6 million. Farming, gathering and hunting, paid employment
Australian Aborigines: 250 000. Formerly nomadic gathering and hunting, now mainly settled; paid employment, state support
Maori: 404 000. Farming, hunting, fishing, paid employment
San ('Bushmen'): 87 000. Formerly nomadic gathering and hunting; now mainly paid employment, state support
dians:
therer-
nployment

Population

Growth of world population by billion and year

World population	*Year*	*Elapsed years*
1 billion	1805	indefinite
2 billion	1926	121
3 billion	1960	34
4 billion	1974	14
5 billion	1987	13
6 billion	1998	11
7 billion	2010	12
8 billion	2023	13
9 billion	2040	17
10 billion	2070	30

The projected slowing down of world population growth to a peak of 10 billion in 2070 is based on the following assumptions: increased use of contraception in developing countries, and an ageing of the global population (with fertile adults making up a smaller percentage of the whole).

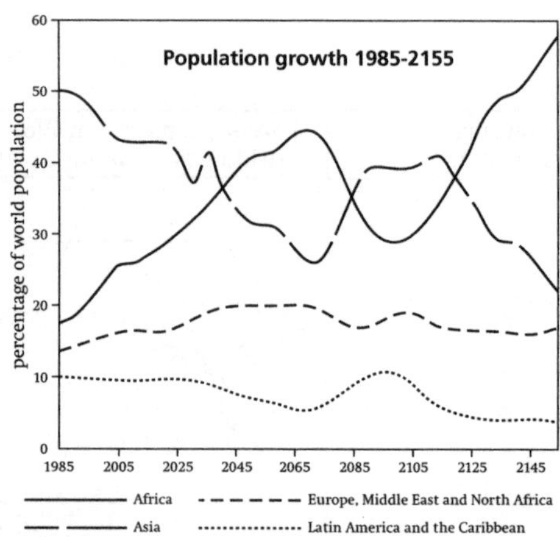

Projected population growth by geographic region, 1985/2025

Region	Population (millions) 1985	Population (millions) 2025	Growth rate (%) 1985–90	Growth rate (%) 2020–5	Birth rate (per 1000) 1985–90	Birth rate (per 1000) 2020–5	Death rate (per 1000) 1985–90	Death rate (per 1000) 2020–5
World	4840	8188	1.71	0.94	26.9	17.6	9.8	8.2
Africa	560	1495	3.05	1.74	45.0	24.1	14.5	6.7
Asia	2819	4758	1.80	0.89	27.4	17.0	9.2	8.1
America	666	1035	1.58	0.72	23.4	15.3	7.9	8.2
Europe	770	863	0.45	0.15	14.7	13.0	10.3	11.5
Oceania	25	36	1.37	0.59	19.6	15.0	8.2	9.1

UK population summary

Thousands

	United Kingdom			*England and Wales*			*Wales*	*Scotland*			*Northern Ireland*		
	Persons	*Males*	*Females*	*Persons*	*Males*	*Females*	*Persons*	*Persons*	*Males*	*Females*	*Persons*	*Males*	*Females*
	Enumerated population: census figures												
1801	–	–	–	8893	4255	4638	587	1608	739	869	–	–	–
1851	22259	10855	11404	17928	8781	9146	1163	2889	1376	1513	1442	698	745
1901	38237	18492	19745	32528	15729	16799	2013	4472	2174	2298	1237	590	647
1911	42082	20357	21725	36070	17446	18625	2421	4761	2309	2452	1251	603	648
1921[a]	44027	21033	22994	37887	18075	19811	2656	4882	2348	2535	1258	610	648
1931[a]	46038	22060	23978	39952	19133	20819	2593	4843	2326	2517	1243	601	642
1951	50225	24118	26107	43758	21016	22742	2599	5096	2434	2662	1371	668	703
1961	52709	25481	27228	46105	22304	23801	2644	5179	2483	2697	1425	694	731
1966[b]	53788	26044	27745	47136	22841	24295	2663	5168	2479	2689	1485	724	761
1971	55515	26952	28562	48750	23683	25067	2731	5229	2515	2714	1536	755	781
1981	55848	27104	28742	49155	23873	25281	2792	5131	2466	2664	1533	750	783
Usually resident													
1981	55089	26803	28286	48522	23625	24897	2750	5035	2428	2607	1532	749	783
	Resident population: mid-year estimates												
1958	51652	24887	26765	45109	21744	23365	2615	5141	2460	2682	1402	684	719
1959	51956	25043	26913	45386	21885	23501	2623	5163	2472	2690	1408	686	722
1960	52372	25271	27102	45775	22097	23678	2629	5178	2482	2696	1420	692	728
1961	52807	25528	27279	46196	22347	23849	2635	5184	2485	2698	1427	696	732
1962	53292	25826	27465	46657	22631	24026	2652	5198	2495	2703	1437	700	737
1963	53625	25992	27633	46973	22787	24186	2664	5205	2500	2705	1447	705	741
1964	53991	26191	27800	47324	22978	24346	2677	5208	2501	2707	1458	711	747
1965	54350	26368	27982	47671	23151	24521	2693	5210	2501	2709	1468	716	752
1966	54643	26511	28132	47966	23296	24671	2702	5201	2496	2704	1476	719	757
1967	54959	26673	28286	48272	23451	24821	2710	5198	2496	2702	1489	726	763
1968	55214	26784	28429	48511	23554	24957	2715	5200	2498	2702	1503	733	770

Thousands

	United Kingdom			*England and Wales*			*Wales*	*Scotland*			*Northern Ireland*		
	Persons	*Males*	*Females*	*Persons*	*Males*	*Females*	*Persons*	*Persons*	*Males*	*Females*	*Persons*	*Males*	*Females*
1969	55461	26908	28553	48738	23666	25072	2722	5208	2503	2706	1514	739	776
1970	55632	26992	28641	48891	23738	25153	2729	5214	2507	2707	1527	747	781
1971	55928	27167	28761	49152	23897	25255	2740	5236	2516	2720	1540	755	786
1972	56097	27259	28837	49327	23989	25339	2755	5231	2513	2717	1539	758	782
1973	56223	27332	28891	49459	24061	25399	2773	5234	2515	2719	1530	756	774
1974	56236	27349	28887	49468	24075	25393	2785	5241	2519	2722	1527	755	772
1975	56226	27361	28865	49470	24091	25378	2795	5232	2516	2716	1524	753	770
1976	56,216	27360	28856	49459	24089	25370	2799	5233	2517	2716	1524	754	770
1977	56190	27345	28845	49440	24076	25364	2801	5226	2515	2711	1523	754	769
1978	56178	27330	28849	49443	24067	25375	2804	5212	2509	2704	1523	754	770
1979	56240	27373	28867	49508	24113	25395	2810	5204	2505	2699	1530	755	773
1980	56330	27411	28919	49603	24156	25448	2816	5194	2501	2693	1533	755	778
1981	56352	27049	28943	49634	24160	25474	2814	5180	2495	2685	1538	754	784
1982	56306	27386	28920	49601	24143	25459	2807	5167	2490	2677	1538	754	784
1983	56347	27417	28931	49654	24176	25478	2808	5150	2485	2665	1543	756	788
1984	56460	27487	28973	49764	24244	25519	2807	5146	2484	2662	1551	760	791
1985	56618	27574	29044	49924	24330	25594	2812	5137	2481	2656	1558	763	795
1986	56763	27647	29116	50075	24403	25672	2821	5121	2475	2646	1567	768	798
1987	56930	27737	29193	50243	24493	25750	2836	5112	2471	2641	1575	773	802
1988	57065	27813	29253	50393	24576	25817	2857	5094	2462	2632	1578	774	804
1989	57236	27907	29330	50562	24669	25893	2873	5091	2460	2630	1583	777	806
1990	57411	28013	29398	50719	24766	25953	2881	5102	2467	2636	1589	780	809

[a] Figures for Northern Ireland are estimated. The population at the census of 1926 was 1257000 (608000 males and 649000 females). [b] Except for Northern Ireland, where a full census was taken, figures are based on the 10 per cent samples census.

Marriage and divorce rates: EC comparison, 1981 and 1989

	Marriages per 1000 eligible population		*Divorces per 1000 existing marriages*	
	1981	1989	1981	1989
United Kingdom	7.1	6.8	11.9	12.6
Belgium	6.5	6.4	6.1	8.6
Denmark	5.0	6.0	12.1	13.6
France	5.8	5.0	6.8	8.4
Germany (Former West)	5.8	6.4	7.2	8.7
Greece	7.3	6.1	2.5	-
Irish Republic	6.0	5.0	0.0	0.0
Italy	5.6	5.4	0.9	2.1
Luxembourg	5.5	5.8	5.9	10.0
Netherlands	6.0	6.1	8.3	8.1
Portugal	7.7	7.1	2.8	-
Spain	5.4	5.6	1.1	-

SOCIAL INSTITUTIONS

Aristocratic ranks

England	*France*	*Holy Roman Empire (Germany)*	*Italy*	*Spain*
king	roi	Kaiser	re	rey
prince	duc	Herzog	duca	duque
duke	prince	Pfalzgraf	principe	principe
marquess	marquis	Markgraf	marchese	marques
earl	comte	Landgraf	conde	conde
viscount	vicomte		visconte	vizconde
baronet				

Honours

Country	Name of honour	Date instituted	History
Denmark	Order of the Dannebrog	1219	One of the most ancient orders in existence and awarded for general merit.
France	Croix de Guerre	1915	Military decoration created in 1915 and 1939 to reward bravery in the two world wars.
	Légion d'Honneur	1802	First order of the French Republic created by Napoleon I as a reward for distinguished civil and military service. Open to all citizens regardless of birth or religion.
Germany	Iron Cross	1813	Instituted first by Prussia and then reinstated by Hitler in 1939. Military decoration awarded for bravery in war time.
	Pour le Mérite	1740	Established by Frederick II the Great. There was a class for military achievement and one for scientific and artistic achievement.
Japan	Chrysanthemum, Order of the	1877	Japan's highest order. Instituted by Emperor Meiji and awarded mainly to members of the Japanese Royal Family, foreign royals, and heads of state. Award exclusive to males.
	Paulownia Sun, Order of the	1888	Founded by Emperor Meiji to reward outstanding military and civil merit. Only awarded to men.
	Rising Sun, Order of the	1875	This was originally the Order of Merit awarded for exceptional civil or military merit.
Netherlands	Order of the House of Orange	1905	The equivalent of the Royal Victorian Order and rewards services to the Royal House.
	Military Order of William	1815	The highest military decoration to military of all ranks and civilians for courageous acts and devotion to duty. Founded by William I.
	Netherlands Lion	1815	An award for patriotism and outstanding devotion to duty, also for scientific and artistic achievements.
United Kingdom	Bath, The Most Honourable Order of the	1725	Order of chivalry formally created by George I in 1725, but traditionally instituted by Henry IV in 1399. The motto of the order is *Tria juncta in uno* (Three joined in one).
	British Empire, The Most Noble Order of the Knight/Dame of the Grand Cross (GBE) Knight/Dame Commander (K/DBE) Commander (CBE) Officer (OBE) Member (MBE)	1917	Founded by George V and the first order of knighthood to be presented to members of both sexes. Appointments made on the recommendations of Government ministers. There are five orders.
	Companions of Honour, Order of the (CH)	1917	Founded by George V to reward men and women for national services. Motto *In action faithful and in honour clear.*
	Distinguished Service Order (DSO)	1886	Military service order in recognition of special services by army and navy officers.
	Garter, The Most Noble Order of the	c. 1344–51	The most ancient order of chivalry, founded by Edward III. Motto *Honi soit qui mal y pense* (Shamed be he who thinks badly of it).
	George Cross (GC)	1940	Named after George VI and awarded 'For Gallantry' (acts of great heroism).
	Merit, Order of (OM)	1902	Founded by Edward VII for eminent service in the military or for distinguished performances in science, the arts and the promotion of culture.
	Royal Victorian Order (RVO) Knight/Dame Grand Cross (GCVO) Knights/Dame Commander (K/DCVO) Commander (CVO) Lieutenant (LVO) Member (MVO)	1896	Knighthood instituted by Queen Victoria to reward distinguished service to the sovereign. There are five orders.
	Thistle, The Most Ancient and Noble Order of the	c. 1460–88	Scottish order of chivalry, probably instituted by James III. Motto *Nemo me impune lacessit* (No-one provokes me with impunity).

Country	Name of honour	Date instituted	History
	Victoria Cross (VC)	1856	Instituted by Queen Victoria. The highest military award in honour of great bravery.
United States	Congressional Medal of Honor	1862	Established by the US Congress and awarded in its name. The country's highest military decoration. Awarded to members of the armed services who, during a military action, risk their lives in acts of bravery beyond the call of duty.
	Legion of Merit, The	1942	Awarded to native American officers and foreigners for exceptional service in peace and war.
	Medal for Merit	1942	Awarded to civilians who have performed an outstanding service in peace or wartime.
	Presidential Medal of Freedom	1963	The highest decoration awarded to civilians in peacetime. The medal is presented in recognition of outstanding achievement in any of a variety of fields, including the arts.
	Purple Heart, The	1782	Originally an award for gallantry. Revived in 1932 and awarded in recognition of wounds received in action.

Forms of address

In the formulae given below, *F* stands for forename and *S* for surname.

Very formal ceremonial styles for closing letters are now seldom used:

'Yours faithfully' is assumed below, unless otherwise indicated.

Forms of spoken address are given only where a special style is followed.

Holders of courtesy titles are addressed according to their rank, but without 'The', 'The Right Hon.' or 'The Most Hon.'

Ranks in the armed forces, and ecclesiastical and ambassadorial ranks, precede titles in the peerage, eg 'Colonel the Earl of –' or 'The Rev the Marquess of –'.

Although the correct forms of address are given below for members of the British Royal Family, it is more normal practice for letters to be addressed to their private secretary, equerry, or lady-in-waiting.

More detailed information about forms of address is to be found in Debrett's *Correct Form* and Black's *Titles and Forms of Address.*

Ambassadors (foreign)
Address on envelope: 'His/Her Excellency the Ambassador of –' or 'His/Her Excellency the – Ambassador'. (The wife of an ambassador is not entitled to style 'Her Excellency'.) *Begin*: 'Your Excellency'. (Within the letter, refer to 'Your Excellency' once, thereafter as 'you'.) *Close*: 'I have the honour to be, Sir/Madam (or according to rank), Your Excellency's obedient servant'. *Spoken address*: 'Your Excellency' at least once, and then 'Sir' or 'Madam' by name.

Archbishop (Anglican communion)
Address on envelope: 'The Most Reverend Lord Archbishop of –'. (The Archbishops of Canterbury and York are Privy Counsellers, and should be addressed as 'The Most Reverend and Right Hon, the Lord Archbishop of –'.) *Begin*: 'Dear Archbishop' or 'My Lord Archbishop'. *Spoken address*: 'Your Grace'. *Begin an official speech*: 'My Lord Archbishop.'

Archbishop (any, US form)
Address on envelope: 'The Most Reverend [F– S–], Archbishop of–'. *Begin*: 'Your Excellency'.

Archbishop (Roman Catholic)
Address on envelope: 'His Grace the Archbishop of –'. *Begin*: 'My Lord Archbishop'. *Close*: 'I remain, Your Grace, Yours faithfully' or 'Yours faithfully'. *Spoken address*: 'Your Grace'.

Archdeacon
Address on envelope: 'The Venerable the Archdeacon of –'. *Begin*: 'Dear Archdeacon' or 'Venerable Sir'. *Spoken address*: 'Archdeacon'. *Begin an official speech*: 'Venerable Sir'.

Baron
Address on envelope: 'The Right Hon. the Lord–'. *Begin*: 'My Lord'. *Spoken address*: 'My Lord'.

Baron's wife (Baroness)
Address on envelope: 'The Right Hon. the Lady [S–]'. *Begin*: 'Dear Madam'. *Spoken address*: 'Madam'.

Baroness (in her own right)
Address on envelope: either as for Baron's wife, or 'The Right Hon. the Baroness [S–]'. Otherwise, as for Baron's wife.

Baronet
Address on envelope: 'Sir [F– S–], Bt'. *Begin*: 'Dear Sir'. *Spoken address*: 'Sir [F–]'.

Baronet's wife
Address on envelope: 'Lady [S–]'. If she has the title 'Lady' by courtesy, 'Lady [F– S–]'. If she has the courtesy style 'The Hon.', this precedes 'Lady'. *Begin*: 'Dear Madam'. *Spoken address*: 'Madam'.

Bishop (Anglican communion)
Address on envelope: 'The Right Reverend the Lord Bishop of –'. (The Bishop of London is a Privy Counseller, so is addressed as 'The Right Rev. and Right Hon. the Lord Bishop of London'. The Bishop of Meath is styled 'The Most Reverend'.) *Begin*: 'Dear Bishop' or 'My Lord'. *Spoken address*: 'Bishop'. *Begin an official speech*: 'My Lord'.

Bishop (Episcopal Church in Scotland)
Address on envelope: 'The Right Reverend [F– S–], Bishop of –'. Otherwise as for a bishop of the Anglican communion. The bishop who holds the position of Primus is addressed as 'The Most Reverend the Primus'. *Begin*: 'Dear Primus'. *Spoken address*: 'Primus'.

Forms of address (continued)

Bishop (Episcopal, US form)
Address on envelope: 'The Right Reverend [F– S–], Bishop of –. *Begin*: 'Right Reverend Sir'.

Bishop (Roman Catholic)
Address on envelope: 'His Lordship the Bishop of –' or 'The Right Reverend [F– S–] Bishop of –'. In Ireland, 'The Most Reverend' is used instead of 'The Right Reverend'. If an auxiliary bishop, address as 'The Right Reverend [F– S–], Auxiliary Bishop of –'. *Begin*: 'My Lord' or (more rarely) 'My Lord Bishop'. *Close*: 'I remain, my Lord' or (more rarely), 'my Lord Bishop', Yours faithfully', or simply 'Yours faithfully'. *Spoken address*: 'My Lord' or (more rarely) 'My Lord Bishop'.

Bishop (Roman Catholic, US form)
Address on envelope: 'The Most Reverend [F– S–], Bishop pf –'. *Begin*: 'Most Reverend Sir' or 'Your Excellency'.

Bishop (Other churches, US form)
Address on envelope: 'The Reverend [F– S–]'. *Begin*: 'Reverend Sir'.

Cabinet Minister *see* **Secretary of State**

Canon (Anglican communion)
Address on envelope: 'The Reverend Canon [F– S–]'. *Begin*: 'Dear Canon' or 'Dear Canon [S–]'. *Spoken address*: 'Canon' or 'Canon [S–]'.

Canon (Roman Catholic)
Address on envelope: 'The Very Reverend Canon [F– S–]'. *Begin*: 'Very Reverend Sir'. *Spoken address*: 'Canon [S–]'.

Cardinal
Address on envelope: 'His Eminence Cardinal [S–]'. If an archbishop, 'His Eminence the Cardinal Archbishop of –'. *Begin*: 'Your Eminence' or (more rarely) 'My Lord Cardinal'. *Close*: 'I remain, Your Eminence (or 'My Lord Cardinal'), Yours faithfully'. *Spoken address*: 'Your Eminence'.

Cardinal (US form)
Address on envelope: 'His Eminence [F–] Cardinal [S–]'. *Begin*: 'Your Eminence'.

Clergy (Anglican communion)
Address on envelope: 'The Reverend [F– S–]'. *Begin*: 'Dear Sir' or 'Dear Mr [S–]'.

Clergy (Roman Catholic)
Address on envelope: 'The Reverend [F– S–]'. If a member of a religious order, the initials of the order should be added after the name. *Begin*: 'Dear Reverend Father'.

Clergy (Other churches)
Address on envelope: 'The Reverend [F– S–]'. *Begin*: 'Dear Sir/Madam' or 'Dear Mr/Mrs etc. [S–]'.

Countess
Address on envelope: 'The Right Hon. the Countess of –'. *Begin*: 'Dear Madam'. *Spoken address*: 'Madam'.

Dean (Anglican)
Address on envelope: 'The Very Reverend the Dean of –'. *Begin*: 'Dear Dean' or 'Very Reverend Sir'. *Spoken address*: 'Dean'. *Begin an official speech*: 'Very Reverend sir'.

Doctor
Physicians, anaesthetists, pathologists and radiologists are addressed as 'Doctor'. In the UK, surgeons, whether they hold the degree of Doctor of Medicine or not, are known as 'Mr/Mrs'. In England and Wales, obstetricians and gynaecologists are addressed as 'Mr/Mrs', but in Scotland, Ireland, and elsewhere as 'Doctor'. In addressing a letter to the holder of a doctorate, the initials DD, MD, etc. are placed after the ordinary form of address, eg 'The Rev John Smith, DD', the 'Rev Dr Smith' and 'Dr John Brown' are also used.

Dowager
Address on envelope: On the marriage of a peer or baronet, the widow of the previous holder of the title becomes 'Dowager' and is addressed 'The Right Hon. the Dowager Countess of –', 'The Right Hon. the Dowager Lady –', etc. If there is already a Dowager still living, she retains this title, the later widow being addressed 'The Most Hon. [F–]. Marchioness of –', 'The Right Hon. [F–], Lady –', etc. However, many Dowagers prefer the style which includes their Christian names to that including the title Dowager. *Begin*, as for a peer's wife.

Duchess
Address on envelope: 'Her Grace the Duchess of –'. *Begin*: 'Dear Madam'. *Spoken address*: 'Your Grace'. (For Royal Duchess, *see* Princess.)

Duke
Address on envelope: 'His Grace the Duke of –'. *Begin*: 'My Lord Duke'. *Spoken address*: 'Your Grace'. (For Royal Duke, *see* Prince.)

Earl
Address on envelope: 'The Right Hon. the Earl of –'. *Begin*: 'My Lord'. *Spoken address*: 'My Lord'. (For Earl's wife, *see* Countess.)

Governor of a colony or **Governor-General**
Address on envelope: 'His Excellency (ordinary designation), Governor(-General) of –'. (The Governor-General of Canada has the rank of 'Right Honourable', which he retains for life.) The wife of a Governor-General is styled 'Her Excellency' within the country her husband administers. *Begin*: according to rank. *Close*: 'I have the honour to be, Sir (or 'My Lord', if a peer), Your Excellency's obedient servant'. *Spoken address*: 'Your Excellency'.

Governor (US, state)
Address on envelope: 'The Honorable [F– S–], Governor of –'. *Begin*: 'Sir/Madam'. *Spoken address*: 'Governor [S–]'.

Judge, High Court
Address on envelope: if a man, 'The Hon. Mr Justice [S–]; if a woman, 'The Hon. Mrs Justice [S–]. *Begin*: 'Dear Sir/Madam'; if on judicial matters, 'My Lord/Lady'. *Spoken address*: 'Sir/Madam'; only on the bench or when dealing with judicial matters should a High Court Judge be addressed as 'My Lord/Lady' or referred to as 'Your Lordship/Ladyship'.

Judge, Circuit
Address on envelope: 'His/Her Honour Judge [S–]'. If a Knight, 'His Honour Judge Sir [F– S–]'. *Begin*: 'Dear Sir/Madam'. *Spoken address*: 'Sir/Madam'; address as 'Your Honour' only when on the bench or dealing with judicial matters.

Judge (US, federal)
Address on envelope: 'The Honorable [F– S–], Judge of the United States District Court of the – District of –'. *Begin*: 'Sir/Madam'. *Spoken address*: 'Judge [S–]'.

Justice of the Peace (England and Wales)
When on the bench, refer to and address as 'Your Wor-

ship'; otherwise according to rank. The letters 'JP' may be added after the person's name in addressing a letter, if desired.

Knight Bachelor
As Baronet, except that 'Bt' is omitted. Knight of the Bath, of St Michael and St George, etc. *Address on envelope*: 'Sir [F– S–], with the initials 'GCB', 'KCB', etc. added. *Begin*: 'Dear Sir'.

Knight's wife
As Baronet's wife, or according to rank.

Lady Mayoress
Address on envelope: 'The Lady Mayoress of –'. *Begin*: 'My Lady Mayoress'. *Spoken address*: '(My) 'Lady Mayoress'.

Lord Mayor
Address on envelope: The Lord Mayors of London, York, Belfast, Cardiff, Dublin and also Melbourne, Sydney, Adelaide, Perth, Brisbane, and Hobart are styled 'The Right Hon. the Lord Mayor of –'. Other Lord Mayors are styled 'The Right Worshipful the Lord Mayor of –'. *Begin*: 'My Lord Mayor', even if the holder of the office is a woman. *Spoken address*: '(My) Lord Mayor'.

Marchioness
Address on envelope: 'The Most Hon. the Marchioness of –'. *Begin*: 'Dear Madam'. *Spoken address*: 'Madam'.

Marquess
Address on envelope: 'The Most Hon. the Marquess of –'. *Begin*: 'My Lord'. *Spoken address*: 'My Lord'.

Mayor
Address on envelope: 'The Worshipful the Mayor of –'; in the case of cities and certain towns, 'The Right Worshipful'. *Begin*: 'Mr Mayor'. *Spoken address*: 'Mr Mayor'.

Mayoress
Address on envelope: 'The Mayoress of –'. *Begin*: 'Madam Mayoress' is traditional, but some now prefer 'Madam Mayor'. *Spoken address*: 'Mayoress' (or 'Madam Mayor').

Member of Parliament
Address on envelope: Add 'MP' to the usual form of address. *Begin*: according to rank.

Monsignor
Address on envelope: 'The Reverend Monsignor [F– S–]'. If a canon, 'The Very Reverend Monsignor (Canon) [F– S–]'. *Begin*: 'Reverend Sir'. *Spoken address*: 'Monsignor [S–]'.

Officers in the Armed Forces
Address on envelope: The professional rank is prefixed to any other rank, eg 'Admiral the Right Hon. the Earl of –', 'Lieut.-Col. Sir [F– S–], KCB'. Officers below the rank of Rear-Admiral, and Marshal of the Royal Air Force, are entitled to 'RN' (or 'Royal Navy') and 'RAF' respectively after their name. Army officers of the rank of Colonel or below may follow their name with the name of their regiment or corps (which may be abbreviated). Officers in the women's services add 'WRNS', 'WRAF', 'WRAC'. *Begin*: according to social rank.

Officers (retired and former)
Address on envelope: Officers above the rank of Lieutenant (in the Royal Navy), Captain (in the Army) and Flight Lieutenant may continue to use and be addressed by their armed forces rank after being placed on the retired list. The word 'retired' (or in an abbreviated form) should not normally be placed after the person's name. Former officers in the women's services do not normally continue to use their ranks.

Pope
Address on envelope: 'His Holiness, the Pope'. *Begin*: 'Your Holiness' or 'Most Holy Father'. *Close*: if a Roman Catholic, 'I have the honour to be your Holiness's most devoted and obedient child' (or 'most humble child'); if not Roman Catholic, 'I have the honour to be (or 'remain') Your Holiness's obedient servant'. *Spoken address*: 'Your Holiness'.

Prime Minister, UK
Address on envelope: according to rank. The Prime Minister is a Privy Counsellor (see separate entry) and the letter should be addressed accordingly. *Begin*, etc. according to rank.

Prince
Address on envelope: If a Duke, 'His Royal Highness the Duke of –'; if not a Duke, 'His Royal Highness the Prince [F–]', if a child of the sovereign; otherwise 'His Royal Highness Prince [F–] of [Kent or Gloucester]'. *Begin*: 'Sir'. Refer to as 'Your Royal Highness'. *Close*: 'I have the honour to remain (or be) Sir, Your Royal Highness's most humble and obedient servant'. *Spoken address*: 'Your Royal Highness' once, thereafter 'Sir'.

Princess
Address on envelope: If a Duchess, 'Her Royal Highness the Duchess of –'; if not a Duchess, the daughter of a sovereign is addressed as 'Her Royal Highness the Princess [F–]', followed by any title she holds by marriage. 'The' is omitted in addressing a princess who is not the daughter of a sovereign. A Princess by marriage is addressed 'HRH Princess [husband's F–] of –'. *Begin*: 'Madam'. Refer to as 'Your Royal Highness'. *Close*: as for Prince, substituting 'Madam' for 'Sir'. *Spoken address*: 'Your Royal Highness' once, thereafter 'Ma'am'.

Privy Counsellor
Address on envelope: If a peer, 'The Right Hon. the Earl of –, PC'; if not a peer, 'The Right Hon. [F– S–]', without the 'PC'. *Begin*: etc. according to rank.

Professor
Address on envelope: 'Professor [F– S–]'; the styles 'Professor Lord [S–]' and 'Professor Sir [F– S–]' are often used, but are deprecated by some people. If the professor is in holy orders, 'The Reverend Professor'. *Begin*: 'Dear Sir/Madam', or according to rank. *Spoken address*: according to rank.

Queen
Address on envelope: 'Her Majesty the Queen'. *Begin*: 'Madam, with my humble duty'. Refer to as 'Your Majesty'. *Close*: 'I have the honour to remain (or 'be'). Madam, Your Majesty's most humble and obedient servant'. *Spoken address*: 'Your Majesty' once, thereafter 'Ma'am'. *Begin an official speech*: 'May it please Your Majesty'.

Rabbi
Address on envelope: 'Rabbi [initial and S–]' or, if a doctor, 'Rabbi Doctor [initial and S–]'. *Begin*: 'Dear Sir'. *Spoken address*: 'Rabbi [S–]' or '[Doctor S–]'.

Secretary of State
Address on envelope: 'The Right Hon. [F– S–], MP. Secretary of State for –', or 'The Secretary of State for –'. Otherwise according to rank.

Viscount
Address on envelope: 'The Right Hon. the Viscount –'. *Begin*: 'My Lord'. *Spoken address*: 'My Lord'.

Viscountess
Address on envelope: 'The Right Hon. the Viscountess –'. *Begin*: 'Dear Madam'. *Spoken address*: 'Madam'.

Heraldry

Heraldry is the granting and devising of pictorial devices (arms) used originally on the shields of knights in armour to distinguish different sides in battle. In the early twelfth century these devices became hereditary in Europe through the male line of descent.

A glossary of terms

armorial bearings	hereditary symbols used to distinguish individuals, institutions and corporations
billet	oblong figure
billette	field with ten or more billets irregularly arranged
blazonry	the science of describing pictorial signs used in heraldry
charges	heraldic signs or symbols
chevron	inverted v-shaped stripe
chief	top third of the shield
compartment	ground or foundation on which supporters stand
crest	object placed on top of helmet and bound to it by the wreath of colours (which shows the two main colours used in the shield)
dexter side	right-hand side
escutcheon	the shield on which a coat of arms is represented
field	basic colour (tincture) or background of the shield
helmet	placed on top of the shield
inescutcheon	small figure shaped like shield in the middle of the shield
lozenge	parallelogram
lozengy	field divided transversely by diagonal lines
mascle	lozenge voided
mantling or lambrequin	this is hung from the helmet and is designed to act as a shield for the wearer. It is painted with the principle colour of the shield
ordinaries	basic charges
orle	inner border not touching the edge of the shield
pile	inverted pyramid
roundel	circular symbol
shield	coat of arms
sinister side	left-hand side
supporters	animals or human figures on either side of the shield
tressure	smaller version of orle

metals

argent	silver
or	gold

Furs

ermine	white field with black spots
ermines	black field with white spots
erminois	gold field with black spots
pean	black field with gold spots
vair	blue and white

Colours

azure	blue
gules	red
murrey	tint between gules and purpure
purpure	purple
sable	black
tenne	orange-tawny
vert	green

Partition lines

impalement or dimidation – shield divided by straight line (top to bottom) into two parts
party per pale – division of field into two equal parts by perpendicular line
party per fess – field divided by horizontal line into two equal parts
party per bend
party per chevron
party per saltire
gyronny of eight

Pale Bend Fess Chief

Chevron Saltire Gyronny of eight

Heraldic descriptions of animals and their posture

addorsed	creatures placed back to back
combattant	two animals fighting on hindlegs
couchant	lying down
displayed	birds with wings extended
dormant	sleeping
at gaze	looking full face
passant	walking
rampant	on hind legs
rampant guardant	on hind legs but full-faced
reguardant	looking back
statant	standing
trippant	at a trot (one foot raised)

Law and crime

Courts

England and Wales

CRIMINAL

House of Lords	judges (5) known as Law Lords or Lords of Appeal in Ordinary head is the Lord Chancellor (the only judge who is also a member of the government)
Court of Appeal	established 1966 to replace Court of Criminal appeal head is known as the Lord Chief Justice
Crown Court	established 1971 to replace Court of Quarter Sessions 92 places in England and Wales where crown court sessions held organised in six circuits – Midlands and Oxford, N Eastern, Northern, S Eastern, Wales and Chester, Western
Magistrates Court	tries around 97% of all criminal cases c. 24 500 lay magistrates

CIVIL

House of Lords	see above
Court of Appeal	judges (3) known as Lord Justices of Appeal head of Civil Division known as Master of the Rolls
High Court	established by the Judicature Acts 173–75 Chancery (11 judges) – deals with trusts and probate matters Queen's Bench (54 judges) – deals with the Judicial Review Family (16 judges) – deals with divorce and ward proceedings
County Court	established 1846 deals with cases of contract and tort where amount does not exceed £5000, landlord and tenant disputes, and matrimonial cases (including divorce)

SPECIALISED CIVIL COURTS

Small Claims Court – deals with low-value debt enforcement
Bankruptcy Court – deals with bankruptcy, but only in London
Restrictive Practices Court – deals with commercial disputes

Scotland

CRIMINAL

High Court of Justiciary in Edinburgh
High Court of Justice
Sheriff Court
District Court

CIVIL

House of Lords
Court of Session (Inner House)
Court of Session (Outer House)
Sheriff Principal Court
Sheriff Court

Northern Ireland

CRIMINAL

House of Lords
N Ireland Court of Appeal
Crown Court

CIVIL

House of Lords
N Ireland Court of Appeal
High Court of Justice
County Court
Magistrates Court

The judiciary and legal representatives: numbers

	1972	1981	1990
England & Wales			
The Judiciary			
Judges[a,b]			
Lord Justice	14	18	27
High Court Judges	70	74	83
Circuit Judges	233	334	427
Recorders	325	446	752
Assistant Recorders			421
District Judges[b]	134	150	223
Magistrates[c]	20 539	25 435	27 011[i]
Legal representatives			
Barristers[d]	2 919	4 685	6 645
Solicitors[e]	26 327	39 795	55 685
Scotland [b]			
The Judiciary			
Judges	19	21	24
Sheriffs[f]		78	101
Stipendiary Magistrates	3	3	4
Justices of the Peace[g]			904
Legal representatives[8]			
Advocates	48	134	276
Solicitors	3 374	5 065	7 087
Northern Ireland[h]			
The Judiciary			
Judges			
High Court Judges		8	10
County Court	5	10	13
Circuit Registrars	0	4	4
Resident Magistrates	17	15	17
Legal representatives			
Barristers	88	203	308
Solicitors		888	1 295

[a] Excludes deputy judges and, for 1972 and 1981, assistant recorders. [b] Figures relate to 31 December each year. [c] Figures relate to 1 January each year. [d] Figures relate to 1 October each year. [e] Number who applied for a practising certificate in year ending 31 October. [f] Numbers not available before local government reorganization in 1975. [g] On rota for court duty, 31 March 1990. [8] Practising. [h] Figures are at 1971, 1981 and 1990. [i] Figures are for 1989.
Source: CSO

Members of the Supreme Court of the United States[a]

Name: apptd. from	*Term of service*	*Date of birth*	*Date of death*
Chief justices			
John Jay, NY	1789–95	1745	1829
John Rutledge, SC	1795	1739	1800
Oliver Ellsworth, CT	1796–1800	1745	1807
John Marshall, VA	1801–35	1755	1835
Roger B. Taney, MD	1836–64	1777	1864
Salmon P. Chase, OH	1864–73	1808	1873
Morrison R. Waite, OH	1874–88	1816	1888
Melville W. Fuller, IL	1888–1910	1833	1910
Edward D. White, LA	1910–21	1845	1921
William H. Taft, CT	1921–30	1857	1930
Charles E. Hughes, NY	1930–41	1862	1948
Harlan F. Stone, NY	1941–46	1872	1946
Frederick M. Vinson, KY	1946–53	1890	1953
Earl Warren, CA	1953–69	1891	1974
Warren E. Burger, VA	1969–86	1907	–
William H. Rehnquist, AZ	1986–	1924	–
Associate justices			
James Wilson, PA	1789–98	1742	1798
John Rutledge, SC	1789–91	1739	1800
William Cushing, MA	1789–1810	1732	1810
John Blair, VA	1789–96	1732	1800
James Iredell, NC	1790–99	1751	1799
Thomas Johnson, MD	1791–93	1732	1819
William Paterson, NJ	1793–1806	1745	1806
Samuel Chase, MD	1796–1811	1741	1811
Bushrod Washington, VA	1798–1829	1762	1829
Alfred Moore, NC	1799–1804	1755	1810
William Johnson, SC	1804–34	1771	1834
Henry B Livingston, NY	1806–23	1757	1823
Thomas Todd, KY	1807–26	1765	1826
Gabriel Duval, MD	1811–35	1752	1844
Joseph Story, MA	1811–45	1779	1845
Smith Thompson, NY	1823–43	1768	1843
Robert Trimble, KY	1826–28	1777	1828
John McLean, OH	1830–61	1785	1861
Henry Baldwin, PA	1830–44	1780	1844
James M. Wayne, GA	1835–67	1790	1867
Philip P. Barbour, VA	1836–41	1783	1841
John Catron, TN	1837–65	1786	1865
John McKinley, AL	1837–52	1780	1852
Peter V. Daniel, VA	1841–60	1784	1860
Samuel Nelson, NY	1845–72	1792	1873
Levi Woodbury, NH	1845–51	1789	1851
Robert C. Grier, PA	1846–70	1794	1870
Benjamin R. Curtis, MA	1851–57	1809	1874
John A. Campbell, AL	1853–61	1811	1889
Nathan Clifford, ME	1858–81	1803	1881
Noah H. Swayne, OH	1862–81	1804	1884
Samuel F. Miller, IA	1862–90	1816	1890
David Davis, IL	1862–77	1815	1886
Stephen J. Field, CA	1863–97	1816	1899
William Strong, PA	1870–80	1808	1895
Joseph P. Bradley, NJ	1870–92	1813	1892
Ward Hunt, NY	1873–82	1810	1886
John M. Harlan, KY	1877–1911	1833	1911
William B. Woods, GA	1880–87	1824	1887
Stanley Matthews, OH	1881–89	1824	1889
Horace Gray, MA	1882–1902	1828	1902
Samuel Blatchford, NY	1882–93	1820	1893
Lucius Q. C. Lamar, MS	1888–93	1825	1893
David J. Brewer, KS	1889–1910	1837	1910
Henry B. Brown, MI	1890–1906	1836	1913
George Shiras, Jr., PA	1892–1903	1832	1924
Howell E. Jackson, TN	1893–95	1832	1895
Edward D. White, LA	1894–1910	1845	1921
Rufus W. Peckham, NY	1896–1909	1838	1909
Joseph McKenna, CA	1898–1925	1843	1926
Oliver W. Holmes, MA	1902–32	1841	1935
William R. Day, OH	1903–22	1849	1923
William H. Moody, MA	1906–10	1853	1917
Horace H. Lurton, TN	1910–14	1844	1914
Charles E. Hughes, NY	1910–16	1862	1948
Willis Van Devanter, WY	1910–37	1859	1941
Joseph R. Lamar, GA	1910–16	1857	1916
Mahlon Pitney, NJ	1912–22	1858	1924
James C. McReynolds, TN	1914–41	1862	1946
Louis D. Brandeis, MA	1916–39	1856	1941
John H. Clarke, OH	1916–22	1857	1945
George Sutherland, UT	1922–38	1862	1942
Pierce Butler, MN	1923–39	1866	1939
Edward T. Sanford, TN	1923–30	1865	1930
Harlan F. Stone, NY	1925–41	1872	1946
Owen J. Roberts, PA	1930–45	1875	1955
Benjamin N. Cardozo, NY	1932–38	1870	1938
Hugo L. Black, AL	1937–71	1886	1971
Stanley F. Reed, KY	1938–57	1884	1980
Felix Frankfurter, MA	1939–62	1882	1965
William O. Douglas, CT	1939–75	1898	1980
Frank Murphy, MI	1940–49	1890	1949
James F. Byrnes, SC	1941–42	1879	1972
Robert H. Jackson, PA	1941–54	1892	1954
Wiley B. Rutledge, IA	1943–49	1894	1949
Harold H. Burton, OH	1945–58	1888	1964
Tom C. Clark, TX	1949–67	1899	1977
Sherman Minton, IN	1949–56	1890	1965
John M. Harlan, NY	1955–71	1899	1971
William J. Brennan, Jr, NJ	1956–90	1906	–
Charles E. Whittaker, MO	1957–62	1901	1973
Potter Stewart, OH	1958–81	1915	1985
Byron R. White, CO	1962–	1917	–
Arthur J. Goldberg, IL	1962–65	1908	–
Abe Fortas, TN	1965–69	1910	1982
Thurgood Marshall, NY	1967–91	1908	–
Harry A. Blackmun, MN	1970–	1908	–
Lewis F. Powell, Jr, VA	1972–87	1907	–
William H. Rehnquist, AZ	1972–86	1924	–
John Paul Stevens, IL	1975–	1920	–
Sandra Day O'Connor, AZ	1981–	1930	–
Antonin Scalia, DC	1986–	1936	–
Anthony M. Kennedy, CA	1988–	1936	–
David H. Souter, NH	1990–	1939	–
Clarence Thomas, DC	1991–	1948	–

[a] The Supreme Court has nine members – a chief justice and eight associate justices – appointed by the President with the advice and consent of the Senate. It is the highest federal court and, in addition to its jurisdiction relating to appeals, it exercises oversight of the constitution through the power of judicial review of the acts of state and federal legislatures, and the executive.

ARMED FORCES

Defence forces and expenditure

Country	Total active duty personnel (1991)[a]	Military expenditure as percentage of GDP[b] (1988)	Country	Total active duty personnel (1991)[a]	Military expenditure as percentage of GDP[b] (1988)
Australia	68 300	2.7	New Zealand	11 300	2.2
Austria	44 000	1.2	Nicaragua	30 500	17.2
Canada	86 600	2.1	Norway	32 700	3.2
China	3 030 000	3.9	Oman	25 500	19.1
Former USSR	3 400 000	11.9	Pakistan	565 000	6.9
Denmark	31 700	2.2	Peru	120 000	4.9
Egypt	420 000	7.8	Philippines	108 500	1.7
France	453 100	3.9	Poland	305 000	8.7
Germany	476 300	2.9	Portugal	61 800	3.3
Greece	158 500	6.5	Romania	200 800	6.5
Hungary	86 500	6.3	Saudi Arabia	76 500	16.5
India	1 265 000	3.5	Singapore	55 500	5.3
Iran	528 000	7.9	South Africa	72 400	4.3
Iraq	382 500	32.0	Spain	257 400	2.2
Israel	141 000	13.8	Sri Lanka	22 000	4.6
Italy	389 600	2.6	Sudan	71 500	2.4
Japan	246 400	1.0	Sweden	63 000	2.8
Jordan	101 300	21.0	Switzerland	3 500	2.1
Kenya	23 600	3.6	Syria	404 000	10.9
Korea, N	1 111 000	20.0	Taiwan	370 000	5.2
Korea, S	750 000	4.3	Thailand	283 000	3.1
Kuwait	8 200	5.1	Turkey	647 400	3.9
Libya	85 000	11.1	USSR *see* CIS		
Luxembourg	800	1.0	United Arab Emirates	44 000	6.8
Malaysia	12 900	2.8			
Mexico	175 000	0.6	United Kingdom	300 100	4.3
Morocco	195 500	6.0	United States	2 029 600	6.3
Mozambique	58 000	8.4	Vietnam	1 041 000	19.4
Netherlands	101 400	3.0			

[a] Figures are approximate [b] Gross Domestic Product

Ranks in the UK armed forces

Army

1. Field Marshal
2. General (Gen.)
3. Lieutenant-General (Lt.-Gen.)
4. Major-General (Maj.-Gen.)
5. Brigadier (Brig.)
6. Colonel (Col.)
7. Lieutenant-Colonel (Lt.-Col.)
8. Major (Maj.)
9. Captain (Capt.)
10. Lieutenant (Lt.)
11. Second Lieutenant (2nd Lt.)

Royal Air Force

1. Marshal of the RAF
2. Air Chief Marshal
3. Air Marshal
4. Air Vice-Marshal
5. Air Commodore (Air Cdre)
6. Group Captain (Gp Capt.)
7. Wing Commander (Wg Cdr.)
8. Squadron Leader (Sqn. Ldr.)
9. Flight Lieutenant (Flt. Lt.)
10. Flying Officer (FO)
11. Pilot Officer (PO)

Navy

1. Admiral of the Fleet
2. Admiral (Adm.)
3. Vice-Admiral (Vice-Adm.)
4. Rear-Admiral (Rear-Adm.)
5. Commodore (1st & 2nd Class) (Cdre)
6. Captain (Capt.)
7. Commander (Cdr.)
8. Lieutenant-Commander (Lt.-Cdr.)
9. Lieutenant (Lt.)
10. Sub-Lieutenant (Sub-Lt.)
11. Acting Sub-Lieutenant (Acting Sub-Lt.)

POLITICS

United Nations membership

Grouped according to year of entry.

1945	Argentina, Australia, Belgium, Belorussian SSR (Byelarus, 1991), Bolivia, Brazil, Canada, Chile, China (Taiwan to 1971), Colombia, Costa Rica, Cuba, Czechoslavakia, Denmark, Dominican Republic, Ecuador, Egypt, El Salvador, Ethiopia, France, Greece, Guatemala, Haiti, Honduras, India, Iran, Iraq, Lebanon, Liberia, Luxembourg, Mexico, Netherlands, New Zealand, Nicaragua, Norway, Panama, Paraguay, Peru, Philippines, Poland, Saudi Arabia, South Africa, Syria, Turkey, Ukranian SSR (Ukraine, 1991), USSR (Russia, 1991), UK, USA, Uruguay, Venezuela, Yugoslavia[a] (to 1992)
1946	Afghanistan, Iceland, Sweden, Thailand
1947	Pakistan, Yemen (N, to 1990)
1948	Burma (Myanmar, 1989)
1949	Israel
1950	Indonesia
1955	Albania, Austria, Bulgaria, Ceylon (Sri Lanka, 1970), Finland, Hungary, Ireland, Italy, Jordan, Cambodia, Laos, Libya, Nepal, Portugal, Romania, Spain
1956	Japan, Morocco, Sudan, Tunisia
1957	Ghana, Malaya (Malaysia, 1963)
1958	Guinea
1960	Cameroon, Central African Republic, Chad, Congo, Côte d'Ivoire, Cyprus, Dahomey (Benin, 1975), Gabon, Madagascar, Mali, Niger, Nigeria, Senegal, Somalia, Togo, Upper Volta (Burkina Faso, 1984), Zaïre
1961	Mauritania, Mongolia, Sierra Leone, Tanganyika (within Tanzania, 1964)
1962	Algeria, Burundi, Jamaica, Rwanda, Trinidad and Tobago, Uganda
1963	Kenya, Kuwait, Zanzibar (within Tanzania, 1964)
1964	Malawi, Malta, Tanzania, Zambia
1965	Maldives, Singapore, The Gambia
1966	Barbados, Botswana, Guyana, Lesotho
1967	Yemen (S, to 1990)
1968	Equatorial Guinea, Mauritius, Swaziland
1970	Fiji
1971	Bahrain, Bhutan, China (People's Republic), Oman, Qatar, United Arab Emirates
1973	Bahamas, German Democratic Republic (within GFR, 1990), German Federal Republic
1974	Bangladesh, Grenada, Guinea-Bissau
1975	Cape Verde, Comoros, Mozambique, Papua New Guinea, São Tomé and Principe, Suriname
1976	Angola, Seychelles, Western Samoa
1977	Djibouti, Vietnam
1978	Dominica, Solomon Islands
1979	St Lucia
1980	St Vincent and the Grenadines, Zimbabwe
1981	Antigua and Barbuda, Belize, Vanuatu
1983	St Christopher and Nevis
1984	Brunei
1990	Liechenstein, Namibia, Yemen (formerly N Yemen and S Yemen)
1991	Estonia, Federated States of Micronesia. Latvia, Lithuania, Marshall Islands, N Korea, S Korea
1992	Armenia, Azerbaijan, Bosnia-Herzegovina, Croatia, Georgia, Kazakhstan, Kyrgysztan, Moldova, San Marino, Slovenia, Tajikistan, Turkmenistan, Uzbekistan

[a] Yugoslavia was excluded from UN membership in 1992 and asked to reapply.

Main bodies of the United Nations

General Assembly	plenary body which controls much of the UN's work, supervises the subsidiary organs, sets priorities and debates major issues of international affairs.
Security Council	has fifteen members, but is dominated by five permanent members (China, France, Russia, UK, USA). Primary role is to maintain international peace and security. Empowered to order mandatory sanctions, call for ceasefires and establish peace-keeping forces.
Secretariat	headed by Secretary General. Staff of 66 000 worldwide answerable to UN only and are engaged in considerable diplomatic work.
International Court of Justice	consists of fifteen judges appointed by the Council and the Assembly. Jurisdiction depends on consent of the states who are a party to a dispute. Also offers advisory opinions to various organs of UN.
Economic and Social Council	elected by the General Assembly. It supervises work of various committees, commissions and expert bodies in the economic and social area, and coordinates work of UN specialized agencies.
Trusteeship Council	oversees the transition of Trust territories to self-government.

Specialized agencies of the United Nations

Abbreviated form	*Full title and location*	*Area of concern*
ILO	International Labour Organization, Geneva	social justice
FAO	Food and Agriculture, Rome	improvement of the production and distribution of agricultural products
UNESCO	United Nations Educational, Scientific and Cultural Organization, Paris	stimulation of popular education and the spread of culture
ICAO	International Civil Aviation Organization, Montreal	encouragement of safety measures in international flight
IBRD	International Bank for Reconstruction and Development, Washington	aid of development through investment
IMF	International Monetary Fund, Washington	promotion of international monetary co-operation
UPU	Universal Postal Union, Berne	uniting members within a single postal territory
WHO	World Health Organization, Geneva	promotion of the highest standards of health for all people
ITU	International Telecommunication Union, Geneva	allocation of frequencies and regulation of procedures
WMO	World Meteorological Organization, Geneva	standardization and utilization of meteorological observations
IFC	International Finance Corporation, Washington	promotion of the international flow of private capital
IMCO	Inter-governmental Maritime Consultative Organization, London	the co-ordination of safety at sea
IDA	International Development Association, Washington	credit on special terms to provide assistance for less developed countries
WIPO	World Intellectual Property Organization, Geneva	protection of copyright, designs, inventions etc
IFAD	International Fund for Agricultural Development, Rome	increase of food production in developing countries by the generation of grants or loans
UNIDO	United Nations Industrial Development Organization, Vienna	promotion of industrialization of developing countries, with special emphasis on manufacturing sector. Provides technical assistance and advice, as well as help with planning
UNICEF[b]	United Nations Children's Fund, New York	provides primary healthcare and education in developing countries
UNHCR[b]	United Nations High Commissioner for Refugees, Geneva	protects rights and interests of refugees, organizes emergency relief and longer term solutions eg. local integration, resettlement or voluntary repatriation
IAEA[a]	International Atomic Energy Association, Vienna	promotion of research and development into peaceful uses of nuclear energy, and oversees system of safeguards and controls governing misuse of nuclear materials for military purposes

[a] Linked to UN but not specialized agency. [b] Specialized bodies established by the General Assembly and supervised jointly with the Economic and Social Council.

United Nations Secretary General

1946–53	Trygve Lie *Norway*
1953–61	Dag Hammarskjöld *Sweden*
1962–71	U Thant *Burma*
1971–81	Kurt Waldheim *Austria*
1982–92	Javier Pérez de Cuéllar *Peru*
1992–	Boutros Boutros Ghali *Egypt*

Commonwealth Secretary General

1965–75	Arnold Smith
1975–90	Shridath S Ramphal
1990–	Emeka Anyaoku

Commonwealth members

The 'Commonwealth' is a free association of independent nations formerly subject to British imperial government, and maintaining friendly and practical links with the UK. In 1931 the Statute of Westminster established the British Commonwealth of Nations; the adjective 'British' was deleted after the Second World War. Most of the states granted independence, beginning with India in 1947, chose to be members of the Commonwealth.

Name of country	Date of joining
Antigua and Barbuda[a]	1981
Australia[a]	1931
Bahamas[a]	1973
Bangladesh[a]	1972
Barbados[a]	1966
Belize[a]	1981
Botswana	1966
Brunei	1984
Canada[a]	1931
Cyprus	1961
Dominica	1978
Gambia, The	1965
Ghana	1957
Grenada[a]	1974
Guyana	1966
India	1947
Jamaica[a]	1962
Kenya	1963
Kiribati	1979
Lesotho	1966
Malawi	1964
Malaysia	1957
Maldives	1982
Malta	1964
Mauritius[a]	1968
Nauru	1968
New Zealand[a]	1931
Nigeria	1960
Pakistan	1947 left 1962, rejoined 1989
Papua New Guinea[a]	1975
St Kitts and Nevis[a]	1983
St Lucia[a]	1979
St Vincent and the Grenadines[a]	1979
Seychelles	1976
Sierra Leone	1961
Singapore	1965
Solomon Islands[a]	1978
Sri Lanka	1948
Swaziland	1968
Tanzania	1961
Tonga	1970
Trinidad and Tobago	1962
Tuvalu[a]	1978
Uganda	1962
United Kingdom	1931
Vanuatu	1980
Western Samoa	1970
Zambia	1964
Zimbabwe	1980

[a] Member states recognizing the Queen, represented by a governor-general, as their Head of State.

Ireland resigned from the association in 1948 and South Africa in 1961.

The European Community

The European Community is a community of twelve states in Western Europe created for the purpose of achieving economic and political integration. While the Community has grown in the 1970s and 1980s and continues to progress towards economic union, political integration still seems a distant possibility.

Name of country	Year of joining	No of seats in European Parliament
Belgium	1958	24
Denmark	1973	16
France	1958	81
Germany	1958	81
Greece	1981	24
Ireland	1973	15
Italy	1958	81
Luxembourg	1958	6
Netherlands	1958	25
Portugal	1986	24
Spain	1986	60
United Kingdom	1973	81

Representation of political parties in the European Parliament*

Party	No of seats
Socialists	179
European People's Party	162
Liberal Democratic Reformists	45
European United Left	29
Greens	27
European Democratic Alliance	21
Rainbow Alliance	15
European Right	14
Coalition Left	13
Independents	13

*The figures represent the political groupings in the parliament since 1989.

European Community policies and policy makers

	Date established	Role
Common Agricultural Policy (CAP)	1962	Basic principles are free trade within the community for agricultural goods, preference for domestic production, control of imports from the rest of the world. Objectives are increased agricultural productivity, reasonable prices for consumers, stability of markets and food supplies.

	Date established	Role
Council of Ministers, Brussels	1974	Composed of foreign ministers from each member state representing national interests within the context of the Community. It is the main body within the Community influencing legislation. Decisions are taken on the basis of unanimity now rather than majority voting.
European Atomic Energy Commission (EURATOM)	1957	Objective is to promote peaceful ways of using atomic energy.
European Coal and Steel Community (ECSC)	1952	Created common framework of laws and institutions to regulate coal and steel industries. Has powers to set quotas and minimum prices. Has abolished currency restrictions, border charges, and discrimination in transport rates.
European Commission, Brussels	1967	This is the bureaucracy of the EC conducting both administrative and political business. Its functions are to uphold the European ideal, propose new policy initiatives and ensure that existing policies are implemented. Comprises seventeen members elected by the member countries. The Commission makes decisions by a majority vote and is directly responsible to the European parliament.
European Court of Justice, Luxembourg	1958	Judges cases involving member states, interprets Community treaties and legislation, decides on whether Community law has been breached by any member states.
European Investment Bank, Luxembourg	1958	Finances capital investment projects to help development of the Community. Each member country appoints a minister to the Board of Governors. Bank's capital is made up from the member states' subscriptions. It is a nonprofit making organisation.
European Monetary System (EMS)	1979	Financial system set up by EC members with the aim of stabilizing and harmonizing currencies. Member states use a special currency – the European Currency Unit (ECU). A percentage of the members' foreign exchange reserve is deposited with the European Monetary Cooperation Fund, and ECUs are received in exchange.
European Parliament, Brussels	1979 (start of direct elections)	The representative assembly of the EC. It has no legislative power but is able to dismiss the Commission if deemed necessary and to reject or amend the Community budget. It has been directly elected since 1979 and elections are held every five years.

International alliances

Name of organization	*Function*
Arab League	Founded 1945 with the aim of encouraging Arab unity. League today has twenty-one member states.
Association of South-East Asian Nations (ASEAN)	Formed 1967 to promote economic cooperation between Indonesia, Malaysia, the Philippines, Thailand, and Singapore. Brunei joined 1984.
Caribbean Community and Common Market (CARICOM)	Established 1973 with three objectives; coordination of foreign policy among member states; provision of common services, cooperation in matters of health, education, culture and industrial relations. There are thirteen member states.
Commonwealth, The	Free association of independent states formerly subject to British imperial rule and maintaining friendly and practical links with the UK.
Council for Mutual Economic Assistance (COMECON)	A body founded by Stalin in 1949 and dominated by the Soviet Union. Its purpose was ostensibly economic integration of the Eastern Bloc as a counterbalance to the economic powers of the EC and EFTA. The ten member states were the USSR, Bulgaria, Cuba, Czechoslovakia, East Germany, Hungary, Mongolia, Poland, Romania, and Vietnam. Disbanded in 1991 and replaced by the Organization for International Economic Cooperation.

International alliances (continued)

Name of organization	*Function*
Council of Europe	Established 1949, an association of European states which has a Committee of Foreign Ministers and a representative Parlimentary Assembly meeting at Strasbourg to discuss matters of concern.
Economic Community of West African States (ECOWAS)	Founded in Lagos 1975 to promote cultural, economic, and social development of West Africa through mutual cooperation. Measures include gradual elimination of trade barriers and improvement of communication and transportation. Supreme authority is invested in the annual summit of all member states' (16) heads of government.
European Economic Community (now commonly referred to as EC)	An association, established in 1958, which is essentially a customs union, with a common external tariff and common market with the removal of barriers to trade among the members.
European Free Trade Association (EFTA)	Established 1960 with aim of securing free trade of industrial goods between members. Also aimed to create single market in N Europe. Relations expanded with non-EC states in recent years, particularly E Europe. Free trade agreements already signed with Czechoslovakia and Turkey. Economic cooperation declarations signed with Bulgaria, Estonia, Latvia, Lithuania, Romania, Slovenia.
League of Nations	An international organization formed in 1919. Main aims were to preserve international peace and security by speedy settlement of disputes and promotion of disarmament. After Second World War it transferred its functions to the United Nations.
Nordic Council	Established 1952 as advisory body on economic and social cooperation, comprising parliamentary delegates from Denmark, Iceland, Norway, Sweden, Finland, Greenland, and Faroe and Åland Islands
North Atlantic Treaty Organization (NATO)	Established 1949, it is a permanent military alliance established originally to defend W Europe against Soviet aggression. Treaty commits members to regard an armed attack on one of them as an attack on all of them, and for all to assist the country attacked by such actions as are deemed necessary.
Organization for Economic Cooperation and Development (OECD)	Set up in 1961 to assist member states to develop economic and social policies aimed at high sustained economic growth with financial stability. It has twenty-four members.
Organization for European Economic Cooperation (OEEC)	Established 1948 by sixteen European countries and by the occupying forces on behalf of W Germany. Formal aims were to promote trade, stability, and expansion. Replaced 1961 by the OECD.
Organization of African Unity (OAU)	Founded 1963 by representatives of thirty-two African governments and dedicated to the eradication of all forms of colonialism in Africa. It had fifty-one members in 1990.
Organization of Arab Petroleum Exporting Countries (OAPEC)	Founded 1968, under the umbrella of OPEC, by Saudi Arabia, Kuwait, and Libya. By 1972 all Arab oil producers had joined.
Organization of Central American States	Established 1951 by Costa Rica, El Salvador, Guatemala, Honduras, and Nicaragua to promote economic, social, and cultural cooperation. In 1965 this was extended to include political and educational cooperation.
Organization of the Petroleum Exporting Countries (OPEC)	Created in 1960 as a permanent inter-governmental organization which aimed to unify and coordinate the policies of members and to determine the best means of protecting their interests.
Warsaw Pact	Consisted of the countries which signed the East European Mutual Assistance Treaty in Warsaw in 1955 – Albania, Bulgaria, Czechoslovakia, East Germany, Hungary, Poland, Romania, and the USSR. Established a unified military command of the armed forces of all the signatories. All members were committed to giving immediate assistance to any other party attacked in Europe. Formally dissolved in 1991.
Western European Union (WEU)	Founded 1955 to coordinate defence and other policies, replacing the European Defence Community. Members include Belgium, France, Germany, Italy, Luxembourg, Netherlands, and the UK. Consists of a Council of Ministers, a representative assembly in the Consultative Assembly of the Council of Europe and a Standing Armaments Committee which works in cooperation with NATO.

Some political systems

Country	*Form of government*	*System of voting*
Argentina	Federal republic Two chambers – Senate and Chamber of Deputies	Simple plurality
Australia	Federal commonwealth Two chambers – Senate and House of Representatives	Alternative vote
Austria	Federal republic Two chambers – Federal Council and National Council	Proportional representation (party list)
Belgium	Parliamentary state and constitutional monarchy Two chambers – Senate and House of Representatives	Proportional representation (party list)
Botswana	Unitary republic One chamber – National Assembly	Simple plurality
Brazil	Federal republic Two chambers – Senate and Chamber of Deputies	Proportional representation (party list)
Canada	Federal commonwealth Two chambers – Senate and House of Commons	Simple plurality
China	People's republic One chamber – National People's Congress	–
Cyprus	Unitary republic One chamber – House of Representatives	Proportional representation (second ballot)
Denmark	Parliamentary state and constitutional monarchy One chamber – Folketing	Proportional representation (party list)
Egypt	Unitary republic One chamber – People's Assembly	Proportional representation (second ballot)
Ethiopia	Unitary republic One chamber – National Assembly	Simple plurality
Finland	Constitutional republic One chamber – Eduskunta	Proportional representation (party list)
France	Constitutional republic Two chambers – Senate and National Assembly	Proportional representation (second ballot)
Germany	Federal republic Two chambers – Bundestag and Bundesrat	Proportional representation (additional member)
Greece	Unitary republic One chamber – Greek Chamber of Deputies	Proportional representation (party list)
India	Federal republic Two chambers – Council of States and House of the People	Simple plurality
Indonesia	Unitary republic One chamber – People's Consultative Assembly	Proportional representation (party list)
Iran	Islamic republic One chamber – Islamic Consultative Assembly	Proportional representation (second ballot)
Iraq	Republic One chamber – National Assembly	Simple plurality
Ireland	Republic Two chambers – Senate and House of Representatives	Proportional representation (single transferable vote)
Israel	Republic One chamber – Knesset	Proportional representation (party list)
Italy	Republic Two chambers – Senate and Chamber of Deputies	Proportional representation (party list)
Jamaica	Parliamentary State Two chambers – Senate and House of Representatives	Simple plurality
Japan	Parliamentary state and monarchy Two chambers – House of Councillors and House of Representatives	Limited vote
Luxembourg	Parliamentary state and constitutional monarchy One chamber – Chamber of Deputies	Proportional representation (party list)
Malaysia	Federation Two chambers – Senate and House of Representatives	Simple plurality
Malta	Unitary republic One chamber – House of Representatives	Proportional representation (single transferable vote)
Mexico	Federal state Two chambers – Senate and Chamber of Deputies	Proportional representation (additional member)
Netherlands	Parliamentary state and constitutional monarchy Two chambers – First Chamber and Second Chamber	Proportional representation (party list)

Some political systems (continued)

Country	*Form of government*	*System of voting*
New Zealand	Parliamentary state One chamber – House of Representatives	Simple plurality
Norway	Parliamentary state and constitutional monarchy One chamber – Storting	Proportional representation (party list)
Pakistan	Federal republic Two chambers – Senate and National Assembly	Simple plurality
Peru	Unitary republic Two chambers – Senate and Chamber of Deputies	Proportional representation (party list)
Philippines	Unitary republic Two chambers – Senate and House of Representatives	Simple plurality
Portugal	Republic One chamber – Assembly of the Republic	Proportional representation (party list)
Russia	Parliamentary state Two chambers – Supreme Soviet and Congress of People's Deputies	Proportional representation (second ballot)
Singapore	Unitary republic One chamber – Parliament	Simple plurality
South Africa	Unitary republic (restricted) Three chambers – House of Assembly (for Whites), House of Representatives (for Blacks), House of Delegates (for Asians)	Simple plurality
Spain	Parliamentary state and constitutional monarchy Two chambers – Senate and Congress of Deputies	Proportional representation (party list)
Sri Lanka	Unitary republic One chamber – National State Assembly	Proportional representation (party list)
Sweden	Parliamentary state and constitutional monarchy One chamber – Riksdag	Proportional representation (party list)
Switzerland	Federal state Two chambers – Nationalrat and Ständerat	Proportional representation (party list)
Turkey	Republic One chamber – Turkish Grand National Assembly	Proportional representation (party list)
Uganda	Unitary republic One chamber – National Assembly	Simple plurality
United Kingdom	Parliamentary state and constitutional monarchy Two chambers – House of Lords and House of Commons	Simple plurality
United States of America	Federal state Two chambers – Senate and House of Representatives	Simple plurality
Venezuela	Federal republic Two chambers – Senate and Chamber of Deputies	Proportional representation (party list)
Zimbabwe	Unitary republic Two chambers – Senate and House of Assembly	One party state

Proportional representation any system of voting designed to ensure that the representation of voters is in proportion to their numbers.

Alternative vote uses single-member constituencies, voter choosing a candidate by marking 1 against his/her name. First preference votes are counted and if one candidate obtains more than 50 per cent of all votes he/she is elected.

Second ballot simple majority election is held and if no one gets more than 50 per cent of total vote, the candidate with fewest votes is eliminated and a second election is held.

Party list political parties fighting the election produce list of candidates, presented in descending order of preference. In many cases, the elector votes for the party of his/her choice and seats are then allocated to each party according to total number of votes received. Names are taken from the lists to fill the seats.

Additional member this system also uses party lists but allows voter to cast two votes, one for the party and one for the candidate. Half the assembly is elected on simple plurality basis, and the other half, using party lists, is chosen so that chamber membership accurately reflects national vote.

Single transferable vote uses multi-member constituencies. All candidates are listed on ballot paper and voter states order of preference. All votes cast are counted and the 'electoral quota' (the minimum number of votes needed to be elected) is calculated. Any candidates with this quota or more is automatically elected.

Limited vote multi-member constituencies each return between three to five members, but voters are allowed only one non-transferable vote. The three to five candidates winning most votes in each constituency are then returned on a simple plurality basis.

Simple plurality also known as 'first-past-the-post' system. The party which gains the majority of votes cast secures all the available assembly seats.

ECONOMY

Selected indices of world agricultural and food production (1979–81 = 100)

Region or country	Total agricultural production 1986	1987	1988	1989	1990	1991[a]	Total food production 1986	1987	1988	1989	1990	1991[a]	Per capita food production 1986	1987	1988	1989	1990	1991[a]
Developed countries	109	108	105	109	111	107	109	108	105	110	111	107	105	103	100	104	104	100
United States	100	100	94	102	105	104	102	100	94	103	105	103	96	94	89	95	96	94
Canada	124	116	103	114	127	125	125	116	104	115	128	126	118	109	96	105	116	113
Europe	109	109	108	110	109	108	109	109	108	110	109	108	107	106	105	107	105	104
Japan	106	102	97	99	99	100	108	104	100	102	102	104	104	99	95	97	97	98
Oceania	109	108	113	112	116	115	107	106	110	109	111	109	99	96	99	95	97	94
South Africa	97	101	105	111	103	105	97	102	105	112	104	105	85	87	88	92	83	82
Former USSR	118	117	117	120	120	107	119	119	119	123	122	108	113	112	110	114	114	98
Less developed countries	122	125	132	136	140	141	123	125	132	136	140	141	109	108	112	113	114	112
South and East Asia[b]	127	130	137	144	150	150	127	130	138	143	149	149	114	114	118	121	124	121
China	135	142	144	149	162	159	135	140	142	148	159	156	125	128	128	131	140	135
India	123	122	138	147	148	150	124	124	139	148	149	151	109	106	117	122	120	120
Indonesia	138	138	144	149	160	163	138	140	147	152	163	166	122	121	125	127	133	133
Korea, South	114	104	111	109	113	105	116	106	113	111	114	107	106	96	103	99	102	94
Malaysia	144	151	162	169	173	178	161	170	183	199	204	209	138	141	148	157	157	157
Pakistan	133	136	141	150	155	162	129	130	136	146	150	156	103	100	101	105	104	105
Philippines	104	103	105	110	114	115	102	102	104	109	114	115	88	85	85	86	88	87
Thailand	114	114	127	132	124	134	112	111	126	130	118	129	100	98	107	110	99	106
Vietnam	130	135	138	149	158	165	128	133	135	147	155	161	113	115	115	121	125	127
Western Asia	123	121	128	118	130	127	126	123	130	119	132	129	104	99	102	91	98	94
Iran	145	142	137	133	153	157	145	143	138	134	153	158	115	110	103	98	110	110
Turkey	114	115	121	113	121	119	115	116	121	112	121	120	99	98	100	91	96	94
Africa[c]	120	119	126	130	130	134	120	119	126	129	130	134	100	96	98	98	96	95
Egypt	133	137	137	140	148	143	140	146	148	153	161	156	120	122	121	122	126	119
Ethiopia	106	102	103	107	110	108	108	102	105	108	110	110	95	88	87	87	87	84
Morocco	160	139	173	176	162	189	160	138	173	175	161	188	137	116	140	139	124	142
Nigeria	126	128	138	149	151	155	126	128	139	149	151	155	104	102	106	111	109	108
Sudan, The	103	93	117	91	90	109	102	90	117	89	90	110	85	73	92	68	87	80
Zaire	119	122	125	128	129	130	119	121	125	127	129	130	99	99	96	97	95	93
Latin America	110	115	121	123	123	113	113	116	123	126	129	128	99	100	104	104	102	102
Argentina	96	98	109	107	105	103	96	99	108	109	105	103	89	89	97	96	92	88
Brazil	110	128	130	138	128	131	115	126	135	142	132	136	101	108	113	117	107	108
Colombia	110	111	118	125	132	134	114	116	123	133	136	137	100	100	105	111	111	110
Mexico	111	111	118	117	119	124	112	111	118	119	121	126	97	95	98	96	96	98
Peru	109	114	124	123	109	112	109	116	126	123	111	115	95	99	105	101	89	90
Venezuela	124	118	121	129	135	135	124	118	121	129	137	138	104	97	97	101	104	101
World	116	116	119	123	125	124	116	116	118	123	125	124	104	103	103	105	105	102

[a]Preliminary. [b]Excludes Japan. [c]Excludes South Africa. Source: Food and Agriculture Organization of the United Nations, *FAO Quarterly Bulletin of Statistics*.

Unemployment

	1990 000s	1981–89 Percentage of labour force[b]	1990	1991	1992	1993	1981–89 Millions	1990	1991	1992	1993
North America	**8000.2**	**7.5**	**5.8**	**7.1**	**7.4**	**6.8**	**9.6**	**8.0**	**9.9**	**10.4**	**9.8**
Canada	1110.3	9.5	8.1	10.3	10.4	10.0	1.2	1.1	1.4	1.4	1.4
United States	6889.9	7.3	5.5	6.7	7.1	6.5	8.4	6.9	8.4	9.0	8.4
Japan	**1325.3**	**2.6**	**2.1**	**2.1**	**2.2**	**2.3**	**1.5**	**1.3**	**1.4**	**1.4**	**1.5**
Central and Western Europe	**6340.7**	**8.2**	**6.3**	**7.0**	**7.7**	**7.7**	**8.0**	**6.3**	**7.1**	**7.9**	**7.9**
Austria	114.8	3.3	3.3	3.7	4.0	4.2	0.1	0.1	0.1	0.1	0.2
Belgium	364.9	11.5	8.7	9.3	9.7	9.6	0.5	0.4	0.4	0.4	0.4
France	2170.5	9.4	8.9	9.4	9.8	9.8	2.2	2.2	2.3	2.4	2.4
Germany	1454.7	6.0	4.9	4.3	4.7	4.8	1.7	1.5	1.3	1.4	1.5
Ireland	179.0	15.0	13.7	15.8	16.9	16.6	0.2	0.2	0.2	0.2	0.2
Luxembourg	2.4	1.4	1.3	1.4	1.4	1.3	0	0	0	0	0
Netherlands	345.0	9.0	6.4	5.9	6.5	6.9	0.5	0.3	0.3	0.4	0.4
Switzerland	22.0	0.6	0.6	1.3	2.5	2.5	0	0	0	0.1	0.1
United Kingdom	1687.5	10.0	5.9	8.3	9.8	9.7	2.8	1.7	2.4	2.8	2.7
Southern Europe	**7505.2**	**12.1**	**11.3**	**11.7**	**11.9**	**12.1**	**7.6**	**7.5**	**7.9**	**8.1**	**8.3**
Greece	280.9	7.0	7.0	8.2	9.4	10.3	0.3	0.3	0.3	0.4	0.4
Italy	2654.4	10.6	11.1	11.0	11.2	11.5	2.4	2.7	2.7	2.7	2.8
Portugal	220.0	7.4	4.7	4.1	5.0	5.4	0.3	0.2	0.2	0.2	0.3
Spain	2441.0	18.8	16.3	16.3	16.1	15.5	2.6	2.4	2.5	2.4	2.3
Turkey	1909.0	11.0	10.0	11.5	11.8	12.2	1.9	1.9	2.2	2.3	2.5
Nordic countries	**543.1**	**4.5**	**4.4**	**6.0**	**7.6**	**7.5**	**0.5**	**0.5**	**0.7**	**0.9**	**0.9**
Denmark	271.7	9.1	9.5	10.4	10.7	10.2	0.3	0.3	0.3	0.3	0.3
Finland	88.2	4.9	3.5	7.6	11.3	10.9	0.1	0.1	0.2	0.3	0.3
Iceland	2.3	0.8	1.8	1.7	2.6	2.4	0	0	0	0	0
Norway	111.8	2.9	5.2	5.5	5.8	5.3	0.1	0.1	0.1	0.1	0.1
Sweden	69.2	2.2	1.5	2.7	4.5	5.2	0.1	0.1	0.1	0.2	0.2
Oceania	**713.9**	**7.1**	**7.1**	**9.7**	**10.6**	**10.2**	**0.6**	**0.7**	**1.0**	**1.1**	**1.1**
Australia	589.9	7.7	6.9	9.6	10.4	9.9	0.6	0.6	0.8	0.9	0.9
New Zealand	124.0	4.6	7.8	10.3	11.8	12.0	0.1	0.1	0.2	0.2	0.2
OECD Europe	**14389.1**	**9.3**	**8.0**	**8.7**	**9.3**	**9.3**	**16.1**	**14.4**	**15.7**	**16.9**	**17.0**
EC	**12071.8**	**9.9**	**8.4**	**8.8**	**9.4**	**9.4**	**13.8**	**12.1**	**12.8**	**13.7**	**13.7**
Total OECD	**24428.5**	**7.5**	**6.2**	**7.1**	**7.5**	**7.3**	**27.8**	**24.4**	**27.9**	**29.9**	**29.4**

[a] For sources and definitions, see *OECD Economic Outlook*, No. 51, June 1992. [b] The rates are not necessarily comparable between countries. Figures relate to unemployment in the Organization for Economic Cooperation and Development (OECD) area.

Inflation and unemployment

	GNP/GDP deflator Percentage change from preceding year			Unemployment rate[a] Percentages		
	1990	*1991*	*1992*	*1990*	*1991*	*1992*
North America						
Canada	3.0	2.7	1.9	8.1	10.3	10.4
United States	4.1	3.6	2.8	5.5	6.7	7.1
Japan	2.1	1.9	1.7	2.1	2.1	2.2
Central and Western Europe						
Austria	2.9	3.8	4.2	3.3	3.7	4.0
Belgium	3.0	3.1	3.1	8.7	9.3	9.7
France	3.1	3.0	3.1	8.9	9.4	9.8
Germany	3.4	4.6	4.5	4.9	4.3	4.7
Ireland[b]	−0.5	2.7	3.5	13.7	15.8	16.9
Luxembourg	2.1	1.6	3.8	1.3	1.4	1.4
Netherlands	2.9	3.3	3.1	6.4	5.9	6.5
Switzerland	5.3	5.2	4.5	0.6	1.3	2.5
United Kingdom	6.4	6.9	5.1	5.9	8.3	9.8
Southern Europe						
Greece	20.5	19.5	14.8	7.0	8.2	9.4
Italy	7.6	7.3	5.3	11.1	11.0	11.2
Portugal	14.3	13.6	11.3	4.7	4.1	5.0
Spain	7.3	6.9	6.0	16.3	16.3	16.1
Turkey	54.4	56.0	59.0	10.0	11.5	11.8
Nordic countries						
Denmark	2.1	3.0	2.3	9.5	10.4	10.7
Finland	5.2	3.5	2.7	3.5	7.6	11.3
Iceland	13.6	8.2	3.7	1.8	1.7	2.6
Norway	4.5	1.5	0.0	5.2	5.5	5.8
Sweden	9.4	7.5	2.3	1.5	2.7	4.5
Oceania						
Australia	4.2	1.3	2.6	6.9	9.6	10.4
New Zealand	5.0	1.3	1.8	7.8	10.3	11.8
Total OECD	4.4	4.1	3.5	6.2	7.1	7.5

[a] Figures for 1991 onwards are estimated and projections. [b] GNP. Source: OECD, Economic Outlook No. 51.

Interest rates

Short-term: Three-month money market rates

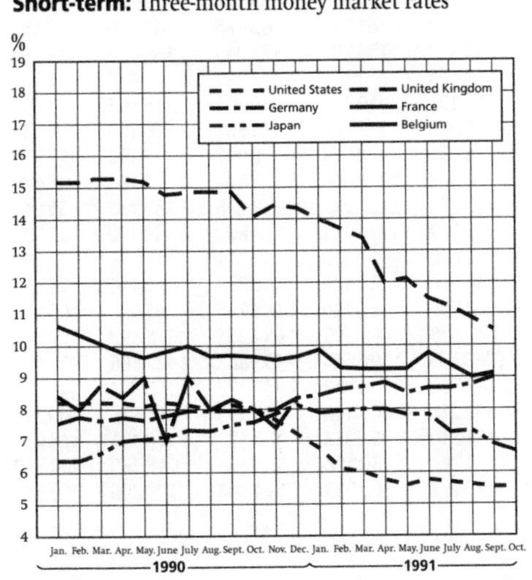

Long-term

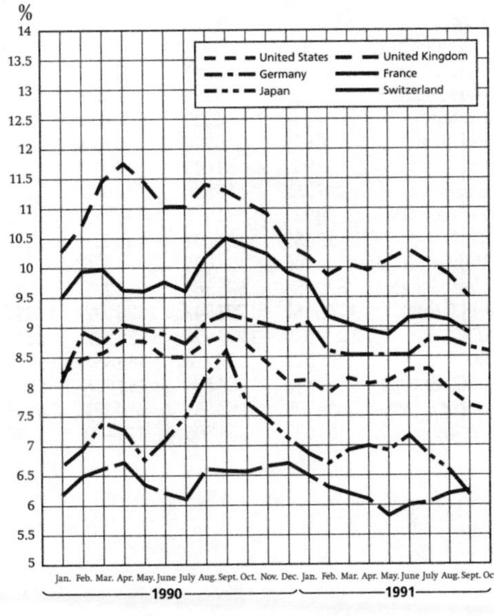

Energy production and consumption

Production of crude oil + NGL (1000 metric tons)

	1982	1983	1984	1985	1986	1987	1988	1989	1990
Australia	19766	19226	23138	26764	27436	27236	27171	24581	27998
Austria	1306	1281	1216	1161	1133	1082	1217	1198	1190
Canada	66467	68215	75885	75767	75662	80320	84038	81708	81554
Denmark	1686	2152	2314	2892	3621	4602	4734	5531	5994
France	2338	2317	2699	3243	3446	3645	3728	3627	3377
Germany	4234	4094	4030	4073	4031	3727	3946	3791	3594
Greece	1032	1241	1320	1322	1333	1221	1118	916	830
Italy	1789	2265	2295	2408	2558	3943	4841	4604	4668
Japan	420	441	426	553	647	621	607	560	553
Netherlands	1894	2900	3433	4069	4995	4663	4271	3814	3976
New Zealand	681	672	864	1282	1427	1370	1634	1829	1891
Norway	24411	30611	35050	38431	42375	49541	56351	74872	82058
Spain	1757	3185	2512	2383	2094	1852	1718	1333	1144
Sweden	14	23	13	8	4	4	3	3	3
Turkey	2333	2203	2087	2110	2394	2627	2569	2876	3712
United Kingdom	103218	114921	125924	127642	127053	123306	114459	91811	91616
United States	477469	479038	490624	493323	477001	462070	453910	424141	411848
OECD total	**710815**	**734785**	**773830**	**787431**	**777210**	**771830**	**766315**	**727195**	**726006**
IEA	708477	732468	771131	784188	773764	768185	762587	723568	722629
EC	117948	133075	144527	148032	149131	146959	138815	115427	115199
OECD Europe	146012	167193	182893	189742	195037	200213	198955	194376	202162
North America	543936	547253	566509	569090	552663	542390	537948	505849	493402
Pacific	20867	20339	24428	28599	29510	29227	29412	26970	30442

Final consumption of oil (1000 metric tons)

	1982	1983	1984	1985	1986	1987	1988	1989	1990
Australia	25575	24041	25146	25373	25769	25927	27469	28635	28893
Austria	8564	8801	8643	8641	9034	9290	9029	8955	9383
Belgium	15358	14431	14393	15280	17362	16977	17446	16851	16781
Canada	65539	62494	62894	62632	63215	65003	67608	69330	66448
Denmark	9190	8851	9012	9351	9287	8870	8329	7867	7789
Finland	9276	8845	8624	8241	9153	9461	9603	9589	9399
France	77343	77444	75186	74864	75072	75362	76008	76355	76618
Germany	96765	97320	99902	100896	106854	103487	104430	97348	102405
Greece	8671	8557	8661	8804	8585	9264	9643	10271	10421
Iceland	498	502	523	519	527	568	597	647	701
Ireland	3586	3432	3474	3486	3561	3636	3524	3702	4013
Italy	59730	60367	60790	59686	59723	61293	62465	63050	62151
Japan	137609	141074	147816	146503	149854	154206	163289	166433	170399
Luxembourg	992	956	964	1027	1105	1275	1297	1439	1580
Netherlands	16640	17983	18329	17676	19196	19097	19284	18895	19396
New Zealand	3509	3390	3508	3460	3559	3800	3885	4138	4334
Norway	7330	7239	7616	7886	8254	8974	8097	7902	7733
Portugal	6625	6210	6439	6401	6662	7004	7806	8164	8629
Spain	32947	33647	33411	32960	33052	33937	38258	37925	38941
Sweden	17252	15640	14615	15249	15919	14832	14802	14100	13702
Switzerland	10921	11970	11529	12572	12615	12516	12571	12676	12597
Turkey	13487	14301	14121	14744	16010	18329	18389	18744	20170
United Kingdom	58700	58080	58826	58439	61759	62140	65795	65951	65592
United States	620754	606367	632277	632551	647028	665395	684258	678899	667372
OECD total	**1306861**	**1291942**	**1326699**	**1327241**	**1363155**	**1390643**	**1433882**	**1427866**	**1425847**
IEA	1229020	1213996	1250990	1251858	1287556	1314713	1357277	1350864	1348528
EC	386547	387278	389387	388870	402218	402342	414285	407818	414316
OECD Europe	453875	454576	455058	456722	473730	476312	487373	480431	488001
North America	686293	668861	695171	695183	710243	730398	751866	748229	734220
Pacific	166693	168505	176470	175336	179182	183933	194643	199206	203626

Production of natural gas (Terajoules = 10^{12}J)

	1982	1983	1984	1985	1986	1987	1988	1989	1990
Australia	448 025	468 474	490 073	522 852	571 092	588 928	610 477	627 770	797 666
Austria	48 196	43 925	46 059	42 249	40 351	42 024	45 524	47 644	46 376
Belgium	1 218	720	1 478	1 591	1 043	1 105	664	523	450
Canada	2 861 188	2 687 109	2 930 295	3 191 627	3 007 437	3 253 860	3 836 221	4 062 975	4 157 425
Denmark			9 450	44 841	77 967	99 244	98 310	124 992	127 277
France	257 074	259 824	246 820	209 382	164 608	152 642	125 478	121 284	117 403
Germany	555 584	592 478	620 149	562 459	515 366	595 606	554 826	546 308	545 985
Greece	3 375	3 215	3 538	3 324	4 555	5 200	6 237	6 290	6 404
Ireland	76 966	82 296	87 282	92 491	62 923	62 815	75 676	85 365	87 127
Italy	549 363	492 598	521 357	536 769	601 505	616 473	626 563	640 451	652 664
Japan	83 991	85 549	87 517	91 293	86 369	88 953	86 025	82 415	83 851
Netherlands	2 533 357	2 691 648	2 716 794	2 838 839	2 603 758	2 611 144	2 307 408	2 522 206	2 540 607
New Zealand	80 617	87 270	115 150	144 851	168 521	162 678	178 157	182 770	181 937
Norway	1 028 772	1 041 391	1 097 348	1 088 677	1 129 393	1 193 171	1 202 853	1 242 770	1 130 703
Spain		2 931	9 295	10 681	15 491	29 630	37 724	66 069	59 228
Switzerland	567	567	544	1 356	1 244	1 011	933	633	511
Turkey	1 482	2 575	1 608	2 026	17 518	11 384	3 792	6 665	8 120
United Kingdom	1 477 735	1 523 736	1 491 242	1 661 741	1 738 971	1 829 288	1 761 317	1 724 074	1 903 539
United States	19 400 350	17 567 532	19 020 959	17 959 454	17 486 128	18 062 977	18 594 050	18 872 910	19 250 285
OECD total	**29 407 860**	**27 633 838**	**29 496 958**	**29 006 503**	**28 294 240**	**29 408 133**	**30 152 235**	**30 964 114**	**31 697 558**
IEA	29 150 786	27 374 014	29 250 138	28 797 121	28 129 632	29 255 491	30 026 757	30 842 830	31 580 155
EC	5 454 672	5 649 446	5 707 405	5 962 118	5 786 187	6 003 147	5 594 203	5 837 562	6 040 684
OECD Europe	6 533 689	6 737 904	6 852 964	7 096 426	6 974 693	7 250 737	6 847 305	7 135 274	7 226 394
North America	22 261 538	20 254 641	21 951 254	21 151 081	20 493 565	21 316 837	22 430 271	22 935 885	23 407 710
Pacific	612 633	641 293	692 740	758 996	825 982	840 559	874 659	892 955	1 063 454

Final consumption of natural gas (Terajoules = 10^{12}J)

	1982	1983	1984	1985	1986	1987	1988	1989	1990
Australia	268 071	279 458	288 868	325 855	351 019	373 259	379 194	392 113	416 329
Austria	109 788	108 049	117 167	124 053	119 026	119 319	117 497	121 946	128 446
Belgium	282 278	281 516	298 715	307 960	289 182	307 094	300 492	309 632	317 260
Canada	1 547 409	1 556 272	1 672 882	1 762 068	1 694 642	1 676 577	1 857 560	1 922 112	1 875 250
Denmark		611	2 290	11 663	24 842	33 007	41 867	45 319	50 990
Finland	19 004	20 553	22 893	22 650	24 665	34 672	34 199	46 846	60 230
France	916 941	967 941	1 043 320	1 082 051	1 100 111	1 118 938	1 080 565	1 096 430	1 124 470
Germany	1 278 578	1 335 635	1 417 736	1 476 059	1 475 980	1 593 526	1 570 262	1 598 672	1 644 549
Greece	1 176	1 231	1 876	2 458	2 734	3 362	4 515	4 300	4 289
Iceland								40	40
Ireland	21 298	18 154	23 363	23 928	34 194	39 084	39 678	43 480	46 721
Italy	861 496	878 446	958 043	1 001 102	1 064 683	1 175 210	1 256 430	1 359 584	1 414 339
Japan	62 241	59 696	64 162	63 104	59 687	57 711	59 851	60 060	60 393
Luxembourg	12 636	11 883	12 824	14 059	14 043	15 181	16 256	18 261	19 533
Netherlands	992 189	1 005 050	1 044 629	1 122 029	1 087 448	1 143 382	1 044 693	1 043 171	1 070 082
New Zealand	26 399	37 268	62 395	61 726	62 353	62 585	64 463	66 475	66 170
Spain	39 833	46 302	55 448	63 793	75 300	95 509	129 498	180 381	201 194
Sweden				2 997	7 009	9 010	10 747	12 729	15 532
Switzerland	44 233	49 289	56 066	58 845	60 466	65 223	66 421	72 621	78 310
Turkey	1 482	2 575	1 608	1 336	1 766	2 043	7 926	19 176	33 062
United Kingdom	1 749 094	1 769 156	1 800 516	1 912 911	1 937 863	2 010 528	1 934 484	1 904 382	1 958 159
United States	13 540 099	12 913 405	13 850 620	13 255 530	12 626 853	13 074 037	14 196 865	14 886 865	14 757 447
OECD total	**21 774 245**	**21 342 490**	**22 795 421**	**22 696 177**	**22 113 866**	**23 009 266**	**24 213 463**	**25 204 595**	**25 342 795**
IEA	20 857 304	20 374 549	21 752 101	21 614 126	21 013 755	21 890 328	23 132 898	24 108 125	24 218 285
EC	6 155 519	6 315 925	6 658 760	7 018 013	7 106 380	7 534 821	7 418 740	7 603 612	7 851 586
OECD Europe	6 330 026	6 496 391	6 856 494	7 227 894	7 319 312	7 765 097	7 655 530	7 876 970	8 167 206
North America	15 087 508	14 469 677	15 523 502	15 017 598	14 321 495	14 750 614	16 054 425	16 808 977	16 632 697
Pacific	356 711	376 422	415 425	450 685	473 059	493 555	503 508	518 648	542 892

OECD Organization for Economic Cooperation and Development
IEA International Energy Agency
EC European Community

Society

Energy production and consumption (continued)

Production of hard coal (1000 metric tons)

	1982	1983	1984	1985	1986	1987	1988	1989	1990
Australia	89453	98267	104583	117504	133383	147718	134807	147804	159417
Belgium	6576	6119	6342	6237	5625	4370	2487	1893	1036
Canada	22379	22583	32063	34310	30542	32651	38585	38794	37672
France	16895	17021	16594	15124	14394	13743	12142	11471	10487
Germany	96318	89620	84868	88849	87125	82380	79319	77451	76553
Ireland	62	75	70	57	54	45	45	43	35
Italy					29	14	40	74	58
Japan	17606	17062	16644	16382	16012	13049	11223	10187	8262
New Zealand	2107	2255	2307	2279	2176	2327	2227	2554	2427
Norway	440	502	451	507	437	399	264	339	311
Portugal	178	185	194	237	236	261	230	258	281
Spain	15423	15419	15289	16091	15895	14101	14205	14525	14743
Sweden	13	13	13	12	12	25	30	–	11
Turkey	4008	3539	3632	3605	3526	3461	3256	3038	2745
United Kingdom	121427	116448	49549	90793	104645	101645	101661	98285	89303
United States	712381	656568	755550	738844	738413	762341	784864	811296	853647
OECD total	**1105266**	**1045676**	**1088149**	**1130831**	**1152494**	**1178530**	**1185385**	**1218012**	**1256988**
IEA	1088371	1028655	1071555	1115707	1138100	1164787	1173243	1206541	1246501
EEC	256879	244887	172906	217388	227993	216559	210129	204000	192496
OECD Europe	261340	248941	177002	221512	231968	2200444	213679	207377	195563
North America	734760	679151	787613	773154	768955	794992	823449	850090	891319
Pacific	109166	117584	123534	136165	151571	163094	148257	160545	170106

Final consumption of hard coal (1000 metric tons)

	1982	1983	1984	1985	1986	1987	1988	1989	1990
Australia	3648	3613	4020	4678	4791	4806	4815	5013	5098
Austria	404	592	835	661	633	538	447	397	405
Belgium	2608	2138	2420	2559	2168	2095	2057	2567	2485
Canada	1510	1382	1495	1723	1675	1708	1797	1729	1671
Denmark	444	296	543	684	599	632	662	639	574
Finland	1093	1088	1145	1256	1096	1264	1108	1377	1379
France	6468	5763	6114	7068	6978	7065	7182	7154	7411
Germany	7211	7495	7825	7481	6950	6923	7105	6809	7057
Greece	491	1054	1333	1443	1408	1364	1396	1276	1380
Iceland	25	37	55	69	74	60	67	71	65
Ireland	1267	1446	1444	1507	1700	1574	1474	1391	1271
Italy	2170	1731	2223	2783	1455	1935	1202	1302	1912
Japan	11745	9468	10419	10859	9777	11009	12942	14245	18961
Luxembourg	259	144	166	176	181	197	161	195	197
Netherlands	290	323	721	770	759	1040	1070	1109	1170
New Zealand	1393	1294	1317	1276	1280	1488	1739	1725	1786
Norway	591	640	682	682	623	660	773	770	734
Portugal	63	144	193	320	575	704	809	839	820
Spain	3773	3740	3715	3585	3452	3247	3379	3306	2762
Sweden	510	570	696	713	704	729	798	930	949
Switzerland	468	427	605	594	516	505	440	439	462
Turkey	1152	1051	1498	1655	1616	1948	2409	2380	2736
United Kingdom	15398	14526	12762	16120	16448	15054	14567	12520	11176
United States	62299	64605	70717	68386	67682	66224	67549	66063	67381
OECD total	**125280**	**123567**	**132943**	**137048**	**133140**	**132769**	**135948**	**134246**	**139842**
IEA	118787	117767	126774	129911	126088	125644	128699	127021	132366
EC	40442	38800	39459	44496	42673	41830	41064	39107	38215
OECD Europe	44685	43205	44975	50126	47935	47534	47106	45471	44945
North America	63809	65987	72212	70109	69357	67932	69346	67792	69052
Pacific	16786	14375	15756	16813	15848	17303	19496	20983	25845

Total production of electricity (gigawatt hours)

	1982	1983	1984	1985	1986	1987	1988	1989	1990
Australia	105 387	106 298	112 308	120 962	126 383	132 670	138 959	147 788	154 571
Austria	42 891	42 625	42 382	44 534	44 653	50 517	49 025	50 174	50 414
Belgium	50 696	52 707	54 657	57 322	58 676	63 367	65 349	67 482	70 846
Canada	387 482	407 981	437 098	459 045	468 593	496 335	505 966	499 538	482 025
Denmark	23 707	22 186	22 620	29 064	30 739	29 449	27 965	22 312	25 745
Finland	41 175	42 197	45 287	49 716	49 266	53 402	53 878	53 817	54 563
France	279 209	296 812	324 509	344 301	362 784	378 309	391 926	406 891	420 155
Germany	366 877	373 813	394 884	408 706	408 266	418 262	431 164	440 896	449 497
Greece	23 272	23 983	24 804	27 740	28 237	30 272	33 394	34 456	35 002
Iceland	3 633	3 828	3 977	3 900	4 114	4 210	4 478	4 537	4 510
Ireland	10 931	11 178	11 593	12 088	12 652	13 064	13 228	13 833	14 515
Italy	184 445	182 880	182 669	185 740	192 330	201 372	203 561	210 750	216 891
Japan	581 358	618 377	648 671	671 952	676 360	719 067	753 728	798 757	857 273
Luxembourg	941	830	896	942	1 022	1 019	1 331	1 372	1 377
Netherlands	60 312	59 650	62 778	62 947	67 158	68 419	69 611	73 050	71 866
New Zealand	24 598	26 138	27 064	27 334	28 169	28 686	29 471	30 578	31 251
Norway	93 156	106 370	106 666	103 292	97 284	104 283	110 019	119 197	121 601
Portugal	15 418	18 161	19 247	18 900	20 355	20 135	22 489	25 808	28 500
Spain	114 569	117 196	120 042	127 363	129 150	133 390	139 571	147 842	150 622
Sweden	100 050	109 391	123 843	137 140	138 651	146 571	146 230	143 091	146 536
Switzerland	53 580	53 137	50 566	56 492	57 564	59 890	60 690	54 767	55 787
Turkey	26 552	27 347	30 613	34 219	39 695	44 353	48 049	52 043	57 543
United Kingdom	272 783	277 474	282 469	297 555	301 590	302 455	308 136	313 825	318 977
United States	2 376 635	2 449 040	2 562 773	2 621 929	2 639 724	2 732 532	2 874 797	2 957 915	2 980 908
OECD total	**5 239 657**	**5 429 599**	**5 692 416**	**5 903 183**	**5 983 415**	**6 232 029**	**6 483 015**	**6 670 719**	**6 800 975**
IEA	4 956 815	5 128 959	5 363 930	5 554 982	5 616 517	5 849 510	6 086 611	6 259 291	6 376 310
EC	1 403 160	1 436 870	1 501 168	1 572 668	1 612 959	1 659 513	1 707 725	1 758 517	1 803 993
OECD Europe	1 764 197	1 821 765	1 904 502	2 001 961	2 044 186	2 122 739	2 180 094	2 236 143	2 294 947
North America	2 764 117	2 857 021	2 999 871	3 080 974	3 108 317	3 228 867	3 380 763	3 457 453	3 462 933
Pacific	711 343	750 813	788 043	820 248	830 912	880 423	922 158	977 123	1 043 095

Final consumption of electricity (gigawatt hours)

	1982	1983	1984	1985	1986	1987	1988	1989	1990
Australia	86 894	87 645	93 457	98 070	104 238	109 068	115 783	122 658	128 034
Austria	33 447	33 987	35 602	37 018	37 380	38 770	40 156	41 453	43 160
Belgium	43 202	44 418	46 555	48 303	49 328	51 822	54 083	55 988	57 984
Canada	309 508	324 015	348 708	364 550	381 490	388 648	407 379	416 235	413 671
Denmark	22 441	22 724	23 846	25 358	26 717	27 691	28 051	28 769	29 290
Finland	38 959	41 985	45 352	48 519	49 516	52 986	55 150	56 635	58 835
France	214 812	226 761	236 827	249 392	264 299	276 089	281 721	293 092	301 912
Germany	317 246	325 337	340 388	349 634	354 238	363 477	369 075	376 501	380 810
Greece	20 146	21 551	22 991	23 833	24 115	25 035	26 898	28 009	28 471
Iceland	3 239	3 364	3 537	3 441	3 602	3 694	4 023	4 092	4 053
Ireland	8 564	8 852	9 254	9 762	10 201	10 590	10 724	11 279	11 868
Italy	161 159	160 460	169 490	173 609	178 993	188 411	198 048	206 837	214 084
Japan	514 960	546 630	574 161	592 713	595 377	631 556	665 669	707 171	758 438
Luxembourg	3 403	3 512	3 745	3 793	3 812	3 893	3 983	4 068	4 127
Netherlands	56 259	57 459	59 485	61 449	62 268	65 136	68 317	70 597	73 506
New Zealand	21 340	22 991	23955	24 233	25 304	25 767	26 666	27 280	27 791
Norway	77 803	82 812	88 738	91 415	90 109	93 187	94 194	94 421	93 833
Portugal	15 332	16 167	16 666	17 644	18 558	19 438	20 783	22 041	23 544
Spain	91 290	95 601	100 093	102 828	105 036	109 215	114 160	122 434	124 932
Sweden	89 423	94 863	103 267	113 076	114 424	119 773	119 846	119 799	120 477
Switzerland	36 731	37 970	39 665	41 321	42 348	43 591	44 327	45 502	46 578
Turkey	22 657	23 581	26 630	28 462	30 812	35 107	38 009	41 259	44 951
United Kingdom	224 756	227 536	232 177	242 564	250 163	258 447	265 231	270 398	274 834
United States	2 010 450	2 073 145	2 205 571	2 253 015	2 274 601	2 376 361	2 492 363	2 565 134	2 626 165
OECD total	**4 424 021**	**4 583 366**	**4 850 160**	**5 004 002**	**5 096 929**	**5 317 752**	**5 544 639**	**5 731 652**	**5 891 348**
IEA	4 205 970	4 353 241	4 609 796	4 751 169	4 829 028	5 037 969	5 258 895	5 434 468	5 585 383
EC	1 178 610	1 210 378	1 261 517	1 308 169	1 347 728	1 399 244	1 441 074	1 490 013	1 525 362
OECD Europe	1 480 869	1 528 940	1 604 308	1 671 421	1 715 919	1 786 352	1 836 779	1 893 174	1 937 249
North America	2 319 958	2 397 160	2 554 279	2 617 565	2 656 091	2 765 009	2 899 742	2 981 369	3 039 836
Pacific	623 194	657 266	691 573	715 016	724 919	766 391	808 118	857 109	914 263

Energy production and consumption (continued)

Production of nuclear energy (gigawatt hours)

	1982	*1983*	*1984*	*1985*	*1986*	*1987*	*1988*	*1989*	*1990*
Belgium	15 664	24 106	27 743	34 601	39 394	41 967	43 102	41 217	42 722
Canada	38 337	48 610	52 210	60 521	71 267	77 261	82 867	79 872	72 886
Finland	16 776	17 720	18 867	19 059	19 059	19 646	19 554	19 090	19 215
France	108 919	144 261	191 234	224 100	254 155	265 520	275 521	303 931	314 081
Germany	63 577	65 833	92 577	125 902	119 580	130 515	145 082	149 390	147 159
Italy	6 804	5 783	6 887	7 024	8 758	174			
Japan	102 430	114 291	134 264	159 578	168 305	187 758	178 659	182 869	202 272
Netherlands	3 897	3 589	3 711	3 899	4 216	3 556	3 675	4 019	3 502
Spain	8 771	10 661	23 086	28 044	37 458	41 271	50 466	56 126	54 273
Sweden	39 045	41 004	50 926	58 561	69 951	67 385	69 424	65 603	68 185
Switzerland	15 133	15 710	18 440	22 558	22 581	23 003	22 792	22 836	23 636
United Kingdom	43 972	49 928	53 979	61 095	59 079	55 238	63 456	71 734	65 747
United States	299 739	311 298	347 292	406 712	438 880	482 586	558 591	561 116	611 473
OECD total	**763 064**	**852 794**	**1 021 216**	**1 211 654**	**1 312 683**	**1 395 880**	**1 513 189**	**1 557 803**	**1 625 151**
IEA	654 145	708 533	829 982	987 554	1 058 528	1 130 360	1 237 668	1 253 872	1 311 070
EC	251 604	304 161	399 217	484 665	522 640	538 241	581 302	626 417	627 484
OECD Europe	322 558	378 595	487 450	584 843	634 231	648 275	693 072	733 946	738 520
North America	338 076	359 908	399 502	467 233	510 147	559 847	641 458	640 988	684 359
Pacific	102 430	114 291	134 264	159 578	168 305	187 758	178 659	182 869	202 272

Production of hydro energy (gigawatt hours)

	1982	*1983*	*1984*	*1985*	*1986*	*1987*	*1988*	*1989*	*1990*
Australia	14 570	12 913	12 890	14 964	15 511	14 744	14 963	15 161	14 785
Austria	30 880	30 589	29 469	31 603	31 680	36 725	36 541	36 146	32 492
Belgium	1 051	1 174	1 318	1 350	1 398	1 469	1 167	975	897
Canada	257 865	266 024	286 196	303 720	310 697	316 288	307 553	291 448	296 919
Denmark	31	39	34	33	29	29	32	27	32
Finland	13 088	13 579	13 246	12 333	12 389	13 795	13 361	13 029	10 931
France	71 298	70 888	67 537	63 663	64 694	72 365	78 216	50 602	57 350
Germany	19 646	18 933	18 470	17 613	18 544	20 587	20 714	19 145	18 366
Greece	3 561	2 340	2 862	2 805	3 348	2 964	2 593	2 147	1 997
Iceland	3 445	3 628	3 779	3 704	3 884	3 957	4 211	4 259	4 204
Ireland	1 203	1 178	1 045	1 180	1 264	1 116	1 205	991	983
Italy	44 081	44 216	45 434	44 595	44 531	42 585	43 547	37 484	35 079
Japan	84 039	87 995	76 723	87 946	86 074	80 846	95 884	97 825	95 835
Luxembourg	494	452	450	510	534	552	825	825	823
Netherlands				3	3	1	2	37	120
New Zealand	17 987	20 198	20 107	19 707	21 788	22 078	23 162	21 999	23 167
Norway	92 888	106 049	106 339	102 946	96 819	103 753	109 544	118 698	121 137
Portugal	6 982	8 134	9 817	10 783	8 542	9 185	12 302	6 079	9 303
Spain	27 394	28 865	33 420	33 033	27 416	28 167	36 233	20 047	26 165
Sweden	55 604	64 066	68 481	71 589	61 494	72 442	70 467	71 921	73 105
Switzerland	37 405	36 362	31 180	33 004	33 925	35 766	36 803	30 790	30 982
Turkey	14 167	11 343	13 426	12 045	11 872	18 618	28 949	17 939	23 148
United Kingdom	5 637	6 459	6 060	6 926	7 001	6 243	6 964	6 569	7 062
United States	312 305	335 451	324 361	283 960	293 752	252 192	225 169	267 714	282 638
OECD total	**1 115 621**	**1 170 875**	**1 172 644**	**1 160 015**	**1 157 189**	**1 156 467**	**1 170 407**	**1 131 857**	**1 167 520**
IEA	1 040 878	1 096 359	1 101 328	1 092 648	1 088 611	1 080 145	1 087 980	1 076 996	1 105 966
EC	181 378	182 678	186 447	182 494	177 304	185 263	203 800	144 928	158 177
OECD Europe	428 855	448 294	452 367	449 718	429 367	470 319	503 676	437 710	454 176
North America	570 170	601 475	610 557	587 680	604 449	568 480	532 722	559 162	579 557
Pacific	116 596	121 106	109 720	122 617	123 373	117 668	134 009	134 985	133 787

Growth industries: the ten highest by output

	Australia 1974–86	*Canada* 1981–86	*France* 1972–85	*Germany* 1978–86	*Japan* 1970–85	*United Kingdom* 1968–84	*United States* 1972–85
1.	Real estate *DFD*	Computers *Exports*	Computers *DFD*	Computers *Exports*	Computers *DFD*	Computers *Exports*	Computers *DFD*
2.	Communications *DFD*	Motor vehicles *Exports*	Communications *DFD*	Aerospace *Exports*	Pharmaceuticals *Tech.*	Real estate *Tech.*	Electronics *DFD*
3.	Utilities *DFD*	Electronics *Exports*	Electronics *Exports/DFD*	Communications *DFD*	Electronics *Exports/DFD*	Electronics *Exports*	Communications *DFD*
4.	Nonferrous Exports	Real estate *DFD*	Pharmaceuticals *DFD*	Real estate *Tech.*	Motor vehicles *Exports*	Finance and insurance *DFD*	Instruments *DFD*
5.	Instruments *DFD*	Pharmaceuticals *DFD*	Aerospace *Exports*	Finance and insurance *DFD*	Communications *DFD*	Mining *Exports*	Social services *DFD*
6.	Pharmaceuticals *DFD*	Plastics *DFD*	Finance and insurance *DFD*	Plastics *Exports*	Instruments *DFD*	Government *DFD*	Finance and insurance *DFD*
7.	Transport services *DFD*	Finance and insurance *DFD*	Social services *DFD*	Electrical machinery *Exports*	Aerospace *Tech*	Pharmaceuticals *DFD*	Trade *DFD*
8.	Mining *Exports*	Communications *DFD*	Utilities *DFD*	Motor vehicles *Exports*	Real estate *DFD*	Communications *DFD*	Real estate *DFD*
9.	Agriculture *DFD/Exports*	Trade *DFD*	Instruments *Exports*	Transport services *Exports*	Government *DFD*	Utilities *DFD*	Plastics *DFD*
10.	Electronics *DFD*	Wood *Exports*	Government *DFD*	Social services *DFD*	Plastics *DFD*	Plastics *DFD*	Aerospace *DFD*

Tech. (technical change), *DFD* (domestic final demand) and *Exports* refer to the primary factor promoting growth in a particular industry.
Source: OECD, STAN input-output database.

RELIGION AND MYTHOLOGY

GODS OF MYTHOLOGY

Principal Greek gods

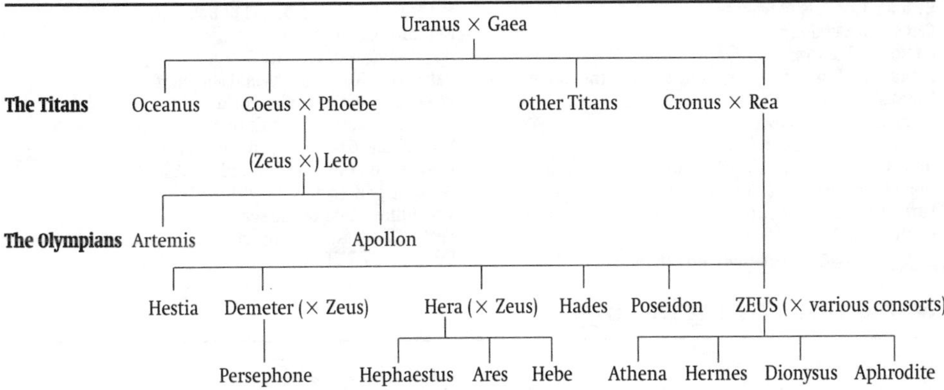

Greek gods of mythology

Aeolus God of the winds
Aphrodite Goddess of love, beauty and, procreation
Apollo God of prophecy, poetry, music, archery, and healing
Ares God of war
Artemis Goddess of the moon, hunting, and fertility
Athene Goddess of wisdom; protectress of Athens
Boreas God of the north wind
Cronus Father of Zeus
Cybele Goddess of fertility, and the mountains
Demeter Goddess of fruit, crops and vegetation
Dionysus God of wine
Eros God of love
Gaea Goddess of the earth
Hades God of the underworld
Hebe Goddess of youth
Hecate Goddess of magic, ghosts, and witchcraft
Helios God of the sun
Hephaestus God of fire
Hera Goddess of marriage and women; queen of heaven
Hermes God of science and commerce; messenger of the gods
Hestia Goddess of the hearth
Iris Goddess of the rainbow; messenger of the gods
Morpheus God of dreams
Nemesis Goddess of vengeance
Nereus Sea god
Nike Goddess of victory
Oceanus Sea god
Pan God of pastures, forests, flocks, and herds
Persephone Goddess of the underworld
Poseidon God of the sea
Rhea Mother of the gods
Selene Moon goddess
Uranus God of the sky
Zeus Overlord of the Olympian gods and goddesses; lord of heaven

Principal Roman gods

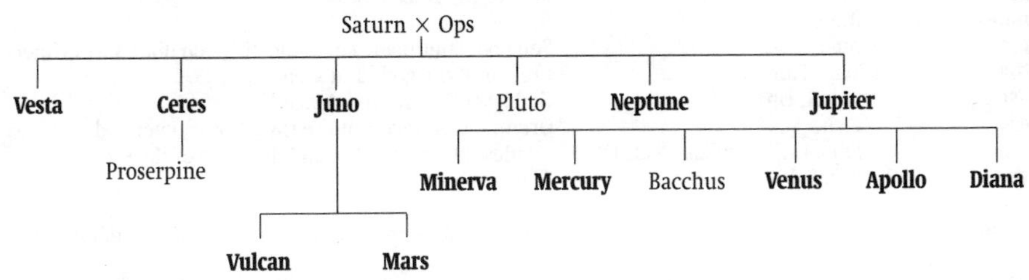

The 12 major gods of Olympus are shown in bold type. Bacchus in some accounts supplants Vesta. Pluto and Proserpine are gods of the Underworld.

Roman gods of mythology

Apollo God of the sun, music, poetry, prophecy, and healing
Bacchus God of wine
Bellona Goddess of war
Ceres Corn goddess
Cupid God of love
Diana Goddess of fertility, hunting, and the moon
Faunus God of prophecy
Flora Goddess of flowers
Janus God of gates and doors
Juno Goddess of marriage and women
Jupiter Supreme god; lord of heaven
Lares Gods of the household and state
Libitina Goddess of funerals
Maia Goddess of growth and increase
Mars God of war
Mercury Messenger god; also god of commerce
Minerva Goddess of wisdom, the arts, and trades
Mithras The sun god; god of light
Neptune God of the sea
Ops Goddess of fertility
Pales Goddess of flocks and shepherds
Pluto God of the underworld
Pomona Goddess of fruit trees and fruit
Proserpine Goddess of the underworld
Saturn God of seed time and harvest
Venus Goddess of beauty and love
Vertumnus God of the seasons
Vesta Goddess of the hearth
Vulcan God of fire

Norse gods of mythology

Aegir God of the sea
Aesir Race of warlike gods, including Odin, Thor, Tyr
Alcis Twin gods of the sky
Balder Son of Odin and favourite of the gods
Bor Father of Odin
Bragi God of poetry
Eir Goddess of medicine
Fafnir Dragon god
Fjorgynn Mother of Thor
Freya Goddess of love and fertility
Frey God of fertility, sun, and rain
Frigg Goddess of married love; wife of Odin
Gefion Goddess who received virgins after death
Heimdall Warden of the gods
Hel Goddess of death; Queen of Niflheim, the land of mists
Hermod Son of Odin
Hoenir Companion to Odin and Loki
Hoder Blind god who killed Balder
Idunn Guardian goddess of the golden apples of youth; wife of Bragi
Kvasir God of wise utterances
Logi Fire god
Loki God of mischief
Mimir God of wisdom
Nanna Goddess wife of Balder
Nehallenia Goddess of plenty
Nerthus Goddess of earth
Njord God of ships and the sea
Norns Goddesses of destiny
Odin (Woden, Wotan) Chief of the Aesir family of gods, the 'father' god; the god of war, learning, and poetry
Otr Otter god
Ran Goddess of the sea
Sif Goddess wife of Thor
Sigyn Goddess wife of Loki
Thor (Donar) God of thunder and sky; good crops
Tyr God of battle, victory
Ull God of the hunt
Valkyries Female helpers of the gods of war
Vanir Race of benevolent gods, including Njord, Frey, Freya
Vidar Slayer of the wolf, Fenvir
Vor Goddess of truth
Weland (Volundr, Weiland, Wayland) Craftsman god

Egyptian gods

	Alternative names	
Amun	Ammon, Amen, Amon	King of the gods
Anubis	Anpu	God of the dead
Aton	Aten	Sun god, later made chief and only god (for a short time)
Atum	Tem, Tum	Creator of the gods and men
Bast	Bastet, Ubasti	Goddess of music and dance
Bes	Bisu	Originally protector of the royal house, later god of recreation
Buto	Edjo, Udjo, Wadjet, Wadjit	Goddess of Lower Egypt and defender of the King
Geb	Keb, Seb	God of the earth
Hapi	Hap, Hep, Apis	God of the Nile
Hathor	Athyr	Originally a personification of the sky, also goddess of love and festivity
Horus	Hor	Originally the god of Lower Egypt, later identified with the reigning King
Isis	Aset, Eset	Queen of the gods
Khenty-Imentiu	Khenti-Amentiu	Warrior god, god of the underworld before Osiris
Khnum	Khnemu	God of the cataract region, earlier associated with the underworld
Khons	Khensu, Khonsu, Chons	Moon god

	Alternative names	
Ma'at	Mayet	Goddess of law, truth, and justice
Min		God of fertility and harvest
Mont	Mentu, Month	War god of Upper Egypt, also lord of the sky with Re
Nefertum	Nefertem, Nefertemu	God of the lotus
Neith	Neit	Goddess of the loom and war
Nekhbet	Nekhebet	Protectress of childbirth
Nut	Neuth, Nuit	Goddess of the sky
Osiris	Usire	Originally fertility god, later supreme god, king of the underworld
Ptah	Phtah	God of fertility, creator of the universe
Re	Phra, Ra	King of the gods, chief state god
Sati	Satet, Satis	Goddess of the inundation and of fertility
Seker	Sokar, Sokaris	God of darkness and decay
Seshat	Sesheta	Goddess of writing and history
Shu		God of light and supporter of the sky
Taurt	Apet, Opet, Tawaret, Thoueris	Goddess of maternity
Thoth	Djhowtey	Moon god

MODERN RELIGIONS

Religion	*Branch/ denomination*	*Sacred texts*	*State religion in*	*Estimated no. of adherents (worldwide)*
Baha'ism		Kitabal-Aqdas, Haft Wadi, Bayan, al-Kalimat al-Maknnah		5 402 000
Buddhism	Therevada Mahayana Tantrism	Tripitaka	Bhutan, Cambodia, Thailand	309 000 000
Christianity	Anglican	Bible	UK (England)	1 783 660 000
	Baptist			
	Church of Christ			
	Lutheran		Denmark, Iceland, Norway, Sweden	
	Methodist			
	Mormon	Book of Mormon		
	Orthodox		Greece	
	Pentecostal			
	Presbyterian		UK (Scotland)	
	Roman Catholic		Argentina, Bolivia, Costa Rica, Dominican Republic, Malta, Paraguay, Peru	
	Unitarian			
Confucianism		The Analects, Su Ching, Shi Ching, Li Chi, I Ching, Lu		5 750 000
Hinduism	Vishnu Shiva Shakti	Rigveda, Yajurveda, Samaveda, Atharveda	Nepal	719 269 000
Islam (Muslim)	Sunni Shi'ah Sufi Ismaili	Koran, Hadith	Afghanistan, Algeria, Bahrain, Bangladesh Comoros, Egypt, Iran, Iraq, Jordan, Kuwait, Libya, Malaysia, Maldives, Mauritania, Morocco, Oman, Pakistan, Qatar, Saudi Arabia, Somalia, Sudan, Tunisia, United Arab Emirates, Yemen	950 726 000
Jainism	Digambara Swetabara	Siddhanta, Pakrit texts		3 724 000
Judaism		Torah, Talmud		17 615 000
Sikhism		Guru Granth Sahib (Adi Granth)		18 460 500
Shintoism		Kojiki, Nohon Shoki		3 162 800
Taoism	Tao Te Ching			190 000 000

Books of the Bible

Old Testament
Law (Pentateuch)
Genesis
Exodus
Leviticus
Numbers
Deuteronomy

Prophets
(FORMER)
Joshua
Judges
Samuel 1 & 2
Kings 1& 2

(LATTER)
Isaiah
Jeremiah
Ezekiel
Book of twelve prophets (Hosea, Joel, Amos, Obadiah, Jonah, Micah, Nahum, Habakkuk, Zephaniah, Haggai, Zechariah, Malachi)

Writings
Psalms
Proverbs
Job
Song of Songs
Ruth
Lamentations
Ecclesiastes
Esther
Daniel
Ezra
Nehemiah
Chronicles 1 & 2

New Testament
Gospels (Matthew, Mark, Luke, John)
Acts of the Apostles
13 Letters attributed to Paul (Romans, Corinthians 1 & 2, Galatians, Ephesians, Philippians, Colossians, Thessalonians 1 & 2, Timothy 1 & 2, Titus, Philemon)
Letter to the Hebrews
7 General or 'Catholic' letters (James, Peter 1 & 2, John 1, 2 & 3, Jude)
Book of Revelation

Apocrypha
Baruch
Additions to the Book of Daniel
Book of Ecclesiasticus
Additions to the Book of Esther
Books of Esdras
Letter of Jeremiah
Book of Judith
Books of the Maccabees
Book of Tobit (Tobias)
Wisdom of Solomon

The Old Testament Apocrypha are a collection of Jewish writings found in the Greek version of the Hebrew bible, but not found in the Hebrew bible itself. Roman Catholics consider them as inspired and authoritative, and deuterocanonical, while Protestants attribute less authority to them.

New Testament Apocrypha are Christian documents similar in title, form, or content to many New Testament works, being called Gospels, Acts, Epistles, or Apocalypses, but are not widely accepted as canonical.

Christian religious vestments

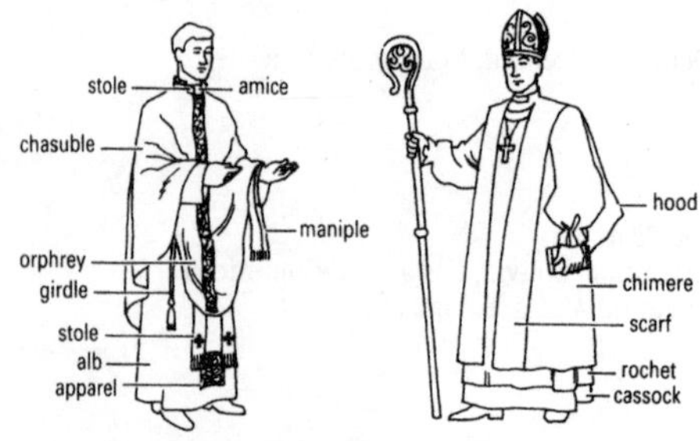

alb A long white garment reaching to the ankles; derived from an ancient tunic.
amice A linen square worn round the back to protect the other vestments; formerly a neckcloth.
apparels Ornamental panels at the foot of the alb, front and back, and on the amice.
cassock The long black gown worn under other vestments; formerly, the daily working costume of the clergy.
chasuble Outer sleeveless vestment worn by a priest or bishop when celebrating Holy Communion; derived from the commonest outdoor garment of classical times.
chimere Worn by bishops over the rochet; of black or scarlet, open in front.
cope In the pre-Christian era, a long cloak; now a costly embroidered vestment, semi-circular in shape, worn by bishops and priests on special occasions.
cotta Similar to the surplice, but shorter, especially in the sleeves; sometimes used by clergy and servers in place of the surplice.
girdle Cord worn about the waist.
hood Worn by clergy at choir offices; a mediaeval head-dress, now worn hanging down the back; denotes a university degree.
maniple Worn over the left arm by bishops, priests, and deacons at the Eucharist; originally a napkin.
orphreys The embroidered strips, customarily cross-shaped, on a chasuble.
rochet Worn by bishops, similar to an alb, but used without girdle or apparels.
stole Once a napkin or towel carried by servants on the left shoulder; now folded and narrow, worn over both shoulders.
surplice Of white linen, reaching to the knees; worn by choir and servers as well as clergy.

Movable Christian feasts, 1990–200

Year	*Ash Wednesday*	*Easter*	*Ascension*	*Whit Sunday*[a]	*Sundays after Trinity*	*First Sunday in Advent*	*Trinity Sunday*	*Corpus Christi*
1990	28 Feb	15 Apr	24 May	3 Jun	24	2 Dec	10 Jun	14 Jun
1991	13 Feb	31 Mar	9 May	19 May	26	1 Dec	26 May	30 May
1992	4 Mar	19 Apr	28 May	7 Jun	23	29 Nov	14 Jun	18 Jun
1993	24 Feb	11 Apr	20 May	30 May	24	28 Nov	6 Jun	10 Jun
1994	16 Feb	3 Apr	12 May	22 May	25	27 Nov	29 May	2 Jun
1995	1 Mar	16 Apr	25 May	4 Jun	24	3 Dec	11 Jun	15 Jun
1996	21 Feb	7 Apr	16 May	26 May	25	1 Dec	2 Jun	6 Jun
1997	12 Feb	30 Mar	8 May	18 May	26	30 Nov	25 May	29 May
1998	25 Feb	12 Apr	21 May	31 May	24	29 Nov	7 Jun	11 Jun
1999	17 Feb	4 Apr	13 May	23 May	25	28 Nov	30 May	3 Jun
2000	8 Mar	23 Apr	1 Jun	11 Jun	23	3 Dec	18 Jun	22 Jun

Ash Wednesday, the first day of Lent, can fall at the earliest on 4 February and at the latest on 10 March.

Palm (Passion) Sunday is the Sunday before Easter; Good Friday is the Friday before Easter; Holy Saturday (often referred to as Easter Saturday) is the Saturday before Easter; Easter Saturday, in traditional usage, is the Saturday following Easter.

Easter Day can fall at the earliest on 22 March at the latest on 25 April. Ascension Day can fall at the earliest on 30 April and at the latest on 3 June. Whit Sunday can fall at the earliest on 10 May and at the latest on 13 June. There are not less than 22 and not more than 27 Sundays after Trinity. The first Sunday of Advent is the Sunday nearest to 30 November.

[a] Whit Sunday commemorates the day of Pentecost.

Major immovable Christian feasts

Jan 1	Solemenity of Mary, Mother of God
Jan 6	Epiphany
Jan 7	Christmas Day (Eastern Orthodox)[a]
Jan 11	Baptism of Jesus
Jan 25	Conversion of Apostle Paul
Feb 2	Presentation of Jesus (Candlemas Day)
Feb 22	The Chair of Peter, Apostle
Mar 25	Annunciation of the Virgin Mary
Jun 24	Birth of John the Baptist
Aug 6	Transfiguration
Aug 15	Assumption of the Virgin Mary
Aug 22	Queenship of Mary
Sep 8	Birthday of the Virgin Mary
Sep 14	Exaltation of the Holy Cross
Oct 2	Guardian Angels
Nov 1	All Saints
Nov 2	All Souls
Nov 9	Dedication of the Lateran Basilica
Nov 21	Presentation of the Virgin Mary
Dec 8	Immaculate Conception
Dec 25	Christmas Day
Dec 28	Holy Innocents

[a] Fixed feasts in the Julian Calendar fall 13 days later than the Gregorian Calendar date.

The dates of Easter, 1900–2099

	0	1	2	3	4	5	6	7	8	9
1900	15	7	**30**	12	3	23	15	**31**	19	11
1910	**27**	16	7	**23**	12	4	23	8	**31**	20
1920	4	**27**	16	1	20	12	4	17	8	**31**
1930	20	5	**27**	16	1	21	12	**28**	17	9
1940	**24**	13	5	25	9	1	21	6	**28**	17
1950	9	**25**	13	5	18	10	1	21	6	**29**
1960	17	2	22	14	**29**	18	10	**26**	14	6
1970	**29**	11	2	22	14	**30**	18	10	**26**	15
1980	6	19	11	3	22	7	**30**	19	3	**26**
1990	15	**31**	19	11	3	16	7	**30**	12	4
2000	23	15	**31**	20	11	27	16	8	**23**	12
2010	4	24	8	**31**	20	5	**27**	16	1	21
2020	12	4	17	9	**31**	20	5	**28**	16	1
2030	21	13	**28**	17	9	**25**	13	5	25	10
2040	1	21	6	**29**	17	9	**25**	14	5	18
2050	10	2	21	6	**29**	18	2	22	14	**30**
2060	18	10	**26**	15	6	**29**	11	3	22	14
2070	**30**	19	10	**26**	15	7	19	11	3	23
2080	7	**30**	19	4	**26**	15	**31**	20	11	3
2090	16	8	**30**	12	4	24	15	**31**	20	12

Numbers in bold type signify Easter falls in the month of April.

Popes

Antipope refers to a pontiff set up in opposition to one asserted to be canonically chosen.

until c. 64	Peter
c. 64–c. 76	Linus
c. 76–c. 90	Anacletus
c. 90–c. 99	Clement I
c. 99–c. 105	Evaristus
c. 105–c. 117	Alexander I
c. 117–c. 127	Sixtus I
c. 127–c. 137	Telesphorus
c. 137–c. 140	Hyginus
c. 140–c. 154	Pius I
c. 154–c. 166	Anicetus
c. 166–c. 175	Soter
175–89	Eleutherius
189–98	Victor I
198–217	Zephyrinus
217–22	Callistus I
217–c. 235	Hippolytus *Antipope*
222–30	Urban I
230–5	Pontian
235–6	Anterus
236–50	Fabian
251–3	Cornelius
251–c. 258	Novatian *Antipope*
253–4	Lucius I
254–7	Stephen I
257–8	Sixtus II
259–68	Dionysius
269–74	Felix I
275–83	Eutychianus
283–96	Caius
296–304	Marcellinus
308–9	Marcellus I
310	Eusebius
311–14	Miltiades
314–35	Sylvester I
336	Mark
337–52	Julius I
352–66	Liberius
355–65	Felix II *Antipope*
366–84	Damasus I
366–7	Ursinus *Antipope*
384–99	Siricius
399–401	Anastasius I
402–17	Innocent I
417–18	Zosimus
418–22	Boniface I
418–19	Eulalius *Antipope*
422–32	Celestine I
432–40	Sixtus III
440–61	Leo I 'the Great'
461–8	Hilarus
468–83	Simplicius
483–92	Felix III (II)
492–6	Gelasius I
496–8	Anastasius II
498–514	Symmachus
498	Laurentius *Antipope*
501–5	
514–23	Hormisdas
523–6	John I
526–30	Felix IV (III)
530–2	Boniface II
530	Dioscorus *Antipope*

533–5	John II
535–6	Agapetus I
536–7	Silverius
537–55	Vigilius
556–61	Pelagius I
561–74	John III
575–9	Benedict I
579–90	Pelagius II
590–604	Gregory I 'the Great'
604–6	Sabinianus
607	Boniface III
608–15	Boniface IV
615–18	Deusdedit (Adeodatus I)
619–25	Boniface V
625–38	Honorius I
640	Severinus
640–2	John IV
642–9	Theodore I
649–55	Martin I
654–7	Eugenius I[a]
657–72	Vitalian
672–6	Adeodatus II
676–8	Donus
678–81	Agatho
682–3	Leo II
684–5	Benedict II
685–6	John V
686–7	Cono
687	Theodore *Antipope*
687–92	Paschal *Antipope*
687–701	Sergius I
701–5	John VI
705–7	John VII
708	Sisinnius
708–15	Constantine
715–31	Gregory II
731–41	Gregory III
741–52	Zacharias
752	Stephen II (not consecrated)
752–7	Stephen II (III)
757–67	Paul I
767–9	Constantine II *Antipope*
768	Philip *Antipope*
768–72	Stephen III (IV)
772–95	Adrian I
795–816	Leo III
816–17	Stephen IV (V)
817–24	Paschal I
824–7	Eugenius II
827	Valentine
827–44	Gregory IV
844	John *Antipope*
844–7	Sergius II
847–55	Leo IV
855–8	Benedict III
855	Anastasius Bibliothecarius *Antipope*
858–67	Nicholas I 'the Great'
867–72	Adrian II
872–82	John VIII
882–4	Marinus I
884–5	Adrian III

885–91	Stephen V (VI)
891–6	Formosus
896	Boniface VI
896–7	Stephen VI (VII)
897	Romanus
897	Theodore II
898–900	John IX
900–3	Benedict IV
903	Leo V
903–4	Christopher *Antipope*
904–11	Sergius III
911–13	Anastasius III
913–14	Lando
914–28	John X
928	Leo VI
928–31	Stephen VII (VIII)
931–5	John XI
936–9	Leo VII
939–42	Stephen IX
942–6	Marinus II
946–55	Agapetus II
955–64	John XII
963–5	Leo VIII
964–6	Benedict V
965–72	John XIII
973–4	Benedict VI
974	Boniface VII *Antipope*
984–5	
974–83	Benedict VII
983–4	John XIV
985–96	John XV
996–9	Gregory V
997–8	John XVI *Antipope*
999–1003	Sylvester II
1003	John XVII
1004–9	John XVIII
1009–12	Sergius IV
1012–24	Benedict VIII
1012	Gregory *Antipope*
1024–32	John XIX
1032–44	Benedict IX
1045	Sylvester III
1045	Benedict IX (second reign)
1045–6	Gregory VI
1046–7	Clement II
1047–8	Benedict IX (third reign)
1048	Damasus II (Poppo)
1048–54	Leo IX (Bruno of Toul)
1055–7	Victor II (Gebhard of Hirschberg)
1057–8	Stephen IX (X) (Frederick of Lorraine)
1058–9	Benedict X (John of Tusculum) *Antipope*
1059–61	Nicholas II (Gerard of Burgundy)
1061–73	Alexander II (Anselm of Lucca)
1061–72	Honorius II (Peter Cadalus) *Antipope*
1073–85	Gregory VII (St Hilderbrand)

1080 1084–1100 Clement III (Guibert of Ravenna) *Antipope*
1086–7 Victor III (Desidenus)
1088–99 Urban II (Odo of Chatillon)
1099–1118 Paschal II (Raneiro da Bieda)
1100–2 Theodoric *Antipope*
1102 Albert *Antipope*
1105–11 Sylvester IV *Antipope*
1118–19 Gelasius II (John of Gaeta)
1118–21 Gregory VIII (Maurice of Braga) *Antipope*
1119–24 Callistus II (Guy of Burgundy)
1124–30 Honorius II (Lamberto dei Fagnani)
1124 Celestine II *Antipope*
1130–43 Innocent II (Gregory Parareschi)
1130–8 Anacletus II *Antipope*
1138 Victor IV[b] *Antipope*
1143–4 Celestine II (Guido di Castello)
1144-5 Lucius II (Gherardo Caccianemici)
1145–53 Eugenius III (Bernardo Paganelli)
1153–4 Anastasius IV (Corrado della Subarra)
1154–9 Adrian IV (Nicholas Breakspear)
1159–81 Alexander III (Orlando Bandinelli)
1159–64 Victor IV[b] (Ottaviano di Monticelli) *Antipope*
1164–8 Paschal III (Guido of Crema) *Antipope*
1168–78 Callistus III (John of Struma) *Antipope*
1179–80 Innocent III (Lando da Sessa)
1181–5 Lucius III (Ubaldo Allucingoli)
1185–7 Urban III (Uberto Crivelli)
1187 Gregory VIII (Alberto di Morra)
1187–91 Clement III (Paolo Scolari)
1191–8 Celestine III (Giacinto Boboni-Orsini)
1198–1216 Innocent III (Lotario de'Conti)
1216–27 Honorius III (Cancio Savelli)
1227–41 Gregory IX (Ugolino di Segni)
1241 Celestine IV (Goffredo Castiglione)
1243–54 Innocent IV (Sinibaldo de' Fieschi)
1254–61 Alexander IV (Rinaldo di Segni)
1261–4 Urban IV (Jacques Pantaléon)
1265–8 Clement IV (Guy le Gros Foulques)
1271–6 Gregory X (Tebaldo Visconti)
1276 Innocent V (Pierre de Champagni)
1276 Adrian V (Ottobono Fieschi)
1276–7 John XXI[c] (Pietro Rebuli-Giuliani)
1277–80 Nicholas III (Giovanni Gaetano Orsini)
1281–5 Martin IV (Simon de Brie)
1285–7 Honorius IV (Giacomo Savelli)
1288–92 Nicholas IV (Girolamo Masci)
1294 Celestine V (Pietro di Morrone)
1294–1303 Boniface VIII (Benedetto Castani)
1303–4 Benedict XI (Niccolo Boccasini)
1305–14 Clement V (Raymond Bertrand de Got)
1316–34 John XXII (Jacques Duèse)
1328–30 Nicholas V (Pietro Rainalducci) *Antipope*
1334–42 Benedict XII (Jacques Fournier)
1342–52 Clement VI (Pierre Roger de Beaufort)
1352–62 Innocent VI (Étienne Aubert)
1362–70 Urban V (Guillaume de Grimoard)
1370–8 Gregory XI (Pierre Roger de Beaufort)
1378–89 Urban VI (Bartolomeo Prignano)
1378–94 Clement VII (Robert of Geneva) *Antipope*
1389–1404 Boniface IX (Pietro Tomacelli)
1394–1423 Benedict XIII (Pedro de Luna) *Antipope*
1404–6 Innocent VII (Cosmato de' Migliorati)
1406–15 Gregory XII (Angelo Correr)
1409–10 Alexander V (Petros Philargi) *Antipope*
1410–15 John XXIII (Baldassare Cossa) *Antipope*
1417–31 Martin V (Oddone Colonna)
1423–9 Clement VIII (Gil Sanchez Muñoz) *Antipope*
1425–30 Benedict XIV (Bernard Garnier) *Antipope*
1431–47 Eugenius IV (Gabriele Condulmer)
1439–49 Felix V (Amadeus VIII of Savoy) *Antipope*
1447–55 Nicholas V (Tommaso Parentuce III)
1455–8 Callistus III (Alfonso de Borja)
1458–64 Pius II (Enea Silvio de Piccolomini)
1464–71 Paul II (Pietro Barbo)
1471–84 Sixtus IV (Francesco della Rovere)
1484–92 Innocent VIII (Giovanni Battista Cibo)
1492–1503 Alexander VI (Rodrigo Borgia)
1503 Pius III (Francesco Todoeschini-Piccolomini)
1503–13 Julius II (Giuliano della Rovere)
1513–21 Leo X (Giovanni de' Medici)
1522–3 Adrian VI (Adrian Dedel)
1523–34 Clement VII (Giulio de' Medici)
1534–49 Paul III (Allessandro Farnese)
1550–5 Julius III (Gianmaria del Monte)
1555 Marcellus II (Marcello Cervini)
1555–9 Paul IV (Giovanni Pietro Caraffa)
1559–65 Pius IV (Giovanni Angelo Medici)
1566–72 Pius V (Michele Ghislieri)
1572–85 Gregory XIII (Ugo Buoncompagni)
1585–90 Sixtus V (Felice Peretti)
1590 Urban VII (Giambattista Castagna)
1590–1 Gregory XIV (Niccolo Sfondrati)
1591 Innocent IX (Gian Antonio Facchinetti)
1592–1605 Clement VIII (Ippolito Aldobrandini)
1605 Leo XI (Alessandro de' Medici-Ottaiano)
1605–21 Paul V (Camillo Borghese)
1621–3 Gregory XV (Alessandro Ludovisi)
1623–44 Urban VIII (Maffeo Barberini)
1644–55 Innocent X (Giambattista Pamfili)
1655–67 Alexander VII (Fabio Chigi)
1667–9 Clement IX (Guilio Rospigliosi)
1670–6 Clement X (Emilio Altieri)
1676–89 Innocent XI (Benedetto Odescalchi)
1689–91 Alexander VIII (Pietro Vito Ottoboni)
1691–1700 Innocent XII (Antonio Pignatelli)
1700–21 Clement XI (Gian

Popes (continued)

	Francesco Albani)
1721–4	Innocent XIII (Michelangelo dei Conti)
1724–30	Benedict XIII (Pietro Francesco Orsini)
1730–40	Clement XII (Lorenzo Corsini)
1740–58	Benedict XIV (Prospero Lambertini)
1758–69	Clement XIII (Carlo Rezzonico)
1769–74	Clement XIV (Lorenzo Ganganelli)
1775–99	Pius VI (Giovanni Angelo Braschi)
1800–23	Pius VII (Luigi Barnaba Chiaramonti)
1823–9	Leo XII (Annibale della Genga)
1829–30	Pius VIII (Francesco Saveno Castiglioni)
1831–46	Gregory XVI (Bartolomeo Alberto Cappellari)
1846–78	Pius IX (Giovanni Maria Mastai Ferretti)
1878–1903	Leo XIII (Vincenzo Gioacchino Pecci)
1903–14	Pius X (Giuseppe Sarto)
1914–22	Benedict XV (Giacomo della Chiesa)
1922–39	Pius XI (Achille Ratti)
1939–58	Pius XII (Eugenio Pacelli)
1958–63	John XXIII (Angelo Giuseppe Roncalli)
1963–78	Paul VI (Giovanni Battista Montini)
1978	John Paul I (Albino Luciani)
1978–	John Paul II (Karol Jozef Wojtyla)

[a] Elected during the banishment of Martin 1 [b] Different individuals [c] There was no John XX

Holy orders

Major orders Bishop, Priest, Deacon, (Sub-deacon)
Minor orders Porter, Lector, Exorcist, Acolyte

In the Roman Catholic church there are now only the orders of Bishop, Priest, Deacon and the ministries of acolyte and lector, following the *motu proprio* of Pope Paul VI, 1973.

Saints' days

The official recognition of Saints, and the choice of a Saint's Day, varies greatly between different branches of Christianity, calendars, and localities. Only major variations are included below, using the following abbreviations:

C Coptic *G* Greek
E Eastern *W* Western

January

1 Basil (E), Fulgentius, Telemachus
2 Basil and Gregory of Nazianzus (*W*), Macarius of Alexandria, Seraphim of Sarov
3 Geneviève
4 Angela of Foligno
5 Simeon Stylites (*W*)
7 Cedda, Lucian of Antioch (*W*), Raymond of Penyafort
8 Atticus (*E*), Gudule, Severinus
9 Hadrian the African
10 Agatho, Marcian
12 Ailred, Benedict Biscop
13 Hilary of Poitiers
14 Kentigern
15 Macarius of Egypt, Maurus, Paul of Thebes
16 Honoratus
17 Antony of Egypt
19 Wulfstan
20 Euthymius, Fabian, Sebastian
21 Agnes, Fructuosus, Maximus (*E*), Meinrad
22 Timothy (*G*), Vincent
23 Ildefonsus
24 Babylas (*W*), Francis de Sales
25 Gregory of Nazianzus (*E*)
26 Paula, Timothy and Titus, Xenophon (*E*)
27 Angela Merici
28 Ephraem Syrus (*E*), Paulinus of Nola, Thomas Aquinas
29 Gildas
31 John Bosco, Marcella

February

1 Bride, Pionius
3 Anskar, Blaise (*W*), Werburga, Simeon (*E*)
4 Gilbert of Sempringham, Isidore of Pelusium, Phileas
5 Agatha, Avitus
6 Dorothy, Paul Miki and companions, Vedast
8 Theodore (*G*), Jerome Emiliani
9 Teilo
10 Scholastica
11 Benedict of Aniane, Blaise (*E*), Caedmon, Gregory II
12 Meletius
13 Agabus (*W*), Catherine dei Ricci, Priscilla (*E*)
14 Cyril and Methodius (*W*), Valentine (*W*)
16 Flavian (*E*), Pamphilus (*E*), Valentine (*G*)
18 Bernadette (*France*), Colman, Flavian (*W*), Leo I (*E*)
20 Wulfric
21 Peter Damian
23 Polycarp
25 Ethelbert, Tarasius, Walburga
26 Alexander (*W*), Porphyrius
27 Leander
28 Oswald of York

March

1 David
2 Chad, Simplicius
3 Ailred
4 Casimir
6 Chrodegang
7 Perpetua and Felicity
8 Felix, John of God, Pontius
9 Frances of Rome, Gregory of Nyssa, Pacian
10 John Ogilvie, Macarius of Jerusalem, Simplicius
11 Constantine, Oengus, Sophronius
12 Gregory (the Great)
13 Nicephorus
14 Benedict (*E*)
15 Clement Hofbauer
17 Gertrude, Joseph of Arimathea (*W*), Patrick
18 Anselm of Lucca, Cyril of Jerusalem, Edward
19 Joseph
20 Cuthbert, John of Parma, Martin of Braga
21 Serapion of Thmuis
22 Catherine of Sweden, Nicholas of Fluë
23 Turibius de Mongrovejo
30 John Climacus

April

1 Hugh of Grenoble, Mary of Egypt (*E*), Melito
2 Francis of Paola, Mary of Egypt (*W*)
3 Richard of Chichester
4 Isidore of Seville
5 Juliana of Liège, Vincent Ferrer
7 Hegesippus, John Baptist de la Salle
8 Agabus (*E*)
10 Fulbert
11 Gemma Galgani, Guthlac, Stanislaus
12 Julius I, Zeno
13 Martin I
15 Aristarchus, Pudus (*E*), Trophimus of Ephesus
17 Agapetus (*E*), Stephen Harding
18 Mme Acarie
19 Alphege, Leo IX
21 Anastasius (*E*), Anselm, Beuno, Januarius (*E*)
22 Alexander (*C*)
23 George
24 Egbert, Fidelis of Sigmaringen, Mellitus
25 Mark, Phaebadius
27 Zita
28 Peter Chanel, Vitalis and Valeria
29 Catherine of Siena, Hugh of Cluny, Peter Martyr, Robert
30 James (the Great) (*E*), Pius V

May

1 Asaph, Joseph the Worker, Walburga
2 Athanasius
3 Phillip and James (the Less) (*W*)
4 Gotthard
5 Hilary of Arles
7 John of Beverley
8 John (*E*), Peter of Tarantaise
10 Antoninus, Comgall, John of Avila, Simon (*E*)
11 Cyril and Methodius (*E*), Mamertus
12 Epiphanius, Nereus and Achilleus, Pancras
14 Matthias (*W*)
16 Brendan, John of Nepomuk, Simon Stock
17 Robert Bellarmine, Paschal Baylon
18 John I
19 Dunstan, Ivo, Pudens (*W*), Pudentiana (*W*)
20 Bernardino of Siena
21 Helena (*E*)
22 Rita of Cascia
23 Ivo of Chartres
24 Vincent of Lérins
25 Aldhelm, Bede, Gregory VII, Mary Magdalene de Pazzi
26 Philip Neri, Quadratus
27 Augustine of Canterbury
30 Joan of Arc

June

1 Justin Martyr, Pamphilus
2 Erasmus, Marcellinus and Peter, Nicephorus (*G*), Pothinus
3 Charles Lwanga and companions, Clotilde, Kevin
4 Optatus, Petrock
5 Boniface
6 Martha (*E*), Norbert
7 Paul of Constantinople (*W*), Willibald
8 William of York
9 Columba, Cyril of Alexandria (*E*), Ephraem (*W*)
11 Barnabas, Bartholomew (*E*)
12 Leo III
13 Anthony of Padua
15 Orsisius, Vitus
17 Alban, Botulph
19 Gervasius and Protasius, Jude (*E*), Romuald
20 Alban
21 Alban of Mainz, Aloysius Gonzaga
22 John Fisher and Thomas More, Niceta, Pantaenus (*C*), Paulinus of Nola
23 Etheldreda
24 Birth of John the Baptist
25 Prosper of Aquitaine
27 Cyril of Alexandria (*W*), Ladislaus
28 Irenaeus
29 Peter and Paul
30 First Martyrs of the Church of Rome

July

1 Cosmas and Damian (*E*), Oliver Plunket
3 Anatolius, Thomas
4 Andrew of Crete (*E*), Elizabeth of Portugal, Ulrich
5 Anthony Zaccaria
6 Maria Goretti
7 Palladius, Pantaenus
8 Kilian, Aquila and Prisca (*W*)
11 Benedict (*W*), Pius I
12 John Gualbert, Veronica
13 Henry II, Mildred, Silas
14 Camillus of Lellis, Deusdedit, Nicholas of the Holy Mountain (*E*)
15 Bonaventure, Jacob of Nisibis, Swithin, Vladimir
16 Eustathius, Our Lady of Mt Carmel
17 Ennodius, Leo IV, Marcellina, Margaret (*E*), Scillitan Martyrs
18 Arnulf, Philastrius
19 Marcrina, Symmachus
20 Aurelius, Margaret (*W*)
21 Lawrence of Brindisi, Praxedes
22 Mary Magdalene
23 Apollinaris, Bridget of Sweden
25 Anne and Joachim (*E*), Christopher, James (the Great) (*W*)
26 Anne and Joachim (*W*)
27 Pantaleon
28 Innocent I, Samson, Victor I
29 Lupus, Martha (*W*), Olave
30 Peter Chrysologus, Silas (*G*)
31 Giovanni Colombini, Germanus, Joseph of Arimathea (*E*), Ignatius of Loyola

August

1 Alphonsus Liguori, Ethelwold
2 Eusebius of Vercelli, Stephen I
4 Jean-Baptise Vianney
6 Hormisdas
7 Cajetan, Sixtus II and companions
8 Dominic
9 Matthias (*G*)
10 Laurence, Oswald of Northumbria
11 Clare, Susanna
13 Maximus (*W*), Pontian and Hippolytus, Radegunde
14 Maximilian Kolbe
15 Arnulf, Tarsicius
16 Roch, Simplicianus, Stephen of Hungary
17 Hyacinth
19 John Eudes, Sebaldus
20 Bernard, Oswin, Philibert
21 Jane Frances de Chantal, Pius X
23 Rose of Lima, Sidonius Apollinaris
24 Bartholomew (*W*), Ouen
25 Joseph Calasanctius, Louis IX, Menas of Constantinople
26 Blessed Dominic of the Mother of God, Zephyrinus
27 Caesarius, Monica
28 Augustine of Hippo
29 Beheading of John the Baptist, Sabina
30 Pammachius
31 Aidan, Paulinus of Trier

September

1 Giles, Simeon Stylites (*E*)
2 John the Faster (*E*)
3 Gregory (the Great)
4 Babylas (*E*), Boniface I
5 Zacharias (*E*)
9 Peter Claver, Sergius of Antioch
10 Finnian, Nicholas of Tolentino, Pulcheria
11 Deiniol, Ethelburga, Paphnutius
13 John Chrysostom (*W*)

Saints' days (continued)

15 Catherine of Genoa, Our Lady of Sorrows
16 Cornelius, Cyprian of Carthage, Euphemia, Ninian
17 Robert Bellarmine, Hildegard, Lambert, Satyrus
19 Januarius (*W*), Theodore of Tarsus
20 Agapetus or Eustace (*W*)
21 Matthew (*W*)
23 Adamnan, Linus
25 Sergius of Rostov
26 Cosmas and Damian (*W*), Cyprian of Carthage, John (*E*)
27 Frumentius (*W*), Vincent de Paul
28 Exuperius, Wenceslaus
29 Michael (*Michaelmas Day*), Gabriel and Raphael
30 Jerome, Otto

October

1 Remigius, Romanos, Teresa of the Child Jesus
2 Leodegar (Leger)
3 Teresa of Lisieux, Thomas de Cantilupe
4 Ammon, Francis of Assisi, Petronius
6 Bruno, Thomas (*G*)
9 Demetrius (*W*), Denis and companions, Dionysius of Paris, James (the Less) (*E*), John Leonardi
10 Francis Borgia, Paulinus of York
11 Atticus (*E*), Bruno (d. 965), Nectarius
12 Wilfrid
13 Edward the Confessor
14 Callistus I, Cosmas Melodus (*E*)
15 Lucian of Antioch (*E*), Teresa of Avila
16 Gall, Hedwig, Lullus, Margaret Mary Alacoque
17 Ignatius of Antioch, Victor
18 Luke
19 John de Bréboeuf and Isaac Jogues and companions, Paul of the Cross, Peter of Alcántara
21 Hilarion, Ursula
22 Abercius
23 John of Capistrano, James
24 Anthony Claret
25 Crispin and Crispinian, Forty Martyrs of England and Wales, Gaudentius
26 Demetrius (*E*)
28 Firmilian (*E*), Simon and Jude
30 Serapion of Antioch
31 Wolfgang

November

1 All Saints, Cosmas and Damian (*E*)
2 Eustace (*E*), Victorinus
3 Hubert, Malachy, Martin de Porres, Pirminius, Winifred
4 Charles Borromeo, Vitalis and Agricola
5 Elizabeth (*W*)
6 Illtyd, Leonard, Paul of Constantinople (*E*)
7 Willibrord
8 Elizabeth (*E*), Willehad
9 Simeon Metaphrastes (*E*)
10 Justus, Leo I (*W*)
11 Martin of Tours (*W*), Menas of Egypt, Theodore of Studios
12 Josaphat, Martin of Tours (*E*), Nilus the Ascetic
13 Abbo, John Chrysostom (*E*), Nicholas I
14 Dubricius, Gregory Palamas (*E*)
15 Albert the Great, Machutus
16 Edmund of Abingdon, Eucherius, Gertrude (the Great), Margaret of Scotland, Matthew (*E*)
17 Elizabeth of Hungary, Gregory Thaumaturgus, Gregory of Tours, Hugh of Lincoln
18 Odo, Romanus
19 Mechthild, Nerses
20 Edmund the Martyr
21 Gelasius
22 Cecilia
23 Amphilochius, Clement I (*W*), Columban, Felicity, Gregory of Agrigentum
25 Clement I (*E*), Mercurius, Mesrob
26 Siricius
27 Barlam and Josaphat
28 Simeon Metaphrastes
29 Cuthbert Mayne
30 Andrew, Frumentius (*G*)

December

1 Eligius
2 Chromatius
3 Francis Xavier
4 Barbara, John Damascene, Osmund
5 Clement of Alexandria, Sabas
6 Nicholas
7 Ambrose
10 Miltiades
11 Damasus, Daniel
12 Jane Frances de Chantal, Spyridon (*E*), Vicelin
13 Lucy, Odilia
14 John of the Cross, Spyridon (*W*)
16 Eusebius
18 Frumentius (*C*)
20 Ignatius of Antioch (*G*)
21 Peter Canisius, Thomas
22 Anastasia (*E*), Chrysogonus (*E*)
23 John of Kanty
26 Stephen (*W*)
27 John (*W*), Fabiola, Stephen (*E*)
29 Thomas à Becket, Trophimus of Arles
31 Sylvester

Buddhism

Founder
Prince Siddhartha Gautama (Buddha) c. 563–483 BC

Date founded
c. 500 BC India

Beliefs
'Four Noble Truths'
All life is permeated by suffering
Source of suffering is desire for existence
This cause can be eliminated
Way of doing this is by treading 'The Eightfold Path'
'The Eightfold Path' leads to 'nirvana' – ultimate state of peace

Major festivals[a]
Buddha's birth
Buddha's enlightenment
Buddha's first sermon
Buddha's death

[a]These take place on different dates in the countries in which Buddhism is practised.

Christianity

Founder
Jesus of Nazareth (Jesus Christ) c.4 BC–AD 30

Date founded
1st century AD

Beliefs
Trinity – God as three in one (Father, Son, Holy Spirit)
God as creator of universe
Original sin
God as judge
Incarnation
Redemption/Salvation
Resurrection

Confucianism

Founder
K'ung Fu-tzu (551–479 BC)

Date founded
6th century BC

Beliefs
Human beings are teachable, improvable, and perfectible
Person can shape his/her own destiny
Self-knowledge and self-realization are attainable through learning
Sense of humanity should infuse society and politics (social participation)
Ritual and tradition

Major Chinese festivals

January/February	Chinese New Year
February/March	Lantern Festival
March/April	Festival of Pure Brightness
May/June	Dragon Boat Festival
July/August	Herd Boy and Weaving Maid
August	All Souls' Festival
September	Mid-Autumn Festival
September/October	Double Ninth Festival
November/December	Winter Solstice

Hinduism

Founder
Aryan invaders of India of Vedic religion

Date founded
c. 1500 BC

Beliefs
Sacred power (Brahman) is sole reality, the creator, transformer, and preserver of everything
Hindu Trinity of Brahma, Visnu, and Siva
Authority of the Veda
Respect for life
Rebirth
Soul emancipated by the Three Margas – duty, knowledge, devotion

Major festivals
S = Sukla, 'waxing fortnight'.
K = Krishna 'waning fortnight'.

Caitra	*S*9	Ramanavami (Birthday of Lord Rama)
Asadha	*S*2	Rathayatra (Pilgrimage of the Chariot at Jagannath)
Sravana	*S*11–15	Jhulanayatra ('Swinging the Lord Krishna')
Sravana	*S*15	Rakshabandhana ('Tying on lucky threads')
Bhadrapada	*K*8	Janamashtami (Birthday of Lord Krishna)
Asvina	*S*7–10	Durga-puja (Homage to Goddess Durga) (*Bengal*)
Asvina	*S*1–10	Navaratri (Festival of 'nine nights')
Asvina	*S*15	Lakshmi-puja (Homage to Goddess Lakshmi)
Asvina	*K*15	Diwali, Dipavali ('String of Lights')
Kartikka	*S*15	Guru Nanak Jananti (Birthday of Guru Nanak)
Magha	*K*5	Sarasvati-puja (Homage to Goddess Sarasvati)
Magha	*K*13	Maha-sivaratri (Great Night of Lord Shiva)
Phalguna	*S*14	Holi (Festival of Fire)
Phalguna	*S*15	Dolayatra (Swing Festival) (*Bengal*)

Islam

Founder
Mohammed (c. 570–632 AD)

Date founded
7th century AD

Beliefs
Unity of God
God as creator and sustainer of the universe
Man superior to nature but still servant of God
Pride is cardinal sin
God always ready to pardon – repentance and redemption possible
Prophets recipients of revelations from God – they, with God, show person the 'right way'

Islam (continued)

Major festivals

1	Muharram	New Year's Day; starts on the day which celebrates Mohammed's departure from Mecca to Medina in AD 622
12	Rabi I	Birthday of Mohammed (Mawlid al-Nabi) AD 572; celebrated throughout month of Rabi I
27	Rajab	'Night of Ascent' (Laylat al-Mi'raj) of Mohammed to Heaven
1	Ramadan	Beginning of month of fasting during daylight hours
27	Ramadan	'Night of Power' (Laylat al-Qadr); sending down of the Koran to Mohammed
1	Shawwal	'Feast of breaking the Fast' ('Id al-Fitr); marks the end of Ramadan
8–13	Dhu-l-Hijja	Annual pilgrimage ceremonies at and around Mecca; month during which the great pilgrimage (Hajj) should be made
10	Dhu-l-Hijja	Feast of the Sacrifice ('Id al-Adha)

Jainism

Founder
Vardhamana Mahavira (599–527 BC)

Date founded
c. 600 BC India

Beliefs
World eternal and uncreated
All phenomena linked by chain of cause and effect
Nonviolence to other living creatures (Ahimsa)
Perfection and purification of soul leads to its emancipation and the ultimate attribute of omniscience
Soul has to pass through various stages of spiritual development before freeing itself of karmic bondages
Right conduct, right knowledge, right belief

Judaism

Founders
Abraham c. 2000 BC and Moses c. 1200 BC

Date founded
c. 2000 BC

Beliefs
Unity of God
God as teacher through instruction of Torah
God as redeemer
Resurrection
Coming of the 'Mashiah' who will establish new age in Israel

Major festivals

1–2	Tishri	Rosh Hashanah (New Year)
3	Tishri	Tzom Gedaliahu (Fast of Gedaliah)
10	Tishri	Yom Kippur (Day of Atonement)
15–21	Tishri	Sukkoth (Feast of Tabernacles)
22	Tishri	Shemini Atzeret (8th Day of the Solemn Assembly)
23	Tishri	Simhat Torah (Rejoicing of the Law)
25	Kislev–2–3 Tevet	Hanukkah (Feast of Dedication)
10	Tevet	Asara be-Tevet (Fast of 10th Tevet)
13	Adar	Taanit Esther (Fast of Esther)
14–15	Adar	Purim (Feast of Lots)
15–22	Nisan	Pesach (Passover)
5	Iyar	Israel Independence Day
6–7	Sivan	Shavuoth (Feast of Weeks)
17	Tammuz	Shiva Asar be-Tammuz (Fast of 17th Tammuz)
9	Av	Tisha be-Av (Fast of 9th Av)

The ancient tribes of Israel

Asher descended from Jacob's eighth son (Z)
Benjamin descended from Jacob's twelfth and youngest son (R)
Dan descended from Jacob's fifth son (B)
Issachar descended from Jacob's ninth or tenth son (L)
Joseph descended from Jacob's eleventh son (R)
Ephraim descended from Joseph's younger son
Manasseh descended from Joseph's elder son
Judah descended from Jacob's fourth son (L)
Levi descended from Jacob's third son (L) (No territory as it was a priestly caste)
Naphtali descended from Jacob's ninth or tenth son (B)
Reuben descended from Jacob's first son (L)
Simeon descended from Jacob's second son (L)
Zebulun descended from Jacob's sixth son (L)

B = borne by Bilhah
L = borne by Leah
R = borne by Rachel
Z = borne by Zilpal

Israel during the period of the Judges – Approximate tribal areas

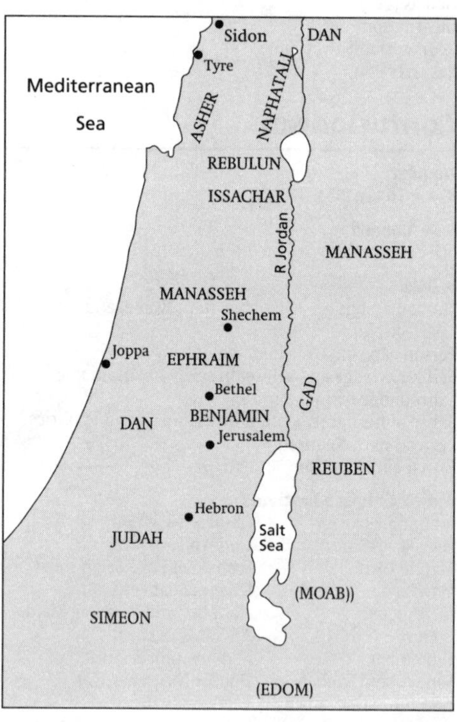

Shintoism

Founder
No founder

Date founded
6th century AD Japan

Beliefs
Polytheistic – belief in 'kami' (deities)
Sincerity arising from awareness of the divine
Spiritual and physical purification
Continuity/communion with ancestry

Major Japanese festivals

1–3	Jan	Oshogatsu (New Year)
3	Mar	Ohinamatsuri (Doll's *or* Girls' Festival)
5	May	Tango no Sekku (Boys' Festival)
7	Jul	Hoshi matsuri *or* Tanabata (Star Festival)
13–31	Jul	Obon (Buddhist All Souls)
15	Nov	Shichi-go-San (Seven-five-three age celebrations for 7 yr old girls, 5 yr old boys and 3 yr old girls)

Sikhism

Founder
Guru Nanak (1469–1539 AD)

Date founded
c. 15th century AD India

Beliefs
Unity of God
Birth, death, and rebirth
Guidance of the Guru to 'moksa' (release) and the way of God
Worship of the Adi Granth

Taoism

Founder
Lao Zi (6th century BC)

Date founded
600 BC China

Beliefs
Interaction of human society and the universe
Divine nature of sovereign
Cult of Heaven
Law of return
State of original purity
Worship of ancestors

Religious symbols

The Trinity

Equilateral triangle · Triangle in circle · Circle within triangle · Trefoil · Triquetra · Triquetra and circle · Interwoven circles

God the Father

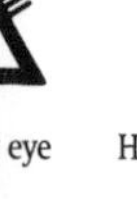

All-seeing eye · Hand of God · Hand of God · Lamb of God · Fish · Dove descending · Sevenfold flame

Old Testament

Menorah (seven branch candlestick) · Abraham · The Ten Commandments · Pentateuch (The Law) · Marked doorposts and lintel (Passover) · Twelve tribes of Israel · Star of David

Crosses

Aiguisée · Avellane · Barbée · Trefly · Canterbury · Celtic · Cercelée · Cross crosslet

Crux ansata · Entrailed · Fleurée · Globical · Graded (Calvary) · Greek · Iona · Jerusalem

Latin · Maltese · Millvine · Papal · Patée · Patée formée · Patonce · Patriarchal (or Lorraine) · Pommel or Pommée

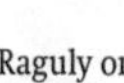

Potent · Raguly or Ragulée · Russian Orthodox · St Andrew's (Saltire) · St Peter's · Tau (St Anthony's)

Monograms

IHC (Latin form) (from Gk IHCOYC 'Jesus') · Chi Rho (from Gk XPICTOC 'Christ')

The Christian Church Year

Advent · Christmas · Epiphany · Lent · Maundy Thursday · Good Friday · Easter Day · Ascension · Pentecost

Other symbols

Ankh (Egyptian) · Yin-yang Tao symbol of harmony · Torii (shinto) · Om (Hinduism, Buddhism, Jainism; sacred syllable) · Ik-onkar (Sikhism; symbol of God) · Swastika (originally symbol of the Sun) · Yantra: Sri Cakra (wheel of fortune)

COMMUNICATIONS

Communications

TRANSPORTATION

Road

Main USA Interstate highways

Odd number Interstates run South-North; even number, West-East.

I5 San Diego–Los Angeles–Sacramento–Seattle–Vancouver, Can
I8 San Diego–Tucson
I10 Los Angeles–Phoenix–San Antonio–Houston–New Orleans–Jacksonville
I15 San Diego–Las Vegas–Salt Lake City–Great Falls
I20 Fort Worth–Dallas–Jackson–Birmingham–Atlanta–Columbia
I25 Albuquerque–Colorado Springs–Denver–Buffalo
I30 Dallas–Little Rock
I35 San Antonio–Austin–Fort Worth–Oklahoma City–Wichita–Kansas City–Des Moines–Minneapolis/St Paul–Duluth
I40 Flagstaff–Albuquerque–Oklahoma City–Little Rock–Memphis–Nashville–Greensboro
I45 Dallas–Houston
I55 New Orleans–Jackson–Memphis–St Louis–Chicago
I59 New Orleans–Birmingham–Chattanooga
I64 St Louis–Louisville–Lexington–Charleston
I65 Mobile–Birmingham–Nashville–Louisville–Indianapolis–Chicago
I70 Denver–Kansas City–St Louis–Indianapolis–Columbus–Philadelphia–Baltimore
I71 Louisville–Cincinatti–Columbus
I74 Davenport–Indianapolis–Cincinatti
I75 Tampa–Atlanta–Cincinatti–Toledo–Detroit
I78 Harrisburg–New York
I80 San Francisco–Salt Lake City–Des Moines–Cleveland–New York
I81 Knoxville–Roanoake–Syracuse
I85 Montgomery–Atlanta–Greensboro–Petersburg
I90 Seattle–Billings–Sioux Falls–Chicago–Cleveland–Boston
I94 Billings–Bismarck–Minneapolis/St Paul–Madison–Milwaukee–Chicago–Detroit
I95 Miami–Jacksonville–Richmond–Washington, DC–Baltimore–New York–Boston–Augusta

British motorways

M1 Belfast–Dungannon (N Ireland)
M1 London–Northampton–Leicester–Nottingham–Sheffield–Leeds
M2 Belfast–Randalstown (N Ireland)
M2 Strood–Faversham (Medway)
M3 London–Basingstoke–Winchester
M4 London–Reading–Newport–Cardiff–Swansea
M5 Birmingham–Bristol–Exeter
M6 Birmingham–Wolverhampton–Stoke-on-Trent–Preston–Lancaster–Carlisle
M8 Edinburgh–Glasgow–Longbank
M9 Edinburgh–Stirling
M10 M1–St Albans spur
M11 London–Cambridge
M18 Rotherham–M62 junction 35 (Goole)
M20 Swanley (London)–Folkestone
M23 Redhill–Crawley
M25 London orbital motorway
M26 Chipstead–M20 junction 3
M27 Portsmouth–Southampton–Cadnam
M32 M4–Bristol spur
M40 London–Oxford–Birmingham
M42 Birmingham–Solihull–Tamworth–Appleby Magna
M45 Watford–Dunchurch
M50 Ross-on-Wye–M5 junction 8
M53 Chester–Wallasey
M54 Telford–M6 junction 10a
M55 Fulwood–Blackpool
M56 Chester–Altringham (N Cheshire)
M57 Liverpool–Aintree
M58 Aintree–Wigan
M61 Manchester–Preston
M62 Liverpool–Manchester–Leeds–North Cave (N Humberside)
M63 Salford–Stockport
M65 Blackburn–Burnley-Colne
M66 Middleton–Ramsbottom
M67 Denton–Mottram in Langendale (Manchester ring)
M69 Leicester–Coventry
M73 M74–Glasgow spur (Maryville–Mollisburn)
M74 Millbank–Maryville
M74 Carlisle–Gretna Green
M80 Longcroft–M9 junction 9 (Haggs)
M85 M90–Perth spur (Perth–Friarton Bridge)
M90 Perth–Inverkeithing
M180 Stainforth–Elsham (S Humberside)
M181 M180 Scunthorpe spur
M271 M27–Totton spur
M275 M27–Portsmouth spur
M606 M62–Bradford spur
M621 M62–Leeds spur
M876 M80–Kincardine Bridge (Banknock-Stenhousemuir)

International E-routes (Euroroutes)

Reference and intermediate roads (class A roads) have two-digit numbers; branch, link, and connecting roads (class B roads, not listed here), have three-digit numbers.

North-South orientated reference roads have two-digit odd numbers ending in the figure 5, and increasing from west to east. East-West orientated roads have two-digit even numbers ending in the figure 0, and increasing from north to south.

Intermediate roads have two-digit odd numbers (for N-S roads) or two-digit even numbers (for E-W roads) falling within the numbers of the reference roads between which they are located.

Only a selection of the towns and cities linked by E-roads are given.

[···] indicates a sea crossing.

West-East orientation

Reference roads

E10 Narvik–Kiruna–Luleå
E20 Shannon–Dublin ··· Liverpool–Hull ··· Esbjerg–Nyborg ··· Korsør-Køge–Copenhagen ··· Malmö–Stockholm ··· Tallin–St Petersburg

International E-routes (Euroroutes) (continued)

E30 Cork–Rosslare ··· Fishguard–London–Felixstowe ··· Hook of Holland–Utrecht–Hanover–Berlin–Warsaw–Smolensk–Moscow
E40 Calais–Brussels–Aachen–Cologne–Dresden–Krakow–Kiev–Rostov na Donu
E50 Brest–Paris–Metz–Nurenberg–Prague–Mukačevo
E60 Brest–Tours–Besançon–Basle–Innsbruck–Vienna–Budapest–Bucharest–Constanţa
E70 La Coruña–Bilbao–Bordeaux–Lyon–Torino–Verona–Trieste–Zagreb–Belgrade–Bucharest–Varna
E80 Lisbon–Coimbra–Salamanca–Pau–Toulouse–Nice–Genoa–Rome–Pescara ··· Dubrovnik–Sofia–Istanbul–Erzincan–Iran
E90 Lisbon–Madrid–Barcelona ··· Mazara del Vallo–Messina ··· Reggio di Calabria–Brindisi ··· Igoumenitsa–Thessaloniki–Gelibolu ··· Lapseki–Ankara–Iraq

Intermediate roads
E06 Olderfjord–Kirkenes
E12 Mo i Rana–Umeå ··· Vaasa–Helsinki
E14 Trondheim–Sundsvall
E16 Londonderry–Belfast ··· Glasgow–Edinburgh
E18 Craigavon–Larne ··· Stranraer–Newcastle ··· Stavanger–Oslo–Stockholm–Kappelskär ··· Mariehamn ··· Turku–Helsinki–Leningrad
E22 Holyhead–Manchester–Immingham ··· Amsterdam–Hamburg–Sassnitz ··· Trelleborg–Norrköping
E24 Birmingham–Ipswich
E26 Hamburg–Berlin
E28 Berlin–Gdańsk
E32 Colchester–Harwich
E34 Antwerp–Bad Oeynhausen
E36 Berlin–Legnica
E42 Dunkirk–Aschaffenburg
E44 Le Havre–Luxembourg–Giessen
E46 Cherbourg–Liège
E48 Schweinfurt–Prague
E52 Strasbourg–Salzburg
E54 Paris–Basle–Munich
E56 Nuremberg–Sattledt
E58 Vienna–Bratislava
E62 Nantes–Geneva–Tortona
E64 Turin–Brescia
E66 Fortezza–Székesfehérvár
E68 Szeged–Braşov
E72 Bordeaux–Toulouse
E74 Nice–Alessandria
E76 Migliarino–Florence
E78 Grosseto–Fano
E82 Porto–Tordesillas
E84 Keşan–Silivri
E86 Krystalopigi–Yefira
E88 Ankara–Refahiye
E92 Igoumenitsa–Volos
E94 Corinth–Athens
E96 Izmir–Sivrihisar
E98 Topbogazi–Syria

North-South orientation

Reference roads
E05 Greenock–Birmingham–Southampton ··· Le Havre–Paris–Bordeaux–Madrid–Algeciras
E15 Inverness–Edinburgh–London–Dover ··· Calais–Paris–Lyon–Barcelona–Algeciras
E25 Hook of Holland–Luxembourg–Strasbourg–Basle–Geneva–Turin–Genoa
E35 Amsterdam–Cologne–Basle–Milan–Rome
E45 Gothenburg ··· Frederikshavn–Hamburg–Munich–Innsbruck–Bologna–Rome–Naples–Villa S Giovanni ··· Messina–Gela
E55 Kemi-Tornio–Stockholm–Helsingborg ··· Helsinger–Copenhagen–Gedser ··· Rostock–Berlin–Prague–Salzburg–Rimini–Brindisi ··· Igoumenitsa–Kalamata
E65 Malmö–Ystrad–Świnouj ście–Prague–Zagreb–Dubrovnik–Bitolj–Antirrion ··· Rion–Kalamata - Kissamos–Chania
E75 Karasjok–Helsinki ··· Gdańsk–Budapest–Belgrade–Athens ··· Chania–Sitia
E85 Černovcy–Bucharest–Alexandropouli
E95 St Petersburg–Moscow–Yalta

Intermediate roads
E01 Larne–Dublin–Rosslare ··· La Coruña–Lisbon–Seville
E03 Cherbourg–La Rochelle
E07 Pau–Zaragoza
E09 Orléans–Barcelona
E11 Vierzon–Montpellier
E13 Doncaster–London
E17 Antwerp–Beaune
E19 Amsterdam–Brussels–Paris
E21 Metz–Geneva
E23 Metz–Lausanne
E27 Belfort–Aosta
E29 Cologne–Sarreguemines
E31 Rotterdam–Ludwigshafen
E33 Parma–La Spezie
E37 Bremen–Cologne
E39 Kristiansand–Aalborg
E41 Dortmund–Altdorf
E43 Würzburg–Bellinzona
E47 Nordkap–Oslo–Copenhagen–Rødby ··· Puttgarden–Lübeck
E49 Magdeburg–Vienna
E51 Berlin–Nurenberg
E53 Plzeň–Munich
E57 Sattledt–Ljubljana
E59 Prague–Zagreb
E61 Klagenfurt–Rijeka
E63 Sodankylä–Naantali ··· Stockholm–Gothenburg
E67 Warsaw–Prague
E69 Tromsø–Tornio
E71 Košice–Budapest–Split
E73 Budapest–Metkovič
E77 Gdańsk–Budapest
E79 Oradea–Calafat ··· Vidin–Thessaloniki
E81 Halmeu–Piteşti
E83 Bjala–Sofia
E87 Tulcea–Eceabat ··· Çanakkale–Antalya
E89 Gerede–Ankara
E91 Toprakkale–Syria
E93 Orel–Odessa
E97 Trabzon–Aşkale
E99 Doğubeyazit–Ş Urfa

European road distances

Road distances between some cities, given in kilometres. To convert to statute miles, multiply number given by 0.6214.

	Athens	Barcelona	Brussels	Calais	Cherbourg	Cologne	Copenhagen	Geneva	Gibraltar	Hamburg	Hook of Holland	Lisbon	Lyons	Madrid	Marseilles	Milan	Munich	Paris	Rome	Stockholm
Barcelona	3313																			
Brussels	2963	1318																		
Calais	3175	1326	204																	
Cherbourg	3339	1294	583	460																
Cologne	2762	1498	206	409	785															
Copenhagen	3276	2218	966	1136	1545	760														
Geneva	2610	803	677	747	853	1662	1418													
Gibraltar	4485	1172	2256	2224	2047	2436	3196	1975												
Hamburg	2977	2018	597	714	1115	460	460	1118	2897											
Hook of Holland	3030	1490	172	330	731	269	269	895	2428	550										
Lisbon	4532	1304	2084	2052	1827	2290	2971	1936	676	2671	2280									
Lyons	2753	645	690	739	789	714	1458	158	1817	1159	863	1778								
Madrid	3949	636	1558	1550	1347	1764	2498	1439	698	2198	1730	668	1281							
Marseilles	2865	521	1011	1059	1101	1035	1778	425	1693	1479	1183	1762	320	1157						
Milan	2282	1014	925	1077	1209	911	1537	328	2185	1238	1098	2250	328	1724	618					
Munich	2179	1365	747	977	1160	583	1104	591	2565	3805	851	2507	724	2010	1109	331				
Paris	3000	1033	285	280	340	465	1176	513	1971	877	457	1799	471	1273	792	856	821			
Rome	817	1460	1511	1662	1794	1497	2050	995	2631	1751	1683	2700	1048	2097	1011	586	946	1476		
Stockholm	3927	2868	1616	1786	2196	1403	650	2068	3886	949	1500	3231	2108	3188	2428	2187	1754	1827	2707	
Vienna	1991	1802	1175	1381	1588	937	1455	1019	2974	1155	1205	2935	1157	2409	1363	898	428	1249	1209	2105

UK road distances

Road distances between British centres are given in statute miles, using routes recommended by the Automobile Association based on the quickest travelling time. To convert to kilometres, multiply number given by 1.6093.

	Aberdeen	Birmingham	Bristol	Cambridge	Cardiff	Dover	Edinburgh	Exeter	Glasgow	Holyhead	Hull	Leeds	Liverpool	Manchester	Newcastle	Norwich	Nottingham	Oxford	Penzance	Plymouth	Shrewsbury	Southampton	Stranraer	York
Birmingham	430																							
Bristol	511	85																						
Cambridge	468	101	156																					
Cardiff	532	107	45	191																				
Dover	591	202	198	121	234																			
Edinburgh	130	293	373	337	395	457																		
Exeter	584	157	81	233	119	248	446																	
Glasgow	149	291	372	349	393	490	45	444																
Holyhead	457	151	232	246	209	347	325	305	319															
Hull	361	136	227	157	246	278	229	297	245	215														
Leeds	336	115	216	143	236	265	205	288	215	163	59													
Liverpool	361	98	178	195	200	295	222	250	220	104	126	72												
Manchester	354	88	167	153	188	283	218	239	214	123	97	43	34											
Newcastle	239	198	291	224	311	348	107	361	150	260	121	91	170	141										
Norwich	501	161	217	62	252	167	365	295	379	309	153	173	232	183	258									
Nottingham	402	59	151	82	170	202	268	222	281	174	92	73	107	71	156	123								
Oxford	497	63	74	82	109	148	361	152	354	218	188	171	164	153	253	144	104							
Penzance	696	272	195	346	232	362	561	112	559	419	411	401	366	355	477	407	265	265						
Plymouth	624	199	125	275	164	290	488	45	486	347	341	328	294	281	410	336	328	193	78					
Shrewsbury	412	48	128	142	110	243	276	201	272	104	164	116	64	69	216	205	724	113	315	242				
Southampton	571	128	75	133	123	155	437	114	436	296	253	235	241	227	319	192	471	67	227	155	190			
Stranraer	241	307	386	361	406	503	130	457	88	332	259	232	234	226	164	393	1048	371	572	502	287	447		
York	325	128	221	153	241	274	191	291	208	190	38	24	100	71	83	185	2108	185	406	340	144	252	228	
London	543	118	119	60	155	77	405	170	402	263	215	196	210	199	280	115	1157	56	283	215	162	76	419	209

International car index marks

A	Austria
ADN	former Yemen PDR
AFG	Afghanistan
AL	Albania
AND	Andorra
AUS	Australia [a]
B	Belgium
BD	Bangladesh [a]
BDS	Barbados [a]
BG	Bulgaria
BH	Belize
BR	Brazil
BRN	Bahrain
BRU	Brunei [a]
BS	Bahamas [a]
BUR	Myanmar (Burma)
C	Cuba
CDN	Canada
CH	Switzerland
CI	Côte d'Ivoire
CL	Sri Lanka [a]
CO	Colombia
CR	Costa Rica
CS	Czechoslovakia
CY	Cyprus [a]
D	Germany
DDR	former E Germany
DK	Denmark
DOM	Dominican Republic
DY	Benin
DZ	Algeria
E	Spain
EAK	Kenya [a]
EAT	Tanzania [a]
EAU	Uganda [a]
EAZ	Tanzania [a]
EC	Ecuador
ES	El Salvador
ET	Egypt
ETH	Ethiopia
F	France
FJI	Fiji [a]
FL	Liechtenstein
FR	Faroe Is
GB	UK [a]
GBA	Alderney [a]
GBG	Guernsey [a]
GBJ	Jersey [a]
GBM	Isle of Man [a]
GBZ	Gibraltar
GCA	Guatemala
GH	Ghana
GR	Greece
GUY	Guyana [a]
H	Hungary
HK	Hong Kong [a]
HKJ	Jordan
I	Italy
IL	Israel
IND	India [a]
IR	Iran
IRL	Ireland [a]
IRQ	Iraq
IS	Iceland
J	Japan [a]
JA	Jamaica [a]
K	Kampuchea
KWT	Kuwait
L	Luxembourg
LAO	Lao PDR
LAR	Libya
LB	Liberia
LS	Lesotho [a]
M	Malta [a]
MA	Morocco
MAL	Malaysia [a]
MC	Monaco
MEX	Mexico
MS	Mauritius [a]
MW	Malawi [a]
N	Norway
NA	Netherlands Antilles
NIC	Nicaragua
NL	Netherlands
NZ	New Zealand [a]
P	Portugal
PA	Panama
PAK	Pakistan [a]
PE	Peru
PL	Poland
PNG	Papua New Guinea [a]
PY	Paraguay
RA	Argentina
RB	Botswana [a]
RC	Taiwan
RCA	Central African Republic
RCB	Congo
RCH	Chile
RH	Haiti
RI	Indonesia [a]
RIM	Mauritania
RL	Lebanon
RM	Madagascar
RMM	Mali
RN	Niger
RO	Romania
ROK	Korea, Republic of
ROU	Uraguay
RP	Philippines
RSM	San Marino
RU	Burundi
RWA	Rwanda
S	Sweden
SD	Swaziland [a]
SF	Finland
SGP	Singapore [a]
SME	Suriname [a]
SN	Senegal
SU	former USSR
SWA	Namibia [a]
SY	Seychelles [a]
SYR	Syria
T	Thailand [a]
TG	Togo
TN	Tunisia
TR	Turkey
TT	Trinidad and Tobago [a]
USA	USA
V	Vatican City
VN	Vietnam
WAG	Gambia
WAL	Sierra Leone
WAN	Nigeria
WD	Dominica [a]
WG	Grenada [a]
WL	St Lucia [a]
WS	W Samoa
WV	St Vincent and the Grenadines [a]
YU	Yugoslavia
YV	Venezuela
Z	Zambia [a]
ZA	South Africa [a]
ZRE	Zaïre
ZW	Zimbabwe [a]

[a] Countries in which the rule of the road is drive on the left; in other countries, drive on the right.

British car index marks

AA	Bournemouth
AB	Worcester
AC	Coventry
AD	Gloucester
AE	Bristol
AF	Truro
AG	Hull
AH	Norwich
AJ	Middlesbrough
AK	Sheffield
AL	Nottingham
AM	Swindon
AN	Reading
AO	Carlisle
AP	Brighton
AR	Chelmsford
AS	Inverness
AT	Hull
AU	Nottingham
AV	Peterborough
AW	Shrewsbury
AX	Cardiff
AY	Leicester
BA	Manchester
BB	Newcastle upon Tyne
BC	Leicester
BD	Northampton
BE	Lincoln
BF	Stoke-on-Trent
BG	Liverpool
BH	Luton
BJ	Ipswich
BK	Portsmouth
BL	Reading
BM	Luton
BN	Manchester
BO	Cardiff
BP	Portsmouth
BR	Newcastle upon Tyne
BS	Inverness
BT	Leeds
BU	Manchester
BV	Preston
BW	Oxford
BX	Haverfordwest
BY	London NW
CA	Chester
CB	Manchester
CC	Bangor
CD	Brighton
CE	Peterborough
CF	Reading
CG	Bournemouth
CH	Nottingham
CJ	Gloucester
CK	Preston
CL	Norwich
CM	Liverpool
CN	Newcastle upon Tyne
CO	Exeter
CP	Huddersfield
CR	Portsmouth
CS	Glasgow
CT	Lincoln
CU	Newcastle upon Tyne
CV	Truro
CW	Preston
CX	Huddersfield
CY	Swansea
DA	Birmingham
DB	Manchester
DC	Middlesbrough
DD	Gloucester
DE	Haverfordwest
DF	Gloucester
DG	Gloucester
DH	Dudley
DJ	Liverpool
DK	Manchester
DL	Portsmouth
DM	Chester
DN	Leeds
DO	Lincoln
DP	Reading
DR	Exeter
DS	Glasgow
DT	Sheffield
DU	Coventry
DV	Exeter

DW Cardiff
DX Ipswich
DY Brighton

EA Dudley
EB Peterborough
EC Preston
ED Liverpool
EE Lincoln
EF Middlesbrough
EG Peterborough
EH Stoke-on-Trent
EJ Haverfordwest
EK Liverpool
EL Bournemouth
EM Liverpool
EN Manchester
EO Preston
EP Swansea
ER Peterborough
ES Dundee
ET Sheffield
EU Bristol
EV Chelmsford
EW Peterborough
EX Norwich
EY Bangor

FA Stoke-on-Trent
FB Bristol
FC Oxford
FD Dudley
FE Lincoln
FF Bangor
FG Brighton
FH Gloucester
FJ Exeter
FK Dudley
FL Peterborough
FM Chester
FN Maidstone
FO Gloucester
FP Leicester
FR Preston
FS Edinburgh
FT Newcastle upon Tyne
FU Lincoln
FV Preston
FW Lincoln
FX Bournemouth
FY Liverpool

GA Glasgow
GB Glasgow
GC London SW
GD Glasgow
GE Glasgow
GF London SW
GG Glasgow
GH London SW
GJ London SW
GK London SW
GL Truro
GM Reading
GN London SW
GO London SW
GP London SW
GR Newcastle upon Tyne
GS Luton
GT London SW
GU London SE
GV Ipswich
GW London SE
GX London SE
GY London SE

HA Dudley
HB Cardiff
HC Brighton
HD Huddersfield
HE Sheffield
HF Liverpool
HG Preston
HH Carlisle
HJ Chelmsford
HK Chelmsford
HL Sheffield
HM London C
HN Middlesbrough
HO Bournemouth
HP Coventry
HR Swindon
HS Glasgow
HT Bristol
HU Bristol
HV London C
HW Bristol
HX London C
HY Bristol

JA Manchester
JB Reading
JC Bangor
JD London C
JE Peterborough
JF Leicester
JG Maidstone
JH Reading
JJ Maidstone
JK Brighton
JL Lincoln
JM Reading
JN Chelmsford
JO Oxford
JP Liverpool
JR Newcastle upon Tyne
JS Inverness
JT Bournemouth
JU Leicester
JV Lincoln
JW Birmingham
JX Huddersfield
JY Exeter

KA Liverpool
KB Liverpool
KC Liverpool
KD Liverpool
KE Maidstone
KF Liverpool
KG Cardiff
KH Hull
KJ Maidstone
KK Maidstone
KL Maidstone
KM Maidstone
KN Maidstone
KO Maidstone
KP Maidstone
KR Maidstone
KS Edinburgh
KT Maidstone
KU Sheffield
KV Coventry
KW Sheffield
KX Luton
KY Sheffield

LA London NW
LB London NW
LC London NW
LD London NW
LE London NW
LF London NW
LG Chester
LH London NW
LJ Bournemouth
LK London NW
LL London NW
LM London NW
LN London NW
LO London NW
LP London NW
LR London NW
LS Edinburgh
LT London NW
LU London NW
LV Liverpool
LW London NW
LX London NW
LY London NW

MA Chester
MB Chester
MC London NE
MD London NE
ME London NE
MF London NE
MG London NE
MH London NE
MJ Luton
MK London NE
ML London NE
MM London NE
MN *not used*
MO Reading
MP London NE
MR Swindon
MS Edinburgh
MT London NE
MU London NE
MV London SE
MW Swindon
MX London SE
MY London SE

NA Manchester
NB Manchester
NC Manchester
ND Manchester
NE Manchester
NF Manchester
NG Norwich
NH Northampton
NJ Brighton
NK Luton
NL Newcastle upon Tyne
NM Luton
NN Nottingham
NO Chelmsford
NP Worcester
NR Leicester
NS Glasgow
NT Shrewsbury
NU Nottingham
NV Northampton
NW Leeds
NX Dudley
NY Cardiff

OA Birmingham
OB Birmingham
OC Birmingham
OD Exeter
OE Birmingham
OF Birmingham
OG Birmingham
OH Birmingham
OJ Birmingham
OK Birmingham
OL Birmingham
OM Birmingham
ON Birmingham
OO Chelmsford
OP Birmingham
OR Portsmouth
OS Glasgow
OT Portsmouth
OU Bristol
OV Birmingham
OW Portsmouth
OX Birmingham
OY London NW

PA Guildford
PB Guildford
PC Guildford
PD Guildford
PE Guildford
PF Guildford
PG Guildford
PH Guildford
PJ Guildford
PK Guildford
PL Guildford
PM Guildford
PN Brighton
PO Portsmouth
PP Luton
PR Bournemouth
PS Aberdeen
PT Newcastle upon Tyne
PU Chelmsford

British car index marks (continued)

PV	Ipswich
PW	Norwich
PX	Portsmouth
PY	Middlesbrough
RA	Nottingham
RB	Nottingham
RC	Nottingham
RD	Reading
RE	Stoke-on-Trent
RF	Stoke-on-Trent
RG	Newcastle upon Tyne
RH	Hull
RJ	Manchester
RK	London NW
RL	Truro
RM	Carlisle
RN	Preston
RO	Luton
RP	Northampton
RR	Nottingham
RS	Aberdeen
RT	Ipswich
RU	Bournemouth
RV	Portsmouth
RW	Coventry
RX	Reading
RY	Leicester
SA	Aberdeen
SB	Glasgow
SC	Edinburgh
SCY	Truro (Isles of Scilly)
SD	Glasgow
SE	Aberdeen
SF	Edinburgh
SG	Edinburgh
SH	Edinburgh
SJ	Glasgow
SK	Inverness
SL	Dundee
SM	Glasgow
SN	Dundee
SO	Aberdeen
SP	Dundee
SR	Dundee
SS	Aberdeen
ST	Inverness
SU	Glasgow
SV	*spare*
SW	Glasgow
SX	Edinburgh
SY	*spare*
TA	Exeter
TB	Liverpool
TC	Bristol
TD	Manchester
TE	Manchester
TF	Reading
TG	Cardiff
TH	Swansea
TJ	Liverpool
TK	Exeter
TL	Lincoln
TM	Luton
TN	Newcastle upon Tyne
TO	Nottingham
TP	Portsmouth
TR	Portsmouth
TS	Dundee
TT	Exeter
TU	Chester
TV	Nottingham
TW	Chelmsford
TX	Cardiff
TY	Newcastle upon Tyne
UA	Leeds
UB	Leeds
UC	London C
UD	Oxford
UE	Dudley
UF	Brighton
UG	Leeds
UH	Cardiff
UJ	Shrewsbury
UK	Birmingham
UL	London C
UM	Leeds
UN	Exeter
UO	Exeter
UP	Newcastle upon Tyne
UR	Luton
US	Glasgow
UT	Leicester
UU	London C
UV	London C
UW	London C
UX	Shrewsbury
UY	Worcester
VA	Peterborough
VB	Maidstone
VC	Coventry
VD	*series withdrawn*
VE	Peterborough
VF	Norwich
VG	Norwich
VH	Huddersfield
VJ	Gloucester
VK	Newcastle upon Tyne
VL	Lincoln
VM	Manchester
VN	Middlesbrough
VO	Nottingham
VP	Birmingham
VR	Manchester
VS	Luton
VT	Stoke-on-Trent
VU	Manchester
VV	Northampton
VW	Chelmsford
VX	Chelmsford
VY	Leeds
WA	Sheffield
WB	Sheffield
WC	Chelmsford
WD	Dudley
WE	Sheffield
WF	Sheffield
WG	Sheffield
WH	Manchester
WJ	Sheffield
WK	Coventry
WL	Oxford
WM	Liverpool
WN	Swansea
WO	Cardiff
WP	Worcester
WR	Leeds
WS	Bristol
WT	Leeds
WU	Leeds
WV	Brighton
WW	Leeds
WX	Leeds
WY	Leeds
YA	Taunton
YB	Taunton
YC	Taunton
YD	Taunton
YE	London C
YF	London C
YG	Leeds
YH	London C
YJ	Brighton
YK	London C
YL	London C
YM	London C
YN	London C
YO	London C
YP	London C
YR	London C
YS	Glasgow
YT	London C
YU	London C
YV	London C
YW	London C
YX	London C
YY	London C

Fastest Cars

Name of car	*Speed*	*Date*	*Type*
Thrust 2 (Rolls-Royce Avon 302)	1019.467 kmh/633.468 mph	1983	Jet-powered
Speed-O-Motive/Spirit 76	696.331 kmh/432.692 mph	1991	Single-piston engine
Bluebird	690.909 kmh/429.054 mph	1964	Gas-turbine engine
Jaguar XJ 220	341 kmh/212.3 mph	1991	Piston-engined
Mercedes C III/3	327.3 kmh/203.3 mph	1978	Diesel-engined
No. 744 *Steamin' Demon*	234.33 kmh/145.607 mph	1985	Steam-powered
Electric car	111.40 kmh/69.21 mph	1991	Electricity-powered

British road signs

Instruction signs

Generally circular; a red border circle indicates a prohibition; blue signs indicate allowed activities.

Entry to 20 mph zone

End of 20 mph zone

School crossing patrol

Maximum speed

National speed limit applies

Stop and give way

Give way to traffic on major road

No vehicles

No entry for vehicular traffic

No right turn

No left turn

No U-turns

No overtaking

Give priority to vehicles from opposite direction

No motor vehicles

No motor vehicles except solo motorcycles, scooters or mopeds

Manually operated temporary 'STOP' sign

No vehicles with over 12 seats except regular scheduled, school and work buses

No cycling

No pedestrians

No goods vehicles over maximum gross weight shown (in tonnes)

No vehicle or combination of vehicles over length shown

No vehicles over height shown

No vehicles over width shown

No vehicles over maximum gross weight shown (in tonnes)

Axle weight limit in tonnes

No stopping (clearway)

Parking restricted to use by people named on sign

No stopping during times shown except for as long as necessary to set down or pick up passengers

Qualifications

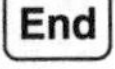
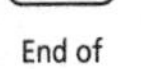

End of restriction

Exception for loading/unloading goods

Exception for regular scheduled, school and work buses

Exception for access to premises and land adjacent to the road where there is no alternative route

British road signs (continued)

Warning signs
Generally triangular.

Distance to 'STOP' line ahead

Crossroads

Junction on bend ahead

T-junction

Staggered junction

Distance to 'Give Way' line ahead

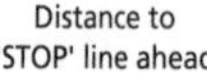

Sharp deviation of route to left (or right if chevrons reversed)

Double bend first to left (symbol may be reversed)

Bend to right (or left if symbol reversed)

Roundabout

Uneven road

REDUCE SPEED NOW

Plate below some signs

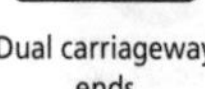

Dual carriageway ends

Road narrows on right (left if symbol reversed)

Road narrows on both sides

Two-way traffic crosses one-way road

Two-way traffic straight ahead

Traffic signals

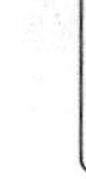

Failure of traffic light signals

Slippery road

Steep hill downwards

Steep hill upwards

Gradients may be shown as a rate ie 20° = 1.5

European road signs

Austria

Umleitung

Diversion

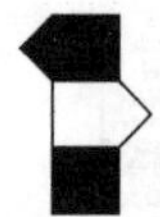

Tram turns at yellow or red

Federal road with priority

25

Federal road without priority

U-turn compulsory

Street lights not on all night

Buses only

Belgium

You may pass right or left

1 15

No parking from 1st to 15th of month

No parking from 16th to end of month

MOEILIJKE DOORGANG

Difficult section of road

Bulgaria

Recommended maximum speed

U-turn allowed

Denmark

Sight-seeing

Pass either side

Beginning of 1 hr parking zone

End of parking zone

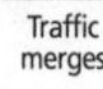

Traffic merges

Compulsory slow lane

Recommended speed in a bend

Finland

Diversion due to road works

8-18

Prohibition applies between 08.00 and 18.00 hours Mon-Fri

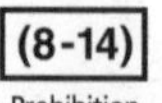

Prohibition applies between 08.00 and 14.00 hours (Saturday)

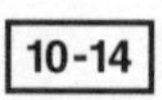

Prohibition applies between 10.00 and 14.00 hours (Sunday)

France

Keep well over to the right

"Priority road" sign

European road signs (continued)

France (continued)

"End of priority" sign

Diversion or relief route

Give way to traffic

Traffic on the roundabout has priority

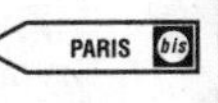

Itineraire Bis (Bison Futé) - Alternative (Holiday) routes

Germany

Diversion

Recommended speed limit

Emergency diversion for motorway traffic

Tram or bus stop

Autobann number

Road number

Parking 2 hours (disc required)

Hungary

Route for heavy vehicles

Lane reserved for buses from 07.00 to 19.00 hrs

Italy

Track for motorcycles

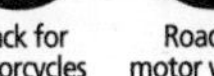
Road for motor vehicles

Restricted parking

Overtaking by vehicles with trailers prohibited

No entry for pedestrians

Stop when meeting public transport bus on mountain road

Easily inflammable forest

Traffic in parallel lanes

Lane reserved for slow vehicles

Netherlands

Cycle track

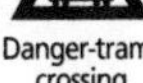
Danger-trams crossing

Built-up area

End of built up area

End of (B) road

2 hours maximum (disc obligatory)

Parking prohibited (see panel)

Stopping prohibited (see panel)

Norway

Tunnel

Passing place (on narrow roads)

Parking prohibited (upper panel) Allowed (lower)

Parking 2 hrs from 08.00-17.00 hrs

Parking 2 hrs from 08.00-18.00 hrs (16.00 hrs Sat)

Portugal

End of parking prohibition

Spain

Recommended maximum speed

Turning permitted

Tourist Accommodation

Sight-seeing

Conpulsory lane for motorcycles

Conpulsory lane for lorries

Sweden

Tunnel

Meeting point (narrow roads)

Slow lane

Width of carriageway

Caution blind person

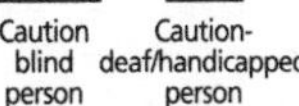

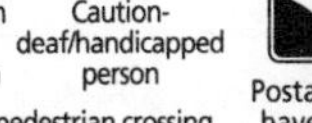
Caution-deaf/handicapped person

e.g. at pedestrian crossing

Switzerland

Postal vehicles have priority

Parking disc compulsory

Slow lane

Motorway

Semi-Motorway

Tunnel (lights compusory)

Flashing red light (level crossing)

Alternately flashing lights (level crossing)

USA road signs

Instruction signs

Stop

4-way stop

Do not enter

Yield

Wrong way

No right turn

No U-turn

One way

Speed limit

Speed zone ahead

Slower traffic keep right

Speed limit with minimum limit posted

School speed limit

Divided highway

Two-way left-turn lanes

No turn on red

Warning signs

Cross road

Side road

Divided highway

Two way traffic

Merge

Railroad crossing

No passing zone

Narrow bridge

Road curves

Right reverse turn

Winding road

Stop ahead

Yield ahead

School crossing

School zone

Pedestrian crossing

Steep downgrade

Slippery when wet

Low clearance

Truck crossing

Deer crossing

Cattle crossing

Farm machinery

No bicycles

Road construction

Flagperson ahead

Freeway exit ramp speed limit

Services signs

Rest area

Telephone

Hospital

Campground

Trailer sites

Rail

UK rail travel times
Intercity routes on British Rail; times are given in hours and minutes for the shortest available weekday services.

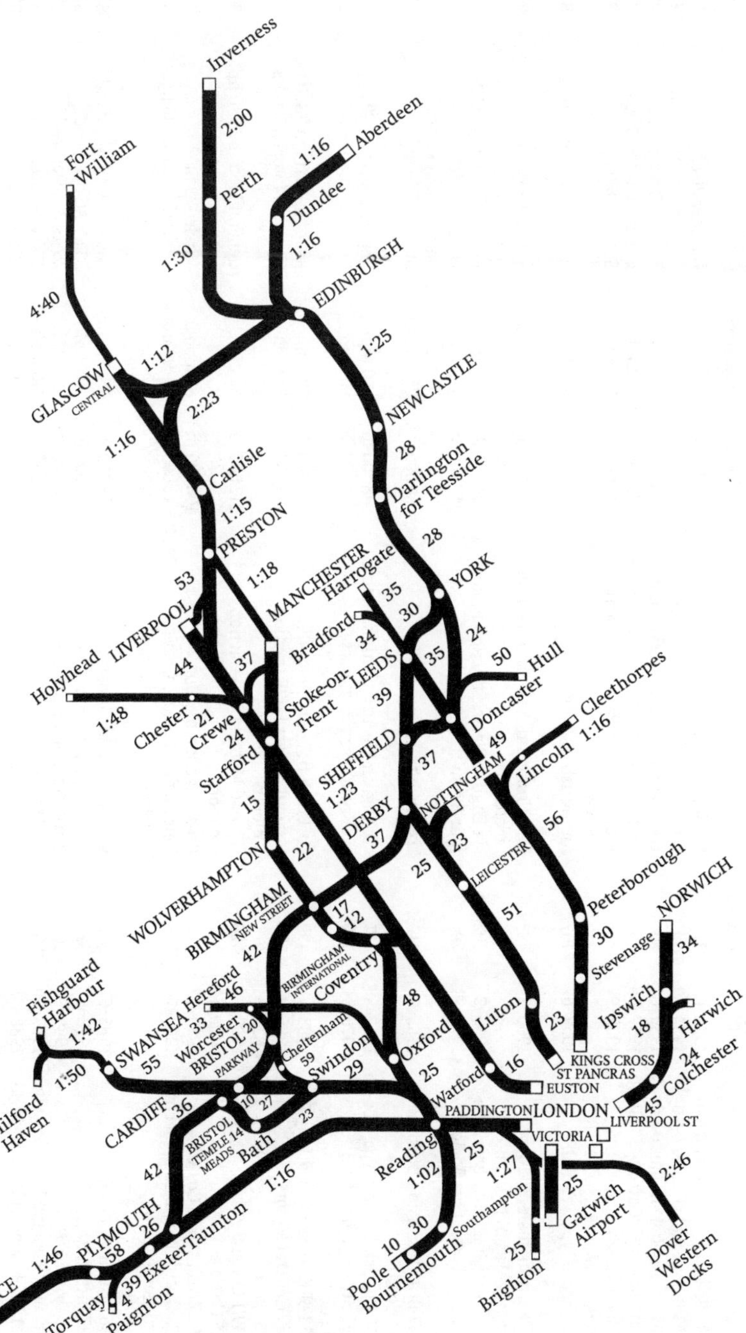

British Rail locomotive classifications

This list gives the details of diesel and electric locomotives operating on BR.

Locomotive	*Built*	*Weight (tonnes)*	*Transmission*	*Maximum tractive effort (lb)*	*Maximum speed (mph)*	*Engine*	*Wheel diameter*
Class 03 British Rail shunter 0-6-0	1958–62	31	Mechanical	15 300 lb	28 mph	Gardner 204 hp	3′7″
Class 08 British Rail shunter 0-6-0	1953–62	50	two English Electric traction motors	35 000 lb	15–20 mph	English Electric 400 hp	4′6″
Class 09 British Rail shunter 0-6-0	1959–62	50	two English Electric traction motors	25 000 lb	27 mph	English Electric 350 hp	4′6″
Class 20 English Electric type 1 Bo-Bo	1957–68	73–4	four English Electric traction motors	42 000 lb	60 mph	English Electric 1 000 hp	3′7″
Class 26 Birmingham Railway Carriage & Wagon type 2 Bo-Bo	1958–9	75	four Crompton-Parkinson traction motors	42 000 lb	60 mph	Sulzer 1 160 hp	3′7″
Class 31 Brush type 2 AIA-AIA	1957–62	107–13	four Brush traction motors	42 800 lb	80–90 mph	English Electric 1 470 hp	3′7″ (driven) 3′3″ (centre)
Class 33 Birmingham Railway Carriage & Wagon type 3 Bo-Bo	1960–2	78–9	four Crompton-Parkinson traction motors	45 000 lb	60–85 mph	Sulzer 1 550 hp	3′7″
Class 37 English Electric type 3 Co-Co	1960–5	102–20	six English Electric traction motors	56 000 lb	80 mph	English Electric 1 750 hp	3′7″
Class 43 HST Power Cars Bo-Bo	1974–82	70	four Brush traction motors	17 980 lb	125 mph	Paxman Valenta Mirrlees Blackstone	3′4″
Class 47 British Rail and Brush type 4 Co-Co	1963–7	117–25	six Brush traction motors	60 000 lb	75–95 mph	Sulzer 2 580 hp	3′9″
Class 50 English Electric type 4 Co-Co	1967–8	117	six English Electric traction motors	48 500 lb	100 mph	English Electric 2 700 hp	3′7″
Class 56 British Rail & Brush type 5 Co-Co	1976–84	125	six Brush traction motors	61 800 lb	80 mph	Rushton-Paxman 3 250 hp	3′9″
Class 58 BREL type 5 Co-Co	1983–7	129	six Brush traction motors	61 800 lb	80 mph	Rushton-Paxman 3 300 hp	3′8″
Class 59 General Motors type 5 Co-Co	1985–9 (USA)	126	General Motors D77B traction motors	113 500 lb	60 mph	General Motors 3 300 hp	3′4″
Class 59/1 General Motors type 5 Co-Co	1990 (Canada)	126	General Motors D77B traction motors	113 500 lb	60 mph	General Motors 3 300 hp	3′4″
Class 60 Brush type 5 Co-Co	1989–92	126	Brush traction motors	106 500 lb	60 mph	Mirrlees 3 100 hp	3′8″
Class 73 British Rail/English Electric electro-diesel Bo-Bo	1962–7	76–7	four English Electric traction motors	34 000–42 000 lb	60–90 mph	English Electric 600 hp	3′4″
						Voltage	
Class 86 British Rail Bo-Bo	1965–6	83–7	four AEI traction motors	46 500–58 000 lb	75–110 mph	660–750 V DC third rail	3′9 1/2″
Class 87 British Rail Bo-Bo	1973–5	83	four GEC traction motors	58 000 lb	110 mph	25 kV AC overhead	3′9 1/2″
Class 89 Brush Co-Co	1986	105	Brush traction motor	46 000 lb	125 mph	25 kV AC overhead	3′9 1/4″
Class 90 BREL General Electric Bo-Bo	1987–90	85	GEC traction motors	43 100 lb	110 mph	25 kV AC overhead	3′9 1/4″
Class 91 BREL General Electric Bo-Bo	1988–91	82	GEC traction motors		140 mph	25 kV AC overhead	3′3 1/4″

Wheel configuration

Basic configurations for steam locomotives operative on British railways 1825–1992.

Tank	*Tender*	
0-4-0	0-4-0	
0-4-2	0-4-2	
0-4-4	0-6-0	
0-6-0	2-4-0	
0-6-2	2-6-0	'Mogul'
0-6-4	2-6-2	
0-8-0	2-8-0	
2-4-0	2-8-2	
2-4-2	2-10-0	
2-6-2	4-2-2	'Single'
2-6-4	4-4-0	
4-4-2	4-4-2	
	4-6-0	
	4-6-2	Pacific
	4-6-4	

Fastest trains

British Rail scheduled train
Edinburgh–London *Scottish Pullman* — 158.9 kmh/98.7 mph (average)

Fastest British locomotive
Class 91 25kV Electric — 260 kmh/162 mph — 1989

Fastest train on a national rail system
TGV (Train à Grande Vitesse), France — 515 kmh/320 mph — 1990

Fastest steam locomotive
LNER 4-6-2 No. 4468, *Mallard*, England — 201.16 kmh/125 mph — 1938

Fastest railed vehicle
Mach 8 unmanned rocket sled, USA — 9 851 kmh/6 121 mph — 1982

Air

Aeroplane classification

Executive/Business jets

Type	*Range*	*Capacity (max seats)*	*Origin*	*Engines (turbofans)*	*Span/length (m)*
BAe 125	Medium	14	UK	2 Viper or 2 TFE731	14.33/15.46 (Series 700)
BAe 1000	Medium/long	15	UK	2 PW305	15.66/16.42
Sabreliner	Short	10	US	2 JT12A or 2 CF700 or 2 TFE731	15.37/14.30 (Series 65)
Swearingen SJ30	Short	6	US	2 FJ44	11/12.9
Beechcraft Model 400 Beechjet/Diamond	Medium	8	US Japan	2 JT15D	13.25/13.15 (Beechjet)
Dassault-Breguet Mystère-Falcon 10/100	Medium		France	2 TFE731	13.08/13.85
IAI 1125 Astra	Medium	6	Israel	2 TFE731	16.05/16.94
Dassault-Breguet Mystère-Falcon 20/200	Medium	10	France	2 CF700 or 2 ATF3-6	16.30/17.15
Dassault-Breguet Falcon-50	Medium/long	9	France	3 TFE731	18.86/18.5
Dassault-Breguet Mystère-Falcon 900	Medium/long	19	France	3 TFE731	19.33/19
Dassault Mystère-Falcon 2000	Medium/long	12	France	2 CFE738	19.3/19.23

Passenger jet airliners

Type	*Range*	*Capacity (max seats)*	*Origin*	*Engines (turbofans)*	*Span/length (m)*
Swept wing, underwing engines					
Boeing 737-100/200	Short/medium	115 (100) 130 (200)	US	2 JT8D	28.35/30.48
Boeing 737-300/400	Short	149 (300) 170 (400)	US	2 CFM56	28.88/33.4 (300) 28.88/36.45 (400)
Boeing 737-500	Medium	108	US	2 CFM56	28.88/36.45
Airbus A320 *	Short/medium	179	European consortium	2 CFM56 or V2500	33.91/35.75
Tu-204	Medium	214	Russia	2 PS-90 or RB211	42/46.22
Airbus A300*	Medium	330	European consortium	2 CF6 or JT9D	44.84/53.62
Airbus A310 *	Medium	240	European consortium	2 CF6 or JT9D	43.9/46.6

Aeroplane classification (continued)

Type	*Range*	*Capacity (max seats)*	*Origin*	*Engines (turbofans)*	*Span/length (m)*
Boeing 767	Medium	255	US	2 RB211, GE CF6-80 PW JTD9-7R4, or PW4050	47.57/48.51 or 54.94
Boeing 757	Medium	204	US	2 RB 211 or PW2037	37.95/47.32
Airbus A330 *	Medium/long	335	European consortium	2 CF6 Trent, or PW4000	60.3/63.5
McDonnell Douglas DC-10	Medium/long	380	US	3 CF6 or JT9D	50.41/55.5
McDonnell Douglas MD-11	Medium/long	405	US	3 PW4360, Trent, or CF6	51.66/61.21
Boeing 777	Long	400	US	2 PW4073, GE 90, or Trent	60.25/63.72
McDonnell Douglas DC8	Medium/long	173	US	4 JT3D	43.41/45.87
DC-8 Super 60		259			45.23/57.12 (Super 63)
Boeing 707	Medium/long	195	US	4 JT3D	44.2/46.61
Ilyushin Il-86 'Camber'	Short	350	Russia	4 Kuznetsov	48.06/59.54
Ilyushin Il-96-300	Medium/long	300	Russia	4 PS-90A	57.66/55.35
Airbus A340 *	Medium/long	335	European consortium	4 CFM56	60.3/63.65
Boeing 747	Medium/long	490	US	4 JT9D, CF6 or RB211	59.64/70.51
Boeing 747-400	Long	630	US	4 CF6, RB211, or PW4256	64.92/70.66
BAe 146	Short	93	UK	4 ALF502	26.34/26.16 (Series 100)

* The Airbus is built jointly by Aérospatiale in France, MBB (Deutsche Airbus) in Germany, and British Aerospace PLC in UK.

Type	*Range*	*Capacity (max seats)*	*Origin*	*Engines (turbofans)*	*Span/length (m)*
Swept wing, rear engines					
Aérospatiale Caravelle	Short	139	France	2 Avon or JT8D	34.30/36.24 (Series 12)
BAe One-Eleven	Short	119	UK	2 Spey	28.5/32.61 (Series 500)
Fokker F28 Fellowship	Short	85	Netherlands	2 Spey	25.07/26.76 (Mk 6000)
Fokker 100	Short	110	Netherlands	2 Tay	28.08/35.53
McDonnell Douglas DC-9	Short	125	US	2 JT8D	28.47/38.28 (Series 40)
McDonnell Douglas MD-80	Short/medium	172	US	2 JT8D	32.85/41.3
Tupolev Tu-134 'Crusty'	Short	72	Russia	2 Soloviev	29/34.35
Tupolev Tu-154 'Careless'	Medium	180	Russia	3 Kuznetsov or Soloviev	37.55/47.9
Boeing 727	Medium	189	US	3 JT8D	32.92/46.69 (200)
Ilyushin Il-62 'Classic'	Long	186	Russia	4 Kuznetsov or Soloviev	43.2/53.12
Yakovlev Yak-42 'Clobber'	Short	120	Russia	3 D-36	34.90/36.38
Delta Wing					
Aérospatiale/BAe Concorde [a]	Long	128	France/UK	4 Olympus 593	25.56/61.66

[a] World's only fully operational supersonic airliner

Regional/Commuter Aircraft (20 passengers or more)

Type	*Range*	*Seats*	*Origin*	*Engines*	*Span/length (m)*
Jets					
Canadair Challenger	Medium	28	Canada	2 ALF502 or CF34	18.83/20.82
Canadair Regional Jet	Short	50	Canada	2 CF34	21.44/26.95
Yakovlev Yak-40 'Codling'	Short	32	Russia	3 Ivchenko	25/20.36
Propeller planes					
Fairchild Metro	Short	20	US	2 TPE331 turboprop	17.37/18.09
Convair CV-240/340/440 Metropolitan	Short	40/44/52	US	2 R-2800 piston	32.12/24.14
Convair 540/580/600/640	Short	56	US	2 Allison 501 or Dart turboprop	32.12/24.14
Martin 4-0-4	Short	40	US	2 R2800 piston	28.44/22.75
Ilyushin Il-14 'Crate'	Short	28	Russia	2 Ash-82 piston	31.69/22.3
Douglas DC-3/Dakota	Short	36	US	2 R-1830 piston	28.96/19.63
Curtiss C-46 Commando	Short	62	US	2 R-2800 piston	32.92/23.26
BAe Jetstream 41	Short	29	UK	2 TPE331 turboprop	18.29/19.25
Gulfstream Aerospace Gulfstream I/I-C	Long	24	US	2 Dart turboprop	23.92/19.43
NAMC YS-11A	Short/medium	60	Japan	2 Dart turboprop	32/26.3
Ilyushin Il-114	Short	60	Russia	2 TV7 turboprop	30/26.31
BAe ATP	Short/medium	64	UK	2 PW126 turboprop	30.63/26
Saab 304A	Short	34	Sweden	2 CT7 turboprop	21.44/19.72
Saab 2000	Short/medium	50	Sweden	2 GMA 2 100A turboprop	24.76/27.93
EMBRAER EMB-110 Bandeirante	Short	21	Brazil	2 PT6A turboprop	15.32/15.08
EMBRAER EMB-120 Brasilia	Short	30	Brazil	2 PW115 turboprop	19.78/20
Aérospatiale N 262/Frégate	Short	26	France	2 Bastan turboprop	21.9/19.28
Fokker F27 Friendship	Short/medium	52	Netherlands	2 Dart turboprop	29/25.06 (Mk 500)
Fokker 50	Short	58	Netherlands	2 PW125 turboprop	29/25.24
Antonov An-24 'Coke'/An-26 'Curl'	Short	50	Ukraine	2 Ivchenko turboprop	29.2/23.53
DH DHC-4A Caribou	Short (STOL)	30	Canada	2 R-2000 piston	29.15/22.13
DH DHC-5E Transporter	Short	44	Canada	2 CT64 turboprops	29.26/24.08
DH DHC-8 Dash 8	Short	40	Canada	2 PW120 turboprop	25.89/22.25
Airtech CN-235	Short	44	Spain/Indonesia	2 CT7 turboprop	25.81/21.35
Avions de Transport Régional ATR42/72	Short	50/74	France/Italy	2 PW120 turboprop	24.57/22.67 (ATR42)
LET L-610	Short	40	Czecho-slovakia	2 M602 or CT-7 turboprop	25.6/21.4
Dornier Do 328	Short	33	Germany	2 PW119 turboprop	20.98/21.22
CASA C-212 Aviocar	Short (STOL)	26	Spain	2 TPE331 turboprop	19/15.16
DH DHC-6 Twin Otter	Short	20	Canada	2 PT6 turboprop	19.81/15.77
Shorts 330-200	Short	30	UK	2 PT6A turboprop	22.76/17.69
Shorts 360	Short	36	UK	2 PT6A turboprop	22.75/21.49

Aeroplane classification (continued)

Vickers Viscount	Short	65	UK	4 Dart turboprop	28.56/25.04
Ilyushin Il-18/Il-20 'Coot'	Medium	122	Russia	4 Ivchenko turboprop	37.4/35.9
Lockheed L-188 Electra	Medium	98	US	4 Allison 501 turboprop	30.18/31.81
Douglas DC-4	Short	44	US	4 R-2000 piston	35.8/28.6
DH DHC Dash 7 (STOL)	Short	50	Canada	4 PT6 turboprop	28.35/24.58

STOL = short take-off and landing

World air distances

Air distances between some major cities, given in statute miles. To convert to kilometres, multiply number given by 1.6093.

[a] Shortest route

	Amsterdam	Anchorage	Beijing	Buenos Aires	Cairo	Chicago	Delhi	Hong Kong	Honolulu	Istanbul	Johannesburg	Lagos	London	Los Angeles	Mexico City	Montreal	Moscow	Nairobi	Paris	Perth	Rome	Santiago	Sydney	Tokyo
Anchorage	4475																							
Beijing	6566	4756																						
Buenos Aires	7153	8329	12000																					
Cairo	2042	6059	6685	7468																				
Chicago	4109	28	7599	5587	6135																			
Delhi	3985	8925	2368	8340	2753	8119																		
Hong Kong	5926	5063	1235	3124	5098	7827	2345																	
Honolulu	8368	2780	6778	8693	9439	4246	7888	5543																
Istanbul	1373	6024	4763	7783	764	5502	2833	5998	9547															
Johannesburg	5606	1042	10108	5725	4012	8705	6765	6728	12892	4776														
Lagos	3161	7587	8030	4832	2443	7065	5196	7541	10367	3207	2854													
London	217	4472	5054	6985	2187	3956	4169	5979	7252	1552	5640	3115												
Los Angeles	5559	2333	6349	6140	7589	1746	8717	7231	2553	6994	10443	7716	5442											
Mexico City	5724	3751	7912	4592	7730	1687	9806	8794	4116	7255	10070	7343	5703	1563										
Montreal	3422	3100	7557	5640	5431	737	7421	8564	4923	4795	8322	5595	3252	2482	2307									
Moscow	1338	4291	3604	8382	1790	5500	2698	4839	8802	1089	6280	4462	1550	6992	6700	4393								
Nairobi	4148	8714	8888	7427	2203	8177	4956	7301	11498	2967	1809	2377	4246	9688	9949	7498	3951							
Paris	261	4683	5108	6892	1995	4140	4089	5987	7463	1394	5422	2922	220	5633	5714	3434	1540	4031						
Perth	9118	8368	4987	9734	7766	11281	5013	3752	7115	7846	5564	10209	9246	9535	11098	12402	8355	7373	12587					
Rome	809	5258	5306	6931	1329	4828	3679	5773	8150	852	4802	2497	898	6340	6601	5431	1478	3349	688	8309				
Santiago	7714	7919	13622	710	8029	5328	12715	3733	8147	10109	5738	6042	8568	5594	4168	5551	10118	7547	461	15129	7548			
Sydney	1039	8522	5689	7760	9196	9324	6495	4586	5078	9883	7601	11700	10565	7498	9061	9980	9425	9410	10150	2037	10149	13092		
Tokyo	6006[a]	3443	1313	13100	6362	6286	3656	1807	3831	5757	8535	9130[a]	6218	5451	7014	6913	4668	8565	6208[a]	4925	6146	11049	4640	
Washington	3854	3430	7930	6097	5859	590	7841	8385	4822	5347	8199	5472	3672	2294	1871	493	4884	7918	3843	11829	4495	5061	9792	6763

Communications

World flying times

Approximate flying times between some major cities. Times quoted (in hours and minutes) are flying time only. In many cases, in order to travel between two points, it is necessary to change aircraft one or more times. Time between flights has not been included.

	Amsterdam	Anchorage	Beijing	Buenos Aires	Cairo	Chicago	Delhi	Hong Kong	Honolulu	Istanbul	Johannesburg	Lagos	London	Los Angeles	Mexico City	Montreal	Moscow	Nairobi	Paris	Perth	Rome	Santiago	Sydney	Tokyo
Anchorage	9.00																							
Beijing	16.50	11.45																						
Buenos Aires	17.45	10.48	28.31																					
Cairo	4.20	13.20	13.15	20.40																				
Chicago	8.35	5.44	15.15	15.40	18.40																			
Delhi	8.15	16.50	6.40	26.20	7.00	20.05																		
Hong Kong	15.15	11.40	3.00	29.35	10.55	17.05	6.05																	
Honolulu	16.42	5.44	10.55	19.00	22.50	9.25	16.50	13.05																
Istanbul	3.15	12.15	15.40	18.45	2.00	12.20	7.35	17.35	21.05															
Johannesburg	13.15	19.50	20.10	12.30	8.55	21.40	23.45	14.55	30.25	16.30														
Lagos	6.40	14.55	22.35	9.55	8.20	14.55	14.55	22.30	23.40	8.05	6.55													
London	1.05	8.30	18.05	16.35	5.35	8.30	10.35	16.05	17.15	3.50	13.10	6.25												
Los Angeles	11.15	6.13	15.25	13.45	21.00	5.00	19.30	15.50	5.15	14.50	24.10	17.25	11.00											
Mexico City	12.27	10.49	18.45	10.25	16.47	5.15	20.42	19.10	8.35	15.42	25.42	19.07	14.35	3.20										
Montreal	7.40	7.91	27.30	16.00	12.35	2.20	17.35	23.05	12.50	10.15	20.10	13.25	7.00	6.40	4.45									
Moscow	3.15	12.15	8.40	22.05	5.25	12.15	7.35	18.00	21.00	4.40	13.30	10.10	3.45	14.45	18.10	10.45								
Nairobi	8.15	17.00	16.00	24.55	4.55	17.00	10.45	12.45	25.45	7.15	3.45	6.20	8.30	19.30	20.42	15.30	12.50							
Paris	1.10	9.00	16.35	15.35	5.05	9.00	10.45	16.40	18.05	3.10	15.50	7.45	1.05	12.50	13.25	6.25	4.00	9.20						
Perth	20.35	17.25	11.15	25.20	17.10	23.00	9.30	8.15	17.25	15.25	14.20	25.55	19.30	19.30	22.50	26.30	19.40	23.00	21.40					
Rome	2.20	12.00	16.10	14.40	3.25	11.35	8.50	15.10	19.13	2.35	12.25	6.55	2.25	14.35	5.35	8.10	4.10	7.20	1.55	20.00				
Santiago	20.50	19.13	22.34	2.10	25.10	17.15	29.05	19.15	8.35	21.00	19.55	24.25	21.55	16.00	12.00	14.50	24.05	29.05	19.45	26.00	18.50			
Sydney	23.05	16.35	16.15	20.45	17.20	21.10	13.50	10.35	11.50	18.40	31.50	28.35	21.55	18.10	18.05	24.50	19.40	31.35	25.05	4.35	23.50	24.30		
Tokyo	11.40	7.20	3.50	28.30	19.40	12.55	9.45	4.20	7.05	14.05	25.00	18.40	11.50	11.55	16.25	18.55	9.25	19.55	16.45	10.05	17.40	27.55	9.15	
Washington	8.55	7.25	25.50	11.00	14.20	1.45	20.10	24.15	10.55	11.25	21.20	14.45	8.10	5.25	7.50	2.50	12.30	17.10	9.25	22.45	12.40	17.40	23.35	12.40

US air distances

Air distances between US cities, given in statute miles. To convert to kilometres, multiply number given by 1.6093.

	Atlanta	Boston	Chicago	Dallas	Denver	Detroit	Houston	Kansas City	Los Angeles	Miami	Minneapolis	New Orleans	New York	Oklahoma City	Omaha	Philadelphia	Phoenix	Pittsburgh	Portland	St Louis	Salt Lake City	San Antonio	San Francisco	Seattle
Boston	946																							
Chicago	606	867																						
Dallas	721	1555	796																					
Denver	1208	1767	901	654																				
Detroit	595	632	235	982	1135																			
Houston	689	1603	925	217	864	1095																		
Kansas City	681	1254	403	450	543	630	643																	
Los Angeles	1946	2611	1745	1246	849	1979	1379	1363																
Miami	595	1258	1197	1110	1716	1146	964	1239	2342															
Minneapolis	906	1124	334	853	693	528	1046	394	1536	1501														
New Orleans	425	1367	837	437	1067	936	305	690	1671	674	1040													
New York	760	187	740	1383	1638	509	1417	1113	2475	1090	1028	1182												
Oklahoma City	761	1505	693	181	500	911	395	312	1187	1223	694	567	1345											
Omaha	821	1282	416	585	485	651	793	152	1330	1393	282	841	1155	418										
Philadelphia	665	281	678	1294	1569	453	1324	1039	2401	1013	980	1094	94	1268	1094									
Phoenix	1587	2300	1440	879	589	1681	1015	1043	370	1972	1270	1301	2143	833	1037	2082								
Pittsburgh	526	496	412	1061	1302	201	1124	769	2136	1013	726	918	340	1010	821	267	1814							
Portland	2172	2537	1739	1637	985	1959	1834	1492	834	2700	1426	2050	2454	1484	1368	2411	1009	2148						
St Louis	484	1046	258	546	781	440	667	229	1592	1068	448	604	892	462	342	813	1262	553	1708					
Salt Lake City	1589	2105	1249	1010	381	1489	1204	919	590	2088	991	1428	1989	865	839	1932	507	1659	630	1156				
San Antonio	875	1764	1041	247	793	1215	191	697	1210	1143	1097	495	1587	407	824	1502	843	1277	1714	786	1086			
San Francisco	2139	2704	1846	1476	956	2079	1636	1498	337	2585	1589	1911	2586	1383	1433	2521	651	2253	550	1735	599	1482		
Seattle	2182	2496	1720	1670	1019	1932	1874	1489	954	2725	1399	2087	2421	1520	1368	2383	1109	2124	132	1709	689	1775	678	
Washington, DC	532	414	590	1163	1464	385	1189	927	2288	919	909	969	229	1158	1000	136	1956	184	2339	696	1839	1361	2419	2307

Communications

International time zones

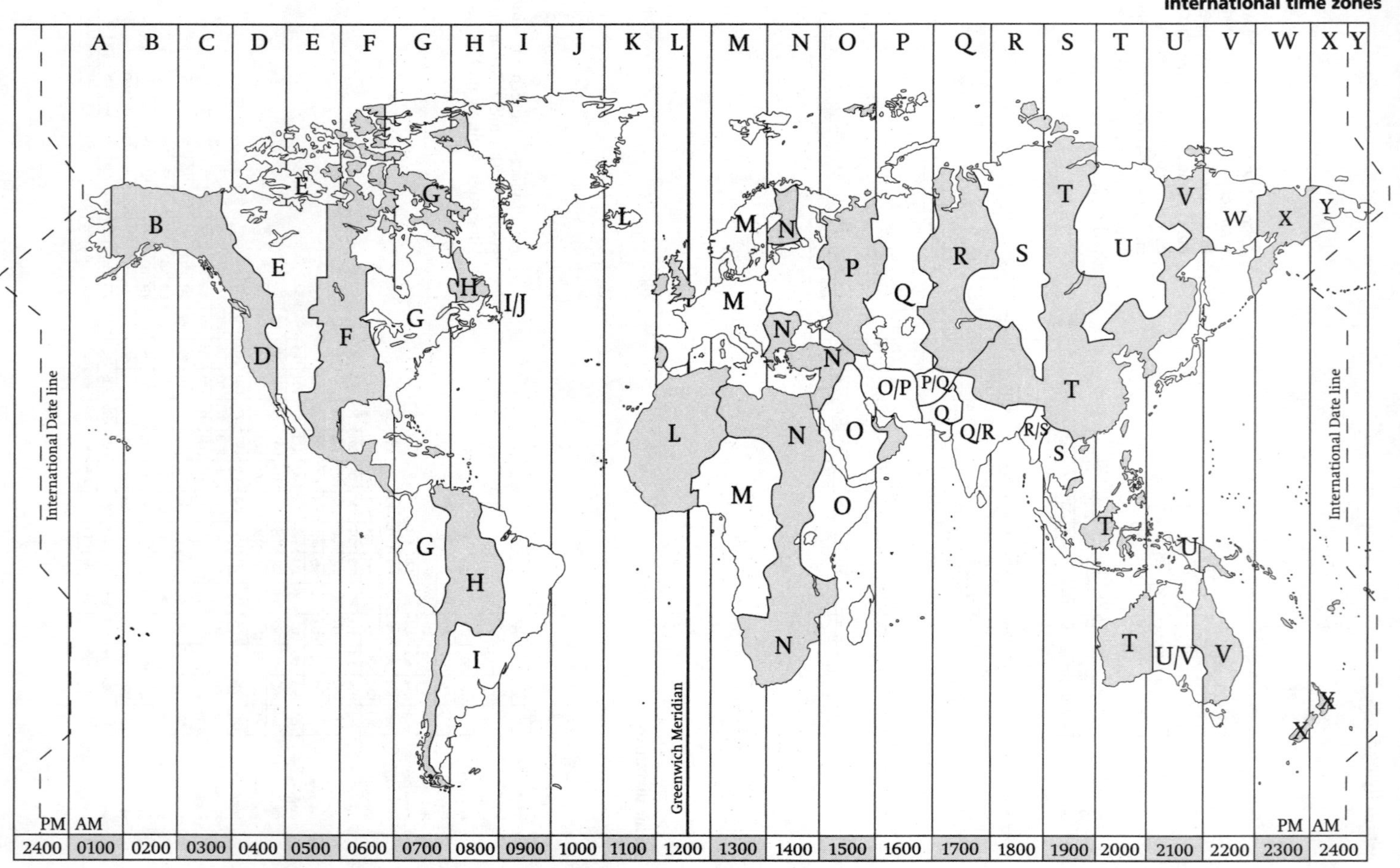

Fastest aeroplanes

A Mach number (Ma) denotes the ratio of the speed of an aircraft to the speed of sound under the same conditions of pressure and density. Mach 1.0 = 1 226kmh/762 mph. Mach 0.5 = 613 kmh/381mph. Mach numbers less than 1 indicate subsonic speed, greater than 1 indicate supersonic speed.

Type	*Aircraft*	*Speed*	*Mach*
Airliner	Aérospatiale/BAe Concorde	2 333 kmh/1 450 mph	2
Autogyro/gyroplane	WA-116F	193.9 kmh/120.3 mph	0.2
Biplane	Italian Fiat CR42B	520 kmh/323 mph	0.4
Bomber	Dassault Mirage IV	2 333 kmh/1 450 mph	2
	General Dynamics FB-111A (swing wing)	3 065 kmh/1 905mph	2.5
	Tupolev Tu-22M (swing wing), *Backfire*	3 065 kmh/1 905mph	2.5
Flying Boat	Martin XP6M-1 Seamaster	911.98 kmh/566.69 mph	0.8
Helicopter	Westland Lynx	400.87 kmh/249.09 mph	0.3
Combat jet	USSR Mikoyan MiG-25 Foxbat-B	3 395 kmh/2 110 mph	3
Reconnaisance jet	USAF Lockheed SR-71A, *Blackbird*	3 529.5 kmh/2 193.17 mph	3
Piston-engine	Grumman F8F Bearcat (modified), *Rare Bear*	850.24 kmh/528.33 mph	0.7
Propeller-driven	USSR Tu-95/142, *Bear*	925 kmh/575 mph	0.8
Ultralight	Gypsy Skycycle	104.6 kmh/65 mph	0.1

Aircraft registration codes

These codes are painted on all aircraft, showing their country of registration.

AP	Pakistan
A2	Botswana
A3	Tonga
A40	Oman
A5	Bhutan
A6	United Arab Emirates
A7	Qatar
A9C	Bahrain
B	China (People's Republic)
B	China/Taiwan (R o C)
C, CF	Canada
CC	Chile
CCCP	former USSR
CN	Morocco
CP	Bolivia
CS	Portugal
CU	Cuba
CX	Uruguay
C2	Nauru
C3	Andorra
C5	The Gambia
C6	The Bahamas
C9	Mozambique
D	Germany
DQ	Fiji
D2	Angola
D4	Cape Verde Islands
D6	Comoros Islands
EC	Spain
EI	Eire
EL	Liberia
EP	Iran
ER	Moldova
ES	Estonia
ET	Ethiopia
EW	Belarus
EY	Tajikistan
EZ	Turkmenistan
F	France
G	Great Britain
HA	Hungary
HB	Switzerland & Lichtenstein
HC	Ecuador
HH	Haiti
HI	Dominican Republic
HK	Colombia
HL	Republic of Korea
HP	Panama
HR	Honduras
HS	Thailand
HV	The Vatican
HZ	Saudi Arabia
H4	Solomon Islands
I	Italy
JA	Japan
JY	Jordan
J2	Djibouti
J3	Grenada
J5	Guinea Bissau
J6	St Lucia
J7	Dominica
J8	St Vincent and the Grenadines
LN	Norway
LV	Argentina
LX	Luxembourg
LY	Lithuania
LZ	Bulgaria
MT	Mongolia
N	USA
OB	Peru
OD	Lebanon
OE	Austria
OH	Finland
OK	Czech Republic
OO	Belgium
OY	Denmark
P	Korea (PDR)
PH	Netherlands
PJ	Netherland Antilles
PK	Indonesia
PP, PT	Brazil
PZ	Suriname
P2	Papua New Guinea
P4	Aruba
RA	Russia
RDPL	Laos, People's Democratic Republic
RP	Philippines
SE	Sweden
SP	Poland
ST	Sudan
SU	Egypt
SX	Greece
S2	Bangladesh
S5	Slovenia
S7	Seychelles
S9	Sao Tomé
TC	Turkey
TF	Iceland
TG	Guatemala
TI	Costa Rica
TJ	Cameroon
TL	Central African Republic
TN	Congo Brazzaville
TR	Gabon
TS	Tunisia
TT	Chad
TU	Côte d'Ivoire
TY	Benin
TZ	Mali
T2	Tuvalu
T3	Kiribati
T7	San Marino
UK	Uzbekistan
UR	Ukraine
VH	Australia
VN	Vietnam
VP-F	Falkland Islands
VP-LA	Anguilla
VP-LM	Montserrat
VP-LV	British Virgin Islands
VQ-T	Turks and Caicos Islands
VR-B	Bermuda
VR-C	Cayman Islands
VR-G	Gibraltar
VR-H	Hong Kong
VT	India

Aircraft registration codes (continued)

V2	Antigua and Barbuda
V3	Belize
V4	St. Kitts and Nevis
V5	Namibia
V7	Marshall Islands
V8	Brunei
XA, XB, XC	Mexico
XT	Burkina Faso
XU	Cambodia
XV	Vietnam
XY	Myanmar (Burma)
YA	Afghanistan
YJ	Vanuatu
YK	Syria
YL	Latvia
YN	Nicaragua
YR	Romania
YS	El Salvador
YU	Yugoslavia
YV	Venezuela
Z	Zimbabwe
ZA	Albania
ZK	New Zealand
ZP	Paraguay
ZS	South Africa
3A	Monaco
3B	Mauritius
3C	Equatorial Guinea
3D	Swaziland
3X	Guinea
4K	Azerbaijan
4R	Sri Lanka
4U	United Nations Organization
4X	Israel
5A	Libya
5B	Cyprus
5H	Tanzania
5N	Nigeria
5R	Madagascar
5T	Mauritania
5U	Niger
5V	Togo
5W	Western Samoa
5X	Uganda
5Y	Kenya
6O	Somalia
6V	Senegal
6Y	Jamaica
7O	Yemen
7P	Lesotho
7Q	Malawi
7T	Algeria
8P	Barbados
8Q	Maldives
8R	Guyana
9A	Croatia
9G	Ghana
9H	Malta
9J	Zambia
9K	Kuwait
9L	Sierra Leone
9M	Malaysia
9N	Nepal
9Q, 9T	Zaire
9U	Burundi
9V	Singapore
9XR	Rwanda
9Y	Trinidad and Tobago

Airline designators

Code	*Airline*	*Country*
AA	American Airlines	US
AC	Air Canada	Canada
AF	Air France	France
AH	Air Algerie	Algeria
AI	Air India	India
AJ	Air Belgium	Belgium
AM	AEROMEXICO	Mexico
AN	Ansett Australia	Australia
AQ	Aloha Airlines	US
AR	Aerolineas Argentinas	Argentina
AS	Alaska Airlines	US
AT	Royal Air Maroc	Morocco
AY	Finnair	Finland
AZ	Al Italia	Italy
BA	British Airways	UK
BB	Sansa	Costa Rica
BD	British Midland	UK
BG	Biman Bangladesh Airlines	Bangladesh
BH	Augusta Airways	Australia
BI	Royal Brunei Airways	Brunei
BJ	Safe Air	New Zealand
BL	Pacific Airways	Vietnam
BM	Belize Air International	Belize
BO	Bouraq Indonesia Airlines	Indonesia
BP	Air Botswana	Botswana
BU	Braathens SAFE	Norway
BW	BWIA International Trinidad and Tobago Airways	Trinidad and Tobago
BY	Britannia Airways	UK
CA	Air China	China
CB	Suckling Airways	UK
CI	China Airlines	Taiwan
CJ	China Northern Airlines	China
CK	Gambia Airways	Gambia
CM	COPA (Compania Panamena de Aviación)	Panama
CO	Continental Airlines	US
CP	Canadian Airlines International	Canada
CS	Continental Micronesia	Mariana Islands
CU	Cubana	Cuba
CX	Cathay Pacific Airways	Hong Kong
CY	Cyprus Airways	Cyprus
CZ	China Southern Airways	China
DL	Delta Airlines	US
DO	Dominicana de Aviación	Dominican Republic
DS	Air Senegal	Senegal
DT	TAAG Angola Airlines	Angola
DU	Hemus Air	Bulgaria
DX	Danair	Denmark
DY	Alyemda-Democratic Yemen Airlines	Yemen Republic
EI	Air Lingus	Ireland
EK	Emirates	United Arab Emirates
ET	Ethiopian Airlines	Ethiopia
EW	Eastwest Airlines	Australia
FC	Berliner Speziel Flug	Germany
FG	Ariana Afghan Airlines	Afghanistan
FI	Icelandair	Iceland
FJ	Air Pacific	Fiji
FO	Western New South Wales Airlines	Australia
FQ	Air Aruba	Aruba
FR	Ryanair (Dublin)	Ireland
GA	Garuda Indonesia	Indonesia
GC	Lina Congo	Congo
GF	Gulf Air Company	Bahrain

Code	Airline	Country
GH	Ghana Airlines	Ghana
GI	Air Guinee	Guinea
GL	Gronlandsfly	Greenland
GN	Air Gabon	Gabon
GR	Aurigny Air Services	Channel Islands
GT	GB Airways	UK
GY	Guyana Airways Corporation	Guyana
HA	Hawaiian Airlines	US
HM	Air Seychelles	Seychelles
HP	America West Airlines	US
HV	Transavia Airlines	Netherlands
HY	Uzbekistan Airways	Uzbekistan
IB	Iberia	Spain
IC	Indian Airlines	India
IE	Solomon Airlines	Solomon Islands
IF	Great China Airlines	China
IL	Istanbul Airways	Turkey
IP	Airlines of Tasmania	Australia
IR	Iranair	Islamic Republic of Iran
IV	Air Gambia	Gambia
IY	Yemenia-Yemen Airways	Yemen
JE	Manx Airlines	Isle of Man
JG	Swedair	Sweden
JL	Japan Airlines	Japan
JM	Air Jamaica	Jamaica
JQ	Trans Jamaica Airlines	Jamaica
JU	JAT Jugoslovenski Aerotransport	Yugoslavia
JY	Jersey European Airways	Channel Islands
KE	Korean Air	Republic of Korea
KL	KLM Royal Dutch Airlines	Netherlands
KM	Air Malta	Malta
KP	Kiwi International Airlines	US
KQ	Kenya Airways	Kenya
KU	Kuwait Airways	Kuwait
KV	Transkei Airways	South Africa
KX	Cayman Airways	Grand Cayman
KY	Waterwings Airways	New Zealand
LA	Lan-Chile	Chile
LC	Loganair	UK
LF	Linjeflyg	Sweden
LG	Luxair	Luxembourg
LH	Lufthansa	Germany
LN	Jamahiriya Libyan Arab Airlines	Libya
LO	LOT Polish Airlines	Poland
LU	Theron Airways	South Africa
LY	El Al Israel Airlines	Israel
LZ	Balkan-Bulgarian Airlines	Bulgaria
MA	Malev Hungarian Airlines	Hungary
MD	Air Madagascar	Madagascar
MH	Malaysia Airlines	Malaysia
MK	Air Mauritius	Mauritius
MN	Commercial Airways	South Africa
MR	Air Mauritania	Mauritania
MS	Egyptair	Egypt
MV	Ansett WA	Australia
NF	Air Vanuatu	Vanuatu
NG	Lauda Air	Austria
NH	All Nippon Airways	Japan
NM	Mount Cook Airlines	New Zealand
NN	Air Martinique	Martinique
NO	Aus-Air	Australia
NQ	Orbi Georgian Airways	Georgia
NR	Norontair	Canada
NU	Southwest Airlines	Japan
NV	Northwest Territorial Airways	Canada
NW	Northwest Airlines	US
NZ	Air New Zealand	New Zealand
OA	Olympic Airways	Greece
OB	Monarch Air	Australia
OG	Air Guadeloupe	Guadeloupe
OK	Czechoslovak Airlines	Czech Republic
OM	Air Mongol	Mongolian People's Republic
ON	Air Nauru	Republic of Nauru
OO	Sky West Airlines	US
OR	Air Comores	Comoros
OS	Austrian Airlines	Austria
OU	Croatia Airlines	Republic of Croatia
OV	Estonian Air	Estonia
PB	Air Burundi	Burundi
PC	Fiji Air	Fiji
PH	Polynesian Airlines	Samoa
PK	Pakistan International Airlines	Pakistan
PL	Aeroperu	Peru
PR	Philippine Airlines	Philippines
PS	Ukraine International Airlines	Ukraine
PU	PLUNA Primeras Lineas Uruguayas de Navigación Aerea	Uruguay
PV	Latvian Airlines	Latvia
PX	Air Niugini	Papua New Guinea
PY	Surinam Airways	Suriname
PZ	LAP Lineas Aereas Paraguayas	Paraguay
QC	Air Zaïre	Zaïre
QF	Qantas Airways	Australia
QL	Lesotho Airways	Lesotho
QM	Air Malawi	Malawi
QU	Uganda Airlines	Uganda
QV	Lao Aviation	Lao PDR
QX	Horizon Airlines	US
QZ	Zambia Airways	Zambia
RA	Royal Nepal Airlines	Nepal
RB	Syrian Arab Airlines	Syria
RG	Varig Brazilian Airlines	Brazil
RJ	Royal Jordanian	Jordan
RK	Air Afrique	Côte d'Ivoire
RO	Tarom	Romania
RY	Air Rwanda	Rwanda
SA	South African Airways	South Africa
SD	Sudan Airways	Sudan
SH	SAHSA Servicio Aero de Honduras	Honduras
SJ	Southern Air	New Zealand
SK	SAS Scandinavian Air	Sweden
SN	Sabena	Belgium
SQ	Singapore Airlines	Singapore
SR	Swissair	Switzerland
SU	Aeroflot	Russia
SV	Saudia	Saudi Arabia
SW	Air Namibia	Namibia
TC	Air Tanzania	Tanzania
TE	Lithuanian Airlines	Lithuania
TG	Thai Airways International	Thailand
TK	Turkish Airlines	Turkey

Airline designators (continued)

Code	Airline	Country
TM	LAM Linhas Aereas de Moçambique	Mozambique
TN	Australian Airlines	Australia
TP	TAP Air Portugal	Portugal
TU	Tunis Air	Tunisia
TW	TWA Trans World Airlines	US
UA	United Airlines	US
UB	Myanma Airlines	Myanmar (Burma)
UI	Norlandair	Iceland
UK	Air UK	UK
UL	Air Lanka	Sri Lanka
UM	Air Zimbabwe	Zimbabwe
UP	Bahamasair	Bahamas
US	US Air	US
UY	Cameroon Airlines	Cameroon
VA	VIASA Venezolana Internacional de Aviación	Venzuela
VE	Avensa	Australia
VH	Air Burkina	Burkina Faso
VJ	Kampuchea Airlines	Cambodia
VN	Vietnam Airlines	Vietnam
VO	Tyrolean Airlines	Austria
VR	Transportes Aereos de Cabo Verde	Cape Verde
VS	Virgin Atlantic Airways	UK
VU	Air Ivoire	Côte d'Ivoire
VX	ACES Aerlineas Centrales de Colombia	Colombia
WG	Taiwan Airlines	Taiwan
WI	Rottnest Airbus	Australia
WJ	Labrador Airways	Canada
WN	Southwest Airlines	US
WR	Royal Tongan Airlines	Tonga
WT	Nigeria Airways	Nigeria
WY	Oman Air	Oman
XX	Aeronaves del Peru	Peru
YJ	National Airlines	South Africa
YK	Cyprus Turkish Airlines	Cyprus
YN	Air Creebec	Canada
YU	Dominair	Dominican Republic
YZ	Transportes Aereos da Guiné Bissau	Guiné Bissau
ZB	Monarch Airlines	UK
ZC	Royal Swazi National Airways	Swaziland
ZP	Virgin Air	Virgin Islands
ZQ	Ansett New Zealand	New Zealand
ZX	Air BC	Canada
2J	Azerbaijan Hava Yollari	Azerbaijan
7E	Nepal Airways	Nepal
7Y	Albanian Airlines	Albania
8Y	Ecuato Guineana de Aviación	Equatorial Guinea
9U	Air Moldova	Republic of Moldova

US local airports

Aberdeen, SD
Abilene, TX
Abingdon, VA
Aiken, SC
Air Park-Dallas
Akron Canton, OH
Akron-Fulton Intl, OH
Akron-Washington County, CO
Alabaster, AL
Alamogordo, NM
Alamosa, CO
Albany County, NY
Albuquerque-Coronado, NM
Albuquerque Intl, NM
Alexandria, MN
Alexandria, IN
Allentown, PA
Allentown-Queen City, PA
Alliance, NE
Alma, GA
Alpine, TX
Alton-St Louis, IL
Altoona, PA
Amarillo Intl, TX
Anchorage Intl, AK
Anchorage-Merrill Field, AK
Anderson, IN
Anderson, SC
Appleton, WI
Ardmore Downtown, OK
Ardmore Municipal, OK
Arlington, TX
Asheboro, NC
Asheville, NC
Ashland, OR
Ashland, WI
Aspen, CO
Astoria, OR
Athens, GA
Atlanta Dekalb-Peachtree, GA
Atlanta Fulton-Brown, GA
Atlantic, IA
Atlantic City, NJ
Atlantic City-Bader, NJ
Auburn, AL
Auburn, ME
Augusta Bush, GA
Augusta Daniel, GA
Augusta State, ME
Aurora, IL
Aurora, CO
Aurora State, OR
Austin, MN
Austin Executive, TX
Austin Mueller, TX
Austin Straubel Intl, WI
Avon Park, FL
Bainbridge, GA
Bakersfield, CA
Ballston Spa, NY
Baltimore-Martin State, MD
Baltimore-Washington Intl, MD
Bangor Intl, ME
Banning, CA
Bardstown, KY
Barre-Montpelier, VT
Barrow, AK
Bartow, FL
Baton Rouge, LA
Battle Creek, MI
Baudette Intl, MN
Beach, ND
Beaufort-Morehead City, NC
Beaumont, TX
Beaumont-Port Arthur, TX
Beaver Falls, PA
Bedford, MA
Bedford, PA
Belfast, ME
Bellingham, WA
Bend Sunriver, OR
Benton Harbor, MI
Bentonville, AR
Berlin, NJ
Bermuda Dunes, CA
Beulah, ND
Beverly, MA
Big Bear City, CA
Big Spring, TX
Big Timber, MT
Billings, MT
Binghamton, NY
Birmingham, AL
Bismarck, ND
Blacksburg, VA
Blanding, UT
Bloomington, IL
Bloomington, IN
Bluefield-Mercer Co, WV
Bluffton, OH
Blytheville Municipal, AR
Boca Raton, FL
Boeing Field/King Co Intl, WA
Boise, ID
Boston-Logan Intl, MA
Bozeman, MT
Bradford, PA
Brainerd, MN
Brandywine, PA
Breckenridge, TX
Bremerton, WA
Bridgeport, CT
Bridgeport, TX
Brooksville, FL
Brownfield, TX

Brownsville, TX
Brunswick, GA
Brunswick McKinnon, GA
Bryan, TX
Buena Vista, CO
Buffalo, NY
Burbank, CA
Burlington, CO
Burlington Intl, VT
Burnet, TX
Butler, PA
Cahokia/St Louis, IL
Calexico Intl, CA
California City, CA
Camden, SC
Canadian, TX
Carbondale Murphysboro, IL
Caribou, ME
Carlsbad, CA
Carlsbad, NM
Carrollton, GA
Cartersville, GA
Carthage, MO
Casa Grande, AZ
Casper, WY
Castroville, TX
Cave Junction, OR
Cedar City, UT
Cedar Rapids, IA
Centennial, CO
Central Nebraska Regional, NE
Centralia, IL
Challis, ID
Chambersburg, PA
Champaign, IL
Chanute, KS
Charles City, IA
Charleston, WV
Charleston Intl, SC
Charleston-Executive, SC
Charlotte Douglas Intl, NC
Charlottesville, VA
Chattanooga-Lovell, TN
Cherokee, IA
Chesapeake, VA
Cheyenne, WY
Chicago Dupage, IL
Chicago Meigs, IL
Chicago Midway, IL
Chicago O'Hare Intl, IL
Chicago Wheeling, IL
Chickasha, OK
Chicopee, MA
Childress, TX
Chino, CA
Chisholm-Hibbing, MN
Cincinatti Blue Ash, OH
Cincinatti Lunken, OH
Circleville, OH
Clarksburg, WV
Clarksdale, MS
Clarksville, TN
Cleburne, TX
Cleveland, MS
Cleveland, OH
Cleveland Cuyahoga, OH
Cleveland Hopkins Intl, OH
Clinton, IA
Cloverdale, CA
Coatsville, PA
Coeur d'Alene, ID
College Park, MD
Colorado City, TX
Colorado Springs, CO
Columbia, CA
Columbia Metro, SC
Columbia Mt Pleasant, TN
Columbia Owens Downtown, SC
Columbia Regional, MO
Columbus, IN
Columbus, NE
Columbus Bolton Fld, OH
Columbus Metro, GA
Columbus–Port Columbus, OH
Concord, CA
Connersville, IN
Conroe–Montgomery Co, TX
Conway, SC
Corpus Christi Intl, TX
Corvallis, OR
Covelo, CA
Covington/Cincinatti, KY
Craig, CO
Crescent City, CA
Crestview, FL
Crete, NE
Cumberland Regional, MD
Cushing, OK
Dalhart, TX
Dallas Addison, TX
Dallas–Fort Worth, TX
Dallas Love, TX
Dallas Redbird, TX
Danbury, CT
Danville, IL
Danville, VA
Davenport, IA
Dayton Cox Intl, OH
Dayton General, OH
Daytona Beach, FL
Decatur, AL
Decatur, IL
Del Rio Intl, TX
Deland, FL
Delano, CA
Delavan, WI
Delaware, OH
Denison, IA
Denton, TX
Denver, CO
Denver Jeffco, CO
Des Moines Intl, IA
Destin, FL
Detroit, MI
Detroit City, MI
Detroit–Grosse Ile, MI
Detroit–Willow Run, MI
Diamond Head, MS
Dickinson, ND
Dodge City, KS
Doersom, PA
Dothan, AL
Douglas, GA
Douglas, WY
Douglas Bisbee, AZ
Downtown Airpark Oklahoma City, OK
Driggs, ID
Dublin, GA
Du Bois, PA
Dubuque, IA
Duluth Intl, MN
Duncan Halliburton Fld, OK
Durango La Plata, CO
Durhamville, NY
Dyersburg, TN
Eagle, CO
Eagle Pass, TX
El Dorado Downtown, AR
El Monte, CA
El Paso Intl, TX
El Paso–W Texas, TX
Elk, OK
Elkin, NC
Elmira, NY
Ely, MN
Ely, NV
Emporia, KS
Erie, PA
Escanaba, MI
Estherville, IA
Eugene Mahlon Sweet, OR
Eureka Murray Field, CA
Evansville, IN
Everett, WA
Fairbanks Intl, AK
Fairhope Point Clear, AL
Fargo, ND
Farmingdale, NY
Farmington, MO
Fayetteville, AR
Fayetteville, NC
Fergus Falls, MN
Findlay, OH
Fitchburg, MA
Flagstaff Pulliam, AZ
Flora, IL
Fort Collins Loveland, CO
Fort Dodge, IA
Fort Lauderdale, FL
Fort Lauderdale Executive, FL
Fort Morgan, CO
Fort Myers, FL
Fort Pierce, FL
Fort Smith, AR
Fort Wayne, IN
Fort Wayne Smith Field, IN
Fort Worth Meacham, TX
Fortuna, CA
Frederick, MD
Frederick, OK
Frenchville, ME
Fresno Air Terminal, CA
Fullerton, CA
Gainesville, FL
Gaithersburg, MD
Galesburg, IL
Gallatin, TN
Galveston, TX
Gary, IN
Gastonia, NC
Georgetown, DE
Gillette, WY
Glendale Municipal, AZ
Glens Falls, NY
Golden Triangle Regional, MS
Goodland, KS
Graham, TX
Grand Canyon, AZ
Grand Junction, CO
Grand Prairie, TX
Grand Rapids, MI
Grand Rapids, MN
Grandview, MO
Grayson County, TX
Great Barrington, MA
Great Falls Intl, MT
Green River, UT
Greeneville, TN
Greensboro, NC
Greenville, KY
Greenville, MS
Greenville Donaldson, SC
Greenville Downtown, SC
Greenwood, MS
Greenwood, SC
Greer, SC
Groton, CT
Grove City, PA
Gulfport, MS
Hagerstown, MD
Hailey, ID
Half Moon Bay, CA
Hammond, LA
Hammonton, NJ
Hancock, MI
Hanover, VA
Harbor Springs, MI
Harlingen, TX
Harrison, AR
Hartford, CT
Hartford, KY
Hartford Springfield, CT
Hartsfield–Atlanta Intl, GA
Hastings, NE
Hawesville, KY
Hawthorne, CA
Hawthorne, NV
Hayden Yampa Valley, CO
Hayward, CA
Hebbronville, TX
Helena, MT
Hendersonville, NC
Hickory, NC
Hilo Intl, HI
Hilton Head, SC
Hobbs, NM
Holbrook, AZ
Holland Tulip City, MI
Hollister, CA

US local airports (continued)

Honolulu Intl, HI
Hornell, NY
Horseshoe Bay, TX
Houma, LA
Houston Clover Field, TX
Houston Ellington Field, TX
Houston Gulf, TX
Houston Hobby, TX
Houston Hooks Memorial, TX
Houston Intercontinental, TX
Houston–W Houston, TX
Huntingburg, IN
Huntington Beach, CA
Huntsville, AL
Huron, SD
Hutchinson, KS
Hutchinson County, TX
Hyannis, MA
Immokalee, FL
Indianapolis Brookside, IN
Indianapolis Greenwood, IN
Indianapolis Intl, IN
Indianapolis–Mt Comfort, IN
Indianapolis Terry, IN
Iowa City, IA
Islip, NY
Ithaca Tompkins County, NY
Jackson, MS
Jackson, WY
Jackson Thompson, MS
Jacksonville, IL
Jacksonville, TX
Jacksonville Craig, FL
Jacksonville Intl, FL
Jamestown, ND
Janesville, WI
Jeffersonville, IN
Johnson City, KS
Johnson County Executive, KS
Johnson County Industrial, KS
Joliet, IL
Jonesboro, AR
Joplin, MO
Josephine County, OR
Juneau, AK
Juneau, WI
Kahului, HI
Kailua-Kona, HI
Kalamazoo, MI
Kalispell, MT
Kalispell City, MT
Kankakee, IL
Kansas City Downtown, MO
Kauai, HI
Kearney, NE
Kelso, WA
Kenai, AK
Kendall Tamiami Executive, FL
Kenosha, WI
Keokuk, IA
Kerrville, TX
Ketchikan Intl, AK
Key West Intl, FL
Killeen, TX
Kingston, NY
Kingsville, TX
Kinston, NC
Kirksville, MO
Kissimmee, FL
Klamath Falls, OR
Knoxville, TN
Knoxville Downtown, TN
Kosciusko, MS
La Crosse, WI
La Grange Callaway, GA
La Porte, TX
La Verne, CA
Laconia, NH
Lafayette, IN
Lafayette, LA
Lafayette, TN
Lake Placid, NY
Lake Tahoe, CA
Lake Wales, FL
Lakeland, FL
Lakeport, CA
Lamar, CO
Lambertville, MI
Lampasas, TX
Lancaster, CA
Lancaster, PA
Lancaster, TX
Lansing, IL
Lansing, MI
Laramie, WY
Laredo Intl, TX
Las Cruces, NM
Las Vegas, NM
Las Vegas, NV
Lawrence, MA
Lawrenceville, IL
Lebanon, NH
Lebanon, TN
Leesburg, VA
Lewisburg, WV
Lewistown, MT
Lexington Blue Grass, KY
Lima, OH
Lincoln, CA
Lincoln, NE
Little Falls, MN
Little Rock, AR
Livermore, CA
Lock Haven, PA
Lompoc, CA
Lone Rock, WI
Long Beach, CA
Longview, TX
Lorain-Elyria, OH
Los Angeles Intl, CA
Los Banos, CA
Louisville, KY
Louisville Standiford, KY
Lubbock Intl, TX
Lubbock Town and Country, TX
Lufkin, TX
Lynchburg, VA
Macon, GA
Madera, CA
Madison, WI
Madisonville, KY
Magnolia, AR
Mammoth June Lakes, CA
Manassas, VA
Manchester, NH
Manhattan, KS
Mankato, MN
Mansfield, LA
Mansfield, OH
Manville, NJ
Marathon, FL
Marianna, FL
Marion, OH
Mariposa-Yosemite, CA
Marquette, MI
Marshall, MN
Marshfield, WI
Mason City, IA
Massena Intl, NY
Mattoon Charleston, IL
Maxton, NC
McAlester, OK
McAllen, TX
McCall, ID
McCook, NE
McGregor, TX
McPherson, KS
Medford, OR
Medina, OH
Melbourne, FL
Melfa, VA
Memphis Intl, TN
Meridian, MS
Mesa Falcon Field, AZ
Miami Intl, FL
Miami Opa Locka, FL
Middle Georgia Regional, GA
Midland Intl, TX
Millersburg, OH
Millinocket, ME
Milwaukee Timmerman, WI
Milwaukee–Gen Mitchell, WI
Mineola, TX
Minneapolis, MN
Minneapolis Anoka-Blaine, MN
Minneapolis–Flying Cloud, MN
Minocqua-Woodruff, WI
Minot Intl, ND
Missoula, MT
Mobile, AL
Mobile-Brookley, AL
Modesto City County, CA
Moline, IL
Monahans, TX
Moncks Corner, SC
Monroe, LA
Monroe, NC
Monroeville, AL
Monterey, CA
Montgomery, AL
Montgomery, NY
Montrose, CO
Morganton, NC
Morrilton Municipal, AR
Morristown, NJ
Morristown, TN
Moses Lake, WA
Moultrie, GA
Moundsville, WV
Mount Pleasant, MI
Mount Pleasant, TX
Mount Pocono, PA
Mount Sterling, KY
Mount Vernon, IL
Mountain Home, AR
Muncie, IN
Murfreesboro, TN
Muscatine, IA
Muscle Shoals, AL
Muskegon, MI
Nantucket, MA
Napa, CA
Nashville, TN
Natchez, MS
Nenana, AK
Neosho, MO
New Braunfels, TX
New Castle, IN
New Castle, PA
New Castle County, DE
New Hanover Intl, NC
New Haven, CT
New Iberia, LA
New Kent County, VA
New Orleans Intl, LA
New Orleans Lakefront, LA
New Roads, LA
New York Kennedy Intl, NY
New York La Guardia, NY
Newark, OH
Newark Intl, NJ
Newnan Coweta, GA
Newport News, VA
Newton, KS
Niagara Falls, NY
Nogales Intl, AZ
Norfolk, NE
Norfolk Intl, VA
Norman, OK
North Las Vegas Air Terminal, NV
North Myrtle Beach, SC
North Platte, NE
Norwood, MA

Novato, CA
Oakdale, CA
Oakland, CA
Ogden, UT
Oklahoma City, OK
Oklahoma City Expressway, OK
Oklahoma City-Sundance, OK
Oklahoma City-Wiley Post, OK
Olive Branch, MS
Olney, TX
Olympia, WA
Omaha Eppley, NE
Omaha Millard, NE
Ontario, CA
Ontario, OR
Orangeburg, SC
Orlando Executive, FL
Orlando Intl, FL
Oroville, CA
Oshkosh, WI
Ottumwa, IA
Owatonna, MN
Owensboro, KY
Owosso, MI
Oxford, CT
Oxford, MS
Oxnard, CA
Paducah, KY
Pahokee, FL
Palacios, TX
Palm Beach Intl, FL
Palm Springs, CA
Pampa, TX
Panama City, FL
Paris, TX
Parkersburg Wood County, WV
Parsons, KS
Pascagoula, MS
Pasco, WA
Paso Robles, CA
Patterson, LA
Pecos, TX
Pendleton, OR
Pensacola, FL
Peoria, IL
Perkasie, PA
Perry, GA
Perryton, TX
Philadelphia, PA
Philadelphia Intl, PA
Phoenix, AZ
Phoenix-Deer Valley, AZ
Phoenix-Goodyear, AZ
Pierre, SD
Pittsburg, KS
Pittsburgh Allegheny Co, PA
Pittsburgh Intl, PA
Pittsburgh Metro, PA
Plainfield, IL
Plainview, TX
Plattsburgh, NY
Plymouth, IN
Plymouth, MA
Pocahontas, IA
Point Lookout, MS
Pompano Beach, FL
Ponca City, OK
Pontiac, MI
Port Angeles, WA
Port Huron, MI
Portland, ME
Portland Hillsboro, OR
Portland Intl, OR
Portland Troutdale, OR
Portsmouth, VA
Prattville, AL
Prescott, AZ
Presque Isle, ME
Price, UT
Princeton, ME
Providence, RI
Provo, UT
Pueblo, CO
Quakertown, PA
Racine, WI
Raleigh County, WV
Raleigh-Durham, NC
Rapid City, SD
Rawlins, WY
Reading, PA
Redding, CA
Redlands, CA
Redmond, OR
Redwood Falls, MN
Reedley, CA
Reidsville, NC
Reno, NV
Reno-Stead, NV
Renton, WA
Rexburg, ID
Rhinelander, WI
Rialto, CA
Richmond Intl, VA
Riverside, CA
Roanoke, VA
Robinson, IL
Rochester, MN
Rochester, NY
Rockford, IL
Rocky Mount, NC
Rolla, ND
Romeoville, IL
Roswell, NM
Roundup, MT
Russell, KS
Russellville, AR
Rutland, VT
Sacramento, CA
Sacramento Metropolitan, CA
Saginaw, MI
Saginaw-Browne, MI
Salina, KS
Salinas, CA
Salisbury, MD
Salisbury, NC
Salt Lake City Intl, UT
San Angelo, TX
San Antonio, TX
San Antonio Intl, TX
San Diego, CA
San Diego Brown Field, CA
San Diego Montgomery, CA
San Francisco Intl, CA
San Jose, CA
San Luis Obispo, CA
Sandusky, OH
Sanford, FL
Sanford, NC
Santa Ana, CA
Santa Barbara, CA
Santa Fe, NM
Santa Maria, CA
Santa Monica, CA
Saranac Lake, NY
Sarasota, FL
Saratoga, WY
Savannah, GA
Scottsbluff, NE
Scottsdale, AZ
Seattle-Tacoma Intl, WA
Sedalia, MO
Selinsgrove, PA
Selma, AL
Selmer, TN
Shamokin, PA
Shawnee, OK
Sheboygan Falls, WI
Sheridan, WY
Shirley, NY
Shreveport, LA
Sidney, MT
Sikeston, MO
Sioux City, IA
Sioux Falls, SD
Slidell, LA
Smyrna, TN
Snyder, TX
Somerset, KY
Somerset, PA
Sonoma County, CA
South Bend, IN
Southern Pines, NC
Southwest Georgia Regional, GA
Sparta, MI
Sparta, TN
Spencer, IA
Spokane Felts Field, WA
Spokane Intl, WA
Springfield, IL
Springfield, KY
Springfield, MO
Springhill, LA
St Anthony, GA
St Cloud, MN
St Francis, KS
St John, NB
St Joseph, MO
St Louis, MO
St Paul, MN
St Petersburg, FL
Stanton, TX
Statesboro, GA
Statesville, NC
Stephenville, TX
Stevens Point, WI
Stewart Intl, NY
Stillwater, OK
Stockton, CA
Stuart, FL
Sugar Land Municipal, TX
Sweetwater, TX
Syracuse, NY
Tacoma, WA
Tallahassee, FL
Tampa, FL
Tampa Intl, FL
Taos, NM
Taylorville, IL
Teterboro, NJ
Texarkana, AR
Tifton, GA
Tillamook, OR
Titusville, FL
Toccoa, GA
Toledo, OH
Tonopah, NV
Topeka, KS
Trenton, NJ
Tri-City Regional, TN
Truckee, CA
Tucson, AZ
Tulsa, OK
Tupelo, MS
Tuscaloosa, AL
Tuskegee, AL
Twentynine Palms, CA
Twin Falls, ID
Tyler, TX
Ukiah, CA
Union City, TN
Valdosta, GA
Van Nuys, CA
Vancouver, WA
Vernal, UT
Vero Beach, FL
Victoria, TX
Waco, TX
Wadsworth, OH
Walla Walla, WA
Walnut Ridge, AR
Walterboro, SC
Wapakoneta, OH
Warsaw, IN
Waseca, MN
Washington, DC
Washington Dulles Intl, DC
Waterloo, IA
Watertown, SD
Watertown, WI
Watertown Intl, NY
Waukegan, IL
Waukesha, WI
Wausau, WI
Wasau-Stevens Point, WI
Wellsville, NY
Wenatchee-Pangborn Memorial, WA
West Bend, WI
West Dover, VT
West Memphis, AR
West Palm Beach, FL

US local airports (continued)

West Plains, MO
Westchester Co White Plains, NY
Westfield, MA
Westhampton Beach, NY
Wichita, KS
Wichita Falls, TX
Wichita Falls Valley, TX
Wildwood, NJ
Wilkes-Barre, PA
Willcox Cochise, AZ
Willimantic, CT
Williston, ND
Willmar, MN
Willoughby, OH
Wilson Industrial Air Center, NC
Winchester, VA
Winslow, AZ
Winston-Salem, NC
Woodward, OK
Worcester, MA
Worland, WY
Xenia, OH
Yakima, WA
Yankton, SD
York, PA
Youngstown, OH
Yuma, AZ
Zanesville, OH

UK local airports

This list comprises only the airports in Britain which offer passenger services. Major international airports are highlighted in bold.

Airport	*Other name*	*Location*	*Type of traffic*
England			
Bembridge		Isle of Wight	Charter, IT services
Birmingham	Elmdon	NE of Birmingham	Scheduled, charter, IT, freight services
Blackpool	Squires Gate	S of Blackpool	Scheduled, charter, IT services
Bournemouth	Hurn	NE of Bournemouth	Scheduled, freight services
Bristol	Lulsgate	SW of Bristol	Scheduled, charter, IT services
Cambridge	Teversham	E of Cambridge	Scheduled, charter, IT services
Carlisle	Crosby	NE of Carlisle	Scheduled services; and light aircraft
Coventry	Baginton	S of Coventry	Scheduled, charter, IT services; club and private aircraft
East Midlands	Castle Donington	SW of Kegworth	Scheduled, charter, IT, freight services; club and private aircraft
Exeter	Clyst Honiton	E of Exeter	Scheduled, charter, IT services
Gatwick		S of London	Scheduled, charter, IT services
Gloucestershire	Staverton	W of Cheltenham	Charter, IT services
Heathrow		W of London	Scheduled services
Humberside	Kirmington	E of Scunthorpe	Scheduled, charter, IT services
Kent International	Manston	NW of Ramsgate	Non-scheduled, charter, IT, freight services
Land's End	St Just	W of Penzance	Scheduled services; club and private aircraft
Leeds/Bradford	Yeadon	W of Leeds	Scheduled, charter, IT services
Liverpool	Speke	SE of Liverpool	Scheduled, charter, IT, mail services; club and private aircraft
London City	STOLport	London	Scheduled services, occasional charter, IT services
Luton		SE of Luton	Scheduled, charter, IT, freight services; club aircraft
Lydd		SW of New Romney	Scheduled, charter, IT services; club and private aircraft
Manchester	Ringway	S of Manchester	Scheduled, charter, IT services; club and private aircraft
Newcastle	Woolsington	NW of Newcastle	Scheduled, charter, IT services
Newquay	St Mawgan	NE of Newquay	Scheduled services occasional company charter flights
Norwich	Horsham St Faith	N of Norwich	Scheduled, charter, IT services
Penzance		E of Penzance	Scheduled helicopter services
Plymouth City		N of Plymouth	Scheduled services; private and club aircraft
Sheffield		NE of Sheffield	Scheduled services
Shoreham		W of Shoreham	Air taxi, private, club, school flights
Southampton	Eastleigh	NE of Southampton	Scheduled, freight services; private and club aircraft
Southend	Rochford	N of Southend	Scheduled, charter, IT, freight services; private and club aircraft
Stansted		E of Bishop's Stortford	Scheduled, charter, IT, freight services
Teesside	Middleton St George	E of Darlington	Scheduled, charter, IT services; school; air taxi; light aircraft
Alderney		SW Alderney	Passenger services
Guernsey		SW of St Peter Port	Scheduled, charter, freight services

Airport	*Other name*	*Location*	*Type of traffic*
Isle of Man	Ronaldsway	SW of Douglas	Scheduled services, occasional charter, IT services
Jersey		NW of St Helier	Scheduled services, occasional charter, IT services
Scilly Isles	St Mary's	E of Hugh Town	Scheduled, helicopter, skybus services
Northern Ireland			
Belfast City	Harbour/Sydenham	Belfast	Scheduled services
Belfast International	Aldergrove	NW of Belfast	Scheduled, charter, IT, freight services
Eglinton		N of Londonderry	Scheduled services; light aircraft
Scotland			
Aberdeen	Dyce	NW of Aberdeen	Scheduled, charter, IT, helicopter services
Barra	North Bay	Barra	Scheduled services; air taxi
Benbecula		NW Benbecula	Scheduled services
Colonsay		Colonsay	Scheduled services
Dundee	Riverside	W of Dundee	Business charter service
Eday		W Orkney	Scheduled services
Edinburgh	Turnhouse	W of Edinburgh	Scheduled, charter, IT, freight services; club and private aircraft
Fair Isle		Shetland	Scheduled services
Fetlar		Shetland	Scheduled services
Glasgow	Abbotsinch	W of Glasgow	Scheduled, charter, IT services
Hoy	Longhope	Orkney	Scheduled services
Inverness	Dalcross	NE of Inverness	Scheduled, non-scheduled, helicopter services
Islay/Port Ellen	Glenegedale	S Islay	Scheduled services
Kirkwall		Orkney	Scheduled services; oil-industry traffic
Machrihanish	Campbeltown	Kintyre	Scheduled services
North Ronaldsay		SW Orkney	Scheduled services
Oronsay		Oronsay	Scheduled services
Papa Stour		S Shetland	Scheduled services
Papa Westray		W Orkney	Scheduled services
Prestwick		S of Kilmarnock	Charter, IT services
Sanday		C Orkney	Scheduled services
Stornoway		E of Stornoway	Scheduled services; transit stop
Stronsay		NW Orkney	Scheduled services
Sumburgh		Shetland	Scheduled, helicopter services; oil-industry traffic
Tingwall	Lerwick	Shetland	Scheduled services
Unst	Baltasound	Shetland	Scheduled services
Westray		N Orkney	Scheduled services
Whalsay		NE Shetland	Scheduled services
Wick		Wick	Scheduled services
Wales			
Cardiff-Wales	Rhoose	SW of Cardiff	Scheduled, charter, IT, freight services

International airports

Abadan	Iran
Abu Dhabi	United Arab Emirates
Adana	Turkey
Adelaide	Australia
Agno	Lugano, Switzerland
Ain el Bay	Constantine, Algeria
Albany County	New York, US
Ålborg Roedslet	Nørresundby, Denmark
Albuquerque	New Mexico, US
Alexandria	Egypt
Alfonso Bonilla Aragon	Cali, Columbia
Alicante	Spain
Almería	Spain
Amarillo	Texas, US
Amborovy	Majunga, Madagascar
Amilcar Cabral International	Sal I, Cape Verde
Aminu	Kano, Nigeria
Anchorage	Alaska, US
Archangel	Russia
Arlanda	Stockholm, Sweden
Arnos Vale	St Vincent
Arrecife	Lanzarote, Canary Islands
Arturo Marino Benitez	Santiago, Chile
Asturias	Spain
Ataturk	Istanbul, Turkey
Auckland	New Zealand
Augusto C Sandino	Managua, Nicaragua
Baghdad	Iraq
Bahrain	Bahrain
Bali/Ngurah Rai	Denpasar, Indonesia
Balice	Cracow, Poland
Bandar Seri Begawan	Brunei
Baneasa	Bucharest, Romania

International airports (continued)

Bangkok	Thailand
Barajas	Madrid, Spain
Barcelona	Spain
Basle-Mulhouse	Basle, Switzerland
Beijing	China
Beira	Mozambique
Beirut	Khaldeh, Lebanon
Belfast	UK
Belgrade	Serbia
Belize City	Belize
Ben Gurion	Tel Aviv, Israel
Benina	Benghazi, Libya
Benito Juarez	Mexico City, Mexico
Berlin-Schonefeld	Berlin, Germany
Berlin-Tegel	Berlin, Germany
Berne	Switzerland
Billund	Denmark
Birmingham	Alabama, US
Blackburne/Plymouth	Montserrat
Blagnac	Toulouse, France
Bole	Addis Ababa, Ethiopia
Bombay	India
Borispol	Kiev, Ukraine
Boukhalef	Tangier, Morocco
Boulogne	France
Bourgas	Bulgaria
Bradley	Hartford, CT, US
Brasília	Brazil
Bremen	Germany
Brisbane	Australia
Brnik	Ljubljana, Slovenia
Bromma	Stockholm, Sweden
Brussels National	Belgium
Buffalo	New York, US
Bujumbura	Burundi
Bulawayo	Zimbabwe
Butmir	Sarajevo, Bosnia-Herzegovina
Cairns	Queensland, Australia
Cairo	Egypt
Calabar	Nigeria
Calcutta	India
Calgary	Canada
Cancún	Mexico
Cannon	Reno, NV, US
Canton	Akron, OH, US
Capodichino	Naples, Italy
Carrasco	Montevideo, Uruguay
Carthage	Tunis, Tunisia
Cebu	Philippines
Jiang Tieshi (Chang Kai-shek)	Taipei, Taiwan
Changi	Singapore
Charleroi (Gossilies)	Belgium
Charles de Gaulle	Paris, France
Charleston	South Carolina, US
Charleston	West Virginia, US
Charlotte	North Carolina, US
Château Bougon	Nantes, France
Christchurch	New Zealand
Ciampino	Rome, Italy
Cologne-Bonn	Cologne, Germany
Columbus	Ohio, US
Congonhas	São Paulo, Brazil
Copenhagen	Kastrup, Denmark
Cork	Ireland
Costa Smeralda	Olbia, Sardinia
Côte d'Azure	Nice, France
Cotonou	Benin
Cristoforo Colombo	Genoa, Italy
Crown Point	Scarborough, Tobago
Cuscatlán	El Salvador
D F Malan	Cape Town, South Africa
Dalaman	Turkey
Dallas/Fort Worth	Texas, US
Damascus	Syria
Dar-es-Salaam	Tanzania
Darwin	Australia
Des Moines	Iowa, US
Detroit-Wayne County	Detroit, MI, US
Deurne	Antwerp, Belgium
Dhahran	Al Khobar, Saudi Arabia
Djibouti	Djibouti
Doha	Qatar
Dois de Julho	Salvador, Brazil
Domodedovo	Moscow, Russia
Don Miguel Hidalgo y Castilla	Guadalaraja, Mexico
Dorval	Montreal, Canada
Douala	Cameroon
Dresden	Germany
Dubai	United Arab Emirates
Dublin	Ireland
Dubrovnik	Croatia
Dulles	Washington, DC, US
Dusseldorf	Germany
Ecterdingen	Stuttgart, Germany
Edmonton	Canada
Eduardo Gomes	Manaus, Brazil
Eindhoven	Netherlands
El Alto	La Paz, Bolivia
El Dorado	Bogotá, Colombia
El Paso	Texas, US
Elat	Israel
Elmas	Cagliari, Italy
Entebbe	Uganda
Entzheim	Strasbourg, France
Eppley Airfield	Omaha, Nebraska, US
Erie	Pennsylvania, US
Ernestso Cortissoz	Barranquilla, Colombia
Esbjerg	Denmark
Esenboga	Ankara, Turkey
Faleolo	Apia, Samoa
Faro	Portugal
Ferihegy	Budapest, Hungary
Findel	Luxembourg
Fiumicino (Leonardo da Vinci)	Rome, Italy
Flesland	Bergen, Norway
Fontanarossa	Catonia, Sicily
Fornebu	Oslo, Norway
Fort de France	Lamentin, Martinique
Fort Lauderdale	Florida, US
Fort Myers	Florida, US
Frankfurt am Main	Germany
Freeport	Bahamas
Frejorgues	Montpellier, France
Fuenterrabía	San Sebastián, Spain
Fuerteventura	Canary Islands
Fuhlsbuttel	Hamburg, Germany
G Marconi	Bologna, Italy

Galileo Galilei	Pisa, Italy
Gatwick	London, UK
G'Bessia	Conakry, Guinea Republic
Gen Abelard L Rodriguez	Tijuana, Mexico
Gen Juan N Alvarez	Acapulco, Mexico
Gen Manuel Marquez de Leon	La Paz, Mexico
Gen Mariano Escobedo	Monterrey, Mexico
Gen Mitchell	Milwaukee, WI, US
Gen Rafael Buelna	Mazatlán, Mexico
Geneva	Switzerland
Gerona/Costa Brava	Gerona, Spain
Gillot	St Denis de la Reunion
Golden Rock	St Kitts
Goleniów	Szczecin, Poland
Glasgow	UK
Granada	Spain
Grantley Adams	Bridgetown, Barbados
Greater Cincinatti	Ohio, US
Greater Pittsburgh	Pennsylvania, US
Guam	Guam
Guararapes	Recife, Brazil
Guarulhos	São Paulo, Brazil
Halifax	Canada
Halim Perdanakusama	Jakarta, Indonesia
Hamilton Kindley Field	Hamilton, Bermuda
Hancock Field	Syracuse, NY, US
Hanover-Langenhagen	Hanover, Germany
Hanoi	Vietnam
Harare	Zimbabwe
Harrisburg	Pennsylvania, US
Hartsfield	Atlanta, Georgia, US
Hassan	Laayoune, Morocco
Hato	Curaçao, Netherlands Antilles
Hahaya	Moroni, Comoros
Hanedi	Tokyo, Japan
Heathrow	London, UK
Hellenikon	Athens, Greece
Henderson Field	Honiari, Solomon Islands
Heraklion	Crete, Greece
Hewanorra	St Lucia
Ho Chi Minh City	Vietnam
Hong Kong	Hong Kong
Hongqiao	Shanghai, China
Honolulu	Hawaii, US
Hopkins	Cleveland, OH, US
Houari Boumedienne	Dar-el-Beida, Algeria
Houston	Texas, US
Ibiza	Balearics, Spain
Indianapolis	Indiana, US
Indira Ghandi	Delhi, India
Inezgane	Agadir, Morocco
Islamabad	Pakistan
Isle Verde	San Juan, Puerto Rico
Izmir	Turkey
Itazuke	Fukuoka, Japan
Ivanka	Bratislava, Slovak Republic
Ivato	Antananarivo, Madagascar
J F Kennedy	New York, US
Jackson Field	Port Moresby, Papua New Guinea
Jacksonville	Florida, US
James M Cox	Dayton, OH, US
Jan Smuts	Johannesburg, South Africa
Jomo Kenyatta	Nairobi, Kenya
Jorge Chavez	Lima, Peru
Jose Marti	Havana, Cuba
Juan Santa Maria	Alajuela, Costa Rica
Kagoshima	Japan
Kalmar	Sweden
Kamazu	Lilongwe, Malawi
Kansas City	Missouri, US
Kaohsiung	Taiwan
Karachi	Pakistan
Karpathos	Karpathos, Greece
Katunayake	Colombo, Sri Lanka
Keflavík	Reykjavík, Iceland
Kent County	Grand Rapids, MI, US
Kerkyra	Corfu, Greece
Key West	Florida, US
Khartoum	Sudan
Khoramaksar	Aden, Yemen
Khwaja Rawash	Kabul, Afghanistan
Kigali	Rwanda
Kimpo	Seoul, South Korea
King Abdul Aziz	Jeddah, Saudi Arabia
King Khaled	Riyadh, Saudi Arabia
Kingsford Smith	Sydney, Australia
Kjevik	Kristiansand, Norway
Klagenfurt	Austria
Komaki	Nagoya, Japan
Kos	Greece
Kota Kinabulu	Sabah, Malaysia
Kotoka	Accra, Ghana
Kranebitten	Innsbruck, Austria
Kuching	Sarawak, Malaysia
Kungsangen	Norrköping, Sweden
Kuwait International	Kuwait
La Aurora	Guatemala City, Guatemala
La Coruna	Spain
La Guardia	New York, US
La Mesa	San Pedro Sula, Honduras
La Parra	Jerez de la Frontera, Spain
Lahore	Pakistan
Landvetter	Gothenburg, Sweden
Larnaca	Cyprus
Las Americas	Santo Domingo, Dominican Republic
Las Palmas	Gran Canaria, Canary Islands
Le Raizet	Point-à-Pitre, Guadeloupe
Leipzig	Germany
Les Angades	Oujda, Morocco
Lesquin	Lille, France
Lester B Pearson	Toronto, Canada
Libreville	Gabon
Lic Gustavo Diaz Ordaz	Puerto Vallarta
Lic Manuel Crecencio Rejon	Mérida, Mexico
Liège (Bierset)	Belgium
Linate	Milan, Italy
Lincoln	Nebraska, US
Lindbergh	San Diego, US
Linz	Austria
Lisbon	Portugal
Little Rock	Arkansas, US
Llabanère	Perpignan, France
Logan	Boston, MA, US
Lomé	Togo
London City	UK
Long Beach	California, US
Los Angeles	California, US
Loshitsa	Minsk, Byelarus
Louis Botha	Durban, South Africa

International airports (continued)

Louisville	Kentucky, US
Lourdes/Tarbes	Juillan, France
Luanda	Angola
Luano	Lubumashi, Zaïre
Lubbock	Texas, US
Luis Munoz Marin	San Juan, Puerto Rica
Lungi	Freetown, Sierra Leone
Luqa	Malta
Lusaka	Zambia
Luxor	Egypt
Maastricht	Netherlands
McCarran	Las Vegas, NV, US
McCoy	Orlando, FL, US
Mactan	Cebu, Philippines
Mahon	Menorca
Mais Gate	Port au Prince, Haiti
Málaga	Spain
Male	Maldives
Malpensa	Milan, Italy
Managua	Nicaragua
Manchester	New Hampshire, US
Manchester	UK
Maputo	Mozambique
Marco Polo	Venice, Italy
Mariscal Sucre	Quito, Ecuador
Maseru	Lesotho
Matsapha	Manzini, Swaziland
Maupertus	Cherbourg, France
Maxglan	Salzburg, Austria
Maya Maya	Brazzaville, Congo
Medina	Saudi Arabia
Meenambakkam	Madras, India
Mehrabad	Teheran, Iran
Melita	Djerba, Tunisia
Memphis	Tennessee, US
Menara	Marrakech, Morocco
Merignac	Bordeaux, France
Miami	Florida, US
Midway	Chicago, IL, US
Mingaladon Yangon	Myanmar, Malaysia
Ministro Pistarini	Buenos Aires, Argentina
Minneapolis/St Paul	Minneapolis, US
Mirabel	Montreal, Canada
Mogadishu	Somalia
Mohamed V	Casablanca, Morocco
Moi	Mombasa, Kenya
Monroe County	Rochester, NY, US
Morelos	Mexico City, Mexico
Münster/Osnabrück	Germany
Murmansk	Russia
Murtala Muhammed	Lagos, Nigeria
Nadi	Fiji
Nagasaki	Japan
Narita	Tokyo, Japan
Narssarsuaq	Greenland
Nashville	Tennessee, US
Nassau	Bahamas
Nauru	Nauru
N'djamena	Chad
N'Djili	Kinshasa, Zaïre
Nejrab	Aleppo, Syria
Newcastle	UK
New Orleans	Louisiana, US
Newark	New Jersey, US
Niamey	Niger
Ninoy Aquino	Manila, Philippines
Nis	Yugoslavia
Norfolk	Virginia, US
Norman Manley	Kingston, Jamaica
North Front	Gibraltar
Nouadhibou	Mauritania
Nouakchott	Mauritania
Novo-Alexeyevka	Tblisi, Georgia
Nuremburg	Germany
Oakland	California, US
Octeville	Le Havrets, France
Odense	Denmark
O'Hare	Chicago, IL, US
Okecie	Warsaw, Poland
Okinawa	Naha, Japan
Oran	Algeria
Orebro	Sweden
Orlando	Florida, US
Orly	Paris, France
Osaka	Japan
Osvaldo Veira	Bissau, Guinea Bissau
Otopeni	Bucharest, Romania
Ougadougou	Burkina Faso
Owen Roberts	Grand Cayman
Pago Pago	Samoa
Palese	Bari, Italy
Palma	Majorca
Pamplona	Spain
Panama City	Panama
Paphos	Cyprus
Papola Casale	Brindisi, Italy
Paradisi	Rhodes, Greece
Patenga	Chittagong, Bangladesh
Penang	Malaysia
Peninsula	Monterey, CA, US
Peretola	Florence, Italy
Perth	Australia
Peshawar	Pakistan
Peterson Field	Colorado Springs, CO, US
Philadelphia	Pennsylvania, US
Piarco	Port of Spain, Trinidad
Pleso	Zagreb, Croatia
Pochentong	Phnom Penh, Cambodia
Point Salines	Grenada
Pointe Noire	Congo
Polonia	Medan, Indonesia
Ponta Delgado	São Miguel, Azores
Port Bouet	Abidjan, Côte d'Ivoire
Port Harcourt	Nigeria
Portland	Maine, US
Portland	Oregon, US
Port Sudan	Sudan
Porto Pedra Rubras	Oporto, Portugal
Praia	Cape Verde
Prestwick	UK
Princess Beatriz	Aruba
Provence	Marseille, France
Pula	Croatia
Pulkovo	St Petersburg, Russia
Punta Arenas	Chile
Punta Raisi	Palermo, Italy
Queen Alia	Amman, Jordan
Raleigh/Durham	North Carolina, US
Ras al Khaimah	United Arab Emirates
Rebiechowo	Gdańsk, Poland
Regina	Canada
Reina Sofia	Tenerife

Rejon	Merida, Mexico
Richmond	Virginia, US
Riem	Munich, Germany
Rio de Janeiro	Brazil
Riyadh	Saudi Arabia
Roberts	Monrovia, Liberia
Rochambau	Cayenne, French Guiana
Robert Mueller Municipal	Austin, TX, US
Ronchi dei Legionari	Trieste, Italy
Rotterdam	Netherlands
Ruzyne	Prague, Czech Republic
Saab	Linkoping, Sweden
St Eufemia	Lamezia Terma, Italy
St Louis	Missouri, US
St Thomas	Virgin Islands
Sainte Foy	Quebec, Canada
Sale	Rabat, Morocco
Salgado Filho	Porto Alegre, Brazil
Salt Lake City	Utah, US
San Antonio	Texas, US
San Diego	California, US
San Francisco	California, US
San Giusto	Pisa, Italy
San Javier	Murcia, Spain
San José	California, US
San Pablo	Seville, Spain
San Salvador	El Salvador
Sanaa	Yemen
Sangster	Montego Bay, Jamaica
Santa Caterina	Funchal, Madeira
Santa Cruz	La Palma, Canary Islands
Santa Isabel	Malabo, Guinea
Santander	Spain
Santiago	Spain
Santos Dumont	Rio de Janeiro, Brazil
São Tomé	São Tomé
Satolas	Lyon, France
Schiphol	Amsterdam, Netherlands
Schwechat	Vienna, Austria
Seeb	Muscat, Oman
Senou	Bamako, Mali
Seychelles	Mahe, Seychelles
Sfax	Tunisia
Shannon	Ireland
Sharjah	United Arab Emirates
Sheremetyevo	Moscow, Russia
Silvio Pettirossi	Asuncion, Paraguay
Simon Bolivar	Caracas, Venezuela
Simon Bolivar	Guayaquil, Ecuador
Sir Seewoosagur Ramgoolam	Plaisance, Mauritius
Sir Seretse Khama	Gaborone, Botswana
Skanes	Monastir, Morocco
Skopje	Macedonia
Sky Harbour	Phoenix, AZ, US
Snilow	Lwow, Ukraine
Sofia	Bulgaria
Sola	Stavanger, Norway
Sondica	Bilbao, Spain
Søndre Strømfjord	Greenland
Spilve	Riga, Latvia
Split	Croatia
Spokane	Washington, US
Stansted	UK
Stapleton	Denver, CO, US
Sturup	Malmö, Sweden
Subang	Kuala Lumpur, Malaysia
Sunan	Pyongyang, North Korea
Tacoma	Washington, US
Tallahassee	Florida, US
Tamatve	Madagascar
Tampa	Florida, US
Tegucigalpa	Toncontin, Honduras
Thalerhof	Graz, Austria
Theodore Francis	Providence, RI, US
Thessalonika	Greece
Timehri	Georgetown, Guyana
Timisoara	Romania
Tirana	Albania
Tito Menniti	Reggio Calabria, Italy
Tontouta	Noumea, New Caledonia
Townsville	Australia
Tribhuyan	Kathmandu, Nepal
Tripoli	Libya
Trivandrum	India
Truax Field	Madison, WI, US
Tucson	Arizona, US
Tullamarine	Melbourne, Australia
Turin	Italy
Turku	Finland
Turnhouse	Edinburgh, UK
Ulemiste	Tallinn, Estonia
Unokovo	Moscow, Russia
Uplands	Ottowa, Canada
V C Bird	Antigua
Vaasa	Finland
Vagar	Faeroe Is
Valencia	Spain
Vancouver	Canada
Vantaa	Helsinki, Finland
Varna	Bulgaria
Verona	Italy
Victoria	British Columbia, Canada
Vigie	St Lucia
Vigo	Spain
Vilnius	Lithuania
Vilo de Porto	Santa Maria, Azores
Viracopos	São Paulo, Brazil
Vitoria	Spain
Washington	Baltimore, MD, US
Wattay	Vientiane, Laos
Wellington	New Zealand
Wichita	Kansas, US
Will Rogers	Oklahoma City, OK, US
Winnipeg	Manitoba, Canada
Yoff	Dakar, Senegal
Yundam	Banjul, Gambia
Zakynthos	Greece
Zia	Dhaka, Bangladesh
Zürich	Switzerland

TELECOMMUNICATIONS

International direct dialling codes

This table gives the international telephone direct dialling codes for most countries.

It is not always possible to dial internationally from every country to every other country, and there are sometimes restrictions and special numbers within a country, for which it is necessary to consult the local telephone directory.

Dialling procedure is as follows:

(a) Dial out, using the access code of the country from which you are making the call; you may need to wait for a dialling tone or announcement (shown by + in the table below).

(b) Then dial the code of the country you are calling, followed by any area or city code, and the subscriber number. (When making an international call, it is usually necessary to omit any initial 0 or 9 of an area/city code.)

Country	*Dialling out code*	*Dialling in code*
Albania	none	355
Algeria	00+	213
Andorra	00	33 628
Angola	none	244
Anguilla	00	1 809
Antigua and Barbuda	011	1 809
Antilles (Netherlands)	00	599
Argentina	00	54
Aruba	00	2978
Ascension Island	00	247
Australia	0011	61
Austria	00	43
Azores	00	351
Bahamas	011	1 809
Bahrain		973
Bangladesh	00	880
Barbados	011	1 809
Belgium	00+	32
Belize	none	501
Benin	none	229
Bermuda	011	1 809
Bhutan	00	975
Bolivia	0800 0044*	591
Botswana	none	267
Brazil	00	55
Brunei Darussalam	00	673
Bulgaria	00	359
Burkina Faso	00	226
Cameroon	00	237
Canada	011	1
Canary Islands	00	34
Cape Verde	00	238
Cayman Islands	00	1 809
Central African Republic	00	236
Chad	00	235
Chile	00	56
China	none	86
Christmas Island	00	672
Cocos Island	00	672
Colombia	90	57
Congo	00	242
Cook Islands	00	682
Costa Rica	00	506
Côte d'Ivoire	00	225
Cuba	none	53
Cyprus	00	357
Czech Republic	00	42
Denmark	009	45
Djibouti	none	253
Dominica	none	1 809
Dominican Republic	1 800 751 2701*	1 809
Ecuador	none	593
Egypt	00	20
El Salvador	0	503
Equatorial Guinea	00	240
Ethiopia	none	251
Falkland Islands	00	500
Faroe Islands	00	298
Fiji	none	679
Finland	990	358
France	19+	33
French Guiana	00	594
French Polynesia	00	689
Gabon	00	241
Gambia	000*	220
Germany, east	06	37
Germany, west	00	49
Ghana	0194*	233
Gibraltar	00	350
Greece	00	30
Greenland	none	299
Grenada	none	1 809
Guadeloupe	00	590
Guam	00	671
Guatemala	00	502
Guinea	00	224
Guinea-Bissau	00	245
Guyana	169*	592
Haiti	none	509
Honduras	00	504
Hong Kong	001	852
Hungary	00+	36
Iceland	90	354
India	900	91
Indonesia	00	62
Iran	00	98
Iraq	00	964
Ireland, Republic of	16	353
Israel	00	972
Italy	00	39
Jamaica	none	1 809
Japan	001	81
Jordan	0	962
Kenya	000	254
Kiribati	00	686
Korea, PDR (North)	00	850
Korea, South	001	82
Kuwait	00	965
Lebanon	00	961
Lesotho	00	266
Liberia	00	231
Libya	00	218

International dialling codes (continued)

Country	*Dialling out code*	*Dialling in code*
Liechtenstein	00	41 75
Luxembourg	00	352
Macao	00	853
Madagascar	none	261
Madeira	00	35191
Malawi	101	265
Malaysia	00	60
Maldives	none	960
Mali	00	223
Malta	00	356
Marshall Islands	00	692
Martinique	00	596
Mauritania	00	222
Mauritius	none	230
Mayotte	00	269
Mexico	98	52
Micronesia	00	691
Monaco	19+	33 93
Montserrat	00	1 809
Morocco	00	212
Mozambique	none	258
Myanmar (Burma)	none	95
Namibia	091	264
Nauru	none	674
Nepal	none	977
Netherlands	09+	31
New Caledonia	00	687
New Zealand	00	64
Nicaragua	none	505
Niger	none	227
Nigeria	009	234
Niue	00	683
Norfolk Island	00	672
Northern Marianas	00	670
Norway	095	47
Oman	00	968
Pakistan	00	92
Palau	00	680
Panama	00	507
Papua New Guinea	31	675
Paraguay	none	595
Peru	00	51
Philippines	00	63
Poland	00	48
Portugal	00	351
Puerto Rico	135	1 809
Qatar	0	974
Réunion	00	262
Romania	none	40
Rwanda	none	250
St Helena	00	290
St Kitts and Nevis	00+	1 809
St Lucia	none	1 809
St Pierre & Miquelon	00	508
St Vincent and the Grenadines	none	1 809
Samoa, American	none	684
Samoa, Western	none	685
San Marino	00	39
São Tomé and Principe	00	239
Saudi Arabia	00	966
Senegal	00	221
Seychelles	0	248
Sierra Leone	none	232
Singapore	005	65
Slovakia	00	42
Solomon Islands	00	677
Somalia	none	252
South Africa	09	27
Spain	07+	34
Sri Lanka	00	94
Suriname	001	597
Swaziland	0992	268
Sweden	009	46
Switzerland	00	41
Syria	00	963
Taiwan	002	886
Tanzania	none	255
Thailand	001	66
Togo	none	228
Tonga	none	676
Trinidad and Tobago	01	1 809
Tunisia	00	216
Turkey	9+9	90
Turks and Caicos Islands	00	1 809
Tuvalu	00	688
Uganda	none	256
United Arab Emirates	00	971
UK	010	44
Uruguay	00	598
USA	011	1
former USSR	810	7
Vanuatu	none	678
Venezuela	00	58
Vietnam	00	84
Virgin Islands (UK)	00	1 809 49
Virgin Islands (US)	00	1 809
Yemen - north, south	00	967, 969
Yugoslavia	99	38
Zaïre	none	243
Zambia	00	260
Zimbabwe	110	263

Afghanistan, Laos and Sudan can be reached only through the international operator.
* denotes 'UK Direct' numbers.

LANGUAGES

Indo-European languages

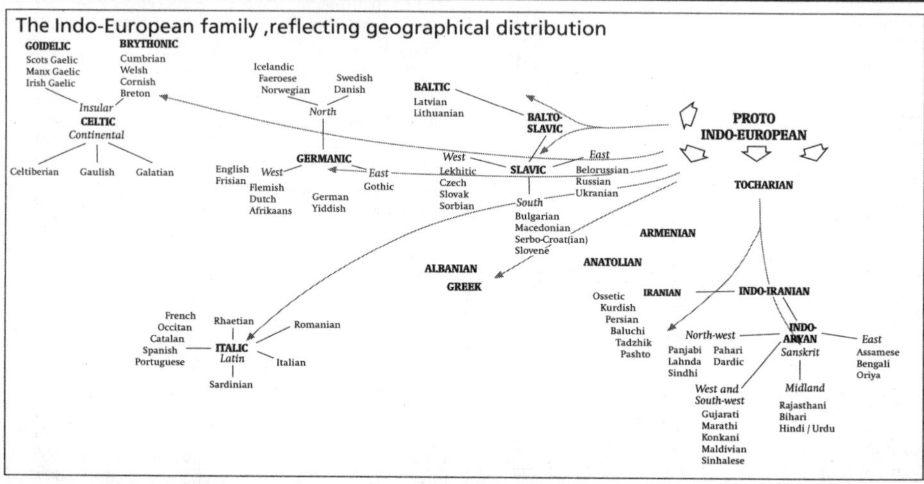

Language families: numbers of speakers

Estimates of the numbers of speakers in the main language families of the world in the 1980s. The list includes Japanese and Korean, which are not clearly related to any other languages.

Main language families

Indo-European	2 000 000 000
Sino-Tibetan	1 040 000 000
Niger-Congo	260 000 000
Afro-Asiatic	230 000 000
Austronesian	200 000 000
Dravidian	140 000 000
Japanese	120 000 000
Altaic	90 000 000
Austro-Asiatic	60 000 000
Korean	60 000 000
Tai	50 000 000
Nilo-Saharan	30 000 000
Amerindian (North, Central, South America)	25 000 000
Uralic	23 000 000
Miao-Yao	7 000 000
Caucasian	6 000 000
Indo-Pacific	3 000 000
Khoisan	50 000
Australian aborigine	50 000
Palaeosiberian	25 000

The top twenty languages

Speaker estimates for the world's top 20 languages (given in millions). The first column lists the languages on the basis of the number of mother-tongue (first-language) speakers they have. The second column gives population estimates for those countries where the language has official status. Note that the totals do not always coincide, since some major languages (such Javanese and Telugu) are not official languages of whole countries, and some languages (such as Malay and Tagalog) are official languages of multilingual countries. The second-column figures are often over-estimates, as by no means everyone in the countries where a second language is recognized (eg India) will be fluent in it; on the other hand, the figures are of some interest as indicators of the way languages are moving.

	Mother-tongue speakers		*Official language populations*
1	Chinese (1 000)	1	English (1 400)
2	English (350)	2	Chinese (1 000)
3	Spanish (250)	3	Hindi (700)
4	Hindi (200)	4	Spanish (280)
5	Arabic (150)	5	Russian (270)
6	Bengali (150)	6	French (220)
7	Russia (150)	7	Arabic (170)
8	Portuguese (135)	8	Portuguese (160)
9	Japanese (120)	9	Malay (160)
10	German (100)	10	Bengali (150)
11	French (70)	11	Japanese (120)
12	Panjabi (70)	12	German (100)
13	Javanese (65)	13	Urdu (85)
14	Bihari (65)	14	Italian (60)
15	Italian (60)	15	Korean (60)
16	Korean (60)	16	Vietnamese (60)
17	Telugu (55)	17	Persian (55)
18	Tamil (55)	18	Tagalog (50)
19	Marathi (50)	19	Thai (50)
20	Vietnamese (50)	20	Turkish (50)

World language families

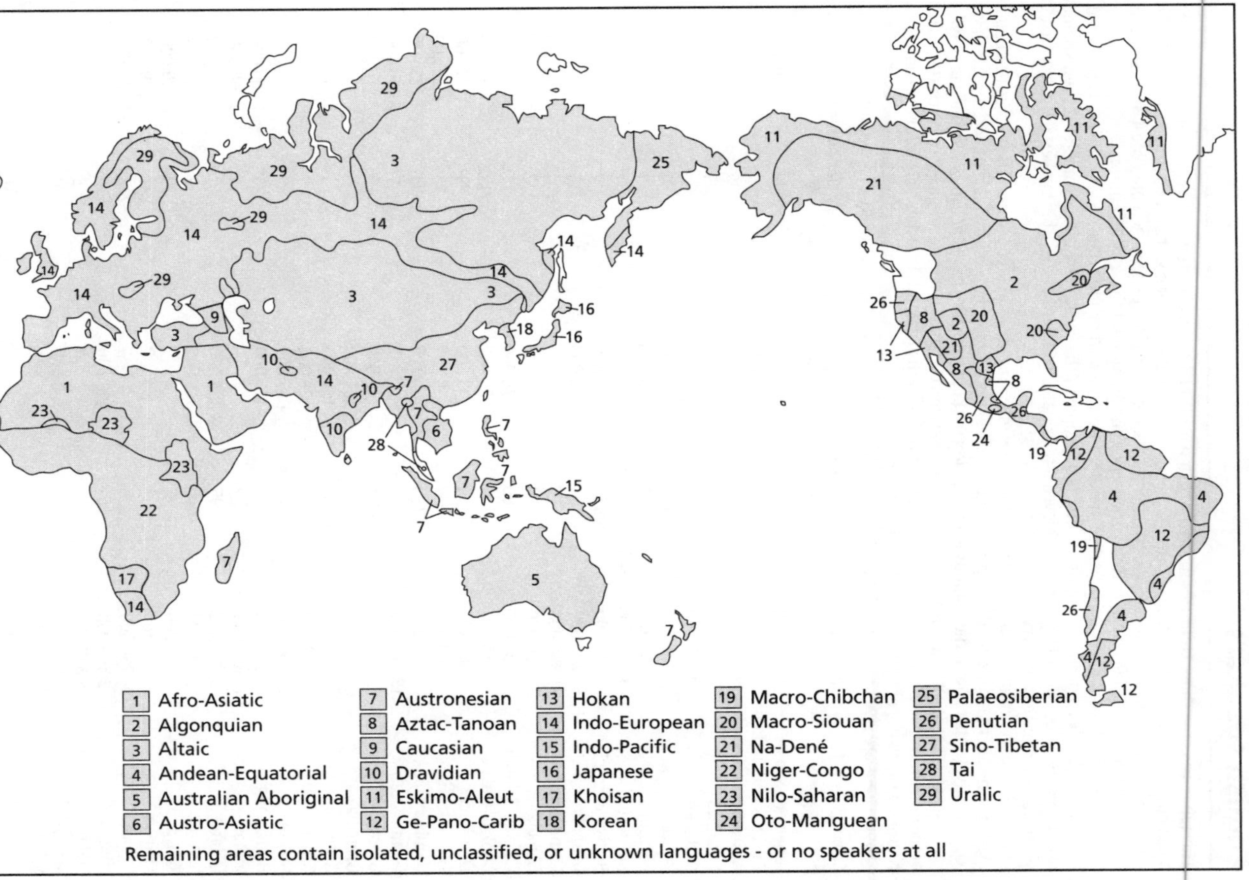

English speakers

This table lists only those countries where English has official or special status. Those who have learned English as a foreign language in countries (eg China, Germany) where it has no such status are not included in the listing.

Areas where English is a creole or creolised pidgin are identified by (c) (eg Sierra Leone). Most of these varieties have been placed in the '*First language*' column, increasing the grand total there by 57 million.

Figures for English as a second language are often unknown (?) or uncertain. Where a total is preceded by ? (eg Botswana) it has been derived from the numbers of people in the country who have completed their secondary education, and who are thus likely to have achieved a reasonable standard of use. This total excludes any first-language speakers listed for that country.

In first-language countries (eg Canada), no totals are given for second-language use when agreed estimates do not exist; as a result, the world total of second-language speakers is probably a considerable underestimate. If we assume (conservatively) that 50% of the remaining population in these countries have English as a second language, the total increases to 145 million. If we also assume (again, conservatively) that in second-language countries (eg Pakistan) 15% of the remaining population might have some command of English, the total reaches 300 million—a commonly quoted figure for world use of English as a second language.

Populations are given for 1990. The world population has been increasing at about 1.7% per annum since this time.

Country	*Population*	*First Language*		*Second language*	
		%	*Total*	*%*	*Total*
American Samoa	39 700	?	?	99	39 300
Antigua and Barbuda	80 600	95 (c)	76 600	?	?
Australia	17 073 000	90	15 365 000	95	1 622 000
Bahamas	253 000	90	228 000	?	?
Barbados	257 000	100 (c)	257 000		
Belize	189 000	65 (c)	123 000	?	?
Bermuda	59 300	95	56 300	?	?
Botswana	1 295 000	?	?	?	?26 000
British Virgin I	12 200	95 (c)	11 600	?	?
Brunei [a]	259 000	4	10 000	?36	?93 200
Cameroon	11 900 000	?	?	50 (c)	5 950 000
Canada	26 620 000	60	15 972 000	?	?
Cayman Islands	26 000	100	26 000		
Cook Islands	19 300	?	?	?13	?2 500
Dominica	82 200	4	3 300	?9	?7 400
Fiji	740 000	?	?	?8	?59 200
Gambia	860 000	? (c)	?	?3	?25 800
Ghana	15 020 000	?	?	7	1 000 000
Gibraltar	300 800	35	10 800	?	?
Grenada	101 000	100 (c)	101 000		
Grenada	101 000	100 (c)	101 000		
Guam	132 000	21	28 000	?	?
Guyana	756 000	75 (c)	567 000	?	?
Hong Kong	5 841 000	2	117 000	25	1 460 000
India[a]	844 000 000	?	?	4	33 760 000
Ireland	3 509 000	95	3 334 000	?	?
Jamaica	2 391 000	97 (c)	2 319 000	?	?
Kenya	2 487 200	?	?	?9	2 239 000
Kiribati	71 100	?	?	?41	?29 200
Lesotho	1 760 000	?	?	?23	?404 800
Liberia	2 595 000	96 (c)	2 500 000	?	?
Malawi	8 830 000	?	?	5	470 000
Malaysia	17 886 000	2	300 000	30	5 366 000
Malta	353 000	20	70 500	?	?
Mauritius	1 080 000	?	?	?11	?119 000
Montserrat	12 000	100 (c)	12 000		
Namibia	1 300 000	10	130 000	?	?
Nauru	9 000	7	600	?	?
New Zealand	3 389	93	3 152 000	?	?
Nigeria	88 500 000	50 (c)	44 250 000	?	?
N Marianas	45 000	90 (c)	40 500	?	?
Pakistan[a]	122 600 000	?	?	2	2 450 00
Palau	14 300	?	?	98	14 000
Papua New Guinea	3 671 000	66 (c)	2 460 000	?	?
Philippines	61 480 000	?	?	50	30 740 000
Puerto Rico	3 336 000	?	?	45	1 500 000
St Kitts	44 100	100	44 100	?	?

Country	Population	First Language %	First Language Total	Second language %	Second language Total
St Lucia	151 000	18	28 000	?	?
St Vincent and the Grenadines	115 000	100 (c)	115 000		
Seychelles [a]	68 700	3	2 000	?	?
Sierra Leone	4 151 000	?95 (c)	3 943 000	?	?
Singapore	2 718 000	?	?	40	1 087 00
Solomon Islands	319 000	?	?	35 (c)	111 600
South Africa	30 797 000	10	3 080 000	15	4 620 000
Suriname [a]	411 000	?	?	80	328 800
Swaziland	770 000	?	?	?4	30 800
Tanzania	24 403 000	?	?	15	3 660 000
Tonga	96 300	?	?	1	1 000
Trinidad and Tobago	1 233 000	50 (c)	616 500	?	?
Tuvalu	9 100	?	?	6	550
Uganda	16 928 000	?	?	?3	507 800
United Kingdom	57 384 000	98	56 236 000	?	?
UK Islands	201 500	100	201 500		
United States [a]	251 394 000	88	221 227 000	?	?
US Virgin I	107 000	80 (c)	86 000	?	?
Vanuatu	147 000	?	?	88	129 000
Western Samoa	186 000	?	?	?57	?106 000
Zambia	8 456 000	?	?	?11	?930 000
Zimbabwe	9 370 000	?	?	?32	?2 998 000
Other dependencies	33 000	60	19 80040	13 200	
Totals	1 660 457 400 (1 661 000 000)		377 120 100 (377 000 000)		101 901 150 (102 000 000)

[a] Countries in which English has a special status. English is an official language in all other countries listed in the table.

English letter frequencies

Here is a selection of frequency orders found in one comparative study of different styles of American English (after A. Zettersten, 1969, p.21):

(a) press reporting

(b) religious writing

(c) scientific writing

(d) general fiction

(e) average rank order, based on a description of 15 categories of text totalling over a million words

(f) order used by Samuel Morse (1791–1872) in compiling the Morse Code

(g) quantities of type found in a printer's office, on which Samuel Morse's frequency ordering was based

Rank order by frequency of use

English sound frequencies

In southern British English (Received Pronunciation) an analysis of the frequency of vowels and consonants in conversation produced the following totals (after D B Fry, 1947).

Consonants	%		%	Vowels	%		%
n	7.58	b	1.97	ə	10.74	ʊ	0.86
t	6.42	f	1.79	ɪ	8.33	ɑː	0.79
d	5.14	p	1.78	e	2.97	aʊ	0.61
s	4.81	h	1.46	aɪ	1.83	ɜ	0.52
l	3.66	ŋ	1.15	ʌ	1.75	ɛə	0.34
ð	3.56	g	1.05	eɪ	1.71	ɪə	0.21
r	3.51	ʃ	0.96	iː	1.65	ɔɪ	0.14
m	3.22	j	0.88	əʊ	1.51	ʊə	0.06
k	3.09	ʤ	0.60	a	1.45		
w	2.81	ʧ	0.41	ɒ	1.37		
z	2.46	θ	0.37	ɔː	1.24		
v	2.00	ʒ	0.10	uː	1.13		

English letter frequencies (continued)

(a)	*(b)*	*(c)*	*(d)*	*(e)*	*(f)*	*(g)*
e	e	e	e	e	e	12000
t	t	t	t	t	t	9000
a	i	a	a	a	a	8000
o	a	i	o	o	i	8000
n	o	o	h	i	n	8000
i	n	n	n	n	o	8000
s	s	s	i	s	s	8000
r	r	r	s	r	h	6400
h	h	h	r	h	r	6200
l	l	l	d	l	d	4400
d	d	c	l	d	l	4000
c	c	d	u	c	u	3400
m	u	u	w	u	c	3000
u	m	m	m	m	m	3000
f	f	f	c	f	f	2500
p	p	p	g	p	w	2000
g	y	g	f	g	y	2000
w	w	y	y	w	g	1700
y	g	b	p	y	p	1700
b	b	w	b	b	b	1600
v	v	v	k	v	v	1200
k	k	k	v	k	k	800
j	x	x	j	x	q	500
x	j	q	x	j	j	400
q	q	j	z	q	x	400
z	z	z	q	z	z	200

English sound frequencies (continued)

The vowel system of Received Pronunciation

/iː/	as in *sea*	/eɪ/	as in *ape*
/ɪ/	as in *him*	/aɪ/	as in *time*
/e/	as in *get*	/ɔɪ/	as in *boy*
/æ/	as in *sat*	/əʊ/	as in *so*
/ʌ/	as in *sun*	/aʊ/	as in *out*
/ɑː/	as in *father*	/ɪə/	as in *deer*
/ɒ/	as in *dog*	/ɛə/	as in *care*
/ɔː/	as in *saw*	/ʊə/	as in *poor*
/ʊ/	as in *put*		
/uː/	as in *soon*		
/ɜː/	as in *bird*		
/ə/	as in *about*		

The consonant system of Received Pronunciation

/p/	as in *pie*	/z/	as in *zoo*
/b/	as in *by*	/ʃ/	as in *shoe*
/t/	as in *tie*	/ʒ/	as in *beige*
/d/	as in *die*	/h/	as in *hi*
/k/	as in *coo*	/m/	as in *my*
/g/	as in *go*	/n/	as in *no*
/ʧ/	as in *chew*	/ŋ/	as in *sing*
/ʤ/	as in *jaw*	/l/	as in *lie*
/f/	as in *fee*	/r/	as in *row*
/v/	as in *view*	/w/	as in *way*
/θ/	as in *thin*	/j/	as in *you*
/ð/	as in *the*		
/s/	as in *so*		

The trancription is the one used by A C Gimson in *An Introduction to the Pronunciation of English* (London, 1980).

Comparative word frequencies

Rank	*French*	*German*	*Written English*	*Spoken English*
1	de	der	the	the
2	le (a)	die	of	and
3	la (a)	und	to	I
4	et	in	in	to
5	les	des	and	of
6	des	den	a	a
7	est	zu	for	you
8	un (a)	das	was	that
9	une (a)	von	is	in
10	du	für	that	it
11	que (p)	auf	on	is
12	dans	mit	at	yes
13	il	sich	he	was
14	à	daß	with	this
15	en	dem	by	but
16	ne	sie	be	on
17	on	ist	it	well
18	qui	im	an	he
19	au	eine	as	have
20	se	DDR	his	for

a = article p = pronoun

Alphabets

The development of the early alphabet

Phoenician	Old Hebrew	Early Greek	Classical Greek	Etruscan	Early Latin	Modern Roman
						Aa
						Bb
						Cc
						Dd
						Ee
						Ff
						Gg
						Hh
						Ii
						Jj
						Kk
						Ll
						Mm
						Nn
						Oo
						Pp
						Qq
						Rr
						Ss
						Tt
						Uu
						Vv
						Ww
						Xx
						Yy
						Zz

A version of the runic alphabet found in Britain

f, u, þ, o, r, k, g, w, h, n, i, j, ï, p, x, s, t, b, c, m, l, ng, œ, d

Alphabetic codes

Semaphore	Letters	Morse	Braille
	A	•–	
	B	–•••	
	C	–•–•	
	D	–••	
	E	•	
	F	••–•	
	G	––•	
	H	••••	
	I	••	
	J	•–––	
	K	–•–	
	L	•–••	
	M	––	
	N	–•	
	O	–––	
	P	•––•	
	Q	––•–	
	R	•–•	
	S	•••	
	T	–	
	U	••–	
	V	•••–	
	W	•––	
	X	–••–	
	Y	–•––	
	Z	––••	

Nato alphabet

Letter	*Code name*	*Pronunciation*
A	Alpha	AL-FAH
B	Bravo	BRAH-VOH
C	Charlie	CHAR-LEE
D	Delta	DELL-TAH
E	Echo	ECK-OH
F	Foxtrot	FOKS-TROT
G	Golf	GOLF
H	Hotel	HOH-TELL
I	India	IN-DEE-AH
J	Juliet	JEW-LEE-ETT
K	Kilo	KEY-LOH
L	Lima	LEE-MAH
M	Mike	MIKE
N	November	NO-VEM-BER
O	Oscar	OSS-CAH
P	Papa	PAH-PAH
Q	Quebec	KEY-BECK
R	Romeo	ROW-ME-OH
S	Sierra	SEE-AIR-RAH
T	Tango	TAN-GO
U	Uniform	YOU-NEE-FORM
V	Victor	VIK-TAH
W	Whiskey	WISS-KEY
X	Xray	ECKS-RAY
Y	Yankee	YANG-KEY
Z	Zulu	ZOO-LOO

Transliteration to the Latin alphabet

Arabic

Letter	Name	Transliteration
ا	'alif	'
ب	ba	b
ت	ta	t
ث	tha	th
ج	jim	j
ح	ha	h
خ	kha	kh
د	dal	d
ذ	dha	th
ر	ra	r
ز	za	z
س	sin	s
ش	shin	sh
ص	sad	s
ض	dad	d
ط	ta	t
ظ	za	z
ع	'ain	'
غ	ghain	gh
ف	fa	f
ق	qaf	q
ك	kaf	k
ل	lam	l
م	mim	m
ن	nun	n
ه	ha	h
و	waw	w
ي	ya	y

Russian

Letter	Name	Transliteration
А	а	a
Б	б	b
В	в	v
Г	г	g
Д	д	d
Е	е	e
Ж	ж	ž, zh
З	з	z
И	и	i
Й	й	j
К	к	k
Л	л	l
М	м	m
Н	н	n
О	о	o
П	п	p
Р	р	r
С	с	s
Т	т	t
У	у	u
Ф	ф	f
Х	х	h, kh, ch
Ц	ц	c, ts
Ч	ч	č, ch
Ш	ш	š, sh
Щ	щ	šč, shch
Ъ	ъ	"
Ы	ы	y
Ь	ь	'
Э	э	è
Ю	ю	ju, yu
Я	я	ja, ya

German

Letter	Name	Transliteration
𝔄	𝔞	a
𝔄̈	𝔞̈	ae
𝔅	𝔟	b
ℭ	𝔠	c
𝔇	𝔡	d
𝔈	𝔢	e
𝔉	𝔣	f
𝔊	𝔤	g
ℌ	𝔥	h
ℑ	𝔦	i
𝔍	𝔧	j
𝔎	𝔨	k
𝔏	𝔩	l
𝔐	𝔪	m
𝔑	𝔫	n
𝔒	𝔬	o
𝔒̈	𝔬̈	oe
𝔓	𝔭	p
𝔔	𝔮	q
ℜ	𝔯	r
𝔖	𝔰	s
𝔗	𝔱	t
𝔘	𝔲	u
𝔘̈	𝔲̈	ue
𝔙	𝔳	v
𝔚	𝔴	w
𝔛	𝔵	x
𝔜	𝔶	y
ℨ	𝔷	z

Hebrew

Letter	Name	Transliteration
א	'aleph	'
ב	beth	b
ג	gimel	g
ד	daleth	d
ה	he	h
ו	waw	w
ז	zayin	z
ח	heth	h
ט	teth	t
י	yodh	y, j
כ ך	kaph	k
ל	lamedh	l
מ ם	mem	m
נ ן	nun	n
ס	samekh	s
ע	'ayin	'
פ ף	pe	p, f
צ ץ	saddhe	s
ק	qoph	q
ר	resh	r
שׁ	shin	sh, ś
שׂ	śin	s
ת	taw	t

Greek

Letter		Name	Transliteration
Α	α	alpha	a
Β	β	beta	b
Γ	γ	gamma	g
Δ	δ	delta	d
Ε	ε	epsilon	e
Ζ	ζ	zeta	z
Η	η	eta	e, e
Θ	θ	theta	th
Ι	ι	iota	i
Κ	κ	kappa	k
Λ	λ	lambda	l
Μ	μ	mu	m
Ν	ν	nu	n
Ξ	ξ	xi	x
Ο	ο	omicron	o
Π	π	pi	p
Ρ	ρ	rho	r
Σ	σ	sigma	s
Τ	τ	tau	t
Υ	υ	upsilon	y
Φ	φ	phi	ph
Χ	χ	chi	ch, kh
Ψ	ψ	psi	ps
Ω	ω	omega	o, o

There is no agreement over the use of a single transliteration system in the case of Arabic, Hebrew, and Russian. The equivalents given here are widely used, but several other possibilities can be found.

Typefaces

The typefaces shown are modern versions of the main groups under which most typefaces may be classified. The dates indicating the introduction of each group are approximate. The roman numbers and names refer to categories in the most recent British Standard for the classification of typefaces, BS 2961 : 1967.

Blackletter c.1450 (IX, Graphic)

ABCDEFGHIJKLMNOPQRSTUVWXYZ
abcdefghijklmnopqrstuvwxyz

14 and 8 pt

Venetian c.1470 (I, Humanist)

ABCDEFGHIJKLMNOPQRSTUVWXYZ
abcdefghijklmnopqrstuvwxyz

14 and 8 pt Centaur

Old Face c.1495 (II, Garalde)

ABCDEFGHIJKLMNOPQRSTUVWXYZ
abcdefghijklmnopqrstuvwxyz

14 and 8 pt Garamond

Transitional c.1757 (III, Transitional)

ABCDEFGHIJKLMNOPQRSTUVWXYZ
abcdefghijklmnopqrstuvwxyz

14 and 8 pt Baskerville

Modern c.1785 (IV, Didone)

ABCDEFGHIJKLMNOPQRSTUVWXYZ
abcdefghijklmnopqrstuvwxyz

14 and 8 pt Bodoni

Grotesque c.1816 (VI, Lineale a, b)

ABCDEFGHIJKLMNOPQRSTUVWXYZ
abcdefghijklmnopqrstuvwxyz

14 and 8 pt Helvetica

Slab-serif c.1830 (V, Slab-serif)

ABCDEFGHIJKLMNOPQRSTUVWXYZ
abcdefghijklmnopqrstuvwxyz

14 and 8 pt Rockwell

Sans-serif c.1918 (VI, Lineale c, d)

ABCDEFGHIJKLMNOPQRSTUVWXYZ
abcdefghijklmnopqrstuvwxyz

14 and 8 pt Gill Sans

Script c.1557 (VIII, Script)

ABCDEFGHIJKLMNOPQRSTUVWXYZ
abcdefghijklmnopqrstuvwxyz

14 and 8 pt

International phonetic alphabet

Consonants

	Bilabial	Labiodental	Dental	Alveolar	Postalveolar	Retroflex	Palatal	Velar	Uvular	Pharyngeal	Glottal
Plosive	p b			t d		ʈ ɖ	c ɟ	k ɡ	q ɢ		ʔ
Nasal	m	ɱ		n		ɳ	ɲ	ŋ	ɴ		
Trill	ʙ			r					ʀ		
Tap or Flap				ɾ		ɽ					
Fricative	ɸ β	f v	θ ð	s z	ʃ ʒ	ʂ ʐ	ç ʝ	x ɣ	χ ʁ	ħ ʕ	h ɦ
Lateral fricative				ɬ ɮ							
Approximant		ʋ		ɹ		ɻ	j	ɰ			
Lateral approximant				l		ɭ	ʎ	ʟ			
Ejective stop	p’			t’		ʈ’	c’	k’	q’		
Implosive	ƥ ɓ			ƭ ɗ			ƈ ʄ	ƙ ɠ	ʠ ʛ		

Where symbols appear in pairs, the one to the right represents a voiced consonant. Shaded areas denote articulations judged impossible.

Vowels

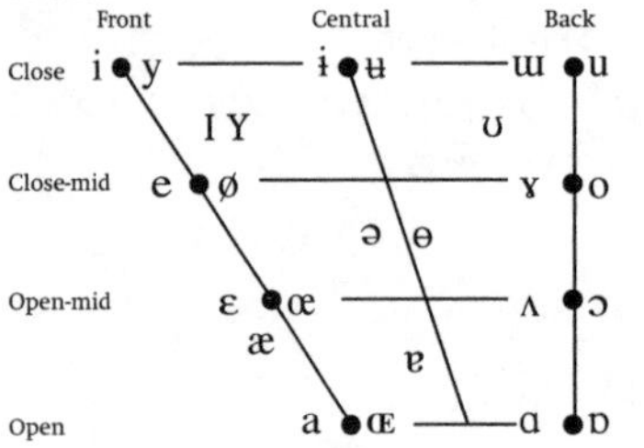

	Front	Central	Back
Close	i y	ɨ ʉ	ɯ u
	ɪ ʏ		ʊ
Close-mid	e ø	ɘ ɵ	ɤ o
		ə	
Open-mid	ɛ œ	ɜ ɞ	ʌ ɔ
	æ	ɐ	
Open	a ɶ		ɑ ɒ

Where symbols appear in pairs, the one to the right represents a rounded vowel.

Suprasegmentals

- ˈ Primary stress ˌfoʊnəˈtɪʃən
- ˌ Secondary stress
- ː Long eː
- ˑ Half-long eˑ
- ˘ Extra-short ĕ
- . Syllable break ɹi.ækt
- | Minor (foot) group
- ‖ Major (intonation group)
- ‿ Linking (absence of break)
- ↗ Global rise
- ↘ Global fall

Tones & word accents

Level		Contour	
e̋ or ˥	Extra high	ě ˩˥	Rising
é ˦	High	ê ˥˩	Falling
ē ˧	Mid	e᷄ ˦˥	High rising
è ˨	Low	e᷅ ˩˨	Low rising
ȅ ˩	Extra low	e᷈ ˧˦˧	Rising-falling etc.
↓	Downstep		
↑	Upstep		

Other symbols

- ʍ Voiceless labial-velar fricative
- w Voiced labial-velar approximant
- ɥ Voiced labial-palatal approximant
- ʜ Voiceless epiglottal fricative
- ʢ Voiced epiglottal fricative
- ʡ Epiglottal plosive
- ɕ ʑ Alveolo-palatal fricatives
- ɜ Additional mid central vowel
- ʘ Bilabial click
- ǀ Dental click
- ! (Post)alveolar click
- ǂ Palatoalveolar click
- ǁ Alveolar lateral click
- ɺ Alveolar lateral flap
- ɧ Simulataneous ʃ and x
- k͡p t͡s Affricates and double articulations can be represented by two symbols joined by a tie if necessary.

Diacritics

̥ Voiceless n̥ d̥	̹ More rounded ɔ̹	ʷ Labialized tʷ dʷ	̃ Nasalized ẽ
̬ Voiced s̬ t̬	̜ Less rounded ɔ̜	ʲ Palatalized tʲ dʲ	ⁿ Nasal release dⁿ
ʰ Aspirated tʰ dʰ	̟ Advanced u̟	ˠ Velarized tˠ dˠ	ˡ Lateral release dˡ
̤ Breathy voiced b̤ a̤	̠ Retracted i̠	ˤ Pharyngealized tˤ dˤ	̚ No audible release d̚
̰ Creaky voiced b̰ a̰	̈ Centralized ë	̴ Velarized or pharyngealized ɫ	
̼ Linguolabial t̼ d̼	̽ Mid-centralized e̽	̝ Raised e̝ (ɹ̝ = voiced alveolar fricative)	
̪ Dental t̪ d̪	̩ Syllabic ɹ̩	̞ Lowered e̞ (β̞ = voiced bilabial approximant)	
̺ Apical t̺ d̺	̯ Non-syllabic e̯	̘ Advanced Tongue Root e̘	
̻ Laminal t̻ d̻	˞ Rhoticity ɚ	̙ Retracted Tongue Root e̙	

Deaf fingerspelling

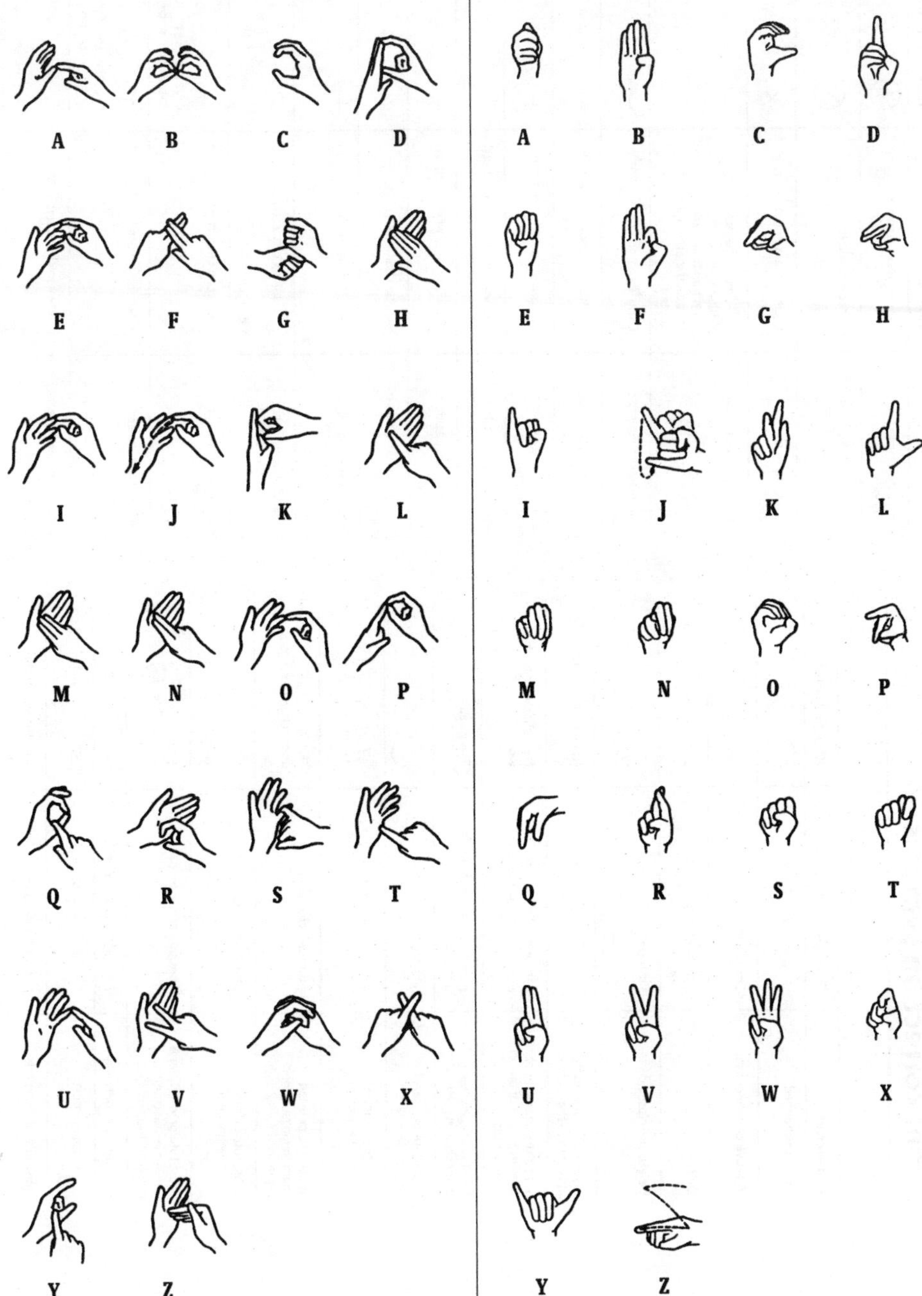

Proof correction symbols

Instruction	Textual mark	Marginal mark
Leave unchanged	- - - - under characters	ⓙ (circled ✓)
Remove extraneous marks	Encircle marks to be removed	×
Delete	/ through character(s) or ⊢—⊣ through words	∂ (delete mark)
Delete and close up	/ through character(s) or ⊢—⊣ (with close-up marks)	∂ with close-up marks
Insert in text the matter indicated in the margin	⋏	New matter followed by ⋏
Substitute character or substitute part of one or more words	/ through character or ⊢—⊣ through word(s)	New character or new word(s)
Substitute ligature e.g. æ for separate letters	⊢—⊣ through characters affected	⌒ e.g. ae (linked)
Substitute or insert full stop or decimal point	/ through character or ⋏	⊙
Substitute or insert comma, semicolon, colon, etc.	/ through character or ⋏	, / ; / ⊙ / (/) /
Substitute or insert character in 'superior' position	/ through character or ⋏	⌐ under character e.g. 2
Substitute or insert character in 'inferior' position	/ through character or ⋏	∟ over character e.g. 2
Substitute or insert single or double quotation marks or apostrophe	/ through character or ⋏	’ ” and/or ’ ” (marked)
Substitute or insert ellipsis	/ through character or ⋏	. . .
Substitute or insert hyphen	/ through character or ⋏	⊢-⊣
Substitute or insert rule	/ through character or ⋏	Give the size of the rule in the marginal mark ⊢1 em⊣ ⊢4 mm⊣
Substitute or insert oblique	/ through character or ⋏	○ with / inside
Wrong fount. Replace by character(s) of correct fount	Encircle character(s)	⊗
Change damaged character(s)	Encircle character(s)	×
Set in or change to italic	—— under character(s) Where space does not permit textual marks, encircle the affected area instead	⊔⊔
Change italic to upright type	Encircle character(s)	⊔⊔ (crossed)
Set in or change to capital letters	≡ under character(s)	≡
Set in or change to small capital letters	= under character(s)	=
Set in or change to bold type	∿∿∿ under character(s)	∿
Set in or change to bold italic type	∿∿∿ (with line) under character(s)	⊔⊔ with ∿
Change capital letters to lower-case letters	Encircle character(s)	≢ (crossed triple lines)
Change small capital letters to lower-case letters	Encircle character(s)	≠
Close up. Delete space between characters or words	⌒ linking characters e.g. a⌒scribe	⌒ ⌣
Insert space between characters	| between characters	Y Give the size of the space when necessary
Insert space between words	Y between words	Y Give the size of the space when necessary
Reduce space between characters	| between characters	⊤ Give the amount by which the space is to be reduced, when necessary

Instruction	Textual mark	Marginal mark
Reduce space between words	between words	Give the amount by which the space is to be reduced, when necessary
Make space appear equal between characters or words	I between characters or words	
Close up to normal interline spacing	(each side of column linking lines)	
Insert space between lines or paragraphs	or	Give the size of the space when necessary
Reduce space between lines or paragraphs	or	Give amount by which the space is to be reduced, when necessary
Start new paragraph		
Run on (no new paragraph)		
Transpose characters or words	between characters or words, numbered when necessary	
Transpose lines		
Transpose a number of lines	3 2 1	Rules extend from the margin into the text with each line to be transposed numbered in the correct sequence
Centre	[enclosing matter to be centred]	[ ]
Indent		Give the amount of the indent
Cancel indent		
Move matter specified distance to the right*	enclosing matter to be moved to the right	

Instruction	Textual mark	Marginal mark
Move matter specified distance to the left*	enclosing matter to be moved to the left	
Set line to specified measure*	and/or	
Set column to specified measure*		
Take over character(s), word(s) or line to next line, column or page		The textual mark surrounds the matter to be taken over and extends into the margin
Take back character(s), word(s) or line to previous line, column or page		The textual mark surrounds the matter to be taken back and extends into the margin
Raise matter*	over matter to be raised under matter to be raised	
Lower matter*	over matter to be lowered under matter to be lowered	
Move matter to position indicated*	Enclose matter to be moved and indicate new position	
Correct vertical alignment	‖	‖
Correct horizontal alignment	Single line above and below misaligned matter	placed level with the head and foot of the relevant line

* Give the exact dimensions when necessary.

Symbols in general use

&	ampersand (and)
&c	et cetera
@	at; per (in costs)
×	by (measuring dimensions eg 3 × 4)
£	pound
$	dollar (also peso, escudo, etc, in certain countries)
¢	cent (also centavo, etc, in certain countries)
©	copyright
®	registered trademark
¶	new paragraph
§	new section
¨	ditto
✱	born (in genealogy)
†	died
✱	hypothetical or unacceptable form (in linguistics)
☠	poison; danger
♂, □	male
♀, ○	female
✠	bishop's name follows
☎	telephone number follows
☜ ☞	this way
✂ ✂	cut here

In astronomy

●	new moon
☽	moon, first quarter
○	full moon
☾	moon, last quarter

In meteorology

▲▲▲	cold front
◗◗◗	warm front
◗▼◗▼	stationary front
◗▲◗▲	occluded front

In cards

♥	hearts
♦	diamonds
♠	spades
♣	clubs

First name preferences

Boys, England and Wales

	1920s		*1950s*		*1960s*		*1970s*		*1980s*
1	John	1	David	1	Paul	1	Stephen	1	Andrew
2	William	2	John	2	David	2	Mark	2	David
3	George	3	Peter	3	Andrew	3	Paul	3	Daniel
4	James	4	Michael	4	Stephen	4	Andrew	4	Christopher
5	Ronald	5	Alan	5	Mark	5	David	5	Stephen
6	Robert	6	Robert	6	Michael	6	Richard	6	Matthew
7	Kenneth	7	Stephen	7	Ian	7	Matthew	7	Paul
8	Frederick	8	Paul	8	Gary	8	Daniel	8	James
9	Thomas	9	Brian	9	Robert	9	Christopher	9	Mark
10	Albert	10	Graham	10	Richard	10	Darren	10	Michael
11	Eric	11	Philip	11	Peter	11	Michael	11	Adam
12	Edward	12	Anthony	12	John	12	James	12	Richard
13	Arthur	13	Colin	13	Anthony	13	Robert	13	Darren
14	Charles	14	Christopher	14	Christopher	14	Simon	14	Robert
15	Leslie	15	Geoffrey	15	Darren	15	Jason	15	Lee

Girls, England and Wales

	1920s		*1950s*		*1960s*		*1970s*		*1980s*
1	Joan	1	Susan	1	Trac(e)y	1	Claire	1	Sarah
2	Mary	2	Linda	2	Deborah	2	Sarah	2	Emma
3	Joyce	3	Christine	3	Julie	3	Nicola	3	Claire
4	Margaret	4	Margaret	4	Karen	4	Emma	4	Kelly
5	Dorothy	5	Carol	5	Susan	5	Joanne	5	Rebecca
6	Doris	6	Jennifer	6	Alison	6	Helen	6	Gemma
7	Kathleen	7	Janet	7	Jacqueline	7	Rachel	7	Rachel
8	Irene	8	Patricia	8	Helen	8	Lisa	8	Lisa
9	Betty	9	Barbara	9	Amanda	9	Rebecca	9	Victoria
10	Eileen	10	Ann	10	Sharon	10	Karen	10	Laura
11	Doreen	11	Sandra	11	Sarah		Michelle	11	Catherine
12	Lilian	12	Pamela	12	Joanne	12	Victoria	12	Nicola
	Vera		Pauline	13	Jane	13	Catherine	13	Michelle
14	Jean	14	Jean	14	Catherine	14	Amanda	14	Joanne
15	Marjorie	15	Jacqueline	15	Angela	15	Trac(e)y	15	Lindsay

Boys, USA

	1920s		*1950s*		*1970s*		*1980s (white)*		*1980s (non-white)*
1	Robert	1	Robert	1	Michael	1	Michael	1	Michael
2	John	2	Michael	2	Robert	2	Christopher	2	Christopher
3	William	3	James	3	David	3	Matthew	3	James

4	James	4	John	4	James	4	David	4	Jason
5	Charles	5	David	5	John	5	Jason	5	Robert
6	Richard	6	William	6	Jeffrey	6	Daniel	6	Anthony
7	George	7	Thomas	7	Steven	7	Robert	7	Brandon
8	Donald	8	Richard	8	Christopher	8	Eric	8	Kevin
9	Joseph	9	Gary	9	Brian	9	Brian	9	David
10	Edward	10	Charles	10	Mark	10	Joseph	10	Charles
11	Thomas	11	Ronald	11	William	11	Ryan	11	Aaron
12	David	12	Dennis	12	Eric	12	James		Brian
13	Frank	13	Steven	13	Kevin	13	Steven		Eric
14	Harold	14	Kenneth	14	Scott	14	John	14	John
15	Arthur	15	Joseph	15	Joseph	15	Jeffrey	15	Darryl

Girls, USA

	1920s		*1950s*		*1970s*		*1980s (white)*		*1980s (non-white)*
1	Mary	1	Linda	1	Michelle	1	Jennifer	1	Tiffany
2	Barbara	2	Mary	2	Jennifer	2	Sarah	2	Crystal
3	Dorothy	3	Patricia	3	Kimberly	3	Nicole	3	Ebony
4	Betty	4	Susan	4	Lisa	4	Jessica	4	Erica
5	Ruth	5	Deborah	5	Tracy	5	Katherine	5	Lakisha
6	Margaret	6	Kathleen	6	Kelly	6	Stephanie	6	Latoya
7	Helen	7	Barbara	7	Nicole	7	Elizabeth	7	Nicole
8	Elizabeth	8	Nancy	8	Angela	8	Amanda	8	Candice
9	Jean	9	Sharon	9	Pamela	9	Melissa	9	Danielle
10	Ann(e)	10	Karen	10	Christine	10	Lindsay	10	Brandi
11	Patricia	11	Carol(e)	11	Dawn	11	Rebecca	11	Jennifer
12	Shirley	12	Sandra	12	Amy	12	Lisa	12	Angela
13	Virginia	13	Diane	13	Deborah	13	Rachel	13	April
14	Nancy	14	Catherine	14	Karen	14	Lauren	14	Kimberly
15	Joan	15	Christine	15	Julie	15	Andrea	15	Stephanie

First name meanings

The meanings of the most popular first names listed above are given here along with a few other well-known names.

Name	*Original meaning*
Aaron	high mountain (Hebrew)
Adam	redness (Hebrew)
Alan	?rock, noble (Celtic)
Albert	noble bright (Germanic)
Alexander	defender of men (Greek)
Alison	French diminutive of Alice; of noble kind
Amanda	fit to be loved (Latin)
Amy	loved (French)
Andrea	female form of Andrew
Andrew	manly (Greek)
Angela	messenger, angel (Greek)
Ann(e)	English form of Hannah
Anthony	Roman family name
April	name of the month
Arthur	?bear, stone (Celtic)
Barbara	strange, foreign (Greek)
Barry	spear, javelin (Celtic)
Beatrice	bringer of joy (Latin)
Benjamin	son of my right hand (Hebrew)
Bernard	bear + brave (Germanic)
Beth	pet form of Elizabeth
Betty	pet form of Elizabeth
Bill/Billy	pet form of William
Bob	pet for of Robert
Brandi	variant of Brandy, from the common noun
Brandon	place name; broom-covered hill (Germanic)
Brian	?hill (?Celtic)
Candice	meaning unknown
Carl	man, husbandman (Germanic)
Carol(e)	form of **Caroline**, Italian female form of **Charles**
Catherine	?pure (Greek)
Charles	man, husbandman (Germanic)
Christine	French form of Christina ultimately from Christian; anointed
Christopher	carrier of Christ (Greek)
Claire	bright, shining (Latin)
Colin	form of Nicholas
Craig	rock (Celtic)
Crystal	female use of the common noun
Daniel	God is my judge (Hebrew)
Danielle	female form of Daniel
Darren	Irish surname
Darryl	surname; uncertain origin
David	?beloved, friend (Hebrew)
Dawn	female use of the common noun
Dean	surname; valley or leader
Deborah	bee (Hebrew)
Dennis	of Dionysus (Greek), the god of wine
Derek	form of Theodoric; ruler of the people (Germanic)
Diane	French form of Diana; divine (Latin)

First name meanings (continued)

Donald	world mighty (Gaelic)
Donna	lady (Latin)
Doreen	from Dora, a short form of Dorothy; gift of God
Doris	woman from Doris (Greek)
Dorothy	gift of God (Greek)
Ebony	female use of the common noun
Edward	property guardian (Germanic)
Eileen	Irish form of ?Helen
Elizabeth	oath/perfection of God (Hebrew)
Emily	Roman family name
Emma	all-embracing (Germanic)
Eric	ruler of all (Norse)
Erica	female form of Eric
Eugenie	French form of Eugene; well-born (Greek)
Frank	pet form of Francis; Frenchman
Frederick	peaceful ruler (Germanic)
Gail	pet form of Abigail; father rejoices (Hebrew)
Gareth	gentle (Welsh)
Gary	?surname; US place name
Gavin	Scottish form of Gawain; hawk + white (Welsh)
Gemma	gem (Italian)
Geoffrey	?peace (Germanic)
George	husbandman, farmer (Greek)
Graham	Germanic place name
Hannah	grace, favour (Hebrew)
Harold	army power/ruler (Germanic)
Harry	pet form of Henry; home ruler (Germanic)
Hayley	English place name; hay-meadow
Heather	plant name
Helen	bright/shining one (Greek)
Ian	modern Scottish form of John
Irene	peace (Greek)
Jacqueline	French female form of Jacques (James)
James	Latin form of Jacob; one who takes by the heel (Hebrew)
Jane	from Latin Johanna, female form of John
Janet	diminutive form of Jane
Jason	form of Joshua; Jehovah is salvation (Hebrew)
Jeffrey	US spelling of Geoffrey
Jean	french form of Johanna, from John
Jennifer	fair/white + yielding/smooth (Celtic)
Jeremy	English form of Jeremiah; Jehova exalts (Hebrew)
Jessica	he beholds (Hebrew)
Joan	contracted form of Johanna, from John
Joanne	French form of Johanna, from John
John	Jehovah has been gracious (Hebrew)
Jonathan	Jehovah's gift (Hebrew)
Joseph	Jehovah adds (Hebrew)
Joyce	?joyful (?Latin)
Julie	French female form of Latin Julius; descended from Jove
Karen	Danish form of Katarina (Catherine)
Katherine	US spelling of Catherine
Kathleen	English form of Irish Caitlin (from Catherine)
Kelly	Irish surname; warlike one
Kenneth	English form of Gaelic; fair one or fire-sprung
Kerry	Irish place name
Kevin	handsome at birth (Irish)
Kimberly	South African place name
Lakisha	La + ?Aisha; woman (Arabic)
Latoya	La + form of Tonya (Antonia)
Laura	bay, laurel (Latin)
Lauren	diminutive of Laura
Lee	Germanic place name; wood, clearing
Leslie	Scottish place name
Lilian	lily (Italian)
Linda	serpent (symbol of wisdom) (Germanic)
Lindsay	Scottish place name
Lisa	pet form of Elizabeth
Margaret	pearl (Greek)
Marjorie	from Marguerite, French form of Margaret
Mark	English form of Marcus, from Mars, god of war
Martin	from Mars, god of war (Latin)
Mary	Greek form of Miriam (Hebrew); unknown meaning
Matthew	gift of the Lord (Hebrew)
Melissa	bee (Greek)
Michael	like the Lord (Hebrew)
Michelle	English spelling of French, Michèle from Michael
Nancy	pet form of Ann
Natalie	birthday of the Lord (Latin)
Neil	champion (Irish)
Nicholas	victory people (Greek)
Nicola	Italian female form of Nicholas
Nicole	French female form of Nicholas
Pamela	?all honey (Greek)
Patricia	noble (Latin)
Paul	small (Latin)
Pauline	French female form of Paul
Peter	stone, rock (Greek)
Philip	fond of horses (Greek)
Rachel	ewe (Hebrew)
Rebecca	?noose (Hebrew)
Richard	strong ruler (Germanic)
Robert	fame bright (Germanic)
Ronald	counsel + power (Germanic)
Ruth	?companion (Hebrew)
Ryan	Irish surname
Sally	pet form of Sarah
Samantha	female form of Samuel; heard/name of God (Hebrew)
Sandra	pet form from Alexandra
Sarah	princess (Hebrew)
Scott	surname from Scotland
Sharon	the plain (Hebrew)
Shaun	English spelling of Irish Sean, from John
Shirley	bright clearing (Germanic)
Simon	form of Simeon; listening attentively (Hebrew)
Stephanie	French female form of Stephen
Stephen	crown (Greek)
Stuart	steward (Germanic)
Susan	short form of Susannah; lily (Hebrew)
Teresa	woman of Theresia (Greek)
Thomas	twin (Hebrew)
Tiffany	manifestation of God (Greek)
Timothy	honouring God (Greek)
Trac(e)y	?pet form of Teresa

Vera	faith (Slavic)
Victoria	victory (Latin)
Vincent	conquer (Latin)
Virginia	maiden (Latin)
Walter	ruling people (Germanic)
Wayne	surname; wagon-maker
William	will + helmet (Germanic)
Zoë	life (Greek)

Common abbreviations

A

AA	Alcoholics Anonymous
AA	Automobile Association
AA(A)	anti-aircraft (artillery)
AAA	Amateur Athletics Association
AAA	American Automobile Association
ABA	Amateur Boxing Association
ABA	American Broadcasting Association
ABC	Australian Broadcasting Corporation
ABM	antiballistic missile
ABTA	Association of British Travel Agents
AC	alternating current
ACAS	Advisory, Conciliation, and Arbitration Service
ACLU	American Civil Liberties Union
ACT	Australian Capital Territory
ACTH	adrenocorticotrophic hormone
ACTU	Australian Council of Trade Unions
AD	anno Domini (in the year of Our Lord)
A-D	analog-to-digital (in computing)
ADH	antidiuretic hormone
ADP	adenosine diphosphate
AEA	Atomic Energy Authority (UK)
AEC	Atomic Energy Commission (USA)
AFC	American Football Conference
AFL/CIO	American Federation of Labor/Congress of Industrial Organizations
AFP	Agence France Presse
AFV	armoured fighting vehicle
AGM	annual general meeting
AGR	advanced gas-cooled reactor
AH	anno Hegirae (in the year of Hegira)
AHF	anti haemophilic factor
AI	artificial intelligence
AID	artificial insemination by donor
AIDS	Acquired Immune Deficiency Syndrome
AIF	Australian Imperial Force
AIH	artificial insemination by husband
ALCM	air-launched cruise missile
ALGOL	algorithmic language
ALP	Australian Labor Party
ALU	arithmetic and logic unit
AM	amplitude modulation
AMA	American Medical Association
AMU	atomic mass unit
ANC	African National Congress
ANS	autonomic nervous system
ANSI	American National Standards Institute
ANZAC	Australian and New Zealand Army Corps
ANZUS	Australia, New Zealand and the United States
AOB	any other business
AONB	Area of Outstanding Natural Beauty
AP	Associated Press
APEX	Association of Professional, Executive, Clerical, and Computer Staff
APL	a programming language
APR	annual percentage rate
APRA	Alianza Popular Revolutionaria Americana (American Popular Revolutionary Alliance)
AR	aspect ratio
ARCIC	Anglican–Roman Catholic International Commission
A/S	Advanced/Supplementary
ASA	American Standards Association
ASCII	American Standards Code for Information Interchange
ASDIC	Admiralty Submarine Detection Investigation Committee
ASEAN	Association of South-East Asian Nations
ASL	American Sign Language
ASLEF	Associated Society of Locomotive Engineers and Firemen
ASLIB	Association of Special Libraries and Information Bureaux
ASM	air-to-surface missile
ASPCA	American Society for the Prevention of Cruelty to Animals
ASSR	Autonomous Soviet Socialist Republic
ASTMS	Association of Scientific, Technical, and Managerial Staffs
ATP	adenosine triphosphate
ATS	Auxiliary Territorial Service
ATV	Associated Television
AU	astronomical unit
AV	audio-visual
AWACS	Airborne Warning and Control System
AWU	Australian Workers' Union

B

B&W	black and white
BAFTA	British Academy of Film and Television Arts
BALPA	British Airline Pilots' Association
BASIC	Beginners All-purpose Symbolic Instruction Code
BASIC	British American Scientific International Commercial (English)
BBC	British Broadcasting Corporation
BC	before Christ
BCD	binary coded decimal
BCG	bacille (bacillus) Calmette Guérin
BCS	Bardeen, Cooper & Schrieffer (theory)
BEF	British Expeditionary Force
BEV	Black English Vernacular
BHP	Broken Hill Proprietary Company
BIA	Bureau of Indian Affairs
BIS	Bank for International Settlements
BLAISE	British Library Automated Information Service
BMA	British Medical Association
BOSS	Bureau of State Security (South Africa)
BP	blood pressure
BSE	bovine spongiform encephalopathy
BSI	British Standards Institution

Common abbreviations (continued)

BST British Summer Time
btu British thermal unit
BUF British Union of Fascists
BUPA British United Provident Association

C

CAB Citizen's Advice Bureau
CACM Central American Common Market
CAD computer-aided design
CAI computer-aided instruction
CAL computer-aided learning
CAM computer-aided manufacture
CAP Common Agricultural Policy
CARICOM Caribbean Community
CARIFTA Caribbean Free Trade Area
CATV cable television
CB citizen's band (radio)
CBE Commander of the (Order of the) British Empire
CBI Confederation of British Industry
CBS Columbia Broadcasting Corporation
CCD charge-coupled device
CCK cholecystokinin-pancreozymin
CCR camera cassette recorder
CCTV closed circuit television
CD Civil Defence
CD compact disk
CDC Centers for Disease Control
CDROM compact disc read-only memory
CDU Christian Democratic Union
CENTO Central Treaty Organization
CERN Organisation Européene pour la Recherche Nucléaire (formerly, Conseil Européen pour la Recherche Nucléaire)
CGS centimetre-gram-second
CGT capital gains tax
CGT Confédération Générale du Travail
CH Companion of Honour
CHAPS Clearing House Automated Clearing System
CHIPS Clearing House Interbank Payments System
CIA Central Intelligence Agency
CID Criminal Investigation Department
CIO Congress of Industrial Organizations
CM Congregation of the Mission
CMG Companion of (the Order of) St Michael & St George
CNAA Council for National Academic Awards
CND Campaign for Nuclear Disarmament
CNES Centre National d'Espace
CNS central nervous system
COBOL Common Business Oriented Language
COMAL Common Algorithmic Language
COMECON Council for Mutual Economic Assistance
CORE Congress of Racial Equality
CP Congregation of the Passion
CPI Consumer Price Index
CP/M control program monitor
CPR cardio-pulmonary resuscitation
CPU central processing unit
CRO cathode-ray oscilloscope
CRT cathode-ray tube
CSE Certificate of Secondary Education
CSF cerebrospinal fluid
CSIRO Commonwealth Scientific and Industrial Research Organisation
CSO colour separation overlay
CTT capital transfer tax
CV cultivar
CVO Commander of the Royal Victorian Order
CVS chorionic villus sampling
CWA County Women's Association
CWS Co-operation Wholesale Society

D

D-A digital-to-analog
DALR dry adiabatic lapse rate
D&C dilation and curettage
DBE Dame Commander of the (Order of the) British Empire
DBMS database management system
DBS direct broadcasting from satellite
DC direct current
DCF discounted cash flow
DCMG Dame Commander Grand Cross of (the Order of) St Michael and St George
DCVO Dame Commander of the Royal Victorian Order
DDT dichloro-diphenyl-trichloroethane
DES Department of Education and Science
DES diethylstilboestrol
DFC Distinguished Flying Cross
DHA District Health Authority
DIA Defence Intelligence Agency
DLP Democratic Labor Party (Australia)
DMSO dimethyl sulphoxide
DNA deoxyribonucleic acid
DOS disk operating system
DSN Deep Space Network
DSO Distinguished Service Order
DST daylight saving time
DTP desk-top publishing

E

EAC European Atomic Commission
EARM electrically alterable read-only memory
EBCDIC extended binary-coded decimal interchange code
EBU European Boxing Union
EBU European Broadcasting Union
EC European Community
ECA European Commission on Agriculture
ECF extracellular fluid
ECG electrocardiograph
ECM European Common Market
ECO European Coal Organization
ECOSOC Economic and Social Council (of the United Nations)
ECOWAS Economic Community of West African States
ECSC European Coal and Steel Community
ECT electroconvulsive therapy
ECTG European Channel Tunnel Group
ECU European currency unit
EDC European Defence Community
EDVAC Electronic Discrete Variable Automatic Computer
EEG electroencephalograph
EEOC Equal Employment Opportunity Commission

EFA European Fighter Aircraft
EFC European Forestry Commission
EFTA European Free Trade Association
EGF epidermal growth factor
EI Exposure Index
ELDO European Launcher Development Organisation
ELF Eritrea Liberation Front
EMF electromotive force
EMS European Monetary System
EMU electromagnetic units
ENIAC Electronic Numeral Indicator and Calculator
EOKA Ethniki Organosis Kipriakou Agonos (National Organisation of Cypriot Struggle)
EP European Parliament
EPA Environmental Protetection Agency
EPR Einstein-Podolsky-Rosen (paradox)
EPR electron paramagnetic resonance
EPROM electronically programmable read-only memory
ERNIE Electronic Random Number Indicator Equipment
ERW enhanced radiation weapon
ESA Environmentally Sensitive Area
ESA European Space Agency
ESC electronic stills camera
ESCU European Space Operations Centre
ESO European Southern Observatory
ESP extra-sensory perception
ESRO European Space Research Organisation
ESTEC European Space Research and Technology Centre
ETU Electricians Trade Union
EUFA European Union Football Associations
EURATOM European Atomic Energy Community

F

FA Football Association
FAA Federal Aviation Administration
FAO Food and Agriculture Organisation
FBI Federal Bureau of Investigation
FCA Farm Credit Administration
FCC Federal Communications Commission
FDIC Federal Deposit Insurance Corporation
FIFA Fédération Internationale de Football Association (International Association Football Federation)
FIMBRA Financial Intermediaries, Managers and Brokers Regulatory Association
FLN Front de Liberation Nationale
FM frequency modulation
FORTRAN formula translation
FPS foot-pound-second
FRELIMO Frente de Libertação de Moçambique
FSH follicle-stimulating hormone
FTC Federal Trade Commission

G

GAR Grand Army of the Republic
GATT General Agreement on Tariffs and Trade
GBE Knight/Dame Grand Cross of (the Order of the) British Empire
GC George Cross
GCC Gulf Co-operation Council
GCE General Certificate of Education
GCHQ Government Communications Headquarters
GCMG Knight/Dame Grand Cross of (the Order of) St Michael and St George
GCSE General Certificate Secondary Education
GCVO Knight/Dame Grand Cross of the Royal Victorian Order
GDI gross domestic income
GDP gross domestic product
GEO geosynchronous Earth orbit
GESP generalized extra-sensory perception
GH growth hormone
GLC gas-liquid chromatography
GLCM ground-launched cruise missile
GM George Medal
GMC General Medical Council
GMT Greenwich Mean Time
GNP gross national product
GnRH gonadotrophin-releasing hormone
GP General Practictioner
GPSS General Purpose System Simulator
GUT grand unified theory

H

HCG human chorionic gonadotrophin

HE His/Her Excellency
HEP hydro-electric power
HF high frequency
HGV heavy goods vehicle
HIH His/Her Imperial Highnes
HIM His/Her Imperial Majesty
HLA human leucocyte antigen
HM His/Her Majesty
HMG His/Hel Majesty's Government
HMI His/Her Majesty's Inspectorate
HMO health maintenance organization
HMS His/Her Majesty's Ship/Service
HMSO His/Her Majesty's Stationery Office
HNC Higher National Certificate
HND Higher National Diploma
HP horsepower
HR House of Representatives
HRH His/Her Royal Highness

I

IAEA International Atomic Energy Agency
IBRD International Bank for Reconstruction and Development
ICAO International Civil Aviation Organization
ICFTU International Confederation of Free Trade Unions
ICI Imperial Chemical Industries
IDA International Development Agency
IFAD International Fund for Agricultural Development
IFC International Finance Corporation
ILO International Labour Organization
IMCO Intergovernmental Maritime Consultative Organization
IMF International Monetary Fund
INLA Irish National Liberation Army
INRI Iesus Nazarenus Rex Iudeorum (Jesus of Nazareth, King of the Jews)
IPA International Phonetic Alphabet
IQ intelligence quotient
IR infrared

Common abbreviations (continued)

IRA Irish Republican Army
IRB Irish Republican Brotherhood
IRBM intermediate-range ballistic missile
ISBN International Standard Book Number
ISO International Organization for Standardization
ISSN International Standard Serial Number
ITA Initial Teaching Alphabet
ITCZ intertropical convergence zone
ITN Independent Television News
ITT International Telephone and Telegraph Corporation
ITU International Telecommunication Union
ITV Independent Television
IUCN International Union for the Conservation of Nature and Natural Resources
IUD intra-uterine device
IUPAC International Union of Pure and Applied Chemistry
IUPAP International Union of Pure and Applied Physics
IVF in vitro fertilisation
IVR International Vehicle Registration
IWW Industrial Workers of the World

J

JET Joint European Torus
JP Justice of the Peace
JPL Jet Propulsion Laboratory

K

KADU Kenya African Democratic Union
KANU Kenya African National Union
KB Knight Bachelor; Knight of the Bath
KBE Knight Commander of the (Order of the) British Empire
KC King's Counsel
KCB Knight Commander of the Bath
KCMG Knight Commander Grand Cross of (the Order of) St Michael and St George
KCVO Knight Commander of The Royal Victorian Order
KG Knight of the Order of the Garter
KGB Komitet Gosudarstvennoye Bezhopaznosti (Committee of State Security)
KKK Ku Klux Klan
KMT Kuomintang
KPC kiloparsec
KT Knight of the Thistle

L

LAFTA Latin American Free Trade Association
LAN local area network
LAUTRO Life Assurance and Unit Trust Companies
LCD liquid-crystal display
LDC less-developed country
LEA Local Education Authority
LED light-emitting diode
LEO low Earth orbit
LFA less favoured area
LH luteinizing hormone
LHRH luteinizing-hormone-releasing hormone
LIFFE London International Financial Futures Exchange
LISP list processing
LMS London Missionary Society
LPG liquefied petroleum gas
LSD lysergic acid diethylamide
LSI large-scale integration
LVO Lieutenant of the Royal Victorian Order

M

MAC multiplexed analogue component
MAO monoamine oxidase
MATV Master Antenna Television
MBE Member of the Order of the British Empire
MCA monetary compensation amount
MCC Marylebone Cricket Club
MDMA methylenedioxymethamphetamine
ME myalgic encephalomyelitis
MH Medal of Honor
MHD magnetohydrodynamics
MICR magnetic ink character recognition
MIRED micro reciprocal degrees
MIRV multiple independently targetted re-entry vehicle
MKSA metre-kilogram-second-ampere
MLR minimum lending rate
MMF magnetomotive force
MMI man-machine interaction
MOH Medal of Honor
MPC megaparsec
MPS marginal propensity to save
MPTP methylphenyltetrahydropyridine
MRA Moral Rearmament
MSC Manpower Services Commission
MSG monosodium glutamate
MSH melanocyte-stimulating hormone
MVD Ministerstvo Vnutrennykh Del (Ministry for Internal Affairs)
MVO Member of the Royal Victorian Order

N

NAACP National Association for the Advancement of Coloured People
NANC non-adrenergic non-cholinergic
NASA National Aeronautics and Space Administration
NASDA National Space Development Agency
NATO North Atlantic Treaty Organisation
NBC National Broadcasting Corporation
NDE near-death experience
NEDO National Economic Development Office
NEP new economic policy
NF National Front
NFC National Football Conference
NGC new general catalogue
NGF nerve growth factor
NHL National Hockey League
NHS National Health Service
NIH National Institutes of Health
NKVD Narodnyi Komissariat Vnutrennikh Del (People's Commissariat of Internal Affairs)
NLRB National Labor Relations Board
NMR nuclear magnetic resonance
NOW National Organization for Women
NPT Non-Proliferation Treaty
NRA National Recovery Administration

NRAO National Radio Astronomy Observatory
NSF National Science Foundation
NSPCC National Society for the Prevention of Cruelty to Children
NTSC National Television System Commission
NUM National Union of Mineworkers
NUT National Union of Teachers
NVC non-verbal communication

O

OAPEC Organization of Arab Petroleum Exporting Countries
OAS Organisation de l'Armée Secrète (Secret Army Organization)
OAS Organization of American States
OAU Organization of African Unity
OB Order of the Bath
OB outside broadcast
OBE Officer of the (Order of the) British Empire
OCARM Order of the Brothers of the Blessed Virgin Mary of Mount Carmel
OCART Order of Carthusians
OCR optical character recognition/reader
OCSO Order of the Reformed Cistercians of the Strict Observance
OD ordnance datum
ODC Order of Discalced Carmelites
ODECA Organizacion de Estados Centro Americanos (Organization of Central American States)
OECD Organization for Economic Co-operation and Development
OEEC Organization for European Economic Co-operation
OEM Original Equipment Manufacturer
OFM Order of Friars Minor
OFMCap Order of Friars Minor Capuchin
OFMConv Order of Friars Minor Conventual
OGPU Otdelenie Gosudarstvenni Politcheskoi Upravi (Special Government Political Administration)
OM Order of Merit
OMCap Order of Friars Minor of St Francis Capuccinorum
OOBE out-of-body experience
OP Order of Preachers
OPEC Organization of Petroleum Exporting Countries
OSA Order of the Hermit Friars of St Augustine
OSB Order of St Benedict
OSFC Order of Friars Minor of St Francis Capuccinorum
OTC over-the-counter (stocks and shares, drugs)
OTEC ocean thermal energy conversion
OU Open University
OXFAM Oxford Committee for Famine Relief

P

PAC Pan-African Congress
PAC political action committee
PAL phase alternation line
PAYE pay as you earn
PC parsec
PC personal computer
PC Poor Clares
PCP phenylcyclohexylpiperidine
PDGF platelet-derived growth factor
PDR precision depth recorder
PEN International Association of Poets, Playwrights, Editors, Essayists, and Novelists
PEP Political and Economic Planning
PF Patriotic Front
PGA Professional Golfers' Association
PH Purple Heart
PIN personal identification number
PK psychokinesis
PKU phenylketonuria
PLA People's Liberation Army
PLC public limited company
PLO Palestine Liberation Organization
PM of F Presidential Medal of Freedom
PNLM Palestine National Liberation Movement
POW prisoner of war
PPI plan position indicator
PR proportional representation
PRO Public Record Office
PRO public relations officer
PROM programmable read-only memory
PSBR public sector borrowing requirement
PTA parent-teacher association
PTFE polytetrafluorethylene
PVA polyvinyl acetate
PVC polyvinyl chloride
PWA Public Works Administration
PWR pressurized-water reactor
PYO pick-your-own

Q

QC Queen's Counsel
QCD quantum chromodynamics
QED quantum electrodynamics

R

RA Royal Academy
R&A Royal & Ancient Golf Club of St Andrews
RAAF Royal Australian Air Force
RADA Royal Academy of Dramatic Art
RAF Royal Air Force
RAM random access memory
RAM Royal Academy of Music
RAN Royal Australian Navy
RDA recommended daily allowance
REM rapid eye movement
RGB red green and blue (colour television)
RHA Regional Health Authority
RISC Reduced instruction set computer
RKKA Rabochekrest'yanshi Krasny (Red Army of Workers and Peasants)
RM Royal Marines
RMS root mean square
RN Royal Navy
RNA ribonucleic acid
RNLI Royal National Lifeboat Institution
ROM read-only memory
RP received pronunciation
RPI retail price index
RPM resale price maintenance
RPM revolutions per minute
RS Royal Society
RSPB Royal Society for the Protection of Birds
RSPCA Royal Society for the Prevention of Cruelty to Animals

Common abbreviations (continued)

RTG radio-isotope thermo-electric generator
RVO Royal Victorian Order

S

SA Sturm Abteilung (Storm Troopers)
SALR saturated adiabatic lapse rate
SALT Strategic Arms Limitation Talks
SAS Special Air Service
SBR styrene butadiene rubber
SCID severe combined immuno-deficiency
SCLC Southern Christian Leadership Conference
SDI selective dissemination of information
SDI strategic defence initiative
SDP Social Democratic Party
SDR special drawing rights
SDS Students for a Democratic Society
SDU Social Democratic Union
SEAQ Stock Exchange Automated Quotations
SEATO South-East Asia Treaty Organization
SEC Securities and Exchange Commission
SECAM Séquence Electronique Couleur avec Mémoire (Electronic Colour Sequence with Memory)
SERPS State earnings-related pension scheme
SHAEF Supreme Headquarters Allied Expeditionary Force
SHAPE Supreme Headquarters Allied Powers, Europe
SHF super-high frequency
SI Système International (International System)
SIB Securities and Investments Board
SIOP single integrated operation plan
SJ Society of Jesus
SLBM submarine-launched ballistic missile
SLCM sea-launched cruise missile
SLDP Social and Liberal Democratic Party
SLE systemic lupus erythematosus
SLR single-lens reflex
SNCC Student Non-Violent Co-ordinating Committee
SNOBOL String-Oriented Symbolic Language
SNP Scottish National Party
SOCist Cistercians of Common Observance
SOE Special Operations Executive
SONAR sound navigation and ranging
SQUID superconducting quantum interference device
SRO self-regulatory organisation
SRO single room occupancy
SS Schutzstaffel (Protective Squad)
SSR Soviet Socialist Republic
SSSI Site of Special Scientific Interest
START Strategic Arms Reduction Talks
STOL short take-off and landing
SWAPO South-West Africa People's Organization
SWS slow wave sleep

T

TAB Totalisator Agency Board
TARDIS time and relative dimensions in space
TASS Telegrafnoe Agentsvo Sovetskovo Soyuza (Telegraph Agency of the Soviet Union)
TCDD tetrachlorodibenzo-p-dioxin
TEFL Teaching English as a Foreign Language
TESL Teaching English as a Second Language
TGWU Transport and General Workers Union
TNT trinitrotoluene
TT Tourist Trophy
TTL through the lens
TUC Trades Union Congress
TV television
TVA Tennessee Valley Authority

U

UAE United Arab Emirates
UAP United Australia Party
UCAR Union of Central African Republics
UCCA University Central Council on Admissions
UDA Ulster Defence Association
UDI Unilateral Declaration of Independence
UEFA Union of European Football Associations
UFO unidentified flying object
UHF ultra-high frequency
UHT ulta-high temperature
UK United Kingdom
UN United Nations
UNCTAD United Nations Conference on Trade and Development
UNDC United Nations Disarmament Commission
UNDP United Nations Development Programme
UNEP United Nations Environment Programme
UNESCO United Nations Economic, Scientific and Cultural Organisation
UNFAO United Nations Food and Agriculture Organization
UNGA United Nations General Assembly
UNHCR United Nations High Commission for Refugees
UNHRC United Nations Human Rights Commissioner
UNICEF United Nations Children's Fund (formerly UN International Children's Emergency Fund)
UNIDO United Nations Industrial Development Organization
UNO United Nations Organization
UNRWA United Nations Relief and Works Agency for Palestine Refugees in the Near East
UNSC United Nations Security Council
UNSG United Nations Secretary General
UNTT United Nations Trust Territory
UPU Universal Postal Union
USA United States of America
USAF United States Air Force
USCG United States Coast Guard
USIS United States Information Service
USSR Union of Soviet Socialist Republics

V

VA Veterans Administration
VAT value-added tax
VC Victoria Cross
VCR video cassette recorder
VD venereal disease
VDU visual display unit
VHF very high frequency
VHS video home system
VIP vasoactive intestinal polypeptide
VLF very low frequency

VLSI	very large scale interpretation
VOA	Voice of America
VSEPR	valence shell electron pair repulsion
VSO	Voluntary Service Overseas
VTOL	vertical take-off and landing
VTR	video tape recorder
	W
WAAC	Women's Auxiliary Army Corps
WAAF	Women's Auxiliary Air Force
WAC	Women's Army Corps
WASP	White Anglo-Saxon Protestant
WBA	World Boxing Association
WBC	World Boxing Council
WCC	World Council of Churches
WEA	Workers' Educational Association
WFTU	World Federation of Trade Unions
WHO	World Health Organization
WI	(National Federation of) Women's Institutes
WIPO	World Intellectual Property Organization
WMO	World Meteorological Organization
WPA	Work Projects Administration
WRAC	Women's Royal Army Corps
WRAF	Women's Royal Air Force
WRNS	Women's Royal Naval Service
WRVS	Women's Royal Voluntary Service
WVS	Women's Voluntary Service
WWF	World Wildlife Fund
	Y
YHA	Youth Hostels Association
YMCA	Young Men's Christian Association
YMHA	Young Men's Hebrew Association
YWCA	Young Women's Christian Associalion
YWHA	Young Women's Hebrew Association

MEDIA

News agencies

	Agency	*Headquartered*
AA	Anadol Ajansi	Ankara
AAP	Australian Associated Press	Sydney
AASA	Agence Arabe Syrienne d'Information	Damascus
ADN	Allgemeiner Deutscher Nachrichtendienst	Berlin
AE	Agence Europe	Brussels
AFP	Agence France Presse	Paris
AIO	Agencia Informativa Orbe de Chile	Santiago
AIP	Agence Ivoirienne de Presse	Abidjan
ALD	Agence Los Diarios	Buenos Aires
ALI	Agencia Lusa de Informacao	Lisbon
AM	Agencia Meridional	Rio de Janeiro
AN	Agencia Nacional	Brasilia
ANA	Athenagence	Athens
ANGOP	Angola Agêcia Naticiosa N'gola Press	Luanda
ANP	Algemeen Nederlands Persbureau	The Hague
ANSA	Agenzia Nazionale Stampa Associate	Rome
ANTARA	Indonesian National News Agency	Jakarta
AP	Associated Press	New York
APA	Austria Presse Agentur	Vienna
APP	Agence Parisienne de Presse	Paris
APP	Associated Press of Pakistan	Islamabad
APS	Agence de Presse Senegalaise	Dakar
APS	Algeria Presse Service	Algiers
ATA	Albanian Telegraphic Agency	Tirana
AUP	Australian United Press	Melbourne
BATRA	Jordan News Agency	Amman
BELGA	Agence Belga	Brussels
BERNAMA	Malaysian National News Agency	Kuala Lumpur
BOPA	Botswana Press Agency	Gaborone
BSS	Bangladesh Sangbad Sangstha	Dhaka
BTA	Bulgarska Telegrafitscheka Agentzia	Sofia
CANA	Caribbean News Agency	Bridgetown
CIP	Centre d'Information de Presse	Brussels
CNA	Central News Agency	Taipei
CNA	Cyprus News Agency	Nicosia
CNS	China News Service	Beijing
COLPRENSA	Colprensa	Bogota
CP	Canadian Press	Toronto
CSTK	Ceskoslovenska Tiskova Kancelar	Prague
DPA	Deutsche Presse Agentur	Hamburg
EFE	Agencia EFE	Madrid
ENA	Eastern News Agency	Dhaka
ETA	Eesti Teadate Agentuur	Tallinn
EXTEL	Exchange and Telegraph Company	London
FIDES	Agenzia Internazionale Fides	Vatican City
GNA	Agence Guinéenne de Presse	Conakry
GNA	Ghana News Agency	Accra
GNA	Guyana News Agency	Georgetown
HHA	Hurriyet Haber Ajasi	Istanbul
HINA	Hrvatska Izvjestajna Novinska Agencija	Zagreb
IC	Inforpress Centroamericana	Guatemala
	Agency	*Headquartered*
INA	Iraqi News Agency	Baghdad
IPS	Inter Press Service	Rome
IRNA	Islamic Republic News Agency	Tehran
ITIM	Associated Israel Press	Tel Aviv
JAMPRESS	Jampress	Kingston
JANA	Jamahiriya News Agency	Tripoli

News agencies (continued)

JIJI	Jiji Tsushin-Sha	Tokyo
JTA	Jewish Telegraphic Agency	Jerusalem
KCNA	Korean Central News Agency	Pyongyang
KNA	Kenya News Agency	Nairobi
KPL	Khao San Pathet Lao	Vientiane
KUNA	Kuwait News Agency	Kuwait City
KYODO	Kyodo Tsushin	Tokyo
LAI	Logos Agencia de Informacion	Madrid
LETA	Latvijas Telegrafa Agentura	Riga
MENA	Middle East News Agency	Cairo
MTI	Magyar Tavariti Iroda	Budapest
NA	Noticias Argentinas	Buenos Aires
NAEWOE	Naewoe Press	Seoul
NAN	News Agency of Nigeria	Lagos
NOTIMEX	Noticias Mexicanas	Mexico City
NOVOSTI	Agentstvo Pechati Novosti	Moscow
NPS	Norsk Presse Service	Oslo
NTB	Norsk Telegrambyra	Oslo
NZPA	New Zealand Press Agency	Wellington
OPA	Orbis Press Agency	Prague
OTTFNB	Oy Suomen Tietoimisto Notisbyran Ab	Helsinki
PA	Press Association	London
PANA	Pan-African News Agency	Dakar
PAP	Polska Agencija Prasowa	Warsaw
PNA	Philippines News Agency	Manila
PPI	Pakistan Press International	Karachi
PRELA	Prensa Latina	Havana
PS	Presse Services	Paris
PTI	Press Trust of India	Bombay
RB	Ritzaus Bureau	Copenhagen
REUTERS	Reuters	London
ROMPRESS	Romanian News Agency	Bucharest
SAPA	South African Press Association	Johannesburg
SDA	Schweizerische Depeschenagentur	Berne
SIP	Svensk Internationella Pressbyran	Stockholm
SLENA	Sierra Leone News Agency	Freetown
SOFIAPRES	Sofia Press Agency	Sofia
SOPAC-NEWS	South Pacific News Service	Wellington
SPA	Saudi Press Agency	Riyadh
SPK	Saporamean Kampuchea	Phnom Penh
STA	Slovenska Tiskovna Agencija	Ljubljana
TANJUG	Novinska Agencija Tanjug	Belgrade
TAP	Tunis Afrique Presse	Tunis
TASS	Telegraph Agency of the Sovereign States	Moscow
TT	Tidningarnes Telegrambyra	Stockholm
UNI	United News of India	New Delhi
UPI	United Press International	New York
UPP	United Press of Pakistan	Karachi
VNA	Vietnam News Agency	Hanoi
XINHUA	Xinhua	Beijing
YONHAP	Yonhap (United) Press Agency	Seoul
ZIANA	Zimbabwe Inter-Africa News Agency	Harare

Government information departments

Afghanistan	Ministry of Information and Culture
American Samoa	Public Information Office
Andorra	Ministry of Tourism and Sport
Angola	Ministry of Information
Antigua & Barbuda	Public Information Division
Argentina	Secretaria de Información Publica (SIP)
Bahamas	Office of the Prime Minister
Bahrain	Ministry of Information
Bangladesh	Press Information Department
Barbados	Barbados Government Information Service (BGIS)
Belau	Public Information Division
Belize	Government Information Service
Benin	Ministry of Culture and Communications
Bermuda	Department of Information Services
Bhutan	Department of Information and Broadcasting
Bolivia	Ministry of Information
Botswana	Department of Information and Broadcasting
Brazil	Serviço Nacional das Informaçaos
Brunei	Department of Broadcasting and Information
Burkina Faso	Ministry of Information and Culture
Burundi	Ministry of Communication
Cambodia	Ministry of Information and Culture
Cameroon	Ministry of Information and Culture
Cape Verde	Ministry of Information, Culture, and Sport
Central African Republic	Ministry of Communication
Chad	Ministry of Information, Culture, and Civic Orientation
Chile	Communications Secretariat; Office of the Minister Secretary-General of the Government
Colombia	Ministry of Communications
Comoros	Ministry of Information and Broadcasting
Congo	Ministry of Information
Costa Rica	General Directorate of Information and the Press
Côte d'Ivoire	Ministry of Communications
Cuba	Publications Office

Country	Office
Cyprus	Press and Information Office
Cyprus, north	Public Information Office
Denmark	Statens Informationstjeneste
Djibouti	Ministry of the Interior
Dominica	Office of the Prime Minister
Ecuador	Secretariat for Public Information
Egypt	Ministry of Information
El Salvador	Centro de Información Nacional
Ethiopia	Ministry of Information and National Guidance
Faroe Islands	Faroes Government
Fiji	Ministry of Information
France	Service d'Information et de Diffusion
Gabon	Ministry of Information, Posts, and Telecommunications
Gambia	Ministry of Information and Tourism
Germany	Press and Information Office of the Federal Government
Ghana	Castle Information Bureau; Secretariat for Information
Gibraltar	General Division
Greece	General Secretariat for Press and Information
Greenland	Greenland Home Government; Ministry for Greenland
Grenada	Ministry of Information
Guam	Governor's Office
Guinea	Department for Information, Culture, and Tourism
Guinea-Bissau	Ministry of Information and Telecommunications
Haiti	Ministry of Information
Hong Kong	Government Information Service
Iceland	Prime Minister's Office
India	Press Information Bureau
Indonesia	Ministry of Information
Iran	Ministry of Information
Iraq	Ministry of Information and Culture
Israel	Government Press Office
Jamaica	Ministry of Information and Culture
Jordan	Ministry of Information
Kenya	Ministry of Information and Broadcasting
Kiribati	Department of Information
Korea, South	Ministry of Public Information
Kuwait	Ministry of Information
Laos	Committee for Information, Press, Radio, and Television and Broadcasting
Latvia	Department of Information
Lebanon	Ministry of Information
Lesotho	Ministry of Information and Broadcasting
Liberia	Ministry of Information
Liechtenstein	Press and Information Office
Lithuania	Information Department
Luxembourg	Ministry of State
Madagascar	Ministry of Information
Malawi	Department of Information
Malaysia	Ministry of Information
Maldives	Department of Information and Broadcasting
Mali	Ministry of Information and Telecommunications
Malta	Department of Information
Marshall Islands	Office of the Chief Secretary
Mauritania	Ministry of Information
Mauritius	Ministry of Communications and Information
Monaco	Directorate of Tourism
Morocco	Ministry of Information
Mozambique	Ministry of Information
Myanmar	Ministry of Information
Namibia	Ministry of Information and Broadcasting
Nauru	Office of the President
Nepal	Department of Information
Netherlands	Foreign Information Service
Nicaragua	Communications Media Bureau
Niger	Ministry of Information
Nigeria	Ministry of Information
Northern Marianas	Governor's Office
Oman	Ministry of Information
Pakistan	Ministry of Information and Broadcasting
Palestine	Information Department (of the Palestine Liberation Organization)
Papua New Guinea	Office of Information
Paraguay	Ministry of the Interior
Peru	Instituto Nacional de Comunicación Social
Philippines	Office of the Press Secretary; Philippine Information Agency
Qatar	Ministry of Information and Culture
Rwanda	L'Office Rwandais d'Information
St Kitts & Nevis	Government Headquarters
St Lucia	Ministry of Information and Broadcasting
St Vincent & the Grenadines	Ministry of Information
San Marino	Secretariat of State for Foreign and Political Affairs
São Tomé & Príncipe	Ministry of Information; Directorate of Information
Saudi Arabia	Ministry of Information
Senegal	Ministry of Culture and Communications
Seychelles	Department of Information and Telecommunications
Sierra Leone	Ministry of Information and Broadcasting
Singapore	Ministry of Communications and Information
Solomon Islands	Government Information Service
Somalia	Ministry of Information and National Guidance
South Africa	Bureau of Information
Spain	Ministry of the Government Spokesperson
Sri Lanka	Department for Broadcasting and Information
Sudan	Ministry and Culture and Information

Government information departments (continued)

Swaziland	Broadcasting and Information Service
Syria	Ministry of Information
Taiwan	Government Information Office
Tanzanian	Ministry of Information and Broadcasting
Thailand	Public Relations Department
Togo	Ministry of Information
Tonga	Government Information Unit
Trinidad & Tobago	Government Information Service
Turkey	General Directorate of Press and Information
Tuvalu	Broadcasting and Information Division
Uganda	Ministry of Information and Broadcasting
United Arab Emirates	Ministry of Information and Culture
United Kingdom	Central Office of Information

Publishing

Newspaper publishers' associations

Argentina	Asociación de Editores de Diarios de Buenos Aires
Australia	Australian Newspapers Council; Country Press Australia; Regional Dailies of Australia
Austria	Verband Österreichischer Zeitungsherausgeber und Zeitungsverleger (VÖZZ)
Bangladesh	Bangladesh Council of Newspapers and News Agencies
Belgium	Belgische Vereniging van de Dagbladuitgevers
Brazil	Associaçïo Brasileira de Imprensa
Canada	Canadian Daily Newspaper Publishers' Association
Chile	Asociación Nacional de la Prensa
Colombia	Asociación Nacional de Medios de Communicación
Denmark	Danske Dagblades Forening (DDF)
El Salvador	Asociación Salvadoreña de Empresarios de Radiodifusión (ASDER)
Finland	Sanomalehtien Liitto/Tindningamas Förbund
France	Fédération Nationale de la Presse Française
Germany	Bundesverband Deutscher Zeitungsverleger
Guinea	Guinean Association of Independent Press Publishers (AGEPI)
Hong Kong	Hsiangkang Hua Wenpaoyeh Hsieh-hui; Newspaper Society of Hong Kong/ Hsiangkang Paoyeh Kunghui
India	Indian Languages Newspapers' Association; Indian Newspaper Society
Indonesia	Serikat Penerbit Suratkabar
Israel	Igud Ha'itonim Hayomiyim Beyisra'el
Italy	Federazione Italiana Editori Giornali; Federazione Nazionale della Stampa Italiana
Japan	Nihon Shimbun Kyokai; Nihon Zasshi Kyokai
Korea, South	Han'guk Shinmun Hypuhoe
Lebanon	Niqabat al-Mukhbirun al-Lubnaniyun
Luxembourg	Association Luxembourgeoise des Editeurs de Journaux
Malaysia	Persatuan Penerbit-Penerbit Akhbar Malaysia
Mexico	Asociación de Diarios Independentes; Asociación de Editores de Periódicos Diarios de la República Mexicana
Netherlands	Vereniging De Nederlandse Dagbladpers
New Zealand	Community Newspapers' Association; Newspaper Publishers' Association of New Zealand
Nigeria	Newspaper Proprietors' Organization of Nigeria
Norway	Norsk Presseforbund; Norsk Avisers Landsforbund
Pakistan	All Pakistan Newspapers Society
Philippines	National Press Club of the Philippines
Portugal	Associaçïo da Imprensa Diária
South Africa	Newspaper Press Union
Spain	Asociación de Editores de Diarios Españoles (AEDE); Federación de Asociaciones de la Prensa de España (FAPE)
Sri Lanka	Sri Lanka Press Association
Sweden	Svenska Tidningsutgivareföreningen
Switzerland	Schweizerischer Verband der Zeitungs und Zeitschriftenverleger/ Association Suisse des Editeurs de Journaux et Periodiques
Thailand	Samakom Nangsupim Hang Prathet Thai
Uganda	Uganda News Editors' and Proprietors' Association
United Kingdom	Newspaper Society; Newspaper Publishers' Association; Scottish Daily Newspaper Society
USA	American Newspaper Publishers' Association (ANPA); American Society of Newspaper Editors (ASNE); National Newspaper Association (NNA)
Uruguay	Asociación de Diarios del Uruguay
Venezuela	Bloque de Prensa Venezolano

Major British newspapers

Paper	Location	Circulation	Issue
Daily Express	London	1 562 829	Daily
Daily Mail	London	1 701 661	Daily
Daily Mirror	London	2 911 098	Daily
Daily Sport	Manchester	210 000	Daily
Daily Star	London	859 474	Daily
Daily Telegraph	London	1 058 676	Daily
European	London	167 457	Daily
Financial Times	London	286 179	Daily
Glasgow Herald	Glasgow	122 101	Daily
Guardian	London	412 654	Daily
Independent	London	376 923	Daily
Independent on Sunday	London	372 187	Weekly
Mail on Sunday	London	1 907 537	Weekly
Morning Star	London	8 500	Daily
News of the World	London	4 845 016[a]	Weekly
Observer	London	554 900	Weekly
People	London	2 278 983	Weekly
Racing Post	London	47 221	Daily
Scotland on Sunday	Edinburgh	72 941	Weekly
Scotsman	Edinburgh	85 903	Daily
Sporting Life	London	79 169	Daily
Sun	London	3 689 931	Daily
Sunday Mirror	London	2 809 637	Weekly
Sunday Post	Dundee	1 198 041	Weekly
Sunday Sport	London	370 559	Weekly
Sunday Telegraph	London	569 039	Weekly
Sunday Times	London	1 147 708	Weekly
Times	London	390 475	Daily
Today	London	470 620	Daily

[a] largest circulation of any paper in Western world

Daily – Monday through Saturday

Best-selling European newspapers

Included are newspapers with circulations of 250 000 and over.

Paper	Location	Circulation	Issue
Austria			
Die Ganze Woche	Vienna	850 000	2 weekly
Kleine Zeitung	Graz	275 000	Weekly
Kurier	Vienna	620 000	Daily & Sun
Neue Kronenzeitung	Vienna	1 000 000	Daily
Belgium			
Antwerpse Post (Dutch/nederlands)	Antwerp	313 327	Weekly
Die Nieuwe Gazet Antwerp (Dutch/nederlands)	Antwerp	298 882	Daily
Visite (Dutch/nederlands)	Berchem	574 355	Monthly
Belgique No 1 (French)	Brussels	530 000	Weekly
L'Echo (French)	Brussels	380 000	Weekly
Groupe AZ (French)	Brussels	1 625 000	Weekly
Groep AZ (Dutch/nederlands)	Brussels	2 800 000	Weekly
Vlan (French)	Brussels	425 000	Weekly
De Gentenaar (Dutch/nederlands)	Ghent	326 000	Daily
Het Nieuwsblad (Dutch/nederlands)	Groot-Bijgaarden	382 397	Daily
De Standaard (Dutch/nederlands)	Groot-Bijgaarden	382 397	Daily
Hier Groep (Dutch/nederlands)	Hasselt	350 000	Weekly
Publi-Hebdo	Liege	382 000	Weekly
Deze Week in (Dutch/nederlands)	Roeselare	840 000	Weekly
Bulgaria			
Duma	Sofia	300 000	Daily
Otechestven Front (Fatherland Front)	Sofia	280 000	Daily
Czech Republic			
Práce (Labour)	Prague	350 000	Daily
Rudé Právo (Red Light)	Prague	340 000	Daily
Éire			
Sunday World	Dublin	263 088	Weekly
France			
Sud-Ouest	Bordeaux	367 860	Daily
La Montagne	Clermont Ferrand	250 288	Daily
L'Est Républicain	Heillecourt	251 236	Daily
Le Progrès	Lyons	353 608	Daily
Nice Matin	Nice	258 205	Daily
Le Figaro	Paris	428 700	Daily
France-Dimanche	Paris	706 338	Weekly
France-Soir	Paris	334 035	Daily
Ici Paris	Paris	422 796	Weekly
Le Journal Dimanche	Paris	360 029	Weekly
Le Monde	Paris	381 549	Daily
Le Parisien	Paris	365 661	Daily
VSD (Vendredi, Samedi, Dimanche)	Paris	261 612	Weekly
Ouest-France	Rennes	739 047	Daily
La Nouvelle République du Centre-Ouest	Tours	271 504	Daily
Le Dauphiné Libéré	Veurey-Voroize	813 209	Daily
Germany			
Super Zeitung	Munich	600 000	Daily
Augsburger Allgemeine	Augsburg	362 000	Daily
BZ-Berlin	Berlin	279 269	Daily
Berliner Zeitung	Berlin	425 000	Daily
Bild Berlin	Berlin	250 000	Daily
Junge Welt	Berlin	330 000	Daily
Express Köln	Cologne	437 104	Daily
Lausitzer Rundschau	Cottbus	291 000	Daily
Sächsische Zeitung	Dresden	513 000	Daily
Rheinische Post	Düsseldorf	391 489	Daily
Das Volk	Erfurt	401 000	Daily
Westdeutsche Allgemeine Zeitung (WAZ)	Essen	1 236 304	Daily

Best-selling European newspapers (continued)

Paper	Location	Circulation	Issue
Frankfurter Allgemeine Zeitung (FAZ)	Frankfurt/ Main	366 703	Daily
Bild	Hamburg	4 416 240	Daily
Die Zeit	Hamburg	488 212	Weekly
Hannoversche Allgemeine Zeitung (HAZ)	Hannover	511 027	Daily
HNA Hessische/ Niedersäch Allgemeine	Kassel	272 249	Daily
Leipziger Volkszeitung	Leipzig	484 000	Daily
Volksstimme	Magdeburg	379 407	Daily
Süddeutsche Zeitung (SZ)	Magdeburg	386 287	Daily
Nürnberger Nachrichten	Nuremburg	325 000	Daily
Nordwest Zeitung	Oldenburg	317 077	Daily
Neue Osnabrücker Zeitung	Osnabruck	299 572	Daily
Ostee Zeitung	Rostock	293 000	Daily
Sonntag Aktuell	Stuttgart	877 140	Weekly
Stuttgarter Zeitung	Stuttgart	509 710	Daily
Südwest Presse	Ulm	367 129	Daily
Hungary			
Népsport (People's Sport)	Budapest	250 000	Daily
Népszabadsag (People's Freedom)	Budapest	450 000	Daily
Reform	Budapest	385 000	Weekly
Vasárnapi Hirek	Budapest	270 595	Weekly
Italy			
Corriere Della Sera	Milan	644 856	Daily
La Gazzetta Dello Sport	Milan	814 889	Daily
Il Sole 24 Ore	Milan	258 771	Daily
Corriere Dello Sport-Stadio	Rome	542 275	Daily
Il Messaggero	Rome	400 000	Daily
La Repubblica	Rome	826 224	Daily
La Stampa	Turin	406 951	Daily
Netherlands			
De Telegraaf	Amsterdam	725 700	Daily
De Volkskrant	Amsterdam	340 038	Daily
Algemeen Dagblad	Rotterdam	417 000	Daily
Norway			
Aftenposten	Oslo	262 892	Daily
Poland			
Gazeta Wyborcza	Warsaw	550 000	Daily
Zycie Warszawy (Warsaw Life)	Warsaw	250 000	Daily
Romania			
Ardevarul	Bucharest	250 000	Daily
România Liberia	Bucharest	400 000	Daily
Slovakia			
Práca	Bratislava	260 300	Daily
Pravda	Bratislava	260 000	Daily
Spain			
ABC	Madrid	280 356	Daily
El Pais	Madrid	377 528	Daily
Sweden			
Göteborg-Posten	Gothenburg	281 000	Daily
Aftonbladet	Stockholm	480 000	Daily
Dagens Nyheter	Stockholm	519 000	Daily
Expressen	Stockholm	575 000	Daily
Turkey			
Milliyet (Nationalism)	Istanbul	250 000	Daily
Sabah (Morning)	Istanbul	506 671	Daily
Russia			
Izvestiya	Moscow	10 130 000	Daily
Komsomolskaya Pravda (Youth Truth)	Moscow	20 354 000	Daily
Moskovskaya Pravda	Moscow	725 000	Daily
Pravda	Moscow	7 700 000	Daily
Rabochaya Tribuna (Worker's Tribune)	Moscow	1 405 000	Daily
Selskaya Zhizn (Country Life)	Moscow	5 772 000	Daily
Sotsialisticheskaya Industriya	Moscow	1 500 000	Daily
Sovetski Sport	Moscow	4 863 000	Daily
Trud (Labour)	Moscow	21 429 000	Daily
Vechernyaya Moskva (Evening News)	Moscow	650 000	Daily

Daily = Monday through Saturday

US newspapers

The highest circulation figures are quoted, whether they be for a paper's Sunday or weekday issue. All papers listed have circulation figures of over 100 000. No free papers are listed.

Paper	Location	Circulation	Issue
Alabama			
News	Birmingham	207 138	Daily
Arizona			
New Times	Phoenix	135 000	Weekly
Republic	Phoenix	517 212	Daily
Star	Tucson	159 698	Daily
Arkansas			
Arkansas Democrat	Little Rock	223 663	Daily
Arkansas Gazette	Little Rock	165 880	Daily
California			
Bee	Fresno	179 731	Daily
Press-Telegram	Long Beach	128 750	Daily
Central News	Los Angeles	210 000	Weekly
Daily News (Japanese)	Los Angeles	215 586	Daily
Daily News	Los Angeles	214 205	Daily & Sun
Herald-Examiner	Los Angeles	303 320	Daily & Sun
Investors Daily	Los Angeles	100 503	Daily
L.A. Times	Los Angeles	1 196 323	Daily & Sun
La Opinion (Spanish)	Los Angeles	105 918	Daily & Sun
Tribune	Oakland	121 537	Daily & Sun

Paper	Location	Circulation	Issue
Press-Enterprise	Riverside	163 246	Daily & Sun
Sacramento Bee	Sacramento	328 018	Daily & Sun
Sun	San Bernadino	100 688	Daily & Sun
Tribune	San Diego	115 673	Daily
Union	San Diego	436 225	Daily & Sun
San Francisco Chronicle	San Francisco	562 887	Daily
San Francisco Examiner	San Francisco	136 346	Daily
Sun Examiner/ Chronicle	San Francisco	716 339	Weekly
Wall Street Journal, western edition	San Francisco	388 013	Daily
Mercury News	San Jose	330 791	Daily & Sun
Register	Santa Ana	406 696	Daily & Sun
Colorado			
Daily Breeze	Torrance	100 000	Daily & Sun
Gazette Telegraph	Colorado Springs	115 883	Daily
Post	Denver	407 561	Daily & Sun
Rocky Mountain News	Denver	407 889	Daily & Sun
Connecticut			
Hartford Courant	Hartford	314 846	Daily & Sun
Register	New Haven	135 569	Daily & Sun
Delaware			
News Journal	Wilmington	139 833	Daily
District of Columbia			
Washington Post	Washington	1 137 034	Daily & Sun
Washington Times	Washington	100 000	Weekly
Florida			
News Journal	Daytona Beach	106 169	Daily & Sun
Sun-Sentinel	Fort Lauderdale	305 804	Daily
News Press	Fort Myers	102 016	Daily & Sun
Florida Times-Union	Jacksonville	245 414	Daily & Sun
Florida Today	Melbourne	106 878	Daily
Miami Herald	Miami	520 075	Daily & Sun
State Paper	Miami	140 000	Daily
Suncoast News	New Port Richey	172 000	2 weekly
Sentinel	Orlando	376 003	Daily
Herald-Tribune	Sarasota	130 872	Daily
Times	St Petersburg	424 432	Daily & Sun
Tribune & Times	Tampa	364 269	Daily & Sun
Palm Beach Post	West Palm Beach	212 129	
Georgia			
Atlanta Constitution	Atlanta	316 793	Mon-Fri
Dekalb News/Sun	Decatur	104 000	Weekly
Macon Telegraph & News	Macon	100 488	Daily & Sun
Illinois			
Chicago Sun Times	Chicago	548 091	Daily
Chicago Tribune	Chicago	1 101 966	Daily & Sun
Wall Street Journal, midwest edition	Chicago	513 653	Daily
Journal Star	Peoria	110 115	Daily & Sun

Paper	Location	Circulation	Issue
Indiana			
Courier	Evansville	116 962	Daily & Sun
Journal-Gazette	Fort Wayne	139 275	Daily & Sun
News	Indianapolis	101 091	Daily
Star	Indianapolis	411 044	Daily & Sun
Iowa			
Register	Des Moines	346 275	Daily & Sun
Kansas			
Wichita Eagle	Wichita	198 906	Daily & Sun
Kentucky			
Herald Leader	Lexington	157 908	Daily & Sun
Courier Journal	Louisville	325 443	Daily & Sun
Louisiana			
Times Picayune	New Orleans	278 990	Daily & Sun
Maryland			
Sun	Baltimore	494 112	Daily
Massachusetts			
The Boston Globe	Boston	791 605	Daily & Sun
Boston Herald	Boston	358 925	Daily & Sun
Christian Science Monitor	Boston	104 314	Mon-Fri
Phoenix	Boston	134 000	Weekly
Patriot Ledger	Quincy	101 639	Daily
Union	Springfield	156 880	Daily
Telegram & Gazette	Worcester	135 891	Daily
Michigan			
Free Press	Detroit	636 182	Daily & Sun
News	Detroit	500 980	Daily & Sun
Journal	Flint	107 940	Daily
Press	Grand Rapids	191 095	Daily & Sun
Minnesota			
Star Tribune	Minneapolis	666 840	Daily & Sun
Pioneer Press Dispatch	St Paul	261 557	Daily
Mississippi			
Clarion Ledger	Jackson	123 052	Daily
Missouri			
Star	Kansas City	322 400	Mon-Fri
Post Dispatch	St Louis	561 630	Daily & Sun
Nebraska			
World Herald	Omaha	284 223	Daily & Sun
Nevada			
Las Vegas Review Journal	Las Vegas	165 078	Daily & Sun
New Jersey			
Asbury Park Press	Asbury Park	228 140	Daily
Courier-Post	Camden-Cherry Hill	101 803	Mon-Fri & Sun
Record	Hackensack	228 158	Daily & Sun
Star-Ledger	Newark	693 183	Daily & Sun
North Jersey Herald News	Passaic	140 260	Daily & Sun
Press	Pleasantville	102 241	Daily & Sun
New Mexico			
Journal	Albuquerque	158 078	Daily & Sun

US newspapers (continued)

Paper	Location	Circulation	Issue
New York			
Times-Union	Albany	173 944	Daily & Sun
News	Buffalo	378 574	Daily & Sun
Newsday	Long Island	714 128	Daily & Sun
Times-Herald Record	Middletown	101 097	Daily & Sun
Daily News	New York	1 401 403	Daily & Sun
New York Post	New York	510 219	Daily
The New York Times	New York	1 686 974	Daily & Sun
Village Voice	New York	147 000	Weekly
Wall Street Journal	New York	1 857 131	Mon-Fri
Suffolk Life	Riverhead	468 000	Weekly
Democrat & Chronicle	Rochester	260 322	Daily & Sun
North Carolina			
Observer	Charlotte	298 749	Daily & Sun
News & Record	Greensboro	130 977	Daily & Sun
News & Observer	Raleigh	184 226	Daily & Sun
Journal	Winston-Salem	107 331	Daily & Sun
Ohio			
Beacon Journal	Akron	222 899	Daily & Sun
The Cincinnati Post	Cincinnati	104 264	Daily
Enquirer	Cincinnati	342 076	Daily & Sun
Plain Dealer	Cleveland	560 871	Daily
Dispatch	Columbus	389 319	Daily & Sun
News	Dayton	230 918	Daily
Blade	Toledo	215 463	Daily & Sun
Vindicator	Youngstown	134 931	Daily & Sun
Oklahoma			
Oklahoman	Oklahoma City	326 284	Daily & Sun
Oregon			
Oregonian	Portland	431 989	Daily & Sun
This Week	Portland	442 000	Weekly
Pennsylvania			
Morning Call	Allentown	181 784	Daily & Sun
Daily News	Philadelphia	225 063	Daily
News Gleaner	Philadelphia	109 000	Weekly
Philadelphia Enquirer (oldest daily in US)	Philadelphia	978 300	Daily & Sun
Times- Northeast	Philadelphia	137 000	Weekly
The Pittsburgh Press	Pittsburgh	554 402	Daily
Post-Gazette	Pittsburgh	162 520	Daily
Rhode Island			
Bulletin	Providence	265 210	Mon-Fri
South Carolina			
News & Courier	Charleston	125 714	Daily
State	Columbia	172 936	Daily & Sun
Tennessee			
News-Free Press	Chattanooga	107 373	Daily & Sun
Commercial Appeal	Memphis	288 866	Daily & Sun
Tennessean	Nashville	264 790	Daily & Sun
Texas			
American Statesman	Dallas	219 857	Daily & Sun
Dallas Morning News	Dallas	585 950	Daily & Sun
Dallas Times Herald	Dallas	340 297	Daily & Sun
Wall Street Journal, southwest edition	Dallas	187 177	Daily
Star-Telegram	Fort Worth	267 558	Daily & Sun
Houston Chronicle	Houston	620 779	Daily & Sun
Houston Post	Houston	370 449	Daily & Sun
Express-News	San Antonio	273 227	Daily & Sun
Light	San Antonio	234 011	Daily & Sun
Utah			
Tribune	Salt Lake City	140 977	Daily & Sun
Virginia			
U.S.A. Today	Arlington	1 748 218	Mon-Fri
News Leader	Richmond	259 093	Daily
Times & World News	Roanoke	126 795	Daily & Sun
Washington			
Post-Intelligencer	Seattle	205 357	Daily
Times	Seattle	233 995	Daily
Chronicle	Spokane	145 507	Daily
News-Tribune	Tacoma	134 866	Daily & Sun
Wisconsin			
Journal	Milwaukee	505 074	Daily & Sun
Sentinel	Milwaukee	176 549	Daily

Daily = Monday through Saturday

Canadian newspapers

All papers listed have circulations of 10 000 or over. In each case the highest circulation figure is given, whether it be for the paper's Sunday or weekly issue.

Paper	Location	Circulation	Issue
Alberta			
Calgary Herald	Calgary	163 206	Daily
Calgary Sun	Calgary	100 466	Daily
Edmonton Journal	Edmonton	190 875	Daily & Sun
Edmonton Sun	Edmonton	125 058	Daily
Daily Herald Tribune	Grand Prairie	11 674	Daily
Lethbridge Herald	Lethbridge	24 720	Daily
News	Medicine Hat	13 942	Daily
Advocate	Red Deer	22 028	Daily
St Albert Gazette	St Albert	10 000	Weekly
British Columbia			
Abbotsford News	Abbotsford	40 700	2 weekly
Chilliwack	Chilliwack	12 700	Weekly
Delta Optimist	Delta	34 500	Weekly
Kamloops Daily News	Kamloops	19 083	Daily
Daily Courier	Kelowna	18 833	Daily
Advance	Langley	10 000	Daily
Daily Free Press	Nanaimo	10 600	Daily

Paper	Location	Circulation	Issue
Citizen	Prince George	21 649	Daily
Richmond Review	Richmond	40 000	2 weekly
North Shore News	Vancouver	58 500	3 weekly
Province	Vancouver	227 432	Mon-Fri & Sun
Vancouver Sun	Vancouver	267 290	Daily
Times-Colonist	Victoria	78 796	Daily
Manitoba			
Sun	Brandon	17 748	Daily & Sun
Carillon	Steinbach	13 000	Weekly
Winnipeg Free Press	Winnipeg	227 290	Daily
New Brunswick			
L'Acadie Nouvelle (French)	Caraquet	14 442	Daily
Le Madawaska (French)	Madawaska	10 000	Weekly
Gleaner	Fredericton	29 775	Daily
Times-Transcript	Moncton	53 344	Daily
Telegraph-Journal	Moncton	61 562	Daily
Newfoundland			
Western Star	Corner Brook	11 240	Daily
Evening Telegram	St John's	57 740	Daily
Nova Scotia			
Chronicle-Herald	Halifax	87 250	Daily
Daily News	Halifax	37 000	Daily & Sun
Mail-Star	Halifax	55 230	Daily
Advertiser	Kentville	10 258	Weekly
Evening News	New Glasgow	11 735	Daily
Cape Breton Post	Sydney	31 741	Daily
Ontario			
Examiner	Barrie	14 742	Daily
Intelligencer	Belleville	19 021	Daily
Expositor	Brantford	32 319	Daily
Recorder & Times	Brockville	16 711	Daily
Burlington Weekend Post	Burlington	40 000	Weekly
Daily Reporter	Cambridge	14 728	Daily
Chatham Daily News	Chatham	16 553	Daily
Standard-Freeholder	Cornwall	18 430	Daily
Daily Mercury	Guelph	19 547	Daily
Hamilton Recorder	Hamilton	20 000	Weekly
Spectator	Hamilton	114 877	Daily
	Burlington	22 282	Daily
Whig Standard	Kingston	42 007	Daily
Kitchener-Waterloo Record	Kitchener	80 917	Daily
Lindsay Daily Post	Lindsay	10 011	Mon-Fri
London Free Press	London	124 879	Daily
Mississauga News	Mississauga	105 000	Weekly
Review	Niagara Falls	23 000	Daily
Nugget	North Bay	24 109	Daily
Packet	Orillia	11 219	Daily
Oshawa Times	Oshawa	20 905	Daily
This Week	Oshawa	60 000	Weekly
Citizen	Ottawa	234 455	Daily
Le Droit (French)	Ottawa	39 762	Daily
Ottawa Sun	Ottawa	40 790	Mon-Fri & Sun

Paper	Location	Circulation	Issue
Sun Times	Owen Sound	24 198	Daily
Examiner	Peterborough	27 089	Mon-Fri
Sarnia Observer	Sarnia	23 979	Daily
Star	Saute Ste Marie	26 757	Daily
Reformer	Simcoe	10 577	Mon-Fri
Standard	St Catharines	43 134	Daily
Times-Journal	St Thomas	10 145	Daily
Beacon Herald	Stratford	13 788	Daily
Sudbury Star	Sudbury	29 483	Daily
Chronicle-Journal	Thunder Bay	38 141	Mon-Fri
Daily Press	Timmins	13 283	Daily
Canadian Jewish News	Toronto	50 587	Weekly
Corriere Canadese (Italian)	Toronto	22 500	Daily
Daily Racing Form	Toronto	10 357	Daily & Sun
Etobicoke Guardian	Etobicoke	66 000	2 weekly
Financial Post	Toronto	186 358	Tues-Sat
Globe & Mail	Toronto	320 000	Daily
Toronto Star	Toronto	767 799	Daily
Toronto Sun	Toronto	500 000	Daily
Welland-Port Colborne Tribune	Welland	17 937	Daily
Windsor Star	Windsor	85 632	Daily
Woodstock-Ingersoll Sentinel Review	Woodstock	10 170	Daily
Québec			
Progrès-Dimanche	Chicoutimi	50 963	Weekly
Le Quotidien	Chicoutimi	31 140	Daily
La Parole	Drummondville	29 000	Weekly
La Voix de l'Est	Granby	15 520	Daily
Le Devoir	Montreal	29 508	Daily
Gazette (English)	Montreal	246 698	Daily
Le Guide de Montreal Nord	Montreal	16 800	Weekly
Le Journal de Montreal	Montreal	345 098	Daily
La Presse	Montreal	310 587	Daily
Le Journal de Québec	Québec	109 353	Daily
Le Soliel	Québec	141 797	Daily
L'Etoile du Lac	Roberval	11 300	Weekly
La Frontière	Rouyn	12 500	Weekly
La Tribune	Sherbrooke	44 590	Daily
L'Eclaireur Progrès-Beauce Nouvelle	St Georges	25 200	Weekly
Le Courrier	St Hyancinthe	13 063	Weekly
Le Canada Français	St Jean	15 417	Weekly
Le Nouvelleiste	Trois Rivieres	49 722	Daily
L'Union des Cantons de l'Est	Victoriaville	12 538	Weekly
Saskatchewan			
Leader-Post	Regina	68 944	Daily
Star-Phoenix	Saskatoon	63 587	Daily
Prince Edward Island			
Guardian	Charlottetown	19 699	Daily
Journal Pioneer	Summerside	11 256	Daily

Daily = Monday through Saturday

Communications

Australian newspapers

All papers listed have circulations of over 10 000. Free papers are not listed.

Paper	Location	Circulation	Issue
Australian Capital Territory			
Canberra Times	Canberra	44 000	Daily
New South Wales			
Border Morning Mail	Albury	25 196	Daily
Richmond River Express Examiner	Casino	13 400	Weekly
Newcastle & Lake Macquarie Post	Newcastle	06 476	Weekly
Newcastle Herald	Newcastle	52 225	Daily
Australian	Sydney	138 497	Daily
Australian Financial Review	Syndey	76 637	Daily
Daily Telegraph Mirror	Sydney	480 000	Daily
Sun-Herald	Sydney	550 354	Weekly
Sunday Telegraph	Sydney	562 000	Weekly
Sydney Morning Herald	Sydney	378 313	Daily
Weekend Australian	Sydney	280 000	Weekly
Advertiser	Parramatta	102 918	Weekly
Bankstown-Canterbury Express	Bankstown	75 000	Weekly
Blacktown Advocate	Blacktown	41 371	Weekly
Farm & Garden	Castle Hill	20 746	Weekly
Hawkesbury Courier	North Richmond	14 700	Weekly
Hornsby & Upper North Shore Advocate	Hornsby	46 547	Weekly
Liverpool-Fairfield Champion	Liverpool	67 450	Weekly
Macarthur Advertiser	Campbell-town	28 369	Weekly
Manly Daily	Manly	80 784	Daily
Mosman & Lower North Shore Daily	Spit Junction	21 179	Daily
North Shore Times	Parramatta	103 980	2 weekly
Northern District Times	Eastwood	51 915	Weekly
Penrith Press	Parramatta	56 542	Weekly
St George & Sutherland Shire Leader	Hurstville	118 383	Weekly
Western Standard	Druitt	25 690	Weekly
Western Suburbs Courier	Waterloo	62 624	Weekly
Northern Daily Leader	Tamworth	11 600	Daily
Daily Advertiser	Wagga Wagga	16 413	Daily
Illawarra Mercury	Wollongong	36 680	Daily
Northern Territory			
Northern Territory News	Darwin	19 500	Daily
Queensland			
Courier-Mail	Brisbane	250 918	Daily
Sun	Brisbane	362 319	Daily
Sunday Mail	Brisbane	348 000	Weekly
Drum	Bundaberg	20 000	Weekly
Cairns Post	Cairns	20 665	Daily
Queensland Times	Ipswich	17 100	Daily
Daily Mercury	Mackay	16 670	Daily
Sunshine Coast Daily	Maroochy-dore	20 787	Daily
Rockhampton Morning Bulletin	Rockhampton	24 000	Daily
Toowoomba Chronicle	Toowoomba	30 644	Daily
Townsville Bulletin	Townsville	25 750	Daily
South Australia			
Adelaide Advertiser	Adelaide	213 341	Daily
News	Adelaide	129 819	Daily
Sunday Mail	Adelaide	268 029	Weekly
City Messenger	Adelaide	24 573	Weekly
Community Courier	Adelaide	33 770	Weekly
Eastern Suburbs Messenger	Adelaide	23 170	Weekly
Elizabeth Salisbury News Review	Adelaide	61 286	Weekly
Guardian	Adelaide	45 640	Weekly
Hills & Valley Gazette	Adelaide	20 582	Weekly
North East Leader	Adelaide	32 882	Weekly
Payneham Messenger	Adelaide	29 570	Weekly
Parkside Messenger	Adelaide	28 932	Weekly
Southern Times	Adelaide	48 415	Weekly
Standard	Adelaide	29 931	Weekly
Weekly Times	Adelaide	41 190	Weekly
Westside	Adelaide	23 315	Weekly
Mount Barker Courier	Adelaide	13 000	Weekly
Tasmania			
Advocate	Burnie	27 293	Daily
Mercury	Hobart	53 864	Daily
Sunday Tasmanian	Hobart	54 753	Weekly
Examiner	Launceton	38 500	Daily
Victoria			
Ballarat Courier	Ballarat	23 595	Daily
Ballarat News	Ballarat	31 000	Weekly
Bendigo Advertiser	Bendigo	16 500	Daily
Geelong Advertiser	Geelong	31 991	Daily
Geelong News	Geelong	46 261	2 weekly
Wimmera Mail-Times	Horsham	10 046	3 weekly
Midland Express	Kyneton	19 907	Weekly
Age	Melbourne	339 905	Daily
Herald-Sun	Melbourne	680 000	Daily
Sunday Age	Melbourne	119 756	Weekly
Sunday Herald Sun	Melbourne	600 000	Weekly
Sunday Observer	Melbourne	90 844	Weekly
Truth	Melbourne	240 433	2 weekly
Weekly Times	Melbourne	118 000	Weekly
Broadmedows Observer	Glenroy	27 767	Weekly
Brunswick Sentinel	Northcote	19 487	Weekly

Paper	Location	Circulation	Issue
Chadstone Progress	Northcote	93 863	Weekly
Coburg Courier	Northcote	28 078	Weekly
Dandenong Journal	Dandenong	34 160	Weekly
Diamond Valley News	Northcote	28 065	Weekly
Doncaster Mirror	Cheltenham	26 297	Weekly
Doncaster & Templestowe News	Northcote	25 974	Weekly
Essendon Gazette	Glenroy	26 598	Weekly
Footsaray & Western Suburbs Advertiser	Dandenong	44 108	Weekly
Frankston Peninsula News	Dandenong	11 801	Weekly
Frankston Standard	Cheltenham	42 273	Weekly
Heidelberger	Northcote	24 831	Weekly
Keilor Messenger	Glenroy	27 022	Weekly
Knox Sherbrooke News	Boronia	39 446	Weekly
Northcote Leader	Northcote	22 789	Weekly
Nunawading Gazette	Blackburn	32 975	Weekly
Progress Press	Blackburn	79 329	Weekly
Ringwood & Croydon Mail	Blackburn	36 315	Weekly
Sandringham & Brighton Advertiser	Cheltenham	23 098	Weekly
Standard Times	Cheltenham	22 836	Weekly
Sunshine Advocate	Dandenong	33 004	Weekly
Waverley Gazette	Glenwaverley	42 048	Weekly
Whittlesea Post	Northcote	19 516	Weekly
Malvern Caulfield Progress	Oakleigh	59 355	Weekly
Berwick City News	Packenham	25 100	Weekly
Warrnambool Standard	Warrnambool	12 900	Daily
Western Australia			
Sunday Times	Perth	324 700	Weekly
West Australia	Perth	252 503	Daily

Daily = Monday through Saturday

New Zealand newspapers

All papers listed have circulation figures of over 10 000.

Paper	Location	Circulation	Issue
National Business Review	Auckland	19 900	Weekly
New Zealand Herald	Auckland	246 458	Daily
North Shore Times Advertiser	Auckland	56 000	3 weekly
Sunday News	Auckland	154 000	Weekly
Sunday Star	Auckland	120 000	Weekly
Marlborough Express	Blenheim	10 400	Daily
Press	Christchurch	95 933	Daily
Star	Christchurch	57 957	Daily
Weekend Star	Christchurch	23 502	Weekly
Otago Daily Times	Dunedin	52 000	Daily
Gisborne Herald	Gisborne	10 582	Daily
Waikato Times	Hamilton	41 090	Daily
Hawke's Bay Herald Tribune	Hastings	20 349	Daily
Southland Times	Invertargill	34 504	Daily
News Gazette	Kawerau	11 000	Weekly
Daily Telegraph	Napier	16 500	Daily
Nelson Evening Mail	Nelson	19 549	Daily
Daily News	New Plymouth	30 454	Daily
Taranaki Herald	New Plymouth	10 410	Daily
Evening Standard	Palmerston North	25 911	Daily
Daily Post	Rotorua	13 992	Daily
Bay of Plenty Times	Tauranga	21 061	Daily
Timaru Herald	Timaru	16 339	Daily
South Waikato News	Tokoroa	10 441	2 weekly
Wanganui Chronicle	Wanganui	16 549	Daily
Contact	Wellington	130 377	Weekly
Dominion	Wellington	87 466	Weekly
Eastern News	Wellington	13 550	Weekly
Evening Post	Wellington	76 770	Daily
Hutt News	Wellington	38 550	Weekly
Independent Herald	Wellington	18 823	Weekly
New Zealand Times	Wellington	89 247	Weekly
Northern Advocate	Whangarei	16 654	Daily

Daily = Monday through Saturday

South African newspapers

All papers listed have circulations of over 10 000.

Paper	Location	Circulation	Issue
Bophuthatswana			
Mafikeng Mail (English)	Mafikeng	10 000	Daily
Mafikeng Mail & Botswana Guardian (English)	Mafikeng	17 000	Weekly
Cape Province			
Argus (English)	Cape Town	102 060	Daily
Die Burger (Afrikaans)	Cape Town	79 113	Daily
Cape Times (English)	Cape Town	60 316	Daily
Weekend Argus (English)	Cape Town	113 614	Weekly
Daily Dispatch (English)	East London	33 505	Daily

Communications

South African newspapers (continued)

Paper	*Location*	*Circulation*	*Issue*
Indaba (black community) (English)	East London	37 108	Weekly
Paarl Post (English & Afrikaans)	Paarl	10 000	Weekly
Eastern Province Herald (English)	Port Elizabeth	28 336	Daily
Evening Post (English)	Port Elizabeth	22 596	Daily
Weekend Post (English)	Port Elizabeth	39 141	Weekly
Gemsbok Kourier (English & Afrikaans)	Roosevelt Park	10 000	Weekly
South (English)	Woodstock	25 000	Weekly
Natal			
Daily News (English)	Durban	100 570	Daily
Ilanga (Zulu)	Durban	142 277	2 weekly
Leader (Indian community) (English)	Durban	15 000	Weekly
Natal Mercury (English)	Durban	62 549	Daily
Post (Natal) (English)	Durban	47 500	Weekly
Sunday Tribune (English)	Durban	124 547	Weekly
Newcastle Advertiser (English & Afrikaans)	Newcastle	18 000	Weekly
Natal Witness (English)	Pietermaritzburg	26 927	Daily
Highway Mail (English)	Pinetown	28 920	Weekly
Northglen News (English)	Pinetown	14 136	Weekly
Orange Free State			
Die Volksblad (Afrikaans)	Bloemfontein	27 268	Daily
Vista (English)	Welkom	26 375	2 weekly
Transvaal			
Benoni City Times en Oosrandse Nuus (English & Afrikaans)	Benoni	23 500	Weekly
Brakpan Herald (English & Afrikaans)	Benoni	12 885	Weekly
Germiston City News (English)	Benoni	28 296	Weekly
Highveld Herald/Die Hoevelder (English & Afrikaans)	Ermelo	15 000	Weekly
Beeld (Afrikaans)	Johannesburg	103 887	Daily
Boksburg Advertiser/ (English & Afrikaans) *Boksburg Volksblad*	Johannesburg	24 150	Weekly
Business Day (English)	Johannesburg	32 871	Mon-Fri
Citizen (English)	Johannesburg	138 512	Daily
City Press (English)	Johannesburg	144 416	Weekly
New Nation (English)	Johannesburg	49 538	Weekly
Randfontein Herald (English & Afrikaans)	Johannesburg	12 016	Weekly
Rapport (English)	Johannesburg	370 565	Weekly
Sowetan (English)	Johannesburg	174 043	Daily
Star (English)	Johannesburg	218 405	Daily
Sunday Star (English)	Johannesburg	97 142	Weekly
Sunday Times (English)	Johannesburg	509 888	Weekly
Die Transvaler (Afrikaans)	Johannesburg	49 580	Daily
Vaderland (Afrikaans)	Johannesburg	150 000	Daily
Vrye Weekblad (Afrikaans)	Johannesburg	14 000	Weekly
Weekly Mail (English)	Johannesburg	31 000	Weekly
Heidelberg Nigel Heraut (English & Afrikaans)	Kempton Park	27 500	Weekly
Western Transvaal Record (English & Afrikaans)	Klerksdrop	11 040	Weekly
Lebowa, Gazankulu & Venda Times (English & N Sesotho)	Pietersburg	16 500	Weekly
Die Noord Transvaaler (Afrikaans)	Pietersburg	18 000	Weekly
Hoofstadv (Afrikaans)	Pretoria	11 855	Daily
Pretoria News (English)	Pretoria	26 880	Daily
De Echo (English & Afrikaans)	Secunda	12 300	Weekly
Springs & Brakpan Advertiser (English & Afrikaans)	Springs	12 994	Weekly
Vanderbijlpark Vaal Weekblad (English & Afrikaans)	Vanderbijlpark	13 268	Weekly
Venda			
Thohoyuandou (English, Afrikaans & Venda)	Venda	33 000	Weekly

Daily = Monday through Saturday

Broadcasting stations and networks

Main terrestrial television broadcasters & stations

Country	*Public service broadcaster*	*Commercial broadcaster*	*Military*
Albania	Radiotelevisione Shqiptar		
Australia	Australian Broadcasting Corporation (ABC) (satellite) Special Broadcasting Service (SBS) (satellite) Imparja Television Pty Ltd (satellite)	6th Metropolitan TV Channel Seven Network (satellite) Nine Network (satellite) Network Ten Australia (satellite)	
Austria	Österreichischer Rundfunk (ORF): ORF FS 1 & ORF FS 2	3 Sat SAT1, RTL, RTL2	
Azores	Radiotelevisão Portuguesa (RTO)		AFRTS (US Air Force)
Belarus	Belaruskaje Telebačanne Ostankino Kanal 1 (OK-1) Rossijskoje Televidenije (RTV)	TV Peterburg (TV-P)	
Belgium	Belgische Radio En Televisie (BRTN) TV1 & TV2 (Dutch) Radio Télévision Belge de la Communaute (French) Culturelle Française (RTBF-TV) Tele-21 (French)	Canal Plus RTL-TVi	
Bosnia & Herzegovina	Televizija Sarajevo		
Bulgaria	Bâlgarska Televizija Russian Television Relay		
Canada	Canadian Broadcasting Corporation/ Société Radio Canada (satellite) Société de Radio-Télévision du Québec TV Ontario (satellite)	City TV (satellite) Canwest Global System (satellite) CTV Television Network Ltd Le Reseau de Télévision (TVA) Télévision Quatre Saisons	
Croatia	Hrvatska Televisija (HTV)		
Czech & Slovak Republics	Československá Televize Česk Televize (CTV) Slovenska Televize (ST)	CT3 (Czech) Channel 3 (Slovavia)	
Denmark	Danmarks Radio (8 channels)	TV-2	
Estonia	Estonian TV Ostankino TV (Moscow) Russian TV	TV-Petersburg (TV-P)	
Faroe Islands	Sjónvarp Føroya		
Finland	Oy Yleisradio AB YLE TV1 & YLE TV 2	MTV Oy Channel 3 Finland (MTV 3)	
France	France 2 France 3 (FR3) La Sept Arte Tele Monte Carlo	Télévision Française 1 (TF1) Canal Plus M6 Metropole TV Tele Toulouse Tele Bleue Tele Lyon Metropole 8 Mont Blanc Aqui TV RTL TV	

Main terrestrial television broadcasters & stations (continued)

Country	*Public service broadcaster*	*Commercial broadcaster*	*Military*
Germany	ARD (Programmdirektion Deutsches Fernsehen)		US Forces Television Germany
	Russian television relays	Vox (Westschienenkanal)	SSVC Television (UK)
	Zweites Deutsches Fernsehen (ZDF)	CFN/RFC-TV (Canada)	Belgium Forces Television
		Deutsches Sportfernsehen (DSF)	French Forces Television
Gibraltar	GBC Television		
Greece	Elliniki Tileorassi-1 (ET-1) Elliniki Tileorassi-2 (ET-2) Elliniki Tileorassi-3 (ET-3) AFN TV	Antenna TV Mega Channel New Channel Kanali 29 7X TeleCity New Television Sky TV	
Hungary	Magyar Televísió		
Iceland	Ríkisútvarpid - Sjónvarp Stöd 2		
Ireland	Radio Telefis Eireann (RTE) Network 2	Ulster TV (overspill) Channel 4 (overspill)	
Italy	Radiotelevisione Italiana RAI Uno RAI Due TV 3 Rundfunkanstalt SüdTirol (RAS)	Canale 5 Circuito 5 Stelle Italia 1 Italia 7 Italia 9 Junior TV Odeon Rete A Rete Quattro Tele Monte Carlo Tele Più 2 Sport Video Music	
Latvia	Latvijas Televizija (LTV)		
Lithuania	Lietuvos Televisija LRT Kauno Direkcija RYTU Lietuvos Televizija Russian television relays	Panevezio Telestudija Kauno Telestukija Plius	
Luxembourg		Tele Luxembourg (RTL) Hei Elei	
Macedonia	Televizija Makedonije TV Makedonije TV Skopje		
Malta	Xandir Television		
Monaco		Tele Monte Carlo	
Montenegro	TV Crne Gore		
Netherlands	Nederlandse Omroepprogrammia Stichting (NOS) NOS 1, 2 & 3		American Forces Network
New Zealand	Television New Zealand Canterbury Television (CTV)	TV3	
Norway	Norsk Rikskringkasting	TV 2 Norway Philips Petroleum 66: TV 1 & 2	

Country	*Public service broadcaster*	*Commercial broadcaster*	*Military*
Poland	Telewizja Polska: TP 1 & 2 Tele-9	Top Kanal Independent TV Echo TV	
Portugal	Radiotelevisão Portuguesa (RTP) RTP 1 & 2	SIC Televisão Independente	
Romania	Radioteleviziumea Românâ TV 1 & 2	SOTI Antenna Independenta	
Russia	Rossijskaja Gosudarstvennaja Teleradiokompanija 'Ostankino' (OK) Ostankino Kanal 1 (OK-1) Ostankino Kanal 4 (OK-4) Vserossijskaja Gosudarstvennaja Teleradiokompanija (VGTRK) Rossijskoje Televidenije (RTV)	TV-Peterburg (TV-P)	
Serbia	TV Srbije–TV Beograd TV Srbije–TV Novi Sad TV Srbile-TV Pristina TV Politika NTV Studio B		
Slovenia	Televizija Slovenia		
South Africa	South African Broadcasting Corporation (SABC-TV) Contemporary Community Value TV Transkei TV	M-Net Television Bophuthatswana Television Trinity Broadcasting – Ciskei MNET Transkei Trinity Broadcasting – Transkei	
Spain	Radiotelevision Española (RTVE) La2 Televisio Valenciana - Canal 9 TV Vasca-Euskal Telebista	Televisio de Catalunya TV3 Canal 33 Television Murciana ETB1 7 ETB2 Tele Madrid TV de Galicia (TVG)	(US Air Force) AFRTS
Sweden	Sveriges Television AB STV 2 Kanal 1 Finnish television relay	TV4 Nordisk Television Co	
Switzerland	Swiss Broadcasting Company (SBC) DRS (German) TSR (French) TSI (Italian)	Telecine Teleclub	
Ukraine	Ukrajinska Telebačennja (UT-1 + 2) Ostankino Kanal 1 (OK-1)		
United Kingdom	British Broadcasting Company (BBC) Independent Television Commission Anglia Television Border Television Carlton Television Ltd Central Independent Telelvision Channel 4 Channel Television Data Broadcasting International Ltd GMTV Ltd Grampian Television Granada Television HTV Wales HTV West	British Sky Broadcasting Independent Television News (ITN) Independent Television Association (ITVA)	

Main terrestrial television broadcasters & stations (continued)

Country	Public service broadcaster	Commercial broadcaster	Military
	London Weekend Television Meridian Broadcasting Ltd Scottish Television Teletext UK Ltd Tyne Tees Television Ulster Television Westcountry Television Ltd Yorkshire Television		
US	Public Broadcasting Service (PBS) TV Marti	ABC Television Division CBS Inc. Fox Television Network National Broadcasting Company	
Yugoslavia (former)	Udruzenje Jugoslovenskih Radiotelevizija		

Major European television broadcasts by satellite

Satellite	Program	Owner
63° E Intelsat 602	M-Net (Johannesburg) SABC-TV (Johannesburg) Channel 3 (Bangkok Entertainment Co) Channel 9 (Mass Comms Org of Thailand) IRIB TV 2 IRIB TV 1 AFRTS-E2 Rete 4 (Italy) Italia 1 Canale 5 (Italy	International
60° E Intelsat 604	Wir in Bayern (Germany) Bayern Journal AFN-Television interSTAR TRT TV4 (Turkey) TRT TV3 TRT TV1 TRT TV2 TV Gap	International
53° E Gorizont 11	Ostanko TV1 MIR-Station	CIS
40° E Gorizont 12	Rossia TV 2 TV 5 Europe (French) RTP International (Portuguese)	CIS
28.5° E Kopernikus (DFS-2)	Wir in Niedersachsen RTL Nord	Germany
23.5° E Kopernikus (DFS-1)	SAT 1 3 Sat ARTE (French/German) VOX Eins Plus RTL Plus n-tv PRO 7 Premiere DSR (16 channels)	Germany
23.5° E Kopernikus (DFS-1) cont.	West-3 Deutschlandfunk DSF (Deutsches Sportfernsehen) Bayerisches Fernsehen (regional German TV)	
19.2° E Astra 1A	Screen Sports RTL Plus (German & English) Scansat TV3 (Swedish) Eurosport Lifestyle TV Sat-1 (German) TV 1000 Succekanalen (Scandinavian) SKY One (English) Teleclub 3-Sat FilmNet (Scandinavian) SKY News (English) RTL-4 (Dutch) Pro 7 (German) MTV SKY Movies Plus	Luxembourg
19.2° E Astra 1B	Premiere The Movie Channel Eins Plus Sky Sports DSF (Deutsches Sportfernsehen) MTV UK Gold JSTV NHK (Japanese) TCC (The Children's Channel) N3 Sky Movies Gold Home Video Channel TV Asia	

Satellite	Program	Owner
19.2° E Astra 1B	Scansat TV 3 (Denmark)	
	CNN International	
	BSkyB	
	Scansat TV3 (Norway)	
16° E Eutelsat II f3	Eurostep (Dutch)	European
	Antenna Tres (Spanish)	
	RTV Zagreb	
	Tele 5 (Spanish)	
	Canal Plus Español (Spanish)	
	Polish Television's Third Program	
	Hungaria TV	
	RTP International	
	HBB-TV/HAS-TV (Turkish)	
	TV 7 Tunisia	
	TV PLUS (Dutch)	
13° E Eutelsat II f1	Eurosport	European
	Super Channel/ Channel e	
	Der Kabelkanal	
	TV 5 Europe	
	RTL-2 (German)	
	Deutsche Welle Fernsehen	
	WorldNet	
	TRT (Turkish)	
	Red Hot Dutch (Adult)	
	Middle East Broadcasting Centre	
	ARD Eins (German)	
	FilmNet Plus (Belgium)	
	FilmNet (Dutch)	
	VisEurope	
	BrightStar	
	WTN/ITN	
	EuroPace	
	TV Sport (France)	
10° E Eutelsat II f1	RAI Uno (Italy)	European
	RAI Due	
	TVE-Internaçional (Spain)	
	Show TV (Turkey)	
	Teleon (Turkey)	
	interSTAR (Turkey)	
	SIP Canal Courses	
	TV Campus	
7° E Eutelsat II f4	ET 1 (Greece)	European
	Kanal 6 (Turkish)	
	CYBC (Cyprus)	
	RTV Beograd (Serbia)	
5° E Tele-X	TV4 (Swedish)	Scandinavian
	NRK (Norwegian TV)	
	TV5 Nordic	
	Kompetenskanalen	
	SSC Tele-X/1	
1° W Intelsat 512	TVN (Norwegian)	International
	Nordisk TV4 (Norway)	
	SVT-2 (Sweden)	
	SVT-1 (Sweden)	
	IBA TV 1 & 2 & 3	
5° W Télécom 2B	RFO/France 2	France
	Métropole 6	
	ARTE	
	Canal Plus	
	TF 1	
	Canal J(eunesse)	
	Canal Jimmy	
	Cine Cinema	
8° W Télécom 2A	Canal Plus	France
	France 2	
	Cine Cinefil	
	Canal J	
	Canal Jimmy	
	MCM Euromusique	
	Planette	
	TV Sport	
11° W Gorizont 7	EBU Moscow	CIS
14° W Gorizont 15	Ostankino TV 1/ Brightside TV	CIS
	Moscow Visnews	
18.5° W Intelsat 515	STV 1	International
	TV Norge	
	TV-4 Norway	
	STV 2	
	TV 2 (Norway)	
19° W TDF 1A/B	Monte Carlo Music	France
	Canal Plus (French)	
	ARTE (French & German)	
	France 2	
19.2° W TV-Sat 1/2	RTL Plus	Germany
	Sat-1	
	3 Sat	
	DSR (16 channels)	
	Eins Plus	
21.5° W Intelsat K	BrightStar	International
27.5° W Intelsat 601	BBC World Service TV	International
	WorldNet	
	Canal France Internationale	
	CNN International	
	TVE (Spain)	
	Bravo	
	The Parliamentary Channel	
	The Children's Channel	
	Discovery Channel	
	KinderNet	
	The Learning Channel	
	Ladbroke Horse Racing	
	Country Music TV Europe	
	Kanal Market (Turkish)	

Major radio broadcasters

Country	*Public service*	*Commercial*	*Military*
Albania	Radiotelevisione Shqiptar Trans World Radio	Radio Valira	
Andorra	Servei de Telecomunicacions d'Andorra (STA) Radio Andorra		
Australia	Australian Broadcasting Corporation (ABC) Domestic Shortwave Service Northern Territory Shortwave Service Public Broadcasting Association of Australia Special Broadcasting Service (SBS)	Federation of Australian Radio Broadcasters	
Austria	Österreichischer Rundfunk (ORF)		
Belarus	Belaruskaje Radyjo		
Belgium	Belgische Radio en Televisie (BRTN) (Dutch) Radio-Télévision Belge de la Communaute Française (RTBF) (French) Belgisches Rundfunk & Fernsehzentrum der Deutschsprachigen Gemeinschaft (BRF)	Radio Contact Radio Nostalgie Network (Dutch) Radio Nostalgie Network (French)	US Forces Network, SHAPE British Forces Broadcasting
Bosnia & Herzegovina	Radiotelevizija Sarajevo		
Bulgaria	Bulgarian National Radio Horizont Christo Botev Orphei Znanie	Radio Express Radio Larik Radio Tanra Radio FM Channel Kom Radio Vesselina Channel TNN Radio Galatea	
Canada	Canadian Broadcasting Corporation/ Société Radio-Canada Radio Canada International CBC Northern Quebec Shortwave Service Sackville Relay Facility		
Croatia	Hrvatska Radio Televizija (HRT)		
Czech & Slovak Republics	Československý Rozhlas Czech & Slovak Radios International	Radio Free Europe	
Denmark	Danmarks Radio		
Estonia	Eesti Raadio		
Faroe Islands	Útvarp Føroya (Danish)		
Finland	Oy Yleisradio AB		
France	Télédiffusion de France (TDF) Radio Télévision Française d'Outre-Mer (RFO) Radio France Internationale France Internationale Radio France Radio Monte Carlo	Sud Radio Europe 1 Radio Monte Carlo NRJ	
Germany	ARD Deutsche Welle Deutschlandsender Kultur	Antenne Bayern Radio Hamburg Radio FFH	Voice of America (VOA) Radio Volga (Russian Armed Forces) American Forces Network Europe (AFN)

Country	Public service	Commercial	Military
Germany cont.	Rias Berlin Radio Moscow relay BBC Berlin relay	OK Radio Europe 1	British Forces Broadcasting Service Canadian Forces Network Radio Forces Françaises de Berlin
Gibraltar	Gibraltar Broadcasting Corporation British Forces Broadcasting Service Gibraltar		Armed Forces Radio Service (US Air Force)
Greece	Elliniki Radiophonia (ERA) Voice of America	Antenna Sky Athina 98.4 Radio Athens	
Hungary	Magyar Radio	Radio Danubius Calypso 873 Radio Bridge	
Iceland	Icelandic National Broadcasting Service Ríkisútvarpid		Navy Broadcasting Service (US Navy)
Ireland	Radio Telefís Éireann Radió Na Gaeltachta	Atlantic 252	
Italy	RAI-Radiotelevisione Italiana	Rundfunk Anstalt SüdTirol (RAS) Radio Tirol Adventist World Radio Europe Nexus International Broadcasting Association	S European Broadcasting (US Armed Forces)
Latvia	Latvijas Radio Liepajas Radio	Radio AA Radio Dejas Radio Sigulda	
Lithuania	Lietuvos Radijas Radio Vilnius LRT Kauno Programų Direkcija Majak relay	Radiocentras M-1 Vilniaus Varpas Znad Wilii Titanika	
Luxembourg		Radio-Télé-Luxembourg	
Macedonia	Radiotelevizija Makedonije		
Malta	Malta Broadcasting Authority Voice of the Mediterranean Deutsche Welle Relay Maltă		
Moldova	Radioteleviziunea Natională Radio Moldova International Radio Moscow relay		
Monaco		Radio Monte Carlo Riviera Radio Trans World Radio	
Montenegro	Radio Podgorica		
Netherlands	NOS Stichting Ether Reclame Ster Nozema RNW		US Forces Network (SHAPE) British Forces Broadcasting Service Canadian Forces Network–Brunssum

Major radio broadcasters (continued)

Country	*Public service*	*Commercial*	*Military*
New Zealand	Radio New Zealand Radio New Zealand International	RNZ Community Net National Radio Net Independent Broadcasters Association	
Norway	Teledirektoratet Norsk Rikskringkasting Foreign Service Svalbard (Spitsbergen)		
Poland	Polskie Radio I Telewizja Rozglosina Harcerska Radio Mazury		
Portugal	Radiodifusão Portuguesa (RDP) RDP International–Radio Portugal Rádio Renascença Lda Emissora Católica Portuguesa Sociedade de Radioretransmissao Ld Radio Trans Europe Voice of America relay	Radio Altitude	American Forces Radio & TV Service
Romania	Radio Romania Radio Romania International RM6	Radio Contact Romania	
Russia	Rossiyskaya Gosudarstvennaya Teleradiokompaniya 'Ostankino' Vserossiyskaya Gosudarsdtvennaya Teleradiokompniya Radio Moscow International Radio Aum Shinrikyo		
Serbia	Radiotelevizija Srbije Radio Beograd Music Radio Youth Radio Radio Politika Radio 'Pingvin' Radio Novi Sad		
Slovenia	Radiotelevizija Slovenia		
South Africa	South African Broadcasting Corporation (SABC) Channel Africa Ciskeian Broadcasting Corporation Transkei Broadcasting Corporation Radio Thohoyandou (Venda Radio)	Home Services Bophuthatswana Broadcasting Radio 702 Capital Radio (Transkei)	
Spain	Ente Publico Radiotelvision Española Radio Nacional de España Radio Exterior de España Sociedad Española de Radiodifusion (SER)	Cadena de Ondas Populares Españolas (COPE) Onda Cero Radio Antena 3 de Radio Cadena Dial Radio Minuto Eusko Irrati Telebista (Basque) Radiotelevision Galicia Radiotelevision de Andalucia Radiotelevision Valencia Canal Sur Radio	
Sweden	Svensk Rundradio AB Sveriges Radio AB Sveriges Utbildningsradio AB		

Country	Public service	Commercial	Military
Switzerland	Swiss Broadcasting Corporation Swiss Radio International United Nations Broadcasting from Geneva Broadcasts from the International Committee of the Red Cross, Geneva		
Ukraine	Derzhavna Teleradiomovna Kompaniya Ukrayiny Radio Ukraine International Radio Moscow relay		
United Kingdom	British Broadcasting Corporation BBC Radio Scotland BBC Radio Wales/Radio Cymru BBC Radio Ulster BBC World Service Voice of America	Independent Radio News Network News Classic FM Independent Music Radio Manx Radio Virgin Radio	British Forces Broadcasting Services
US	National Public Radio Voice of America VOA Europe Radio Marti United Nations Radio BBC relays	ABC Radio Networks CBS Radio Division NBC Radio Mutual Radio Network National Black Network Sheridan Broadcasting Network C-Span Audio Networks KCBI International International Broadcast Station KGEI Radio Station KJES KTBN KVOH Radio Earth International, Inc Radio Miami International WEWN Catholic Radio Service WHRI World Harvest Radio WMLK World International Broadcasters, Inc Worldwide Christian Radio WRNO Worldwide World Service of the Christian Science Monitor World Wide Gospel Radio, Inc WYFR–Family Radio Organization of the American States	US Armed Forces Radio & Television Service
Vatican City State	Vatican Radio		
Yugoslavia (former)	Udruženje Jugoslovenskih Radiotelevizija (JRT) Radiotelevizija Srbije Radiotelevizija Crne Gore Foreign Service–Radio Jugoslavija		

British national radio stations

BBC Radio

Radio 1	pop & rock music
Radio 2	popular music, comedy, arts, entertainment
Radio 3	classical music, documentaries, arts, cricket (seasonal)
Radio 4	news, documentaries, drama, entertainment
Radio 5	sport, education, children's programmes, World Service

BBC World Service

World Service in English
African Service: Swahili, Somali, Hausa
Arabic Service
Central European Service: Czech, Slovak, Hungarian, Polish, Finnish
Eastern Service: Bengali, Burmese, Hindi, Nepali, Pahto, Persian, Sinhalese, Tamil, Urdu
Far Eastern Service: Cantonese, Mandarin, Indonesian, Thai, Vietnamese
French & Portuguese Service
German Service
Latin American Service: Spanish, Portuguese
Russian & Ukrainian Service
Southeast European Service: Bulgarian, Romanian, Serbian, Croatian, Slovene, Greek , Turkish
BBC English (broadcasts series of English-language teaching courses worldwide)
BBC Monitoring (overseas and regional radio and television news)
Topical Tapes – provides tapes of programmes for use by overseas radio stations & produces 'Calling the Falklands'
BBC Transcription – produces & sells recorded BBC programmes to overseas radio stations

National regional radio

Radio Scotland
Radios Aberdeen, Highland & Orkney
Radio Ulster
Radio Wales
Radio Cymru (Welsh)

Independent national radio stations

Classic FM
Independent Music Radio
Virgin Radio

SCIENCE AND TECHNOLOGY

MATHEMATICS

Signs and symbols

$+$	plus; positive; underestimate
$-$	minus; negative; overestimate
$\pm$	plus or minus; positive or negative; degree of accuracy
$\mp$	minus or plus; negative or positive
$\times$	multiplies (colloq. 'times') (6×4)
$\cdot$	multiplies (colloq. 'times') ($6\cdot4$); scalar product of two vectors (**A·B**)
$\div$	divided by ($6\div4$)
/	divided by; ratio of (6/4)
—	divided by; ratio of ($^6/_4$)
!	factorial ($4!=4\times3\times2\times1$)
$=$	equals
$\neq$, $\neq$	not equal to
$\equiv$	identical with
$\not\equiv$, $\not\equiv$	not identical with
$\triangleq$	corresponds to
:	ratio of (6:4)
::	proportionately equals (1:2::2:4)
$\approx$	approximately equal to; equivalent to; similar to
$>$	greater than
$\gg$	much greater than
$\ngtr$	not greater than
$<$	less than
$\ll$	much less than
$\nless$	not less than
$\geqslant$, $\geqq$, $\gtreqqless$	equal to or greater than
$\leqslant$, $\leqq$, $\lesseqqgtr$	equal to or less than
$\propto$	directly proportional to
( )	parentheses
[ ]	brackets
{ }	braces
—	vinculum: division ($\overline{a-b}$); chord of circle or length of line ($\overline{AB}$); arithmetic mean ($\overline{X}$)

∞	infinity
$\rightarrow$	approaches the limit
$\sqrt{}$	square root
$\sqrt[3]{}$, $\sqrt[4]{}$	cube root, fourth root, etc.
%	per cent
$'$	prime; minute(s) of arc; foot/feet
$''$	double prime; second(s) of arc; inch(es)
$\frown$	arc of circle
$^\circ$	degree of arc
$\angle$, $\angle^s$	angle(s)
$\veebar$	equiangular
$\perp$	perpendicular
$\parallel$	parallel
○, Ⓢ	circle(s)
$\triangle$, △ with s	triangle(s)
$\square$	square
▭	rectangle
▱	parallelogram
$\cong$	congruent to
$\therefore$	therefore
$\because$	because
$\overset{m}{=}$	measured by
Δ	increment
Σ	summation
Π	product
$\int$	integral sign
∇	del: differential operator
$\cup$	union
$\cap$	intersection
$\in$	is an element of
$\subset$	strict inclusion
$\supset$	contains
$\Rightarrow$	implies
$\Leftarrow$	implied by
$\Leftrightarrow$	implies and is implied by

Important formulae

Circumference, area and volume

The value of π is approximately 3·1416

Circle

circumference = $2\pi r = \pi d$
area = $\pi r^2 = {}^1/_4\pi d^2$

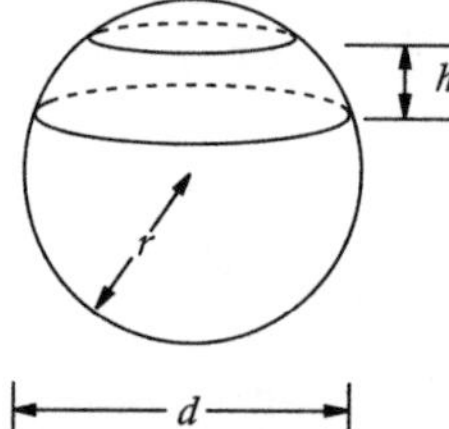

Sphere

surface area = $4\pi r^2 = \pi d^2$.
volume = ${}^4/_3\,\pi r^3 = {}^1/_6\,\pi\, d^3$.
surface area of zone bounded by parallel planes = $2\pi rh$.

Prism, including cylinder

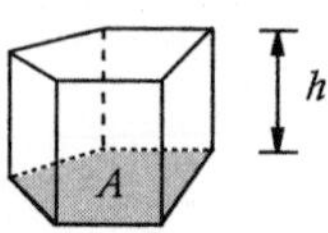

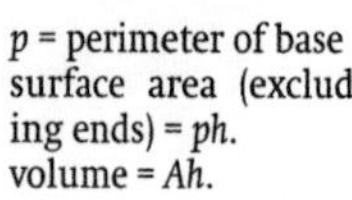

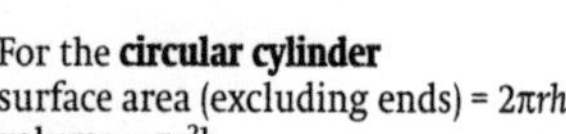

p = perimeter of base
surface area (excluding ends) = ph.
volume = Ah.

For the **circular cylinder**
surface area (excluding ends) = $2\pi rh$.
volume = $\pi r^2 h$.

Pyramid, including cone

volume = ${}^1/_3 Ah$.

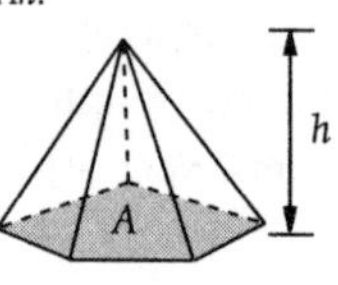

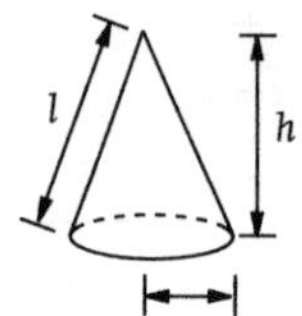

For the **circular cone**
surface area (excluding base) = πrl.
volume = ${}^1/_3\,\pi r^2 h$.

Parallelogram

Area = bh.

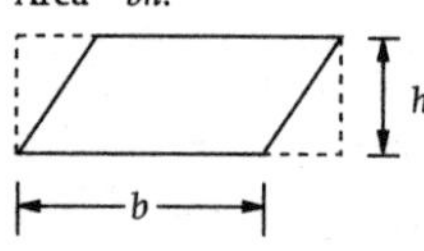

Triangle

Area = ${}^1/_2 bh$.

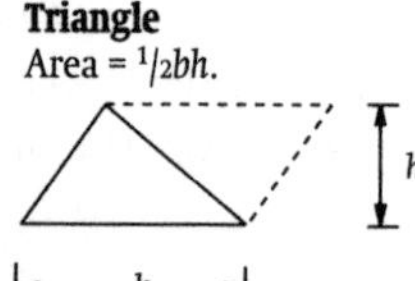

Trapezium

Area = ${}^1/_2\,(a+b)h$.

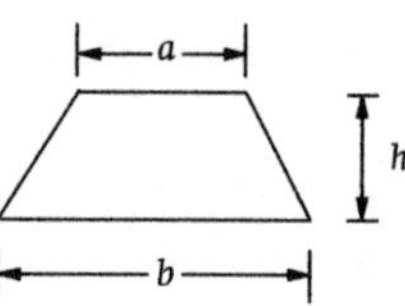

Algebra

Series

$\sum_{i=1}^{n} i = {}^1/_2 n(n+1)$ (an **arithmetic progression**); $\sum_{i=1}^{n} i^2 = {}^1/_6\, n(n+1)(2n+1)$; $\sum_{i=1}^{n} i^3 = {}^1/_4 n^2(n+1)^2$.

Logarithms

$\log_b x = \log_c x/\log_c b$; in particular, $\log_b x = \ln x/\ln b$.

To any base, $\log 1 = 0$; $\log(xy) = \log x + \log y$; $\log(x/y) = \log x - \log y$; $\log x^k = k\log x$.

Factorials

$0! = 1$, $(i+1)! = (i+1)\times i!$ for $i = 0, 1, 2, \ldots$

For large values of n, **Stirling's approximation** is $\ln(n!) \approx {}^1/_2 \ln(2\pi) + (n + {}^1/_2)\ln n - n + {}^1/_{12n}$

Binomial coefficients (*i* denotes a natural number)

For any real n, $\binom{n}{i} = \dfrac{n\,(n-1)\ldots(n-i+1)}{i!}$.

This may be calculated from the inductive definition $\binom{n}{0} = 1$, $\binom{n}{i+1} = \dfrac{n-i}{i+1}\binom{n}{i}$ for $i = 0, 1, 2, \ldots$

The 'Pascal triangle' rule: $\binom{n+1}{i} = \binom{n}{i-1} + \binom{n}{i}$.

If n is also a natural number, and if ${}_nC_i$ denotes the number of subsets of i elements contained in a set of n elements, then ${}_nC_i = \binom{n}{i} = \frac{n!}{i!(n-i)!}$

The binomial theorem: If n is a natural number, $(b+a)^n = \sum_{i=0}^{n} \binom{n}{i} b^{n-i}a^i$.

Quadratic functions and equations

Completing the square: If $a \neq 0$, $ax^2 + bx + c = a\left(x + \frac{b}{2a}\right)^2 + \frac{4ac - b^2}{4a}$,

so that

$$ax^2 + bx + c = 0 \Leftrightarrow x = \frac{-b \pm \sqrt{(b^2 - 4ac)}}{2a}.$$

Cubic equations,

If $a \neq 0$, and the roots of $ax^3 + bx^2 + cx + d = 0$ are α, β, γ, then

$$\alpha + \beta + \gamma = -b/a, \quad \beta\gamma + \gamma\alpha + \alpha\beta = c/a, \alpha\beta\gamma = -d/a.$$

Complex numbers

The **modulus-argument form** of z is $z = [r,\theta] = r(\cos\theta + j\sin\theta) = r\exp(\theta j)$, where r, θ are real.

The **product rule** $[r, \theta] \times [s, \phi] = [rs, \theta + \phi]$.

De Moivre's theorem for integral index: $[1,\theta]^n = [1,n\theta]$, or $(\cos\theta + j\sin\theta)^n = \cos n\theta + j\sin n\theta$.

The roots of $z^n = 1$ are $z = [1, 2\pi k/n] = \exp\{2\pi(k/n)j\}$ for $k = 0, 1, 2, ..., n-1$. In particular, the roots of $z^3 = 1$ are ω, ω^2, where $\omega = \cos \tfrac{2}{3}\pi + j\sin\tfrac{2}{3}\pi = -\tfrac{1}{2} + (\tfrac{1}{2}\sqrt{3})j$, so that $\omega^3 = 1$ and $1 + \omega + \omega^2 = 0$.

Vectors

Products

If the vectors **a**, **b** are represented by column matrices $\begin{bmatrix} a_1 \\ a_2 \\ a_3 \end{bmatrix}, \begin{bmatrix} b_1 \\ b_2 \\ b_3 \end{bmatrix}$ of their components with respect to a rectangular system of right-handed axes, or as $a_1\mathbf{i} + a_2\mathbf{j} + a_3\mathbf{k}$, $b_1\mathbf{i} + b_2\mathbf{j} + b_3\mathbf{k}$, then $\mathbf{a} \cdot \mathbf{b} = a_1b_1 + a_2b_2 + a_3b_3$;

$$\mathbf{a} \times \mathbf{b} = \begin{bmatrix} a_2b_3 - a_3b_2 \\ a_3b_1 - a_1b_3 \\ a_1b_2 - a_2b_1 \end{bmatrix} = (a_2b_3 - a_3b_2)\,\mathbf{i} + (a_3b_1 - a_1b_3)\,\mathbf{j} + (a_1b_2 - a_2b_1)\,\mathbf{k}.$$

Scalar triple product: $[\mathbf{a} \cdot \mathbf{b} \cdot \mathbf{c}] = \mathbf{a} \cdot (\mathbf{b} \times \mathbf{c}) = \mathbf{b} \cdot (\mathbf{c} \times \mathbf{a}) = \mathbf{c} \cdot (\mathbf{a} \times \mathbf{b}) = \det \begin{bmatrix} a_1 & b_1 & c_1 \\ a_2 & b_2 & c_2 \\ a_3 & b_3 & c_3 \end{bmatrix}$.

Vector triple product: $\mathbf{a} \times (\mathbf{b} \times \mathbf{c}) = (\mathbf{a} \cdot \mathbf{c})\,\mathbf{b} - (\mathbf{a} \cdot \mathbf{b})\,\mathbf{c}$; $(\mathbf{a} \times \mathbf{b}) \times \mathbf{c} = (\mathbf{a} \cdot \mathbf{c})\,\mathbf{b} - (\mathbf{b} \cdot \mathbf{c})\,\mathbf{a}$.

Trigonometry

Formulae involving sines

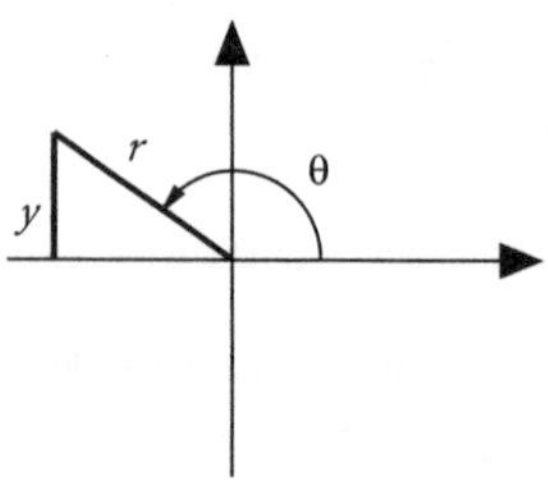

Coordinates: $y = r \sin\ \theta.$

For any angle θ:

$$\sin(90° - \theta) = \cos\ \theta,$$
$$\sin(180° - \theta) = \sin\ \theta,$$
$$\sin(360° - \theta) = -\sin\ \theta.$$

In a right-angled triangle:

$$\text{sine (angle)} = \frac{\text{opposite side}}{\text{hypotenuse}}.$$

Formulae involving cosines

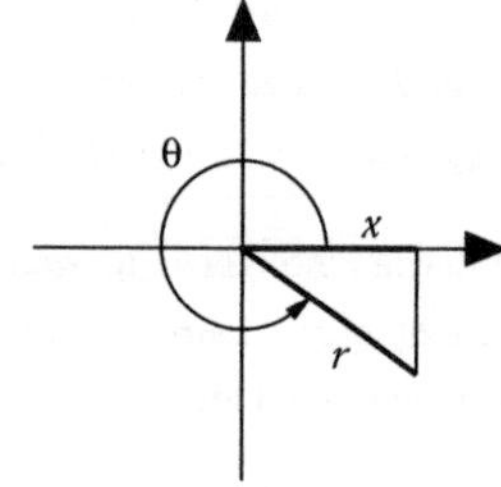

Coordinates: $x = r \cos \theta.$

For any angle θ:

$$\cos(90° - \theta) = \sin \theta,$$
$$\cos(180° - \theta) = -\cos\ \theta,$$
$$\cos(360° - \theta) = \cos\ \theta.$$

In a right-angled triangle:

$$\text{cosine (angle)} = \frac{\text{adjacent side}}{\text{hypotenuse}}.$$

Formulae involving tangents

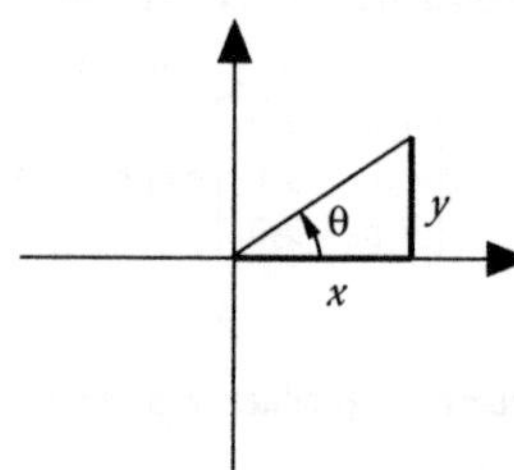

Coordinates: $y = x \tan\ \theta.$

For any angle θ:

$$\tan\theta = \frac{\sin\ \theta}{\cos\ \theta}$$
$$\tan(90° - \theta) = \frac{1}{\tan\ \theta}$$
$$\tan(180° - \theta) = -\tan\ \theta,$$
$$\tan(360° - \theta) = -\tan\ \theta.$$

In a right-angled triangle:

$$\text{tangent (angle)} = \frac{\text{opposite side}}{\text{adjacent side}}.$$

$\sec\theta = \frac{1}{\cos\theta}$, $\tan\theta = \frac{\sin\theta}{\cos\theta}$ $[\theta \neq (k + {}^1/_2)\,\pi\,]$;

$\operatorname{cosec}\theta$ (or $\csc\theta$) $= \frac{1}{\sin\theta}$, $\cot\theta = \frac{1}{\tan\theta} = \frac{\cos\theta}{\sin\theta}$ $[\theta \neq k\,\pi]$.

Pythagoras formulae: $\cos^2\theta + \sin^2\theta = 1$; $1 + \tan^2\theta = \sec^2\theta$; $\cot^2\theta + 1 = \operatorname{cosec}^2\theta$.

Additional formulae: $\sin(\theta \pm \phi) = \sin\theta\cos\phi \pm \cos\theta\sin\phi$; $\cos(\theta \pm \phi) = \cos\theta\cos\phi \mp \sin\theta\sin\phi$;

$\tan(\theta \pm \phi) = \frac{\tan\theta \pm \tan\phi}{1 \mp \tan\theta\tan\phi}$.

Triangle formulae: In the triangle *ABC*,

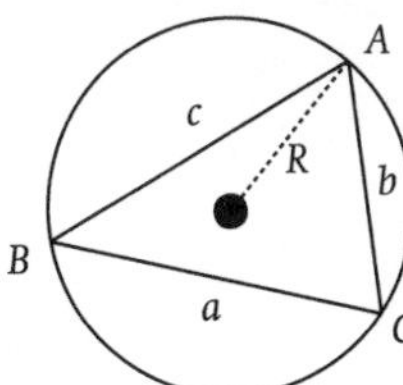

$$\frac{a}{\sin A} = \frac{b}{\sin B} = \frac{c}{\sin C} = 2R \text{ (the **sine rule**);}$$

$$a^2 = b^2 + c^2 - 2bc\cos A, \quad \text{or } \cos A = \frac{b^2 + c^2 - a^2}{2bc}, \text{ (the **cosine rule**)}$$

Calculus

Chain rule: If $y = f(u)$ and $u = g(x)$, then $\frac{dy}{dx} = \frac{dy}{du} \times \frac{du}{dx}$

Taylor's polynomial approximation

For small h $\quad f(a+h) \approx f(a) + f'(a)\cdot h + \frac{1}{2!} f''(a)\cdot h^2 + \dots + \frac{1}{n!} f^{(n)}(a)\cdot h^n.$

The remainder (error) can be expressed as $\frac{1}{(n+1)!} f^{(n+1)}(\xi)\cdot h^{n+1}$, where ξ is some number between a and $a + h$.

Power series with intervals of validity

$(1+x)^m = \sum_{i=0}^{\infty} \binom{m}{i} x^i$ for $|x| < 1$. and sometimes also for $x = 1$ and/or $x = -1$.

$\ln(1+x) = \sum_{i=0}^{\infty} (-1)^{i+1} \frac{x^i}{i}$ for $-1 < x \leqslant 1$.

$e^x = \sum_{i=0}^{\infty} \frac{x^i}{i!}$ for all x.

Indefinite integrals (In the following we take $a > 0$ and omit the additive constant.)

$f(x)$	$\int f(x)\,dx$	$f(x)$	$\int f(x)\,dx$
$x^n \ (n \neq -1)$	$x^{n+1}/(n+1)$	$\sin x$	$-\cos x$
$1/x$	$\ln\|x\|,\ x \neq 0$	$\cos x$	$\sin x$
$\frac{1}{x^2+a^2}$	$\frac{1}{a}\tan^{-1}\frac{x}{a}$	$\tan x$	$\ln\|\sec x\|$

Integration by parts: $\int u \frac{dv}{dx}\,dx = uv - \int \frac{du}{dx}\, v\,dx.$

Curvature: $\kappa = \frac{d\psi}{ds} = \frac{x'y'' - x''y'}{[(x')^2 + (y')^2]^{3/2}}.$

NUMERICAL METHODS

Simpson's rule, in which n must be *even*, giving an *odd* number of ordinates:

$\int_{x_0}^{x_n} f(x)\,dx \approx {}^1/_3 h\,[(y_0 + y_n) + 4\,(y_1 + y_3 + \dots + y_{n-1}) + 2\,(y_2 + y_4 + \dots + y_{n-2})]$.

Newton–Raphson method: If p_n is an approximation to a root of $f(x) = 0$, then

$$p_{n+1} = p_n - \frac{f(p_n)}{f'(p_n)}$$

is generally a better one. The error is approximately

$$\frac{[f(p_n)]^2 f''(p_n)}{2\,[f'(p_n)]^3}$$

Conics

Name of curve	*Standard form of equation*	*Standard parametric forms*	*Eccentricity e*	*Foci F and F'*	*Directrices d and d'*	*Asymptotes*
Parabola	$y^2 = 4ax$	$(ap^2, 2ap)$	1	$(a, 0)$	$x = -a$	none
Ellipse	$\frac{x^2}{a^2} + \frac{y^2}{b^2} = 1$	$(a\cos\theta, b\sin\theta)$	$\frac{\sqrt{(a^2 - b^2)}}{a} < 1$	$(\pm ae, 0)$	$x = \pm\frac{a}{e}$	none
Circle	$x^2 + y^2 = a^2$	$(a\cos\theta, a\sin\theta)$	0	$(0, 0)$	none	none
Hyperbola	$\frac{x^2}{a^2} - \frac{y^2}{b^2} = 1$	$(a\sec\phi, b\tan\phi)$ or $(\pm a\cosh u, b\sinh u)$	$\frac{\sqrt{(a^2 + b^2)}}{a} > 1$	$(\pm ae, 0)$	$x = \pm\frac{a}{e}$	$\frac{x}{a} \pm \frac{y}{b} = 0$

Probability

$P(A \text{ and } B) + P(A \text{ and } {\sim}B) = P(A)$; $P(A \text{ or } B) = P(A) + P(B) - P(A \text{ and } B)$.

Conditional probability: $P(A|B) = P(A \text{ and } B)/P(B)$.

Bayes' theorem: $P(A|B) = \dfrac{P(B|A) \times P(A)}{P(B|A) \times P(A) + P(B|{\sim}A) \times P({\sim}A)}$.

Parameters

Mean $\mu = E(X) = \Sigma x_i p(x_i)$ or $\int x\phi(x)\,dx$ (evaluated over the possibility space).
Variance $\sigma^2 = V(X) = E((X-\mu)^2) = E(X^2) - \mu^2 = \Sigma x_i^2 p(x_i) - \mu^2$ or $\int x^2\phi(x)\,dx - \mu^2$.

Expectation

For a single random variable, $E(aX + b) = aE(X) + b$, $V(aX+b) = a^2 V(X)$.
For two random variables, $E(X \pm Y) = E(X) \pm E(Y)$, $V(X \pm Y) = V(X) + V(Y) \pm 2\text{cov}(X, Y)$,
where the covariance $\text{cov}(X,Y) = E((X - \mu_X)(Y - \mu_Y)) = E(XY) - \mu_X\mu_Y$.
If X, Y are independent, $\text{cov}(X, Y) = 0$ so that $V(X \pm Y) = V(X) + V(Y)$.

Particular probability models

Discrete

	Parameter	*Probability p(i)*	*Probability generator*	*Mean*	*Variance*	*Meaning of p(i)*
Binomial $B(n, a)$	P (success) = a P (failure) = b $[a + b = 1]$	$\dfrac{n!\,a^i b^j}{i!\,j!}$ $[i + j = n]$	$(b + at)^n$	na	nab	probability of i successes in n independent trials
Geometric		ab^{i-1} $[i \geqslant 1]$	$at/(1 - bt)$	$1/a$	b/a^2	probability that the first success occurs at the ith trial
Poisson	Mean λ in unit interval	$\dfrac{\lambda^i e^{-\lambda}}{i!}$ $[i \geqslant 0]$	$e^{\lambda(t-1)}$	λ	λ	probability of i occurrences in unit interval

Statistics

Statistical measures

If n is the sample size and $f(x_i)$ the frequency of occurrence of the value x_i in the sample (so that $n = \Sigma f(x_i)$), then:

Sample mean m (or $\bar{x}$) $= \dfrac{1}{n}\sum_i x_i f(x_i)$.

Conic sections

Cone (sometimes double) cut by a plane in (*a*) a single point (*b*) a pair of straight lines (*c*) a hyperbola (*d*) a parabola (*e*) a circle (*f*) an ellipse

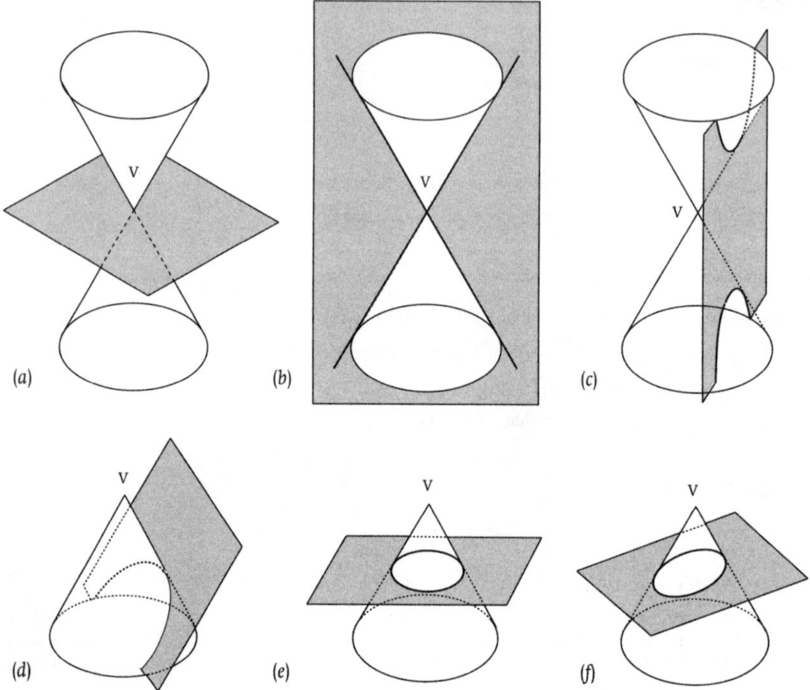

Pythagoras' theorem

A mathematical proposition advanced by Pythagoras, that in any right-angled triangle, the square on the hypotenuse is equal to the sum of the squares on the other two sides. The converse of the theorem is also true: in any triangle in which the square on the longest side is equal to the sum of the squares on the other two sides, the angle opposite the longest side is a right angle. Although known to the Babylonians, tradition ascribes to Pythagoras himself the first proof, probably based on the first diagram. The commoner proof (the second diagram), proving first that the area of square *ABXY* is equal to that of the rectangle *APRS*, was given by Euclid.

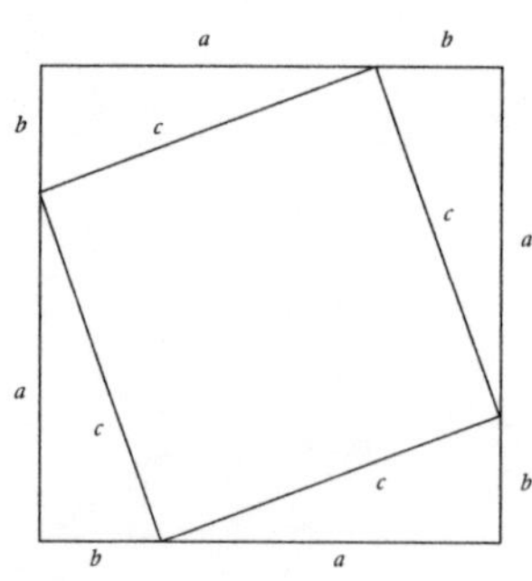

Pythagoras' theorem: $c^2 = a^2 + b^2$

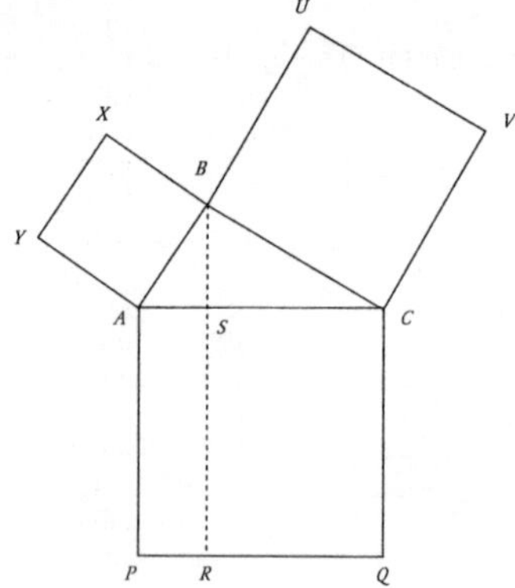

Pythagoras' theorem: $AC^2 = AB^2 + BC^2$

MEASUREMENT

Basic SI units

The SI (Système International d'Unitiés) system of units has seven basic units from which all derived units are obtained. Multiples and submultiples of the basic units may be used with approved prefixes.

1. metre *(unit of length) symbol:* m
The metre is the length equal to 1 650 763.73 wavelengths in vacuum corresponding to the quantized electron transition between energy levels $2p^{10}$ and $5d^5$ of the krypton-86 atom.

2. kilogram *(unit of mass) symbol:* kg
The kilogram is the unit of mass equal to the mass of the international prototype kilogram kept at Sèvres, France.

3. second *(unit of time) symbol:* s
The second is the duration of 9 192 631 770 periods of the radiation corresponding to the quantized electron transition between two hyperfine levels of the ground state of the caesium-133 atom.

4. ampere *(unit of electric current) symbol:* A
The ampere is that constant electric current which, if maintained in two straight parallel conductors of infinite length, of negligible cross-section and placed 1 metre apart in vacuum, would produce between these conductors a force equal to 2×10^{-7} newton/ metre.

5. kelvin *(unit of temperature) symbol:* K
The kelvin, unit of thermodynamic temperature is the fraction 1/273.16 of the thermodynamic temperature of the triple point of water.

6. candela *(unit of luminous intensity) symbol:* cd
The candela is the luminous intensity, in a perpendicular direction, of a surface 1/600 000 metre^2 of a black body at the freezing point of platinum at a pressure of 101 325 newton/metre^2.

7. mole *(unit of amount of substance) symbol:* mol
The mole is the amount of substance containing as many elementary units as there are carbon atoms in 0.012 kilogram of carbon-12. The elementary unit may be an atom, molecule, ion or electron.

Two supplementary units are also used:

radian *(unit of plane angle) symbol:* rad
The radian is the unit of measurement of angle and is the angle subtended at the centre of a circle by an arc equal in length to the circle radius.

steradian *(unit of solid angle) symbol:* sr
The steradian is the unit of measurement of solid angle and is the solid angle subtended at the centre of a circle by a spherical cap equal in area to the square of the circle radius.

SI conversion factors

This table gives the conversion factors for many British and other units which are still in common use, showing their equivalents in terms of the International System of Units (SI). The column labelled 'SI equivalent' gives the SI value of one unit of the type named in the first column, e.g. 1 calorie is 4.187 joules. The column labelled 'Reciprocal' allows conversion the other way, e.g. 1 joule is 0.239 calories. (All values are to three decimal places.) As a second example, 1 dyne is 10 μN = 10×10^{-6} N = 10^{-5} N; so 1 newton is $0.1 \times 10^{+6} = 10^5$ dyne. Finally, 1 torr is 0.133 kPa = 0.133×10^3 Pa; so 1 Pa is 7.501×10^{-3} torr.

Unit name	*Symbol*	*Quantity*	*SI equivalent*	*Unit*	*Reciprocal*
acre		area	0.405	hm^2	2.471
ångström[a]	Å	length	0.1	nm	10
astronomical unit	AU	length	0.150	Tm	6.684
atomic mass unit	amu	mass	1.661×10^{-27}	kg	6.022×10^{26}
bar	bar	pressure	0.1	MPa	10
barn	b	area	100	fm^2	0.01
barrel (US) = 42 US gal	bbl	volume	0.159	m^3	6.290
British thermal unit	Btu	energy	1.055	kJ	0.948
calorie	cal	energy	4.187	J	0.239
cubic foot	ft^3	volume	0.028	m^3	35.315
cubic inch	in^3	volume	16.387	cm^3	0.061
cubic yard	yd^3	volume	0.765	m^3	1.308
curie[a]	Ci	activity of radionuclide	37	GBq	0.027
degree = 1/90 rt angle	°	plane angle	π/180	rad	57.296
degree Celsius	°C	temperature	1	K	1
degree Centigrade	°C	temperature	1	K	1
degree Fahrenheit	°F	temperature	5/9	K	1.8
degree Rankine	°R	temperature	5/9	K	1.8
dyne	dyn	force	10	μN	0.1
electronvolt	eV	energy	0.160	αJ	6.241
erg	erg	energy	0.1	μJ	10
fathom (6ft)		length	1.829	m	0.547
fermi	fm	length	1	fm	1
foot	ft	length	30.48	cm	0.033
foot per second	ft s^{-1}	velocity	0.305	m s^{-1}	3.281
			1.097	km h^{-1}	0.911
gallon (UK)[a]	gal	volume	4.546	dm^3	0.220

Unit name	Symbol	Quantity	SI equivalent	Unit	Reciprocal
gallon (US)[a] = 231in^3	gal	volume	3.785	dm^3	0.264
gallon (UK) per mile		consumption	2.825	dm^{3}km^{-1}	0.354
gauss	Gs, G	magnetic flux density	100	μT	0.01
grade = 0.01 rt angle	rt angle	plane angle	π/200	rad	63.662
grain	gr	mass	0.065	g	15.432
hectare[a]	ha	area	1	hm^2	1
horsepower	hp	power	0.746	kW	1.341
inch	in	length	2.54	cm	0.394
kilogram-force	kgf	force	9.807	N	0.102
knot[a]		velocity	1.852	km h^{-1}	0.540
light year	l.y.	length	9.461×10^{15}	m	1.057×10^{-16}
litre	l	volume	1	dm^3	1
Mach number	Ma	velocity	1193.3	km h	8.380×10^{-4}
maxwell	Mx	magnetic flux	10	nWb	0.1
metric carat		mass	0.2	g	5
micron	μ	length	1	μm	1
mile (nautical)[a]		length	1.852	km	0.540
mile (statute)		length	1.609	km	0.621
mile per hour (mph)	mile h^{-1}	velocity	1.609	km h^{-1}	0.621
minute = (1/60)°		plane angle	π/10 800	rad	3437.75
oersted	Oe	magnetic field strength	1/(4π)	kA m^{-1}	4π
ounce (avoirdupois)	oz	mass	28.349	g	0.035
ounce (troy) = 480 gr		mass	31.103	g	0.032
parsec	pc	length	30857	Tm	0.0000324
phot	ph	illuminance	10	klx	0.1
pint (UK)	pt	volume	0.568	dm^3	1.760
poise	p	viscosity	0.1	Pa s	10
pound	lb	mass	0.454	kg	2.205
pound force	lbf	force	4.448	N	0.225
pound force/in		pressure	6.895	kPa	0.145
poundal	pdl	force	0.138	N	7.233
pounds per square inch	psi	pressure	6.895×10^3	k Pa	0.145
rad[a]	rad	absorbed dose	0.01	Gy	100
rem[a]	rem	dose equivalent	0.01	Sv	100
right angle = π/2 rad		plane angle	1.571	rad	0.637
röntgen[a]	R	exposure	0.258	mC kg^{-1}	3.876
second = (1/60)'	"	plane angle	π/648	mrad	206.265
slug		mass	14.594	kg	0.068
solar mass	M	mass	1.989×10^{30}	kg	5.028×10^{-31}
square foot	ft^2	area	9.290	dm^2	0.108
square inch	in^2	area	6.452	cm^2	0.155
square mile (statute)	mi^2	area	2.590	km^2	0.386
square yard	yd^2	area	0.836	m^2	1.196
standard atmosphere	atm	pressure	0.101	MPa	9.869
stere	st	volume	1	m^3	1
stilb	sb	luminance	10	kcd m^{-2}	0.1
stokes	St	viscosity	1	cm^{2}s^{-1}	1
therm = 10^5 Btu		energy	0.105	GJ	9.478
ton = 2240 lb		mass	1.016	Mg	0.984
ton-force	tonf	force	9.964	kN	0.100
ton-force/in^2		pressure	15.444	MPa	0.065
tonne	t	mass	1	Mg	1
torr, or mmHg	torr	pressure	0.133	kPa	7.501
X unit		length	0.100	pm	10
yard	yd	length	0.915	m	1.094

[a]In temporary use with SI.

SI prefixes

Factor	Prefix	Symbol	Factor	Prefix	Symbol	Factor	Prefix	Symbol
10^{18}	exa	E	10^2	hecto	h	10^{-9}	nano	n
10^{15}	peta	P	10^1	deca	da	10^{-12}	pico	p
10^{12}	tera	T	10^{-1}	deci	d	10^{-15}	femto	f
10^9	giga	G	10^{-2}	centi	c	10^{-18}	atto	a
10^6	mega	M	10^{-3}	milli	m			
10^3	kilo	k	10^{-6}	micro	μ			

Common measures

Metric units		Imperial equivalent
Length		
	1 millimetre	0.03937 in
10 mm	1 centimetre	0.39 in
10 cm	1 decimetre	3.94 in
100 cm	1 metre	39.37 in
1000 m	1 kilometre	0.62 mi
Area		
	1 square millimetre	0.0016 sq in
	1 square centimetre	0.155 sq in
100 sq cm	1 square decimetre	15.5 sq in
10 000 sq cm	1 square metre	10.76 sq ft
10 000 sq m	1 hectare	2.47 acres
Volume		
	1 cubic centimetre	0.016 cu in
1 000 cu cm	1 cubic decimetre	61.024 cu in
1 000 cu dm	1 cubic metre	35.31 cu ft
		1.308 cu yds
Liquid volume		
	1 litre	1.76 pints
100 litres	1 hectolitre	22 gallons
Weight		
	1 gram	0.035 oz
1 000 g	1 kilogram	2.2046 lb
1 000 kg	1 tonne	0.0842 ton

Imperial units		Metric equivalent
Length		
	1 inch	2.54 cm
12 in	1 foot	30.48 cm
3 ft	1 yard	0.9144 m
1 760 yd	1 mile	1.6093 km
Area		
	1 square inch	6.45 sq cm
144 sq in	1 square foot	0.0929 m^2
9 sq ft	1 square yard	0.836 m^2
4 840 sq yd	1 acre	0.405 ha
640 acres	1 square mile	259 ha
Volume		
	1 cubic inch	16.3871 cm^2
1 728cu in	1 cubic foot	0.028 m^2
27 cu ft	1 cubic yard	0.765 m^2
Liquid volume		
	1 pint	0.57 litre
2 pints	1 quart	1.14 litres
4 quarts	1 gallon	4.55 litres
Weight		
	1 ounce	28.3495 g
16 oz	1 pound	0.4536 kg
14 lb	1 stone	6.35 kg
8 stones	1 hundredweight	50.8 kg
20 cwt	1 ton	1.016 tonnes

Conversion factors

Imperial to metric			*Multiply by*
Length			
inches	→	millimetres	25.4
inches	→	centimetres	2.54
feet	→	metres	0.3048
yards	→	metres	0.9144
statute miles	→	kilometres	1.6093
nautical miles	→	kilometres	1.852
Area			
square inches	→	square centimetres	6.4516
square feet	→	square metres	0.0929
square yards	→	square metres	0.8361
acres	→	hectares	0.4047
square miles	→	square kilometres	2.5899
Volume			
cubic inches	→	cubic centimetres	16.3871
cubic feet	→	cubic metres	0.0283
cubic yards	→	cubic metres	0.7646
Capacity			
UK fluid ounces	→	litres	0.0284
US fluid ounces	→	litres	0.0296
UK pints	→	litres	0.5682
US pints	→	litres	0.4732
UK gallons	→	litres	4.546
US gallons	→	litres	3.7854
Weight			
ounces (avoirdupois)	→	grams	28.3495
ounces (troy)	→	grams	31.1035
pounds	→	kilograms	0.4536
tons (long)	→	tonnes	1.016

Metric to imperial			*Multiply by*
Length			
millimetres	→	inches	0.0394
centimetres	→	inches	0.3937
metres	→	feet	3.2806
metres	→	yards	1.9036
kilometres	→	statute miles	0.6214
kilometres	→	nautical miles	0.54
Area			
square centimetres	→	square inches	0.155
square metres	→	square feet	10.764
square metres	→	square yards	1.196
hectares	→	acres	2.471
square kilometres	→	square miles	0.386

Volume			*Multiply by*
cubic centimetres	→	cubic inches	0.061
cubic metres	→	cubic feet	35.315
cubic metres	→	cubic yards	1.308

Capacity			
litres	→	UK fluid ounces	35.1961
litres	→	US fluid ounces	33.8150
litres	→	UK pints	1.7598
litres	→	US pints	2.1134
litres	→	UK gallons	0.2199
litres	→	US gallons	0.2642

Weight			
grams	→	ounces (avoirdupois)	0.0353
grams	→	ounces (troy)	0.0322
kilograms	→	pounds	2.2046
tonnes	→	tons (long)	0.9842

Conversion tables: length

in	*cm*
1/8	0.3
1/4	0.6
3/8	1
1/2	1.3
5/8	1.6
3/4	1.9
7/8	2.2
1	2.5
2	5.1
3	7.6
4	10.2
5	12.7
6	15.2
7	17.8
8	20.3
9	22.9
10	25.4
11	27.9
12	30.5
13	33
14	35.6
15	38.1
16	40.6
17	43.2
18	45.7
19	48.3
20	50.8
21	53.3
22	55.9
23	58.4
24	61
25	63.5
26	66
27	68.6
28	71.1
29	73.7
30	76.2
40	101.6
50	127
60	152.4
70	177.8
80	203.2
90	228.6
100	254

Exact conversion:
1 in = 2.540 cm

cm	*in*
1	0.39
2	0.79
3	1.18
4	1.57
5	1.97
6	2.36
7	2.76
8	3.15
9	3.54
10	3.94
11	4.33
12	4.72
13	5.12
14	5.51
15	5.91
16	6.3
17	6.69
18	7.09
19	7.48
20	7.87
21	8.27
22	8.66
23	9.06
24	9.45
25	9.84
26	10.24
27	10.63
28	11.02
29	11.42
30	11.81
31	12.2
32	12.6
33	12.99
34	13.39
35	13.78
36	14.17
37	14.57
38	14.96
39	15.35
40	15.75
50	19.69
60	23.62
70	27.56
80	31.5
90	35.43
100	39.37

Exact conversion:
1 cm = 0.3937 in

in	*mm*
1/8	3.2
1/4	6.4
3/8	9.5
1/2	12.7
5/8	15.9
3/4	19
7/8	22.2
1	25.4
2	50.8
3	76.2
4	101.6
5	127
6	152.4
7	177.8
8	203.2
9	228.6
10	254
11	279.4
12	304.8
13	330.2
14	355.6
15	381

Exact conversion:
1mm = 0.0394 in

mm	*in*
1	0.04
2	0.08
3	0.12
4	0.16
5	0.2
6	0.24
7	0.28
8	0.31
9	0.35
10	0.39
11	0.43
12	0.47
13	0.51
14	0.55
15	0.59
16	0.63
17	0.67
18	0.71
19	0.75
20	0.79
25	0.98
50	1.97
100	3.94

Exact conversion:
1 in = 25.40 cm

ft	*m*
1	0.3
2	0.6
3	0.9
4	1.2
5	1.5
6	1.8
7	2.1
8	2.4
9	2.7
10	3.0
15	4.6
20	6.1
25	7.6
30	9.1
35	10.7
40	12.2
45	13.7
50	15.2
75	22.9
100	30.5
200	61.0
300	91.4
400	121.9
500	152.4
600	182.9
700	213.4
800	243.8
900	274.3
1 000	304.8
1 500	457.2
2 000	609.6
2 500	762.0
3 000	914.4
3 500	1 066.8
4 000	1 219.2
5 000	1 524.0
10 000	3 048.0

Exact conversion:
1 ft = 0.3048 m

m	*ft*
1	3.3
2	6.6
3	9.8
4	13.1
5	16.4
6	19.7
7	23.0
8	26.2
9	29.5
10	32.8
15	49.2
20	65.5
25	22.9
30	98.4
35	114.8
40	131.2
45	147.6
50	164.0
75	246.1
100	328.1
200	656.2
300	984.3
400	1 312.3
500	1 640.4
600	1 968.5
700	2 296.6
800	2 624.7
900	2 952.8
1 000	3 280.8
1 500	4 921.3
2 000	6 561.7
2 500	8 202.1
3 000	9 842.5
3 500	11 482.9
4 000	13 123.4
5 000	16 404.2
10 000	32 808.4

Exact conversion:
1 m = 3.2808 ft

yd	*m*
1	0.9
2	1.8
3	2.7
4	3.7
5	4.6
6	5.5
7	6.4
8	7.3
9	8.2
10	9.1
15	13.7
20	18.3
25	22.9
30	27.4
35	32.0
40	36.6
45	41.1
50	45.7
75	68.6
100	91.4
200	182.9
220	201.2
300	274.3
400	365.8
440	402.3
500	457.2
600	548.6
700	640.1
800	731.5
880	804.7
900	823.0
1 000	914.4
1 500	1 371.6
2 000	1 828.8
2 500	2 286.0
5 000	4 572.0
10 000	9 144.0

Exact conversion:
1 yd = 0.9144 m

m	*yd*
1	1.1
2	2.2
3	3.3
4	4.4
5	5.5
6	6.6
7	7.7
8	8.7
9	9.8
10	10.9
15	16.4
20	21.9
25	27.3
30	32.8
35	38.3
40	43.7
45	49.2
50	54.7
75	82.0
100	109.4
200	218.7
220	240.6
300	328.1
400	437.4
440	481.2
500	546.8
600	656.2
700	765.5
800	874.9

Science and technology

m	yd
880	962.4
900	984.2
1 000	1 093.6
1 500	1 640.4
2 000	2 187.2
2 500	2 734.0
5 000	5 468.1
10 000	10 936.1

Exact conversion:
1 m = 1.0936 yd

*mi**	*km*
1	1.6
2	3.2
3	4.8
4	6.4
5	8.0
6	9.7
7	11.3
8	12.9
9	14.5
10	16.1
15	24.1
20	32.2
25	40.2
30	48.3
35	56.3
40	64.4
45	72.4
50	80.5
55	88.5
60	96.6
65	104.6
70	112.7
75	120.7
80	128.7
85	136.8
90	144.8
95	152.9
100	160.9
200	321.9
300	482.8
400	643.7
500	804.7
750	1 207.0
1 000	1 609.3
2 500	4 023.4
5 000	8 046.7

*Statute miles
Exact conversion:
1 mi = 1.6093 km

km	*mi*
1	0.6
2	1.2
3	1.9
4	2.5
5	3.1
6	3.7
7	4.3
8	5.0
9	5.6
10	6.2
15	9.3
20	12.4
25	15.5
30	18.6
35	21.7
40	24.9
45	28.0
50	31.1
55	34.2
60	37.3
65	40.4
70	43.5
75	46.6
80	49.7
85	52.8
90	55.9
95	59.0
100	62.1
200	124.3
300	186.4
400	248.5
500	310.7
750	466.0
1 000	621.4
2 500	1 553.4
5 000	3 106.9

Exact conversion:
1 km = 0.6214 mi

Conversion tables: area

sq in	*sq cm*
1	6.45
2	12.90
3	19.35
4	25.81
5	32.26
6	38.71
7	45.16
8	51.61
9	58.06
10	64.52
11	70.97
12	77.42
13	83.87
14	90.32
15	96.77
16	103.23
17	109.68
18	116.13
19	122.58
20	129.03
25	161.29
50	322.58
75	483.87
100	645.16
125	806.45
150	967.74

Exact conversion:
1 in^2 = 6.4516 cm^2

sq cm	*sq in*
1	0.16
2	0.31
3	0.47
4	0.62
5	0.78
6	0.93
7	1.09
8	1.24
9	1.40
10	1.55
11	1.71
12	1.86
13	2.02
14	2.17
15	2.33
16	2.48
17	2.64
18	2.79
19	2.95
20	3.10
25	3.88
50	7.75
75	11.63
100	15.50
125	19.38
150	23.25

Exact conversion:
1 cm^2 = 0.155 in^2

sq ft	*sq m*
1	0.09
2	0.19
3	0.28
4	0.37
5	0.46
6	0.56
7	0.65
8	0.74
9	0.84
10	0.93
11	1.02
12	1.11
13	1.21
14	1.30
15	1.39
16	1.49
17	1.58
18	1.67
19	1.77
20	1.86
25	2.32
50	4.65
75	6.97
100	9.29
250	23.23
500	46.45
750	69.68
1 000	92.90

Exact conversion:
1 ft^2 = 0.0929 m^2

sq m	*sq ft*
1	10.8
2	21.5
3	32.3
4	43.1
5	53.8
6	64.6
7	75.3
8	86.1
9	96.9
10	107.6
11	118.4
12	129.2
13	139.9
14	150.7
15	161.5
16	172.2
17	183
18	193.8
19	204.5
20	215.3
25	269.1
50	538.2
75	807.3
100	1 076.4
250	2 691
500	5 382
750	8 072.9
1 000	10 763.9

Exact conversion:
1 m^2 = 10.7639 ft^2

acre	*hectares*
1	0.40
2	0.81
3	1.21
4	1.62
5	2.02
6	2.43
7	2.83
8	3.24
9	3.64
10	4.05
11	4.45
12	4.86
13	5.26
14	5.67
15	6.07
16	6.47
17	6.88
18	7.28
19	7.69
20	8.09
25	10.12
50	20.23
75	30.35
100	40.47
250	101.17
500	202.34
750	303.51
1 000	404.69
1 500	607.03

Exact conversion:
1 acre =
0.4047 hectare

hectares	*acre*
1	2.5
2	4.9
3	7.4
4	9.9
5	12.4
6	14.8
7	17.3
8	19.8
9	22.2
10	24.7
11	27.2
12	29.7
13	32.1
14	34.6
15	37.1
16	39.5
17	42
18	44.5
19	46.9
20	49.4
25	61.8
50	123.6
75	185.3
100	247.1
250	617.8
500	1 235.5
750	1 853.3
1 000	2 471.1
1 500	3 706.6

Exact conversion:
1 hectare =
2.471 acres

sq mi	*sq km*
1	2.6
2	5.2
3	7.8
4	10.4
5	12.9
6	15.5
7	18.1
8	20.7
9	23.3
10	25.9
11	28.5
12	31.1
13	33.7
14	36.3
15	38.8
16	41.4
17	44.0
18	46.6
19	49.2
20	51.8
21	54.4
22	57.0
23	59.6
24	62.2
25	64.7
30	77.7
40	103.6
50	129.5
60	155.4
70	181.3
80	207.2
90	233.1
100	259.0
200	518.0
300	777.0
400	1 036.0
500	1 295.0
600	1 554.0
700	1 813.0
800	2 072.0
900	2 331.0
1 000	2 590.0
1 500	3 885.0
2 000	5 180.0
2 500	6 475.0
3 000	7 770.0
3 500	9 065.0
4 000	10 360.0
5 000	12 950.0
7 500	19 424.9
10 000	25 899.9

sq km	*sq mi*
1	0.39
2	0.77
3	1.16
4	1.54
5	1.93
6	2.32

Conversion tables: area (continued)

7	2.70	16	6.18	25	9.65	200	77.22	1500	579.2	Exact conversions:
8	3.09	17	6.56	30	11.58	300	115.83	2000	772.2	1 sq mi =
9	3.47	18	6.95	40	15.44	400	154.44	2500	965.3	2.589999 sq km
10	3.86	19	7.34	50	19.31	500	193.05	3000	1158.3	1 sq km =
11	4.25	20	7.72	60	23.17	600	231.66	3500	1351.4	0.3861 sq ml
12	4.63	21	8.11	70	27.03	700	270.27	4000	1544.4	
13	5.02	22	8.49	80	30.89	800	308.88	5000	1930.5	
14	5.41	23	8.88	90	34.75	900	347.49	7500	2895.8	
15	5.79	24	9.27	100	38.61	1000	386.1	10000	3861.0	

Conversion tables: volume

cu in	*cu cm*	*cu cm*	*cu in*	*cu ft*	*cu m*	*cu m*	*cu ft*	*cu yd*	*cu m*	*cu m*	*cu yd*
1	16.39	1	0.61	1	0.03	1	35.3	1	0.76	1	1.31
2	32.77	2	1.22	2	0.06	2	70.6	2	1.53	2	2.62
3	49.16	3	1.83	3	0.08	3	105.9	3	2.29	3	3.92
4	65.55	4	2.44	4	0.11	4	141.3	4	3.06	4	5.23
5	81.93	5	3.05	5	0.14	5	176.6	5	3.82	5	6.54
6	93.32	6	3.66	6	0.17	6	211.9	6	4.59	6	7.85
7	114.71	7	4.27	7	0.20	7	247.2	7	5.35	7	9.16
8	131.10	8	4.88	8	0.23	8	282.5	8	6.12	8	10.46
9	147.48	9	5.49	9	0.25	9	317.8	9	6.88	9	11.77
10	163.87	10	6.10	10	0.28	10	353.1	10	7.65	10	13.08
11	180.26	11	6.71	11	0.31	11	388.5	11	8.41	11	14.39
12	196.64	12	7.32	12	0.34	12	423.8	12	9.17	12	15.70
13	213.03	13	7.93	13	0.37	13	459.1	13	9.94	13	17.00
14	229.42	14	8.54	14	0.40	14	494.4	14	10.70	14	18.31
15	245.81	15	9.15	15	0.42	15	529.7	15	11.47	15	19.62
20	327.74	20	12.20	20	0.57	20	706.3	20	15.29	20	26.16
50	819.35	50	30.50	50	1.41	50	1765.7	50	38.23	50	65.40
100	1638.71	100	61.00	100	2.83	100	3531.5	100	76.46	100	130.80
Exact conversions: 1 in^3 = 16.3871 cm^3		1 cm^3 = 0.0610 in^3		1 ft^3 = 0.0283 m^3		1 m^3 = 35.3147 ft^3		1 yd^3 = 0.7646 m^3		1 m^3 = 1.3080 yd^3	

Conversion tables: capacity

Liquid measure

UK fluid ounces	*litres*	*UK fluid ounces*	*litres*	*litres*	*UK fluid ounces*	*US fluid ounces*	*UK pints*	*litres*	*US pints*	*litres*	*litres*	*UK pints*	*US pints*
1	0.0284	1	0.0296	1	35.2	33.8	1	0.57	1	0.47	1	1.76	2.11
2	0.0568	2	0.0592	2	70.4	67.6	2	1.14	2	0.95	2	3.52	4.23
3	0.0852	3	0.0888	3	105.6	101.4	3	1.70	3	1.42	3	5.28	6.34
4	0.114	4	0.118	4	140.8	135.3	4	2.27	4	1.89	4	7.04	8.45
5	0.142	5	0.148	5	176.0	169.1	5	2.84	5	2.37	5	8.80	10.57
6	0.170	6	0.178	6	211.2	202.9	6	3.41	6	2.84	6	10.56	12.68
7	0.199	7	0.207	7	246.4	236.7	7	3.98	7	3.31	7	12.32	14.79
8	0.227	8	0.237	8	281.6	270.5	8	4.55	8	3.78	8	14.08	16.91
9	0.256	9	0.266	9	316.8	304.3	9	5.11	9	4.26	9	15.84	19.02
10	0.284	10	0.296	10	352.0	338.1	10	5.68	10	4.73	10	17.60	21.13
11	0.312	11	0.326	11	387.2	372.0	11	6.25	11	5.20	11	19.36	23.25
12	0.341	12	0.355	12	422.4	405.8	12	6.82	12	5.68	12	21.12	25.36
13	0.369	13	0.385	13	457.5	439.6	13	7.38	13	6.15	13	22.88	27.47
14	0.397	14	0.414	14	492.7	473.4	14	7.95	14	6.62	14	24.64	29.59
15	0.426	15	0.444	15	527.9	507.2	15	8.52	15	7.10	15	26.40	31.70
20	0.568	20	0.592	20	703.9	676.3	20	11.36	20	9.46	20	35.20	105.67
50	1.42	50	1.48	50	1759.8	1690.7	50	28.41	50	23.66	50	87.99	211.34
100	2.84	100	2.96	100	3519.6	3381.5	100	56.82	100	47.32	100	175.98	422.68
Exact conversions: 1 fl oz = 0.0284 l		1 fl oz = 0.0296 l		1 l = 35.1961 UK fl oz 1 l = 33.8140 US fl oz			1 UK pt = 0.5682 l 1 UK pt = 1.20 US pt		1 US pt = 0.4732 l 1 US pt = 0.83 UK pt		1 l = 1.7598 UK pt, 2.1134 US pt 1 US cup = 8 US fl oz		

Conversion tables: capacity (continued)

UK gall	litres
1	4.55
2	9.09
3	13.64
4	18.18
5	22.73
6	27.28
7	31.82
8	36.37
9	40.91
10	45.46
11	50.01
12	54.55
13	59.10
14	63.64
15	68.19
16	72.74
17	77.28
18	81.83
19	86.37
20	90.92
21	95.47
22	100.01
23	104.56
24	109.10
25	113.65
50	227.30
75	340.96
100	454.61

Exact conversion:
1 UK gall = 4.546 l

litres	UK gall	US gall
1	0.22	0.26
2	0.44	0.53
3	0.66	0.79
4	0.88	1.06
5	1.10	1.32
6	1.32	1.58
7	1.54	1.85
8	1.76	2.11
9	1.98	2.38
10	2.20	2.64
11	2.42	2.91
12	2.64	3.17
13	2.86	3.43
14	3.08	3.70
15	3.30	3.96
16	3.52	4.23
17	3.74	4.49
18	3.96	4.76
19	4.18	5.02
20	4.40	5.28
21	4.62	5.55
22	4.84	5.81
23	5.06	6.08
24	5.28	6.34
25	5.50	6.60
50	11.00	13.20
75	16.50	19.81
100	22.00	26.42

Exact conversion: 1 l = 0.220 UK gall
1 l = 0.2642 US gall

US gall	litres
1	3.78
2	7.57
3	11.36
4	15.14
5	18.93
6	22.71
7	26.50
8	30.28
9	34.07
10	37.85
11	41.64
12	45.42
13	49.21
14	52.99
15	56.78
16	60.57
17	64.35
18	68.14
19	71.92
20	75.71
21	79.49
22	83.28
23	87.06
24	90.85
25	94.63
50	189.27
75	283.90
100	378.54

Exact conversion:
1 US gall = 3.7854 l

UK gall	US gall
1	1.2
2	2.4
3	3.6
4	4.8
5	6
6	7.2
7	8.4
8	9.6
9	10.8
10	12
11	13.2
12	14.4
13	15.6
14	16.8
15	18
20	24
25	30
50	60

Exact conversion:
1 UK gall=
1.200929 US gall

US gall	UK gall
1	0.8
2	1.7
3	2.5
4	3.3
5	4.2
6	5
7	5.8
8	6.7
9	7.5
10	8.3
11	9.2
12	10
13	10.8
14	11.7
15	12.5
16	13.3
17	14.1
18	15
19	15.8
20	16.6
25	20.8
50	41.6
75	62.4
100	83.3

Exact conversion:
1 US gall =
0.832688 UK gall

Other liquid capacity measures

UK quarts	litres
1	1.14
2	2.27
3	3.41
4	4.55
5	5.68
10	11.36

Exact conversion:
1 UK quart = 1.1365 l

US quarts	litres
1	0.95
2	1.89
3	2.84
4	3.78
5	4.73
10	9.46

Exact conversion:
1 US quart = 0.9463 l

litres	US quarts	UK quarts
1	0.88	1.06
2	1.76	2.11
3	2.64	3.17
4	3.52	4.23
5	4.40	5.28
10	8.80	10.57

Exact conversions: 1 l = 0.220 UK gall
1 l = 1.0567 US quarts

cu in	litres
1	0.016
2	0.033
3	0.049
4	0.066
5	0.082
10	0.164

Exact conversion:
1 in^3 = 0.0164 l

cu in	litres
1	28.3
2	56.6
3	84.9
4	113.3
5	141.6
10	283.1

Exact conversion:
1 ft^3 = 28.3161 l

litres	cu in	cu ft
1	61	0.03
2	122	0.07
3	183	0.11
4	244	0.14
5	305	0.18
10	610	0.35

Exact conversions: 1 l = 61.0255 in^3
= 0.0353 ft^3

Conversion tables capacity (continued)

Petrol consumption

Use UK table and US table independently.

per UK gall		*per litre*	
mi	*km*	*mi*	*km*
30	48	6.6	10.61
35	56	7.7	12.38
40	64	8.8	14.15
45	72	9.9	15.92
50	80	11	17.69

per US gall		*per litre*	
mi	*km*	*mi*	*km*
30	48	7.9	12.78
35	56	9.3	14.91
40	64	10.6	17.04
45	72	11.9	19.17
50	80	13.2	21.30

Dry capacity measures

UK bushels	*cu m*	*litres*
1	0.037	36.4
2	0.074	72.7
3	0.111	109.1
4	0.148	145.5
5	0.184	181.8
10	0.369	363.7

Exact conversions:
1 UK bushel = 0.0369 m^3
1 UK bushel = 36.3677 l

US bushels	*cu m*	*litres*
1	0.035	35.2
2	0.071	70.5
3	0.106	105.7
4	0.141	140.9
5	0.175	176.2
10	0.353	352.4

Exact conversions:
1 US bushel = 0.9353 m^3
1 US bushel = 35.2381 l

cu m	*UK bushels*	*US bushels*
1	27.5	28.4
2	55.0	56.7
3	82.5	85.1
4	110	113
5	137	142
10	275	284

Exact conversions:
1 m^3 = 27.4962 UK bu
1 m^3 = 28.3776 US bu

litres	*UK bushels*	*US bushels*
1	0.027	0.028
2	0.055	0.057
3	0.082	0.085
4	0.110	0.114
5	0.137	0.142
10	0.275	0.284

Exact conversions:
1 l = 0.0275 UK bu
1 l = 0.0284 US bu

UK pecks	*litres*	*US pecks*	*litres*
1	9.1	1	8.8
2	18.2	2	17.6
3	27.3	3	26.4
4	36.4	4	35.2
5	45.5	5	44
10	90.9	10	88.1

Exact conversion:
1 UK pk = 9.0919 l

Exact conversion:
1 US pk = 8.8095 l

litres	*UK pecks*	*US pecks*
1	0.110	0.113
2	0.220	0.226
3	0.330	0.339
4	0.440	0.454
5	0.550	0.567
10	1.100	1.135

Exact conversions:
1 l = 0.1100 UK pk
1 l = 0.1135 US pk

US quarts	*cu m*	*litres*
1	1 101	1.1
2	2 202	2.2
3	3 304	3.3
4	4 405	4.4
5	5 506	5.5
10	11 012	11

Exact conversions:
1 US qt = 1101.2209 cm^3
1 US qt = 1.1012 l

US pints	*cu m*	*litres*
1	551	0.55
2	1 101	1.10
3	1 652	1.65
4	2 202	2.20
5	2 753	2.75
10	5 506	5.51

Exact conversions:
1 US pt = 550.6105 cm^3
1 US pt = 0.5506 l

Conversion tables: weight

ounces[a]	*grams*
1	28.3
2	56.7
3	85
4	113.4
5	141.7
6	170.1
7	198.4
8	226.8
9	255.1
10	283.5
11	311.7
12	340.2
13	368.5
14	396.9
15	425.2
16	453.6

[a] avoirdupois

Exact conversion:
1 oz (avdp) = 28.3495 g

grams	*ounces*
1	0.04
2	0.07
3	0.11
4	0.14
5	0.18
6	0.21
7	0.25
8	0.28
9	0.32
10	0.35
20	0.71
30	1.06
40	1.41
50	1.76
60	2.12
70	2.47
80	2.82
90	3.18
100	3.53

Exact conversion:
1 g = 0.0353 oz (avdp)

pounds	*kilograms*
1	0.45
2	0.91
3	1.36
4	1.81
5	2.27
6	2.72
7	3.18
8	3.63
9	4.08
10	4.54
11	4.99
12	5.44
13	5.90
14	6.35
15	6.80
16	7.26
17	7.71
18	8.16
19	8.62
20	9.07
25	11.34
30	13.61
35	15.88
40	18.14
45	20.41
50	22.68
60	27.24
70	31.78
80	36.32
90	40.86
100	45.36
200	90.72
250	113.40
500	226.80
750	340.19
1 000	453.59

Exact conversion:
1 lb = 0.454 kg

kilograms	*pounds*
1	2.2
2	4.4
3	6.6
4	8.8
5	11
6	13.2
7	15.4
8	17.6
9	19.8
10	22
11	24.3
12	26.5
13	28.7
14	30.9
15	33.1
16	35.3
17	37.5
18	39.7
19	41.9
20	44.1
25	55.1
30	66.1
35	77.2
40	88.2
45	99.2
50	110.2
60	132.3
70	154.4
80	176.4
90	198.5
100	220.5
200	440.9
250	551.2
500	1 102.3
750	1 653.5
1 000	2 204.6

Exact conversion:
1 kg 2.205 lb

stones	*pounds*
1	14
2	28
3	42
4	56
5	70
6	84
7	98
8	112
9	126
10	140
11	154
12	168
13	182
14	196
15	210
16	224
17	238
18	252
19	266
20	280

Exact conversions:
1 st = 14 lb
1 lb = 0.07 st

stones	*kilograms*
1	6.35
2	12.70
3	19.05
4	25.40
5	31.75
6	38.10
7	44.45
8	50.80
9	57.15
10	63.50

Exact conversions:
1 st = 6.350 kg
1 kg = 0.1575 st

Hundredweights:
long, UK 112 lb; short, US 100 lb

UK cwt	*kilograms*
1	50.8
2	102
3	152
4	203
5	254
10	508
15	762
20	1 016
50	2 540
75	3 810
100	5 080

Exact conversion:
1 UK cwt = 50.8023 kg

UK cwt	*US cwt*
1	1.12
2	2.24
3	3.36
4	4.48
5	5.6
10	11.2
15	16.8
20	22.4
50	56
75	84
100	102

Exact conversion:
1 UK cwt = 1.1199 US cwt

US tons	*tonnes*
1	0.91
2	1.81
3	2.72
4	3.63
5	4.54
10	9.07
15	13.61
20	18.14
50	45.36
75	68.04
100	90.72

Exact conversion:
1 US ton = 0.9072 tonne

US cwt	*kilograms*
1	45.4
2	90.7
3	136
4	181
5	227
10	454
15	680
20	907
50	2 268
75	3 402
100	4 536

Exact conversion:
1 US cwt = 45.3592 kg

UK tons	*tonnes*
1	1.02
2	2.03
3	3.05
4	4.06
5	5.08
10	10.16
15	15.24
20	20.32
50	50.80
75	76.20
100	101.61

Exact conversion:
1 UK ton = 1.0160 tonnes

UK tons	*US tons*
1	1.12
2	2.24
3	3.36
4	4.48
5	5.6
10	11.2
15	16.8
20	22.4
50	56
75	84
100	102

Exact conversion:
1 UK ton = 1.1199 US tons

Conversion tables: weight (continued)

kilograms	*UK cwt*	*US cwt*
1	0.0197	0.022
2	0.039	0.044
3	0.059	0.066
4	0.079	0.088
5	0.098	0.11
10	0.197	0.22
15	0.295	0.33
20	0.394	1.44
50	0.985	1.10
75	1.477	1.65
100	1.970	2.20

Exact conversions:
1 kg = 0.0197 UK cwt
= 0.0220 US cwt

US cwt	*UK cwt*
1	0.89
2	1.79
3	2.68
4	3.57
5	4.46
10	8.93
15	13.39
20	17.86
50	44.64
75	66.96
100	89.29

Exact conversion:
1 US cwt =
0.8929 UK cwt

Tons: long, UK 2240lb; short, US 2000 lb

tonnes	*UK tons*	*US tons*
1	0.98	1.10
2	1.97	2.20
3	2.95	3.30
4	3.94	4.40
5	4.92	5.50
10	9.84	11.02
15	14.76	16.53
20	19.68	22.05
50	49.21	55.11
75	73.82	82.67
100	98.42	110.23

Exact conversions:
1 tonne = 0.9842 UK ton
= 1.1023 US tons

US tons	*UK tons*
1	0.89
2	1.79
3	2.68
4	3.57
5	4.46
10	8.93
15	13.39
20	17.86
50	44.64
75	66.96
100	89.29

Exact conversion:
1 US ton = 0.8929
UK ton

Conversion table: tyre pressures

lb per sq in	*kg per sq cm*
10	0.7
15	1.1
20	1.4
24	1.7
26	1.8
28	2
30	2.1
40	2.8

Conversion table: oven temperatures

Gas Mark	*Electricity* °C	°F	*Rating*
1/2	120	250	Slow
1	140	275	
2	150	300	
3	170	325	
4	180	350	Moderate
5	190	375	
6	200	400	Hot
7	220	425	
8	230	450	Very hot
9	260	500	

Temperature conversion

To convert	*To*	*Equation*
°Fahrenheit	°Celsius	−32, × 5, ÷ 9
°Fahrenheit	°Rankine	+ 459.67
°Fahrenheit	°Réaumur	− 32, × 4, ÷ 9
°Celsius	°Fahrenheit	× 9, ÷ 5, + 32
°Celsius	Kelvin	+ 273.15
°Celsius	°Réaumur	× 4, ÷ 5
Kelvin	°Celsius	− 273.15
°Rankine	°Fahrenheit	−459.67
°Réaumur	°Fahrenheit	× 9, ÷ 4, + 32
°Réaumur	°Celsius	× 5, ÷ 4

Carry out operations in sequence.

Temperature scales

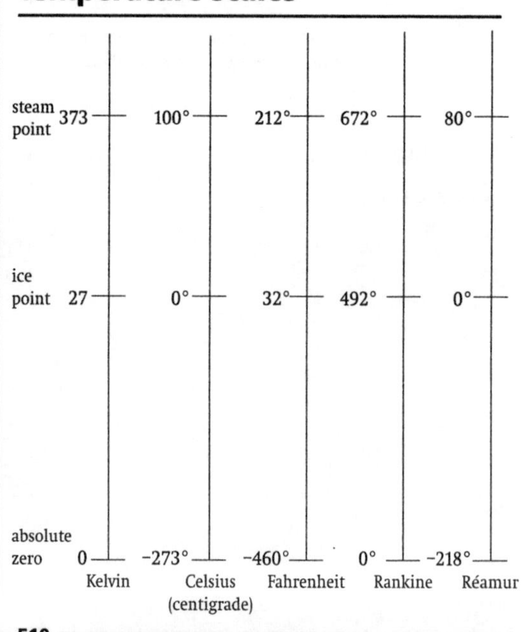

Conversion tables: temperature

Degrees Fahrenheit (F) → Degrees Celsius (Centigrade) (C)

°F	°C	°F	°C	°F	°C	°F	°C	°F	°C	°F	°C
1	−17.2	36	2.2	71	21.7	106	41.1	141	60.5	177	80.5
2	−16.7	37	2.8	72	22.2	107	41.7	142	61.1	178	81.1
3	−16.1	38	3.3	73	22.8	108	42.2	143	61.7	179	81.7
4	−15.5	39	3.9	74	23.3	109	42.8	144	62.2	180	82.2
5	−15.0	40	4.4	75	23.9	110	43.3	145	62.8	181	82.8
6	−14.4	41	5.0	76	24.4	111	43.9	146	63.3	182	83.3
7	−13.9	42	5.5	77	25.0	112	44.4	147	63.9	183	83.9
8	−13.3	43	6.1	78	25.5	113	45.0	148	64.4	184	84.4
9	−12.8	44	6.7	79	26.1	114	45.5	149	65.0	185	85.0
10	−12.2	45	7.2	80	26.7	115	46.1	150	65.5	186	85.5
11	−11.6	46	7.8	81	27.2	116	46.7	151	66.1	187	86.1
12	−11.1	47	8.3	82	27.8	117	47.2	152	66.7	188	86.7
13	−10.5	48	8.9	83	28.3	118	47.8	153	67.2	189	87.2
14	−10.0	49	9.4	84	28.9	119	48.3	154	67.8	190	87.8
15	−9.4	50	10.0	85	29.4	120	48.9	155	68.3	191	88.3
16	−8.9	51	10.5	86	30.0	121	49.4	156	68.9	192	88.8
17	−8.3	52	11.1	87	30.5	122	50.0	157	69.4	193	89.4
18	−7.8	53	11.7	88	31.1	123	50.5	158	70.0	194	90.0
19	−7.2	54	12.2	89	31.7	124	51.1	159	70.5	195	90.5
20	−6.7	55	12.8	90	32.2	125	51.7	160	71.1	196	91.1
21	−6.1	56	13.3	91	32.8	126	52.2	161	71.7	197	91.7
22	−5.5	57	13.9	92	33.3	127	52.8	162	72.2	198	92.2
23	−5.0	58	14.4	93	33.9	128	53.3	163	72.8	199	92.8
24	−4.4	59	15.0	94	34.4	129	53.9	164	73.3	200	93.3
25	−3.9	60	15.5	95	35.0	130	54.4	165	73.9	201	93.9
26	−3.3	61	16.1	96	35.5	131	55.0	166	74.4	202	94.4
27	−2.8	62	16.7	97	36.1	132	55.5	167	75.0	203	95.0
28	−2.2	63	17.2	98	36.7	133	56.1	168	75.5	204	95.5
29	−1.7	64	17.8	99	37.2	134	56.7	169	76.1	205	96.1
30	−1.1	65	18.3	100	37.8	135	57.2	170	76.7	206	96.7
31	−0.5	66	18.9	101	38.3	136	57.8	171	77.2	207	97.2
32	0	67	19.4	102	38.9	137	58.3	172	77.8	208	97.8
33	0.5	68	20.0	103	39.4	138	58.9	173	78.3	209	98.3
34	1.1	69	20.5	104	40.0	139	59.4	174	78.9	210	98.9
35	1.7	70	21.1	105	40.5	140	60.0	175	79.4	211	99.4
								176	80.0	212	100.0

Degrees Celsius (Centigrade) (C) → Degrees Fahrenheit (F)

°C	°F	°C	°F	°C	°F	°C	°F	°C	°F	°C	°F
1	33.8	18	64.4	35	95.0	52	125.6	69	156.2	86	186.8
2	35.6	19	66.2	36	96.8	53	127.4	70	158.0	87	188.6
3	37.4	20	68.0	37	98.6	54	129.2	71	159.8	88	190.4
4	39.2	21	69.8	38	100.4	55	131.0	72	161.6	89	192.2
5	41.0	22	71.6	39	102.2	56	132.8	73	163.4	90	194.0
6	42.8	23	73.4	40	104.0	57	134.6	74	165.2	91	195.8
7	44.6	24	75.2	41	105.8	58	136.4	75	167.0	92	197.6
8	46.4	25	77.0	42	107.6	59	138.2	76	168.8	93	199.4
9	48.2	26	78.8	43	109.4	60	140.0	77	170.6	94	201.2
10	50.0	27	80.6	44	111.2	61	141.8	78	172.4	95	203.0
11	51.8	28	82.4	45	113.0	62	143.6	79	174.2	96	204.8
12	53.6	29	84.2	46	114.8	63	145.4	80	176.0	97	206.6
13	55.4	30	86.0	47	116.6	64	147.2	81	177.8	98	208.4
14	57.2	31	87.8	48	118.4	65	149.0	82	179.6	99	210.2
15	59.0	32	89.6	49	120.2	66	150.8	83	181.4	100	212.0
16	60.8	33	91.4	50	122.0	67	152.6	84	183.2		
17	62.6	34	93.2	51	123.8	68	154.4	85	185.0		

Numerical equivalents

Arabic	Roman	Greek	Binary numbers
1	I	α′	1
2	II	β′	10
3	III	γ′	11
4	IV	δ′	100
5	V	ε′	101
6	VI	ζ′	110
7	VII	ξ′	111
8	VIII	η′	1000
9	IX	θ′	1001
10	X	ι′	1010
11	XI	ια′	1011
12	XII	ιβ′	1100
13	XIII	ιγ′	1101
14	XIV	ιδ′	1110
15	XV	ιε′	1111
16	XVI	ιζ′	10000
17	XVII	ιξ′	10001
18	XVIII	ιη′	10010
19	XIX	ιθ′	10011
20	XX	κ′	10100
30	XXX	λ′	11110
40	XL	μ′	10100
50	L	ν′	110010
60	LX	ξ′	111100
70	LXX	ο′	1000110
80	LXXX	π′	1010000
90	XC	͵ο′	1011010
100	C	ρ′	1100100
200	CC	σ′	11001000
300	CCC	τ′	100101100
400	CD	υ′	110010000
500	D	φ′	111110100
1000	M	͵α	1111101000
5000	$\overline{\text{V}}$	͵ε	1001110001000
10000	$\overline{\text{X}}$	͵ι	10011100010000
100000	$\overline{\text{C}}$	͵ρ	11000011010100000

Fraction	Decimal
1/2	0.5000
1/3	0.3333
2/3	0.6667
1/4	0.2500
3/4	0.7500
1/5	0.2000
2/5	0.4000
3/5	0.6000
4/5	0.8000
1/6	0.1667
5/6	0.8333
1/7	0.1429
2/7	0.2857
3/7	0.4286
4/7	0.5714
5/7	0.7143
6/7	0.8571
1/8	0.1250
3/8	0.3750
5/8	0.6250
7/8	0.8750
1/9	0.1111
2/9	0.2222
4/9	0.4444
5/9	0.5555
7/9	0.7778
8/9	0.8889
1/10	0.1000
3/10	0.3000
7/10	0.7000
9/10	0.9000
1/11	0.0909
2/11	0.1818
3/11	0.2727
4/11	0.3636
5/11	0.4545
6/11	0.5454
7/11	0.6363

Fraction	Decimal
8/11	0.7272
9/11	0.8181
10/11	0.9090
1/12	0.0833
5/12	0.4167
7/12	0.5833
11/12	0.9167
1/16	0.0625
3/16	0.1875
5/16	0.3125
7/16	0.4375
9/16	0.5625
11/16	0.6875
13/16	0.8125
15/16	0.9375
1/20	0.0500
3/20	0.1500
7/20	0.3500
9/20	0.4500
11/20	0.5500
13/20	0.6500
17/20	0.8500
19/20	0.9500
1/32	0.0312
3/32	0.0938
5/32	0.1562
7/32	0.2187
9/32	0.2812
11/32	0.3437
13/32	0.4062
15/32	0.4687
17/32	0.5312
19/32	0.5937
21/32	0.6562
23/32	0.7187
25/32	0.7812
27/32	0.8437
29/32	0.9062
31/32	0.9687

%	Decimal	Fraction
1	0.01	1/100
2	0.02	1/50
3	0.03	3/100
4	0.04	1/25
5	0.05	1/20
6	0.06	3/50
7	0.07	7/100
8	0.08	2/25
8 1/3	0.089	1/12
9	0.09	9/100
10	0.1	1/10
11	0.11	11/100
12	0.12	3/25
12 1/2	0.125	1/8
13	0.13	13/100
14	0.14	7/50
15	0.15	3/20
16	0.16	4/25
16 2/3	0.167	1/6
17	0.17	17/100
18	0.18	9/50
19	0.19	19/100
20	0.20	1/5
21	0.21	21/100
22	0.22	11/50
23	0.23	23/100
24	0.24	6/25
25	0.25	1/4
26	0.26	13/50
27	0.27	27/100
28	0.28	7/25
29	0.29	29/100
30	0.30	3/10
31	0.31	31/100
32	0.32	8/25
33	0.33	33/100
33 1/3	0.333	1/3
34	0.34	17/50
35	0.35	7/20
36	0.36	9/25
37	0.37	37/100
38	0.38	19/50
39	0.39	39/100
40	0.40	2/5
41	0.41	41/100
42	0.42	21/50
43	0.43	43/100
44	0.44	11/25
45	0.45	9/20
46	0.46	23/50
47	0.47	47/100
48	0.48	12/25
49	0.49	49/100
50	0.50	1/2
55	0.55	11/20
60	0.60	3/5
65	0.65	13/20
70	0.70	7/10
75	0.75	3/4
80	0.80	4/5
85	0.85	17/20
90	0.90	9/10
95	0.95	19/20
100	1.00	1

Multiplication table

	2	**3**	**4**	**5**	**6**	**7**	**8**	**9**	**10**	**11**	**12**	**13**	**14**	**15**	**16**	**17**	**18**	**19**	**20**	**21**	**22**	**23**	**24**	**25**
2	4	6	8	10	12	14	16	18	20	22	24	26	28	30	32	34	36	38	40	42	44	46	48	50
3	6	9	12	15	18	21	24	27	30	33	36	39	42	45	48	51	54	57	60	63	66	69	72	75
4	8	12	16	20	24	28	32	36	40	44	48	52	56	60	64	68	72	76	80	84	88	92	96	100
5	10	15	20	25	30	35	40	45	50	55	60	65	70	75	80	85	90	95	100	105	110	115	120	125
6	12	18	24	30	36	42	48	54	60	66	72	78	84	90	96	102	108	114	120	126	132	138	144	150
7	14	21	28	35	42	49	56	63	70	77	84	91	98	105	112	119	126	133	140	147	154	161	168	175
8	16	24	32	40	48	56	64	72	80	88	96	104	112	120	128	136	144	152	160	168	176	184	192	200
9	18	27	36	45	54	63	72	81	90	99	108	117	126	135	144	153	162	171	180	189	198	207	216	225
10	20	30	40	50	60	70	80	90	100	110	120	130	140	150	160	170	180	190	200	210	220	230	240	250
11	22	33	44	55	66	77	88	99	110	121	132	143	154	165	176	187	198	209	220	231	242	253	264	275
12	24	36	48	60	72	84	96	108	120	132	144	156	168	180	192	204	216	228	240	252	264	276	288	300
13	26	39	52	65	78	91	104	117	130	143	156	169	182	195	208	221	234	247	260	273	286	299	312	325
14	28	42	56	70	84	98	112	126	140	154	168	182	196	210	224	238	252	266	280	294	308	322	336	350
15	30	45	60	75	90	105	120	135	150	165	180	195	210	225	240	255	270	285	300	315	330	345	360	375
16	32	48	64	80	96	112	128	144	160	176	192	208	224	240	256	272	288	304	320	336	352	368	384	400
17	34	51	68	85	102	119	136	153	170	187	204	221	238	255	272	289	306	323	340	357	374	391	408	425
18	36	54	72	90	108	126	144	162	180	198	216	234	252	270	288	306	324	342	360	378	396	414	432	450
19	38	57	76	95	114	133	152	171	190	209	228	247	266	285	304	323	342	361	380	399	418	437	456	475
20	40	60	80	100	120	140	160	180	200	220	240	260	280	300	320	340	360	380	400	420	440	460	480	500
21	42	63	84	105	126	147	168	189	210	231	252	273	294	315	336	357	378	399	420	441	462	483	504	525
22	44	66	88	110	132	154	176	198	220	242	264	286	308	330	352	374	396	418	440	462	484	506	528	550
23	46	69	92	115	138	161	184	207	230	253	276	299	322	345	368	391	414	437	460	483	506	529	552	575
24	48	72	96	120	144	168	192	216	240	264	288	312	336	360	384	408	432	456	480	501	528	552	576	600
25	50	75	100	125	150	175	200	225	250	275	300	325	350	375	400	425	450	475	500	525	550	575	600	625

Squares, cubes and roots

No.	*Square*	*Cube*	*Square root*	*Cube root*
1	1	1	1.000	1.000
2	4	8	1.414	1.260
3	9	27	1.732	1.442
4	16	64	2.000	1.587
5	25	125	2.236	1.710
6	36	216	2.449	1.817
7	49	343	2.646	1.913
8	64	512	2.828	2.000
9	81	729	3.000	2.080
10	100	1 000	3.162	2.154
11	121	1 331	3.317	2.224
12	144	1 728	3.464	2.289

No.	*Square*	*Cube*	*Square root*	*Cube root*
13	169	2 197	3.606	2.351
14	196	2 744	3.742	2.410
15	225	3 375	3.873	2.466
16	256	4 096	4.000	2.520
17	289	4 913	4.123	2.571
18	324	5 832	4.243	2.621
19	361	6 859	4.359	2.668
20	400	8 000	4.472	2.714
25	625	15 625	5.000	2.924
30	900	27 000	5.477	3.107
40	1 600	64 000	6.325	3.420
50	2 500	125 000	7.071	3.684

International paper sizes

A series

	mm	in
A0	841 × 1189	33.11 × 46.81
A1	594 × 841	23.39 × 33.1
A2	420 × 594	16.54 × 23.29
A3	297 × 420	11.69 × 16.54
A4	210 × 297	8.27 × 11.69
A5	148 × 210	5.83 × 8.27
A6	105 × 148	4.13 × 5.83
A7	74 × 105	2.91 × 4.13
A8	52 × 74	2.05 × 2.91
A9	37 × 52	1.46 × 2.05
A10	26 × 37	1.02 × 1.46

B series

	mm	in
B0	1000 × 1414	39.37 × 55.67
B1	707 × 1000	27.83 × 39.37
B2	500 × 707	19.68 × 27.83
B3	353 × 500	13.90 × 19.68
B4	250 × 353	9.84 × 13.90
B5	176 × 250	6.93 × 9.84
B6	125 × 176	4.92 × 6.93
B7	88 × 125	3.46 × 4.92
B8	62 × 88	2.44 × 3.46
B9	44 × 62	1.73 × 2.44
B10	31 × 44	1.22 × 1.73

C series

	mm	in
C0	917 × 1 297	36.00 × 51.20
C1	648 × 917	25.60 × 36.00
C2	458 × 648	18.00 × 25.60
C3	324 × 458	12.80 × 18.00
C4	229 × 324	9.00 × 12.80
C5	162 × 229	6.40 × 9.00
C6	114 × 162	4.50 × 6.40
C7	81 × 114	3.20 × 4.50
DL	110 × 220	4.33 × 8.66
C7/6	81 × 162	3.19 × 6.38

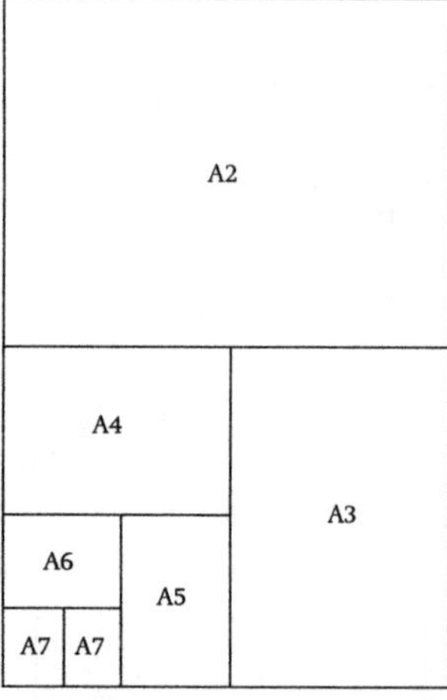

All sizes in these series have sides in the proportion of 1: $\sqrt{2}$.
A series is used for writing paper, books and magazines. **B** series for posters. **C** series for envelopes.

PHYSICS

Basic equations

Density

density = $\frac{\text{mass}}{\text{volume}}$ volume = $\frac{\text{mass}}{\text{density}}$

mass = volume × density

Velocity

$v = u + at$

where v is the final velocity, u the original velocity, a the acceleration, and t the time taken

Pressure

pressure = $\frac{\text{force}}{\text{area}}$ $P = \frac{F}{A}$

Energy

potential energy = weight × height above ground
kinetic energy = $\frac{1}{2} mv^2$
where m is the mass and v is the velocity

Waves

speed = frequency × wavelength $v = f\lambda$

Electricity

charge = current × time
(coulombs) (amperes) (seconds)

resistance (ohms) = $\frac{\text{voltage (volts)}}{\text{current (amperes)}}$ $R = \frac{V}{I}$

$V = I \times R$

Electrical power

power = voltage × current = $P = V \times I$
(watts) (volts) (amperes)

$V = \frac{P}{I}$ and $I = \frac{P}{V}$

Forces of nature

	Gravity	Electro-magnetism	Weak nuclear force	Strong nuclear force
Range m	infinite	infinite	10^{-18} (sub-atomic)	10^{-15} (sub-atomic)
Relative strength	6×10^{-39}	1/137	10^{-5}	1
Examples of application	orbit of Earth around Sun	force between electrical charges	radio-active β-decay	binds atomic nucleus together

Elementary particles

Fundamental particles (matter particles)

electrons
muons
neutrinos
quarks
taus

Force particles

gluons
gravitons
photons
W and *Z* bosons

Some common physical qualities and their units

Physical quantity	Symbol	SI unit	SI Symbol
acceleration, deceleration	*a*	metre/second^2 kilometre/hour/second	m s^{-2} km h^{-1} s^{-1}
angular velocity	ω	radian/second	rad s^{-1}; s^{-1}
capacitance	*C*	farad (coulomb/volt)	F (CV^{-1})
coefficient of viscosity	η	poise, dekapoise (newton second/metre^2) (kilogram/metre/second)	 N s m^{-2} kgm^{-1}s^{-1}
density	ρ	kilogram/metre^3 kilogram/millilitre	kgm^{-3} kgm^{-1}
displacement, distance	*S*	metre	m
electric charge	*Q*, *q*	coulomb	C
electric current	*I*, *i*	ampere (coulomb/second)	A C s^{-1}
electrical energy	-	megajoule, kilowatt-hour	MJ kWh
electric intensity, field strength	*E* (= −d*V*/d*r*)	newton/coulomb volt/metre	N C^{-1} V m^{-1}
electric p.d.	*V*	volt (joule/coulomb)	V (J C^{-1})
electrical power	-	watt (joule/second)	W (J s^{-1})
electromotive force (e.m.f.)	*E*	volt (watt/ampere)	V (WA^{-1})
electrical conductance	*S*	siemen, ohm $^{-1}$	AV^{-1}
electrical resistance	*R*	ohm (volt/ampere)	Ω (V A^{-1})
electric permittivity	ε	farad/metre	F m^{-1}
frequency	*f*	hertz (cycles/second)	Hz (s^{-1})
force	F	newton (kilogram metre/second^2)	N (kg m s^{-2})
gravitational, intensity, field strength	-	newton/kilogram	N kg^{-1}
heat capacity of a body	*ms*	joule/kelvin	J K^{-1}
inductance	*L*	henry volt second/ampere) (weber/ampere)	H (V s A^{-1}) (Wb A^{-1})
induced emf	*e*	volt (weber/second)	V (Wb s^{-1})
magnetic field strength	*H*	ampere/metre	A m^{-1}
magnetic flux	φ	weber	Wb
magnetic flux density	*B*	tesla (weber/metre^2)	T (Wb m^{-2})
magnetic permeability	μ	henry/metre	Hm^{-1}
mass	*m*	kilogram	kg
mechanical power	-	watt (joule/second)	W (J s^{-1})
moment of intertia	*I*	kilogram metre^2	kg m^2
momentum	*mv*	kilogram metre/second	kg m s^{-1}
pressure	*P*	pascal (newton/metre^2)	Pa N m^{-2}
quantity of substance	-	mole	mol
specific heat capacity	*s*	joule/kilogram/kelvin	J kg^{-1} K^{-1}
specific latent heats of fusion, vaporization	*L*	joule/kilogram	J kg^{-1}
surface tension	*T*, γ	newton/metre	N m^{-1}
torque, moment of force, moment of couple	-	newton metre	N m
velocity gradient	d*v*/d*r*	metre/second/metre	(m s^{-1} m^{-1})
velocity, speed	*u*, *v*	metre/second kilometre/hour	m s^{-1} km h^{-1} s^{-1}
volume	*V*	metre^3 millilitre	m^3 ml
wavelength	λ	metre	m
weight	*W*	newton, kilogram-force	N kgf
work, energy	-	joule (newton metre)	J (N m)

Newton's laws

First law: the velocity of an object does not change unless a force acts on it.
Second law: a force F applied to an object of mass *m* causes an acceleration *a* according to $F = ma$.
Third law: every action has an equal and opposite reaction.

Newton's law of gravitation

$F = Gm_1m_2/r^2$ where *F* is the force between objects of mass m_1 and m_2 separated by distance *r*, and *G* is the Gravitational constant.

Einstein's principle of relativity

All physical laws are the same in all frames of reference in uniform motion with respect to one another.

If the energy of a body changes by amount *E* then its mass must change by E/c^2 where *c* is the velocity of light (or, expressed in its better-known form, $E=mc^2$).

Magnetism

A magnetic field is a region of magnetic influence around a magnet, moving charge, or current-carrying wire; denoted by *B* (unit, tesla), the magnetic flux density, and by *H* (unit, ampere/metre), the magnetic field strength.

Lines of magnetic field circulate around current-carrying wire.

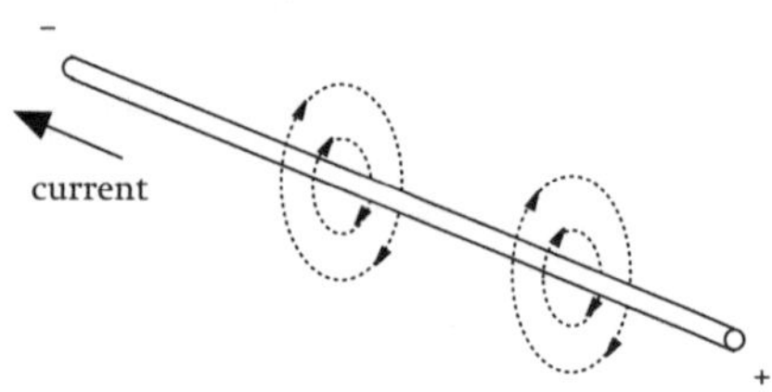

Circuit symbols

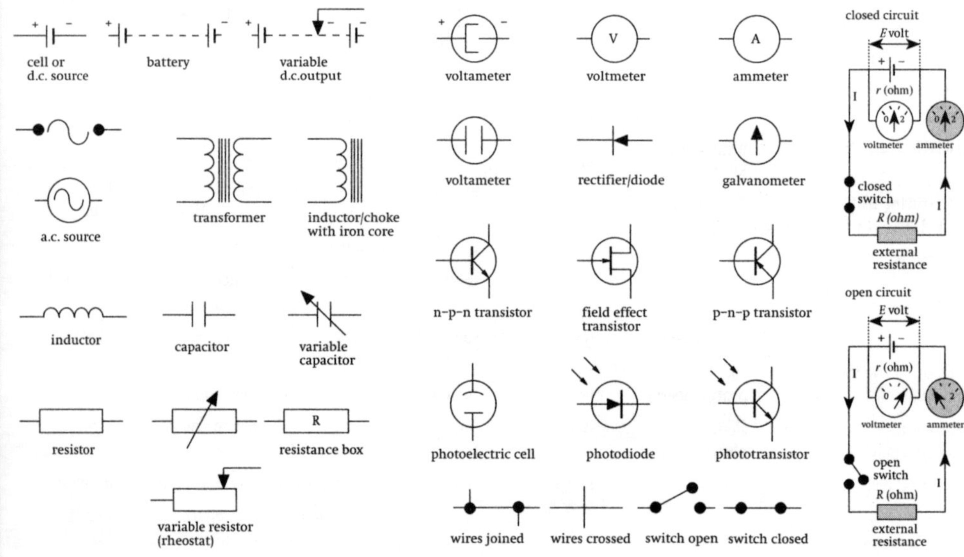

Optics

A reflection at a mirror. The law of reflection says that angles A an B are the same.

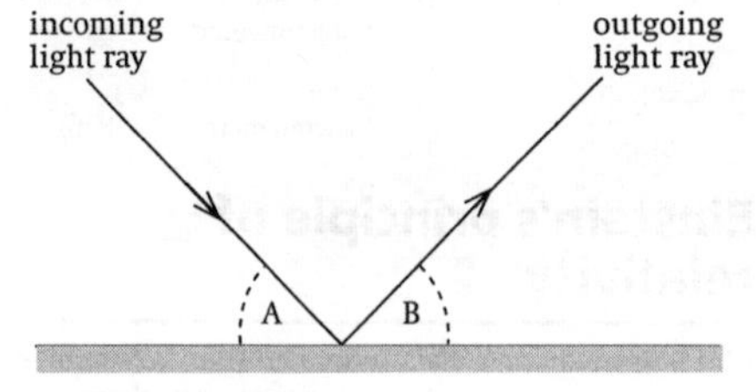

A double-convex converging lens.

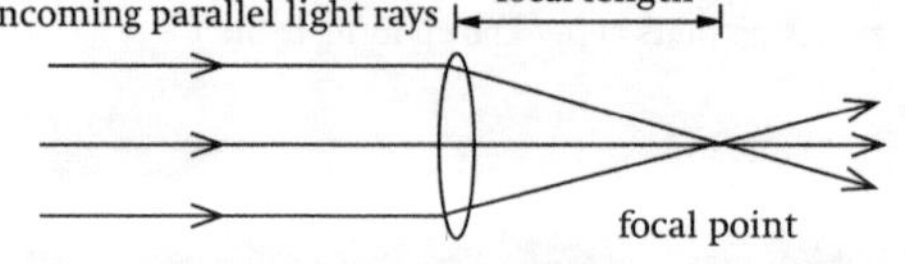

A double-concave diverging lens.

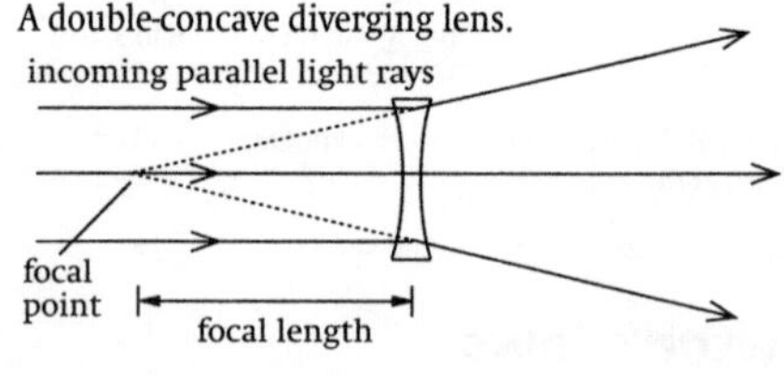

A basic telescope. A long focal length objective lens and a short focal length eyepiece are required.

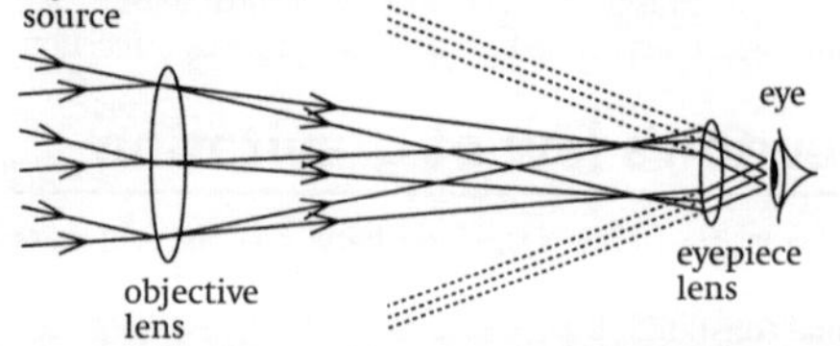

A basic compound microscope. The object lens forms an enlarged real image of the object, which is then viewed via the eyepiece. A short focal length objective lens and eyepiece are required. A 'virtual image' is an image which cannot be projected on to a screen.

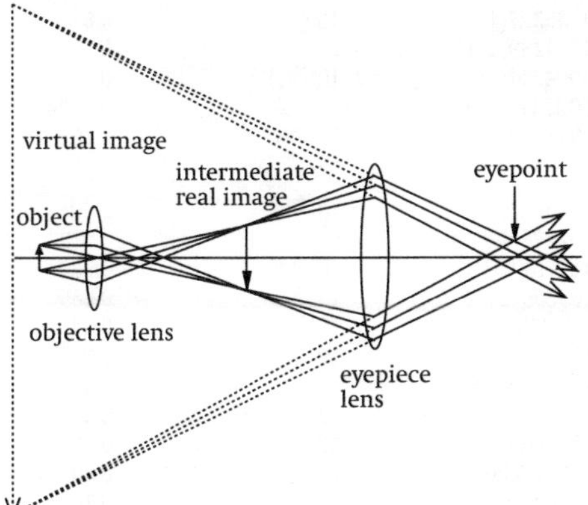

A beam of white light falling on to a prism splits into constituent colours (wavelengths), since the bending of light at an air–glass surface depends on the light wavelength, and white light comprises a mixture of colours. The white light is *dispersed* into a spectrum: the spectrum is really a continuous range of colours, not simply six as shown. With lenses, the actual bending of light occurs only at air–glass interfaces.

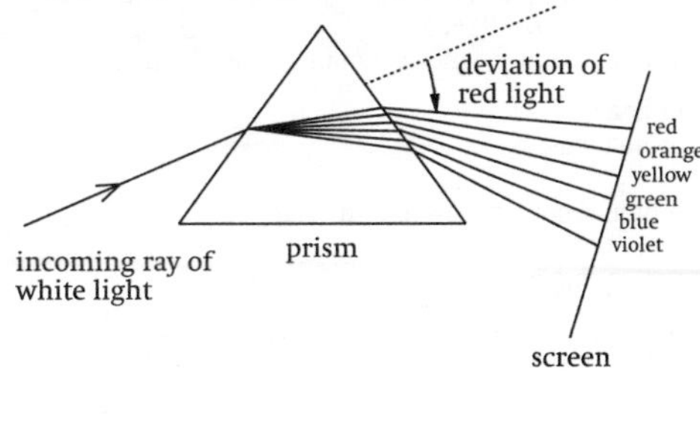

Physical constants

1986 recommended values of the main fundamental physical constants of physics and chemistry, based on a least-squares adjustment with 17 degrees of freedom. The digits in parentheses are the one-standard-deviation uncertainty in the last digits of the given value. (After Cohen and Taylor, 1987)

Quantity	*Symbol*	*Value*	*Units*	*Relative uncertainty*
Universal constants				
speed of light in vacuum	c	299 792 458	m s^{-1}	(exact)
permeability of vacuum	μ_0	$4\pi \times 10^{-7}$	N A^{-2}	
		= 12.566370614...	10^{-7} N A^{-2}	(exact)
permittivity of vacuum $1/\mu_0 c^2$	ε_0	8.854187187...	10^{-12} F m^{-1}	(exact)
Newtonian constant of gravitation	G	6.67259(85)	10^{-11} m^{3}kg^{-1} s^{-2}	128
Planck constant	$\hbar$	6.6260755(40)	10^{-34} J s	0.60
$h/2\pi$		1.05457266(63)	10^{-34} J s	0.60
Electromagnetic constants				
elementary charge	e	1.60217733(49)	10^{-19} C	0.30
	e/h	2.41798836(72)	10^{14} A J^{-1}	0.30
magnetic flux quantum, $h/2e$	Φ_0	2.06783461(61)	10^{-15} Wb	0.30
Josephson frequency–voltage quotient	$2e/h$	4.8359767(14)	10^{-14} Hz V^{-1}	0.30
Bohr magneton, $e\hbar/2m_e$	μ_B	9.2740154(31)	10^{-24} J T^{-1}	0.34
nuclear magneton, $e\hbar/2m_p$	μ_N	5.0507866(17)	10^{-27} J T^{-1}	0.34
Atomic constants				
fine-structure constant, $\mu_0 c e^2/2h$	α	7.29735308(33)	10^{-3}	0.045
	α^{-1}	137.0359895(61)		0.045
Rydberg constant, $m_e c\alpha^2/2h$	R_∞	10 973 731.534(13)	m^{-1}	0.0012
Bohr radius, $\alpha/4\pi R_\infty$	a_0	0.529177249(24)	10^{-10} m	0.045
quantum of circulation	$h/2m_e$	3.63694807(33)	10^{-4} m^{2}s^{-1}	0.089
	h/m_e	7.27389614(65)	10^{-4} m^{2}s^{-1}	0.089
Electron				
electron mass	m_e	9.1093897(54)	10^{-31} kg	0.59
		5.48579903(13)	10^{-4} u	0.023
electron–muon mass ratio	m_e/m_μ	4.83633218(71)	10^{-3}	0.15
electron–proton mass ratio	m_e/m_p	5.44617013(11)	10^{-4}	0.020
electron specific charge	$-e/m_e$	−1.75881962(53)	10^{11} Ckg^{-1}	0.30
Compton wavelength, $h/m_e c$	λ_c	2.42631058(22)	10^{-12} m	0.089
$\lambda_c/2\pi = \alpha a_0 = \alpha^2/4\pi R_\infty$	λ_c	3.86159323(35)	10^{-13} m	0.089
classical electron radius, $\alpha^2 a_0$	r_e	2.81794092(38)	10^{-15} m	0.13
electron magnetic moment	μ_e	928.47701(31)	10^{-26} J T^{-1}	0.34
electron g factor, $2(1+a_e)$	g_e	2.002319304386(20)		1×10^{-5}
electron–proton magnetic moment ratio	μ_e/μ_p	658.2106881(66)		0.010

Physical constants (continued)

Quantity	*Symbol*	*Value*	*Units*	*Relative uncertainty (ppm)*
Muon				
muon mass	m_μ	1.8835327(11)	10^{-28}kg	0.61
		0.113428913(17)	u	0.15
muon magnetic moment	μ_μ	4.4904514(15)	10^{-26} JT^{-1}	0.33
muon g factor, $2(1+a_\mu)$	g_μ	2.002331846(17)		0.0084
muon-proton magnetic moment ratio	μ_μ/μ_p	3.18334547(47)		0.15
Proton				
proton mass	m_p	1.6726231(10)	10^{-27}kg	0.59
		1.007276470(12)	u	0.012
proton Compton wavelength, h/m_pc	$\lambda_{C,p}$	1.32141002(12)	10^{-15}m	0.089
$\lambda_{C,p}/2\pi$	$\lambda_{C,p}$	2.10308937(19)	10^{-16}m	0.089
proton magnetic moment	μ_p	1.41060761(47)	10^{-26} J T^{-1}	0.34
in Bohr magnetons	μ_p/μ_B	1.521032202(15)	10^{-3}	0.010
in nuclear magnetons	μ_p/μ_N	2.792847386(63)		0.023
proton gyromagnetic ratio	γ_p	26 752.2128(81)	10^4 s^{-1} T^{-1}	0.30
	$\gamma_p/2\pi$	42.577469(13)	MHz T^{-1}	0.30
uncorrected (H_20, sph., 25°C)	γ'_p	26 751.525581)	10^4 s^{-1} T^{-1}	0.30
	$\gamma'_p/2\pi$	42.576375(13)	MHz T^{-1}	0.30
Neutron				
neutron mass	m_n	1.6749286(10)	10^{-27}kg	0.59
		1.008664904(14)	u	0.014
neutron Compton wavelength, h/m_nc	$\lambda_{C,n}$	1.31959110(12)	10^{-15}m	0.089
$\lambda_{C,n}/2\pi$	$\lambda_{C,n}$	2.10019445(19)	10^{-16}m	0.089
Physico-chemical constants				
Avogadro constant	N_A, L	6.0221367(36)	10^{23} mol^{-1}	0.59
atomic mass constant $m_u = {}^1/_{12}m$ (^{12}C)	m_u	1.6605402(10)	10^{-27}kg	0.59
Faraday constant, N_Ae	F	96 485.309(29)	C mol^{-1}	0.30
molar gas constant	R	8.314510(70)	J mol^{-1} K^{-1}	8.4
Boltzmann constant R/N_A	k	1.380658(12)	10^{-23} J K^{-1}	8.5
molar volume (ideal gas), RT/p				
T = 273.15 K, p = 101 325 Pa	V_m	0.02241410(19)	m^3 mol^{-1}	8.4
Stefan-Boltzmann constant, $(\pi^2/60)\ k^4/\hbar^3 c^2$	σ	5.67051(19)	10^{-8} W m^{-2} K^{-4}	34
first radiation constant, $2\pi hc^2$	C_1	3.7417749(22)	10^{-16} W m^2	0.60
second radiation constant, hc/k	C_2	0.01438769(12)	m K	8.4

The electromagnetic spectrum

Wavelength		Band		Frequency	Temperature of black-body radiation maximum
1 000 km					
	extremely low frequency	ELF		1 kHz	
100 km					
	very low frequency	VLF		10 kHz	
10 km					
	low frequency	LF		100 kHz	
1 km					
	medium frequency	MF	am Radio	1 MHz	
100 m					
	high frequency	HF		10 MHz	
10 m					
	very high frequency	VHF	fm radio, television	100 MHz	
1 m					
	ultra high frequency	UHF		1 GHz	
10 cm					
	super high frequency	SHF	Microwave	10 GHz	
1 cm					
	extremely high frequency	EHF		100 GHz	1 K
1 mm					
		Submillimetre or far infrared		1 THz	10 K
100 μm					
				10 THz	100 K
10 μm		Infrared			
				100 THz	1 000 K
1 μm					
		Visible			
				10^{15}Hz	10^4K
100 nm		Ultraviolet			
				10^{16}Hz	10^5K
10 nm					
				10^{17}Hz	10^6K
1 nm		X-rays			
				10^{18}Hz	10^7K
100 pm					
				10^{19}Hz	10^8K
10 pm		Gamma rays			
				10^{20}Hz	10^9K
1 pm					

Radioactivity units

The activity of a radioactive source is expressed in *becquerels*, Bq, where 1Bq is one decay per second. Particles from different substances may be produced in similar numbers but with very different energies. This is taken into account using a second unit, the *gray*, Gy, which measures the energy deposited in some object by the radiation: the *absorbed dose*. Different types of radiation cause different degrees of biological damage, even if the total energy deposited is the same; for example, 1Gy of alpha radiation causes 20 times as much damage as 1Gy of beta radiation. This potential for causing harm is expressed as *dose equivalent*, units sievert, Sv, which is the product of absorbed dose in Gy and a *relative biological effectiveness* (RBE) factor. Radiation limits for working places and the environment are expressed in Sv. Names, definitions, and units are summarised in the table.

Name	*Definition*	*Unit*	*Old unit*
activity	rate of disintegrations	Bq	Ci (curie)
absorbed dose	energy deposited in object, divided by mass of object	Gy	rad
dose equivalent	absorbed dose × RBE	Sv	rem

RBE	*Radiation*
20	alpha
10	neutron
1	beta, gamma, X-ray

Sound intensity level

Source	*Sound intensity level (dB)*
jet aircraft	120
heavy machinery	90
busy street	70
conversation	50
whisper	20

dB = decibels

CHEMISTRY

Table of elements

Atomic weights are taken from the 1983 list of the International Union of Pure and Applied Chemistry. For radioactive elements, the mass number of the most stable isotope is given in square brackets.

Symbol	Element	Atomic No.	Weight
Ac	actinium	89	[227]
Ag	silver	47	107.8682
Al	aluminium	13	26.98154
Am	americium	95	[243]
Ar	argon	18	39.948
As	arsenic	33	74.9216
At	astatine	85	[210]
Au	gold	79	196.9665
B	boron	5	10.811
Ba	barium	56	137.33
Be	beryllium	4	9.01218
Bi	bismuth	83	208.9804
Bk	berkelium	97	[247]
Br	bromine	35	79.904
C	carbon	6	12.011
Ca	calcium	20	40.078
Cd	cadmium	48	112.41
Ce	cerium	58	140.12
Cf	californium	98	[251]
Cl	chlorine	17	35.453
Cm	curium	96	[249]
Co	cobalt	27	58.9332
Cr	chromium	24	51.9961
Cs	cesium/caesium	55	132.9054
Cu	copper	29	63.546
Dy	dysprosium	66	162.50
Er	erbium	68	167.26
Es	einsteinium	99	[252]
Eu	europium	63	151.96
F	fluorine	9	18.998403
Fe	iron	26	55.847
Fm	fermium	100	[257]
Fr	francium	87	[223]
Ga	gallium	31	69.723
Gd	gadolinium	64	157.25
Ge	germanium	32	72.59
H	hydrogen	1	1.00794
He	helium	2	4.002602
Hf	hafnium	72	178.49
Hg	mercury	80	200.59
Ho	holmium	67	164.9304
I	iodine	53	126.9045
In	indium	49	114.82
Ir	iridium	77	192.22
K	potassium	19	39.0983
Kr	krypton	36	83.80
La	lanthanum	57	138.9055
Li	lithium	3	6.941
Lr	lutetium	71	174.967
Lw	lawrencium	103	[260]
Md	mendelevium	101	[258]
Mg	magnesium	12	24.305
Mn	manganese	25	54.9380
Mo	molybdenum	42	95.94
N	nitrogen	7	14.0067
Na	sodium	11	22.98977
Nb	niobium	41	92.9064
Nd	neodymium	60	144.24
Ne	neon	10	20.179
Ni	nickel	28	58.69
No	nobelium	102	[259]
Np	neptunium	93	[237]
O	oxygen	8	15.9994
Os	osmium	76	190.2
P	phosphorus	15	30.97376
Pa	protactinium	91	[231]
Pb	lead	82	207.2
Pd	palladium	46	106.42
Pm	promethium	61	[145]
Po	polonium	84	[209]
Pr	praseodymium	59	140.9077
Pt	platinum	78	195.08
Pu	plutonium	94	[244]
Ra	radium	88	[226]
Rb	rubidium	37	85.4678
Re	rhenium	75	186.207
Rh	rhodium	45	102.9055
Rn	radon	86	[222]
Ru	ruthenium	44	101.77
S	sulphur/sulfur	16	32.066
Sb	antimony	51	121.75
Sc	scandium	21	44.95591
Se	selenium	34	78.96
Si	silicon	14	28.0855
Sm	samarium	62	150.36
Sn	tin	50	118.710
Sr	strontium	38	87.62
Ta	tantalum	73	180.9479
Tb	terbium	65	158.9254
Tc	technetium	43	[99]
Te	tellurium	52	127.60
Th	thorium	90	232.0381
Ti	titanium	22	47.88
Tl	thallium	81	204.383
Tm	thulium	69	168.9342
U	uranium	92	238.0289
Une	unnilennium	109	[266]
Unh	unnilhexium	106	[263]
Unp	unnilpexium	105	[262]
Unq	unnilquadium	104	[261]
Uns	unnilseptium	107	[262]
V	vanadium	23	50.9415
W	tungsten	74	183.85
Xe	xenon	54	131.29
Y	yttrium	39	88.9059
Yb	ytterbium	70	173.04
Zn	zinc	30	65.39
Zr	zirconium	40	91.224

Periodic table of elements

1	2											3	4	5	6	7	8
1 H Hydrogen 1.00794																1 H Hydrogen 1.00794	2 He Helium 4.00260
3 Li Lithium 6.941	4 Be Beryllium 9.01218											5 B Boron 10.81	6 C Carbon 12.011	7 N Nitrogen 14.0067	8 O Oxygen 15.9994	9 F Fluorine 18.998403	10 Ne Neon 20.179
11 Na Sodium 22.98977	12 Mg Magnesium 22.98977					*Transition series*						13 Al Aluminium 26.98154	14 Si Silicon 28.0855	15 P Phosphorus 30.97376	16 S Sulphur 32.06	17 Cl Chlorine 35.453	18 Ar Argon 39.948
19 K Potassium 39.0983	20 Ca Calcium 40.08	21 Sc Scardium 44.9559	22 Ti Titanium 47.88	23 V Vanadium 50.9415	24 Cr Chromium 51.996	25 Mn Manganese 54.9380	26 Fe Iron 55.847	27 Co Cobalt 58.9332	28 Ni Nickel 58.69	29 Cu Copper 63.546	30 Zn Zinc 65.38	31 Ga Gallium 69.72	32 Ge Germanium 72.59	33 As Arsenic 74.9216	34 Se Selenium 78.96	35 Br Bromine 79.904	36 Kr Krypton 83.80
37 Rb Rubidium 85.4678	38 Sr Strontium 87.62	39 Y Yttrium 88.9059	40 Zr Zirconium 91.22	41 Nb Niobium 92.9064	42 Mo Molybdenum 95.94	43 Tc Technetium (98)	44 Ru Ruthenium 101.07	45 Rh Rhodium 102.9055	46 Pd Palladium 106.42	47 Ag Silver 107.8682	48 Cd Cadmium 112.41	49 In Indium 114.82	50 Sn Tin 118.69	51 Sb Antimony 121.75	52 Te Tellenum 127.60	53 I Iodine 126.9045	54 Xe Xenon 131.29
55 Cs Caesium 132.9054	56 Ba Barium 137.33	57–71 Lathanide series (rare earth elements) ★	72 Hf Hafnium 178.49	73 Ta Tantalum 180.7479	74 W Tungsten 180.7479	75 Re Rhenium 186.207	76 Os Osmium 190.2	77 Ir Iridium 192.2	78 Pt Platinum 195.08	79 Au Gold 196.9665	80 Hg Mercury 200.59	81 Tl Thallium 204.383	82 Pb Lead 207.2	83 Bi Bismuth 208.9804	84 Po Polonium (209)	85 At Astatine (210)	86 Rn Radon (222)
87 Fr Francium (223)	88 Ra Radium 226.0254	89–103 Actinide series (radioactive rare earth elements) ☆	104 Unq Unnilquadium (261)	105 Unp Unnilpentium (262)	106 Unh Unnilhexium (263)	107 Uns Unnilseptium (262)		108 Une Unnilennium (266)									

★	57 La Lanthanum 138.9055	58 Ce Cerium 140.12	59 Pr Praseodymium 140.9077	60 Nd Neodymium 144.24	61 Pm Promethium (145)	62 Sm Samarium 150.36	63 Eu Europium 151.96	64 Gd Gadolinium 157.25	65 Tb Terbium 158.9254	66 Dy Dysprosium 162.50	67 Ho Holmium 164.9304	68 Er Erbium 167.26	69 Tm Thulium 168.9342	70 Yb Ytterbium 173.04	71 Lu Lutetium 174.967
☆	89 Ac Actinium 227.0278	90 Th Thorium 232.0381	91 Pa Protactinium 231.0359	92 U Uranium 238.0289	93 Np Neptunium 237.0482	94 Pu Plutonium (244)	95 Am Americium (243)	96 Cm Curium (247)	97 Bk Berkelium (247)	98 Cf Californium (252)	99 Es Einsteinium (254)	100 Fm Fermium (257)	101 Md Mendelevium (258)	102 No Nobelium (259)	103 Lr Lawrencium (260)

Key: 86 Rn Radon (222)

- Atomic number — 86
- Symbol — Rn
- Element name — Radon
- Atomic weight (most stable isotope of radioactive elements in parentheses) — (222)

Science and technology

Physical properties of metals

Metal	*Electron structure*	*Electronegativity*	*Atomic number*	*Melting point (°C)*	*Boiling point (°C)*
Aluminium (Al)	$(Ne)3s^2 3p^1$	1.5	13	659	2447
Barium (Ba)	$(Xe)6s^2$	0.9	56	710	1637
Beryllium (Be)	$(He)2s^2$	1.5	4	1283	2477
Caesium(Cs)	$(Xe)6s'$	0.7	55	29	685
Calcium (Ca)	$(Ar)4s^2$	1.0	20	850	1492
Chromium (Cr)	$(Ar)3d^5 4s'$	1.6	24	2176	2915
Cobalt (Co)	$(Ar)3d^7 4s^2$	1.8	27	1768	3150
Copper (Cu)	$(Ar)3d^{10} 4s'$	1.9	29	1356	2855
Iron (Fe)	$(Ar)3d^6 4s^2$	1.8	26	1812	3160
Lead (Pb	$(Xe)5d^{10} 6s^2 6p^2$	1.8	82	328	1751
Lithium (Li)	$(He)2s^1$	1.0	3	181	1331
Magnesium (Mg)	$(Ne)3s^2$	1.2	12	650	117
Manganese (Mn)	$(Ar)3d^5 4s^2$	1.5	25	1517	2314
Nickel (Ni)	$(Ar)3d^8 4s^2$	1.8	28	1728	3110
Potassium (K)	$(Ar)4s^1$	0.8	19	63	766
Rubidium (Rb)	$(Kr)5s^1$	0.8	37	39	701
Sodium (Na)	$(Ne)3s^1$	0.9	11	98	890
Strontium (Sr)	$(Kr)5s^2$	1.0	38	770	1367
Tin (Sn)	$(Kr)4d^{10} 5s^2 5p^2$	1.8	50	232	2690
Titanium (Ti)	$(Ar)3d^2 4s^2$	1.5	22	1673	2750
Vanadium (V)	$(Ar)3d^3 4s^2$	1.6	23	2190	3650
Zinc (Zn)	$(Ar)3d^{10} 4s^2$	1.6	30	693	1181

Symbols used in chemistry

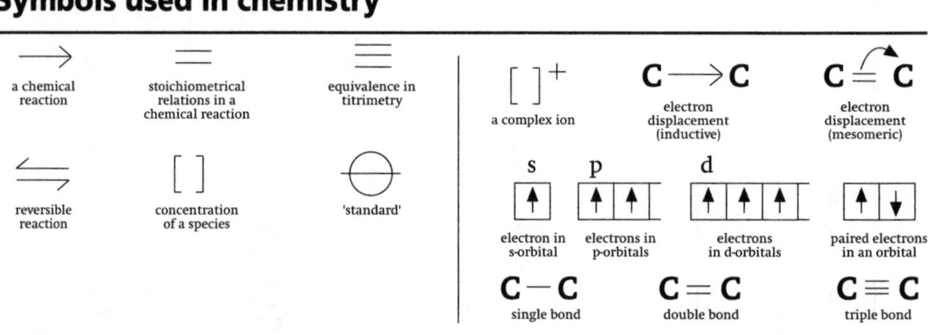

Polymers

Polymer	*Repeat unit*	*Properties and uses*
Polyamides		
Nylon-6,6	$-NH-(CH_2)_6-NH-CO-(CH_2)_4-CO-$	Textile fibre, threads, ropes Moulded gears and electrical insulation
Nylon-6,10	$-NH-(CH_2)_6-NH-CO-(CH_2)_8-CO-$	Sports equipment Bristles for brushes
Nomex	$-NH-C_6H_4-NH-CO-C_6H_4-CO-$	Heat resistant polymer in space suits Also for parachute cords
Polyesters and polycarbonates		
Terylene, Dacron	$-O-CH_2-CH_2-O-CO-C_6H_4-CO-$	Textile fibre Basis for magnetic tape and photographic film

Polymer	*Repeat unit*	*Properties and uses*
Lexan	$-O-C_6H_4-C(CH_3)_2-C_6H_4-O-C(=O)-$	Tough and transparent Bullet proof windows, safety glass Food containers Car components
Polyethers		
Polyglycol 166	$-O-CH_2-CH(CH_2Cl)-$	Making urethanes and speciality elastomers, eg for oil and fuel hoses, oil-well equipment
Delrin, Celcon	$-O-CH_2-$	Tough plastic for gears, pipes, pens
Phenol-based		
Bakelite	OH; $-CH_2-$; OH; $-CH_2-$; CH_2 (phenol rings linked by CH_2 groups)	Hard thermosetting polymer Telephones, buttons, electrical insulators
Poly(melamine formaldehyde)	triazine ring with three N substituents linked by $-CH_2-$ groups	Laminated surfaces, eg table tops, cupboards
Polyurethanes		
Polyurethane	$-(CH_2)_3-NH-C(=O)-O-$	Foam rubber, synthetic leather
Lycra	$-NH-C(=O)-NH-C_6H_4-CH_2-C_6H_4-NH-C(=O)-O-(CH_2)_{32}-C(=O)-$	Expanded foam rubber, carpet underlays, clothing
Alkenes		
ABS[a] polymers contain these four types of repeat unit	$-CH_2-CH(CN)-$; $-CH_2-CH=CH-CH_2-$; $-CH_2-CH(CH=CH_2)-$; $-CH_2-CH(C_6H_5)-$	Tough structural plastic or rubber Telephones, pipes, many moulded articles
Polybutadiene (butadiene rubber)	$-CH_2-CH=CH-CH_2-$	Alternative to natural rubber Footwear, tyres, toys

Polymer	*Repeat unit*	*Properties and uses*
Neoprene	$—CH_2—CCl{=}CH—CH_2—$	Adhesive golf ball covers, liquid seals
Polythene[b] (polyethene)	$—CH_2—CH_2—$	Tough plastic Fibres, thin films, extrusion moulded objects, toys, bottles
Butyl rubber	$—CH_2—C(CH_3)_2—$	Tyre inner tubes, raincoats, seals
Natural rubber (poly (*cis*-1,4-isoprene))	$—CH_2—C(CH_3){=}CH—CH_2—$	After vulcanisation, used in car, and other, tyres
PTFE (poly(tetra-fluoroethene), Teflon)	$—CF_2—CF_2—$	Highly water repellent Nonstick cooking ware Industrial uses where very low friction needed
Polystyrene	$—CH_2—CH(C_6H_5)—$	Transparent, glass-like Wide variety of moulded and expanded objects Packing and insulation
Perspex (poly(methyl methacrylate))	$—CH_2—C(CN)(C{=}O—O—CH_3)—$	Transparent, glass-like Windows, fibre optics, illuminated signs
PVC (polyvinyl chloride)	$—CH_2—CHCl—$	Hard inflexible polymer With plasticiser, used in tubing, thin films, car seat covers, floor tile
Alkynes		
Polyethyne (polyacetylene)	$—CH—CH—$ (delocalised electrons)	With iodine, an electrically conducting polymer
Inorganic		
Silicone rubber	$—O—Si(CH_3)_2—$	Seals, hoses, waterproofing, 'silicone grease'
Carbon fibres	Carbon layers with layers parallel to axis of fibre	Very high strength fibres, e.g. in aeroplane and boat building
Polythiazyl	$—S{=}N—$	An electrically conducting polymer Semiconductor at very low temperatures

[a] ABS = acrylonitrile–butadiene–styrene
[b] There are two main types of polyethene; low density polyethene (LDPE) has considerable branching; high density polyethene (HDPE) has no branching.

Hazardous substances symbols

harmful/ irritant

toxic

radioactive

flammable

corrosive

oxidising/ supports fire

explosive

TECHNOLOGY

Major technological inventions

Date	*Invention*	*Inventor/Discoverer*
1752	lightning conductor	Benjamin Franklin
1764	spinning jenny	James Hargreaves
1768	spinning frame	Richard Arkwright
1769	condenser (steam engine)	James Watt
1774	telegraph (electric)	Georges Louis Lesage
1775	steam ship	Jacques Perrier
1776	submarine	David Bushnell
1779	spinning mule	Samuel Crompton
1780	circular saw	Gervinus
1783	hot air balloon	Jacques and Joseph Montgolfier
1784	safety lock	Joseph Bramah
1785	chemical bleaching	Claude Berthollet
1792	cotton gin	Eli Whitney
	gas lighting	William Murdoch
1795	preserving jar (foods)	Francois Appert
1798	lithography	Alois Senefelder
1799	sheet paper making machine	Louis Robert
1800	electric battery	Alessandro Volta
1802	wood-planing machine	Joseph Bramah
1804	locomotive	Richard Trevithick
1807	conveyor belt	Oliver Evans
1810	canning	Nicholas Appert
1812	photographic lens	William H Wollaston
1813	power loom	William Horrocks
1823	waterproof material	Charles Macintosh
1824	cement	Joseph Aspdin
1829	typewriter	William Burt
1831	electric generator	Michael Faraday
1834	harvesting machine	Cyril McCormick
1835	revolver	Samuel Colt
	computer	Charles Babbage
1838	photography (on paper)	William Henry Fox Talbot
1839	bicycle	Kirkpatrick Macmillan
1843	underground railway	Charles Pearson
1845	hydraulic crane	W G Armstrong
1846	sewing machine	Elias Howe
	rotary printing press	Richard Hoe
1850	synthetic oil	James Young
	refrigerator	James Harrison and Alexander Twining
1851	mechanical lift	Elisha Otis
1854	hydraulic lift	Elisha Otis
1855	celluloid	Alexander Parks
	steel production	Henry Bessemer
1856	synthetic dye	William Henry Perkin
1876	microphone	Alexander Graham Bell
1861	colour photography	James Clerk Maxwell
1866	telegraph (transatlantic)	Willliam Thompson (Lord Kelvin)
1867	pasteurisation	Louis Pasteur
1868	tungsten steel	Robert Mushet
	traffic lights	J P Knight
1871	pneumatic drill	Samuel Ingersoll
1872	electric typewriter	Thomas Edison
1873	barbed wire	Joseph Glidden
1876	telephone	Alexander Graham Bell
1877	electric welding	Elisha Thomson
	gramophone	Thomas Edison
1878	electric railway	Ernst Werner von Siemens
1879	electric lamp	Thomas Edison
1880	pendulum seismograph	James Ewing, Thomas Gray, Sir John Milne
1882	electric flat iron	Harry W Seeley
1883	automatic machine gun	Sir Hiram (Stevens) Maxim
1884	fountain pen	Lewis Waterman
	car (internal combustion engine)	Gottlieb Daimler
1885	adding machine	William Burroughs
	petrol engine	Gottlieb Daimler
	motorcycle	Gottlieb Daimler
1886	car (petrol engine)	Karl Benz
1887	celluloid film	Goodwin
1888	pneumatic tyre	John Boyd Dunlop
	alternating-current motor	Nikola Tesla
	gramophone record	Emil Berliner
1889	photographic film	George Eastman
1892	escalator	Jesse Reno
1894	automatic loom	J H Northrop
	cinematograph	Auguste and Louis Lumière
	turbine ship	Charles Parsons
1895	X-ray	Wilhelm Röntgen
	safety razor	King C Gillette
1898	diesel engine	Rudolf Diesel
1900	cellophane	J E Brandenburger
	airship	Graf Ferdinand von Zeppelin
1901	radio	Guglielmo Marconi
	vacuum cleaner (electric)	Hubert Cecil Booth

Major technological inventions (continued)

Date	Invention	Inventor/Discoverer
1902	windscreen wipers	Mary Anderson
1903	electrocardiagraph	Wilhelm Einthoven
	aeroplane	Orville and Wilbur Wright
1906	freeze-drying	Arsene D'Arsonval and Georges Bordas
1907	electric washing machine	Hurley Machine Co.
	facsimile machine (fax)	Arthur Korn
	bakelite	Leo Bakeland
1911	neon light	Georges Claude
1913	stainless steel	Harry Brearley
1924	loudspeaker	Rice-Kellogg
1926	television	John Logie Baird
	liquid fuel rocket	Robert Goddard
1933	electron microscope	Max Knoll and Ernst Ruska
1934	cat's eyes	Percy Shaw
1935	parking meter	Carlton C Magee
1937	turbo jet	Frank Whittle
1938	ball-point pen	Laszlo and Georg Biró
	nylon	Wallace Carrothers
	xerography	Charles Carson
1939	helicopter	Igor Sikorsky
	atom bomb	Otto Frisch, Niels Bohr and Rudolf Peierls
1941	terylene	J R Whinfield and J T Dickson
1942	turbo-prop engine	Max Mueller
1944	digital computer	Harvard University
1945	microwave oven	Percy Le Baron Spencer
1948	transistor	William Shockley, John Bardeen and Walter Brattain
1950	gas-turbine powered car	Rover Motor Co.
1954	solar battery	Bell Telephone Co.
1956	video recorder	Ampex Co.
1959	hovercraft	Christopher Cockerell
	microchip	Kilby and Robert Noyce
1960	laser	Charles Townes
1967	laser surgery operating theatre	Cincinatti, US
1969	Concorde supersonic	Britain–France
1969	test tube baby	Robert Edwards, Patrick Steptoe
1969	V/STOL harrier	Hawker Siddeley
1970	747 Jumbo jet	Boeing
1971	microprocessor	Marcian Hoff
1972	pocket calculator	
1976	industrial robot	
	space shuttle	NASA
1978	TGV high speed train	France
1979	walkman	Sony
	compact disc	Philips and Sony
1981	personal computer	IBM
1985	battery powered vehicle (C5)	Clive Sinclair
1986	laser instruments for heart and eye surgery	
	pocket telephone	
1987	digital audio tape	
1988	video walkman	Sony

The world's tallest structures

Name of structure	Location	Year	Height m	Height ft
Warszawa Radio Mast	Konstantynow, Poland	1974	646	2120
KTHI-TV	North Dakota, US	1963	629	2063
CN Tower	Toronto,Canada	1975	553	1815
Ostankino TV Tower	Nr Moscow, Russia	1967	537	1762
WRBL-TV & WTVM	Georgia, US	1963	533	1749
WBIR-TV	Tennessee, US	1963	533	1749
Moscow TV Tower	Moscow, Russia		528	1732
KFVS-TV	Missouri, US	1960	510	1672
WSPD-TV	Kentucky, US		499	1638
WGAN-TV	Maine, US	1959	493	1619
KSWS-TV	New Mexico, US	1956	490	1610
WKY-TV	Oklahoma, US		487	1600
KW-TV	Oklahoma, US	1954	479	1572
Bren Tower	Nevada, US	1962	465	1527
Sears Tower	Chicago, Illinois, US	1974	443	1454
World Trade Centre	New York City, US	1973	412	1350
Empire State Building	New York City, US	1930	381	1200
Empire State Building	New York City, US	1988	368	1250
Bank of China	Hong Kong	1973	346	1136
John Hancock Centre	Chicago, Illinois, US	1968	343	1127
Chrysler Building	New York City, US	1930	319	1046
Library Tower	Los Angeles, US	1989	310	1017
Texas Commercial Plaza	Houston, Texas, US	1981	305	1000
Allied Bank Plaza	Houston,Texas, US	1983	302	991

The world's highest dams

Name	*Date completed*	*Place*	*Height ft*	*m*
Bhakra	1963	India	741	226
Chicoasen	1981	Mexico	869	265
Chirkey	1977	Ukraine	764	233
Chivor	1975	Columbia	778	237
Contra	1965	Switzerland	722	220
Dabaklamm	uncompleted	Austria	722	220
El Cajon	1984	Honduras	741	226
Grande Dixence	1962	Switzerland	935	285
Guavio	1989	Columbia	820	250
Hoover	1936	Arizona/ Nevada, US	726	221
Inguri	1984	Georgia, US	892	272
Kinshau	1985	India	830	253
Mauvoisin	1957	Switzerland	777	237
Mica	1972	Canada	794	242
Mihoesti	1983	Romania	794	242
Nurek	1980	Tadzhikistan	984	300
Oroville	1968	California	770	235
Rogun	1985	Tadzhikistan	1066	325
Sayano-Shushenk	1980	Russia	794	242
Tehri	uncompleted	India	856	261
Vaiont	1961	Italy	869	265

The world's longest tunnels

Name	*Date completed*	*Place*	*Length km*	*mi*
Aki	1975	Japan	12.8	8
Apennine	1934	Italy	17.7	11
Cascade	1929	US	14.5	9
Channel	1994 (scheduled)	UK/France	49.9	31
Chesaspeake Bay	1964	US	28	17.65
Dai-shimizu	1979	Japan	22.5	14
Flathead	1970	US	12.8	8
Frejus (Mont Cenis)	1871	France/Italy	12.8	8
Hokuriku	1962	Japan	14.5	9
Kammon	1975	Japan	19.3	12
Lotschberg	1913	Switzerland	14.5	9.03
Mersey	1934	UK	4	2.5
Mont Blanc	1965	France/Italy		
Moscow subway	1990	Russia	37.9	23.5
Mount MacDonald	1989	Canada	14.6	9.1
Rokko (rail)	1972	Japan	16	10
Rove	1927	France	7.12	4.42
San Fransisco Subway	1971	US	5.8	3.6
Seikan	1985	Japan	53.9	33.49
Shin Shimizu	1961	Japan	12.8	8
Simplon I and II	1906, 1922	Switzerland/ Italy	19.3	12
St Gotthard (rail)	1882	Switzerland	14.9	9.26

The world's longest bridges

Name	*Date completed*	*Place*	*Length ft*	*m*
Akashi-Kaikyo	uncompleted	Japan	12828	83910
Ambassador	1929	Detroit, US	1850	564
Angostura	1967	Venezuela	5507	1678
Bendorf	1965	Koblenz, Germany	3378	1030
Bosporus	1973	Istanbul, Turkey	3524	1074
Commodore John Bay	1974	Pennsylvania, US	1644	501
Forth Road Bridge	1964	Scotland, UK	3000	900
George Washington Bridge	1931	New York City, US	3500	1067
Golden Gate	1937	San Francisco, US	4200	1280
Humber	1981	UK	4626	1410
Kincardine	1936	Scotland, UK	2696	822
Little Belt	1970	Denmark	1968	600
Luzhniki	1959	Russia	6650	2027
Mackinac	1957	Michigan, US	3800	1158
Minami-Bisan-Seto	1988	Japan	3609	1100
New Gorge	1977	Virginia, US	12596	3839
Oakland Bay (Transbay)	1936	San Francisco, US	1400	426.7
Osland Island	1972	Sweden	19882	6060
Philadelphia-Camden	1926	US	1750	533
Quebec rail	1917	Canada	1850	549
Rio Nileroi	1972	Brazil	3363	1025
Salazar	1966	Lisbon, Portugal	3323	1013
Save Bridge	1970	Mozambique	2860	872
Second Lake Washington	1963	Seattle, US	12596	3839
Seto-Ohashi	1988	Japan	43374	13220
Skarnsundet	1991	Norway	1739	530
Sydney Harbour	1932	Sydney, Australia	1650	503
Tatara	1997 (scheduled)	Japan	2920	890
Tay II	1887	Scotland, UK	11653	3552
Tete	1971	Mozambique	2360	872
Verrazano-Narrows	1964	New York Harbor, US	4260	1298
Yokohama Bay	1989	Japan	2805	855

COMPUTERS

Programming languages

Language	Full name	Description
Ada		A high-level procedural language designed for programming computers for real-time applications. More specifically, where the computer is controlling the behaviour of military devices.
ALGOL	(ALGOrithmic Language)	One of the first languages developed for mathematical and scientific use. It introduced a number of new concepts and has been very influential in the design of other languages.
Assembly language		A low-level language that is a notation for representing machine code in human-readable form.
BASIC	(Beginners' All-purpose Symbolic Instruction Code)	A simple high-level language that can be used for general-purpose computing, especially on microcomputers. Designed for beginners.
C		Provides all the structure of a high-level language with certain low-level features that do not require the programmer to use assembly language. It is fast and portable and is the language in which the UNIX operating system was developed.
C++		An object-oriented language that is a descendent of C but in the tradition of ALGOL.
COBOL	(COmmon Business Oriented Language)	A high-level language that is the standard for all business data processing.
FORTRAN	(FORmula TRANslation)	A high-level language widely used for scientific computing; current standard is FORTRAN 77, but dates from 1956.
Hypertalk		A scripting language that is the basis of Hypercard.
LISP	(LISt Processing)	A high-level functional language with the imperative features designed for the processing of non-numeric data. Used for symbolic manipulation and in Artificial Intelligence.
LOGO		A graphics language used mainly for teaching small children.
Machine code		A low-level language into which all high-level languages must be translated before they can run. They are specific to machines and are in fact a series of machine-readable instructions.
ML	(Meta Language)	A high-level functional language used mainly for research purposes.
Modula 2		A high-level imperative language, derived from Pascal, in which programs may be written in modular form, i.e. built up from independently written modules.
Pascal		A high-level imperative language descended from ALGOL, and originally designed for teaching purposes.
PROLOG	(PROgramming in LOGic)	A high-level declarative language, designed for use in Artificial Intelligence.
Smalltalk		One of the first object-oriented languages, developed at Xerox Palo Alto Research Center.

The development of computers

Name of instrument	*Inventor*	*Date developed*	*Comments*
Abacus		Middle Ages	Calculations performed with sliding counters
Mechanical adding machine	Blaise Pascal, France	1642	
Stepped reckoner	Gottfried Leibniz, Germany	1673	Mechanical instrument able to multiply, divide and extract square roots as well as add
Analytical engine	Charles Babbage, Britain	1830	First automatic computer. Able to combine arithmetic processes with decisions based on own computations
Boolean algebra	George Boole, Britain	mid 19th century	Boole discovered analogy of algebraic symbols and those of logic. Binary logic operations brought about electronic computer switching theory and procedures
Data processing cards	Hermann Hollerith, US	1890	Introduction of perforated cards with pattern of holes which could be read by machine designed to sort and manipulate the data represented by the holes
Prototype of electromechanical digital computer	John Atanasoff, US	1939	
Calculator	Howard Aiken, US	1939	
Automatic Sequence Controlled calculator (Harvard Mark I)	Howard Aiken, US	1944	Series of instructions coded on punched paper tape entered and output recorded on cards or by electric typewriter
Colossus	Alan Turing, Britain	1943	Special purpose electronic computer designed to decipher codes
ENIAC (Electronic Numerical integrator and Calculator)	J Presper Eckert and John W Mauchly	1946	Marked the beginning of the first generation of modern computers. This was the first all purpose electronic digital computer
Transistor	Shockley, Bardeen and Brattain	1948	Reliable with low power consumption
EDSAC	Cambridge University	1949	First working version of a stored-program computer i.e. instructions stored in computer's memory
EDVAC (Electronic Discrete Variable Automatic Computer)	John Neumann	1950	Stored-program computer
UNIVAC (Universal Automatic Computer)	Eckert and Mauchly	1951	Used memory system made of mercury delay lines which gave access time of 500 microseconds. First computer able to handle numerical and alphabetical data with equal ease
Harvard Mark III		mid 1950s	Magnetic drum memory provided large storage capacity
Integrated circuit (IC)		1960s/70s	IC allowed construction of large-scale (mainframe) computers with high operating speeds
LSI (Large-scale Integration)		1960s/70s	Thousands of transistors and related devices could be packed onto a single integrated circuit
RAM (Random Access Memory)		1960s/70s	RAM chip used in constructing semiconductor memory units
PDP–8	DEC (Digital Equipment)	1963	First minicomputer
IBM System/360	IBM	1964	First family of compatible computers launched

The development of computers (continued)

Name of instrument	*Inventor*	*Date developed*	*Comments*
Control Data CD6000		1965	First supercomputer developed
Intel 4004	Marian Hoff, US	1971	First microprocessor. (An integrated circuit with all arithmetic, logic and control circuitry necessary to serve the central processing unit (CPU).)
Altair 8800		1975	First personal computer
Xerox Start System		1981	First windows, icons, menus and pointing devices system developed
Optical microchip		1988	Used light instead of electricity
Water-scale silicon memory chip		1989	Able to store 200 million characters
Windows	Microsoft	1990	Windows 3 released, a windowing environment for computers

ARTS AND CULTURE

LITERATURE

Novelists

Name	Dates	Place of birth	Selected works
Achebe, Chinua (Albert Chinualumogu)	1930–	Ogidi, Nigeria	*Things Fall Apart* (1959), *Anthills of the Savannah* (1988)
Ackroyd, Peter	1949–	London	*The Last Testament of Oscar Wilde* (1983), *Chatterton* (1988)
Adams, Douglas (Noel)	1952–	Essex	*The Hitch Hiker's Guide to the Galaxy* (1979)
Adams, Richard (George)	1920–	Newbury, Berkshire	*Watership Down* (1972). *Shardik* (1974), *The Girl in a Swing* (1980)
Alcott, Louisa M(ay)	1832–88	Germantown, Pennsylvania	*Little Women* (1868)
Amis, Kingsley (William)	1922–	London	*Lucky Jim* (1954), *That Uncertain Feeling* (1955), *Jake's Thing* (1978), *The Old Devils* (1986)
Amis, Martin	1949–	Oxford	*The Rachel Papers* (1973), *London Fields* (1990), *Time's Arrow* (1991)
Angelou, Maya (Marguerita Johnson)	1928–	St Louis, Missouri	*I Know Why The Caged Bird Sings* (1969), *All God's Children Need Travelling Shoes* (1986)
Archer, Jeffrey (Howard)	1940–	Somerset	*Not a Penny More, Not a Penny Less* (1975), *Kane and Abel* (1979), *First Among Equals* (1984), *A Twist in the Tale* (1989)
Asimov, Isaac	1920–92	Petrovichi, USSR	*Foundation* (1951), *The Disappearing Man and other stories* (1985), *Nightfall* (1990)
Atwood, Margaret (Eleanor)	1939–	Ottowa, Canada	*The Handmaid's Tale* (1986), *Cat's Eye* (1989)
Austen, Jane	1775–1817	Steventon, Hampshire	*Sense and Sensibility* (1811), *Pride and Prejudice* (1813), *Mansfield Park* (1814), *Emma* (1816), *Persuasion* (1818)
Auster, Paul	1947–	Newark, New Jersey	*The New York Trilogy* (1985-6), *Moon Palace* (1989), The *Music of Chance* (1990)
Bainbridge, Beryl	1934–	Liverpool	*The Dressmaker* (1973), *Injury Time* (1977), *Forever England* (1986)
Baldwin, James (Arthur)	1924–87	Harlem, New York City	*Go Tell It On the Mountain* (1953), *Another Country* (1962)
Ballard, J(ames) G(raham)	1930–	Shanghai, China	*The Drowned World* (1962), *The Terminal Beach* (1964), *Empire of the Sun* (1984)
Balzac, Honoré de	1799–1850	Tours	*La Comédie humaine* (1827– 47), *Illusions perdues* (1837– 43)
Banks, lain	1954–	Fife, Scotland	*The Wasp Factory*(1984), *The Bridge* (1986)
Barnes, Djuna	1892–1982	New York	*Nightwood* (1936)
Barnes, Julian	1946–	Leicester	*Flaubert's Parrot* (1984), *Staring at the Sun* (1986), *A History of the World in 10$^1/_2$ Chapters* (1989), *The Porcupine* (1992)
Barstow, Stan(ley)	1928–	Horbury, Yorkshire	*A Kind of Loving* (1961)
Bates, H(erbert) E(rnest)	1906–74	Northamptonshire	*The Two Sisters* (1926), *The Jacaranda Tree* (1949), *The Darling Buds of May* (1958), *Oh, To Be in England* (1963)
Bawden, Nina	1925–	London	*The Birds on the Trees* (1970), *Walking Naked* (1981), *The Ice House* (1983)
Beckett, Samuel (Barclay)	1906–89	Dublin	*Murphy* (1938), *Malone Dies* (1951), *The Unnameable* (1953)
Bedford, Sybille (née Schoenebach)	1911–	Charlottenburg, Germany	*A Legacy* (1956), *Jigsaw: An Unsentimental Education* (1989)
Bellow, Saul	1915–	Quebec, Canada	*Herzog* (1964), *Humboldt's Gift* (1974), *The Dean's December* (1982)
Bennett, Arnold	1867–1931	Hanley, Staffordshire	*Anna of the Five Towns* (1902), *Clayhanger* series (1910–18)
Binchy, Maeve	1940–	Dublin	*Light a Penny Candle* (1982), *Echoes* (1985), *Firefly Summer* (1987), *Circle of Friends* (1990)
Blackmore, R(ichard) D(oddridge)	1825–1900	Longworth, Oxfordshire	*Lorna Doone* (1969)
Böll, Heinrich	1917–	Cologne	*And Never Said a Solitary Word* (1953), *The Unguarded House* (1954), *The Bread of Our Early Years* (1955)
Borges, Jorge Luis	1899–1986	Buenos Aires	*Fictions* (1945), *El Aleph* (1949), *Labyrinths* (1953)
Bowen, Elizabeth (Dorothea Cole)	1899–1973	Dublin	*The Death of the Heart* (1938), *The Heat of the Day* (1949)
Bowles, Paul	1910–	New York City	*The Sheltering Sky* (1949)

Novelists (continued)

Name	*Dates*	*Place of birth*	*Selected works*
Boyd, William	1952–	Accra, Ghana	*A Good Man in Africa* (1982), *An Ice Cream War* (1983), *Brazzaville Beach* (1990)
Bradbury, Malcolm (Stanley)	1932–	Sheffield	*Eating People Is Wrong* (1959), *The History Man* (1975)
Bradbury, Ray	1920–	Waukegan, Illinois	*Fahrenheit 451* (1953), *Something Wicked This Way Comes* (1962)
Bradford, Barbara Taylor	1933–	Leeds	*A Woman of Substance* (1979), *Hold the Dream* (1985)
Bragg, Melvyn	1939–	Carlisle	*The Hired Man* (1969), *A Time To Dance* (1989), *The Maid of Buttermere* (1987), *A Time to Dance* (1989)
Brittain, Vera	1893–1970	Stoke-on-Trent	*Testament of Youth* (1938), *Testament of Friendship* (1940)
Brontë, Anne	1820–49	Thornton, Yorkshire	*Agnes Grey* (1847), *The Tenant of Wildfell Hall* (1848)
Brontë, Charlotte	1816–55	Thornton, Yorkshire	*Jane Eyre* (1847), *Shirley* (1849), *Villette* (1853)
Brontë, Emily	1818–48	Thornton, Yorkshire;	*Wuthering Heights* (1847)
Brookner, Anita	1938–	London	*Hotel du Lac* (1984), *Family and Friends* (1985), *Brief Lives* (1991)
Buchan, John	1875–1940	Scotland	*The Thirty-Nine Steps* (1915)
Buck, Pearl (née Sydenstricher)	1892–1973	Hillsborough, Virginia	*The Good Earth* (1913), *Pavillion of Women* (1946)
Bulgakov, Mikhail	1891–1940	Kiev	*The Master and Margarita* (1928-40), *The White Guard* (1925), *Heart of a Dog* (1925)
Bunyan, John	1628–88	Elstow, nr Bedford	*The Pilgrim's Progress* (1678, 1684)
Burgess, Anthony (John Anthony Burgess Wilson)	1917–	Manchester	*A Clockwork Orange* (1962), *Earthly Powers* (1980), *Kingdom of the Wicked* (1985), *Any Old Iron* (1989)
Burroughs, William S(eward)	1914–	St Louis, Missouri	*The Naked Lunch* (1959), *The Soft Machine* (1961), *The Wild Boys* (1971), *Exterminator!* (1974), *Cities of the Red Night* (1981)
Butler, Samuel	1835–1902	Langar Rectory, Nottinghamshire	*Erewhon* (1872), *The Way of All Flesh* (1903)
Byatt, A(ntonia) S(usan)	1936–	Sheffield	*The Shadow of a Sun* (1964), *The Virgin in the Garden* (1978), *Possession* (1989)
Caldwell, Erskine	1903–87	Georgia	*Tobacco Road* (1932), *God's Little Acre* (1933), *Journeyman* (1935)
Calvino, Italo	1923–87	Santiago de Las Vegas, Cuba	*Invisible Cities* (1972), *The Castle of Crossed Destinies* (1969), *If on a Winter's Night a Traveller* (1981)
Camus, Albert	1913–60	Mondovi, Algeria	*The Outsider* (1942), *The Plague* (1948), *The Fall* (1957)
Canetti, Elias	1905–	Russe, Bulgaria	*Auto da Fé* (1935), *Crowds and Power* (1960), *A Torch in my Ear* (1980)
Capote, Truman	1924–84	New Orleans	*Other Voices, Other Rooms* (1948), *Breakfast at Tiffany's* (1958), *In Cold Blood* (1966)
Carey, Peter	1943–	Bacchus Marsh, Victoria	*Bliss* (1981), *Illywhacker* (1985), *Oscar and Lucinda* (1988), *The Tax Inspector* (1991)
Carroll, Lewis (Charles Lutwidge Dodgson)	1832–98	Daresbury, Cheshire	*Alice's Adventures in Wonderland* (1865), *Through the Looking Glass and What Alice Found There* (1871), *The Hunting of the Snark* (1876)
Carter, Angela	1940–92	London	*The Magic Toyshop* (1967), *The Infernal Desire Machines of Dr Hoffman*, (1972), *Nights at the Circus* (1984), *Wise Children* (1991)
Cartland, (Mary) Barbara (Hamilton)	1901–	Birmingham	*The Husband Hunters* (1976), *Wings on My Heart* (1954), *The Castle Made for Love* (1985)
Cary, (Arthur) Joyce (Lunel)	1888–1957	Londonderry	*The Horse's Mouth* (1944)
Cather, Willa (Silbert)	1876–1947	Winchester, Virginia	*O Pioneers!* (1913), *My Antonia* (1918), *One of Ours* (1922), *The Professor's House* (1925), *My Mortal Enemy* (1926), *Death Comes for the Archbishop* (1927), *Sapphira and the Slave Girl* (1940)
Chandler, Raymond	1888–1959	Chicago	*The Big Sleep* (1939), *Farewell, My Lovely* (1940), *The High Window* (1942), *The Lady in the Lake* (1943), *The Long Goodbye* (1953)
Chatwin, Bruce	1940–1989		*In Patagonia* (1977), *On the Black Hill* (1982), *Utz* (1988)
Chesterton, G(ilbert) K(eith)	1874–1936	London	*The Innocence of Father Brown* (1911)

Name	*Dates*	*Place of birth*	*Selected works*
Christie, Dame Agatha (Mary Clarissa)	1890–1976	Torquay, Devon	*Murder on the Orient Express* (1934), *Death on the Nile* (1937), *Ten Little Niggers* (1939), *Curtain* (1975)
Clarke, Arthur C(harles)	1917–	Minehead, Somerset	*Childhood's End* (1953), *The Fountains of Paradise* (1979), *The Garden of Rama* (1991)
Cleland, John	1709–89	London	*Fanny Hill* (1748–9)
Coetzee, J(ohn) M(ichael)	1940–	Cape Town	*Life and Times of Michael K* (1983)
Collins, Wilkie	1824–89	London	*The Woman in White* (1860), *No Name* (1862), *Armadale* (1866), *The Moonstone* (1868)
Compton-Burnett, Ivy	1884–1969	Pinner, Middlesex	*A House and its Head* (1935), *A Family and a Fortune* (1939), *Manservant and Maidservant* (1947)
Conrad, Joseph (originally Jozef Teodor Konrad Nalecz Korzeniowski)	1857–1924	Berdichev, Ukraine	*Lord Jim* (1900), *Heart of Darkness* (1902), *Nostromo* (1904), *The Secret Agent* (1907), *Chance* (1914)
Cookson, Catherine (Ann)	1906–	Tyne Dock, County Durham	*Tilly Trotter* (1956), *The Glass Virgin* (1969)
Cooper, James Fenimore	1789–1851	Burlington, New Jersey	*The Pioneers* (1823), *The Last of the Mohicans* (1826)
Cooper, Jilly	1937–	Hornchurch, Essex	*Men and Supermen* (1972), *Class* (1979), *Riders* (1985), *Rivals* (1988), *Polo* (1990)
Crane, Stephen	1871–1900	Newark, New Jersey	*The Red Badge of Courage* (1895)
Davies, Robertson	1913–	Thamesville, Ontario	*Tempest Tost* (1951), *Leaven of Malice* (1952), *A Mixture of Frailties* (1958), *What's Bred In the Bone* (1986)
De Beauvoir, Simone	1908–86	Paris	*The Second Sex* ((1949), *Les Mandarins* (1954), *Memoirs of a Dutiful Daughter* (1959)
Defoe, Daniel	1660–1731	Stoke Newington, London	*Robinson Crusoe* (1719), *Moll Flanders* (1722), *A Journal of the Plague Year* (1722)
Deighton, Len (Leonard Cyril)	1929–	London	*The Ipcress File* (1962), *Funeral in Berlin* (1964), *Spy Hook* (1988), *Spy Line* (1989), *Spy Sinker* (1990)
DeLillo, Don	1936–	New York City	*End Zone* (1972), *Ratner's Star* (1976), *The Names* (1982), *White Noise* (1985)
De Quincey, Thomas	1785–1859	Manchester	*Confessions of an English Opium Eater* (1822)
Dibdin, Michael	1947–		*Dirty Tricks* (1991), *Cabal* (1992), *The Dying of the Light* (1993)
Dickens, Charles	1812–70	Landport, Portsmouth	*Oliver Twist* (1837–9), *David Copperfield* (1849–50), *Bleak House* (1852–3), *Great Expectations* (1860–1)
Dinesen, Isak (Karen Blixen)	1885–1962	Rungsted, Denmark	*Seven Gothic Tales* (1934), *Out of Africa* (1937)
Doctorow, E(dgar) L(awrence)	1931–	New York City	*Ragtime* (1975)
Dos Passos, John (Roderigo)	1896–1970	Chicago	*Manhattan Transfer* (1925), *USA* (1930)
Dostoevsky, Fyodor Mikhailovich	1821–81	Moscow	*Crime and Punishment* (1866), *The Idiot* (1868–9) *The Brothers Karamazov* (1880)
Doyle, Sir Arthur Conan	1859–1930	Edinburgh	*The Memoirs of Sherlock Holmes* (1894), *The Hound of the Baskervilles* (1902), *The Lost World* (1912)
Drabble, Margaret	1939–	Sheffield	*The Millstone* (1965), *Jerusalem the Golden* (1967), *The Ice Age* (1977), *A Natural Curiosity* (1989)
Dreiser, Theodore	1871–1945	Terre Haute, Indiana	*Sister Carrie* (1900), *Jennie Gerhardt* (1911)
Du Maurier, Dame Daphne	1907–89	London	*Rebecca* (1938), *My Cousin Rachel* (1951)
Durrell, Gerald Malcolm	1925–90	Jamshedpur, India	*The Overloaded Ark* (1953), *My Family and Other Animals* (1956)
Durrell, Lawrence (George)	1912–90	Julundur, India	*Prospero's Cell* (1945), *'Alexandria Quartet'* (1957–60)
Eco, Umberto	1932–	Alessandria, Piedmont	*The Name of the Rose* (1980), *Foucault's Pendulum* (1989)
Eliot, George (originally Mary Ann, later Marian Evans)	1819–80	Arbury, Warwickshire	*Adam Bede* (1858), *The Mill on the Floss* (1860), *Silas Marner* (1861), *Middlemarch* (1871-2), *Daniel Deronda* (1874-6)
Ellis, Alice Thomas (Anna Margaret Haycraft, née Lindholm)	1932–	Liverpool	*The Sin Eater* (1977), *The 27th Kingdom* (1982), *The Inn at the Edge of the World* (1990)
Faulkner, William Harrison	1897–1962	Oxford, Mississippi	*Sartoris* (1929), *The Sound and the Fury* (1929), *Absalom, Absalom!* (1936)

Novelists (continued)

Name	*Dates*	*Place of birth*	*Selected works*
Fielding, Henry	1707–54	Sharpham Park, nr Glastonbury	*Joseph Andrews* (1742), *Tom Jones* (1749)
Fitzgerald, F(rancis) Scott (Key)	1896–1940	St Paul, Minnesota	*The Great Gatsby* (1925), *Tender is the Night* (1934)
Fitzgerald, Penelope (Mary) (née Knox)	1916–	Lincoln	*The Bookshop* (1978), *Offshore* (1979), *The Gate of Angels* (1990)
Flaubert, Gustave	1821–80	Rouen	*Madame Bovary* (1857), *Salammbo* (1862), *Sentimental Education* (1869), *Bouvard et Pécuchet* (1881)
Fleming, lan	1908–64	Lancaster	*Casino Royale* (1953), *From Russia with Love* (1957), *Dr No* (1958), *Goldfinger* (1959), *The Man with the Golden Gun* (1965)
Ford, Ford Madox (Ford Hermann Hueffer)	1873–1939	Merton, Surrey	*The Fifth Queen* (1906), *The Good Soldier* (1915), *Parade 's End* (1924–8)
Forester, C(ecil) S(cott)	1899–1966	Cairo	*The Happy Return* (1937), *The African Queen* (1935)
Forster, E(dward) M(organ)	1879–1970	London	*A Room with a View* (1908), *Howards End* (1910), *A Passage to India* (1922–4), *Maurice* (1913, published 1971)
Forsyth, Frederick	1938–	Ashford, Kent	*The Day of the Jackal* (1971), *The Odessa File* (1972), *The Fourth Protocol* (1984)
Fowles, John (Robert)	1926–	Leigh-on-Sea	*The Collector* (1963), *The Magus* (1965, revised 1977), *The French Lieutenant's Woman* (1969)
France, Anatole (Jacques-Anatole-François Thibault)	1844–1922	Paris	*Le Crime de Sylvestre Bonnard* (1881), *Les Dieux ont Soif* (1912)
Fraser, Antonia (Lady Antonia Pinter)	1932–	London	*Mary Queen of Scots* (1969), *Quiet as a Nun* (1977), *A Splash of Red* (1981)
French, Marilyn	1929–	New York City	*The Women's Room* (1977), *The Bleeding Heart* (1980), *Her Mother's Daughter* (1987)
Gaddis, William	1922–	New York City	*JR* (1975), *Carpenter's Gothic* (1985)
Galsworthy, John	1867-1933	Coombe, Surrey	*The Forsyte Saga* (1906-31)
García Márquez, Gabriel	1928–	Aracataca, Columbia	*One Hundred Years of Solitude* (1970), *Chronicle of a Death Foretold* (1982), *Love in the Time of Cholera* (1985), *The General in his Labyrinth* (1989)
Gaskell, Mrs Elizabeth	1810–65	London	*Cranford* (1853), *North and South* (1855)
Genet, Jean	1910–86	Paris	*Our Lady of the Flowers* (1944), *The Miracle of the Rose* (1946)
Gibbons, Stella (Dorothea)	1902–89	London	*Cold Comfort Farm* (1933)
Gide, André (Paul Guillaume)	1860–1951	Paris	*The Immoralist* (1902), *Strait is the Gate* (1909), *The Vatican Cellars* (1914), *The Pastoral Symphony* (1919), *The Counterfeiters* (1925)
Gilchrist, Ellen	1935–		*The Annunciation* (1983), *I Cannot Get You Close Enough* (1990), *Net of Jewels* (1993)
Goethe, Johann Wolfgang von	1749–1832	Frankfurt-am-Main	*The Sorrows of Young Werther* (1774), *Wilhelm Meister's Apprenticeship* (1796), *Elective Affinities* (1809)
Gogol, Nikolai Vasilievich	1809–52	Sorochinstsi, Poltava	*The Overcoat* (1835), *Diary of a Madman* (1835), *Dead Souls* (1842), *The Odd Women* (1893)
Golding, William (Gerald)	1911–93	St Columb Minor, Cornwall	*Lord of the Flies* (1954), *The Spire* (1964), *Rites of Passage* (1980), *The Paper Men* (1984), *Close Quarters* (1987), *Fire Down Below* (1989)
Goldsmith, Oliver	1728–74	Pallasmore, County Longford	*The Vicar of Wakefield* (1766)
Gordimer, Nadine	1923–	Springs, Transvaal	*Occasion for Loving* (1963), *A Guest of Honour* (1970), *The Conservationist* (1974), *A Sport of Nature* (1987)
Gorky, Maxim (Aleksei Maksimovich Peshkov)	1868–1936	Nizhni Novgorod (New Gorky)	*The Mother* (1906–7), *Childhood* (1913), *The Life of Klim Samgin* (1925–36)
Grahame, Kenneth	1859–1932	Edinburgh	*The Wind in the Willows* (1908)
Grass, Günter (Wilhelm)	1927–	Danzig	*The Tin Drum* (1959), *Cat and Mouse* (1961), *The Meeting at Telgte* (1979)
Graves, Robert (von Ranke)	1895–1985	Wimbledon	*No Decency Left* (1932), *The Real David Copperfield* (1933), *I, Claudius* (1934)
Greene, (Henry) Graham	1904–91	Berkhamstead, Hertfordshire	*Brighton Rock* (1938), *The Power and the Glory* (1940), *The Third Man* (1950), *The Honorary Consul* (1973)
Haggard, Sir Henry Rider	1856–1925	Norfolk	*King Solomon's Mines* (1885), *She: A History of Adventure* (1887)

Name	Dates	Place of birth	Selected works
Hammett, (Samuel) Dashiell	1894–1961	Maryland	*The Maltese Falcon* (1930), *The Thin Man* (1934)
Hamsun, Knut	1859–1952	Oudsrandsdal, Valley, Norway	*Hunger* (1890), *Mysteries* (1892), *Pan* (1894), *Victoria* (1898), *Growth of the Soil* (1917)
Hardy, Thomas	1840–1928	Higher Bockhampton, Dorset	*Far from the Madding Crowd* (1874), *The Mayor of Casterbridge* (1886), *Tess of the D'Urbervilles* (1891), *Jude the Obscure* (1895)
Hartley, L(eslie) P(oles)	1895–1972	Whittlesey, Cambridgeshire	*The Go-Between* (1953)
Heller, Joseph	1923–	Brooklyn, New York	*Catch 22* (1961), *Something Happened* (1974), *Picture This* (1988)
Hemingway Ernest (Millar)	1899–1961	Chicago, Illinois	*A Farewell to Arms* (1929), *For Whom the Bell Tolls* (1940), *The Old Man and the Sea* (1952)
Hesse, Herman	1877–1962	Calw, Württemberg	*Siddhartha* (1922), *Steppenwolf* (1927), *The Glass Bead Game* (1943)
Highsmith, Patricia	1921–	Fort Worth	*Strangers on a Train* (1950), *The Talented Mr Ripley* (1955), *Ripley Under Ground* (1971), *Ripley Under Water* (1991)
Hoban, Russell (Conwell)	1925–	Lansdale, Pennsylvania	*Turtle Diary* (1975), *Riddley Walker* (1980), *Pilgermann* (1983)
Holt, Victoria (Eleanor Alice Burford Hibbert) also writes as Philippa Carr, Jean Plaidy	1906–93	London	*Catherine de 'Medici* (1969 – as JP), *Will You Love Me in September* (1981 – as PC), *The Captive* (1989 – as VH)
Hugo,Victor (Marie)	1802–85	Besançon	*Notre Dame de Paris* (1831), *Les Miserables* (1862)
Hulme, Keri	1947–	Christchurch, New Zealand	*The Bone People* (1983), *Lost Possessions* (1985)
Hurston, Zora Neale	1903–60	Eatonville, Florida	*Their Eyes Were Watching God* (1937), *Moses: Man of the Mountain* (1939)
Huxley, Aldous (Leonard)	1894–1963	Godalming, Surrey	*Brave New World* (1932), *Eyeless in Gaza* (1936), *Island* (1962)
Irving, John	1942–	Exeter, New Hampshire	*The World According to Garp* (1978), *The Hotel New Hampshire* (1981), *A Prayer for Owen Meany* (1989)
Isherwood, Christopher (William Bradshaw)	1904–	Disley, Cheshire	*Mr Norris Changes Trains* (1935), *Goodbye to Berlin* (1939), *Down There on a Visit* (1962)
Ishiguro, Kazuo	1954–	Japan	*An Artist of the Floating World* (1986), *The Remains of the Day* (1989)
Jacobson, Dan	1929–	Johannesburg	*A Dance in the Sun* (1950), *Evidence of Love* (1960), *The Rape of Tamar* (1970)
James, Henry	1843–1916	New York	*The Portrait of a Lady* (1881), *The Bostonians* (1886), *The Turn of the Screw* (1898), *The Awkward Age* (1899), *The Ambassadors* (1903), *The Golden Bowl* (1904)
Jerome, Jerome K(lapka)	1859–1927	Walsall, Staffordshire	*Three Men in a Boat* (1889)
Jhabvala, Ruth Prawer	1927–	Cologne, Germany	*Heat and Dust* (1975), *In Search of Love and Beauty* (1983)
Johnston, Jennifer	1930–	Dublin	*The Captains and the Kings* (1972), *How Many Miles to Babylon* (1974), *The Invisible Worm* (1991)
Joyce, James (Augustine Aloysius)	1882–1941	Dublin	*Dubliners* (1914), *A Portrait of the Artist as a Young Man* (1914-15), *Ulysses* (1922), *Finnegan's Wake* (1939)
Kafka, Franz	1883–1924	Prague	*The Metamorphosis* (1916), *The Trial* (1925), *The Castle* (1926), *America* (1927)
Kazantzakis, Nikos	1883–1957	Heraklion, Crete	*Zorba The Greek* (1946)
Keillor, Garrison	1942–	Anoka, Minnesota	*Lake Wobegone Days* (1983), *Leaving Home* (1987), *WLT: A Radio Romance* (1992)
Kelman, James	1946–	Glasgow	*The Busconductor Hines* (1984), *A Chancer* (1985), *Greyhound for Breakfast* (1987), *A Disaffection* (1989)
Keneally, Thomas	1935–	Sydney	*A Dutiful Daughter* (1971), *Schindler's Ark* (1982)
Kerouac, Jack	1922–69	Lowell, Massachusetts	*On The Road* (1957)
Kesey, Ken	1935–	La Junta, Colorado	*One Flew Over The Cuckoo's Nest* (1962)
King, Stephen	1947–	Portland, Maine	*Carrie* (1974), *The Shining* (1977), *Christine* (1983), *Misery* (1987)
Kingsley, Charles	1819–75	Holne, Decon	*Westward Ho! (1855)*, (1855), *The Heroes* (1856), *The Water Babies* (1863)
Kipling, Rudyard	1865–1936	Bombay	*The Jungle Book* (1894), *Kim* (1901), *Just So Stories* (1902)
Koestler, Arthur	1905–83	Budapest	*Darkness at Noon* (1940), *Arrival and Departure* (1943)
Kundera, Milan	1929–	Brno	*Life is Elsewhere* (1973), *The Book of Laughter and Forgetting* (1979), *The Unbearable Lightness of Being* (1984), *Immortality* (1991)

Novelists (continued)

Name	*Dates*	*Place of birth*	*Selected works*
Laclos, Pierre Choderlos de	1741–1803	Amiens	*Les Liaisons Dangereuses* (1782)
La Fayette, Marie Madeleine Pioche de Lavergne, Comtesse de	1634–93	Paris	*Zaide* (1670), *La Princesse de Clèves* (1678)
Lampedusa, Giuseppe Tomasi di	1896–1957	Palermo, Sicily	*The Leopard* (1958)
Lawrence, D(avid) H(erbert)	1885–1930	Eastwood, Nottinghamshire	*Sons and Lovers* (1913), *The Rainbow* (1915), *Women in Love* (1920), *Lady Chatterley's Lover* (1928)
Le Carré, John (David John Moore Cornwell)	1931–	Poole, Dorset	*Tinker, Tailor, Soldier, Spy* (1974), *Smiley's People* (1980), *The Little Drummer Girl* (1983), *The Russia House* (1989)
Lee, Harper	1926–	Monroeville, Alabama	*To Kill A Mocking Bird* (1960)
Lee, Laurie	1914–	Slad, Gloucestershire	*Cider With Rosie* (1959), *As I Walked Out One Midsummer Morning* (1969)
Lehmann, Rosamond (Nina)	1903–90	London	*Dusty Answer* (1927), *Invitation To Waltz* (1932), *The Ballad and the Source* (1944), *The Echoing Grove* (1953)
Leroux, Gaston	1868–1927	France	*The Phantom of the Opera* (1911)
Lessing, Doris	1919–	Kermanshah, Iran	*The Grass is Singing* (1950), *The Golden Notebook* (1962), *Canopus in Argus Archives* (1979-83), *The Fifth Child* (1988)
Levi, Primo	1919–87	Turin	*If This is a Man* (1947), *The Periodic Table* (1984)
Lewis, (Harry) Sinclair	1885–1951	Sauk Center, Minnesota	*Main Street* (1920), *Babbitt* (1922), *Martin Arrowsmith* (1925), *Elmer Gantry* (1927)
Lively, Penelope (Margaret)	1933–	Cairo, Egypt	*The Road to Lichfield* (1977), *Moon Tiger* (1987), *City of the Mind* (1991)
Llosa, Mario Vargas	1936–	Arequipa, Peru	*The City of Dogs* (1964), *Aunt Julia and the Scriptwriter* (1977)
Lodge, David	1935–	London	*Changing Places* (1975), *Small World* (1984), *Nice Work* (1988)
London, Jack (Griffith)	1876–1916	San Francisco	*The Call of the Wild* (1903), *White Fang* (1907), *Martin Eden* (1909)
Lurie, Alison	1926–	Chicago	*Love and Friendship* (1962), *The War Between the Tates* (1974), *The Truth About Lorin Jones* (1988)
Macauley, Rose	1881–1958	Rugby, Warwickshire	*Dangerous Ages* (1921), *The Towers of Trebizond* (1956)
Mailer, Norman	1923–	Long Beach, New Jersey	*The Naked and the Dead* (1949), *Barbary Shore* (1951), *An American Dream* (1965), *The Executioner's Song* (1979)
Malraux, André	1901–76	Paris	*La Condition Humaine* (1933)
Mann, Thomas	1875–1955	Lübeck	*Death in Venice* (1912), *The Magic Mountain* (1924), *Dr Faustus* (1947)
Mansfield, Katherine (Katherine Mansfield Beauchamp)	1888–1923	Wellington, New Zealand	*Prelude* (1918), *Bliss* (1920), *The Garden Party* (1922)
Mars-Jones, Adam	1954–	London	*Lantern Lecture* (1981), *The Darker Proof* (1987)
Maugham, Somerset	1874–1965	Paris	*Of Human Bondage* (1915), *The Moon and Sixpence* (1919), *The Razor's Edge* (1945)
Maupassant, Guy de	1850-93	Miromesnil	*Bel-ami* (1885)
Maupin, Armistead	1944–	Washington D.C.	*Tales of the City* (1978), *More Tales of the City* (1980), *Further Tales of the City* (1982), *Significant Others* (1988), *Sure of You* (1990), *Maybe The Moon* (1992)
Mauriac, François	1885–1970	Bordeaux	*Le Baiser aux Lepreux* (1922), *Thérèse Desqueyroux* (1927)
McCullers, Carson	1917–67	Columbus, Georgia	*The Heart is a Lonely Hunter* (1940), *The Member of the Wedding* (1940), *The Ballad of the Sad Café* (1951)
McEwan, Ian (Russell)	1948–	Aldershot, Hampshire	*First Love, Last Rites* (1975), *The Cement Garden* (1978), *The Child in Time* (1987), *The Innocent* (1990), *Black Dogs* (1992)
McGahern, John	1934–	Dublin	*The Leavetaking* (1975), *The Pornographer* (1979), *Amongst Women* (1990)
Melville, Hermann	1819–91	New York	*Typee* (1846), *Omoo* (1847), *Moby Dick* (1851)
Meredith, George	1828–1909	Portsmouth	*The Egoist* (1879), *Diana of the Crossways* (1883)
Miller, Henry Valentine	1891–1980	New York	*Tropic of Cancer* (1934), *Tropic of Capricorn* (1938)
Mishima, Yukio (Hiraoka Kimitake)	1925–70	Tokyo	*Confessions of a Mask* (1960), *The Temple of the Golden Pavillion* (1959), *The Sea of Fertility* (1969–71)

Name	Dates	Place of birth	Selected works
Mitchell, Margaret	1900–49	Atlanta, Georgia	*Gone with the Wind* (1936)
Mitford, Nancy	1904–73	London	*Love in a Cold Climate* (1949), *Don't Tell Alfred* (1960)
Mo, Timothy	1950–	Hong Kong	*The Monkey King* (1978), *Sour Sweet* (1982), *An Insular Possession* (1986)
Moore, Brian	1921–	Belfast	*Judith Hearne* (1955)
Mosley, Nicholas	1923–	London	*Spaces of the Dark* (1951), *Accident* (1965), *Hopeful Monsters* (1991)
Murdoch, Iris	1919–	Dublin	*The Bell* (1958), *The Sea,The Sea* (1978), *The Philosopher's Pupil* (1983), *The Book and the Brotherhood* (1987)
Nabokov, Vladimir	1899–1977	St Petersburg	*Lolita* (1955)
Naipaul, V(idiadhar) S(urajprasad)	1932–	Trinidad	*A House for Mr Biswas* (1961), *In a Free State* (1971), *A Bend in the River* (1979)
Nesbit, E(dith)	1858–1924	London	*Five Children and It* (1902), *The Railway Children* (1906)
Oates, Joyce Carol	1938–	New York	*A Garden of Earthly Delights* (1967), *Them* (1969), *Wonderland* (1971)
O'Brien, Edna	1932–	Tuamgranay, County Clare	*The Country Girls* (1960), *August is a Wicked Month* (1964), *A Pagan Place* (1971)
Okri, Ben	1959–	Minna, Nigeria	*The Famished Road* (1991), *Songs of Enchantment* (1993)
Orczy, Baroness (Mrs Montague Barstow)	1865–1947	Tarnaörs, Hungary	*The Scarlet Pimpernel* (1905)
Orwell, George (Eric Arthur Blair)	1903–50	Bengal	*Down and Out in Paris and London* (1933), *Animal Farm* (1945), *Nineteen Eighty-Four* (1949)
Pasternak, Boris	1890–1960	Moscow	*Doctor Zhivago* (1957)
Paton, Allan	1903–88	Pietermaritzburg, Natal	*Cry, the Beloved Country* (1948)
Peacock, Thomas Love	1785–1866	Weymouth, Dorset	*Headlong Hall* (1816), *Nightmare Abbey* (1818), *Crotchet Castle* (1883)
Peake, Mervyn (Laurence)	1911–68	Kuling, China	*Titus Groan* (1946), *Gormenghast* (1950), *Titus Alone* (1959)
Plath, Sylvia	1932–63	Boston	*The Bell Jar* (1963)
Powell, Anthony	1905–	London	*A Dance to the Music of Time* (1951–75), *The Fisher King* (1986)
Priestley, J(ohn) B(oyntron)	1894–1984	Bradford	*The Good Companions* (1929), *Angel Pavement* (1930)
Proust, Marcel	1871–1922	Paris	*Remembrance of Things Past* (1913–27)
Pushkin, Alexander (Sergeyevich)	1799–1837	Moscow	*The Prisoner of the Caucasus* (1821), *Eugene Onegin* (1828), *Boris Gudunov* (1831)
Pynchon, Thomas	1937–	Long Island	*V* (1963), *The Crying of Lot 49* (1966), *Gravity's Rainbow* (1973), *Vineland* (1990)
Radcliffe, Anne	1764–1823	London	*The Mysteries of Udolpho* (1794), *The Italian* (1797)
Rendell, Ruth	1930–	London	*A Judgement in Stone* (1977), *The Killing Doll* (1980), *Heartstones* (1987)
Rhys, Jean (Ella Gwendoline Rhys Williams)	1894–1979	Dominica, West Indies	*Wide Sargasso Sea* (1966), *Tigers Are Better Looking* (1968)
Richardson, Samuel	1689–1761	nr Derby	*Pamela* (1740), *Clarissa* (1747-8), *Sir Charles Grandison* (1753–4)
Richler, Mordecai	1931–	Montreal	*The Apprenticeship of Duddy Kravitz* (1959), *Solomon Gursky Was Here* (1989)
Roth, Philip	1933–	Newark, New Jersey	*Portnoy's Complaint* (1969), *My Life As a Man* (1974), *The Counterlife* (1986)
Rubens, Bernice	1928–	Cardiff	*The Elected Member* (1970), *Our Father* (1987), *Kingdom Come* (1990)
Rushdie, Salman	1947–	Bombay	*Midnight's Children* (1981), *Shame* (1983), *The Satanic Verses* (1988), *Haroun and the Sea of Stories* (1990)
Sackville-West, Vita	1892–1962	Knole, Kent	*The Edwardians* (1930), *All Passion Spent* (1931), *Signposts in the Sea* (1961)
Sade, Donatien Alphonse François, Comte de (known as Marquis)	1740–1814	Paris	*Justine* (1791), *La Philosphie dans le Boudoir* (1793), *Juliette* (1798), *Les Crimes de L'Amour* (1800)
Salinger, J(erome) D(avid)	1919–	New York	*The Catcher in the Rye* (1951), *Franny and Zooey* (1961)
Sand, Georges (Amandine Aurore Lucille Dupin)	1804–76	Paris	*Lelia* (1833), *La Petite Fadette* (1849)

Novelists (continued)

Name	*Dates*	*Place of birth*	*Selected works*
Sartre, Jean-Paul	1905–80	Paris	*Nausea* (1949), *The Roads to Freedeom* (1945–7)
Scott, Paul (Mark)	1920–78	London	*The Jewel in the Crown* (1966), *Staying On* (1977)
Scott, Sir Walter	1771–1832	Edinburgh	*The Lady of the Lake* (1810), *Waverley* (1814), *Rob Roy* (1817), *The Bride of Lammermoor* (1819)
Seth, Vikram	1952–	Calcutta	*From Heaven Lake* (1983), *The Golden Gate* (1986), *A Suitable Boy* (1993)
Sharpe, Tom (Thomas Ridley)	1928–	London	*Blott on the Landscape* (1975), *Porterhouse Blue* (1978), *Wilt* (1976)
Shelley, Mary (Wollstonecroft)	1797–1851	London	*Frankenstein* (1818)
Schreiner, Olive	1855–1920	Wittebergen, S Africa	*The Story of an African Farm* (1883)
Shute, Neville (Neville Shute Norway)	1899–1960	Ealing	*A Town Like Alice* (1950)
Sillitoe, Alan	1928–	Nottingham	*Saturday Night, Sunday Morning* (1958), *The Loneliness of the Long Distance Runner* (1959)
Sinclair, Upton	1878–1968	Baltimore	*The Jungle* (1906), *Dragon's Teeth* (1942)
Singer, Isaac Bashevis	1904–91	Radzymin, Poland	*The Family Moskat* (1950), *Satan in Goray* (1955), *The Slave* (1962)
Smollett, Tobias	1721–71	Cardross, Dunbartonshire	*The Adventures of Roderick Random* (1748), *The Adventures of Peregrine Pickle* (1751)
Solzhenitsyn, Alexander Isayevich	1918–	Kislovodsk, Caucasus	*One Day in the Life of Ivan Denisovich* (1962), *The First Circle* (1969), *The Gulag Archipelago* (1973–5)
Spark, Muriel	1918–	Edinburgh	*The Ballad of Peckham Rye* (1960), *The Prime of Miss Jean Brodie* (1962), *The Girls of Slender Means* (1963)
Stein, Gertrude	1874–1946	Allegheny, Pennsylvania	*Three Lives* (1900), *Tender Buttons* (1914)
Steinbeck, John Ernest	1902–68	Salinas, California	*Of Mice and Men* (1937), *The Grapes of Wrath* (1939), *East of Eden* (1952)
Stendhal (Henri Marie Beyle)	1788–1842	Grenoble	*The Red and The Black* (1830), *The Charterhouse of Parma* (1839)
Sterne, Lawrence	1713–68	Clonmel, Tipperary	*Tristram Shandy* (1759-67), *A Sentimental Journey* (1768)
Stevenson, Robert Louis (Balfour)	1850–94	Edinburgh	*Treasure Island* (1883), *Kidnapped* (1886), *The Strange Case of Dr Jekyll and Mr Hyde* (1886)
Stoker, Bram	1847–1912	Dublin	*Dracula* (1897)
Stowe, Harriet Beecher	1811–96	Litchfield, Connecticut	*Uncle Tom's Cabin* (1852)
Süskind, Patrick	1949–		*Perfume* (1985)
Swift, Graham	1949–	London	*The Sweet Shop Owner* (1980), *Waterland* (1984)
Swift, Jonathan	1667–1745	Dublin	*Gulliver's Travels* (1726)
Thackery, William Makepeace	1811–63	Calcutta	*Vanity Fair* (1847-8), *Pendennis* (1848-50), *The History of Henry Esmond* (1852)
Theroux, Paul	1941–	Medford, Massachusetts	*The Mosquito Coast* (1981), *Doctor Slaughter* (1984), *My Secret History* (1989)
Thomas, D(onald) M(ichael)	1935–	Redruth, Cornwall	*The White Hotel* (1981), *Ararat* (1983), *Lying Together* (1990)
Tolkien, J(ohn) R(onald) R(euel)	1892–1973	Bloemfontein, S Africa	*The Hobbit* (1937), *The Lord of the Rings* (1954–5)
Tolkin, Michael			*The Player* (1988), *Among the Dead* (1993)
Tolstoy, Count Leo Nikolayevich	1828–1910	Yasnaya Polyana, Central Russia	*War and Peace* (1863-9), *Anna Karenina* (1873-7)
Toole, John Kennedy	1937–69	New Orleans	*A Confederacy of Dunces* (1980), *The Neon Bible* (1989)
Townsend, Sue	1946–	Leicester	*The Secret Diary of Adrian Mole* (1982), *The Queen and I* (1992)
Tremain, Rose	1943–	London	*The Cupboard* (1981), *Restoration* (1989), *Sacred Country* (1992)
Trollope, Anthony	1815–82	London	*Barchester Towers* (1857), *The Way We Live Now* (1875)
Turgenev, Ivan (Sergeyevich)	1818–83	Orel province, Russia	*Fathers and Sons* (1862)
Tutola, Amos	1920–	Abeokuta, Nigeria	*The Palm-Wine Drinkard* (1952)
Twain, Mark (Samuel Longhorn Clemens)	1835–1910	Florida, Missouri	*The Adventures of Tom Sawyer* (1876), *The Prince and the Pauper* (1882), *The Adventures of Huckleberry Finn* (1884), *A Connecticut Yankee in King Arthur's Court* (1889)
Tyler, Anne	1941–	Minneapolis	*The Accidental Tourist* (1985), *Breathing Lessons* (1989), *Saint Maybe* (1991)

Name	*Dates*	*Place of birth*	*Selected works*
Updike, John (Hoyer)	1932–	Shillington, Pennsylvania	*Rabbit, Run* (1960), *The Centaur* (1963), *Couples* (1968), *Rabbit Redux* (1971), *Roger's Version* (1986)
Van der Post, Sir Laurence	1906–	Philippolis, S Africa	*Flamingo Feather* (1955), *Journey into Russia* (1964), *A Far Off Place* (1974)
Verne, Jules	1828–1905	Nantes	*Voyage to the Centre of the Earth* (1864), *Twenty Thousand Leagues Under the Sea* (1870)
Vidal, Gore (Eugene Luther Vidal, Jr)	1925–	West Point, New York	*The Season of Comfort* (1949), *Myra Beckenridge* (1968), *Kalki* (1978)
Vonnegut, Kurt	1922–	Indianapolis, Indiana	*Cat's Cradle* (1963), *Slaughterhouse-Five* (1969), *Hocus Pocus* (1990)
Walker, Alice	1944–	Eatonville, Georgia	*The Colour Purple* (1983)
Warner, Marina	1946–	London	*In A Dark Wood* (1977), *The Skating Party* (1982), *The Lost Father* (1988)
Warner, Rex	1905–86	Birmingham	*The Wild Goose Chase* (1937), *The Professor* (1938), *The Aerodrome* (1941)
Waugh, Evelyn (Arthur St John)	1903–66	Hampstead	*Decline and Fall* (1928), *A Handful of Dust* (1934), *Brideshead Revisited* (1945)
Weldon, Fay	1933–	Alvechurch, Worcestershire	*Down Among Women* (1971), *Female Friends* (1975), *Life and Loves of a She-Devil* (1983)
Wells, H(erbert) G(eorge)	1866–1946	Bromley, Kent	*The Time Machine* (1895), *The Invisible Man* (1897), *The War of the Worlds* (1898), *The History of Mr Polly* (1910)
Welty, Eudora	1909–	Jackson, Mississippi	*A Curtain of Green* (1941), *The Golden Apples* (1949), *The Ponder Heart* (1954), *The Optimist's Daughter* (1972)
Wesley, Mary	1912–	Englefield Green, Berkshire	*The Camomile Lawn* (1984), *A Sensible Life* (1990)
Wharton, Edith	1862–1937	New York	*The House of Mirth* (1905), *Ethan Frome* (1911), *The Age of Innocence* (1920)
White, Antonia (Eirene Adeline Botting)	1899–1980	London	*Frost in May* (1933)
White, Edmund	1940–	U.S.	*A Boy's Own Story* (1982), *The Beautiful Room is Empty* (1988)
White, Patrick (Victor Martindale)	1912–	London	*Voss* (1957), *The Vivisector* (1970), *A Fringe of Leaves* (1976)
Wilde, Oscar	1854–1900	Dublin	*The Picture of Dorian Gray* (1895)
Wilder, Thornton (Niven)	1897–1976	Madison, Wisconsin	*The Bridge On San Luis Rey* (1927), *The Woman of Andros* (1930), *Heaven's My Destination* (1935)
Wilson, A(ndrew) N(orman)	1950–	London	*Kindly Light* (1979), *Wise Virgin* (1982), *Daughters of Albion* (1991)
Wilson, Sir Angus (Frank Johnstone)	1913–91	Bexhill, Sussex	*Anglo-Saxon Attitudes* (1956), *The Old Men At The Zoo* (1961)
Winterson, Jeanette	1959–	Lancashire	*Oranges Are Not The Only Fruit* (1987), *The Passion* (1987), *Sexing The Cherry* (1989), *Written on the Body* (1992)
Wodehouse, P(elham) G(renville)	1881–1975	Guildford, Surrey	*My Man Jeeves* (1919), *The Inimitable Jeeves* (1923), *Carry On, Jeeves* (1925)
Wolfe, Tom (Thomas Kennerley)	1931–	Richmond, Virginia	*The Right Stuff* (1979), *The Bonfire of the Vanities* (1988)
Woolf, Virginia	1882–1941	London	*Mrs Dalloway* (1925), *To The Lighthouse* (1927), *Orlando* (1928), *A Room of One's Own* (1929), *The Waves* (1931)
Wright, Richard	1908–60	Natchez, Mississippi	*Native Son* (1940)
Wyndham, John (John Wyndham Parkes Lucas Benon Hariss)	1903–69	Knowle, Warwickshire	*The Day of the Triffids* (1955), *The Midwich Cuckoos* (1957)
Zola, Emile	1840–1902	Paris	*Thérèse Raquin* (1867), *Les Rougon-Macquart* (1871-93), *Germinal* (1885)

Booker Prize (UK)

1971	V S Naipaul *In a Free State*
1972	John Berger *G*
1973	J G Farrell *The Siege of Krishnapur*
1974	Nadine Gordimer *The Conservationist*
	Stanley Middleton *Holiday*
1975	Ruth Prawer Jhabvala *Heat and Dust*
1976	David Storey *Saville*
1977	Paul Scott *Staying On*
1978	Iris Murdoch *The Sea, The Sea*
1979	Penelope Fitzgerald *Offshore*
1980	William Golding *Rites of Passage*
1981	Salman Rushdie *Midnight's Children*
1982	Thomas Keneally *Schindler's Ark*
1983	J M Coetzee *Life and Times of Michael K*
1984	Anita Brookner *Hotel du Lac*
1985	Keri Hulme *The Bone People*
1986	Kingsley Amis *The Old Devils*
1987	Penelope Lively *Moon Tiger*
1988	Peter Carey *Oscar and Lucinda*
1989	Kazuo Ishiguro *The Remains of the Day*
1990	A S Byatt *Possession*
1991	Ben Okri *The Famished Road*
1992	Barry Unsworth *Sacred Hunger*
	Michael Ondaatje *The English Patient*

Nobel Prize in literature

1901	René François Armand Sully-Prudhomme
1902	Theodor Mommsen
1903	Bjørnsterne Martinius Bjørnson
1904	Frédéric Mistral
	José Echegaray y Eizaguirre
1905	Henryk Sienkiewicz
1906	Giosuè Carducci
1907	Rudyard Kipling
1908	Rudolf Christoph Eucken
1909	Selma Ottiliana Lovisa Lagerlöf
1910	Paul Johann von Heyse
1911	Count Maurice Maeterlinck
1912	Gerhart Hauptmann
1913	Rabindranath Tagore
1914	*No award*
1915	Romain Rolland
1916	(Karl Gustav) Verner von Heidenstam
1917	Karl Gjellerup
	Henrik Pontoppidan
1918	*No award*
1919	Carl Friedrich Georg Spitteler
1920	Knut Hamsun
1921	Anatole France
1922	Jacinto Benavente
1923	William Butler Yeats
1924	Władysław Stanisław Reymont
1925	George Bernard Shaw
1926	Grazia Deledda
1927	Henri Bergson
1928	Sigrid Undset
1929	Thomas Mann
1930	(Harry) Sinclair Lewis
1931	Erik Axel Karlfeldt
1932	John Galsworthy
1933	Ivan Alexeievich Bunin
1934	Luigi Pirandello
1935	*No award*
1936	Eugene Gladstone O'Neill
1937	Roger Martin du Gard
1938	Pearl Buck
1939	Frans Eemil Sillanpää
1943	*No award*
1944	Johannes Vilhelm (JV) Jensen
1945	Gabriela Mistral
1946	Hermann Hesse
1947	André (Paul Guillaume) Gide
1948	T S (Thomas Stearns) Eliot
1949	William Faulkner
1950	Bertrand (Arthur William, 3rd Earl) Russell
1951	Pär (Fabian) Lagerkvist
1952	François Mauriac
1953	Winston (Leonard Spencer) Churchill
1954	Ernest (Millar) Hemingway
1955	Halldór Laxness
1956	Juan Ramón Jiménez
1957	Albert Camus
1958	Boris (Leonidovich) Pasternak
1959	Salvatore Quasimodo
1960	Saint-John Perse
1961	Ivo Andrić
1962	John (Ernest) Steinbeck
1963	George Seferis
1964	Jean-Paul Sartre, *declined*
1965	Mikhail (Alexandrovich) Sholokhov
1966	Shmuel Yosef Agnon
	Nelly (Leonie) Sachs
1967	Miguel Angel Asturias
1968	Kawabata Yasunari
1969	Samuel Beckett
1970	Alexander (Isayevich) Solzhenitsyn
1971	Pablo (Neftali Reyes) Neruda
1972	Heinrich Böll
1973	Patrick White
1974	Eyvind Johnson
	Harry (Edmund) Martinson
1975	Eugenio Montale
1976	Saul Bellow
1977	Vicente Aleixandre
1978	Isaac Bashevis Singer
1979	Odysseus Elytis
1980	Czesław Miłosz
1981	Elias Canetti
1982	Gabriel Garcia Márquez
1983	William (Gerald) Golding
1984	Jaroslav Seifert
1985	Claude (Eugène Henri) Simon
1986	Wole Soyinka
1987	Joseph Brodsky
1988	Naguib Mahfouz
1989	Camilo José Cela
1990	Octavio Paz
1991	Nadine Gordimer

Pulitzer Prize in fiction

1917	*No award*
1918	Ernest Poole *His Family*
1919	Booth Tarkington *The Magnificent Ambersons*
1920	*No award*
1921	Edith Wharton *The Age of Innocence*
1922	Booth Tarkington *Alice Adams*
1923	Willa Cather *One of Ours*
1924	Margaret Wilson *The Able McLaughlins*
1925	Edna Ferber *So Big*
1926	Sinclair Lewis *Arrowsmith*
1927	Louis Bromfield *Early Autumn*
1928	Thornton Wilder *The Bridge of San Luis Rey*
1929	Julia Peterkin *Scarlet Sister Mary*
1930	Oliver LaFarge *Laughing Boy*
1931	Margaret Ayre Barnes *Years of Grace*
1932	Pearl S Buck *The Good Earth*
1933	T S Stribling *The Store*
1934	Caroline Miller *Lamb in His Bosom*
1935	Josephine Winslow Johnson *Now in November*
1936	Harold L Davis *Honey in the Horn*
1937	Margaret Mitchell *Gone with the Wind*
1938	John Phillips Marquand *The Late George Apley*
1939	Marjorie Kinnan Rawlings *The Yearling*
1940	John Steinbeck *The Grapes of Wrath*
1941	*No award*
1942	Ellen Glasgow *In This Our Life*
1943	Upton Sinclair *Dragon's Teeth*
1944	Martin Flavin *Journey in the Dark*
1945	John Hersey *A Bell for Adano*
1946	*No award*
1947	Robert Penn Warren *All the King's Men*
1948	James Michener *Tales of the South Pacific*
1949	James Gould Cozzens *Guard of Honor*
1950	A B Guthrie Jr *The Way West*
1951	Conrad Richter *The Town*
1952	Herman Wouk *The Caine Mutiny*
1953	Ernest Hemingway *The Old Man and the Sea*
1954	*No award*
1955	William Faulkner *A Fable*
1956	MacKinlay Kantor *Andersonville*
1957	*No award*
1958	James Agee *A Death in the Family*
1959	Robert Lewis Taylor *The Travels of Jaime McPheeters*
1960	Allen Drury *Advise and Consent*
1961	Harper Lee *To Kill a Mockingbird*
1962	Edwin O'Connor *The Edge of Sadness*
1963	William Faulkner *The Reivers*
1964	*No award*
1965	Shirley Ann Grau *The Keepers of the House*
1966	Katherine Anne Porter *The Collected Stories*
1967	Bernard Malamud *The Fixer*
1968	William Styron *The Confessions of Nat Turner*
1969	Navarre Scott Momaday *House Made of Dawn*
1970	Jean Stafford *Collected Stories*
1972	Wallace Stegner *Angle of Repose*
1973	Eudora Welty *The Optimist's Daughter*
1975	Michael Shaara *The Killer Angels*
1976	Saul Bellow *Humboldt's Gift*
1978	James Alan McPherson *Elbow Room*
1979	John Cheever *The Stories of John Cheever*
1980	Norman Mailer *The Executioner's Song*
1981	John Kennedy Toole *A Confederacy of Dunces*
1982	John Updike *Rabbit is Rich*
1983	Alice Walker *The Color Purple*
1984	William Kennedy *Ironweed*
1985	Alison Lurie *Foreign Affairs*
1986	Larry McMurtry *Lonesome Dove*
1987	Peter Taylor *A Summons to Memphis*
1988	Toni Morrison *Beloved*
1989	Anne Tyler *Breathing Lessons*
1990	Oscar Hijuelos *The Mambo Kings Play Songs of Love*
1991	John Updike *Rabbit at Rest*
1992	Jane Smiley *A Thousand Acres*

Poets

Name	*Dates*	*Place of birth*	*Selected works*
Adcock, Fleur	1934–	Papakura, New Zealand	*The Eye of the Hurricane* (1964), *The Incident Book* (1986)
Apollinaire, Guillaume	1880–1918	Rome	*Alcools* (1913), *Calligrammes* (1918)
Arnold, Matthew	1822–88	Laleham, Middlesex	*The Strayed Reveller* (1849), *Poems* (1852), *Poems* (1853), *Merope* (1858), *New Poems* (1867)
Auden, W(ystan) H(ugh)	1907–1973	York	*Another Time* (1940), *The Sea and the Mirror* (1944), *The Age of Anxiety* (1947)
Baudelaire, Charles	1821–67	Paris	*Les Fleurs du Mal* (1857)
Belloc, Hilaire	1870–1953	St Cloud, France	*Cautionary Tales* (1907), *Sonnets and Verse* (1923)
Betjeman, John	1906–84	Highgate	*Mount Zion* (1931), *New Bats in Old Belfries* (1945), *A Nip in the Air* (1972)
Blake, William	1757–1827	London	*The Marriage of Heaven and Hell* (1793), *The Vision of the Daughter of Albion* (1793), *Songs of Innocence and Experience* (1794), *Milton* (1810)
Blunden, Edmund	1896–1974	London	*The Waggoner and Other Poems* (1920), *The Shepherd and Other Poems of Peace and War* (1922), *English Poems* (1929), *Collected Poems* (1930), *After the Bombing and Other Short Poems* (1950), *A Hong Kong House* (1962)

Poets (continued)

Name	*Dates*	*Place of birth*	*Selected works*
Blunt, Wilfrid Scawen	1840–1922	Petworth, Sussex	*Sonnets and Songs by Proteus* (1875), *In Vinculis* (1899)
Bocaccio, Giovanni	1313–75	Florence	*The Decameron, Filostrato*
Brooke, Rupert	1887–1915	Rugby	*Poems* (1911), *1914 and Other Poems* (1915), *Complete Poems* (1946)
Browning, Elizabeth Barrett	1806–61	Coxhoe Hall, Durham	*Sonnets from the Portuguese* (1850), *Aurora Leigh* (1855)
Browning, Robert	1812–89	Camberwell	*Bells and Pomegranates, Dramatic Lyrics, Men and Women* (1855), *The Ring and the Book* (1868-9)
Burns, Robert	1759–96	Alloway, Ayr	*Poems Chiefly in the Scottish Dialect* (1786), *Tam O'Shanter* (1790)
Byron, George Gordon	1788–1824	London	*Hours of Idleness* (1807), *Childe Harolde* (1817), *Don Juan* (1819-24)
Chaucer, Geoffrey	1343–1400	London	*Troilus and Criseyde* (c.1385), *The Canterbury Tales* (1387–1400)
Coleridge, Samuel Taylor	1722–1834	Ottery St Mary, Devon	*Kubla Khan* (1797), *The Rime of the Ancient Mariner* (1798), *Christabel* (1798), *Sybylline Leaves* (1817), *Collected Poems* (1817)
Cowper, William	1731–1800	Great Berkhampstead, Hertfordshire	*The Task* (1785)
cummings, e(dward) e(estlin)	1894–1962	Cambridge, Massachusetts	*Tulips and Chimneys* (1923), *XLI Poems* (1925), *is 5* (1926)
Dante, Alighieri	1265–1321	Florence	*Divine Comedy* (1321)
Day Lewis, Cecil	1904–72	Ballintogher, Sligo	*Overtures to Death* (1938), *The Aeneid of Virgil* (1952)
De la Mare, Walter	1873–1956	Charleston, Kent	*The Listeners* (1912), *The Burning Glass and Other Poems* (1945)
Dickinson, Emily	1830–86	Amherst, Massachusetts	*Poems* (1890)
Donne, John	1572–1631	London	*Satires and Elegies* (1590s), *Holy Sonnets* (1610–11)
Dryden, John	1631–1700	Aldwinckle All Saints, Northamptonshire	*Astrea Redux* (1660), *Absalom and Achitophel* (1681), *MacFlecknoe* (1684)
Dunn, Douglas	1942–	Inchinnann	*Love or Nothing* (1974), *Elegies* (1985)
Eliot, T(homas) S(tearns)	1888–1965	St Louis, Missouri	*Prufrock and Other Observations* (1917), *The Waste Land* (1922), *Ash Wednesday* (1930), *Four Quartets* (1944)
Éluard, Paul (Eugene Grindal)	1895–1952	Saint-Denis	*La Vie Immediate* (1934), *Poesie et Verité* (1942)
Emerson, Ralph Waldo	1803–84	Boston	*Complete Works* (1903-4)
Fitzgerald, Edward	1809–83	Bredfield, Suffolk	*The Rubáiyát of Omar Khayyám* (1859)
Frost, Robert	1874–1963	San Francisco	*North of Boston* (1914), *Mountain Interval* (1916), *New Hampshire* (1923), *In The Clearing* (1962)
Ginsberg, Allen	1926–	Newark, New Jersey	*Howl and Other Poems* (1956), *Empty Mirror* (1961), *The Fall of America* (1973)
Goethe, Johann Wolfgang von	1749–1832	Frankfurt	*Römische Elegien* (1795), *Der west-östliche Divan* (1819)
Graham, W(illiam) S(ydney)	1918–86	Greenock, Renfrewshire	*Cage Without Grievance* (1942), *The Seven Journeys* (1944), *The White Threshold* (1949), *The Nightfishing* (1955), *Implements in their Place* (1977), *Collected Poems* (1979), *Aimed at Nobody* (1993)
Graves, Robert (van Ranke)	1895–1985	London	*Fairies and Fusiliers* (1917)
Hardy, Thomas	1840–1928	Higher Bockhampton, Dorset	*Wessex Poems* (1898), *Poems of the Past and Present* (1902), *Satires of Circumstance, Lyrics and Reveries* (1914), *Moments of Vision and Miscellaneous Verse* (1917), *Human Shows, Far Phantasies, Songs and Trifles* (1925)
Harrison, Tony	1937–	Leeds	*Mysteries* (1985), *V* (1985), *The Gaze of the Gorgon* (1992)
Heaney, Seamus	1939–	County Derry	*Death of a Naturalist* (1966), *Door into Dark* (1969), *Field Work* (1979)
Heine, Henrich	1797–1856	Düsseldorf	*Buch der Lieder* (1827)
Herbert, George	1593–1633	Montgomery	*The Temple* (1633)
Hopkins, Gerard Manley	1844–89	London	*The Wreck of the Deutschland* (1876)
Hughes, Ted	1930–	Mytholmroyd, Yorkshire	*The Hawk in the Rain* (1957), *Lupereal* (1960), *Seasons Songs* (1976), *Moortown* (1979)
Keats, John	1795–1821	London	*Endymion* (1818), *Lamia and Other Poems* (1820)
Lamartine, Alphonse de	1790–1869	Mâcon	*Meditations Poétiques* (1829), *Harmonies Poétiques et Religieuses* (1830), *Recueillements Poétiques* (1839)

Name	*Dates*	*Place of birth*	*Selected works*
Langland, William	1332–1400	Ledbury, Hertfordshire	*Piers Plowman* (1362–99)
Larkin, Philip	1922–1985	Coventry	*The North Ship* (1945), *The Whitsun Weddings* (1964), *High Windows* (1974)
Lear, Edward	1812–88	London	*A Book of Nonsense* (1845), *Laughable Lyrics* (1877), *Queery Leary Nonsense* (1911), *Teapots and Quails* (1953)
Longfellow, Henry	1807–82	Portland, Maine	*Voices and the Night* (1839), *Ballads and Other Poems* (1842), *Hiawatha* (1855), *Divina Comedia* (1872)
MacDiarmid, Hugh (Christopher Murray Grieve)	1892–1978	Langholm, Dumfriesshire	*A Drunk Man Looks at the Thistle* (1926)
MacNiece, (Frederick) Louis	1907–63	Belfast	*Blind Fireworks* (1929), *Solstices* (1961)
Mallarmé, Stéphane	1842–98	Paris	*Herodiade* (1864), *Prélude à L'Apres-midi d'un Faune* (1865), *Poésies* (1887)
Marvell, Andrew	1621–78	Yorkshire	*Elegy* (1649), *Upon Appleton House* (c. 1652-3), *To His Coy Mistress* (pre–1653)
Masefield, John	1878–1967	Ledbury, Herefordshire	*The Everlasting Mercy* (1911), *Dauber* (1913), *Collected Poems* (1923)
Millay, Edna St Vincent	1892–1950	Rockland, Maine	*Renascence and Other Poems* (1917), *A Few Figs From Thistles* (1920), *The Harp-Weaver and Other Poems* (1923)
Milton, John	1608–74	London	*Paradise Lost* (1667)
Moore, Marianne	1887–1972	St Louis, Missouri	*Poems* (1921), *Observations* (1924), *Collected Poems* (1951), *O, to be a Dragon* (1959), *Tell Me, Tell Me: Granite, Steel and Other Topics* (1966)
Muir, Edwin	1887–1959	Deerness, Orkney	*First Poems* (1925), *Chorus of the Newly Dead* (1926), *Variations on a Time Theme* (1934), *The Labyrinth* (1949), *New Poems* (1949–51)
Muldoon, Paul	1951–	County Armagh	*New Weather* (1973), *Mules* (1977), *Why Brownlee Left* (1980), *Quoof* (1984), *Madoc:A Mystery* (1990)
Nash, (Frederick) Ogden	1902–71	New York	*Free Wheeling* (1931)
Nerval, Gérard de	1808–55	Paris	*Les Chimères* (1854)
O'Hara, Frank (Francis Russell)	1926–66	Baltimore	*A City Winter and Other Poems* (1952), *Lunch Poems* (1964)
Owen, Wilfred (Edward Salter)	1893–1918	Oswestry, Shropshire	*Poems* (1920, 1931), *Collected Poems* (1963)
Parker, Dorothy	1893–1967	New Jersey	*Enough Rope* (1926), *Sunset Gun* (1928), *Death and Taxes* (1931), *Not so Deep as a Well* (1936)
Paulin, Tom	1949–	Leeds	*A Sense of Justice* (1977), *The Strange Museum* (1980), *Liberty Tree* (1983), *Fivemiletown* (1987)
Paz, Octavio	1914–	Mexico City	*Salamander* (1958–61) , *Collected Poems* (1988)
Petrarch (Francesco Petrarca)	1304–74	Arezzo	*Rime Sparse*
Plath, Sylvia	1932–63	Boston	*The Colossus and Other Poems* (1960), Ariel (1965), *Crossing the Water* (1971), *Winter Trees* (1972)
Pound, Ezra (Weston Loomir)	1885–1972	Haile, Idaho	*The Cantos* (1917, 1948, 1959)
Pushkin, Aleksandr	1799–1837	Moscow	*Eugen Onegin* (1828), *Ruslam and Lyudmilla* (1820)
Raine, Craig	1944–	Shildon, Essex	*A Martian Sends a Postcard Home* (1979), *Rich* (1984)
Raine, Kathleen	1908–	London	*Stone and Flower* (1943)
Rilke, Rainer Maria	1875–1926	Prague	*Die Sonettean Orpheus* (1923)
Rimbaud, Arthur	1854–91	Charleville, Ardennes	*Les Illuminations* (1886)
Rosetti, Christina	1830–94	London	*Goblin Market* (1862), *The Prince's Progress* (1872), *A Pageant and Other Poems* (1881)
Sassoon, Siegfried	1886–1967	Kent	*Counter-Attack and Other Poems* (1917), *The Road to Ruin* (1933)
Schiller, Johann Christoph Friedrich von	1759–1805	Marbach	*Die Künstler* (The Artists), *An die Freude* (Ode to Joy)
Shelley, Percy Bysshe	1792–1822	Sussex	*Prometheus Unbound* (1820), *The Mask of Anarchy* (1819), *Ode to the West Wind* (1819), *The Triumph of Life*
Sitwell, Edith	1887–1964	Scarborough	*Facade* (1922), *Colonel Fantock* (1926)

Poets (continued)

Name	*Dates*	*Place of birth*	*Selected works*
Smith, Stevie (Florence Margaret Smith)	1902–71	Hull	*Not Waving But Drowning* (1957)
Spender, Stephen	1909–	London	*Poems* (1933)
Spenser, Edmund	1552–99	London	*The Shepheardes Calender* (1579), *The Faerie Queene* (1590)
Stevens, Wallace	1879–1955	Reading, Pennsylvania	*Harmonium* (1923), *Transport to Summer* (1947)
Tate, James	1943–	Kansas City	*The Lost Pilot* (1967), *The Oblivion Ha-Ha* (1970), *Absences* (1971), *Distance From Loved Ones* (1990)
Tennyson, Alfred, Lord	1809–92	Somersby Rectory, Lincolnshire	*Poems* (1832), *The Princess* (1847), *In Memoriam* (1850), *Idylls of the King* (1859), *Maud* (1885)
Thomas, Dylan	1914–53	Swansea	*Twenty-five Poems* (1936), *Deaths and Entrances* (1946), *In Country Sleep and Other Poems* (1952), *Under Milk Wood* (1952)
Valéry, Paul	1871–1945	Cette	*La Jeune Parque* (1917), *Charmes* (1922)
Vega, Lope de	1562–1635	Madrid	*La Dragentea* (1598)
Verlaine, Paul	1844–96	Metz	*Fêtes Galantes* (1869), *Sagesse* (1881)
Walcott, Derek	1930–	Castries, St Lucia	*In a Green Night* (1962), *The Castaway* (1965), *The Gulf* (1970), *Another Life* (1973), *Omeras* (1989), *The Odyssey* (1989)
Warren, Robert Penn	1905–89	Guthrie, Kentucky	*Brother to Dragons* (1953), *Promises: Poems 1954-56* (1957), *Now and Then: Poems 1976–78* (1978), *Portrait of a Father* (1988)
Whitman, Walt	1819–92	New York	*Leaves of Grass* (1855–89)
Williams, William Carlos	1883–1963	New Jersey	*The Tempers* (1913), *Sour Grapes* (1921), *The Desert Music and Poems* (1954), *Journey to Love* (1955), *Pictures from Breughel and Other Poems* (1962)
Wordsworth, William	1770–1850	Cockermouth	*Lyrical Ballads* (1798), *The Prelude* (1799, 1805, 1850), *The Excursion* (1814)
Yeats W(illiam) B(utler)	1865–1939	County Dublin	*The Wanderings of Oisin and Other Poems* (1889), *The Wind Among the Reeds* (1892), *The Wild Swans at Coole* (1917), *Michael Robartes and the Dancer* (1921), *The Winding Stair and Other Poems* (1933)

Poets Laureate

1617	Ben Jonson*	1730	Colley Cibber	1896	Alfred Austin
1638	Sir William Davenant*	1757	William Whitehead	1913	Robert Bridges
1668	John Dryden	1785	Thomas Warton	1930	John Masefield
1689	Thomas Shadwell	1790	Henry Pye	1968	Cecil Day Lewis
1692	Nahum Tate	1813	Robert Southey	1972	Sir John Betjeman
1715	Nicholas Rowe	1843	William Wordsowrth	1984	Ted Hughes
1718	Laurence Eusden	1850	Alfred, Lord Tennyson		

* The post was not officially established until 1668.

Pulitzer Prize in poetry

1917	*No award*
1918	Sara Teasdale *Love Songs*
1919	Carl Sandburg *Corn Huskers*
	Margaret Widdemer *Old Road to Paradise*
1920	*No award*
1921	*No award*
1922	Edwin Arlington Robinson *Collected Poems*
1923	Edna St Vincent Millay *The Harp Weaver and Other Poems*
1924	Robert Frost *New Hampshire: a Poem with Notes and Grace Notes*
1925	Edwin Arlington Robinson *The Man Who Died Twice*
1926	Amy Lowell *What's O'Clock?*
1927	Leonora Speyer *Fiddler's Farewell*
1928	Edwin Arlington Robinson *Tristram*
1929	Stephen Vincent Benét *John Brown's Body*
1930	Conrad Aiken *Selected Poems*
1931	Robert Frost *Collected Poems*
1932	George Dillon *The Flowering Stone*
1933	Archibald MacLeish *Conquistador*
1934	Robert Hillyer *Collected Verse*
1935	Audrey Wurdemann *Bright Ambush*
1936	R P Tristram Coffin *Strange Holiness*
1937	Robert Frost *A Further Range*
1938	Marya Zaturenska *Cold Morning Sky*
1939	John Gould Fletcher *Selected Poems*
1940	Mark Van Doren *Collected Poems*

1941	Leonard Bacon *Sunderland Capture*
1942	William Benét *The Dust Which is God*
1943	Robert Frost *A Witness Tree*
1944	Stephen Vincent Benét *Western Star*
1945	Karl Shapiro *V-Letter and Other Poems*
1946	No award
1947	Robert Lowell *Lord Weary's Castle*
1948	W H Auden *The Age of Anxiety*
1949	Peter Viereck *Terror and Decorum*
1950	Gwendolyn Brooks *Annie Allen*
1951	Carl Sandburg *Complete Poems*
1952	Marianne Moore *Collected Poems*
1953	Archibald MacLeish *Collected Poems 1917–1952*
1954	Theodore Roethke *The Waking*
1955	Wallace Stevens *Collected Poems*
1956	Elizabeth Bishop *Poems – North & South*
1957	Richard Wilbur *Things of This World*
1958	Robert Penn Warren *Promises: Poems 1954–56*
1959	Stanley Kunitz *Selected Poems 1928–1958*
1960	W D Snodgrass *Heart's Needle*
1961	Phyllis McGinley *Times Three: Selected Verse from Three Decades*
1962	Alan Dugan *Poems*
1963	William Carlos Williams *Pictures from Breughel*
1964	Louis Simpson *At the End of the Open Road*
1965	John Berryman *77 Dream Songs*
1966	Richard Eberhart *Selected Poems*
1967	Ann Sexton *Live or Die*
1968	Anthony Hecht *The Hard Hour*
1969	George Oppen *Of Being Numerous*
1970	Richard Howard *Untitled Subjects*
1971	W S Merwin *The Carrier of Ladders*
1972	James Wright *Collected Poems*
1973	Maxine Winokur Kumin *Up Country*
1974	Robert Lowell *The Dolphin*
1975	Gary Snyder *Turtle Island*
1976	John Ashbery *Self-Portrait in a Convex Mirror*
1977	James Merrill *Divine Comedies*
1978	Howard Nemerov *Collected Poems*
1979	Robert Penn Warren *Now and Then*
1980	Donald Justice *Selected Poems*
1981	James Schuyler *The Morning of the Poem*
1982	Sylvia Plath *The Collected Poems*
1983	Galway Kinnell *Selected Poems*
1984	Mary Oliver *American Primitive*
1985	Carolyn Kizer *Yin*
1986	Henry Taylor *The Flying Change*
1987	Rita Dove *Thomas and Beulah*
1988	William Meredith *Partial Accounts; New and Selected Poems*
1989	Richard Wilbur *New and Selected Poems*
1990	Charles Simic *The World Doesn't End*
1991	Mona van Duyn *Near Changes*
1992	James Tate *Selected Poems*

THEATRE

Playwrights

Name	*Dates*	*Place of birth*	*Selected works*
Aeschylus	c.525–426 BC	Eleusis, nr Athens	*Persians* (c.472 BC), *Seven Against Thebes* (c.467 BC), *Oresteia* (458 BC)
Albee, Edward	1928–	Washington DC	*The American Dream* (1961), *Who's Afraid of Virginia Woolf?* (1962)
Anouilh, Jean	1910–87	Bordeaux	*Antigone* (1944), *L'Alouette* (1953), *Beckett* (1960)
Arden, John	1930–	Barnsley	*All Fall Down* (1955), *The Waters of Babylon* (1957), *Serjeant Musgrave's Dance* (1959)
Aristophanes	c.448–380 BC	Athens	*Clouds* (c.423 BC), *Wasps* (c.422 BC), *Birds* (c.414 BC), *Lysistrata* (c.411 BC), *Frogs* (c.405 BC)
Ayckbourn, Alan	1939–	London	*Absurd Person Singular* (1972), *The Norman Conquests* (1973), *A Chorus of Disapproval* (1985), *A Woman in Mind* (1986), *Man of the Moment* (1990)
Barnes, Peter	1931–	Stroud	*The Bewitched* (1974), *Laughter* (1978), *Red Noses* (1985)
Barrie, Sir J(ames) M(atthew)	1860–1937	Kirriemuir, Angus	*Peter Pan* (1904), *What Every Woman Knows* (1908)
Beckett, Samuel	1906–89	Foxrock, nr Dublin	*Waiting for Godot* (1955), *Endgame* (1961), *Happy Days* (1961)
Bennett, Alan	1934–	Yorkshire	*Beyond the Fringe* (1960), *Forty Years On* (1968), *Getting On* (1971), *Habeas Corpus* (1973), *The Madness of George III* (1991)
Berkoff, Stephen	1937–	London	*East* (1975), *Greek* (1979), *Decadence* (1981)
Bond, Edward	1934–	London	*Saved* (1965), *Lear* (1972), *The Sea* (1973), *The Fool* (1975)
Brecht, Bertolt	1898–1956	Augsburg	*Galileo* (1938-9), *Mother Courage* (1941), *The Good Person of Sezuan* (1943), *Caucasian Chalk Circle* (1949)
Brenton, Howard	1942–	Portsmouth	*Christie in Love* (1969), *Revenge* (1969), *The Romans in Britain* (1980), *Pravda* (with David Hare) (1985)
Čapek, Karel	1890–1938	Bohemia	*RUR* (1920), *The Makropulos Affair* (1923)
Chekov, Anton	1860–1904	Tagarog	*The Seagull* (1895), *Uncle Vanya* (1900), *Three Sisters* (1901), *The Cherry Orchard* (1904)
Churchill, Caryl	1938–		*Cloud Nine* (1978), *Top Girls* (1982), *Serious Money* (1987)

Playwrights (continued)

Name	*Dates*	*Place of birth*	*Selected works*
Cocteau, Jean	1889–1963	Maisons-Lafitte, nr Paris	*Orphée* (1926), *La Machine Infernale* (1934)
Congreve, William	1670–1729	Bardsey, nr Leeds	*The Way of the World* (1700)
Corneille, Pierre	1606–84	Rouen	*Le Cid* (1637), *Horace* (1640), *Cinna* (1641), *Polyeucte* (1643)
Coward, Noel	1899–1973	Teddington, Middlesex	*Hay Fever* (1925), *Private Lives* (1933), *Blithe Spirit* (1941)
Delaney, Shelagh	1939–	Salford	*A Taste of Honey* (1958)
Eliot, T S	1888–1965	St Louis, Missouri	*Murder in the Cathedral* (1935), *The Cocktail Party* (1950), *The Family Reunion* (1939)
Euripedes	c.485–406 BC	Phyla, Attica	*Medea* (c. 431 BC), *Electra* (c. 422-416 BC), *Iphigenia in Tauris* (c. 414 BC), *Bacchae* (?, produced posthumously)
Fo, Dario	1926–	Lombardy	*Accidental Death of an Anarchist* (1970), *Can't Pay, Won't Pay* (1978)
Ford, John	1586–1640	Devonshire	*'Tis Pity She's a Whore* (1633)
Frayn, Michael	1933–	London	*The Two of Us* (1970), *Donkey's Years* (1976), *Noises Off* (1982)
Friel, Brian	1929–	Omagh	*Philadelphia, Here I Come !* (1964), *Lovers* (1967), *The Freedom of the City* (1973), *Translations* (1980), *Dancing at Lughnasa* (1991)
Fry, Christopher	1907–		*The Lady's Not for Burning* (1948)
Fugard, Athol	1932–	Middelburg, Cape Province	*Sizwe Bansi is Dead* (1972), *Statement After an Arrest Under the Immortality Act* (1972), *A Lesson From Aloes* (1979), *Master Harold... and the Boys* (1982), *The Road to Mecca* (1984)
Genet, Jean	1910–86	*Paris*	*Les Bonnes (The Maids)* (1948), *Le Balcon (The Balcony)* (1956)
Giraudoux, Jean	1882–1944	Bellac	*Amphitryon 38* (1929), *La Guerre de Troie n'aura pas Lieu* (1935)
Goethe, Johann Wolfgang von	1749–1832	Frankfurt	*Faust I* (1808), *Faust II* (1832)
Goldsmith, Oliver	1728–74	Pallas, Ireland	*She Stoops to Conquer* (1773)
Gray, Simon	1936–		*Burley* (1971)
Griffiths, Trevor	1935–	Manchester	*Occupations* (1970), *The Party* (1973), *Comedians* (1975)
Hampton, Christopher	1946–	Fayal, Azores	*The Philanthropist* (1970), *Savages* (1973), *Tales from Hollywood* (1983), *Les Liasons Dangereuses* (1985)
Hare, David	1947–	Bexhill	*Teeth 'n' Smiles* (1975), *Plenty* (1978), *Pravda* (with Howard Brenton) (1985), *The Secret Rapture* (1988), *Racing Demon* (1990)
Hauptmann, Gerhard	1862–1946	Obersalzbrunn	*Vor Sonnenaufgang (Before Sunrise)* (1889), *The Weavers* (1892)
Hellman, Lillian	1907–84	New Orleans	*The Little Foxes* (1939)
Ibsen, Henrik	1828–1906	Skien, Norway	*Peer Gynt* (1867), *A Doll's House* (1879), *Hedda Gabler* (1890), *The Master Builder* (1892)
Ionesco, Eugène	1912–	Romania	*La Cantatrice Chauve (The Bald Prima Donna)* (1948), *Rhinoceros* (1960)
Jonson, Ben	1572–1637	Westminster	*Every Man His Humour* (1598), *Sejanus* (1603), *Volpone* (1606), *The Alchemist* (1610), *Bartholomew Fair* (1614)
Lorca, Frederico Garcia	1899–1936	Fuente Vaqueros, Spain	*Blood Wedding* (1933), *The House of Bernarda Alba* (1945)
Mamet, David	1947–	Chicago	*Sexual Perversity in Chicago* (1974), *American Buffalo* (1975), *Glengarry Glen Ross* (1983)
Marlowe, Christopher	1564–1593	Canterbury	*Tamburlaine the Great* (1587), *Dr Faustus* (1588), *The Jew of Malta* (1589), *Edward II* (1592)
Middleton, Thomas	c.1580–1627	London	*The Changeling* (1622), *Women Beware Women* (c.1625)
Miller, Arthur	1915–	New York	*All My Sons* (1947), *Death of a Salesman* (1949), *The Crucible* (1952), *View From the Bridge* (1955), *The Misfits* (1961)
Molière (Jean-Baptiste Poquelin)	1622–73	Paris	*Le Bourgeois Gentilhomme* (1660), *Tartuffe* (1664), *Le Misanthrope* (1666), *Le Malade Imaginaire* (1673)
Musset, Alfred de	1810–57	Paris	*Fantasio* (1834), *On Ne Badine Pas Avec L'Amour* (1834), *Lorenzaccio* (1834)
Nichols, Peter (Richard)	1927–	Bristol	*A Day In the Death of Joe Egg* (1967), *Privates on Parade* (1977)
O'Casey, Sean	1880–1964	Dublin	*Juno and the Paycock* (1924), *The Plough and the Stars* (1926)
O'Neill, Eugene	1888–1953	New York	*Long Day's Journey into Night* (1941)
Orton, Joe	1933–67	Leicester	*Entertaining Mr Sloane* (1964), *Loot* (1965), *What the Butler Saw* (1969)
Osborne, John	1929–	London	*Look Back in Anger* (1956), *The Entertainer* (1957), *A Patriot for Me* (1965), *Déjàvu* (1991)

Pinero, Arthur Wing	1855–1934	London	*The Second Mrs Tanquerey* (1893), *Trelawny of the Wells* (1898)
Name	*Dates*	*Place of birth*	*Selected works*
Pinter, Harold	1930–	London	*The Birthday Party* (1958), *The Caretaker* (1960), *The Homecoming* (1965), *No Man's Land* (1975), *Betrayal* (1978)
Pirandello, Luigi	1867–1936	Agrigento, Sicily	*Six Characters in Search of an Author* (1921), *Henry IV* (1922)
Poliakoff, Stephen	1952–	London	*The Carnation Gang* (1973), *Hitting Town* (1975), *City Sugar* (1975), *Breaking the Silences* (1984)
Priestley, J(ohn B(oynton)	1894–1984	Bradford	*Dangerous Corner* (1932), *Time and the Conways* (1937), *When We Are Married* (1938), *An Inspector Calls* (1947),
Racine, Jean (Baptiste)	1639–99	La Ferté-Milon	*Andromaque* (1667), *Bérénice* (1670), *Phèdre* (1677)
Rattigan, Terence	1911–77	London	*French Without Tears* (1936), *The Winslow Boy* (1946), *The Browning Version* (1948), *The Deep Blue Sea* (1952), *Ross* (1960)
Rostand, Edmond de	1868–1918	Marseilles	*Cyrano de Bergerac* (1897)
Sartre, Jean-Paul	1905–80	Paris	*Les Mouches (The Flies)* (1943), *Huis Clos* (1945), *Les Séquestrés D'Altona (The Condemned of Altona)* (1961)
Schiller, Johann Christoph Friedrich von	1759–1805	Marbach	*The Robbers* (1781), *Wallenstein* (1799), *Maria Stuart* (1800)
Shaffer, Peter Levin	1926–	Liverpool	*Five Finger Exercise* (1958), *The Royal Hunt of the Sun* (1964), *Equus* (1973), *Amadeus* (1979), *Yonadab* (1985), *Lettuce and Lovage* (1987)
Taylor, Cecil P(hilip)	1928–81	Galsgow	*Good* (1981)
Shakespeare, William	1564–1616	Stratford-Upon-Avon	For complete list of plays see box p550.
Shaw, George Bernard	1856–1950	Dublin	*Arms and the Man* (1894), *Man and Superman* (1903), *Pygmalion* (1913), *Heartbreak House* (1920), *Saint Joan* (1924)
Shepherd, Sam	1943–	Sheridan, Illinois	*La Turista* (1966), *The Tooth of Crime* (1972), *Fool For Love* (1979), *A Lie of the Mind* (1985), *The States of Shock* (1991)
Sheridan, Richard Brinsley	1751–1816	Dublin	*The Rivals* (1775), *The School for Scandal* (1777)
Sherrif, R(obert) C(ederic)	1896–1973	Kingston-upon-Thames	*Journey's End* (1929)
Simon, Neil	1927–	New York	*Barefoot in the Park* (1963), *The Odd Couple* (1965), *Plaza Suite* (1968), *The Last of the Red Hot Lovers* (1969), *California Suite* (1976), *Lost in Yonkers* (1992)
Sophocles	c.496–406 BC	Colonus, nr Athens	*Antigone* (c.442 BC), *Oedipus Tyrannus* (c.420 BC), *Electra* (c.409 BC), *Philoctetes* (c.409 BC)
Soyinka, Wole	1934–	Abeskata, Nigeria	*The Swamp Dwellers* (1958), *The Bacchae of Euripedes* (1973)
Stoppard, Tom	1937–	Zlin, Czechoslovakia	*Rosenkrantz and Gildenstern are Dead* (1966), *The Real Inspector Hound* (1968), *Travesties* (1974), *Jumpers* (1972), *Arcadia* (1993)
Storey, David	1933–	Wakefield	*The Contractor* (1970), *Home* (1970), *The Changing Room* (1972)
Strindberg, August	1849–1912	Stockholm	*Miss Julie* (1888), *Master Olof* (1877), *The Dance of Death* (1901)
Synge J(ohn), M(illington)	1871–1909	Dublin	*The Playboy of the Western World* (1907)
Terson, Peter	1932–	Tyneside	*A Night to Make the Angels Weep* (1964), *Zigger, Zagger* (1967), *Strippers* (1984)
Travers, Ben	1886–1980	Hendon	*Rookery Nook* (1926), *Thark* (1927)
Webster, John	1578–1632	London	*The White Devil* (1612), *The Duchess of Malfi* (c.1613)
Wesker, Arnold	1932–	London	*Chicken Soup With Barley* (1958), *Roots* (1959), *I'm Talking About Jerusalem* (1960), *Chips With Everything* (1962)
Wilde, Oscar (Fingal O'Flahertie Wills)	1854–1906	Dublin	*Lady Windermere's Fan* (1892), The *Importance of Being Earnest* (1895), *Salomé* (1896)
Wilder, Thornton	1897–1975	Wisconsin	*Our Town* (1938), *The Merchant of Yonkers* (1938), *The Skin of Our Teeth* (1942)
Williams, Tennessee (Thomas Lanier Williams)	1911–83	Mississippi	*The Glass Menagerie* (1944), *A Streetcar Named Desire* (1947), *Cat on a Hot Tin Roof* (1955), *Sweet Bird of Youth* (1959)
Wycherley, William	1641–1715	Clive, nr Shrewsbury	*The Country Wife* (1665), *The Plain Dealer* (1676)

Shakespeare: the plays

Early comedies	*Written*	*Well-known characters*
The Comedy of Errors	1590–4	Antipholus, Dromio, Adriana
Love's Labour's Lost	1590–4	Armado, Berowne, Costard
The Two Gentlemen of Verona	1592–3	Proteus, Valentine, Julia, Sylvia
The Taming of the Shrew	1592	Petruchio, Katharina, Sly
Histories		
Henry VI Part I	1589–90	Henry, Talbot, Joan of Arc
Henry VI Part II	1590–1	Henry, Margaret, Jack Cade
Henry VI Part III	1590–1	Henry, Margaret, Richard of Gloucester
Richard III	1592–3	Richard, Margaret, Clarence, Anne
King John	1595–7	John, Constance, Arthur, Bastard
Richard II	1595	Richard, John of Gaunt, Bolingbroke
Henry IV Part I	1596	Henry, Hal, Hotspur, Falstaff
Henry IV Part II	1597	Henry, Hal, Falstaff, Mistress Quickly
Henry V	1599	Henry (formerly Hal), Pistol, Nym, Katherine
Henry VIII	1613	Henry, Katherine, Wolsey
Middle comedies		
A Midsummer Night's Dream	1595	Oberon, Titania, Puck, Bottom
The Merchant of Venice	1596–8	Bassanio, Portia, Shylock, Jessica
The Merry Wives of Windsor	1597	Falstaff, Mistress Quickly, Shallow
As You Like It	1599	Rosalind, Orlando, Touchstone, Jacques
Twelfth Night	1600–2	Orsino, Olivia, Viola, Malvolio, Feste, Sir Andrew Aguecheek
Dark comedies		
Much Ado About Nothing	1598	Beatrice, Benedick, Dogberry, Verges
All's Well That Ends Well	1602–3	Bertram, Helena, Parolles
Measure for Measure	1604–5	Duke, Angelo, Isabella, Mariana
Tragedies		
Romeo and Juliet	1595–6	Romeo, Juliet, Mercutio, the Nurse
Hamlet	1600–1	Hamlet, Ophelia, the Ghost, the Grave-Digger
Othello	1604	Othello, Desdemona, Iago, Cassio
King Lear	1605–6	Lear, Cordelia, the Fool, Kent, Edgar/Poor Tom
Macbeth	1605–6	Macbeth, Lady Macbeth, Banquo/Ghost, the Three Witches
Greek and Roman plays		
Titus Andronicus	1590–4	Andronicus, Aaron, Lavinia
Julius Caesar	1599	Caesar, Brutus, Cassius, Antony
Troilus and Cressida	1601–2	Troilus, Cressida, Pandarus
Timon of Athens	1605–9	Timon, Apemantus
Antony and Cleopatra	1606–7	Antony, Cleopatra, Enobarbus
Coriolanus	1607–8	Coriolanus, Volumnia
Late comedies		
Pericles	1607–8	Pericles, Marina
Cymbeline	1609–10	Imogen, Iachimo
The Winter's Tale	1611	Leontes, Perdita, Florizel, Autolycus
The Tempest	1613	Prospero, Miranda, Ferdinand, Ariel, Caliban

Theatre personalities

Name	*Dates*	*Place of birth*	*Occupation*
Abbott, George	1887–	New York	Director/playwright/producer
Abington, Frances	1737–1818	London	Actress
Ackerman, Robert Allan	1945–		Director
Agate, James (Evershed)	1877–1947	Manchester	Critic
Aitken, Maria	1945–	Dublin	Actress/director
Alexander, Bill	1948–	Hunstanton	Actor/director
Alleyn, Edward	1566–1626	London	Actor
Allgood, Sara	1883–1950	Dublin	Actress
Anderson, Dame Judith (originally Frances Margaret Anderson)	1898–1992	Adelaide	Actress

Name	*Dates*	*Place of birth*	*Occupation*
Antoine, André	1858–1943	Limoges	Actor
Appia, Adolphe	1862–1928	Geneva	Designer
Arliss, George (originally Augustus George Andrews)	1868–1946	London	Actor
Arnaud, Yvonne Germaine	1892–1958	Boredeaux	Actress
Artaud, Antonin	1896–1948	Marseilles	Dramatist/actor/director/theorist
Ashcroft, Dame Peggy (properly Edith Margaret Emily)	1907–1991	London	Actress
Attenborough, Sir Richard	1923–	Cambridge	Actor
Aylmer, Sir Felix Edward	1889–1979		Actor
Bancroft, Sir Squire	1841–1926	London	Actor/manager
Barber, Frances	1957–	Wolverhampton	Actress
Barrymore, Ethel	1879–1959	Philadelphia	Actress
Barton, John	1928–	London	Director
Baylis, Lilian	1874–1937	London	Theatrical manager
Benson, Sir Frank Robert	1858–1939	Alresford, Hampshire	Actor/Manager
Bergman, Ingmar	1918–	Stockholm	Director
Berkoff, Steven	1937–	London	Dramatist/actor/director
Bernhardt, Sarah (properly Henriette Rosine Bernard)	1844–1923	Paris	Actress
Bjornson, Maria	1949–	Paris	Stage designer
Blakely, Colin	1930–87	Bangor, Co Down	Actor
Blin, Roger	1907–84	Neuilly, Paris	Director
Bloom, Claire	1931–	London	Actress
Bogdanov, Michael	1938–	London	Director
Booth, Edwin Thomas	1833–93	Harford County, Maryland	Actor
Bracegirdle, Anne	c.1673–1748	London	Actress
Branagh, Kenneth	1960–	Belfast	Actor/director
Briers, Richard	1934–	Croydon, Surrey	Actor
Bron, Eleanor		Stanmore, Middlesex	Actress/director
Brook, Peter (Stephen Paul)	1925–	London	Director
Brustein, Robert	1927–	New York	Critic/director
Burbage, Richard	c.1567–1619	London	Actor. Builder of the Globe Theatre, 1599
Callow, Simon	1949–	London	Actor/director
Campbell, Mrs Patrick (née Beatrice Stella Tanner)	1865–1940	Kensington	Actress
Carte, Richard D'Oyly	1844–1901	London	Impresario
Casson, Sir Lewis	1875–1969	Birkenhead	Actor-manager
Chaikin, Joseph	1935–	Brooklyn	Director/actor/producer
Charleson, Ian	1949–90	Edinburgh	Actor
Cheeseman, Peter	1932–	Portsmouth	Director/artistic director
Chereau, Patrice	1944–	France	Director
Chevalier, Albert	1862–1923	London	Actor
Cibber, Colley	1671–1757	London	Actor /dramatist
Cibber, Mrs (née Susannah Maria Arne)	1714–66	London	Actress
Clements, Sir John Selby	1910–88	London	Actor/director
Clurman, Harold Edgar	1901–80	New York City	Director/critic
Cochran, Sir Charles Blake	1872–1951	Lindfield, Sussex	Producer
Compton, Fay	1894–1978	London	Actress
Cooney, Ray	1932–	London	Dramatist/director/producer
Copeau, Jacques	1879–1949	France	Director/manager
Copley, John (Michael Harold)	1933–	Brimingham	Producer
Cornell, Katherine	1898–1974	Berlin	Actress/producer/manager
Courtenay, Tom	1937–	Hull	Actor
Courtneidge, Dame Cicely (Esmerelda)	1883–1980	Sydney	Actress
Coward, Sir Noel (Pierce)	1899–1973	Teddington	Actor/director/dramatist
Craig, Edward Gordon	1872–1966	Stevenage	Actor/stage designer
Crawford, Michael	1942–	Salisbury, Wiltshire	Actor

Theatre personalities (continued)

Name	*Dates*	*Place of birth*	*Occupation*
Croft, Michael	1922–	Manchester	Director
Crowley, Bob	1954–		Stage designer
Cusack, Cyril	1910–	Durban	Actor /director
Cusack, Sinead	1948–	Dublin	Actress
Cushman, Robert	1943–	London	Critic/director
Daubeny, Sir Peter	1921–75		Impresario/theatre manager
Davies, Howard	1945–	Reading	Director
Debureau, Jean Gaspard	1796–1846	Bohemia	Actor
De La Tour, Frances	1944–	Bovingdon, Hertfordshire	Actress
Dench, Judi	1934–	York	Actress
Devine, George	1910–65		Actor/stage director
Dexter, John	1925–90	Derby	Director
Draper, Ruth	1889–1956	New York	Monologist and diseuse
Dudley, William	1947–	London	Stage designer
Du Maurier, Sir Gerald	1873–1934	London	Actor-manager
Dunlop, Frank	1927–	Leeds	Stage director
Duse, Eleonora	1859–1924	Venice	Actress
Eddington, Paul	1927–	London	Actor
Egan, Peter	1946–	London	Actor/director
Espert, Nuria	1935–		Actress/director
Evans, Dame Edith	1888–1976	London	Actress
Eyre, Richard	1943–	Barnstaple	Director
Finlay, Frank	1926–	Farnworth, Lancashire	Actor
Finney, Albert	1936–	Salford	Actor
Forbes-Robertson, Sir Johnston	1853–1937	London	Actor
Forrest, Edwin	1806–72	Philadelphia	Actor
Gambon, Michael	1940–	Dublin	Actor
Garrick, David	1717–79	Hereford	Actor
Gielgud, Sir John	1904–		Actor
Grotowski, Jerzy	1933–	Rzeszów, Poland	Stage director
Guinness, Sir Alec	1914–	Southborne	Actor
Guthrie, Sir William Tyrone	1900–71	Tunbridge Wells	Producer
Gwyn, Eleonor (known as Nell)	c.1650–87	Hereford	Actress
Hall, Sir Peter	1930–	Bury St Edmund's	Director
Hancock, Sheila	1933–	Blackgang, Isle of Wight	Actress
Hands, Terry	1941–	Aldershot	Stage director
Hardwicke, Sir Cedric (Webster)	1893–1964	Lye, Worcestershire	Actor
Hare, Robertson	1891–1979	London	Actor
Harewood, George Henry Hubert Lascelles, 7th Earl of	1923–	Harewood, nr Leeds	Arts patron
Harris, Julie	1925–	Michigan	Actress
Harris, Rosemary	1930–	Ashby, Suffolk	Actress
Harvey, Sir John Martin	1863–1944	Wivenhoe, Essex	Actor-manager
Hawthorne, Nigel	1929–	Coventry	Actor
Hayes, Helen	1900–	Washington	Actress
Higgins, Clare	1957–	Yorkshire	Actress
Hijikata, Tatsumi	1928–86	Akita province	Performance artist
Hiller, Dame Wendy	1912–	Bramhall, Cheshire	Actress
Holm, Ian	1931–	Ilford, Essex	Actor
Hordern, Sir Michael	1911–	Berkhampstead	Actor
Horniman, Anne Elizabeth Fredericka	1860–1937	Forest Hall, London	Theatre manager
Houseman, John (originally Jaques Haussmann)	1902–89	Bucharest	Actor/stage director
Irving, Sir Henry (John Henry Brodribb)	1838–1905	Keinton-Mandeville, Somerset	Actor
Jackson, Glenda	1936–	Birkenhead	Actress
Jacobi, Derek	1938–	London	Actor
Jacobs, Sally	1932–	London	Designer
Jefferson, Joseph	1829–1905	Philadelphia	Actor

Name	*Dates*	*Place of birth*	*Occupation*
Johnson, Dame Celia	1908–82	Richmond, Surrey	Actress
Jouvet, Louis	1887–1951	Finistère	Director/actor
Kazan, Elia	1909–	Constantinople	Director
Kean, Edmund	1789–1833	London	Actor
Kemble, Frances ('Fanny')	1809–93	London	Actress
Kemp, Lindsay	1939–	Lewis, Hebrides	Mime artist/actor/director
Kendal, Felicity	1946–	Olton, Warwickshire	Actress
Kendal, Dame Madge	1848–1935	Cleethorpes	Actress
Kerr, Walter Francis	1913–	Evanston, Illinois	Critic
Kingsley, Ben	1943–	Snaiton, Yorkshire	Actor
Langtry, Lilly (properly Emilie Charlotte Le Breton)	1853–1929	Jersey	Actress
Lapotaire, Jane	1944–	Ipswich	Actress
Lawrence, Gertrude	1898–1952	London	Actress
Lecoq, Jacques	1921–	Paris	Mime artist/director
Lehmann, Beatrix	1903–79	Bourne End, Buckinghamshire	Actress/director-producer
Lenya, Lotte (originally Karoline Wilhelmine Blamauer)	1898–1981	Hitzing, Vienna	Actress
Littlewood, Joan	1914–	London	Stage director
Lloyd, Marie	1870–1922	London	Actress
Lloyd Webber, Andrew	1948–	London	Musicals composer
Lunt, Alfred	1892–1977	Milwaukee	Actor
Lyubimov, Yuri	1917–	Russia	Stage director
Mackintosh, Cameron	1946–	Enfield, Middlesex	Producer
Macrae, John Duncan	1905–67		Actor
Macready, William Charles	1793–1873	London	Actor
Marceau, Marcel	1923–	Strasbourg	Mime artist
McCowen, Alec	1925–	Tunbridge Wells	Actor
McEwan Geraldine	1932–	Old Windsor	Actress
McKellen, Sir Ian	1939–	Burnley	Actor
McKenzie, Julia	1941–		Actress
Menken, Adah Isaacs (Adah Berthe Theodore)	1835–68	New Orleans	Actress
Merman, Ethel	1909–84	Long Island, New York	Actress
Meyerhold, Vsevold Emillevich	1874–1940	Penza	Actor/director
Miles, Bernard, Baron	1907–	Uxbridge	Actor/stage director
Miller, Jonathan Wolfe	1934–	London	Director
Mirren, Helen	1946–		Actress
Mnouchkine, Arianne	1938–	France	Stage director
Morley, Sheridan	1941–	Ascot	Critic
Noble, Adrian	1950–		Director
Nunn, Trevor	1940–	Ipswich	Director
Olivier, Laurence	1907–89	Dorking	Actor/director
Papp, Joseph (originally Papirofsky)	1922–	Brooklyn, New York	Stage director/producer
Pennington, Michael	1943–		Actor
Perry, Antoinette	1888–1946	Denver	Actress/director
Piscator, Erwin	1893–1966	Ulm, Germany	Stage director
Plowright, Joan	1929–	Brigg, Lincolnshire	Actress
Porter, Eric	1928–	London	Actor
Prince, Hal (Harold Smith)	1928–	New York City	Stage director/producer
Prowse, Philip	1937–		Director
Quayle, Sir Anthony	1913–89	Ainsdale	Actor
Redgrave, Sir Michael	1908–85	Bristol	Actor
Redgrave, Vanessa	1937–	London	Actress
Rees, Roger	1944–	Aberystwyth	Actor
Reinhardt, Max	1873–1942	Baden, nr Vienna	Theatre manager
Ricardson, Ian	1934–	Edinburgh	Actor
Richardson, Sir Ralph	1902–83	Cheltenham	Actor
Rix, Sir Brian	1924–	Cottingham	Actor
Robson, Dame Flora	1902–	South Shields	Actress
Rossiter, Leonard	1926–84	Liverpool	Actor
Routledge, Patricia	1929–	Birkenhead	Actress

Theatre personalities (continued)

Name	*Dates*	*Place of birth*	*Occupation*
Scofield, Paul	1922–	Hurstpierpoint, Sussex	Actor
Sher, Anthony	1949–	South Africa	Actor
Smith, Dame Maggie	1934–	Ilford, Essex	Actress
Sondheim, Stephen	1930–	New York City	Musicals composer
Speaight, Robert William	1904–76		Actor
Stafford-Clark, Max	1941–	Cambridge	Director
Stanislavsky (Konstantin Sergeivitch Alexeyev)	1865–1938	Moscow	Actor/producer/teacher
Stapleton, Maureen	1925–	New York	Actress
Steadman, Alison	1946–	Liverpool	Actress
Stein, Peter	1937–	Berlin	Director
Stevenson, Juliet	1956–		Actress
Strasberg, Lee (originally Israel Strassberg)	1901–82	Budzanow	Actor/director/teacher
Strehler, Giorgio	1921–	Italy	Director
Suzman, Janet	1939–	S Africa	Actress
Terry, Dame Ellen	1848–1928	Coventry	Actress
Thacker, David	1950–		Actor
Thorndike, Dame Cybil	1882–1976	Gainsborough	Actress
Threlfell, David	1953–	Manchester	Actor
Tinker, Jack	1938–	Oldham	Critic
Tree, Sir Herbert Beerbohm	1853–1917	London	Actor-manager
Tutin, Dorothy	1931–	London	Actress
Tynan, Kenneth	1927–1980	Birmingham	Critic
Wall, Max (Maxwell George Lorimer)	1908–90	London	Actor
Walter, Harriet	1950–		Actress
Wanamaker, Sam	1919–	Chicago	Actor/director
Wardle, Irving	1929–	Bolton	Critic
Warner, Deborah	1959–	Avon	Director
Weigel, Helene	1900–72	Austria	Actress. Founded the Berliner Ensemble, 1948, with husband Bertolt Brecht
Whitelaw, Billie	1932–	Coventry	Actress
Wilson, Snoo	1948–	Reading	Director
Wilton, Penelope	1946–	Scarborough	Actress
Wood, John		Derbyshire	Actor
Wood, Peter Lawrence	1927–	Colyton, Devon	Director
Zefirelli, Franco	1923–	Florence	Director
Ziegfeld, Florenz	1867–1932	Chicago	Theatre manager/producer

Pulitzer Prize in drama

1918	*No award*
1919	Jesse Lynch Williams *Why Marry?*
1920	*No award*
1921	Eugene O'Neill *Beyond the Horizon*
1922	Zona Gale *Miss Lulu Bett*
1923	Eugene O'Neill *Anna Christie*
1924	Owen Davis *Icebound*
1925	Hatcher Hughes *Hell-Bent for Heaven*
1926	Sidney Howard *They Knew What They Wanted*
1927	George Kelly *Craig's Wife*
1928	Paul Green *In Abraham's Bosom*
1929	Eugene O'Neill *Strange Interlude*
1930	Elmer Rice *Street Scene*
1931	Marc Connelly *The Green Pastures*
1932	Susan Glaspell *Alison's House*
1933	George S Kaufman *Morris Ryskind and Ira Gershwin: Of Thee I Sing*
1934	Maxwell Anderson *Both Your Houses*
1935	Sidney Kingsley *Men in White*
1936	Zöe Akins *The Old Maid*
1937	Robert E Sherwood *Idiot's Delight*
1938	George S Kaufman and Moss Hart *You Can't Take It With You*
1939	Thornton Wilder *Our Town*
1940	Robert E Sherwood *Abe Lincoln in Illinois*
1941	William Saroyan *The Time of Your Life*
1942	Robert E Sherwood *There Shall Be No Night*
1943	No award
1944	Thornton Wilder *The Skin of Our Teeth*
1945	*No award*
1946	Mary Chase *Harvey*
1947	Russell Crouse and Howard Lindsay *State of the Union*
1948	*No award*
1949	Tennessee Williams *A Streetcar Named Desire*
1950	Arthur Miller *Death of a Salesman*
1951	Richard Rogers, Oscar Hammerstein II and Joshua Logan *South Pacific*

1952	*No award*
1953	Joseph Kramm *The Shake*
1954	William Inge *Picnic*
1955	John Patrick *Teahouse of the August Moon*
1956	Tennessee Williams *Cat on a Hot Tin Roof*
1957	Frances Goodrich and Albert Hackett *The Diary of Anne Frank*
1958	Eugene O'Neill *Long Day's Journey into Night*
1959	Ketti Frings *Look Homeward Angel*
1960	Archibald Macleish *JB*
1961	George Abbott, Jerome Weidman, Sheldon Harnick and Jerry Bock *Fiorello*
1962	Tad Mosel *All the Way Home*
1963	Frank Loesser and Abe Burrows *How to Succeed in Business Without Really Trying*
1964	*No award*
1965	*No award*
1966	Frank D Gilroy *The Subject Was Roses*
1967	*No award*
1968	Edward Albee *A Delicate Balance*
1969	*No award*
1970	Howard Sackler *The Great White Hope*
1971	Charles Gordone *No Place to Be Somebody*
1972	Paul Zindel *The Effect of Gamma Rays on Man-in-the-Moon Mangolds*
1973	*No award*
1974	Jason Miller *The Championship Season*
1975	*No award*
1976	*No award*
1977	Michael Bennett, James Kirkwood, Nicholas Dante, Marvin Hamlisch, Edward Kleban *A Chorus Line*
1978	Michael Cristofer *The Shadow Box*
1979	Donald L Coburn *The Gin Game*
1980	Sam Shepard *Burned Child*
1981	Lanford Wildon *Talley's Folly* Beth Henley *Games of the Heart*
1982	Charles Fuller *A Soldier's Play*
1983	Marsha Norman *'Night, Mother*
1984	David Mamet *Glengarry Glen Ross*
1985	Stephen Sondhiem and James Lapine *Sunday in the Park with George*
1986	*No award*
1987	August Wilson *Fences*
1988	Alfred Uhry *Driving Miss Daisy*
1989	Wendy Wasserstein *The Heidi Chronicles*
1990	August Wilson *The Piano Lesson*
1991	Neil Simon *Lost in Yonkers*
1992	Robert Schenkhan *The Kentucky Cycle*

Musicals

Show	*Date*	*Composer(s)*	*Lyricist(s)*	*Librettist(s)*
A Chorus Line	1975	Marvin Hamlisch	Edward Kleban	James Kirkwood & Nicholas Dante
A Funny Thing Happened on the Way to the Forum	1962	Stephen Sondheim	Stephen Sondheim	Bert Shevelove & Larry Gelbart
A Little Night Music	1973	Stephen Sondheim	Stephen Sondheim	Hugh Wheeler
Annie	1976	Charles Strouse	Martin Charnin	Thomas Meehan
Annie Get Your Gun	1946	Irving Berlin	Herbert & Dorothy Fields	Herbert & Dorothy Fields
Anyone Can Whistle	1964	Stephen Sondheim	Stephen Sondheim	Arthur Laurents
Anything Goes	1934	Cole Porter	Cole Porter	Guy Bolton & PG Wodehouse
Blood Brothers	1983	Willy Russell	Willy Russell	Willy Russell
Brigadoon	1947	Frederick Loewe	Alan Jay Lerner	Alan Jay Lerner
Cabaret	1966	John Kander	Freb Ebb	Joe Masteroff
Camelot	1960	Frederick Loewe	Alan Jay Lerner	Alan Jay Lerner
Candide	1956	Leonard Bernstein	Richard Wilbur	Lillian Hellman
Carmen Jones	1943	George Bizet, adapted by Meilhac & Halevy	Oscar Hammerstein II	Oscar Hammerstein II
Carousel	1945	Richard Rogers	Oscar Hammerstein II	Oscar Hammerstein II
Cats	1981	Andrew Lloyd Webber	TS Eliot, adapted by Trevor Nunn	TS Eliot, adapted by Trevor Nunn
Chess	1986	Bjorn Ulvaeus & Benny Anderson	Tim Rice	Tim Rice
Chicago	1975	John Kander	Fred Ebb	Fred Ebb & Bob Fosse
Company	1970	Stephen Sondheim	Stephen Sondheim	George Furth
Do I Hear a Waltz?	1965	Richard Rogers	Stephen Sondheim	Arthur Laurents
Evita	1978	Andrew Lloyd Webber	Tim Rice	Tim Rice
Fiddler on the Roof	1964	Jerry Bock	Sheldon Harnick	Joseph Stein
Follies	1971	Stephen Sondheim	Stephen Sondheim	James Goldman
42nd Street	1980	Harry Warren	Al Dubin	Michael Stewart & Mark Bramble
Funny Girl	1964	Jule Styne	Bob Merrill	Isobel Lennart
Godspell	1971	Stephen Schwartz	Stephen Schwartz	John-Michael Tebelak
Grease	1972	Jim Jacobs & Warren Casey	Jim Jacobs & Warren Casey	Jim Jacobs & Warren Casey
Guys & Dolls	1950	Frank Loesser	Frank Loesser	Abe Burrows & Jo Swerling

Musicals (continued)

Show	*Date*	*Composer(s)*	*Lyricist(s)*	*Librettist(s)*
Gypsy	1959	Jule Styne	Stephen Sondheim	Arthur Laurents
Hair	1967	Galt MacDermot	Galt MacDermot	Gerome Ragni & James Rado
Half a Sixpence	1963	David Heneker	David Heneker	Beverley Cross
Hello Dolly	1964	Jerry Herman	Jerry Herman	Michael Stewart
How to Succeed in Business Without Really Trying	1961	Frank Loesser	Frank Loesser	Abe Burrows, Jack Weinstock & Willie Gilbert
Into the Woods	1987	Stephen Sondheim	Stephen Sondheim	James Lapine
Irma La Douce	1956	Margaret Monnot	Margaret Monnot	Alexandre Breffort
Jesus Christ Superstar	1971	Andrew Lloyd Webber	Tim Rice	Tim Rice
Joesph and the Amazing Technicolor Dreamcoat	1968	Andrew Lloyd Webber	Tim Rice	Tim Rice
Kismet	1953	Aleksandr Borodin, arr by Robert Wright & George Forrest	Robert Wright & George Forrest	Charles Lederer & Luther Davis
Kiss Me Kate	1947	Cole Porter	Cole Porter	Samuel & Bella Spewack
La Cage aux Folles	1983	Jerry Herman	Jerry Herman	Harvey Fierstein
Lady Be Good	1924	George Gerschwin	Ira Gerschwin	Guy Bolton & Fred Thompson
Lady in the Dark	1941	Kurt Weill	Ira Gerschwin	Moss Hart
Les Misérables	1980 (1985)	Claude-Michel Schönburg	Alain Boublil & Jean-Marc Natel (English lyrics Herbert Kretzmer)	Alain Boublil & Jean-Marc Natel
Little Shop of Horrors	1982	Alan Menken	Howard Ashman	Howard Ashman
Mame	1966	Jerry Herman	Jerry Herman	Jerome Lawrence & Robert E Lee
Me and My Girl	1937	Noel Gay	L. Arthur Rose & Douglas Farber	L. Arthur Rose & Douglas Farber
Miss Saigon	1990	Claude-Michel Schönburg	Alain Boublil & Richard Maltby Jr	Alain Boublil & Richard Maltby Jr
My Fair Lady	1956	Frederick Loewe	Alan Jay Lerner	Alan Jay Lerner
Of Thee I Sing	1931	George Gerschwin	Ira Gerschwin	George S Kaufman & Murray Ryskind
Oh, Kay!	1926	George Gerschwin	Ira Gerschwin	Guy Bolton & PG Wodehouse
Oklahoma	1943	Richard Rogers	Oscar Hammerstein II	Oscar Hammerstein II
Oliver!	1960	Lionel Bart	Lionel Bart	Lionel Bart
On The Town	1944	Leonard Bernstein	Betty Comden & Adolph Green	Betty Comden & Adolph Green
On the Twentieth Century	1978	Cy Coleman	Betty Comden & Adolph Green	Betty Comden & Adolph Green
On Your Toes	1936	Richard Rogers	Lorenz Hart	Richard Rogers, Lorenz Hart & George Abbott
Paint Your Wagon	1951	Frederick Loewe	Alan Jay Lerner	Alan Jay Lerner
Pal Joey	1940	Richard Rogers	Lorenz Hart	John O'Hara
Phantom of the Opera	1987	Andrew Lloyd Webber	Charles Hart	Andrew Lloyd Webber & Richard Stilgoe
Salad Days	1954	Julian Slade	Julian Slade & Dorothy Reynolds	Julian Slade & Dorothy Reynolds
Show Boat	1927	Jerome Kern	Oscar Hammerstein II	Oscar Hammerstein II
South Pacific	1949	Richard Rogers	Oscar Hammerstein II	Oscar Hammerstein II & Joshua Logan
Starlight Express	1984	Andrew Lloyd Webber	Richard Stilgoe	Andrew Lloyd Webber & Richard Stilgoe
Stop the World – I Want to Get Off	1961	Leslie Bricuse & Anthony Newley	Leslie Bricuse & Anthony Newley	Leslie Bricuse & Anthony Newley
Sunday in the Park with George	1984	Stephen Sondheim	Stephen Sondheim	James Lapine
Sweeney Todd	1979	Stephen Sondheim	Stephen Sondheim	Hugh Wheeler
Sweet Charity	1966	Cy Coleman	Dorothy Fields	Neil Simon
The Boyfriend	1953	Sandy Wilson	Sandy Wilson	Sandy Wilson
The King and I	1951	Richard Rogers	Oscar Hammerstein II	Oscar Hammerstein II

Show	Date	Composer(s)	Lyricist(s)	Librettist(s)
The Most Happy Fella	1956	Frank Loesser	Frank Loesser	Frank Loesser
The Music Man	1957	Meredith Wilson	Meredith Wilson	Meredith Wilson
The Rocky Horror Show	1973	Richard O'Brien	Richard O'Brien	Richard O'Brien
The Sound of Music	1959	Richard Rogers	Oscar Hammerstein II	Howard Lindsey & Russell Crouse
West Side Story	1957	Leonard Bernstein	Stephen Sondheim	Arthur Laurents
Wonderful Town	1953	Leonard Bernstein	Betty Comden & Adolph Green	Joseph Fields & Jerome Chadarov

FILM AND TELEVISION

Film and television personalities

Name	Dates	Place of birth	Selected works
Adjani, Isabelle	1955–	Paris	*The Story of Adele H* (1975), *Nosferatu* (1978), *Possession* (1980), *Quartet* (1981), *One Deadly Summer* (1983), *Subway* (1985), *Ishtar* (1987), *Camille Claudel* (1988), *La Reine Margot* (1992)
Agutter, Jenny	1952–	Taunton	*The Railway Children* (1970), *Walkabout* (1970), *Logan's Run* (1976), *Equus* (1977), *An American Werewolf in London* (1981), *Child's Play 2* (1990)
Aimée, Anouk (Françoise Sorya)	1934–	Paris	*Les Amants de Verone* (1949), *La Dolce Vita* (1960), *Lola* (1961), *Un Homme et Une Femme* (1966), *Justine* (1969)
Alda, Alan	1936–	New York City	*Paper Lion* (1968), *Catch 22* (1970), *M*A*S*H* (TV, 1972-83), *California Suite* (1978), *Same Time Next Year* (1978), *The Four Seasons* (1981), *Sweet Liberty* (1986), *A New Life* (1988), *Crimes and Misdemeanours* (1990), *Betsy's Wedding* (1990)
Allen, Woody (Allen Stuart Konigsberg)	1935–	Brooklyn, New York	Director/screenplay writer/actor. *Play it Again Sam* (1972), *Sleeper* (1973), *Love and Death* (1975), *Annie Hall* (1977), *Manhattan* (1979), *Broadway Danny Rose* (1984), *Purple Rose of Cairo* (1985), *Hannah and Her Sisters* (1986), *Crimes and Misdemeanour* (1990), *Husbands and Wives* (1992)
Almodovar, Pedro	1951–	Calzada de Calatrava	Director. *Women on the Verge of a Nervous Breakdown* (1988), *Tie Me Up ! Tie Me Down !* (1990), *High Heels* (1991)
Altman, Robert	1925–	Kansas City	Director.*The James Dean Story, McCabe and Mrs Miller* (1971), *The Long Goodbye* (1973), *Popeye* (1980), *Vincent and Theo* (1990), *The Player* (1992)
Andress, Ursula	1936–	Berne	*Dr No* (1963), *She* (1965), *What's New Pussycat* (1965), *Casino Royale* (1967), *The Clash of the Titans* (1981)
Andrews, Julie (Julia Elizabeth Wells)	1935–	Walton-on-Thames, Surrey	*Mary Poppins* (1964), *The Sound of Music* (1965), *Star !* (1968), *Victor/Victoria* (1982), *Duet for One* (1987)
Anderson, Lindsay	1923–	Bangalore, India	*This Sporting Life* (1963), *If...* (1968), *O Lucky Man* (1973), *Britannia Hospital* (1982)
Antonioni, Michelangelo	1912–	Ferrara	Director. *L'Avventura* (1959, *The Adventure*), *La Notte* (1961, *The Night*), *Blow-up* (1966), *Zabriskie Point* (1969), *The Oberwald Mystery* (1980)
Ashcroft, Dame Peggy	1907–91	Croydon	*The Thirty-Nine Steps* (1935), *Quiet Wedding* (1940), *A Passage to India* (1984), *The Jewel in the Crown* (TV, 1984), *Madame Sousatzka* (1988)
Astaire, Fred (Fred Austerlitz)	1899–1977	Omaha, Nebraska	*Top Hat* (1935), *Follow the Fleet* (1936), *Easter Parade* (1948)

Film and television personalities (continued)

Name	*Dates*	*Place of birth*	*Selected works*
Atkinson, Rowan	1955–	Northumberland	*Blackadder* (TV, 1984), *Blackadder II* (TV, 1985), *Blackadder III* (1986), *Blackadder Goes Forth* (TV, 1989), *The Tall Guy* (1989)
Attenborough, Sir Richard	1923–	Cambridge	*In Which We Serve* (1942), *Brighton Rock* (1947). Directed *Oh What A Lovely War* (1969), *A Bridge Too Far* (1977), *Ghandi* (1982), *A Chorus Line* (1985), *Cry Freedom* (1987), *Chaplin* (1992)
August, Bille	1948–	Sweden	Director. *Pelle The Conqueror* (1987), *The Best Intentions* (1992)
Akroyd, Dan	1952–	Ottowa	*The Blues Brothers* (1980), *Ghostbusters* (1984), *Spies Like Us* (1986), *My Stepmother is an Alien* (1989), *Driving Miss Daisy* (1989)
Bacall, Lauren (Betty Perske)	1924–	New York City	*The Big Sleep* (1946), *Dark Passage* (1947), *Key Largo* (1948)
Ball, Lucille	1910–89	Celaron, New York	*Ziegfield Follies* (1946), *I Love Lucy* (TV, 1951–5)
Bancroft, Anne (Anna Maria Italiano)	1931–	Bronx, New York	*The Miracle Worker* (1962), *The Graduate* (1968), *Silent Movie* (1976), *The Elephant Man* (1980), *84 Charing Cross Road* (1986), *Torch Song Trilogy* (1988)
Bankhead, Tallulah	1902–68	Huntsville, Texas	*Tarnished Lady* (1931), *Lifeboat* (1944), *A Royal Scandal* (1945)
Bardot, Brigitte	1934–	Paris	*Et Dieu Créa La Femme* (1956, *And God Created Woman*), *Si Don Juan Était Une Femme* (1973, *If Don Juan Were A Woman*)
Barrault, Jean-Louis	1910–	Le Vesinet	*Les Enfants du Paradis* (1945, *The Children of Paradise*), *La Ronde* (1950), *The Longest Day* (1962)
Barrymore, Ethel	1882–1959	Philadelphia	*Rasputin and the Empress* (1932), *None But the Lonely Heart* (1944)
Barrymore, John	1882–1942	Philadelphia	*Grand Hotel* (1932), *Dinner At Eight* (1933), *Midnight* (1939)
Basinger, Kim	1953–	Athens, Georgia	*Never Say Never Again* (1983), *9 1/2 Weeks* (1985), *Blind Date* (1987), *Batman* (1989), *My Stepmother is an Alien* (1989)
Bates, Alan	1934–	Allestree, Derbyshire	*A Kind of Loving* (1962), *Whistle Down the Wind* (1962), *Zorba the Greek* (1965), *Far From the Madding Crowd* (1967), *Women in Love* (1969), *Hamlet* (1990)
Beatty, Warren	1937–	Richmond, Virginia	*Splendour in the Grass* (1961), *All Fall Down* (1962), *Bonnie and Clyde* (1967), *Reds* (1981), *Dick Tracy* (1990), *Bugsy* (1991)
Belmondo, Jean-Paul	1933–	Neuilly-sur-Seine	*A Bout de Souffle* (1959, *Breathless*), *Un Singe en Hiver* (1962), *That Man From Rio* (1964)
Bergman, Ingmar	1918–	Uppsala	Director. *Smiles of a Summer Night* (1955), *The Seventh Seal* (1956), *Wild Strawberries* (1957), *Herbsonate* (1978), *Fanny and Alexander* (1983)
Bergman, Ingrid	1915–82	Stockholm	*Intermezzo* (1939), *Casablanca* (1942), *For Whom The Bell Tolls* (1943), Gaslight (1944), *Anstasia* (1956), *Autumn Sonata* (1978), *A Woman Called Golda* (TV, 1982)
Besson, Luc	1959–	Paris	Director. *Subway* (1985), *The Big Blue* (1988), *Nikita* (1990)
Bloom, Claire	1931–	London	*Look Back In Anger* (1959), *The Haunting* (1963), *The Spy Who Came in From the Cold* (1966)
Bertolucci, Bernado	1940–	Parma	Director. *Last Tango in Paris* (1972), *The Last Emperor* (1987), *The Sheltering Sky* (1990)
Bogarde, Dirk (Derek van den Bogaerde)	1921–	London	*Victim* (1961), *The Servant* (1963), *The Damned* (1969), *Death in Venice* (1971)
Bogart, Humphrey	1899–1957	New York City	*The Maltese Falcon* (1941), *Casablanca* (1942), *The Big Sleep* (1946), *The Treasure of the Sierra Madre* (1948), *The African Queen* (1951)
Bogdanovich, Peter	1939–	Kingston, New York	Director. *The Last Picture Show* (1971), *Paper Moon* (1973), *What's Up Doc ?* (1972), *Nickleodeon* (1976), *Mask* (1985), *Noises Off* (1992)

Name	*Dates*	*Place of birth*	*Selected works*
Bonham-Carter, Helena	1966–	London	*A Room With a View* (1985), *Hamlet* (1990), *Howard's End* (1992)
Boorman, John	1933–	Shepperton	Director. *Deliverance* (1972), *Excalibur* (1981), *Hope and Glory* (1987)
Bow, Clara	1901–65	New York City	*Mantrap* (1926), *It* (1927), *Wings* (1927)
Boyer, Charles	1899–1978	Figeac	*Mayerling* (1936), *The Garden of Allah* (1936), *The Mad Woman of Chaillot* (1969), *Stavisky* (1974)
Branagh, Kenneth	1960–	Belfast	*A Month in the Country* (1988), *Henry V* (1989), *Dead Again* (1991), *Peter's Friends* (1992)
Brandauer, Klaus Maria von	1944–	Alt Aussee	*Mephisto* (1980), *Out of Africa* (1985), *The Russia House* (1990)
Brando, Marlon	1924–	Omaha, Nebraska	*A Streetcar Named Desire* (1951), *The Wild One* (1953), *On The Waterfront* (1954), *Guys and Dolls* (1955), *Mutiny on the Bounty* (1962), *The Godfather* (1972), *Last Tango in Paris* (1972), *Apocalypse Now* (1979), *The Freshman* (1990)
Bresson, Robert	1907–	Auvergne	Director. *Anges du Péché* (1943, *Angels of Sin*), *Le Journal d'un Curé de Campagne* (1951, *Diary of a Country Priest*), *Un Condamné à Mort s'est Échappé* (1956, *A Man Condemned*)
Bridges, Jeff	1949–	Los Angeles	*The Last Picture Show* (1971), *Against All Odds* (1983), *Jagged Edge* (1985), *The Fabulous Baker Boys* (1989), *The Fisher King* (1991), *The Vanishing* (1992)
Broderick, Matthew	1963–	New York City	*Biloxi Blues* (1988), *Torch Song Trilogy* (1988), *The Freshman* (1990)
Bronson, Charles (Charles Buchinski)	1920–	Ehrenfield, Pennsylvania	*The Magnificent Seven* (1960), *This Property is Condemned* (1966), *The Dirty Dozen* (1967), *Death Wish* (1974)
Brooks, Louise (Leslie Gettman)	1906–85	Cherryvale, Kansas	*Pandora's Box* (1929), *Diary of a Lost Girl* (1930)
Brooks, Mel (Melvin Kaminski)	1926–	New York City	Director. *Blazing Saddles* (1974), *Silent Movie* (1976), *High Anxiety* (1978), *History of the World Part One* (1981)
Buñuel, Luis	1900–83	Calanda	Director. *Un Chien Andalou* (1928, *An Adalusian Dog*), *L'Age D'Or* (1930, *The Golden Age*), *Los Olvidados* (1950, *The Young and the Damned*), *That Obscure Object of Desire* (1977)
Burton, Richard	1925–84	Pontrhydfen, Wales	*My Cousin Rachel* (1952), *Look Back in Anger* (1959), *Cleopatra* (1962), *The Night of the Iguana* (1964), *Who's Afraid of Virginia Woolf* (1966), *Where Eagles Dare* (1969), *1984* (1984)
Cage, Nicholas (Nicholas Coppola)	1964–	Long Beach, California	*Rumblefish* (1983), *The Cotton Club* (1984), *Birdy* (1985), *Peggy Sue Got Married* (1986), *Raising Arizona* (1987), *Moonstruck* (1987), *Wild At Heart* (1990)
Cagney, James	1899–1986	New York City	*Public Enemy* (1931), *Lady Killer* (1933), *A Midsummer Night's Dream* (1935), *Yankee Doodle Dandee* (1942)
Caine, Michael (Maurice Micklewhile)	1933–	London	*Zulu* (1963), *The Ipcress File* (1965), *Alfie* (1966), *The Man Who Would Be King* (1975), *The Eagle Has Landed* (1976), *Dressed to Kill* (1980), *Educating Rita* (1983), *Hannah and Her Sisters* (1986)
Callow, Simon	1945–	London	*Amadeus* (1984), *A Room With A View* (1985), *Maurice* (1987)
Capra, Frank	1897–	Palermo	Director. *It Happened One Night* (1934), *Mr Deed Goes to Town* (1936), *You Can't Take It With You* (1938), *Arsenic and Old Lace* (1942), *It's A Wonderful Life* (1946)
Carné, Marcel	1909–	Paris	Director. *Quai des Brumes* (1938, *Port of Shadows*), *Le Jour se Lève* (1939, *Daybreak*), *Les Enfants du Paradis* (1944, *Children of Paradise*)
Cassavetes, John	1929–89	New York City	Director. *The Dirty Dozen* (1967), *Rosemary's Baby* (1969), *The Fury* (1978), *Whose Life is it Anyway ?* (1981), *Tempest* (1983)

Film and television personalities (continued)

Name	*Dates*	*Place of birth*	*Selected works*
Chabrol, Claude	1930–	Paris	*Le Beau Serge* (1958, *Handsome Serge*), *Les Cousins* (1959), *Les Biches* (1968, *The Does*), *Le Boucher* (1970, *The Butcher*), *Les Noces Rouges* (1973, *Blood Wedding*)
Chaney, Lon	1883–1930	Colorado Springs	*The Hunchback of Notre Dame* (1923), *The Phantom of the Opera* (1925)
Chaplin, Charlie (Sir Charles Spencer Chaplin)	1889–1977	London	*The Kid* (1921), *The Goldrush* (1925), *City Lights* (1931), *Modern Times* (1936), *The Great Dictator* (1940)
Chevalier, Maurice	1888–1972	Paris	*The Innocents of Paris* (1929), *One Hour With You* (1932), *Gigi* (1958)
Christie, Julie	1941–	Assam, India	*Billy Liar* (1963), *Doctor Zhivago* (1965), *Fahrenheit 451* (1966), *Far From the Madding Crowd* (1967), *The Go-Between* (1971), *Don't Look Now* (1974), *Heat and Dust* (1982)
Clair, René (René Lucien Chomette)	1898–1981	Paris	Director. *Sous les Toits de Paris* (1929), *And Then There Were None* (1945), *Les Belles de Nuit* (1952), *Porte des Lilas* (1956)
Cleese, John	1939–	Weston-Super-Mare	*Monty Python's Flying Circus* (TV, 1969–74), *Monty Python and the Holy Grail* (1974), *Fawlty Towers* (TV, 1975 & 1979), *The Life of Brian* (1979), *The Time Bandits* (1982), *The Meaning of Life* (1983), *Clockwise* (1985), *A Fish Called Wanda* (1988)
Clift, Montgomery	1920–66	Omaha, Nebraska	*Red River* (1946), *A Place in the Sun* (1951), *From Here To Eternity* (1953), *Suddenly Last Summer* (1968)
Close, Glenn	1947–	Greenwich, Connecticut	*The World According to Garp* (1982), *The Big Chill* (1983), *Jagged Edge* (1985), *Fatal Attraction* (1987), *Dangerous Liaisons* (1988), *Reversal of Fortune* (1990), *Hamlet* (1990)
Cohen, Ethan and Joel	1958– 1955–	St Louis Park, Minnesota	Directors, screenplay writers and producers. *Blood Simple* (1984), *Raising Arizona* (1987), *Miller's Crossing* (1990), *Barton Fink* (1991)
Colbert, Claudette (Lily Claudette Chaucoin)	1905–	Paris	*It Happened One Night* (1934), *Tovarich* (1937), *The Palm Beach Story* (1942)
Connery, Sean	1930–	Edinburgh	*Dr No* (1963), *From Russia With Love* (1964), *Goldfinger* (1965), *You Only Live Twice* (1967), *Diamonds Are Forever* (1971), *The Man Who Would Be King* (1975), *The Name of the Rose* (1986), *The Untouchables* (1987), *Indiana Jones and The Last Crusade* (1989), *Hunt for Red October* (1990), *The Russia House* (1990)
Cooper, Gary (Frank)	1901–61	Helena, Montana	*The Winning of Barbara Worth* (1926), *A Farewell to Arms* (1932), *For Whom the Bell Tolls* (1943), *High Noon* (1952)
Coppola, Francis Ford	1939–	Detroit	Director. *The Godfather* (1972), *Apocalypse Now* (1979), *The Cotton Club* (1984), *Peggy Sue Got Married* (1987)
Courtenay, Tom	1937–	Hull	*The Loneliness of the Long Distance Runner* (1962), *Billy Liar* (1963), *Dr Zhivago* (1965), *The Dresser* (1983)
Crawford, Joan (Lucille Le Sueur)	1906–77	San Antonio, Texas	*Our Darling Daughters* (1928), *Mildred Pierce* (1945), *Possessed* (1947), *Whatever Happened to Baby Jane* (1962)
Cronenberg, David	1943–	Toronto	*The Dead Zone* (1983), *The Fly* (1985), *Dead Ringers* (1988), *Naked Lunch* (1991)
Crosby, Bing (Harry Lillis Crosby)	1904–77	Tacoma, Washington	*Anything Goes* (1936), *Road to Singapore* (1940), *Road to Morocco* (1942), *A Connecticut Yankee in King Arthur's Court* (1949), *White Christmas* (1954), *High Society* (1956)
Cruise, Tom	1962–	Syracuse, New York	*Risky Business* (1984), *Top Gun* (1985), *The Colour of Money* (1986), *Rain Man* (1988), *Born on the Fourth of July* (1989), *Days of Thunder* (1990), *Far and Away* (1992), *A Few Good Men* (1992)

Name	*Dates*	*Place of birth*	*Selected works*
Crystal, Billy	1947–	Long Beach, New York	*Throw Momma From the Train* (1987), *The Princess Bride* (1988), *When Harry Met Sally* (1989), *City Slickers* (1991)
Cukor, George D(ewey)	1899–1983	New York City	Director. *Girls About Town* (1931), *Little Women* (1933), *Gaslight* (1944), *A Star is Born* (1954), *My Fair Lady* (1964)
Curtis, Tony (Bernard Schwarz)	1925–	New York City	*Some Like it Hot* (1959), *Spartacus* (1960), *The Boston Strangler* (1968)
Curtiz, Michael (Mihály Kerlész)	1888–1962	Budapest	Director. *Captain Blood* (1935), *Charge of the Light Brigade* (1936), *The Adventures of Robin Hood* (1938), *Yankee Doodle Dandee* (1942), *Casablanca* (1943), *Mildred Pierce* (1945), *White Christmas* (1954)
Cushing, Peter	1913–	Kenley, Surrey	*The Man in the Iron Mask* (1939), *The Curse of Frankenstein* (1957), *Dracula* (1958), *The Hound of the Baskervilles* (1959)
Dafoe, Willem	1955–	Appleton, Wisconsin	*Heaven's Gate* (1980), *Platoon* (1986), *The Last Temptation of Christ* (1988), *Mississippi Burning* (1989), *Born on the Fourth of July* (1989), *Wild at Heart* (1990), *Light Sleeper* (1992), *Body of Evidence* (1992)
Dalton, Timothy	1946–	Wales	*Wuthering Heights* (1970), *Mary Queen of Scots* (1971), *The Living Daylights* (1987), *Licence to Kill* (1989)
Dance, Charles	1946–	Rednal, Worcestershire	*The Jewel in the Crown* (TV, 1984), *Plenty* (1985), *Good Morning Babylon* (1987), *White Mischief* (1987), *Pascali's Island* (1988)
Davis, Bette	1908-89	Lowell, Massachusetts	*Bad Sister* (1931), *Dangerous* (1935), *Jezebel* (1938), *Whatever Happened to Baby Jane* (1962)
Davis, Geena	1957–	Wareham, Massachusetts	*Tootsie* (1982), *The Fly* (1986), *The Accidental Tourist* (1989), *Earth Girls Are Easy* (1989), *Thelma and Louise* (1991)
Davis, Judy	1956–	Perth	*My Brilliant Career* (1979), *A Passage To India* (1987), *Barton Fink* (1991), *Husbands and Wives* (1992)
Day, Doris (Doris von Kappelhoff)	1924–	Cincinnati, Ohio	*Calamity Jane* (1953), *Young at Heart* (1954), The *Pyjama Game* (1957), *Pillow Talk* (1959)
Day-Lewis, Daniel	1958–	London	*Ghandi* (1983), *My Beautiful Launderette* (1985), *Room With A View* (1985), *The Unbearable Lightness of Being* (1988), *My Left Foot* (1989), *The Last of the Mohicans* (1992), *Age of Innocence* (1992)
Dean, James	1931–55	Marion, Indiana	*East of Eden* (1955), *Rebel Without A Cause* (1955), *Giant* (1956)
De Havilland, Olivia	1916–	Tokyo	*Midsummer Night's Dream* (1955), *The Adventures of Robin Hood* (1938), *Gone With The Wind* (1939), *The Dark Mirror* (1946), *The Heiress* (1949)
Delon, Alain	1935–	Paris	*The Leopard* (1962), *Swann in Love* (1984)
De Mille, Cecil B(lount)	1881–1959	Ashfield, Massachusetts	Director. *The Squaw Man* (1913), *The Ten Commandments* (1923), *The Plainsman* (1937), *The Greatest Show On Earth* (1952)
Demme, Jonathan	1944–	Long Island, New York	Director. *Something Wild* (1987), *Married To The Mob* (1988), *The Silence of the Lambs* (1991)
Dench, Dame Judy	1934–	York	*Four in the Morning* (1966), *A Fine Romance* (TV, 1981-4), *A Room With A View* (1985), *84 Charing Cross Road* (1987), *A Handful of Dust* (1988), *Henry V* (1989)
Deneuve, Catherine	1943–	Paris	*Repulsion* (1965), *Belle de Jour* (1967), *Tristana* (1970), *The Hunger* (1983), *Indochine* (1992)
De Niro, Robert	1943–	New York City	*Mean Streets* (1973), *Taxi Driver* (1976), *The Deer Hunter* (1978), *Raging Bull* (1980), *Angel Heart* (1987), *Midnight Run* (1988), *Goodfellas* (1990), *Awakenings* (1990), *Cape Fear* (1991), *Night and the City* (1992), *This Boy's Life* (1992)

Film and television personalities (continued)

Name	Dates	Place of birth	Selected works
Dennehy, Brian	1940–	Bridgeport, Connecticut	*First Blood* (1982), *Gorky Park* (1983), *Legal Eagles* (1986), *Belly of An Architect* (1987), *Presumed Innocent* (1990)
De Palma, Brian	1940–	Newark, New Jersey	Director. *Dressed To Kill* (1980), *Scarface* (1983), *Body Double* (1984), *The Untouchables* (1987)
Depardieu, Gerard	1948–	Chateauroux	*Loulou* (1980), *The Last Metro* (1980), *The Return of Martin Guerre* (1981), *Danton* (1982), *Jean de Florette* (1986), *Under the Sun of Satan* (1987), *Cyrano de Bergerac* (1990), *Green Card* (1990), *Merci La Vie* (1991), *Mon Père, Ce Héros* (1991), *Tous Les Matins du Monde* (1991), *Germinal* (1992)
Dietrich, Marlene (Maria Magdelena von Losch)	1901–92	Berlin	*Der Blaue Engel* (1930, *The Blue Angel*), *Blond Venus* (1932), *Shanghai Express* (1932), *The Devil is A Woman* (1935), *Desire* (1936), *Notorious* (1956), *Judgement at Nuremberg* (1961)
Dillon, Matt	1964–	Larchmont, New York	*Rumblefish* (1983), *The Flamingo Kid* (1984), *Target* (1985), *Kansas* (1988), *Drugstore Cowboy* (1989), *Singles* (1992)
Disney, Walt	1901–66	Chicago	Artist and film producer. *Snow White and the Seven Dwarfs* (1937), *Pinocchio* (1940), *Fantasia* (1940), *Dumbo* (1941)
Donat, Robert	1905–58	Withington	*The Count of Monte Cristo* (1934), *The Thirty-Nine Steps* (1935), *The Citadel* (1938), *Goodbye Mr Chips* (1939), *Inn of the Sixth Happiness* (1958)
Douglas, Kirk (Issur Danielovitch Demsky)	1916–	Amsterdam, New York	*The Strange Love of Martha Ivers* (1946), *Lust for Life* (1956), *Gunfight at the OK Coral* (1957), *Paths of Glory* (1957), *Spartacus* (1960), *The Man From Snowy River* (1982)
Douglas, Michael	1944–	New Jersey	*The China Syndrome* (1980), *Romancing the Stone* (1984), *The Jewel of the Nile* (1985), *Fatal Attraction* (1987), *Wall Street* (1987), *War of the Roses* (1989), *Basic Instinct* (1992), *Falling Down* (1992)
Dreyfuss, Richard	1947–	Brooklyn, New York	*The Apprenticeship of Duddy Kravitz* (1974), *Jaws* (1975), *Close Encounters of the Third Kind* (1977), *Whose Life is it Anyway ?* (1981), *Down and Out in Beverley Hills* (1986), *Stakeout* (1987), *Tin Men* (1987), *Moon Over Parador* (1988), *Always* (1989)
Dunaway, Faye	1941–	Bascom, Florida	*Bonnie and Clyde* (1967), *Chinatown* (1974), *The Towering Inferno* (1974), *The Eyes of Laura Mars* (1978), *The Champ* (1979), *Mommie Dearest* (1981), *Barfly* (1987), *The Handmaid's Tale* (1990)
Eastwood, Clint	1930–	San Francisco	*A Fistful of Dollars* (1964), *The Good, The Bad and the Ugly* (1966), *Play Misty For Me* (1971), *Dirty Harry* (1972). Director *Bird* (1987), *Unforgiven* (1992)
Eisenstein, Serge (Mikhailovich)	1898–1948	Riga	Director. *The Battleship Potemkin* (1925), *October* (1927), *Alexander Nevski* (1938), *Ivan The Terrible* (1944)
Elliot, Denholm	1922–1992	London	*A Bridge Too Far* (1977), *Raiders of the Lost Ark* (1981), *Trading Places* (1983), *A Private Function* (1984), *A Room With A View* (1985), *Defence of the Realm* (1985), *Maurice* (1987), *Indiana Jones and the Last Crusade* (1989)
Everett, Rupert	1960–	Norfolk	*Another Country* (1984), *Dance With A Stranger* (1985), *The Comfort of Strangers* (1990)
Fairbanks, Douglas Sr (Douglas Elton Ullman)	1883–1939	Denver, Colorado	*The Mark of Zorro* (1920), *The Three Musketeers* (1921), *Robin Hood* (1922), *The Thief of Baghdad* (1924)
Fairbanks, Douglas Jr	1907–	New York City	*Catherine the Great* (1934), *The Prisoner of Zenda* (1937), *Sinbad the Sailor* (1947)

Name	*Dates*	*Place of birth*	*Selected works*
Farrow, Mia	1945–	Los Angeles	*Rosemary's Baby* (1968), *The Great Gatsby* (1973), *A Midsummer Night's Sex Comedy* (1982), *The Purple Rose of Cairo* (1985), *Hannah and Her Sisters* (1986), *New York Stories* (1989), *Alice* (1991), *Husbands and Wives* (1992)
Fassbinder, Reiner Werner	1945–82	Bad Wörishofen, Germany	Director. *Die Bitteren Tränen der Petra von Kant* (1972, *The Bitter Tears of Petra von Kant), Die Ehe von Maria von Braun* (1978, *The Marraige of Maria von Braun*)
Fellini, Federico	1920–	Rimini	Director. *La Strada* (1954, *The Road*), *Fellini's Roma* (1972), *Amarcord* (1974, *I Remember), La Dolce Vita* (1960, *The Sweet Life*)
Fields, W C (William Claude Dunkenfeld)	1879–1946	Philadelphia	*It's A Gift* (1934), *The Old-Fashioned Way* (1934), *David Copperfield* (1935), *My Little Chickadee* (1940), *Never Give A Sucker An Even Break* (1941)
Finney, Albert	1936–	Salford	*Saturday Night and Sunday Morning* (1960), *Tom Jones* (1963), *Shoot the Moon* (1981), *Annie* (1982), *The Dresser* (1983), *The Green Man* (TV, 1990), *Miller's Crossing* (1990), *The Playboys* (1992)
Firth, Peter	1953–	Bradford	*Equus* (1983), *A Letter To Breshnev* (1985)
Flaherty, Robert	1884–1951	Iron Mountain, Michigan	Documentary film-maker. *Nanook of the North* (1922), *Moana* (1926), *Tabu* (1931). Director *Elephant Boy* (1937), *Louisiana Story* (1948)
Flynn, Errol	1909–59	Hobart, Tasmania	*In the Wake of the Bounty* (1933), *Captain Blood* (1935), *The Charge of the Light Brigade* (1936), *The Adventures of Robin Hood* (1938)
Fonda, Henry	1905–82	Grand Island, Nebraska	*Young Mr Lincoln* (1939), *The Grapes of Wrath* (1940), *Twelve Angry Men* (1957), *On Golden Pond* (1981)
Fonda, Jane	1937–	New York City	*Barbarella* (1968), *They Shoot Horses, Don't They?* (1969), *Coming Home* (1978), *The Electric Horseman* (1979), *The China Syndrome* (1980), *Nine To Five* (1981), *On Golden Pond* (1981), *The Morning After* (1986), *Old Gringo* (1989)
Ford, Harrison	1942–	Chicago	*Star Wars* (1977), *The Empire Strikes Back* (1980), *Raiders of the Lost Ark* (1981), *Blade Runner* (1982), *Indiana Jones and the Temple of Doom* (1984), *Witness* (1985), *Mosquito Coast* (1986), *Frantic* (1988), *Working Girl* (1988), *Indiana Jones and the Last Crusade* (1989), *Presumed Innocent* (1990), *Regarding Henry* (1991), *Patriot Games* (1992)
Ford, John	1895–1973	Cape Elizabeth, Maine	Director. *Stagecoach* (1935), *The Grapes of Wrath* (1940), *How Green was my Valley* (1941), *The Quiet Man* (1952)
Forman, Milos	1932–	Caslav	*Lásky Jedné Plavovlásky* (1965, *A Blonde in Love*), *Horí Mà Panenko* (1967, *The Fireman's Ball), One Flew Over the Cuckoo's Nest* (1975), *Amadeus* (1984)
Forsyth, Bill	1946–	Glasgow	Director. *That Sinking Feeling* (1979), *Gregory's Girl* (1981), *Local Hero* (1983)
Foster, Jodie (Ariane Munker)	1962–	Bronx, New York	*Alice Doesn't Live Here Anymore* (1974), *Bugsy Malone* (1976), *Taxi Driver* (1976), *The Little Girl Who Lives Down the Lane* (1976), *The Accused* (1988), *Silence of the Lambs* (1991), *Little Man Tate* (1991), *Shadows and Fog* (1992), *Somersby* (1992)
Gabin, Jean (Jean-Alexis Moncorgé)	1904–76	Paris	*Pépé le Moko* (1936), *Quai des Brumes* (1938, *Port of Shadows*), *Le Jour Se Lève* (1939, *Daybreak*)
Gable, Clark	1901–60	Cadiz, Ohio	*It Happened One Night* (1934), *Mutiny on the Bounty* (1935), *Gone With the Wind* (1939), *The Misfits* (1961)
Gambon, Michael	1940–	Dublin	*Turtle Diary* (1985), *The Singing Detective* (TV, 1986), *Paris By Night* (1989), *The Cook, The Thief, His Wife and Her Lover* (1989)

Film and television personalities (continued)

Name	*Dates*	*Place of birth*	*Selected works*
Garbo, Greta (Greta Lovisa Gustafsson)	1905–90	Stockholm	*Grand Hotel* (1932), *Anna Karenina* (1935), *Camille* (1936), *Ninotchka* (1939)
Gardner, Ava (Lucy Johnson)	1922–90	Smithfield, North Carolina	*The Barefoot Contessa* (1954), *The Sun Also Rises* (1957), *The Night of the Iguana* (1964)
Garland, Judy (Frances Gumm)	1922–69	Grand Rapids, Minnesota	*The Wizard of Oz* (1939), *Babes in Arms* (1939), *Meet Me in St Louis* (1944), *Easter Parade* (1948), *A Star is Born* (1954)
Gere, Richard	1949–	Philadelphia	*American Gigolo* (1980), *An Officer and a Gentleman* (1982), *Breathless* (1983), *The Cotton Club* (1984), *No Mercy* (1985), *Pretty Woman* (1990), *Somersby* (1992)
Gibson, Mel	1956–	Peekskill, New York	*Tim* (1979), *Mad Max* (1979), *Gallipoli* (1981), *The Year of Living Dangerously* (1982), *Lethal Weapon* (1987), *Hamlet* (1990), *Forever Young* (1992)
Gielgud, Sir John	1904–	London	*Oh What A Lovely War* (1969), *Brideshad Revisited* (TV, 1981), *Gandhi* (1982), *Prospero's Books* (1991)
Gilliam, Terry	1940–	Minneapolis	Director. *Jabberwocky* (1977), *The Time Bandits* (1980), *Brazil* (1985), *The Adventures of Baron Munchausen* (1988), *The Fisher King* (1991)
Gish, Lilian (Lilian de Guiche)	1896–1993	Springfield, Ohio	*Birth of A Nation* (1914), *Intolerance* (1916), *Orphans of the Storm* (1922)
Godard, Jean-Luc	1930–	Paris	Director. *A Bout de Souffle* (1959, *Breathless*), *Vivre Sa Vie* (1962, *My Life to Live*), *Weekend* (1968), *Sauve Qui Peut* (1980, *Slow Motion*), *Detective* (1984)
Goldberg, Whoopi (Caryn Johnson)	1949–	Manhattan, New York	*The Colour Purple* (1985), *Jumping Jack Flash* (1986), *Ghost* (1990), *Sister Act* (1992), *The Player* (1992)
Goldblum, Jeff	1952–	Pittsburgh	*Death Wish* (1974), *Invasion of the Bodysnatchers* (1978), *The Right Stuff* (1983), *The Big Chill* (1983), *The Fly* (1985), *The Tall Guy* (1989), *Earth Girls Are Easy* (1989), *Jurassic Park* (1993)
Goodman, John	1953–	St Louis, Missouri	*True Stories* (1986), *The Big Easy* (1987), *Sea of Love* (1990), *Always* (1990), *Barton Fink* (1991)
Granger, Stewart (James Lablanche Stewart)	1913–93	London	*The Man in Grey* (1943), *Love Story* (1944), *King Solomon's Mines* (1950), *Beau Brummell* (1954), *The Wild Geese* (1977)
Grant, Cary (Archibald Alexander Leech)	1904–86	Bristol	*The Awful Truth* (1937), *His Girl Friday* (1940), *Arsenic and Old Lace* (1944), *Notorious* (1946), *To Catch A Thief* (1953), *North by Northwest* (1959)
Greenaway, Peter	1942–	London	Director. *The Draughtsman's Contract* (1982), *The Belly of An Architect* (1987), *Drowning By Numbers* (1988), *The Cook, The Thief, His Wife and Her Lover* (1989), *Prospero's Books* (1991)
Grenfell, Joyce	1910–75	London	*The Happiest Days of Your Life* (1949), *Laughter in Paradise* (1951), *The Bells of St Trinians* (1954)
Griffith, D(avid) W(ark)	1875–1948	Floydsfork, Kentucky	Director. *The Birth of a Nation* (1915), *Intolerance* (1916)
Griffith, Melanie	1957–	New York City	*Something Wild* (1987), *Working Girl* (1988), *Pacific Heights* (1990), *Bonfire of the Vanities* (1990)
Guiness, Sir Alec	1914–	London	*Oliver Twist* (1948), *Kind Hearts and Coronets* (1949), *The Lavender Hill Mob* (1951), *The Man in the White Suit* (1951), *The Ladykillers* (1955), *The Bridge on the River Kwai* (1957), *Our Man in Havana* (1960), *Tunes of Glory* (1962), *Lawrence of Arabia* (1962), *Doctor Zhivago* (1966), *Tinker, Tailor, Solier, Spy* (TV, 1979), *Smiley"s People* (TV, 1981), *A Passage to India* (1984), *Little Dorrit* (1987), *A Handful of Dust* (1988), *Kafka* (1991)

Name	Dates	Place of birth	Selected works
Hackman, Gene	1931–	San Bernadino, California	*Bonnie and Clyde* (1967), *French Connection* (1971), *The Poseidon Adventure* (1972), *Young Frankenstein* (1974), *A Bridge Too Far* (1978), *Superman* (1978), *Mississippi Burning* (1989), *Postcards From the Edge* (1990), *Unforgiven* (1992)
Hancock, Tony	1924–68	Birmingham	*Educating Archie* (Radio, 1951), *Hancock's Half Hour* (TV, 1954)
Hanks, Tom	1957–	Oakland, California	*Splash !* (1984), *Big* (1988), *The Burbs* (1989), *Turner and Hooch* (1990), *Bonfire of the Vanities* (1991)
Harlow, Jean (Harlean Carpentier)	1911–37	Kansas City	*Hell's Angels* (1930), *Platinum Blonde* (1931), *Bombshell* (1933)
Harris, Richard	1930–	County Limerick	*The Guns of Navarone* (1961), *Mutiny on the Bounty* (1962), *This Sporting Life* (1963), *Camelot* (1967), *A Man Called Horse* (1969), *The Wild Geese* (1978), *The Field* (1990)
Harrison, Sir Rex (Reginald Carey Harrison)	1908–90	Houghton, Lancashire	*Storm in a Teacup* (1937), *Blithe Spirit* (1945), *The Constant Husband* (1958), *My Fair Lady* (1964), *Dr Doolittle* (1967)
Hauer, Rutger	1944–	Amsterdam	*Blade Runner* (1982), *The Osterman Weekend* (1983), *The Hitcher* (1985)
Hawks, Howard	1896–1977	Goshen, Indiana	Director. *The Road to Glory* (1925), *The Dawn Patrol* (1930), *The Big Sleep* (1946)
Hawn, Goldie (Jeanne)	1945–	Washington DC	*Cactus Flower*(1969), *There's A Girl in my Soup* (1970), *Private Benjamin* (1980), *Bird on a Wire* (1990), *Housesitter* (1992), *Death Becomes Her* (1992)
Hayworth, Rita (Margarita Carmen Cansino)	1918–87	New York City	*Gilda* (1946), *Separate Tables* (1958)
Hepburn, Audrey	1929–93	Brussels	*Roman Holiday* (1953), *Funny Face* (1957), *Breakfast at Tiffany's* (1961), *My Fair Lady* (1964), *Wait Until Dark* (1967), *Robin and Marian* (1976), *Always* (1991)
Hepburn, Katherine	1907–	Hartford, Connecticut	*Morning Glory* (1933), *The Philadelphia Story* (1940), *The African Queen* (1951), *Long Day's Journey into Night* (1962), *Guess Who's Coming to Dinner* (1967), *The Lion in Winter* (1968), *Suddenly Last Summer* (1968), *On Golden Pond* (1981)
Hershey, Barbara	1948–	Hollywood, California	*The Right Stuff* (1983), *The Natural* (1984), *Hannah and Her Sisters* (1986), *The Last Temptation of Christ* (1988), *Beaches* (1988), *Naked Lunch* (1991)
Herzog, Werner (Walter Stipetic)	1942–	Sachrang	Director. *Aguirre, der Zorn Gottes* (1973, *Aguirre, Wrath of God*), *Jeder Für Sich und Gott Gegen Alle* (1974, *The Mystery of Kaspar Hauser*), *Nosferatu, The Vampyre* (1979)
Heston, Charlton (John Charles Carter)	1923–	Evanston, Illinois	*Dark City* (1950), *The Greatest Show on Earth* (1951), *The Ten Commandments* (1956), *Ben Hur* (1956), *The Awakening* (1980)
Hill, George Roy	1922–	Minneapolis	Director. *Butch Cassidy and the Sundance Kid* (1969), *Slaughterhouse 5* (1972), *The Sting* (1973), *The World According to Garp* (1982)
Hitchcock, Sir Alfred (Joseph)	1899–1980	London	Director. *The Thirty-Nine Steps* (1935), *The Lady Vanishes* (1938), *Rebecca* (1940), *Psycho* (1960), *The Birds* (1963), *Frenzy* (1972)
Hoffman, Dustin	1937–	Los Angeles	*The Graduate* (1967), *Midnight Cowboy* (1969), *Marathon Man* (1976), *All The President's Men* (1976), *Kramer vs Kramer* (1979), *Tootsie* (1982), *Rain Man* (1989), *Dick Tracy* (1990), *Billy Bathgate* (1991), *Hook* (1991)
Holden, William	1918–82	O'Fallon, Illinois	*Sunset Boulevard* (1950), *The Bridge on the River Kwai* (1957), *Casino Royale* (1967), *The Wild Bunch* (1969)

Film and television personalities (continued)

Name	*Dates*	*Place of birth*	*Selected works*
Hope, Bob (Leslie Townes Hope)	1903-	Eltham, London	*Road to Singapore* (1940), *My Favourite Blonde* (1942), *Road to Morocco* (1942), *Road to Hong Kong* (1961)
Hopkins, Anthony	1941-	Port Talbot, Wales	*The Elephant Man* (1980), *The Bounty* (1983), *84 Charing Cross Road* (1986), *Silence of the Lambs* (1991), *Howard's End* (1992), *Dracula* (1992)
Hopper, Denis	1936–	Dodge City, Kansas	*Rebel without a Cause* (1955), *Giant* (1956), *Cool Hand Luke* (1967), *Easy Rider* (1969), *Apocalypse Now* (1979), *Blue Velvet* (1986), *River's Edge* (1986)
Hordern, Sir Michael	1911–	Berkhampstead	*The Constant Husband* (1955), *A Funny Thing Happened on the Way to the Forum* (1966), *The Missionary* (1982), *Paradise Postponed* (TV, 1986), *The Fool* (1990)
Hoskins, Bob	1942–	Bury St Edmunds, Suffolk	*Pennies from Heaven* (TV, 1978), *The Long Good Friday* (1980), *The Honorary Consul* (1983), *The Cotton Club* (1984), *Brazil* (1985), *Sweet Liberty* (1985), *Mona Lisa* (1986), *Who Framed Roger Rabbit* (1988), *Shattered* (1991), *Hook* (1991)
Howard, Leslie (Leslie Howard Stainer)	1893–1943	London	*Scarlet Pimpernel* (1935), *Gone With The Wind* (1939)
Howard, Trevor	1915–88	Cliftonville, Kent	*Brief Encounter* (1946), *The Third Man* (1949), *Mutiny on the Bounty* (1962), *The Charge of the Light Brigade* (1968), *Ryan's Daughter* (1970), *Gandhi* (1982), *White Mischief* (1987)
Hudson, Rock (Roy Scherer, Jr)	1925–85	Winnetka, Illinois	*Magnificent Obsession* (1954), *Giant* (1956), *Pillow Talk* (1959), *Ice Station Zebra* (1968)
Hurt, John	1940–	Chesterfield, Derbyshire	*A Man for All Seasons* (1966), *The Naked Civil Servant* (TV, 1975), *Midnight Express* (1978), *Alien* (1979), *The Elephant Man* (1980), *1984* (1984), *White Mischief* (1987), *Scandal* (1989)
Hurt, William	1950–	Washington DC	*The Janitor* (1981), *Body Heat* (1981), *The Big Chill* (1983), *Gorky Park* (1983), *Kiss of the Spider Woman* (1985), *Children of a Lesser God* (1986), *Broadcast News* (1987), *The Accidental Tourist* (1989), *Alice* (1990), *The Doctor* (1991)
Huston, Angelica	1952–	Ireland	*The Last Tycoon* (1976), *Prizzi's Honour* (1985), *The Dead* (1987), *A Handful of Dust* (1988), *The Witches* (1990), *The Grifters* (1990), *The Adams Family* (1991), *Bitter Moon* (1992)
Huston, John	1906–87	Nevada, Missouri	Director. *The Maltese Falcon* (1941), *The African Queen* (1951), *Moby Dick* (1956), *The Dead* (1987)
Irons, Jeremy	1948–	Cowes	*The French Lieutenant's Woman* (1981), *Brideshead Revisited* (TV, 1981), *Swann in Love* (1984), *The Mission* (1985), *Dead Ringers* (1988), *Reversal of Fortune* (1990), *Kafka* (1991), *Waterland* (1992), *Damage* (1992)
Ivory, James (Francis)	1928–	Berkeley, California	Director. *Heat and Dust* (1982), *The Bostonians* (1984), *A Room With A View* (1985), *Maurice* (1987), *Mr and Mrs Bridge* (1990), *Howard's End* (1992)
Jackson, Glenda	1936–	Liverpool	*Women in Love* (1969), *Sunday Bloody Sunday* (1971), *A Touch of Class* (1972), The *Turtle Diary* (1985), *Business As Usual* (1987), *The Rainbow* (1989)
Jackson, Gordon	1923–89	Glasgow	*Whisky Galore* (1948), *The Great Escape* (1962), *The Ipcress File* (1965), *The Prime of Miss Jean Brodie* (1969), *Upstairs, Downstairs* (TV, 1970-5), *The Medusa Touch* (1977), *The Professionals* (TV, 1977-81), *A Town Like Alice* (TV, 1980), *The Shooting Party* (1980)
Jarman, Derek	1942–	Northwood, Middlesex	*Jubilee* (1977), *Caravaggio* (1985), *Edward II* (1991), *Wittgenstein* (1993)

Name	Dates	Place of birth	Selected works
Johnson, Dame Celia	1908–82	Richmond, Surrey	*In Which We Serve* (1942), *The Happy Breed* (1944), *Brief Encounter* (1945), *The Prime of Miss Jean Brodie* (1969)
Jordan, Neil	1950–	Sligo	Director. *Angel* (1982), *Company of Wolves* (1984), *Mona Lisa* (1986), *High Spirits* (1988), *The Crying Game* (1992)
Karloff, Boris (William Pratt)	1887–1969	London	*Frankenstein* (1931)
Kasdan, Lawrence	1949–	Miami Beach, Florida	Director. *Body Heat* (1981), *The Big Chill* (1983), *Silverado* (1985), *The Accidental Tourist* (1989), *Love You to Death* (1990), *Grand Canyon* (1991)
Kaufman, Philip	1936–	Chicago	Director. *Invasion of the Body Snatchers* (1978), *The Right Stuff* (1983), *The Unbearable Lightness of Being* (1988), *Henry and June* (1990)
Kaye, Danny (Daniel Kominski)	1913–87	New York City	*Up In Arms* (1944), *Wonder Man* (1944), *The Secret Life of Walter Mitty* (1946), *Hans Christian Anderson* (1952)
Kazan, Elia (Elia Kazanjoglous)	1909–	Constantinople	*Gentlemen's Agreement* (1948), *On the Waterfront* (1954)
Keaton, Buster (Joseph Francis Keaton)	1895–1966	Pickway, Kansas	*The Butcher Boy* (1917), *The Navigator* (1924), *The General* (1926), *It's A Mad, Mad, Mad, Mad World* (1963)
Keaton, Diane	1946–	Los Angeles	*The Godfather* (1972), *Sleeper* (1973), *Annie Hall* (1977), *Manhattan* (1979), *Reds* (1981), *Mrs Soffel* (1984), *Baby Boom* (1987)
Keaton, Michael	1951–	Carapolis, Pennsylvania	*Beetlejuice* (1988), *Batman* (1989), *The Dream Team* (1989), *Pacific Heights* (1990), *Batman Returns* (1992)
Kelly, Gene	1912–	Pittsburgh	*For Me and My Gal* (1942), *An American in Paris* (1951), *Singin' in the Rain* (1952)
Kelly, Grace	1928–82	Philadelphia	*High Noon* (1952), *Dial M for Murder* (1954), *Rear Window* (1954), *To Catch a Thief* (1955), *High Society* (1956)
Kerr, Deborah (Deborah Jane Kerr Trimmer)	1921–	Helensburgh, Scotland	*The Life and Death of Colonel Blimp* (1943), *Perfect Strangers* (1945), *Black Narcissus* (1947), *The King and I* (1956), *Separate Tables* (1958), *The Night of the Iguana* (1964), *Casino Royale* (1967)
Kingsley, Ben (Krishna Banji)	1943–	Snaiton, Yorkshire	*Gandhi* (1982), *Turtle Diary* (1985), *Pascali's Island* (1988)
Kinski, Klaus (Claus Gunther Nakszynski)	1926–	Sopot, Gdańsk	*For A Few Dollars More* (1965), *Dr Zhivago* (1965), *Nosferatu* (1979), *Fitzcarraldo* (1982)
Kinski, Natassja	1960–	Berlin	*Tess* (1979), *Cat People* (1982), *One from the Heart* (1982), *Paris Texas* (1984)
Kline, Kevin	1947–	St Louis, Missouri	*Sophie's Choice* (1983), *The Big Chill* (1983), *Cry Freedom* (1987), *A Fish Called Wanda* (1988), *Love You to Death* (1990), *Chaplin* (1992)
Korda, Sir Alexander (Sándor Laszlo Korda)	1893–1956	Turkeye, Hungary	Director. *The Private Life of Henry VIII* (1932), *The Thief of Baghdad* (1940), *The Third Man* (1949), *Richard III* (1956)
Kubrick, Stanley	1928–	New York City	Director. *Spartacus* (1960), *Lolita* (1962), *Dr Strangelove* (1964), *2001: A Space Odyssey* (1965), *A Clockwork Orange* (1971), *The Shining* (1980), *Full Metal Jacket* (1987)
Kurosawa, Akira	1910–	Tokyo	Director. *Rashomon* (1951), *The Seven Samurai* (1954), *Kagemushi* (1980), *Ran* (1985)
Lambert, Christopher	1957–	New York City	*Greystoke* (1984), *Subway* (1985), *Highlander* (1985), *The Sicilian* (1987)
Lancaster, Burt (Stephen Burton)	1913–	New York City	*From Here To Eternity* (1953), *Gunfight at the OK Coral* (1957), *Birdman of Alcatraz* (1962), *Local Hero* (1983), *Field of Dreams* (1988)
Lang, Fritz	1890–1976	Vienna	Director. *Metropolis* (1926), *Fury* (1936)
Lange, Jessica	1949–	Cloquet, Minnesota	*King Kong* (1976), *The Postman Always Rings Twice* (1981), *Tootsie* (1982), *Music Box* (1989), *Cape Fear* (1991), *Night and the City* (1991)
Laughton, Charles	1899–1962	Scarborough	*The Private Life of Henry VIII* (1932), *Mutiny on the Bounty* (1935), *Hobson's Choice* (1954)

Film and television personalities (continued)

Name	*Dates*	*Place of birth*	*Selected works*
Laurel and Hardy			
Oliver Hardy	1892–1957	Atlanta, Georgia	*Putting Pants on Philip* (1927), *The Battle of the Century* (1927), *Two Tars* (1928), *The Perfect Day* (1929), *The Music Box* (1932), *Babes in Toyland* (1934), *Way out West* (1937), *The Flying Deuces* (1939), *Atoll K* (1950)
Stan Laurel	1890–1965	Ulveston, Lancashire	
Laurie, Piper (Rosetta Jacobs)	1932–	Detroit	*The Hustler* (1961), *Carrie* (1976), *Tender is the Night* (TV, 1985), *Children of a Lesser God* (1986), *Twin Peaks* (TV, 1991)
Lean, David	1908–	Croyden, Greater London	Director. *Blithe Spirit* (1945), *Brief Encounter* (1945), *Great Expectations* (1946), *Oliver Twist* (1948), *The Bridge on the River Kwai* (1957), *Lawrence of Arabia* (1962), *Doctor Zhivago* (1965), *A Passage to India* (1984)
Lee, Christopher	1922–	London	*The Curse of Frankenstein* (1956), *Dracula* (1958), *The Mummy* (1959), *The Three Musketeers* (1973), *The Man with the Golden Gun* (1974), *Howling II* (1985)
Lee, Spike	1957–	Atlanta, Georgia	Director. *She's Gotta Have it* 1986), *Do the Right Thing* (1989), *Mo Better Blues* (1990), *Malcolm X* (1992)
Leigh, Vivien (Vivien Mary Hartley)	1913–67	Darjeeling, India	*Fire Over England* (1937), *Gone With the Wind* (1945), *Lady Hamilton* (1941), *Anna Karenina* (1941), *A Streetcar Named Desire* (1951)
Lemmon, Jack (John Uhler Lemmon III)	1925–	Boston	*Some Like it Hot* (1959), *The Great Race* (1965), *The Odd Couple* (1968), *The China Syndrome* (1979), *JFK* (1991), *The Player* (1992), *Glengarry Glen Ross* (1992)
Levinson, Barry	1942–	Baltimore	Director. *Diner* (1982), *The Natural* (1984), *Tin Men* (1987), *Good Morning Vietnam* (1987), *Rain Man* (1988) , *Bugsy* (1991)
Lloyd, Harold (Clayton)	1893–1971	Burchard, Nebraska	*High and Dizzy* (1920), *Safety Last* (1923), *The Freshman* (1925), *Welcome Danger* (1929)
Lockwood, Margaret (Margaret Day)	1916–90	Karachi, India	*Lorna Doone* (1934), *The Lady Vanishes* (1938), *The Wicked Lady* (1945)
Loren, Sophia (Sofia Scicolone)	1934–	Rome	*The Pride and the Passion* (1957), *Two Women* (1961)
Losey, Joseph (Walton)	1909–84	La Crosse, Wisconsin	Director. *The Boy with the Green Hair* (1945), *The Servant* (1963), *The Go-Between* (1971)
Lubitsch, Ernst	1892–1947	Berlin	Director. *The Love Parade* (1929), *Ninotchka* (1939)
Lynch, David	1946–	Missoula, Montana	Director. *Eraserhead* (1976), *The Elephant Man* (1980), *Blue Velvet* (1986), *Wild at Heart* (1990), *Twin Peaks* (TV 1990-1), *Twin Peaks: Fire Walk With Me* (1992)
MacLaine, Shirley (Shirley Beaty)	1934–	Richmond, Virginia	*The Trouble with Harry* (1955), *Irma La Douce* (1963), *Sweet Charity* (1969) *Terms of Endearment* (1983), *Madame Sousatzka* (1988), *Postcards From the Edge* (1990)
Malkovich, John	1953–	Christopher, Illinois	*The Killing Fields* (1984), *Places in the Heart* (1984), *Empire of the Sun* (1987), *Dangerous Liaisons* (1988), *The Sheltering Sky* (1990)
Malle, Louis	1932–	Thumeries, France	Director, producer, screenwriter. *Les Amants* (1958, *The Lovers*), *Zazie dans le Métro* (1960), *Lacômbe Lucien* (1974), *Pretty Baby* (1978), *Atlantic City* (1990, *My Dinner with André* (1981), *Au revoir, Les enfants* (1987)
Mankiewicz, Joseph Leo	1909–	Wilkes-Barre, Pennsylvania	Director. *All About Eve* (1950), *The Barefoot Contessa* (1954), *Guys and Dolls* (1954), *Suddenly Last Summer* (1959)
Mansfield, Jayne (Vera Jayne Palmer)	1933–67	Bryn Mawr, Pennsylvania	*The Girl Can't Help It* (1957), *Too Hot to Handle* (1960)

Name	Dates	Place of birth	Selected works
Martin, Steve	1945–	Waco, Texas	*Dead Men Don't Wear Plaid* (1982), *The Man With Two Brains* (1983), *The Little Shop of Horrors* (1986), *Planes, Trains and Automobiles* (1987), *Roxanne* (1987), *Dirty Rotten Scoundrels* (1989), *Parenthood* (1989) *LA Story* (1991) , *Grand Canyon* (1991)
Marx Brothers, The			*The Cocoanuts* (1929), *Monkey Business*, (1931), *Horse Feathers* (1932), *Duck Soup* (1933) *A Day at the Races* (1937)
Chico (Leonard Marx)	1886–1961	New York City	
Harpo (Adolph Marx)	1888–1964		
Groucho (Julius Henry Marx)	1890–1977		
Zeppo (Herbert Marx)	1901–		
Mason, James	1909–84	Huddersfield	*Fanny by Gaslight* (1944), *The Wicked Lady* (1946) *A Star is Born* (1954), *Lolita* (1962), *Georgy Girl* (1966), *Heaven Can Wait* (1978), *The Boys From Brazil* (1978), *The Shooting Party* (1984)
Mastroianni, Marcello	1924–	Fontana Liri	*White Nights* (1957), *La Dolce Vita* (1960), *Otto e Mezzo* (1963), *Black Eyes* (1987)
Matthau, Walter	1920–	New York City	*The Odd Couple* (1968), *Hello Dolly* (1969), *Cactus Flower* (1969), *Pirates* (1986)
Maura, Carmen	1945–	Madrid	*Dark Habits* (1983),*What Have I Done to Deserve This?* (1964), *Law of Desire* (1987), *Women on the Verge of a Nervous Breakdown* (1988)
McQueen, Steve (Terence Steve McQueen)	1930–80	Slater, Missouri	*The Magnificent Seven* (1960), *The Great Escape* (1962), *The Cincinnati Kid* (1965), *Getaway* (1972), *Papillon* (1973), *Towering Inferno* (1974)
Mercouri, Melina (Anna Amalia Mercouri)	1923–	Athens	*Never on Sunday* (1960), *Topkapi* (1964), *Gaily, Gaily* (1969)
Midler, Bette	1945–	Honolulu, Hawaii	*Down and Out in Beverly Hills* (1986), *Ruthless People* (1986), *Outrageous Fortune* (1987), *Beaches* (1988), *Scenes From the Mall* (1991)
Mills, Hayley	1946–	London	*Tiger Bay* (1959),*Whistle Down the Wind* (1961)
Mills, Sir John	1908–	Felixstowe, Suffolk	*In Which We Serve* (1942), *Great Expectations* (1946), *The History of Mr Polly* (1972), *Ryan's Daughter* (1970)
Minnelli, Liza	1946–	Los Angeles	*Cabaret* (1972), *Stepping Out* (1991)
Mirren, Helen	1945–	London	*Cal* (1984), *Heavenly Pursuits* (1985), *Mosquito Coast* (1986), *The Cook, The Thief, His Wife and Her Lover* (1989), *The Comfort of Strangers* (1990)
Mitchum, Robert	1917–	Bridgeport, Connecticut	*Cape Fear* (1962), *Ryan's Daughter* (1970), *Farewell My Lovely* (1975), *The Big Sleep* (1978), *War and Remembrance* (TV, 1987), *Cape Fear* (1991)
Monroe, Marilyn (Norma Jean Mortensen or Baker)	1926–62	Los Angeles	*Gentlemen Prefer Blondes* (1953), *The Seven year Itch* (1955), *Some Like it Hot* (1959), *The Misfits* (1960)
Montand, Yves (Ivo Levi)	1921–91	Monsumagno, Italy	*The Wages of Fear* (1953), *Let's Make Love* (1962), *Jean de Florette* (1986), *Manon des Sources* (1986)
Moore, Demi (Demi Guines)	1962–	Roswell, New Mexico	*St Elmo's Fire* (1986), *Ghost* (1990), *The Butcher's Wife* (1991), *A Few Good Men* (1992), *Indecent Proposal* (1992)
Moore, Roger	1927–	London	*The Saint* (TV, 1963-8), *Live and Let Die* (1973), *The Man with the Golden Gun* (1974), *The Spy Who Loved Me* (1977), *The Wild Geese* (1978), *For Your Eyes Only* (1981), *Octopussy* (1983), *A View to a Kill* (1985)
Moreau, Jeanne	1928–	Paris	*Les Amants* (1958), *Jules et Jim* (1961), *Journal d'une Femme de Chambre* (1964), *Nikita* (1990)
Murphy, Eddie	1961–	Brooklyn, New York	*48 Hours* (1982), *Trading Places* (1983), *Beverly Hills Cop* (1985), *Coming to America* (1988), *Another 48 Hours* (1990)
Neeson, Liam	1952–	Ballymena, Northern Ireland	*Excalibur* (1981), *Suspect* (1987), *The Dead Pool* (1988), *Husbands and Wives* (1992)
Neill, Sam	1948–	New Zealand	*The Final Conflict* (1981), *Reilly Ace of Spies* (TV, 1983), *Plenty* (1985), *Kane and Abel* (TV, 1988), *A Cry in the Dark* (1988), *The Hunt for Red October* (1990), *Jurassic Park* (1993)

Film and television personalities (continued)

Name	*Dates*	*Place of birth*	*Selected works*
Newman, Paul	1925–	Cleveland, Ohio	*The Long Hot Summer* (1958), *Cat on a Hot Tin Roof* (1958), *The Hustler* (1961), *Butch Cassidy and the Sundance Kid* (1969), *The Sting* (1973), *The Verdict* (1982), *The Colour of Money* (1986), *Mr and Mrs Bridge* (1990)
Nicholson, Jack	1937–	Neptune, New Jersey	*Easy Rider* (1969), *Chinatown* (1974), *One Flew Over the Cuckoo's Nest* (1975), *The Shining* (1980), *The Postman Always Rings Twice* (1981), *Terms of Endearment* (1983) *Prizzi's Honour* (1985), *The Witches of Eastwick* (1987), *Batman* (1989), *A Few Good Men* (1992)
Niven, David (James David Graham Niven)	1910–83	London	*Wuthering Heights* (1939), *Raffles* (1940), *Around the World in Eighty Days* (1956), *Separate Tables* (1958), *The Guns of Navarone* (1961), *The Pink Panther* (1964), *Casino Royale* (1967), *Trail of the Pink Panther* (1982), *Curse of the Pink Panther* (1982)
Nolte, Nick	1940–	Omaha, Nebraska	*48 Hours* (1982), *Down and Out in Beverly Hills* (1986), *Cape Fear* (1991), *Prince of Tides* (1991), *The Player* (1992)
O'Neal, Ryan (Patrick Ryan O'Neal)	1941–	Los Angeles	*Love Story* (1970), *What's Up Doc?* (1972), *Paper Moon* (1973), *Nickleodeon* (1976)
O'Toole, Peter	1932–	Kerry, Connemara	*Lawrence of Arabia* (1962), *Goodbye Mr Chips* (1969), *The Stunt Man* (1980), *The Last Emperor* (1987)
Oldman, Gary	1959–	New Cross, London	*Sid and Nancy* (1986), *Prick up Your Ears* (1987), *Track 29* (1988), *JFK* (1991), *Dracula* (1992)
Olivier, Sir Laurence	1907–89	Dorking	*Wuthering Heights* (1939), *Rebecca* (1940), *Henry V* (1944), *Hamlet* (1948), *Richard III* (1956), *The Prince and the Showgirl* (1958), *The Entertainer* (1960), *Marathon Man* (1976), *A Bridge Too Far* (1977), *Brideshead Revisited* (TV, 1981)
Ophuls or Opüls, Max (Max Oppenheimer)	1902–57	Saarbrücken	Director. *La Ronde* (1950), *Lola Montez* (1955)
Pabst, G(eorg) W(ilhelm)	1895–1967	Raudnitz	Director. *Die Liebe der Jeanne Ney* (1927, *The Love of Jeanne Ney*), *Westfront 1918* (1930), *Der Letzte Akt* (1955, *The Last Act*)
Pacino, Al (Alfredo Pacino)	1940–	New York City	*The Godfather* (1972), *Scarface* (1983), *Sea of Love* (1990), *Dick Tracy* (1990), *Frankie and Johnny* (1991), *Glengarry Glen Ross* (1992), *Scent of a Woman* (1992)
Palin, Michael	1943–	Sheffield	*Monty Python's Flying Circus* (TV, 1969-74), *Monty Python and the Holy Grail* (1974),*The Life of Brian* (1978), *The Meaning of Life* (1982), *A Private Function* (1984), *A Fish Called Wanda* (1968), *Around the World in 80 Days* (TV, 1990), *Pole to Pole* (TV, 1992)
Parker, Alan	1944–	London	Director. *Bugsy Malone* (1976), *Midnight Express* (1978), *Birdy* (1985), *Angel Heart* (1987), *Mississippi Burning* (1988), *The Commitments* (1991)
Pasolini, Pier Paulo	1922–75	Bologna	Director. *The Gospel According to St Matthew* (1964), *The Decameron* (1972), *The Canterbury Tales* (1973)
Peck, Gregory (Eldred)	1916–	La Jolla, California	*Spellbound* (1945), *The Man in the Grey Flannel Suit* (1956), *Cape Fear* (1962), *To Kill a Mocking Bird* (1963), *The Omen* (1976) *Old Gringo* (1989), *Cape Fear* (1991)
Peckinpah, Sam	1925–84	Fresno, California	Director. *The Deadly Companions* (1961), *Major Dundee* (1965), *The Wild Bunch* (1969)

Name	*Dates*	*Place of birth*	*Selected works*
Pfeiffer, Michelle	1957–	Santa Ana, California	*Sweet Liberty* (1982) *The Witches of Eastwick* (1987), *Dangerous Liaisons* (1988), *The Fabulous Baker Boys* (1989), *The Russia House* (1990), *Frankie and Johnny* (1991), *Batman Returns* (1992)
Phoenix, River	1970–	Madras, Oregon	*Mosquito Coast* (1986), *Running on Empty* (1988), *Indiana Jones and the Last Crusade* (1989), *Love You to Death* (1990), *My Own Private Idaho* (1991)
Pickford, Mary (Gladys Mary Smith)	1893–1979	Toronto	*Rebecca of Sunnybrook Farm* (1917), *Poor Little Rich Girl* (1917), *Pollyanna* (1919), *Little Lord Fauntleroy* (1921)
Plowright, Joan	1929–	Scunthorpe Brigg, Lincolnshire	*The Entertainer* (1960), *Drowning By Numbers* (1988), *Love You to Death* (1990)
Plummer, Christopher	1927–	Toronto	*The Sound of Music* (1965), *The Man Who Would be King* (1975), *The Return of the Pink Panther* (1975), *Where the Heart Is* (1990)
Poitier, Sidney	1924–	Miami, Florida	*Cry, The Beloved Country* (1952), *The Blackboard Jungle* (1955), *Porgy and Bess* (1959), *Lilies of the Field* (1963), *In The Heat of the Night* (1967), *To Sir With Love* (1967)
Polanski, Roman	1933–	Paris	Director. *No'z w Wodzie* (1962, *Knife in the Water*), *Rosemary's Baby* (1968), *Repulsion* (1965), *Macbeth* (1971), *Tess* (1979), *Frantic* (1988), *Bitter Moon* (1992)
Pollack, Sydney	1934–	South Bend, Indiana	Director. *They Shoot Horses Don't They?* (1969), *The Electric Horseman* (1979), *Tootsie* (1982), *Out of Africa* (1985)
Powell, Michael	1905–90	Canterbury	Director. *The Thief of Baghdad* (1940), *Black Narcissus* (1947), *The Tales of Hoffman* (1951), *Peeping Tom* (1960), *The Boy Who Turned Yellow* (1972)
Powell, Robert	1944–	Salford, Lancashire	*Jesus of Nazareth* (TV, 1977), *The 39 Steps* (1978), *Pygmalion* (TV, 1981)
Preminger, Otto	1906–	Vienna	Director. *Laura* (1944), *Carmen Jones* (1954), *Bonjour Tristesse* (1959), *Porgy and Bess* (1959), *Exodus* (1960), *The Human Factor* (1979)
Pudovkin, Vsevoied (Ilarionovich)	1893–1953	Penza, Russia	Director. *Konets Sankt-Peterburga* (1927, *The End of St Petersburg*), *Potomok Chingis-Khan* (1928, *Storm over Asia*), *Dezetir* (1933, *Deserter*)
Quaid, Dennis	1954–	Houston, Texas	*The Big Easy* (1986), *Suspect* (1987), *Great Balls of Fire* (1989), *Postcards From the Edge* (1990)
Rampling, Charlotte	1946–	Sturmer, Essex	*Georgy Girl* (1966), *Angel Heart* (1987), *Paris By Night* (1988)
Rathbone, Basil (Philip St John)	1892–1967	Johannesburg	*David Copperfield* (1935), *Anna Karenina* (1935), *Captain Blood* (1935), *The Hound of the Baskervilles* (1939), *The Adventures of Sherlock Holmes* (1939)
Ray, Satyajit	1921–92	Calcutta	Director. *Pather Panchali* (1954, *On The Road*), *Aparajito* (1956, *The Unvanquished*), *Apur Sansar* (1959, *The World of Apu*), *The Kingdom of Diamonds* (1980), *Pickoo* (1982), *The Home Around the World* (1984)
Redford, Robert	1936–	Santa Barbara, California	*Barefoot in the Park* (1968), *Butch Cassidy and the Sundance Kid* (1969), *The Sting* (1973), *All the President's Men* (1976), *Out of Africa* (1986), *Indecent Proposal* (1993). Director *Ordinary People* (1980), *A River Runs Through It* (1993)
Redgrave, Sir Michael	1908–85	Bristol	*The Lady Vanishes* (1938), *The Dam Busters* (1955), *The Quiet American* (1958), *The Innocents* (1961)
Redgrave, Vanessa	1937–	London	*The Bostonians* (1984), *Wetherby* (1985), *Prick Up Your Ears* (1987), *The Ballad of the Sad Café* (1991), *Howard's End* (1992)
Reed, Sir Carol	1906–76	London	Director. *The Fallen Idol* (1948), *The Third Man* (1949)

Film and television personalities (continued)

Name	*Dates*	*Place of birth*	*Selected works*
Reed, Oliver	1938–	London	*The Damned* (1962), *Women in Love* (1969), *Castaway* (1987)
Reeve, Christopher	1952–	New York City	*Superman* (1978), *Superman II* (1980), *Superman III* (1983), *The Bostonians* (1984)
Reeves, Keanu	1965–	Beirut, Lebanon	*Dangerous Liaisons* (1988), *Bill and Ted's Excellent Adventure* (1989), *Parenthood* (1989), *Love You to Death* (1990), *My Own Private Idaho* (1991), *Dracula* (1992)
Reiner, Rob	1945–	The Bronx, New York	Director. *This is Spinal Tap* (1984), *Stand By Me* (1987), *The Princess Bride* (1988), *When Harry Met Sally* (1989), *Misery* (1990), *A Few Good Men* (1992)
Renoir, Jean	1894–1979	Paris	Director. *La Grande Illusion* (1937, *Grand Illusion*), *La Règle du Jeu* (1939, *The Rules of the Game*)
Resnais, Alan	1922–	Vannes, France	*Van Gogh* (1948), *Guernica* (1950), *Hiroshima, Mon Amour* (1959, *Hiroshima My Love*),*L'Année Dernière à Marienbad* (1961, *Last Year at Marienbad*), *Mon Oncle d'Amérique* (1980, *My American Uncle*), *La Vie est un Roman* (1983, *Life is a Novel*), *Melo* (1986)
Richardson, Miranda	1958–	Liverpool	*Dance With a Stranger* (1984), *Blackadder II* (TV, 1986), *Empire of the Sun* (1987), *A Month in the Country* (1988), *Damage* (1992)
Richardson, Sir Ralph	1902–83	Cheltenham	*Anna Karenina* (1948),*The Fallen Idol* (1948), *Richard III* (1956), *Long Day's Journey Into Night* (1962), *Dr Zhivago* (1966)
Riefenstahl, Leni	1902–	Berlin	Film-maker. *Triumph des Willens* (1935, *Triumph of the Will*), *Olympia* (1938)
Robbins, Tim	1958–	New York City	*Bull Durham* (1988), *Jacob's Ladder* (1990), *The Player* (1992), *Bob Roberts* (1992)
Roberts, Julia	1967–	Smyrna, Georgia	*Mystic Pizza* (1988), *Pretty Woman* (1990), *Sleeping With the Enemy* (1191) *Dying Young* (1991), *Hook* (1991), *The Player* (1992)
Robinson, Edward G (Emmanuel Goldberg)	1893–1973	Bucharest	*Little Caesar* (1930), *Double Indemnity* (1944), *All My Sons* (1948), *The Cincinnati Kid* (1965)
Roeg, Nicholas Jack	1928–	London	Director. *Walkabout* (1971), *Don't Look Now* (1973), *The Man Who Fell to Earth* (1976), *Bad Timing* (1980), *Castaway* (1986), *Black Widow* (1988), *Track 29* (1988)
Rogers, Ginger (Virginia Katherine McMath)	1911–	Missouri	*Flying Down to Rio* (1933), *The Gay Divorcee* (1934), *Top Hat* (1935), *Follow The Fleet* (1936)
Rooney, Mickey (Joe Yule, Jr)	1920–	Brooklyn, New York	*A Midsummer Night's Dream* (1935), *Babes in Arms* (1939), *Summer Holiday* (1948), *Breakfast at Tiffany's* (1961) *It's a Mad, Mad, Mad, Mad World* (1963)
Rossellini, Isabella	1952–	Rome	*White Nights* (1985), *Blue Velvet* (1985), *Cousins* (1989), *Wild at Heart* (1990)
Rossellini, Roberto	1906–77	Rome	Director. *Roma, città aperta* (1945, *Rome, Open City*) *Paisà* (1946, *Paisan*) *Germania, anno zero* (1947, *Germany, Year Zero*), *Il Generale della Rovere* (1959, *General della Rovere*)
Rourke, Mickey	1956–	Schenectady, New York	*Rumble Fish* (1983), *9½ weeks* (1985), *Angel Heart* (1987), *Wild Orchid* (1990)
Russell, Jane	1921–	Bernidji, Minnesota	*The Outlaw* (1943), *The Paleface* (1948), *Gentlemen Prefer Blondes* (1953)
Russell, Ken	1927–	Southampton	Director. *Women in Love* (1969), *The Music Lovers* (1971), *The Devils* (1971), *Gothic* (1987), *The Rainbow* (1989)
Russell, Kurt	1951–	Springfield, Massachusetts	*Silkwood* (1983), *Tequila Sunrise* (1988) *Backdraft* (1991)
Rutherford, Dame Margaret	1892–1972	London	*Blithe Spirit* (1945), *The Happiest Days of Your Life* (1950), *Murder She Said* (1961), *Murder Most Foul* (1964)

Name	*Dates*	*Place of birth*	*Selected works*
Ryan, Meg	1962–	Fairfield, Connecticut	*Top Gun* (1985), *El Presidio* (1988), *When Harry Met Sally* (1989), *The Doors* (1991)
Ryder, Winona	1971–	Winona, Michigan	*Beetlejuice* (1988), *Heathers* (1989), *Great Balls of Fire* (1989), *Dracula* (1992)
Saint, Eva Marie	1924–	Newark, New Jersey	*On the Waterfront* (1954), *North by Northwest* (1959)
Sarandon, Susan (Susan Abigail Tomalin)	1946–	New York City	*The Hunger* (1983), *The Witches of Eastwick* (1987), *Bull Durham* (1988), *White Palace* (1991), *Thelma and Louise* (1991), *Light Sleeper* (1991)
Schlesinger, John	1926–	London	Director. *A Kind Of Loving* (1962), *Billy Liar* (1963), *Far From the Madding Crowd* (1967), *Midnight Cowboy* (1969), *Sunday, Bloody Sunday* (1971), *Marathon Man* (1976), *Yanks* (1979), *Madame Sousatzka* (1989)
Schwarzenegger, Arnold	1947–	Graz, Austria	*Conan the Barbarian* (1982), *Conan the Destroyer* (1984), *The Terminator* (1984), *Total Recall* (1990), *Kindergarten Cop* (1990), *Teminator 2: Judgement Day* (1991), *Last Action Hero* (1992)
Scofield, Paul	1922–	Hurstpierpoint, Sussex	*A Man For All Seasons* (1966), *Hamlet* (1990)
Scorcese, Martin	1942–	Queens, New York	Director. *Mean Streets* (1973), *Taxi Driver* (1976), *Raging Bull* (1980), *The Mission* (1986), *The Last Temptation of Christ* (1988), *Goodfellas* (1990), *Cape Fear* (1991), *Age of Innocence* (1992)
Scott, George C(ampbell)	1927–	Wise, Virginia	*Anatomy of a Murder* (1959), *The Hustler* (1962), *Dr Strangelove* (1963), *Patton* (1970), *The Changeling* (1980), *Oliver Twist* (1982), *The Excorcist III* (1990)
Scott, Ridley	1937–	South Shields	Director. *Alien* (1979), *Blade Runner* (1982), *No Way Out* (1989), *Thelma and Louise* (1991)
Segal, George	1934–	New York City	*Who's Afraid of Virginia Woolf?* (1966), *The Owl and the Pussycat* (1979), *The Last Married Couple in America* (1979), *Look Who's Talking* (1989)
Sellers, Peter	1925–80	Southsea	*The Ladykillers* (1959), *I'm Alright Jack* (1959), *Dr Strangelove* (1963), *The Pink Panther* (1963), *A Shot in the Dark* (1964), *Return of The Pink Panther* (1975), *The Pink Panther Strikes Again* (1976), *Revenge of The Pink Panther* (1978)
Sennett, Mack (Michael Sinott)	1880–1960	Richmond, Quebec	Producer. *The Keystone Cops* (1912), *Sennett Bathing Beauties* (1920)
Sharif, Omar (Michael Shalhouz)	1932–	Alexandria, Egypt	*Lawrence of Arabia* (1962) *Doctor Zhivago* (1965) *Funny Girl* (1968), *The Tamarind Seed* (1974), *Return to Eden* (1982)
Sheen, Charlie (Carlos Irwin Estevez)	1965–	Santa Monica, California	*Wall Street* (1987), *Platoon* (1987)
Sheen, Martin (Ramon Estevez)	1940–	Dayton, Ohio	*Catch 22* (1970), *The Little Girl Who Lives Down the Lane* (1976), Apocalypse Now (1979), *Gandhi* (1982), *The Dead Zone* (1983), *Wall Street* (1987)
Shepherd, Cybil	1950–	Memphis, Tennessee	*The Last Picture Show* (1971), *Taxi Driver* (1976), *The Lady Vanishes* (1979), *Moonlighting* (TV, 1985-9), *Alice* (1991)
Signoret, Simone (Simone Henriette Charlotte Kaminker)	1921–85	Wiesbaden	*La Ronde* (1950), *Les Diaboliques* (1952), *Room at the Top* (1959), *Ship of Fools* (1965)
Sim, Alistair	1900–76	Edinburgh	*The Happiest Days of Your Life* (1950), *Scrooge* (1951), *Laughter in Paradise* (1951), *The Belles of St Trinians* (1954)
Simmons, Jean	1929–	London	*Great Expectations* (1946), *Black Narcissus* (1946), *Hamlet* (1948), *The Blue Lagoon* (1948), *Spartacus* (1960)
Sinatra, Frank (Francis Albert Sinatra)	1915–	Hoboken, New Jersey	*From Here to Eternity* (1953), *The Man With the Golden Arm* (1955), *The Manchurian Candidate* (1962)

Film and television personalities (continued)

Name	*Dates*	*Place of birth*	*Selected works*
Slater, Christian	1969–	New York City	*The Name of the Rose* (1986), *Heathers* (1989), *Pump up the Volume* (1990), *Robin Hood, Prince of Thieves* (1991)
Smith, Dame Maggie	1934–	Ilford, Essex	*The Prime of Miss Jean Brodie* (1969), *Travels with my Aunt* (1972), *A Private Function* (1984), *A Room With a View* (1985), *The Lonely Passion of Judith Hearne*
Spader, James	1960–	Boston, Massachusetts	*Pretty in Pink* (1986), *Sex, Lies and Videotape* (1989), *The Rachel Papers* (1989), *Bad Influence* (1990), *White Palace* (1991), *The Music of Chance* (1993)
Spielberg, Steven	1947–	Cincinnati, Ohio	Director. *Duel* (1972) *Jaws* (1975), *Close Encounters of the Third Kind* (1977), *Raiders of the Lost Ark* (1981), *ET* (1982), *The Colour Purple* (1985), *Indiana Jones and the Temple of Doom* (1984), *Empire of the Sun* (1987), *Indiana Jones and the Last Crusade* (1989), *Hook* (1992), *Jurassic Park* (1993)
Stallone, Sylvester	1946–	New York City	*Rocky* (1976) *Part II* (1979), *III* (1982), *IV* (1985), *V* (1990), *First Blood* (1981), *Rambo* (1985), *Over the Top* (1987), *Rambo III* (1988), *Tango and Cash* (1990), *Cliffhanger* (1992)
Stamp, Terence	1939–	Stepney	*The Collector* (1965), *Far From the Madding Crowd* (1967), *Superman* (1978), *Superman II* (1980), *Company of Wolves* (1985), *Legal Eagles* (1986), *Wall Street* (1987)
Stanton, Harry Dean	1926–	Kentucky	*Cool Hand Luke* (1967), *The Godfather – Part II* (1974), *Alien* (1979), *Repo Man* (1984), *Paris, Texas* (1984)
Steiger, Rod (Rodney Stephen Steiger)	1925–	Westhampton, New York	*On the Waterfront* (1954), *Oklahoma!* (1955), *Al Capone* (1958), *Dr Zhivago* (1965), *In the Heat of the Night* (1967), *American Gothic* (1988)
Sternberg, Josef von (Jonas Stern)	1894–1969	Vienna	*Der Blaue Engel* (1930, *The Blue Angel*), *The Devil is a Woman* (1935)
Stewart, James	1908–	Indiana, Pennsylvania	*You Can't Take it With You* (1938), *The Philadelphia Story* (1940), *It's a Wonderful Life* (1946), *Rear Window* (1954), *Vertigo* (1958), *Anatomy of a Murder* (1959)
Stone, Oliver	1946–	New York City	*Platoon* (1987), *Wall Street* (1987), *Born on the Fourth of July* (1989), *The Doors* (1991), *JFK* (1991)
Streep, Meryl (Mary Louise Streep)	1949–	Summit, New Jersey	*The Deer Hunter* (1978), *Kramer vs Kramer* (1979), *The French Lieutenant's Woman* (1981), *Sophie's Choice* (1982), *Silkwood* (1983), *Plenty* (1985) *Out of Africa* (1986), *A Cry in the Dark* (1988), *Postcards From the Edge* (1990)
Streisand, Barbra	1942–	Brooklyn, New York	*Funny Girl* (1968), *Hello Dolly* (1969), *What's up Doc?* (1972), *The Way We Were* (1973), *A Star Is Born* (1976) *Yentl* (1983), *Nuts* (1987), *Prince of Tides* (1991)
Stroheim, Erich (Oswald) von	1886–1957	Vienna	Director. *Blind Husbands* (1919), *Greed* (1923), *La Grande Illusion* (1930), *Sunset Boulevard* (1955)
Sutherland, Donald	1934–	St John, New Brunswick	*The Dirty Dozen* (1967), *The Eagle Has Landed* (1977), *Invasion of the Body Snatchers* (1978), *Ordinary People* (1980), *Backdraft* (1991)
Suzman, Janet	1939–	Johannesburg	*Nicholas and Alexandra* (1972), *Voyage of the Damned* (1976), *The Draughtsman's Contract* (1982), *Leon, the Pig Farmer* (1992)
Swanson, Gloria (Gloria May Josephine Svensson)	1897–1983	Chicago	*Male and Female* (1919), *Manhandled* (1924), The *Trespasser* (1929), *Sunset Boulevard* (1950)
Tandy, Jessica	1909–	London	*The Birds* (1963),*The World According to Garp* (1982), *Still of the Night* (1982), *The Bostonians* (1984), *Cocoon* (1985), *The House on Carroll Street* (1988), *Driving Miss Daisy* (1989)

Name	Dates	Place of birth	Selected works
Tati, Jacques (Jacques Tatischeff)	1908–82	Pecq	Director. *Jour de Fête* (1947, *The Big Day*), *Les Vacances de Mr Hulot* (1953, *Mr Hulot's Holiday*), *Mon Oncle* (1958, *My Uncle*)
Taylor, Elizabeth (Rosemond)	1932–	London	*The Father of the Bride* (1950), *Cat on a Hot Tin Roof* (1958), *Butterfield 8* (1960), *Cleopatra* (1962), *Who's Afraid of Virginia Woolf* (1966), *Suddenly Last Summer* (1968), *The Mirror Crack'd* (1981), *Young Toscanini* (1988)
Temple, Shirley	1928–	Santa Monica, California	*Stand Up and Cheer* (1934), *Bright Eyes* (1934), *Heidi* (1937), *The Little Princess* (1939)
Thomas, Terry (Thomas Terry Hoar Stevens)	1911–90	Finchley, London	*Private's Progress* (1956), *I'm All Right Jack* (1959), *It's a Mad, Mad, Mad, Mad World* (1963), *Those Magnificent Men in Their Flying Machines* (1965), *Don't Look Now* (1968)
Tracy, Spencer (Bonadventure)	1900–67	Milwaukee	*Up The River* (1930), *Captains Courageous* (1937), *Boys' Town* (1938), *Woman of the Year* (1942), *State of the Union* (1948), *Father of the Bride* (1950), *Bad Day at Black Rock* (1955), *Judgement at Nuremberg* (1961), *Guess Who's Coming to Dinner* (1967)
Travolta, John	1954–	Englewood, New Jersey	*Saturday Night Fever* (1977), *Grease* (1978), *Staying Alive* (1983), *Perfect* (1985), *Look Who's Talking* (1989)
Truffaut, François	1932–84	Paris	Director. *Les Quatres Cents Coups* (1959, *The 400 Blows*), *Tirez sur le Pianiste* (1960, *Shoot the Pianist*), *Jules et Jim* (1962), *La Nuit Américaine* (1972, *Day for Night*), *L'Enfant Sauvage* (1969) *Le Dernier Metro* (1980), *Vivement Dimanche* (1983, *Lively Sunday*)
Turner, Kathleen	1954–	Springfield, Missouri	*Body Heat* (1981), *Romancing the Stone* (1984), *The Jewel of the Nile* (1985), *Prizzi's Honour* (1985), *Peggy Sue Got Married* (1986), *The Accidental Tourist* (1989), *The War of the Roses* (1989)
Turturro, John	1957–	Brooklyn, New York	*Raging Bull* (1980), *Hannah and Her Sisters* (1986), *Do the Right Thing* (1989), *Miller's Crossing* (1990), *Barton Fink* (1991)
Ustinov, Peter (Alexander)	1921–	London	*Quo Vadis* (1951), *Spartacus* (1960), *Topkapi* (1964), *Death on the Nile* (1978), *Appointment with Death* (1988)
Vadim, Roger (Roger Vadim Plemiannikov)	1928–	Paris	Director. *Et Dieu Créa La Femme* (1956, *And God Created Woman*), *Les Liaisons Dangereuses* (1959), *Barbarella* (1968), *La Vice et la Vertue* (1962)
Valentino, Rudolph (Rodolpho Alfonso di Valentino d'Antonguolla)	1895–1926	Castellaneta	*The Four Horsemen of the Apocalypse* (1919), *The Sheikh* (1921), *Blood and Sand* (1922)
Vidor, King	1894–1982	Galveston, Texas	Director. *The Turn in the Road* (1919), *The Big Parade* (1925), *Hallelujah* (1929), *Northwest Passage* (1940), *War and Peace* (1956), *Solomon and Sheba* (1959)
Visconti, Count Luchino	1906–76	Milan	Director. *Ossessione* (1942, *Obsession*), *La Terra Trema* (1947, *The Earth Trembles*), *Il Gattopardo* (1963, *The Leopard*), *Morte a Venezia* (1971, *Death in Venice*)
Von Sydow, Max	1929–	Lund	*The Seventh Seal* (1956), *The Greatest Story Ever Told* (1965), *Hannah and Her Sisters* (1986), *Pelle the Conqueror* (1988), *Awakenings* (1990), *The Father* (1990), *The Ox* (1991), *The Touch* (1992)
Wajda, Andrzej	1926–	Suwałki, Poland	Director. *Pokolenie* (1954, *A Generation*), *Czlowiek z marmary* (1977, *Man of Marble*), *Czlowiek z Zelaza* (1981, *Man of Iron*)
Walken, Christopher	1943–	Astoria, New York	*The Deer Hunter* (1978), *The Dogs of War* (1981), *The Dead Zone* (1983), *A View to a Kill* (1984), *Biloxi Blues* (1988), *The Comfort of Strangers* (1990), *Batman Returns* (1992)

Film and television personalities (continued)

Name	*Dates*	*Place of birth*	*Selected works*
Walters, Julie	1950–	Birmingham	*Educating Rita* (1983), *Prick up Your Ears* (1987), *Personal Services* (1987), *Just Like A Woman* (1991)
Washington, Denzel	1954–	Mt Vernon, New York	*Cry Freedom* (1987), *Mo' Better Blues* (1990), *Mississippi Masala* (1991), *Malcolm X* (1992)
Wayne, John (Marion Michael Morrison)	1907–79	Winterset, Iowa	*Stagecoach* (1939), *Red River* (1948), *She Wore a Yellow Ribbon* (1949), *The Quiet Man* (1952), *True Grit* (1969)
Weaver, Sigourney	1949–	New York City	*Alien* (1979), *The Janitor* (1981), *The Year of Living Dangerously* (1982), *Ghostbusters* (1984), *Aliens* (1986), *Gorillas in the Mist* (1988), *Working Girl* (1988), *Aliens III* (1992)
Weir, Peter	1944–	Sydney	Director. *Picnic at Hanging Rock* (1975), *Gallipoli* (1981), *The Year of Living Dangerously* (1982), *Witness* (1985), *Mosquito Coast* (1986), *Dead Poet's Society* (1989), *Green Card* (1990)
Welles, Orson	1915–85	Kenosha, Washington	Director, screenplay writer, actor. *Citizen Kane* (1941), *The Magnificent Ambersons* (1942), *Lady from Shanghai* (1948), *Macbeth* (1948), *The Third Man* (acting only, 1949), *Othello* (1952), *Touch of Evil* (1958), *Chimes at Midnight* (1966)
West, Mae	1892–1980	New York City	*Night After Night* (1932), *I'm No Angel* (1933), *My Little Chickadee* (1939), *Myra Breckinridge* (1970)
Wilder, Billy (Samuel Wilder)	1906–	Vienna	Director. *The Major and The Minor* (1942), *The Lost Weekend* (1945), *Sunset Boulevard* (1955), *The Apartment* (1960), *The Private Life of Sherlock Holmes* (1970), *Fedora* (1978)
Wilder, Gene (Jerome Silberman)	1935–	Milwaukee	*Bonnie and Clyde* (1967), *Blazing Saddles* (1974), *Young Frankenstein* (1974), *The Frisco Kid* (1979), *Stir Crazy* (1982), *Haunted Honeymoon* (1986)
Williams, Robin	1952–	Chicago	*Popeye* (1980), *The World According to Garp* (1982), *Good Morning Vietnam* (1987), *Dead Poets Society* (1989), *Awakenings* (1990), *The Fisher King* (1991), *Hook* (1991), *Toys* (1992)
Winger, Deborah	1955–	Columbus, Ohio	*An Officer and a Gentleman* (1982), *Terms of Endearment* (1983), *Legal Eagles* (1985), *Betrayed* (1988), *The Sheltering Sky* (1990)
Winters, Shelley (Shirley Schrift)	1922–	St Louis, Missouri	*A Double Life* (1948), *The Night of the Hunter* (1955), *Lolita* (1962)
Wood, Natalie (Natasha Gurdin)	1938–81	San Francisco	*Rebel Without a Cause* (1955), *Splendour in the Grass* (1961), *West Side Story* (1961), *This Property is Condemned* (1966), *Bob and Carol and Ted and Alice* (1969)
Woodward, Joanne	1930–	Thomasville, Georgia	*The Long Hot Summer* (1958), *The Glass Menagerie* (1987), *Mr and Mrs Bridge* (1990)
Wyler, William	1902–81	Mulhausen, Alsace	Director. *Mrs Miniver* (1942), *The Best Years of our Lives* (1946), *Friendly Persuasion* (1956), *Ben Hur* (1959), *Funny Girl* (1968)
Zefirelli, Franco	1922–	Florence	Director. *Romeo and Juliet* (1968), *La Traviata* (1982), *Othello* (1986), *Hamlet* (1990)
Zinnemann, Fred	1907–	Vienna	Director. *High Noon* (1952), *From Here to Eternity* (1953), *A Man for All Seasons* (1966)

Motion picture Academy Awards (Oscars)

1928
Picture *Wings*, Paramount
Director Frank Borzage, *Seventh Heaven*; Lewis Milestone, *Two Arabian Nights*
Actress Janet Gaynor, *Seventh Heaven, Street Angel, Sunrise*
Actor Emil Jannings, *The Way of All Flesh, The Last Command*

1929
Picture *The Broadway Melody*, MGM
Director Frank Lloyd, *The Divine Lady*
Actress Mary Pickford, *Coquette*
Actor Warner Baxter, *In Old Arizona*

1930
Picture *All Quiet on the Western Front*, Universal
Director Lewis Milestone, *All Quiet on the Western Front*
Actress Norma Shearer, *The Divorcee*
Actor George Arliss, *Disraeli*

1931
Picture *Cimarron*, RKO Radio
Director Norman Taurog, *Skippy*
Actress Marie Dressler, *Min and Bill*
Actor Lionel Barrymore, *A Free Soul*

1932
Picture *Grand Hotel*, MGM
Director Frank Borzage, *Bad Girl*
Actress Helen Hayes, *The Sin of Madelon Claudet*
Actor Fredric March, *Dr Jekyll and Mr Hyde*, and Wallace Beery, *The Champ*

1933
Picture *Cavalcade*, Fox
Director Frank Lloyd, *Cavalcade*
Actress Katharine Hepburn, *Morning Glory*
Actor Charles Laughton, *The Private Life of Henry VIII*

1934
Picture *It Happened One Night*, Columbia
Director Frank Capra, *It Happened One Night*
Actress Claudette Colbert, *It Happened One Night*
Actor Clark Gable, *It Happened One Night*

1935
Picture *Mutiny on the Bounty*, MGM
Director John Ford, *The Informer*
Actress Bette Davis, *Dangerous*
Actor Victor McLaglen, *The Informer*

1936
Picture *The Great Ziegfeld*, MGM
Director Frank Capra, *Mr. Deeds Goes to Town*
Actress Luise Rainer, *The Great Ziegfeld*
Actor Paul Muni, *The Story of Louis Pasteur*
Supporting Actress Gale Sondergaard, *Anthony Adverse*
Supporting Actor Walter Brennan, *Come and Get It*

1937
Picture *The Life of Emile Zola*, Warner Bros
Director Leo McCarey, *The Awful Truth*
Actress Luise Rainer, *The Good Earth*
Actor Spencer Tracy, *Captains Courageous*
Supporting Actress Alice Brady, *In Old Chicago*
Supporting Actor Joseph Schildkraut, *The Life of Emile Zola*

1938
Picture *You Can't Take it With You*, Columbia
Director Frank Capra, *You Can't Take it With You*
Actress Bette Davis, *Jezebel*
Actor Spencer Tracy, *Boys Town*
Supporting Actress Fay Bainter, *Jezebel*
Supporting Actor Walter Brennan, *Kentucky*

1939
Picture *Gone with the Wind*, Selznick MGM
Director Victor Flemming, *Gone with the Wind*
Actress Vivien Leigh, *Gone with the Wind*
Actor Robert Donat, *Goodbye Mr Chips*
Supporting Actress Hattie McDaniel, *Gone with the Wind*
Supporting Actor Thomas Mitchell, *Stagecoach*

1940
Picture *Rebecca*, Selznick UA
Director John Ford, *The Grapes of Wrath*
Actress Ginger Rogers, *Kitty Foyle*
Actor James Stewart, *The Philadelphia Story*
Supporting Actress Jane Darwell, *The Grapes of Wrath*
Supporting Actor Walter Brennan, *The Westerner*

1941
Picture *How Green Was My Valley*, 20th Century Fox
Director John Ford, *How Green Was My Valley*
Actress Joan Fontaine, *Suspicion*
Actor Gary Cooper, *Sergeant York*
Supporting Actress Mary Astor, *The Great Lie*
Supporting Actor Donald Crisp, *How Green Was My Valley*

1942
Picture *Mrs Miniver*, MGM
Director William Wyler, *Mrs Miniver*
Actress Greer Garson, *Mrs Miniver*
Actor James Cagney, *Yankee Doodle Dandy*
Supporting Actress Teresa Wright, *Mrs Miniver*
Supporting Actor Van Heflin, *Johnny Eager*

1943
Picture *Casablanca*, Warner Bros
Director Michael Curtiz, *Casablanca*
Actress Jennifer Jones, *The Song of Bernadette*
Actor Paul Lukas, *Watch on the Rhine*
Supporting Actress Katina Paxinou, *For Whom the Bell Tolls*
Supporting Actor Charles Coburn, *The More the Merrier*

1944
Picture *Going My Way*, Paramount
Director Leo McCarey, *Going My Way*
Actress Ingrid Bergman, *Gaslight*
Actor Bing Crosby, *Going My Way*
Supporting Actress Ethel Barrymore, *None But the Lonely Heart*
Supporting Actor Barry Fitzgerald, *Going My Way*

1945
Picture *The Lost Weekend*, Paramount
Director Billy Wilder, *The Lost Weekend*
Actress Joan Crawford, *Mildred Pierce*
Actor Ray Milland, *The Lost Weekend*
Supporting Actress Anne Revere, *National Velvet*
Supporting Actor James Dunn, *A Tree Grows in Brooklyn*

1946
Picture *The Best Years of Our Lives*, Goldwyn-RKO Radio
Director William Wyler, *The Best Years of Our Lives*
Actress Olivia de Havilland, *To Each His Own*

Motion picture Academy Awards (Oscars) (continued)

Actor Fredric March, *The Best Years of Our Lives*
Supporting Actress Anne Baxter, *The Razor's Edge*
Supporting Actor Harold Russell, *The Best Years of Our Lives*

1947
Picture *Gentleman's Agreement*, 20th Century Fox
Director Elia Kazan, *Gentleman's Agreement*
Actress Loretta Young, *The Farmer's Daughter*
Actor Ronald Colman, *A Double Life*
Supporting Actress Celeste Holm, *Gentleman's Agreement*
Supporting Actor Edmund Gwenn, *Miracle on 34th Street*

1948
Picture *Hamlet*, Rank-Two Cities-UI
Director John Huston, *Treasure of Sierra Madre*
Actress Jane Wyman, *Johnny Belinda*
Actor Laurence Olivier, *Hamlet*
Supporting Actress Claire Trevor, *Key Largo*
Supporting Actor Walter Huston, *Treasure of Sierra Madre*

1949
Picture *All the King's Men*, Rossen-Columbia
Director Joseph L Mankiewicz, *A Letter to Three Wives*
Actress Olivia de Havilland, *The Heiress*
Actor Broderick Crawford, *All the King's Men*
Supporting Actress Mercedes McCambridge, *All the King's Men*
Supporting Actor Dean Jagger, *Twelve O'Clock High*

1950
Picture *All About Eve*, 20th Century Fox
Director Joseph L Mankiewicz, *All About Eve*
Actress Judy Holliday, *Born Yesterday*
Actor José Ferrer, *Cyrano de Bergerac*
Supporting Actress Josephine Hull, *Harvey*
Supporting Actor George Sanders, *All About Eve*

1951
Picture *An American in Paris*, MGM
Director George Stevens, *A Place in the Sun*
Actress Vivien Leigh, *A Streetcar Named Desire*
Actor Humphrey Bogart, *The African Queen*
Supporting Actress Kim Hunter, *A Streetcar Named Desire*
Supporting Actor Karl Malden, *A Streetcar Named Desire*

1952
Picture *The Greatest Show on Earth*, DeMille-Paramount
Director John Ford, *The Quiet Man*
Actress Shirley Booth, *Come Back, Little Sheba*
Actor Gary Cooper, High Noon
Supporting Actress Gloria Grahame, *The Bad and the Beautiful*
Supporting Actor Anthony Quinn, *Viva Zapata*

1953
Picture *From Here to Eternity*, Columbia
Director Fred Zinnemann, *From Here to Eternity*
Actress Audrey Hepburn, *Roman Holiday*
Actor William Holden, *Stalag 17*
Supporting Actress Donna Reed, *From Here to Eternity*
Supporting Actor Frank Sinatra, *From Here to Eternity*

1954
Picture *On the Waterfront*, Horizon-American Corp, Columbia
Director Elia Kazan, *On the Waterfront*
Actress Grace Kelly, *The Country Girl*
Actor Marlon Brando, *On the Waterfront*
Supporting Actress Eva Marie Saint, *On the Waterfront*
Supporting Actor Edmond O'Brien, *The Barefoot Contessa*

1955
Picture *Marty*, Hecht and Lancaster, United Artists
Director Delbert Mann, *Marty*
Actress Anna Magnani, *The Rose Tattoo*
Actor Ernest Borgnine, *Marty*
Supporting Actress Jo Van Fleet, *East of Eden*
Supporting Actor Jack Lemmon, *Mister Roberts*

1956
Picture *Around the World in 80 Days*, Michael Todd Co, Inc-UA
Director George Stevens, *Giant*
Actress Ingrid Bergman, *Anastasia*
Actor Yul Brynner, *The King and I*
Supporting Actress Dorothy Malone, *Written on the Wind*
Supporting Actor Anthony Quinn, *Lust for Life*

1957
Picture *The Bridge on the River Kwai*, Horizon Picture, Columbia
Director David Lean, *The Bridge on the River Kwai*
Actress Joanne Woodward, *The Three Faces of Eve*
Actor Alec Guinness, *The Bridge on the River Kwai*
Supporting Actress Miyoshi Umeki, *Sayonara*
Supporting Actor Red Buttons, *Sayonara*

1958
Picture *Gigi*, Arthur Freed Productions Inc, MGM
Director Vincente Minnelli, *Gigi*
Actress Susan Hayward, *I Want to Live!*
Actor David Niven, *Separate Tables*
Supporting Actress Wendy Hiller, *Separate Tables*
Supporting Actor Burl Ives, *The Big Country*

1959
Picture *Ben Hur*, MGM
Director William Wyler, *Ben Hur*
Actress Simone Signoret, *Room at the Top*
Actor Charlton Heston, *Ben Hur*
Supporting Actress Shelley Winters, *The Diary of Anne Frank*
Supporting Actor Hugh Griffith, *Ben Hur*

1960
Picture *The Apartment*, Mirisch Co Inc, United Artists
Director Billy Wilder, *The Apartment*
Actress Elizabeth Taylor, *Butterfield 8*
Actor Burt Lancaster, *Elmer Gantry*
Supporting Actress Shirley Jones, *Elmer Gantry*
Supporting Actor Peter Ustinov, *Spartacus*

1961
Picture *West Side Story*, Mirisch Pictures Inc, and B and P Enterprises Inc, United Artists
Director Robert Wise and Jerome Robbins, *West Side Story*
Actress Sophia Loren, *Two Women*
Actor Maximillian Schell, *Judgment at Nuremberg*
Supporting Actress Rita Moreno, *West Side Story*
Supporting Actor George Chakiris, *West Side Story*

1962
Picture *Lawrence of Arabia*, Horizon Pictures Ltd, Columbia
Director David Lean, *Lawrence of Arabia*
Actress Anne Bancroft, *The Miracle Worker*
Actor Gregory Peck, *To Kill a Mockingbird*
Supporting Actress Patty Duke, *The Miracle Worker*
Supporting Actor Ed Begley, *Sweet Bird of Youth*

1963
Picture *Tom Jones*, A Woodfall Production, UA-Lopert Pictures
Director Tony Richardson, *Tom Jones*
Actress Patricia Neal, *Hud*
Actor Sidney Poitier, *Lilies of the Field*
Supporting Actress Margaret Rutherford, *The VIPs*
Supporting Actor Melvyn Douglas, *Hud*

1964
Picture *My Fair Lady*, Warner Bros
Director George Cukor, *My Fair Lady*
Actress Julie Andrews, *Mary Poppins*
Actor Rex Harrison, *My Fair Lady*
Supporting Actress Lila Kedrova, *Zorba the Greek*
Supporting Actor Peter Ustinov, *Topkapi*

1965
Picture *The Sound of Music*, Argyle Enterprises Production, 20th Century Fox
Director Robert Wise, *The Sound of Music*
Actress Julie Christie, *Darling*
Actor Lee Marvin, *Cat Ballou*
Supporting Actress Shelley Winters, *A Patch of Blue*
Supporting Actor Martin Balsam, *A Thousand Clowns*

1966
Picture *A Man for All Seasons*, Highland Films Ltd Production, Columbia
Director Fred Zinnemann, *A Man for All Seasons*
Actress Elizabeth Taylor, *Who's Afraid of Virginia Woolf?*
Actor Paul Scofield, *A Man for All Seasons*
Supporting Actress Sandy Dennis, *Who's Afraid of Virginia Woolf?*
Supporting Actor Walter Matthau, *The Fortune Cookie*

1967
Picture *In the Heat of the Night*, Mirisch Corp Productions, United Artists
Director Mike Nichols, *The Graduate*
Actress Katharine Hepburn, *Guess Who's Coming to Dinner*
Actor Rod Steiger, *In the Heat of the Night*
Supporting Actress Estelle Parsons, *Bonnie and Clyde*
Supporting Actor George Kennedy, *Cool Hand Luke*

1968
Picture *Oliver!* Columbia Pictures
Director Sir Carol Reed, *Oliver!*
Actress Katharine Hepburn, *The Lion in Winter* and Barbra Streisand, *Funny Girl*
Actor Cliff Robertson, *Charly*
Supporting Actress Ruth Gordon, *Rosemary's Baby*
Supporting Actor Jack Albertson, *The Subject Was Roses*

1969
Picture *Midnight Cowboy*, Jerome Hellman-John Schlesinger Production, United Artists
Director John Schlesinger, *Midnight Cowboy*
Actress Maggie Smith, *The Prime of Miss Jean Brodie*
Actor John Wayne, *True Grit*
Supporting Actress Goldie Hawn, *Cactus Flower*
Supporting Actor Gig Young, *They Shoot Horses Don't They?*

1970
Picture *Patton*, Frank McCarthy-FranklinJ Schaffner Production, 20th Century Fox
Director Franklin J Schaffner, *Patton*
Actress Glenda Jackson, *Women in Love*
Actor George C Scott, *Patton*
Supporting Actress Helen Hayes, *Airport*
Supporting Actor John Mills, *Ryan's Daughter*

1971
Picture *The French Connection*, D'Antoni Productions, 20th Century Fox
Director William Friedkin, *The French Connection*
Actress Jane Fonda, *Klute*
Actor Gene Hackman, *The French Connection*
Supporting Actress Cloris Leachman, *The Last Picture Show*
Supporting Actor Ben Johnson, *The Last Picture Show*

1972
Picture *The Godfather*, Albert S Ruddy Production, Paramount
Director Bob Fosse, *Cabaret*
Actress Liza Minnelli, *Cabaret*
Actor Marlon Brando, *The Godfather*
Supporting Actress Eileen Heckart, *Butterflies Are Free*
Supporting Actor Joel Gray, *Cabaret*

1973
Picture *The Sting*, Universal-Bill Phillips-George Roy Hill Production, Universal
Director George Roy Hill, *The Sting*
Actress Glenda Jackson, *A Touch of Class*
Actor Jack Lemmon, *Save the Tiger*
Supporting Actress Tatum O'Neal, *Paper Moon*
Supporting Actor John Houseman, *The Paper Chase*

1974
Picture *The Godfather, Part II*, Coppola Co Production, Paramount
Director Francis Ford Coppola, *The Godfather, Part II*
Actress Ellen Burstyn, *Alice Doesn't Live Here Anymore*
Actor Art Carney, *Harry and Tonto*
Supporting Actress Ingrid Bergman, *Murder on the Orient Express*
Supporting Actor Robert De Niro, *The Godfather, Part II*

1975
Picture *One Flew Over the Cuckoo's Nest*, Fantasy Films Production, United Artists
Director Milos Forman, *One Flew Over the Cuckoo's Nest*
Actress Louise Fletcher, *One Flew Over the Cuckoo's Nest*
Actor Jack Nicholson, *One Flew Over the Cuckoo's Nest*
Supporting Actress Lee Grant, *Shampoo*
Supporting Actor George Burns, *The Sunshine Boys*

1976
Picture *Rocky*, Robert Chartoff-Irwin Winkler Production, United Artists
Director John G Avildsen, *Rocky*
Actress Faye Dunaway, *Network*
Actor Peter Finch, *Network*
Supporting Actress Beatrice Straight, *Network*
Supporting Actor Jason Robards, *All the President's Men*

Motion picture Academy Awards (Oscars) (continued)

1977
Picture *Annie Hall*, Jack Rollins-Charles H Joffe Production, United Artists
Director Woody Allen, *Annie Hall*
Actress Diane Keaton, *Annie Hall*
Actor Richard Dreyfuss, *The Goodbye Girl*
Supporting Actress Vanessa Redgrave, *Julia*
Supporting Actor Jason Robards, *Julia*

1978
Picture *The Deer Hunter*, Michael Cimino Film Production, Universal
Director Michael Cimino, *The Deer Hunter*
Actress Jane Fonda, *Coming Home*
Actor Jon Voight, *Coming Home*
Supporting Actress Maggie Smith, *California Suite*
Supporting Actor Christopher Walken, *The Deer Hunter*

1979
Picture *Kramer vs Kramer*, Stanley Jaffe Production, Columbia Pictures
Director Robert Benton, *Kramer vs Kramer*
Actress Sally Field, *Norma Rae*
Actor Dustin Hoffman, *Kramer vs Kramer*
Supporting Actress Meryl Streep, *Kramer vs Kramer*
Supporting Actor Melvyn Douglas, *Being There*

1980
Picture *Ordinary People*, Wildwood Enterprises Production, Paramount
Director Robert Redford, *Ordinary People*
Actress Sissy Spacek, *Coal Miner's Daughter*
Actor Robert De Niro, *Raging Bull*
Supporting Actress Mary Steenburgen, *Melvin and Howard*
Supporting Actor Timothy Hutton, *Ordinary People*

1981
Picture *Chariots of Fire*, Enigma Productions, Ladd Company/Warner Bros
Director Warren Beatty, *Reds*
Actress Katharine Hepburn, *On Golden Pond*
Actor Henry Fonda, *On Golden Pond*
Supporting Actress Maureen Stapleton, *Reds*
Supporting Actor John Gielgud, *Arthur*

1982
Picture *Gandhi*, Indo-British Films Production/Columbia
Director Richard Attenborough, *Gandhi*
Actress Meryl Streep, *Sophie's Choice*
Actor Ben Kingsley, *Gandhi*
Supporting Actress Jessica Lange, *Tootsie*
Supporting Actor Louis Gossett Jr, *An Officer and a Gentleman*

1983
Picture *Terms of Endearment*, Paramount
Director James L Brooks, *Terms of Endearment*
Actress Shirley MacLaine, *Terms of Endearment*
Actor Robert Duvall, *Tender Mercies*
Supporting Actress Linda Hunt, *The Year of Living Dangerously*
Supporting Actor Jack Nicholson, *Terms of Endearment*

1984
Picture *Amadeus*, Orion Pictures
Director Milos Forman, *Amadeus*
Actress Sally Field, *Places in the Heart*
Actor F Murray Abraham, *Amadeus*
Supporting Actress Dame Peggy Ashcroft, *A Passage to India*
Supporting Actor Haing S Ngor, *The Killing Fields*

1985
Picture *Out of Africa*, Universal
Director Sydney Pollack, *Out of Africa*
Actress Geraldine Page, *The Trip to Bountiful*
Actor William Hurt, *Kiss of the Spider Woman*
Supporting Actress Anjelica Huston, *Prizzi's Honor*
Supporting Actor Don Ameche, *Cocoon*

1986
Picture *Platoon*, Orion Pictures
Director Oliver Stone, *Platoon*
Actress Marlee Matlin, *Children of a Lesser God*
Actor Paul Newman, *The Color of Money*
Supporting Actress Dianne Wiest, *Hannah and Her Sisters*
Supporting Actor Michael Caine, *Hannah and Her Sisters*

1987
Picture *The Last Emperor*, Columbia Pictures
Director Bernardo Bertolucci, *The Last Emperor*
Actress Cher, *Moonstruck*
Actor Michael Douglas, *Wall Street*
Supporting Actress Olympia Dukakis, *Moonstruck*
Supporting Actor Sean Connery, *The Untouchables*

1988
Picture *Rain Man*, United Artists
Director Barry Levington, *Rain Man*
Actress Jodie Foster, *The Accused*
Actor Dustin Hoffman, *Rain Man*
Supporting Actress Geena Davis, *The Accidential Tourist*
Supporting Actor Kevin Kline, *A Fish Called Wanda*

1989
Picture *Driving Miss Daisy*, Warner Brothers
Director Oliver Stone, *Born on the Fourth of July*
Actress Jessica Tandy, *Driving Miss Daisy*
Actor Daniel Day-Lewis, *My Left Foot*
Supporting Actress Brenda Fricker, *My Left Foot*
Supporting Actor Denzel Washington, *Glory*

1990
Picture *Dances With Wolves*, Orion
Director Kevin Costner, *Dances With Wolves*
Actress Kathy Bates, *Misery*
Actor Jeremy Irons, *Reversal of Fortune*
Supporting Actress Whoopi Goldberg, *Ghost*
Supporting Actor Joe Pesci, *Goodfellas*

1991
Picture *The Silence of the Lambs*, Orion
Director Jonathan Demme, *The Silence of the Lambs*
Actress Jodie Foster, *The Silence of the Lambs*
Actor Anthony Hopkins, *The Silence of the Lambs*
Supporting Actress Mercedes Ruehl, *The Fisher King*
Supporting Actor Jack Palance, *City Slickers*

1992
Picture *Unforgiven*
Director Clint Eastwood, *Unforgiven*
Actress Emma Thompson, *Howard's End*
Actor Al Pacino, *Scent of a Woman*
Supporting Actress Marisa Tomei, *My Cousin Vinny*
Supporting Actor Gene Hackman, *Unforgiven*

International film festivals

Exact dates of these festivals may vary but the months indicated remain generally the same.

*Denotes a festival recognized by the International Federation of Film Producers Association

Country	*Festival*	*Time of year*
Australia	Australian International Film Festival	September
	Melbourne	June
	Sydney*	June
Austria	Austrian Film Days	September
	Viennale (Vienna)	March
Belgium	Antwerp	March
	Belgian Film Festival (Brussels)	January
	Flanders (Ghent)	October
Brazil	Rio de Janeiro	November
	Sao Paulo	October
Bulgaria	Varna	June
Burkina Faso	Pan African Film Festival	February–March
Canada	Banff TV Festival	June
	Montreal World Film Festival	August
	Toronto	September
	Vancouver	September–October
Colombia	Cartagena	April
Cuba	New Latin American Cinema	December
Czech Republic	Karlovy Vary*	July
	Prague Television Festival	June
Egypt	Cairo	December
England	Birmingham Film and Television Festival	October–November
	Bristol Film and Television Festival	September
	Cambridge	July
	London Film Festival	November–December
Finland	Midnight Sun	June
	Tampere Film Festival	February
France	Amiens	November
	Annecy (animation)	May–June (alternate years)
	Avoriaz (fantasy and horror)	January
	Biarritz (Iberian, Latin American)	September
	Cannes*	May
	Cherbourg	October
	Clermont-Ferrand (shorts)	February
	Cognac	April
	Deauville (American films)	September
	Grenoble (thrillers)	October
	Paris	March–April
	Rouen	March
	Strasbourg	March
Germany	Berlin*	February
	Hof	October
	Munich	June
Greece	Thessaloniki	October
India	Indian International Film Festival	January
Ireland	Cork*	September–October
	Dublin	October
Israel	Jerusalem	June–July
Italy	Bergamo (horror)	July
	Pesaro International Festival of New Cinema	June
	Pordenone (silents)	October
	Festival dei Popoli, Florence	November–December
	San Remo	March
	Trieste Science-Fiction Festival	July
	Venice Film Festival	September
Japan	Tokyo	September
Monaco	Monte Carlo Film Festival	January–February
Netherlands	Dutch Film Days and Film Market	September
	Rotterdam Film International	March
New Zealand	Wellington	July

International film festivals (continued)

Country	*Festival*	*Time of year*
Poland	Gdańsk	September
	Katowice (scientific/technical)	November
	Krakow* (shorts)	June
Portugal	Porto Fantasy Film Festival	February
Russia	Moscow	July
	Teleforum, Moscow	September
Scotland	Edinburgh	August–September
Spain	Barcelona	November
	Madrid (Imagfic)	March–April
	San Sebastian*	September
	Sitges (horror)	September–October
Sweden	Gothenburg	January–February
	Malmo	September
Switzerland	Locarno*	August
	Nyon* (documentaries)	October
	Vevey	August
Taiwan	Taipei	October
United States	AFI/European Community Film Festival, Los Angeles	June
	AFI/LA Film Festival	April
	American Film Market, LA	February–March
	Boston	September
	Chicago	October
	Cinetex, Las Vegas	September
	Filmfest DC, Washington	April–May
	Hawaii, Honolulu	November
	Miami	February
	Mill Valley Film and Video Festival	October
	NATPE, New Orleans	January
	New York*	September–October
	Palm Springs	January
	Portland	February
	Santa Barbara International Film Festival	March
	San Francisco International Film Festival*	April–May
	Seattle International Film Festival	May–June
	Sundance Film Festival, Park City Utah	January
	Women in Film, LA	October
Yugoslavia	Belgrade	January–February
	Pula (national)	July
	Zagreb* (animation)	June

MUSIC

Musical symbols, terms and abbreviations

SYMBOLS

The staff or stave

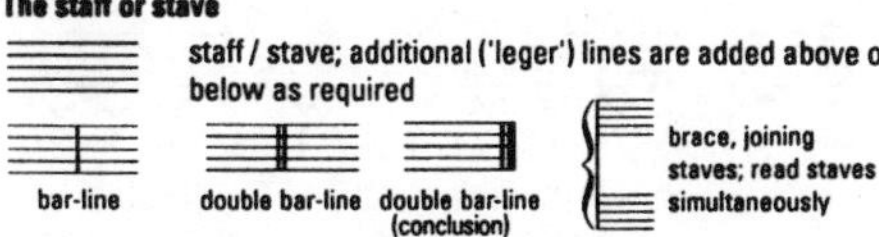

Clefs

These are in common use (the note Middle C is shown in each case):

In older music the C clef is found on any of the five lines of the staff

Accidentals

♯ sharp, raising the pitch of a note by a semitone
× double sharp, raising the pitch of a note by two semitones
♭ flat, lowering the pitch of a note by a semitone
♭♭ double flat, lowering the pitch of a note by two semitones
♮ natural, cancelling the effect of a previous accidental

Note lengths

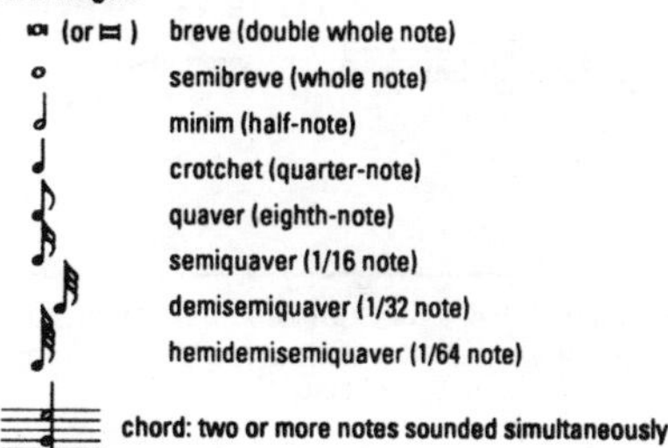

Ties (⌒, ‿) are used to combine the lengths of two or more notes of the same pitch; dots are used to extend the length of a note by one-half, eg:

Beams are often used to group together quavers (eighth-notes) or shorter notes into larger units, eg:

Time signatures

The lower figure indicates the unit of measurement, the upper figure the number of these units in a bar, eg:

2/2 (or ¢) two minims (half-notes) or their equivalent in a bar
4/4 (or C) four crotchets (quarter-notes) or their equivalent in a bar
3/8 three quavers (eighth-notes) or their equivalent in a bar
9/16 nine semiquavers (1/16-notes) or their equivalent in a bar

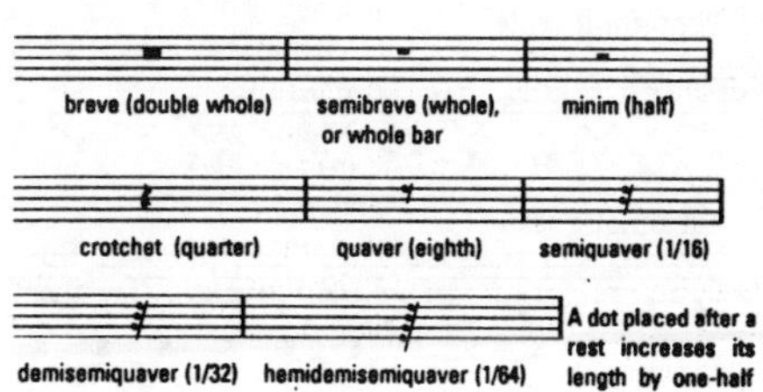

Articulation and expression

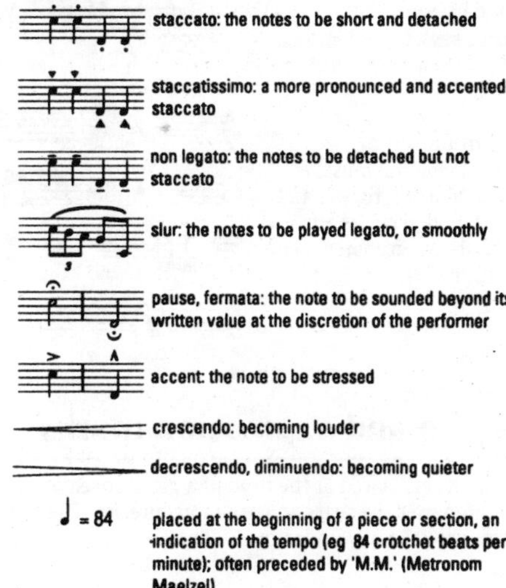

♩ = 84 placed at the beginning of a piece or section, an indication of the tempo (eg 84 crotchet beats per minute); often preceded by 'M.M.' (Metronom Maelzel)

Ornaments

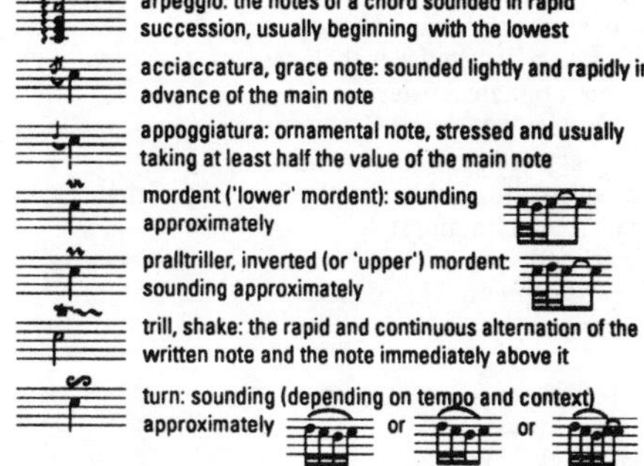

Musical scales and keys

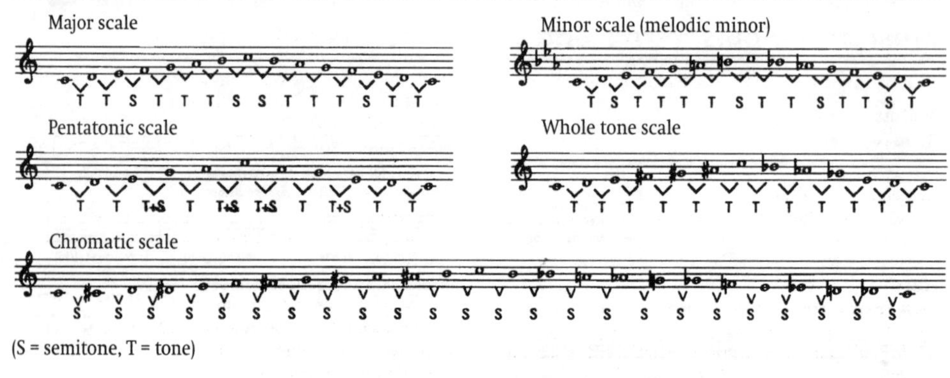

Key signatures
(Major keys: capital letters; minor keys; lower-case letters)

Repetition
In instrumental music repeated notes, figures and even whole sections are often shown in abbreviated form, eg:

Tempo and expression marks

Italian terms placed at the head of a piece or section to indicate its tempo and general expression have changed in meaning over the years and are rarely precise. The following list gives some indication of how the more common terms are generally understood today.

adagio slow
agitato agitated
allegro lively, fast
allegretto rather lively
andante 'going'; at a moderate pace
andantino a little quicker than *andante*
animate animated, lively
appassionato impassioned
assai 'very' (*allegro assai* very fast)
brio 'spirit', 'fire' (*allegro con brio* fast energetic)
cantabile in a singing style
dolente sadly
energico energetic, vigorous
espressivo expressive
feroce fierce
fuoco 'fire' (*con fuoco* with fire)
furioso furious
giocoso light, humerous
grave slow, solemn
grazioso graceful
larghetto fairly slow
largo slow, broad
legato smoothly
leggiero light
lento slow
maestoso majestic
marciale in the style of a march
marziale in a military style
meno 'less' (*meno mosso* slower)
moderato moderate, at a moderate pace
molto 'much', 'very' (*molto lento* very slow)
moto 'motion' (*con moto* quickly)
pesante heavy, ponderous
piacevole pleasant, agreeable
piu 'more' (*piu mosso* faster)
poco 'little' (*poco adagio* rather slowly)
presto very fast
prestissimo faster than *presto*
quasi 'as if', 'almost' (*andante, quasi allegretto*)
risoluto resolute, in a determined manner
scherzando in a jocular style
semplice simple, in an unforced style
sotto voce extremely quiet
strepitoso loud, noisy, boisterous
tanto, troppo 'so much', 'too much' (*allegro non tanto* fast but not very fast; *lento ma non troppo* slow, but not becoming too slow)
veloce rapid
vivace lively, very fast
vivo vigorous, brisk

Other terms and abbreviations

This section lists only those symbols and terms that might be found in a musical score.

a tempo in time (ie reverting to the original speed)
accel (accelerando) getting gradually faster
alla breve in a time signature where minims or semibreves and the metrical units
allarg. (allargando) broadening, getting slower and (usually) louder
arco with the bow
cal. (calando) dying away
colla voce 'with the voice', follow closely the singer's tempo
col legno 'with the wood', play a string instrument with the stick of the bow
con sordino with the mute
cresc. (crescendo) becoming louder
D C, da capo (al fine) return to the start of the piece or movement (and play to the end marked *fine*)
decresc. (decrescendo) becoming quieter
dim. (diminuendo) becoming quieter
dol (dolce) sweetly
D S, dal segno return to and repeat from the sign (usually $)
f (forte) loud; *ff (fortissimo), fff* increasing degrees of loudness
Fine see *D C* above
fz (forzato) accented
gliss. (glissando) slide quickly from one note to another
GP 'General pause', a rest for the whole ensemble
MM metronom maelzel
marc. (marcato) stressed, accented
mf (mezzo forte) moderately loud
mp (mezzo piano) moderately quiet
ossia 'or', 'alternatively'
ottava, 8va, 8 play a passage an octave higher or lower, *coll ottava, col 8va, col 8:* play the written notes together with their octaves
p (piano) quiet, soft; *pp (pianissimo), ppp* increasing (but imprecise) degrees of softness
ped. depress the sustaining (loud) pedal on a piano, release indicated by *
pizz. (pizzicato) 'plucked' with the finger, rather than bowed
rall. (rallentando) getting slower
rinf., rfz, rf getting suddenly louder
rit., ritard. (ritardando) getting slower
rubato with a freedom of tempo, but not impairing the overall flow of the music
segno see *D S* above
senza sordino without the mute
sf, sfz, (sforzando, sforzato) strongly accented
simile play in the same manner as before
smorz. (smorzando) fading away
sost. (sostenuto) sustained
stacc. (stoccato) short and detached
string. (stringendo) getting much faster
ten. (tenuto) linger slightly on the note
tre. corde see *una corda* below
una corda depress the soft pedal on the piano, release indicated by *tre corde*
V S (volti subito) turn the page quickly

World orchestras

Name	*Date founded*	*Location*
Academy of Ancient Music	1973	London
Academy of St Martin-in-the Fields	1959	London
Berliner Philharmonic	1882	Germany
Boston Symphony	1881	Boston
BBC Northern Symphony Orcestra	1934	
BBC Scottish Symphony	1935	Glasgow
BBC Symphony	1930	London
BBC Welsh Symphony	1935	Cardiff
Bournemouth Symphony	1893	Bournemouth
Chicago Symphony	1891	Chicago
City of Birmingham Symphony	1920	Birmingham
City of Glasgow Philharmonic		Glasgow
Cleveland Symphony	1918	Cleveland
Concertgebouw	1888	Amsterdam
Detroit Symphony	1914	Detroit
English Chamber	1948	London
Hallé	1858	Manchester
Israel Philharmonic	1936	Tel Aviv
Leningrad Philharmonic	1921	St Petersburg
London Philharmonic	1932	London
London Symphony	1904	London
Los Angeles Philharmonic	1919	Los Angeles
Melbourne Symphony	1906	Melbourne
La Scala, Milan	1778	Milan
NBC Symphony	1937–54	New York
National Symphony	1931	Washington DC
New Orleans Philharmonic Symphony	1936	New Orleans
New York Philharmonic	1842	New York
New York Symphony	1878	New York
Northern Sinfonia	1958	Newcastle-Upon-Tyne
Orchestre Symphonique de Monréal	1842	Montreal
Oslo Philharmonic	1919	Oslo
The Philharmonia	1945	London
Pittsburgh Symphony	1926	Pittsburgh
Royal Liverpool Philharmonic	1840	Liverpool
Royal Philharmonic	1946	London
San Francisco Symphony	1911	San Francisco
Santa Cecelia Academy	1895	Rome
Scottish Chamber	1974	Edinburgh
Scottish National	1891	Glasgow
Seattle Symphony	1903	Seattle
Staatskapelle	1923	Dresden
Sydney Symphony	1934	Sydney
Vienna Philharmonic	1842	Vienna
Vienna Symphony	1900	Vienna

Brass instruments

French horn trumpet cornet trombone tuba

Percussion instruments

timpani side drum bass drum cymbals

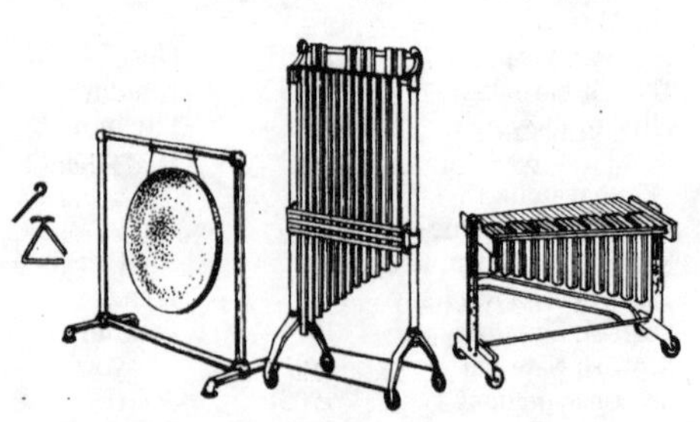

triangle tam-tam tubular bells xylophone

String instruments

violin viola

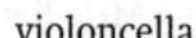

violoncella

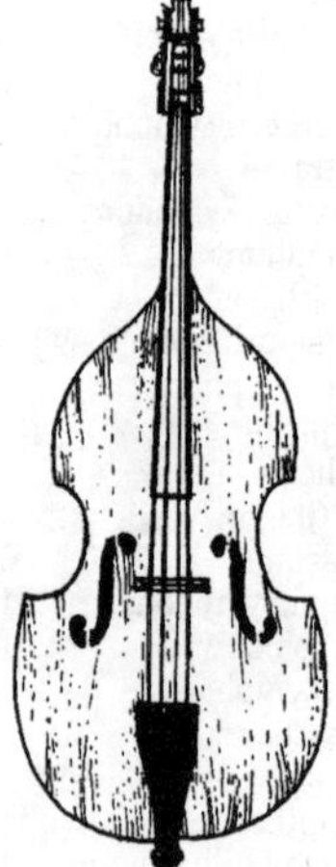

double bass

Arts and culture

Woodwind instruments

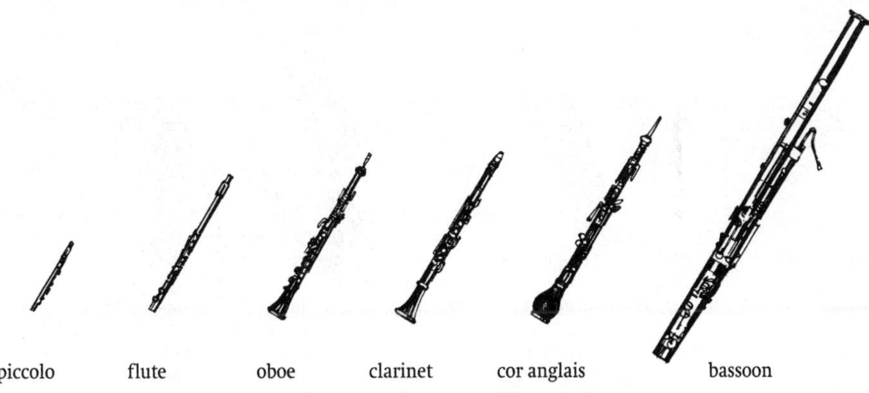

Composers

Name	*Dates*	*Place of birth*	*Selected works*
Albinoni, Tommaso	1671–1751	Venice	String concertos; *concerti grossi; Adagio* for organ and strings in G minor
Bach, Johann Sebastian	1685–1750	Eisenach, Germany	Oratorios – *St John Passion, St Matthew Passion, Christmas Oratorio;* Mass in B minor; Brandenburg Concertos nos.1-6; Keyboard – *The Well-Tempered Clavier, Goldberg Variations;* Organ – *Toccata and Fugue* in D minor
Barber, Samuel	1910–81	West Chester, Pennsylvania	*Dover Beach* (for voice and strings); *Adagio for Strings*
Bartók, Béla	1881–1945	Nagyszentmiklos, Hungary (now Sinnicolau Mare, Romania)	Opera – *Duke Bluebeard's Castle;* Ballet – *The Wooden Prince, The Miraculous Mandarin;* Orchestral – *Kossuth, Dance Suite, Concerto for Orchestra, Music for Strings, Percussion and Celesta,* 3 Piano Concertos; 6 string quartets
Beethoven, Ludwig van	1770–1827	Bonn	Symphonies – no.3 in E flat major *(Eroica),* no.5 in C minor, no.6 in F major *(Pastoral),* no. 9 in D minor *(Choral);* Piano concertos – no.5 in E flat major *(Emperor);* Violin Concerto in D major; Triple Concerto in C major; Overtures – *Leonora* nos.1,2 and 3, *Egmont, Ruins of Athens;* Opera – *Fidelio;* Mass in D major *(Missa Solemnis);* Piano Sonatas – no.8 *(Pathétique),* no.14 *(Moonlight),* no.23 – *(Appassionata),* no.29 *(Hammerklavier);* String Quartets – nos.7-9 *(Rasumowsky),* nos.12-16, *Grosse Fuge*
Bellini, Vincenzo	1801–35	Catania, Sicily	Opera – *La Sonnambula, Norma*
Bennett, Richard Rodney	1936–	Broadstairs, Kent	Opera – *The Mines of Sulphur , Penny for a Song; Spells* (for voice and orchestra); Saxophone Concerto
Berg, Alban	1885–1935	Vienna	Opera – *Wozzeck, Lulu;* Orchestral – *Three Pieces,* Chamber Concerto, Violin Concerto
Berio, Luciano	1925–	Imperia, Italy	*Sinfonia* (for voice and orchestra); *Sequenza* (pieces for various instruments)
Berlioz, Hector	1803–69	La Cote-St-André, Isere	Opera – *Les Troyens, Béatrice et Benedict;* Orchestral – *Harold in Italy, Symphonie Fantastique;* For voice and orchestra – *Requiem, Roméo et Juliette, La Damnation de Faust, Les Nuits d'Été*
Birtwistle, Sir Harrison	1934–	Accrington, Lancashire	Opera – *Punch and Judy, The Mask of Orpheus, Gawain;* Orchestral – *Earth Dances*
Bizet, Georges (Alexandre Cesar Leopold Bizet)	1838–75	Paris	Opera – *The Pearl Fishers, The Fair Maid of Perth, Carmen;* Orchestral – *L'Arlésienne*
Bloch, Ernst	1880–1959	Geneva	Opera – *Macbeth;* Orchestral – *Israel Symphony, Shelomo;* For voice and orchestra – *Sacred Service*
Borodin, Alexander Porphyrevich	1833–87	St Petersburg	Opera – *Prince Igor;* Orchestral – Symphony no.2 in B minor, *In the Steppes of Central Asia*
Boulez, Pierre	1925–	Montbrison, France	*Pli selon pli* (for voice and orchestra); *Éclats* (for chamber orchestra)

Composers (continued)

Name	*Dates*	*Place of birth*	*Selected works*
Brahms, Johannes	1833–97	Hamburg	Violin Concerto, Concerto for Violin and Cello, (orchestral), Piano Quintet, F, Clarinet Quintet (chamber music), *Ein Deutsches Requiem* (choral)
Bridge, Frank	1879–1941	Brighton	*Love Went a-Riding* (song); Orchestral – *The Sea, Oration*
Britten, Benjamin, Baron Britten of Aldeburgh	1913–76	Lowestoft	Opera – *Peter Grimes, Albert Herring, Billy Budd, The Turn of the Screw, A Midsummer Night's Dream, Death in Venice;* Orchestral – *Simple Symphony, Variations on a Theme of Frank Bridge, Sinfonia da Requiem, Young Persons Guide to the Orchestra;* For voice and orchestra – *Cantata Academica, War Requiem, Our Hunting Fathers*
Bruch, Max	1838–1920	Cologne	3 Violin Concertos; *Scottish Fantasy* (for violin and orchestra)
Bruckner, Anton	1824–96	Ansfelden, Austria	Symphonies – no. 4 in E flat major *(Romantic)*, no.7 in E major, no.8 in C minor, no.9 in D minor (unfinished)
Busoni, Ferruccio	1866–1924	Empoli, Italy	Opera – *Arlecchino, Turandot, Doktor Faust;* Orchestral – *Berceuse élégiaque;* Piano – *Indian Diary*
Byrd, William	1543–1623	Lincoln (probably)	3 Masses; Keyboard – *My Ladye Nevells Booke*
Cage, John	1912–92	Los Angeles	Variations I–VI (for any number of performers and objects); 4'33" (silent – for any instrument(s))
Carter, Elliott	1908–	New York	4 String Quartets; Orchestral – Double Concerto for Harpsichord and Piano, *A Symphony of Three Orchestras*
Chopin, Frederic	1810–49	Zelazowa Wola, Poland	2 Piano Concertos; For solo piano – 3 Piano Sonatas, numerous *Ballades, Scherzos, Études, Nocturnes, Préludes, Valses, Polonaises, Mazurkas*
Copland, Aaron	1900–	Brooklyn	Ballets – *Billy the Kid, Rodeo, Appalachian Spring;* Orchestral – *A Lincoln Portrait, Fanfare for the Common Man*
Couperin, François	1668–1733	Paris	For Harpsichord – *Pièces de Clavecin* (Books I–IV)
Debussy, Claude	1862–1918	St Germain-en-Laye, France	Opera – *Pelléas et Mélisande;* Ballet – *Jeux; Orchestral – Prélude à l'après-midi d'un faune, Nocturnes, La Mer;* Chamber – String Quartet, Cello Sonata, Violin Sonata; Piano – *Préludes* (Books I and II)
Delibes, Léo	1836–91	St Germain-du-Val, France	Ballets – *Coppélia, Sylvia;* Opera – *Lakmé*
Delius, Frederick	1862–1934	Bradford, Yorkshire	Opera – *A Village Romeo and Juliette;* Orchestral – *Brigg Fair, In a Summer Garden, On Hearing the First Cuckoo in Spring;* For voice, chorus and orchestra – *Sea Drift, A Mass of Life*
Donizetti, Gaetano	1797–1848	Bergamo, Italy	Opera – *L'Elisir d'Amore, Lucia di Lammermoor*
Dukas, Paul	1865–1935	Paris	Orchestral – *The Sorcerer's Apprentice*
Dvořák, Antonín	1841–1904	Nelahozeves, Czechoslovakia	Orchestral – Symphonies (no.6 in D major, no.8 in G major, no.9 in E minor – *From the New World*), *Slavonic Dances*, Violin Concerto, Cello Concerto
Elgar, Sir Edward	1857–1934	Broadheath, nr Worcester	Orchestral – *Variations on an Original Theme (Enigma Variations), Pomp and Circumstance Marches, Cockaigne, Falstaff,* Violin Concerto, Cello Concerto, Symphony no.1; For voice, chorus and orchestra – *Dream of Gerontius*
Falla, Manuel de	1876–1946	Cadiz	Ballet – *The Three-Cornered Hat;* Orchestral – *Nights in the Gardens of Spain*
Fauré, Gabriel	1845–1924	Pamiers	Opera – *Pénélope;* For voice, chorus and orchestra – *Requiem;* Songs *(Après un rêve, Les Roses d'Ispahan, Clair de Lune)*
Franck, César	1822–90	Liège	Orchestral – *Symphonic Variations*, Symphony in D minor; For chorus and orchestra – *Psyché*
Gershwin, George	1898–1937	Brooklyn, New York	Opera – *Porgy and Bess;* Orchestral – *Rhapsody in Blue, An American in Paris*
Glass, Philip	1937–	Baltimore	Opera – *Einstein on the Beach, Akhnaten;* Film soundtrack – *Koyaanisqatsi*
Glazunov, Alexander	1865–1936	St Petersburg	Orchestral – Symphony no.1, *The Seasons*
Glinka, Mikhail	1804–57	Smolensk	Opera – *A Life for the Tsar, Ruslan and Lyudmila*
Gluck, Christoph	1714–87	Erasbach	Opera – *Orfeo, Alceste, Iphigénie en Aulide, Iphigénie en Tauride*
Górecki, Henryk	1933–	Czernica, Poland	Orchestral – Symphony no. 3 *(Symphony of Sorrowful Songs);* Chamber – *Genesis*
Gounod, Charles	1818–93	Paris	Opera – *Faust, Roméo et Juliette;* Songs *(Ave Maria)*
Grieg, Edvard	1843–1907	Bergen	Orchestral – Piano Concerto in A minor, *Peer Gynt* (Suites 1 and 2)

Name	Dates	Place of birth	Selected works
Handel, Georges Frideric	1685–1759	Halle	Orchestral – *Water Music, Music for Royal Fireworks;* Oratorios – *Saul, Messiah, Belshazzar, Solomon*
Haydn, Franz Joseph	1732–1809	Rohrau, Austria	Oratorios – *The Creation, The Seasons;* Symphonies – nos.82–87 *(Paris),* nos.93–104 *(London);* String Quartets – nos.50–56 *(Seven Last Words from the Cross),* no.61 *(Razor)*
Hindemith, Paul	1895–1963	Hanau, Germany	Orchestral – *Mathis der Maler* (Symphony); *Trauermusik* (for viola and strings); *Symphonic Metamorphosis of Themes by Carl Maria von Weber*
Holst, Gustav	1874–1934	Cheltenham	Orchestral – Suite, *The Planets; Egdon Heath*
Honegger, Arthur	1892–1955	Le Havre	Oratorio – *Jeanne d'Arc au Bûcher;* Orchestral – *Pacific 231*
Ives, Charles	1874–1954	Danbury, Connecticut	Orchestral – *Holidays Symphony, The Unanswered Question, Central Park in the Dark,* Symphonies 1–3, *Variations on 'America'*
Janáček, Leoš	1854–1928	Hukvaldy, Czechoslovakia	Opera – *Jenufa, Kata Kabanova, The Cunning Little Vixen, From the House of the Dead;* Orchestral – *Sinfonietta, Taras Bulba;* For voice, chorus, organ and orchestra – *Glagolitic Mass;* 2 String Quartets; Piano Sonata *(I.X.1905)*
Khachaturian, Aram	1903–78	Tbilisi	Ballet – *Gayane, Spartacus*
Kodály, Zoltan	1882–1967	Kecskemét, Hungary	Opera – *Háry János;* For voice, chorus and orchestra – *Psalmus Hungaricus*
Léhar, Ferencz	1870–1948	Komarom, Hungary	Operetta – *The Merry Widow, The Land of Smiles*
Ligeti, György	1923–	Discöszentmáron, Hungary	Opera – *Le Grand Macabre;* Orchestral – *Atmosphères, Melodien*
Liszt, Franz	1811–86	Raiding, Hungary	Orchestral – *A Faust Symphony, Mazeppa;* Piano – *Années de Pèlerinages* (Books I–III), *Mephisto Waltz* no.2, Sonata in B minor, *Hungarian Rhapsodies*
Lully, Jean-Baptiste	1632–87	Florence	*Le Bourgeois Gentilhomme* (comedy-ballet, after Molière); many operas
Mahler, Gustav	1860–1911	Kalist, Austria (now Czechoslovakia)	Symphonies – no.2 in C minor *(Resurrection),* no.3 in D minor, no.5 in C sharp minor, no. 6 in A minor *(Tragic),* no.8 in E flat major *(Symphony of a Thousand),* no.9 in D major; *Das Lied von der Erde* (song symphony); Song cycles – *Lieder eines fahrenden Gesellen, Kindertotenlieder;* Songs – *Des Knaben Wunderhorn*
Mascagni, Pietro	1863–1945	Leghorn, Italy	Opera – *Cavalleria Rusticana*
Maxwell Davies, Sir Peter	1934–	Salford	Opera – *Taverner, The Martyrdom of St Magnus;* For the Theatre – *Eight Songs for a Mad King;* Orchestral – *1st Fantasia on In Nomine of John Taverner, Sinfonia*
Mendelssohn, Felix	1809–47	Hamburg	Orchestral – Symphony no.3 in A minor *(Scotch),* Symphony no.4 in A major *(Italian),* 2 Piano Concertos, Violin Concerto in E minor, Overture, *A Midsummer Night's Dream,* Overture, *Hebrides (Fingal's Cave);* Piano – *Songs Without Words* (Books I–VIII)
Messiaen, Olivier	1908–92	Avignon	Orchestral – *Turangalîla-symphonie, Oiseaux Exotiques;* Piano *Vingt Regards sur l'enfant Jésus;* Organ – *Nativité du Seigneur;* Chamber – *Quatuor pour la fin du temps*
Milhaud, Darius	1892–1974	Aix-en-Provence	Opera – *Christophe Colomb;* Ballet – *Le Boeuf sur le Toit, La Création du Monde;* Orchestral – *Saudades do Brazil , Suite Provençal*
Monteverdi, Claudio	1567–1643	Cremona, Italy	Opera – *Orfeo;* Church Music – *Vespers of 1610 (Vespro della Beata Vergine)*
Mozart, Wolfgang Amadeus	1756–91	Salzburg	Opera – *Die Entführung aus dem Serail, Le Nozze di Figaro, Don Gionanni, Così fan tutte, Die Zauberflöte;* Orchestral – Symphonies (nos.35–41), Serenades *(Gran Partita, Eine Kleine Nachtmusik),* Concertos (no.21 for piano – *Elvira Madigan,* for viola and violin – *Sinfonia Concertante,* for clarinet in A major, for flute and harp in C major); Church Music – *Coronation Mass, Requiem*
Mussorgsky, Modest	1839–81	Karevo, Russia	Opera – *Boris Godunov ;* Orchestral – *Night on the Bare Mountain;* Piano – *Pictures at an Exhibition*
Nielsen, Carl	1865–1931	Norre-Lyndelse, Denmark	Opera – *Saul and David;* Symphonies – no.1 in G minor, no.3 *(Sinfonia Espansiva),* no.4 *(The Inextinguishable),* no.5
Offenbach, Jaques	1819–80	Cologne	Opera – *Orpheus in the Underworld, The Tales of Hoffmann*
Orff, Carl	1895-1981	Munich	Carmina Burrana (for voice, boy's choir, chorus and orchestra)

Composers (continued)

Name	*Dates*	*Place of birth*	*Selected works*
Palestrina, Giovanni Pierluigi da	c.1525–94	Palestrina, nr Rome	many masses and motets
Poulenc, Francis	1899–1963	Paris	Opera – *Les Dialogues des Carmélites, La Voix humaine,* Ballet – *Les Biches;* Concerto in G minor for organ, strings and timpani; Chamber – Violin Sonata, Cello Sonata; Choral – *4 Motets pour un temps de pénitence*
Prokofiev, Sergei Sergeyevitch	1891–1953	Sontsovka, Ukraine	Opera – *Love for Three Oranges;* Ballet – *The Age of Steel, Romeo and Juliet, Cinderella;* Symphonies – no.1 in D major *(Classical),* no.5 in B flat major, no.7 in C sharp minor; *Peter and the Wolf* (for narrator and orchestra); Film scores – *Lieutenant Kijé, Alexander Nevsky;* 5 Piano Concertos
Puccini, Giacomo	1858–1924	Lucca, Italy	Opera – *Manon Lescaut, La Bohème, Tosca, Madama Butterfly, Turandot*
Purcell, Henry	1659–95	London	Opera – *Dido and Aeneas;* Choral – *Come ye sons of art, away , Ode on St Cecilia's Day, Thou knowest, Lord, the Secrets of our Hearts*
Rachmaninov, Sergei Vasileyevich	1873–1943	Semyonovo, Russia	Orchestral – 4 Piano Concertos, 3 Symphonies, *The Isle of the Dead, Rhapsody on a Theme of Paganini, Symphonic Dances*
Rameau, Jean-Philippe	1683–1764	Dijon	Opera – *Castor et Pollux;* many pieces for harpsichord
Ravel, Maurice	1875–1937	Ciboure, France	Opera – *L'Heure Espagnole, L'Enfant et les Sortilèges;* Ballet – *Daphnis et Chloé, Boléro;* Orchestral – *Alborada del gracioso, Rapsodie Espagnole, Ma Mère l'Oye, La Valse,* Piano Concerto for Left Hand, Piano Concerto in G major; Chamber – String Quartet, *Introduction and Allegro* for harp, flute, clarinet and string quartet; Piano – *Pavane pour une infante défunte, Miroirs, Valses nobles et sentimentales, Le Tombeau de Couperin*
Reich, Steve	1936–	New York	*Drumming* (for percussion instruments and voices); Orchestral – *Four Sections*
Rimsky-Korsakov, Nikolai	1844–1908	Tikhvin-Novgorod, Russia	Opera – *The Golden Cockerel;* Orchestral – *Capriccio Espagnol, Scheherazade*
Rodrigo, Joáquin	1902–	Sagunto, Spain	Concierto de Aranjuez (for guitar and orchestra)
Rossini, Gioacchino	1792–1868	Pesaro, Italy	Opera – *The Barber of Seville, Otello, William Tell*
Saint-Saëns, Camille	1835–1921	Paris	Opera – *Samson et Dalila;* Orchestral – Symphony no.3 *(Organ),* 3 Piano Concertos, *Carnaval des Animaux* (for piano and orchestra)
Satie, Erik	1866–1925	Honfleur, France	Ballet – *Parade;* Solo Piano – *3 Gymnopédies, 6 Gnossiennes, Morceaux en forme de poire*
Scarlatti, Alessandro	1660–1725	Palermo	many operas, oratorios and masses
Schoenberg, Arnold	1874–1951	Vienna	Opera – *Moses und Aron;* Orchestral – *5 Orchestral Pieces,* Chamber Symphony no.1; For voice, chorus and orchestra – *Gurrelieder;* For voice and chamber orchestra – *Pierrot Lunaire;* Chamber – *Verklärte Nacht* (for string sextet)
Schubert, Franz	1797–1828	Vienna	Symphonies – no.5 in B flat major, no.8 in B minor *(Unfinished),* no.9 in C major *(Great);* Chamber – String Quartet no.14 in D minor *(Death and the Maiden),* Piano Quintet in A major *(Trout),* Octet in F major; Song-cycles – *Winterreise, Schwanengesang;* many songs
Schumann, Robert	1810–56	Zwickau, Germany	Orchestral – Symphony no.1 *(Spring),* no.3 *(Rhenish),* Piano Concerto in A minor, Cello Concerto in A minor; Solo Piano – *Fantasiestücke, Études Symphoniques, Kinderscenen, Waldscenen, Albumblätter*
Shostakovich, Dmitri	1906–75	St Petersburg	Opera – *The Nose, Lady Macbeth of Mtsensk;* Ballet – *The Age of Gold;* Symphonies – no.1 in F minor, no.4 in C minor, no.5 in D minor, no.7 in C major *(Leningrad),* no.10 in E minor, no.13 in B flat minor *(Babi-Yar),* no.15 in A major; 2 Piano Concertos; 2 Violin Concertos; 2 Cello Concertos; String Quartets – no.8 in C minor, no.10 in A flat major; Solo Piano – *24 Preludes and Fugues*
Sibelius, Jean	1865–1957	Hameenlinna, Finland	Orchestral – Symphonies, no.1 in E minor, no.2 in D major, no.5 in E flat major, *Finlandia* (symphonic piece), *Karelia Overture*

Name	*Dates*	*Place of birth*	*Selected works*
Smetana, Bedřich	1824–1884	Litomyšl, Czechoslovakia	Opera – *The Bartered Bride, Dalibor;* Orchestral – *Má Vlast*
Sousa, John Philip	1854–32	Washington DC	Marches – *Stars and Stripes, Liberty Bell, Hands across the Sea*
Stockhausen, Karlheinz	1928–	Burg Modrath	Opera – *Donnerstag aus Licht;* Orchestral – *Spiel, Punkte, Gruppen;* Instrumental – *Kontra-Punkte, Zeitmasze, Zyklus;* Electronic – *Gesang der Jünglinge*
Strauss, Johann II	1825–99	Vienna	Opera – *Die Fledermaus;* many waltzes – *Blue Danube, Roses from the South, Tales from the Vienna Woods*
Strauss, Richard	1864–1949	Munich	Opera – *Salomé, Elektra, Der Rosenkavalier, Ariadne auf Naxos, Capriccio;* Orchestral – *Symphonia Domestica, An Alpine Symphony;* Symphonic Poems – *Don Juan, Death and Transfiguration, Till Eulenspiegels lustige Streiche, Also Sprach Zarathustra, Don Quixote, Ein Heldenleben, Metamorphosen;* Song-cycle – *Four Last Songs*
Stravinsky, Igor	1882–1971	Oranienbaum (now Lomonosov, Russia)	Opera – *Oedipus Rex, The Rake's Progress;* Ballet – *The Firebird, Petrushka, The Rite of Spring, Pulcinella, Jeu de cartes, Orpheus;* Theatre – *The Soldier's Tale;* Orchestral – Symphony in C, *Symphony in Three Movements, Symphonies of Wind Instruments,* Violin Concerto, *Ebony Concerto* (for clarinet); Liturgical – *Symphony of Psalms,* Mass, *Canticum Sacrum*
Suk, Joseph	1874–1935	Krecovice, Czechoslovakia	*Asrael Symphony*
Sullivan, Sir Arthur	1842–1900	London	Operetta – *HMS Pinafore, The Pirates of Penzance, Iolanthe, The Mikado, The Yeomen of the Guard, The Gondoliers*
Szymanowski, Karol	1882–1937	Tymoshovka, Ukraine	Orchestral – Symphony no.2 in B flat, Symphony no.3 *(Song of the Night), Symphonie Concertante* (for piano and orchestra), 2 Violin Concertos, *Stabat Mater* (for voice, women's chorus and orchestra)
Tallis, Thomas	c.1505–85	Greenwich	Liturgical music – *Spem in alium* (40-part motet)
Tchaikovsky, Peter Ilyich	1840–93	Kamsko-Votkinsk, Russia	Opera – *Eugene Onegin, Queen of Spades;* Ballet – *Swan Lake, Sleeping Beauty, Nutcracker;* Orchestral – Symphony no.4 in F minor, Symphony no.5 in E minor, Symphony no.6 in B minor *(Pathetic), Manfred Symphony, Romeo and Juliet* (Overture)
Telemann, Georg Philipp	1681–1767	Magdeburg, Germany	c. 600 overtures, also many operas, oratorios and concertos
Tippett, Sir Michael	1905–	London	Opera – *The Midsummer Marriage, The Ice Break;* Oratorio – *A Child of Our Time;* Orchestral – *Fantasia Concertante on a Theme of Corelli*
Vaughan Williams, Ralph	1872–1958	Down Ampney, Gloucestershire	Opera – *The Pilgrim's Progress;* Orchestral – *A Sea Symphony, A London Symphony, A Pastoral Symphony,* Symphony no.4 in F minor, *Sinfonia Antarctica, The Wasps* (Overture), *Fantasia on a Theme by Thomas Tallis, The Lark Ascending* (for violin and orchestra)
Verdi, Giuseppe	1813–1901	Roncole	Opera – *Nabucco, Macbeth, Rigoletto, Il trovatore, La traviata, Simon Boccanegra, A Masked Ball, The Force of Destiny, Don Carlos , Aida, Otello, Falstaff;* Orchestral – *Requiem*
Villa-Lobos, Heitor	1887–1959	Rio de Janeiro	*Bachianas Brasileiras* (9 chamber pieces)
Vivaldi, Antonio	1678–1741	Venice	c. 230 violin concertos – *Le quattro stagioni (The Four Seasons);* orchestral concertos; bassoon, cello, oboe and flute concertos; many operas and cantatas
Wagner, Richard	1813–83	Leipzig	Opera – *Rienzi , Der fliegende Holländer, Tannhäuser, Lohengrin, Der Ring des Nibelungen (Das Rheingold, Die Walküre, Siegfried, Götterdämmerung), Tristan und Isolde, Die Meistersinger von Nürnberg, Parsifal;* Orchestral – *Siegfried Idyll*
Walton, Sir William	1902–83	Oldham	*Façade* (for reciter and chamber orchestra), Orchestral – Symphony no.1 in B flat major, Viola Concerto in B minor; Coronation Marches *(Crown Imperial, Orb and Sceptre);* For Chorus and Orchestra – *Belshazzar's Feast;* Film Scores – *Henry V, Hamlet, Battle of Britain, Richard III*
Weber, Carl Maria von	1786–1826	Eutin, in Oldenburg, Germany	Opera – *Der Freischütz, Euryanthe, Die drei Pintos, Oberon*
Webern, Anton von	1883–1945	Vienna	Orchestral – *Passacaglia, 6 Pieces, 5 Pieces;* Choral – *Das Augenlicht*

Composers (continued)

Name	*Dates*	*Place of birth*	*Selected works*
Weill, Kurt	1900–50	Dessau, Germany	Opera – *The Threepenny Opera, Rise and Fall of the City of Mahagonny, Happy End;* Ballet – *Seven Deadly Sins;* Orchestral – 2 Symphonies, Violin Concerto, *The Berlin Requiem*
Wolf, Hugo	1860–1903	Windischgraz, Austria	Opera – *Der Corregidor;* Orchestral – *Italian Serenade;* Songs – *Spanish Songbook, Italian Songbook*
Zemlinsky, Alexander von	1871–1942	Vienna	Opera – *Eine florentinische Tragödie;* Ballet – *Das gläserne Herz;* Orchestral – *Lyric Symphony*

Operatic works

Name of work	*Date*	*Composer*	*Librettist*
Aida	1871	Verdi	Ghislanzoni
Alceste	1767	Gluck	Calzabigi
Arabella	1933	Richard Strauss	Hofmannsthal
Barber of Seville	1816	Rossini	Sterbini
Bartered Bride, The	1866	Smetana	Sabini
Beggar's Opera	1728	Gay	Gay
Billy Budd	1951	Britten	Forster/Crozier
Bohème, La	1896	Puccini	Giacosa/Illica
Boris Godunov	1974	Mussorgsky	Mussorgsky
Carmen	1875	Bizet	Meilhac/Halevy
Cavalleria Rusticana	1890	Mascagni	Menasci/ Targioni-Tozetti
Clemenza di Tito, La	1791	Mozart	Mazzolà
Coronation of Poppea	1642	Monteverdi	Busenello
Cosi Fan Tutte	1790	Mozart	Da Ponte
Cunning Little Vixen, The	1924	Janáček	Janáček
Damnation of Faust, The	1846	Berlioz	Berlioz
Death in Venice	1973	Britten	Piper
Dido and Aeneas	1689	Purcell	Tate
Don Giovanni	1787	Mozart	Da Ponte
Duke Bluebeard's Castle	1918	Bartók	Balasz
Elektra	1909	Richard Strauss	Hofmannsthal
Eugene Onegin	1879	Tchaikovsky	Tchaikovsky/ Shilovsky
Falstaff	1893	Verdi	Wagner
Faust	1859	Gounod	Barbier/Carré
Fidelio	1805	Beethoven	Sonnleithner
Fledermaus, Die	1874	Johann Strauss II	Haffner/Genee
Flying Dutchman, The	1843	Wagner	Wagner
Freischütz, Der	1821	Weber	Kind
Golden Cockerel, The	1909	Rimsky-Korsakov	Byelsky
Idomeneo	1781	Mozart	Varesco
Jenůfa	1904	Janáček	Janáček
Juilius Caesar in Egypt	1724	Handel	Haym
Kátya Kabanová	1921	Janàček	Janàček
King Priam	1962	Tippett	Tippett
Les Huguenots	1836	Meyerbeer	Scribe
Lohengrin	1850	Wagner	Wagner
Love for Three Oranges, The	1920	Prokofiev	Prokofiev
Lucia di Lammermoor	1835	Donizetti	Cammarano
Lulu	1937	Berg	Berg
Macbeth	1847	Verdi	Piave
Madame Butterfly	1904	Puccini	Giacoso/Illica
Magic Flute, The	1791	Mozart	Schikaneder
Manon Lescaut	1893	Puccini	Giacoso/Illica
Marriage of Figaro, The	1786	Mozart	Da Ponte
Mask of Orpheus, The	1986	Birtwistle	Zinovieff
Meistersinger, Die	1868	Wagner	Wagner
Midsummer Marriage	1955	Tippett	Duncan
Midsummer Night's Dream, A	1960	Britten	Britten/Pears
Mikado, The	1885	Sullivan	Gilbert
Nabucco	1842	Verdi	Solera
Oedipus Rex	1927	Stravinsky	Cocteau
Orfeo	1607	Monteverdi	Striggio
Orpheus and Eurydice	1762	Gluck	Calzabigi
Orpheus in the Underworld	1858	Offenbach	Cremeux/Halevy
Otello	1887	Verdi	Boito
Pagliacci	1892	Leoncavallo	Leoncavallo
Paradise Lost	1978	Penderecki	Fry
Parsifal	1882	Wagner	Wagner
Pelléas et Mélissande	1902	Debussy	Maeterlinck
Peter Grimes	1945	Britten	Slater
Pilgrim's Progress, The	1951	Vaughan Williams	Vaughan Williams/Wood
Porgy and Bess	1935	Gershwin	Ira Gershwin/ Heyward
Prince Igor	1890	Borodin	Borodin
Rake's Progress, The	1951	Stravinsky	Auden/Kallman
Rape of Lucretia, The	1946	Britten	Duncan
Rigoletto	1851	Verdi	Piave
Ring of the Nibelung, The	1876	Wagner	Wagner
Rosenkavalier, Der	1911	Richard Strauss	Hofmannsthal
Rossignol, Le	1914	Stravinsky	Stravinsky/ Mitusov

Name of work	Date	Composer	Librettist
Salomé	1905	Richard Strauss	Wilde/Lachmann
Samson and Dalila	1877	Saint-Saëns	Lemaire
Tales of Hoffman, The	1881	Offenbach	Barbier
Tannhäuser	1845	Wagner	Wagner
Threepenny Opera The	1928	Weill	Brecht/ Hauptmann
Tosca	1900	Puccini	Giacosa/Illica
Traviata, La	1853	Verdi	Piave
Tristan and Isolde	1865	Wagner	Wagner
Trojans, The (Les Troyens)	1863	Berlioz	Berlioz
Trovatore, Il	1853	Verdi	Cammarano
Turandot	1926	Puccini	Adami/Simoni
Turn of the Screw, The	1954	Britten	Piper
William Tell	1829	Rossini	De Jouy/Bis/ Marrast
Wozzeck	1925	Berg	Berg

Opera singers

Name	Dates	Place of birth	Range
Allen, Thomas	1944–	Seaham	Baritone
Ameling, Elly	1938–	Rotterdam	Soprano
Anderson, Marian	1902–93	Philadelphia	Contralto
Austral, Florence	1892–1968	Richmond, Melbourne	Soprano
Bailey, Norman	1933–	Birmingham	Baritone
Baker, Dame Janet	1933–	Hatfield, Yorkshire	Mezzo-soprano
Barstow, Josephine	1940–	Sheffield	Soprano
Bartolio, Cecilia	1966–	Rome	Mezzo-soprano
Battistini, Mattia	1856–1928	Contigliano, Italy	Baritone
Bergonzi, Carlo	1924–	Polisene, Italy	Tenor
Berganza, Teresa	1935–	Madrid	Mezzo-soprano
Björling, Jussi	1911–60	Stora Tuna, Sweden	Tenor
Borgatti, Giuseppe	1871–1950	Cento, Italy	Tenor
Borgioli, Dino	1891–1960	Florence	Tenor
Bowman, James	1941–	Oxford	Counter-tenor
Butt, Dame Clara	1872–1936	Southwick, Sussex	Contralto
Caballé, Montserrat	1933–	Barcelona	Soprano
Callas, Maria (Maria Ann Sofia Cecelia Kalogeropoulos)	1923–77	New York	Soprano
Carreras, José	1946–	Barcelona	Tenor
Caruso, Enrico	1873–1921	Naples	Tenor
Chaliapin, Fyodor	1873–1938	Kazan, Russia	Bass
Deller, Alfred	1912–79	Margate	Counter-tenor
De Los Angeles, Victoria	1923–	Barcelona	Soprano
Domingo, Placido	1941–	Madrid	Tenor
Evans, Sir Geraint	1922–92	Pontypridd, S Wales	Baritone
Ewing, Maria	1950–	Detroit	Mezzo-soprano
Farrar, Geraldine	1882–1967	Meltrose, Massachusetts	Soprano
Ferrier, Kathleen	1912–53	Higher Walton, Lancashire	Contralto
Fischer-Dieskau, Dietrich	1925–	Berlin	Baritone
Flagstad, Kirsten	1895–1962	Hamar, Norway	Soprano
Forrester, Maureen	1930–	Montreal	Contralto
Freni, Mirella	1936–	Modena, Italy	Soprano
Gedda, Nicolai	1925–	Stockholm	Tenor
Gigli, Beniamino	1880–1957	Recanati, Italy	Tenor
Gobi, Tito	1913–84	Bassano del Grappa, Italy	Baritone
Hendricks, Barbara	1948–	Stephens, Arizona	Soprano
Hotter, Hans	1909–	Offenbach-am-Main, Germany	Bass-baritone
Kollo, René	1937–	Berlin	Tenor
Kraus, Alfredo	1927–	Las Palmas	Tenor
Lehmann, Lotte	1888–1976	Perleberg, Germany	Soprano
Lind, Jenny	1820–87	Stockholm	Soprano
Ludwig, Christa	1924–	Berlin	Mezzo-soprano
Luxon, Benjamin	1937–	Camborne, Cornwall	Baritone
Martinelli, Giovanni	1885–1969	Montagnana, Italy	Tenor
McCormack, John	1884–1945	Athlone, Ireland	Tenor
Melba, Dame Nellie	1861–1931	Richmond, nr Melbourne	Soprano
Migenes-Johnson Julia	1945–	New York	Soprano
Milanov, Zinka	1906–89	Zagreb	Soprano
Nilsson, Birgit	1918–	Karup, Sweden	Soprano
Norman, Jessye	1945–	Augusta, Georgia	Soprano
Patti, Adelina	1843–1919	Madrid	Soprano
Pavarotti, Luciano	1935–	Modena, Italy	Tenor
Pears, Sir Peter	1910–86	Farnham, Surrey	Tenor
Pinza, Ezio	1892–1957	Rome	Bass
Ponselle, Rosa	1897–1981	Meriden, Connetticut	Soprano
Popp, Lucia	1939–	Lihorska, Czechoslovakia	Soprano
Prey, Hermann	1929–	Berlin	Baritone
Price, Leontyne	1927–	Laurel, Mississippi	Soprano

Opera singers (continued)

Name	Dates	Place of birth	Range
Schumann, Elisabeth	1888–1952	Merseburg, Germany	Soprano
Schwarzkopf, Elisabeth	1915–	Jarotschin, nr Poznań	Soprano
Scotto, Renata	1933–	Savona, Italy	Soprano
Shirley-Quirk, John	1931–	Liverpool	Baritone
Söderström, Elisabeth	1927–	Stockholm	Soprano
Stratas, Teresa	1938–	Toronto	Soprano
Studer, Cheryl	1955–	Midland, Michigan	Soprano
Sutherland, Dame Joan	1926–	Sydney	Soprano
Tauber, Richard	1892–1948	Linz	Tenor
Tear, Robert	1939–	Barry, Glamorgan	Tenor
Tebaldi, Renata	1922–	Pesaro, Itlay	Soprano
Te Kanawa, Dame Kiri	1944–	Gisborne, New Zealand	Soprano
Tetrazzini, Luisa	1871–1938	Milan	Soprano
Teyte, Dame Maggie	1888–1976	Wolverhampton	Soprano
Turner, Dame Eva	1892–1990	Oldham	Soprano
Van Dam, José	1940–	Brussels	Baritone
Vickers, Jon	1926–	Prince Albert, Saskatchewan	Tenor

Jazz personalities

Name	Dates	Place of birth	Instrument
Armstrong, Louis	1901–71	New Orleans	Trumpet/cornet/vocal
Baker, Chet	1929–88	Yale, Oklahoma	Trumpet/flugelhorn/vocal
Barber, Chris	1930–	Hertfordshire	Trombone/bass trumpet/vocal
Basie, William 'Count'	1904–84	Red Bank	Piano/organ
Bechet, Sidney	1897–1959	New Orleans	Soprano, tenor and bass saxophones/clarinet/piano
Beiderbecke, Bix	1903–31	Davenport	Cornet
Blakey, Art	1919–90	Pittsburgh	Drums
Bley, Carla	1938–	Oakland, California	Piano
Braxton, Anthony	1945–	Chicago	Alto saxophone/clarinet/flute
Brubeck, Dave	1920–	Concord, California	Piano
Calloway, Cab	1906–	New York	Vocal
Charles, Ray	1930–	Albany	Vocal/piano
Cherry, Don	1936–	Oklahoma City	Trumpet/flute
Christian, Charlie	1916–42	Dallas	Guitar
Clark, Kenny	1914–85	Pittsburgh	Drums
Coleman, Ornette	1930–	Fort Worth	Alto and soprano saxophones/vocal
Coltrane, John	1926–67	Hamlet	Soprano, alto and tenor saxophones/flute
Corea, Chick	1941–	Chelsea (US)	Piano/keyboards
Dankworth, John	1927–	London	Alto saxophone
Davis, Miles	1926–92	Alton	Trumpet
Desmond, Paul	1924–77	San Francisco	Alto saxophone
Dolphy, Eric	1928–64	Los Angeles	Flute/alto saxophone/bass clarinet/clarinet
Eldridge, Roy	1911–89	Pittsburgh	Trumpet
Ellington, Duke	1899–1974	Washington	Piano
Evans, Bill	1929–80	Plainfield	Piano
Evans, Gil (Ian Ernest Gilmore Green)	1912–88	Toronto	Piano
Fitzgerald, Ella	1918–	Newport News	Vocal
Gabarek, Jan	1947–	Mysen, Norway	Soprano, tenor and bass saxophones/flute
Gaillard, Slim	1916–91	Detroit	Vocal
Garner, Erroll	1926–77	Pittsburgh	Piano
Getz, Stan	1927–91	Philadelphia	Soprano, tenor and baritone saxophones
Gillespie, Dizzy	1917–93	Cheraw	Trumpet/piano/vocal
Goodman, Benny	1909–86	Chicago	Clarinet
Gordon, Dexter	1923–89	Los Angeles	Soprano and tenor saxophones
Grappelli, Stephane	1908–	Paris	Violin
Hamilton, Chico	1921–	Los Angeles	Drums
Hamilton, Scott	1954–	Providence, Rhode Island	Tenor saxophone
Hampton, Lionel	1909–	Louisville	Vibraphone
Hancock, Herbie	1940–	Chicago	Piano

Name	Dates	Place of birth	Instrument
Hawkins, Coleman	1901–69	Saint Joseph	Tenor saxophone/vocal
Herman, Woody	1913–87	Milwaukee	Alto saxophone/clarinet/vocal
Hines, Earl	1903–83	Duquesne	Piano/vocal
Hodges, Johnny	1907–70	Massachusetts	Soprano and alto saxophone
Holliday, Billie	1915–59	Baltimore	Vocal
Ibrahim, Abdullah (Dollar Brand)	1934–	Cape Town	Piano
Jackson, Milt	1923–	Detroit	Vibraphone
Jarrett, Keith	1945–	Allentown	Piano/organ/soprano saxophone
Johnson, J J	1924–	Indianapolis	Trombone
Jones, Elvin	1927–	Pontiac	Drums
Kenton, Stan	1912–79	Wichita, Kansas	Piano/vocal
Konitz, Lee	1927–	Chicago	Soprano and alto saxophones
Lacy, Steve	1934–	New York	Soprano saxophone
Lyttleton, Humphrey	1921–	Eton	Trumpet/cornet/clarinet
Marsalis, Wynton	1961–	New Orleans	Trumpet
McLaughlin, John	1942–	Yorkshire	Guitar
Merrill, Helen	1930–	New York	Vocal
Metheny, Pat	1954–	Lee's Summit	Guitar
Mingus, Charles	1922–79	Nogales	Double bass/piano
Monk, Thelonius	1917–82	Rocky Mount	Piano
Montgomery, Wes	1925–68	Indianapolis	Guitar/bass guitar
Moreton, Jelly Roll (Frederick LaMenthe)	1885-1941	Gulfport	Piano
Mulligan, Gerry	1927–	New York	Soprano and baritone saxophones/piano
Navarro, Theodore 'Fats'	1923–50	Key West, Florida	Trumpet
O'Day, Anita	1919–	Chicago	Vocal
Oliver, King	1895–1938	New Orleans	Cornet/trumpet
Parker, Charlie	1920–55	Kansas City	Alto and tenor saxophones
Pepper, Art	1925–82	Gardena, California	Alto and tenor saxophones/clarinet
Peterson, Oscar	1925–	Montreal	Piano
Pettiford, Oscar	1922–60	Okmulgee, Oklahoma	Double bass/cello
Powell, Bud	1924–1966	New York	Piano
Rheinhardt, Django	1910–53	Liverchies, Belgium	Guitar
Rich, Buddy	1917–87	New York	Drums/vocal
Roach, Max	1925–	New York	Drums
Rollins, Sonny	1930–	New York	Soprano and tenor saxophones
Shaw, Artie	1910–	New York	Clarinet
Shepp, Archie	1937–	Fort Lauderdale	Soprano, alto and tenor saxophones
Shorter, Wayne	1933–	Newark	Soprano and tenor saxophones
Simone, Nina	1933–	North Carolina	Vocal
Smith, Bessie	1894–1937	Chattanooga	Vocal
Smith, Tommy	1967–	Luton	Tenor saxophone
Solal, Martial	1927–	Algiers	Piano
Surman, John	1944–	Tavistock	Soprano and baritone saxophones/bass clarinet/piano
Tatum, Art	1910–56	Toledo	Piano
Taylor, Cecil	1930–	New York	Piano/vocal
Terry, Clark	1920–	St Louis	Trumpet/flugelhorn
Thielmans, Jean-Baptiste 'Toots'	1922–	Brussels	Harmonica
Tracey, Stan	1926–	London	Piano
Tristano, Lennie	1919–78	Chicago	Piano
Tyner, McCoy	1938–	Philadelphia	Piano/flute
Vaughan, Sarah	1924–90	Newark	Vocal
Walker, T-Bone	1910–75	Linden	Guitar
Waller, Thomas 'Fats'	1904–43	New York	Piano/organ/vocal
Washington, Dinah	1924–63	Alabama	Vocal
Weber, Eberhard	1940–	Stuttgart	Double bass
Webster, Ben	1909–73	Missouri	Tenor saxophone
Williams, Tony	1945–	Chicago	Drums
Young, Lester	1909–59	Woodville	Tenor saxophone

Classic pop and rock groups/singers

Name	*Country of origin*	*Group members**	*Period*	*Major hits*
Abba	Sweden	Benny Anderson (keyboards,vocals) Bjorn Ulvaeus (guitar, vocals) Agnetha Faltskog (vocals) Frida Lyngstad (vocals)	1970s–80s	*Waterloo, Mamma Mia, Fernando, Knowing Me Knowing You, Dancing Queen, The Name of the Game, Take a Chance on Me, I Have a Dream , Super Trouper, The Winner Takes it All*
Animals, The	Britain	Eric Burden (vocals) Alan Price (keyboards) Hilton Valentine ((guitar) Chas Chandler (bass) John Steel (drums)	1960s	*House of the Rising Sun, I'm Crying Don't Let Me Be Misunderstood, Bring it on Home to Me, We've Gotta Get Out of This Place, It's My Life, Don't Bring Me Down*
Band, The	Canada	Robbie Robertson (guitar, vocals) Richard Manuel (piano, vocals) Garth Hudson (organ) Rick Danko (bass, vocals) Levon Helm (drums, vocals)	1960s–70s	*Up on Cripple Creek, Rag Mama Rag, Stage Fright* Albums : *The Band, Cahoots, Before the Flood, The Last Waltz*
Beach Boys, The	US	Brian Wilson (bass, keyboards,vocals) Mike Love (vocals) Carl Wilson (guitar, vocals) Al Jardine (guitar, vocals) Denis Wilson (drums, vocals)	1960s–70s	*Get Around, When I Grow Up, Do You Wanna Dance, Help Me Rhonda, California Girls, Barbara Ann, Surfin' USA, God Only Knows, Wouldn't It Be Nice, Good Vibrations, Then I Kissed Her, Heroes and Villains, Darlin', Do It Again, I Can Hear Music, Rock and Roll Music, Lady Lynda*
Beatles, The	Britain	John Lennon (vocals, rhythm guitar) Paul McCartney (vocals, bass) George Harrison (vocals, lead guitar) Ringo Starr (vocals, drums)	1960s	*Please Please Me, From Me to You, She Loves You, I Want to Hold Your Hand, Can't Buy Me Love, A Hard Day's Night, I Feel Fine, Eight Days A Week, Ticket to Ride, Help!, Yesterday, Day Tripper, We Can Work it Out, Paperback Writer, Yellow Submarine, Eleanor Rigby, Penny Lane, Strawberry Fields Forever, All You Need is Love, Hello Goodbye, Lady Madonna, Hey Jude, Get Back, The Ballad of John and Yoko, Let it Be* Albums : *Sergeant Pepper's Lonely Hearts Club Band*
Bee Gees, The	Britain	Barry Gibb (vocals, guitar) Maurice Gibb (vocals, bass) Robin Gibb (vocals)	1950s–present	*To Love Somebody, I've Gotta Get a Message to You, How Deep is Your Love, Stayin' Alive, Saturday Night Fever, Tragedy, You Win Again*
Berry, Chuck	US		1950s–present	*Maybellene, Roll over Beethoven, School Day, Rock and Roll Music, Sweet Little Sixteen, Johnny Be Good, Carol, No Particular Place to Go, My Ding-A-Ling*
Black Sabbath	Britain	Tony Iommi (guitar) 'Geezer' Butler (bass) Ozzy Osbourne (vocals) Bill Ward (drums)	1970s	*Paranoid, Never Say Die, Neon Knights.* Albums: *Paranoid, Black Sabbath Vol. 4, Sabbath Bloody Sabbath, Master of Reality, Sabotage, Technical Ecstasy, Heaven and Hell, Mob Rules, Born Again*
Blondie	US	Debbie Harry (vocals) Chris Stein (guitar) Jimmy Destri (keyboards) Gary Valentine (bass) Clem Burke (drums)	1970s–80s	*Denis, (I'm Always Touched by Your) Presence Dear, Picture This, Hanging on the Telephone, Heart of Glass, Sunday Girl, Dreaming, Atomic, Call Me, The Tide is High, Rapture, French Kissin' in the USA*

Name	Country of origin	Group members	Period	Major hits
Bowie, David	Britain		1970s–present	*Space Oddity, Aladdin Sane, The Jean Genie, Time, Sound and Vision, Ashes to Ashes, Fashion, Let's Dance, China Girl, Modern Love, Absolute Beginners*
Brown, James	US		1950s–present	*Papa's Got a Brand New Bag, I Got You (I Feel Good), It's a Man's Man's Man's World, I Got the Feelin', Say it, Loud - I'm Back and I'm Proud, Give it Up or Turn it Loose, Mother Popcorn, Get Up, I Feel Like Being a Sex Machine, Super Bad, Get on the Good Foot*
Byrds, The	US	Roger (Jim) McGuinn, (vocals, guitar) Gene Clark (vocals, percussion) David Crosby (vocals, guitar) Chris Hillman (vocals, bass) Michael Clarke (drums)	1960s–70s	*Mr Tambourine Man, All I Really Want to Do, Turn! Turn! Turn!, Eight Miles High, Chestnut Mare*
Carpenters, The	US	Richard Carpenter (vocals, drums) Karen Carpenter (vocals,keyboards)	1970s–80s	*Close to You, We've Only Just Begun, For All We Know, Rainy Days and Mondays, Hurting Each Other, It's Going to Take Some Time, Goodbye to Love, Sing, Please Mr Postman, Only Yesterday, Calling Occupants of Interplanetary Craft*
Clapton, Eric	Britain		1960s–present	*Layla, I Shot the Sheriff, Lay Down Sally, Wonderful Tonight, Forever Man, Cocaine, Knocking on Heaven's Door, Behind the Mask, Tears in Heaven*
Clash, The	Britain	Joe Strummer (vocals, guitar) Mick Jones (guitar) Paul Simonon (bass) Nicky 'Topper' Headon (drums)	1970s–80s	*Tommy Gun, Bankrobber, Rock the Casbah, Should I Stay or Should I Go?*
Cochran, Eddie	US		1950s	*Sittin' in the Balcony, Summertime Blues, C'Mon Everybody, Somethin' Else, Three Steps to Heaven, Hallelujah I Love Her So*
Collins, Phil	Britain		1980s–present	*In the Air Tonight, I Missed Again, You Can't Hurry Love, Against All Odds, Easy Lover, Sussudio, One More Night, Separate Lives, Take Me Home, Groovy Kind of Love, Two Hearts, Another Day in Paradise, I Wish it Would Rain*
Commodores, The	US	Lionel Richie (vocals, keyboards) William King (trumpet) Thomas McClary (lead guitar) Milan Williams (keyboards, trombone, guitar, drums) Ronald La Praed (bass, trumpet) Walter (Clyde) Orange (vocals, drums)	1970s–80s	*Machine Gun, Slippery When Wet, Sweet Love, Just To Be Close To You, Easy, Brickhouse, Three Times A Lady, Sail On, Still, Nightshift*
Cream	Britain	Eric Clapton (vocals, guitar) Jack Bruce (vocals, bass) Ginger Baker (drums)	1960s	*I Feel Free, Strange Brew, Sunshine of Your Love, White Room, Badge*
Diamond, Neil	US		1960s–	*Cherry Cherry, I Got the Feelin', You Got to Me, Girl You'll Be A Woman Soon, Sweet Caroline, Holly Holy, Cracklin' Rosie, I Am ... I Said, Stones, Song Sung Blue, Longfellow Serenade, Beautiful Noise, You Don't Bring Me Flowers, Forever in Blue Jeans, Love on the Rocks*

Classic pop and rock groups/singers (continued)

Name	*Country of origin*	*Group members*	*Period*	*Major hits*
Diddley, Bo	US		1950s–60s	*Bo Diddley, I'm a Man, Who Do You Love, Road Runner, Hey Good Lookin'*
Dire Straits	Britain	Mark Knopfler (guitar, vocals) John Illsley (bass) Hal Lindes (guitar) Pick Withers (drums) Alan Clark (keyboards)	1970s–80s	*Sultans of Swing, Romeo and Juliet, Telegraph Road, Private Investigations, Money for Nothing, Walk of Life*
Doors, The	US	Jim Morrison (vocals) Ray Manzarek (keyboards) Robbie Krieger (guitar) John Densmore (drums)	1960s–70s	*Light My Fire, Love Me Two Times, Hello I Love You, Touch Me, Love Her Madly, Riders on the Storm*
Dylan, Bob	US		1960s–present	*Blowin' in the Wind, The Times They Are a-Changin', Subterranean Homesick Blues, Like a Rollin' Stone, Positively 4th Street, Can You Please Crawl Out Your Window, Rainy Day Woman, Just Like a Woman, Lay Lady Lay, Knockin' on Heaven's Door, Baby Stop Crying*
Eagles, The	US	Glenn Frey (guitar, vocals) Bernie Leadon (guitar, vocals) Randy Meisner (bass, vocals) Don Henley (drums, vocals)	1970s	*Take it Easy, Witchy Woman, The Best of My Love, One of These Nights, Lyin' Eyes, Hotel California, New Kid in Town, Life in the Fast Lane, Life's Been Good, Heartache Tonight*
Eurythmics, The	Britain	Annie Lennox (vocals) Dave Stewart (keyboards, guitar)	1980s	*Sweet Dreams, Love is a Stranger, Right By Your Side, Here Comes The Rain Again, Who's That Girl, Would I Lie To You, There Must Be An Angel, Sisters Are Doing It For Themselves, It's Alright, Thorn In My Side*
Everley Brothers,	US	Don Everley (vocals, guitar) Phil Everley (vocals, guitar)	1950s–60s	*Bye Bye Love, Wake Up Little Susie, All I The Have to Do is Dream, Devoted to You, Bird Dog, Problems, A Message to Mary, I Kissed You, Let It Be Me, Cathy's Clown, When Will I Be Loved, Like Strangers, Walk Right Back, Ebony Eyes, Temptation, Crying in the Rain, That's Old-Fashioned, That'll Be The Day, Love is Strange*
Fleetwood Mac	UK/US	Mick Fleetwood (drums) John McVie (bass) Christine McVie (keyboards, vocals) Lindsey Buckingham (guitars, vocals) Stevie Nicks (vocals)	1960s–80s	*Albatross, Man of the World, Oh Well, The Green Manalishi, Over My Head, Go Your Own Way, Don't Stop, Dreams, You Make Loving Fun, Tusk, Sara,Trouble, Hold Me, Oh Diane, Big Love, Seven Wonders, Little Lies, Everywhere*
Four Tops, The	US	Levi Stubbs (vocals) Renaldo 'Obie' Benson (vocals) Abdul 'Duke' Fakir (vocals) Lawrence Paynton (vocals)	1960s–80s	*I Can't Help Myself, It's the Same Old Song, Loving You is Sweeter Than Ever, Reach Out I'll Be There, Bernadette, Seven Rooms of Gloom, Walk Away Renée, If I Were A Carpenter, What is a Man, Do What You Gotta Do, I Can't Help Myself, River Deep Mountain High, So Deep Within You, Ain't No Woman, When She was My Girl, Don't Walk Away, Loco in Acapulco*

Name	*Country of origin*	*Group members*	*Period*	*Major hits*
Franklin, Aretha	US		1960s–80s	*I Never Loved a Man, Do Right Woman- Do Right Man, Respect, Baby I Love You, Natural Woman, Since You've Been Gone, I Say A Little Prayer, The House That Jack Built, Chain of Fools, Don't Play That Song, Bridge Over Troubled Water, A Brand New Me, Spanish Harlem, Rock Steady, Who's Zoomin' Who, Sisters Are Doing it For Themselves, I Knew You Were Waiting*
Gabriel, Peter	Britain		1980s	*Games Without Frontiers, Sledgehammer, In Your Eyes, Don't Give Up*
Gaye, Marvin	US		1960s–80s	*How Sweet It Is, Ain't That Peculiar, It Takes Two, You're All I Need To Get By, I Heard It Through The Grapevine, Too Busy Thinking About My Baby, The Onion Song, Abraham, Martin and John, What's Going On, Mercy Mercy Mercy, Let's Get It On, You Are Everything, Sexual Healing*
Genesis	Britain	Tony Banks (keyboards) Mike Rutherford (guitars) Phil Collins (drums, vocals)	1960s–present	*Follow You, Follow Me, Turn It On Again, Paperlate, Mama, That's All, In Too Deep, Throwing It All Away, Land of Confusion, Tonight Tonight Tonight*
Grateful Dead, The	US	Jerry Garcia (lead guitar) Bob Weir (rhythm guitar) Ron 'Pigpen' McKernan (organ, harmonica) Phil Lesh (bass) Bill Kreutzmann (drums)	1960s–present	*Touch of Grey* Albums: *Grateful Dead, Workingman's Dead, Europe '72, Wake of the Flood, Blues for Allah, Terrapin Station, Dead Set, In the Dark*
Haley, Bill, and his Comets	US	Bill Haley (vocals, guitar) Frannie Beecher (lead guitar) Al Pompilli (bass) Rudi Pompilli (saxophone) Ralph Jones (drums)	1950s	*Shake, Rattle and Roll, Rock Around the Clock, Rock-a-Beatin' Boogie, See You Later Alligator, The Saints Rock'n'Roll, Rockin' Through The Rye, Razzle Dazzle, Rip it Up*
Hendrix, Jimi	US		1960s	*Hey Joe, Purple Haze, The Wind Cries Mary, Burning of the Midnight Lamp, Axis: Bold As Love, All Along The Watchtower, Voodoo Chile*
Hollies, The	Britain	Allan Clarke (vocals) Graham Nash (guitar) Tony Hicks (guitar) Erick Haydock (bass) Bobby Elliott (drums)	1960s–70s	*Just Like Me, Searchin', Stay, Here I Go Again, We're Through, Yes I Will, I'm Alive, Look Through Any Window, I Can't Let Go, Bus Stop, Stop Stop Stop, On a Carousel, Carrie-Anne, Jennifer Eccles, Listen To Me, Sorry Suza, He Ain't Heavy He's My Brother, I Can't Tell the Bottom From the Top, The Air That I Breathe*
Holly, Buddy, and the Crickets	US	Buddy Holly (vocals, guitar) Sonny Curtis (guitar) Joe B. Mauldin (bass) Jerry Allison (drums)	1950s	*That'll Be The Day, Peggy Sue, Oh Boy!, Listen to Me, Maybe Baby*

Classic pop and rock groups/singers (continued)

Name	*Country of origin*	*Group members*	*Period*	*Major hits*
Houston, Whitney	US		1980s	*Saving All My Love for You, How Will I Know, Greatest Love of All, I Wanna Dance With Somebody, Didn't We Almost Have It All, So Emotional, One Moment in Time, I'm Your Baby Tonight, I'll Always Love You, I Have Nothing*
Jackson, Michael	US		1970s–present	*Don't Stop 'Til You Get Enough, Rock With You, She's Out of My Life, One Day in Your Life, The Girl is Mine, Billie Jean, Beat It, Wanna Be Startin' Somethin', Say Say Say, Thriller, PYT, I Just Can't Stop Loving You, Bad, The Way You Make Me Feel, Dirty Diana, Another Part of Me, Smooth Criminal, Leave Me Alone*
Jacksons, The	US	Jackie Jackson (vocals) Tito Jackson (vocals) Jermaine Jackson (vocals) Marlon Jackson (vocals) Michael Jackson (vocals)	1960s–80s	*I Want You Back, ABC, The Love You Save, I'll Be There, Mama's Pearl, Never Can Say Goodbye, Dancing Machine, Enjoy Yourself, Show You the Way to Go, Blame It on the Boogie, Shake Your Body, Can You Feel It, State of Shock, Torture*
Jam, The	Britain	Paul Weller (vocals, bass) Bruce Foxton (guitar) Rick Buckler (drums)	1970s–80s	*In the City, All Around the World, Down in the Tube Station at Midnight, Eton Rifles, Going Underground, Start, Funeral Pyre, Absolute Beginners, Town Called Malice, Just Who is the Five O'Clock Hero, The Bitterest Pill, Beat Surrender*
Jefferson Airplane /Starship	US	Grace Slick (vocals) Marty Balin (vocals) Paul Kantner (guitar) Jorma Kaukonen (guitar) Jack Casady (bass guitar) Spencer Dryden (drums)	1960s–70s	*White Rabbit, Miracles, With Your Love, Count on Me, Runaway, Jane, Hearts*
Jethro Tull	Britain	Ian Anderson (vocals, flute) Mick Abrahams (guitar) Glen Connick (bass) Clive Bunker (drums)	1960s–present	*Living in the Past, The Witch's Promise/Teacher, Life Is A Long Song, Bungle in the Jungle, Thick as a Brick, Too Old To Rock and Roll – Too Young to Die*
Joel, Billy	US		1970s–present	*New York State of Mind, Say Hollywood, Just The Way You Are, Goodbye to She's Always a Woman, My Life, It's Still Rock'n'Roll to Me, Tell Her About It, Uptown Girl, An Innocent Man, The Longest Time, We Didn't Start the Fire*
John, Elton	Britain		1970s–	*Your Song, Rocket Man, Crocodile Rock, Daniel, Saturday Night's Alright for Fighting, Goodbye Yellow Brick Road, Candle in the Wind, Don't Let the Sun Go Down on Me, Don't Go Breaking My Heart, Sorry Seems to be the Hardest Word, Song for Guy, Blue Eyes, I Guess That's Why They Call It The Blues, I'm Still Standing, Sad Songs, Nikita, Sacrifice*

Name	*Country of origin*	*Group members*	*Period*	*Major hits*
Jones, Tom	Britain		1960s–present	*It's Not Unusual, What's New, Pussycat? Green Green Grass of Home, Detroit City, Funny Familiar Forgotten Feelings, I'll Never Fall in Love Again, I'm Coming Home, Delilah, Help Yourself, Love Me Tonight, Daughter of Darkness, A Boy From Nowhere, Kiss*
King, B.B.	US		1950s–80s	*Three O'Clock Blues, You Didn't Want Me, The Thrill is Gone, Hold On*
King, Carole	US		1960s–80s	*It Might As Well Rain Until September, It's Too Late/I Feel the Earth, Sweet Seasons, Jazzman, Nightingale*
Kinks, The	Britain	Roy Davies (vocals, guitar) Dave Davies (vocals, guitar) Pete Quaire (bass) Mick Avory (drums)	1960s–80s	*You Really Got Me, All Day and All of the Night, Tired of Waiting for You, See My Friend, Till the End of the Day, Sunny Afternoon, Dead End Street, Waterloo Sunset, Autumn Almanac, Lola, Come Dancing*
Knight, Gladys, and the Pips	US	Gladys Knight (vocals) Merald 'Bubba' Knight (vocals) William Guest (vocals) Edward Pattern (vocals)	1960s–80s	*Every Beat of My Heart, Take Me in Your Arms and Love Me, I Heard It Through the Grapevine, Just Walk in My Shoes, Help Me Make It Through the Night, Neither One of Us, Midnight Train to Georgia, I've Got to Use My Imagination, On and On, The Way We Were, Best Thing That Ever Happened To Me, Come Back and Finish What You Started*
Led Zeppelin	Britain	Robert Plant (vocals) Jimmy Page (guitar) John Paul Jones (bass) John Bonham (drums)	1960s–1980s	*Whole Lotta Love, Stairway to Heaven, Black Dog, Kashmir, Dazed and Confused, Delta Blues*
Lennon, John	Britain		1960s–80s	*Give Peace A Chance, Instant Karma, Power to the People, Imagine, Whatever Gets You Through the Night, Dream, Starting Over, Woman, Jealous Guy*
Lewis, Jerry Lee	US		1950s–present	*Whole Lotta Shakin', Great Balls of Fire, Breathless, High School Confi dential, What'd I Say, Good Golly Miss Molly, Chantilly Lace*
Little Richard	US		1950s–present	*Tutti Frutti, Long Tall Sally, Rip it Up, She's Got It, The Girl Can't Help It, Lucille, Jenny Jenny, Keep a-Knockin', Good Golly Miss Molly, Baby Face, Bama Lama Bama Loo*
McCartney, Paul	Britain		1970s–present	Songs with Wings : *Another Day, Mary Had a Little Lamb, Hi Hi Hi, My Love, Live and Let Die, Helen Wheels, Jet, Band on the Run, Listen to What The Man Said, Silly Love Songs, Let 'Em In, Mull of Kintyre, With a Little Luck.* McCartney's solo songs : *Wonderful Christmastime, Ebony and Ivory, The Girl Is Mine, Say Say Say, Pipes of Peace, No More Lonely Nights, We All Stand Together, My Brave Face*

Classic pop and rock groups/singers (continued)

Name	*Country of origin*	*Group members*	*Period*	*Major hits*
Madness	Britain	Graham 'Suggs' McPherson (vocals) Mike Barson (keyboards) Chris Foreman (guitar) Mark Bedford (bass) Lee Thompson (saxophone, vocals) Dan Woodgate (drums) Carl 'Chas Smash' Smyth (horns)	1980s	*One Step Beyond, My Girl, Night Train to Cairo, Baggy Trousers, Embarrassment, Return of the Los Palmas Seven, Grey Day, It Must Be Love, House of Fun, Driving in My Car, Our House, Tomorrow, Wings of a Dove, The Sun and the Rain*
Madonna	US		1980s–	*Like a Virgin, Material Girl, Holiday, Crazy for You, Angel, Dress You Up, Live To Tell, True Blue, Papa Don't Preach, Open Your Heart, La Isla Bonita, Who's That Girl, Express Yourself, Like a Prayer, Cherish, Dear Jessie, Vogue, I'm Breathless, Hanky Panky, Justify My Love*
Mamas and Papas, The	US	John Phillips (vocals) Denny Doherty (vocals) Cass Elliot (vocals) Michelle Gilliam (vocals)	1960s	*California Dreamin', Monday Monday, I Saw Her Again, Dedicated to the One I Love, San Francisco, Dream a Little Dream of Me*
Marley, Bob, and the Wailers	Jamaica	Bob Marley (vocals, guitar) Peter Tosh (vocals, guitar) Bunny Wailer (vocals, percussion) Carlton Barrett (drums) Aston 'Family Man' Barrett (bass)	1970s	*No Woman No Cry, Exodus, Jamming, Is This Love, Satisfy My Soul, Could You Be Loved, Buffalo Soldier*
Michael, George	Britain		1980s–present	*Careless Whisper, I Knew You Were Waiting, I Want Your Sex, Faith, Father Figure, One More Try, Praying for Time, Freedom!, Too Funky, Somebody to Love*
Monkees, The	US	Davy Jones (vocals, guitar) Mike Nesmith (vocals, guitar) Peter Tork (vocals, keyboards, bass guitar) Micky Dolenz (drums)	1960s	*Hey Hey We're the Monkees, Last Train to Clarksville, I'm a Believer, A Little Bit of Me, A Little Bit of You, Alternate Title, Pleasant Valley Sunday, Valleri*
Morrison, Van	Ireland		1960s–present	*Brown Eyed Girl, Domino, Blue Money, Wild Night, Jackie Wilson Said*
Newman, Randy	US		1960s–present	*Short People* Albums: *Little Criminals, Born Again*
Orbison, Roy	US		1950s–60s, 1980s	*Pretty Woman, Only the Lonely, Blue Angel, I'm Hurtin', Running Scared, Cryin', Dream By, Falling, Blue Bayou, It's Over, Pretty Paper, Too Soon To Know, You Got It*
Osmonds, The	US	Alan Osmond (vocals) Wayne Osmond (vocals) Merrill Osmond (vocals) Jay Osmond (vocals) Donny Osmond (vocals)	1970s	*One Bad Apple, Yo-Yo, Down By the Lazy River, Let Me In, I Can't Stop, Love Me for a Reason, The Proud One, Crazy Horses*
Pink Floyd	Britain	Roger Waters (vocals, bass) Rick Wright (keyboards) David Gilmour (vocals, guitar) Nick Mason (drums)	1960s–present	*Arnold Layne, See Emily Play, Another Brick in the Wall, Not Now John* Albums: *The Piper at the Gates of Dawn, A Saucerful of Secrets, Ummagumma, Dark Side of the Moon, Wish You Were Here, Animals, The Wall, The Final Cut*

Name	Country of origin	Group members	Period	Major hits
Pitney, Gene	US		1960s–80s	*24 Hours From Tulsa, Somethin's Gotten Hold of My Heart, Backstage, A Town Without Pity, 24 Sycamore, Maria Elena*
Pogues, The	Britain	Shane McGowan (vocals, guitar) Jem Finer (banjo) James Fearnley (accordian) Spider Stacy (tin whistle) Caitlin O'Riordan (bass) Andrew Ranken (drums)	1980s–present	*A Pair of Brown Eyes, Dirty Old Town, The Irish Rover, A Fairytale of New York*
Police, The	Britain	Sting [Gordon Sumner] (vocals, bass) Andy Summers (vocals, guitar) Stewart Copeland (drums, percussion, vocals)	1970s–80s	*Roxanne, Can't Stand Losing You, Message In a Bottle, Walking on the Moon, So Lonely, Don't Stand So Close To Me, Invisible Sun, Every Little Thing She Does is Magic, Every Breath You Take*
Presley, Elvis	US		1950s–70s	*Baby Let's Play House , Heartbreak Hotel, Blue Suede Shoes, Hound Dog, I Want You I Need You I Love You, Don't Be Cruel, Love Me Tender, All Shook Up, Teddy Bear, Jailhouse Rock, Don't, Hard-Headed Woman, A Big Hunk of Love, Stuck On You, It's Now or Never, Are You Lonesome Tonight, Surrender, His Latest Flame, Can't Help Falling In Love, Good Luck Charm, She's Not You, Return to Sender, Devil in Disguise, Crying in the Chapel, Suspicious Minds, Don't Cry Daddy, The Wonder of You, I Just Can't Help Believing American Trilogy, In the Ghetto*
Pretenders, The	Britain	Chrissie Hynde (vocals) Pete Farndon (bass) James Honeyman-Scott (guitar) Martin Chambers (drums)	1970s–present	*Stop Your Sobbing, Brass in Pocket (I'm Special), Talk of the Town, Message of Love, I Go to Sleep, Back on the Chain Gang, Don't Get Me Wrong, Learning to Crawl, Packed*
Prince	US		1980s–present	*Little Red Corvette, 1999, When Doves Cry, Purple Rain, Let's Go Crazy, Kiss, Girls and Boys, Sign of the Times, U Got The Look, Alphabet St, Batdance*
Queen	Britain	Freddie Mercury (vocals) (d.1992) Brian May (guitar) John Deacon (bass) Roger Taylor (drums)	1970s–90s	*Seven Seas of Rye, Killer Queen, Now I'm Here, Bohemian Rhapsody, You're My Best Friend, Somebody To Love, We Are The Champions, We Will Rock You, Fat Bottomed Girls, Don't Stop Me Now, Crazy Little Thing Called Love, Another One Bites the Dust, Flash, Under Pressure, Radio GaGa, I Want To Break Free, A Kind of Magic, The Great Pretender, I Want It All, Innuendo*
Redding, Otis	US		1960s	*I've Been Loving You Too Long, Mr Pitiful, Pain in My Heart, My Girl, Try a Little Tenderness, The Dock of the Bay*
Reed, Lou	US		1970s	*Walk on the Wild Side, Soul Man*
REM	US	Michael Stripe (vocals) Peter Buck (guitar) Mike Mills (bass) Bill Berry (drums)	1980s–present	*Radio Free Europe, It's the End of the World As We Know It, The One I Love, Stand, Losing My Religion, The Greenhouse Effect*

Classic pop and rock groups/singers (continued)

Name	*Country of origin*	*Group members*	*Period*	*Major hits*
Richard, Cliff	Britain		1950s–present	*Move It, Livin' Lovin' Doll, Mean Streak, Living Doll, A Voice in the Wilderness, Fall In Love With You, Please Don't Tease, Nine Times Out of Ten, I Love You, Theme For A Dream, A Girl Like You, When The Girl In Your Arms Is The Girl In Your Heart, It'll Be Me, The Next Time, Batchelor Boy, Summer Holiday, Lucky Lips, Don't Talk To Him, I'm The Lonely One, On The Beach, I Could Easily Fall, The Minute You're Gone, Wind Me Up, Vision, In the Country, The Day I Met Marie, All My Love, Congratulations, Big Ship, Goodbye Sam Hello Samantha, PowerTo All Our Friends, Devil Woman, We Don't Talk Anymore, Carrie, Dreaming, Wired for Sound, Daddy's Home, Silhouette, Saviour's Day*
Richie, Lionel	US		1980s–present	*Endless Love, Truly, All Night Long, Running in the Night, Hello, Stuck On You, Penny Lover, Say You Say Me, Dancing on the Ceiling, Ballerina Girl*
Robinson, Smokey,	US		1950s–present	Smokey Robinson and The Miracles songs: *Sheree Baby, Shop Around, You've Really Got A Hold On Me, I Second That Emotion, Tracks of my Tears, The Tears of a Clown, I Don't Blame You At All* Smokey Robinson solo songs: *Love Machine, Being with You*
Rolling Stones, The	Britain	Mick Jagger (vocals, harmonica) Keith Richard (rhythm guitar) Brian Jones (lead guitar) Bill Wyman (bass) Charlie Watts (drums) Mick Taylor (lead guitar 1969–74) Ron Wood (lead guitar 1974–present)	1960s–present	*Come On, I Wanna Be Your Man, Not Fade Away, It's All Over Now, Little Red Rooster, Time Is On My Side, The Last Time, Satisfaction, Get Off Of My Cloud, 19th Nervous Breakdown, Paint It Black, Out of Time, Have You Seen Your Mother Baby Standin' In The Shadows?, Let's Spend the Night Together, Jumpin' Jack Flash, Honky Tonk Woman, Brown,Sugar, Fool To Cry, Miss You, Emotional Rescue, Start Me Up, Harlem Shuffle, Under Cover of the Night*
Ross, Diana	US		1970s–present	*Ain't No Mountain High Enough, I'm still Waiting, Touch Me in The Morning, All of My Life, You Are Everything, Theme from Mahogany, One Love In My Lifetime, Upside Down, My Old Piano, It's My Turn, Endless Love, Chain Reaction*

Name	*Country of origin*	*Group members*	*Period*	*Major hits*
Roxy Music	Britain	Bryan Ferry (vocals) Andy MacKay (saxophone, woodwind) Phil Manzanera (guitar) Brian Eno (keyboards) Rik Kenton (bass) Thompson (drums)	1970s–90s	*Virginia Plain, Pyjamarama, Street Life, Love Is The Drug, Dance Away, Angel Eyes, Over You, Oh Yeah, Avalon, The Same Old Scene, Avalon, The Same Old Scene,* Paul *Jealous Guy, More Than This*
Sex Pistols, The	Britain	Johnny Rotten (vocals) Steve Jones (guitar) Sid Vicious (bass) Paul Cook (drums)	1970s	*God Save The Queen, Pretty Vacant, Holidays in the Sun, Something Else, C'Mon Everybody, Silly Thing*
Shadows, The	Britain	Hank Marvin (lead guitar) Bruce Welch (rhythm guitar) Brian Bennett (drums) Jet Harris (bass 1958–62, left band) Tony Meehan (drums 1958–61, replaced by Bennett)	1960s–present	*Apache, Man of Mystery, The Stranger, The Frightened City, Kon-Tiki, Wonderful Land, Guitar Tango, Dance On, Foot Tapper, Atlantis, Shindig, The Rise and Fall of Aingel Bunt, Don't Make My Baby Blue, Riders in the Sky*
Simon and Garfunkel	US	Paul Simon (vocals, guitar) Art Garfunkel (vocals)	1960s–70s	*The Sound of Silence, Homeward Bound, I am a Rock, Scarborough Fair, 58th Street Bridge Song, Mrs Robinson, The Boxer, Bridge Over Troubled Water*
Simon, Paul	US		1970s–present	*Kodachrome, Loves Me Like A Rock, Slip Slidin' Away, Late in the Evening, Fifty Ways to Leave Your Lover, American Theme, You Can Call Me Al*
Simple Minds	Britain	Jim Kerr (vocals) Charlie Burchill (guitar) Mike McNeil (keyboards) John Giblin (bass) Mel Gaynor (drums)	1980s–present	*Promised You a Miracle, Waterfront, Don't You Forget About Me, Sanctify Yourself, All the Things She Said, Belfast Child*
Simply Red	Britain	Mick Hucknall (vocals) Sylvan Richardson (guitar) Fritz McIntyre (keyboards) Tony Bowers (bass) Chris Joyce (drums) Tim Kellett (horns)	1980s–present	*Holding Back The Years, Money's Too Tight To Mention, The Right Thing, If You Don't Know Me By Now*
Smiths, The	Britain	Morrissey (vocals) Johnny Marr (guitar) Andy Rourke (bass) Mike Joyce (drums)	1980s	*What Difference Does It Make, Heaven Knows I'm Miserable Now, William It Was Really Nothing, Panic, Shoplifters of the World Unite, Sheila Take a Bow, Girlfirend in a Coma*
Springfield, Dusty	Britain		1960s–present	*I Only Want To Be With You, I Just Don't Know What To Do With Myself, Wishin' and Hopin', You Don't Have To Say You Love Me, Island of Dreams, Say I Won't Be There, Losing You, In the Middle of Nowhere, Some of Your Lovin', All I See Is You, I Close My Eyes and Count to Ten, Son of a Preacher Man, What Have I Done To Deserve This, In Private*
Springsteen, Bruce	US		1970s–present	*The River, Hungry Heart, Fire, Dancing in the Dark, Cover Me, Born in the USA, I'm On Fire, Born to Run*

Classic pop and rock groups/singers (continued)

Name	*Country of origin*	*Group members*	*Period*	*Major hits*
Status Quo	Britain	Francis Rossi (guitar, vocals) Rick Parfitt (guitar, vocals) Alan Lancaster (bass) John Coghlan (drums)	1960s–present	*Pictures of Matchstick Men, Ice in the Sun, Paper Plane, Caroline, Break the Rules, Down Down, Roll Over Lay Down, Rain, Mystery Song, Wild Side of Life, Again and Again, Whatever You Want, Lies, Somethin' 'Bout You Baby I Like, Dear John, The Wanderer, Rockin' All Over The World, Rollin' Home, In The Army Now, Burning Bridges*
Stewart, Rod	Britain		1970s–present	*Maggie May, You Wear It Well, Oh No Not My Baby, Sailing, Tonight's The Night, The Killing of Georgie, I Don't Want to Talk About It, You're In My Heart, Hotlegs, D'Ya Think I'm Sexy, Tonight I'm Yours, Young Turks, Baby Jane, What Am I Gonna Do, Infatuation, Some Guys Have All the Luck, Every Beat of My Heart, Downtown Train, It Takes Two, Rhythm of the Heart*
Sting	Britain		1980s–present	*Spread a Little Happiness, Russians, We'll Be Together, An Englishman in New York*
Stranglers, The	Britain	Hugh Cornwell (vocals, guitar) Dave Greenfield (keyboards) Jean-Jacques Burnel (bass) Jet Black (drums)	1970s–present	*Peaches, Something Better Change, No More Heroes, Five Minutes, Nice'n'Sleazy, Golden Brown, European Female, Skin Deep, All Day and All of the Night*
Summer, Donna	US		1970s–present	*Love to Love You Baby, I Feel Love, I Remember Yesterday, Down Deep, Last Dance, MacArthur Park, Heaven Knows, Hot Stuff, Bad Girls, Dim All the Lights, No More Tears, On The Radio, The Wanderer, State of Independence, She Works Hard for the Money, This Time I Know It's For Real, I Don't Wanna Get Hurt*
Supremes, The	US	Diana Ross (vocals) Mary Wilson (vocals) Florence Ballard (vocals)	1960s–70s	*Where Did Our Love Go, Baby Love, Come See About Me, Stop! In The Name of Love, Back In My Arms Again, I Hear a Symphony, You Can't Hurry Love, You Keep Me Hangin' On, Love Is Here And Now You're Gone, The Happening, In And Out Of Love, Love Child, I'm Gonna Make You Love Me, I Second That Emotion, Someday We'll Be Together, Up The Ladder to the Roof, Stoned Love, Floy Joy, River Deep Mountain High*
T-Rex	Britain	Marc Bolan (vocals, guitar) Steve Peregrine Took (percussion)	1960s–70s	*Ride a White Swan, Hot Love, Get It On, Jeepster, Telegram Sam, Metal Guru, Children of the Revolution, Solid Gold Easy Action, Twentieth Centruy Boy, The Groover, Truck On, Teenage Dream, I Love to Boogie*

Name	*Country of origin*	*Group members*	*Period*	*Major hits*
Talking Heads	US	David Byrne (guitar, vocals) Tina Weymouth (bass) Jerry Harrison (keyboards) Chris Frantz (drums)	1970s–present	*Psycho Killer, Once in a Lifetime, Burning Down the House, Road to Nowhere, And She Was*
Temptations, The	US	Eddie Kendricks (vocals) Otis Williams (vocals) Paul Williams (vocals) Melvin Franklin (vocals) David Ruffin (vocals)	1960s–present	*The Way You Do The Things You Do, My Girl, Ain't Too Proud to Beg, Beauty is Only Skin Deep, You're My Everythng, Get Ready, Papa Was a Rollin' Stone, Treat Her Like a Lady*
10CC	Britain	Graham Gouldman (vocals, guitar) Eric Stewart (vocals, guitar) Lol Creme (vocals, guitar) Kevin Godley (vocals, drums)	1970s	*Rubber Bullets, The Dean and I, Wall Street Shuffle, Life Is A Minestrone, I'm Not In Love, Art For Art's Sake, I'm Mandy Fly Me, Things We Do For Love, Good Morning Judge, Dreadlock Holiday*
Turner, Tina	US		1960s–present	Ike and Tina Turner songs : *It's Gonna Work Out Fine, River Deep Mountain High, Proud Mary* Tina Turner solo songs : *Let's Stay Together, What's Love Got To Do With It, Better Be Good To Me, We Don't Need Another Hero, The Best, I Don't Wanna Lose You, Steamy Windows, Private Dancer*
U2	Ireland	Bono (vocals) The Edge (guitar) Adam Clayton (bass) Larry Mullen, Jr (drums)	1980s–present	*New Year's Day, Sunday Bloody Sunday, Two Hearts Beat As One, Pride, The Unforgettable Fire, The Streets Have No Name, With or Without You, I Still Haven't Found What I'm Looking For, Desire, Angel of Harlem, When Love Comes to Town, All I Want Is You*
Waits, Tom	US		1970s–present	*Ol' 55, Downtown Train, Sea of Love*
Warwick, Dionne	US		1960s–present	*Anyone Who Had a Heart, Walk On By, A Messge to Martha, I Say a Little Prayer, Do You Know The Way To San José, This Girl's In Love With You, You've Lost That Lovin' Feeling, I'll Never Fall In Love Again, Then Came You, I'll Never Love This Way Again, Déjà Vu, Heartbreaker, All The Love In The World, That's What Friends Are For*
White, Barry	US		1970s–present	*I'm Gonna Love You Just A Little More, Baby, Never Gonna Give You Up, I'm Under the Influence of Love, Can't Get Enough of Your Love Babe, You're The First The Last My Everything, What Am I Gonna Do With You, Let The Music Play, You See The Trouble With Me, It's Ecstasy When You Lay Down Next To Me*
Who, The	Britain	Pete Townshend (guitar) Roger Daltrey (vocals) John Entwhistle (bass) Keith Moon (drums)	1960s–80s	*Can't Explain, Anyway Anyhow Anywhere, My Generation, Substitute, I'm A Boy, Happy Jack, Pictures of Lily, I Can See For Miles, Pinball Wizard, Won't Get Fooled Again, Squeeze Box, Who Are You, You Better You Bet*

Classic pop and rock groups/singers (continued)

Name	*Country of origin*	*Group members*	*Period*	*Major hits*
Wonder, Stevie	US		1960s–present	*Fingertips - Pt 2, Uptight, A Place in the Sun, I Was Made to Love Her, For Once in My Life, My Cherie Amour, Yester-Me, Yester-You, Yesterday, Never Had A Dream Come True, Signed Sealed Delivered I'm Yours, You Are the Sunshine of My Life, Superstition, Living for the City, He's Misstra Know It All, I Wish, Sir Duke, Master Blaster, I Ain't Gonna Stand For It, Lately, Happy Birthday, Jammin', Ebony and Ivory, I Just Called to Say I Love You, Part-Time Lover*
Young, Neil	Canada		1960s–	Albums: *After The Goldrush, Harvest, Time Fades Away, Rust Never Sleeps, American Stars'n'Bars, Comes A Time, Live Rust, Trans*
Zappa, Frank	US		1960s–present	*Memories of El Monte* Albums: *Absolutely Free, Hot Rats, Burnt Weeny Sandwich, Weasels Ripped My Flesh, Over-Nite Sensation, Apostrophe, Sheik Yerbouti*

*Group members are given for the best-known line-up.

International music festivals

Festival	*Date founded*	*Location*	*Time of year*
Aldeburgh Festival	1948	Aldeburgh, Suffolk	Summer
Aspen Music Festival	1949	Aspen, Colorado	Summer
Bayreuth Festival (Richard Wagner Festival)	1876	Bayreuth, Bavaria	Summer
Berkshire Festival	1937	Stockbridge, Massachusetts	Summer
Glyndebourne Festival	1934	nr Lewes, East Sussex	Summer
Llangollen International Music Eisteddfod	1947	Llangollen, Clwyd, N Wales	Summer
Marlboro Music Festival	1951	Malboro, Vermont	Summer
Montreux International Jazz Festival	1967	Montreux, Switzerland	Summer
Newport Jazz Festival	1954	Newport, Rhode Island (until 1971, then in NYC)	Summer
Salzburg Festival	1920	Salzburg	Summer
Sante Fe Opera	1957	Santa Fe, New Mexico	Summer
Spoleto Festival (Festival of the Two Worlds)	1958	Spoleto, Italy	Summer

Pulitzer Prize in music

1943	*Secular Cantata No 2, A Free Song* William Schuman
1944	*Symphony No 4* (Op. 34) Howard Hanson
1945	*Appalachian Spring* Aaron Copland
1946	*The Canticle of the Sun* Leo Sowerby
1947	*Symphony No 3* Charles Ives
1948	*Symphony No 3* Walter Piston
1949	*Louisiana Story* music Virgil Thomson
1950	*The Consul* Gian Carlo Menotti
1951	Music for opera *Giants in the Earth* Douglas Stuart Moore
1952	*Symphony Concertante* Gail Kubik
1954	*Concerto for Two Pianos and Orchestra* Quincy Porter
1955	*The Saint of Bleecker Street* Gian Carlo Menotti
1956	*Symphony No 3* Ernest Toch
1957	*Meditations on Ecclesiastes* Norman Dello Joio
1958	*Vanessa* Samuel Barber
1959	*Concerto for Piano and Orchestra* John La Montaine
1960	*Second String Quartet* Elliott Carter
1961	*Symphony No 7* Walter Piston
1962	*The Crucible* Robert Ward
1963	*Piano Concerto No 1* Samuel Barber

1966	*Variations for Orchestra* Leslie Bassett
1967	*Quartet No 3* Leon Kirchner
1968	*Echoes of Time and the River* George Crumb
1969	*String Quartet No 3* Karel Husa
1970	*Time's Encomium* Charles Wuorinen
1971	*Synchronisms No 6 for Piano and Electronic Sound* Mario Davidowsky
1972	*Windows* Jacob Druckman
1973	*String Quartet No 3* Elliott Carter
1974	*Notturno* Donald Martino
1975	*From the Diary of Virginia Woolf* Dominick Argento
1976	*Air Music* Ned Rorem
1977	*Visions of Terror and Wonder* Richard Wernick
1978	*Déjà Vu for Percussion Quartet and Orchestra* Michael Colgrass
1979	*Aftertones of Infinity* Joseph Schwantner
1980	*In Memory of a Summer Day* David Del Tredici
1981	*Not awarded*
1982	*Concerto for Orchestra* Roger Sessions
1983	*Three Movements for Orchestra* Ellen T Zwilich
1984	*Canti del Sole* Bernard Rands
1985	*Symphony River Run* Stephen Albert
1986	*Wind Quintet IV* George Perle
1987	*The Flight into Egypt* John Harbison
1988	*12 New Etudes for Piano* William Bolcom
1989	*Whispers Out of Time* Roger Reynolds
1990	*Duplicates: A Concerto for Two Pianos and Orchestra* Mel Powell
1991	*Symphony* Shulamit Ran
1992	*The Face of the Night, The Heart of the Dark* Wayne Peterson
	Special award
1992	*Maus* Art Spiegelmann

National anthem/song

Country	*Title*	*Composer*	*Adopted*
Australia	*Advance Australia Fair*	Peter Dodds McCormick	1977
Canada	*O Canada*	Calixa Lavallée	1980
France	*La Marseillaise*	Claude-Joseph Rouget de Lisle	1795
Japan	*Kimigayo ('His Majesty's Reign')*	Hayashi Hiromori	not offically adopted
West Germany	*Deutschland-lied ('Song of Germany')*	Haydn	1950
UK	*God Save the Queen/King*	not known	18th-c
US	*The Star Spangled Banner*	John Stafford Smith	1931
Former USSR	*Gimn Soretskogo Soyuza ('Hymn of the Soviet Union')*	not known	1944

National tune. The official anthem is *God Save the Queen/King* played when a regal or vice-regal personage is present.

DANCE

Dance personalities

Name	*Dates*	*Place of birth*	*Occupation*
Ailey, Alvin	1931–89	Texas	Dancer, choreographer (ballet). Formed the Alvin Ailey American Dance Theatre in 1958
Ailian, Dai	1916–	Trinidad	Dancer, choreographer (ballet). 1959 cofounder of Central Ballet of China
Alonso, Alicia	1921–	Havana	Dancer, choreographer. Founder of Ballet de Cuba. 1948 formed the Alicia Alonso Company
Alston, Richard	1948–	Sussex	Choreographer (modern dance)
Amagatsu, Yushio	1948–		Choreographer (modern dance)
Argentina, La (Antonia Mercé)	1890–1936	Buenos Aires	Ballerina
Armitage, Karole	1954–	Madison, Wisconsin	Dancer, choreographer (ballet)
Ashton, Sir Frederick (Wiliam Mallandaine)	1904–88	Guayaquil, Ecuador	Dancer, choreographer (ballet)
Babilée Jean (Jean Gutman)	1923–	Paris	Dancer, choreographer (ballet)
Balanchine, George (Georgi Melitonovich Balachivadze)	1904–83	St Petersburg	Dancer, choreographer
Baryshnikov, Mikhail Nikolayevich	1948–	Riga	Dancer (ballet)
Bausch, Pina	1940–	Solingen, Germany	Dancer, choreographer, director (ballet)
Beauchamp, Pierre	1637–1705	Versailles	Dancer, choreographer, ballet master
Béjart, Maurice	1927–	Marseilles	Founder of Ballet Béjart 1953 (modern ballet)
Benesh, Rudolph	1916–75	London	Dancer notator
Bennett, Michael	1943–87	Buffalo, New York	Dancer, choreographer (musical)
Berkeley, Busby	1895–1976	Los Angeles	Choreographer (film)
Bessmertnova, Natalia	1941–	Moscow	Ballerina

Dance personalities (continued)

Name	*Dates*	*Place of birth*	*Occupation*
Bolm, Adolph	1884–1951	St Petersburg	Dancer, choreographer, teacher (ballet)
Borovansky, Edouard	1902–59	Prerov	Dancer, choreographer, ballet director
Bournonville, August	1805–79	Copenhagen	Choreographer
Brown, Trisha	1936–	Aberdeen, Washington	Choreographer. Cofounder of Judson Dance Company, 1962 (experimental dance)
Bruce, Christopher	1945–	Leicester	Choreographer (ballet/modern dance)
Bruhn, Eric	1928–86	Copenhagen	Dancer, ballet director
Bujones, Fernando	1955–	Florida	Dancer (ballet)
Butcher, Rosemary	1947–	Bristol	Choreographer (experimental dance)
Camargo, Maria Anna de	1710–70	Brussels	Ballerina
Clark, Michael	1962–	Aberdeen	Dancer, choreographer (ballet/modern dance)
Cohan, Robert	1925–	Brooklyn, New York	Choreographer, dancer, director (modern dance)
Cranko, John	1927–73	Rustenburg, S Africa	Dancer, choreographer and director (ballet)
Culberg, Birgit Ragnhild	1908–	Nyköping, Sweden	Dancer, choreographer and director (ballet)
Cunningham, Merce	1919–	Centralia, Washington	Dancer, choreographer, director, teacher (modern dance)
Danilova, Alexandra (Dionysievna)	1904–	Peterhof	Dancer (ballet)
Dantzig, Rudi von	1933–	Amsterdam	Dancer, choreographer, ballet director
Davies, Siobhan	1950–	London	Choreographer, dancer. Formed Siobhan Davies Company, 1988 (contemporary dance)
Dean, Laura	1945–	New York	Dancer, choreographer, teacher (ballet/modern dance)
De Basil, Colonel Wassili	1881–1951	Kaunas	Ballet impresario
Demille, Agnes	1909–	New York City	Choreographer (ballet)
Diaghilev, Sergei (Pavlovich)	1872–1920	Novgorod	Ballet impresario and founder of Ballets Russes
Dolin, Anthony (Patrick Healey-Kay)	1904–83	Slinfold, Sussex	Dancer, choreographer. Cofounder of the Markova-Dolin Ballet
Dowell, Anthony	1943–	London	Dancer (ballet)
Duncan, Isadora	1877–1927	San Francisco	Dancer, choreographer (ballet)
Dunham, Katherine	1912–	Chicago	Dancer (ballet)
Dunn, Douglas	1942–	Palo, Alto, California	Dancer, choreographer (experimental dance)
Dupond, Patrick	1959–	Paris	Dancer (ballet)
Falco, Louis	1942–		Dancer, choreographer (contemporary dance)
Farrell, Suzanne	1945–	Cincinatti, Ohio	Dancer (ballet)
Feld, Eliot	1942–	Brooklyn, New York	Dancer, choregrapher (ballet/modern dance)
Fokine, Michel (Mikhail Mikhaylovich Fokine)	1882–1942	St Petersburg	Dancer, choreographer (creator of modern ballet)
Fonteyn, Dame Margot (Margaret Hokham)	1919–91	Reigate	Ballerina
Forsythe, William	1949–	New York City	Dancer, choreographer (contemporary dance)
Fosse, Bob	1927–87	Chicago	Choreographer (film and theatre)
France, Celia	1921–	London	Dancer (ballet). 1951 National Ballet of Canada founded under her directorship
Franklin, Frederic	1914–	Liverpool	Dancer, teacher, ballet director
Fuller, Loie	1862–1928	Illinois	Dancer, choreographer (performance art)
Gable, Christopher	1940–	London	Dancer (ballet)
Gielgud, Maina	1945–	London	Dancer, artistic director, teacher (modern dance)
Gilpin, John	1830–83	Southsea	Dancer (ballet)
Gordon, David	1936–	Brooklyn, New York	Choreographer (experimental dance)
Graham, Martha	1849–91	Pittsburgh, Pennsylvania	Dancer, teacher, choreographer (modern dance)
Grahn, Lucile	1819–1907	Copenhagen	Ballerina
Grant, Alexander	1925–	Wellington, New Zealand	Dancer (ballet)
Grey, Dame Beryl (Mrs Beryl Svenson)	1927–	London	Ballerina
Grigorovich, Yuri (Nikolayevich)	1927–	St Petersburg	Dancer, teacher, choreographer (ballet)
Hawkins, Erick	1909–	Colorado	Dancer, choreographer, teacher (ballet/modern dance)

Name	*Dates*	*Place of birth*	*Occupation*
Haydée, Marcia (Marcia Salavery Pereira de Silva)	1939–	Niteroi, Brazil	Ballerina
Helpmann, Sir Robert (Murray)	1909–86	Mount Gambier, Australia	Dancer, choreographer (ballet)
Hightower, Rosella	1920–		Dancer, teacher (ballet)
Holm, Hanya (Johanna Eckert)	1893–1992	Worms	Dancer, choreographer, teacher (modern dance)
Humphrey, Doris	1895–1958	Oak Park, Illinois	Dancer, choreographer, teacher (modern dance)
Ivanov, Lev (Ivanovich)	1834–1901	Moscow	Choreographer (ballet)
Jamison, Judith	1943–	Philadelphia	Dancer
Joffrey, Robert (Abdullah Jaffa Anver Bey Khan)	1930–88	Seattle	Dancer, choreographer, teacher, ballet director
Jooss, Kurt	1901–79	Waaseralfingen	Choreographer (ballet)
Kain, Karen	1951–	Hamilton, Ontario	Ballerina
Karsavina, Tamara (Platonovna)	1885–1978	St Petersburg	Ballerina
Kaye, Nora	1920–87	New York	Ballerina
Kidd, Michael	1949–	Brooklyn, New York	Dancer, choreographer, director (modern ballet/musical)
Kirkland, Gelsey	1953–	Bethlehem, Pennsylvania	Dancer (ballet)
Kirstein, Lincoln	1907–	Rochester, New York	Impresario and ballet director
Kylian, Jiri	1947–	Prague	Dancer, choreographer (ballet)
Laban, Rudolf von	1879–1958	Pozsony, Hungary (now Bratislava, Slovakia)	Dancer, choreographer, dance theoretician (modern dance)
Lander, Harald	1905–71	Copenhagen	Dancer, choreographer, teacher (modern ballet)
Larrieu, Daniel	1957–	Marseilles	Dancer, choreographer (modern ballet)
Legat, Nicolai	1869–1937	St Petersburg	Dancer, choreographer, teacher and ballet master
Lifar, Serge	1905–86	Kiev	Dancer, choreographer (ballet)
Limon, Jose	1908–72	Culiacan, Mexico	Dancer, choreographer, teacher (modern dance)
Lophukov, Fyodor	1886–1973	St Petersburg	Dancer, choreographer, teacher (modern ballet/modern dance)
MacDonald, Elaine	1943–	Tadcaster	Ballerina
Macmillan, Sir Kenneth	1929–92	Dunfermline	Dancer, choreographer, ballet company director. Artistic director of Royal Ballet from 1970 and principal choreographer from 1977
Makarova, Nataliya (Romanovna)	1940–	St. Petersburg	Ballerina
Manen, Hans van	1932–	Amstel, Netherlands	Dancer, choreographer, director (ballet)
Marin, Maguy	1951–	Toulouse	Dancer, choreographer (modern ballet)
Markova, Dame Alicia (Lilian Alicia Marks)	1910	London	Prima ballerina
Martins, Peter	1946–	Copenhagen	Dancer (ballet)
Massine, Leonide	1896–1979	Moscow	Dancer, choreographer (ballet)
Messerer, Asaf	1903–	Viln	Dancer, teacher, choreographer (ballet)
Mitchell, Arthur	1934–	New York	Dancer, choreographer, director. Founder of Dance Theater of Harlem, 1971 (ballet/modern dance)
Moiseyev, Igor Alexandrovich	1906–	Kiev	Dancer, choreographer, ballet director. Founded the State Ensemble of Classical Ballet, 1967
Mordkin, Mikhail	1880–1944	Moscow	Dancer, teacher (ballet)
Morris, Mark	1956–	Seattle	Dancer, choreographer. Founded Mark Morris Dance Group, 1980 (modern dance)
Murphy, Graeme	1951–	Melbourne	Dancer, choreographer, ballet director (ballet/contemporary dance)
Nijinska, Bronislava	1891–1972	Minsk	Dancer, choreographer (ballet)
Nijinsky, Vaslav	1890–1950	Kiev	Dancer, choreographer (ballet/modern ballet)
North, Robert	1945–	Charlestown, S Carolina	Dancer, choreographer (contemporary dance)
Noverre, Jean-Georges	1727–1810	Paris	Dancer, choreographer, ballet master
Nureyev, Rudolf (Hametovich)	1938–1993	Irkutsk, Siberia	Dancer (ballet). Director at Paris Opera from 1983

Dance personalities (continued)

Name	*Dates*	*Place of birth*	*Occupation*
Panov, Valeri	1938–	Vitebsk	Dancer (ballet)
Pavlova, Anna	1881–1931	St Petersburg	Ballerina
Paxton, Steve	1939–	Tucson, Arizona	Dancer, choreographer (experimental dance)
Petipa, Marius	1818–1910	Marseilles	Dancer, choreographer, ballet master. Created *The Sleeping Beauty* and *Swan Lake*
Petit, Roland	1924–	Paris	Choreographer and dancer. Founded Ballets de Paris de Roland Petit, 1948, and Ballet de Marseille, 1972
Petronio, Stephen	1956–	New Jersey	Dancer, choreographer (experimental dance)
Plisetskaya, Maya (Mikhaylovna)	1925–	Moscow	Ballerina
Praagh, Peggy van	1910–90	London	Dancer, teacher, ballet director
Rainer, Yvonne	1934–	San Francisco	Dancer, choreographer (experimental dance)
Rambert, Dame Marie (Cyvia Rambam)	1888–1982	Warsaw	Dancer, teacher. Founded Ballet Rambert, 1935 (ballet/modern dance)
Reitz, Dana	1948–	New York	Dancer, choreographer (ballet)
Robbins, Jerome	1918–	New York City	Dancer, choreographer, director (musical)
Saint-Leon, (Charles Victor) Arthur	1821–70	Paris	Choreographer (ballet)
Sallé, Marie	1707–56	Paris	Ballerina
Schaufuss, Peter	1949–	Copenhagen	Dancer (ballet)
Seymour, Lynn	1939–	Wainright, Canada	Ballerina
Shearer, Moira (Moira King)	1926–	Dunfermline	Ballerina
Sibley, Dame Antoinette	1939–	Bromley	Ballerina
Sokolow, Anna	1912–	Hartford, Connecticut	Dancer, choreographer, teacher (modern dance)
Spoerli, Heinz	1941–	Basel	Dancer, choreographer, ballet director
Takei, Kei	1939–	Tokyo	Post-modern dancer and choreographer
Taylor, Paul (Belville)	1930–	Pittsburgh	Choreographer (modern dance)
Tetley, Glen	1926–	Cleveland, Ohio	Dancer, choreographer (contemporary ballet)
Tharp, Twyla	1941–	Portland, Indiana	Dancer, choreographer (modern dance)
Tudor, Anthony (William Cook)	1908–87	London	Choreographer (ballet)
Ulanova, Galina (Sergeyevna)	1910–	St Petersburgh	Ballerina
Valois, Dame Ninette (Edris Stannus) de	1898–	Co. Wicklow, Ireland	Ballerina. Founder of Sadler's Wells Ballet, 1931
Villella, Edward	1936–	New York	Dancer (ballet)
Wagoner, Dan	1932–	Springfield, W Virginia	Dancer, choreographer (modern dance)
Wigman, Mary (Marie Wiegmann)	1886–1973	Hanover	Dancer, choreographer, teacher (modern dance)
Zakharov, Rostislav	1907–84	Astrakhan	Dancer, choreographer, teacher, ballet director

Ballets

Ballet	*Composer*	*Choreographer*	*First performed*
Anastasia	Tchaikovsky	Macmillan	1971
Apollon Musagète	Stravinsky	Bolm	1928
Appalachian Spring	Copland	Graham	1944
L'Après-midi D'un Faune	Debussy	Nijinsky	1912
Bayadère, La	Minkus	Petipa	1877
Biches, Les	Poulenc	Nijinska	1924
Billy the Kid	Copland	Loring	1938
Bolero	Ravel	Nijinska	1928
Boutique Fantastique, La	Rossini	Massine	1919
Burrow, The	Martin	Macmillan	1958
Cain and Abel	Panufnik	Macmillan	1968
Carmen	Bizet	Petit	1949
Chant du Rossignol, Le	Stravinsky	Massine	1920
Cinderella	Prokofiev	Zakharov	1945
Concerto Barocco	Bach	Balanchine	1941
Coppélia	Delibes	Saint-Leon	1870
Don Quixote	Minkus	Petipa	1869
Elite Syncopations	Joplin	Macmillan	1974
Enigma Variations	Elgar	Ashton	1968
Fille Mal Gardée, La	Various (traditional French songs)	Dauberval	1789
Firebird, The	Stravinsky	Fokine	1910
Four Seasons, The	Verdi	Macmillan	1975
Giselle	Adam	Coralli/Perrot	1841

Ballet	Composer	Choreographer	First performed
Gods Go A-Begging, The	Handel	Balanchine	1928
Hamlet	Tchaikovsky	Helpmann	1942
Harlequinade	Drigo	Balanchine	1965
Hermanas, Las	Martin	Macmillan	1963
Illuminations	Britten	Ashton	1950
Invitation, The	Seiber	Macmillan	1960
Isadora	Rodney Bennett	Macmillan	1981
Ivan The Terrible	Prokofiev	Grigorovich	1975
Jeune Homme et La Mort, Le	Bach	Petit	1946
Knight Errant	Strauss (Richard)	Tudor	1968
Judas Tree, The	Elias	Macmillan	1992
Labyrinth	Schubert	Massine	1941
Lady and the Fool, The	Verdi	Cranko	1954
Lady of the Camelias	Chopin	Neumeier	1978
Lament of the Waves	Masson	Ashton	1970
Legend of Joseph	Strauss (Richard)	Fokine	1914
Luna, La	Bach	Béjart	1991
Malade Imaginaire, Le	Rota	Béjart	1976
Manon	Massenet	Macmillan	1974
Masques, Les	Poulenc	Ashton	1933
Mathilde	Wagner	Béjart	1965
Mayerling	Liszt	Macmillan	1978
Midsummer Night's Dream	Mendelssohn	Balanchine	1962
Month in the Country, A	Chopin	Ashton	1976
Night Journey	Schumann	Graham	1947
Night Shadow	Rieti	Balanchine	1946
Nocturne	Delius	Ashton	1936
Nutcracker, The	Tchaikovsky	Ivanov	1892
Ondine	Henze	Ashton	1958
Onegin	Tchaikovsky	Cranko	1965
Orpheus	Stravinsky	Balanchine	1948
Papillons, Les	Schumann	Fokine	1913
Parade	Satie	Massine	1917
Patineurs, Les	Meyerbeer	Ashton	1937
Petrushka	Stravinsky	Fokine	1911
Pineapple Poll	Sullivan	Cranko	1951
Present Histories	Schubert	Tuckett	1991
Prince Igor	Borodin	Ivanov	1890
Prince of the Pagodas, The	Britten	Cranko	1957
Prodigal Son, The	Prokofiev	Balanchine	1929
Rake's Progress, The	Gordon	De Valois	1935
Rendez-Vous, Les	Auber	Ashton	1933
Rhapsody	Rachman -inov	Ashton	1980
Rite of Spring, The	Stravinsky	Nijinsky	1913
Rituals	Bartok	Macmillan	1975
Romeo and Juliet	Prokofiev	Psota	1938
Rooms	Hopkins	Sokolow	1955
Russian Soldier, The	Prokofiev	Fokine	1942
Saisons, Les	Glazunov	Petipa	1900
Scènes de Ballet	Stravinsky	Dolin	1944
Scotch Symphony	Mendelssohn	Balanchine	1952
Serenade	Tchaikovsky	Balanchine	1934
Seven Deadly Sins	Weill	Balanchine	1933
Sheherezade	Rimsky-Korsakov	Fokine	1910
Sleeping Beauty, The	Tchaikovsky	Petipa	1890
Song of the Earth	Mahler	Macmillan	1965
Spectre de la Rose, Le	Weber	Fokine	1911
Stoics Quartet	Mendelssohn	Burrows	1991
Summerspace	Feldman	Cunningham	1958
Swan Lake	Tchaikovsky	Reisinger	1877
Sylphides, Les	Chopin	Fokine	1907
Symphonic Variations	Franck	Ashton	1946
Symphonie Fantastique	Berlioz	Massine	1936
Symphony in C	Bizet	Balanchine	1991
Tales of Hoffmann	Offenbach	Darrell	1972
Taming of the Shrew	Scarlatti-Stolze	Cranko	1969
Three-Cornered Hat, The	De Falla	Massine	1919
Vainqueurs, Les	Wagner	Béjart	1969
Valse, La	Ravel	Nijinska	1929
Variations	Stravinsky	Balanchine	1966
Voluntaries	Poulenc	Tetley	1973
Walk to the Paradise Garden, The	Delius	Ashton	1972

Dance companies

Name	Date founded	Location
Alvin Ailey Dance Company	1958	New York
American Ballet Theater	1940	New York
Australian Ballet, The	1962	Melbourne
Australian Dance Theatre	1965	Adelaide
Ballet des Champs-Elysées	1944	Paris
Ballet Jooss	1933	Cambridge, UK
Ballets de Paris	1948	France
Ballet Rambert	1926	London
Ballet Russe de Monte Carlo	1938	Monte Carlo
Ballets Russes de Sergei Diaghilev (now known as Kirov Ballet)	1909–29	St Petersburg
Ballets Suedois	1920	France

Dance companies (continued)

Name	*Date founded*	*Location*
Ballet Théâtre Contemporain	1968	Amiens
Ballet du Xième Siecle (formerly Ballet Béjart, 1953)	1960	Brussels moved to Lausanne, 1988)
Ballet West	1968	Salt Lake City, Utah
Birmingham Royal Ballet (formerly the Sadler's Wells Royal Ballet)	1946	Birmingham
Bolshoi Ballet	1776	Moscow
Borovansky Ballet	1942	Melbourne
Boston Ballet	1964	Boston
Dance Theater of Harlem	1971	New York
English National Ballet (originally London Festival Ballet)	1950	London
Feld Ballet NY	1974	New York
Grands Ballets Canadiens, Les	1956	Montreal
Houston Ballet	1968	Houston
Joffrey Ballet	1954	New York
Jose Limon Dance Company	1946	New York
Kirov Ballet	1935	St Petersburg
Lar Lubovitch Dance Company	1968	New York
London City Ballet	1978	London
London Contemporary Dance Theatre	1967	London
Maly Ballet	1915	St Petersburg
Martha Graham Dance Company	1927	New York
Merce Cunningham Dance Company	1952	New York
Miami City Ballet	1986	Miami
National Ballet	1962	Washington
National Ballet of Canada	1951	Toronto
National Ballet of Cuba	1948	Havana
National Ballet of Mexico	1949	Mexico City
Netherlands Dance Theatre	1959	The Hague
New York City Ballet	1948	US
Nikolais Dance Theatre	1951	New York
Northern Ballet	1969	Manchester
Pennsylvania Ballet	1963	Philadelphia
Pilobolus Dance Theatre	1971	Vermont
Pittsburgh Ballet Theater	1970	Pittsburgh
Royal Ballet	1931	Covent Garden, London
Royal Danish Ballet	16th-c	Copenhagen
Royal New Zealand Ballet Company (as from 1984)	1961	Wellington
Royal Swedish Ballet	17th-c	Stockholm
Royal Winnipeg Ballet	1938	Canada
San Francisco Ballet	1933	US
School of American Ballet (now the American Ballet)	1933	New York
Scottish Ballet	1956	Glasgow
Stanislavsky Ballet	1929	Moscow
Stuttgart Ballet	17th-c	Germany
Washington Ballet	1962	Washington
Western Theatre Ballet	1957	Bristol

DESIGN

Personalities

Name	*Dates*	*Nationality*	*Field of work*
Aalto, Alvar	1898–1976	Finnish	Furniture, particularly bentwood designs
Ashbee, Charles Robert	1863–1942	British	Arts and Crafts designer, particularly jewellery, also wallpaper, pottery and carpets. Founded the Guild of Handicraft, 1888
Baillie Scott, Mackay Hugh	1865–1945	British	Stained glass, ironwork, mosaics, furniture and wallpaper
Barnsley, Sidney	1865–1926	British	Furniture
Behrens, Peter	1868–1940	Austrian	Furniture, glass, cutlery, fabrics. Designer for AEG
Bell, Vanessa	1879–1961	British	Murals and interiors
Berlage, Hendrik Petrus	1856–1934	Dutch	Interior design, furniture, ironwork
Bindesboll, Thorvald	1846–1908	Danish	Ceramics
Brandt, Edgar	1880–1960	French	Metalwork
Brandt, Marianne	1893–	German	Metalwork and lighting. Designed the Kandem bedside table light
Brangwyn, Frank	1867–1956	British	Graphics
Breuer, Marcel	1902–81	Hungarian	Furniture
Bugatti, Carlo	1855–1940	Italian	Furniture
Burges, William	1827–81	British	Furniture (Yatman cabinet, Great Bookcase) and interior design
Burne-Jones, Sir Edward	1833–98	British	Stained glass and tapestries
Charpentier, Alexandre	1856–1909	French	Posters, furniture, metalwork, ceramics, interiors

Name	*Dates*	*Nationality*	*Field of work*
Chermayeff, Serge	1900–	Russian	Furniture, carpets, decorative work
Cliff, Clarice	1899–1972	British	Ceramics
Cooper, John Paul	1869–1933	British	Silversmith and jeweller
Crane, Walter	1845–1915	British	Illustrator and book designer
Czeschka, Carl Otto	1878–1960	Austrian	Jewellery, embroidery, stained glass
Daum, Auguste and Antonin	1853–1909 1864–1930	French	Glasswork
Day, Lewis F	1845–1910	British	Stained glass, wallpaper, textiles, jewellery, furniture
Deck, Theodore	1823–91	French	Pottery
Decoeur, Emile	1876–1953	French	Ceramics
Delaherche, Auguste	1857–1940	French	Ceramics
Doat, Taxile	1851–1938	French	Ceramics
Dorn, Marion	1900–64	American	Textiles
Dresser, Christopher	1834–1904	British	Silver plate, ceramics, glass, furniture, textiles
Dufrene, Maurice	1876–1955	French	Interior design
Dufy, Raoul	1877–1953	French	Textiles
Dunand, Jean	1877–1942	Swiss	Furniture, metalwork, lacquerwork
Eames, Charles	1907–78	American	Furniture
Eastlake, Charles	1836–1906	British	Furniture
Elmslie, George Grant	1871–1952	Scottish	Furniture, metalwork, stained glass, embroidery
Erp, Dirk van	1860–1933	American	Metalworker
Erté (Romain de Tirtoff)	1892–	Russian	Graphics
Fabergé, Carl	1846–1920	Russian	Jewellery
Farge, John La	1835–1910	American	Stained glass
Feure, Georges De	1869–1928	French	Interiors, furniture, porcelain, glass
Finch, Alfred William	1854–1930	Belgian	Ceramics
Fisher, Alexander	1864–1936	British	Enamelling
Follot, Paul	1877–1941	French	Jewellery, textiles, interiors, furniture, ceramics. Designed the 'Pomone' dinner service for Wedgwood
Frankl, Paul	1886–1958	Austrian	Furniture
Fry, Roger	1866–1934	British	Founder of the Omega workshop, producing furniture, textiles, stained glass and pottery
Gaillard, Eugene	1862–1933	French	Textiles, furniture, interiors
Gallé, Emile	1846–1904	French	Glass and furniture
Gate, Simon	1883–1943	Swedish	Glass
Gaudi, Antonio	1859–1926	Spanish	Metalwork and furniture
Gill, Eric	1882–1903	British	Sculpture and typography
Gimson, Ernest	1864–1919	British	Furniture
Gomperz, Lucie Marie	1902–	Austrian	Pottery
Grant, Duncan	1885–1978	British	Murals
Grasset, Eugène	1841–1917	Swiss	Textiles, wallpapers, stained glass, ceramics, jewellery
Gray, Eileen	1879–1976	British	Lacqueur work
Greene, Charles Sumner	1868–1957	American	Furniture
Gropius, Walter	1883–1969	German	Furniture. Director of Bauhaus
Grueby, William H	1867–1925	American	Pottery
Guimard, Hector	1867–1942	French	Ironwork, decorative work. Designed the Paris metro entrance signs
Gulberg, Elsa	1886–na	Swedish	Textiles
Hald, Edward	1883–na	Swedish	Glass
Hansen, Frieda	1855–1931	Norwegian	Textiles
Heal, Ambrose	1872–1959	British	Furniture
Hoffmann, Josef	1870–1956	Czech	Furniture (Kubus chair), metalwork, textiles, jewellery. Founder of the Wiener Werkstatte, 1903
Holiday, Henry	1839–1927	British	Stained glass
Horta, Victor	1861–1947	Belgian	Interiors
Jensen, Georg	1866–1935	Danish	Silver and jewellery
Joel, Betty	1896–na	British	Furniture and textiles
Knox, Archibald	1864–1933	British	Silver
Koehler, Florence	1861–1944	American	Jewellery
Krog, Arnold	1856–1931	Danish	Ceramics
Lalique, Réné	1860–1945	French	Goldsmith. Jewellery and glass
Leach, Bernard	1887–1979	British	Ceramics
Lethaby, William	1857–1931	British	Furniture
Livemont, Privat	1861–1936	Belgian	Graphics

Personalities (continued)

Name	*Dates*	*Nationality*	*Field of work*
Lurcat, Jean	1892–1966	French	Ceramics and tapestry
Mackintosh, Charles Rennie	1868–1928	Scottish	Interiors, furniture, cutlery, stained glass, jewellery
Mackmurdo, Arthur	1851–1942	British	Metalwork, furniture, wallpaper, embroidery. Founder of the Century Guild, 1884
Mathews, Arthur and Lucia	1860–1945 1870–1955	American	Murals. Founded the Furniture Shop and Philopolis magazine
Morgan, William de	1839–1917	British	Ceramics
Morris, William	1834–-96	British	Wallpaper, textiles, carpets, tapestry, typography. Leader of the Arts and Crafts Movement
Moser, Koloman	1868–1918	Austrian	Graphics
Mucha, Alphonse	1860–1939	Czech	Art and poster design
Munthe, Gerhard	1849–1929	Norwegian	Furniture
Muthesius, Hermann	1861–1927	German	Interiors and furniture. Founder of the Deutscher Werkbund, 1907
Nash, Paul	1889–1946	British	Textiles, upholstery, posters
Nilsson, Wiven	1870–1942	Swedish	Silver
Nordstrom, Patrick	1870–1929	Swedish	Pottery
Obseiger, Robert	1884–1940	Austrian	Pottery
Olbrich, Josef Maria	1867–1908	Austrian	Cofounder of the Vienna Secession
Pabst, Daniel	1826–1910	American	Furniture and cabinet making
Parrish, Maxfield	1870–1966	American	Graphics and poster design
Peche, Dagobert	1887–1923	Austrian	Art, metalwork
Pick, Frank	1878–1941	British	Poster design and typography. Responsible for design for the London Underground
Poiret, Paul	1879–1944	French	Interior design, costume design
Ponti, Gio	1891–1979	Italian	Furniture
Prutscher, Otto	1880–1949	Austrian	Furniture and jewellery
Puiforcat, Jean	1897–1945	French	Silversmith
Quarti, Eugenio	1867–1931	Italian	Furniture
Redon, Odilon	1840–1916	French	Lithography, etching
Riegel, Ernst	1871–1946	German	Goldsmith and silversmith
Riemerschmied, Richard	1868–1957	German	Interiors, furniture, porcelain, glass, cutlery. Founder member of Deutscher Werkbund
Rietveld, Gerritt Thomas	1888–1964	Dutch	Furniture
Robineau, Adelaide	1865–1929	American	Ceramics. Edited the *Keramic Studio*
Rohe, Ludwig Mies van der	1886–1969	German	Furniture. Last head of Bauhaus
Rohlfs, Charles	1853–1936	American	Furniture
Rousseau, Clement	1872–na	French	Furniture
Ruskin, John	1819–1900	British	Social critic and inspiration for the Arts and Crafts Movement
Russell, Gordon	1892–1980	British	Furniture
Ryggen, Hannah	1894–1970	Norwegian	Textiles
Serrurier-Bovy, Gustave	1858–1910	Belgian	Ironwork, furniture, wallpaper, stained glass
Staite-Murray, William	1861–1910	British	Ceramics
Stam, Mart	1899–na	Dutch	Designed the first cantilever chair
Stickley, Gustav	1857–1942	American	Furniture. Founded *The Craftsman* magazine, 1901
Taylor, William Howson	1876–1935	British	Ceramics. Founded the Ruskin Pottery, 1898
Tiffany, Louis Comfort	1848–1933	American	Jewellery, stained glass, art glass, interiors
Voysey, Charles Annesley	1857–1941	British	Wallpaper and textile pattern design, furniture, tableware, lighting
Wagenfeld, Wilhelm	1900–	German	Goldsmith. Metalwork, glass, porcelain
Webb, Philip	1831–1915	British	Furniture
Wilson, Henry	1864–1934	British	Silversmith
Wimmer, Joseph Eduard	1882–1961	Austrian	Metalwork. Codirector of the Wiener Werkstatte
Wolfe, Elsie de	1865–1950	American	Interior design
Wolfers, Philippe	1858–1929	Belgian	Jewellery
Zen, Carlo	1851–1918	Italian	Cabinet maker
Zen, Pietro	1879–1950	Italian	Furniture

na = not available

FASHION

Fashion designers

Name	Dates	Place of birth
Alaia, Azzedine	na	Busto Arsizio
Amies, Sir (Edwin) Hardy	1909–	London
Armani, Giorgio	1935–	Piacenza
Ashley, Laura	1925–85	Merthyr Tydfil
Azagury, Jacques	1958–	Casablanca
Balenciaga, Cristobal	1895–1972	Guetaria, Spain
Balmain, Pierre (Alexandre Claudius)	1914–82	St Jean de Maurienne
Banks, Jeff	1943–	Ebbw Vale, Wales
Beene, Geoffrey	1927–	Haynesville, Louisiana
Beretta, Anne-Marie	1937–	Beziers, France
Blass, Bill	1922–	Fort Wayne, Indiana
Bohan, Marc (Roger Maurice Louis)	1926–	Paris
Cacharel, Jean (Louis Henri Bousquet)	1932–	Nîmes
Capucci, Roberto	1929–	Rome
Cardin, Pierre	1922–	Venice
Cerruti, Nino (Antonio)	1930–	Biella, Italy
Chanel, Gabrielle (Coco)	1883–1971	Saumur
Conran, Jasper	1959–	London
Courrèges, André	1923–	Pau, France
De la Renta, Oscar	1932–	Santo Domingo
Desses, Jean (Jean Dimitrie Verginie)	1904–70	Alexandria
Dior, Christian	1905–57	Granville, Normandy
Erté (Romain de Tirtoff)	1892–	St Petersburg
Fiorucci, Elio	1935–	Milan
Fortuny, Mariano (Mariano Fortuny y Madrazo)	1871–1949	Granada
Galliano, John (Charles)	1960–	Gibraltar
Gaultier, Jean-Paul	1952–	Paris
Givenchy, Hubert James Marcel Taffin de	1927–	Beauvais
Halston (Roy Halston Frowick)	1932–	Des Moines, Iowa
Hamnett, Katherine	1952–	Gravesend, Kent
Hartnell, Sir Normann	1901–78	Honiton, Devon
Hechter, Daniel	1938–	Paris
Herrera, Caroline	1939–	Venezuela
Jackson, Betty	1940–	Backup, Lancashire
Karan, Donna	1948–	Forest Hills, New York
Kenzo, Takada	1940–	Kyoto
Klein, Anne Hannah (Hannah Golofski)	1921–74	New York
Klein, Calvin (Richard)	1942–	New York
Lacroix, Christian	1951–	Arles
Lagerfeld, Karl	1939–	Hamburg
Lanvin, Jeanne	1867–1946	Brittany
Lapidus, Ted	1929–	Paris
Laroche, Guy	1923–89	La Rochelle, nr Bordeaux
Lauren, Ralph (Ralph Lifschitz)	1939–	New York City
Lelong, Lucien	1889–1958	Paris
Mainbocher (Main Rousseau Bocher)	1891–1976	Chicago
Maxwell, Vera (Vera Huppe)	1901–	New York
Michiko, Koshino	1950–	Osaka
Missoni, Tai Otavio	1921–	Yugoslavia
Miyake, Issy	1935–	Hiroshima
Molyneux, Edward Henry	1891–1974	London
Montana, Claude	1949–	Paris
Moschino, Franco	1950–	Italy
Mugler, Thierry	1948–	Strasbourg
Muir, Jean (Elizabeth)	1933–	London
Oldfield, Bruce	1950–	London
Ozbek, Rifat	1955–	Istanbul
Patou, Jean	1880–1936	Normandy
Poiret, Paul	1879–1944	Paris
Pucci, Emilio , Marchese di Barsento	1914–	Naples
Quant, Mary	1934–	London
Rabanne, Paco (Francisco de Rabaneda-Cuervo)	1934–	San Sebastian
Reger, Janet	1935–	London
Rhodes, Zandra	1940–	Chatham, Kent
Ricci, Nina (Maria Nielli)	1883–1970	Turin
Rochas, Marcel	1902–55	Paris
Saint-Laurent, Yves (Henri Donat Mathieu)	1936–	Oran, Algeria
Scherrer, Jean-Louis	1936–	Paris
Schiaparelli, Elsa	1890–1973	Rome
Simonetta (Duchesa Simonetta Colonna di Cesaro)	1922–	Rome
Stavropoulos, George	1920–	Tripolis, Greece
Stiebel, Victor	1907–76	Durban
Strauss, Levi	na	Bavaria
Tarlazzi, Angelo	1945–	Ascoli Piceno, Italy
Ungaro, Emmanuel (Maffeolti)	1933–	Aix-en-Provence
Valentino (Valentino Garavani)	1933–	Voghera, Italy
Versace, Gianni	1946–	Calabria
Von Furstenburg, Diane (Diane Michelle Halfin)	1946–	Brussels
Westwood, Vivienne	1941–	Tintwhistle
Worth, Charles Frederick	1825–95	Bourn, Lincolnshire
Yamamoto, Yohji	1943–	Tokyo

na = not available

Clothes care

Do not iron

Can be ironed with *cool* iron (up to 110°C)

Can be ironed with *warm* iron (up to 150°C)

Can be ironed with *hot* iron (up to 200°C)

Hand wash only

Can be washed in a washing machine. The number shows the most effective washing temperature (in °C)

Reduced (medium) washing conditions

Much reduced (minimum) washing conditions (for wool products)

Do not wash

Can be tumble dried (one dot within the circle means a low temperature setting; two dots for higher temperatures)

Do not tumble dry

Do not dry clean

Dry cleanable (letter indicates which solvents can be used)
A: all solvents

Dry cleanable
F: white spirit and solvent 11 can be used

Dry cleanable
P: perchloroethylene (tetrachloroethylene), white spirt, solvent 113 and solvent 11 can be used

Dry cleanable, if special care taken

Chlorine bleach may be used with care

Do not use chlorine bleach

International clothing sizes

Size equivalents are approximate, and may display some variation between manufacturers.

Women's suits/dresses

UK	*US*	*UK/Continent*
8	6	36
10	8	38
12	10	40
14	12	42
16	14	44
18	16	46
20	18	48
22	20	50
24	22	52

Women's hosiery

UK/US	*UK/Continent*
8	0
$8\frac{1}{2}$	1
9	2
$9\frac{1}{2}$	3
10	4
$10\frac{1}{2}$	5

Adults' shoes

UK	*US/(ladies)*	*UK/Continent*
4	$5\frac{1}{2}$	37
$4\frac{1}{2}$	6	38
5	$6\frac{1}{2}$	38
$5\frac{1}{2}$	7	39
6	$7\frac{1}{2}$	39
$6\frac{1}{2}$	8	40
7	$8\frac{1}{2}$	41
$7\frac{1}{2}$	$8\frac{1}{2}$	42
8	$9\frac{1}{2}$	42
$8\frac{1}{2}$	$9\frac{1}{2}$	43
9	$10\frac{1}{2}$	43
$9\frac{1}{2}$	$10\frac{1}{2}$	44
10	$11\frac{1}{2}$	44
$10\frac{1}{2}$	$11\frac{1}{2}$	45
11	12	46

Children's shoes

UK/US	*UK/Continent*
0	15
1	17
2	18
3	19
4	20
5	22
6	23
7	24
8	25
$8\frac{1}{2}$	26
9	27
10	28
11	29
12	30
13	32

Men's suits and overcoats

UK/US	*Continental*
36	46
38	48
40	50
42	52
44	54
46	56

Men's shirts

UK/US	*UK/Continent*
12	30–31
$12\frac{1}{2}$	32
13	33
$13\frac{1}{2}$	34–35
14	36
$14\frac{1}{2}$	37
15	38
$15\frac{1}{2}$	39–40
16	41
$16\frac{1}{2}$	42
17	43
$17\frac{1}{2}$	44–45

Men's socks

UK/US	*UK/Continent*
$9\frac{1}{2}$	38–39
10	39–40
$10\frac{1}{2}$	40–41
11	41–42
$11\frac{1}{2}$	42–43

International pattern sizes

Young junior/teenage

Size	Bust cm	Bust in	Waist cm	Waist in	Hip cm	Hip in	Back waist length cm	Back waist length in
5/6	71	28	56	22	79	31	34.5	13½
7/8	74	29	58	23	81	32	35.5	14
9/10	78	30½	61	24	85	33½	37	14½
11/12	81	32	64	25	89	35	38	15
13/14	85	33½	66	26	93	36½	39	15⅜
15/16	89	35	69	27	97	38	40	15¾

Misses

Size	Bust cm	Bust in	Waist cm	Waist in	Hip cm	Hip in	Back waist length cm	Back waist length in
6	78	30½	58	23	83	32½	39.5	15½
8	80	31½	61	24	85	33½	40	15¾
10	83	32½	64	25	88	34½	40.5	16
12	87	34	67	26½	92	36	41.5	16¼
14	92	36	71	28	97	38	42	16½
16	97	38	76	30	102	40	42.5	16¾
18	102	40	81	32	107	42	43	17
20	107	42	87	34	112	44	44	17¼

Half-size

Size	Bust cm	Bust in	Waist cm	Waist in	Hip cm	Hip in	Back waist length cm	Back waist length in
10½	84	33	69	27	89	35	38	15
12½	89	35	74	29	94	37	39	15¼
14½	94	37	79	31	99	39	39.5	15½
16½	99	39	84	33	104	41	40	15¾
18½	104	41	89	35	109	43	40.5	15⅞
20½	109	43	96	37½	116	45½	40.5	16
22½	114	45	102	40	122	48	41	16⅛
24½	119	47	108	42½	128	50½	41.5	16¼

Women's

Size	Bust cm	Bust in	Waist cm	Waist in	Hip cm	Hip in	Back waist length cm	Back waist length in
38	107	42	89	35	112	44	44	17¼
40	112	44	94	37	117	46	44	17⅜
42	117	46	99	39	122	48	44.5	17½
44	122	48	105	41½	127	50	45	17⅝
46	127	50	112	44	132	52	45	17¾
48	132	52	118	46½	137	54	45.5	17⅞
50	137	54	124	49	142	56	46	18

ARCHITECTURE

The orders of architecture

Composite — Corinthian — (Greek) Doric — Ionic — Tuscan

Architects

Name	*Dates*	*Place of birth*	*Selected works*
Aalto, Alvar	1898–1976	Kuortane, Finland	Designed public and industrial buildings, and some furniture
Abercrombie, Sir (Leslie) Patrick	1879–1957	Ashton-upon-Mersey	Pioneer of town planning. His major work was the replanning of London – County of London Plan (1943) and Greater London Plan (1944)
Adam, Robert	1728–92	Kircaldy, Fife	He was architect of the King's works in 1761–9. Examples of his work are Home House in London's Portland Square, Landsdown House, Derby House, and Register House in Edinburgh
Alberti, Leon Battista	1404–72	Genoa	One of the most brilliant figures of the Renaissance who worked in Florence from 1428
Alessi, Galeazzo	1512–72	Perugia	Gained recognition in Europe for his designs for churches and palaces in Genoa
Ammanti, Bartolommeo	1511–92	Settignano	Designed the Ducal Palace at Lucca and part of the Pitti palace and the Ponte Sta Trinita in Florence
Archer, Thomas	1668–1743	Tanworth	Baroque architect responsible for the churches of St John's, Westminster (1714) and St Paul's, Deptford (1712). He also designed part of Chatsworth House
Arnolfo di Cambio	1232–1302	Colle di Valdelsa, Tuscany	Major work is the design of Florence Cathedral
Asplund, Erik Gunnar	1885–1940	Stockholm	Major works are concentrated in Stockholm: the Stockholm City Library (1924–7), the Woodland Chapel, Skandia Cinema. He was responsible for most of the exhibits in the Stockholm Exhibition of 1930
Baker, Sir Herbert	1862–1946	Kent	Designed Groote Schur, near Cape Town, the Union Government buildings in Pretoria, and worked with Edward Lutyens on the design of New Delhi, India. In Britain he designed the new Bank of England and South Africa House, and Rhodes House in Oxford
Barry, Charles	1795–1860	London	Palace of Westminster (1840)
Basevi, George	1794–1845	London	In classic revivalist style he designed the Fitzwilliam Museum, Cambridge, laid out part of Belgravia and designed a number of country houses and Gothic churches
Behrens, Peter	1868–1940	Hamburg	Designed the AEG turbine assembly works in glass and steel. Also designed workers houses in Stuttgart and Vienna, and the German embassy in St Petersburg
Berlage, Hendrick Petrus	1856–1934	Amsterdam	Designed the Amsterdam Bourse (1903), Holland House, London (1914) and the Gemeente Museum in the Hague (1934)
Blacket, Edmund Thomas	1817–83	Southwark	Government architect for New South Wales in 1849, but returned to private practice in 1854 and designed the New South Wales University. He adopted Victorian Gothic style for his work on ecclesiastical buildings, including Sydney and Perth cathedrals, but classical forms for his commercial projects , such as banks and hotels
Borromini, Francesco	1599–1667	Bissone, Lake Lugano	San Carlo alle Quattro Fontane (1637–41)
Boullée, Etienne-Louis	1728–99	Paris	He became architect to the King of Prussia in 1762. His pre-Revolution Neo-Classical work includes the Hotel de Brunoy, Paris (1772)
Boyd, Robin Penleigh	1919–71	Melbourne	Influential critical works shaped the future direction of Australian architecture
Bramante, Donato	c.1444–1514	nr Urbino	Renovation of the Vatican and St Peter's (1505–6)
Breuer, Marcel (Lajos)	1902–81	Pécs	Student of the Bauhaus from 1921 and took charge of the furniture workshop in 1924. His architectural works were designed with Bernard Zehfuss and Pier Luigi Nervi and include the UNESCO building in Paris

Name	Dates	Place of birth	Selected works
Brosse, Salomon de	1571–1626	Verneuil-sur-Oise	Designed the Luxembourg Palace, Paris (1615–20) and Louis XIII's hunting lodge at Versailles (1624–26)
Brunelleschi, Filippo	1377–1446	Florence	Dome of Florence Cathedral (1417–34)
Burges, William	1827–81	London	Architecture employed strong medieval style. Designed Castell Coch (1876–81) as a hunting lodge for the third marquess of Bute, Cardiff Castle (1868–81), Cork Cathedral (1862–76) and a house in Park Place (1870s)
Burton, Decimus	1800–81	London	Planned the Regent's Park colosseum and in 1825 designed the new layout of Hyde Park and the Triumphal Arch at Hyde Park Corner. Also designed the Palm House at Kew Gardens (1844–48)
Butterfield, William	1814–1900	London	Leading exponent of the Gothic revival and the architect of Keble College, Oxford, St Augustine's College, Canterbury, the chapel and quad at Rugby and St Albans, Holborn
Campen, Jacob van	1595–1657	Haarlem	Built the first classical building in Holland. Most celebrated work was the Maurithuis in The Hague (1633). Other works include the Amsterdam Theatre (1637) and Amsterdam Town Hall (1647–55)
Candela, Felix	1910–	Spain	One of the world's foremost designers of reinforced concrete hyperbolic paraboloid shell roofs. His works include the Sports Palace for the Olympic Games in Mexico City (1968)
Casson, Sir Hugh	1910–	London	Directed the architecture of the Festival of Britain (1948)
Chambers, Sir William	1726–96	Stockholm	Designed Somerset House (1776) and the pagoda in Kew Gardens
Chermayeff, Serge	1900–	Caucasus	Designed De La Warr Pavilion at Bexhill-on-Sea (1933–35)
Churriguera, Done Jose	1650–1725	Salamanca	Royal architect to Charles II and developed the Churrigueresque style. Designed Salamanca Cathedral
Coates, Wells Wintemute	1895–1958	Tokyo	Leading figure in the modern movement of architecture. Responsible for the design of the BBC studios and the EKCO laboratories as well as many other buildings in Britain and Canada
Cockerell, Charles Robert	1788–1863	London	Designed the Taylorian Institute and Ashmolean Museum at Oxford
Costa, Lucio	1902–	Toulouse	Designed the award-winning Eduardo Gunile apartments. Drew up plans for city of Brasilia
Dance, George	1695–1768	London	Newgate Prison (1770–83)
Doshi, Balkrishna Vithaldas	1927–	Poona, India	Worked as a senior designer with Le Corbusier. Works include the City Hall, Toronto (1958), the Indian Institute of Management (1962–74) in Ahmedabad, and Vidyadhar Nagar New Town, Jaipur
Dudok, Willem Marinus	1884–1974	Amsterdam	Became city architect of Hilversum in 1915. His most famous work s are the Hilversum Town Hall (1928–30) and the Bijenkorf department store in Rotterdam
Erickson, Arthur Charles	1924–	Vancouver	His work on the Simon Fraser University buildings (1963) in British Columbia brought him international recognition. He also designed the Lethbridge University (1971) in Alberta, the Museum of Anthropology, British Columbia (1971–77) and the Roy Thomson Hall, Toronto (1976–80)
Fischer von Erlach, Johann Bernard	1656–1723	Graz, Austria	Designer of churches and palaces, notably the Karlskirche in Vienna and the University Church at Salzburg
Fontana, Carlo	1638–1714	Rancate, nr Como	Worked as a papal architect in Rome where he designed many major works such as the fountain in the Piazza di San Petro. He also designed Loyola College in Spain and the Palazzo Durazzo at Genoa

Architects (continued)

Name	*Dates*	*Place of birth*	*Selected works*
Fontana, Domenico	1543–1607	Melide, nr Lugano	Papal architect in Rome, employed on the Lateran Palace, the Vatican Library and St Peter's Dome
Foster, Norman	1935–	Manchester	Works include the Willis Faber Dumas building, Ipswich (1975), Sainsbury Centre, University of East Anglia (1978), Hong Kong and Shanghai Bank, Hong Kong (1979–85)
Fowke, Albert	1823–65	Belfast	Planned the Albert Hall, London, and produced the original designs for the Victoria and Albret Museum. Also planned the Royal Scottish Museum in Edinburgh
Francesco di Giorgio	1439–1502	Siena	Chief architect of Siena Cathedral
Gabriel, Jacques Ange	1698–1782	Paris	Court architect to Louis XV he designed the Petit Trianon (1768) and also laid out the Place de la Concorde (1753)
Garnier, Tony	1869–1948	Lyon	His theoretical work, Une Cité Industrielle, made a major contribution to the development of 20th century urban architecture. His works include the Grange Blanche hospital (1911–27) and the Stadium (1913–18) in Lyon, and the Hôtel de Ville in Boulogne-Bilancourt (1931–33)
Gaudi, (I Cornet) Antonio	1852–1929	Riudoms, Catalonia	Exponent of Catalan 'modernism', also famous for the Church of the Holy Family in Barcelona
Gilbert, Cass	1859–1934	Zanesville, Ohio	Remembered as the architect of the first skyscraper, the 66 floor Woolworth Building in New York (1912). Designed many public buildings, including the US Customs House in New York City (1907), the Supreme Court building in Washington DC (1935,) and the campuses of the universities of Minnesota (Minneapolis) and Texas (Austin)
Griffin, Walter Burley	1876–1937	Maywood, Illinois	Director of design and construction of the city of Canberra. His plans for the design of the city were adopted in 1925. Designed a number of notable buildings and Castlecrag Estate in north Sydney
Gropius, Walter	1883–1969	Berlin	Founder of Bauhaus movement
Guarini, Guarino	1624–83	Modena	Designed several churches in Turin; San Lorenzo (1668–80) and Capella della SS Sindone (1668), also the Palazzo Carignano (1679), as well as palaces for Bavaria and Baden
Guimard, Hector Germain	1867–1942	Lyon	The most important art nouveau architect in Paris before the first world war. Designed the Castel Béranger apartment block (1894–98) and is famous for the Paris Metro signs of the 1900s
Hamilton, Thomas	1784–1858	Glasgow	Designs include the Burns Monument, Galloway (1820), Royal High School, Edinburgh (1823–29), Royal College of Physicians Hall (1844–45), Edinburgh
Hardwick, Philip	1792–1870	London	Designer of Euston station, Lincoln's Inn Hall and Library, Goldsmith's Hall and Limerick Cathedral
Haussmann, George Eugene, Baron	1809–91	Paris	Restructured Paris by widening streets, laying out boulevards and parks, and building bridges
Hawksmoor, Nicholas	1661–1736	East Drayton, Nottinghamshire	His work includes the London churches St Mary Woolnorth, St George's (Bloomsbury),and Christ Church (Spitalfields)
Hoffmann, Josef	1870–1956	Pirnitz, Austria	Leader of the Vienna Secession and founded the Wiener Werkstatte in 1903. His architectural achievements include the Purkersdorf Sanatorium (1903–5) and Stociet House in Brussels (1905–11). He was city architect for Vienna from 1920
Holland, Henry	1746–1806	Ledbury	Designed old Carlton House in London, the original Brighton Pavilion and Brook's Club

Name	Dates	Place of birth	Selected works
Hood, Raymond Matthewson	1881–1934	Rhode Island	The leading designer of skyscrapers in the 1930s. Designed the American Radiator building, New York (1924), the Daily News building (1929–30), the Rockerfeller Center (1930–40) and the McGraw-Hill building (1931)
Horta, Victor, Baron	1861–1947	Ghent	Regarded as the originator of Art Nouveau. In Brussels his works include the Maison Tassel (1892–3), the Maison Solray (1894–1900) and the Maison du Peuple (1895–99). He also designed the first department store there, L'Innovation (1901)
Howard, Sir Ebenezer	1850–1928	London	Founder of the Garden City movement
Jacobsen, Arne	1902–71	Copenhagen	Main public building in Copenhagen was the SAS skyscraper (1955). He also designed St Catharine's College, Oxford
Johnson, Philip Cortelyou	1906–	Cleveland, Ohio	Designed the Seagram building , New York City (1945), New York State Theater, Lincoln Center (1964), Amon Carter Museum of Western Art, Texas (1961) and the American Telephone and Telegraph Company (1978–84)
Jones, Inigo	1573–1652	London	Introduced the Palladian style to England.His designs include the Queen's House at Greenwich (1616) and the Banqueting House in Westminster (1619–22)
Kahn, Louis Isadore	1901–74	Saaremaa, Estonia	Pioneer of functionalist architecture. Designed the Richards Medical Research Building in Pennsylvania (1957–61), the City Tower Municipal Building in Philadelphia, Yale University Art Gallery (1953), Salk Institute, La Jolla, California (1959–65), the Indian Institute of Management, Ahmedabad, (with Doshi), and the Paul Mellon Center, Yale (1969–72)
Kent, William	1684–1748	Bridlington	Designed many public buildings in London, including the Royal Mews, Trafalgar Square, the Treasury buildings and the Horse Guards block in Whitehall
Larsen, Henning	1925–		His buildings include the University of Trondheim, institutes of the Freie Universität and the Danish Embassy in Riadh
Lasdun, Sir Denys	1914–	London	His most well-known buildings include the Royal College of Musicians (1958–64), the University of East Anglia (1962–8), the National Theatre, London (1965–76), European Investment Bank, Luxembourg (1975) and the Institute of Education (1970–8)
Le Corbusier (Charles Edouard Jeanneret)	1887–1965	La-Chaux-de-Fonds	First building was the Unite d'Habitation, Marseilles (1945–50). Designed the plans for the city of Chandigarh, the capital of the Punjab. First use of piloti (stilts) in his designs was the Swiss Pavilion on the campus of the Cité Universitaire, Paris
Ledoux, Claude Nicholas	1736–1806	Dormans, Champagne	Architect to Louis XVI, his major works include the Chateau at Louveciennes, the Saltworks at Arc-et-Senans (1775–80), theatre at Besançon (1771–3)
Lescot, Pierre	c.1510–78	Paris	Major work is the Louvre, Paris
Loos, Adolf	1870–1933	Brno	One of the major architects of the 'Modern Movement'. He settled in Vienna in 1896
Lutyens, Sir Edwin	1869–1944	London	His best-known projects are Castle Drogo (1910–30), the Cenotaph in Whitehall and the laying out of New Delhi, India (1912–30)
Mackintosh, Charles Rennie	1868–1928	Glasgow	Became a leader of the 'Glasgow style', a movement related to Art Nouveau. As well as interiors and furniture, his designs include the Glasgow School of Art (1896–9 and 1906–9)
Maderno, Carlo	1556–1629	Capalgo, Italy	Appointed architect to St Peter's in 1603 where he added a large facade (1606–12). Other important works are Sta Susanna (1597–1603) and the Palazzo Barberini (1628–38)

Architects (continued)

Name	*Dates*	*Place of birth*	*Selected works*
Mansard or Mansart, François	1598–1666	Paris	He brought a simplified adaptation of the Baroque style into France and made fashionable the high-pitched type of roof which bears his name
Mendelsohn, Erich	1887–1953	Olszlyn, Poland	Designed the Einstein Tower in Potsdam, and various hospitals and stores, also the Hebrew University in Jerusalem. From 1941 he worked in the United States designing synagogues and hospitals
Mies van der Rohe, Ludwig	1886–1969	Aachen	His designs include the German pavilion for the Barcelona Exhibition (1928) and the Seagram Building , New York (1956–9)
Nash, John	1752–1835	London	Designed Regent's Park and Marble Arch, recreated Buckingham Palace and laid out Trafalgar Square and St James Park
Nervi, Pier Luigi	1891–1979	Sondrio, Italy	Designed the Stadium for the Olympic games in Rome (1960) and San Francisco Cathedral (1970)
Neumann, Balthasar	1687–1753	Eger, Germany	Designed many outstanding examples of the Baroque style, notably Würzburg Palace and Schloss Bruchsal
Niemeyer, Oscar	1907–	Rio de Janeiro	Works include the Church of São Francisco, Pampulha (1942–44), the Exhibition Hall, São Paulo (1953), and in Brasilia the President's Palace, the Cathedrals and Law Courts
Oud, Jacobus Johann Pieter	1890–1963	Purmerend, Netherlands	Launched the review *de Stijl* and became a pioneer of modern architecture based on simplified forms. He became city architect to Rotterdam in 1918
Palladio, Andrea	1508–80	Vicenza	Developed the style now known as 'Palladian' based on classical Roman principles. He remodelled the basilica at Vicenza and designed many villas, palaces and churches, particularly in Venice
Pei, Ieoh Meng	1917–	Canton	Major projects include Mile High Center, Denver, the John Hancock Tower, Boston and the glass pyramid at the Louvre
Peruzzi, Baldassare Tommaso	1481–1536	Ancajano	Designed the Villa Farnesina, the Ossoli Palace and the Palazzo Massimo in Rome
Piranesi, Giovanni Battista	1720–78	Venice	Major influence on Neo-Classicism
Playfair, William Henry	1789–1857	Edinburgh	Designed most of Edinburgh's most important buildings, including the National Gallery of Scotland, the Royal Scottish Academy, and Donaldson's Hospital
Poelzig, Hans	1869–1936	Berlin	Expressionist architect who served as the city architect for Dresden between 1916 and 1920. Early projects included the Luban Chemical Works, Posen and the Water Tower and Exhibition Hall, Posen (1911–12). Later works were the remodelling of the Grosses Schauspielhaus, Berlin (1919), Salzburg Festival Theatre (1920–2), and the I G Farben Headquarters, Frankfurt (1928–31)
Pugin, Augustus	1812–52	London	Designed a large part of the decorations and sculpture for the new Houses of Parliament (1836–7) and did much to revive Gothic architecture in Britain
Rietveld, Gerrit Thomas	1888–1964	Utrecht	Works include the Schrode House, Utrecht (1924) and the Van Gogh Museum, Amsterdam (completed posthumously 1973)
Rogers, Richard	1933–	Florence	Architect of often controversial works, examples of which include the Centre Pompidou, Paris (1971–9) and Lloyds of London (1979–85)
Saarinnen, Eero	1910–61	Kirkonnumi, Finland	His designs for Expressionist buildings include the Trans-World Airline Kennedy Terminal, New York
Sangallo, Antonio Giamberti da	1485–1546	Florence	Leading architect of the High Renaissance in Rome, designing the Palazzo Palma-Bassadini, Rome (c. 1520), and the Palazzo Farnese, Rome (1534–46)

Name	Dates	Place of birth	Selected works
Scott, Sir George Gilbert	1811–78	Gawcott, Buckinghamshire	The leading practical architect of the British Gothic Revival, as seen in the Albert Memorial (1862–3), St Pancras Station and Hotel (1865) and Glasgow University (1865)
Scott, Sir Giles Gilbert	1880–1960		Designed the Anglican cathedral in Liverpool (1924), the new buildings at Clare College, Cambridge and Cambridge University Library (1931–4), the new Bodleian Library, Oxford (1936–46). He designed the new Waterloo Bridge (1939–45) and was responsible for the rebuilding of the House of Commons after the second world war
Shaw, (Richard) Norman	1831–1912	Edinburgh	Major works include the Old Swan House, Chelsea (1876), New Scotland Yard (1888), the Gaiety Theatre, Aldwych (1902) and the Picadilly Hotel (1905)
Smirke, Sir Robert	1781–1867		Significant buildings include Covent Garden Theatre (1809), the British Museum (1823–47). He also designed the General Post Office (1824–9) and the College of Physicians (1825)
Soane, Sir John	1753–1837	Goring, Oxfordshire	His designs include The Bank of England (1792–1833) and Dulwich College Art Gallery (1811–14)
Soufflot, Jacques	1709–80	Irancy	Leading exponent of Neo-Classicism, designing the Panthéon and École de Droit, Paris, the Hotel Dieu, Lyon and Rennes Cathedral
Spence, Sir Basil	1907–76	Bombay	The leading post-war architect; examples of his work include the pavilion for the Festival of Britain (1951) and the new Coventry Cathedral (1951)
Sullivan, Louis	1856–1924	Boston	His experimental, functional skeleton constructions of skyscrapers and office blocks, particularly the Gage Building and stock exchange, earned him the title of the 'Father of Modernism'
Tait, Thomas Smith	1882–1954		Prominent architect of the inter-war period, designing Adelaide House (1921–4) and the Daily Telegraph offices (1927) in London, and St Andrew's House, Edinburgh (1934)
Tange, Kenzo	1913–	Tokyo	Works include the Hiroshima Peace Centre (1949–55), the Shizoka Press and Broadcasting Centre (1966–7) and the National Gymnasium for the 1964 Olympic Games
Utzon, Jørn	1918–	Copenhagen	Designer of the Sydney Opera House, the Kuwait House of Parliament, Copenhagen's Bagvae Church and Paustian's House of Furniture
Vignola, Giacomo da	1507–73	Vignola	In Rome he designed the Villa di Papa Giulio and the Church of the Gesù
Viollet-le-Duc, Eugene	1814–79	Paris	Restored the cathedrals of Notre Dame, Amiens and Laon, and the Chateau de Pierrefonds
Vitruvius (Marco Vitruvius Pollio)	1st-c AD	Rome	Architect and engineer. He wrote the *De Architectura*, the only extant Roman treatise on this subject
Wagner, Otto	1841–1918	Vienna	Considered the founder of the 'modern movement'. His most influential works include Karlsplatz station (1898–9) and Am Steinhof Church (1905–7). His main hall of the K K Sportsparkasse (1904–6) was regarded as the first example of modern architecture in the 20th century
Waterhouse, Alfred	1830–1905	Liverpool	Built the romanesque Natural History Museum in London (1873–81) and from his great use of red brick came the name 'red-brick university'
Webb, Sir Aston	1849–1930	London	Designed the Admiralty Arch, Imperial College of Science and many other buildings in London
Wood, John (the Elder)	1705–1754	Bath	Responsible for many of the well-known streets and buildings of Bath–North and South Parades, Queen Square, the Circus and Prior Park

Architects (continued)

Name	*Dates*	*Place of birth*	*Selected works*
Wren, Sir Christopher	1632–1723	East Knoyle, Wiltshire	After the Great Fire of London he drew up plans for rebuilding the whole city , but the plans were never implemented. He designed the new St Paul's Cathedral in 1669 and then many other public buildings such as the Greenwich Observatory, the Ashmolean Library, Oxford, part of Hampton Court, The Sheldonian Theatre, Oxford, the Royal Exchange, the Temple Bar, and Greenwich Hospital
Wright, Frank Lloyd	1867–1959	Richland Center, Wisconsin	One of the leading designers of private dwellings, planned in conformity with the natural features of the land. Among his larger works is the Guggenheim Museum of Art in New York
Wyatt, James	1746–1813	Burton Constable, Staffordshire	Designed the London Pantheon (1772), but his best known work is the Gothic-Revival Fonthill Abbey (1796–1807)

PAINTING

Artists

Name	*Dates*	*Place of birth*	*Selected works*
Albani, Francesco	1578–1660	Bologna	Altarpieces in the Chapel of the Annunciation, Quirinal Palace and the choir of St Maria della Pace, frescoes in the chapel of St Diego, church of St Giacomo degli Spagnuoli, *Dance of the Amorini*
Angelico, Fra (Guido di Petro)	c.1395–1455	Vicchio, Tuscany	San Marco frescoes, Florence, *Last Judgement , Orvieto, Coronation of the Virgin, Glory, Pietas,*
Antonello da Messina	1430–79	Sicily	San Cassiano altarpiece, *Annunciation*
Bacon, Francis	1909–	Dublin	*Studio of Velazquez*
Bassano, Jacopo da	c.1510–92	Bassano	*Adoration of the Magi, Crucifixion*
Beardsley, Aubrey	1872–98	Brighton	*Isolde, Salome, Morte d'Arthur*
Bellini, Giovanni	c.1430–1516	Venice	San Giobbe altarpiece, *Madonna with Baptist and another Saint, Bacchanale, Pieta, The Doge Loredano*
Blake, William	1757–1827	London	Illustrations to the Book of Job
Bonnard, Pierre	1867–1947	Paris	*Nude in the Bath, Skating Rink, Red Bodice, La Toilette, Woman in Black Stockings*
Bosch, Hieronymus	1450–1516	Hertogenbosch	*The Garden of Delights, The Last Judgement*
Botticelli, Sandro	1445–1510	Florence	*Birth of Venus, Primavera, Nativity, Mars and Venus*
Boucher, François	1703–70	Paris	*Birth of Venus*
Boudin, Eugene	1824–98	Honfleur	*Deauville, Harbour at Trouville, Corvette Russe*
Braque, Georges	1882–1963	Argenteuil-sur-Seine	*Piano and Lute, House at L'Estaque, Still Life*
Breugel, Pieter (the Elder)	1528–69	Breda	*Massacre of the Innocents, Peasant Wedding, Hunters in the Snow, The Triumph of Death*
Bronzino, Agnolo Filippo	1503–72	Monticelli	*Cupid, Time and Folly, Portrait of Lucrezia Panciatichi*
Canaletto (Giovanni Antonio Canal)	1697–1768	Venice	*The Stonemason's Yard, Venice: Piazza San Marco and the Colonnade of the Procurate Nuove, Scene in Venice; The Piazzetta Entrance to the Grand Canal*
Caravaggio (Michelangelo Merisi)	1571–1610	Milan	*Madonna of the Rosary, Death of the Virgin, Supper at Emmaus, Deposition of Christ, The Conversion of St Paul, The Entombment, The Calling of St Matthew*
Carpaccio, Vittore	c.1460–c.1525	Venice	*Young Knight in a Landscape, Stories of St Ursula, The Presentation in the Temple*
Cézanne, Paul	1839–1906	Aix-en-Provence	*The Bathers, La Maison du Pendu, Les Grandes Baigneuses, The Blue Vase, Man Standing with Hands on Hips*
Chagall, Marc	1887–1985	Vitebsk	*Self-Portrait with Seven Fingers, The Newspaper Seller, Paris Through the Window*
Constable, John	1776–1837	East Bergholt, Suffolk	*The Haywain, Weymouth Bay, Borrowdale, White Horse, Valley Farm, Cornfield*

Name	Dates	Place of birth	Selected works
Corot, Jean-Baptiste-Camille	1796–1875	Paris	*The Bridge at Nantes, The Studio, Chartres Cathedral, Danse des Nymphes, Le Bûcheron, Orphée, Homère et les Bergers, Joueur de Flûte*
Correggio, Antonio	1489–1534	Correggio	*Adoration of the Shepherds, Madonna of St Francis, Madonna of St Sebastian, Jupiter and Io, Nativity, Jupiter and Antiope, Education of Cupid, Danae, Ecce Homo*
Courbet, Gustave	1819–77	Ornans	*The Painter's Studio, Funeral at Ornans, Girls on the Banks of the Seine, Peasants of Flazey*
Dali, Salvador	1904–89	Figueras	*Persistence of Memory, Christ of St John of the Cross*
Daumier, Honoré	1808–79	Marseilles	*La Rue Transnonain, The Washerwoman, Ecce Homo, Third-Class Carriage*
David, Jacques Louis	1748–1825	Paris	*Oath of the Horatii, The Death of Socrates, Portrait of Madame Recamier*
Degas, Edgar	1834–1917	Paris	*Absinthe Drinker, Bellelli Family, Miss Lola at the Cirque Fernando, Dancer at the Bar, Cotton-brokers Office*
Delacroix, Eugène	1798–1863	Charenton-Saint-Maurice	*Women of Algiers, Liberty Guiding the People, The Massacre at Chios*
Delaunay, Robert	1885–1941	Paris	*Eiffel Tower, Fenêtres*
Dix, Otto	1891–1969	Gera	*The Hall of Mirrors, The Artist's Parents, Pimp and Girls, Two Sacrifices of Capitalism, Saul and David, Crucifixion*
Dufy, Raoul	1877–1953	Le Havre	*Nice, Bois de Boulogne, Deauville*
Dürer, Albrecht	1471–1528	Nuremburg	*Self-Portrait, Lamentation on the Dead Christ, Melancolia*
Ernst, Max	1891–1976	Bruhl	*The Elephant Celebes, The Hat Makes the Man, Two Children are Threatened By a Nightingale, Oedipus, Une Semaine de Bonté*
Fantin-Latour, Henri	1836–1904	Grenoble	*Hommage à Delacroix, Still Life, L' Anniversaire*
Fragonard, Jean-Honoré	1732–1806	Grasse	*La Belle Serveuse, The Swing, Bacchante Endormie, La Chemise Enlevée*
Francesca, Piero della	1415–92	Borgo San Sepolcro	*Annunciation, Flagellation, Brera Madonna, Annunciation*
Gainsborough, Thomas	1727–88	Sudbury, Suffolk	*The Morning Walk, Lady Brisco, Lord and Lady Howe, Mrs Portman, Blue Boy*
Gauguin, Paul	1848–1903	Paris	*The Moon and the Earth, La Belle Angele, Whence do we come ? What are we ? Where doe we go ?, The Yellow Christ, Vision after the Sermon, Nevermore*
Gentile da Fabriano	c.1370–c.1427	Fabriano	*Adoration of the Magi*
Giotto	1267–1337	Vespignano	*Stefaneschi Triptych, The Lamentation, Death of the Knight of Celano, The Betrayal, The Lives of Christ and the Virgin*
Goya, Francisco	1746–1828	Saragossa	*The Execution of the Rebels, Stilt Walkers, Blind Guitarist*
Greco, El (Domenikos Theotkopoulos)	1541–1614	Crete	*Baptism, Pentecost, Resurrection, Assumption of the Virgin*
Grünewald, Mathias	1480–1528	Würzburg	*Crucifixion,* Isenheim altarpiece
Hals, Frans	c.1580–1666	Antwerp	*Portrait of a Married Couple, Merry Drinkers, Banquet of the Officers of St George, The Laughing Cavalier, Gypsy Girl*
Hiroshige, Ando	1797–1858	Edo, Japan	*Ukiyo-e, (Pictures of the Floating World), Fifty-three Stages on the Tōkaidō Progress, Portrait of an Artist*
Hodler, Ferdinand	1853–1918	Berne	*Night, The Elect, Eurhythmy, Day, The Battle of Nafels*
Hogarth, William	1607–1764	London	*Marriage à la Mode, Harlot's Progress, Rake's Progress*
Hokusai, Katsushika	1760–1849		*The Great Wave of Kanagawa, Hundred Views of Mount Fuji*
Holbein, Hans (the Younger)	1467–1543	Augsburg	*Portrait of Erasmus of Rotterdam, The Ambassadors*
Hopper, Edward	1882–1967	New York	*Window at Night, Early Sunday Morning, House by the Railroad, Room in Brooklyn, Nighthawks, Second Story Sunlight*
Hunt, William Henry	1790–1864	London	*Peaches and Grapes, Old Pollard, Wild Flowers*
Ingres, Jean Auguste Dominique	1780–1867	Montauban	*Napoleon on the Imperial Throne, Oedipus and the Sphinx, The Dream of Ossian, La Grande Odalisque, Apotheosis of Homer*
John, Augustus	1878–1961	Tenby	*Smiling Woman,* portraits of James Joyce, G B Shaw, Mme Suggia and Dylan Thomas
Kandinsky, Wassily	1866–1944	Moscow	*Landscape with Red Spot, Painting with a Black Arch, Improvisation V, The Abstract Watercolour, White Line, Blue Segment, Dominant Curve, Affirmed Pink*

Artists (continued)

Name	*Dates*	*Place of birth*	*Selected works*
Kirchner, Ernst	1880–1938	Aschaffenburg	*Five Women in the Street, Self-Portrait with Model, Woman at the Mirror*
Klee, Paul	1879–1940	Munchenbuchsee	*Red-Green Gardens, Around the Fish, Goldfish Wife, Twittering Machine*
Klein, Yves	1928–62	Nice	*Anthropometries*
Klimt, Gustav	1862–1918	Baumgarten, Austria	*The Kiss, Frau Fritza Riedler, Frau Adele Bloch-Bauer, Beethoven Frieze, Jurisprudence*
Klinger, Max	1857–1920	Leipzig	*The Judgement of Paris, Pietà, Christ in Olympus, Fantasy on Brahms, Eve of the Future, A Life, Of Death*
Kokoschka, Oskar	1886–1980	Pochlarn, Austria	*The Tempest, Knight Errant, Portrait of Dr Tietze and his Wife, Ambassador Maysky*
Laurencin, Marie	1885–1957	Paris	*The Assembly*
Leonardo da Vinci	1452–1519	Vinci, Florence	*Madonna Benois, Madonna Litta, Mona Lisa, The Virgin of the Rocks, Last Supper*
Lichtenstein, Roy	1923–	New York	*M-Maybe, Hopeless, New York City*
Lippi, Fra Filippo	c.1406–69	Florence	*Annunciation, Tarquinia Madonna, The Virgin and the Saints, The Vision of St Bernard, The Adoration of the Magi*
Lorenzetti, Pietro	c.1280/90 –c.1348	Siena	*Deposition, Birth of the Virgin*
Lowry, Lawrence Stephen	1887–1976	Manchester	*Coming from the Mill*
Macke, August	1887–1914	Meschede	*The Storm, Woman with a Green Jacket, The Zoo*
Magritte, René	1898–1967	Lessines	*Ceci n'est pas une Pipe, Duration Knifed, Le Plaisir, The Wind and the Song, The Human Condition*
Manet, Edouard	1832–83	Paris	*Déjeuner sur L'Herbe, Olympia, Portrait of Emile Zola, A Bar at the Folies-Bergères*
Mantegna, Andrea	1431–1506	Padua	*Agony in the Garden, Dead Christ, Martyrdom of St Sebastian,* San Zeno altarpiece
Masson, André	1896–1987	Balagny	*Fish in Sand, Dead Horses*
Matisse, Henri	1869–1954	Cateau-Cambresis	*The Yellow Curtain, Girl Swimming in the Aquarium, The Red Room, Portrait of Madame Matisse with a Green Streak, The Snail, Woman with the Hat*
Michelangelo, (Buonarotti)	1475–1564	Caprese	*Tondo Doni, Birth of Eve, Universal Judgement, Holy Family of the Tribune, The Last Judgement*
Millais, Sir John Everett	1829–96	Southampton	*Ophelia, Gambler's Wife, The Boyhood of Raleigh, Bubbles*
Millet, Jean-Francois	1814–75	Gruchy	*The Winnower, The Sower, Angelus*
Miró, Joán	1893–1983	Barcelona	*Dutch Interior, The Ploughed Field, Person Throwing a Stone at a Bird*
Modigliani, Amedeo	1884–1920	Leghorn	*Red Nude, Portrait of Madame Anna Zborowska, Reclining Nude*
Mondrian, Piet	1872–1944	Amersfoort	*Composition with Red, Yellow and Blue, Tree*
Monet, Claude	1840–1926	Giverny	*Rouen Cathedral, Waterlillies, Women in the Garden, Impression: Sunrise*
Morisot, Berthe	1841–95	Bourges	*The Artist's Sister, Madame Pontillon, Seated on the Grass, The Artist's Sister Edma and their Mother*
Moroni, Giovanni Battista	1525–78	Bondo	*The Tailor*
Munch, Edvard	1863–1944	Loten	*The Scream, Angst, Girls on the Bridge, The Dance of Life, White Night, Marat's Death, Inttell–Self-Portrait*
Nicholson, Ben	1894–1982	Denham	*White Relief*
Nolan, Sir Sidney	1917–92	Melbourne	*Boy and the Moon, Kelly, Leda and the Swan*
Noland, Kenneth	1924–	Asheville, Carolina	*Gift*
Nolde, Emil (Emil Hansen)	1867–1956	Nolde, Schleswig-Holstein	*Dance Round the Golden Calf, Red and Yellow Roses, The Life of Christ, Marsh Landscape*
O'Keefe, Georgia	1887–1986	Sun Prairie, Wisconsin	*Blue and Green Music, Black Iris, 'Near Abiquiu, New Mexico'*
Pechstein, Max	1881–1955	Zwickau	*Still Life with African Mask, Indian and Woman*
Picasso, Pablo	1881–1973	Malaga	*The Accordian Player, Les Demoiselles d'Avignon, Bottle of Vieux Marc, Guernica, Girl with a Mandolin, Two Women Running on the Beach*
Pisanello, Antonio	1395–1455	San Visilio	*Vision of St Eustache, The Madonna with Saints Anthony and George, Margherita Gonzaga, Lionello d'Este*

Name	Dates	Place of birth	Selected works
Pissarro, Camille	1830–1903	St Thomas, W Indies	*Entrance to the Village of Voisins, Boulevard Montmartre, Place du Théâtre Français, Bridge at Bruges, 'Orchard with Flowering Fruit Trees, Springtime, Pontoise', Peasant Girl with a Stick*
Pollock, Jackson	1912–56	Cody, Wyoming	*Number 1, Convergence, Number 12, Lucifer*
Poussin, Nicolas	1594–1665	Les Andelys	*Triumph of Neptune, Autumn, The Adoration of the Golden Calf*
Raphael (Raffaello Sanzio)	1483–1520	Urbino	*Conestabile Madonna, Holy Family, Sistine Madonna, Madonna of the Meadow, The Three Graces, Madonna and Child Enthroned with Saints, La Belle Jardinière, Coronation of the Virgin, Transfiguration, Madonna of Foligno, School of Athens*
Rembrandt (Harmenszoon) van Rijn	1606–69	Leiden	*Self-Portrait with Saskia, Self-Portrait, Flora, The Night Watch, The Jewish Bride, Syndics of the Cloth Drapers' Guild, Dr Tulp's Anatomy Lesson*
Renoir, Pierre Auguste	1841–1919	Limoges	*Le Moulin de la Galette, La Grenouillère, The Two Sisters, Luncheon of the Boating Party*
Roberti, Ercole de	1450–96	Ferrara	Santa Maria in Porto altarpiece, *Madonna, Pietà*
Rossetti, Dante Gabriel	1828–82	London	*Beata Beatrix, The Annunciation, The Girlhood of Mary Virgin, Ecce Ancilla Domini*
Rothko, Mark	1903–70	Dangavpils, Latvia	*Number 10, Light Red Over Black*
Rousseau, Henri (le Douanier)	1844–1910	Laval	*The Sleeping Gypsy, Carnival Evening, Myself : Portrait Landscape, Yadivigha's Dream, The Hungry Lion*
Rousseau, Théodore	1812–67	Paris	*Path through the Forest of L'Isle Adam, Effet d'Orage, Forest of Compiègne*
Rubens, Pieter Paul	1577–1640	Siegen	*Deposition, Henry IV Receiving the Portrait of Maria de' Medici, Allegory of War, Descent from the Cross, The Crucifixion of St Peter*
Sargent, John Singer	1856–1925	Florence	*Madame Gautreau, Madam X, The Wyndham Sisters, 'Carnation, Lily, Lily, Rose', Mountain Fire*
Schiele, Egon	1890–1918	Tullin	*Self-Portrait, The Self-Seer, The Cardinal and the Nun, Embrace*
Schwitters, Kurt	1887–1948	Hanover	*The Constellation, Picture with Light Centers, Merzbilden*
Seurat, Georges	1859–99	Paris	*Bathers at Asnières, Sunday Afternoon on the Island of La Grande Jatte, La Baignade, Les Poseuses, Le Cirque*
Signac, Paul	1863–1935	Paris	*The Seine at Asnières, View of the Port of Marseilles*
Signorelli, Luca	c.1441–1523	Cortona	*The Preaching of the Anti-Christ, Last Judgement*
Sisley, Alfred	1839–99	Paris	*Flood at Port Marley, The Boat During the Flood*
Spencer, Sir Stanley	1891–1959	Cookham, Berkshire	*Resurrection: Port Glasgow, Shipbuilding on the Clyde, The Resurrection*
Steer, Philip Wilson	1860–1942	Birkenhead	*Self-Portrait, The Music Room, Portrait of Mrs Hammersley*
Tanguy, Yves	1900–55	Paris	*Fear, Mama Papa is Wounded*
Tiepolo, Giovanni Battista	1696–1770	Venice	*Thetis Comforting Achilles, The Sacrifice of Isaac, Madonna of Carmelo and the Souls of Purgatory, The Banquet of Cleopatra, The Martyrdom of St Sebastian, Time Revealing Truth*
Tintoretto (Jacopi Robusti)	1518–94	Venice	*Miracles of St Mark, Discovery of the Body of St Mark, The Last Supper, The Miracle of the Loaves and Fishes, The Golden Calf, Entombment*
Titian (Tiziano Vecelli)	1490–1576	Pieve di Cadore	*Pietà, Presentation of the Virgin in the Temple, Isabella d'Este, The Gypsy Madonna, Madonna of Frari, Assumption of the Virgin*
Toulouse-Lautrec, Henri	1864–1901	Albi	*Au Moulin Rouge, Les Deux Amis, The Bar, At the Races*
Turner, Joseph Mallord William	1775–1851	London	*Calais Pier, Fall of an Avalanche in the Grisons, Norham Castle, Hannibal Crossing the Alps, Burning of the Houses of Parliament*
Utrillo, Maurice	1883–1955	Paris	*Church at Chatillon, Sacré-Coeur de Montmartre*
Van Dyck, Anthony	1599–1641	Antwerp	*Iconographica, The Deposition, Le Roi à la Chasse*
Van Eyck, Jan	1390–1441	Maastricht	*Arnolfini Wedding Portrait, Adoration of the Lamb*
Van Gogh, Vincent	1853–90	Groot Zundert	*The Night Café, Starry Night, The Potato Eaters, Sunflowers, The Bridge, The Chair and the Pipe*
Velazquez, Diego	1599–1660	Seville	*The Drinkers, Christ in the House of Martha, The Coronation of the Virgin, The Toilet of Venus*
Vermeer, Jan	1632–75	Delft	*A Girl Asleep, Young Woman Reading a Letter, The Letter, The Kitchen Maid, View of Delft, The Love Letter, The Lacemaker*

Artists (continued)

Name	*Dates*	*Place of birth*	*Selected works*
Veronese, Paulo	c.1528–88	Verona	*Feast in the House of Levi, Mars and Venus United by Love, Venice Crowned Queen of the Sea, The Marriage Feast at Cana, The Adoration of the Magi*
Vuillard, Edouard	1868–1940	Cuiseaux	*Under the Trees, Jardin de Paris, Woman Sweeping*
Warhol, Andy	1928–87	Pittsburgh, Pennsylvania	*Campbell's Soup, Marilyn Monroe, Dick Tracy, 100 Soup Cans*
Watteau, Antoine	1684–1721	Valenciennes	*L'Indifférente, Enseigne de Gersaint, Fêtes Galantes, Embarquement pour Cythère*
Whistler, James Abbott McNeill	1834–1903	Lowell, Massachusetts	*Portrait of the Artist's Mother, Old Battersea Bridge, The White Girl, Cremorne Gardens, No.2, Three Figures: Pink and Grey*
Witz, Konrad	1400–46	Rotweil	*Annunciation, Christ Walking on the Water, Miraculous Draft of Fishes*

SCULPTURE

Sculptors

Name	*Dates*	*Place of birth*	*Selected works*
Agostino di Ducchio	1418–81	Forence	Tempio Malatestiano decorations, oratory of St Bernadino, Perugia
Andre, Carl	1935–	Massachusetts	*Equivalents, Cedar Piece*
Arp, Hans (Jean)	1887–1966	Strasbourg	*Shell and Head*
Barlach, Ernst	1870–1938	Wedel	*The Avenger, Death*
Bernini, Gian Lorenzo	1598–1680	Naples	*Fontana dei Quattro Fiumi*, Rome, dome of San Carlo alle Quattro Fontane, *Appollo and Daphne, Conaro* Chapel
Brancusi, Constantin	1876–1957	Hobitza	*Bird in Space, The Kiss, Torso of a Young Man*
Brunelleschi, Filippo	1377–1446	Florence	Dome of Florence cathedral, *Sacrifice of Isaac*
Calder, Alexander	1898–1976	Philadelphia	*Joesphine Baker, Romulus and Remus, The Horse, Spring, A Universe, Hanging Mobile, Lobster Trap and Fish Tail, Constellation with Red Object*
Canova, Antonio	1757–1822	Possagno	*Cupid and Psyche, Winged Cupid, Venus and Adonis, Psyche Holding a Butterfly, Penitent Magdalen, Perseus with the Head of the Medusa*
Cellini, Benvenuto	1500–71	Florence	*Perseus with the Head of the Medusa, Nymph, Neptune and Ceres*
Donatello (Donato) di Niccolo	c.1386–1466	Florence	*David, Judith and Holofernes, Cantoria, Magdalen, Gattamelata*
Duchamp, Marcel	1887–1968	Blanville	*The Bride Stripped Bare by her Bachelors, Fountain, Bicycle Wheel*
Duchamp Villon, Ramond	1876–1918	Damville	*Horse, Baudelaire, Maggy, The Seated Woman*
Epstein, Sir Jacob	1880–1959	New York	*Rima, Genesis, Ecce Homo, Christ in Majesty, St Michael and the Devil*
Ghiberti, Lorenzo	c.1378–1455	Florence	*Sacrifice of Isaac, John the Baptist, St Matthew, The Gates of Paradise*
Giacommetti, Alberto	1901–66	Stampo	*Suspended Square, Observing Head, Torso, Cubist Composition, Three Figures Outdoors, Tall Figures, City Square, Chariot*
Giambologna, Jean de Bologne	1529–1608	Douai	*Rape of the Sabine Women, Mercury, Fountain of Neptune, Samson and a Philistine, Altar of Liberty*
Gill, Eric (Arthur Eric Rowton Gill)	1882–75	Brighton	*Stations of the Cross, Mankind, Mother and Child, Prospero and Ariel, The Creation of Adam*
Hepworth, Dame Barbara	1903–75	Wakefield	*Figure of a Woman, Large and Small Forms, Reclining Figure, Wave, Four Squares, Orpheus*
Judd, Donald	1929–	Excelsior Spring	*Eight Modular Unit V-Channel Piece*
Laurens, Henri	1885–1954	Paris	*The Farewell, Head of a Young Girl, Still Life*
Leonardo da Vinci	1452–1519	Vinci	*St John the Baptist*
Leoncillo (Leoncillo Leonardi)	1915–1968	Spoleto	*St Sebastian*

Name	Dates	Place of birth	Selected works
Lipchitz, Jaques	1891–1973	Druskininkai	*Sailor with a Guitar, Harpist, The Couple, Prayer, Prometheus Strangling the Vulture II*
Maitani, Lorenzo	c.1275–1330	Orvieto	*Creation of the Animals, Eagle of St John, Angel of St Matthew*
Marini, Marino	1901–80	Pistoia	*The Dancer, Horse and Rider, Portrait of Igor Stravinsky*
Martini, Arturo	1889–1947	Treviso	*Water Drinker, Moonlight, Thirst, Girl Swimming Under Water, Corporate Justice*
Michelangelo (Buonarroti)	1475–1564	Caprese	*Pietá, Madonna of the Steps, Victory*
Moore, Henry	1898–1986	Castleford	*Recumbent Figure, Fallen Warrior, Mother and Child, Family Group, Reclining Figure, King and Queen, Seated Figure Against Curved Wall*
Morris, Robert	1931–	Kansas City	*Untitled, In the Realm of the Carceral*
Parmiggiani, Claudio	1943–	Luzzara	*Sineddoche*
Pisano, Andrea	1270–1348	Pontedera	*The Baptism of Christ,* Bell Tower of Florence Cathedral
Pisano, Giovanni	1245–1317	Pisa	*Annunciation, Nativity, Annunciation to the Shepherds,* tomb sculpture for Margaret of Luxembourg
Rodin, Auguste	1887–1917	Paris	*L'Homme au Nez Cassé, Le Baiser, Le Penseur, Les Bourgeois de Calais, The Vanquished, The Age of Bronze*
Rossellino, Antonio	1427–79	Florence	Bust of Florentine Matteo Palmieri, bust of Giovanni Chellini, *Madonna and Child, Shrine of the Marcolino de Forli*
Schlemmer, Oska	1888–1943	Stuttgart	*Triadic Ballet, Abstrakte Rindplastik*
Segal, George	1925–	New York	*Rock'n Roll Combo, The Truck, The Laundromat, Hot Dog Stand*
Sluter, Claus	1350–1405	Haarlem	Bust of Christ, *Well of Moses,* chapel of Chartreuse de Champnol, Dijon, tomb of Philip the Bold, Duke of Burgundy
Tinguely, Jean	1925–91	Fribourg	*Machines à Peindre, Study for an End of the World, Metamécanique No., Homage to New York*

PHOTOGRAPHY

Photographers

Name	Dates	Place of birth
Adams, Ansel	1902–84	San Francisco
Arbus, Diane	1923–71	New York City
Bailey, David	1938–	London
Beaton, Sir Cecil	1904–80	London
Bourke-White, Margaret	1906–71	New York City
Brady, Matthew	1823–96	Lake George, New York
Brandt, Bill	1904–83	London
Brassaï (Gyula Halasz)	1899–1984	Brasso, Transylvania
Cameron, Julia Margaret	1815–79	Calcutta
Capa, Robert (André Friedmann)	1913–54	Budapest
Cartier-Bresson, Henri	1908–	Paris
Cunningham, Imogen	1883–1976	Portland, Oregon
Curtis, Edward Sheriff	1868–1952	Madison, Wisconsin
Daguerre, Louis Jacques Mandé	1789–1851	Cormeilles
Eisenstaedt, Alfred	1898–	Tczew, Poland (formerly Dirschau)
Evans, Frederick	1853–1943	Whitechapel, London
Evans, Walker	1903–75	St. Louis, Missouri
Fenton, Roger	1819–69	Lancashire
Firth, Francis	1822–98	Chesterfield
Godwin, Fay Simmonds	1931–	Berlin
Hardy, Bert	1913–	London
Hill, David Octavius	1802–70	Perth, Scotland
Hine, Lewis	1874–1940	Oshkosh, Wisconsin
Karsh, Yousef	1908–	Mardin (Turkey)
Kertész, André	1894–1985	Budapest
Lange, Dorothea	1895–1965	Hoboken, New Jersey
Lartigue, Jacques-Henri	1894–1986	Curbvoie, France
Martin, Paul	1864–1942	Herbenville, France
McBean, Angus Rowland	1904–	Newbridge, Monmouth
Moholy-Nagy, László	1895–1946	Bucsborsod, Hungary
Muybridge, Eadweard (Edward James Muggeridge)	1830–1904	Kingston-on-Thames
Nadar (Gaspard-Felix Tournachon)	1820–1910	Paris
Nilsson, Lennart	1922–	Strängnäs, Sweden
Parer, Damien	1912–44	Malvern, Victoria
Parkinson, Norman (Ronald William Parkinson Smith)	1913–90	London

Photographers (continued)

Name	*Dates*	*Place of birth*
Ray, Man (Emanuel Rabinovich)	1870–1976	Philadelphia
Robinson, Henry Peach	1830–1901	Ludlow
Saint Joseph, John Kenneth Sinclair	1912–	Worcestershire
Sander, August	1876–1964	Herdorf, Germany
Sheeler, Charles	1883–1965	Philadelphia
Steichen, Edward Jean	1879–1973	Luxembourg
Stieglitz, Alfred	1864–1946	Hoboken, New Jersey
Strand, Paul	1890–1976	New York City
Sutcliffe, Frank Meadow	1853–1941	Whitby, Yorkshire
Weston, Edward	1886–1958	Highland Park, Illinois
White, Minor	1908–76	Minneapolis

KNOWLEDGE

Museums and art galleries of the world

Country	*Location*	*Museum*	*Date established*
Afghanistan	Kabul	Kabul Museum	1922
Albania	Tirane	Albanian National Culture Museum	
Argentina	Buenos Aires	National History Museum	1889
Algeria	Algiers	National Museum of Algiers	1930
Armenia	Yerevan	Armenian State Historical Museum	
		Armenian State Picture Gallery	1921
Australia	Sydney	Australian Museum	1827
	Canberra	Australian National Gallery	1975
	Melbourne	Museum of Victoria	1854
Austria	Salzburg	Residence Gallery	1789
	Vienna	Kunsthistorisches Museum	1891
		Belvedere Gallery	18th-c
		Schönbrunn Palace	1569, museum in 1922
Bahamas	Nassau	Bahamia Museum	
Bahrain	Manama	Bahrain Museum	1970
Bangladesh	Dhaka	Bangladesh National Museum	1913
Barbardos	St Ann's Garrison	Barbados Museum and Historical Society	1933
Belarus	Minsk	Belarussian State Art Museum	1939
Belgium	Antwerp	Ruben's House	17th-c
		Royal Museum of Fine Art	1890
	Brussels	Erasmus House	1515
Bhutan	Paro	National Museum	1968
Bolivia	La Paz	National Museum	1846
Brazil	Rio de Janerio	National Museum	1818
Brunei	Kota Batu	Brunei Museum	1965
Bulgaria	Sofia	National Art Gallery	1948
Canada	Quebec	McCord Museum of Canadian History	1919
	Montreal	Montreal Museum of Fine Arts	1860
	Vancouver	Vancouver Art Gallery	1931
Chile	Santiago	National Historical Museum	1911
China	Beijing	Museum of Chinese History	1920
Colombia	Carrera	National Museum	1823
Costa Rica	San Jose	National Museum of Costa Rica	1887
Croatia	Zagreb	Croatian Historical Museum	1844
Cuba	Havana	National Museum	1913
Cyprus	Nicosia	The Cyprus Museum	1883
Czech Republic	Prague	National Museum	1818
		National Gallery	1796
Denmark	Copenhagen	National Museum	1807
Dominican Republic	Santo Domingo	National Fine Arts Gallery	1943
Ecuador	Quito	Civic Museum of Arts and History	1930
Egypt	Cairo	Egyptian Museum	1857
El Salvador	San Salvador	National Museum	1976
Estonia	Tallinn	Art Museum of Estonia	1919
		Estonian History Museum	1864
Ethiopia	Addis Abbaba	Museum of the Institute of Ethiopian Studies	1963
Finland	Helsinki	Museum of Applied Arts	1873
France	Beauvais	National Tapestry Gallery	1964
	Fontainebleau	The Royal Palace of Fontainebleau	12th-c
	Paris	Auguste Rodin Museum	1915
		The Louvre	1791
		Museé d'Orsay	1986
		Museum of Modern Art at the Pompidou centre	1976
		Museum of Technology	1794
		Picasso Museum	1985
	Saint-Germain-en-Laye	Museum of National Antiquities	16th-c
	Versailles	Château de Versailles	1837
Georgia	Tbilisi	Georgian State Museum	1852
Germany	Berlin	Bauhaus Archives and Museum of Design	1969
		Berlin Museum	1962
		Deutsches Historisches Museum	1987
		Haus der Wannsee-Konferenz	1992

Museums and art galleries of the world (continued)

Country	*Location*	*Museum*	*Date established*
	Frankfurt	Goethe Museum	1859
	Hamburg	Altona Museum	1863
		Hamburg Art Gallery	1869
	Mainz	Roman-Germanic Central Museum	1852
	Munich	Deutsches Museum	1925
		Bavarian National Museum	1859
Greece	Athens	National Archaeological Museum	1866
		Museum of Cycladic Art	1986
		Acropolis Museum	1865
	Heraklion (Crete)	Archaeological Museum	1904
	Olympia	Museum of Ancient Olympia	1888
Grenada	St George's	Grenada National Museum	1976
Guatemala	Guatemala City	National Museum of History	1975
Guyana	George Town	Guyana Museum	1853
Haiti	Port-au-Prince	National Museum	1983
Hong Kong	Tsimshatsui	Hong Kong Museum of History	1975
Hungary	Budapest	Hungarian National Museum	1802
Iceland	Reykjavik	National Museum	1863
India	New Delhi	National Museum of India	1949
Indonesia	Jakarta	National Museum	1778
Iran	Teheran	Iran Bastan Museum	1946
Iraq	Baghdad	Archaeological Museum of Iraq	
Ireland	Dublin	National Museum of Ireland	1731
		National Gallery of Ireland	1864
Israel	Tel Aviv	Eretz-Israel Museum	1948
	Jerusalem	Israel Museum	1965
Italy	Bologna	Archaeological Museum	1881
		Museum of the Middle Ages and Renaissance	1985
		National Art Gallery	1882
	Florence	Accademia Gallery	1784
		Museum of the History of Science	1929
		Bardini Museum	1924
		Bargello Museum	1857
		Uffizi Gallery	1581
	Milan	Brera Art Gallery	1776
		Leonardo da Vinci Museum of Science and Technology	1953
	Naples	National Archaeological Museum	18th-c
Rome	Borghese Gallery	1902	
		Vatican Museums	
		National Museum of Popular Art	1923
	Siena	Siena Museum	
	Turin	Sabauda Gallery	1832
	Venice	Accademia Gallery	1807
		Peggy Guggenheim Collection	1980
		Treasury of St Mark's	
Japan	Tokyo	National Museum	1871
Jordan	Amman	Folklore Museum	1972
		Popular Life Museum	1973
Kazakhstan	Alma Ata	Central State Museum of Kazakhstan	
Kyrgyzstan	Bishkek	State Historical Museum of Kyrgyzstan	
Korea, North	Pyongyang	Korean Central Historical Museum	
Korea, South	Seoul	National Museum of Korea	1908
Kuwait	Kuwait City	Kuwait National Museum	1957
Laos	Vientiane	National Museum	1965
Latvia	Riga	Latvian Historical Museum	1869
		State Museum of Latvian and Russian Art	
Lebanon	Beirut	National Museum of Lebanon	1920
Liechtenstein	Vaduz	Liechtenstein Museum	1954
Lithuania	Vilnius	Museum of History and Ethnography of Lithuania	1855
		Art Museum of Lithuania	1941
Luxembourg	Luxembourg-Ville	Luxembourg Museum	1845
Malaysia	Kuala Lumpur	National Museum of Malaysia	1963
Maldives	Dhivehi	National Museum	1952

Country	*Location*	*Museum*	*Date established*
Mexico	Mexico City	National Museum of Archaeology	1964
Monaco	Monaco-Ville	Oceanographic Museum	1910
Morocco	Rabat	Museum of Antiquities	1917
Nepal	Katmandu	National Museum of Nepal	1928
Netherlands	Amsterdam	Rijksmuseum	1817
		Rijksmuseum Vincent Van Gogh	1973
		Stedelijk Museum	1893
	Utrecht	Catherine Convent State Museum	1921
New Zealand	Auckland	Auckland City Art Gallery	1888
		Auckland Institute and Museum	1852
	Wellington	Museum of New Zealand Te Papa Tongarewa	1992
Nicaragua	Managua	National Museum of Nicaragua	1896
Norway	Bergen	Bergen Art Gallery	1925
	Oslo	Edvard Munch Museum	1963
		National Gallery	1836
		National Museum of Contemporary Art	1902
Oman	Muscat	Oman Natural History Museum	1983
Pakistan	Islamabad	National Museum of Pakistan	1950
Panama	Apdo	Museum of the History of Panama	1977
Paraguay	Asuncion	National Museum of Fine Arts	1887
Peru	Lima	National Museum of History	1836
Philippines	Manila	National Museum of the Philippines	1901
Poland	Warsaw	National Museum	1862
Portugal	Lisbon	National Museum of Natural History	1859
		Museum of Popular Art	1948
Qatar	Doha	Qatar National Museum	1975
Romania	Bucharest	National History Museum of Romania	1968
		National Museum of Art	1950
Russia	Moscow	Pushkin Museum of Fine Arts	1912
	St Petersburg	Hermitage Museum	1764
		State Russian Museum	1898
Saudi Arabia	Riyadh	Museum of Archaeology and Ethnography	1978
Singapore	Singapore City	National Museum	1849
Spain	Barcelona	Catalan Museum of Art	1929
		Ethnological Museum	1948
		Picasso Museum	1963
	Bilbao	Museum of Fine Art	1914
	Madrid	Prado Museum	1819
		National Museum of Ethnology	1940
	Seville	Museum of the Alcazar of Seville	
		Museum of Fine Art	1835
	Valencia	Museum of Fine Art	1839
Sri Lanka	Colombo	Colombo National Museum	1877
Surinam	Paramaribo	Stichting Suranaams Museum	1947
Sweden	Stockholm	National Museum of Antiquities	1647
		Nordic Museum	1873
Switzerland	Basle	Basle Historical Museum	1894
	Geneva	Museum of Art and History	1910
	Zürich	Swiss National Museum	1898
		House of Art	1910
Syria	Damascus	National Museum	1919
Tajikistan	Dushanbe	Tajik Historical State Museum	
Thailand	Bangkok	National Museum	1926
Trinidad & Tobago	Port of Spain	National Museum and Art Gallery	1898
Tunisia	Tunis	National Museum of Bardo	1888
Turkey	Istanbul	Topkapi Palace Museum	
		Hagia Sophia Museum	1934
		Museum of the Ancient Orient	
		Archaeological Museum	1891
Turkmenistan	Ashkhabad	Turkmen State United Museum of History and Ethnography	1899
Ukraine	Kiev	Kiev State Historical Museum	1934
United Arab Emirates	Abu Dhabi	Al-Ain Museum	1971
Uruguay	Montevideo	National Historical Museum	1900

Museums and art galleries of the world (continued)

Country	*Location*	*Museum*	*Date established*
United Kingdom	Bradford	National Museum of Photography, Film and Television	1983
	Cambridge	Fitzwilliam Museum	1848
	Cardiff	National Museum of Wales	1907
	Edinburgh	National Gallery of Scotland	1859
		Royal Museum of Scotland	1854
		Scottish National Portrait Gallery	1882
	Glasgow	Kelvingrove Art Gallery & Museum	1902
		Burrell Collection	1944
	London	British Museum	1824
		Imperial War Museum	1815
		National Gallery	1838
		National Maritime Museum	1934
		National Portrait Gallery	1896
		Natural History Museum	1963
		Tate Gallery	1897
		Victoria & Albert Museum	1850
	Oxford	Ashmolean Museum	1683
USA	Boston	Museum of Fine Arts	1924
	Chicago	Field Museum of Natural History	1893
	Dallas	Dallas Museum of Fine Arts	1903
	Detroit	Henry Ford Museum	1929
	Los Angeles (Malibu)	John Paul Getty Museum	1953
	New York	Solomon R Guggenheim Museum	1937
		Metropolitan Museum of Art	1870
		Museum of Modern Art	1929
	Philadelphia	Philadelphia Museum of Art	1876
	San Francisco	MH de Young Memorial Museum	1895
	Washington Smithsonian Institution	National Air and Space Museum	1946
		National Museum of American Art	1846
		National Museum of American History	
Uzbekistan	Tashkent	Tashkent Historical Museum of the People of Uzbekistan	1876
Venezuela	Los Caobos	Museum of Fine Arts	1938
Vietnam	Hanoi	Vietnam History Museum	1958

Presidents of the Royal Academy

1768–92	Joshua Reynolds
1792–1805	Benjamin West
1805–6	James Wyatt
1806–20	Benjamin West
1820–30	Thomas Lawrence
1830–50	Martin Archer Shee
1850–66	Charles Eastlake
1866–78	Francis Grant
1878–96	Frederick, 1st Baron Leighton
1896	John Millais
1896–1919	Edward Poynter
1919–24	Aston Webb
1924–8	Frank Dicksee
1928–33	William Llewellyn
1938–44	Edwin Lutyens
1944–9	Alfred Munnings
1949–54	Gerald Festus Kelly
1954–6	Albert Edward Richardson
1956–66	Charles Wheeler
1966–76	Thomas Monnington
1976–84	Hugh Casson
1984–	Roger de Grey

Presidents of the Royal Society

1662–77	William, 2nd Viscount Brouncker
1677–80	Joseph Williamson
1680–2	Christopher Wren
1682–3	John Hoskins
1683–4	Cyril Wyche
1684–6	Samuel Pepys
1686–9	John, Earl of Carbery
1689–90	Thomas Herbert, Earl of Pembroke
1690–5	Robert Southwell
1695–8	Charles Montagu, 1st Earl of Halifax
1698–1703	John, 1st Baron Somers
1703–27	Isaac Newton
1727–41	Hans Sloane
1741–52	Martin Folkes
1752–64	George, Earl of Macclesfield
1764–8	Lord Morton
1768–72	James West
1772–8	John Pringle
1778–1820	Joseph Banks
1820–7	Humphrey Davy
1827–30	Davies Gilbert
1830–8	Augustus Frederick, Duke of Sussex
1838–47	Marquis of Northampton
1847–54	William Parsons, 3rd Earl of Rosse
1854–8	Lord Wrothesley
1858–61	Benjamin Brodie
1861–71	Edward Sabine
1871–3	George Airy
1873–8	Joseph Hooker
1878–83	William Spottiswoode
1883–5	Thomas H Huxley
1885–90	George Stokes
1890–5	William Thomson, 1st Baron Kelvin
1895–1900	Joseph, Lord Lister
1900–5	William Huggins
1905–8	John William Strutt, 3rd Baron Rayleigh
1908–13	Archibald Geikie
1913–15	William Crookes
1915–20	Joseph Thomson
1920–5	Charles Sherrington
1925–30	Ernest, 1st Baron Rutherford
1930–5	Frederick Hopkins
1935–40	William Bragg
1940–5	Henry Dale
1945–50	Robert Robinson
1950–5	Edgar, 1st Baron Adrian
1955–60	Cyril Hinshelwood
1960–5	Howard, Baron Florey
1965–70	Patrick Stuart, Baron Blackett
1970–5	Alan Hodgkin
1975–80	Alexander, Baron Todd
1980–5	Andrew Huxley
1985–90	George, Lord Porter
1990–	Michael Atiyah

Nobel prizes 1981–92

Year	*Peace*	*Literature*	*Economic Science*	*Chemistry*	*Physics*	*Physiology/Medicine*
1981	Office of the UN High Commissioner for Refugees	Elias Canetti	James Tobin	Kenrichi Fukui Roald Hoffman	Nicolaas Bloembergen Arthur L Schaalow Kai M Siegbahn	Roger W Sperry David H Hubel Torsten N Wiesel
1982	Alfonso García Robles Alva Myrdal	Gabriel García Márquez	George J Stigler	Aaron Klug	Kenneth G Wilson	Sune K Bergström Bengt I Samuelsson John R Vane
1983	Lech Wałesa	William Golding	Gerard Debreu	Henry Taube	Subrahmanyan Chandrasekhar William A Fowler	Barbara McClintock
1984	Desmond Tutu	Jaroslav Seifert	Richard Stone	Robert B Merrifield	Carlo Rubbia Simon van der Meer	Niels K Jerne Georges J F Köhler César Milstein
1985	International Physicians for the Prevention of Nuclear War	Claude Simon	Franco Modigliani	Herbert Hauptman Jerome Karle	Klaus von Klitzing	Joseph L Goldstein Michael S Brown
1986	Elie Wiesel	Wole Soyinka	James M Buchanan	Dudley R Herschbach Yuan Tseh Lee John C Polanyi	Gerd Binnig Heinrich Rohrer Ernst Ruska	Stanley Cohen Rita Levi-Montalcini
1987	Oscar Arias Sánchez	Joseph Brodsky	Robert M Solow	Charles Pedersen Donald Cram Jean-Marie Lehn	George Bednorz Alex Müller	Susumu Tonegawa
1988	UN Peacekeeping Forces	Naguib Mahfouz	Maurice Allais	Johann Deisenhofer Robert Huber Hartmut Michel	Leon Lederman Melvin Schwartz Jack Steinberger	James Black Gertrude Elion George Hitchings
1989	Tenzin Ciyatso (Dalai Lama)	Camilo José Cela	Trygve Haavelmo	Sydney Altman Thomas Cech	Hans Dehmelt Wolfgang Paul Norman Ramsay	J Michael Bishop Harold E Varmus
1990	Mikhail Gorbachev	Octavio Paz	Harry M Markovitz Merton Miller William Sharpe	Elias James Corey	Jerome Friedman Henry Kendall Richard Taylor	Joseph E Murray E Donnall Thomas
1991	Aung San Suu Kyi	Nadine Gordimer	Ronald Coase	Richard Ernst	Pierre-Gilles de Gennes	Erwin Nehrer Bert Sakmann
1992	Rigoberta Menchú	Derek Walcott	Gary S Becker	Rudolph A Marcus	George Charpak	Edmond H Fisher Edwin G Krebs

Universities of the world

Country	City	University	Date founded	Approximate number of students
Austria	Graz	Karl-Franzens-Universität	1585	27300
		Technische Universität Graz	1811	12300
		Hochschule für Musik und Darstellende Kunst in Graz (University of Music and Dramatic Art in Graz)	1963	1600
	Innsbruck	Leopold-Franzens Universität Innsbruck	1669	24700
	Klagenfurt	Universität Klagenfurt	1970	5000
	Linz	Johannes Kepler Universität Linz	1966	12000
		Hochschule für Künstlerische und Industrielle Gestaltung (University of Art and Industrial Design)	1947	500
	Leoben	Montanuniversität Leoben (Leoben University of Mining and Metallurgy)	1840	2000
	Salzburg	Universität Salzburg	1622; closed 1810, reconstituted 1962	12000
		Hochschule für Musik und Darstellende Kunst 'Mozarteum' in Salzburg ('Mozarteum' University of Music and Dramatic Art Salzburg)	1841	1500
	Vienna	Universität Wien	1365	68000
		Technische Universität Wien	1815	18500
		Universität für Bodenkultur Wien (Vienna Agricultural University)	1872	6500
		Wirtschaftsuniversität Wien (Vienna University of Economics and Business Administration)	1898	19000
		Veterinärmedizinische Universität Wien	1767	2700
		Akademie der Bildende Künste (Academy of Fine Arts)	1692	560
		Hochschule für Angewandte Kunst in Wien (University of Applied Arts in Vienna)	1868	1100
		Hochschule für Musik und Darstellende Kunst (University of Music and Dramatic Art)	1909	3000
Belgium	Brussels	Catholic University of Brussels	1991	911
		Free University of Brussels (Flemish)	1834, present status 1970	7500
		Free University of Brussels (French)	1834, present status 1970	17300
	Ghent	University of Ghent	1817	16000
	Liège	University of Liège	1425, present	12200
	Louvain	Catholic University of Louvain (Flemish)	status 1970	25200
	Louvain-le-Neuve	Catholic University of Louvain (French)	1425, present status 1970	19900
	Mons	University of Mons	1965	3500
Czech Republic	Brno	Univerzita Masarykova (Masaryk University)	1919	11300
		Vysoká Škola Veterinární A Farmaceutická v Brně (University of Veterinary Science and Pharmacy in Brno)	1918	1100
		Vysoké Učení Technické v Brně (Technical University of Brno)	1899	14600
		Vysoká Škola Zemědělska (University of Agriculture)	1919	3300
	Liberec	Vysoká Škola Strojní a Textilní Liberci (Technical University of Mechanical and Textile Engineering in Liberec)	1953	2900
	Olomouc	Univerzita Palackého v Olomouci (Palacky University)	1573, reopened 1946	5600
	Ostrava	Vysoká Škola Báňská v Ostravě (Technical University of Mining and Metallurgy of Ostrava)	1716	6500
	Pardubice	Vysoká Škola Chemicko-Technologická v Pardubicích (Institute of Chemical Technology in Pardubice)	1950	975

Universities of the world (continued)

Country	*City*	*University*	*Date founded*	*Approximate number of students*
Czech Republic	Plzen	Západočeská Univerzita (University of West Bohemia)	1949, present name 1991	4100
	Prague	České Vysoké Učení Technické v Praze (Czech Technical University)	1707, reorganized 1960	15000
		Univerzita Karlova (Charles University)	1348	30000
		Vysoká Škola Chemicko-Technologická v Praze (University of Chemistry and Technology, Prague)	1807	2500
		Vysoká Škola Ekonomická (Prague University of Economics)	1953	11000
		Vysoká Škola Zemědělska v Praze (Prague Agricultural University)	1906	4900
	Nitra	Vysoka Skola Pol'Nohospodarska (College of Agriculture)	1946	4000
	Zvolen	Vysoka Skola Lesnicka a Drevarska (College of Forestry and Wood Technology)	1807, reorganized 1952	1200
Denmark	Aalborg	Aalborg Universitets Center	1974	9000
	Aarhus	University of Aarhus	1928	13000
		Jutland Open University	1982	864
	Copenhagen	University of Copenhagen	1479	26300
		Technical University of Denmark	1829	5600
	Fredericksburg	Royal Veterinary and Agricultural University	1856	3200
	Odense	University of Odense	1964	5600
Finland	Åbo	Åbo Akademi (Finland-Swedish University of Åbo)	1918	5200
	Helsinki	Helsingin Yliopisto/Helsingfors Universitet	1911	26600
		Teknillinen Korkeakoulu (Helsinki University of Technology)	1908	11500
	Joensuu	Jeonsuun Yliopisto (Jeonsuu University)	1969	5700
	Jyväskylä	Jyväskylän Yliopisto	1966	8600
	Kuopio	Kuopion Yliopisto (University of Kuopio)	1966	2300
	Rovaniemi	Lapin Yliopisto (University of Lapland)	1979	1700
	Lappeenranta	Lappeenrannan Teknillinen Korkeakoulu (Lappeenranta University of Technology)	1969	2500
	Oulu	Oulun Yliopisto	1958	10000
	Tampere	Tampereen Tenknillinen Korkeakoulu (Tampere University of Technology)	1965	5500
		Tampereen Yliopisto (University of Tampere)	1925	15200
	Turku	Turun Yliopisto (Turka University)	1920	11800
	Vaasa	Vaasan Yliopisto (University of Vaasa)	1968	2300
France	Aix-en-Provence	Université d'Aix-Marseille III (Université de Droit, d'Economie et des Sciences)	1973	19200
	Angers	Université d'Angers	1971	14000
	Amiens	Université de Picardie	1965	18000
	Avignon	Université d'Avignon	1973	5200
	Besançon	Université de Franche-Comté	1423 at Dôle, 1691 at Besançon	19300
	Bordeaux	Université de Bordeaux II		14500
	Brest	Université de Bretagne Occidentale		16600
	Caen	Université de Caen	1432, reorganized 1985	23000
	Chambéry	Université de Savoie (Chambéry)	1970	7900
	Clermont-Ferrand	Université de Clermont-Ferrand I	1976, present status 1985	9600
	Clermont-Ferrand	Université de Clermont-Ferrand II (Université Blaise Pascal)	1810, present status 1984	14800
	Corti	Université de Corse 1 Università de Corsica	1976, opened 1981	
	Créteil	Université de Paris XII (Paris-Val-de-Marne)	1970	18000
	Dijon	Université de Bourgogne		24000
	Grenoble	Université de Grenoble I (Université Joseph Fourier)		15000

Country	City	University	Date founded	Approximate number of students
	Grenoble	Université de Grenoble II (Université Pierre Mendès- France)	1970	18 500
	Grenoble	Université de Grenoble III (Université Stendhal)	1810	6 800
	Le Havre	Université du Havre	1984	4 400
	Le Mans	Université du Maine	1969	8 600
	Lille	Université de Lille II (Droit et Santé)	1969	17 400
	Limoges	Université de Limoges	1808, reopened 1965	11 600
	Lyons	Université Lyon II		19 900
	Lyons	Université Lyon III (Université Jean Moulin)	1973	16 000
	Marseilles	Université d'Aix-Marseille I (Université de Provence)	1970	18 700
	Marseilles	Université d'Aix-Marseille II	1973	19 100
	Metz	Université de Metz	1971	12 100
	Montpellier	Université de Montpellier I	1970	18 000
	Montpellier	Université de Montpellier II (Université des Sciences et Techniques de Languedoc)		11 000
	Montpellier	Université de Montpellier III (Université Paul Valéry)	1970	15 500
	Mont-Saint-Aignan	Université de Rouen	1966	21 300
	Mulhouse	Université de Haute-Alsace	1975	2 000
	Nancy	Université de Nancy I	1970	16 300
	Nancy	Université de Nancy II	1970	18 500
	Nanterre	Université de Paris X (Paris-Nanterre)		32 500
	Nantes	Université de Nantes	1962	28 000
	Nice	Université de Nice	1971	22 500
	Orléans	Université d'Orléans	1961	13 200
	Orsay	Université de Paris XI (Paris-Sud)	1970	28 000
	Paris	Université de Paris I (Panthéon-Sorbonne)	1971	36 800
	Paris	Université de Paris II (Université Panthéon-Assas)	1970	18 600
	Paris	Université de Paris III (Sorbonne-Nouvelle)	1970	
	Paris	Université de Paris IV (Paris-Sorbonne)	1970	23 700
	Paris	Université de Paris V (René Descartes)	1970	32 300
	Paris	Université de Paris VI (Pierre et Marie Curie)		
	Paris	Université de Paris VII	1970	30 000
	Paris	Université de Paris IX (Paris-Dauphine)	1968	6 700
	Pau	Université de Pau et des Pays de l'Adour	1970	12 100
	Perpignan	Université de Perpignan	1971	4 500
	Poiters	Université de Poitiers	1432	25 000
	Reims	Université de Reims Champagne-Ardenne	1548	23 500
	Rennes	Université de Rennes I		23 500
	Rennes	Université de Rennes II (Université de Haute Bretagne)		13 000
	St Denis	Université de Paris VIII (Vincennes à St-Denis)	1969	23 500
	St-Étienne	Université Jean Monnet (Université de St-Étienne)	1969, present name 1991	12 600
	Strasbourg	Université de Strasbourg I (Université Louis Pasteur)	1971	17 500
		Université de Strasbourg II (Sciences Humaines)	1538	11 000
		Université de Strasbourg III (Université Robert Schumann)		8 300
	Talence	Université de Bordeaux I		18 600
	Talence	Université de Bordeaux III		14 800
	Toulon/La Garde	Université de Toulon et du Var	1970	5 200
	Toulouse	Université de Toulouse I (Sciences Sociales)	1229	16 400
		Université de Toulouse II (Le Mirail)		21 300
		Université de Toulouse III (Université Paul Sabatier)	1969	26 800
	Tours	Université de Tours (Université François Rabelais)	1970	22 000
	Valenciennes	Université de Valenciennes et du Hainaut-Cambresis	1964	9 000
	Versailles	Université Versailles/Saint Quentin-en-Yvelines	1991	4 400

Universities of the world (continued)

Country	*City*	*University*	*Date founded*	*Approximate number of students*
France	Villeneuve d'Ascq	Université de Lille I (Université des Sciences et Techniques de Lille Flandres Artois)	1855 as Faculty of Sciences, present status 1971	19 100
	Villeneuve d'Ascq	Université de Lille III (Sciences Humaines, Lettres et Arts)	1560, present status 1985	23 900
	Villetaneuse	Université de Paris XIII (Pais-Nord)	1970	13 400
	Villeurbanne	Université Lyon I (Université Claude-Bernard)	1970	23 000
Germany	Aachen	Rheinisch-Westfälische Technische Hochschule Aachen	1870, university status 1880	37 000
	Augsburg	Universität Augsburg	1970	14 700
	Bamberg	Otto Friedrich Universität Bamberg	1647	7 500
	Bayreuth	Universität Bayreuth	1972	8 500
	Berlin	Humboldt-Universität zu Berlin	1809	21 000
	Berlin	Freie Universität Berlin	1948	62 000
	Berlin	Technische Universität Berlin	Bauakademie (f.1799) and Gewerbeakademie (f.1821), amalgamated 1879 as Technische Hoch-schule; opened under present title 1946	38 000
	Bielefeld	Universität Bielefeld	1969	16 000
	Bochum	Ruhr-Universität Bochum	1961	37 000
	Bonn	Rheinische Friedrich-Wilhelms-Universität Bonn	founded 1786; refounded 1818	38 000
	Braunschweig	Technische Universität Carolo Wilhelmina zu Braunschweig	1745, present title 1968	17 000
	Bremen	Universität Bremen	1971	15 600
	Chemnitz	Technische Universität (Karl-Marx-Stadt) Chemnitz	1836	6 200
	Clausthal-Zellerfeld	Technische Universität Clausthal	1775, university status 1968	4 200
	Darmstadt	Technische Hochschule Darmstadt	1836, university status 1895	18 400
	Dortmund-Eichlinghafen	Universität Dortmund	1966	22 300
	Dresden	Technische Universität Dresden	1828, university status 1961	12 000
	Duisburg	Universität Duisburg Gesamthochschule	1972	14 500
	Düsseldorf	Heinrich-Heine-Universität Düsseldorf	1965 (formerly Medizinische Akademie f. 1907)	17 800
	Eichstätt	Katholische Universität Eichstätt	1972 (founded originally 1574)	3 000
	Erlangen	Friedrich-Alexander-Universität Erlangen-Nürnberg	1743	28 000
	Essen	Universität Essen-Gesamtshochschule	1972	20 500
	Frankfurt am Main	Johann Wolfgang Goethe-Universität Frankfurt	1914	34 300
	Freiburg	Albert Ludwigs Universität	1457	23 600
	Giessen	Justus-Liebig-Universität Giessen	1607	20 500
	Göttingen	George-August-Universität Göttingen	1737	30 000
	Greifswald	Ernst Moritz Arndt Universität	1456	4 000
	Freiburg	Albert-Ludwigs-Universität Freiburg	1457	23 600
	Halle	Martin Luther-Universität Halle-Wittenberg	1502 Wittenberg; 1694 Halle; 1817 Halle-Wittenberg	
	Hamburg	Universität Hamburg		43 000
	Hannover	Universität Hannover	1831	29 900
	Heidelberg	Ruprecht-Karls-Universität Heidelberg	1386	27 500
	Hohenheim (Stuttgart)	Universität Hohenheim	1818	6 200
	Jena	Friedrich-Schiller Universität	1558	6 500

Country	*City*	*University*	*Date founded*	*Approximate number of students*
	Kaiserslautern	Universität Kaiserslautern	1975	10000
	Karlsruhe	Universität Fridericiana Karlsruhe	1825	21200
	Kassel	Gesamthochschule Kassel	1970	14900
	Kiel	Christian-Albrechts Universität zu Kiel	1665	20000
	Konstanz	Universität Konstanz	1966	8900
	Cologne	Universität zu Köln	1388	54000
	Leipzig	Universität Leipzig	1409	
	Luneburg	Universität Luneburg	1946	5400
	Mainz	Johannes Gutenburg-Universität Mainz	1477; closed 1816; reopened 1946	27000
	Mannheim	Universität Mannheim	1907, university status 1967	13000
	Marburg	Philipps-Universität Marburg	1527	16900
	Munich	Ludwig-Maximilians-Universität München	1472	60000
	Munich	Technische Universität München	1868	24100
	Münster	Westfälische Wilhelms-Universität Münster	1780	45900
	Oldenburg	Universität Carl von Ossietzky Oldenburg	1974	11000
	Osnabruck	Universität Osnabrück	1973	13000
	Hagen	Open University	1974	50000
	Paderborn	Universität-Gesamthochschule Paderborn	1972	16300
	Passau	Universität Passau	1972	8500
	Regensburg	Universität Regensburg	1962	13000
	Rostock	Universität Rostock	1419	7900
	Saarbrücken	Universität Des Saarlandes	1948	20000
	Siegen	Universität-Gesamthochschule Siegen	1972	12500
	Stuttgart	Universität Stuttgart	1829, university status 1967	21400
	Trier	Universität Trier	1970	10300
	Tübingen	Eberhard-Karls-Universität Tübingen	1477	24800
	Ulm	Universität Ulm	1967	6100
	Wuppertal	Bergische Universität-Gesamthochschule Wuppertal	1972	17700
	Würzburg	Bayerische-Julius-Maximilians-Universität Würzburg	1582	18200
Greece	Athens	National and Capodistrian University of Athens	1837	45000
		National Technical University of Athens	1836	8000
		University of the Aegean	1984	1400
	Crete	University of Crete	1973	1000
		Technical University of Crete	1977	850
	Ioannina	University of Ioannina	1964, independent status 1970	9100
	Komotini	'Demokritos' University of Thrace	1973	6000
	Patras	University of Patras	1964	8900
	Thessaloniki	University of Macedonia	1957	6200
		Aristotelian University of Thessaloniki	1925	65000
Hungary	Budapest	Eötvös Loránd Tudományegyetem (Loránd Eötvös University)	1635	11000
		Semmelweis Orvostudományi Egyetem	1769, independent 1951	5000
		Budapesti Közgazdaságtudományi Egyetem (Budapest University of Economic Sciences)	1948	4600
		Orvostovábbképzö Egyetem (Postgraduate Medical University)	1987	10000
		Állatorvostudományi Egyetem (University of Veterinary Sciences)	1787	550
		Budapesti Müszaki Egyetem (Technical University of Budapest)	1871	9300
		Kertészeti És Élelmiszeripari Egyetem (University of Horticulture and Food Technology)	1853	1800
	Debrecen	Kossuth Lajos Tudományegyetem	1912	2600
		Debreceni Orvostudományi Egyetem (University Medical School of Debrecen)	1951	1100

Universities of the world (continued)

Country	*City*	*University*	*Date founded*	*Approximate number of students*
Hungary		Debreceni Agrártudományi Egyetem (Debrecen University of Agrarian Sciences)	1868	1400
	Gödollö	Agrártudományi Egyetem (University of Agricultural Sciences)	1945	3500
	Keszthely	Pannon Agrártudományi Egyetem (Pannon University of Agricultural Sciences)	1797	1400
	Miskolc	Miskolci Egyetem (Miskolc University)	1949	2800
	Pécs	Pécsi Jannus Pannonius Tudományegyetem (Janus Pannonius University of Pécs)	1367	3800
		Pécsi Orvostudományi Egyetem (Medical University of Pecs)	1951	1500
	Szeged	Szent-Györgi Albert Orvostudományi Egyetem (Albert Szent-Györgi Medical University)	1951	2100
		József Attila Tudományegyetem (Attila József University)	1872	4300
	Sopron	Erdészeti Es Faipari Egyetem (University of Forestry and Wood Science)	1808	840
	Veszprém	Veszprémi Egyetem (Veszprem University)	1949	1500
Ireland	Cork	University College Cork[1]	1845 as Queen's College; 1908	7100
	Dublin	University of Dublin Trinity College	1592	9800
		National University of Ireland	1908	
		University College Dublin[1]	1909	12500
		Dublin City University	1975, university status 1989	4500
	Galway	University College Galway[1]	1845 as Queen's College; 1908	6100
	Limerick	University of Limerick	1970, university status 1989	6200
Italy	Ancona	Università degli Studi di Ancona	1969	7900
	L'Aquila	Università degli Studi dell' Aquila	1952	8200
	Bari	Università degli Studi di Bari	1924	42400
	Bologna	Università degli Studi di Bologna	11th-c	59100
	Brescia	Università degli Studi di Brescia	1982	7800
	Cagliari, Sardinia	Università di Cagliari	1606	18000
	Camerino	Università di Camerino	1336, university status 1727	6000
	Commenda di Rende	Università di Calabria	1972	11000
	Campobasso	Università degli Studi del Molise	1982	
	Cassino	Università degli Studi di Cassino	1982	
	Catania	Università di Catania	1434	45500
	Ferrara	Università degli Studi di Ferrara	1391	6000
	Florence	Università degli Studi di Firenze	1321	46300
	Fisciano (Salerno)	Università degli Studi di Salerno	1970	
	Genoa	Università degli Studi di Genova	1471	30400
	Lecce	Università degli Studi di Lecce	1956	13000
	Macerata	Università degli Studi di Macerata	1290	7100
	Messina	Università degli Studi di Messina	1548	28000
	Milan	Università degli Studi di Milano	1924	89200
	Milan	Politecnico di Milano	1863	45800
	Milan	Catholic University of the Sacred Heart	1920, present status 1924	28200
	Milan	Università Commerciale Luigi Bocconi	1902	10900
	Modena	Università degli Studi di Modena	1175	8100
	Naples	Università degli Studi di Napoli	1224	100000
	Padua	Università degli Studi di Padova	1222	53800
	Palermo	Università degli Studi di Palermo	1777	20000
	Parma	Università degli Studi	962	22600

[1] The National University of Ireland has three constituent Colleges.

Country	City	University	Date founded	Approximate number of students
	Pavia	Università degli Studi di Pavia	1361	26600
	Perugia	Università degli Studi di Perugia	1200	19200
	Perugia	Università Italiana per Stranieri	1921	7000
	Pisa	Università degli Studi di Pisa	1343	28000
	Reggio Calabria	Università di Reggio Calabria	1982	
	Rome	Università degli Studi di Roma 'La Sapienza'	1303	180000
	Rome	Università degli Studi di Roma 'Tor Vergata'	1970	
	Sassari	Università degli Studi di Sassari	1562	9500
	Siena	Università degli Studi di Siena	1240	11000
	Trento	Università degli Studi di Trento	1962	10200
	Trieste	Università degli Studi di Trieste	1938	18500
	Turin	Università degli Studi di Torino	1404	42500
	Turin	Politecnico di Torino	1859	18200
	Udine	Università degli Studi di Udine	1977	8000
	Urbino	Università degli Studi di Urbino	1506	16500
	Venice	Università degli Studi di Venezia	1868	18000
	Verona	Università degli Studi di Verona	1982	13800
	Viterbo	Università degli Studi della Tuscia	1981	
Netherlands	Amsterdam	University of Amsterdam	1632	27000
		Free University, Amsterdam	1880	12000
	Delft	Delft University of Technology	1842	14500
	Eindhoven	Eindhoven University of Technology	1956	7000
	Enschede	Twente University of Technology	1961	7000
	Groningen	University of Groningen	1614	18000
	Heerlen	Open University	1984	50000
	Leiden	Leiden University	1575	17900
	Maastricht	University of Limburg	1976	7000
	Nijmegen	Catholic University, Nijmegen	1923	13000
	Rotterdam	Erasmus University, Rotterdam	1973	18000
	Tilburg	Tilburg University	1927	9000
	Utrecht	Utrecht University	1636	23000
	Wageningen	Agricultural University	1918	6000
Norway	Bergen	Universitetet I Bergen	1948	13600
	Oslo	Universitetet I Oslo	1811	32000
	Tromsø	Universitetet I Tromsø	1968	3800
	Trondheim	Universitetet I Trondheim	1968	14500
Poland	Białystok	Politechnika Białostocka (Białystok Technical University)	1949	2600
	Częstochowa	Politechnika Częstochowska (Częstochowa Technical University)	1949	2000
	Gdańsk	Uniwersytet Gdański (University of Gdańsk)	1970	12300
		Politechnika Gdańska (Technical University of Gdańsk)	1945	5700
	Gliwice	Politechnika Slaska Im. W. Pstrowskiego (Silesian Technical University)	1945	8000
	Katowice	Uniwerystet Słaski (Silesian University)	1968	13400
	Kielce	Politechnika Świętokrzyska (Kielce University of Technology)	1965	2100
	Krakow	Uniwersytet Jagielloński (Jagiellonian University)	1364	9600
		Akademia Gorniczo-Hutnicza Im. Stanislawa Staszica W Krakowie (Stanislaw Staszic Academy of Mining and Metallurgy)	1919	7500
		Politechnika Krakowska Im. Tadeusza Kościuszki (Cracow Technical University)	1945	5100
	Łódz	Uniwersytet Łódzki (University of Łódz)	1945	14200
		Politechnika Łódzka (Łódz Technical University)	1945	8200
	Lublin	Katolicki Uniwersytet Lubelski (Catholic University of Lublin)	1918	7100
		Uniwersytet Marii Curie-Skłodowskiej (Marie-Curie Skłodowska University)	1944	15800
		Politechnika Lubelska (Technical University of Lublin)	1953	3300

Universities of the world (continued)

Country	*City*	*University*	*Date founded*	*Approximate number of students*
Poland	Poznań	Uniwersytet Im Adama Mickiewicza w Poznaniu (Adam Mickiewicz University in Poznań)	1919	15 300
		Politechnika Poznańska (Poznań Technical University)	1919	4 200
	Rzeszów	Politechnika Rzeszowska (Rzeszów Technical University)	1974	3 700
	Szczecin	Uniwersytet Szczeciński (Szczecin University)	1985	9 500
		Politechnika Szczecinska (Szczecin Technical University)	1946	2 400
	Toruń	Uniwersytet Mikołaja Kopernika w Toruniu (Nicholas Copernicus University in Toruń)	1945	10 000
	Warsaw	Uniwersytet Warszawski (University of Warsaw)	1818	25 400
		Politechnika Warszawska (Warsaw University of Technology)	1826	12 500
	Wrocław	Uniwersytet Wrocławski	1702, rebuilt 1945	14 600
		Politechnika Wrocławska (Wrocław Technical University)	1945	6 800
Portugal	Braga	Universidade de Minho	1973	7 800
	Coímbra	Universidade de Coímbra	1290	13 000
	Corvilla	Universidade de Beira Interior	1986	3 000
	Évora	Universidade de Évora	1973, university status 1979	2 200
	Lisbon	Universidade Autónoma de Lisboa 'Luis de Camões'	1977	5 000
		Universidade Católica Portuguesa	1968	9 200
		New University of Lisbon	1973	9 100
		Universidade Técnica de Lisboa	1930	15 900
		Universidade Lusíada	1986	8 900
	Porto	Universidade de Porto	1911	18 000
Slovak Republic	Bratislava	Univerzita Komenského Bratislava (Comenius University of Bratislava)	1919	15 900
		Slovenská Technická Univerzita v Bratislave (Slovak Technical University)	1938	12 100
		Vysoká Ekonomicka v Bratislave (School of Economics in Bratislava)	1940	7 400
	Košice	Univerzita Pavla Jozefa Šafárika (Safarik University)	1959	6 100
		Vysoká Škola Veterinárská Košiciach (University of Veterinary Medicine in Košice)	1949	750
		Technická Univerzita v Košiciach (Košice Technical University)	1952	6 400
	Žilina	Vysoká Škola Dopravy a Spojov (University of Transport and Telecommunications)	1953	4 900
Spain	Alcalá de Henares (Madrid)	Universidad de Alcalá de Henares	1977	15 700
	Alicante	Universidad de Alicante	1979	19 500
	Barcelona	Universitat de Barcelona	1450	80 500
	Barcelona Bellaterra (Barcelona)	Universitat Autónoma de Barcelona	1968	33 400
	Bilbao	Universidad de Deusto	1886	15 000
		University of the Basque Country	1968, reorganized 1980	50 500
	Cáceres	Universidad de Extremadura	1973	12 300
	Cádiz	Universidad de Cádiz	1979	14 900
	Ciudad Real	Universidad de Castilla-la-Mancha	1982	18 600
	Córdoba	Universidad de Córdoba	1972	14 000
	Granada	Universidad de Granada	1526	56 200
	La Laguna, Canary Is	Universidad de La Laguna	1792	21 200
	León	Universidad de León	1979	10 300
	Madrid	Universidad Complutense de Madrid	1508	24 150

Country	*City*	*University*	*Date founded*	*Approximate number of students*
		Universidad Pontificia 'Comillas'	1890 in Santander; moved to Madrid 1960	16 800
		Universidad Autónoma de Madrid	1968	28 000
		Open University	1972	88 000
		Universidad Carlos III de Madrid	1989	4 000
	Málaga	Universidad de Málaga	1972	23 000
	Murcia	Universidad de Murcia	1915	26 400
	Palma de Mallorca	Universitat de Les Illes Balears	1978	9 500
	Las Palmas Canary Is	Universidad de Las Palmas de Gran Canaria	1980	10 000
	Pamplona	Universidad de Navarra	1952	15 300
	Oviedo	Universidad de Oviedo	1608	36 900
	Salamanca	Universidad Pontificia de Salamanca	1134 as Ecclesiastical School, university status 1219; defunct by end 18th-c, restored 1940	8 500
		Universidad de Salamanca	1218, reorganized 1254	27 600
	Santander	Universidad de Cantabria	1972, as Universidad de Santander	12 000
	Seville	Universidad de Sevilla	1502	56 900
	Valencia	Universitat de València	1510	55 300
	Valladolid	Universidad de Valladolid	13th-c	42 500
	Zaragoza	Universidad de Zaragoza	1583	40 000
Sweden	Gothenburg	Chalmers Tekniska Högskola (Chalmers University of Technology)	1829	4 500
		Göteborgs Universitet	1891	22 000
	Karlstad	Högskolan Karlstad (Karlstad University)	1977	4 300
	Linköping	Universitet Linköping	1970	11 000
	Luleå	Högskolan I Luleå	1971	5 200
	Lund	Lunds Universitet	1666	30 000
	Örebro	Högskolan I Örebro	1967	5 000
	Stockholm	Kungliga Tekniska Högskolan (Royal Institute of Technology)	1827	8 500
		Stockholms Universitet	1877, state university 1960	26 000
	Uppsala	Sveriges Lantbruksuniversitet (Swedish University of Agricultural Sciences)	1977	2 500
		Uppsala Universitet	1477	18 000
	Umeå	Umeå Universitet	1963	10 000
	Växjö	Högskolan Växjö (Växjö University)	1967	3 600
Switzerland	Basel	Universität Basel	1460	6 800
	Bern	Universität Bern	1834	8 000
	Fribourg	Université de Fribourg	1889	5 900
	Geneva	Université de Genève	1559	12 900
	Lausanne	Université de Lausanne	1537	6 700
		École Polytechnique Fédérale de Lausanne	1853	3 900
	Neuchâtel	Université de Neuchâtel	1909	2 900
	Zürich	Universität Zürich	1833	21 100
		Eidgenössische Technische Hochschule Zürich (Swiss Federal Institute of Technology)	1855	11 200
United Kingdom	Aberdeen	University of Aberdeen	1495	8 000
		Robert Gordon University	1885[1]	4 600 full-time, 1 300 part-time
	Aberystwyth	University College of Wales	1872	4 000
	Bangor	University College of North Wales	1884	4 200
	Bath	University of Bath	1966	5 000
	Bedford	Cranfield Institute of Technology	1969	2 091
	Belfast	The Queen's University of Belfast	1908	7 867
	Birmingham	Aston University	1966	4 700
		The University of Birmingham	1900	9 700

Universities of the world (continued)

Country	*City*	*University*	*Date founded*	*Approximate number of students*
United Kingdom		University of Central England in Birmingham	1971[1]	7800 full-time; 7000 part-time
	Bradford	University of Bradford	1966[1]	5300
	Brighton	University of Brighton	1970[1]	7500
		The University of Sussex	1961	6600
	Bristol	The University of Bristol	1909	9200
		University of the West of England	1969[1]	7000 full-time; 5000 part-time
	Buckingham	University of Buckingham	1983[1]	900
	Chelmsford and Cambridge	Anglia Polytechnic University	1905[1] as Chelmsford School of Science and Art, university status 1992	10700, incl. part-time
	Cambridge	The University of Cambridge		14000
		Christ's	1505	
		Churchill	1960	
		Clare	1326	
		Clare Hall	1966	
		Corpus Christi	1352	
		Darwin	1964	
		Downing	1800	
		Emmanuel	1584	
		Fitzwilliam	1966	
		Girton	1869	
		Gonville & Caius	1348	
		Homerton	1824	
		Hughes Hall	1885	
		Jesus	1496	
		King's	1441	
		Lucy Cavendish	1965	
		Magdalene	1542	
		New Hall	1954	
		Newnham	1871	
		Pembroke	1347	
		Peterhouse	1284	
		Queens'	1448	
		Robinson	1977	
		St Catharine's	1473	
		St Edmund's	1896	
		St John's	1511	
		Selwyn	1882	
		Sidney Sussex	1596	
		Trinity	1546	
		Trinity Hall	1350	
		Wolfson	1965	
	Canterbury	University of Kent at Canterbury	1965	5500
	Cardiff	The University of Wales	1893	24449
		University of Wales College of Cardiff	1988	11000
		University of Wales College of Medicine	1931, present status 1984	1300
	Colchester	The University of Essex	1964	4600
	Coleraine	University of Ulster	1985	11140
	Coventry	Coventry University	1970[1]	8300
	Coventry	The University of Warwick	1965	11000
	Dundee	University of Dundee	1967	5500
	Durham	The University of Durham	1832	5500
	Edinburgh	University of Edinburgh	1583	14000
		Heriot-Watt University	1966	8000
		Napier University	1964[1]	5500 full-time; 3500 part-time
	Exeter	The University of Exeter	1955	6800

Country	City	University	Date founded	Approximate number of students
	Glasgow	University of Glasgow	1451	13460
		Glasgow Polytechnic (awaiting university title)	Queen's College 1875; Glasgow Polytechnic 1971[1]; merged 1992	Queen's College 1773; Glasgow Polytechnic 4000 full-time; 2700 part-time
		University of Strathclyde	1964	8500
	Guildford	University of Surrey	1966	5000
	Hatfield	University of Hertfordshire	1952[1]	8000
	Huddersfield	University of Huddersfield	1841[1]	6800 full-time; 2900 part-time
	Hull	The University of Hull	1954	7000
		University of Humberside	1978[1]	8000
	Kingston-upon-Thames	Kingston University	1970[1]	12700
	Lampeter	St David's College, Lampeter	1827, present status 1971	1100
	Lancaster	The University of Lancaster	1964	4500
	Leeds	The University of Leeds	1904	11500
		Leeds Metropolitan University	1970[1]	9000 full-time; 7200 part-time
	Leicester	The University of Leicester	1957	6800
		De Montfort University	1969[1]	6300 full-time; 2300 part-time
	Liverpool	The University of Liverpool	1903	12100
		Liverpool John Moores University	1970[1]	15500
	London	City University	1966	5 000
		City of London University	1970[1]	15000
		University of East London	1970[1]	6500 full-time; 3000 part-time
		The University of London	1836	66000 internal; 22400 external
		Birkbeck College	1823	
		Goldsmiths' College	1904	
		Imperial College of Science, Technology, and Medicine	1907	
		Institute of Education	1902; controlled by London University since 1932; School of London University since 1987	
		King's College London	1829	
		London School of Economics and Political Science	1895	
		Queen Mary and Westfield College	Queen Mary 1887; Westfield 1882; merged 1989	
	(Egham)	Royal Holloway and Bedford New College	Royal Holloway 1886; Bedford 1849; merged 1985	
		Royal Veterinary College	1791	
		School of Oriental and African Studies	1916	
		School of Pharmacy	1842	
		University College London	1826	
	(Ashford)	Wye College	1447	
		Middlesex University	1973[1]	5000 full-time; 4000 sandwich; 2000 part-time
		University of North London	1971[1]	10800
		South Bank University	1970[1]	11000
		University of Westminster	1970[1]	5000 full-time; 6500 part-time; 18000 short course
	Loughborough	Loughborough University of Technology	1966	5900

Universities of the world (continued)

Country	*City*	*University*	*Date founded*	*Approximate number of students*
	Manchester	Victoria University of Manchester	1851	16500
		University of Manchester Institute of Science and Technology	1824	
		Manchester Metropolitan University	1970[1]	10700 full-time; 2800 sandwich; 7000 part-time
	Middlesbrough	University of Teesside	1929[1]	7800
	Milton Keynes	The Open University	1969	195000
	Newcastle	University of Northumbria at Newcastle	1969[1]	9200 full-time; 4400 part-time
	Newcastle under Lyme	The University of Keele	1962	3100
	Newcastle upon Tyne	The University of Newcastle upon Tyne	1851	8500
	Norwich	The University of East Anglia	1964	5800
	Nottingham	City University Nottingham	1970[1]	11000 full-time; 4700 part-time
		The University of Nottingham	1948	10500
	Oxford	The University of Oxford		14000
		All Souls	1438	
		Balliol	1263	
		Brasenose	1509	
		Christ Church	1546	
		Corpus Christi	1517	
		Exeter	1314	
		Green	1979	
		Hertford	1874	
		Jesus	1571	
		Keble	1868	
		Lady Margaret Hall	1878	
		Linacre	1962	
		Lincoln	1427	
		Magdalen	1458	
		Merton	1263	
		New College	1379	
		Nuffield	1937	
		Oriel	1326	
		Pembroke	1624	
		Queen's	1340	
		Rewley House	1990	
		St Anne's	1952	
		St Antony's	1950	
		St Catherine's	1962	
		St Cross	1965	
		St Edmund Hall	c.1278	
		St Hilda's	1938	
		St Hugh's	1886	
		St John's	1555	
		St Peter's	1929	
		Somerville	1879	
		Trinity	1554	
		University	1249	
		Wadham	1612	
		Wolfson	1966	
		Worcester	1714	
		Oxford Brookes University	1970[1]	6400 full-time; 2900 part-time
	Paisley	University of Paisley	1897	4000 full-time; 1000 part-time
	Plymouth	University of Plymouth	1970[1]	7700 full-time; 1100 part-time

Country	City	University	Date founded	Approximate number of students
	Pontypridd	University of Glamorgan	1913[1] as mining college	4 900 full-time; 1 600 part-time
	Poole	Bournemouth University	1961 as Dorset Institute of Higher Education[1]	8 300
	Portsmouth	University of Portsmouth	1870[1]	8 700 full-time; 1 800 part-time
	Preston	University of Central Lancashire	1956[1]	7 500 full-time; 4 800 part-time
	Reading	The University of Reading	1926	9 600
	Salford	University of Salford	1967	4 300
	Sheffield	The University of Sheffield	1905	9 600
		Sheffield Hallam University	1969[1]	12 200 full-time; 4 800 part-time
	Southampton	The University of Southampton	1952	7 800
	St Andrews	University of St Andrews	1411	4 600
	Stirling	University of Stirling	1967	4 000
	Stoke-on-Trent	Staffordshire University	1970[1]	3 700 full-time; 1 900 sandwich; 2 400 part-time
	Sunderland	University of Sunderland	1969[1]	4 400 full-time; 1 400 part-time
	Swansea	University College, Swansea	1920	5 800
	Uxbridge	Brunel University	1966	4 800
	W London	Thames Valley University	1991[2]	5 900 full-time; 9 000 part-time
	Wolverhampton	University of Wolverhampton	1969[1]	7 362 full-time; 4 885 part-time
	Woolwich	University of Greenwich	1890[1]	12 000
	York	The University of York	1963	4 600

[1] Founded as a polytechnic or other college; university status applied for in 19192; 1991–2 enrolment figures
[2] Formerly Ealing College of Higher Education

Country	State	University	Location	Date founded
United States	Alabama	Auburn University	Auburn University	1856
		Tuskegee University	Tuskegee	1881
		University of Alabama	Tuscaloosa	1831
		University of Alabama at Birmingham	Birmingham	1969
		University of Alabama in Huntsville	Huntsville	1950
		University of South Alabama	Mobile	1963
	Alaska	University of Alaska Anchorage	Anchorage	1954
		University of Alaska Fairbanks	Fairbanks	1917
	Arizona	Arizona State University	Tempe	1885
		Northern Arizona University	Flagstaff	1899
		University of Arizona	Tucson	1885
	Arkansas	University of Arkansas	Fayetteville	1871
		University of Arkansas at Little Rock	Little Rock	1927
		University of Arkansas at Pine Bluff	Pine Bluff	1873
	California	California Institute of Technology	Pasadena	1891
		California Polytechnic State University	San Luis Obispo	1901
		California Polytechnic State University	Pomona	1938
		California State University	Bakersfield	1970
		California State University	Chico	1887
		California State University, Dominguez Hills	Carson	1960
		California State University	Fresno	1911
		California State University	Fullerton	1957
		California State University	Hayward	1957
		California State University	Long Beach	1949
		California State University	Los Angeles	1847
		California State University	Northridge	1958
		California State University	Sacramento	1947
		California State University	San Bernardino	1965

Universities of the world (continued)

Country	*State*	*University*	*Location*	*Date founded*
United States		Loyola Marymount University	Los Angeles	1911
		National University	San Diego	1971
		Pomona College	Claremont	1887
		San Diego State University	San Diego	1897
		San Francisco State University	San Francisco	1899
		San Jose State University	San Jose	1857
		Santa Clara University	Santa Clara	1851
		Stanford University	Stanford	1891
		University of California at Berkeley	Berkeley	1868
		University of California, Davis	Davis	1906
		University of California, Irvine	Irvine	1965
		University of California, Los Angeles	Los Angeles	1919
		University of California, Riverside	Riverside	1954
		University of California, San Diego	La Jolla	1959
		University of California, Santa Barbara	Santa Barbara	1891
		University of California, Santa Cruz	Santa Cruz	1965
		University of Southern California	Los Angeles	1880
	Colorado	Colorado School of Mines	Golden	1874
		Colorado State University	Fort Collins	1862
		Metropolitan State College	Denver	1965
		University of Colorado at Boulder	Boulder	1876
		University of Northern Colorado	Greeley	1890
	Connecticut	Central Connecticut State University	New Britain	1849
		Fairfield University	Fairfield	1942
		Southern Connecticut State University	New Haven	1893
		University of Connecticut	Storrs	1881
		Wesleyan University	Middletown	1831
		Yale University	New Haven	1701
	Delaware	University of Delaware	Newark	1743
	District of Columbia	American University	Washington	1893
		Catholic University of America	Washington	1887
		Gallaudet University	Washington	1856
		Georgetown University	Washington	1789
		George Washington University	Washington	1821
		Howard University	Washington	1867
		University of the District of Columbia	Washington	1976
	Florida	Florida Atlantic University	Boca Raton	1961
		Florida International University	Miami	1965
		Florida State University	Tallahassee	1857
		Nova University	Fort Lauderdale	1964
		University of Central Florida	Orlando	1963
		University of Florida	Gainsville	1853
		University of Miami	Coral Gables	1925
		University of South Florida	Tampa	1956
	Georgia	Emory University	Atlanta	1836
		Georgia Institute of Technology	Atlanta	1885
		Georgia Southern University	Statesboro	1906
		Georgia State University	Atlanta	1913
		University of Georgia	Athens	1785
	Hawaii	University of Hawaii at Hilo	Hilo	1970
		University of Hawaii at Manoa	Honolulu	1907
	Idaho	Boise State University	Boise	1932
		University of Idaho	Moscow	1889
	Illinois	DePaul University	Chicago	1898
		Eastern Illinois University	Charleston	1895
		Illinois State University	Normal	1857
		Loyola University Chicago	Chicago	1870
		Northern Illinois University	De Kalb	1895
		Northeastern Illinois University	Chicago	1961
		Northwestern University	Evanston	1851
		Southern Illinois University of Carbondale	Carbondale	1869
		Southern Illinois University at Edwardsville	Edwardsville	1957
		University of Chicago	Chicago	1891
		University of Illinois at Chicago	Chicago	1965
		University of Illinois at Urbana – Champaign	Urbana	1867

Country	State	University	Location	Date founded
		Western Illinois University	Macomb	1899
	Indiana	Ball State University	Muncie	1918
		Indiana State Univesity	Terre Haute	1865
		Indiana State University Kokomo	Kokomo	1945
		Indiana University at South Bend	South Bend	1922
		Indiana University at Bloomington	Bloomington	1820
		Indiana University Northwest	Gary	1959
		Indiana University of Pennsylvania	Indiana	1875
		Indiana University – Purdue Univesity at Fort Wayne	Fort Wayne	1917
		Indiana University – Purdue University at Indianapolis	Indianapolis	1969
		Indiana University Southeast	New Albany	1941
		Purdue University	West Lafayette	1869
		Purdue University Calumet	Hammond	1951
		Purdue University North Central	Westville	1967
		University of Notre Dame	Notre Dame	1842
		Valparaiso University	Valparaiso	1859
	Iowa	Drake University	Des Moines	1881
		Grinnell College	Grinnell	1846
		Iowa State University of Science and Technology	Ames	1858
		University of Iowa	Iowa City	1947
		University of Northern Iowa	Cedar Falls	1876
	Kansas	Kansas State University	Manhattan	1863
		University of of Kansas	Lawrence	1866
		Wichita State University	Wichita	1895
	Kentucky	Bellarmine College	Louisville	1950
		University of Kentucky	Lexington	1865
		University of Louisville	Louisville	1798
		Western Kentucky University	Bowling Green	1906
	Louisiana	Louisiana State University and A&M College	Baton Rouge	1860
		Louisiana Technical University	Ruston	1894
		Loyola University New Orleans	New Orleans	1912
		Northeast Louisiana University	Monroe	1931
		Southern University and A&M College	Baton Rouge	1880
		Tulane University	New Orleans	1834
		University of New Orleans	New Orleans	1958
		University of Southwestern Louisiana	Lafayette	1898
	Maine	Bowdoin College	Brunswick	1794
		University of Maine	Orono	1865
		University of Southern Maine	Portland	1878
	Maryland	Johns Hopkins University	Baltimore	1876
		Towson State University	Towson	1866
		University of Maryland Baltimore County	Baltimore	1966
		University of Maryland College Park	College Park	1856
		University of Maryland University College	College Park	1947
		Washington College	Chestertown	1782
	Massachusetts	Amherst College	Amherst	1821
		Boston College	Chestnut Hill	1863
		Boston University	Boston	1839
		Brandeis University	Waltham	1948
		College of the Holy Cross	Worcester	1843
		Harvard University	Cambridge	1636
		Massachusetts Institute of Technology	Cambridge	1861
		Northeastern University	Boston	1898
		Smith College	Northampton	1871
		Tufts University	Medford	1852
		University of Lowell	Lowell	1894
		University of Massachusetts at Amherst	Amherst	1863
		University of Massachusetts at Boston	Boston	1964
		Wellesley College	Wellesley	1870
		Wheaton College	Norton	1834
		Williams College	Williamstown	1793
	Michigan	Central Michigan University	Mount Pleasant	1892
		Eastern Michigan University	Ypsilanti	1849
		Ferris State University	Big Rapids	1884

Universities of the world (continued)

Country	*State*	*University*	*Location*	*Date founded*
United States		Grand Valley State University	Allendale	1960
		Michigan State University	East Lansing	1855
		Oakland University	Rochester	1957
		University of Michigan	Ann Arbor	1817
		University of Michigan – Dearborn		1959
		University of Michigan – Flint		1956
		Wayne State University	Detroit	1868
		Western Michigan University	Kalamazoo	1903
	Minnesota	Mankato State University	Mankato	1867
		St Cloud State University	St Cloud	1869
		University of Minnesota, Twin Cities Campus	Minneapolis	1851
	Mississippi	Mississippi State University	Mississippi State	1878
		University of Mississippi	University	1844
		University of Southern Mississippi	Hattiesburg	1910
	Missouri	Central Missouri State University	Warrensburg	1871
		Saint Louis University	St Louis	1818
		Southwest Missouri State University	Springfield	1905
		Stephens College	Columbia	1833
		University of Missouri – Columbia	Columbia	1839
		University of Missouri – Kansas City	Kansas City	1933
		University of Missouri – Rolla	Rolla	1870
		University of Missouri – St Louis	St Louis	1963
		Washington University	St Louis	1853
	Montana	Montana State University	Bozeman	1893
		University of Montana	Missoula	1893
	Nebraska	Creighton University	Omaha	1878
		University of Nebraska at Kearney	Kearney	1903
		University of Nebraska at Omaha	Omaha	1908
		University of Nebraska – Lincoln	Lincoln	1869
	Nevada	University of Nevada, Las Vegas	Las Vegas	1957
		University of Nevada, Reno	Reno	1874
	New Hampshire	Dartmouth College	Hanover	1769
		University of New Hampshire	Durham	1866
		Drew University	Madison	1866
	New Jersey	Fairleigh-Dickinson University, Teaneck-Hackensack Campus	Teaneck	1954
		Kean College of New Jersey	Union	1855
		Montclair State College	Upper Montclair	1908
		Princeton University	Princeton	1746
		Rutgers, State University of New Jersey, Douglas College	New Brunswick	1918
		Rutgers, State University of New Jersey, Livingston College	New Brunswick	1969
		Rutgers, State University of New Jersey, Newark College of Arts and Science	Newark	1946
		Rutgers, State University of New Jersey, Rutgers College	New Brunswick	1766
		Rutgers, State University of New Jersey, University College – New Brunswick	New Brunswick	1934
		Seton Hall University	South Orange	1856
		William Paterson College of New Jersey	Wayne	1855
	New Mexico	New Mexico State University	Las Cruces	1888
		University of New Mexico	Albuquerque	1889
	New York	Adelphi University	Garden City	1896
		Barnard College	New York	1889
		Baruch College of the City University of New York	New York	1968
		Brooklyn College of the City University of New York	New York	1930
		City College of the City University of New York	New York	1847
		Clarkson University	Potsdam	1896
		Colgate University	Hamilton	1819
		College of Staten Island of the City University of New York	New York	1955
		Columbia College	New York	1754

Country	State	University	Location	Date founded
		Columbia University School of Engineering and Applied Science	New York	1864
		Columbia University School of General Studies	New York	1754
		Cooper Union for the Advancement of Science and Art	New York	1859
		Cornell University	Ithaca	1865
		Fashion Institute of Technology	New York	1944
		Fordham University	New York	1841
		Hamilton College	Clinton	1812
		Hartwick College	Oneonta	1797
		Hofstra University	Hempstead	1935
		Hunter College of the City University of New York	New York	1870
		Ithaca College	Ithaca	1892
		Juilliard School	New York	1905
		Long Island University, Brooklyn Campus	Brooklyn	1926
		Long Island University, CW Post Campus	Brookville	1954
		New York Institute of Technology	Old Westbury	1955
		New York University	New York	1831
		Pace University	New York	1906
		Parsons School of Design, New School for Social Research	New York	1896
		Pratt Institute	Brooklyn	1887
		Queens College of the City University of New York	Flushing	1937
		Rensselaer Polytechnic Institute	Troy	1824
		Rochester Institute of Technology	Rochester	1829
		Sarah Lawrence College	Bronxville	1926
		Skidmore College	Saratoga Springs	1903
		St John's University	Jamaica	1870
		State University of New York at Albany	Albany	1844
		State University of New York at Binghamton	Binghamton	1946
		State University of New York at Buffalo	Buffalo	1946
		State University of New York at Stony Brook	Brook	1957
		State University of New York, College at Brockport	Brockport	1867
		State University of New York, College at Buffalo	Buffalo	1867
		State University of New York, College at Cortland	Cortland	1868
		State University of New York, College at Fredonia	Fredonia	1826
		State University of New York, College at Geneseo	Geneseo	1867
		State University of New York, College at New Paltz	New Paltz	1828
		State University of New York, College at Old Westbury	Old Westbury	1965
		State University of New York, College at Oneonta	Oneonta	1889
		State University of New York, College at Oswego	Oswego	1861
		State University of New York, College at Plattsburgh	Plattsburgh	1889
		State University of New York, College at Potsdam	Potsdam	1816
		State University of New York, Empire State College	Saratoga Springs	1971
		Syracuse University	Syracuse	1870
		Union College	Schenectady	1795
		State University of New York, Regents College	Albany	1971
		Vassar College	Poughkeepsie	1861
		Yeshiva University	New York	1886
	North Carolina	Appalachian State University	Boone	1899
		Duke University	Durham	1838
		East Carolina University	Greenville	1907
		North Carolina State University	Raleigh	1887
		University of North Carolina at Asheville	Asheville	1927
		University of North Carolina at Chapel Hill	Chapel Hill	1795
		University of North Carolina at Charlotte	Charlotte	1946
		University of North Carolina at Greensboro	Greensboro	1891
		University of North Carolina at Wilmington	Wilmington	1947
		Wake Forest University	Winston-Salem	1834

Universities of the world (continued)

Country	*State*	*University*	*Location*	*Date founded*
United States	North Dakota	University of North Dakota	Grand Forks	1883
	Ohio	Bowling Green State University	Bowling Green	1910
		Case Western Reserve University	Cleveland	1826
		Cleveland State University	Cleveland	1964
		John Carroll University	University Heights	1886
		Kent State University	Kent	1910
		Miami University	Oxford	1809
		Oberlin College	Oberlin	1833
		Ohio State University	Columbus	1870
		Ohio University	Athens	1804
		University of Akron	Akron	1870
		University of Cincinnati	Cincinnati	1819
		University of Dayton	Dayton	1850
		University of Toledo	Toledo	1872
		Wright State University	Dayton	1964
		Xavier University	Cincinnati	1831
		Youngstown State University	Youngstown	1908
	Oklahoma	Central State University	Edmond	1890
		Oklahoma State University	Stillwater	1890
		Oral Roberts University	Tulsa	1963
		University of Oklahoma	Norman	1890
	Oregon	Oregon State University	Corvallis	1868
		Portland State University	Portland	1946
		University of Oregon	Eugene	1872
	Pennsylvania	Bryn Mawr College	Bryn Mawr	1885
		Bucknell University	Lewisburg	1846
		Carnegie Mellon University	Pittsburgh	1900
		Dickinson College	Carlisle	1773
		Drexel University	Philadelphia	1891
		Duquesne University	Pittsburgh	1878
		Haverford College	Haverford	1833
		La Salle University	Philadelphia	1863
		Lehigh University	Bethlehem	1865
		Moravian College	Bethlehem	1742
		Pennsylvania State University, University Park Campus	University Park	1855
		Swarthmore College	Swarthmore	1864
		Temple University	Philadelphia	1884
		Temple University, Ambler Campus	Ambler	1910
		University of Pittsburgh	Pittsburgh	1787
		University of Pittsburgh at Johnstown	Johnstown	1927
		Villanova University	Villanova	1842
		Washington and Jefferson College	Washington	1781
		West Chester University of Pennsylvania	West Chester	1871
	Rhode Island	Brown University	Providence	1764
		Rhode Island School of Design	Providence	1877
		University of Rhode Island	Kingston	1892
	South Carolina	The Citadel, The Military College of South Carolina	Charleston	1842
		Clemson University	Clemson	1889
		Converse College	Spartanburg	1889
		University of South Carolina	Columbia	1801
		University of South Carolina at Spartanburg	Spartanburg	1967
		University of South Carolina – Coastal Carolina College	Conway	1954
	Tennessee	East Tennessee State University	Johnson City	1911
		Memphis State University	Memphis	1912
		Middle Tennessee State University	Murfreesboro	1911
		University of Tennessee at Chattanooga	Chattanooga	1886
		University of Tennessee at Martin	Martin	1927
		University of Tennessee, Knoxville	Knoxville	1794
		Vanderbilt University	Nashville	1873
	Texas	Abilene Christian University	Abilene	1906
		Baylor University	Waco	1845
		Lamar University	Beaumont	1923

Country	State	University	Location	Date founded
		Rice University	Houston	1912
		Sam Houston State University	Huntsville	1879
		Southern Methodist University	Dallas	1911
		Southwest Texas State University	San Marcos	1899
		Stephen F Austin State University	Nacogdoches	1923
		Texas A&M University	College Station	1876
		Texas Technical University	Lubbock	1923
		Trinity University	San Antonio	1869
		University of Houston	Houston	1927
		University of Houston Clear Lake	Houston	1971
		University of Houston Downtown	Houston	1974
		University of North Texas	Denton	1890
		University of Texas at Arlington	Arlington	1895
		University of Texas at Austin	Austin	1883
		University of Texas at Dallas	Richardson	1969
		University of Texas at El Paso	El Paso	1913
		University of Texas at San Antonio	San Antonio	1969
		University of Texas at Tyler	Tyler	1972
		University of Texas – Pan American	Edinburg	1927
	Utah	Brigham Young University	Provo	1875
		University of Utah	Salt Lake City	1850
		Utah State University	Logan	1888
		Weber State College	Ogden	1889
	Vermont	University of Vermont	Burlington	1791
	Virginia	College of William and Mary	Williamsburg	1693
		George Mason University	Fairfax	1957
		Hampden-Sydney College	Hampden-Sydney	1776
		James Madison University	Harrisonburg	1908
		Liberty University	Lynchburg	1971
		Old Dominion University	Norfolk	1930
		University of Virginia	Charlottesville	1810
		Virginia Commonwealth University	Richmond	1838
		Virginia Polytechnic Institute and State University	Blacksburg	1872
		Washington and Lee University	Lexington	1749
	Washington	Gonzaga University	Spokane	1887
		University of Washington	Seattle	1861
		Washington State University	Pullman	1892
	West Virginia	Marshall University	Hungtinton	1837
		West Virginia University	Morgantown	1867
	Wisconsin	Marquette University	Milwaukee	1881
		University of Wisconsin – Eau Claire	Eau Claire	1916
		University of Wisconsin – Green Bay	Green Bay	1968
		University of Wisconsin – La Crosse	La Crosse	1909
		University of Wisconsin – Madison	Madison	1848
		University of Wisconsin – Milwaukee	Milwaukee	1956
		University of Wisconsin – Oshkosh	Oshkosh	1871
		University of Wisconsin – Parkside	Kenosha	1968
		University of Wisconsin – Platteville	Platteville	1866
		University of Wisconsin – River Falls	River Falls	1874
		University of Wisconsin – Stevens Point	Stevens Point	1894
		University of Wisconsin – Stout	Menomonie	1891
		University of Wisconsin – Whitewater	Whitewater	1868
	Wyoming	University of Wyoming	Laramie	1886

SPORTS AND GAMES

OLYMPIC GAMES

First modern Olympic games took place in 1896, founded by Frenchman Baron de Coubertin; held every four years; women first competed in 1900. First separate Winter Games celebration in 1924; beginning in 1994, Winter Games take place between Summer Games celebrations.

Venues

	Summer Games	*Winter Games*
1896	Athens, Greece	–
1900	Paris, France	–
1904	St Louis, USA	–
1908	London, UK	–
1912	Stockholm, Sweden	–
1920	Antwerp, Belgium	–
1924	Paris, France	Chamonix, France
1928	Amsterdam, Netherlands	St Moritz, Switzerland
1932	Los Angeles, USA	Lake Placid, NY, USA
1936	Berlin, Germany	Garmisch-Partenkirchen, Germany
1948	London, UK	St Moritz, Switzerland
1952	Helsinki, Finland	Oslo, Norway
1956	Melbourne, Australia	Cortina, Italy
1960	Rome, Italy	Squaw Valley, CA, USA
1964	Tokyo, Japan	Innsbruck, Austria
1968	Mexico City, Mexico	Grenoble, France
1972	Munich, West Germany	Sapporo, Japan
1976	Montreal, Canada	Innsbruck, Austria
1980	Moscow, USSR	Lake Placid, NY, USA
1984	Los Angeles, USA	Sarajevo, Yugoslavia
1988	Seoul, South Korea	Calgary, Canada
1992	Barcelona, Spain	Albertville, France
1994		Lillehammer, Norway
1996	Atlanta, USA	

Olympic games were also held in 1906 in Athens, Greece, to commemorate the 10th anniversary of the birth of the modern Games.

The 1956 equestrian events were held at Stockholm, Sweden, due to quarantine laws in Australia.

Leading medal winners (including 1992)

Summer Games		*Gold*	*Silver*	*Bronze*	*Total*
1	USA	783	594	512	1889
2	Germany[a]	343	357	362	1062
3	USSR	395	323	299	1017
	Unified Team (1992)	45	38	29	112
4	Great Britain	178	225	218	621
5	France	161	172	193	526
6	Sweden	132	146	173	451
7	Italy	153	126	132	411
8	Hungary	135	124	143	402
9	Finland	98	77	112	287

Winter Games		*Gold*	*Silver*	*Bronze*	*Total*
1	Germany[a]	75	72	64	211
2	USSR	79	57	59	195
	Unified Team (1992)	9	6	8	23
3	Norway	63	66	59	188
4	USA	47	51	36	134
5	Austria	34	45	40	119
6	Finland	36	44	37	117
7	Sweden	37	25	34	96
8	Switzerland	24	25	27	76
9	Canada	16	15	20	51

The USSR dissolved in 1991. The newly formed Unified Team, consisting of 12 of the former soviet republics, gained the most medals in the 1992 Summer Games and the second highest number of medals in the 1992 Winter Games.

[a]This figure includes East Germany's total (shown below) for the years 1968–88 when West and East Germany competed as two nations.

	Gold	Silver	Bronze	Total
Summer	153	129	127	409
Winter	39	36	35	110

COMMONWEALTH GAMES

First held as the British Empire Games in 1930; take place every four years and between Olympic celebrations; became the British Empire and Commonwealth Games in 1954; the current title adopted in 1970.

Venues

1930 Hamilton, Canada
1934 London, England
1938 Sydney, Australia
1950 Auckland, New Zealand
1954 Vancouver, Canada
1958 Cardiff, Wales
1962 Perth, Australia
1966 Kingston, Jamaica
1970 Edinburgh, Scotland
1974 Christchurch, New Zealand
1978 Edmonton, Canada
1982 Brisbane, Australia
1986 Edinburgh, Scotland
1990 Auckland, New Zealand
1994 Victoria, Canada

Leading medal winners (including 1990)

Nation		*Gold*	*Silver*	*Bronze*	*Total*
1	England	420	368	368	1156
2	Australia	397	374	382	1153
3	Canada	287	301	299	887
4	New Zealand	94	121	161	376
5	Scotland	56	74	109	239
6	South Africa	60	44	47	151
7	Wales	32	39	60	131
8	India	37	36	31	104
9	Kenya	35	24	33	92
10	Northern Ireland	15	20	34	69

ANGLING

World fresh water championship

First held in 1957; takes place annually.

Recent winners, individual

1979 Gérard Heulard (France)
1980 Wolf-Rüdiger Kremkus (W Germany)
1981 David Thomas (England)
1982 Kevin Ashurst (England)
1983 Wolf-Rüdiger Kremkus (W Germany)
1984 Bobby Smithers (Ireland)
1985 David Roper (England)
1986 Lud Wever (Netherlands)
1987 Clive Branson (Wales)
1988 Jean-Pierre Fouquet (France)
1989 Tom Pickering (England)
1990 Bob Nudd (England)
1991 Bob Nudd (England)
1992 David Wesson (Australia)

Recent winners, team

1979 France
1980 W Germany
1981 France
1982 Netherlands
1983 Belgium
1984 Luxembourg
1985 England
1986 Italy
1987 England
1988 England
1989 Wales
1990 France
1991 England
1992 Italy

Most wins: Individual (3), Robert Tesse (France) 1959–60, 1965. Team (12), France, 1959, 1963–4, 1966, 1968, 1972, 1974–5, 1978–9, 1981, 1990.

World fly fishing championship

First held in 1981; takes place annually

Winners, individual

1981 C. Wittkamp (Netherlands)
1982 Viktor Diez y Diez (Spain)
1983 Segismondo Fernandez (Spain)
1984 Tony Pawson (England)
1985 Leslaw Frasik (Poland)
1986 Slivoj Svoboda (Czechoslovakia)
1987 Brian Leadbetter (England)
1988 John Pawson (England)
1989 Wladyslaw Trzebuinia (Poland)
1990 Franciszek Szajnik (Poland)
1991 Brian Leadbetter (England)
1992 Pierluigi Cocito (Italy)

Winners, team

1981 Netherlands
1982 Italy
1983 Italy
1984 Italy
1985 Poland
1986 Italy
1987 England
1988 England
1989 Poland
1990 Czechoslovakia
1991 New Zealand
1992 Italy

Most wins: Individual (2), Brian Leadbetter (England) 1987, 1991. Team (5), Italy, 1982–84, 1986, 1992.

ARCHERY

World championships

First held in 1931; took place annually until 1959; since then, every two years.

Recent winners, individual (men)

1969 Hardy Ward (USA)
1971 John Williams (USA)
1973 Vikto Sidoruk (USSR)
1975 Darrell Pace (USA)
1977 Richard McKinney (USA)
1979 Darrell Pace (USA)
1981 Kysti Laasonen (Finland)
1983 Richard McKinney (USA)
1985 Richard McKinney (USA)
1987 Vladimir Yesheyev (USSR)
1989 Stanislav Zabrodsky (USSR)
1991 Simon Fairweather (Australia)

Recent winners, team (men)

1969 USA
1971 USA
1973 USA
1975 USA
1977 USA
1979 USA
1981 USA
1983 USA
1985 South Korea
1987 South Korea
1989 USSR
1991 South Korea

Most wins: Individual (4), Hans Deutgen (Sweden) 1947–50. Team (14), USA, 1957–83.

Recent winners, individual (women)

1969 Dorothy Lidstone (Canada)
1971 Emma Gapchenko (USSR)
1973 Linda Myers (USA)
1975 Zebiniso Rustamova (USSR)
1977 Luann Ryon (USA)
1979 Kim Jin-ho (South Korea)
1981 Natalia Butuzova (USSR)
1983 Kim Jin-ho (South Korea)
1985 Irina Soldatova (USSR)
1987 Ma Xiaojun (China)
1989 Kim Soo-nyung (South Korea)
1991 Kim Soo-nyung (South Korea)

Recent winners, team (women)

1969 USSR
1971 Poland
1973 USSR
1975 USSR
1977 USA
1979 South Korea
1981 USSR
1983 South Korea
1985 USSR
1987 USSR
1989 South Korea
1991 South Korea

Most wins: Individual (7), Janina Kurkowska (Poland) 1931–4, 1936, 1939, 1947. Team (8), USA, 1952, 1957–9, 1961, 1963, 1965, 1977.

Olympic games

Gold medal winners, 1992

Individual (men)
Sebastien Flute (France)

Team (men)
Spain

Individual (women)
Cho Youn Jeong (South Korea)

Team (women)
South Korea

ATHLETICS

Performance times are given in seconds, or minutes:seconds, or hours:minutes:seconds. Distances are given in metres. Performances in the decathlon, pentathlon and heptathlon are given in points.

World championships

First held in Helsinki, Finland in 1983, then in Rome, Italy in 1987, and Tokyo, Japan in 1991.

Event winners (men)

100 m
1983 Carl Lewis (USA) 10.07
1987 Carl Lewis (USA) 9.93[a]
1991 Carl Lewis (USA) 9.86

200 m
1983 Calvin Smith (USA) 20.14
1987 Calvin Smith (USA) 20.16
1991 Michael Johnson (USA) 20.01

400 m
1983 Bert Cameron (Jamaica) 45.05
1987 Thomas Schlönlebe (E Germany) 44.33
1991 Antonio Pettigrew (USA) 44.57

800 m
1983 Willi Wülbeck (W Germany) 1:43.65
1987 Billy Konchellah (Kenya) 1:43.06
1991 Billy Konchellah (Kenya) 1:43.99

1500 m
1983 Steve Cram (Great Britain) 3:41.59
1987 Abdi Bile (Somalia) 3:36.80
1991 Noureddine Morceli (Algeria) 3:32.84

5000 m
1983 Eamonn Coghlan (Ireland) 13:28.53
1987 Saïd Aouita (Morocco) 13:26.44
1991 Yobes Ondieki (Kenya) 13:14.45

10000 m
1983 Alberto Cova (Italy) 28:01.04
1987 Paul Kipkoech (Kenya) 27:38.63
1991 Moses Tanui (Kenya) 27:38.74

Marathon
1983 Rob de Castella (Australia) 2:10:03
1987 Douglas Wakiihuri (Kenya) 2:11:48
1991 Hiromi Taniguchi (Japan) 2:14:57

3000 m steeplechase
1983 Patriz Ilg (W Germany) 8:15.06
1987 Francesco Panetta (Italy) 8:08.57
1991 Moses Kiptanui (Kenya) 8:12.59

110 m hurdles
1983 Greg Foster (USA) 13:42
1987 Greg Foster (USA) 13:21
1991 Greg Foster (USA) 13:06

400 m hurdles
1983 Edwin Moses (USA) 47.50
1987 Edwin Moses (USA) 47:46
1991 Samuel Matete (Zambia) 47:64

High jump
1983 Gennadiy Avdeyenko (USSR) 2.32
1987 Patrik Sjöberg (Sweden) 2.38
1991 Charles Austin (USA) 2.38

Pole vault
1983 Sergey Bubka (USSR) 5.70
1987 Sergey Bubka (USSR) 5.85
1991 Sergey Bubka (USSR) 5.92

Long jump
1983 Carl Lewis (USA) 8.55
1987 Carl Lewis (USA) 8.67
1991 Mike Powell (USA) 8.95

Triple jump
1983 Zdzislaw Hoffmann (Poland) 17.42
1987 Khristo Markov (Bulgaria) 17.92
1991 Kenny Harrison (USA) 17.78

Shot
1983 Edward Sarul (Poland) 21.39
1987 Werner Günthör (Switzerland) 22.23
1991 Werner Günthör (Switzerland) 21.67

Discus
1983 Imrich Bugár (Czechoslovakia) 67.72
1987 Jürgen Schult (E Germany) 68.74
1991 Lars Riedel (Germany) 66.20

Hammer
1983 Sergey Litvinov (USSR) 82.68
1987 Sergey Litvinov (USSR) 83.06
1991 Yuriy Sedykh (USSR0 81.70

Javelin
1983 Detlef Michel (GDR) 89.48[b] (E Germany)
1987 Seppo Räty (Finland) 83.54
1991 Kimmo Kinnunen (Finland) 90.82

Decathlon
1983 Daley Thompson (Great Britain) 8666
1987 Torsten Voss (E Germany) 8680
1991 Dan O'Brien (USA) 8812

4 × 100 m relay
1983 USA 37.86
1987 USA 37.90
1991 USA 37.50

4 × 400 m relay
1983 USSR 3:00.79
1987 USA 2:57.29
1991 Great Britain 2:57.53

20 km walk
1983 Ernesto Canto (Mexico) 1:20:49
1987 Maurizio Damilano (Italy) 1:20:45
1991 Maurizio Damilano (Italy) 1:19:37

50 km walk
1983 Ronald Weigel (E Germany) 3:43:08
1987 Hartwig Gauder (E Germany) 3:40:53
1991 Aleksandr Potashov (USSR) 3:53:09

[a]Ben Johnson (Canada) stripped of this title following IAAF ruling on illegal drug-taking.
[b]Old specification javelin

Athletics, world championships (continued)

Event winners (women)

100 m
1983 Marlies Göhr (E Germany) 10.97
1987 Silke Gladisch (E Germany) 10.90
1991 Katrin Krabbe (Germany) 10.99

200 m
1983 Marita Koch (E Germany) 22.13
1987 Silke Gladisch (E Germany) 21.74
1991 Katrin Krabbe (Germany) 22.09

400 m
1983 Jarmila Kratochvilová (Czechoslovakia) 47.99
1987 Olga Bryzgina (USSR) 49.38
1991 Marie-José Pérec (France) 49.13

800 m
1983 Jarmila Kratochvílová (Czechoslovakia) 1:54.68
1987 Sigrun Wodars (E Germany) 1:55.26
1991 Lilia Nurutdinova (USSR) 1:57.50

1 500 m
1983 Mary Decker (USA) 4:00.90
1987 Tatyana Samolenko (USSR) 3:58.56
1991 Hassiba Boulmerka (Algeria) 4:02.21

3 000 m
1983 Mary Decker (USA) 8:34.62
1987 Tatyana Samolenko (USSR) 8:38.73
1991 Tatyana Dorovskikh (USSR) 8:35.82

10 000 m
1983 *not held*
1987 Ingrid Kristiansen (Norway) 31:05.85
1991 Liz McColgan (Great Britain) 31:14.31

Marathon
1983 Grete Waitz (Norway) 2:28:09
1987 Rosa Mota (Portugal) 2:25:17
1991 Wanda Panfil (Poland) 2:29:53

100 m hurdles
1983 Bettine Jahn (E Germany) 12.35
1987 Ginka Zagorcheva (Bulgaria) 12.34
1991 Lyudmila Narozhilenko (USSR) 12.59

400 m hurdles
1983 Yekaterina Fesenko (USSR) 54.14
1987 Sabine Busch (E Germany) 53.62
1991 Tatyana Ledovskaya (USSR) 53.11

High jump
1983 Tamara Bykova (USSR) 2.01
1987 Stefka Kostadinova (Bulgaria) 2.09
1991 Heike Henkel (Germany) 2.05

Long jump
1983 Heike Daute (E Germany) 7.27[a]
1987 Jackie Joyner-Kersee (USA) 7.36
1991 Jackie Joyner -Kersee (USA) 7.32

Shot
1983 Helena Fibingerová (Czechoslovakia) 21.05
1987 Natalya Lisovskaya (USSAR) 21.24
1991 Huang Zhihong (China) 20.83

Discus
1983 Martina Opitz (E Germany) 68.94
1987 Martina Hellmann (E Germany) 71.62
1991 Tsvetanka Khristova (Bulgaria) 71.02

Javelin
1983 Tiina Lillak (Finland) 70.82
1987 Fatima Whitbread (Great Britain) 76.64
1991 Xu Demei (China) 68.78

Heptathlon
1983 Ramona Neubert (E Germany) 6770
1987 Jackie Joyner-Kersee (USA) 7128
1991 Sabine Braun (Germany) 6672

10 km walk
1987 Irina Strakhova (USSR) 44:12
1991 Alina Ivanova (USSR) 42:57

4 × 100 m relay
1983 E Germany 41.76
1987 USA 41.58
1991 Jamaica 41.94

4 × 400 m relay
1983 E Germany 3:19.73
1987 E Germany 3:18.63
1991 USSR 3:18.43

[a]wind-assisted

Olympic games

Event winners (men)

100 m
1896 Thomas Burke (USA) 12.0
1900 Francis Jarvis (USA) 11.0
1904 Archie Hahn (USA) 11.0
1906 Archie Hahn (USA) 11.2
1908 Reginald Walker (S Africa) 10.8
1912 Ralph Craig (USA) 10.8
1920 Charles Paddock (USA) 10.8
1924 Harold Abrahams (Great Britain) 10.6
1928 Percy Williams (Canada) 10.8
1932 Eddie Tolan (USA) 10.3
1936 Jesse Owens (USA) 10.3
1948 Harrison Dillard (USA) 10.3
1952 Lindy Remigino (USA) 10.4
1956 Bobby Morrow (USA) 10.5
1960 Armin Hary (W Germany) 10.2
1964 Bob Hayes (USA) 10.06
1968 James Hines (USA) 9.95
1972 Valeriy Borzov (USSR) 10.14
1976 Hasely Crawford (Trinidad) 10.06
1980 Allan Wells (Great Britain) 10.25
1984 Carl Lewis (USA) 9.99
1988 Carl Lewis (USA) 9.92
1992 Linford Christie (Great Britain) 9.96

200 m
1900 John Walter Tewksbury (USA) 22.2
1904 Archie Hahn (USA) 21.6
1908 Robert Kerr (Canada) 22.6
1912 Ralph Craig (USA) 21.7
1920 Allen Woodring (USA) 22.0
1924 Jackson Scholz (USA) 21.6
1928 Percy Williams (Canada) 21.8
1932 Eddie Tolan (USA) 21.2
1936 Jesse Owens (USA) 20.7
1948 Melvin Patton (USA) 21.1
1952 Andrew Stanfield (USA) 20.7
1956 Bobby Morrow (USA) 20.5
1960 Livio Berruti (Italy) 20.6

1964 Henry Carr (USA) 20.36
1968 Tommie Smith (USA) 1983
1972 Valeriy Borzov (USSR) 20.00
1976 Donald Quarrie (Jamaica) 20.3
1980 Pietro Mennea (Italy) 20.19
1984 Carl Lewis (USA) 19.80
1988 Joe DeLoach (USA) 19.75
1992 Michael Marsh (USA) 20.01

400 m
1896 Thomas Burke (USA) 54.2
1900 Maxey Long (USA) 49.4
1904 Harry Hillman (USA) 49.2
1906 Paul Pilgrim (USA) 53.2
1908 Wyndham Halswelle (Great Britain) 50.0
1912 Charles Reidpath (USA) 48.2
1920 Bevil Rudd (S Africa) 49.6
1924 Eric Liddell (Great Britain) 47.6
1928 Ray Barbuti (USA) 47.8
1932 Bill Carr (USA) 46.28
1936 Archie Williams (USA) 46.66
1948 Arthur Wint (Jamaica) 46.2
1952 George Rhoden (Jamaica) 46.09
1956 Charles Jenkins (USA) 46.86
1960 Otis Davis (USA) 45.07
1964 Michael Larrabee (USA) 45.15
1968 Lee Evans (USA) 43.86
1972 Vincent Matthews (USA) 44.66
1976 Alberto Juantoreno (Cuba) 44.26
1980 Viktor Markin (USSR) 44.60
1984 Alonzo Babers (USA) 44.27
1988 Steve Lewis (USA) 43.87
1992 Quincy Watts (USA) 43.50

800 m
1896 Edwin Flack (Australia) 2:11.0
1900 Alfred Tycoe (Great Britain) 2:01.2
1904 James Lightbody (USA) 1:56.0
1906 Paul Pilgrim (USA) 2:01.5
1908 Mel Sheppard (USA) 1:52.8
1912 James Meredith (USA) 1:51.9
1920 Albert Hill (Great Britain) 1:53.4
1924 Douglas Lowe (Great Britain) 1:52.4
1928 Douglas Lowe (Great Britain) 1:51.8
1932 Tom Hampson (Great Britain) 1:49.70
1936 John Woodruff (USA) 1:52.9
1948 Malvin Whitfield (USA) 1:49.2
1952 Malvin Whitfield (USA) 1:49.34
1956 Thomas Courtney (USA) 1:47.75
1960 Peter Snell (New Zealand) 1:46.48
1964 Peter Snell (New Zealand) 1:45.1
1968 Ralph Doubell (Australia) 1:44.40
1972 David Wottle (USA) 1:45.86
1976 Alberto Juantorena (Cuba) 1:43.50
1980 Steven Ovett (Great Britain) 1:45.40
1984 Joaquim Cruz (Brazil) 1:43.00
1988 Paul Ereng (Kenya) 1:43.45
1992 William Tanui (Kenya) 1:43.66

1500 m
1896 Edwin Flack (Australia) 4:33.2
1900 Charles Bennett (Great Britain) 4:06.2
1904 James Lightbody (USA) 4:05.4
1906 James Lightbody (USA) 4:12.0
1908 Mel Sheppard (USA) 4:03.4
1912 Arnold Jackson (Great Britain) 3:56.8
1920 Albert Hill (Great Britain) 4:01.8
1924 Paavo Nurmi (Finland) 3:53.6
1928 Harri Larva (Finland) 3:53.2
1932 Luigi Beccali (Italy) 3:51.20
1936 Jack Lovelock (New Zealand) 3:47.8
1948 Henry Eriksson (Sweden) 3:49.8
1952 Josef Barthel (Luxembourg) 3:45.28
1956 Ron Delany (Ireland) 3:41.49
1960 Herbert Elliott (Australia) 3:35.6
1964 Peter Snell (New Zealand) 3:38.1
1968 Kipchoge Keino (Kenya) 3:34.91
1972 Pekkha Vasala (Finland) 3:36.33
1976 John Walker (New Zealand) 3:39.17
1980 Sebastian Coe (Great Britain) 3:38.40
1984 Sebastian Coe (Great Britain) 3:32.53
1988 Peter Rono (Kenya) 3:35.96
1992 Fermin Cacho (Spain) 3:40.12

5000 m
1912 Hannes Kolehmainen (Finland) 14.36.6
1920 Joseph Guillemot (France) 14:55.6
1924 Paavo Nurmi (Finland) 14.31.2
1928 Ville Ritola (Finland) 14:38.0
1932 Lauri Lehtinen (Finland) 14:29.91
1936 Gunnar Höckert (Finland) 14:22.2
1948 Gaston Reiff (Belgium) 14:17.6
1952 Emil Zátopek (Czechoslovakia) 14:06.72
1956 Vladimir Kuts (USSR) 13:39.86
1960 Murray Halberg (New Zealand) 13:43.4
1964 Robert Schul (USA) 13:48.8
1968 Mohamed Gammoudi (Tunisia) 14:05.0
1972 Lasse Viren (Finland) 13:26.42
1976 Lasse Viren (Finland) 13:24.76
1980 Miruts Yifter (Ethiopia) 13:20.91
1984 Saïd Aouita (Morocco) 13:05.59
1988 John Ngugi (Kenya) 13:11.70
1992 Dieter Baumann (Germany) 13:12.52

10 000 m
1912 Hannes Kolehmainen (Finland) 31:20.8
1920 Paavo Nurmi (Finland) 31:45.8
1924 Ville Ritola (Finland) 30:23.1
1928 Paavo Nurmi (Finland) 30:18.8
1932 Janusz Kusocinski (Poland) 30:11.4
1936 Ilmari Salminen (Finland) 30:15.4
1948 Emil Zátopek (Czechoslovakia) 29:59.6
1952 Emil Zátopek (Czechoslovakia) 29:17.0
1956 Vladimir Kuts (USSR) 28:45.60
1960 Pyotr Bolotnikov (USSR) 28:32.18
1964 William Mills (USA) 28:24.4
1968 Naftali Temu (Kenya) 29:27.45
1972 Lasse Viren (Finland) 27:38.35
1976 Lasse Viren (Finland) 27:40.38
1980 Miruts Yifter (Ethiopia) 27:42.69
1984 Alberto Cova (Italy) 27:47.54
1988 Brahim Boutayeb (Morocco) 27:21.46
1992 Khalid Skah (Morocco) 27:46.70

Marathon*
1896 Spyridon Louis (Greece) 2:58:50.0 *(40km)*
1900 Michel Théato (France) 2:59:45.0 *(40.26km)*
1904 Thomas Hicks (USA) 3:28:35.0 *(40km)*
1906 William Sherring (Canada) 2:51:23.6 *(41.86km)*
1908 John Hayes (USA) 2:55:18.4
1912 Kenneth McArthur (S Africa) 2:36:54.8 *(40.2km)*
1920 Hannes Kolehmainen (Finland) 2:32:35.8 *(42.75km)*
1924 Albin Stenroos (Finland) 2:41:22.6
1928 Mohamed Boughéra El Ouafi (France) 2:32:57.0
1932 Juan Carlos Zabala (Argentina) 2:31:36.0
1936 Kitei Son (Japan) 2:29:19.2[a]
1948 Delfo Cabrera (Argentina) 2:34:51.6

Athletics, Olympic games (continued)

1952 Emil Zátopek (Czechoslovakia) 2:23:03.2
1956 Alain Mimoun (France) 2:25:00.0
1960 Abebe Bikila (Ethiopia) 2:15:16.2
1964 Abebe Bikila (Ethiopia) 2:12:11.2
1968 Mamo Wolde (Ethiopia) 2:20:26.4
1972 Frank Shorter (USA) 2:12:19.8
1976 Waldemar Cierpinski (E Germany) 2:09:55
1980 Waldemar Cierpinski (E Germany) 2:11:03
1984 Carlos Lopes (Portugal) 2:09:21
1988 Gelindo Bordin (Italy) 2:10:32
1992 Hwang Young-jo (S Korea) 2:13:23

*Unless shown as otherwise above, the Marathon is run over a distance of 42km 195m/26mi 385yd.

110 m hurdles

1896 Thomas Curtis (USA) 17.6
1900 Alvin Kraenzlein (USA) 15.4
1904 Fred Schule (USA) 16.0
1906 Robert Leavitt (USA) 16.2
1908 Forrest Smithson (USA) 15.0
1912 Fred Kelly (USA) 15.1
1920 Earl Thomson (Canada) 14.8
1924 Daniel Kinsey (USA) 15.0
1928 Sydney Atkinson (S Africa) 14.8
1932 George Saling (USA) 14.57
1936 Forrest Towns (USA) 14.2
1948 William Porter (USA) 13.9
1952 Harrison Dillard (USA) 13.91
1956 Lee Calhoun (USA) 13.70
1960 Lee Calhoun (USA) 13.98
1964 Hayes Jones (USA) 13.67
1968 Willie Davenport (USA) 13.33
1972 Rodney Milburn (USA) 13.24
1976 Guy Drut (France) 13.30
1980 Thomas Munkelt (E Germany) 13.39
1984 Roger Kingdom (USA) 13.20
1988 Roger Kingdom (USA) 12.98
1992 Mark McKoy (Canada) 13.12

400 m hurdles

1900 Walter Tewksbury (USA) 57.6
1904 Harry Hillman (USA) 53.0
1908 Charles Bacon (USA) 55.0
1920 Frank Loomis (USA) 54.0
1924 Morgan Taylor (USA) 52.6
1928 Lord Burghley (Great Britain) 53.4
1932 Robert Tisdall (Ireland) 51.67
1936 Glenn Hardin (USA) 52.4
1948 Roy Cochran (USA) 51.1
1952 Charles Moore (USA) 51.06
1956 Glenn Davis (USA) 50.29
1960 Glenn Davis (USA) 49.51
1964 Rex Cawley (USA) 49.69
1968 David Hemery (Great Britain) 48.12
1972 John Akii-Bua (Uganda) 47.82
1976 Edwin Moses (USA) 47.63
1980 Volker Beck (E Germany) 48.70
1984 Edwin Moses (USA) 47.75
1988 Andre Phillips (USA) 47.19
1992 Kevin Young (USA) 46.78

Steeplechase*

1900 George Orton (Canada) 7:34.4 *(2500m)*
1900 John Rimmer (Great Britain) 12:58.4 *(4000m)*
1904 James Lightbody (USA) 7:39.6 *(2590m)*
1908 Arthur Russell (Great Britain) 10:47.8 *(3200m)*
1920 Percy Hodge (Great Britain) 10:00.4
1924 Ville Ritola (Finland) 9:33.6
1928 Toivo Loukola (Finland) 9:21.8
1932 Volmari Iso-Hollo (Finland) 10:33.4**
1936 Volmari Iso-Hollo (Finland) 9:03.8
1948 Tore Sjöstrand (Sweden) 9:04.6
1952 Horace Ashenfelter (USA) 8:45.68
1956 Christopher Brasher (Great Britain) 8:41.35
1960 Zdzislaw Kryszkowiak (Poland) 8:34.31
1964 Gaston Roelants (Belgium) 8:30.8
1968 Amos Biwott (Kenya) 8:51.0
1972 Kipchoge Keino (Kenya) 8:23.64
1976 Anders Gärderud (Sweden) 8:08.02
1980 Bronislaw Malinowski (Poland) 8:09.70
1984 Julius Korir (Kenya) 8:11.80
1988 Julius Kariuki (Kenya) 8:05.51
1992 Matthew Birir (Kenya) 8:08.94

*Unless shown otherwise above, distance is 3000m.
**Athletes ran an extra lap in error – distance 3460m.

High jump

1896 Ellery Clark (USA) 1.81
1900 Irving Baxter (USA) 1.90
1904 Samuel Jones (USA) 1.80
1906 Con Leahy (Ireland)[b] 1.77
1908 Harry Porter (USA) 1.90
1912 Alma Richards (USA) 1.93
1920 Richard Landon (USA) 1.94
1924 Harold Osborn (USA) 1.98
1928 Robert King (USA) 1.94
1932 Duncan McNaughton (Canada) 1.97
1936 Cornelius Johnson (USA) 2.03
1948 John Winter (Austrialia) 1.98
1952 Walter Davis (USA) 2.04
1956 Charles Dumas (USA) 2.12
1960 Robert Shavlakadze (USSR) 2.16
1964 Valeriy Brumel (USSR) 2.18
1968 Dick Fosbury (USA) 2.24
1972 Jüri Tamak (USSR) 2.23
1976 Jacek Wszola (Poland) 2.25
1980 Gerd Wessig (E Germany) 2.36
1984 Dietmar Mögenburg (W Germany) 2.35
1988 Gennadiy Avdeyenko (USSR) 2.38
1992 Javier Sotomayor (Cuba) 2.34

Pole vault

1896 William Hoyt (USA) 3.30
1900 Irving Baxter (USA) 3.30
1904 Charles Dvorak (USA) 3.50
1906 Fernand Gonder (France) 3.40
1908 Edward Cooke & Alfred Gilbert (USA) 3.71
1912 Harry Babock (USA) 3.95
1920 Frank Foss (USA) 4.09
1924 Lee Barnes (USA) 3.95
1928 Sabin Carr (USA) 4.20
1932 Bill Miller (USA) 4.31
1936 Earle Meadows (USA) 4.35
1948 Guinn Smith (USA) 4.30
1952 Robert Richards (USA) 4.55
1956 Robert Richards (USA) 4.56
1960 Donald Bragg (USA) 4.70
1964 Frederick Hansen (USA) 5.10
1968 Bob Seagren (USA) 5.40
1972 Wolfgang Nordwig (E Germany) 5.50
1976 Tadeusz Slusarski (Poland) 5.50
1980 Wladyslaw Kozakiewicz (Poland) 5.78
1984 Pierre Quinon (France) 5.75
1988 Sergey Bubka (USSR) 5.90
1992 Maksim Tarassov (Unified Team) 5.80

Long jump
1896 Ellery Clark (USA) 6.35
1900 Alvin Kraenzlein (USA) 7.18
1904 Myer Prinstein (USA) 7.34
1906 Myer Prinstein (USA) 7.20
1908 Francis Irons (USA) 7.48
1912 Albert Gutterson (USA) 7.60
1920 William Pettersson (Sweden) 7.15
1924 William De Hart Hubbard (USA) 7.44
1928 Edward Hamm (USA) 7.73
1932 Edward Gordon (USA) 7.64
1936 Jesse Owens (USA) 8.06
1948 William Steele (USA) 7.82
1952 Jerome Biffle (USA) 7.57
1956 Gregory Bell (USA) 7.83
1960 Ralph Boston (USA) 8.12
1964 Lynn Davies (Great Britain) 8.07
1968 Bob Beamon (USA) 8.90
1972 Randy Williams (USA) 8.24
1976 Arnie Robinson (USA) 8.35
1980 Lutz Dombrowski (E Germany) 8.54
1984 Carl Lewis (USA) 8.54
1988 Carl Lewis (USA) 8.72
1992 Carl Lewis (USA) 8.67

Triple jump
1896 James Connolly (USA) 13.71
1900 Myer Prinstein (USA) 14.47
1904 Myer Prinstein (USA) 14.35
1906 Peter O'Connor (Ireland)[b] 14.07
1908 Tim Ahearne (Ireland)[b] 14.91
1912 Gustaf Lindblom (Sweden) 14.76
1920 Viho Tuulos (Finland) 14.50
1924 Anthony Winter (Australia) 15.52
1928 Mikio Oda (Japan) 15.21
1932 Chuhei Nambu (Japan) 15.72
1936 Naoto Tajima (Japan) 16.00
1948 Arne Åhman (Sweden) 15.40
1952 Adhemar Ferreira da Silva (Brazil) 16.22
1956 Adhemar Ferreira da Silva (Brazil) 16.35
1960 Jozef Schmidt (Poland) 16.81
1964 Jozef Schmidt (Poland) 16.85
1968 Viktor Saneyev (USSR) 17.39
1972 Viktor Saneyev (USSR) 17.35
1976 Viktor Saneyev (USSR) 17.29
1980 Jaak Uudmäe (USSR) 17.35
1984 Al Joyner (USA) 17.26
1988 Khristo Markov (Bulgaria) 17.61
1992 Mike Conley (USA) 18.17[c]

Shot
1896 Robert Garrett (USA) 11.22
1900 Richard Sheldon (USA) 14.10
1904 Ralph Rose (USA) 14.80
1906 Martin Sheridan (USA) 12.32
1908 Ralph Rose (USA) 14.21
1912 Patrick McDonald (USA) 15.34
1920 Ville Pörhölä (Finland) 14.81
1924 Clarence Houser (USA) 14.99
1928 John Kuck (USA) 15.87
1932 Leo Sexton (USA) 16.00
1936 Hans Woellke (Germany) 16.20
1948 Wilbur Thompson (USA) 17.12
1952 Parry O'Brien (USA) 17.41
1956 Parry O'Brien (USA) 18.57
1960 William Nieder (USA) 19.68
1964 Dallas Long (USA) 20.33
1968 Randy Matson (USA) 20.54
1972 Wladyslaw Komar (Poland) 21.18
1976 Udo Beyer (E Germany) 21.05
19890 Vladimir Kiselyov (USSR) 21.35
1984 Alessandro Andrei (Italy) 21.26
1988 Ulf Timmermann (E Germany) 22.47
1992 Mike Stulce (USA) 21.70

Discus
1896 Robert Garrett (USA) 29.15
1900 Rudolf Bauer (Hungary) 36.04
1904 Martin Sheridan (USA) 39.28
1906 Martin Sheridan (USA) 41.46
1904 Martin Sheridan (USA) 40.89
1912 Armas Taipale (Finland) 45.21
1920 Elmer Niklander (Finland) 44.68
1924 Clarence Houser (USA) 46.15
1928 Clarence Houser (USA) 47.32
1932 John Anderson (USA) 49.49
1936 Ken Carpenter (USA) 50.48
1948 Adolfo Consolini (Italy) 52.78
1952 Sim Iness (USA) 55.03
1956 Al Oerter (USA) 56.36
1960 Al Oerter (USA) 59.18
1964 Al Oerter (USA) 61.00
1968 Al Oerter (USA) 64.78
1972 Ludvik Danek (Czechloslovakia) 64.40
1976 Mac Wilkins (USA) 67.50
1980 Viktor Rashchupkin (USSR) 66.64
1984 Rolf Danneberg (W Germany) 66.60
1988 Jürgen Schult (E Germany) 68.82
1992 Romas Ubartas (Lithuania) 65.12

Hammer
1900 John Flanagan (USA) 49.73
1904 John Flanagan (USA) 51.23
1908 John Flanagan (USA) 51.92
1912 Matt McGrath (USA) 54.74
1920 Patrick Ryan (USA) 52.87
1924 Fred Tootell (USA) 53.29
1928 Patrick O'Callaghan (Ireland) 51.39
1932 Patrick O'Callaghan (Ireland) 53.92
1936 Karl Hein (Germany) 56.49
1948 Imre Németh (Hungary) 56.07
1952 József Csermak (Hungary) 60.34
1956 Harold Connolly (USA) 63.19
1960 Vasiliy Rudenkov (USSR) 67.10
1964 Romuald Klim (USSR) 69.74
1968 Gyula Zsivótzky (Hungary) 73.36
1972 Anatoliy Bondarchuk (USSR) 75.50
1976 Yuriy Sedykh (USSR) 77.52
1980 Yuriy Sedykh (USSR) 81.80
1984 Juha Tiainen (Finland) 78.08
1988 Sergey Litvinov (USSR) 84.80
1992 Andrey Abduyvaliyev (Unified Team) 82.54

Javelin*
1906 Erik Lemming (Sweden) 53.90
1908 Erik Lemming (Sweden) 54.82
1912 Erik Lemming (Sweden) 60.64
1920 Jonni Myyrä (Finland) 65.78
1924 Jonni Myyrä (Finland) 62.96
1928 Erik Lundkvist (Sweden) 66.60
1932 Matti Järvinen (Finland) 72.71
1936 Gerhard Stöck (Germany) 71.84
1948 Tapio Rautavaara (Finland) 69.77
1952 Cyrus Young (USA) 73.78
1956 Egil Danielsen (Norway) 85.71
1960 Viktor Tsibulenko (USSR) 84.64
1964 Pauli Nevala (Finland) 82.66
1968 Janis Lusis (USSR) 90.10

Athletics, Olympic games (continued)

1972 Klaus Wolfermann (W Germany) 90.48
1976 Miklós Németh (Hungary) 94.58
1980 Dainis Kula (USSR) 91.20
1984 Arto Harkönen (Finland) 86.76
1988 Tápio Korjus (Finland) 84.28
1992 Jan Zelezny (Czechoslovakia) 89.66

• New javelin specification introduced in 1984.

Decathlon*
1904 Thomas Kiely (Ireland) 6036
1912 Jim Thorpe (USA) 6564
1920 Helge Lövland (Norway) 5804
1924 Harold Osborn (USA) 6476
1928 Paavo Yrjölä (Finland) 6587
1932 James Bausch (USA) 6735
1936 Glenn Morris (USA) 7254
1948 Robert Mathias (USA) 6628
1952 Robert Mathias (USA) 7592
1956 Milton Campbell (USA) 7614
1960 Rafer Johnson (USA) 7926
1964 Willi Holdorf (W Germany) 7794
1968 Bill Toomey (USA) 8144
1972 Nikolay Avilov (USSR) 8466
1976 Bruce Jenner (USA) 8634
1980 Daley Thompson (Great Britain) 8522
1984 Daley Thompson (Great Britain) 8847
1988 Christian Schenk (E Germany) 8488
1992 Robert Zmelik (Czechoslovakia) 8611

*All points given here are rescored using 1984 tables

20 000 m walk
1956 Leonid Spirin (USSR) 1:31:27.4
1960 Vladimir Golubnichiy (USSR) 1:34:07.2
1964 Kenneth Matthews (Great Britain) 1:29:34.0
1968 Vladimir Golubnichiy (USSR) 1:33:58.4
1972 Peter Frenkel (E Germany) 1:26:42.4
1976 Daniel Bautista (Mexico) 1:24:40.6
1980 Maurizio Damilano (Italy) 1:23:35.5
1984 Ernesto Canto (Mexico) 1:23:13
1988 Jozef Pribilinec (Czechoslovakia) 1:19:57
1992 Daniel Plaza (Spain) 1:21:45

50 000 m walk
1932 Thomas Green (Great Britain) 4:50:10.0
1936 Harold Whitlock (Great Britain) 4:30:41.1
1948 John Ljunggren (Sweden) 4:41:52.0
1952 Giuseppe Dordoni (Italy) 4:28:07.8
1956 Norman Read (New Zealand) 4:30:42.8
1960 Don Thompson (Great Britain) 4:25:30.0
1964 Abdon Pamich (Italy) 4:11:12.4
1968 Christophe Höhne (E Germany) 4:20:13.6
1972 Bernd Kannenberg (E Germany) 3:56:11.6
1980 Hartwig Gauder (E Germany) 3:49:24
1984 Raúl Gonzales (Mexico) 3:47:26
1988 Vyacheslav Ivanenko (USSR) 3:38:29
1992 Andrei Perlov (Unified Team) 3:50:13

4 × 100 m relay
1912 Great Britain 42.4
1920 USA 42.2
1924 USA 41.0
1928 USA 41.0
1932 USA 40.1
1936 USA 39.8
1948 USA 40.6
1952 USA 40.26
1956 USA 39.59
1960 W Germany 39.66
1964 USA 39.06
1968 USA 38.23
1972 USA 38.19
1976 USA 38.83
1980 USSR 38.26
1984 USA 37.83
1988 USSR 38.19
1992 USA 37.40

4 × 400 m relay
1912 USA 3:16.6
1920 Great Britain 3:22.2
1924 USA 3:16.0
1928 USA 3:14.2
1932 USA 3:08.14
1936 Great Britain 3:09.0
1948 USA 3:10.4
1952 Jamaica 3:04.04
1956 USA 3:04.80
1960 USA 3:02.37
1964 USA 3:00.71
1968 USA 2:56.16
1972 Kenya 2:59.83
1976 USA 2:58.66
1980 USSR 3:01.08
1984 USA 3:57.91
1988 USA 2:56.16
1992 USA 2:55.74

Event winners (women)

100 m
1928 Elizabeth Robinson (USA) 12.2
1932 Stanislawa Walasiewicz (Poland) 11.9
1936 Helen Stephens (USA) 11.5
1948 Fanny Blankers-Koen (Netherlands) 11.9
1952 Marjorie Jackson (Australia) 11.65
1956 Betty Cuthbert (Australia) 11.82
1960 Wilma Rudolph (USA) 11.08
1964 Wyomia Tyus (USA) 11.49
1968 Wyomia Tyus (USA) 11.08
1972 Renate Stecher (E Germany) 11.07
1976 Annegret Richter (W Germany) 11.08
1980 Lyudmila Kondratyeva (USSR) 11.06
1984 Evelyn Ashford (USA) 10.97
1988 Florence Griffith-Joyner (USA) 10.54[c]
1992 Gail Devers (USA) 10.82

200 m
1948 Fanny Blankers-Koen (Netherlands) 24.4
1952 Marjorie Jackson (Australia) 23.89
1956 Betty Cuthbert (Australia) 23.55
1960 Wilma Rudolph (USA) 24.03
1964 Edith Maguire (USA) 23.05
1968 Irena Szewinska (Poland) 22.58
1972 Renate Stecher (E Germany) 22.40
1976 Bärbel Eckert (E Germany) 22.37
1980 Bärbel Wöckel (E Germany) 22.03
1984 Valerie Brisco-Hooks (USA) 21.81
1988 Florence Griffith-Joyner (USA) 21.34
1992 Gwen Torrence (USA) 21.81

400 m
1964 Betty Cuthbert (Australia) 52.01
1968 Colette Besson (France) 52.03
1972 Monika Zehrt (E Germany) 51.08
1976 Irena Szewinska (Poland) 49.29
1980 Marita Koch (E Germany) 48.88
1984 Valerie Brisco-Hooks (USA) 48.83

1988 Olga Bryzgina (USSR) 48.65
1992 Marie-José Pérec (France) 48.83

800 m
1928 Lina Radke (Germany) 2:16.8
1960 Lyudmila Shevtsova (USSR) 2:04.50
1964 Ann Packer (Great Britain) 2:01.1
1968 Madeline Manning (USA) 2:00.92
1972 Hilde Falck (W Germany) 1:58.55
1976 Tatyana Kazankina (USSR) 1:54.94
1980 Nadezhda Olizarenko (USSR) 1:53.43
1984 Doina Melinte (Romania) 1:57.60
1988 Sigrun Wodars (E Germany) 1:56.10
1992 Ellen van Langen (Netherlands) 1:55.54

1500 m
1972 Lyudmila Bragina (USSR) 4:01:38
1976 Tatyana Kazankina (USSR) 4:05.48
1980 Tatyana Kazankina (USSR) 3:56.56
1984 Gabriella Doria (Italy) 4:03.25
1988 Paula Ivan (Romania) 3:53.96
1992 Hassiba Boulmerka (Algeria) 3:55:30

3000 m
1984 Maricica Puica (Romania) 8:35.96
1988 Tatyana Samolenko (USSR) 8:26.53
1992 Yelena Romanova (Unified Team) 8:46.04

10 000 m
1988 Olga Bondarenko (USSR) 31:05.21
1992 Derartu Tulu (Ethiopia) 31:06.02

Marathon
1984 Joan Benoit (USA) 2:24:62
1988 Rosa Mota (Portugal) 2:25:40
1992 Valentina Yegorova (Unified Team) 2:32:41

80 m hurdles
1932 Mildred Didrikson (USA) 11.7
1936 Trebisonda Valla (Italy) 11.75
1948 Fanny Blankers-Koen (Netherlands) 11.2
1952 Shirley Strickland (Australia) 11.03
1956 Shirley Strickland (Australia) 10.96
1960 Irina Press (USSR) 10.94
1964 Karin Balzer (E Germany) 10.54
1968 Maureen Caird (Australia) 10.39

100 m hurdles
1972 Annelie Ehrhardt (E Germany) 12.59
1976 Johanna Schaller (E Germany) 12.77
1980 Vera Komisova (USSR) 12.56
1984 Benita Fitzgerald-Brown (USA) 12.84
1988 Yordanka Donkova (Bulgaria) 12.38
1992 Paraskevi Patoulidou (Greece) 12.64

400 m hurdles
1984 Nawal El Moutawakil (Morocco) 54.61
1988 Debbie Flintoff-King (Australia) 53.17
1992 Sally Gunnell (Great Britain) 53.23

High jump
1928 Ethel Catherwood (Canada) 1.59
1932 Jean Shiley (USA) 1.65
1936 Ibolya Csák (Hungary) 1.60
1948 Alice Coachman (USA) 1.68
1952 Esther Brand (S Africa) 1.67
1956 Mildred McDaniel (USA) 1.76
1960 Iolanda Balas (Romania) 1.85
1964 Iolanda Balas (Romania) 1.90
1968 Miloslava Rezková (Czechoslovakia)1.82
1972 Ulrike Meyfarth (W Germany) 1.92
1976 Rosemarie Ackermann (E Germany) 1.93
1980 Sara Simeoni (Italy) 1.97
1984 Ulrike Meyfarth (W Germany) 2.02
1988 Louise Ritter (USA) 2.03
1992 Heike Henkel (Germany) 2.02

Long jump
1948 Olga Gyarmati (Hungary) 5.69
1952 Yvette Williams (New Zealand) 6.24
1956 Elzbieta Krzesinska (Poland) 6.35
1960 Vyera Krepkina (USSR) 6.37
1964 Mary Rand (Great Britain) 6.76
1968 Viorica Viscopoleanu (Romania) 6.82
1972 Heide Rosendahl (W Germany) 6.78
1976 Angela Voigt (E Germany) 6.72
1980 Tatyana Kolpakova (USSR) 7.06
1984 Anisoara Stanciu (Romania) 6.96
1988 Jackie Joyner-Kersee (USA) 7.40
1992 Heike Drechsler (Germany) 7.14

Shot
1948 Micheline Ostermeyer (France) 13.75
1952 Galina Zybina (USSR) 15.28
1956 Tamara Tishkyevich (USSR) 16.59
1960 Tamara Press (USSR) 17.32
1964 Tamara Press (USSR) 18.14
1968 Margitta Gummel (E Germany) 19.61
1972 Nadezhda Chizhova (USSR) 21.03
1976 Ivanka Khristova (Bulgaria) 21.16
1980 Ilona Slupianek (E Germany) 22.41
1984 Claudia Losch (W Germany) 20.48
1988 Natalya Lisovskaya (USSR) 22.24
1992 Svetlana Krivelyova (Unified Team) 21.06

Discus
1928 Helena Konopacka (Poland) 39.62
1932 Lillian Copeland (USA) 40.58
1936 Gisela Mauermayer (Germany) 47.63
1948 Micheline Ostermeyer (France) 41.92
1952 Nina Ponomaryeva (USSR) 51.42
1956 Olga Fikotová (Czechoslovakia) 53.69
1960 Nina Ponomaryeva (USSR) 55.10
1964 Tamara Press (USSR) 57.27
1968 Lia Manoliu (Romania) 58.28
1972 Faina Melnik (USSR) 66.62
1976 Evelin Schlaak (E Germany) 69.00
1980 Evelin Jahl (E Germany) 69.96
1984 Ria Stalmach (Netherlands) 65.36
1988 Martina Hellmann (E Germany) 72.30
1992 Maritza Marten (Cuba) 70.06

Javelin
1932 Mildred Didrikson (USA) 43.68
1936 Tilly Fleischer (Germany) 45.18
1948 Herma Bauma (Australia) 45.57
1952 Dana Zátopková (Czechoslovakia) 50.47
1956 Inese Jaunzeme (USSR) 53.86
1960 Elvira Ozolina (USSR) 55.98
1964 Mihaela Penes (Romania) 60.54
1968 Angéla Németh (Hungary) 60.36
1972 Ruth Fuchs (E Germany) 63.88
1976 Ruth Fuchs (E Germany) 65.94
1980 Maria C. Colón (Cuba) 68.40
1984 Tessa Sanderson (Great Britain) 69.56
1988 Petra Felke (E Germany) 74.68
1992 Silke Renk (Germany) 68.34

Athletics, Olympic games (continued)

Pentathlon
1964 Irina Press (USSR) 4702
1968 Ingrid Becker (W Germany) 4559
1972 Mary Peters (Great Britain) 4801
1976 Sigrun Siegl (E Germany) 4745
1980 Nadezhda Tkachenko (USSR) 5083

Heptathlon
1984 Glynis Nunn (Australia) 6387
1988 Jackie Joyner-Kersee (USA) 7291
1992 Jackie Joyner-Kersee (USA) 7044

10 km walk
1992 Chen Yueling (China) 44:32

4 × 100 m relay
1928 Canada 48.4
1932 USA 46.86
1936 USA 46.9
1948 Netherlands 47.5
1952 USA 46.14
1956 Australia 44.65
1960 USA 44.72
1964 Poland 43.69
1968 USA 42.87
1972 W Germany 42.81
1976 E Germany 42.55
1980 E Germany 41.60
1984 USA 41.65
1988 USA 41.98
1992 USA 42.11

4 × 400 m relay
1972 E Germany 3:22.95
1976 E Germany 3:19.23
1980 USSR 3:20.12
1984 USA 3:18.29
1988 USSR 3:15.18
1992 Unified Team 3:20.20

[a] Real name Sohn Kee-chung of Korea
[b] Competing as member of Great Britain team
[c] Wind-assisted

Marathon

Run over 42km 195m/26mi 385yd; a distance which became standard from 1924. Women first competed officially in 1972.

Boston
The world's oldest annual race; first held in 1897.

Men
1981 Toshihiko Seko (Japan)
1982 Alberto Salazar (USA)
1983 Greg Meyer (USA)
1984 Geoff Smith (Great Britain)
1985 Geoff Smith (Great Britain)
1986 Rob de Castella (Australia)
1987 Toshihiko Seko (Japan)
1988 Ibrahim Hussein (Kenya)
1989 Abebe Mekonnen (Ethiopia)
1990 Gelindo Bordin (Italy)
1991 Ibrahim Hussein (Kenya)
1992 Ibrahim Hussein (Kenya)

Most wins: (7), Clarence De Mar (USA) 1911, 1922–4, 1927–8, 1930.

Women
1981 Allison Roe (New Zealand)
1982 Charlotte Teske (W Germany)
1983 Joan Benoit (USA)
1984 Lorraine Moller (New Zealand)
1985 Lisa Weidenbach (USA)
1986 Ingrid Kristiansen (Norway)
1987 Rosa Mota (Portugal)
1988 Rosa Mota (Portugal)
1989 Ingrid Kristiansen (Norway)
1990 Rosa Mota (Portugal)
1991 Wanda Panfil (Poland)
1992 Olga Markova (Russia)

Most wins: (3), Rosa Mota (Portugal), as above.

London
First run in 1981.

Men
1981 Dick Beardsley (USA) and Inge Simonsen (Norway)
1982 Hugh Jones (Great Britain)
1983 Mike Gratton (Great Britain)
1984 Charlie Spedding (Great Britain)
1985 Steve Jones (Great Britain)
1986 Toshihiko Seko (Japan)
1987 Hiromi Taniguchi (Japan)
1988 Henrik Jørgensen (Denmark)
1989 Douglas Wakihuri (Kenya)
1990 Allister Hutton (Great Britain)
1991 Yakov Tolstikov (USSR)
1992 António Pinto (Portugal)
1993 Eamonn Martin (Great Britain)

Most wins: (no one more than 1).

Women
1981 Joyce Smith (Great Britain)
1982 Joyce Smith (Great Britain)
1983 Grete Waitz (Norway)
1984 Ingrid Kristiansen (Norway)
1985 Ingrid Kristiansen (Norway)
1986 Grete Waitz (Norway)
1987 Ingrid Kristiansen (Norway)
1988 Ingrid Kristiansen (Norway)
1989 Véronique Marot (Great Britain)
1990 Wanda Panfil (Poland)
1991 Rosa Mota (Portugal)
1992 Katrin Dörre (Germany)
1993 Katrin Dörre (Germany)

Most wins: (4), Ingrid Kristiansen (Norway), as above.

New York
First run in 1970.

Men
1981 Alberto Salazar (USA)
1982 Alberto Salazar (USA)
1983 Rod Dixon (New Zealand)
1984 Orlando Pizzolato (Italy)
1985 Orlando Pizzolato (Italy)
1986 Gianni Poli (Italy)
1987 Ibrahim Hussein (Kenya)
1988 Steve Jones (Great Britain)
1989 Juma Ikangaa (Tanzania)

1990 Douglas Wakihuri (Kenya)
1991 Salvador Garcia (Mexico)
1992 Willie Mtolo (South Africa)

Most wins: (4), Bill Rodgers (USA) 1976–9

Women
1981 Allison Roe (New Zealand)
1982 Grete Waitz (Norway)
1983 Grete Waitz (Norway)
1984 Grete Waitz (Norway)
1985 Grete Waitz (Norway)
1986 Grete Waitz (Norway)
1987 Priscilla Welch (Great Britain)
1988 Grete Waitz (Norway)
1989 Ingrid Kristiansen (Norway)
1990 Wanda Panfil (Poland)
1991 Liz McColgan (Great Britain)
1992 Liz McColgan (Great Britain)

Most wins: (9), Grete Waitz (Norway) 1978–80, 1982–6, 1988

BADMINTON

World championships

First held in 1977; initially took place every three years, since 1983 every two years.

Singles winners (men)
1980 Rudo Hartono (Indonesia)
1983 Icuk Sugiarto (Indonesia)
1985 Han Jian (China)
1987 Yang Yang (China)
1989 Yang Yang (China)
1991 Zhao Jianhua (China)

Singles winners (women)
1980 Wiharjo Verawatay (Indonesia)
1983 Li Lingwei (China)
1985 Han Aiping (China)
1987 Han Aiping (China)
1989 Li Lingwei (China)
1991 Tang Jiuhong (China)

Most titles: (4), Park JooBong (South Korea), men's doubles 1985, 1991, mixed doubles 1989, 1991.

Thomas cup

An international event for men's teams: inaugurated in 1949, now held every two years.

Recent winners
1967 Malaysia
1970 Indonesia
1973 Indonesia
1976 Indonesia
1979 Indonesia
1982 China
1984 Indonesia
1986 China
1988 China
1990 China
1992 Malaysia

Most wins: (8), Indonesia, 1958, 1961, 1964, 1970, 1973, 1976, 1979, 1984.

Uber cup

An international event for women's teams; first held in 1957, now held every two years.

Recent winners
1966 Japan
1969 Japan
1972 Japan
1975 Indonesia
1978 Japan
1981 Japan
1984 China
1986 China
1988 China
1990 China
1992 China

Most wins: (5), Japan and China, as above.

All-England championship

Badminton's premier event prior to the inauguration of the World Championships; first held in 1899.

Recent winners, singles (men)
1982 Morten Frost (Denmark)
1983 Luan Jin (China)
1984 Morten Frost (Denmark)
1985 Zhao Jianhua (China)
1986 Morten Frost (Denmark)
1987 Morten Frost (Denmark)
1988 Ib Frederikson (Denmark)
1989 Yang Yang (China)
1990 Zhao Jianhua (China)
1991 Ardi Wiranata (Indonesia)
1992 Liu Jun (China)

Recent winners, singles (women)
1982 Zang Ailing (China)
1983 Zang Ailing (China)
1984 Li Lingwei (China)
1985 Han Aiping (China)
1986 Yun-Ja Kim (Korea)
1987 Kirsten Larsen (Denmark)
1988 Gu Jiaming (China)
1989 Li Lingwei (China)
1990 Susi Susanti (Indonesia)
1991 Susi Susanti (Indonesia)
1992 Tang Jiuhong (China)

Most titles: (21: 4 singles, 9 men's doubles, 8 mixed doubles), George Thomas (England) 1903–28.

Olympic games

Gold medal winners, 1992
Singles (men)
Alan Budi Kusuma (Indonesia)

Singles (women)
Susi Susanti (Indonesia)

BASEBALL

There are two leagues in the North American Major League – the National League (NL) and the American League (AL). Each league consists of two divisions (Eastern and Western) and each league championship is settled in a best-of-seven series between the leaders of these divisions.

World Series

First held in 1903; takes place each October, the best of seven games; professional baseball's leading event, the end-of-season meeting between the 'Pennant' winners of the National League and the American League.

1903 Boston (AL) 5, Pittsburgh (NL) 3
1904 No series
1905 New York (NL) 4, Philadelphia (AL) 1
1906 Chicago (AL) 4, Chicago (NL) 2
1907 Chicago (NL) 4, Detroit (AL) 0; 1 tie
1908 Chicago (NL) 4, Detroit (AL) 1
1909 Pittsburgh (NL) 4, Detroit (AL) 3
1910 Philadelphia (AL) 4, Chicago (NL) 1
1911 Philadelphia (AL) 4, New York (NL) 2
1912 Boston (AL) 4, New York (NL) 3; 1 tie
1913 Philadelphia (AL) 4, New York (NL) 1
1914 Boston (NL) 4, Philadelphia (AL) 0
1915 Boston (AL) 4, Philadelphia (NL) 1
1916 Boston (AL) 4, Brooklyn (NL) 1
1917 Chicago (AL) 4, New York (NL) 2
1918 Boston (AL) 4, Chicago (NL) 2
1919 Cincinnati (NL) 5, Chicago (AL) 3
1920 Cleveland (AL) 5, Brooklyn (NL) 2
1921 New York (NL) 5, New York (AL) 3
1922 New York (NL) 4, New York (AL) 0; 1 tie
1923 New York (AL) 4, New York (NL) 2
1924 Washington (AL) 4, New York (NL) 3
1925 Pittsburgh (NL) 4, Washington (AL) 3
1926 St Louis (NL) 4, New York (AL) 3
1927 New York (AL) 4, Pittsburgh (NL) 0
1928 New York (AL) 4, St Louis (NL) 0
1929 Philadelphia (AL) 4, Chicago (NL) 1
1930 Philadelphia (AL) 4, St Louis (NL) 2
1931 St Louis (NL) 4, Philadelphia (AL) 3
1932 New York (AL) 4, Chicago (NL) 0
1933 New York (NL) 4, Washington (AL) 1
1934 St Louis (NL) 4, Detroit (AL) 3
1935 Detroit (AL) 4, Chicago (NL) 2
1936 New York (AL) 4, New York (NL) 2
1937 New York (AL) 4, New York (NL) 1
1938 New York (AL) 4, Chicago (NL) 0
1939 New York (AL) 4, Cincinnati (NL) 0
1940 Cincinnati (NL) 4, Detroit (AL) 3
1941 New York (AL) 4, Booklyn (NL) 1
1942 St Louis (NL) 4, New York (AL) 1
1943 New York (AL) 4, St Louis (NL) 1
1944 St Louis (NL) 4, St Louis (AL) 2
1945 Detroit (AL) 4, Chicago (NL) 3
1946 St Louis (NL) 4, Boston (AL) 3
1947 New York (AL) 4, Brooklyn (NL) 3
1948 Cleveland (AL) 4, Boston (NL) 2
1949 New York (AL) 4, Brooklyn (NL) 1
1950 New York (AL) 4, Philadelphia (NL) 0
1951 New York (AL) 4, New York (NL) 2
1952 New York (AL) 4, Brooklyn (NL) 3
1953 New York (AL) 4, Brooklyn (NL) 2
1954 New York (NL) 4, Cleveland (AL) 0
1955 Brooklyn (NL) 4, New York (AL) 3
1956 New York (AL) 4, Brooklyn (NL) 3
1957 Milwaukee (NL) 4, New York (AL) 3
1958 New York (AL) 4, Milwaukee (NL) 3
1959 Los Angeles (NL) 4, Chicago (AL) 2
1960 Pittsburgh (NL) 4, New York (AL) 3
1961 New York (AL) 4, Cincinnati (NL) 1
1962 New York (AL) 4, San Francisco (NL) 3
1963 Los Angeles (NL) 4, New York (AL) 0
1964 St Louis (NL) 4, New York (AL) 3
1965 Los Angeles (NL) 4, Minnesota (AL) 3
1966 Baltimore (AL) 4, Los Angeles (NL) 0
1967 St Louis (NL) 4, Boston (AL) 3
1968 Detroit (AL) 4, St Louis (NL) 3
1969 New York (NL) 4, Baltimore (AL) 1
1970 Baltimore (AL) 4, Cincinnati (NL) 1
1971 Pittsburgh (NL) 4, Baltimore (AL) 3
1972 Oakland (AL) 4, Cincinnati (NL) 3
1973 Oakland (AL) 4, New York (NL) 3
1974 Oakland (AL) 4, Los Angeles (NL) 1
1975 Cincinnati (NL) 4, Boston (AL) 3
1976 Cincinnati (NL) 4, New York (AL) 0
1977 New York (AL) 4, Los Angeles (NL) 2
1978 New York (AL) 4, Los Angeles (NL) 2
1979 Pittsburgh (NL) 4, Baltimore (AL) 3
1980 Philadelphia (NL) 4, Kansas City (AL) 2
1981 Los Angeles (NL) 4, New York (AL) 2
1982 St Louis (NL) 4, Milwaukee (AL) 3
1983 Baltimore (AL) 4, Philadelphia (NL) 1
1984 Detroit (AL) 4, San Diego (NL) 1
1985 Kansas City (AL) 4, St Louis (NL) 3
1986 New York (NL) 4, Boston (AL) 3
1987 Minnesota (AL) 4, St Louis (NL) 3
1988 Los Angeles (NL) 4, Oakland (AL) 1
1989 Oakland (AL) 4, San Francisco (NL) 0
1990 Cincinnati (NL) 4, Oakland (AL) 0
1991 Minnesota (AL) 4, Atlanta (NL) 3
1992 Toronto (AL) 4, Atlanta (NL 2)

Most wins: (22), New York Yankees (AL), 1923, 1927–8, 1932, 1936–9, 1941, 1943, 1947, 1949–53, 1956, 1958, 1961–2, 1977–8.

World amateur championship

Instituted in 1938; since 1974 held every two years.

Recent winners

1973 Cuba & USA (shared)
1974 USA
1976 Cuba
1978 Cuba
1980 Cuba
1982 South Korea
1984 Cuba
1986 Cuba
1988 Cuba
1990 Cuba
1992 Cuba

Most wins: (21), Cuba, 1939–40, 1942–43, 1950, 1952–3, 1961, 1969–73, 1976, 1978, 1980, 1984, 1986, 1988, 1990, 1992.

Olympic games

Became an Olympic event in 1992.

1992 Cuba

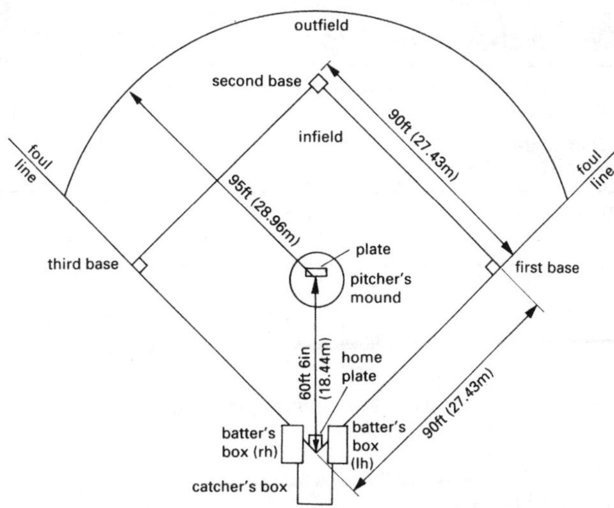

Baseball diamond

BASKETBALL

In the USA the game's governing body is the National Basketball Association (NBA) which comprises two 'conferences': Eastern (Atlantic Division and Central Division) and Western (Midwest Division and Pacific Division). At the end of the season (currently played over 82 games) each conference title is decided in a series of play-offs involving the divisional leaders and the next six best teams; the two conference title-holders compete in a best-of-seven series for the NBA Championship.

National Basketball Association championship

First held in 1947; the major competition in professional basketball in the USA.

1947 Philadelphia 4, Chicago 1
1948 Baltimore 4, Philadelphia 2
1949 Minneapolis 4, Washington 2
1950 Minneapolis 4, Syracuse 2
1951 Rochester 4, New York 3
1952 Minneapolis 4, New York 3
1953 Minneapolis 4, New York 1
1954 Minneapolis 4, Syracuse 3
1955 Syracuse 4, Ft Wayne 3
1956 Philadelphia 4, Ft Wayne 4
1957 Boston 4, St Louis 3
1958 St Louis 4, Boston 2
1959 Boston 4, Minneapolis 0
1960 Boston 4, St Louis 3
1961 Boston 4, St Louis 1
1962 Boston 4, LA Lakers 3
1963 Boston 4, LA Lakers 2
1964 Boston 4, San Francisco 1
1965 Boston 4, LA Lakers 1
1966 Boston 4, LA Lakers 3
1967 Philadelphia 4, San Francisco 2
1968 Boston 4, LA Lakers 2
1969 Boston 4, LA Lakers 3
1970 New York 4, LA Lakers 3
1971 Milwaukee 4, Baltimore 0
1972 LA Lakers 4, New York 1
1973 New York 4, LA Lakers 1
1974 Boston 4, Milwaukee 3
1975 Golden State 4, Washington 0
1976 Boston 4, Phoenix 2
1977 Portland 4, Philadelphia 2
1978 Washington 4, Seattle 3
1979 Seattle 4, Washington 1
1980 LA Lakers 4, Philadelphia 2
1981 Boston 4, Houston 2
1982 LA Lakers 4, Philadelphia 2
1983 Philadelphia 4, LA Lakers 0
1984 Boston 4, LA Lakers 3
1985 LA Lakers 4, Boston 2
1986 Boston 4, Houston 2
1987 LA Lakers 4, Boston 2
1988 LA Lakers 4, Detroit 3
1989 Detroit 4, LA Lakers 0
1990 Detroit 4, Portland 1
1991 Chicago 4, LA Lakers 1
1992 Chicago 4, Portland 1

Most wins: (16), Boston Celtics, 1967, 1959–66, 1968–9, 1974, 1976, 1981, 1984, 1986.

Basketball (continued)

World championship

First held 1950 for men, 1953 for women; generally now takes place every four years.

Winners (men)

1954 USA
1959 Brazil
1963 Brazil
1967 USSR
1970 Yugoslavia
1974 USSR
1978 Yugoslavia
1982 USSR
1986 USA
1990 Yugoslavia

Most wins: (3), USSR and Yugoslavia, as above.

Winners (women)

1957 USA
1959 USSR
1964 USSR
1967 USSR
1971 USSR
1975 USSR
1979 USA
1983 USSR
1987 USA
1991 USA

Most wins: (6), USSR, as above.

Olympic games

Became an Olympic event for men in 1936, for women in 1976.

Winners (men)

1936 USA
1948 USA
1952 USA
1956 USA
1960 USA
1964 USA
1968 USA
1972 USSR
1976 USA
1980 Yugoslavia
1984 USA
1988 USSR
1992 USA

Most wins: (10), USA, as above.

Winners (women)

1976 USSR
1980 USSR
1984 USA
1988 USA
1992 Unified Team

Most wins: (2), USA and USSR, as above.

BIATHLON

World championships

First held in 1958; take place annually; the Olympic champion is the automatic world champion in Olympic years; women's championship first held in 1984.

Recent winners, individual (men)

15 km (10 km before 1988)

1979 Frank Ullrich (E Germany)
1980 Frank Ullrich (E Germany)
1981 Frank Ullrich (E Germany)
1982 Eirik Kvalfoss (Norway)
1983 Eirik Kvalfoss (Norway)
1984 Eirik Kvalfoss (Norway)
1985 Frank-Peter Rötsch (E Germany)
1986 Valeriy Medvetsev (USSR)
1987 Frank-Peter Rötsch (E Germany)
1988 Frank-Peter Rötsch (E Germany)
1989 Frank Luck (E Germany)
1990 Mark Kirchner (E Germany)
1991 Mark Kirchner (Germany)
1992 Mark Kirchner (Germany)

20 km

1979 Klaus Siebert (E Germany)
1980 Anatoliy Alyabyev (USSR)
1981 Heikki Ikola (Finland)
1982 Frank Ullrich (E Germany)
1983 Frank Ullrich (E Germany)
1984 Peter Angerer (W Germany)
1985 Yuriy Kashkarov (USSR)
1986 Valeriy Medevetsev (USSR)
1987 Frank-Peter Rötsch (E Germany)
1988 Frank-Peter Rötsch (E Germany)
1989 Eric Kvalfoss (Norway)
1990 Valeriy Medvetsev (USSR)
1991 Mark Kirchner (Germany)
1992 Yevgeniy Redkine (Unified Team)

Most individual titles: (6), Frank Ullrich (E Germany), 1978 10 km, and as above.

4 x 7.5 km relay (First held 1965)

1979 E Germany
1980 USSR
1981 E Germany
1982 E Germany
1983 USSR
1985 USSR
1986 USSR
1987 E Germany
1988 USSR
1989 E Germany
1990 Italy
1991 Germany
1992 Germany

Most wins (including Olympic years): (15) USSR 1968–74, 1976–77, 1980, 1983–86, 1988.

Recent winners, individual (women)

7.5 km (5 km before 1988)

1984 Venera Cherhyshova (USSR)
1985 Sanna Gronlid (Norway)
1986 Kaya Parva (USSR)
1987 Yelena Golovina (USSR)
1988 Petra Schaaf (W Germany)
1989 Anne-Elinor Elvebakk (Norway)
1990 Anne-Elinor Elvebakk (Norway)
1991 Grete Ingeborg Nykkelmo (Norway)
1992 Anfissa Restzova (Unified Team)

15 km (10 km before 1988)

1984 Venera Chernyshova (USSR)
1985 Kaya Parva (USSR)
1986 Eva Korpela (Sweden)
1987 Sanna Gronlid (Norway)
1988 Anne-Elinor Elvebakk (Norway)
1989 Petra Schaaf (W Germany)
1990 Svetlana Davydova (USSR)
1991 Petra Schaaf (Germany)
1992 Antje Misersky (Germany)

Most individual titles: (3), Anne-Elinor Elvebakk (Norway) and Petra Schaaf (Germany), as above.

3 x 7.5 km relay (3 x 5 km before 1989)

1984 USSR
1985 USSR
1986 USSR
1987 USSR
1988 USSR
1989 USSR
1990 USSR
1991 USSR
1992 France

Most wins: (8), USSR, as above.

BILLIARDS

World professional championship

First held in 1870, organized on a challenge basis; became a knockout event in 1909; discontinued in 1934; revived in 1951 as a challenge system; reverted to a knockout event in 1980.

Recent winners
1982 Rex Williams (England)
1983 Rex Williams (England)
1984 Mark Wildman (England)
1985 Ray Edmonds (England)
1986 Robbie Foldvari (Australia)
1987 Norman Dagley (England)
1988 Norman Dagley (England)
1989 Mike Russell (England)
1990 *Not held*
1991 Mike Russell (England)
1992 Geet Sethi (India)

Most wins: knockout (6), Tom Newman (England), 1921–2, 1924–7; challenge (8), John Roberts, Jnr (England), 1870–85.

BOBSLEIGHING AND TOBOGGANING/LUGE

World championships

First held in 1930 (four-man) and in 1931 (two-man); Olympic champions automatically become world champions.

Recent winners, two-man
1980 Erich Schärer/Josef Benz (Switzerland)
1981 Bernard Germeshausen/Hans-Jürgen Gerhardt (E Germany)
1982 Erich Schärer/Josef Benz (Switzerland)
1983 Ralf Pichler/Urs Leuthold (Switzerland)
1984 Wolfgang Hoppe/Dietmar Schauerhammer (E Germany)
1985 Wolfgang Hoppe/Dietmar Schauerhammer (E Germany)
1986 Wolfgang Hoppe/Dietmar Schauerhammer (E Germany)
1987 Ralf Pichler/Celest Poltera (Swizerland)
1988 Janis Kipurs/Vladimir Kozlov (USSR)
1989 Wolfgang Hoppe/Bogdan Musiol (E Germany)
1990 Gustav Weder/Bruno Gerber (Switzerland)
1991 Rudi Lochner/Markus Zimmermann (Germany)
1992 Gustav Weder/Donad Acklin (Switzerland)

Recent winners, four-man
1980 E Germany
1981 E Germany
1982 Switzerland
1983 Switzerland
1984 E Germany
1985 E Germany
1986 Switzerland
1987 Switzerland
1988 Switzerland
1989 Switzerland
1990 Switzerland
1991 Germany
1992 Austria

Most wins: Two-man (8), Eugenio Monti (Italy) 1957–61, 1963, 1966, 1968. Four-man (15), Switzerland, 1939, 1947, 1954–5, 1957, 1971, 1973, 1975, 1982–3, 1986–90.

Luge world championships

First held in 1955; annually until 1981, then every two years; the Olympic champion automatically becomes the world champion.

Recent winners, men's single-seater
1976 Detlef Günther (E Germany)
1977 Hans Rinn (E Germany)
1978 Paul Hildgartner (Italy)
1979 Detlef Günther (E Germany)
1980 Bernhard Glass (E Germany)
1981 Sergey Danilin (USSR)
1983 Miroslav Zajonc (Canada)
1985 Michael Walter (E Germany)
1987 Markus Prock (Austria)
1989 Georg Hackl (W Germany)
1990 Georg Hackl (W Germany)
1991 Arnold Huber (Italy)

Most wins: (3), Thomas Köhler (E Germany), 1962, 1964, 1967.

Recent winners, women's single-seater
1976 Margrit Schumann (E Germany)
1977 Margrit Schumann (E Germany)
1978 Vera Sosulya (USSR)
1979 Melitta Sollmann (E Germany)
1980 Vera Sosulya (USSR)
1981 Melitta Sollman (E Germany)
1983 Steffi Martin (E Germany)
1985 Steffi Martin (E Germany)
1987 Cerstin Schmidt (E Germany)
1989 Susi Erdmann (E Germany)
1990 Gabriele Kohlisch (E Germany)
1991 Susi Erdmann (Germany)

Most wins: (5), Margrit Schumann (E Germany), 1973–7.

Olympic games, luge

Winners, men's single-seater
1984 Paul Hildgartner (Italy)
1988 Jens Müller (E Germany)
1992 Georg Hackl (Germany)

Winners, pairs (men)
1984 W Germany
1988 E Germany
1992 Germany

Most wins: Singles (no one more than 1). Pairs (5), E Germany, 1968, 1972, 1976, 1980, 1988.

Winners, women's single-seater
1984 Steffi Martin (E Germany)
1988 Steffi Martin Walter (E Germany)
1992 Doris Neuner (Austria)

Most wins: (2) Steffi Martin Walter (E Germany), as above.

BOWLS

World championships

Instituted for men in 1966 and for women in 1969; held every four years.

Men's singles
1966 David Bryant (England)
1972 Malwyn Evans (Wales)
1976 Doug Watson (South Africa)
1980 David Bryant (England)
1984 Peter Bellis (New Zealand)
1988 David Bryant (England)
1992 Tony Allcock (England)

Men's pairs
1966 Australia
1972 Hong Kong
1976 South Africa
1980 Australia
1984 USA
1988 New Zealand
1992 Scotland

Men's triples
1966 Australia
1972 USA
1976 South Africa
1980 England
1984 Ireland
1988 New Zealand
1992 Israel

Men's fours
1966 New Zealand
1972 England
1976 South Africa
1980 Hong Kong
1984 England
1988 Ireland
1992 Scotland

Leonard Trophy
Team award, given to the nation with the best overall performances in the men's world championship.

Winners
1966 Australia
1972 Scotland
1976 South Africa
1980 England
1984 Scotland
1988 England
1992 Scotland

Most wins: (5) David Bryant (Singles as above, triples 1988, team 1980).

Women's singles
1969 Gladys Doyle (Papua New Guinea)
1973 Elsie Wilke (New Zealand)
1977 Elsie Wilke (New Zealand)
1981 Norma Shaw (England)
1985 Merle Richardson (Australia)
1988* Janet Ackland (Wales)
1992 Margaret Johnston (Ireland)

Women's pairs
1969 South Africa
1973 Australia
1977 Hong Kong
1981 Ireland
1985 Australia
1988* Ireland
1992 Ireland

Women's triples
1969 South Africa
1973 New Zealand
1977 Wales
1981 Hong Kong
1985 Australia
1988* Australia
1992 Scotland

Women's fours
1969 South Africa
1973 New Zealand
1977 Australia
1981 England
1985 Scotland
1988* Australia
1992 Scotland

Women's team
1969 South Africa
1973 New Zealand
1977 Australia
1981 England
1985 Australia
1988* England
1992 Scotland

Most wins: (3), Merle Richardson (Fours 1977; Singles and Pairs 1985).

*The women's event was advanced to December 1988 (Australia)

World indoor championships

First held in 1979; takes place annually.

Winners
1981 David Bryant (England)
1982 John Watson (Scotland)
1983 Bob Sutherland (Scotland)
1984 Jim Baker (Ireland)
1985 Terry Sullivan (Wales)
1986 Tony Allcock (England)
1987 Tony Allcock (England)
1988 Hugh Duff (Scotland)
1989 Richard Coursie (Scotland)
1990 John Price (Wales)
1991 Richard Coursie (Scotland)
1992 Ian Schuback (Australia)

Most wins: (3), David Bryant (England), 1979, 1980, 1981.

Waterloo Handicap

First held in 1907 and annually at Blackpool's Waterloo Hotel; the premier event of Crown Green Bowling.

Recent winners
1981 Roy Nicholson
1982 Dennis Mercer
1983 Stan Frith
1984 Steve Ellis
1985 Tommy Johnstone
1986 Brian Duncan
1987 Brian Duncan
1988 Ingham Gregory
1989 Brian Duncan
1990 John Bancroft
1991 John Eccles
1992 Brian Duncan

Most wins: (5), Brian Duncan, 1979 and as above.

BOXING

World heavyweight champions

Undisputed
1882 John L Sullivan (USA)
1892 James J Corbett (USA)[a]
1897 Bob Fitzsimmons (Great Britain)
1899 James J Jefferies (USA)
1905 Marvin Hart (USA)
1906 Tommy Burns (Can)
1908 Jack Johnson (USA)
1915 Jess Willard (USA)
1919 Jack Dempsey (USA)
1926 Gene Tunney (USA)
1930 Max Schmeling (Germany)
1932 Jack Sharkey (USA)
1933 Primo Carnera (Italy)
1934 Max Baer (USA)
1935 James J Braddock (USA)
1937 Joe Louis (USA)
1949 Ezzard Charles (USA)
1951 Jersey Joe Walcott (USA)
1952 Rocky Marciano (USA)
1956 Floyd Patterson (USA)
1959 Ingemar Johansson (Sweden)
1960 Sonny Liston (USA)
1964 Cassius Clay (USA)*
1970 Joe Frazier (USA)
1973 George Foreman (USA)
1974 Muhammad Ali (USA)*
1978 Leon Spinks (USA)
1987 Mike Tyson (USA)

[a]The first world heavyweight champion under Queensberry rules with gloves.

World heavyweight champions (continued)

In recent years, 'world champions' have been recognized by up to four different governing bodies.

Champions since 1978		*Recognizing body*
1978	Muhammad Ali (USA)*	WBA
1978	Larry Holmes (USA)	WBC
1979	John Tate (USA)	WBA
1980	Mike Weaver (USA)	WBA
1982	Mike Dokes (USA)	WBA
1983	Gerry Coetzee (South Africa)	WBA
1984	Larry Holmes (USA)	IBF
1984	Tim Witherspoon (USA)	WBC
1984	Pinklon Thomas (USA)	WBC
1984	Greg Page (USA)	WBA
1985	Michael Spinks (USA)	IBF
1985	Tony Tubbs (USA)	WBA
1986	Tim Witherspoon (USA)	WBA
1986	Trevor Berbick (Canada)	WBC
1986	Mike Tyson (USA)	WBC
1986	James Smith (USA)	WBA
1987	Tony Tucker (USA)	IBF
1987	Mike Tyson (USA)	WBA/WBC
1987	Mike Tyson (USA)	UND
1989	Francesco Damiani (Italy)	WBO
1990	James (Buster) Douglas (USA)	WBA/WBC/IBF
1990	Evander Holyfield (USA)	WBA/WBC/IBF
1991	Ray Mercer (USA)	WBO
1992	Riddick Bowe (USA)	WBA/WBC/IBF
1992	Michael Mourer (USA)	WBO
1992	Lennox Lewis (Great Britain)	WBC

*Cassius Clay changed his name to Muhammed Ali upon joining the Black Muslims.

IBF = International Boxing Federation
UND = Undisputed Champion
WBA = World Boxing Association
WBC = World Boxing Council
WBO = World Boxing Organization

The weight divisions in professional boxing

Name	*Maximum weight*
Heavyweight	any weight
Cruiserweight/junior-heavyweight	88 kg/195 lb
Light-heavyweight	79 kg/175 lb
Super-middleweight	77 kg/170 lb
Middleweight	73 kg/160 lb
Light-middleweight/junior-middleweight	70 kg/154 lb
Welterweight	67 kg/147 lb
Light-welterweight/junior-welterweight	64 kg/140 lb
Lightweight	61 kg/135 lb
Junior-lightweight/super-featherweight	59 kg/130 lb
Featherweight	57 kg/126 lb
Super-bantamweight/junior-featherweight	55 kg/122 lb
Bantamweight	54 kg/118 lb
Super-flyweight/junior-bantamweight	52 kg/115 lb
Flyweight	51 kg/112 lb
Light-flyweight/junior-flyweight	49 kg/108 lb
Mini-flyweight/straw-weight/minimum weight	under 48 kg/105 lb

CANOEING

Olympic games

Single kayak, 1000 m (men)

1936 Gregor Hradetzky (Austria)
1948 Gert Fredriksson (Sweden)
1952 Gert Fredriksson (Sweden)
1956 Gert Fredriksson (Sweden)
1960 Erik Hansen (Denmark)
1964 Rolf Peterson (Sweden)
1968 Mihaly Hesz (Hungary)
1972 Aleksandr Shaparenko (USSR)
1976 Rüdiger Helm (E Germany)
1980 Rüdiger Helm (E Germany)
1984 Alan Thompson (New Zealand)
1988 Greg Barton (USA)
1992 Clint Robinson (Australia)

Single kayak, 500 m (women)

1948 Keren Hoff (Denmark)
1952 Sylvi Saimo (Finland)
1956 Elisaveta Dementyeva (USSR)
1960 Antonina Seredina (USSR)
1964 Lyudmila Khvedosyuk (USSR)
1968 Lyudmila Pinayeva (USSR)
1972 Yulia Ryabchinskaya (USSR)
1976 Carola Zirzow (E Germany)
1980 Birgit Fischer (E Germany)
1984 Agneta Andersson (Sweden)
1988 Vania Gecheva (USSR)
1992 Brigit Schmidt (Germany)

Most wins: Men (3), Gert Fredriksson as above. No woman has won more than one title.

CHESS

World champions

World champions have been recognized since 1886; first women's champion recognized in 1927.

Recent champions (men)

1948–57	Mikhail Botvinnik (USSR)
1957–8	Vassiliy Smyslov (USSR)
1958–60	Mikhail Botvinnik (USSR)
1960–1	Mikhail Tal (USSR)
1961–3	Mikhail Botvinnik (USSR)
1963–9	Tigran Petrosian (USSR)
1969–72	Boris Spassky (USSR)
1972–5	Bobby Fischer (USA)
1975–85	Anatoliy Karpov (USSR)
1985–	Gary Kasparov (USSR/Azerbaijan)

Longest reigning champion: 27 years, Emanuel Lasker (Germany) 1894–1921.

Champions (women)

1927–44	Vera Menchik-Stevenson (UK)
1950–3	Lyudmila Rudenko (USSR)
1953–6	Elizabeta Bykova (USSR)
1956–8	Olga Rubtsova (USSR)
1958–62	Elizaveta Bykova (USSR)
1962–78	Nona Gaprindashvili (USSR)
1978–91	Maya Chiburdanidze (USSR)
1991–	Xie Jun (China)

Longest reigning champion: 17 years, Vera Menchik-Stevenson (UK), as above.

Chess notation

The opening position

QR	QN	QB	Q	K	KB	KN	KR
♜	♞	♝	♛	♚	♝	♞	♜
♟	♟	♟	♟	♟	♟	♟	♟
♙	♙	♙	♙	♙	♙	♙	♙
♖	♘	♗	♕	♔	♗	♘	♖
QR	QN	QB	Q	K	KB	KN	KR

Abbreviations

B	Bishop
K	King
KB	King's bishop
KN	King's knight
KR	King's rook
N	Knight
P	Pawn
Q	Queen
QB	Queen's bishop
QN	Queen's knight
QR	Queen's rook
R	Rook

Descriptive notation

Black

QR1 QR8	**QN1** QN8	**QB1** QB8	**Q1** Q8	**K1** K8	**KB1** KB8	**KN1** KN8	**KR1** KR8
QR2 QR7	**QN2** QN7	**QB2** QB7	**Q2** Q7	**K2** K7	**KB2** KB7	**KN2** KN7	**KR2** KR7
QR3 QR6	**QN3** QN6	**QB3** QB6	**Q3** Q6	**K3** K6	**KB3** KB6	**KN3** KN6	**KR3** KR6
QR4 QR5	**QN4** QN5	**QB4** QB5	**Q4** Q5	**K4** K5	**KB4** KB5	**KN4** KN5	**KR4** KR5
QR5 QR4	**QN5** QN4	**QB5** QB4	**Q5** Q4	**K5** K4	**KB5** KB4	**KN5** KN4	**KR5** KR4
QR6 QR3	**QN6** QN3	**QB6** QB3	**Q6** Q3	**K6** K3	**KB6** KB3	**KN6** KN3	**KR6** KR3
QR7 QR2	**QN7** QN2	**QB7** QB2	**Q7** Q2	**K7** K2	**KB7** KB2	**KN7** KN2	**KR7** KR2
QR8 QR1	**QN8** QN1	**QB8** QB1	**Q8** Q1	**K8** K1	**KB8** KB1	**KN8** KN1	**KR8** KR1

White

Each file is named by the piece on the first rank; ranks are numbered 1–8 away from the player.

x	captures (Q x P = Queen takes Pawn)
–	moves to (Q–KB4)
ch	check (R–QB3 ch)
dis ch	discovered check
dbl ch	double check
e.p.	en passant
mate	checkmate
0–0	castles, King's side
0–0–0	castles, Queen's side
!	good move (P x R!)
!!	very good move
!!!	outstanding move
?	bad move
!?	good or bad move (depends on response of the other player)

Algebraic notation

Black

a8	b8	c8	d8	e8	f8	g8	h8
a7	b7	c7	d7	e7	f7	g7	h7
a6	b6	c6	d6	e6	f6	g6	h6
a5	b5	c5	d5	e5	f5	g5	h5
a4	b4	c4	d4	e4	f4	g4	h4
a3	b3	c3	d3	e3	f3	g3	h3
a2	b2	c2	d2	e2	f2	g2	h2
a1	b1	c1	d1	e1	f1	g1	h1

White

Each square is named by a combination of file letter and rank number.

Chess pieces in other languages

French

B	fou (fool)
K	roi (king)
N	cavalier (horseman)
P	pion (pawn)
Q	dame, reine (lady), (queen)
R	tour (tower)

German

B	Läufer (runner)
K	König (king)
N	Springer (jumper)
P	Bauer (peasant)
Q	Königin (queen)
R	Turm (tower)

CONTRACT BRIDGE

World team championship

The game's biggest championship; men's contest (The Bermuda Bowl) first held in 1951, and now takes place every two years; women's contest (The Venice Cup) first held in 1974, and since 1985 is concurrent with the men's event.

Bermuda Bowl winners (men)

1973	Italy	1981	USA
1974	Italy	1983	USA
1975	Italy	1985	USA
1976	USA	1987	USA
1977	USA	1989	Brazil
1979	USA	1991	Iceland

Most wins: (13), Italy, 1957–9, 1961–3, 1965–7, 1969, 1973–5.

Venice Cup winners (women)

1974	USA	1985	UK
1976	USA	1987	Italy
1978	USA	1989	USA
1981	UK	1991	USA
1983	*not held*		

Most wins: (5), USA, as above.

World team olympiad

First held in 1960; takes place every four years.

Winners (men)

1960	France	1980	France
1964	Italy	1984	Poland
1968	Italy	1988	USA
1972	Italy	1992	France
1976	Brazil		

Winners (women)

1960	United Arab Emirates	1976	USA
		1980	USA
		1984	USA
1964	UK	1988	Denmark
1968	Sweden	1992	Austria
1972	Italy		

Most wins: Men (3), Italy and France, as above. Women (3), USA, as above.

CRICKET

World cup

First played in England in 1975; held every four years; the 1987 competition was the first to be played outside England, in India and Pakistan.

Winners

1975	West Indies	1987	Australia
1979	West Indies	1992	Pakistan
1983	India		

County championship

The oldest cricket competition in the world; first won by Sussex in 1827; not officially recognized until 1890, when a proper points system was introduced.

Recent winners

1981 Nottinghamshire
1982 Middlesex
1983 Essex
1984 Essex
1985 Middlesex
1986 Essex
1987 Nottinghamshire
1988 Worcestershire
1989 Worcestershire
1990 Middlesex
1991 Essex
1992 Essex

Most outright wins: (29), Yorkshire, 1893, 1896, 1898, 1900–2, 1905, 1908, 1912, 1919, 1922–5, 1931–3, 1935, 1937–9, 1946, 1959–60, 1962–3, 1966–8.

Sunday league

First held in 1969; known as the John Player League 1969–86; Refuge Assurance League 1987–1991.

Recent winners

1981 Essex
1982 Sussex
1983 Yorkshire
1984 Essex
1985 Essex
1986 Hampshire
1987 Worcestershire
1988 Worcestershire
1989 Lancashire
1990 Derbyshire
1991 Nottinghamshire
1992 Middlesex

Most wins: (3), Kent, 1972–3, 1976; Essex, as above; Lancashire 1969–70, 1989, Hampshire 1975, 1978, 1986; Worcestershire 1971, 1987, 1988.

NatWest Bank trophy

First held in 1963; known as the Gillette Cup until 1981.

Recent winners

1981 Derbyshire
1982 Surrey
1983 Somerset
1984 Middlesex
1985 Essex
1986 Sussex
1987 Nottinghamshire
1988 Middlesex
1989 Warwickshire
1990 Lancashire
1991 Hampshire
1992 Northamptonshire

Most wins: (5), Lancashire, 1970–2, 1975, 1990.

Benson and Hedges cup

First held in 1972.

Recent winners

1981 Somerset
1982 Somerset
1983 Middlesex
1984 Lancashire
1985 Leicestershire
1986 Middlesex
1987 Yorkshire
1988 Hampshire
1989 Nottinghamshire
1990 Lancashire
1991 Worcestershire
1992 Hampshire
1993 Derbyshire

Most wins: (3), Kent, 1973, 1976, 1978; Leicestershire, 1972, 1975, 1985.

Cricket (continued)

Sheffield Shield

Australia's leading domestic competition; contested inter-state since 1891.

Recent winners
1982 South Australia
1983 New South Wales
1984 Western Australia
1985 New South Wales
1986 New South Wales
1987 Western Australia
1988 Western Australia
1989 Western Australia
1990 New South Wales
1991 Victoria
1992 Western Australia

Most wins: (40), New South Wales, 1896–7, 1900, 1902–7, 1909, 1911–12, 1914, 1920–1, 1923, 1926, 1929, 1932–3, 1938, 1940, 1949–50, 1952, 1954–62, 1965–6, 1983, 1985–6, 1990.

Cricket field positions

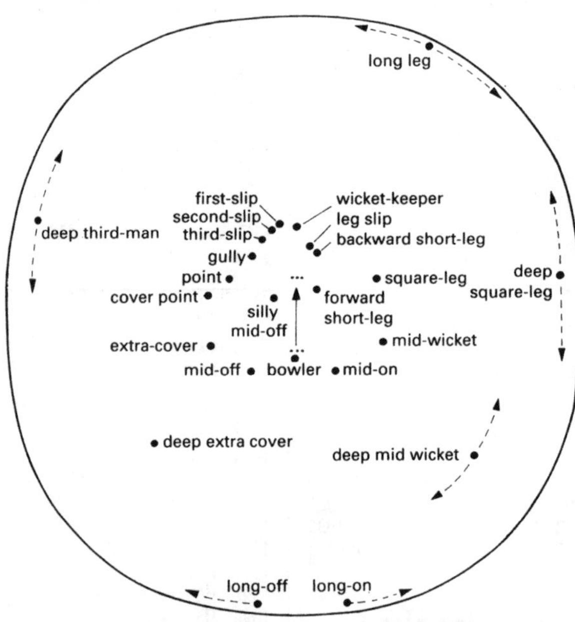

CROQUET

McRobertson Shield

Croquet's leading tournament; held spasmodically since 1925; contested by teams from Great Britain, New Zealand and Australia.

Winners
1925 Great Britain
1928 Australia
1930 Australia
1935 Australia
1937 Great Britain
1950 New Zealand
1956 Great Britain
1963 Great Britain
1969 Great Britain
1974 Great Britain
1979 New Zealand
1982 Great Britain
1986 New Zealand
1990 Great Britain

Most wins: (8), Great Britain, as above.

World singles championships

Inaugurated in 1989; held at Hurlingham.

Winners
1989 Joe Hogan (New Zealand)
1990 Robert Fulford (Great Britain)
1991 John Walters (Great Britain)
1992 Robert Fulford (Great Britain)

Most wins: (2), Robert Fulford (UK) as above.

CROSS-COUNTRY RUNNING

World championships

First international championship held in 1903, but only included runners from England, Ireland, Scotland and Wales; recognized as an official world championship from 1973; first women's race in 1967.

Recent winners, individual (men)
1982 Mohamed Kedir (Ethiopia)
1983 Bekele Debele (Ethiopia)
1984 Carlos Lopes (Portugal)
1985 Carlos Lopes (Portugal)
1986 John Ngugi (Kenya)
1987 John Ngugi (Kenya)
1988 John Ngugi (Kenya)
1989 John Ngugi (Kenya)
1990 Khalid Skah (Morocco)
1991 Khalid Skah (Morocco)
1992 John Ngugi (Kenya)

Recent winners, team (men)

1982	Ethiopia	1988	Kenya
1983	Ethiopia	1989	Kenya
1984	Ethiopia	1990	Kenya
1985	Ethiopia	1991	Kenya
1986	Kenya	1992	Kenya
1987	Kenya		

Most wins: Individual (5), John Ngugi (Kenya), as above. Team (45), England, between 1903 and 1980.

Recent winners, individual (women)
1982 Maricica Puica (Romania)
1983 Grete Waitz (Norway)
1984 Maricica Puica (Romania)
1985 Zola Budd (England)
1986 Zola Budd (England)
1987 Annette Sergent (France)
1988 Ingrid Kristiansen (Norway)
1989 Annette Sergent (France)
1990 Lynn Jennings (USA)
1991 Lynn Jennings (USA)
1992 Lynn Jennings (USA)

Recent winners, team (women)

1982	USSR	1988	USA
1983	USA	1989	USSR
1984	USA	1990	USSR
1985	USA	1991	Kenya
1986	England	1992	Kenya
1987	USA		

Most wins: Individual (5), Doris Brown (USA), 1967–71; Grete Waitz (Norway), 1978–81, 1983. Team (8), USA, 1968–9, 1975, 1979, 1983–5, 1987, also 1988–9.

CURLING

World championships

First men's championship held in 1959; first women's championship in 1979; takes place annually.

Recent winners (men)

1979	Norway	1986	Canada
1980	Canada	1987	Canada
1981	Switzerland	1988	Norway
1982	Canada	1989	Canada
1983	Canada	1990	Canada
1984	Norway	1991	Scotland
1985	Canada		

Recent winners (women)

1979 Switzerland
1980 Canada
1981 Sweden
1982 Denmark
1983 Switzerland
1984 Canada
1985 Canada
1986 Canada
1987 Canada
1988 W Germany
1989 Canada
1990 Norway
1991 Norway

Most wins: Men (20), Canada, 1959–64, 1966, 1968–72, 1980, 1982–3, 1985–7, 1989, 1990. Women (6), Canada, as above.

CYCLING

Tour de France

World's premier cycling event; first held in 1903.

Recent winners

1981 Bernard Hinault (France)
1982 Bernard Hinault (France)
1983 Laurent Fignon (France)
1984 Laurent Fignon (France)
1985 Bernard Hinault (France)
1986 Greg LeMond (USA)
1987 Stephen Roche (Ireland)
1988 Pedro Delgado (Spain)
1989 Greg LeMond (USA)
1990 Greg LeMond (USA)
1991 Miguel Induráin (Spain)
1992 Miguel Induráin (Spain)

Most wins: (5), Jacques Anquetil (France), 1957, 1961–4; Eddy Merckx (Belgium), 1969–72, 1974; Bernard Hinault (France), 1978–9, 1981–2, 1985.

World road race championships

Men's race first held in 1927; takes place annually. First women's race in 1958; takes place annually, but not in Olympic years.

Recent winners (professional men)

1981 Freddy Maertens (Belgium)
1982 Giuseppe Saroni (Italy)
1983 Greg LeMond (USA)
1984 Claude Criquielion (Belgium)
1985 Joop Zoetemelk (Netherlands)
1986 Moreno Argentin (Italy)
1987 Stephen Roche (Ireland)
1988 Maurizio Fondriest (Italy)
1989 Greg LeMond (USA)
1990 Rudy Dhaemens (Belgium)
1991 Gianni Bugno (Italy)
1992 Gianni Bugno (Italy)

Recent winners (women)

1981 Ute Enzenauer (W Germany)
1982 Mandy Jones (Great Britain)
1983 Marianne Berglund (Sweden)
1985 Jeannie Longo (France)
1986 Jeannie Longo (France)
1987 Jeannie Longo (France)
1989 Jeannie Longo (France)
1990 Catherine Marsal (France)
1991 Leontein van Moorseel (Netherlands)

Most wins: Men (3), Alfredo Binda (Italy), 1927, 1930, 1932: Rik Van Steenbergen (Belgium), 1949, 1956–7; Eddy Merckx (Belgium), 1967, 1971, 1974. Women (4), Yvonne Reynders (Belgium) 1959, 1961, 1963, 1966; Jeannie Longo (France), as above.

Olympic games

Gold medal winners, 1992 (men)

Individual road race
Fabio Casartelli (Italy)

Sprint
Jens Fiedler (Germany)

4000 m individual pursuit
Chris Boardman (Great Britain)

Gold medal winners, 1992 (women)

Individual road race
Kathryn Watt (Australia)

Sprint
Erika Salumyae (Estonia)

3000 m individual pursuit
Petra Rossner (Germany)

CYCLO-CROSS

World championships

First held in 1950 as an open event; separate professional and amateur events since 1967.

Recent winners, professional

1980 Roland Liboton (Belgium)
1981 Johannes Stamsnijder (Netherlands)
1982 Roland Liboton (Belgium)
1983 Roland Liboton (Belgium)
1984 Roland Liboton (Belgium)
1985 Klaus-Peter Thaler (W Germany)
1986 Albert Zweifel (Switzerland)
1987 Klaus-Peter Thaler (W Germany)
1988 Pascal Richard (Switzerland)
1989 Danny De Bie (Belgium)
1990 Henk Baars (Netherlands)
1991 Radomir Simunek (Czechoslovakia)
1992 Mike Kluge (Germany)

Recent winners, amateur

1980 Fritz Saladin (Switzerland)
1981 Milos Fisera (Czechoslovakia)
1982 Milos Fisera (Czechoslovakia)
1983 Radomir Simunek (Czechoslovakia)
1984 Radomir Simunek (Czechoslovakia)
1985 Mike Kluge (W Germany)
1986 Vito di Tano (Italy)
1987 Mike Kluge (W Germany)
1988 Karol Camrola (Czechoslovakia)
1989 Ondrej Glaja (Czechoslovakia)
1990 Andreas Buesser (Switzerland)
1991 Thomas Frischknecht (Switzerland)
1992 Daniele Pontoni (Italy)

Most wins: Professional (7), Eric de Vlaeminck (Belgium), 1966, 1968–73. Amateur (5), Robert Vermiere (Belgium), 1970–1, 1974–5, 1977.

DARTS

World professional championship

First held at Nottingham in 1978.

Winners
1979 John Lowe (England)
1980 Eric Bristow (England)
1981 Eric Bristow (England)
1982 Jocky Wilson (Scotland)
1983 Keith Deller (England)
1984 Eric Bristow (England)
1985 Eric Bristow (England)
1986 Eric Bristow (England)
1987 John Lowe (England)
1988 Bob Anderson (England)
1989 Jocky Wilson (Scotland)
1990 Phil Taylor (England)
1991 Dennis Priestley (England)
1992 Phil Taylor (England)
1993 John Lowe (England)

Most wins: (5), Eric Bristow, as above.

World cup

A team competition first held at Wembley in 1977; takes place every two years.

Winners (team)
1979 England
1981 England
1983 England
1985 England
1987 England
1989 England
1991 England

Winners (individual)
1979 Nicky Virachkul (USA)
1981 John Lowe (England)
1983 Eric Bristow (England)
1985 Eric Bristow (England)
1987 Eric Bristow (England)
1989 Eric Bristow (England)
1991 John Lowe (England)

Most wins: Team (7), England, as above. Individual (4), Eric Bristow (England), as above.

DRAUGHTS

World championship

Held on a challenge basis; the champion since 1979 has been M Tinsley (USA); he has defended the title five times.

British Open championship

The leading championship in Britain; first held in 1926; now takes place every two years.

Recent winners
1970 I Edwards (Great Britain)
1972 G Davies (Great Britain)
1974 J McGill (Great Britain)
1976 A Huggins (Great Britain)
1978 J McGill (Great Britain)
1980 T Watson (Great Britain)
1982 T Watson (Great Britain)
1984 A Long (USA)
1986 H Delvin (Great Britain)
1988 De Oldbury (Great Britain)

EQUESTRIAN EVENTS

World championships

Show jumping championships first held in 1953 (for men) and 1965 (for women); since 1978 they have competed together and on equal terms; team competition introduced in 1978; three day event and dressage championships introduced in 1966; all three now held every four years.

Winners, show jumping (men)
1953 Francisco Goyoago (Spain)
1954 Hans-Günter Winkler (W Germany)
1955 Hans-Günter Winkler (W Germany)
1956 Raimondo D'Inzeo (Italy)
1960 Raimondo D'Inzeo (Italy)
1966 Pierre d'Oriola (France)
1970 David Broome (Great Britain)
1974 Hartwig Steenken (W Germany)

Winners, show jumping (women)
1965 Marion Coakes (Great Britain)
1970 Janou Lefèbvre (France)
1974 Janou Tissot (France)

Winners, individual
1978 Gerd Wiltfang (W Germany)
1982 Norbert Koof (W Germany)
1986 Gail Greenough (Canada)
1990 Eric Navet (France)

Winners (team)
1982 France
1986 USA
1990 France

Winners, three day event, individual
1970 Mary Gordon-Watson (Great Britain)
1974 Bruce Davidson (USA)
1978 Bruce Davidson (USA)
1982 Lucinda Green (Great Britain)
1986 Virginia Leng (Great Britain)
1990 Blyth Tait (New Zealand)

Winners, three day event, team
1970 Great Britain
1974 USA
1978 Canada
1982 Great Britain
1986 Great Britain
1990 New Zealand

Winners, dressage, individual
1970 Yelene Petouchkova (USSR)
1974 Reiner Klimke (W Germany)
1978 Christine Stückelberger (Switzerland)
1982 Reiner Klimke (W Germany)
1986 Anne Grethe Jensen (Denmark)
1990 Nicole Uphoft (W Germany)

Winners, dressage, team
1970 USSR
1974 W Germany
1978 W Germany
1982 W Germany
1986 W Germany
1990 W Germany

Olympic games

Gold medal winners, 1992, individual

Three day event
Matthew Ryan (Australia)

Dressage
Nicole Uphoff (Germany)

Jumping
Ludger Beerbaum (Germany)

Gold medal winners, 1992, team

Three day event Australia
Dressage Germany
Jumping Netherlands

FENCING

World championships

Held annually since 1921 (between 1921–35, known as European Championships); not held in Olympic years.

Recent winners, foil, individual (men)

1975 Christian Noel (France)
1977 Alexander Romankov (USSR)
1978 Didier Flament (France)
1979 Alexander Romankov (USSR)
1981 Vladimir Smirnov (USSR)
1982 Alexander Romankov (USSR)
1983 Alexander Romankov (USSR)
1985 Mauro Numa (Italy)
1986 Andrea Borella (Italy)
1987 Mathias Gey (W Germany)
1989 Alexandr Koch (W Germany)
1990 Philippe Omnes (France)
1991 Ingo Weissenborn (Germany)

Recent winners foil, team (men)

1975 France
1977 W Germany
1978 Poland
1979 USSR
1981 USSR
1982 USSR
1983 W Germany
1985 Italy
1986 Italy
1987 USSR
1989 USSR
1990 Italy
1991 Cuba

Most wins: Individual (5), Alexander Romankov (USSR), 1974, 1977, 1979, 1982–3. Team (15), USSR (between 1959–89).

Recent winners, foil, individual (women)

1975 Ecaterina Stahl (Romania)
1977 Valentina Sidorova (USSR)
1978 Valentine Sidorova (USSR)
1979 Cornelia Hanisch (W Germany)
1981 Cornelia Hanisch (W Germany)
1982 Naila Giliazova (USSR)
1983 Dorina Vaccaroni (Italy)
1985 Cornelia Hanisch (W Germany)
1986 Anja Fichtel (W Germany)
1987 Elisabeta Tufan (Romania)
1989 Olga Velitschko (USSR)
1990 Anja Fichtel (W Germany)
1991 Giovanna Trillini (Italy)

Recent winners, foil, team (women)

1975	USSR	1985	W Germany
1977	USSR	1986	USSR
1978	USSR	1987	Hungary
1979	USSR	1989	W Germany
1981	USSR	1990	Italy
1982	Italy	1991	Cuba
1983	Italy		

Most wins: Individual (3), Helène Mayer (Germany), 1929, 1931, 1937; Ilona Elek (Hungary), 1934–5, 1951; Ellen Müller-Preiss (Austria), 1947, 1949, 1950; Cornelia Hanisch, as above. Team (15), USSR (between 1956–86).

Recent winners epée, individual (men)

1975 Alexander Pusch (W Germany)
1977 Johan Harmenberg (Sweden)
1978 Alexander Pusch (W Germany)
1979 Philippe Riboud (France)
1981 Zoltan Szekely (Hungary)
1982 Jenö Pap (Hungary)
1983 Ellmar Bormann (W Germany)
1985 Philippe Boisse (France)
1986 Philippe Riboud (France)
1987 Volker Fischer (W Germany)
1989 Manuel Pereira (Spain)
1990 Thomas Gerull (W Germany)
1991 Andrei Shuvalov (USSR)

Recent winners, epée, team (men)

1975	Sweden	1985	W Germany
1977	Sweden	1986	W Germany
1978	Hungary	1987	W Germany
1979	USSR	1989	Italy
1981	USSR	1990	Italy
1982	France	1991	USSR
1983	France		

Most wins: Individual (3), Georges Buchard (France), 1927, 1931, 1933; Alexei Nikanchikov (USSR), 1966–7, 1970. Team (11), Italy (between 1931–58 and 1989–90); France (between 1934–83).

Recent winners, epée, individual (women)

1989 Anja Straub (Switzerland)
1990 Taime Chappe (Cuba)
1991 Mariann Horváth (Hungary)

Recent winners, epée, team (women)

1989 Hungary
1990 W Germany
1991 Hungary

Recent winners, sabre, individual (men)

1975 Vladimir Nazlimov (USSR)
1977 Pal Gerevich (Hungary)
1978 Viktor Krovopuskov (USSR)
1979 Vladimir Nazlimov (USSR)
1981 Mariusz Wodke (Poland)
1982 Viktor Krovopuskov (USSR)
1983 Vasiliy Etropolski (Bulgaria)
1985 György Nebald (Hungary)
1986 Sergey Mindirgassov (USSR)
1987 Jean-François Lamour (France)
1989 Grigoriy Kirienko (USSR)
1990 György Nébald (Hungary)
1991 Grigoriy Kirienko (USSR)

Recent winners sabre, team (men)

1975 USSR
1977 USSR
1978 Hungary
1979 USSR
1981 Hungary
1982 Hungary
1983 USSR
1985 USSR
1986 USSR
1987 USSR
1989 USSR
1990 USSR
1991 Hungary

Most wins: Individual (3), Aladar Gerevich (Hungary), 1935, 1951, 1955; Jerzy Pawlowski (Poland) 1957, 1965–6; Yokov Rylsky (USSR), 1958, 1961, 1963. Team (18), Hungary (between 1930–91).

Olympic games

Gold medal winners, 1992 (men)

Individual foil
Philip Omnes (France)

Team foil
Germany

Individual epée
Eric Srecki (Hungary)

Team epée
Germany

Individual sabre
Bence Szabo (Hungary)

Team sabre
Unified Team

Gold medal winners, 1992 (women)

Individual foil
Giovanna Tullini (Italy)

Team foil
Italy

FOOTBALL (AMERICAN)

National Football League (NFL)

In its existing form since 1970, the NFL consists of two 'conferences': the American Football Conference (AFC) and the National Football Conference (NFC).
Each of these comprises three divisions (Eastern, Central and Western) which are made up of either four or five teams. The season is played over sixteen games, with the championship of each conference being decided by two rounds of play-offs involving the three winners of the divisions, plus a number of 'wild cards', ie the best of the rest.

Superbowl

First held in 1967 between champions of the National Football league (NFL) and the American Football League (AFL); takes place each January; since 1971 an end of season meeting between the champions of the AFC and the NFC.

1967 Green Bay Packers (NFL) 35, Kansas City Chiefs (AFL) 10
1968 Green Bay Packers (NFL) 33, Oakland Raiders (AFL) 14
1969 New York Jets (AFL) 16, Baltimore Colts (NFL) 7
1970 Kansas City Chiefs (AFL) 23, Minnesota Vikings (NFL) 7
1971 Baltimore Colts (AFC) 16, Dallas Cowboys (NFC) 13
1972 Dallas Cowboys (NFC) 24, Miami Dolphins (AFC) 3
1973 Miami Dolphins (AFC) 14, Washington Redskins (NFC) 7
1974 Miami Dolphins (AFC) 24, Minnesota Vikings (NFL) 7
1975 Pittsburgh Steelers (AFC) 16, Minnesota Vikings (NFC) 6
1976 Pittsburgh Steelers (AFC) 21, Dallas Cowboys (NFC) 17
1977 Oakland Raiders (AFC) 32, Minnesota Vikings (NFC) 14
1978 Dallas Cowboys (NFL) 27, Denver Broncos (AFC) 10
1979 Pittsburgh Steelers (AFC) 35, Dallas Cowboys (NFC) 31
1980 Pittsburgh Steelers (AFC) 31, Los Angeles Rams (NFC) 19
1981 Oakland Raiders (AFC) 27, Philadelphia Eagles (NFC) 10
1982 San Francisco 49ers (NFC) 26, Cincinnati Bengals (AFC) 21
1983 Washington Redskins (NFC) 27, Miami Dolphins (AFC) 17
1984 Los Angeles Raiders (AFC) 38, Washington Redskins (NFC) 9
1985 San Francisco 49ers (NFC) 38, Miami Dolphins (AFC) 16
1986 Chicago Bears (NFC) 46, New England Patriots (AFC) 10
1987 New York Giants (NFC) 39, Denver Broncos (AFC) 20
1988 Washington Redskins (NFC) 42, Denver Broncos (AFC) 10
1989 San Francisco 49ers (NFC) 20, Cincinnati Bengals (AFC) 10
1990 San Francisco 49ers (NFC) 55, Denver Broncos (AFC) 10
1991 New York Giants (NFC) 20, Buffalo Bills (AFC) 19
1992 Washington Redskins (NFC) 37, Buffalo Bills (AFC) 24
1993 Dallas Cowboys (NFL) 52, Buffalo Bills (AFC) 17

Most wins: (4), Pittsburgh Steelers 1975–6, 1979–80; (2) San Francisco 49ers 1982, 1985, 1989–90.

American football field

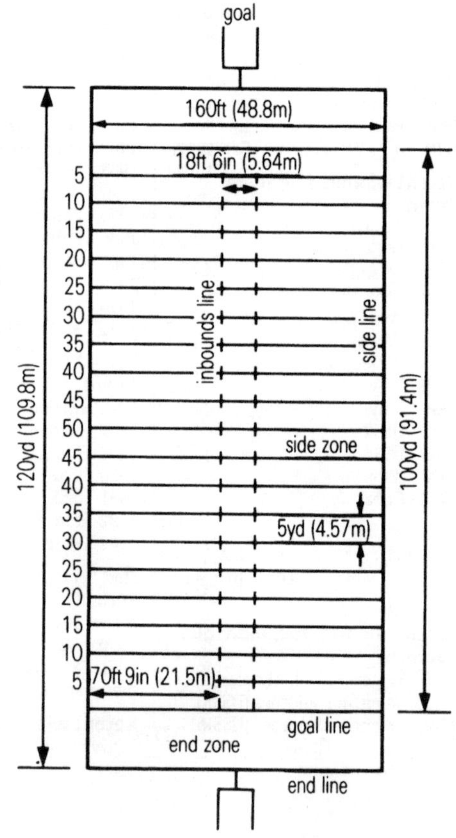

Sports and games

FOOTBALL (ASSOCIATION FOOTBALL/SOCCER)

FIFA World Cup

Association Football's premier event; first contested for the Jules Rimet Trophy in 1930; Brazil won it outright after winning for the third time in 1970; since then teams have competed for the FIFA (*Fédération Internationale de Football Association*) World Cup; held every four years.

	Winner	*Score*	*Runner-up*	*Final held in*
1930	Uruguay	4–2	Argentina	Montevideo
1934	Italy	2–1	Czechoslovakia	Rome
1938	Italy	4–2	Hungary	Paris
1950	Uruguay	2–1	Brazil	Rio de Janeiro
1954	W Germany	5–2	Sweden	Stockholm
1958	Brazil	5–2	Hungary	Berne
1962	Brazil	3–1	Czechoslovakia	Santiago
1966	England	4–2	W Germany	London
1970	Brazil	4–1	Italy	Mexico City
1974	W Germany	2–1	Netherlands	Munich
1978	Argentina	3–1	Netherlands	Buenos Aires
1982	Italy	3–1	W Germany	Madrid
1986	Argentina	3–2	W Germany	Mexico City
1990	W Germany	1–0	Argentina	Rome

Most wins: (3), Brazil, Italy and W Germany, as above.

European championship

Held every four years since 1960; qualifying group matches held over the two years preceding the final.

	Winner	*Score*	*Runner-up*	*Final held in*
1960	USSR	2–1	Yugoslavia	Paris
1964	Spain	2–1	USSR	Madrid
1968[a]	Italy	2–1	Yugoslavia	Rome
1972	W Germany	3–0	USSR	Brussels
1976[b]	Czechoslovakia	2–2	W Germany	Belgrade
1980	W Germany	2–1	Belgium	Rome
1984	France	2–0	Spain	Paris
1988	Netherlands	2–0	USSR	Munich
1992	Denmark	2–0	Germany	Gothenburg

[a] Replay after 1–1 draw
[b] Czechoslovakia won 5–2 on penalties
Most wins: (2), W Germany, as above.

South American championship

First held in 1916, for South American national sides; discontinued in 1967, but revived eight years later; now played every two years.

Recent winners

1956	Uruguay	1975	Peru
1957	Argentina	1979	Paraguay
1959[a]	Argentina	1983	Uruguay
1959[a]	Uruguay	1987	Uruguay
1963	Bolivia	1989	Brazil
1967	Uruguay	1991	Argentina

a There were two tournaments in 1959.
Most wins: (13), Uruguay, 1916–17, 1920, 1923–4, 1926, 1935, 1942, 1956, 1959, 1967, 1983, 1987.

Association football field

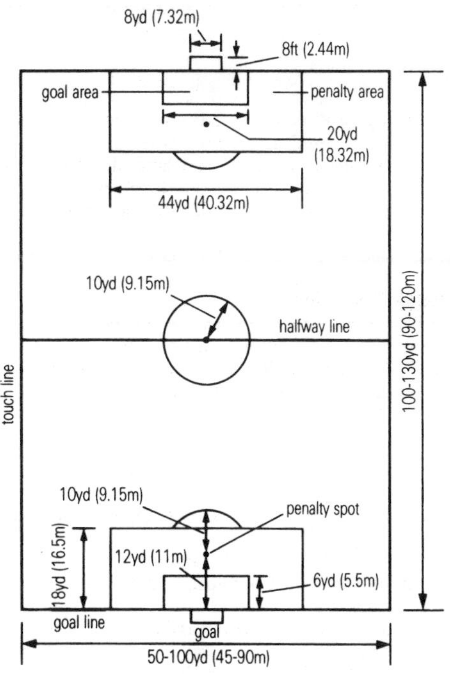

European Champions Cup

The leading club competition in Europe; open to the League champions of countries affiliated to UEFA (Union of European Football Associations); commonly known as the 'European Cup'; inaugurated in the 1955–6 season; played annually.

Recent winners

	Winner	*Score*	*Runner-up*
1975	Bayern Munich	2–0	Leeds United
1976	Bayern Munich	1–0	St Etienne
1977	Liverpool	3–1	BM/gladbach
1978	Liverpool	1–0	FC Bruges
1979	Nottingham Forest	1–0	Malmo
1980	Nottingham Forest	1–0	SV Hamburg
1981	Liverpool	1–0	Real Madrid
1982	Aston Villa	1–0	Bayern Munich
1983	SV Hamburg	1–0	Juventus
1984[a]	Liverpool	1–1	AS Roma
1985	Juventus	1–0	Liverpool
1986[b]	Steaua Bucharest	0–0	Barcelona
1987	FC Porto	2–1	Bayern Munich
1988[c]	PSV Eindhoven	0–0	Benfica
1989	AC Milan	4–0	Steaua Bucharest
1990	AC Milan	1–0	Benfica
1991[d]	Red Star Belgrade	0–0	Olympique Marseilles
1992	Barcelona	1–0	Sampdoria
1993	Olympique Marseilles	1–0	AC Milan

[a] Liverpool won 4–2 on penalties
[b] Steaua won 2–0 on penalties
[c] Eindhoven won 6–5 on penalties
[d] Red Star won 5–3 on penalties

Most wins: (6), Real Madrid (Spain), 1956–60, 66.

European Cup-Winners' Cup

Annual club competition, open to the main cup winners from all the UEFA countries; inaugurated in 1961, when the final was played over two legs. Since 1962 there has been a single game final.

Recent winners

1981	Dynamo Tiblisi	1988	Mechelen
1982	Barcelona	1989	Barcelona
1983	Aberdeen	1990	Sampdoria
1984	Juventus	1991	Manchester United
1985	Everton	1992	Werder Bremen
1986	Dynamo Kiev	1993	Parma
1987	Ajax		

Most wins: (3), Barcelona, 1979, 1982, 1989.

UEFA Cup

Originally the International Industries Fairs Inter-Cities Cup (more commonly the 'Fairs Cup'); was first contested in 1955: became the UEFA Cup in 1971. Each participating nation is allotted a certain number of team places. The final is played over two legs.

Recent winners

1981	Ipswich Town	1988	Bayer Leverskusen
1982	IFK Gothenburg	1989	Napoli
1983	Anderlecht	1990	Juventus
1984	Tottenham Hotspur	1991	Inter-Milan
1985	Real Madrid	1992	Ajax
1986	Real Madrid	1993	Juventus
1987	IFK Gothenburg		

Most wins: (3), Barcelona, 1958, 1960, 1966.

Football League

The oldest league in the world, founded in 1888; consists of four divisions; the current complement of 92 teams achieved in 1950. Prior to the start of the 1992–93 season the 22 teams of the 1st division voted to form the FA Premier League; divisions 2, 3 and 4 becoming League divisions 1, 2 and 3 respectively; the system of promotion and relegation remaining unchanged.

League champions

1888–89	Preston North End
1889–90	Preston North End
1890–91	Everton
1891–92	Sunderland
1892–93	Sunderland
1893–94	Aston Villa
1894–95	Sunderland
1895–96	Aston Villa
1896–97	Aston Villa
1897–98	Sheffield United
1898–99	Aston Villa
1899–1900	Aston Villa
1900–01	Liverpool
1901–02	Sunderland
1902–03	Sheffield Wednesday
1903–04	Sheffield Wednesday
1904–05	Newcastle United
1905–06	Liverpool
1906–07	Newcastle United
1907–08	Manchester United
1908–09	Newcastle United
1909–10	Aston Villa
1910–11	Manchester United
1911–12	Blackburn Rovers
1912–13	Sunderland
1913–14	Blackburn Rovers
1914–15	Everton
1919–20	West Bromwich Albion
1920–21	Burnley
1921–22	Liverpool
1922–23	Liverpool
1923–24	Huddersfield Town
1924–25	Huddersfield Town
1925–26	Huddersfield Town
1926–27	Newcastle United
1927–28	Everton
1928–29	Sheffield Wednesday
1929–30	Sheffield Wednesday
1930–31	Arsenal
1931–32	Everton
1932–33	Arsenal
1933–34	Arsenal
1934–35	Arsenal
1935–36	Sunderland
1936–37	Manchester City
1937–38	Arsenal
1938–39	Everton
1946–47	Liverpool
1947–48	Arsenal
1948–49	Portsmouth
1949–50	Portsmouth
1950–51	Tottenham Hotspur
1951–52	Manchester United
1952–53	Arsenal
1953–54	Wolverhampton Wanderers
1954–55	Chelsea
1955–56	Manchester United
1956–57	Manchester United
1957–58	Wolverhampton Wanderers
1958–59	Wolverhampton Wanderers
1959–60	Burnley
1960–61	Tottenham Hotspur

1961–62	Ipswich Town
1962–63	Everton
1963–64	Liverpool
1964–65	Manchester United
1965–66	Liverpool
1966–67	Manchester United
1967–68	Manchester City
1968–69	Leeds United
1969–70	Everton
1970–71	Arsenal
1971–72	Derby County
1972–73	Liverpool
1973–74	Leeds United
1974–75	Derby County
1975–76	Liverpool
1976–77	Liverpool
1977–78	Nottingham Forest
1978–79	Liverpool
1979–80	Liverpool
1980–81	Aston Villa
1981–82	Liverpool
1982–83	Liverpool
1983–84	Liverpool
1984–85	Everton
1985–86	Liverpool
1986–87	Everton
1987–88	Liverpool
1988–89	Arsenal
1989–90	Liverpool
1990–91	Arsenal
1991–92	Leeds United
1992–93	Manchester United

Most wins: (18), Liverpool, 1901, 1906, 1922–3, 1947, 1964, 1966, 1973, 1976–7, 1979–80, 1982–4, 1986, 1988, 1990.

Football Association Challenge Cup

The world's oldest club knockout competition (the 'FA cup'), held annually, it is open to both League and non-League teams; first contested in the 1871–2 season; first final at the Kennington Oval on 16 March 1872; first winners were the Wanderers. Played at Wembley since 1923.

	Winners	*Score*	*Runner-up*
1871–72	Wanderers	1–0	Royal Engineers
1872–73	Wanderers	2–0	Oxford University
1873–74	Oxford University	2–0	Royal Engineers
1874–75	Royal Engineers	1–1, 2–0	Old Etonians
1875–76	Wanderers	1–1, 3–0	Old Etonians
1876–77	Wanderers	2–1	Oxford University
1877–78	Wanderers	3–1	Royal Engineers
1878–79	Old Etonians	1–0	Clapham Rovers
1879–80	Clapham Rovers	1–0	Oxford University
1880–81	Old Carthusians	3–0	Old Etonians
1881–82	Old Etonians	1–0	Blackburn Rovers
1882–83	Blackburn Olympic	2–1	Old Etonians
1883–84	Blackburn Rovers	2–1	Queen's Park Rangers
1884–85	Blackburn Rovers	2–0	Queen's Park Rangers
1885–86	Blackburn Rovers	0–0, 2–0	West Bromwich Albion
1886–97	Aston Villa	2–0	West Bromwich Albion
1887–88	West Bromwich Albion	2–1	Preston North End
1888–89	Preston North End	3–0	Wolverhampton Wanderers
1889–90	Blackburn Rovers	6–1	Sheffield Wednesday
1890–91	Blackburn Rovers	3–1	Notts County
1891–92	West Bromwich Albion	3–0	Aston Villa
1892–93	Wolverhampton Wanderers	1–0	Everton
1893–94	Notts County	4–1	Bolton Wanderers
1894–95	Aston Villa	1–0	West Bromwich Albion
1895–96	Sheffield Wednesday	2–1	Wolverhampton Wanderers
1896–97	Aston Villa	3–2	Everton
1897–98	Nottingham Forest	3–1	Derby County
1898–99	Sheffield United	4–1	Derby County
1899–1900	Bury	4–0	Southampton
1900–01	Tottenham Hotspur	2–2, 3–1	Sheffield United
1901–02	Sheffield United	1–1, 2–1	Southampton
1902–03	Bury	6–0	Derby County
1903–04	Manchester City	1–0	Bolton Wanderers
1904–05	Aston Villa	2–0	Newcastle United
1905–06	Everton	1–0	Newcastle United
1906–07	Sheffield Wednesday	2–1	Everton
1907–08	Wolverhampton Wanderers	3–1	Newcastle United
1908–09	Manchester United	1–0	Bristol City
1909–10	Newcastle United	1–1, 2–0	Barnsley
1910–11	Bradford City	0–0, 1–0	Newcastle United
1911–12	Barnsley	0–0, 1–0	West Bromwich Albion
1912–13	Aston Villa	1–0	Sunderland
1913–14	Burnley	1–0	Liverpool
1914–15	Sheffield United	3–0	Chelsea
1919–20	Aston Villa	1–0	Huddersfield Town
1920–21	Tottenham Hotspur	1–0	Wolverhampton Wanderers
1921–22	Huddersfield Town	1–0	Preston North End
1922–23	Bolton Wanderers	2–0	West Ham United
1923–24	Newcastle United	2–0	Aston Villa
1924–25	Sheffield United	1–0	Cardiff City
1925–26	Bolton Wanderers	1–0	Manchester City
1926–27	Cardiff City	1–0	Arsenal
1927–28	Blackburn Rovers	3–1	Huddersfield Town
1928–29	Bolton Wanderers	2–0	Portsmouth
1929–30	Arsenal	2–0	Huddersfield Town
1930–31	West Bromwich Albion	2–1	Birmingham City
1931–32	Newcastle United	2–1	Arsenal

Football Association Challenge Cup (continued)

	Winners	*Score*	*Runner-up*
1932–33	Everton	3–0	Manchester City
1933–34	Manchester City	2–1	Portsmouth
1934–35	Sheffield Wednesday	4–2	West Bromwich Albion
1935–36	Arsenal	1–0	Sheffield United
1936–37	Sunderland	3–1	Preston North End
1937–38	Portsmouth	4–1	Wolverhampton Wanderers
1945–46	Derby County	4–1	Charlton Athletic
1946–47	Charlton Atheltic	1–0	Burnley
1947–48	Manchester United	4–2	Blackpool
1948–49	Wolverhampton Wanderers	3–1	Leicester City
1949–50	Arsenal	2–0	Liverpool
1950–51	Newcastle United	2–0	Blackpool
1951–52	Newcastle United	1–0	Arsenal
1952–53	Blackpool	4–3	Bolton Wanderers
1953–54	West Bromwich Albion	3–2	Preston North End
1954–55	Newcastle United	3–1	Manchester City
1955–56	Manchester City	3–1	Birmingham City
1956–57	Aston Villa	2–1	Manchester United
1957–58	Bolton Wanderers	2–0	Manchester United
1958–59	Nottingham Forest	2–1	Luton Town
1959–60	Wolverhampton Wanderers	3–0	Blackburn Rovers
1960–61	Tottenham Hotspur	2–0	Leicester City
1961–62	Tottenham Hotspur	3–1	Burnley
1962–63	Manchester United	3–1	Leicester City
1963–64	West Ham United	3–2	Preston North End
1964–65	Liverpool	2–1	Leeds United
1965–66	Everton	3–2	Sheffield Wednesday
1966–67	Tottenham Hotspur	2–1	Chelsea
1967–68	West Bromwich Albion	1–0	Everton
1968–69	Manchester City	1–0	Leicester City
1969–70	Chelsea	2–2, 2–1	Leeds United
1970–71	Arsenal	2–1	Liverpool
1971–72	Leeds United	1–0	Arsenal
1972–73	Sunderland	1–0	Leeds United
1973–74	Liverpool	3–0	Newcastle United
1974–75	West Ham United	2–0	Fulham
1975–76	Southampton	1–0	Manchester United
1976–77	Manchester United	2–1	Liverpool
1977–78	Ipswich Town	1–0	Arsenal
1978–79	Arsenal	3–2	Manchester United
1979–80	West Ham United	1–0	Arsenal
1980–81	Tottenham Hotspur	1–1, 3–2	Manchester City
1981–82	Tottenham Hotspur	1–1, 1–0	Queen's Park Rangers
1982–83	Manchester United	2–2, 4–0	Brighton & Hove Albion
1983–84	Everton	2–0	Watford
1984–85	Manchester United	1–0	Everton
1985–86	Liverpool	3–1	Everton
1986–87	Coventry City	3–2	Tottenham Hospur
1987–88	Wimbledon	1–0	Liverpool
1988–89	Liverpool	3–2	Everton
1989–90	Manchester United	3–3, 1–0	Crystal Palace
1990–91	Tottenham Hotspur	2–1	Nottingham Forest
1991–92	Liverpool	2–0	Sunderland
1992–93	Arsenal	1–1, 2–1	Sheffield Wednesday

Most wins: (8) Tottenham Hotspur, 1901, 1921, 1961–2, 1967, 1981–2, 1991.

Football League Cup

Inaugurated in 1961, it is competed for by the 92 clubs of the Football League. From 1982 to 1986 it was known as the Milk Cup; 1986–90, the Littlewoods Cup; 1990–92 the Rumbelows Cup, and in 1992–3 the Coca-Cola Cup.

Recent winners

1981	Liverpool
1982	Liverpool
1983	Liverpool
1984	Liverpool
1985	Norwich City
1986	Oxford United
1987	Arsenal
1988	Luton Town
1989	Nottingham Forest
1990	Nottingham Forest
1991	Sheffield Wednesday
1992	Manchester United
1993	Arsenal

Most wins: (4), Liverpool, as above; Nottingham Forest 1978–9, 1989–90.

Clubs of the English Football League

Team	Nickname	Ground
Aldershot	Shots	Recreation Ground
Arsenal	Gunners	Highbury
Aston Villa	Villa	Villa Park
Barnet		Underhill
Barnsley		Oakwell
Birmingham City	Blues	St Andrews
Blackburn Rovers		Ewood Park
Blackpool	Tangerines	Bloomfield Road
Bolton Wanderers	Trotters	Burnden Park
Bournemouth	Cherries	Dean Court
Bradford City	Bantams	Valley Parade
Brentford	Bees	Griffin Park
Brighton and Hove Albion	Seagulls	Goldstone Ground
Bristol City	Robins	Ashton Gate
Bristol Rovers	Pirates	Tiverton Park
Burnley	Clarets	Turf Moor
Bury	Shakers	Gigg Lane
Cambridge United	'U's	Abbey Stadium
Cardiff City	Bluebirds	Ninian Park
Carlisle United		Brunton Park
Charlton Athletic	Valiants	The Valley
Chelsea	Blues	Stamford Bridge
Chester City		Moss Rose
Chesterfield	Spireites	Saltergate
Colchester United	'U's	Layer Road
Coventry City	Sky Blues	Highfield Road
Crewe Alexandra	Railwaymen	Gresty Road
Crystal Palace	Eagles	Selhurst Park
Darlington	Quakers	Feethams
Derby County	Rams	Baseball Ground
Doncaster Rovers		Belle Vue
Everton	Toffeemen	Goodison Park
Exeter City	Grecians	St James Park
Fulham	Cottagers	Craven Cottage
Gillingham	Gills	Priestfield
Grimsby Town	Mariners	Blundell Park
Halifax Town	Shaymen	The Shay
Hartlepool United	Pool	Victoria Ground
Hereford United		Edgar Street
Huddersfield Town	Terriers	Leeds Road
Hull City	Tigers	Boothferry Park
Ipswich Town		Portman Road
Leeds United	Peacocks	Elland Road
Leicester City		Filbert Street
Leyton Orient	'O's	Brisbane Road
Lincoln City	Imps	Sincil Bank
Liverpool	Reds	Anfield
Luton Town	Hatters	Kenilworth Road
Manchester City	Blues	Maine Road
Manchester United	Reds	Old Trafford
Mansfield Town	Stags	Field Mill
Middlesbrough	Boro	Ayresome Park
Millwall	Lions	The Den
Newcastle United	Magpies	St James' Park
Northampton Town	Cobblers	County Ground
Norwich City	Canaries	Carrow Road
Nottingham Forest	Reds	City Ground
Nottingham County	Magpies	Meadow Lane
Oldham Athletic	Latics	Boundary Park
Oxford United	'U's	Manor Ground
Peterborough United	Posh	London Road
Plymouth Argyle	Pilgrims	Home Park
Portsmouth	Pompey	Fratton Park
Port Vale		Vale Park
Preston North End	Lillywhites	Deepdale
Queens Park Rangers	'R's	Loftus Road
Reading	Royals	Elm Park
Rochdale		Spotland
Rotherham United	Millers	Millmoor
Scarborough		Seamer Road
Scunthorpe United	Irons	Glanford Park
Sheffield United	Blades	Bramall Lane
Sheffield Wednesday	Owls	Hillsborough
Shrewsbury Town	Shrews	Gay Meadow
Southampton	Saints	The Dell
Southend United	Shrimpers	Roots Hall
Stockport County		Edgeley Park
Stoke City	Potters	Victoria Ground
Sunderland	Black Cats	Roker Park
Swansea City	Swans	Vetch Field
Swindon Town	Robins	County Ground
Torquay United	Gulls	Plainmoor
Tottenham Hotspur	Spurs	White Hart Lane
Transmere Rovers		Prenton Park
Walsall	Saddlers	Bescot Stadium
Watford	Hornets	Vicarage Road
West Bromwich Albion	Baggies	The Hawthorns
West Ham United	Hammers	Upton Park
Wigan Athletic	Latics	Springfield Park
Wimbledon	Dons	Plough Lane
Wolverhampton Wanderers	Wolves	Molineux
Wrexham	Robins	Racecourse Ground
Wycombe Wanderers	Blues	Adams Park
York City		Bootham Crescent

Scottish Football League

Formed in 1890, with a second division added in 1893. The present format (Premier Division, Division 1, Division 2) was arrived at in 1975.

Recent winners

1981–82	Celtic	1987–88	Celtic
1982–83	Dundee United	1988–89	Rangers
1983–84	Aberdeen	1989–90	Rangers
1984–85	Aberdeen	1990–91	Rangers
1985–86	Celtic	1991–92	Rangers
1986–87	Rangers	1992–93	Rangers

Most wins: (43), Rangers.

Scottish FA Cup

First played in 1874; held at Hampden Park.

Recent winners

1981	Rangers	1988	Celtic
1982	Aberdeen	1989	Celtic
1983	Aberdeen	1990	Aberdeen
1984	Aberdeen	1991	Motherwell
1985	Celtic	1992	Rangers
1986	Aberdeen	1993	Rangers
1987	St Mirren		

Most wins: (29), Celtic.

Sports and games

FOOTBALL (AUSTRALIAN)

Australian Football League

Known as the Victoria Football League until 1987, when teams from Western Australia and Queensland joined the league. The top prize is the annual VFL Premiership Trophy.

Premiership Trophy

First contested in 1897 and won by Essendon.

Recent winners
1981 Carlton
1982 Carlton
1983 Hawthorn
1984 Essendon
1985 Essendon
1986 Hawthorn
1987 Carlton
1988 Hawthorn
1989 Hawthorn
1990 Collingwood
1991 Hawthorn
1992 West Coast Eagles

Most wins: (15), Carlton, 1906–8, 1914–15, 1938, 1945, 1947, 1968, 1970, 1972, 1979, 1981–2, 1987.

Australian football field

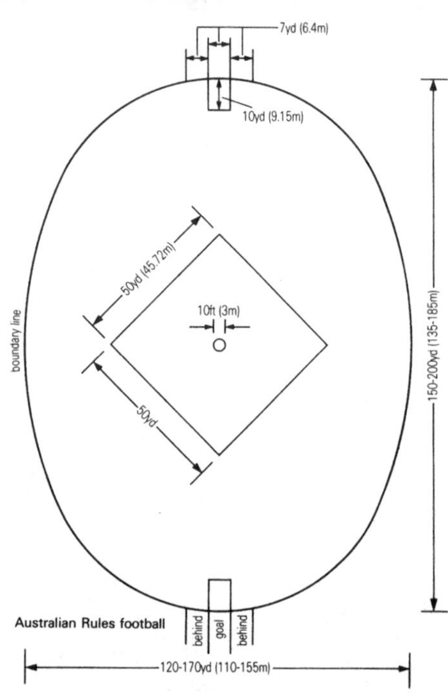

FOOTBALL (GAELIC)

All-Ireland championship

First held 1887; takes place in Dublin on the third Sunday in September each year.

Recent winners
1979 Kerry
1980 Kerry
1981 Kerry
1982 Offaly
1983 Dublin
1984 Kerry
1985 Kerry
1986 Kerry
1987 Meath
1988 Meath
1989 Cork
1990 Cork
1991 Down
1992 Donegal

Most wins: (30), Kerry, 1903–4, 1909, 1913–14, 1924, 1926, 1929–32, 1937, 1939–41, 1946, 1953, 1955, 1959, 1962, 1969–70, 1975, 1978–81, 1984–86.

GLIDING

World championships

First held in 1937; current classes are Open, Standard and 15 metres; the Open class is the principal event, held every two years until 1978 and again since 1981.

Recent winners, open category
1968 Harro Wödl (Austria)
1970 George Moffat (USA)
1972 Göran Ax (Sweden)
1974 George Moffat (USA)
1976 George Lee (Great Britain)
1978 George Lee (Great Britain)
1981 George Lee (Great Britain)
1983 Ingo Renner (Australia)
1985 Ingo Renner (Australia)
1987 Ingo Renner (Australia)
1989 Claude Lopitaux (France)
1991 Janusz Centka (Poland)

Most wins: (3), George Lee and Ingo Renner, as above.

GOLF

British Open

First held at Prestwick in 1860, and won by Willie Park; takes place annually; regarded as the world's leading golf tournament.

Recent winners
1981 Bill Rogers (USA)
1982 Tom Watson (USA)
1983 Tom Watson (USA)
1984 Severiano Ballesteros (Spain)
1985 Sandy Lyle (Great Britain)
1986 Greg Norman (Australia)
1987 Nick Faldo (Great Britain)
1988 Severiano Ballesteros (Spain)
1989 Mark Calcavecchia (USA)
1990 Nick Faldo (Great Britain)
1991 Ian Baker-Finch (Australia)
1992 Nick Faldo (Great Britain)

[a] Greg Norman (Australia)

Most wins: (6), Harry Vardon (Great Britain), 1896, 1898–9, 1903, 1911, 1914.

United States Open

First held at Newport, Rhode Island, in 1895, and won by Horace Rawlins; takes place annually.

Recent winners
1981 David Graham (Australia)
1982 Tom Watson (USA)
1983 Larry Nelson (USA)
1984 Fuzzy Zoeller (USA)
1985 Andy North (USA)
1986 Ray Floyd (USA)
1987 Scott Simpson (USA)
1988 Curtis Strange (USA)
1989 Curtis Strange (USA)
1990 Hale Irwin (USA)
1991 Payne Stewart (USA)
1992 Tom Kite (USA)
1993 Lee Janzen (USA)

Most wins: (4), Willie Anderson (USA), 1901, 1903–5; Bobby Jones (USA), 1923, 1926, 1929–30; Ben Hogan (USA), 1948, 1950–1, 1953; Jack Nicklaus (USA), 1962, 1967, 1972, 1980.

US Masters

First held in 1934; takes place at the Augusta National course in Georgia every April.

Recent winners
1981 Tom Watson (USA)
1982 Craig Stadler (USA)
1983 Severiano Ballesteros (Spain)
1984 Ben Crenshaw (USA)
1985 Bernhard Langer (W Germany)
1986 Jack Nicklaus (USA)
1987 Larry Mize (USA)
1988 Sandy Lyle (Great Britain)
1989 Nick Faldo (Great Britain)
1990 Nick Faldo (Great Britain)
1991 Ian Woosnam (Great Britain)
1992 Fred Couples (USA)
1993 Bernard Langer (Germany)

Most wins: (6), Jack Nicklaus (USA), 1963, 1965–6, 1972, 1975, 1986.

United States PGA championship

The last of the season's four 'Majors'; first held in 1916, and a match-play event until 1958; takes place annually.

Recent winners
1981 Larry Nelson (USA)
1982 Ray Floyd (USA)
1983 Hal Sutton (USA)
1984 Lee Trevino (USA)
1985 Hubert Green (USA)
1986 Bob Tway (USA)
1987 Larry Nelson (USA)
1988 Jeff Sluman (USA)
1989 Payne Stewart (USA)
1990 Wayne Grady (USA)
1991 John Daly (USA)
1992 Nick Price (South Africa)
1993 Paul Azinger (USA)

Most wins: (5), Walter Hagen (USA), 1921, 1924–7; Jack Nicklaus (USA), 1963, 1971, 1973, 1975, 1980.

Ryder Cup

The leading international team tournament; first held at Worcester, Massachusetts, in 1927; takes place every two years between teams from the USA and Europe (Great Britain 1927–71; Great Britain and Ireland 1973–7).

Recent winners

1971	USA	18½–13½
1973	USA	19–13
1975	USA	21–11
1977	USA	12½–7½
1979	USA	17–11
1981	USA	18½–9½
1983	USA	14½–13½
1985	Europe	16½–11½
1987	Europe	15–13
1989	Drawn	14–14
1991	USA	14½–13½

Wins: (22), USA between 1927 and 1991. (3), Great Britain, 1929, 1933, 1957. (2), Europe, 1985, 1987. (2), Drawn, 1969, 1989.

GREYHOUND RACING

Greyhound Derby

The top race of the British season, first held in 1927; run at the White City every year (except 1940) until its closure in 1985; since then all races run at Wimbledon.

Recent winners
1979 Sarah's Bunny
1980 Indian Joe
1981 Parkdown Jet
1982 Laurie's Panther
1983 I'm Slippy
1984 Whisper Wishes
1985 Pagan Swallow
1986 Tico
1987 Signal Spark
1988 Hit the Lid
1989 Lartigue Note
1990 Slippy Blue
1991 Ballinderry Ash
1992 Farloe Melody

Most wins: (2), Mick the Miller, 1929–30; Patricia's Hope, 1972–3.

GYMNASTICS

World championships

First held in 1903; took place every four years, 1922–78; since 1979, every two years.

Recent winners, individual combined exercises (men)
1966 Mikhail Voronin (USSR)
1970 Eizo Kenmotsu (Japan)
1974 Shigeru Kasamatsu (Japan)
1978 Nikolai Adrianov (USSR)
1979 Aleksandr Ditiatin (USSR)
1981 Yuriy Korolev (USSR)
1983 Dmitri Belozerchev (USSR)
1985 Yuriy Korolev (USSR)
1987 Dmitri Belozerchev (USSR)
1989 Igor Korobichensky (USSR)
1991 Grigoriy Misutin (USSR)

Recent winners, team (men)
1966 Japan
1970 Japan
1974 Japan
1978 Japan
1979 USSR
1981 USSR
1983 China
1985 USSR
1987 USSR
1989 USSR
1991 USSR

Most wins: Individual (2), Marco Torrès (France), 1909, 1913; Peter Sumi (Yugoslavia), 1922, 1926; Yuriy Korolev and Dmitri Belozerchev, as above. Team (8), USSR, 1954, 1958, and as above.

Recent winners, individual combined exercises (women)
1966 Vera Caslavska (Czechoslovakia)
1970 Ludmila Tourischeva (USSR)
1974 Ludmila Tourischeva (USSR)
1978 Yelena Mukhina (USSR)
1979 Nelli Kim (USSR)
1981 Olga Bitcherova (USSR)
1983 Natalia Yurchenko (USSR)
1985 Yelena Shoushounova (USSR) and Oksana Omeliantchuk (USSR)
1987 Aurelia Dobre (Romania)
1989 Svetlana Boginskaya (USSR)
1991 Kim Zmeskal (USA)

Gymnastics (continued)

Recent winners, team (women)
1966 Czechoslovakia
1970 USSR
1974 USSR
1978 USSR
1979 Romania
1981 USSR
1983 USSR
1985 USSR
1987 Romania
1989 USSR
1991 USSR

Most wins: Individual (2), Vlasta Dekanová (Czechoslovakia), 1934, 1938; Larissa Latynina (USSR), 1958, 1962; Ludmila Tourischeva, as above. Team (10), USSR, 1954, 1958 and as above.

Olympic games

Gold medal winners, 1992 combined exercises (men)
Individual
Vitally Sheherbo (Unified Team)

Team
Unified Team

Gold medal winners, 1992 combined exercises (women)
Individual
Tatjana Gutsu (Unified Team)

Team
Unified Team

HANDBALL

World championships

First men's championships held in 1938, both indoors and outdoors (latter discontinued in 1966); first women's outdoor championships in 1949, (discontinued in 1960); first women's indoor championships in 1957.

Winners, indoors (men)
1938 Germany
1954 Sweden
1958 Sweden
1961 Romania
1964 Romania
1967 Czechoslovakia
1970 Romania
1974 Romania
1978 W Germany
1982 USSR
1986 Yugoslavia
1990 Sweden

Winners, outdoors (men)
1938 Germany
1948 Sweden
1952 W Germany
1955 W Germany
1959 E/W Germany (combined)
1963 E Germany
1966 W Germany

Most wins: Indoors (4), Romania, as above. Outdoors (4), W Germany (including 1 as combined E/W German team), as above.

Winners, indoors (women)
1957 Czechoslovakia
1962 Romania
1965 Hungary
1971 E Germany
1973 Yugoslavia
1975 E Germany
1979 E Germany
1982 USSR
1986 USSR
1990 USSR

Winners, outdoors (women)
1949 Hungary
1956 Romania
1960 Romania

Most wins: Indoors (3), E Germany, as above. Outdoors (2), Romania, as above.

Olympic games

Gold medal winners, 1992
Men Unified Team
Women South Korea

HANG GLIDING

World championships

First held officially in 1976; since 1979, take place every two years.

Winners, individual (class 1)
1976 Christian Steinbach (Austria)
1979 Josef Guggenmose (W Germany)
1981 Pepe Lopez (Brazil)
1983 Steve Moyes (Australia)
1985 John Pendry (Great Britain)
1987 Rich Duncan (Australia)
1989 Robert Whittall (Great Britain)
1991 Tomás Schanek (Czechoslovakia)

Winners (team)
1976 Austria
1979 France
1981 Great Britain
1983 Australia
1985 Great Britain
1987 Australia
1989 Great Britain
1991 Great Britain

Most wins: Individual, no person has more than one. Team (4), Great Britain, as above.

HOCKEY

World Cup

Men's tournament first held in 1971, and every four years since 1978; women's tournament first held in 1974, and now takes place every three years.

Recent winners (men)

1973 Netherlands
1975 India
1978 Pakistan
1982 Pakistan
1986 Australia
1990 Netherlands

Most wins: (3), Pakistan, as above, plus 1971.

Recent winners (women)

1976 W Germany
1978 Netherlands
1981 W Germany
1983 Netherlands
1986 Netherlands
1990 Netherlands

Most wins: (5), Netherlands, as above, plus 1974.

Olympic games

Regarded as hockey's leading competition; first held in 1908; included at every celebration since 1928; women's competition first held in 1980.

Recent winners (men)

1948 India
1952 India
1956 India
1960 Pakistan
1964 India
1968 Pakistan
1972 W Germany
1976 New Zealand
1980 India
1984 Pakistan
1988 Great Britain
1992 Germany

Recent winners (women)

1980 Zimbabwe
1984 Netherlands
1988 Australia
1992 Spain

Most wins: Men (8), India, 1928, 1932, 1936 and as above. Women, no nation has won the title more than once.

Hockey field

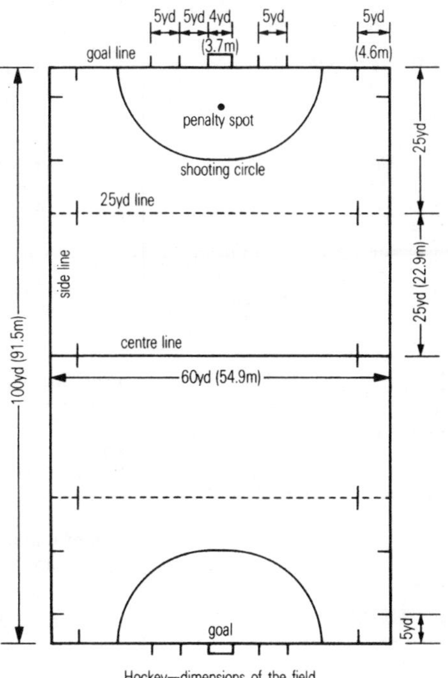

Hockey—dimensions of the field

HORSE RACING

The English Classics are five races run from April to September each year for three-year-olds: The Derby; Oaks; One Thousand Guineas; Two Thousand Guineas, and St Leger.

The Derby

The 'Blue Riband' of the Turf; run at Epsom over $1^1/_2$ miles; first run in 1780.

Recent winners

Horse (Jockey)

1981 Shergar (Walter Swinburn)
1982 Golden Fleece (Pat Eddery)
1983 Teenoso (Lester Piggott)
1984 Secreto (Christy Roche)
1985 Slip Anchor (Steve Cauthen)
1986 Shahrastani (Walter Swinburn)
1987 Reference Point (Steve Cauthen)
1988 Kahyasi (Ray Cochrane)
1989 Nashwan (Willie Carson)
1990 Quest for Fame (Pat Eddery)
1991 Generous (Alan Munro)
1992 Dr Devious (John Reid)
1993 Commander-In-Chief (Michael Kinane)

Most wins: Jockey (9), Lester Piggott, 1954, 1957, 1960, 1968, 1970, 1972, 1976–7, 1983.

The Oaks

Raced at Epsom over $1^1/_2$ miles; for fillies only; first run in 1779.

Recent winners

Horse (Jockey)

1981 Blue Wind (Lester Piggott)
1982 Time Charter (Billy Newnes)
1983 Sun Princess (Willy Carson)
1984 Circus Plume (Lester Piggott)
1985 Oh So Sharp (Steve Cauthen)
1986 Midway Lady (Ray Cochrane)
1987 Unite (Walter Swinburn)
1968 Diminuendo (Steve Cauthen)
1989 Aliysa (Walter Swinburn)
1990 Salsabil (Willie Carson)
1991 Jet Ski Lady (Christy Roche)
1992 User Friendly (George Duffield)
1993 Intrepedity (Michael Roberts)

Most wins: Jockey (9), Frank Buckle, 1797–9, 1802–3, 1805, 1817–18, 1823.

Horse racing (continued)

One Thousand Guineas

Run over 1 mile at Newmarket; for fillies only; first run in 1814.

Recent winners

Horse (Jockey)

1981 Fairy Footsteps (Lester Piggott)
1982 On the House (John Reid)
1983 Ma Biche (Freddy Head)
1984 Pebbles (Philip Robinson)
1985 Oh So Sharp (Steve Cauthen)
1986 Midway Lady (Ray Cochrane)
1987 Miesque (Freddy Head)
1988 Ravinella (Gary Moore)
1989 Musical Bliss (Walter Swinburn)
1990 Salsabil (Willie Carson)
1991 Shadayid (Willie Carson)
1992 Hatoof (Walter Swinburn)
1993 Sayyedati (Ray Cochrane)

Most wins: Jockey (7), George Fordham, 1859, 1861, 1865, 1868–9, 1881, 1883.

Two Thousand Guineas

Run at Newmarket over 1 mile; first run in 1809.

Recent winners

Horse (Jockey)

1981 To-Agori-Mou (Greville Starkey)
1982 Zino (Freddy Head)
1983 Lomond (Pat Eddery)
1984 El Gran Senor (Pat Eddery)
1985 Shadeed (Lester Piggott)
1986 Dancing Brave (Greville Starkey)
1987 Don't Forget Me (Willie Carson)
1988 Doyoun (Walter Swinburn)
1989 Nashwan (Willie Carson)
1990 Tirol (Michael Kinane)
1991 Mystiko (Michael Roberts)
1992 Rodrigo de Triano (Lester Piggott)
1993 Zafonic (Pat Eddery)

Most wins: Jockey (9), Jem Robinson, 1825, 1828, 1831, 1833, 1847–8.

St Leger

The oldest of the five English classics; first run in 1776; raced at Doncaster annually over 1 mile 6 furlongs 127 yards.

Recent winners

Horse (Jockey)

1981 Cut Above (Joe Mercer)
1982 Touching Wood (Paul Cook)
1983 Sun Princess (Willie Carson)
1984 Commanche Run (Lester Piggott)
1985 Oh So Sharp (Steve Cauthen)
1986 Moon Madness (Pat Eddery)
1987 Reference Point (Steve Cauthen)
1988 Minster Son (Willie Carson)
1989 Michelozzo (Steve Cauthen)
1990 Snurge (Richard Quinn)
1991 Toulon (Pat Eddery)
1992 User Friendly (George Duffield)

Most wins: Jockey (9), Bill Scott, 1821, 1825, 1828–9, 1938–41, 1846.

Grand National

Steeplechasing's most famous race; first run at Maghull in 1836; at Aintree since 1839; war-time races at Gatwick 1916–18.

Recent winners

Horse (Jockey)

1981 Aldaniti (Bob Champion)
1982 Grittar (Mr Dick Saunders)
1983 Corbiere (Ben De Haan)
1984 Hallo Dandy (Neale Doughty)
1985 Last Suspect (Hywel Davies)
1986 West Tip (Richard Dunwoody)
1987 Maori Venture (Steve Knight)
1988 Rhyme 'N' Reason (Brendan Powell)
1989 Little Polveir (Jimmy Frost)
1990 Mr Frisk (Marcus Armytage)
1991 Seagram (Nigel Howke)
1992 Party Politics (Carl Llewellyn)
1993* Void

*after a 2nd false start, the field was not called back
'Mr' denotes that the jockey is an amateur rider.

Most wins: Jockey (5), George Stevens, 1856, 1863–4, 1869–70. Horse (3), Red Rum 1973–4, 1977.

Prix de l'Arc de Triomphe

The leading end of season race in Europe; raced over 2 400 metres at Longchamp, France; first run in 1920.

Recent winners

Horse (Jockey)

1981 Gold River (Gary Moore)
1982 Akiyda (Yves Saint-Martin)
1983 All Along (Walter Swinburn)
1984 Sagace (Yves Saint-Martin)
1985 Rainbow Quest (Pat Eddery)
1986 Dancing Brave (Pat Eddery)
1987 Trempolino (Pat Eddery)
1988 Tony Bin (John Reid)
1989 Caroll House (Michael Kinane)
1990 Saumarez (Gerald Mossé)
1991 Suave Dancer (Cash Asmussen)
1992 Subotica (Thierry Jarnet)

Most wins: Jockey (4), Jacko Doyasbère, 1942, 1944, 1950–1; Freddy Head, 1966, 1972, 1976, 1979; Yves Saint-Martin, 1970, 1974, as above. Horse (2), Ksar, 1921–2; Motrico, 1930, 1932; Corrida, 1936–7; Tantième, 1950–1; Ribot, 1955–6; Alleged 1977–8.

The American Triple Crown comprises three races for three-year olds; The Kentucky Derby, Preakness Stakes and Belmont Stakes.

Kentucky Derby

Raced at Churchill Downs, Louisville over 1 mile 2 furlongs; first run in 1875.

Recent winners

Horse (Jockey)

1981 Pleasant Colony (Jorge Velasquez)
1982 Gato Del Sol (Eddie Delahoussaye)
1983 Sunny's Halo (Eddie Delahoussaye)
1984 Swale (Laffit Pincay, Jr)
1985 Spend A Buck (Angel Cordero, Jr)
1986 Ferdinand (Willie Shoemaker)
1987 Alysheba (Chris McCarron)
1988 Winning Colors (Gary Stevens)
1989 Sunday Silence (Pat Valenzuela)
1990 Unbridled (Craig Perret)
1991 Strike The Gold (Chris Antley)
1992 Lil E Tee (Pat Day)

Most wins: Jockey (5), Eddie Arcaro, 1938, 1941, 1945, 1948, 1952; Bill Hartack, 1957, 1960, 1962, 1964, 1969.

Preakness Stakes

Raced at Pimlico, Baltimore, Maryland over 1 mile $1^1/_2$ furlongs; first run in 1873.

Recent winners
Horse (Jockey)

1981 Pleasant Colony (Jorge Velasquez)
1982 Aloma's Ruler (Jack Kaenel)
1983 Deputed Testimony (Don Miller, Jr)
1984 Gate Dancer (Angel Cordero, Jr)
1985 Tank's Prospect (Pat Day)
1986 Snow Chief (Alex Solis)
1987 Alysheba (Chris McCarron)
1988 Risen Star (Eddie Delahoussaye)
1989 Sunday Silence (Pat Valenzuela)
1990 Summer Squall (Pat Day)
1991 Hansel (Jerry Bailey)
1992 Pine Bluff (Chris McCarron)

Most wins: Jockey (6), Eddie Arcaro, 1941, 1948, 1950–1, 1955, 1957.

Belmont Stakes

Raced at Belmont Park, New York over 1 mile 4 furlongs; first run in 1867 at Jerome Park.

Recent winners
Horse (Jockey)

1981 Summing (George Martens)
1982 Conquistador Cielo (Laffit Pincay, Jr)
1983 Caveat (Laffit Pincay, Jr)
1984 Swale (Laffit Pincay, Jr)
1985 Creme Fraiche (Eddie Maple)
1986 Danzig Connection (Chris McCarron)
1987 Bet Twice (Craig Perrett)
1988 Risen Star (Eddie Delahoussaye)
1989 Easy Goer (Pat Day)
1990 Go And Go (Michael Kinane)
1991 Hansel (Jenny Bailey)
1992 A.P. Indy (Eddie Delahoussaye)

Most wins: Jockey (6), Jimmy McLaughlin, 1882–4, 1886–8; Eddie Arcaro, 1941–2, 1945, 1948, 1952, 1955.

HURLING

All-Ireland championship

First contested in 1887; played on the first Sunday in September each year.

Recent winners

1979 Kilkenny
1980 Galway
1981 Offaly
1982 Kilkenny
1983 Kilkenny
1984 Cork
1985 Offaly
1986 Cork
1987 Galway
1988 Galway
1989 Tipperary
1990 Cork
1991 Tipperary
1992 Limerick

Most wins: (27), Cork, 1890, 1892–4, 1902–3, 1919, 1926, 1928–9, 1931, 1941–4, 1946, 1952–4, 1966, 1970, 1976–8, 1984, 1986, 1990.

ICE HOCKEY

World championship

First held in 1930; takes place annually (except 1980); up to 1968 Olympic champions also regarded as world champions.

Recent winners

1981 USSR
1982 USSR
1983 USSR
1984 USSR
1985 Czechoslovakia
1986 USSR
1987 Sweden
1988 USSR
1989 USSR
1990 USSR
1991 Sweden
1992 Sweden

Most wins: (24), USSR, 1954, 1956, 1963–71, 1973–5, 1978–9, and as above.

Stanley Cup

The most sought-after trophy at club level; the end-of-season meeting between the winners of the two conferences in the National Hockey League in the USA and Canada.

Recent winners

1981 New York Islanders
1982 New York Islanders
1983 New York Islanders
1984 Edmonton Oilers
1985 Edmonton Oilers
1986 Montreal Canadiens
1987 Edmonton Oilers
1988 Edmonton Oilers
1989 Calgary Flames
1990 Edmonton Oilers
1991 Pittsburgh Penguins
1992 Pittsburgh Penguins
1993 Montreal Canadiens

Most wins: (24), Montreal Canadiens, 1916, 1924, 1930–1, 1944, 1946, 1953, 1956–60, 1965–6, 1968–9, 1971, 1973, 1976–9, 1986, 1993.

Olympic games

Gold medal winners

1972 USSR
1976 USSR
1980 USA
1986 USSR
1988 USSR
1992 Unified Team

ICE SKATING

World championships

First men's championships in 1896; first women's event in 1906; pairs first contested in 1908; ice dance officially recognized in 1952.

Recent winners (men)

1982 Scott Hamilton (USA)
1983 Scott Hamilton (USA)
1984 Scott Hamilton (USA)
1985 Alexander Fadayev (USSR)
1986 Brian Boitano (USA)
1987 Brian Orser (Canada)
1988 Brian Boitano (USA)
1989 Kurt Browning (Canada)
1990 Kurt Browning (Canada)
1991 Kurt Browning (Canada)
1992 Viktor Petrenko (Unified Team)

Most wins: (10), Ulrich Salchow (Sweden), 1901–5, 1907–11.

Recent winners (women)

1982 Elaine Zayak (USA)
1983 Rosalynn Sumners (USA)
1984 Katarina Witt (E Germany)
1985 Katarina Witt (E Germany)
1986 Debbie Thomas (USA)
1987 Katarina Witt (E Germany)
1988 Katarina Witt (E Germany)
1989 Midori Ito (Japan)
1990 Jill Trenany (USA)
1991 Kristi Yamaguchi (USA)
1992 Kristi Yamaguchi (USA)

Most wins: (10), Sonja Henie (Norway), 1927–36.

Recent winners (pairs)

1982 Sabine Baess/Tassilo Thierbach (E Germany)
1983 Yelena Valova/Oleg Vasiliev (USSR)
1984 Barbara Underhill/Paul Martini (Canada)
1985 Yelena Valova/Oleg Vasiliev (USSR)
1986 Yekaterina Gordeeva/Sergey Grinkov (USSR)
1987 Yekaterina Gordeeva/Sergey Grinkov (USSR)
1988 Yelena Valova/Oleg Vasiliev (USSR)
1989 Yekaterina Gordeeva/Sergey Grinkov (USSR)
1990 Yekaterina Gordeeva/Sergey Grinkov (USSR)
1991 Natalya Mishkutienok/Artur Dmitriev (USSR)
1992 Natalya Mishkutienok/Artur Dmitriev (Unified Team)

Most wins: (10), Irina Rodnina (USSR), 1969–72 (with Aleksey Ulanov), 1973–8 (with Aleksander Zaitsev).

Recent winners, ice dance

1982 Jayne Torvill/Christopher Dean (Great Britain)
1983 Jayne Torvill/Christopher Dean (Great Britain)
1984 Jayne Torvill/Christopher Dean (Great Britain)
1985 Natalya Bestemianova/Andrey Bukin (USSR)
1986 Natalya Bestemianova/Andrey Bukin (USSR)
1987 Natalya Bestemianova/Andrey Bukin (USSR)
1988 Natalya Bestemianova/Andrey Bukin (USSR)
1989 Marina Klimova/Sergey Ponomarenko (USSR)
1990 Marina Klimova/Sergey Ponomarenko (USSR)
1991 Maia Usova/Alexandr Zhulin (USSR)
1992 Marina Klimova/Sergey Ponomarenko (Unified Team)

Most wins: (6), Aleksander Gorshkov and Lyudmila Pakhomova (USSR), 1970–4, 1976.

JUDO

World championships

First held in 1956, now contested every two years; current weight categories established in 1979; women's championship instituted in 1980.

Recent winners, open (men)

1979 Sumio Endo (Japan)
1981 Yasuhiro Yamashita (Japan)
1983 Hitoshi Saito (Japan)
1985 Yoshimi Masaki (Japan)
1987 Naoya Ogawa (Japan)
1989 Naoya Ogawa (Japan)
1991 Naoya Ogawa (Japan)

Recent winners, over 95 kg (men)

1979 Yasuhiro Yamashita (Japan)
1981 Yasuhiro Yamashita (Japan)
1983 Yasuhiro Yamashita (Japan)
1985 Yung-Chul Cho (Korea)
1987 Grigori Vertichev (USSR)
1989 Naoya Ogawa (Japan)
1991 Sergey Kosorotow (USSR)

Recent winners, under 95 kg (men)

1979 Tengiz Khubuluri (USSR)
1981 Tengiz Khubuluri (USSR)
1983 Valeriy Divisenko (USSR)
1985 Hitoshi Sugai (Japan)
1987 Hitoshi Sugai (Japan)
1989 Koba Kurtanidze (Japan)
1991 Stéphane Traineau (France)

Recent winners, under 85 kg (men)

1979 Detlef Ultsch (E Germany)
1981 Bernard Tchoullouyan (France)
1983 Detlef Ultsch (E Germany)
1985 Peter Seisenbacher (Austria)
1987 Fabien Canu (France)
1989 Fabien Canu (France)
1991 Hirotaka Okada (Japan)

Recent winners, under 78 kg (men)

1979 Shozo Fujii (Japan)
1981 Neil Adams (Great Britain)
1983 Nobutoshi Hikage (Japan)
1985 Nobutoshi Hikage (Japan)
1987 Hirotaka Okada (Japan)
1989 Kim Byung-ju (S Korea)
1991 Daniel Lascau (Germany)

Recent winners, under 71 kg (men)

1979 Kyoto Katsuki (Japan)
1981 Chon-Hak Park (Korea)
1983 Kidetoshi Nakanishi (Japan)
1985 Byeong-Keun Ahn (Korea)
1987 Mike Swain (USA)
1989 Toshihiko Koga (Japan)
1991 Toshihiko Koga (Japan)

Recent winners, under 65 kg (men)

1979 Nikolai Soludkhin (USSR)
1981 Katsuhiko Kashiwazaki (Japan)

1983 Nikolai Soludkhin (USSR)
1985 Yuriy Sokolov (USSR)
1987 Yosuke Yamamoto (Japan)
1989 Drago Becanovic (Yugoslavia)
1991 Udo Quellmalz (Germany)

Recent winners, under 60 kg (men)

1979 Thierry Ray (France)
1981 Yasuhiko Moriwaki (Japan)
1983 Khazret Tletseri (USSR)
1985 Shinji Hosokawa (Japan)
1987 Kim Jae-Yup (S Korea)
1989 Amiran Totikashvili (USSR)
1991 Tadanori Koshino (Japan)

Most titles: (4), Yashiro Yamashita (Japan), 1981 (Open), 1979, 1981, 1983 (over 95 kg); Shozo Fujii (Japan), 1971, 1973, 1975 (under 80 kg), 1979 (under 78 kg).

Recent winners, open (women)

1980 Ingrid Berghmans (Belgium)
1982 Ingrid Berghmans (Belgium)
1984 Ingrid Berghmans (Belgium)
1986 Ingrid Berghmans (Belgium)
1987 Gao Fengliang (China)
1989 Estella Rodriguez (Cuba)
1991 Zhuang Xiaoyan (China)

Recent winners, over 72 kg (women)

1980 Margarita de Cal (Italy)
1982 Natalina Lupino (France)
1984 Maria-Teresa Motta (Italy)
1986 Gao Fengliang (China)
1987 Gao Fengliang (China)
1989 Gao Fengliang (China)
1991 Moon Ji-Yoon (S Korea)

Recent winners, under 72 kg (women)

1980 Jocelyne Triadou (France)
1982 Barbara Classen (W Germany)
1984 Ingrid Berghmans (Belgium)
1986 Irene de Kok (Netherlands)
1987 Irene de Kok (Netherlands)
1989 Ingrid Berghmans (Belgium)
1991 Kim Mi-Jeono (S Korea)

Recent winners, under 66 kg (women)

1980 Edith Simon (Austria)
1982 Brigitte Deydier (France)
1986 Brigitte Deydier (France)
1987 Alexandra Schreiber (W Germany)
1989 Emanuela Pierantozzi (Italy)
1991 Emanuela Pierantozzi (Italy)

Recent winners, under 61 kg (women)

1980 Anita Staps (Netherlands)
1982 Martine Rotheir (France)
1984 Natasha Hernandez (Venezuela)
1986 Diane Bell (Great Britain)
1987 Diane Bell (Great Britain)
1989 Catherine Fleury (France)
1991 Frauke Eickhoff (Germany)

Recent winners, under 56 kg (women)

1980 Gerda Winklbauer (Austria)
1982 Béatrice Rodriguez (France)
1984 Ann-Maria Burns (USA)
1986 Ann Hughes (Great Britain)
1987 Catherine Arnaud (France)
1989 Catherine Arnaud (France)
1991 Miriam Blasco Soto (Spain)

Recent winners, under 52 kg (women)

1980 Edith Hrovat (Austria)
1982 Loretta Doyle (Great Britain)
1984 Kaori Yamaguchi (Japan)
1986 Dominique Brun (France)
1987 Sharon Rendle (Great Britain)
1989 Sharon Rendle (Great Britain)
1991 Alessandra Giungi (Italy)

Recent winners, under 48 kg (women)

1980 Jane Bridge (Great Britain)
1982 Karen Briggs (Great Britain)
1984 Karen Briggs (Great Britain)
1986 Karen Briggs (Great Britain)
1987 Zhangyun Li (China)
1989 Karen Briggs (Great Britain)
1991 Cécille Nowak (France)

Most titles: (6), Ingrid Berghmans (Belgium), 1980, 1982, 1984, 1986 (open), 1984, 1989 (under 72 kg).

KARATE

World championships

First held in Tokyo 1970; takes place every two years since 1980, when women first competed; there is a team competition plus individual competitions – Kumite (seven weight categories for men and three for women) and Kata.

Team winners

1970 Japan
1972 France
1975 Great Britain
1977 Netherlands
1980 Spain
1982 Great Britain
1984 Great Britain
1986 Great Britain
1988 Great Britain
1990 Great Britain

Most wins: (6), Great Britain, as above.

LACROSSE

World championships

First held for men in 1967; for women in 1969; taken place every four years since 1974; since 1982 the women's event has been called the World Cup.

Winners (men)

1967 USA
1974 USA
1978 Canada
1982 USA
1986 USA
1990 USA

Most wins: (5), USA, as above.

Winners (women)

1969 Great Britain
1974 USA
1978 Canada
1982 USA
1986 Australia
1989 USA

Most wins: (3), USA, as above.

Iroquois Cup

The sport's best known trophy; contested by English club sides annually since 1890.

Recent winners

1979 Cheadle
1980 South Manchester
1981 Cheadle
1982 Sheffield University
1983 Sheffield University
1984 Cheadle
1985 Cheadle
1986 Heaton Mersey
1987 Stockport
1988 Mellor
1989 Stockport
1990 Cheadle
1991 Cheadle
1992 Cheadle

Most wins: (17), Stockport, 1897–1901, 1903, 1905, 1911–13, 1923–4, 1926, 1928, 1934, 1987, 1989.

MODERN PENTHATHLON

World championships

Held annually since 1949 with the exception of Olympic years, when the Olympic champions automatically become world champions.

Recent winners, individual

1979 Robert Nieman (USA)
1980 Anatoliy Starostin (USSR)
1981 Janusz Pyciak-Peciak (Poland)
1982 Daniele Masala (Italy)
1983 Anatoliy Starostin (USSR)
1984 Daniele Masala (Italy)
1985 Attila Mizser (Hungary)
1986 Carlo Massullo (Italy)
1987 Joel Bouzou (France)
1988 Janos Martinek (Hungary)
1989 László Fábián (Hungary)
1990 Gianluca Tiberti (Italy)
1991 Arkadiusz Skrzypasjek (Poland)
1992 Arkadiusz Skrzypasjek (Poland)

Recent winners, team

1979 USA
1980 USSR
1981 Poland
1982 USSR
1983 USSR
1984 Italy
1985 USSR
1986 Italy
1987 Hungary
1988 Hungary
1989 Hungary
1990 USSR
1991 USSR
1992 Poland

Most wins: Individual (6), Andras Balczo (Hungary), 1963, 1965–9, 1972. Team (18), USSR, 1956–9, 1961–2, 1964, 1969, 1971–4, 1980, 1982–3, 1985, 1990, 1991.

MOTOR CYCLING

World championships

First organized in 1949; current titles for 500 cc, 250 cc, 125 cc, 80 cc and Sidecar; Formula One and Endurance world championships also held annually; the most prestigious title is the 500 cc category.

Recent winners, 500 cc

1981 Marco Lucchinelli (Italy)
1982 Franco Uncini (Italy)
1983 Freddie Spencer (USA)
1984 Eddie Lawson (USA)
1985 Freddie Spencer (USA)
1986 Eddie Lawson (USA)
1987 Wayne Gardner (Australia)
1988 Eddie Lawson (USA)
1989 Eddie Lawson (USA)
1990 Wayne Rainey (USA)
1991 Wayne Rainey (USA)
1992 Wayne Rainey (USA)

Most wins: (8), Giacomo Agostini (Italy), 1966–72, 1975.

Most world titles: (15), Giacomo Agostini (Italy), 500 cc as above, 350 cc 1968–74.

Isle of Man TT races

The most famous of all motor cycle races; take place each June; first held 1907; principal race is the Senior TT.

Recent winners, senior TT

1981 Mick Grant (Great Britain)
1982 Norman Brown (Great Britain)
1983 Rob McElnea (Great Britain)
1984 Rob McElnea (Great Britain)
1985 Joey Dunlop (Ireland)
1986 Roger Burnett (Great Britain)
1987 Joey Dunlop (Ireland)
1988 Joey Dunlop (Ireland)
1989 Steve Hislop (Great Britain)
1990 Carl Fogarty (Great Britain)
1991 Steve Hislop (Great Britain)
1992 Steve Hislop (Great Britain)

Most senior TT wins: (7), Mike Hailwood (Great Britain), 1961, 1963–7, 1979.

MOTOR RACING

World championship

A Formula One drivers' world championship instituted in 1950; constructor's championship instituted in 1958.

Recent winners

1981 Nelson Piquet (Brazil) Brabham
1982 Keke Rosberg (Finland) Williams
1983 Nelson Piquet (Brazil) Brabham
1984 Niki Lauda (Austria) McLaren
1985 Alain Prost (France) McLaren
1986 Alain Prost (France) McLaren
1987 Nelson Piquet (France) Williams
1988 Ayrton Senna (Brazil) McLaren
1989 Alain Prost (France) McLaren
1990 Ayrton Senna (Brazil) McLaren
1991 Ayrton Senna (Brazil) McLaren
1992 Nigel Mansell (Great Britain) Williams

Most wins: Driver (5), Juan Manuel Fangio (Argentina), 1951, 1954–7. Constructor (8), Ferrari, 1964, 1975–7, 1979, 1982–3.

Le Mans 24-Hour Race

The greatest of all endurance races; first held in 1923.

Recent winners

1981 Jacky Ickx (Belgium)
Derek Bell (Great Britain)
1982 Jacky Ickx (Belgium)
Derek Bell (Great Britain)
1983 Vern Schuppan (Austria)
Al Holbert (USA)
Hurley Haywood (USA)
1984 Klaus Ludwig (W Germany)
Henri Pescarolo (France)
1985 Klaus Ludwig (W Germany)
'John Winter'* (W Germany)
Paolo Barilla (Italy)
1986 Hans Stück (W Germany)
Derek Bell (Great Britain)
Al Holbert (USA)
1987 Hans Stück (W Germany)
Derek Bell (Great Britain)
Al Holbert (USA)
1988 Jan Lammers (Netherlands)
Johnny Dumfries (Great Britain)
Andy Wallace (Great Britain)
1989 Jochen Mass (W Germany)
Manuel Reuter (W Germany)
Stanley Dickens (Sweden)
1990 John Neilsen (Denmark)
Price Cobb (USA)
Martin Brundle (Great Britain)
1991 Volker Weidler (Germany)
Johnny Herbert (Great Britain)
Bertrand Gochot (Belgium)
1992 Derek Warwick (Great Britain)
Mark Blundell (Great Britain)
Yannick Dalmas (France)

*pseudonym

Most wins: (6), Jacky Ickx (Belgium), 1969, 1975–7, 1981–2.

Indianapolis 500

First held in 1911; raced over the Indianapolis Raceway as part of the Memorial Day celebrations at the end of May each year.

Recent winners

1981 Bobby Unser (USA)
1982 Gordon Johncock (USA)
1983 Tom Sneva (USA)
1984 Rick Mears (USA)
1985 Danny Sullivan (USA)
1986 Bobby Rahal (USA)
1987 Al Unser (USA)
1988 Rick Mears (USA)
1989 Emerson Fittipaldi (Brazil)
1990 Arie Luyendyk (Netherlands)
1991 Rick Mears (USA)
1992 Al Unser Jr (USA)
1993 Emerson Fittipaldi (Brazil)

Most wins: (4), A J Foyt (USA), 1961, 1964, 1967, 1977; Al Unser (USA), 1970–1, 1978, 1987; Rick Mears (USA), 1979, 1984, 1988, 1991.

Monte Carlo rally

The world's leading rally; first held in 1911.

Recent winners

1980 Walter Röhrl/Christian Geistdorfer (W Germany)
1981 Jean Ragnotti/Jean-Marc André (France)
1982 Walter Röhrl/Christian Geistdorfer (W Germany)
1983 Walter Röhrl/Christian Geistdorfer (W Germany)
1984 Walter Röhrl/Christian Geistdorfer (W Germany)
1985 Ari Vatanen (Finland)/Terry Harryman (Great Britain)
1986 Henri Toivonen (Finland)/ Sergio Cresto (Italy)
1987 Mikki Biasion/Tigiano Siviero (Italy)
1988 Bruno Saby/Jean-Francois Fauchille (France)
1989 Mikki Biasion/Tigiano Siviero (Italy)
1990 Didier Auriol/Bernard Occelli (France)
1991 Carlos Sainz/Luis Moya (Spain)
1992 Didier Auriol/Bernard Occelli (France)

Most wins: (4), Sandro Munari (Italy), 1972, 1975–7; Walter Röhrl (W Germany), as above. Most successful co-driver: 4 wins Christian Geistdorfer, all with Walter Röhrl.

NETBALL

World championships

First held in 1963, then every four years.

Winners

1963 Australia
1967 New Zealand
1971 Australia
1975 Australia
1979 Australia, New Zealand, Trinidad & Tobago (*shared*)
1983 Australia
1987 New Zealand
1991 Australia

Most wins: (6), Australia, as above.

ORIENTEERING

World championships

First held in 1966; takes place every two years (to 1978, and since 1979).

Winners, individual (men)

1966 Age Hadler (Norway)
1968 Karl Johansson (Sweden)
1970 Stig Berge (Norway)
1972 Age Hadler (Norway)
1974 Bernt Frilen (Sweden)
1976 Egil Johansen (Norway)
1978 Egil Johansen (Norway)
1979 Oyvin Thon (Norway)
1981 Oyvin Thon (Norway)
1983 Morten Berglia (Norway)
1985 Kari Sallinen (Finland)
1987 Kent Olsson (Sweden)
1989 Peter Thoresen (Norway)
1991 Jörgen Mårtensson (Sweden)

Winners, individual (women)

1966 Ulla Lindqvist (Sweden)
1968 Ulla Lindqvist (Sweden)
1970 Ingrid Hadler (Norway)
1972 Sarolta Monspart (Finland)
1974 Mona Norgaard (Denmark)
1976 Lia Veijalainen (Finland)
1978 Anne Berit Eid (Norway)
1979 Outi Bergonstrom (Finland)
1981 Annichen Kringstad (Norway)
1983 Annichen Kringstad Svensson (Norway)
1985 Annichen Kringstad Svensson (Norway)
1987 Arja Hannus (Sweden)
1989 Marita Skogum (Sweden)
1991 Katalin Olah (Hungary)

Most wins: Men (2), Age Hadler (Norway), Egil Johansen (Norway), Oyvin Thon (Norway), as above. Women (3), Annichen Kringstad (Norway), as above.

Winners, relay (men)

1966	Sweden	1979	Sweden
1968	Sweden	1981	Norway
1970	Norway	1983	Norway
1972	Sweden	1985	Norway
1974	Sweden	1987	Norway
1976	Sweden	1989	Norway
1978	Norway	1991	Switzerland

Winners, relay (women)

1966	Sweden	1979	Finland
1968	Norway	1981	Sweden
1970	Sweden	1983	Sweden
1972	Finland	1985	Sweden
1974	Sweden	1987	Norway
1976	Sweden	1989	Sweden
1978	Finland	1991	Sweden

Most wins: Men (7), Norway, as above. Women (9) Sweden, as above.

POLO

Cowdray Park Gold Cup

First held in 1956, replacing the Champion Cup; the British Open Championship for club sides; so named because played at Cowdray Park, Sussex.

Recent winners

1979 Songhai
1980 Stowell Park
1981 Falcons
1982 Southfield
1983 Falcons
1984 Southfield
1985 Maple Leafs
1986 Tramontona
1987 Tramontona
1988 Tramontona
1989 Tramontona
1990 Hildon
1991 Tramontona
1992 Black Bears

Most wins: (5), Stowell Park, 1973–4, 1976, 1978, 1980; Tramontona as above.

POWERBOAT RACING

World championships

Instituted in 1982; held in many categories, with Formula One and Formula Two being the principal competitions; Formula Two, known as Formula Grand Prix, was discontinued in 1989.

Winners, Formula One

1982 Roger Jenkins (Great Britain)
1983 Renato Molinari (Italy)
1984 Renato Molinari (Italy)
1985 Bob Spalding (Great Britain)
1986 Gene Thibodaux (USA)
1987 Ben Robertson (USA)
1990 John Hill (Great Britain)
1991 Jonathan Jones (Great Britain)

Most wins: (2), Renato Molinari (Italy), as above.

Winners, Formula Two/Formula Grand Prix

1982 Michael Werner (W Germany)
1983 Michael Werner (W Germany)
1984 John Hill (Great Britain)
1985 John Hill (Great Britain)
1986 Jonathan Jones (Great Britain) and Buck Thornton (USA) (*shared*)
1987 Bill Seebold (USA)
1988 Chris Bush (USA)
1989 Jonathan Jones (Great Britain)

Most wins: (2), Michael Werner (W Germany); John Hill (Great Britain), Jonathan Jones (Great Britain), as above.

RACKETS

World championship

Organized on a challenge basis, the first champion in 1820 was Robert Mackay (Great Britain).

Recent winners

1929–37 Charles Williams (Great Britain)
1937–47 Donald Milford (Great Britain)
1947–54 James Dear (Great Britain)
1954–72 Geoffrey Atkins (Great Britain)
1972–73 William Surtees (USA)
1973–74 Howard Angus (Great Britain)
1975–81 William Surtees (USA)
1981–84 John Prenn (Great Britain)
1984–86 William Boone (Great Britain)
1986–88 John Prenn (Great Britain)
1988– James Male (Great Britain)

Longest reigning champion: 18 years, Geoffrey Atkins, as above.

REAL TENNIS

World championship

The first world champion was M Clerge (France) c. 1740, regarded as the first world champion of any sport. Held on a challenge basis; first held for women in 1985, and then every two years.

Recent winners (men)

1916–28 Fred Covey (Great Britain)
1928–55 Pierre Etchebaster (France)
1955–57 James Dear (Great Britain)
1957–59 Albert Johnson (Great Britain)
1959–69 Northrup Knox (USA)
1969–72 Pete Bostwick (USA)
1972–75 Jimmy Bostwick (USA)
1976–81 Howard Angus (Great Britain)
1981–87 Chris Ronaldson (Great Britain)
1987– Wayne Davis (Australia)

Longest reigning champion: 33 years, Edmond Barre (France), 1829–62.

Winners (women)

1985 Judy Clarke (Australia)
1987 Judy Clarke (Australia)
1989 Penny Fellows (Great Britain)
1991 Penny Fellows Lumley (Great Britain)

ROLLER SKATING

World championships

Figure skating world championships were first organized in 1947.

Recent winners, combined (men)
1979 Michael Butzke (E Germany)
1980 Michael Butzke (E Germany)
1981 Michael Butzke (E Germany)
1982 Michael Butzke (E Germany)
1983 Joachim Helmle (W Germany)
1984 Michele Biserni (Italy)
1985 Michele Biserni (Italy)
1986 Michele Tolomini (Italy)
1987 Sandro Guerra (Italy)
1988 Sandro Guerra (Italy)
1989 Sandro Guerra (Italy)
1990 Samo Kokorovec (Italy)
1991 Sandro Guerra (Italy)

Most wins: (5), Karl-Heinz Losch (W Germany), 1958–9, 1961–2, 1966.

Recent winners, combined (women)
1979 Petre Schneider (W Germany)
1980 Petre Schneider (W Germany)
1981 Petre Schneider (W Germany)
1982 Claudia Bruppacher (W Germany)
1983 Claudia Bruppacher (W Germany)
1984 Claudia Bruppacher (W Germany)
1985 Chiara Sartori (Italy)
1986 Chiara Sartori (Italy)
1987 Chiara Sartori (Italy)
1988 Rafaella Del Vinaccio (Italy)
1989 Rafaella Del Vinaccio (Italy)
1990 Rafaella Del Vinaccio (Italy)
1991 Rafaella Del Vinaccio (Italy)

Most wins: (4), Astrid Bader (W Germany), 1965–8; Rafaela Del Vinaccio (Italy), as above.

Recent winners, pairs
1979 Ray Chapatta/Karen Mejia (USA)
1980 Paul Price/Tina Kniesley (USA)
1981 Paul Price/Tina Kniesley (USA)
1982 Paul Price/Tina Kniesley (USA)
1983 John Arishita/Tammy Jeru (USA)
1984 John Arishita/Tammy Jeru (USA)
1985 John Arishita/Tammy Jeru (USA)
1986 John Arishita/Tammy Jeru (USA)
1987 Fabio Trevisani/Monica Mezzardi (Italy)
1988 Fabio Trevisani/Monica Mezzardi (Italy)
1989 David De Motte/Nicky Armstrong (USA)
1990 Larry McGrew/Tammy Jeru (USA)
1991 Larry McGrew/Tammy Jeru (USA)

Most wins: (6), Tammy Jeru (USA), as above (4 with John Arishita).

Recent winners, dance
1979 Dan Littel/Florence Arsenault (USA)
1980 Torsten Carels/Gabriele Achenback (E Germany)
1981 Mark Howard/Cindy Smith (USA)
1982 Mark Howard/Cindy Smith (USA)
1983 David Golub/Angela Famiano (USA)
1984 David Golub/Angela Famiano (USA)
1985 Martin Hauss/Andrea Steudte (W Germany)
1986 Scott Myers/Anna Danks (USA)
1987 Rob Ferendo/Lori Walsh (USA)
1988 Peter Wulf/Michela Mitzlaf (W Germany)
1989 Greg Goody/Jodee Viola (USA)
1990 Greg Goody/Jodee Viola (USA)
1991 Greg Goody/Jodee Viola (USA)

Most wins: (3), Jane Puracchio (USA), 1973, 1975–6; Dan Littel and Florence Arsenault (USA), 1977–9, Greg Goody and Jodee Viola (USA), as above.

ROWING

World championships

First held for men in 1962 and for women in 1974; Olympic champions assume the role of world champion in Olympic years; principal events are the single sculls.

Recent winners, single sculls (men)
1981 Peter-Michael Kolbe (W Germany)
1982 Rudiger Reiche (E Germany)
1983 Peter-Michael Kolbe (W Germany)
1984 Perrti Karppinen (Finland)
1985 Perrti Karppinen (Finland)
1986 Peter-Michael Kolbe (W Germany)
1987 Thomas Lange (E Germany)
1988 Thomas Lange (E Germany)
1989 Thomas Lange (E Germany)
1990 Yuri Janson (USSR)
1991 Thomas Lange (Germany)
1992 Thomas Lange (Germany)

Most wins: (5), Thomas Lange (Germany), as above.

Recent winners, sculls (women)
1981 Sanda Toma (Romania)
1982 Irina Fetissova (USSR)
1983 Jutta Hampe (E Germany)
1984 Valeria Racila (Romania)
1985 Cornelia Linse (E Germany)
1986 Jutta Hampe (E Germany)
1987 Magdelena Georgieva (Bulgaria)
1988 Jutta Behrendt (E Germany)
1989 Elisabeta Lipa (Romania)
1990 Brigit Peter (E Germany)
1991 Silke Laumann (Canada)
1992 Elisabeta Lipa (Romania)

Most wins: (5), Christine Hahn (neé Scheiblich) (E Germany), 1974–8.

University Boat Race

An annual contest between the crews from the Oxford and Cambridge University rowing clubs; first contested in 1829; the current course is from Putney to Mortlake.

Recent winners

1981 Oxford	1986 Cambridge	1988 Oxford
1982 Oxford	1987 Oxford	1991 Oxford
1983 Oxford	1988 Oxford	1992 Oxford
1984 Oxford	1989 Oxford	1993 Cambridge
1985 Oxford	1990 Oxford	

Wins: 70, Cambridge; 68, Oxford; 1 dead-heat (1877).

Diamond Sculls

Highlight of Henley Royal Regatta held every July; first contested in 1884.

Recent winners
1981 Chris Baillieu (Great Britain)
1982 Chris Baillieu (Great Britain)
1983 Steve Redgrave (Great Britain)
1984 Chris Baillieu (Great Britain)
1985 Steve Redgrave (Great Britain)
1986 Bjarne Eltang (Denmark)
1987 Peter-Michael Kolbe (W Germany)
1988 Hamish McGlashan (Australia)
1989 Vaclav Chalupa (Czechoslovakia)
1990 Eric Verdonk (New Zealand)
1991 Wim van Belleghem (Belgium)
1992 Rorie Henderson (Great Britain)

Most wins: (6), Stuart Mackenzie (Great Britain), 1957–62.

RUGBY LEAGUE

World Cup/International championship

First contested in 1954 between Great Britain, France, New Zealand and Australia. In 1975, England and Wales replaced Great Britain. The competition was discontinued after the 1977 World Cup, but was revived in 1988.

Winners

1954	Great Britain	1972	Great Britain
1957	Australia	1975	Australia
1960	Great Britain	1977	Australia
1968	Australia	1988	Australia
1970	Australia	1992	Australia

Most wins: (7) Australia, as above.

League championship

The original Northern Union was formed in 1895–6, and was won by Manningham. Since then there have been many changes to the rules and structure of the league, which from 1906 to 1973 featured a Championship Play-off. The present structure, with Divisions One and Two, dates from the 1973–4 season.

Recent winners

1981–82	Leigh	1987–88	Widnes
1982–83	Hull	1988–89	Widnes
1983–84	Hull Kingston Rovers	1989–90	Wigan
1984–85	Hull Kingston Rovers	1990–91	Wigan
1985–86	Halifax	1991–92	Wigan
1986–87	Wigan	1992–93	Wigan

Challenge Cup final

First contested in 1897 and won by Batley; first final at Wembley Stadium in 1929.

Recent winners

1981	Widnes	1988	Wigan
1982	Hull	1989	Wigan
1983	Featherstone Rovers	1990	Wigan
1984	Widnes	1991	Wigan
1985	Wigan	1992	Wigan
1986	Castleford	1993	Wigan
1987	Halifax		

Most wins: (14), Wigan, 1924, 1929, 1948, 1951, 1958–9, 1965, plus as above.

Premiership trophy

End-of-season knockout competition involving the top eight teams in the first division; first contested at the end of the 1974–5 season.

Recent winners

1981	Hull Kingston Rovers	1988	Widnes
1982	Widnes	1989	Widnes
1983	Widnes	1990	Widnes
1984	Hull Kingston Rovers	1991	Hull
1985	St Helens	1992	Wigan
1986	Warrington	1993	Wigan
1987	Wigan		

Most wins: (6), Widnes, 1980, plus as above.

Regal trophy

A knockout competition, first held in 1971–2. Formerly known as the John Player Special Trophy, it adopted its current name/title in 1989–90.

Recent winners

1982	Hull	1988	St Helens
1983	Wigan	1989	Wigan
1984	Leeds	1990	Wigan
1985	Hull Kingston Rovers	1991	Warrington
1986	Wigan	1992	Widnes
1987	Wigan	1993	Wigan

Most wins: (6), Wigan, as above.

Sydney Premiership

The principal competition in Australia, first held in 1908. The culmination of the competition is the Grand Final; the winning team receives the Winfield Cup.

Recent Winners
1980 Canterbury-Bankstown
1981 Parramatta
1982 Parramatta
1983 Parramatta
1984 Canterbury-Bankstown
1985 Canterbury-Bankstown
1986 Parramatta
1987 Manly-Warringah
1988 Canterbury-Bankstown
1989 Canberra
1990 Canberra
1991 Penrith
1992 Brisbane Broncos

RUGBY UNION

World Cup

The first Rugby Union World Cup was staged in 1987; New Zealand were crowned the first champions after beating France in the final. Australia beat England in the final of the second competition, in 1991.

Five Nations championship

A round-robin competition involving England, Ireland, Scotland, Wales and France; first contested in 1884.

Recent winners

1982	Ireland	1988	France and Wales
1983	France and Ireland	1989	France
1984	Scotland	1990	Scotland
1985	Ireland	1991	England
1986	France and Scotland	1992	England
1987	France	1993	France

Most outright wins: (21), Wales, 1893, 1900, 1902, 1905, 1908–9, 1911, 1922, 1931, 1936, 1950, 1952, 1956, 1965–6, 1969, 1971, 1975–6, 1978–9.

County championship

First held in 1889.

Recent winners

1982	Lancashire	1988	Lancashire
1983	Gloucestershire	1989	Durham
1984	Gloucestershire	1990	Lancashire
1985	Middlesex	1991	Cornwall
1986	Warwickshire	1992	Lancashire
1987	Yorkshire	1993	Lancashire

Most wins: (15) Gloucestershire, 1910, 1913, 1920–2, 1930–2, 1937, 1972, 1974–6, 1983–4.

Pilkington Cup

An annual knockout competition for English club sides; first held in the 1971–2 season. Known as the John Player Special Cup until 1988.

Recent winners

1982	Gloucester and Moseley (*shared*)	1988	Harlequins
		1989	Bath
1983	Bristol	1990	Bath
1984	Bath	1991	Harlequins
1985	Bath	1992	Bath
1986	Bath	1993	Leicester
1987	Bath		

Most wins: (7) Bath, as above.

Rugby Union football field

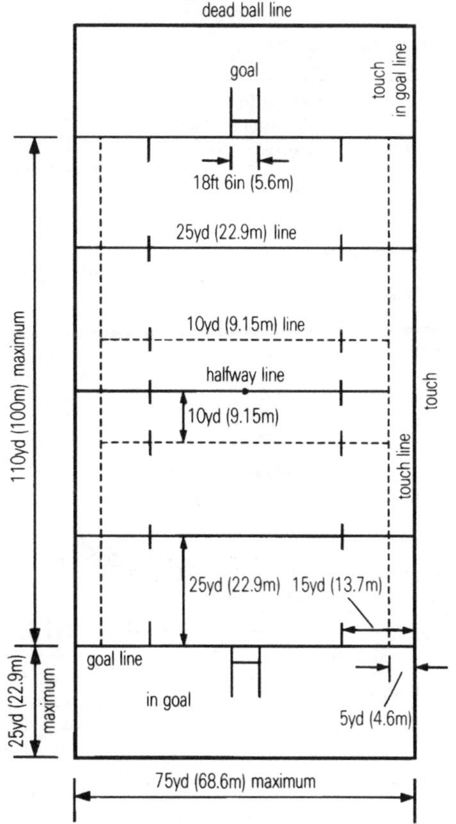

Schweppes Welsh Cup

The knockout tournament for Welsh clubs; first held in 1971–2.

Recent winners

1982	Cardiff	1988	Llanelli
1983	Pontypool	1989	Neath
1984	Cardiff	1990	Neath
1985	Llanelli	1991	Llanelli
1986	Cardiff	1992	Llanelli
1987	Cardiff	1993	Llanelli

Most wins: (9), Llanelli, 1973–6, 1985, 1988, 1991–3.

SHOOTING

Olympic games

The Olympic competition is the highlight of the shooting calendar; winners in all categories since 1980 are given below.

Free pistol (men)
1980 Aleksander Melentyev (USSR)
1984 Xu Haifeng (China)
1988 Sorin Babil (Romania)
1992 Konstantine Loukachik (Unified Team)

Rapid fire pistol (men)
1980 Corneliu Ion (Romania)
1984 Takeo Kamachi (Japan)
1988 Afanasi Kouzmine (USSR)
1992 Ralf Shumann (Germany)

Small bore rifle, three position (men)
1980 Viktor Vlasov (USSR)
1984 Malcolm Cooper (Great Britain)
1988 Malcolm Cooper (Great Britain)
1992 Gratchia Petrikiane (Unified Team)

Running game target (men)
1980 Igor Sokolov (USSR)
1984 Li Yuwei (China)
1988 Tor Heiestad (Norway)
1992 Michael Jakositz (Germany)

Trap (mixed)
1980 Luciano Giovanetti (Italy)
1984 Luciano giovanetti (Italy)
1988 Dmitri Monakov (USSR)
1992 Peter Hrdlicka (Czechoslovakia)

Skeet (mixed)
1980 Hans Rusmussen (Denmark)
1984 Matthew Dryke (USA)
1988 Axel Wegner (E Germany)
1992 Zhang Shan (China)

Small bore rifle, prone (men)
1980 Karoly Varga (Hungary)
1984 Edward Etzel (USA)
1988 Miroslav Varga (Czechoslovakia)
1992 Lee Eun Chul (S Korea)

Air rifle (men)
1984 Philippe Heberle (France)
1988 Goran Maksimovic (Yugoslavia)
1992 Iouri Fedkine (Unified Team)

Air pistol (men)
1988 Taniou Kiriakoy (USSR)
1992 Wang Yifu (China)

Sport pistol (women)
1984 Linda Thom (Canada)
1988 Nino Saloukvadze (USSR)
1992 Marina Logvinenko (Unified Team)

Air rifle (women)
1984 Pat Spurgin (USA)
1988 Irina Chilova (USSR)
1992 Yeo Kab-Soon (S Korea)

Small bore rifle (women)
1984 Wu Xiaoxuan (China)
1988 Silvia Sperber (W Germany)
1992 Lauri Melli (USA)

Air pistol (women)
1988 Jasna Sekuric (Yugoslavia)
1992 Marina Logrinenko (Unified Team)

SKIING

World Cup

A season-long competition first organized in 1967; champions are declared in downhill, slalom, giant slalom and super-giant slalom, as well as the overall champion; points are obtained for performances in each category.

Recent overall winners (men)
1982 Phil Mahre (USA)
1983 Phil Mahre (USA)
1984 Pirmin Zurbriggen (Switzerland)
1985 Marc Girardelli (Luxembourg)
1986 Marc Girardelli (Luxembourg)
1987 Pirmin Zurbriggen (Switzerland)
1988 Pirmin Zurbriggen (Switzerland)
1989 Marc Girardelli (Luxembourg)
1990 Pirmin Zurbriggen (Switzerland)
1991 Marc Girardelli (Luxembourg)
1992 Paul Accola (Switzerland)

Recent overall winners (women)
1982 Erika Hess (Switzerland)
1983 Tamara McKinney (USA)
1984 Erika Hess (Switzerland)
1985 Michela Figini (Switzerland)
1986 Maria Walliser (Switzerland)
1987 Maria Walliser (Switzerland)
1988 Michela Figini (Switzerland)
1989 Vreni Schneider (Switzerland)
1990 Petra Kronberger (Austria)
1991 Petra Kronberger (Austria)
1992 Petra Kronberger (Austria)

Most wins: Men (4), Gustavo Thoeni (Italy), 1971–3, 1975; Pirmin Zurbriggen (Switzerland), as above; Marc Girardelli (Luxembourg), as above. Women (6), Annemarie Moser-Pröll (Austria), 1971–5, 1979.

Olympic games

Gold medal winners, 1992
Men's Alpine combination
Josef Polig (Italy)

Women's Alpine combination
Petra Kronberger (Austria)

SNOOKER

World Professional championship

Instituted in the 1926–7 season; a knockout competition open to professional players who are members of the World Professional Billiards and Snooker Association; played at the Crucible Theatre, Sheffield.

Recent winners
1981 Steve Davis (England)
1982 Alex Higgins (N Ireland)
1983 Steve Davis (England)
1984 Steve Davis (England)
1985 Dennis Taylor (N Ireland)
1986 Joe Johnson (England)
1987 Steve Davis (England)
1988 Steve Davis (England)
1989 Steve Davis (England)
1990 Stephen Hendry (Scotland)
1991 John Parrott (England)
1992 Stephen Hendry (Scotland)

Most wins: (15), Joe Davis (England). 1927–40, 1946.

Rothmans Grand Prix

Originally the Professional Players Tournament; under present name since 1984; a ranking tournament.*

Winners
1982 Ray Reardon (Wales)
1983 Tony Knowles (England)
1984 Dennis Taylor (N Ireland)
1985 Steve Davis (England)
1986 Jimmy White (England)
1987 Stephen Hendry (Scotland)
1988 Steve Davis (England)
1989 Steve Davis (England)
1990 Stephen Hendry (Scotland)
1991 Stephen Hendry (Scotland)
1992 Jimmy White (England)

Most wins: (3), Steve Davis (England), Stephen Hendry (Scotland), as above.

British Open

Became a ranking tournament* in 1985.

Recent winners
1980 Alex Higgins (N Ireland)
1981 Steve Davis (England)
1982 Steve Davis (England)
1983 Ray Reardon (Wales)
1984 Steve Davis (England)
1985 Silvino Francisco (S Africa)
1986 Steve Davis (England)
1987 Jimmy White (England)
1988 Stephen Hendry (Scotland)
1989 Tony Meo (England)
1990 Bob Chaperon (Canada)
1991 Stephen Hendry (Scotland)
1992 Jimmy White (England)

Most wins: (4), Steve Davis (England), as above.

Benson and Hedges Masters

First contested in 1975 and won by John Spencer; held at the Wembley Conference Centre, it is the most prestigious non-ranking tournament of the season.

Recent winners
1982 Steve Davis (England)
1983 Cliff Thorburn (Canada)
1984 Jimmy White (England)
1985 Cliff Thorburn (Canada)
1986 Cliff Thorburn (Canada)
1987 Dennis Taylor (N Ireland)
1988 Steve Davis (England)
1989 Stephen Hendry (Scotland)
1990 Stephen Hendry (Scotland)
1991 Stephen Hendry (Scotland)
1992 Stephen Hendry (Scotland)

Most wins: (4), Stephen Hendry (Scotland), as above.

World Amateur championship

First held in 1963; originally took place every two years, but annual since 1984.

Recent winners
1976 Doug Mountjoy (Wales)
1978 Cliff Wilson (Wales)
1980 Jimmy white (England)
1982 Terry Parson (Wales)
1984 O. B. Agrawal (India)
1985 Paul Mifsud (Malta)
1986 Paul Mifsud (Malta)
1987 Darren, Morgan (Wales)
1988 James Wattana (Thailand)
1989 Ken Doherty (Ireland)
1990 Steven O'Connor (Ireland)
1991 Noppodol Noppachorn (Thailand)
1992 Neil Mosley (England)

Most wins: (2), Gary Owen (England), 1963, 1966; Ray Edmonds (England), 1972, 1974; Paul Mifsud, as above.

*A ranking tournament ia a tournament at which players may gather world ranking points.

SOFTBALL

World championships

First held for women in 1965 and for men the following year; now held every four years.

Winners (men)
1966 USA
1968 USA
1972 Canada
1976 Canada, New Zealand, USA (*shared*)
1980 USA
1984 New Zealand
1988 USA
1992 Canada

Most wins: (5), USA, as above.

Winners (women)
1965 Australia
1970 Japan
1974 USA
1978 USA
1982 New Zealand
1986 USA

Most wins: (3), USA, as above.

SPEEDWAY

World championships

Individual championships inaugurated in 1936; team championship instituted in 1960; first official pairs world championship in 1970 (threes from 1991).

Recent winners, individual
1981 Bruce Penhall (USA)
1982 Bruce Penhall (USA)
1983 Egon Muller (W Germany)
1984 Erik Gundersen (Denmark)
1985 Erik Gundersen (Denmark)
1986 Hans Nielsen (Denmark)
1987 Hans Nielsen (Denmark)
1988 Erik Gundersen (Denmark)
1989 Hans Nielsen (Denmark)
1990 Per Jonsson (Sweden)
1991 Jan Pedersen (Denmark)
1992 Gary Havelock (England)

Most wins: (6), Ivan Mauger (New Zealand), 1968–70, 1972, 1977, 1979.

Recent winners, pairs
1981 Bruce Penhall/Bobby Schwartz (USA)
1982 Dennis Sigalos/Bobby Schwartz (USA)
1983 Kenny Carter/Peter Collins (England)
1984 Peter Collins/ Chris Morton (England)
1985 Erik Gundersen/Tommy Knudsen (Denmark)
1986 Erik Gunderson/Hans Nielsen (Denmark)
1987 Erik Gundersen/Hans Nielsen (Denmark)
1988 Erik Gundersen/Hans Nielsen (Denmark)
1989 Eril Gundersen/Hans Nielsen (Denmark)
1990 Hans Nielsen/Jan Pedersen (Denmark)
1991 Hans Nielsen/Jan Pedersen/Tommy Knudsen (Denmark)
1992 Greg Hancock/Sam Ermolenko/ Ronnie Correy (USA)

Most wins: (6), Hans Nielsen (Denmark), as above.

Speedway (continued)

Recent winners, team

1981 Denmark
1982 USA
1983 Denmark
1984 Denmark
1985 Denmark
1986 Denmark
1987 Denmark
1988 Denmark
1989 England
1990 USA
1991 Denmark
1992 USA

Most wins: (9), Great Britain/England, 1968, 1971–5, 1977, 1980, 1989.

SQUASH

World Open championship

First held in 1976; held annually for men, every two years for women, until 1990, since when it has been annual.

Recent winners (men)

1981 Jahangir Khan (Pakistan)
1982 Jahangir Khan (Pakistan)
1983 Jahangir Khan (Pakistan)
1984 Jahangir Khan (Pakistan)
1985 Jahangir Khan (Pakistan)
1986 Ross Norman (New Zealand)
1987 Jansher Khan (Pakistan)
1988 Jahangir Khan (Pakistan)
1989 Jansher Khan (Pakistan)
1990 Jansher Khan (Pakistan)
1991 Rodney Martin (Australia)
1992 Jansher Khan (Pakistan)

Most wins: (6), Jahangir Khan (Pakistan), as above.

Recent winners (women)

1979 Heather McKay (Australia)
1981 Rhonda Thorne (Australia)
1983 Vicky Cardwell (Australia)
1985 Sue Devoy (New Zealand)
1987 Sue Devoy (New Zealand)
1989 Martine Le Moignan (Great Britain)
1990 Sue Devoy (New Zealand)
1991 Sue Devoy (new Zealand)
1992 Sue Devoy (New Zealand)

Most wins: (5), Sue Devoy (New Zealand), as above.

SURFING

World professional championship

A season-long series of Grand Prix events; first held in 1970.

Recent winners (men)

1979 Mark Richards (Australia)
1980 Mark Richards (Australia)
1981 Mark Richards (Australia)
1982 Mark Richards (Austrailia)
1983 Tom Carroll (Australia)
1984 Tom Carroll (Australia)
1985 Tommy Curren (USA)
1986 Tommy Curren (USA)
1987 Damien Hardman (Australia)
1988 Barton Lynch (Australia)
1989 Martin Potter (Great Britain)
1990 Tommy Curren (USA)
1991 Damien Hardman (Australia)
1992 Kelly Slater (USA)

Recent winners (women)

1979 Margo Oberg (Hawaii)
1980 Lyne Boyer (Hawaii)
1981 Margo Oberg (Hawaii)
1982 *not held*
1983 Margo Oberg (Hawaii)
1984 Kim Mearig (USA)
1985 Frieda Zamba (USA)
1986 Frieda Zamba (USA)
1987 Wendy Botha (S Africa)
1988 Frieda Zamba (USA)
1989 Wendy Botha (S Africa)
1990 Pam Burridge (Australia)
1991 Wendy Botha (Australia)
1992 Wendy Botha (Australia)

Most wins: Men (5), Mark Richards (Australia), 1975, 1979–82. Women (4), Wendy Botha (Australia, ex-S Africa), as above.

SWIMMING AND DIVING

World Championships

First held in 1973, the World Championships have since taken place in 1975, 1978, 1982, 1986 and 1991.

World champions, 1991 (men)

50 m freestyle	Tom Jager (USA)
100 m freestyle	Matt Biondi (USA)
200 m freestyle	Giorgio Lamberti (Italy)
400 m freestyle	Jörg Hoffmann (Germany)
1500 m freestyle	Jörg Hoffmann (Germany)
100 m backstroke	Jeff Rouse (USA)
200 m backstroke	Martin López-Zubero (Spain)
100 m breaststroke	Norbert Rosza (Hungary)
200 m breaststroke	Mike Barrowman (USA)
100 m butterfly	Anthony Nesty (Surinam)
200 m butterfly	Melvin Stewart (USA)
200 m individual medley	Tamás Darnyi (Hungary)
400 m individual medley	Tamás Darnyi (Hungary)
4 x 100 m freestyle medley	USA
4 x 200 m freestyle medley	Germany
4 x 100 m medley relay	USA
1 m springboard diving	Edwin Jongejans (Netherlands)
Platform diving	Sun Shewei (China)

World champions, 1991 (women)

50 m freestyle	Zhuang Yong (China)
100 m freestyle	Nicola Haislett (USA)
200 m freestyle	Hayley Lewis (Australia)
400 m freestyle	Janet Evans (USA)
800 m freestyle	Janet Evans (USA)
100 m backstroke	Krisztina Egerszegi (Hungary)
200 m backstroke	Krisztina Egerszegi (Hungary)
100 m breaststroke	Linley Frame (Australia)
200 m breaststroke	Elena Volkova (USSR)
100 m butterfly	Qian Hong (China)
200 m butterfly	Summer Sanders (USA)
200 m individual medley	Lin Li (China)
400 m individual medley	Lin Li (China)
4 x 100 m freestyle medley	USA
4 x 200 m freestyle medley	Germany
4 x 100 m medley relay	USA
1 m springboard diving	Gao Min (China)
Platform diving	Fu Mingxia (China)
Synchronized swimming	
Solo	Silvie Frechette (Canada)
Duet	USA
Team	USA

Olympic games

Gold medal winners, 1992 (men)

50 m freestyle	Aleksandr Popov (Unified Team)
100 m freestyle	Aleksandr Popov (Unified Team)
200 m freestyle	Yevgeniy Sadoviy (Unified Team)
400 m freestyle	Yevgeniy Sadoviy (Unified Team)
1 500 m freestyle	Kieren Perkins (Australia)
100 m breaststroke	Nelson Diebel (USA)
200 m breaststroke	Mike Barrowman (USA)
100 m butterfly	Pablo Moralos (USA)
200 m butterfly	Mel Stewart (USA)
100 m backstroke	Mark Tewksbury (Canada)
200 m backstroke	Martin López-Zubero (Spain)
200 m individual medley	Tamás Darnyi (Hungary)
400 m individual medley	Tamás Darnyi (Hungary)
400 m freestyle relay	(USA)
800 m freestyle relay	(Unified Team)
400 m medley relay	(USA)

Gold medal winners, 1992 (women)

50 m freestyle	Yang Wenyl (China)
100 m freestyle	Zhuang Yong (China)
200 m freestyle	Nicole Haislett (USA)
400 m freestyle	Dagmar Hase (Germany)
800 m freestyle	Janet Evans (USA)
100 m breaststroke	Yelena Rudkovskaya (Unified Team)
200 m breaststroke	Kyoko Iwasaki (Japan)
100 m backstroke	Krisztina Egerszegi (Hungary)
200 m backstroke	Krisztina Egerszegi (Hungary)
100 m butterfly	Qian Hong (China)
200 m butterfly	Summer Sanders (USA)
200 m individual medley	Lin Li (China)
400 m individual medley	Krisztina Egerszegi (Hungary)
400 m freestyle relay	(USA)
400 m medley relay	(USA)

TABLE TENNIS

World championships

First held in 1926 and every two years since 1957.

Recent winners, Swaythling Cup (men's team)

1971	China	1983	China
1973	Sweden	1985	China
1975	China	1987	China
1977	China	1989	Sweden
1979	Hungary	1991	Sweden
1981	China		

Recent winners, Corbillon Cup (women's team)

1971	Japan	1983	China
1973	S Korea	1985	China
1975	China	1987	China
1977	China	1989	China
1979	China	1991	China
1981	China		

Most wins: Swaythling Cup (12), Hungary, 1926, 1928–31, 1933 (twice), 1935, 1938, 1949, 1952, 1979. Corbillon Cup (9), China, 1965, 1975, 1977, 1979, 1981, 1983, 1985, 1987, 1989.

Recent winners (men)

1971	Stellan Bengtsson (Sweden)
1973	Hsi En-Ting (China)
1975	Istvan Jonyer (Hungary)
1977	Mitsuru Kohno (Japan)
1979	Seiji Ono (Japan)
1981	Guo Yuehua (China)
1983	Guo Yuehua (China)
1985	Jiang Jialiang (China)
1987	Jiang Jialiang (China)
1989	Jan-Ove Waldner (Sweden)
1991	Jörgen Persson (Sweden)

Most wins: (5), Viktor Barna (Hungary), 1930, 1932–5.

Table tennis, world championships (continued)

Recent winners (women)

1971 Lin Hui-Ching (China)
1973 Hu Yu-Lan (China)
1975 Pak Yung-Sun (N Korea)
1977 Pak Yung-Sun (N Korea)
1979 Ge Xinai (China)
1981 Ting Ling (China)
1983 Cao Yanhua (China)
1985 Cao Yanhua (China)
1987 He Zhili (China)
1989 Qiao Hong (China)
1991 Deng Yaping (China)

Most wins: (6), Angelica Rozeanu (Romania), 1950–55.

Recent winners, doubles (men)

1971 Istvan Jonyer/Tiber Klampar (Hungary)
1973 Stellan Bengtsson/Kjell Johansson (Sweden)
1975 Gabor Gergely/Istvan Jonyer (Hungary)
1977 Li Zhenshi/Liang Geliang (China)
1979 Dragutin Surbek/Anton Stipancic (Yugoslavia)
1981 Cai Zhenhua/Li Zhenshi (China)
1983 Dragutin Surbek/Zoran Kalinic (Yugoslavia)
1985 Mikael Applegren/Ulf Carlsson (Sweden)
1987 Chen Longcan/Wei Quinguang (China)
1989 Joerg Rosskopf/Stefen Fetzner (W Germany)
1991 Peter Karlson/Thomas von Scheele (Sweden)

Most wins: (8), Viktor Barna (Hungary/England), 1929–33 (won two titles 1933), 1935, 1939.

Recent winners, doubles (women)

1971 Cheng Min-Chih/Lin Hui-Ching (China)
1973 Maria Alexandru (Romania)/ Miho Hamada (Japan)
1975 Maria Alexandru (Romania)/ Shoko Takashima (Japan)
1977 Pak Yong Ok (N Korea)/Yang Yin (China)
1979 Zhang Li/Zhang Deying (China)
1981 Zhang Deying/Cao Yanhua (China)
1983 Shen Jianping/Dai Lili (China)
1985 Dai Lili/Geng Lijuan (China)
1987 Yang Young-Ja/Hyun Jung-Hwa (Korea)
1989 Quio Hong/Deng Yaping (China)
1991 Chen Zhie/Gao Jun (China)

Most wins: (7), Maria Mednyanszky (Hungary), 1928, 1930–5.

Recent winners, mixed doubles

1971 Chang Shih-Ling/Lin Hui-Ching (China)
1973 Liang Geliang/Li Li (China)
1975 Stanislav Gomozkov/Anna Ferdman (USSR)
1977 Jacques Secretin/Claude Bergeret (France)
1979 Liang Geliang/Ge Xinai (China)
1981 Xie Saike/Huang Junqun (China)
1983 Guo Yuehua/Ni Xialian (China)
1985 Cai Zhenua/Coa Yanhua (China)
1987 Hui Jun/Geng Lijuan (China)
1989 Yoo Nam-Kyu/Hyun Jung-Hwa (S Korea)
1991 Wang Tao/Liu Wei (China)

Most wins: (6), Maria Mednyanszky (Hungary), 1927–8, 1930–1, 1933 (two titles).

Olympic games

Gold medal winners, 1992

Men's singles
Jan-Ove Waldner (Switzerland)

Men's doubles
Lu Lin/Wang Tao (China)

Women's singles
Deng Yaping (China)

Women's doubles
Deng Yaping/Qiao Hong (China)

TENNIS (LAWN)

Wimbledon Championships

The All-England Championships at Wimbledon are lawn tennis's most prestigious championships; first held in 1877.

Recent winners, men's singles

1981 John McEnroe (USA)
1982 Jimmy Connors (USA)
1983 John McEnroe (USA)
1984 John McEnroe (USA)
1985 Boris Becker (W Germany)
1986 Boris Becker (W Germany)
1987 Pat Cash (Australia)
1988 Stefan Edberg (Sweden)
1989 Boris Becker (W Germany)
1990 Stefan Edberg (Sweden)
1991 Michael Stich (Germany)
1992 Andre Agassi (USA)
1993 Pete Sampras (USA)

Most wins: (7), William Renshaw (Great Britain) 1881–6, 1889.

Recent winners, women's singles

1981 Chris Evert-Lloyd (USA)
1982 Martina Navratilova (USA)
1983 Martina Navratilova (USA)
1984 Martina Navratilova (USA)
1985 Martina Navratilova (USA)
1986 Martina Navratilova (USA)
1987 Martina Navratilova (USA)
1988 Steffi Graf (W Germany)
1989 Steffi Graf (W Germany)
1990 Martina Navratilova (USA)
1991 Steffi Graf (Germany)
1992 Steffi Graf (Germany)
1993 Steffi Graf (Germany)

Most wins: (9), Martina Navratilova (Czechoslovakia/USA), 1978, 1979, plus as above.

Recent winners, men's doubles

1981 Peter Fleming/John McEnroe (USA)
1982 Peter McNamara/Paul McNamee (Australia)
1983 Peter Fleming/John McEnroe (USA)
1984 Peter Fleming/John McEnroe (USA)
1985 Heinz Gunthardt (Switzerland)/Balazs Taroczy (Hungary)
1986 Joakim Nystrom/Mats Wilander (Sweden)
1987 Ken Flach/Robert Seguso (USA)
1988 Ken Flach/Robert Seguso (USA)
1989 John Fitzgerald (Australia)/Anders Jarryd (Sweden)
1990 Rick Leach/Jim Pugh (USA)
1991 John Fitzgerald (Australia)/ Anders Jarryd (Sweden)
1992 John McEnroe (USA)/Michael Stich (Germany)
1993 Todd Woodbridge/Mark Woodforde (Australia)

Most wins: (8), Lawrence Doherty/Reg Doherty (Great Britain), 1897–1901, 1903–5.

Recent winners, women's doubles

1981 Martina Navratilova/Pam Shriver (USA)
1982 Martina Navratilova/Pam Shriver (USA)
1983 Martina Navratilova/Pam Shriver (USA)
1984 Martina Navratilova/Pam Shriver (USA)
1985 Kathy Jordan/Elizabeth Smylie (Australia)
1986 Martina Navratilova/Pam Shriver (USA)
1987 Claudia Kohde-Kilsch (W Germany)/ Helena Sukova (Czechoslovakia)
1988 Steffi Graf (W Germany)/Gabriela Sabatini (Argentina)
1989 Jana Novotna/Helena Sukova (Czechoslovakia)
1990 Jana Novotna/Helena Sukova (Czechoslovakia)
1991 Larissa Savchenko/Natalya Zvereva (USSR)
1992 Gigi Fernandez (USA)/Natalya Zvereva (Belarus)
1993 Gigi Fernandez (USA)/Natalya Zvereva (Belarus)

Most wins: (12), Elizabeth Ryan (USA), 1914, 1919–23, 1925–7, 1930, 1933–4.

Recent winners, mixed doubles

1981 Betty Stove (Netherlands)/Frew McMillan (S Africa)
1982 Anne Smith (USA)/Kevin Curren (S Africa)
1983 Wendy Turnbull (Australia)/John Lloyd (Great Britain)
1984 Wendy Turnbull (Australia)/John Lloyd (Great Britain)
1985 Martina Navratilova (USA)/Paul McNamee (Australia)
1986 Kathy Jordan/Ken Flach (USA)
1987 Jo Durie/Jeremy Bates (Great Britain)
1988 Sherwood Stewart/Zina Garrison (USA)
1989 Jim Pugh (USA)/Jana Novotna (Czechoslovakia)
1990 Rick Leach/Zina Garrison (USA)
1991 John Fitzgerald/Elizabeth Smylie (Australia)
1992 Cyril Suk (Czech Republic)/Lavisa Savchenko (Latvia)
1993 Mark Woodforde (Australia)/Martina Navratilova (USA)

Most wins: (7), Elizabeth Ryan (USA), 1919, 1921, 1923, 1927–8, 1930, 1932.

Tennis court

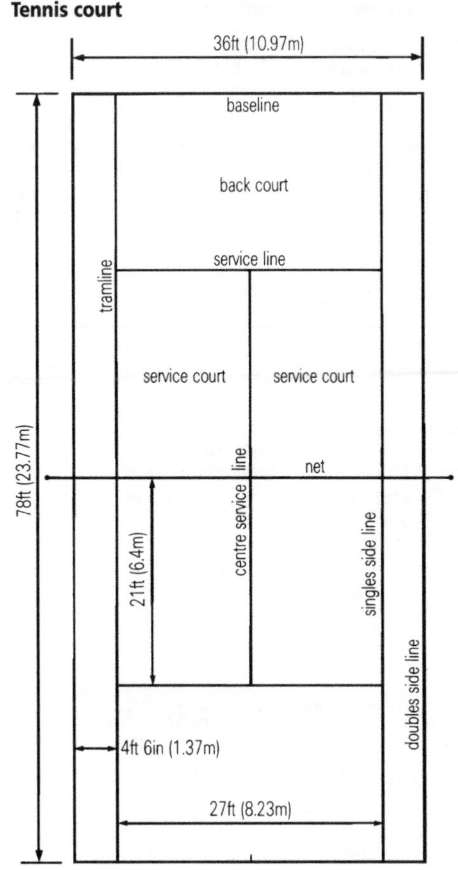

United States Open

First held in 1891 as the United States Championship; became the United States Open in 1968.

Recent winners, men's singles

1981 John McEnroe (USA)
1982 Jimmy Connors (USA)
1983 Jimmy Connors (USA)
1984 John McEnroe (USA)
1985 Ivan Lendl (Czechoslovakia)
1986 Ivan Lendl (Czechoslovakia)
1987 Ivan Lendl (Czechoslovakia)
1988 Mats Wilander (Sweden)
1989 Boris Becker (W Germany)
1990 Peter Sampras (USA)
1991 Stefan Edberg (Sweden)
1992 Stefan Edberg (Sweden)

Recent winners, women's singles

1981 Tracy Austin (USA)
1982 Chris Evert-Lloyd (USA)
1983 Martina Navratilova (USA)
1984 Martina Navratilova (USA)
1985 Hana Mandlikova (Czechoslovakia)
1986 Martina Navratilova (USA)
1987 Martina Navratilova (USA)
1988 Steffi Graf (W Germany)

Tennis (lawn) (continued)

1989 Steffi Graf (W Germany)
1990 Gabriela Sabatini (Argentina)
1991 Monica Seles (Yugoslavia)
1992 Monica Seles (Yugoslavia)

Most wins: Men (7), Richard Sears (USA), 1881–7; Bill Larned (USA), 1901–2, 1907–11; Bill Tilden (USA), 1920–5, 1929. Women (7), Molla Mallory (neé Bjurstedt) (USA), 1915–16, 1928, 1920–2, 1926; Helen Wills-Moody (USA), 1923–5, 1927–9, 1931.

Davis Cup

International team competition organized on a knockout basis; first held in 1900; contested on a challenge basis until 1972.

Recent winners

1981	USA	1987	Sweden
1982	USA	1988	W Germany
1983	Australia	1989	W Germany
1984	Sweden	1990	USA
1985	Sweden	1991	France
1986	Australia	1992	USA

Most wins: (29), USA, 1900, 1902, 1913, 1920–6, 1937–8, 1946–9, 1954, 1958, 1963, 1968–72, 1978–9, 1981–2, 1990.

TENPIN BOWLING

World championships

First held in 1923 by the International Bowling Association; since 1954 organized by the Fédération Internationale des Quillieurs (FIQ); since 1963, when women first competed, held every four years.

Recent winners, individual (men)

1954 Göska Algeskog (Sweden)
1955 Nils Bäckström (Sweden)
1958 Kaarlo Asukas (Finland)
1960 Tito Reynolds (Mexico)
1963 Les Zikes (USA)
1967 David Pond (Great Britain)
1971 Ed Luther (USA)
1975 Bud Staudt (USA)
1979 Ollie Ongtawco (Philippines)
1983 Armando Marino (Colombia)
1987 Rolland Patrick (France)
1991 Ma Ying-chei (Taiwan)

Recent winners, individual (women)

1963 Helen Shablis (USA)
1967 Helen Weston (USA)
1971 Ashie Gonzales (Puerto Rico)
1975 Annedore Haefker (W Germany)
1979 Lita de la Roas (Philippines)
1983 Lena Sulkanen (Sweden)
1987 Edda Piccini (Italy)
1991 Martha Beckel (Germany)

Most wins: No one has more than one.

TRAMPOLINING

World championships

First held in 1964 and annually until 1968; since then, every two years.

Recent winners, individual (men)

1970 Wayne Miller (USA)
1972 Paul Luxon (Great Britain)
1974 Richard Tison (France)
1976 Richard Tison (France)/Yevgeni Yanes (USSR) (*shared*)
1978 Yevgeni Yanes (USSR)
1980 Stewart Matthews (Great Britain)
1982 Carl Furrer (Great Britain)
1984 Lionel Pioline (France)
1986 Lionel Pioline (France)
1988 Vadim Krasnoshapka (USSR)
1990 Aleksandr Moskalenko (USSR)
1992 Aleksandr Moskalenko (Russia)

Most wins: (2), David Jacobs (USA), 1967–8; Wayne Miller (USA), 1966, 1970; Richard Tison (France), as above; Yevgeni Yanes (USSR), as above; Lionel Pioline (France), as above, Aleksandr Moskalenko (Russia), as above.

Recent winners, individual (women)

1970 Renee Ransom (USA)
1972 Alexandra Nicholson (USA)
1974 Alexandra Nicholson (USA)
1976 Svetlana Levina (USSR)
1978 Tatyana Anisimova (USSR)
1980 Ruth Keller (Switzerland)
1982 Ruth Keller (Switzerland)
1984 Sue Shotton (Great Britain)
1986 Tatyana Lushina (USSR)
1988 Rusadan Khoperia (USSR)
1990 Yelena Merkulova (USSR)
1992 Yelena Merkulova (Russia)

Most wins: (5), Judy Wills (USA), 1964–8.

TUG OF WAR

World championships

Instituted in 1975, held every two years; contested at 560 kg from 1982.

Winners

	720 kg	*640 kg*	*560 kg*	*Catchweight (no specification)*
1975	England	England	–	–
1976	England	England	–	–
1977	England	Wales	–	–
1978	England	England	–	–
1980	England	England	–	–
1982	England	Ireland	Switzerland	–
1984	Ireland	Ireland	England	England
1985	Switzerland	Switzerland	Switzerland	–
1986	Ireland	Ireland	England	–
1988	Ireland	England	England	–
1990	Ireland	Ireland	Switzerland	–

Most titles: (15), England, as above.

VOLLEYBALL

World championships

Inaugurated in 1949; first women's championships in 1952; now held every four years, but Olympic champions are also world champions in Olympic years.

Recent winners (men)

1970	E Germany	1982	USSR
1972	Japan	1984	USA
1974	Poland	1986	USA
1976	Poland	1988	USA
1978	USSR	1990	Italy
1980	USSR	1992	Brazil

Recent winners (women)

1970	USSR	1982	China
1972	USSR	1984	China
1974	Japan	1986	China
1976	Japan	1988	USSR
1978	Cuba	1990	USSR
1980	USSR	1992	Cuba

Most wins: Men (9), USSR, 1949, 1952, 1960, 1962, 1964, 1968, 1978, 1980, 1982. Women (8), USSR, 1952, 1956, 1960, 1968, 1970, 1972, 1980, 1988.

WALKING

Lugano Trophy

The principal road walking trophy; contested every two years by men's national teams; first held in 1961.

Recent winners

1973 E Germany
1975 USSR
1977 Mexico
1979 Mexico
1981 Italy
1983 USSR
1985 E Germany
1987 USSR
1989 USSR
1991 Italy

Most wins: (5), E Germany, 1965, 1967, 1970, 1973, 1985.

Eschborn Cup

The women's equivalent of the Lugano Trophy; first held in 1979; takes place every two years.

Winners

1981	USSR	1987	USSR
1983	China	1989	USSR
1985	China	1991	USSR

Most wins: (4), USSR, as above.

WATER POLO

World championship

First held in 1973, and every four years since 1978; was included in the world swimming championships; since 1991 has been held separately. First women's event held in 1986.

Winners (men)

1973	Hungary	1982	USSR
1975	USSR	1986	Yugoslavia
1978	Italy	1991	Yugoslavia

Winners (women)

1986 Australia
1991 Netherlands

Most wins: Men (2), USSR, Yugoslavia, as above.

World Cup

Inaugurated in 1979 and held every two years; women's event unofficial until 1989.

Winners (men)

1979	Hungary	1987	Yugoslavia
1981	USSR	1989	Yugoslavia
1983	USSR	1991	USA
1985	W Germany		

Most wins: (2), USSR, Yugoslavia, as above.

Winners (women)

1979 USA
1981 Canada
1988 Netherlands
1989 Netherlands
1991 Netherlands

Most wins: (3), Netherlands, as above.

WATER SKIING

World championships

First held in 1949; take place very two years; competitions for slalom, tricks, jumps, and the overall individual title.

Recent winners, overall (men)

1971 George Athans (Canada)
1973 George Athans (Canada)
1975 Carlos Suarez (Venezuela)
1977 Mike Hazelwood (Great Britain)
1979 Joel McClintock (Canada)
1981 Sammy Duvall (USA)
1983 Sammy Duvall (USA)
1985 Sammy Duvall (USA)
1987 Sammy Duvall (USA)
1989 Patrice Martin (France)
1991 Patrice Martin (France)

Most wins: (4), Sammy Duvall (USA), as above.

Recent winners, overall (women)

1971 Christy Weir (USA)
1973 Lisa St John (USA)
1975 Liz Allan-Shetter (USA)
1977 Cindy Todd (USA)
1979 Cindy Todd (USA)
1981 Karin Roberge (USA)
1983 Ana-Maria Carrasco (Venezuela)
1985 Karen Neville (Australia)
1987 Deena Brush (USA)
1989 Deena Mapple (USA)
1991 Karen Neville (Australia)

Most wins: (3), Willa McGuire (USA), 1949–50, 1955; Liz Allan-Shetter (USA), 1965, 1969, 1975.

WEIGHTLIFTING

World championships

First held in 1898; 11 weight divisions; the most prestigious is the 110 kg plus category (formerly known as Super Heavyweight); Olympic champions are automatically world champions in Olympic years.

Recent champions (over 110 kg)

1981 Anatoliy Pisarenko (USSR)
1982 Anatoliy Pisarenko (USSR)
1983 Anatoliy Pisarenko (USSR)
1984 Dean Lukin (Australia)
1985 Antonio Krastev (Bulgaria)
1986 Antonio Krastev (Bulgaria)
1987 Aleksandr Kurlovich (USSR)
1988 Aleksandr Kurlovich (USSR)
1989 Aleksandr Kurlovich (USSR)
1990 Leonid Taranenko (USSR)
1991 Aleksandr Kurlovich (USSR)
1992 Aleksandr Kurlovich (Unified Team)

Most titles (all categories): (8), John Davies (USA), 82.5 kg 1938; over 82.5 kg 1946–50; over 90 kg 1951–2; Tommy Kono (USA), 67.5 kg 1952; 75 kg 1953, 1957–9; 82.5 kg 1954–6; Vasiliy Alexseyev (USSR), over 110 kg 1970–7.

WRESTLING

World championships

Graeco-Roman world championships first held in 1921; first freestyle championships in 1951; each style contests 10 weight divisions, the heaviest being the 130 kg (formerly over 100 kg) category; Olympic champions become world champions in Olympic years.

Recent winners, freestyle (super-heavyweight/over 100 kg)

1981 Salman Khasimikov (USSR)
1982 Salman Khasimikov (USSR)
1983 Salman Khasimikov (USSR)
1984 Bruce Baumgartner (USA)
1985 David Gobedzhishvilli (USSR)
1986 Bruce Baumgartner (USA)
1987 Khadartsv Aslam (USSR)
1988 David Gobedzhishvilli (USSR)
1989 Ali Reiza Soleimani (Iran)
1990 David Gobedzhishvilli (USSR)
1991 Andreas Schroder (Germany)
1992 Bruce Baumgartner (USA)

Recent winners, graeco-Roman (super-heavyweight/over 100 kg)

1981 Refik Memisevic (Yugoslavia)
1982 Nikolai Denev (Bulgaria)
1983 Jevgeniy Artiochin (USSR)
1984 Jeffrey Blatnick (USA)
1985 Igor Rostozotskiy (USSR)
1986 Thomas Johansson (Sweden)
1987 Igor Rostozotskiy (USSR)
1988 Aleksandr Karelin (USSR)
1989 Aleksandr Karelin (USSR)
1990 Aleksandr Karelin (USSR)
1991 Aleksandr Karelin (USSR)
1992 Aleksandr Karelin (Unified Team)

Most titles (all weight divisions): Freestyle (10), Aleksander Medved (USSR), 90 kg 1962–4, 1966; 100 kg 1967–8, over 100 kg 1969–72. Greco-Roman (7), Valeriy Rezantsev (USSR), 90 kg 1970–6.

YACHTING

America's Cup

One of sport's famous trophies; first won by the schooner Magic in 1870; now held approximately every four years, when challengers compete in a series of races to find which of them races against the holder; all 25 winners up to 1983 were from the United States.

Recent winners

1958 *Columbia* (USA) (Briggs Cunningham)
1962 *Weatherly* (USA) (Emil Mosbacher)
1964 *Constellation* (USA) (Bob Bavier)
1967 *Intrepid* (USA) (Emil Mosbacher)
1970 *Intrepid* (USA) (Bill Ficker)
1974 *Courageous* (USA) (Ted Hood)
1977 *Courageous* (USA) (Ted Turner)
1980 *Freedom* (USA) (Dennis Conner)
1983 *Australia II* (Australia) (John Bertrand)
1987 *Stars & Stripes* (USA) (Dennis Conner)
1988 *Stars & Stripes* (USA) (Dennis Conner)[a]
1992 *America 3* (USA) (Bill Koch)

[a] *Stars & Stripes* won a special challenge match but on appeal the race was awarded to *New Zealand* skippered by Davis Barnes. However, after much legal wrangling, the cup was retained by *Stars & Stripes*.

Most wins: (Skipper) (3), Charlie Barr (USA), 1899, 1901, 1903; Harold Vanderbilt (USA), 1930, 1934, 1937; Dennis Conner (USA), as above.

Admiral's Cup

A two-yearly series of races in the English Channel, around Fastnet rock and at Cowes; national teams of three boats per team; first held in 1957.

Recent winners

1969	USA	1981	Great Britain
1971	Great Britain	1983	W Germany
1973	W Germany	1985	W Germany
1975	Great Britain	1987	New Zealand
1977	Great Britain	1989	Great Britain
1979	Australia	1991	France

Most wins: (9), Great Britain, 1957, 1959, 1963, 1965, 1971, 1975, 1977, 1981, 1989.

International racing yacht classes

Class	*Crew*	*Type of craft*
Finn	1	Centre-board dinghy
Flying Dutchman	2	Centre-board dinghy
International 470	2	Centre-board dinghy
International Soling	3	Keel boat
International Star	2	Keel boat
International Tornado	2	Catamaran
Windglider	1	Single board

GOVERNING BODIES IN SPORT

AAA Amateur Athletic Association
AAU Amateur Athletic Union (USA)
ACU Auto Cycle Union
AIBA International Amateur Boxing Federation
ASA Amateur Swimming Association
BDO British Darts Organisation
FA Football Association
FEI International Equestrian Federation
FIA International Automobile Association
FIAC International Amateur Cycling Federation
FIBA International Basketball Federation
FIBT International Bobsleigh and Tobogganing Federation
FIC International Canoeing Federation
FIDE International Chess Federation
FIE International Fencing Federation
FIFA International Football Association Federation
FIG International Gymnastic Federation
FIH International Hockey Federation
FILA International Amateur Wrestling Federation
FIM International Motorcycling Federation
FINA International Amateur Swimming Federation
FIQ International Bowling Federation
FIRA International Amateur Rugby Federation
FIS International Ski Federation
FIT International Trampoline Federation
FITA International Archery Federation
FIVB International Volleyball Federation
GAA Gaelic Athletic Association
IAAF International Amateur Athletic Federation
IBA International Baseball Association
IBF International Badminton Federation
IBF International Boxing Federation
IBSF International Billiards and Snooker Federation Association
ICF International Curling Federation
IHF International Handball Federation
IIHF International Ice Hockey Federation
IJF International Judo Federation
IOC International Olympic Committee
IRFB International Rugby Football Board
ISRF International Squash Rackets Federation
ISU International Skating Union
ITF International Tennis Federation
ITTF International Table Tennis Federation
IWF International Weightlifting Federation
IWSF International Water Ski Federation
IYRU International Yacht Racing Union
LPGA Ladies Professional Golfers' Association
LTA Lawn Tennis Association
MCC Marylebone Cricket Club
NBA National Basketball Association (USA)
NCAA National Collegiate Athletic Association (USA)
NFL National Football League (USA)
NHL National Hockey League (USA)
PGA Professional Golfers' Association
RFU Rugby Football Union
RL Rugby League
TCCB Test and County Cricket Board
UEFA Union of European Football Associations
UIPMB International Union of Modern Pentathlon and Biathlon
UIT International Shooting Union
USGA United States Golf Association
USPGA United States Professional Golfers' Association
WBA World Boxing Association
WBC World Boxing Council
WBO World Boxing Organisation
WPBSA World Professional Billiards and Snooker Association
WWSU World Water Skiing Union

INDEX

Guide to the Index

The alphabetical arrangement of this index is letter-by-letter. The order follows the English alphabet, ignoring capital letters, accents, diacritics, or apostrophes.

In cases where a series of headwords have the same spelling, general topics are ordered before people, and people precede places.

Rulers are listed chronologically, ordering them by country if their names are the same (e.g. *Charles I of England* would precede *Charles I of Spain*, and these would be followed by *Charles II*).

When a number of people have the same name, monarchs are given before saints and popes, and these are followed by lay people. Compound names (e.g. *John of Gaunt)* appear later than single-element surnames (e.g. *John, Elton*), and are taken in strict letter-by-letter order, including grammatical words (e.g. *John of Gaunt* precedes *John the Baptist*).

Entries involving numbers are located on the basis of their spoken form (e.g. *10* will be found under 'ten').

Names beginning with *St* are ordered under *Saint*, and all *Mc* prefixes are ordered as if they were *Mac*.

Cross-references between index entries are shown with the symbol >>.

Conventional abbreviations are used for American states; these are explained on pp. 345–6.

Most of the entries consist of a single reference to a page in the first part of this book. In a few cases, sets of references have been compiled on points of possible interest.

Index

Index

Index

Index

Index

ACKNOWLEDGEMENTS

We would like to thank the following for their help in the preparation of this book:

Geoffrey Briggs, NASA; British Rail; British Standards Institution; British Telecom; Dr Michael Brooke, Cambridge; Professor A. Brown and Mrs P. Brown, Oxford; Calmann and King; Carol-June Cassidy; Central Statistical Office; Civil Aviation Authority; Department of Health; Food and Agriculture Organization; Dr J.T. Houghton, Hadley Climate Centre; International Monetary Fund; International Phonetic Association; Organization for Economic Co-operation and Development; Maureen Storey; World Health Organization; UNESCO.

The following Cambridge University Press titles were used in the preparation of data for this book:

M. Brooke and T. Birkhead (eds.) *The Cambridge Encyclopedia of Ornithology* (Cambridge University Press, 1991)
D. Crystal (ed.) *The Cambridge Encyclopedia* (Cambridge University Press, 1992)
D. Crystal *The Cambridge Encyclopedia of Language* (Cambridge University Press, 1991)
D. Crystal (ed.) *The Cambridge Paperback Encyclopedia* (Cambridge University Press, 1993)
J.T. Houghton, G.J. Jenkins and J.J. Ephraums (eds.) *Climate Change The Scientifc Assessment* (Cambridge University Press, 1990)
S. Jones, R. Martin and D. Pilbeam (eds.) *The Cambridge Encyclopedia of Human Evolution* (Cambridge University Press, 1992)
R.J. Lincoln and G.A. Boxhall *The Cambridge Illustrated Dictionary of Natural History* (Cambridge University Press, 1990)
K. Nicholls and A. Nicholls (eds.) *The Cambridge Guide to the Museums of Europe* (Cambridge University Press, 1991)
A. Sherratt (ed.) *The Cambridge Encyclopedia of Archaeology* (Cambridge University Press, 1980)
N. Smart *The World's Religions* (Cambridge University Press, 1992)
D. Smith (ed.) *The Cambridge Encyclopedia of Earth Sciences* (Cambridge University Press, 1982)

Thank you also to the following for their work on the index:
Hilary Crystal; Geoff Leeming; Teresa Regan; Ann Rowlands